k_s Cost of retained earnings
k_{sL} Cost of equity of a levered firm
k_{sU} Cost of equity of an unlevered firm
M/B   Market-to book ratio
MCC   Marginal cost of capital
n   (1) Number of periods or years
     (2) Number of shares outstanding
NPV   Net present value
NWC   Net working capital
P   (1) Price of a share of stock
     (2) Price per unit of output
     (3) Probability of occurrence
P/E   Price/earnings ratio
PI   Profitability index
PV   Present value
PVIF   Present value interest factor for a lump sum
PVIFA   Present value interest factor for an annuity
Q   Unit sales
r   (1) Rate of return on new investment
     (2) IRR of a project
     (3) Correlation coefficient
R_F Rate of return on a riskless security
ROA   Return on assets
ROE   Return on equity
RP   Risk premium
S   (1) Dollar sales
     (2) Total market value of equity
SML   Security Market Line
Σ Summation sign (capital sigma)
σ Standard deviation (lower case sigma)
T   Tax rate
t   Time, when used as a subscript
TIE   Times-interest-earned ratio
V   (1) Value
     (2) Variable cost per unit
V_L Total market value of a levered firm
V_U Total market value of an unlevered firm
YTM   Yield to maturity

Financial Management
Theory and Practice

Fourth Edition

Financial Management
Theory and Practice

Fourth Edition

Eugene F. Brigham
University of Florida

in collaboration with

Louis C. Gapenski
University of Florida

The Dryden Press
Chicago   New York   Philadelphia   San Francisco
Montreal   Toronto   London   Sydney
Tokyo   Mexico City   Rio de Janeiro   Madrid

Acquisitions Editor: Elizabeth Widdicombe
Developmental Editor: Judy Sarwark
Project Editor: Cate Rzasa
Managing Editor: Jane Perkins
Design Director: Alan Wendt
Production Manager: Mary Jarvis

Copy Editor: Lorraine Wolf
Compositor: The Clarinda Company
Text Type: 10/12 Palatino

Library of Congress Cataloging in Publication Data

Brigham, Eugene F., 1930–
  Financial management.

  Includes bibliographies and index.
  1. Corporations—Finance.   I. Title.
HG4026.B669   1985   658.1'5   84-21060
ISBN 0-03-071693-4

Printed in the United States of America
567-032-987654321

Address orders:
383 Madison Avenue
New York, NY 10017

Address editorial correspondence:
One Salt Creek Lane
Hinsdale, IL 60521

CBS COLLEGE PUBLISHING
The Dryden Press
Holt, Rinehart and Winston
Saunders College Publishing

The Dryden Press Series in Finance

Brigham
Financial Management: Theory and Practice,
Fourth Edition

Brigham
Fundamentals of Financial Management, *Third Edition*

Brigham and Crum
Cases in Managerial Finance, *Fifth Edition*

Brigham and Gapenski
Intermediate Financial Management

Brigham and Johnson
Issues in Managerial Finance, *Second Edition*

Campsey and Brigham
Introduction to Financial Management

Clayton and Spivey
The Time Value of Money

Fama and Miller
The Theory of Finance

Gitman
Personal Finance, *Third Edition*

Greer and Farrell
Contemporary Real Estate: Theory and Practice

Greer and Farrell
Investment Analysis for Real Estate Decisions

Harrington
Case Studies in Financial Decision Making

Johnson and Johnson
Commercial Bank Management

Kidwell and Peterson
Financial Institutions, Markets, and Money,
Second Edition

Lorie and Brealey
Modern Developments in Investment Management,
Second Edition

Mayo
Investments: An Introduction

Mayo
Finance

Myers
Modern Developments in Financial Management

Pettijohn
PROFIT

Reilly
Investment Analysis and Portfolio Management,
Second Edition

Reilly
Investments

Tallman and Neal
Financial Analysis and Planning Package

Weston and Brigham
Essentials of Managerial Finance, *Seventh Edition*

Weston and Copeland
Managerial Finance, *Eighth Edition*

Preface

Financial management has changed greatly in recent years. Strong inflationary pressures have pushed interest rates to unprecedented heights, and the resulting high and volatile cost of capital has led to profound changes in corporate financial policies and practices. Academic researchers have made a number of significant theoretical advances. At the same time, business practitioners are making increasing use of financial theory, and feedback from the "real world" has led to modifications and improvements in academic financial theory. Finally, computers, especially personal computers, are being used increasingly and effectively to analyze financial decisions. This usage has made it more important than ever that financial problems be set up in a form suitable for quantitative analysis. To a large extent, these trends have dictated the revisions made in the fourth edition of *Financial Management: Theory and Practice.*

The book begins with basic concepts, focusing on security markets and the valuation process, and then goes on to show how the principles of financial management can be used to help maximize the value of a firm. This organization has three important advantages:

1. Explaining early in the book how financial markets operate, and how security prices are determined within these markets, gives students a basic appreciation of how financial management can affect the value of the firm. Also, this organization gives students an early familiarity with the time value of money, valuation, and risk analysis, which in turn permits us to use and reinforce these key concepts throughout the book.

2. Structuring the book around market and valuation concepts provides a unifying theme that is missing in many texts. Some finance texts develop a series of topics in modular form, then attempt to integrate them in later chapters. The organization used in *Financial Management* gives students a better and more comprehensive understanding of how the topics interact.

3. Students—even those who do not plan to major in finance—generally find the study of investments interesting. They enjoy working with stock and bond values, rates of return, and the like. Because people's ability to learn a subject is a function of their interest and motivation, and because *Financial Management* begins with a discussion of security prices and markets, the book's organization is good from a pedagogic standpoint.

Intended Market and Use

Financial Management is designed primarily for use as an introductory MBA text, although it can be used as an undergraduate introductory text either with exceptionally good students or where the introductory course is taught over two terms. In the past, the book has also been used in the second undergraduate corporate finance course, following the use of an easier book in the first course. *Financial Management* can still be used in this manner, but our new book, *Intermediate Financial Management*, is preferable for the second undergraduate course.

There is too much material in the text to cover everything thoroughly in one term, and it is certainly not possible to go over everything in class. However, we have tried to write the book in a manner that permits students, especially MBAs, to read on their own and understand those parts that are not covered in class. In our introductory MBA course, we have taken two somewhat different approaches. At times, we have covered only the material in Chapters 1–15, plus Chapters 18–23, or 21 chapters in total. At other times, we have covered the entire text. Obviously, the depth of coverage is less when we cover more material, but in both situations, we expect students to learn most of the assigned materials by reading the book, and we concentrate on the more difficult materials in class.

We have also made a special effort to make the text useful as a reference book. It is important that students have materials available that they can use in subsequent case courses and apply in on-the-job situations after graduation. Based on a study of the leading casebooks, plus our own experience in consulting assignments, in work with executive development programs, and in discussions with numerous financial executives, we have tried to put into the book what students need to know to deal with most real-world financial decisions.

Major Changes in the Fourth Edition

Updates. We updated the entire book to reflect recent changes in tax laws, interest rates, bankruptcy proceedings, takeovers, and the like. The biggest update, by far, is in the tax area, especially depreciation allowances. We changed most examples and end-of-chapter problems to reflect ACRS depreciation schedules.

Introductory Examples. A real-world example that highlights the key issues in each chapter is presented at the beginning of the chapter. These examples both motivate students to read the chapters and help them see, as they go through each of the chapters, where we are headed.

End-of-Chapter Problems. Most end-of-chapter problems have been revised and extended. Also, the first question at the end of each chapter now lists the key terms in the chapter. This serves both as a quick self-test for students and as a speedy summary/review of the chapter's basic coverage. Further, a set of fairly difficult self-test problems, with detailed solutions, is given at the end of the more quantitative chapters. These problems serve (1) to test students' ability to set up problems for solution and (2) to explain the solution setup for those who need help.

Level. Both the breadth and depth of coverage have been extended. Therefore, the fourth edition of *Financial Management (FM)* is a somewhat "higher level" book than the third edition. However, because of our efforts to clarify our explanations of the more difficult concepts, the fourth edition is not necessarily more difficult than the previous one.

If you felt that the last edition of *FM* was challenging enough for your students and are concerned that this new, more rigorous edition may be too difficult, we urge you to consider using the third edition of *Fundamentals of Financial Management* (1983, Dryden Press). *Fundamentals* is close in level to the basic chapters in the third edition of *FM*, but quite a bit easier than the fourth edition. One of the reasons for *FM*'s revision was to differentiate it further from *Fundamentals*, so that they present clear alternatives.

Organization. We made some significant changes in the organization of the book to improve its flow. Here is the new structure:

    I. **Introduction.** The introduction, which was expanded from two to three chapters, now includes a discussion of agency theory, as well as more material on types of securities, capital markets, and the economic environment. The new materials on securities and security price changes over time in Chapters 2 and 3 provide a better lead-in to the valuation and risk chapters that follow.

   II. **Valuation and the Cost of Capital.** This section contains four chapters which progress from time value, to valuation models, to risk/return relationships, to the cost of capital. The major change here is the shift in the cost of capital chapter from Chapter 15 to Chapter 7.

 III. **Capital Budgeting.** This important subject is expanded from two to three chapters. Also, having covered cost of capital earlier in the book, we now discuss the effects of capital budgeting on the cost of capital in the capital budgeting section. Note also that microcomputer models are introduced in an appendix in this section.

IV. **Capital Structure and Dividend Policy.** Here we discuss strategic policy decisions regarding how the firm is to be financed. We stress how the target capital structure and the target dividend payout ratio are established.

V. **Types of Long-Term Capital.** Part V moves on from strategic long-term financing policies to implementation. Investment banking, common and preferred stock, long-term debt, leasing, and options-related securities, including a discussion of the Black-Scholes model, are presented in this section. Because these chapters now follow cost of capital and capital structure, their level has been raised somewhat.

VI. **Working Capital Management.** This material has been moved from Chapters 8–10 to Chapters 18–21. The new placement greatly improves the flow of the book by permitting us to complete our strategic, long-run analysis before moving into tactical, operational decision analysis, which is what working capital management is all about. Note also that this section has been expanded from three to four chapters, and greater emphasis is now given to overall working capital policy.

VII. **Financial Analysis and Planning.** In the last edition, this material was presented in Chapters 6 and 7. However, such early placement made it difficult for students to appreciate why ratios were targeted at specific levels, and to understand the intricacies of financial planning. With the topics' new placement, following all the asset and liability management chapters, students can better understand the logic of ratio analysis and grasp the forecasting/planning models. Also, by placing planning and analysis later in the book, we can use it to tie together earlier parts of the course.

VIII. **Special Topics.** Mergers, bankruptcy/reorganizations, multinational finance, and pension fund management are presented in this section. Executive reviewers of the third edition of *Financial Management* suggested that the most glaring omission was a chapter on pension fund management, which today has become one of the most critical areas of financial management. We rectified that and also greatly strengthened the other chapters in this section.

Financial Calculators and Microcomputers. In the third edition, we offered only the traditional approach to time value of money. In this edition, we have expanded that discussion to show how financial calculators can be used to solve most compound interest problems. Also, rapid advances in computer hardware and software are revolutionizing financial management. Powerful personal computers are now available to any business that can afford to hire a business student, and new software programs make it easy to do things that were not feasible a few years ago. Today, a business that does not use microcomputers in its financial planning process is about as competitive as a student who tries to take a finance exam without a financial calculator. Therefore, wherever possible, we have included examples of how computers can be used to help make better financial decisions. This orients students toward the kind of business environment they will face upon graduation; moreover, students can often understand the underlying financial theory better after working through a computer model of the problem than they could using the older methods.

Obviously, everyone does not have access to a personal computer or a mainframe terminal; therefore, (1) the text is written so that it requires no computer orientation whatever, and (2) it does not include any problems that require computer solutions. However, we do provide an appendix which introduces electronic spreadsheets (*VisiCalc* and *Lotus 1-2-3*). Additionally, we include both spreadsheet and *IFPS* models in the Instructor's Manual, along with diskettes, on the following subjects: (1) capital budgeting, (2) capital structure, (3) debt refunding, (4) leasing, (5) cash budgeting, and (6) financial forecasting/analysis.

Ancillary Materials

The package of ancillary materials which accompanies *Financial Management* is the most complete one available with any finance text. The additional items available to aid both students and instructors include the following:

1. Study Guide. This supplement outlines the key sections of the text, gives some self-test questions for each chapter, and provides a set of solved problems similar to those in the text. The Study Guide for the third edition was designed for use with both *FM* and *Fundamentals*. The new one is designed specifically for *FM*.

2. Casebooks. A revised edition of *Cases in Managerial Finance*, fifth edition (1983, Dryden Press), by Eugene F. Brigham and Roy L. Crum, is well suited for use with this text. In addition, a new collection of Harvard-type cases by Diana Harrington, *Case Studies in Financial Decision Making*, also coordinated with this text, is available from The Dryden Press.

3. Readings Books. A number of readings books, including *Issues in Managerial Finance*, second edition (1980, Dryden Press), edited by Eugene F. Brigham and Ramon E. Johnson, can be used as supplements to *FM*.

4. Test Bank. A Test Bank with more than 600 class-tested questions/problems in objective format is now available both in book form and on computer diskettes (Apple II and IBM PC). The Computerized Test Bank is also available on magnetic tape. The Test Bank questions are, in general, more challenging than those in most test banks, and they are well suited for exams. (Most other test banks are more suitable for quizzes than for midterm and final exams.)

5. Transparencies. A comprehensive set of acetate transparencies, designed to highlight key materials in each chapter and keyed to extensive lecture notes in the Instructor's Manual, is available from The Dryden Press to instructors who adopt the text.

6. Instructor's Manual. A complete, 300-page manual is available to instructors who adopt the book. The manual contains (1) answers to all text questions, (2) solutions to all text problems, (3) extensive lecture notes that focus on more difficult topics and are keyed to the transparency acetates, and (4) several write-ups of personal computer solutions (or "template models") to key financial problems in a form suitable for reproduction.

7. Diskette with Models. A diskette with actual programs for computer solutions is available to instructors. These models work with *VisiCalc, Lotus 1-2-3,* and *IFPS/Personal,* and they correspond to the text examples and appendices provided in the Instructor's Manual.

8. Financial Management with *Lotus 1-2-3* (CBS College Publishing). The *Lotus 1-2-3* spreadsheet program is currently the best-selling financial analysis package available for use with personal computers. Paul D. Cretien, Susan E. Ball, and Eugene F. Brigham are writing a supplemental book that explains how many commonly encountered problems in financial management can be analyzed with electronic spreadsheets. The supplement will also provide a series of "template models" that address most types of decision areas in finance.

Acknowledgments

We would like to thank the 14 professors who reviewed the third edition of *FM* and who provided us with detailed comments and suggestions for this revision: Keith Boles, Severin Carlson, William Damon, Sankar De, Samuel Hadaway, Joseph Kiernan, Joan Lamm, Edward Lawrence, D. J. Masson, John Settle, Stephen Smith, Sue Visscher, Jonathan Welch, and Dennis Zocco. In addition, we appreciate the marketing feedback on the draft manuscript provided by Roger Miller, William Nelson, and Jaye Smith. A great many people helped with the book during its first three editions, and we would like to thank them here:

Michael Adler	Peter Bacon	Roger Bey
Ed Altman	Thomas Bankston	John Bildersee
Robert Angell	Charles Barngrover	Russ Boisjoly
Vincent Apilado	William Beedles	Kenneth Boudreaux
Bob Aubey	Moshe Ben-Horim	Donald Boyd
Guilford Babcock	Bill Beranek	Patricia Boyer

Mary Broske	Ramon Johnson	R. Potter
Bill Brueggeman	Ray Jones	R. Powell
B. J. Campsey	Gus Kalogeras	Chris Prestopino
Bob Carleson	Michael Keenan	Howard Puckett
Stephen Celec	Don Knight	Herbert Quigley
Donald Chance	Jaroslaw Komarynsky	George Racette
S. K. Choudhury	Harold Krogh	Bob Radcliffe
Lal Chugh	Charles Kroncke	Bill Rentz
Phil Cooley	Larry Lang	Charles Rini
David Crary	P. Lange	John Ritchie
Brent Dalrymple	Howard Lanser	Dexter Rowell
Fred Dellva	Wayne Lee	James Sachlis
Mark Dorfman	John Lewis	Mary Jane Scheuer
David Durst	Charles Linke	Carl Schweser
Edward Dyl	Jim Longstreet	Sol Shalit
A. Edwards	Bob Magee	Ron Shrieves
John Ezzell	Phil Malone	Joe Sinkey
Mike Ferri	Terry Martell	Don Sorenson
John Finnerty	Andy McCollough	Kenneth Stanley
Dan French	Larry Merville	Don Stevens
James Garvin	James Millar	Glen Strasburg
Adam Gehr	Carol Moerdyk	Al Sweetser
Walt Goulet	Bob Moore	Philip Swensen
Edwin Grossnickle	Frederic Morrissey	Ernest Swift
John Groth	Tim Nantell	Gary Tallman
Manak Gupta	Bill Nelson	Craig Tapley
Donald Hakala	Bob Nelson	Russ Taussig
Robert Haugen	Tom O'Brien	George Trivoli
Robert Hehre	Dennis O'Connor	Mel Tysseland
George Hettenhouse	Jim Pappas	Howard Van Auken
Haws Heymann	Jim Pettijohn	Pretorius Van den Dool
Kendall Hill	Rich Pettit	Pieter Vanderburg
Pearson Hunt	Dick Pettway	Paul Vanderheiden
Kose John	Hugo Phillips	Jim Verbrugge
Craig Johnson	John Pinkerton	Tony Wingler
Keith Johnson	Gerald Pogue	Don Woods

In addition, all or major parts of the book were reviewed by the following executives: James Dunn, Financial Vice President, GT&E; Larry Hastie, former Treasurer, Bendix Corporation; Victor Leavengood, Treasurer, General Telephone of Florida; Archie Long, former Comptroller, General Motors; and James Taggart, Financial Vice President, Tampa Electric Company.

Special thanks are due to Roy Crum, who coauthored the chapter on multinational finance; to Russ Fogler, who coauthored the chapter on pension funds; to Art Herrmann, who coauthored the bankruptcy chapter; to Dilip Shome, who coauthored the capital structure chapter; and to Susan Ball and Paul Cretien, who worked on the computer programs discussed in both the text and the Instructor's Manual.

Several of our students at the University of Florida worked through all or major parts of the book and ancillaries to help us remove errors and confusing sections; included are Susan Ball and Debbie Kriebel. Melissa Davis, Bob Karp, Sue Shiels, Terry Sicherman, and Eric Smith typed and helped proof the various manuscripts. The Dryden Press staff, especially Mary Jarvis, Jane Perkins, Cate Rzasa, Judy Sarwark, Bill Schoof, Alan Wendt, Liz Widdicombe, and Lorraine Wolf, helped greatly with all phases of the revision.

Last, but certainly not least, we owe a special debt to Fred Weston, both for teaching us much of what we know about finance and for permitting us to draw from our coauthored texts.

Errors in the Text

At this point in the preface, authors of most books say something like this: "We appreciate all the help we received from the people listed above, but any remaining errors are, of course, our own responsibility." And in many books there are plenty of remaining errors. Having experienced difficulties with errors ourselves, both as students and as instructors, we resolved to avoid this problem in *Financial Management*. As a result of the error detection procedures used, we are convinced that it is virtually free of mistakes.

Some of our colleagues suggested that if we are so confident about the book's accuracy, we should offer a reward to people who find errors. With this in mind, but primarily because we want to detect any remaining errors in order to correct them in subsequent printings, we hereby offer a reward of $5 per error (misspelled word, arithmetic mistake, and the like) to the first person who reports it to us. (Any error that has follow-through effects is counted as two errors only.) Two accounting students have set up a foolproof audit system to make sure we pay off. Accounting students tend to be skeptics!

Conclusion

Finance is, in a real sense, the cornerstone of the enterprise system, so good financial management is vitally important to the economic health of business firms, and hence to the nation and the world. Because of its importance, finance should be widely and thoroughly understood, but this is easier said than done. The field is relatively complex, and it is undergoing constant change in response to shifts in economic conditions. All of this makes finance stimulating and exciting, but also challenging and sometimes perplexing. We sincerely hope that *Financial*

Management will meet its own challenge by contributing to a better understanding of the financial system.

Eugene F. Brigham
Louis C. Gapenski

Graduate School of Business Administration
University of Florida
Gainesville, Florida 32611

November 1984

Contents

Financial Management
Theory and Practice
Fourth Edition

Introduction

I

An Overview of Financial Management

1

In 1964, Eastern Airlines' stock sold for over $60 per share, while Delta's sold for $20. In the 1980s, Eastern dropped below $4, while Delta was up to $50. Delta's earnings and dividends increased steadily over the years; Eastern paid its last dividend in 1969 and it has recently been losing money. Further, Delta's employees have reasonably secure, well-paid positions, while Eastern has been laying off people and slashing the salaries of those who remain.

Although many factors helped to cause these divergent results, financial management has exerted a major influence. Eastern has traditionally used a great deal of debt, while Delta has financed primarily with common equity. (In 1984, Delta had about 50 percent equity and 50 percent debt; Eastern had about 12 percent equity and 88 percent debt.) The dramatic increase in interest rates (the prime business loan rate rose from 6 percent in the 1960s to 21 percent in the early 1980s) greatly increased Eastern's costs and lowered its profits, but it had only a minor effect on Delta. Further, when the airlines saw the need to buy new, fuel-efficient planes, because fuel prices had risen by over 1,000 percent, Delta could do so, but Eastern could not. Finally, when the airlines were deregulated in the late 1970s, Delta was strong enough to expand into developing markets and to cut prices as necessary to attract business, but Eastern was not.

Similar stories could be told about hundreds of companies in scores of industries—autos, computers, insurance, banking, or you-name-it. One company does well while another goes under, and a major reason for the divergent results is a difference in some basic financial policy. In this chapter, we shall outline the major types of financial decisions that must be made. Then, in the remainder of the book, we shall examine how these decisions should be made.

The field of *financial management* has undergone significant changes over the years. When finance first emerged as a separate field of study in the early 1900s, the emphasis was on the legal aspects of such matters as mergers, consolidations, the formation of new firms, and the various types of securities issued by corporations. Industrialization was sweeping the country, and the critical problem firms faced was obtaining capital for expansion. The capital markets were relatively primitive, making transfers of funds from individual savers to businesses difficult. The earnings and asset values reported in accounting statements were unreliable, while stock trading by insiders and manipulators caused prices to fluctuate wildly. Consequently, investors were reluctant to purchase stocks and bonds. As a result of these environmental conditions, finance in the early 1900s concentrated heavily on legal issues relating to the issuance of securities.

The emphasis remained on securities through the 1920s. However, radical changes occurred during the depression of the 1930s, when an unprecedented number of business failures caused finance to focus on bankruptcy and reorganization, on corporate liquidity, and on governmental regulation of securities markets. Finance was still a descriptive, legalistic subject, but the emphasis shifted from expansion to survival.

During the 1940s and early 1950s, finance continued to be taught as a descriptive, institutional subject, viewed from the outside rather than from the standpoint of management. However, methods of financial analysis designed to help firms maximize their profits and stock prices were beginning to receive attention.

The evolutionary pace toward rigorous analysis quickened during the late 1950s. Also, the major emphasis began to shift from the right-hand side of the balance sheet (liabilities and capital) to asset analysis. Computers were beginning to be used, and models were developed to help manage inventories, cash, accounts receivable, and fixed assets. Increasingly, the focus of finance shifted from the outsider's to the insider's point of view, as financial decisions within the firm were recognized as the critical issue in corporate finance. Descriptive, institutional materials on capital markets and financing instruments were still studied, but these topics were considered within the context of corporate financial decisions.

The 1960s and 1970s witnessed a renewed interest in the liabilities and capital side of the balance sheet, with a focus (1) on the optimal mix of securities and (2) on the way individual investors make investment decisions, or *portfolio theory*, and its implications for corporate finance. Corporate financial management is designed to help general management take actions that will maximize the value of the firm and the wealth of its stockholders; therefore, sound corporate financial decisions are dependent upon how investors are likely to react to them. *This was recognized in the 1960s and 1970s, and with this recognition came a merging of investments with corporate finance.*

Thus far in the 1980s, three issues have received emphasis: (1) inflation and how to deal with it, (2) deregulation of financial institutions and a trend away from specialized institutions and toward broadly diversified financial service corporations, and (3) a dramatic increase in the use of computers for the analysis of financial decisions. We have had to work inflation into the fabric of both financial theories and financial decision processes. Inflation has led to the creation of new financial institutions and industries—for example, money market funds and the interest rate futures markets. Older institutions have been forced into major structural changes, and it is getting harder and harder to tell a bank from a savings and loan, or an insurance company from a brokerage firm. Bank of America owns a stock brokerage firm; Merrill Lynch offers checking account services; and Sears, Roebuck is one of the largest U.S. financial institutions. Regarding computers, technological developments in the hardware and telecommunications areas, and the development of software packages that make otherwise very difficult numerical analyses relatively easy, are bringing about fundamental changes in the way managers manage. Data storage, transmittal, and retrieval abilities are reducing the "speculation" aspects of management and, at the same time, desk-top microcomputers are enabling financial managers to obtain relatively precise estimates of the effects of various courses of action.

Increasing Importance of Financial Management

These evolutionary changes have greatly increased the importance of financial management. In earlier times, the marketing manager would project sales, the engineering and production staffs would determine the assets necessary to meet these demands, and the financial manager's job was simply to raise the money needed to purchase the plant, equipment, and inventories. This mode of operation is no longer prevalent. Today, decisions are made in a much more coordinated manner, with the financial manager having direct responsibility for the control process.

Northeast Utilities can be used to illustrate this change. A few years ago, Northeast's economic forecasters would project power demand on the basis of historic trends and give these forecasts to the engineers, who would then proceed to build the new plants necessary to meet the forecasted demand. The finance group simply had the task of raising the capital the engineers told them was needed. However, inflation, environmental regulations, and other factors combined to double or even triple plant construction costs, and this caused a corresponding increase in the need for new capital. At the same time, rising fuel costs caused dramatic increases in electricity prices, which lowered demand and made some of the new construction unnecessary. Thus, Northeast found itself building plants that it did not need and, at the same time, unable to raise the capital necessary to pay for them. The price of the company's stock declined from $20 to $5. As a result of this experience, Northeast Utilities (and most other companies) now places far more emphasis on the planning and control process, and this has greatly increased the importance of the finance staff.

The direction in which business is moving, as well as the increasing importance of finance, was described recently in *Fortune*. After pointing out that well over half of today's top executives had majored in business administration, versus about 25 percent a few years earlier, *Fortune* continued:

> Career patterns have followed the educational trends. Like scientific and technical schooling, nuts-and-bolts business experience seems to have become less important. The proportion of executives with their primary experience in production, operations, engineering, design, and research and development has fallen from a third of the total to just over a quarter. And the number of top officers with legal and financial backgrounds has increased more than enough to make up the difference. Lawyers and financial men now head two out of five corporations.
>
> It is fair to assume the changes in training, and in the paths that led these men to the top, reflect the shifting priorities and needs of their corporations. In fact, the expanding size and complexity of corporate organizations, coupled with their continued expansion overseas, have increased the importance of financial planning and controls. And the growth of government regulation and of obligations companies face under law has heightened the need for legal advice. The engineer and the production man have become, in consequence, less important in management than the finance man and the lawyer.
>
> Today's chief executive officers have obviously perceived the shift in emphasis, and many of them wish they had personally been better prepared for it. Interestingly enough, a majority of them say they would have benefited from additional formal training, mainly in business administration, accounting, finance, and law.[1]

These same trends are evident at lower levels within firms of all sizes, as well as in nonprofit and governmental organizations. Thus, it is becoming increasingly important for people in marketing, accounting, production, personnel, and other areas to understand finance in order to do a good job in their own fields. Marketing people, for instance, must understand how marketing decisions affect and are affected by funds availability, by inventory levels, by excess plant capacity, and so on. Accountants, to cite another example, must understand how accounting data are used in corporate planning and viewed by investors. The function of accounting is to provide quantitative financial information for use in making economic decisions, while the main functions of financial

---

[1]Charles G. Burck, "A Group Profile of the Fortune 500 Chief Executive," *Fortune*, May 1976, 173.

management are to plan for, acquire, and utilize funds in order to max-imize the efficiency and value of the enterprise.[2]

Thus, there are financial implications in virtually all business decisions, and nonfinancial executives simply must know enough finance to work these impli-cations into their own specialized analyses.[3] This point is amplified in the following section.

The Place of Finance in a Business Organization

Organization structures vary from firm to firm, but Figure 1-1 gives a fairly typical picture of the role of finance within a business. The chief financial officer—who has the title of vice-president: finance—reports to the president. Key subordinates are the treasurer and the controller. The treasurer has direct responsibility for managing the firm's cash and mar-

Figure 1-1
Place of Finance in a Typical Business Organization

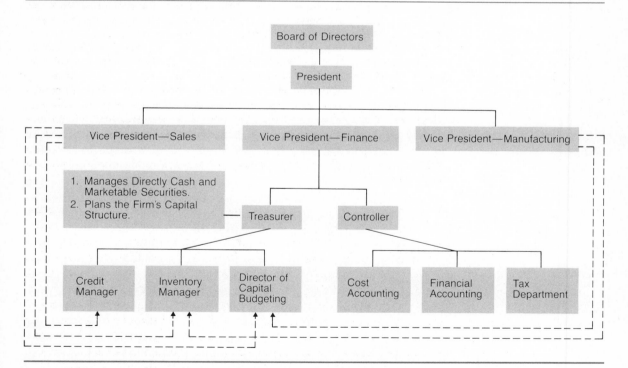

[2]American Institute of Certified Public Accountants, *Statement of the Accounting Principles Board #4* (New York, October 1970).

[3]It is an interesting fact that the course "Financial Analysis for Nonfinancial Executives" has the highest enrollment in most executive development programs.

ketable securities, for planning the financial structure, for selling stocks and bonds to raise capital, and for overseeing the corporate pension fund. Under the treasurer (but in some firms under the controller) are the credit manager, the inventory manager, and the director of capital budgeting (who analyzes decisions relating to investments in fixed assets). The controller is responsible for the activities of the accounting and tax departments.

The Goals of the Firm

Decisions are not made in a vacuum but, rather, with some objective in mind. *Throughout this book, we operate on the assumption that management's primary goal is to maximize the wealth of its stockholders.* As we shall see, this translates into *maximizing the price of the common stock*. Firms do, of course, have other objectives—managers, who make the actual decisions, are interested in their own personal satisfaction, in employees' welfare, and in the good of the community and of society at large. Still, for the reasons set forth below, *stock price maximization is the most important goal of most firms (except public utilities)*, and it is a reasonable operating objective upon which to build decision rules in a book such as this one.

Managerial Incentives to Maximize Shareholder Wealth

Stockholders own the firm and elect the management team. Management in turn is supposed to operate in the best interests of the stockholders. We know, however, that because the stock of most large firms is widely held, the managers of such firms have a great deal of autonomy. This being the case, might not managements pursue goals other than maximization of stockholder wealth? For example, some argue that the management of a large, well-entrenched corporation could work to keep stockholder returns at a "fair" or "reasonable" level and then devote part of its efforts and resources to public service activities, employee benefits, higher executive salaries, or golf.

Similarly, an entrenched management might avoid risky ventures, even when the possible gains to stockholders were high enough to warrant taking the gamble. The theory behind this argument is that stockholders are generally well diversified, holding portfolios of many different stocks, so if one company takes a chance and loses, the stockholders lose only a small part of their wealth. Managers, on the other hand, are not diversified, so setbacks affect them more seriously. Accordingly, some maintain that corporate managers tend to "play it safe" rather than aggressively seek to maximize the prices of their firms' stocks.

It is extremely difficult to determine whether a particular management team is trying to maximize shareholder wealth or is merely attempting to keep stockholders satisfied while pursuing other goals. For example, how can we tell whether voluntary employee or community benefit programs are in the long-run best interests of the stockholders? Are relatively high executive salaries really necessary to attract and retain excellent managers who in turn will keep the firm ahead of its competition? When a risky venture is turned down, does this reflect management conservatism, or is it a correct judgment regarding the risks of the venture versus its potential rewards?

It is impossible to give definitive answers to these questions. However, we do know that the managers of a firm operating in a competitive market will be forced to undertake actions that are reasonably consistent with shareholder wealth maximization. If managers depart from this goal, they run the risk of being removed from their jobs in a takeover or proxy fight.[4] Thus, while managers may have other goals in addition to stock price maximization, there are reasons to view this as the dominant goal for most firms. We shall return to this point later in the chapter.

Social Responsibility

Another issue that deserves consideration is social responsibility: Should businesses operate strictly in the stockholders' best interest, or are firms also partly responsible for the welfare of employees, customers, the communities in which they operate, and indeed for society at large? In tackling this question, consider first those firms whose rates of return on investment are close to normal, that is, close to the average for all firms. If some companies attempt to be social do-gooders, thereby increasing their costs over what they otherwise would have been, and if the other businesses in the industry do not follow suit, then the socially oriented firms would probably be forced by competition to abandon their efforts. Thus, any socially responsible acts that raise costs will be difficult, if not impossible, in industries subject to keen competition.

What about oligopolistic firms with profits above normal levels—can they not devote resources to social projects? Undoubtedly, they can; many large, successful firms do engage in community projects, employee benefit programs, and the like to a greater degree than would appear to be called for by pure profit or wealth maximization goals.[5]

---

[4]A *takeover* is a bid by one company to buy the stock of another, while a *proxy fight* involves an attempt to gain control by getting stockholders to vote a new management group into office. Both actions are facilitated by low stock prices, so self-preservation can lead management to try to keep the stock value as high as possible. However, it is quite clear from the actions taken by some managements in resisting takeover attempts that they are far more interested in their own survival as managers than in the interests of stockholders in general. The general view is that takeovers would never present a serious threat to an entrenched management team if that team had succeeded in maximizing the firm's value, for people attempt to take over undervalued, bargain companies, not fully valued ones. Still, takeover experience does make it crystal clear that many, if not most, managers are more interested in their own personal positions than in maximizing shareholder wealth per se. We shall address this issue at more length later in the chapter.

[5]Even firms such as these often find it necessary to justify such programs at stockholder meetings by stating that these programs contribute to long-run profit maximization.

Still, publicly owned firms are constrained in such actions by capital market factors. Suppose a saver who has funds to invest is considering two alternative firms. One firm devotes a substantial part of its resources to social actions, while the other concentrates on profits and stock prices. Most investors are likely to shun the socially oriented firm, thus putting it at a disadvantage in the capital market. After all, why should the stockholders of one corporation subsidize society to a greater extent than stockholders of other businesses? For this reason, even highly profitable firms (unless they are closely held rather than publicly owned) are generally constrained against taking unilateral cost-increasing social actions.

Does all this mean that firms should not exercise social responsibility? Not at all—it simply means that most cost-increasing actions may have to be put on a *mandatory* rather than a voluntary basis, at least initially, to insure that the burden of such action falls uniformly across all businesses. Thus, such social benefit programs as fair hiring practices, minority training, product safety, pollution abatement, and antitrust actions are most likely to be effective if realistic rules are established initially and then enforced by government agencies. Of course, it is critical that industry and government cooperate in establishing the rules of corporate behavior, that the costs as well as the benefits of such actions be accurately estimated and taken into account, and that firms follow the spirit as well as the letter of the law in their actions. In such a setting, the rules of the game become constraints. Throughout the book, we shall assume that managers are stock price maximizers who operate subject to a set of socially imposed constraints.

Stock Price Maximization and Social Welfare

If firms attempt to maximize stock prices, is this good or bad for society? In general, it is good. Aside from such illegal actions as attempting to form monopolies, violating safety codes, and failing to meet pollution control requirements—all of which are constrained by the government—*the same actions that maximize stock prices also benefit society*. First, stock price maximization requires efficient, low-cost operations that produce the desired quality and quantity of output at the lowest possible cost. Second, stock price maximization requires the development of products that consumers want and need, so the profit motive leads to new technology, new products, and new jobs. Finally, stock price maximization necessitates efficient and courteous service, adequate stocks of merchandise, and well-located business establishments, because these factors are all necessary to make sales, and sales are necessary for profits. *Therefore, the types of actions that help a firm increase the price of its stock are also directly beneficial to society at large.* This is why profit-motivated, free-enterprise economies have been so much more successful than socialistic and other types of economic systems. Since financial management plays a crucial role in the operation of successful firms, and since successful firms are absolutely necessary for a healthy, productive economy, it is easy to see why finance is important from a social standpoint.[6]

The Agency Problem

In a very important article, Michael Jensen and William Meckling defined an *agency relationship* as a contract under which one or more persons (the principals) hire another person (the agent) to perform some service on their behalf, and then delegate some decision-making authority to the agent.[7] Within the financial management framework, agency relationships exist (1) between stockholders and managers and (2) between bondholders (or creditors generally) and stockholders. These relationships are discussed in the following sections.

Stockholders versus Managers

Jensen and Meckling contend that an agency problem arises whenever a manager owns less than 100 percent of the firm's common stock. If a firm is solely owned and managed by a single individual, we can assume that the owner-manager will take every possible action to increase his or her own welfare. Most of the actions taken would probably be to increase personal wealth, but some could also lead to increases in leisure or perquisites.[8] If the owner-manager relinquishes a portion of his or her ownership by selling some of the firm's stock to outsiders, a potential conflict of interests will arise. For example, the manager may now decide (1) to lead a more relaxed life and not work as strenuously to maximize shareholder wealth, because less of this wealth will go to him or her, or (2) to consume more perquisites, because part of the costs of the perquisites now fall on the outside stockholders. This potential conflict between two parties, the principals (outside shareholders) and the agent (manager), is called an *agency problem*.

To insure that the manager acts in the best interests of the outside shareholders, these shareholders will have to incur *agency costs*, which

---

[6]People sometimes argue that firms, in their efforts to raise profits and stock prices, increase product prices and gouge the public. In a reasonably competitive economy, which we have, prices are constrained by competition and consumer resistance. If a firm raises its prices beyond reasonable levels, it will simply lose its market share. Even giant firms like General Motors lose business to the Japanese and Germans, as well as to Ford and Chrysler, if they do not set prices that merely cover production costs plus a ''normal'' profit. Of course, firms *want* to earn more, and they constantly try to cut costs, develop new products, and so on, and thereby earn above-normal profits. Yet, if they are successful and do earn above-normal profits, these very profits will attract competition and eventually drive prices down, so the main beneficiary is the consumer.

[7]See Michael C. Jensen and William H. Meckling, ''Theory of the Firm: Managerial Behavior, Agency Costs, and Ownership Structure,'' *Journal of Financial Economics*, October 1976, 350-360. The discussion of agency theory which follows draws heavily from their work.

[8]*Perquisites* are executive fringe benefits such as luxurious offices, use of corporate planes and yachts, personal assistants, and so on.

may take several forms: (1) expenditures to monitor managerial actions, (2) expenditures to bond the manager, (3) expenditures to structure the organization so that the possibility of undesirable managerial behavior is limited, and (4) opportunity costs associated with lost profit opportunities because the organizational structure does not permit managers to take actions on as timely a basis as would be possible if the managers were also the owners.

There are two extreme positions regarding how to solve the agency problem. First, if the manager were compensated only with shares of the firm's stock, then agency costs would be low, because the manager would have less incentive to take excessive leisure or perquisites. However, it would be difficult to hire managers under these terms. At the opposite extreme, owners could monitor closely every managerial activity, but this solution would be extremely costly and inefficient. The optimal solution lies somewhere between the extremes, where executive compensation is tied to performance, but some monitoring is also done. Several mechanisms which tend to force managers to act in the shareholders' best interests are discussed next. These include (1) the managerial labor market, (2) the threat of firing, (3) the threat of takeover, and (4) the proper structuring of managerial incentives.

Managerial Labor Market. It has been argued that the managerial labor market exerts a great deal of influence on managerial behavior, perhaps even enough to make the agency problem unimportant and not worth worrying about.[9] The argument goes like this: Managers' wealth is composed of both current wealth and the present value of future income. The better the managerial performance, as measured by stock prices, the greater will be the salary that the manager will command, both in his or her current employment and in future employment. Thus, if the capital markets (stock prices) provide efficient signals concerning managerial performance, and if the managerial labor market correctly values managerial performance, then the manager's own desire for personal wealth will provide a strong incentive for him or her to act in the shareholders' best interests.

The Threat of Firing. Until recently, the probability of a large firm's management being ousted by its stockholders was so remote that little threat was posed. This situation existed because ownership of most firms was so widely distributed, and management's control over the proxy mechanism so strong, that it was almost impossible for dissident stockholders to gain enough votes to overthrow the managers. How-

---

[9]See Eugene F. Fama, "Agency Problems and the Theory of the Firm," *Journal of Political Economy*, April 1980, 288-307.

ever, stock ownership is being increasingly concentrated in the hands of large institutions rather than individuals, and the institutional money managers have the clout, if they choose to use it, to exercise considerable influence over a firm's operations. To illustrate, consider the case of GAF Corporation, a leading producer of building materials and industrial chemicals, with 1983 sales of $699 million. Its stock price was as high as $41 in 1965, after which it began a long slide, and by 1980 it was selling at below $8. At that point, institutions began to buy heavily, and their ownership increased from 15 to 40 percent. Many bought shares on the expectation that GAF's chairman, Jesse Werner, would retire at the end of 1981 and that the company would be broken up or taken over. This expectation was fueled by the fact that Mr. Werner, who became chairman in 1964, announced in 1980 that GAF would sell eight marginally profitable businesses representing about half its sales. Analysts figured that this would make the company cash-rich and a likely takeover candidate and that the price of its stock would rise. Indeed, the stock price did more than double, from $7.75 in 1980 to $16.375 in 1981.

But Mr. Werner decided to keep his job. He obtained a new five-year contract and announced that the firm would reinvest internally most of the $212 million it had received from the sale of several unprofitable divisions. These actions caused GAF's stock price to drop back below $9.

All this prompted Samuel Heyman, a Connecticut shopping center owner who held 4.2 percent of GAF's stock, to wage a proxy fight. On April 28, 1983, at the annual meeting, Mr. Heyman received proxies representing about 60 percent of the shares, so he was able to oust Mr. Werner. The victory for the dissidents was made possible because of the support of large institutional holders. "You've got to outperform the market," explained one money manager. "If your clients have many money managers, and you're performing poorly, the meter starts running. And pretty soon you get cut from the list." Another money manager said, "There is little patience with poor management." So, whereas individual investors may be uninformed, lazy, or simply willing to "vote with their feet" by selling shares in companies whose performance is sub-par, institutional investors are more likely to work actively to oust an inefficient management. Recognizing this fact, people like Mr. Heyman are now more likely to "run against" an entrenched management than would have been true some years ago.

The Threat of Takeover. Hostile takeovers (where management does not want the firm to be taken over) are most likely to occur when a firm's stock is undervalued relative to its potential, reflecting poor managerial decisions. In a hostile takeover, the managers of the acquired firm are generally fired, and even if any are able to stay on, they lose the autonomy that they had prior to the acquisition. Thus, to avoid takeover, managers have an incentive to take actions which maximize share price. In the words of one company president, "If you want to keep control, don't let your company's stock sell at a bargain price."

Actions to increase the firm's stock price and keep it from being a bargain are obviously good from the standpoint of the stockholders, but other tactics that managers can take to ward off a hostile takeover may not be. Two examples of questionable tactics are (1) poison pills and (2) greenmail. A "poison pill" is an action which a firm can take which practically kills it and thus makes it unattractive to potential suitors. Examples include Scott Industries' sale of its most attractive assets and Lenox's threat to issue a huge quantity of convertible preferred stock. "Greenmail," which is like blackmail, occurs when this sequence of events takes place: (1) A potential acquirer (firm or individual) buys a block of stock in a company, (2) the target company's management becomes frightened that the acquirer will make a tender offer and take control of the company, and (3) to head off a possible takeover, management offers to pay greenmail, buying the stock of the potential raider at a price above the existing market price without offering the same deal to other stockholders. A good example of greenmail was Texaco's 1984 buy-back of 13 million shares of its stock from the Bass Brothers organization at a price of $50 at a time when the stock sold in the market at less than $40. As this book goes to press (summer 1984), the SEC and Congress are considering legislation to protect stockholders from poison pills, greenmail, and the like.

Structuring Managerial Incentives. More and more, firms are tying managers' compensation to the company's performance, and research suggests that this motivates managers to operate in a manner consistent with stock price maximization.[10]

Performance plans have become an accepted management tool. In the 1950s and 1960s, most of these plans involved stock options on the theory that allowing management to purchase stock at a fixed price would provide an incentive for managers to take actions which would maximize the stock's price. However, this type of managerial incentive lost favor because in the 1970s the options generally did not pay off. The whole stock market was relatively flat, and stock prices did not necessarily reflect companies' earnings growth. Incentive plans ought to be based on those factors over which managers have control, and since they cannot control the general stock market, stock option plans proved to have a weakness as an incentive device. Therefore, while 61 of the 100 largest U.S. firms used stock options as their sole incentive compen-

---

[10]See Wilbur G. Lewellen, "Management and Ownership in the Large Firm," *Journal of Finance*, May 1969, 299-322. Lewellen concluded that managers seem to make decisions that are largely oriented toward stock price maximization, and economic events since his study was published suggest that the incentives for price maximization are even stronger today than they were during the period his data covered.

sation in 1970, not even one of the largest 100 companies relied exclusively on stock options in 1983.

The main tool now is *performance shares*, which are shares of stock given to executives on the basis of performance as measured by earnings per share, return on assets, return on equity, and so on. For example, Honeywell uses growth in earnings per share as its primary performance measure. The firm has two overlapping four-year performance periods, beginning two years apart. At the beginning of each period, the participating executives are allocated a certain number of performance shares, say 10,000 shares for the president down to 1,000 shares for a lower-ranking manager. If the company achieves, say, a targeted 13 percent annual average growth in earnings per share, the managers will earn 100 percent of their shares. If the corporate performance is above the target, they can earn even more shares, up to a maximum of 130 percent, which requires a 16 percent growth rate. However, if growth is below 13 percent, they get less than 100 percent of the shares, and below a 9 percent growth rate, they get zero.

Notice that performance shares have a value even if the company's stock price does nothing because of a poor general stock market, whereas under similar conditions, stock options could have no value even though managers had been successful in boosting earnings. Of course, the *value* of the shares received is dependent on market price performance, because 1,000 shares of Honeywell stock are a lot more valuable if the stock sells for $200 than if it sells for only $100.

All incentive compensation plans—executive stock options, performance shares, profit-based bonuses, and so forth—are supposed to accomplish two purposes. First, they offer executives incentives to act on those factors under their control in a manner that will contribute to stock price maximization. Second, the existence of such performance plans helps companies attract and retain top-level executives. Well-designed plans certainly can accomplish these goals.

Leveraged Buyouts. One other type of action that represents a potential conflict between management and stockholders is a *leveraged buyout*, a term used to describe the situation when management itself (1) arranges a line of credit, (2) makes a tender offer for the stock not already owned by the management group, and (3) "takes the company private" after it buys the outstanding shares. Dozens of such buyouts of New York Stock Exchange listed companies have occurred recently, and a potential conflict clearly exists whenever one is contemplated. For example, suppose Firm A's management decides to make a leveraged buyout offer to the outside stockholders. It would then be in management's best interests to have the stock price *minimized*, not maximized, prior to the offer. Aware of this, most managements who contemplate leveraged buyouts obtain outside opinions as to the value of the stock. Further, if the price offered by management is too low, another party will step in and make a competing offer. Nevertheless, management does have more information about the company than anyone else, and leveraged buyouts do constitute a type of agency problem.

Stockholders versus Creditors

The second agency problem arises because of potential conflicts between stockholders and creditors. Creditors lend funds to the firm at rates which are based on (1) the riskiness of the firm's existing assets; (2) expectations concerning the riskiness of future asset additions; (3) the firm's existing capital structure, that is, the amount of debt financing it uses; and (4) expectations concerning future capital structure changes. These are the factors that determine the riskiness of the firm's cash flows, and hence the safety of its debt issues, so the creditors set their required rates of return, and hence the cost of debt to the firm, on these expectations.

Now suppose the stockholders, acting through management, cause the firm to take on new projects that have greater risks than were anticipated by the creditors. This would cause the required rate of return on the firm's debt to increase, which in turn would cause the value of the outstanding debt to fall.[11] If the riskier capital investments turn out to be successful, all of the benefits would go to the stockholders, because the creditors get only a fixed return. What we would have, from the stockholders' point of view, is a game of "heads I win, tails you lose," which is not a good game from the creditors' standpoint. Similarly, if the firm increases its leverage in an effort to boost profits, then the value of the old debt will decrease because the old debt's bankruptcy protection will be lessened by the issuance of the new debt. In both of these situations, stockholders would be expropriating wealth from the firms' creditors.

Does this mean that stockholders, through their managers/agents, should try to expropriate wealth from the firm's creditors? In general, the answer is no. First, because such attempts have been made in the past, creditors today protect themselves against such stockholder actions through restrictions in credit agreements. Second, if creditors perceive that the firm is trying to maximize shareholder wealth at the creditors' expense, they will either refuse to deal further with the firm or else require much higher than normal rates of return to compensate for the risks of such possible exploitation. Thus, firms which try to deal unfairly with creditors either lose access to the debt markets or are saddled with higher interest rates and consequently lower returns on equity, and generally with a decrease in the long-run value of the stock.

In view of these constraints, it follows that the goal of maximizing shareholder wealth is also consistent with fair play with creditors. Stock-

---

[11]Basically, the higher the required rate of return on an existing debt issue, the lower its value. In Chapter 5 we will present some models which illustrate this point.

holder wealth depends on continued access to capital markets, and access depends on fair play and abiding by both the letter and the spirit of contracts and agreements. Therefore, the managers, as agents of both the creditors and the shareholders, must act in a manner which is fairly balanced between the interests of both classes of security holders.

Additionally, because of other constraints and sanctions, management actions which would expropriate wealth from the firm's employees, customers, suppliers, or community will ultimately be to the detriment of shareholders. We conclude, then, that in our society the goal of shareholder wealth maximization in the long run also implies the fair treatment of all other groups whose economic position is affected by the performance, and hence value, of the firm.

Managerial Actions to Maximize Shareholder Wealth

Assuming that a firm's management team does indeed seek to maximize the long-run value of its stock, what types of actions should it take? First, consider the question of stock prices versus profits: Will profit maximization also result in stock price maximization? In answering this question, we must analyze the matter of total corporate profits versus earnings per share (EPS). For example, suppose Company X had 1 million shares outstanding and earned $2 million, or $2 per share, and you owned 100 shares of the stock, so your share of the total profits was $200. Now suppose the company sold another 1 million shares and invested the funds received in assets which produced $1 million of income. Total income would rise to $3 million, but earnings per share would decline from $2 to $3,000,000/2,000,000 shares = $1.50. Now your share of the firm's earnings would be only $150, down from $200. You (and the other original stockholders) would have suffered an earnings dilution, even though total corporate profits had risen. Therefore, other things held constant, *if management is interested in the well-being of its existing stockholders, it should concentrate on earnings per share rather than on total corporate profits.*

Will maximization of expected earnings per share always maximize stockholder welfare, or should other factors be considered? Think about the *timing of the earnings.* Suppose one project would cause earnings per share to rise by $0.20 per year for 5 years, or $1.00 in total, while another project would have no effect on earnings for 4 years but would increase earnings by $1.25 in the fifth year. Which project is better? In other words, is $0.20 per year for 5 years as good as $1.25 in Year 5? The answer depends on which project adds the most to the value of the stock, which in turn depends on the time value of money to investors. Thus, timing is an important reason to concentrate on wealth as measured by the price of the stock rather than on earnings alone.

Still another issue relates to *risk.* Suppose one project is expected to increase earnings per share by $1.00, while another is expected to raise earnings by $1.20 per share. The first project is not very risky; if it is undertaken, earnings will almost certainly rise by about $1.00 per share. The other project is quite risky, so while our best guess is that earnings will rise by $1.20 per share, we must recognize the possibility that there may be no increase whatsoever. Depending on how averse stockholders are to risk, the first project may be preferable to the second.

The riskiness inherent in projected earnings per share (EPS) also depends on *how the firm is financed*. As we shall see, many firms go bankrupt every year, and the greater the use of debt, the greater the threat of bankruptcy. *Consequently, while the use of debt financing may increase projected EPS, debt also increases the riskiness of these projected earnings.*

Still another issue is the matter of paying dividends to stockholders versus retaining earnings and reinvesting them in the firm, thereby causing the earnings stream to grow over time. Stockholders like cash dividends, but they also like the growth in EPS that results from plowing earnings back into the business. The financial manager must decide exactly how much of the current earnings should be paid out as dividends rather than retained and reinvested—this is called the *dividend policy decision*. The optimal dividend policy is the one that maximizes the firm's stock price.

We see, then, that the firm's stock price is dependent on the following factors:

1. projected earnings per share,
2. riskiness of these projected earnings,
3. timing of the earnings stream,
4. manner of financing the firm, and
5. dividend policy.

Every significant corporate decision should be analyzed in terms of its effect on these factors, and hence on the price of the firm's stock. For example, suppose Rocky Mountain Coal is considering opening a new mine. If the mine is opened, can it be expected to increase EPS? Is there a chance that costs will exceed estimates, that prices and output will fall below projections, and that EPS will be reduced because the new mine was opened? How long will it take for the new mine to start showing a profit? How should the capital required to open the mine be raised? If debt is used, how much will this increase Rocky Mountain's riskiness? Should the firm reduce its current dividends and use the cash thus saved to finance the project, or should it maintain its dividends and finance the mine with external capital? Financial management is designed to help answer such questions as these, plus many more.

The Economic Environment

Although managers can take actions which affect the values of their firms' stocks, there are additional factors which influence stock prices. Included among them are external constraints, the general level of eco-

Figure 1-2
Summary of Major Factors Affecting Stock Prices

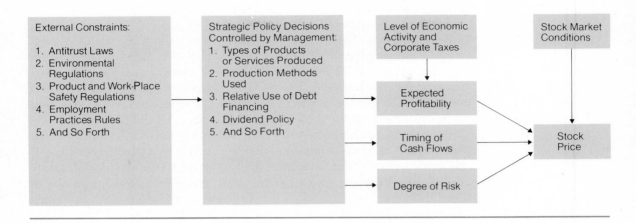

nomic activity, taxes, and conditions in the stock market. Figure 1-2 diagrams these general relationships. Working within the set of external constraints shown in the box at the extreme left, management makes a set of long-run strategic policy decisions which chart a future course for the firm. These policy decisions, along with the general level of economic activity and the level of corporate income taxes, influence the firm's expected profitability, the timing of its earnings, the eventual transfer of earnings to stockholders in the form of dividends, and the degree of uncertainty (or risk) inherent in projected earnings and dividends. Profitability, timing, and risk all affect the price of the firm's stock, but so does another factor, the state of the stock market as a whole, for all stock prices tend to move up and down together to some extent.

Organization of the Book

Part I contains chapters with fundamental background materials and concepts upon which the book builds. Finance cannot be studied in a vacuum—financial decisions are made within an economic and social environment which has a profound influence on these decisions. Therefore, this background is provided in Chapters 1, 2, and 3.

The specific tasks of financial managers include (1) coordinating the planning process, (2) administering the control process, (3) handling the specialized finance functions such as raising capital, and (4) analyzing strategic long-term investment decisions which have a major influence on the firm's long-run future. To perform these tasks properly, it is necessary to estimate stockholders' reactions to alternative actions or events and to know the firm's cost of capital. Accordingly, the major goal of

Part II is to develop a set of *valuation models* which can be used to gain insights into how different actions are likely to affect the value of the firm's securities and the cost of its capital. Therefore, some basic concepts and models are developed in Chapters 4 through 7 for use throughout the remainder of the book.

Beginning with Part III, we move into the execution phase of the long-range strategic planning process. In Chapters 8, 9, and 10, we consider the vital subject of long-term investment decisions, or capital budgeting. Since major capital expenditures take years to plan and execute, and since decisions in this area are generally not reversible and affect operations for many years, their impact on the value of the firm is obvious.

Part IV sets forth the conceptual framework for an analysis of how the firm should raise the capital needed to finance its capital expenditures. Here we consider two fundamentally important issues—capital structure and dividend policy. Capital structure is, essentially, the firm's mix of debt and equity, while dividend policy relates to the issue of how much of its earnings the firm should retain and invest versus pay out to the stockholders as dividends.

Part V focuses on the specific types of long-term capital available to the firm, and it addresses these three questions: What are the principal sources and forms of long-term capital? How are the terms on each type of security established? And how can the financial manager negotiate the best price for each type of capital?

In Part VI, we examine current, ongoing operations as opposed to long-term strategic decisions. From accounting, we know that assets which are expected to be converted to cash within a year, such as inventories and accounts receivable, are called *current assets*, and liabilities which must be paid off within a year are called *current liabilities*. The management of current assets and current liabilities is known as *working capital management*, and Part VI deals with this topic.

In Parts I through VI, we focus on specific decisions which have a major impact on the firm's position and value. Then, in Part VII, we show how these separate pieces are pulled together and analyzed as a cohesive whole. Here we first discuss the analysis of financial statements to determine the firm's current strengths and weaknesses, and then we go on to look at the planning and control process.

Finally, in Part VIII, we consider some subjects that, while important, are best studied within the general framework of financial management as developed in Parts I through VII. Included here are mergers, bankruptcy, multinational operations, and pension fund management.

Summary

This chapter has provided an overview of financial management. We began with a brief review of the evolution of finance as an academic discipline, tracing developments from 1900 to the present. We next examined the place of finance in the firm, and we saw that the financial manager has been playing an increasingly important role in the organization. We also considered the goals of financial management, and we concluded that *the key goal in most publicly owned firms is stock price maximization.*

However, there does exist the potential for conflicts of interest between shareholders and managers, and between shareholders and creditors. These conflicts are called *agency problems.* There are a number of incentives to motivate managers to act in the best interest of stockholders, including (1) the managerial labor market, (2) the threat of firing, (3) the threat of takeovers, and (4) properly structured managerial compensation packages. Thus, in a competitive economy, where managers serve at the pleasure of stockholders, stock price maximization must, in general, be the dominant goal.

The book's organization reflects this primary goal. First, we discuss the economic and social environment, and then we develop valuation models that can be used to show how corporate actions affect stock prices. Then, in the remainder of the book, we examine actions that management can take to help maximize the price of the firm's stock.

Questions

1-1 Define each of the following terms:
   a. Profit maximization; stockholder wealth maximization
   b. Earnings per share; price per share
   c. Social responsibility
   d. Normal profits; normal rate of return
   e. Dividend policy
   f. Agency problem; agency costs
   g. Proxy fight
   h. Takeover, tender offer
   i. Performance shares
   j. Leveraged buyout
   k. Poison pill; greenmail

1-2 Would the "normal" rate of return on investment be the same in all industries? Would "normal" rates of return change over time? Explain.

1-3 Would the role of the financial manager be likely to increase or decrease in importance relative to other executives if the rate of inflation increased? Explain.

1-4 Should stockholder wealth maximization be thought of as a long-run or a short-run goal; for example, if one action would probably increase the firm's stock price from a current level of $20 to $25 in 6 months and then to $30 in 5 years, but another action would probably keep the stock at $20 for several years but then increase it to $40 in 5 years, which action would be better? Can you think of actual examples which might have these general tendencies?

1-5 Drawing on your background in accounting, can you think of any accounting procedure differences which might make it difficult to establish the relative performance of different firms?

1-6   Would the management of a firm in an oligopolistic or in a competitive industry be more likely to engage in what might be called "socially conscious" practices? Explain your reasoning.

1-7   What is the difference between stock price maximization and profit maximization? Would profit maximization not lead to stock price maximization?

1-8   If you were running a large, publicly owned corporation, would you make decisions to maximize stockholder's welfare or your own interests? What are some actions stockholders could take to insure that your interests and theirs coincided? What are some other factors which might influence your actions?

1-9   The president of Union Manufacturing Corporation made this statement in the company's annual report: "Union's primary goal is to increase the value of the common stockholders' equity over time." Later on in the report, the following announcements were made:

a. The company contributed $1 million to the symphony orchestra in the headquarters' city.

b. The company is spending $300 million to open a new plant in South America. No revenues will be produced by the plant for 3 years, so earnings will be depressed during this period versus what they would have been had the decision been made not to open the new plant.

c. The company is increasing its relative use of debt. Whereas assets were formerly financed with 40 percent debt and 60 percent equity, henceforth the financing mix will be 50-50.

d. The company uses a great deal of electricity in its manufacturing operations, and it generates most of this power itself. Plans are to utilize nuclear fuel, rather than coal, to produce electricity in the future.

Discuss how each of these factors might affect Union's stock price.

Selected Additional References

For a good summary of financial management, see

Pogue, Gerald A., and Kishore Lall, "Corporate Finance: An Overview," *Sloan Management Review*, Spring 1974, 19-38.

For alternative views on firms' goals and objectives, see the following articles:

Anthony, Robert N., "The Trouble with Profit Maximization," *Harvard Business Review*, November-December 1960, 126-134.

Donaldson, Gordon, "Financial Goals: Management versus Stockholders," *Harvard Business Review*, May-June 1963, 116-129.

Elliot, J. Walter, "Control, Size, Growth, and Financial Performance in the Firm," *Journal of Financial and Quantitative Analysis*, January 1972, 1309-1320.

Seitz, Neil, "Shareholder Goals, Firm Goals and Firm Financing Decisions," *Financial Management*, Autumn 1982, 20-26.

The following articles extend our discussion of the agency problem:

Barnea, Amir, Robert A. Haugen, and Lemma W. Senbet, "Market Imperfections, Agency Problems, and Capital Structure: A Review," *Financial Management*, Summer 1981, 7-22.

Hand, John H., William P. Lloyd, and Robert B. Rogow, "Agency Relationships in the Close Corporation," *Financial Management*, Spring 1982, 25-30.

For a general review of the state of the art in academic finance, together with an extensive bibliography of key research articles, see

Beranek, William, "Research Directions in Finance," *Quarterly Review of Economics and Business*, Spring 1981, 6-24.

Cooley, Philip L., and J. Louis Heck, "Significant Contributions to Finance Literature," *Financial Management*, Tenth Anniversary Issue, 1981, 23-33.

Weston, J. Fred, "Developments in Finance Theory," *Financial Management*, Tenth Anniversary Issue, 1981, 5-22.

For more information on managerial compensation, see

Cooley, Philip L., and Charles E. Edwards, "Ownership Effects on Managerial Salaries in Small Business," *Financial Management*, Winter 1982, 5-9.

Lewellen, Wilbur G., and Blaine Huntsman, "Managerial Pay and Corporate Performance," *American Economic Review*, September 1970, 710-720.

Business Organizations, Financial Statements, and Taxes

2

Companies such as Hewlett-Packard often begin life as proprietorships, then convert to partnerships, and finally evolve into corporations. Why would this pattern emerge? How does form of organization affect the risk, returns, and growth opportunities—and hence the market value—of a business firm?

We all know that taxes are a necessary evil, but how does our tax system operate, and how does it affect business income, the cash flows businesses pass on to their owners, and hence their stock prices? Are there legitimate actions which firms can take to minimize the tax bite and, consequently, raise their after-tax incomes? As we shall see, taxes take a large share of firms' incomes, and when business incomes are passed on to investors in the form of interest, dividends, and capital gains, the government takes a further bite. Because of this, a knowledge of the tax system is essential to sound financial decisions.

Financial management cannot be studied in a vacuum—if the value of a firm is to be maximized, the financial manager must understand the legal environment in which financial decisions are made. Further, value depends on the *usable income* available to investors, and this means the *after-tax income*. Accordingly, this chapter presents some background information on forms of business organizations, the major types of business securities, and the federal income tax system.[1]

---

[1]This chapter contains essential information, but many business students will have been exposed to some or all of it in economics, accounting, or business law courses. Even if they have not, the material is both straightforward and descriptive. Therefore, some instructors may require students to cover Chapter 2 on their own.

Alternative Forms of Business Organization

There are three major forms of business organization: the sole proprietorship, the partnership, and the corporation. In terms of numbers, about 80 percent of business firms are operated as sole proprietorships, while the remainder are divided equally between partnerships and corporations. By dollar value of sales, however, about 80 percent of business is conducted by corporations, about 13 percent by sole proprietorships, and about 7 percent by partnerships. Since most business is conducted by corporations, we shall concentrate on them in this book, but it is important to understand the differences among each of the three forms, as well as the advantages and disadvantages of each.

Sole Proprietorship

A *proprietorship* is a business owned by one individual. Going into business as a single proprietor is very simple—one merely begins business operations. However, most cities require even the smallest establishments to be licensed, and occasionally state licenses are required as well.

The proprietorship has several important advantages for small operations. It is easily and inexpensively formed, since no formal charter for operations is required, and a proprietorship is subject to few government regulations. Further, the business pays no corporate income taxes; however, all earnings of the firm, whether they are reinvested in the business or withdrawn, are subject to personal income taxes.

The proprietorship also has important limitations. First, as we shall see shortly, it is difficult for a proprietorship to obtain large sums of capital. Second, the proprietor has unlimited personal liability for business debts. And third, the life of a business organized as a proprietorship is limited to the life of the individual who created it. For all of these reasons, the individual proprietorship is restricted primarily to small business operations. *However, businesses are frequently started as proprietorships and then converted to corporations if and when their growth causes the disadvantages of the proprietorship form to outweigh its advantages.*

Partnership

A *partnership* exists whenever two or more persons associate to conduct a business. Partnerships may operate under different degrees of formality, ranging from informal, oral understandings to formal agreements filed with the secretary of the state in which the partnership does business. The major advantage of a partnership is its low cost and ease of formation. The disadvantages are similar to those associated with proprietorships: (1) unlimited liability, (2) limited life of the organization, (3) difficulty of transferring ownership, and (4) difficulty of raising large amounts of capital. The tax treatment of a partnership is similar to that for proprietorships, and when compared to that of a corporation, this can be either an advantage or a disadvantage, depending on the situation; this point is discussed later in the chapter.

Regarding liability, the partners must all risk their personal assets, even those not invested in the business, for under partnership law, the partners are liable for the business's debts. This means that if any partner is unable to meet his or her pro rata claim in the event the partnership goes bankrupt, the remaining partners must take over the unsatisfied claims, drawing on their personal assets if necessary.[2]

The first three disadvantages—unlimited liability, impermanence of the organization, and difficulty of transferring ownership—combine to cause the fourth, the difficulty partnerships have in attracting substantial amounts of capital. This is no particular problem for a slow-growing business, but if a business's products really catch on, and it needs to raise large amounts of capital to expand and thus capitalize on its opportunities, the difficulty in attracting large amounts of capital becomes a real drawback. Thus, companies such as Hewlett-Packard and Apple Computer generally begin life as proprietorships or partnerships, but at some point they find it necessary to convert into corporations.

Corporation

A *corporation* is a legal entity or "person" created by a state. It is separate and distinct from its owners and managers. This separateness gives the corporation three major advantages: (1) It has an *unlimited life*—it can continue after its original owners and managers are deceased. (2) It permits *easy transferability of ownership interest* in the firm, since ownership interests can be divided into shares of stock, which can be transferred far more easily than can partnership interests. (3) It permits *limited liability*. To illustrate, if you invested $10,000 in a partnership which then went bankrupt owing a considerable sum of money, you could be assessed for a share of these debts. Thus, an investor in a partnership is exposed to unlimited liability. On the other hand, if you invested $10,000 in the stock of a corporation, your potential loss on the investment would be $10,000—your liability would be limited to the amount of your investment in the business.[3]

While a proprietorship or a partnership can commence operations without much paperwork, setting up a corporation is a bit more involved. The incorporators must prepare a charter and a set of bylaws. The *charter* includes the following information: (1) name of the proposed corporation, (2) type of activities it will pursue, (3) amount of capital

---

[2] However, it is possible to limit the liabilities of some of the partners by establishing a *limited partnership*, wherein certain partners are designated *general partners* and others *limited partners*. Limited partnerships are quite common in the area of real estate investment, but they do not work well with most types of businesses.

[3] In the case of small corporations, the limited liability feature is often a fiction, since bankers and credit managers frequently require personal guarantees from the stockholders of small, weak businesses.

stock, (4) number of directors, and (5) names and addresses of directors. The charter is filed with the secretary of the state in which the firm will be headquartered, and when it is approved, the corporation is officially in existence.

The *bylaws* are a set of rules drawn up by the founders of the corporation to aid in governing the internal management of the company. Included are such points as (1) how directors are to be elected (all elected each year or, say, one-third each year); (2) whether the existing stockholders shall have the first right to buy any new shares the firm issues; and (3) what provisions there are for management committees, such as an executive committee or a finance committee, and their duties. Also included is the procedure for changing the bylaws themselves, should conditions require it. Lawyers have standard form charters and bylaws in their word processors, and can set up a corporation with very little effort. For about $500—less if you find a hungry young lawyer fresh out of law school—a business can be incorporated.

The value of any business other than a very small one will probably be maximized if the business is organized as a corporation. The reasons are as follows:

1. Limited liability reduces risk to investors, and the lower the firm's risk, other things held constant, the higher its value.

2. Value is dependent on growth opportunities, which in turn are dependent on a firm's ability to attract capital. Since corporations can attract capital more easily than unincorporated businesses, they have superior growth opportunities.

3. The value of an asset also depends on its *liquidity*, which means the ease of selling the asset and converting it to cash. Since an investment in the stock of a corporation is much more liquid than a similar investment in a proprietorship or partnership, this too means that the corporate form of organization can enhance the value of a business.

4. Corporations are taxed differently than proprietorships and partnerships, and under certain conditions, the tax laws favor corporations. This point is discussed in detail later in the chapter.

Since most firms are managed with value maximization in mind, it is easy to see why most business is conducted by corporations.

Business Securities

Irrespective of its form of organization, any business must have *assets* if it is to operate, and in order to acquire assets, the firm must raise *capital*. Capital comes in two basic forms, *debt* and *equity*. There are many different types of debt—long-term and short-term, interest-bearing and non-interest-bearing, secured and unsecured, and so on. Similarly, there are different types of equity. The equity of a proprietorship is called *proprietor's interest* or *proprietor's net worth*, and for a partnership, the word *partner* is inserted in lieu of *proprietor*. For a corporation, equity is represented by *preferred stock* and *common stockholders' equity*. Common equity, in turn, includes both *paid-in capital* and *retained earnings*.

Table 2-1 shows a simplified balance sheet for Teletron Electronics Company, a large electronic components manufacturer, as of December 31, 1984. Teletron began life in 1951 as a proprietorship, then became a partnership, and finally converted to a corporation in 1962. Its 1984 sales were $401 million, and the $280 million of assets shown in Table 2-1 were necessary to support these sales. Teletron and other companies obtain the bulk of the funds used to buy assets (1) by buying on credit from their suppliers (accounts payable); (2) by borrowing from banks, insurance companies, pension funds, and other institutions; (3) from the sale of preferred and common stock to investors; and (4) by "saving money" as reflected in the retained earnings account.[4] Also, since wages and taxes are not paid on a daily basis, Teletron obtains some "credit" from its labor force and from the government in the form of accrued wages and taxes.

Table 2-1
Teletron Electronics Company:
Balance Sheet as of December 31, 1984
(Thousands of Dollars)

Assets		Claims on Assets	
Cash and marketable securities	$ 12,081	Accounts payable	$ 23,818
		Notes payable to banks	30,000
Accounts receivable	50,262	Accrued wages and taxes	2,568
Inventories	91,611	Other current liabilities	5,151
Prepaid expenses and other current assets	1,605	Total current liabilities	$ 61,537
Total current assets	$155,559	Long-term bonds	107,015
Net fixed assets	124,718	Preferred stock (111,500 shares)	11,150
		Common stockholders' equity:	
		Common stock and paid-in capital (1,706,351 shares)	10,375
		Retained earnings	90,200
		Total common equity	$100,575
Total assets	$280,277	Total claims	$280,277

---

[4]Corporate saving occurs whenever a company pays dividends which are less than its net income. The savings that have accumulated since the company began are reported as retained earnings on its balance sheet.

The first claim against Teletron's income and assets is by its creditors—all those claims items listed on the balance sheet above preferred stock. However, the creditors' claims are limited to fixed amounts; for example, most of the long-term debt bears interest at a rate of 9 percent per year, so the bondholders, in total, get interest of about 0.09 x $107,015,000 = $9,631,350 per year. If Teletron did extremely well and had profits of, say, $80 million, the bondholders would still get only $9.6 million. However, if Teletron lost money, the bondholders would nevertheless get their $9.6 million—assets would be sold, the cash would be used to pay the bond interest, and common equity would be reduced. Further, if the company's situation were so bad that it simply could not generate the cash needed to make the required payments to the bondholders and other creditors, then as a rule (1) it would be forced into bankruptcy, (2) the assets would be sold off (generally at less than the values stated on the balance sheet), and (3) the creditors would have first claim on the proceeds from the bankruptcy liquidation.

The preferred stockholders stand next in line, after the creditors, for the firm's income and assets. Teletron has 111,500 shares of preferred stock, each with a par value of $100. This preferred pays a dividend of $8.125 per year, or 8.125 percent on its $100 par value. The preferred dividends must be paid before any dividends can be paid on the common, and in the event of bankruptcy, the preferred must be paid off in full before anything goes to the common stockholders.[5]

Teletron has 1,706,351 shares of common stock outstanding. Investors actually paid about $6.08, on the average, for these shares ($10,375,000/ 1,706,351 = $6.08), but the company has saved (or retained) $90,200,000/ 1,706,351 = $52.86 per share since it was incorporated in 1962. Therefore, stockholders, on the average, have a total investment of $6.08 + $52.86 = $58.94 per share in the company; this is the stock's *book value*.

Teletron's debt and preferred stock is held primarily by its suppliers, five banks, and some institutions such as life insurance companies and pension funds: The debt is rarely if ever traded, since this particular set of investors tends to hold debt until it matures. Teletron's common stock, on the other hand, is listed on an exchange and is traded fairly actively. Individuals own about 65 percent of the stock, while institu-

---

[5]The status of the different types of investors, and bankruptcy proceedings in general, are discussed in more detail in Chapters 14, 15, and 25. As a general rule, here is the order of priority of different claimants in the event of bankruptcy: (1) secured creditors for the proceeds from the sale of the specific assets securing specific loans, such as a building which secures a mortgage; (2) federal and state governments for accrued taxes; (3) employees for accrued wages and unfunded pension benefits; (4) other creditors; (5) preferred stockholders; and (6) common stockholders. Further, contracts can and are written to give certain of the "other creditors" priority over others. This priority system has a major effect on the riskiness and consequently on the rates of return on different classes of securities.

tions own the remaining 35 percent; these are typical percentages. In the fall of 1984, the stock traded in the general range of $60 to $70 per share, and it has ranged from a high of $75 to a low of $10 over the past 12 years. The price rises and falls depending on (1) how the company is doing at a given point in time, (2) what is happening to other stock prices, and (3) most important, how investors expect the company to do in the future. The *market value* (or price) does not depend directly on, and is usually different from, the book value. We will return to the question of stock price valuation in Chapter 5.

The Federal Income Tax System

The value of any financial asset, such as stocks or bonds, and most real assets, such as plants or even whole firms, depends on the stream of *usable* income produced by the asset. Usable income means income *after taxes*. Proprietorship and partnership income must be reported and taxed as personal income to the owners. Most corporations must first pay taxes on their own income, and stockholders must then pay taxes on corporate after-tax income distributed to them as dividends. Therefore, consideration must be given to both *personal* and *corporate* income taxes.

Federal income tax rates for individuals go up to 50 percent, and when state income taxes are included, the marginal tax rate on an individual's income can approach 70 percent. Business income is also taxed heavily. The income from partnerships and proprietorships is reported by the individual owners and consequently taxed at rates going up to about 70 percent, while corporate profits are subject to federal income tax rates of up to 46 percent, in addition to state income taxes. Because of the magnitude of the tax bite, taxes play an important role in many financial decisions.

Taxes are so complicated that university law schools offer master's degrees in taxation to practicing lawyers, many of whom also have CPA licenses. In a field complicated enough to warrant such detailed study, we can only cover the highlights. This is all that is really necessary, because business people and investors should and do rely on tax specialists rather than trust their own limited knowledge. Still, it is important to know the basic elements of the tax system as a starting point for discussions with tax experts.

Individual Income Taxes

Individuals pay taxes on wages and salaries, on investment income (dividends, interest, and profits from the sale of securities), and on the profits of proprietorships and partnerships. Our tax rates are *progressive*; that is, the higher the income, the larger the percentage paid in taxes.

Table 2-2
Individual Tax Rates in 1984

	Single Individuals			Married Couples Filing Joint Returns		
If Your Taxable Income Is	You Pay this Amount on the Base of the Bracket (Tax on Base)	Plus this Percentage on the Excess over the Base (Marginal Rate)		If Your Taxable Income Is	You Pay this Amount on the Base of the Bracket (Tax on Base)	Plus this Percentage on the Excess over the Base (Marginal Rate)
Up to $2,300	No tax	—		Up to $3,400	No tax	—
$2,300 to $3,400	$ 0	11%		$3,400 to $5,500	$ 0	11%
$3,400 to $4,400	121	12		$5,500 to $7,600	231	12
$4,400 to $6,500	241	14		$7,600 to $11,900	483	14
$6,500 to $8,500	535	15		$11,900 to $16,000	1,085	16
$8,500 to $10,800	835	16		$16,000 to $20,200	1,741	18
$10,800 to $12,900	1,203	18		$20,200 to $24,600	2,497	22
$12,900 to $15,000	1,581	20		$24,600 to $29,900	3,465	25
$15,000 to $18,200	2,001	23		$29,900 to $35,200	4,790	28
$18,200 to $23,500	2,737	26		$35,200 to $45,800	6,274	33
$23,500 to $28,800	4,115	30		$45,800 to $60,000	9,772	38
$28,800 to $34,100	5,705	34		$60,000 to $85,600	15,168	42
$34,100 to $41,500	7,507	38		$85,600 to $109,400	25,920	45
$41,500 to $55,300	10,319	42		$109,400 to $162,400	36,630	49
$55,300 to $81,800	16,115	48		Over $162,400	62,600	50
Over $81,800	28,835	50				

Table 2-2 gives the current tax rates for single individuals and married couples filing joint returns under the rate schedules that existed in 1984.[6]

Here are the highlights of the table:

1. *Taxable income* is defined as gross income less a set of deductions which are spelled out in the instructions to the tax forms people must file (Forms 1040, 1040A, or 1040EZ).

2. The *marginal tax rate* is the tax on the last unit of income; marginal tax rates are zero on the first units of income, but they rise to 50 percent.

3. One can calculate *average tax rates* from the data in the table. For example, if Jane Vincent, a single individual, had a taxable income of $30,000 in 1984, then her tax bill would be $5,705 + 0.34($30,000 − $28,800) = $5,705 + 0.34($1,200) = $6,113. Her *average tax rate* would be $6,113/$30,000 = 0.204 = 20.4% versus a *marginal rate* of 34 percent. If Jane received a raise of $1,000, to $31,000, she would have to pay $340 of it as taxes, so her net raise would be $660.

4. It is not shown in the table, but Congress committed itself (though it could change its mind) to *index tax rates* beyond 1984 to avoid the *bracket*

---

[6]It should be noted that Congress changes the tax laws fairly often. The provisions given here are those for 1984 as they existed in the fall of 1984.

creep which occurred during the 1970s and which de facto raised tax rates substantially.[7]

Taxes on Dividend and Interest Income. Dividend and interest income received by individuals from corporate securities is taxed at rates going up to 50 percent. Since corporations pay dividends out of earnings that have already been taxed, there is *double taxation* of corporate income. However, the first $100 of dividend income ($200 for married couples filing joint returns) is *excluded* from personal income taxes.

It should be noted that under U.S. tax laws, interest on state and local government bonds, called *municipals* or *"munis,"* is not subject to federal income taxes. Thus, investors get to keep more of the interest paid on municipal bonds than on bonds issued by corporations or by the U.S. government. This means that a lower-yielding muni can provide the same after-tax return as a higher-yielding corporate bond. For example, a taxpayer in the 34 percent marginal tax bracket would receive as much after-tax income by owning a 6.6 percent state bond as by owning a 10 percent corporate or U.S. Treasury bond:

$$
\begin{aligned}
\text{After-tax yield} &= \text{Before-tax yield} - \text{Taxes} \\
&= \text{Before-tax yield} - (\text{Before-tax yield})T \\
&= \text{Before-tax yield}(1 - T) \\
&= 10\%(1 - 0.34) \\
&= 10\%(0.66) = 6.6\%.
\end{aligned}
$$

Here T is the investor's marginal tax rate. This exemption from federal taxes stems from the separation of federal and state powers, and its primary purpose is to help state and local governments borrow at lower rates than would otherwise be available to them.

Capital Gain versus Ordinary Income. Assets such as stocks, bonds, and real estate are defined as *capital assets*. If you buy a capital asset and later sell it for more than your purchase price, the profit is defined as a *capital gain*. If you suffer a loss, it is called a *capital loss*.

---

[7]*Bracket creep* occurs when progressive tax rates combine with inflation to cause a greater share of each taxpayer's income to go to the government. For example, if you were single and had a 1984 taxable income of $10,800, your tax bill would be $1,203. Now suppose inflation causes prices to double, and your income, being tied to a cost of living index, rises to $21,600. Because our tax rates are progressive, your taxes (at 1984 rates) would jump to $3,621. Your after-tax income has thus increased from $9,597 to $17,979 but, since prices have doubled, your real income has *declined* from $9,597 to $8,990 (calculated as one-half of $17,979). You are in a higher tax bracket, so you are paying a higher percentage of your real income in taxes. If this happens to everyone, and if Congress fails to change tax rates sufficiently, then real individual incomes decline because the federal government is taking a larger share of the national product. This is called the federal government's "inflation dividend," and it helps explain why congressional liberals have not been too concerned about inflation, since it has given them more of the nation's real income to dispense. Bracket creep was a real problem during the 1970s, but President Reagan's tax program, and especially the plan to index rates, will stop it unless Congress rescinds that part of the current tax act.

An asset sold within 6 months of the time it was purchased produces a *short-term gain or loss*, while an asset held for more than 6 months produces a *long-term gain or loss*.[8] Thus, if you buy 100 shares of GM stock for $70 per share and sell it for $80, you make a capital gain of 100 × $10, or $1,000. However, if you sell the stock for $60, you will have a $1,000 capital loss. If you hold the stock for more than 6 months, the gain or loss is long-term; otherwise, it is short-term.

Long-term capital gains are generally taxed at only 40 percent of the rate which applies to short-term gains (or other ordinary income). Under the law, 60 percent of all long-term gains are excluded from taxable income, so taxes are paid on only 40 percent of long-term gains income. Thus, if an individual had $1,000 of short-term capital gains (or dividends) and was in the 34 percent marginal tax bracket, his or her gains tax would be $340, while if the gain had been long-term, the tax would have been only 0.34($1,000 − $600) = $136. Because of this 60 percent exclusion, the effective long-term gains tax rate is only 40 percent of the ordinary tax rate.[9]

The fact that capital gains income is taxed at a lower rate than dividend or interest income has an important bearing on financial management. As we shall see, most businesses have at least some flexibility in providing returns to investors in the form of capital gains rather than dividends. Since the tax treatment of income from an asset has a significant effect on the value of the asset, personal income taxes must be taken into account by a firm seeking to maximize the value of its stock.

Corporate Income Taxes

The corporate tax structure, contained in Table 2-3, is relatively simple. To illustrate, if a small firm (one with $1.4 million or less in taxable income) had $200,000 of taxable income, its 1984 tax bill would be $71,750:

$$\text{Taxes} = 0.15(\$25,000) + 0.18(\$25,000) + 0.30(\$25,000)$$
$$+ 0.40(\$25,000) + 0.46(\$100,000)$$
$$= \$3,750 + \$4,500 + \$7,500 + \$10,000 + \$46,000$$
$$= \$71,750.$$

Alternatively, a large firm's federal income taxes on its first $200,000 of income would be 0.46($200,000) = $92,000. Thus, the corporate tax rate for a small firm is very progressive on income up to $100,000, but it is constant thereafter, while the effective tax rate for a large firm is a con-

---

[8]The Deficit Reduction Act of 1984 reduced the capital gains holding period from over 1 year to over 6 months. This reduction is on a "trial basis," and is scheduled to expire on December 31, 1987, unless renewed by Congress.

[9]Some complexities in long-term capital gains (and losses) are not discussed here. The interested reader is referred to *Federal Tax Course* (Englewood Cliffs, N. J.: Prentice-Hall, 1985).

Table 2-3
Corporate Tax Rates in 1984

	Tax Rates[a]	
Taxable Income	Small Firm	Large Firm
1st $25,000	15%	46%
2nd $25,000	18	46
3rd $25,000	30	46
4th $25,000	40	46
Over $100,000	46	46

[a]A firm with total taxable income of $1.4 million or less is classified as a small firm. A large firm has over $1.4 million in taxable income.

stant 46 percent. Also, note that the marginal corporate tax rate is 46 percent for all firms earning over $100,000 in pre-tax income.

Interest and Dividend Income Received by a Corporation. Interest income received by a corporation is taxed as ordinary income at regular corporate tax rates. However, 85 percent of the dividends received by one corporation from another is excluded from taxable income. The remaining 15 percent of dividends received is taxed at the ordinary tax rate. Thus, a corporation earning over $100,000 and paying a 46 percent marginal tax rate would pay $(0.15)(0.46) = 0.069 = 6.9\%$ of its dividend income as taxes. If this firm had $10,000 in pre-tax dividend income, its after-tax dividend income would be $9,310:

$$
\begin{aligned}
\text{After-tax income} &= \text{Before-tax income} - \text{Taxes} \\
&= \text{Before-tax income} - (\text{Before-tax income})(\text{Effective tax rate}) \\
&= \text{Before-tax income}(1 - \text{Effective tax rate}) \\
&= \$10,000[1 - (0.15)(0.46)] \\
&= \$10,000(1 - 0.069) \\
&= \$10,000(0.931) = \$9,310.
\end{aligned}
$$

If this corporation passes its own after-tax income on to its stockholders as dividends, the income is ultimately subjected to *triple taxation*: (1) The original corporation is first taxed, (2) the second corporation is then taxed on the dividends it received, and (3) the individuals who receive the final dividends are taxed again. This is the reason for the 85 percent exclusion on intercorporate dividends.

Notice that if a corporation has surplus funds which can be invested in marketable securities, the tax factor favors investment in stocks, which pay dividends, rather than bonds, which pay interest. For example, suppose a firm had $100,000 to invest, and it could buy bonds that paid interest of $10,000 per year or stock that paid dividends of $10,000. If the firm were in the 46 percent tax bracket, its tax on the interest would be $0.46(\$10,000) = \$4,600$, and its after-tax income would be

$5,400. If it bought stock, its tax would be 0.46[(0.15)($10,000)] = $690, and its after-tax income would be $9,310. Other factors might lead the firm to invest in bonds, but the tax factor favors stock investments when the investor is a corporation. Also note that corporations are restricted in their use of borrowed funds to purchase another firm's preferred or common stock. Without such restrictions firms could engage in *tax arbitrage* whereby the interest on borrowed funds reduces taxable income on a dollar for dollar basis, but taxable income is only increased by $0.15 per dollar of dividend income. Thus, current tax laws reduce the 85 percent dividend exclusion in proportion to the amount of borrowed funds used to purchase the stock.

Interest and Dividends Paid by a Corporation. A firm's operations can be financed with either debt or equity capital. If it uses debt, it must pay interest on this debt, while if it uses equity, it will pay dividends to the equity investors (stockholders). The interest paid by a corporation is deducted from its operating income to obtain its taxable income, but dividends paid are not deductible. Thus, interest is paid with before-tax dollars, while dividends are paid with after-tax dollars.

To illustrate, Table 2-4 shows the situation for a firm whose assets produced $25,000 of income in 1984 before taxes. If the firm were financed entirely by debt and had interest payments of $25,000, then its taxable income would be zero, taxes would be zero, and investors would receive the entire $25,000. (The term *investors* includes both stockholders and bondholders.) If the firm had no debt and was therefore financed only by stock, the $25,000 would be taxable income to the corporation, the tax would be $25,000(0.15) = $3,750, and investors would receive only $21,250 versus $25,000 under debt financing. Of course, it is generally not possible to finance exclusively with debt capital, and the risk of doing so would offset the benefits of the higher expected income. *Still, the fact that interest is a deductible expense has a profound effect on the way businesses are financed—our tax system favors debt financing over equity financing.* This point is discussed in more detail in Chapters 11 and 12.

Table 2-4
Cash Flows to Investors under
Bond and Stock Financing

	Use Bonds	Use Stock
Before-tax income	$25,000	$25,000
Interest	25,000	0
Taxable income	$ 0	$25,000
Taxes (15%)	0	3,750
After-tax income	$ 0	$21,250
Income to investors	$25,000	$21,250

Corporate Capital Gains. Corporate long-term capital gains are taxed at rates lower than ordinary income, just as with individuals. A firm could generate capital gains by the sale of financial assets (stock, bonds, and so on) which it held as part of an investment portfolio, but firms could also realize capital gains on their capital assets such as land, plant, and equipment. (Remember that a capital gain occurs when an asset is sold for more than its purchase price.) As with individuals, to qualify as a long-term capital gain, the asset must be held for more than 6 months. The laws governing corporate capital gains are even more complex than those pertaining to individual capital gains. We will discuss corporate capital gains again in Chapter 9, where we discuss capital budgeting cash flows.

Corporate Loss Carry-Back and Carry-Forward. Ordinary corporate operating losses can be carried back to each of the preceding 3 years and forward for the following 15 years, and used to offset taxable income in those years. For example, an operating loss in 1984 can be used to reduce taxable income in 1981, 1982, or 1983, and then any remaining losses can be carried forward and used in 1985, 1986, and so on, to the year 1999. The loss must be first applied to the earliest year, then to the next earliest year, and so on.

To illustrate, suppose Manhattan Manufacturing, Inc., had a $1 million *pre-tax* profit in 1981, 1982, and 1983, and then in 1984, it had a bad year and lost $6 million. Manhattan would use the carry-back feature to recompute taxes for 1981, using $1 million of the 1984 operating losses to reduce the 1981 pre-tax profit to zero. This would permit the company to recover the amount of taxes paid in 1981, so Manhattan would receive a refund in 1985 of 1981 taxes because of the loss experienced in 1984. Since $5 million of unrecovered losses would still be available, Manhattan would repeat this procedure for 1982 and 1983. Thus, Manhattan would pay zero taxes for 1984 and would receive in 1985 a refund of taxes paid from 1981 through 1983. The firm would still have $3 million of unrecovered losses to carry forward (subject to the 15-year limit) until the entire $6 million loss had been used to offset taxable income. The purpose of permitting this loss averaging is, of course, to avoid penalizing corporations whose incomes fluctuate significantly from year to year.

Improper Accumulation to Avoid Payment of Dividends. Corporations could refrain from paying dividends to permit their stockholders to avoid personal income taxes on dividends. To prevent this, the tax code states that earnings accumulated by a corporation are subject to penalty rates *if the purpose of the accumulation is to enable stockholders to avoid the personal income tax.* Of income not paid out in dividends, a cumulative total of $250,000 (the balance sheet item ''retained earnings'') is by law exempted from the improper accumulation tax.[10] This is a benefit primarily to small corporations.

Although there is a penalty rate on all amounts over $250,000 *shown to be unnecessary to meet the reasonable needs of the business*, many companies do indeed have legitimate reasons for retaining earnings over $250,000 and are thus not subject to the penalty rate. Earnings during a given year may be retained and used to pay off debt, to finance growth, or to provide the corporation with a cushion against possible cash drains caused by losses. How much a firm should properly accumulate for uncertain contingencies is a matter of judgment. We shall consider this matter again in Chapter 13, which deals with corporate dividend policy.

Consolidated Corporate Tax Returns. If a corporation owns 80 percent or more of another corporation's stock, it can aggregate income and file one consolidated tax return. Thus, losses in one company can be used to offset profits in another. (Similarly, one division's losses can be used to offset another division's profits.) No business ever wants to incur losses (you can go broke losing $1 to save 46 cents in taxes), but tax offsets do make it more feasible for large, multidivisional corporations to undertake risky new ventures or ventures that will suffer losses during a developmental period.

Taxation of Small Businesses: S Corporations

The Internal Revenue Code provides that small businesses which meet certain restrictions as spelled out in the code may be set up as corporations and thus receive the benefits of the corporate form of organization—especially limited liability—yet still be taxed as proprietorships or as partnerships rather than as corporations. These corporations are called *S corporations* (formerly Subchapter S corporations). There are several reasons for a small firm's electing to be taxed as an S corporation, including the following:

1. If an S firm is profitable, its income is reported on a pro rata basis as taxable income to its stockholders, who may then withdraw funds without the payment of further taxes. This avoids the double taxation that occurs when a corporation reports income, pays taxes, and then pays dividends that are taxable income to its stockholders. (Of course, if the owners are already in high personal tax brackets from other income, and if they do not plan to withdraw profits from the business, then they may elect not to use the S option.)

2. If the firm has operating losses, its stockholders can claim these losses on a pro rata basis as deductions against their ordinary income. This is an especially attractive feature for a new business that incurs heavy

---

[10]The limit is $150,000 for certain personal service corporations.

start-up costs and whose stockholders are in high marginal tax brackets because of income from other sources.

3. If the firm has investment tax credits, these credits can be passed along to the stockholders. (Investment tax credits are discussed later in the chapter.) Again, this is especially important for small, new firms that are making heavy capital investments yet whose income is insufficient to utilize fully the tax credits generated by these investments, but whose owners have outside income that can be offset by the firm's tax credits.

Many factors other than taxes bear on the question of whether or not a firm should be organized as a corporation. However, the existence of S corporations make it possible for most small businesses to have the benefits of a corporation yet avoid double taxation problems.

Suppose a firm buys a milling machine for $100,000 and uses it for 5 years. The cost of the goods produced by the machine must include a charge for the machine, and this charge is called *depreciation*. Depreciation reduces profits as calculated by the accountants and reported to investors, but it is not a cash outflow, and it is termed a *noncash expense*. Depreciation also reduces taxable income and, hence, the firm's tax bill.

    Congress has recently made sweeping changes in the way depreciation is calculated for tax purposes. The old methods of accelerated depreciation (double declining balance and sum-of-years'-digits) were replaced by a simpler procedure known as the *Accelerated Cost Recovery System (ACRS, which is pronounced "acres")*. We now describe the highlights of ACRS as it existed in 1984, as well as some other relevant tax code features.

Tax Implications of Capital Investment

The cost of an asset is expensed gradually over its depreciable life for tax purposes. Historically, an asset's depreciable life was determined by its estimated useful economic life; it was intended that an asset would be fully depreciated at approximately the same time that it reached the end of its useful economic life. However, ACRS totally abandoned this practice and set simpler guidelines which created several classes of assets, each with a more-or-less arbitrarily prescribed life, called a *recovery period* or *class life*. These ACRS class lives bear no necessary relationship to expected economic lives.

    A major effect of the ACRS system has been to shorten the depreciable lives of assets, thus giving businesses larger tax deductions and increasing cash flows available for reinvestment. Table 2-5 describes what types of property fit into the different class life groups, and Table 2-6 sets forth the ACRS recovery allowances (depreciation rates) for the var-

Tax Depreciation Life

Table 2-5
Classes and Asset Lives under ACRS

Class	Type of Property	Optional Recovery Period for Straight Line Depreciation
3-year	Automobiles, tractor units, light-duty trucks, and certain special manufacturing tools.	3, 5, or 12 years
5-year	Personal property that is not 3-year or 10-year property. Includes most equipment, office furniture, and fixtures.	5, 12, or 25 years
10-year	Certain real property, certain public utility property, and theme park structures. Includes manufactured homes and mobile homes.	10, 25, or 35 years
18-year[a]	All real property, such as buildings, other than any designated as 10-year property.	18, 35, or 45 years

[a]Some low-income housing is depreciated over 15 years rather than 18 years. Also, note that land cannot be depreciated.

ious classes of investment property. Consider Table 2-5 first. The first column gives the ACRS class life, while the second column describes the types of assets which fall into each category. Although the prescribed class lives are normally used for tax purposes, ACRS does provide the option of figuring tax depreciation on a straight line basis using three alternative lives, as shown in the third column. With the straight line method, a uniform annual depreciation charge is allowed. The annual depreciation charge is equal to the cost of the asset divided by the years of the recovery life chosen. The ACRS recovery allowances as set by Congress always equal or exceed the straight line rates. Therefore, a firm will always obtain a faster depreciation write-off if it uses the ACRS recovery allowances than if it uses one of the optional straight line alternatives. Only companies which expect to lose money in the early years of a project's life, and hence to have no tax liability for a period of time, should elect the straight line option. Use of the straight line method would give these firms more depreciation allowances in later years when, it is to be hoped, they will be earning profits and will need tax deductions.

Computing ACRS Depreciation

Under earlier depreciation methods, the rate at which the value of an asset actually declined was estimated, and this rate was then used as the basis for tax depreciation. Thus, different assets were depreciated along different paths over time. The ACRS method, however, sets forth prescribed depreciation rates, called *recovery allowance percentages*, for all assets within each class. These rates, as set forth in 1984, are shown in Table 2-6. The yearly recovery, or depreciation expense, is determined by multiplying the asset's *depreciable basis* by the applicable recovery al-

Table 2-6
Recovery Allowances for Property
Placed in Service after December 31, 1980[a]

Ownership Year	Class of Investment			
	3-Year	5-Year	10-Year	18-Year
1	25%	15%	8%	4%
2	38	22	14	8
3	37	21	12	7
4		21	10	7
5		21	10	6
6			10	6
7			9	6
8			9	6
9			9	5
10			9	5
11				5
12				5
13				5
14				5
15				5
16				5
17				5
18				5
	100%	100%	100%	100%

[a]Congress developed these recovery allowance percentages based on the 150 percent declining balance method, with a switch to straight line depreciation at some point in the asset's life. For example, consider the 10-year recovery allowances. The straight line allowance would be 10 percent per year, so the 150 percent declining balance multiplier is $1.5 \times 10\% = 15\%$. However, the half-year convention applies, so the ACRS allowance for Year 1 is 7.5 percent, rounded to 8 percent. For Year 2, there is 92 percent of the depreciable basis remaining to be depreciated, so the recovery allowance is $0.15(92\%) = 13.8\%$, rounded to 14 percent. After 3 years, straight line depreciation exceeds the declining balance depreciation, so a switch is made to straight line. This switch gives an allowance of $66\%/7 = 9.43\%$, which is rounded to 10 percent for 3 years and to 9 percent for the final 4 years to eliminate fractional percentages.

lowance percentage. In the remainder of this section, we discuss some additional features of the ACRS system, discuss the computation of an asset's depreciable basis, and illustrate the calculation of annual depreciation expense.

Half-Year Convention. The ACRS recovery percentages as shown in Table 2-6 employ the *half-year convention*; that is, they assume that all assets are put into service at mid-year, and hence generate a half-year's depreciation, irrespective of when the asset actually goes into service. This feature hurts companies that put assets into service in the first half of the year, but it is beneficial to companies that acquire assets during the second half. To understand why this is so, consider two firms which purchase depreciable assets in 1984. Firm J places its new asset into service on January 1, while Firm D's asset goes into service on December 31. Under the earlier methods of calculating depreciation, which were based on the actual portion of the year the asset was in service, Firm J would have obtained a full year's depreciation, but Firm D could have expensed only one day's depreciation for 1984. However, under the ACRS method, each firm receives six months' depreciation. Clearly, this convention *hurts* Firm J, since it receives only six months' depreciation for an asset that is in service for a full year, and it *helps* Firm D, since it, too, receives six months' depreciation although its asset has been in service only one day.

Depreciable Basis. The *depreciable basis* is a critical element of ACRS since each year's allowance (depreciation expense) depends on the asset's depreciable basis and ACRS class life. The depreciable basis under ACRS is not adjusted for *salvage value*, which is the estimated market value of the asset at the end of its useful life. However, the depreciable basis is affected by (1) Section 179 expensing and (2) the investment tax credit.

Section 179 Expensing. *Section 179* of the tax code permits a business to write off as an expense, rather than to capitalize and depreciate, up to a total of $5,000 of capital expenditures per year. This feature is especially important to smaller firms—the write-off would have no material effect on GM or IBM, but it would benefit a small company. If an asset has a capitalized cost of more than the allowable Section 179 expense, and if the company takes its Section 179 expense for the year on that asset, then its cost basis for calculating depreciation and the investment tax credit (ITC) is reduced by the amount of the expense taken.

For example, assume that in 1984 a company pays $80,000 for a new computer system. In addition, the freight charges are $5,000, and $15,000 must be spent for installation. Thus, the capitalized cost, which is also the original depreciable basis, is $80,000 + $5,000 + $15,000 = $100,000. The company could elect to expense $5,000 of the depreciable basis under Section 179. If it did, its 1984 tax deductions would increase by $5,000, but the depreciable basis of the computer system would be reduced to $100,000 − $5,000 = $95,000. Additionally, the investment tax credit would apply to the adjusted basis of $95,000 rather than to the original basis of $100,000.

Investment Tax Credit. The *Investment Tax Credit (ITC)* provides for a direct reduction of taxes, and it is designed to stimulate business investment.[11] The credit applies only to depreciable personal property with a

---

[11]In addition to investment tax credits, there are also tax credits for research and development, for job training and employment programs, and for other specific expenditures. A discussion of these credits goes beyond the scope of this text.

life of 3 years or more, and currently the ITC is 6 percent for assets in the 3-year class and 10 percent for assets in the 5- and 10-year classes. Nearly all new property except land and buildings qualifies for the ITC. The dollar tax deduction is determined by multiplying the capitalized cost of the asset, less the amount of Section 179 expense, by the applicable ITC percentage.

There are four other points to bear in mind regarding the ITC: (1) The depreciable basis of an asset, that is, the amount to which the ACRS recovery allowances are applied, is reduced by one-half the amount of the ITC. This reduction is in addition to the adjustment for Section 179 expensing.[12] (2) If an asset is sold prior to meeting the minimum qualifying life, the firm will have to repay, and the IRS will "recapture," some of the ITC. (3) The ITC is limited to the first $25,000 of tax liability plus 85 percent of the remainder of the tax liability. Thus, if a company's income is low in a year when it makes large capital expenditures, it may not be able to use all of its ITC. (4) If the credit during a given year exceeds the limitations noted in Point 3, the excess may be carried back to the 3 prior years and then forward for the next 15 years.[13]

ACRS and ITC Illustration. Assume that a stamping machine which falls into the 5-year class life and which costs $50,000 is placed into service on March 1, 1985. An ITC of $5,000 is taken, but no Section 179 expensing will be applied to this asset. Salvage value is not considered, but one-half of the ITC, or $2,500, must be deducted to determine the depreciable basis, which is therefore $47,500. Each year's recovery (depreciation expense) is determined by multiplying the depreciable basis by the applicable recovery percentage. Thus, the depreciation expense for 1985 is $0.15(\$47,500) = \$7,125$. Similarly, the depreciation expense is $10,450 for 1986, and $9,975 per year for 1987, 1988, and 1989. The total depreciation expense is $47,500, which is the depreciable basis of the machine.

Now assume that the stamping machine is sold after 4 years. To qualify for the full 10 percent ITC, the asset must be kept for at least 5 years. Since the asset was only in service for 4 out of 5 years, or 80 percent of the required period, 20 percent of the ITC, or $1,000, would have to be repaid.

---

[12]The Tax Code also provides an alternative ITC method. Rather than taking a 6 percent ITC on 3-year property, along with a 3 percent reduction in depreciable basis, the firm could take a 4 percent ITC with no reduction in depreciable basis. Similarly, the firm can take an 8 percent ITC on property that falls into the other classes with no reduction in depreciable basis. Since the method presented within the paragraph generally provides somewhat greater benefits to the firm, we will take the full ITC in our illustrations throughout the text.

[13]The carry-back and carry-forward of the ITC effectively transfers the credit from less profitable years to more profitable years. Leases, which we discuss in Chapter 17, permit the transfer of the ITC from low-profit to high-profit firms.

Straight Line Option. As discussed above, under most circumstances, it is advantageous to use the ACRS recovery allowances rather than any of the optional straight line recovery lives. However, if the straight line method is used, there are some important points to remember. First, the same method and recovery period must be used for all property in the same class placed into service in the same year. Second, as with the ACRS recovery allowances, salvage value is not considered when calculating the depreciation expense. Third, the half-year convention is applicable—regardless of when the asset is placed into service, only one-half of the straight line depreciation expense is allowed in the first year. However, if the asset is held for the entire recovery period, then the other half-year amount can be taken in the year following the end of the recovery period.

Summary

This chapter presented some background information on forms of business organization, business securities, and income taxes. First, we saw that firms may be organized as *proprietorships*, as *partnerships*, or as *corporations*. The first two types are easy and inexpensive to form. However, corporations have a major advantage in terms of risk reduction, growth possibilities, and investment liquidity, and these features make it possible to maximize the value of any business except very small ones by using the corporate form of organization. Accordingly, corporations are the dominant form of business.

The capital raised to acquire business assets consists of *debt* and *equity*. The debtholders, or creditors, have first claim against the earnings of the business, but these claims are limited to fixed amounts. The common equity holders are the owners of the business; thus, they have claims against all remaining earnings. The specific dollar amounts invested by both creditors and equity holders is reflected in the business's balance sheet.

The value of any asset is dependent on the effective income it produces for its owner. *Effective income* means *after-tax income*. Since corporate income is taxed at rates going up to 46 percent, and since personal income is subjected to additional federal tax of up to 50 percent, the tax consequences of various decisions have a most important impact on a firm's value. It is not necessary to memorize everything about taxes—indeed, this would be impossible. However, you should know the basic differences between corporate and personal taxes, that interest is a tax deduction to the payer of the interest, that capital gains and operating income are taxed differently, and so on. These matters will come up throughout the book as we examine various types of financial decisions.

Finally, we discussed the tax implications of capital investment. Corporate tax laws permit fixed assets to be depreciated over time, and the annual depreciation expense is tax deductible. The current depreciation system is called the *Accelerated Cost Recovery System (ACRS)*. As we shall see in Chapter 9, when we discuss capital budgeting cash flow estimation, tax depreciation rules have a major impact on the profitability of capital investments.

2-1 Define each of the following terms: *Questions*
    a. Proprietorship; partnership; corporation
    b. Retained earnings
    c. Equity
    d. Progressive tax system
    e. Marginal and average tax rates
    f. Bracket creep
    g. Capital gain
    h. Tax loss carry-back and carry-forward
    i. Improper accumulation
    j. ACRS depreciation; half-year convention
    k. Investment tax credit (ITC); recapture
    l. S corporation
    m. Section 179 expense

2-2 What are the three principal forms of business organization? What are the advantages and disadvantages of each?

2-3 Suppose you owned 100 shares of General Motors stock and the company just earned $6 per share. Suppose further that GM could either pay all its earnings out as dividends (in which case you would receive $600) or retain the earnings in the business, buy more assets, and cause the price of the stock to go up by $6 per share (in which case the value of your stock would rise by $600).
    a. How would the tax laws influence what you, as a typical stockholder, would want the company to do?
    b. Would your choice be influenced by how much other income you had? Might the desires of a 45-year-old doctor differ from those of a pension fund manager or a retiree with respect to corporate dividend policy?
    c. How might the corporation's decision with regard to dividend policy influence the price of its stock?

2-4 What does *double taxation of corporate income* mean?

2-5 If you were starting a business, what tax considerations might cause you to prefer to set it up as a proprietorship or a partnership rather than as a corporation?

2-6 Explain how the federal income tax structure affects the choice of financing (debt versus equity) used by U.S. business firms.

2-7 How can the federal government influence the level of business investment by adjusting the ITC?

2-8 For someone planning to start a new business, is the average or the marginal tax rate more relevant?

2-1 The Bryant Metals Company had a 1984 income of $200,000 from operations after all operating costs but before (1) interest charges of $10,000, (2) dividends paid of $20,000, and (3) income taxes. What is Bryant's income tax liability?   *Problems*

2-2   The Charles River Corporation had $200,000 of taxable income from operations in 1984.

    a. What is the company's federal income tax bill for the year?

    b. Assume the firm receives an additional $20,000 interest income from some bonds it owns. What is the tax on this interest income?

    c. Now assume that the firm does not receive the interest income but that it does receive an additional $20,000 as dividends on some stock it owns. What is the tax on this dividend income?

2-3   The Matrix Company has made $200,000 before taxes for each of the last 15 years, and it expects to make $200,000 a year before taxes in the future. However, this year (1984), Matrix incurred a loss of $1,200,000. Matrix will claim a tax credit at the time it files its 1984 income tax returns and will receive a check from the U.S. Treasury. Show how it calculates this credit, and then indicate Matrix's tax liability for each of the next 5 years. Assume a 50 percent tax rate on *all* income to ease the calculations.

2-4   Robert Gould has operated his small repair shop as a sole proprietorship for several years, but recent changes in the corporate tax structure have led him to consider incorporating.

    Gould is married and has two children. His family's only income, an annual salary of $40,000, is from operating the business. He reinvests any additional earnings in the business. His itemized deductions are $6,100, and with four exemptions, he has total exemptions of $4 \times \$1,000 = \$4,000$, so his taxable income, given a salary of $40,000, would be $40,000 - \$6,100 - \$4,000 = \$29,900$. Gould estimates that his proprietorship earnings before salary and taxes for the period 1985 to 1987 will be:

Year	Income before Salary and Taxes
1985	$50,000
1986	70,000
1987	90,000

    a. What will his total taxes (corporate plus personal) be under:

      1. a corporate form of organization?

      2. a proprietorship?

    b. Should Gould incorporate? Discuss.

2-5   Jill Triffs has this situation for the year 1984: salary: $50,000; dividend income: $10,000; interest on IBM bonds: $5,000; interest on state of Florida bonds: $8,000; proceeds of $12,500 from sale of 100 shares of IBM stock purchased in 1981 at a cost of $6,000; and proceeds of $12,500 from sale of 100 shares of IBM stock purchased in October of 1984 at a cost of $12,000. Jill gets one exemption ($1,000), and she has itemized deductions of $4,000; these amounts will be deducted from her gross income to determine her taxable income.

    a. What is Jill's tax liability for 1984?

    b. What are her marginal and average tax rates?

    c. If she had some money to invest, and was offered a choice of Florida bonds with a yield of 7 percent, or more IBM bonds with a yield of 11 percent, which should she choose, and why? Assume the bonds are similar in terms of risk, maturity, and liquidity (marketability).

d. At what marginal tax rate would Jill be indifferent to the choice between the Florida and IBM bonds?

2-6 The Apex Corporation commenced operations on January 1, 1984. Here are some data on the company: Sales revenues in 1984 were $1,000,000. Labor and materials costs were $700,000. On January 1, the company purchased $100,000 of equipment which had a 5-year ACRS class life, plus $7,500 of 10-year class life assets on which it took an immediate write-off under Section 179. Apex received $10,000 of dividends on some stock the company owned, and it received $10,000 of interest on some bonds it owned. Also, on January 1, the company issued $500,000 of long-term bonds which carried an interest rate of 12 percent, and it paid its shareholders a dividend of $40,000 during 1984.

a. What is the depreciation expense in each year on the 5-year class life equipment? What is the Section 179 depreciation expense in 1984?

b. What is Apex's 1984 liability?

c. Suppose Apex has forecasted higher costs and lower revenues for the first few years of its operations, so when you developed the income statement, you found a loss, and hence no taxes. Would this mean the company would lose the tax credit? How would you recommend that it handle the situation? Assume for purposes of this question that losses were projected for 5 years, and after this start-up period, substantial profits were projected.

Selected Additional References

For additional insights into the optimal form of business, see

Maer, C. M., Jr., and R. A. Francis, "Whether to Incorporate," *Business Lawyer*, April 1967, 127-142.

The following articles provide additional information on the effect of corporate taxes on business behavior:

Angell, Robert J., and Tony Wingler, "A Note on Expensing Versus Depreciating under the Accelerated Cost Recovery System," *Financial Management*, Winter 1982, 34-35.

Comiskey, Eugene E., and James R. Hasselback, "Analyzing the Profit and Tax Relationship," *Financial Management*, Winter 1973, 57-62.

McCarty, Daniel E., and William R. McDaniel, "A Note on Expensing versus Depreciating under the Accelerated Cost Recovery System: Comment," *Financial Management*, Summer 1983, 37-39.

Skadden, Donald H., ed., *A New Tax Structure for the United States* (Indianapolis, Ind.: Bobbs-Merrill, 1978).

For a good reference guide to tax issues, see

Federal Tax Course (Englewood Cliffs, N. J.: Prentice-Hall, published annually).

Financial Markets, Institutions, and Interest Rates

3

"Money Men Are Minding the Store: The Financial Brains Have Taken Charge in Retailing." This headline appeared in a recent issue of *The New York Times*. The article went on to explain how financial executives were taking over the top spots of major U.S. retailing chains from marketing executives and the reasons behind this shift of power. The primary reason is that finance people best understand the markets wherein companies raise capital for expansion and where stock prices, which the firms seek to maximize, are established.

Another article, this one in *Business Week*, illustrates the impact that financial timing can have. Caterpillar Company executives had recently decided to delay a $300 million bond issue on the grounds that the 10.5 percent interest rate the company would have had to pay was too high. Subsequently, interest rates rose sharply rather than falling as the Caterpillar executives had expected, and a year later, with rates at 15 percent, they finally had to go ahead with the issue—at an additional cost of $13.5 million per year.

Caterpillar was a victim of bad luck (or bad forecasting), but rising interest rates have been far more painful to many other companies. For example, Washington Savings and Loan Association, one of the largest Miami companies, borrowed money on a short-term basis and loaned it out on a long-term, fixed rate basis. This was profitable as long as short-term rates were lower than long-term rates, but in 1982 short rates rose above long rates, and Washington S&L found itself with an asset portfolio that was yielding about 11 percent and liabilities which had an average cost of about 14 percent. To avoid bankruptcy, Washington S&L had to be merged into a stronger firm; many of Washington's managers were demoted or fired.

To some extent, the problems of Caterpillar, Washington S&L, and the thousands of other companies that have been hurt by high interest rates were the result of bad luck—it is hard to predict interest rates. However, some of these problems might have been avoided had these firms' financial managers had a better understanding of financial markets and institutions, and of the way interest rates are established in these markets. These topics are discussed in this chapter.

The Financial Markets

Business firms, as well as individuals and government units, often need to raise capital. For example, suppose Tampa Electric Company forecasts an increase in the demand for electricity in its service area and decides to build a new power plant. It almost certainly will not have the $500 million necessary to pay for the plant, so it will have to raise this capital in the market. Or suppose Mr. Jones, the proprietor of a local hardware store, decides to expand into appliances. Where will he get the money to buy the initial inventory of TV sets, washers, and freezers? Similarly, if the Smith family wants to buy a home that costs $60,000, but they have only $20,000 in savings, how can the Smiths raise the additional $40,000? Or if the City of Sacramento wants to borrow $20 million to finance a new sewer plant, while the federal government needs some $180 billion to cover its 1984 deficit, each of them needs sources for raising this capital.

On the other hand, some individuals and firms have incomes which are greater than their current expenditures, so they have funds available to invest. For example, Edgar Rice has an income of $36,000, but his expenses are only $30,000, and in 1984, Xerox Corporation had accumulated about $500 million of excess cash which it could make available for investment.

Entities wanting to borrow money are brought together with those having surplus funds in the *financial markets*. Note that "markets" is plural—there are a great many different financial markets in a developed economy. Each market deals with a somewhat different type of security, serves a different set of customers, or operates in a different part of the country. Some of the major types of markets follow:

1. *Physical asset markets* and *financial asset markets* must be distinguished. *Physical asset markets* (also called "tangible" or "real" asset markets) include those for wheat, autos, real estate, computers, machinery, and so on. *Financial markets* deal in stocks, bonds, notes, mortgages, and other *claims on assets*.

2. *Spot markets* and *futures markets* are terms which refer to whether the assets are being bought or sold for "on the spot" delivery (literally, within a few days) or for delivery at some future date such as six months or a year in the future. The futures markets (which could include the options markets) are growing in importance, but we shall not discuss them until much later in the text.

3. *Money markets* are defined as the markets for debt securities with short-term maturities (less than one year). The New York money market

is the world's largest, and it is dominated by the major U.S. banks, although branches of foreign banks are also active there. London, Tokyo, and Paris are other major money market centers.

4. *Capital markets* are defined as the markets for long-term debt and for corporate stocks. The New York Stock Exchange, which handles both the stocks and the bonds of the largest corporations, is a prime example of a capital market. The stocks and bonds of smaller corporations are handled in other segments of the capital market.

5. *Mortgage markets* deal with loans on residential, commercial, and industrial real estate, and on farmland.

6. *Consumer credit markets* involve loans on autos and appliances, as well as loans for education, vacations, and so on.

7. *World, national, regional, and local markets* also exist. Thus, depending on an organization's size and scope of operations, it can borrow all around the world, or it may be confined to strictly local, even neighborhood, markets.

8. *Primary markets* are the markets in which newly issued securities are bought and sold for the first time. If IBM were to sell a new issue of common stock to raise capital, this would be a primary market transaction.

9. *Secondary markets* are those in which existing, outstanding securities are bought and sold. Thus, Jane Vincent would sell the 100 shares of IBM stock which she currently owns in the secondary market. The New York Stock Exchange is a secondary market, since it deals with "used," as opposed to new, stocks and bonds.

Other classifications could be made, but this breakdown is sufficient to show that there are many types of financial markets.

A healthy economy is vitally dependent on efficient transfers of funds from savers to firms and individuals who need capital, that is, on *cost-efficient financial markets*. Without efficient transfers, the economy simply could not function: Tampa Electric could not raise capital, so Tampa's citizens would have no electricity; the Smith family would not have adequate housing; Edgar Rice would have no place to invest his savings; and so on. Obviously, our levels of employment and productivity, and hence our standard of living, would be much lower, so it is absolutely essential that our financial markets function efficiently—not only quickly, but also at a low cost.[1]

---

[1]When organizations such as the United Nations design plans to aid developing nations, just as much attention must be paid to the establishment of cost-efficient financial markets as to electrical power, transportation, and communications systems. Economic efficiency is simply impossible without a good system for allocating capital within the economy.

Financial Institutions

Transfers of capital between savers and those who need capital take place in the three different ways diagrammed in Figure 3-1:

1. *Direct transfers* of money and securities.

2. Transfers through an *investment banking house*, such as Merrill Lynch, which serves as a middleman and facilitates the issuance of securities.

3. Transfers through a *financial intermediary*, such as a bank or mutual fund, which obtains funds from savers and then issues its own securities in exchange. Intermediaries literally transform money capital from one form to another, which increases general market efficiency.

For simplicity, we assume that the entity which needs capital is a business, and specifically a corporation, although it is easy enough to visualize the demander-of-capital as a potential home purchaser, a government unit, and so on.

Direct transfers of funds from savers to businesses are possible and do occur on occasion, but it is generally more efficient for a business to obtain the services of a specialized financial institution called an *investment banker*. Merrill Lynch, Salomon Brothers, and E. F. Hutton are examples of financial institutions which offer investment banking services. Such organizations (1) help corporations design securities with the features that will be most attractive to investors, (2) buy these securities from the corporation, and (3) then resell them to savers in the primary markets. Thus, the investment bankers are *middlemen* in the process of transferring capital from savers to businesses.

The *financial intermediaries* shown in the third section of Figure 3-1 do more than simply transfer money and securities between firms and savers—the intermediaries literally create new financial products. Since the intermediaries are generally large, they gain economies of scale in analyzing the creditworthiness of potential borrowers, in processing and collecting loans, and in pooling risks and thus helping individual savers avoid "putting all their financial eggs in one borrower's basket." Further, a system of specialized intermediaries can enable savings to do more than just draw interest—for example, people can put money into banks and get both interest and a convenient way of making payments (checking), put money into life insurance companies and get both interest and protection against early death, and so on.

In the United States and other developed nations, a large set of specialized, highly efficient financial intermediaries has evolved. The situation is, however, changing rapidly, and different types of institutions are performing services that were formerly reserved for other institutions, causing institutional distinctions to become blurred. Still, there is a degree of institutional identity, and here are the major classes of intermediaries:

1. *Commercial banks*, which are the traditional "department stores" of finance, serve a wide variety of savers and those with needs for funds.

Figure 3-1
Diagram of the Capital Formation Process

1. Direct Transfers

2. Indirect Transfers through Investment Bankers

3. Indirect Transfers through a Financial Intermediary

Historically, the commercial banks have been the major institutions which handled checking accounts and through which the Federal Reserve System expanded or contracted the money supply. Today, however, some of the other institutions discussed below also provide checking services and significantly influence the effective money supply. Conversely, commercial banks now provide an ever wider range of services such as "discount" brokerage services and insurance.

2. *Savings and loan associations (S&Ls)*, which serve individual savers and residential and commercial mortgage borrowers, take the funds of many small savers and then lend this money to home buyers and other types of borrowers. The savers are provided a degree of liquidity that would be absent if they bought the mortgages or other securities directly, so perhaps the most significant economic function of the S&Ls is to "create liquidity" which would otherwise be lacking. Also, the S&Ls have more expertise in analyzing credit, setting up loans, and making collections than individual savers could possibly have, so the S&Ls reduce the cost and increase the feasibility of making real estate loans. Finally, the S&Ls hold large, diversified portfolios of loans and other assets and thus spread risks in a manner that would be impossible if small savers were making direct loans. Because of these factors, savers benefit by being able to invest their savings in more liquid, better managed, and less risky accounts, while borrowers benefit by being able to obtain more capital, and at lower costs, than would otherwise be possible.

3. *Mutual savings banks*, which are similar to S&Ls, operate primarily in the northeastern states, accept savings primarily from individuals, and lend mainly on a long-term basis to home buyers and consumers.

4. *Credit unions* are cooperative associations whose members have a common bond such as being employees of the same firm. Members' savings are loaned only to other members, generally for auto purchases, home improvements, and the like.

5. *Pension funds* are retirement plans funded by corporations or government agencies for their workers, and administered primarily by the trust departments of commercial banks or by life insurance companies. Pension funds invest primarily in bonds, stocks, mortgages, and real estate.

6. *Life insurance companies* take savings in the form of annual premiums, then invest these funds in stocks, bonds, real estate, and mortgages, and finally make payments to the beneficiaries of the insured parties upon their deaths. In recent years, life insurance companies have also offered a variety of tax-deferred savings plans which provide benefits to the participants when they retire.

7. *Mutual funds* are corporations which accept dollars from savers and then use these dollars to buy stocks, long-term bonds, or short-term debt instruments issued by businesses or government units. These organizations pool funds and thus reduce risks by diversification. They also gain economies of scale, which lower the costs of analyzing securities, managing portfolios, and trading in the stock and bond markets. Different funds are designed to meet the objectives of different types of savers. Hence, we have bond funds for those who desire safety; stock funds for savers who are willing to accept significant risks in the hope of very high returns; and still other funds that are used as interest-bearing checking accounts (the *money market funds*). There are literally hundreds of different mutual funds, with dozens of different goals and purposes.

The financial institutions have historically been heavily regulated, with the major purpose of this regulation being to insure the safety of the institutions for the protection of their savers. However, these regulations—which have taken the form of prohibitions on nationwide branching, restrictions on the types of assets the institutions can buy, ceilings on the interest rates they can pay, and limitations on the types of services they can provide—have tended to impede the free flow of capital from surplus to deficit areas and thus have hurt the efficiency of our capital markets. Recognizing this fact, Congress has authorized some major changes, and more will be coming along.

The major result of the developing changes is a blurring of the distinctions among the different types of institutions. Indeed, the trend in the United States today is toward huge *financial service corporations*, which own banks, S&Ls, investment banking houses, insurance companies, pension plan operations, and mutual funds, and which have branches across the country and, indeed, around the world. Sears, Roebuck is, interestingly, one of the largest—if not the largest—financial service corporations. It owns Allstate Insurance, Dean Witter (a brokerage and investment banking firm), Coldwell Banker (the largest real estate brokerage firm), a huge credit card business, and a host of other related businesses. Other major companies, most of which started in one area and have now diversified to cover the full financial spectrum, include Transamerica, Merrill Lynch, American Express, Citicorp, BankAmerica, and Prudential.

The Stock Market

As has been noted, secondary markets are the markets where outstanding, previously issued securities are traded. By far the most active market—and the most important one to financial managers—is the *stock market*. It is here that the price of each firm's stock is established. Since the primary goal of financial management is to contribute to the maximization of the firm's stock price, a knowledge of the market in which this price is established is clearly essential for anyone involved in managing a business.

The Stock Exchanges

There are two basic types of stock markets—the *organized exchanges*, which are typified by the New York Stock Exchange (NYSE) and the American Stock Exchange (AMEX), and the less formal *over-the-counter markets*. Since the organized exchanges have actual physical market locations and are easier to describe and understand, we shall consider them first.

The organized security exchanges are tangible, physical entities. Each of the larger ones occupies its own building, has specifically designated members, and has an elected governing body—its board of governors. Members are said to have "seats" on the exchange, although everybody stands up. These seats, which are bought and sold, represent the right to trade on the exchange. In 1968, seats on the NYSE sold at a record high of $515,000, but in 1979 they sold for as little as $40,000. They were back up to $425,000 in April of 1984.

Most of the larger investment banking houses operate *brokerage departments* which own seats on the exchanges and designate one or more of their officers as members. The exchanges are open on all normal working days, with the members meeting in a large room equipped with telephones and other electronic equipment that enable each brokerage house member to communicate with the firm's offices throughout the country.

Like other markets, security exchanges facilitate communication between buyers and sellers. For example, Merrill Lynch (the largest brokerage firm), might receive an order in its Atlanta office from a customer who wants to buy 100 shares of General Motors stock. Simultaneously, E. F. Hutton's Denver office might receive an order from a customer wishing to sell 100 shares of GM. Each broker communicates by wire with the firm's representative on the NYSE. Other brokers throughout the country are also communicating with their own exchange members. The exchange members with *sell orders* offer the shares for sale, and they are bid for by the members with *buy orders*. Thus, the exchanges operate as *auction markets*.[2]

The Over-the-Counter Market

In contrast to the organized security exchanges, the over-the-counter market is a nebulous, intangible organization. An explanation of the term *over-the-counter* will help clarify exactly what this market is. The exchanges operate as auction markets—buy and sell orders come in more or less simultaneously, and the exchanges are used to match these orders. But if a stock is traded less frequently, perhaps because it is the stock of a new or a small firm, few buy and sell orders come in, and matching them within a reasonable length of time would be difficult. To avoid this problem, some brokerage firms maintain an inventory of such stocks. They buy when individual investors wish to sell, and sell when investors want to buy. At one time, the inventory of securities was kept in a safe, and when bought and sold, the stocks were literally passed over the counter.

Today, over-the-counter markets are defined as all facilities that provide for security transactions not conducted on the organized ex-

---

[2]The NYSE is actually a modified auction market, where people (through their brokers) bid for stocks. Originally, a hundred or so years ago, brokers would literally shout, "I have 100 shares of Union Pacific for sale; how much am I offered?" and then sell to the highest bidder. If a broker had a buy order, he or she would shout, "I want to buy 100 shares of Union Pacific; who'll sell at the best price?" The same general situation still exists, although the exchanges now have members known as *specialists*, who facilitate the trading process by keeping an inventory of shares of the stocks in which they specialize. If a buy order comes in at a time when no sell order arrives, the specialist will sell off some inventory. Similarly, if a sell order comes in, the specialist will buy and add to inventory. The specialist sets a *bid price* (the price the specialist will pay for the stock) and an *asked price* (the price at which shares will be sold out of inventory). The bid and asked prices are set at levels designed to keep the inventory in balance. If many buy orders start coming in because of favorable developments, or sell orders because of unfavorable events, the specialist will raise or lower prices to keep supply and demand in balance.

Also, it should be noted that special facilities are available to help institutional investors such as mutual funds or pension funds sell large blocks of stock without depressing their prices. In esssence, brokerage houses which cater to institutional clients are made aware that a block of stock is available, and they line up purchasers before the stock is put on the market. Similarly, when a firm has a major announcement which is likely to cause its stock price to change sharply, it will ask the exchanges to halt trading in its stock until the announcement has been made and digested by investors. Thus, when Texaco in 1984 announced that it planned to acquire Getty Oil, trading was halted for one day in both Texaco and Getty stock.

changes. These facilities consist (1) of the relatively few dealers who hold inventories of over-the-counter securities and who are said to "make a market" in these securities, (2) of the thousands of brokers who act as agents in bringing these dealers together with investors, and (3) of the computers, terminals, and electronic network which facilitates communications between dealers and brokers. The dealers who make a market in a particular stock continuously post a price at which they are willing to buy the stock (the *bid price*) and a price at which they will sell shares (the *asked price*). These prices, which are changed as supply and demand conditions change, can be read off computer screens all across the country. The spread between bid and asked prices represents the dealer's markup, or profit.

In terms of numbers of issues, the majority of stocks are traded over-the-counter. However, because the stocks of larger companies are listed on the exchanges, it is estimated that two-thirds of the dollar volume of stock trading takes place on the exchanges.

From the NYSE's inception in the 1800s until the 1970s, the vast majority of all stock trading occurred on the Exchange and was conducted by member firms. The Exchange established a set of minimum brokerage commission rates, and no NYSE member firm could charge a commission lower than the set rate. This was a monopoly, pure and simple. However, in the 1970s, the Securities and Exchange Commission (SEC), with strong prodding from the antitrust division of the Justice Department, forced the NYSE to abandon its fixed commissions. Commission rates declined dramatically, falling in some cases as much as 80 percent from former levels. These changes were a boon to the investing public, but not to the brokerage industry. A number of brokerage houses went bankrupt, and others were forced to merge with stronger firms. Many Wall Street experts predict that, once the dust settles, the number of "full service" brokerage houses will have declined from literally thousands in the 1960s to perhaps 20 large, strong, nationwide companies, all of which are units of diversified financial services corporations. On the other hand, deregulation has spawned a large number of small "discount" brokers, many of which are affiliated with banks or savings and loans.

Some Trends in Security Trading Procedures

Information on transactions both on the exchanges and in the over-the-counter market is available in daily newspapers. We cannot delve deeply into the matter of financial reporting—this is more properly the field of investment analysis—but it is useful to explain the basics of the stock market reporting system.

Table 3-1, taken from a daily newspaper, is a section of the stock market page which lists stocks on the NYSE. For each stock listed, it pro-

Stock Market Reporting

Table 3-1
Stock Market Transactions, December 7, 1983

52 Weeks High	52 Weeks Low	Stock	Div.	Yld %	P-E Ratio	Sales 100s	High	Low	Close	Net Chg.
17 ¾	8 ½	AAR	.44	3.1	18	7	14 ⅛	14	14	− ⅛
52 ⅜	29 ½	ACF	1.40	2.8	39	225	50 ⅝	50 ¼	50 ¼	− ½
18 ⅝	18 ¼	AMCA		..	..	1	u18 ¾	18 ¾	18 ¾	+ ⅛
18 ⅞	14 ¾	AMF	.50	3.2	..	380	16	15 ½	15 ⅝	+ ⅛
39 ⅛	18 ½	AMR Cp		..	16	5937	37 ⅜	36 ⅝	36 ¾	+ ⅜
19 ½	15	AMRpf	2.18	11.	..	34	19 ⅜	19 ¼	19 ¼	....
40 ¼	24 ⅞	AMRpf	2.13	5.6	..	96	38 ¾	38 ¼	38 ¼	+ ⅛
16 ¼	3 ⅛	APL		..	22	24	15 ¼	15	15 ¼	....

vides specific data on the trading that took place on December 7, 1983, as well as other, more general information. Similar information is available on stocks listed on the other exchanges, and also on stocks traded over-the-counter. Stocks are listed alphabetically, from AAR Industries to Zurn Industries; the data in Table 3-1 were taken from the top of the listing. The two columns on the left show the highest and lowest prices in which the stocks have sold during the past year; AAR, the first company shown, has traded in the range from $17 ¾ to $8 ½ (or from $17.75 to $8.50) during the preceding 52 weeks. The figure just to the right of the company's abbreviated name is the dividend; AAR had a current indicated annual dividend rate of $0.44 per share and a dividend yield (which is the dividend divided by the closing stock price) of 3.1 percent. Next comes the ratio of the stock's price to its annual earnings (the P-E ratio), followed by the volume of trading for the day; 700 shares of AAR stock were traded on December 7, 1983. Following the volume come the high and the low prices for the day, and then the closing price. On December 7, AAR traded as high as $14 ⅛ and as low as $14, while the last trade was at $14. The last column gives the change from the closing price on the previous day. AAR was down ⅛, or $0.125, so the previous close must have been $14 ⅛ (since $14 ⅛ − ⅛ = $14, the indicated closing price on December 7).

There are two other points to note in Table 3-1: (1) The "pf" following the stock name of the lower two AMR listings tells us that these are issues of preferred rather than common stock. Incidentally, AMR Corporation is the name of the company that owns American Airlines. (2) The "u" preceding AMCA's daily high indicates that the $18 ¾ price is a new 52-week high. Note that the reported yearly high and low listing does not include the current trading day.

Essentially the same information is given for stocks which are traded on other exchanges and in the over-the-counter markets.

Corporate bonds are traded much less frequently than common stock, *Bond Markets* and over 95 percent of the bond trading which does occur takes place in the over-the-counter market. The reason is that, unlike stocks, most bonds are owned by and traded among the large financial institutions (for example, life insurance companies, mutual funds, and pension funds, which deal in very large blocks of securities). It is relatively easy for the over-the-counter bond dealers to arrange the transfer of large blocks of bonds among the relatively few holders of the bonds. It would be impossible to conduct similar operations in the stock market among the literally millions of large and small stockholders.

Information on bond trades in the over-the-counter market is not published. However, a representative group of bonds is listed and traded on the bond division of the NYSE. Information on NYSE bond trades is published daily, and it reflects reasonably well the conditions in the larger over-the-counter market. Table 3-2 gives a section of the bond market page of *The Wall Street Journal* on trading for December 7, 1983.

Table 3-2
NYSE Bond Market Transactions, December 7, 1983

Bonds	Coupon Rate and Maturity Year		Current Yield	Volume	High	Low	Close	Net Change
AlaP	9	2000	13.	61	71 ½	71 ¼	71 ⅜	+ ¼
AlaP	8 ½	01	13.	43	67 ⅝	67 ⅛	67 ⅝	....
AlaP	7 ⅞	02	12.	63	64	64	64	− ½
AlaP	7 ¾	02	12.	20	63 ¼	63 ⅛	63 ⅛	− ⅛
AlaP	9 ¾	04	13.	35	75	74 ⅞	75	− ½
AlaP	10 ½	05	13.	6	81	81	81	....
AlaP	8 ¾	07	13.	5	68	67 ⅜	67 ⅜	− ⅝
AlaP	8 ⅝	87	9.7	2	89 ½	89 ½	89 ½	− ½
AlaP	9 ¼	07	13.	10	71 ½	71 ½	71 ½	....
AlaP	9 ½	08	13.	33	73 ⅞	72	72 ¼	− 1 ¼
AlaP	9 ⅝	08	13.	9	74 ½	74 ½	74 ½	+ ½
AlaP	12 ⅝	10	13.	5	96	96	96	....
AlaP	15 ¼	10	14.	52	108 ½	107 ⅛	107 ⅛	− 1 ⅜
AlaP	14 ¾	91	14.	1	106 ½	106 ½	106 ½	....
AlaP	17 ⅜	11	15.	54	114 ½	112 ½	112 ½	+ 1 ⅞
AlaP	18 ¼	89	16.	152	112 ½	111	112 ½	+ 1

Notes:

a. All of the Alabama Power bonds had 30-year maturities when they were issued except the 18¼s of 1989, which were issued in 1981 with an 8-year maturity.

b. This listing contains only those Alabama Power bonds which were actually traded on the NYSE on December 7, 1983. The company has additional issues outstanding that were not traded on that date.

A total of 1,050 issues were traded on that date, but we show only the bonds of Alabama Power Company.

The bonds of Alabama Power and other companies generally have a par value of $1,000—this is how much the company borrowed and how much it must someday repay. However, for trading and reporting purposes, bonds are quoted as percentages of par. Looking at the first bond listed, we see that there is a 9 just after the company's name; this indicates that the bond is of the series which pays 9 percent interest, or 0.09($1,000) = $90 of interest per year.[3] Nine percent is defined as the bond's *coupon rate*. The 2000 indicates that this bond must be repaid in the year 2000; it is not shown in the table, but this bond was issued in 1970 and hence had a 30-year maturity when it was issued. The 13 in the fourth column is the bond's *current yield*, which is defined as the annual interest payment divided by the closing price of the bond: Current yield = $90/$713.75 = 12.6%, rounded to 13 percent. (Current yields above 9.9 percent are reported to the nearest whole percent.) The 61 in the fifth column indicates that 61 of the 9s of 2000 were traded on December 7, 1983. Since the prices shown are expressed as a percentage of par, the high was 71 ½ percent of $1,000, or $715; the low was $712.50; and the bond closed at $713.75, up $2.50 from the previous day's close.

Alabama Power has been growing, and it has been selling bonds almost every year to finance its growth. As we shall see later in the chapter, interest rates vary over time, and companies generally set their coupon rates at levels which reflect the "going rate of interest" on the day they are issued. If the rates were set lower, investors simply would not buy the bonds, or not pay the $1,000 par value, and the company could not borrow the money it needed. Bonds are listed in the paper, and hence in Table 3-2, in order of the dates on which they were originally issued. Thus, the fact that the coupon rates shown in the table are rising as we move down the list reflects the fact that interest rates have generally risen in recent years.

A bond's price reflects how much investors are willing to pay for it, given (1) its riskiness as well as the interest the bond pays relative to interest rates available elsewhere in the economy. Alabama Power's 9s of 2000 were worth $1,000 when they were issued in 1970, but people were not willing to pay $1,000 in 1983 for a bond which would only provide $90 of interest per year because $1,000 would buy a new bond which would pay about $130 of interest per year. Thus, the 9s of 2000 have fallen in price from $1,000 in 1970 to $714 in 1983 as a result of the increase in competitive interest rates.

---

[3]The Alabama Power bonds, like most in the United States, pay interest semiannually; therefore, the company would send a check for $45 each six months to the holder of one of the 9s of 2000.

In the next section, we shall see how and why interest rates change, and in Chapter 5 we will examine the precise way bond prices are established, given the level of interest rates in the economy.

Interest Rates

Capital in a free economy is allocated through the price system. *The interest rate is the price paid to borrow capital, while in the case of equity capital, investors expect compensation in the form of dividends and capital gains.* The factors which affect the supply of and the demand for investment capital, and hence the level of interest rates, are discussed in this section.

The two most fundamental factors which affect the general level of interest rates are (1) production opportunities and (2) time preferences for consumption. To see how these factors operate, visualize an isolated island community where the people live on fish. They have a certain stock of fishing gear which permits them to survive in reasonably good shape, but they would like to have more fish. Now suppose Mr. Crusoe had a bright idea for a new type of fishnet that would enable him to double his daily catch. However, it would take him a year to perfect his design, build his net, and learn how to use it efficiently, and Mr. Crusoe would probably starve before he could put his new net into operation. Therefore, he might suggest to Ms. Robinson, Mr. Friday, and several others that if they would give him one fish each day for a year, he would return two fish a day during all of the next year. If someone accepted the offer, then the fish which Ms. Robinson or one of the others gave to Mr. Crusoe would constitute *savings*; these savings would be *invested* in the fishnet; and the extra fish the net produced would constitute a *return on the investment.*

Obviously, the more productive Mr. Crusoe thought the new fishnet would be, the higher would be his expected return on the investment, and the more he could offer to pay Ms. Robinson and Mr. Friday for their savings. In the example, we assumed that Mr. Crusoe thought he would be able to pay, and thus he offered, a 100 percent rate of return— he offered to give back two fish for every one he received. He might have tried to attract savings for less. For example, he might have decided to offer only 1.5 fish next year for every one he received this year, which would represent a 50 percent rate of return to Ms. Robinson or the other potential savers. How attractive this offer would be to potential savers would depend in large part on the savers' time preferences for consumption. For example, Ms. Robinson might be thinking of retirement, and she might be willing to trade fish today for fish in the future on a one-for-one basis. On the other hand, Mr. Friday might have a wife and several young children and need his current fish, so he might be unwilling to "lend" a fish today except in exchange for three fish next year. Mr. Friday would be said to have a high *time preference for consump-*

tion, and Ms. Robinson a low time preference. Note also that if the whole population were living right at the subsistence level, then time preferences for current consumption would necessarily be high, aggregate savings would be low, interest rates would be high, and capital formation would be difficult.

In a more complex society, there are many businesses like Mr. Crusoe's, many products, and many savers like Ms. Robinson and Mr. Friday. Further, people use money as a medium of exchange rather than barter with fish. Still, the interest rate paid to savers depends in a basic way on (1) *the rate of return producers can expect to earn on invested capital* and (2) *consumers'/savers' time preferences for current versus future consumption*. Producers' expected returns set an upper limit on how much they can pay for savings, while consumers' time preferences for consumption establish how much consumption they are willing to defer and hence to save at different levels of interest offered by producers.[4]

Interest Rate Levels

Capital in a free economy is allocated through the price system. Firms with the most profitable investment opportunities can pay the most for capital, so they tend to attract it away from inefficient firms or from those whose products are not in demand. Of course, our economy is not completely free in the sense of being influenced only by market forces. Thus, the federal government has agencies which help individuals or groups as stipulated by Congress to obtain credit on favorable terms. Among those eligible for this kind of assistance are small businesses, certain minorities, firms willing to build plants in areas with high unemployment, and so on. Still, most capital in the U.S. economy is allocated through the price system.

Figure 3-2 shows how supply and demand interact to determine interest rates in two capital markets. Markets A and B represent two of the many capital markets in existence. The going interest rate, k, is 10 percent for the low-risk securities in Market A. Borrowers whose credit is strong enough to qualify for this market can obtain funds at a cost of 10 percent, and investors who want to put their money to work at low risk can obtain a 10 percent return. Riskier borrowers must obtain higher-cost funds in Market B. There, investors who are more willing to take risks invest with the expectation of receiving a 12 percent return but also with the realization that they might receive much less.

If the demand for funds in a market declines, as it typically does during a business recession, the demand curve will shift to the left (or down) as shown by Curve D_2 in Market A. The market clearing, or equi-

---

[4]The term "producers" is really too narrow. A better word might be "borrowers," which would include home purchasers, people borrowing to go to college, or even people borrowing to buy autos or to pay for vacations. Also, the wealth of the society influences people's ability to save, and hence their time preferences for current consumption versus future consumption.

Figure 3-2
Interest Rates as a Function of Supply and Demand for Funds

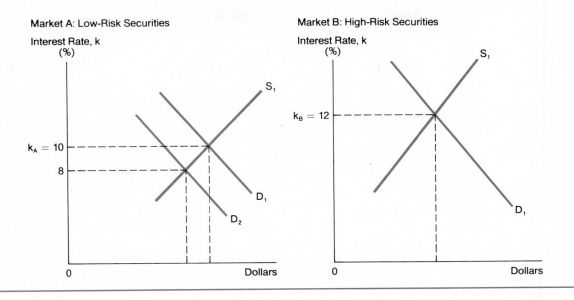

Market A: Low-Risk Securities

Interest Rate, k
(%)

$k_A = 10$

8

0   Dollars

S_1

D_1

D_2

Market B: High-Risk Securities

Interest Rate, k
(%)

$k_B = 12$

0   Dollars

S_1

D_1

librium, interest rate in this example will decline to 8 percent. You can also visualize what would happen if the Federal Reserve tightened credit: The supply curve, S_1, would shift to the left, and this would raise interest rates and lower the current level of borrowing in the economy.

Capital markets are interdependent. For example, assuming that Markets A and B were in equilibrium before the demand shift to D_2 in Market A, then investors were willing to accept the higher risk in Market B in exchange for a risk premium of $12\% - 10\% = 2\%$. After the shift to D_2, the risk premium would immediately increase to $12\% - 8\% = 4\%$. In all likelihood, this much larger premium would induce some of the lenders in Market A to shift to Market B. This, in turn, would cause the supply curve in Market A to shift to the left (or up) and that in Market B to shift to the right. This transfer of capital between markets would raise interest rates in Market A and lower them in Market B, and bring the risk premium back closer to the original level (2 percent).

There are many, many capital markets in the United States. U.S. firms also raise capital throughout the world, while foreign borrowers obtain capital in the United States. There are markets in the United States for real estate loans; farm loans; business loans; federal, state, and local government loans; and consumer loans. Within each category, there are also regional markets, as well as submarkets. For example, in real estate there are separate markets for first and second mortgages and for loans on owner-occupied homes, apartments, office buildings, shopping centers, vacant land, and so on. Within the business sector, there are doz-

Figure 3-3
Long- and Short-Term Interest Rates, 1953-1984

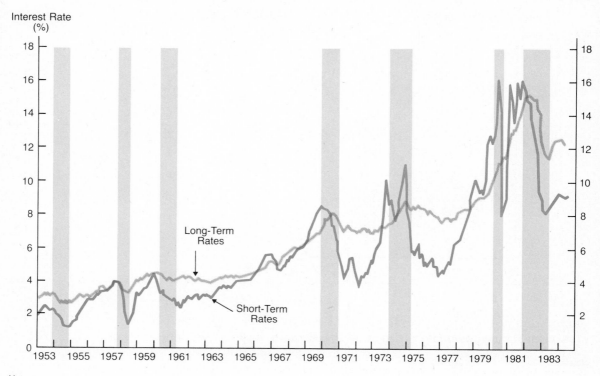

Interest Rate
(%)

Long-Term Rates

Short-Term Rates

Notes:
a. The shaded areas designate business recessions.
b. Short-term rates are measured by four- to six-month loans to very large, strong corporations, and long-term rates by AAA corporate bonds.
Source: *Federal Reserve Bulletin.*

ens of types of debt, and also several sharply differentiated markets for common stocks as opposed to debt.

There are as many prices as there are types of capital, and these prices change over time as shifts occur in supply and demand conditions. Figure 3-3 shows how long- and short-term interest rates to business borrowers have varied over the last 31 years. Notice that short-term interest rates are especially prone to rise during booms and then fall during recessions. (The shaded areas of the chart indicate recessions.) When the economy is expanding, firms need capital, and this pressure to borrow pushes rates up. Also, inflationary pressures are strongest during business booms, so at such times the Federal Reserve tends to tighten the money supply, which also exerts an upward pressure on rates. Just the reverse holds true during recessions—the Fed increases the money supply, slack business reduces the demand for credit, and the result is a

Figure 3-4
Relationship between Annual Inflation Rates and Long-Term Interest Rates,
1953-1983

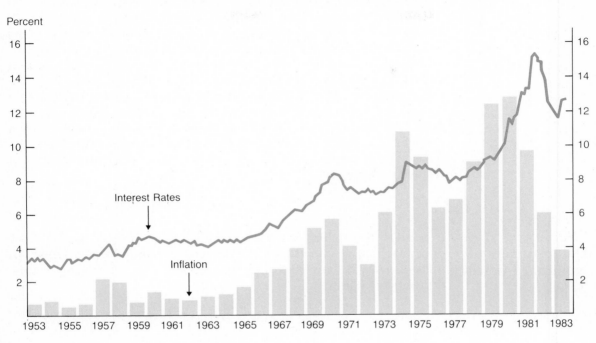

Notes:
a. Interest rates are those on AAA long-term corporate bonds.
b. Inflation is measured as the annual rate of change in the Consumer Price Index (CPI).
Source: *Federal Reserve Bulletin.*

drop in interest rates. In addition, inflationary pressures are normally weakest during recessions, and this too helps keep interest rates down.

These tendencies do not hold exactly—the early part of the 1974-1975 recession is a case in point. The price of oil increased dramatically in 1974, exerting inflationary pressures on other prices and raising fears of serious, long-term inflation. These fears pushed rates to high levels. Investors "looked over the valley" of the 1974-1975 recession, forecasted a continued problem with inflation, and demanded an inflation premium that kept long-term rates high by historic standards.[5]

The relationship between inflation and long-term interest rates is highlighted in Figure 3-4, which plots rates of inflation along with long-

[5]Short-term rates are responsive to current economic conditions, while long-term rates primarily reflect long-run expectations for inflation. As a result, short-term rates are sometimes above and sometimes below long-term rates. The relationship between long-term and short-term rates is called the *term structure of interest rates*. This topic is discussed in a later section.

term interest rates. From 1960 through 1964, when the average rate of inflation was 1.4 percent, interest rates on AAA-rated bonds ranged from 4 to 5 percent. As the war in Vietnam accelerated in the mid-1960s, the rate of inflation increased, and interest rates began to rise. The rate of inflation dropped after 1970, and so did long-term interest rates. However, the lifting of wage and price controls, in conjunction with the Arab oil embargo and a quadrupling of oil prices in 1974, caused a spurt in the price level, which drove interest rates to new record highs in 1974 and 1975. Inflationary pressures eased in late 1975 and 1976, but then rose again after 1976. In 1980, inflation rates hit the highest level on record, and fears of continued double-digit inflation pushed interest rates up to historic highs. In 1984, as this is written, the current inflation rate has dropped to the 4-5 percent level, but investors' fears of a renewal of double-digit inflation are keeping long-term interest rates at relatively high levels.

The Determinants of Nominal Interest Rates

In general, the nominal interest rate on a debt security, k, is composed of a pure rate of interest, k*, plus several premiums which reflect (1) inflation and (2) the riskiness of the security.[6] This relationship can be expressed as follows:

$$k = k^* + IP + DP + LP + MP.$$

Here

$$k^* = \text{pure rate of interest.}$$
$$IP = \text{inflation premium.}$$
$$DP = \text{default risk premium.}$$
$$LP = \text{liquidity premium.}$$
$$MP = \text{maturity risk premium.}$$

We discuss each of these components in the following sections.

The Pure Rate of Interest

The *pure rate of interest*, *k**, is the equilibrium interest rate on a riskless security if there were no expected inflation. Thus, the pure rate is also a "real, risk-free rate," and it may be thought of as the rate of interest on short-term U.S. Treasury securities in an inflation-free world. The pure rate is not static—it changes over time depending on economic condi-

---

[6]The term *nominal* as it is used here means the *stated* rate as opposed to the *real* rate, which is adjusted for inflation. If you bought a 10-year Treasury bond in April 1984, the stated, or nominal, rate would be about 12.5 percent, but if inflation averages 8 percent over the next 10 years, your real rate would be about 12.5% − 8.0% = 4.5%. In Chapter 4, we will use the term nominal in yet another way, to distinguish between stated rates and effective rates when compounding occurs more frequently than once a year.

tions. It is a function of (1) the rate of return borrowers can expect to earn on their real assets, and (2) consumers'/savers' time preferences for current versus future consumption. Borrowers' expected returns on real asset investment set an upper limit on how much they can afford to pay for borrowed funds, while consumers' time preferences for consumption establish how much consumption they are willing to defer and, hence, the amount of funds they will lend at different levels of interest. It is very difficult to measure k* precisely; many experts think that in the United States it has fluctuated in the range of 2 to 4 percent in recent years.

Inflation has a major impact on interest rates. Inflation can erode the purchasing power of the dollar and lower the real rate of return on investments. Investors are well aware of all this, so when they lend money, they add an *inflation premium* to the rate they would have been willing to accept in the absence of inflation. For a short-term, default-free U.S. Treasury bill, the actual interest rate charged, $k_{T\text{-bill}}$, would be the pure rate, k*, plus the inflation premium (IP):

Inflation Premium

$$k_{T\text{-bill}} = k^* + IP.$$

Therefore, if the pure rate of interest were $k^* = 4\%$, and if inflation were expected to be 5 percent (and hence $IP = 5\%$) over the next year, the rate of interest on 1-year T-bills would be 9 percent. On January 5, 1984, the expected 1-year inflation rate was about 6 percent, and the yield on 1-year T-bills was 9.5 percent, which implies that the pure rate on that date was 3.5 percent.

It is important to note that the rate of inflation built into interest rates is the *rate of inflation expected in the future*, not the rate experienced in the past. Thus, the latest reported figures might show an annual rate of 4 percent, but if people on the average expect a 5 percent inflation rate in the future, then 5 percent would be built into the current rate of interest. Note also that the inflation rate reflected in the interest rate on any security is the *average rate of inflation expected over the security's life*. Thus, the inflation rate built into a 1-year bond is the expected inflation rate for the next year, but the inflation rate built into a 30-year bond is the average rate of inflation expected over the next 30 years.[7]

---

[7]To be theoretically precise, we should use a *geometric average*. Also, note that since millions of investors are active in the market, it is impossible to determine exactly the consensus expected inflation rate. However, survey data are available which give us a reasonably good idea of what investors expect over the next few years. For example, in 1980 the University of Michigan's Survey Research Center reported that people expected inflation over the next year to be 11.9 percent, and the average rate of inflation expected over the next 5 to 10 years was 10.5 percent. However, the economy cooled in 1981 and 1982, and inflationary expectations dropped to 4 percent for 1983 and to the range of 6 to 7 percent for the next 5 to 10 years. As inflationary expectations dropped, so did the rate of interest.

Expectations for future inflation are closely related to, but not perfectly correlated with, rates experienced in the recent past. Therefore, if the inflation rate reported for the past few months increased, people would tend to raise their expectations for future inflation, and this change in expectations would cause an increase in interest rates as shown in Figure 3-4.

Default Risk Premium

The risk that a borrower will not pay the interest or principal on a loan on a timely basis, which means that the borrower might go into *default*, also affects the interest rate built into the transaction: the greater the default risk, the higher the interest rate lenders charge. Treasury securities have no default risk, and hence they carry the lowest taxable interest rates in the United States. For corporate bonds, the higher the bond's rating, the lower is its default risk and, consequently, the lower its interest rate.[8] Here are some representative interest rates on long-term bonds during December 1983:[9]

U.S. Treasury	11.44%
AAA	12.57
AA	12.76
A	13.21

The difference between the interest rate on a T-bond and that on a corporate bond *with similar maturity, liquidity, and other features* is defined as the *default risk premium (DP)*. Therefore, if the bonds listed above were otherwise similar, the default risk premium would be DP = 12.57% − 11.44% = 1.13 percentage points for AAA corporate bonds, 1.32 percentage points for AA, and 1.77 percentage points for A corporate bonds.

Liquidity Premium

A security which is highly *liquid* can be sold and converted to spendable cash on short notice. Active markets, which provide liquidity, exist for government bonds, for the stocks and bonds of the larger corporations, and for the securities of certain financial intermediaries. If a security is *not* liquid, investors will add a *liquidity premium (LP)* when they establish the equilibrium interest rate on the security. It is very difficult to measure liquidity premiums, but a differential of at least one and probably two percentage points exists between the least liquid and the most liquid financial assets of similar default risk and maturity.

---

[8]Bond ratings, and bonds' riskiness in general, will be discussed in Chapter 15. For now, merely note that bonds rated AA are judged to have more default risk than bonds rated AAA, A bonds are more risky than AA bonds, and so on.

[9]*Federal Reserve Bulletin*, January 1984, Table 1.35.

U.S. Treasury securities are free of default risk in the sense that one can be virtually certain that the government will pay interest on its bonds and will pay them off when they mature. Therefore, the default risk premium on Treasury securities is essentially zero. Further, active markets exist for Treasury securities, so their liquidity premiums are also close to zero. Thus, as a *first approximation*, the rate of interest on a Treasury bond should be equal to the pure rate, k*, plus the inflation premium, IP. However, an adjustment is needed. As we saw previously in our discussion of Alabama Power's bonds, the prices of long-term bonds decline sharply whenever interest rates rise, and since interest rates can and do occasionally rise, all long-term bonds, even Treasury bonds, have an element of risk called *interest rate risk*. As a general rule, the bonds of any organization, from the U.S. government to International Harvester, have more interest rate risk the longer the maturity of the bond.[10] Therefore, a *maturity risk premium (MP)*, which is higher the longer the years to maturity, must be included in the required interest rate.

Maturity Risk Premium

The effect of maturity risk premiums is to raise interest rates on long-term bonds relative to those on short-term bonds. This premium, like the others, is extremely difficult to measure, but (1) it seems to vary over time, rising when interest rates are more volatile and uncertain, and falling when rates are more stable, and (2) in recent years, the maturity risk premium on 30-year T-bonds appears to have generally been in the range of 1 to 2 percentage points.

We should mention that while long-term bonds have interest rate risk, short-term bonds that have a maturity shorter than the desired holding period have *reinvestment rate risk*. When the bonds mature and the funds must be reinvested, or "rolled over," a decline in interest rates would mean reinvestment at a lower rate, and hence a decline in interest income. Thus, although the principal is preserved, the interest earned over the holding period would vary from year to year depending on the intervening reinvestment rates.

A study of Figure 3-3 reveals that at certain times such as 1983, short-term interest rates were lower than long-term rates, while at other times such as 1980, short rates were above long rates. The relationship between long and short rates is important to corporate treasurers who must decide whether to borrow by issuing long- or short-term debt. It is

The Term Structure of Interest Rates

---

[10]For example, if you had bought a 30-year Treasury bond for $1,000 in 1972, when the long-term interest rate was 7 ⅜ percent, and held it until January 1984, when long-term rates were about 11.8 percent, the value of your bond would have declined to $675. Had you invested in short-term bills in 1972 and subsequently reinvested your principal each time the bills matured, you would still have $1,000. This point will be discussed in detail in Chapter 5.

Figure 3-5
U.S. Treasury Bond Interest Rates on Different Dates

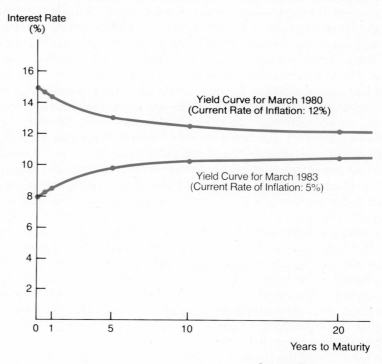

Term to Maturity	Interest Rate	
	March 1980	March 1983
6 months	15.03%	8.32%
1 year	14.03	9.04
5 years	13.47	10.08
10 years	12.75	10.51
20 years	12.49	10.80

also important to investors who must decide whether to buy long- or short-term bonds. Thus, it is essential to understand (1) how long- and short-term rates are related to one another and (2) what causes shifts in their relative positions.

To begin, we can look up in a source such as *The Wall Street Journal* or the *Federal Reserve Bulletin* the interest rates on bonds of various maturities at a given point in time. For example, Figure 3-5 presents interest rates for Treasury issues of different maturities on two dates. The set of data for a given date, when plotted on a graph such as that in Figure 3-5, is defined as *the term structure of interest rates*, or *the yield curve*, on that date. The yield curve changes over time as interest rates rise and fall. In

March of 1980, short-term rates were higher than long-term rates, so the yield curve on that date was *downward sloping*. However, in March of 1983, short-term rates were lower than long-term rates, so the yield curve at that time was *upward sloping*. Had we drawn the yield curve during June of 1980, it would have been essentially horizontal, for long-term and short-term bonds on that date had about the same rate of interest. (See Figure 3-3.)

Figure 3-5 shows yield curves for U.S. Treasury securities, but we could have constructed them for corporate bonds. For example, we could have developed yield curves for IBM, General Motors, Eastern Airlines, or any other company that borrows money over a range of maturities. Had we constructed such curves and plotted them on Figure 3-5, the corporate yield curves would have been above those for Treasury securities on the same date because of the addition of default risk premiums, but they would have had the same general shape as the Treasury curves. Also, the more risky the corporation, the higher is its yield curve; thus, Eastern's curve would have been above that of IBM.

In a stable economy such as we had in the 1950s and 1960s, where (1) inflation fluctuated in the 1 to 3 percent range, (2) the expected future rate of inflation was about equal to the current rate, and (3) the Federal Reserve did not actively intervene in the markets, the yield curve was relatively low, and it generally had a slight upward slope to reflect maturity effects. People often speak of such an upward sloping yield curve as being a *normal yield curve*, and a yield curve which slopes downward is called an *inverted*, or *abnormal, curve*.

Term Structure Theories

Three major theories have been proposed to explain the term structure of interest rates. They are (1) the expectations theory; (2) the liquidity preference theory; and (3) the market segmentation, or preferred habitat, theory. In this section, we discuss the three theories, using U.S. Treasury securities as an illustration, but note that the theories are equally applicable to corporate debt securities.

The Expectations Theory

The *expectations theory* postulates that the term structure of interest rates is based solely on investors' expectations of future inflation rates. Investors at any point in time have a set of expectations about the rate of inflation in each future year. A number of governmental and private organizations forecast future interest rates and give (or sell) these forecasts to investors. Most brokerage houses make inflation forecasts available to their customers, and they are reported in *Business Week, The Wall Street Journal,* and other publications. We will illustrate the expectations theory using riskless securities, but the same principles apply to all debt securities.

The short-term interest rate that is expected to exist on riskless securities at the beginning of any given future year is estimated by adding the rate of inflation expected during that year to the pure rate, k*, say 3 percent. Therefore, if in late 1985 most investors expected a zero rate of inflation during 1986, then the market-clearing interest rate on 1-year Treasury bills should be 3 percent. If inflation for 1986 had been expected to be 9 percent, then the interest rate on 1-year Treasury bills should be 12 percent. The rates expected for 1987, 1988, and so on, as anticipated in late 1985, could also be estimated; these anticipated rates are called *forward rates*. Finally, given the estimated set of future 1-year interest rates, or forward rates, the long-term rate as it exists in late 1985, according to the expectations theory, is the geometric average of these 1-year forward rates.

The following example illustrates the process. It is not complicated, but it can be confusing unless approached in a careful, step-by-step manner.

Step 1: Inflation Adjustment. Assume that on January 1, 1985, you have $1, which you plan to hold for one year. How much will it be worth, in beginning-of-year dollars, on December 31, 1985, if the rate of inflation, I, during 1985 is 6 percent, or 0.06? The answer is 94 cents:

$$\text{Value in beginning-of-year dollars} = \frac{\$1}{1 + I} = \frac{\$1}{1.06} = \$0.9434.$$

Step 2: Offsetting Inflation. What rate of interest, k, would you have to earn on your $1 to end up on December 31, 1985, with as much purchasing power as you had on January 1, 1985; that is, to end up with $1 rather than 94 cents in January 1, 1985, dollars? The answer is found by solving for k in this equation:

$$\$1 = \frac{\$1(1 + k)}{(1 + I)}$$

$$\$1 = \frac{\$1(1 + k)}{1.06}$$

$$1.06 = 1 + k$$

$$k = 1.06 - 1.00$$

$$= 0.06 = 6\%.$$

Thus, if your money earned 6 percent, you would exactly "break even" in the battle against inflation.[11]

---

[11]Of course, most of us would have to pay taxes on the interest earned, so we would really have to earn 6 percent *after taxes* to break even in a world with 6 percent inflation.

Step 3: The Real Rate of Return. What *nominal rate of interest, k,* would you have to earn on your money (disregarding taxes) in order to earn a k* percent real rate of return? In general, this equation may be used:[12]

$$k = k^* + I + k^*(I). \qquad (3\text{-}1)$$

With $I = 6\%$ as in our example, the nominal rate required to produce $k^* = 3\%$ must be 9.18 percent:

$$k = 0.03 + 0.06 + (0.03)(0.06)$$
$$= 0.03 + 0.06 + 0.0018$$
$$= 0.0918 = 9.18\%.$$

Thus, if you started with $1 (or $1 million) and earned an interest rate of 9.18 percent during a year when inflation was 6 percent, then your real rate of return would be 3 percent:

$$\frac{\text{Ending nominal dollars}}{1 + \text{Inflation rate}} = \frac{\$1(1.0918)}{1.06} = \begin{array}{l}\$1.03 \text{ in beginning-}\\ \text{of-year dollars}\end{array}.$$

As a practical matter, the cross-product term, or $k^*(I) = 0.0018 = 0.18\%$ in the example, is generally dropped on the grounds that it is so small that we do not need to worry about it, at least when inflation rates are low. Also, our ability to estimate expected inflation does not warrant four decimal places of accuracy. Therefore, as a reasonable approximation, the nominal interest rate on 1-year Treasury bills can be estimated as follows:

$$k = k^* + I. \qquad (3\text{-}1a)$$

---

[12]The proof of Equation 3-1 is developed in the following set of equations. Our goal is to find the nominal rate, k, which provides a given real rate, k*, after inflation of I. We want to end up with $1 + $k*, or $1(1 + k*), after one year, with dollars expressed in beginning-of-year terms. We will actually end up with $1(1 + k) in nominal, or end-of-year, dollars. Dividing $1(1 + k) by (1 + I) converts the end-of-year dollars to beginning-of-year values. Therefore, we can set $1(1 + k*) equal to $1(1 + k)/(1 + I), and then solve for k to find the nominal k needed to produce a real return k* given an inflation rate of I percent:

$$\$1(1 + k^*) = \frac{\$1(1 + k)}{1 + I}$$
$$(1 + k^*)(1 + I) = (1 + k)$$
$$k = (1 + k^*)(1 + I) - 1 \qquad (3\text{-}1)$$
$$= 1 + k^* + I + k^*(I) - 1$$
$$= k^* + I + k^*(I).$$

Note that, since we are dealing with Treasury securities, the real rate, RR, is equal to the pure rate, or RR = k*. If we were discussing corporate bonds with default and liquidity risk, then RR = k* + DP + LP. Also, note that the expectations theory does not recognize the existence of maturity risk premiums.

Step 4: Multiple Time Periods. Thus far, we have considered only 1-year bills. Our goal, however, is to show how the interest rates on long-term notes and bonds such as those maturing in 5, 10, or 20 years are related to the set of expected future 1-year bill rates. As a general rule, Equation 3-1a holds reasonably well for interest rates on bonds of any maturity *provided the inflation rate used is the geometric average expected inflation rate over the life of the bond in question.* To illustrate, we would find the interest rate on a 3-year bond, k, assuming that k* = 3% and that inflation is expected to be 6, 7, and 8 percent during the next 3 years, as follows:

1. Find the geometric average inflation rate:

$$
\begin{aligned}
\text{Average inflation rate} &= [(1 + I_1)(1 + I_2) \, . \, . \, . \, (1 + I_n)]^{1/n} - 1.0 \\
&= [(1.06)(1.07)(1.08)]^{1/3} - 1.0 \\
&= (1.22494)^{0.3333} - 1.0 \\
&= 0.06997 = 6.997\%.
\end{aligned}
$$

2. Apply Equation 3-1a:

$$
k = k^* + I = 3\% + 6.997\% = 9.997\%.
$$

If you bought a 3-year bond with a nominal yield of 9.997 percent, it would provide a return equivalent to the return you would expect if you adopted the strategy of investing in a series of three 1-year bills:[13]

$$
\begin{aligned}
&\text{Value of \$1 at the end of 3} \\
&\text{years if you buy a 3-year bond} = \$1(1.09997)^3 = \$1.33. \\
&\text{which yields 9.997\% per year}
\end{aligned}
$$

$$
\begin{aligned}
&\text{Value of \$1 at the end of 3 years} \\
&\text{if you buy a series of 1-year bills} = \$1(1.09)(1.10)(1.11) = \$1.33. \\
&\text{which yield 3\% + I, or} \\
&\text{9\%, 10\%, and 11\%}
\end{aligned}
$$

Given the assumed 1-year inflation rates and, therefore, interest rates over the next 3 years, if the interest rate on a 3-year bond were anything other than 9.997 percent, a disequilibrium would exist. For example, if the rate on a 3-year bond were 8 percent, then you and others would refuse to buy this bond, choosing instead to invest in the series of 1-year bills with a higher expected total return. Conversely, if the rate were 11 percent on the 3-year bond, there would be an excess demand for them. This would push their price up and their yield down until an

---

[13]We will discuss compounding in detail in Chapter 4. For now, recognize that the value of $1 at the end of some holding period, when invested in interest-bearing securities, is $1 times a factor for each year held, where the factor is 1 plus the interest rate earned in that year.

equilibrium was established at k = 9.997%. (However, we must remember that the realized returns after the 3 years were up would probably not be the same for the two strategies. If inflation and consequently future 1-year rates turn out to be higher than were expected, the short-term investment strategy would yield more than the long-term strategy, and vice versa.) Note that the yield curve in our example would be upward sloping, or normal, because the current 1-year rate is 9 percent and the 3-year rate is 9.997 percent. If we had set up the example with the inflation rate expected to decrease over time, then the resulting yield curve would have been downward sloping, or inverted.

To summarize, the pure expectations theory postulates that interest rates are based solely on expectations about future inflation, so changes in interest rates, according to the expectations theory, are dependent primarily on changes in expectations about future inflation. Further, if inflation rates are expected to increase, the yield curve will be upward sloping, and vice versa if inflation is expected to decline. Empirical studies support the expectations theory to a large extent, but the empirical evidence also suggests that factors in addition to inflation also affect interest rates. These factors are considered in the following two theories.

The Liquidity, or Maturity, Preference Theory

The *liquidity preference theory* states that, other things held constant, investors prefer short-term bills to long-term bonds, and, accordingly, that rates on long-term bonds will generally be above the level called for by the expectations theory. We will see in Chapter 5 (1) that the value of outstanding bonds will fall if interest rates rise, and (2) that such losses are much greater on long-term bonds than on short-term bills. For example, suppose the going rate of interest on both 1-year bills and 30-year bonds was 10 percent. If you owned one of each, then each would pay you 0.10($1,000) = $100, your securities would sell for $1,000 each, and the total value of your investment would be $2,000.

Now suppose the expected rate of inflation increased, from 7 to 17 percent, causing the going rate of interest to rise from 10 to 20 percent. The value of your 1-year bill would decline from $1,000 to $916.67, which would be bad, but the value of your 30-year bond would fall to $502.11, which would be terrible.[14]

This decline in the values of outstanding fixed-income securities as a result of an increase in interest rates *is greater the longer the maturity of the bond*. Since investors prefer less risk to more, other things held constant, it follows that investors would, at the same expected rate of return, prefer to own short- rather than long-term bonds. Therefore, long-term interest rates should have a tendency to exceed short-term rates, other things held constant. This is the basis of the liquidity preference theory.

---

[14]Again, these values are found using formulas developed in Chapter 5.

Figure 3-6
Effect of Interest Rate Risk on the Yield Curve

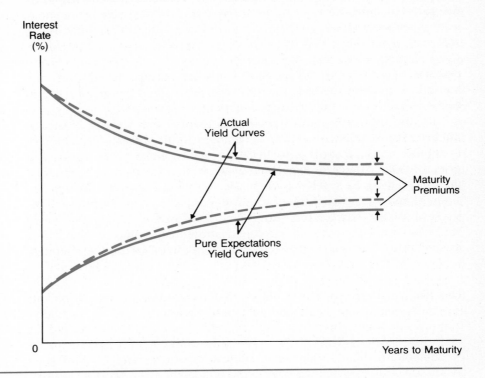

The implications of liquidity (or maturity) preference for the yield curve are shown in Figure 3-6. The solid lines represent two yield curves that might exist on two different dates if the pattern of rates were determined by the expectations theory only, while the dashed lines show how maturity premiums increase the interest rates on longer-term bonds. We have no way of knowing exactly how large the maturity premium is, or exactly how it increases as the term to maturity of a bond lengthens. However, the limited evidence which is available suggests that relatively long-term bonds (bonds that mature in 20 to 30 years) have maturity premiums in the range of 1 to 2 percentage points over the rate called for by the pure expectations theory.[15]

---

[15]See J. Houston McCulloch, "An Estimate of the Liquidity Premium," *Journal of Political Economy*, January 1975, 95-199.

Some lenders are required by law or custom to lend primarily on a short-term basis—banks are an example. Other lenders, such as pension funds and life insurance companies, prefer to operate in the long-term market because they have long-term liabilities. At the same time, some borrowers need short-term money (for instance, retailers borrowing money to build inventories prior to the Christmas season), while other borrowers need long-term capital (for example, people buying homes). Therefore, according to the *market segmentation theory,* if more funds are available in the short-term end of the market relative to demand than in the long-term market, then interest rates will be lower in the short-term and higher in the long-term market than predicted by the expectations and liquidity preference theories. Thus, the yield curve will, under these conditions, slope upward more steeply than would be called for by the other theories. Since, at any given time, it is possible for either long-term or short-term money to be in relatively tight supply, the market segmentation, or "preferred habitat," phenomenon could cause the yield curve to slope either up or down.

A number of empirical tests of term structure theories have been conducted. All three theories—expectations, maturity (or liquidity) preference, and market segmentation—apparently affect yield curves. However, further discussions of interest rate theories and empirical tests are best deferred for money and capital markets courses.

*Market
Segmentation
Theory*

In addition to inflation expectations and preferences for certain maturities, there are other factors which influence the general level of interest rates.

Other Factors which Influence Interest Rate Levels

*Federal Reserve
Policy*

As you probably learned in your studies of economics, (1) the growth in the money supply has a major effect on both the level of economic activity and the rate of inflation, and (2) in the United States, the Federal Reserve System controls the money supply. If the Fed wants to stimulate the economy, it increases the money supply growth rate. The initial effect of such an action is to cause interest rates to decline, but the action may also lead to an increase in the expected rate of inflation, which in turn pushes interest rates up. The reverse holds if the Fed tightens the money supply.

To illustrate, in 1981, inflation was quite high, so the Fed tightened up on the money supply. The Fed deals primarily in the short-term end of the market, so this tightening had the direct effect of pushing short-term interest rates up sharply. At the same time, the very fact that the Fed was taking strong action to reduce inflation led to a decline in expectations for long-run inflation, which led to a drop in long-term bond yields. Short-term rates decreased shortly thereafter.

During periods when the Fed is actively intervening in the markets, the yield curve will be distorted. Short-term rates will be temporarily "too high" if the Fed is tightening credit, and "too low" if it is easing credit. Long-term rates are not affected as much by Fed intervention, except to the extent that such intervention affects expectations for long-term inflation.

Business Cycles

Figure 3-3, presented earlier, can be examined to see how recessions have influenced rates. Here are the key points revealed by the graph:

1. Because inflation has generally been increasing since 1953, the general tendency has been toward higher interest rates.

2. Until 1966, short-term rates were almost always below long-term rates. Thus, in those years the yield curve was almost always "normal" in the sense that it was upward sloping, as the liquidity preference theory suggests it should be if inflation is constant.

3. The shaded areas in the graph represent recessions. During recessions, the demand for money falls, and, at the same time, the Federal Reserve tends to increase the money supply in an effort to stimulate the economy. As a result, there is a tendency for interest rates to decline during recessions.

4. In recessions, short-term rates fall much more rapidly than long-term rates. This occurs because (1) the Fed operates mainly in the short-term sector, and hence Federal Reserve intervention has its major effect here, and (2) long-term rates reflect the average expected inflation rate over the next 20 to 30 years, and this expectation generally does not change much even though the current rate of inflation may be low because of a recession.

Interest Rate Levels and Stock Prices

Interest rates have a direct effect on corporate profits: Interest is a cost, so the higher the rate of interest, the lower a firm's profits, other things held constant. Interest rates affect stock prices because of their effects on profits but, more important, because of competition in the marketplace between stocks and bonds. If interest rates rise sharply, investors can get a higher return on their money in the bond market, which induces the sale of stocks in order to transfer funds from the stock market to the bond market. Such transfers obviously depress stock prices.

To illustrate, suppose you had $100,000 invested in Midwest Power stock and were receiving dividends of 12 percent, or $12,000, per year. Suppose further that Midwest Power's bonds returned 9 percent, so you could switch and receive $9,000 per year, but you choose not to do so because you want to earn the extra $3,000 that the stock pays. (The $3,000, or 3 percent, differential reflects a risk premium.) Now suppose interest rates double, causing Midwest Power's bond prices to decline and their yields to rise to 18 percent. If the stock were still yielding 12 percent, then you could switch to bonds and increase your income from $12,000 to $18,000. You (and other stockholders) would call your broker and try to sell the stock and buy the bonds. However, the influx of sell orders would depress the price of the stock relative to that of the bond, probably before you could complete the transaction. Thus, changes in interest rates have a major effect on stock prices.

The yield curve for March 1983 in Figure 3-5 shows how much the U.S. government had to pay in 1983 to borrow money for 1 year, 5 years, 10 years, and so on. A business borrower would have had to pay somewhat more, but we shall assume for the moment that we are back in 1983 and the yield curve shown for that year also applies to your company. Now suppose you have decided (1) to build a new plant with a 20-year life which will cost $1 million and (2) to raise the $1 million by selling an issue of debt (or borrowing) rather than by selling stock. If you borrowed in 1983 on a short-term basis, say for one year, your interest cost for that year would be only 9.04 percent, or $90,400, while if you used long-term (20-year) financing, your cost would be 10.8 percent, or $108,000. Therefore, at first glance, it would seem that you should have used short-term debt.

Interest Rates and Business Decisions

However, this could prove to be a horrible mistake. If you use short-term debt, you will have to renew your loan every year, and the rate charged on each new loan will reflect the then-current short-term rate. Interest rates could return to their March 1980 levels, so by 1987 you could be paying 14 percent, or $140,000 per year. These high interest payments would cut into and perhaps eliminate your profits. Your reduced profitability could easily increase your firm's risk to the point where your bond rating would be lowered, causing lenders to increase the risk premium built into the interest rate they charge you, which in turn would force you to pay even higher rates. These very high interest rates would further reduce your profitability, worrying lenders even more, and making them reluctant to renew your loan. If your lenders refused to renew the loan and demanded payment, as they have every right to do, you might have trouble raising the cash. If you had to make price cuts to convert physical assets to cash, you might incur heavy operating losses or even bankruptcy.

On the other hand, if you used long-term financing in 1983, your interest costs would remain constant at $108,000 per year, so an increase in interest rates in the economy would not hurt you. You might even be able to buy up some of your bankrupted competitors at bargain prices—bankruptcies increase dramatically when interest rates rise.

Does all this suggest that firms should always avoid short-term debt? Not necessarily. If you borrowed on a long-term basis for 10.8 percent in March 1983, and if the Administration's economic program works, inflation will fall sharply in the next few years, and so will interest rates. In that event, your company would be at a major disadvantage if its debt were locked in at 10.8 percent while its competitors (who used short-term debt in 1983 and thus rode interest rates down in subsequent years) had a borrowing cost of only 5 or 6 percent. On the other hand, the Administration's program might not work, and large federal deficits might drive inflation and interest rates up to new record levels. In that case, you would wish you had borrowed long-term in 1983.

Finance would be easy if we could predict future interest rates accurately. Unfortunately, predicting future interest rates with consistent accuracy is somewhere between difficult and impossible—people who make a living by selling interest rate forecasts say it is difficult; many others (including us) say it is impossible.

Even if it is not possible to predict future interest rate *levels*, it is easy to predict that interest rates will *fluctuate*—they always have, and they always will. This being the case, sound financial policy calls for using a mix of long- and short-term debt, as well as equity, in such a manner that the firm can survive in most interest rate environments. Further, the optimal financial policy depends in an important way on the nature of the firm's assets—the easier it is to sell off assets and thus to pay off debts, the more feasible it is to use large amounts of short-term debt. We will return to this issue later in the book.

Summary

In this chapter, we discussed the nature of financial markets, the types of institutions that operate in these markets, how prices and interest rates are determined, and some of the ways in which interest rates affect business decisions.

The *pure interest rate, k^*,* is determined by (1) the *returns on investment available to producers* and (2) *consumers' time preferences* for current consumption as opposed to saving for future consumption. To establish the nominal interest rate for a given security, k, we must add to the pure rate some premiums which reflect *expected inflation* over the life of the security (IP), the *default risk* inherent in the security (DP), the degree of *liquidity* of the security (LP), and the *maturity* of the security (MP):

$$k = k^* + IP + DP + LP + MP.$$

Interest rates fluctuate over time. Long-term rates change primarily because of changes in the rate of expected inflation, while short-term rates reflect both expected inflation and Federal Reserve intervention in the markets.

The *term structure* of interest rates, or the *yield curve*, describes the relationship between long- and short-term interest rates. Three major theories have been proposed to explain term structure: (1) the *expectations theory*, (2) the *liquidity preference theory*, and (3) the *market segmentation theory*. It appears that all three theories have some merit, but no single theory fully describes observed phenomena.

Interest rate levels have a profound effect on stock prices. Higher interest rates mean (1) higher interest expenses, and thus lower corporate income, and (2) higher returns in the bond market. Both of these factors tend to depress stock prices.

Finally, interest rate levels have a significant influence on financial policy. Since interest rate levels are difficult, if not impossible, to predict, sound financial policy calls for using a mix of short- and long-term debt, and equity, and for positioning the firm to survive in any future interest rate environment.

3-1   Define each of the following terms: *Questions*
a. Money market; capital market
b. Primary market; secondary market
c. Financial intermediary
d. Investment banking house
e. NYSE
f. Over-the-counter market
g. Mutual fund; money market fund
h. Production opportunities; consumption time preferences
i. Pure rate of return; real risk-free rate of interest
j. Bond ratings
k. Default risk premium (DP)
l. Inflation premium (IP)
m. Liquid asset; liquidity premium (LP)
n. Interest rate risk; maturity risk premium (MP)
o. Reinvestment rate risk
p. Term structure of interest rates; yield curve
q. "Normal" yield curve; inverted yield curve
r. Expectations theory; liquidity, or maturity preference, theory; market segmentation theory

3-2   Suppose interest rates on residential mortgages of equal risk were 14 percent in California and 16 percent in New York. Could this differential persist? What forces might tend to equalize rates? Would differences in borrowing costs for businesses of equal risk located in California and New York be more or less likely than mortgage rate differentials? Would differentials in the cost of money for New York and California firms be more likely to exist if the firms being compared were very large or if they were very small? What are the implications of all this for the pressure now being put on Congress to permit banks to engage in nationwide branching?

3-3   What would happen to the standard of living in the United States if people lost faith in the safety of our financial institutions? Explain.

3-4   How does a cost-efficient capital market hold down the prices of goods and services?

3-5   Which fluctuate more, long-term or short-term interest rates? Why?

3-6   You feel that the economy is just entering a recession. Your firm must raise capital immediately, and debt will be used. Would it be better to borrow on a long-term or a short-term basis? Explain.

3-7   Suppose the population of Area A is relatively young, while that of Area B is relatively old, but everything else about the two areas is equal.
      a. Would interest rates be the same or different in the two areas? Explain.
      b. Would a trend toward nationwide branching by banks and S&Ls, and the development of diversified financial corporations, affect your answer to Part a?

3-8   Suppose a new type of computer-controlled industrial robot were developed which was quite expensive but which would, in time, triple the productivity of the labor force. What effect would this have on interest rates?

3-9   Suppose a new and much more liberal Congress and administration were elected, and their first order of business was to change the Federal Reserve System and force the Fed to expand greatly the money supply. What effect would this have
      a. On the level and slope of the yield curve immediately after the announcement?
      b. On the level and slope of the yield curve that would probably exist two or three years in the future?

3-10 The federal government (1) encouraged the development of the S&L industry; (2) forced the industry to make long-term, fixed interest rate mortgages; and (3) forced the S&Ls to obtain most of their capital as deposits that were withdrawable on demand.
      a. Would S&Ls be better off in a world with a "normal" or an inverted yield curve?
      b. If federal actions such as deficit spending and expansion of the money supply produced a sharp increase in inflation, why might this necessitate a federal "bailout" of the S&L industry?

3-11 Suppose interest rates on Treasury bonds rose from 12 to 17 percent. Other things held constant, what do you think would happen to the price of an average company's common stock?

Self-Test Problem   ST-1 Assume that it is now January 1, 1985. The rate of inflation is expected to average 5 percent over 1985. However, increased government deficits and renewed vigor in the economy are expected to push inflation rates higher. Investors expect the inflation rate to be 6 percent in 1986, 7 percent in 1987, and 8 percent in 1988. The pure rate, k^*, is currently 3 percent. Assume that no maturity risk premiums are required on bonds with 5 years or less to maturity. The current interest rate on 5-year T-bonds is 10 percent.

    a. What is the arithmetic average expected inflation rate over the next 4 years? What is the geometric average?

    b. According to the expectations theory, what is the prevailing interest rate on 4-year T-bonds?

    c. What is the implied expected inflation rate in 1989, or Year 5?

Problems

3-1 Suppose you and most other investors expect the rate of inflation to be 10 percent next year, to fall to 5 percent during a recession in the following year, and then to run at a rate of 8 percent thereafter. Assume that the pure rate, k^*, is 2 percent, and that maturity risk premiums on Treasury securities rise from zero on very short-term bonds (those that mature in a few days) by 0.30 percentage points for each year to maturity, up to a limit of 1.5 percentage points on 5-year or longer-term T-bonds.

    a. Calculate the interest rate on 1, 2, 3, 4, 5, 10, and 20-year Treasury securities, and plot the yield curve.

    b. Now suppose IBM, an AAA company, had bonds with the same maturities as the Treasury bonds. As an approximation, plot an IBM yield curve on the same graph with the Treasury bond yield curve (Hint: Think about the default risk premium on IBM's long-term versus its short-term bonds.)

3-2 Look in *The Wall Street Journal* or some other paper which publishes interest rates on U.S. Treasury securities. Identify some Treasury bonds which mature at various dates in the future, record the years to maturity and the interest rate, and then plot a yield curve. (Note: Some of the bonds—for example, the 3 percent issue which matures in February 1995—will show very low yields. Disregard them—these are "flower bonds," which are generally owned by older people and are associated with funerals because they can be turned in and used at par value to pay estate taxes. They always sell at close to par and have a yield which is close to the coupon yield, irrespective of the "going rate of interest." Also, the yields quoted in the *Journal* are not for the same point in time for all bonds, so random variations will appear. An interest rate series that is purged of flower bonds and random variations, and hence one which provides a better picture of the true yield curve, can be obtained from the *Federal Reserve Bulletin*.

3-3 Look up the prices of IBM's stock and bonds in *The Wall Street Journal* or some other newspaper.

    a. What was the stock's price range over the last year?

    b. What is IBM's dividend? What is its dividend yield?

    c. What change occurred in IBM's stock price the day the newspaper was published?

    d. If IBM were to sell a new issue of $1,000 par value long-term bonds, approximately what coupon interest rate would it have to set on the bonds if it wanted to bring them out at par?

    e. If you had $10,000 and wanted to invest it in IBM, what return would you get if you bought the bonds, and what return if you bought IBM's stock? (Hint: Think about capital gains when you answer the stock part of this question.)

3-4   If the rate of interest on 2-year bonds is 9.4 percent and the rate on 1-year bills is 12 percent, what is the expected rate on 1-year bills one year from now? (Assume that the real rate is 2 percent.) What does this suggest about the expected rate of inflation?

3-5   In late 1980, the U.S. Commerce Department released new figures which showed that inflation was running at an annual rate of close to 15 percent. However, many investors expected the new Reagan administration to be more effective in controlling inflation than the Carter administration had been. At the time, the prime rate of interest was 21 percent, a record high. However, many observers felt that the extremely high interest rates and generally tight credit, which were brought on by the Federal Reserve System's attempts to curb the inflation rate, would shortly bring about a recession, which would in turn lead to a decline in the inflation rate and also in the rate of interest. Assume that at the beginning of 1981 the expected rate of inflation for 1981 was 12 percent; for 1982, 10 percent; for 1983, 8 percent; and for 1984 and thereafter, 6 percent.

   a. What was the average expected inflation rate over the 5-year period 1981-1985?
   b. What average *nominal* interest rate would, over the 5-year period, produce a 2 percent real rate of return?
   c. Assuming a pure rate of 2 percent, estimate the interest rate in January 1981 on bonds that mature in 1, 2, 5, 10, and 20 years, and draw a yield curve based on these data.
   d. Describe the general economic conditions that could be expected to produce an upward sloping curve.
   e. If the consensus view of investors in early 1981 had been that the expected rate of inflation for every future year was 10 percent, that is, $I_t = I_{t+1} = 10\%$ for $t = 1$ to ∞, what do you think the yield curve would have looked like? Consider all the factors that are likely to affect the curve. Does your answer here make you question the yield curve you drew in Part c?

3-6   Assume that it is now January 1, 1985. The real rate of return is estimated to be 2 percent. A 3-year bond bought today would yield $k = 10.638\%$. A 1-year bond purchased today would yield $k = 14\%$. A 1-year bond purchased one year from today (on January 1, 1986) is expected to carry an interest rate of 10 percent. What is the expected rate of inflation in the third year, according to the expectations theory?

Solution to Self-Test Problem

ST-1
a.   Arithmetic average = (5% + 6% + 7% + 8%)/4 = 26%/4 = 6.50%.
         Geometric average = $[(1.05)(1.06)(1.07)(1.08)]^{1/4} - 1.0$
                           $= (1.28618)^{0.25} - 1.0$
                           $= 1.06494 - 1.0$
                           $= 0.06494 = 6.494\%.$

b. $k_{\text{T-bond}} = k^* + I = 0.03 + 0.06494 = 0.09494 = 9.494\%.$

         Or, more precisely:

$$k_{T\text{-bond}} = k^* + I + k^*(I)$$
$$= 0.03 + 0.06494 + 0.03(0.06494)$$
$$= 0.09689 = 9.689\%.$$

c. If the 5-year T-bond rate is 10 percent, then the inflation rate is expected to average approximately $10\% - 3\% = 7\%$ over the next 5 years. Thus, the Year 5 implied inflation rate is 9.048 percent:

$$0.07 = [(1.05)(1.06)(1.07)(1.08)(1 + I_5)]^{1/5} - 1.0$$
$$(1.07)^5 = (1.05)(1.06)(1.07)(1.08)(1 + I_5)$$
$$1.40255 = 1.28618(1 + I_5)$$
$$1.09048 = 1 + I_5$$
$$I_5 = 0.09048 = 9.048\%.$$

Or, more precisely, the expected 5-year inflation rate is 6.796 percent:

$$0.10 = 0.03 + I + 0.03I$$
$$1.03I = 0.07$$
$$I = 0.07/1.03 = 0.06796.$$

Therefore,

$$(1.06796)^5 = 1.28618(1 + I_5)$$
$$1.38923 = 1.28618(1 + I_5)$$
$$1.08012 = 1 + I_5$$
$$I_5 = 0.08012 = 8.012\%.$$

Two of the most widely used textbooks on interest rates and financial markets are

Robinson, Ronald I., and Dwayne Wrightsman, *Financial Markets: The Accumulation and Allocation of Wealth* (New York: McGraw-Hill, 1980).

Van Horne, James C., *Financial Market Rates and Flows* (Englewood Cliffs, N.J.: Prentice-Hall, 1984).

For current empirical data and a forecast of monetary conditions, see the most recent edition of this annual publication:

Salomon Brothers, *Supply and Demand for Credit* (New York).

The classic works on term structure theories include the following:

Culbertson, John M., "The Term Structure of Interest Rates," *Quarterly Journal of Economics,* November 1957, 489-504.

Fisher, Irving, "Appreciation and Interest," *Publications of the American Economic Association,* August 1896, 23-29 and 91-92.

Hicks, J. R., *Value and Capital* (London: Oxford University Press, 1946).

Lutz, F. A., "The Structure of Interest Rates," *Quarterly Journal of Economics,* November 1940, 36-63.

Modigliani, Franco, and Richard Sutch, "Innovations in Interest Rate Policy," *American Economic Review,* May 1966, 178-197.

For additional information on financial institutions, see

Campbell, Tim S., *Financial Institutions, Markets, and Economic Activity* (New York: McGraw-Hill, 1982).

Gup, Benton E., *The Management of Financial Institutions* (Boston: Houghton Mifflin, 1984).

Selected Additional References

Valuation and the Cost of Capital

II

Time Value of Money

4

In 1984, the managers of AT&T's pension plan were offered the opportunity to buy J. C. Penney & Company bonds which cost $519.37 per bond, paid *zero* interest during their lifetime, but then paid $1,000 when they matured five years later, in 1989. At the same time, AT&T's fund managers were offered "regular" Penney bonds which cost $1,000, paid interest of $150 per year, and then returned the $1,000 purchase price at maturity in 1989. Should the AT&T managers buy the zero coupon bonds or the "regular" bonds?

A father, concerned about the rapidly rising cost of a college education, is planning a savings program to put his daughter through college. She is 13 years old, plans to enroll at the university 5 years from now, and should take 4 years to complete her education. Currently, the cost per year (for everything—food, clothing, tuition, books, transportation, and so forth) is $8,000, but a 10 percent inflation rate in these costs is forecasted. The daughter recently received $5,000 from her grandfather's estate; this money is invested in a bank account which pays 12 percent interest, compounded annually. How much will the father have to save each year between now and the time his daughter starts college in order to put her through school?

Suppose that in January 1984, General Motors' engineers informed top management that they had just made a breakthrough which would permit them to produce an electric auto capable of operating at an energy cost of about 3 cents per mile versus an energy cost of about 5 cents for a comparable gasoline-powered car. If GM were to produce the electric car, the company should be able to regain its market share previously lost to the Japanese. However, the investment required to complete development of the new batteries, design the new car, and tool up for production would amount to $5 billion per year for 5 years, starting immediately. Cash flows from the $25 billion investment should amount to $3 billion per year for 15 years, starting 5 years from now, or $45 billion in total. Assuming these cost and cash flow estimates are correct (and they are obviously subject to more forecasting errors than if GM simply bought $25 billion of Treasury bonds), should management give the go-ahead for full-scale electric car production?

These are a few of the many different kinds of questions that can only be answered after an analysis based on the concepts set forth in this chapter.

In Chapter 1, we saw that the primary goal of management is to maximize the value of a firm's stock. We also saw that stock values depend, in part, on the timing of the cash flows investors expect to receive—a dollar expected soon is worth more than a dollar expected in the far future. These concepts are extended and made more precise in this chapter, where we show how the timing of cash flows affects asset values and rates of return.

The principles of the time value of money as developed here also have many other applications, ranging from setting up schedules for paying off loans to making decisions about whether to acquire new equipment. *In fact, of all the techniques used in finance, none is more important than the time value of money.* Since this concept is used throughout the remainder of the book, it is vital to understand the material in this chapter thoroughly before going on to other topics.[1]

Future Value

A dollar in hand today is worth more than a dollar to be received next year because, if you had it now, you could invest it, earn interest, and end up next year with more than one dollar. To illustrate, suppose you had $100 and deposited it in a bank savings account that paid 5 percent interest compounded annually. How much would you have at the end of 1 year? Let us define terms as follows:

PV = present value of your account, or the beginning amount, $100.

---

[1]This chapter, and indeed the entire book, is written on the assumption that many students do not have financial calculators. The cost of these calculators is falling rapidly, however, so the assumption is becoming increasingly questionable. As a result, financial calculator solutions are set forth in footnotes to each of the major sections. Students are urged to obtain financial calculators and learn how to use them, for they—and not clumsy, rounded, and incomplete tables—are used exclusively in well-run, efficient businesses.

Even though financial calculators are efficient, they do pose a danger: People sometimes learn how to use them in a "cookbook" fashion without understanding the logical processes that underlie financial mathematics. Then, when confronted with a new type of problem, they do not understand the process well enough to set it up. Therefore, you are urged not only to get a good calculator and learn how to use it, but also to work through the illustrative problems "the long way" to insure that you understand the concepts involved.

k = interest rate the bank pays you = 5% per year, or, expressed as a decimal, 0.05. On financial calculators, the term i is frequently used rather than k.

I = dollars of interest you earn during the year = PV(k).

FV_n = future value, or ending amount, of your account at the end of n years. Whereas PV is the value now, at the *present* time, FV_n is the value n years into the future, after compound interest has been earned. Note also that FV_0 is the future value *zero* years into the future, which is the *present*, so FV_0 = PV.

n = number of years or, more generally, periods, involved in the transaction.

In our example, n = 1, so FV_n = FV_1, and it is calculated as follows:

$$
\begin{aligned}
FV_1 &= PV + I \\
&= PV + PV(k) \\
&= PV(1 + k).
\end{aligned} \tag{4-1}
$$

We can now use Equation 4-1 to find how much your account is worth at the end of one year:

$$FV_1 = \$100(1 + 0.05) = \$100(1.05) = \$105.$$

Your account earned $5 of interest (I = $5), so you have $105 at the end of the year.

Now suppose you leave your funds on deposit for 5 years; how much will you have at the end of the fifth year? The answer is $127.63; this value is worked out in Table 4-1. Notice that the Table 4-1 value for FV_2, the value of the account at the end of Year 2, is equal to

$$FV_2 = FV_1(1 + k) = PV(1 + k)(1 + k) = PV(1 + k)^2.$$

Continuing, we see that FV_3, the balance after 3 years, is

$$FV_3 = FV_2(1 + k) = PV(1 + k)^3.$$

Table 4-1
Compound Interest Calculations

Year	Beginning Amount, PV	×	(1 + k)	=	Ending Amount, FV_n
1	$100.00		1.05		$105.00
2	105.00		1.05		110.25
3	110.25		1.05		115.76
4	115.76		1.05		121.55
5	121.55		1.05		127.63

Table 4-2
Future Value of $1 at the End of n Periods:

$$FVIF_{k,n} = (1 + k)^n$$

Period (n)	1%	2%	3%	4%	5%	6%	7%	8%	9%	10%
1	1.0100	1.0200	1.0300	1.0400	1.0500	1.0600	1.0700	1.0800	1.0900	1.1000
2	1.0201	1.0404	1.0609	1.0816	1.1025	1.1236	1.1449	1.1664	1.1881	1.2100
3	1.0303	1.0612	1.0927	1.1249	1.1576	1.1910	1.2250	1.2597	1.2950	1.3310
4	1.0406	1.0824	1.1255	1.1699	1.2155	1.2625	1.3108	1.3605	1.4116	1.4641
5	1.0510	1.1041	1.1593	1.2167	**1.2763**	1.3382	1.4026	1.4693	1.5386	1.6105
6	1.0615	1.1262	1.1941	1.2653	1.3401	1.4185	1.5007	1.5869	1.6771	1.7716
7	1.0721	1.1487	1.2299	1.3159	1.4071	1.5036	1.6058	1.7138	1.8280	1.9487
8	1.0829	1.1717	1.2668	1.3686	1.4775	1.5938	1.7182	1.8509	1.9926	2.1436
9	1.0937	1.1951	1.3048	1.4233	1.5513	1.6895	1.8385	1.9990	2.1719	2.3579
10	1.1046	1.2190	1.3439	1.4802	1.6289	1.7908	1.9672	2.1589	2.3674	2.5937

In general, FV_n, the future value at the end of n years, is found as follows:

$$FV_n = PV(1 + k)^n. \tag{4-2}$$

Applying Equation 4-2 to our 5-year, 5 percent case, we obtain

$$
\begin{aligned}
FV_5 &= \$100(1.05)^5 \\
&= \$100(1.2763) \\
&= \$127.63,
\end{aligned}
$$

which is the same as the value worked out in Table 4-1.

If an electronic calculator is available, it is easy enough to calculate $(1 + k)^n$ directly.[2] However, tables have been constructed for values of $(1 + k)^n$ for wide ranges of k and n. Table 4-2 is illustrative; a more complete table, with more years and more interest rates, is given in Table A-3 at the end of the book. Notice that we have used the term *period* rather than *year* in Table 4-2. As we shall see later in the chapter, compounding can occur over periods of time different from one year. Thus, while compounding is often on an annual basis, it can be quarterly, semiannually, monthly, or for any other period.

---

[2]For example, to calculate $(1 + k)^n$ for k = 5% = 0.05 and n = 5 years, we multiply $(1 + k)$ = (1.05) times (1.05), multiply this product by (1.05), and so on:

$$(1 + k)^5 = (1.05)(1.05)(1.05)(1.05)(1.05) = 1.2763.$$

This same result is obtained using the exponential function of a calculator, y^x. Here y = (1.05); x = 5; and $(1.05)^5$ = 1.2763. If you have a financial calculator, simply punch in n = 5, k = i = 5, and PV = 1, and then punch the FV button to obtain the factor 1.2763. Alternatively, you could punch in n = 5, k = i = 5, and PV = 100, and then hit the FV button to find the final answer, $127.63.

We define the term *future value interest factor for k,n (FVIF_{k,n})* to equal $(1 + k)^n$. Therefore, Equation 4-2 can be written as $FV_n = PV(FVIF_{k,n})$. It is necessary only to go to an appropriate interest table (4-2 or A-3) to find the proper interest factor. For example, the correct interest factor for our 5-year, 5 percent illustration can be found in Table 4-2. We look down the period column to 5 and then across this row to the 5 percent column to find the interest factor, 1.2763. Then, using this interest factor, we find the value of $100 after 5 years as $FV_5 = PV(FVIF_{5\%,5 \text{ years}}) = \$100(1.2763) = \$127.63$, which is identical to the value obtained by the long method in Table 4-1.

Figure 4-1 shows how $1 (or any other sum) grows over time at various rates of interest. The 5 and 10 percent curves are based on the values given in Table 4-2. The higher the rate of interest, the faster is the rate of growth. The interest rate is, in fact, a growth rate; if a sum is deposited and earns 5 percent, then the funds on deposit grow at the rate of 5 percent per period.

Graphic View of the Compounding Process: Growth

Figure 4-1
Relationship between Future Value Interest Factors,
Interest Rates, and Time

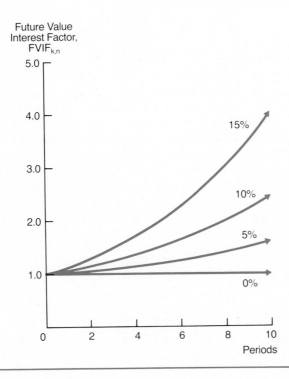

Present Value

Suppose you are offered the alternative of receiving either $127.63 at the end of 5 years or X dollars today. There is no question that the $127.63 will be paid in full (perhaps the payer is the United States government). Having no current need for the money, you would deposit the X dollars in a bank account that pays 5 percent interest. (Five percent is defined to be your *opportunity cost*, or the rate of interest you could earn on alternative investments of equal risk.) What value of X would make you indifferent in your choice between X dollars today and the promise of $127.63 five years hence?

From Table 4-1 we saw that the initial amount of $100 growing at 5 percent a year yields $127.63 at the end of 5 years. Thus, you should be indifferent to the choice between $100 today and $127.63 at the end of 5 years. The $100 is defined as the present value, or PV, of $127.63 due in 5 years when the opportunity cost is 5 percent. Therefore, if X is anything less than $100, you would prefer the promise of $127.63 in 5 years to X dollars today; if X were greater than $100, you would prefer X.

In general, the present value of a sum due n years in the future is the amount which, if it were on hand today, would grow to equal the future sum. Since $100 would grow to $127.63 in 5 years at a 5 percent interest rate, $100 is defined to be the present value of $127.63 due 5 years in the future when the appropriate interest rate is 5 percent.

Finding present values—or *discounting*, as it is commonly called—is simply the reverse of compounding, and Equation 4-2 can be transformed into a present value formula:

$$FV_n = PV(1 + k)^n, \qquad (4\text{-}2)$$

which, when solved for PV, gives

$$PV = \frac{FV_n}{(1 + k)^n} = FV_n(1 + k)^{-n} = FV_n\left[\frac{1}{(1 + k)}\right]^n. \qquad (4\text{-}3)$$

Tables have been constructed for the term in brackets for various values of k and n; Table 4-3 is an example. For a more complete table, see Table A-1 in Appendix A at the end of the book. For the illustrative case being considered, look down the 5 percent column in Table 4-3 to the fifth row. The figure shown there, 0.7835, is the *present value interest factor (PVIF$_{k,n}$)* used to determine the present value of $127.63 payable in 5 years, discounted at 5 percent:[3]

$$
\begin{aligned}
PV &= FV_5(PVIF_{5\%,5 \text{ years}}) \\
&= \$127.63(0.7835) \\
&= \$100.
\end{aligned}
$$

---

[3]Again, you could use a regular calculator to find PVIF and a financial calculator to find the PV of $100. With a financial calculator, just punch in n, k = i, and FV and then hit the PV button to find the PV.

Table 4-3
Present Value of $1 Due at the End of n Periods:

$$PVIF_{k,n} = \frac{1}{(1 + k)^n} = \left[\frac{1}{(1 + k)}\right]^n$$

Period (n)	1%	2%	3%	4%	5%	6%	7%	8%	9%	10%
1	.9901	.9804	.9709	.9615	.9524	.9434	.9346	.9259	.9174	.9091
2	.9803	.9612	.9426	.9246	.9070	.8900	.8734	.8573	.8417	.8264
3	.9706	.9423	.9151	.8890	.8638	.8396	.8163	.7938	.7722	.7513
4	.9610	.9238	.8885	.8548	.8227	.7921	.7629	.7350	.7084	.6830
5	.9515	.9057	.8626	.8219	**.7835**	.7473	.7130	.6806	.6499	.6209
6	.9420	.8880	.8375	.7903	.7462	.7050	.6663	.6302	.5963	.5645
7	.9327	.8706	.8131	.7599	.7107	.6651	.6227	.5835	.5470	.5132
8	.9235	.8535	.7894	.7307	.6768	.6274	.5820	.5403	.5019	.4665
9	.9143	.8368	.7664	.7026	.6446	.5919	.5439	.5002	.4604	.4241
10	.9053	.8203	.7441	.6756	.6139	.5584	.5083	.4632	.4224	.3855

Figure 4-2 shows how interest factors for discounting decrease as the discounting period increases. The curves in the figure were plotted with data taken from Table A-1; they show that the present value of a sum to be received at some future date decreases (1) as the payment date is extended further into the future and (2) as the discount rate increases.

Graphic View of the Discounting Process

Figure 4-2
Relationship between Present Value Interest Factors,
Interest Rates, and Time

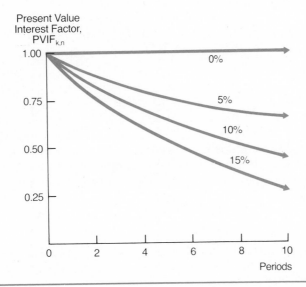

If relatively high discount rates apply, funds due in the future are worth very little today, and even at relatively low discount rates, the present values of funds due in the distant future are quite small.

Future Value versus Present Value

Notice that Equation 4-2, the basic equation for compounding, was developed from the logical sequence set forth in Table 4-1; the equation merely presents in mathematical form the steps outlined in the table. The present value interest factor ($PVIF_{k,n}$) in Equation 4-3, the basic equation for discounting or finding present values, was found as the *reciprocal* of the future value interest factor ($FVIF_{k,n}$) for the same k,n combination:

$$PVIF_{k,n} = \frac{1}{FVIF_{k,n}}.$$

For example, since the *future value* interest factor for 5 percent over 5 years is seen in Table 4-2 to be 1.2763, the *present value* interest factor for 5 percent over 5 years must be the reciprocal of 1.2763:

$$PVIF_{5\%,5 \text{ years}} = \frac{1}{1.2763} = 0.7835.$$

The $PVIF_{k,n}$ found in this manner does, of course, correspond with the $PVIF_{k,n}$ shown in Table 4-3.

The reciprocal nature of the relationship between present value and future value permits us to find present values in two ways—by multiplying or by dividing. Thus, the present value of $1,000 due in 5 years and discounted at 5 percent may be found as

$$PV = FV_n(PVIF_{k,n}) = FV_5\left(\frac{1}{1+k}\right)^5 = \$1,000(0.7835) = \$783.50,$$

or as

$$PV = \frac{FV_n}{FVIF_{k,n}} = \frac{FV_5}{(1+k)^5} = \frac{\$1,000}{1.2763} = \$783.50.$$

To conclude this comparison of present and future values, compare Figures 4-1 and 4-2. Notice that the vertical intercept is at 1.0 in each case, but future value interest factors rise, while present value interest factors decline.[4]

---

[4]Notice that Figure 4-2 is not a mirror image of Figure 4-1. The curves in Figure 4-1 approach ∞ as n increases; in Figure 4-2 the curves approach zero, not −∞.

An annuity is defined as a series of payments of a fixed amount for a specified number of periods. If payments, which are given the symbol PMT, occur at the end of each period, as they typically do, then we have an *ordinary annuity,* or a *deferred annuity,* as it is sometimes called. If payments are made at the beginning of each period, then we have an *annuity due.* Since ordinary (or deferred) annuities are far more common in finance, when the word *annuity* is used in this book, you may assume that payments are received at the end of each period unless otherwise indicated.

Future Value of an Annuity

A promise to pay $1,000 a year for 3 years is a 3-year annuity, and if each payment is made at the end of the year, it is an *ordinary annuity.* If you were to receive such an annuity and were to deposit each annual payment in a savings account paying 4 percent interest, how much would you have at the end of 3 years? The answer is shown graphically as a *time line* in Figure 4-3. The first payment is made at the end of Year 1, the second at the end of Year 2, and the third at the end of Year 3. Thus, the first payment is compounded over 2 years; the second payment is compounded for 1 year; and the last payment is not compounded at all. When the future values of each of the payments are added, their total is the sum of the annuity. In the example, this total is $3,121.60.

Ordinary Annuities

Expressed algebraically, with S_n, the sum of the annuity, defined as the future value of an annuity over n periods, PMT as the periodic payment, and $FVIFA_{k,n}$ as the future value interest factor for an annuity, the formula is

$$
\begin{aligned}
S_n &= PMT(1 + k)^{n-1} + PMT(1 + k)^{n-2} + \cdots + PMT(1 + k)^1 + PMT(1 + k)^0 \\
&= PMT[(1 + k)^{n-1} + (1 + k)^{n-2} + \cdots + (1 + k)^1 + (1 + k)^0] \\
&= PMT \sum_{t=1}^{n} (1 + k)^{n-t} \\
&= PMT[FVIFA_{k,n}].
\end{aligned}
$$

Figure 4-3
Time Line for an Ordinary Annuity:
Future Value with k = 4%

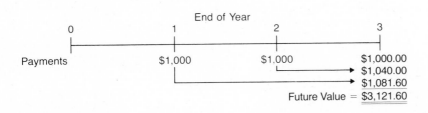

Table 4-4
Sum of an Annuity of $1 per Period for n Periods:

$$FVIFA_{k,n} = \sum_{t=1}^{n}(1 + k)^{n-t} = \frac{(1 + k)^n - 1}{k}$$

Number of Periods (n)	1%	2%	3%	4%	5%	6%	7%	8%	9%	10%
1	1.0000	1.0000	1.0000	1.0000	1.0000	1.0000	1.0000	1.0000	1.0000	1.0000
2	2.0100	2.0200	2.0300	2.0400	2.0500	2.0600	2.0700	2.0800	2.0900	2.1000
3	3.0301	3.0604	3.0909	**3.1216**	3.1525	3.1836	3.2149	3.2464	3.2781	3.3100
4	4.0604	4.1216	4.1836	4.2465	4.3101	4.3746	4.4399	4.5061	4.5731	4.6410
5	5.1010	5.2040	5.3091	5.4163	5.5256	5.6371	5.7507	5.8666	5.9847	6.1051
6	6.1520	6.3081	6.4684	6.6330	6.8019	6.9753	7.1533	7.3359	7.5233	7.7156
7	7.2135	7.4343	7.6625	7.8983	8.1420	8.3938	8.6540	8.9228	9.2004	9.4872
8	8.2857	8.5830	8.8923	9.2141	9.5491	9.8975	10.2598	10.6366	11.0285	11.4359
9	9.3685	9.7546	10.1591	10.5828	11.0266	11.4913	11.9780	12.4876	13.0210	13.5795
10	10.4622	10.9497	11.4639	12.0061	12.5779	13.1808	13.8164	14.4866	15.1929	15.9374

The expression in brackets, $FVIFA_{k,n}$, has been calculated for various combinations of k and n.[5] An illustrative set of these annuity interest factors is given in Table 4-4.[6] A full set of annuity present value factors is given in Table A-4 of Appendix A. To find the answer to the 3-year, $1,000 annuity problem, simply refer to Table 4-4, look down the 4 percent column to the row of the third period, and multiply the factor

----

[5]The third step in the equation is simply a shorthand expression in which sigma (Σ) signifies "sum up" or add the values of n factors. If $t = 1$, then $(1 + k)^{n-t} = (1 + k)^{n-1}$; if $t = 2$, then $(1 + k)^{n-t} = (1 + k)^{n-2}$; and so on until $t = n$, the last year the annuity provides any returns. The symbol

simply says, "Go through the following process: Let $t = 1$ and find the first factor. Then let $t = 2$ and find the second factor. Continue until each individual factor has been found, and then add these individual factors to find the value of the annuity factor."

[6]The equation given with Table 4-4 recognizes that an FVIFA factor is the sum of a geometric progression. The proof of this equation is given in Appendix 4B. Notice that it is easy to use the equation to develop annuity factors; this is especially useful if you need the FVIFA for some interest rate not given in the tables, for example, 6.5 percent. The equation is also useful for finding factors for fractional periods—for example, 2.5 years—but one needs a calculator with an exponential function for this.

Note also that one could, with a financial calculator, find S_n directly. Just punch in $n = 3$, $k = i = 4$, and $PMT = 1,000$, and then hit the FV button to get the answer, $S_n = $3,121.60$. Financial calculators also handle fractional years and interest rates with no trouble.

3.1216 by $1,000. The answer is the same as the one derived by the long method illustrated in Figure 4-3:

$$S_n = PMT(FVIFA_{k,n})$$
$$S_3 = \$1,000(FVIFA_{4\%,3 \text{ years}})$$
$$= \$1,000(3.1216) = \$3,121.60.$$

Notice that for all positive interest rates, the $FVIFA_{k,n}$ for the sum of an annuity is always equal to or greater than the number of periods the annuity runs. Also note that the entry for each period n in Table 4-4 is equal to 1.0 plus the sum of the entries in Table 4-2 up to Period n − 1. For example, the entry for Period 3 under the 4 percent column in Table 4-4 is equal to 1.000 + 1.0400 + 1.0816 = 3.1216.

Annuity Due

Had the three $1,000 payments in the previous example each been made at the beginning of the year, the annuity would have been an *annuity due*. In terms of Figure 4-3, each payment would have been shifted to the left, so there would have been $1,000 under Period 0 and a zero under Period 3. Thus, each payment would be compounded for one extra year.

We can modify Equation 4-4 to handle annuities due as follows:

$$S_n(\text{Annuity due}) = PMT(FVIFA_{k,n})(1 + k). \qquad \textbf{(4-4a)}$$

Each payment is compounded for one extra year, and multiplying $PMT(FVIFA_{k,n})$ times $(1 + k)$ takes care of this extra compounding. Applying Equation 4-4a to the previous example, we obtain

$$S_n(\text{Annuity due}) = \$1,000(3.1216)(1.04) = \$3,246.46$$

versus $3,121.60 for the ordinary annuity.[7] Since its payments come in faster, the annuity due is more valuable.

Present Value of an Annuity

Suppose you were offered the following alternatives: (1) a 3-year annuity with payments of $1,000 at the end of each year or (2) a lump sum payment today. You have no need for the money during the next 3 years, so if you accept the annuity, you would simply deposit the payments in a savings account paying 4 percent interest. Similarly, the lump sum payment would be deposited in an account paying 4 percent, compounded annually. How large must the lump sum payment be to make

[7]Note that some financial calculators have a switch or an entry marked "Due" or "Beginning" that permits you to convert from ordinary annuities to annuities due.

Figure 4-4
Time Line for an Ordinary Annuity:
Present Value with k = 4%

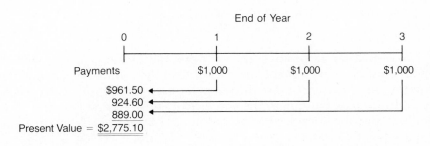

it equivalent to the annuity? The time line shown in Figure 4-4 will help explain the problem.

The present value of the first payment is $PMT[1/(1 + k)]$, the second is $PMT[1/(1 + k)]^2$, and so on. Defining the present value of an annuity of n periods as A_n, and with $PVIFA_{k,n}$ defined as the present value interest factor for an annuity, we may write the following equation in its several equivalent forms:

$$A_n = PMT\left(\frac{1}{1 + k}\right)^1 + PMT\left(\frac{1}{1 + k}\right)^2 + \cdots + PMT\left(\frac{1}{1 + k}\right)^n$$

$$= PMT\left[\frac{1}{(1 + k)} + \frac{1}{(1 + k)^2} + \cdots + \frac{1}{(1 + k)^n}\right] \qquad \text{(4-5)}$$

$$= PMT \sum_{t=1}^{n}\left(\frac{1}{1 + k}\right)^t$$

$$= PMT(PVIFA_{k,n}).$$

Again, tables have been worked out for $PVIFA_{k,n}$. Table 4-5 is illustrative; a more complete listing is found in Table A-2 in Appendix A.[8] From Table 4-5, the $PVIFA_{k,n}$ for a 3-year, 4 percent annuity is found to be 2.7751. Multiplying this factor by the $1,000 annual payment gives $2,775.10, the present value of the annuity. This value is identical to the long-method answer shown in Figure 4-4:[9]

$$A_n = PMT(PVIFA_{k,n})$$
$$A_3 = \$1{,}000(PVIFA_{4\%,3 \text{ years}})$$
$$= \$1{,}000(2.7751) = \$2{,}775.10.$$

---

[8]The second and third versions of the equation given at the top of Table 4-5 are derived in Appendix 4B.

[9]Again, the problem can be solved directly with a financial calculator. Just punch in n = 3, k = i = 4, and PMT = 1,000, and then hit the PV button to find A_n = $2,775.09. The penny difference results from rounding.

Table 4-5
Present Value of an Annuity of $1 per Period
for n Periods:

$$PVIFA_{k,n} = \sum_{t=1}^{n} \frac{1}{(1 + k)^t} = \frac{1 - \dfrac{1}{(1 + k)^n}}{k} = \frac{1}{k} - \frac{1}{k(1 + k)^n}$$

Number of Periods (n)	1%	2%	3%	4%	5%	6%	7%	8%	9%	10%
1	0.9901	0.9804	0.9709	0.9615	0.9524	0.9434	0.9346	0.9259	0.9174	0.9091
2	1.9704	1.9416	1.9135	1.8861	1.8594	1.8334	1.8080	1.7833	1.7591	1.7355
3	2.9410	2.8839	2.8286	**2.7751**	2.7232	2.6730	2.6243	2.5771	2.5313	2.4869
4	3.9020	3.8077	3.7171	3.6299	3.5460	3.4651	3.3872	3.3121	3.2397	3.1699
5	4.8534	4.7135	4.5797	4.4518	4.3295	4.2124	4.1002	3.9927	3.8897	3.7908
6	5.7955	5.6014	5.4172	5.2421	5.0757	4.9173	4.7665	4.6229	4.4859	4.3553
7	6.7282	6.4720	6.2303	6.0021	5.7864	5.5824	5.3893	5.2064	5.0330	4.8684
8	7.6517	7.3255	7.0197	6.7327	6.4632	6.2098	5.9713	5.7466	5.5348	5.3349
9	8.5660	8.1622	7.7861	7.4353	7.1078	6.8017	6.5152	6.2469	5.9952	5.7590
10	9.4713	8.9826	8.5302	8.1109	7.7217	7.3601	7.0236	6.7101	6.4177	6.1446

Notice that the entry for each value of n in Table 4-5 is equal to the sum of the entries in Table 4-3 up to and including Period n. For example, the PVIFA for 4 percent, 3 periods, as shown in Table 4-5, could have been calculated by summing values from Table 4-3:

$$0.9615 + 0.9246 + 0.8890 = 2.7751.$$

Notice also that for all positive interest rates, $PVIFA_{k,n}$ for the *present value* of an annuity is always less than the number of periods the annuity runs, whereas $FVIFA_{k,n}$ for the *sum* of an annuity is equal to or greater than the number of periods.

Present Value of an Annuity Due

Had the payments in the preceding example occurred at the beginning of each year, the annuity would have been an *annuity due*. In terms of Figure 4-4, each payment would have been shifted to the left, so $1,000 would have appeared under the 0, and a zero would have appeared under the 3. Each payment occurs one period earlier, so it has a higher PV. To account for these shifts, we modify Equation 4-5 as follows to find the present value of an annuity due:

$$A_n(\text{Annuity due}) = PMT(PVIFA_{k,n})(1 + k). \qquad \textbf{(4-5a)}$$

Our illustrative 3-year annuity, with payments made at the beginning of each year, thus has a present value of $2,886.10 versus a value of $2,775.10 on an ordinary annuity basis:

$$A_3 = \$1,000(2.7751)(1.04)$$
$$= \$2,775.10(1.04)$$
$$= \$2,886.10.$$

Since each payment comes earlier, an annuity due is worth more than an ordinary annuity.

Perpetuities

Most annuities call for payments to be made for some definite period of time—for example, $1,000 per year for 3 years. However, some annuities go on indefinitely; here the payments constitute an *infinite series*, and the series is defined as a *perpetuity*. The value of a perpetuity is found by applying Equation 4-6:[10]

$$\text{Present value of a perpetuity} = \frac{\text{Payment}}{\text{Discount rate}} = \frac{\text{PMT}}{\text{k}}. \qquad \text{(4-6)}$$

To illustrate, after the Napoleonic Wars, in 1815, the British government sold a huge bond issue and used the proceeds to pay off many smaller issues that had been floated in prior years to pay for the wars. Since the purpose of the new bonds was to consolidate past debts, the bonds were called "consols." Suppose each consol promised to pay $90 interest per year in perpetuity. (Actually, interest was stated in pounds.) What would each bond be worth if the going rate of interest, or the discount rate, were 8 percent? The answer is $1,125:

$$\text{Value} = \$90/0.08 = \$1,125.$$

Perpetuities are discussed further in Chapter 5, where procedures for finding the values of various types of securities (stocks and bonds) are analyzed.

Present Value of an Uneven Series of Payments

The definition of an annuity includes the words *fixed amount*—in other words, annuities involve situations where cash flows are *identical* in every period. Although many financial decisions do involve constant cash flows, some important decisions are concerned with uneven flows of cash. In particular, common stocks are typically expected to pay an

---

[10]The derivation of Equation 4-6 is given in Appendix 4B.

Table 4-6
Present Value of an Uneven Stream of Payments

Year	Payment	$\times$	$PVIF_{6\%,n}$	$=$	PV of Individual Payments
1	$ 100		0.9434		$ 94.34
2	200		0.8900		178.00
3	200		0.8396		167.92
4	200		0.7921		158.42
5	200		0.7473		149.46
6	0		0.7050		0
7	1,000		0.6651		665.10
				PV = Sum =	$1,413.24

increasing series of dividends over time. Consequently, it is necessary to expand our analysis to deal with varying payment streams.

The PV of an uneven stream of future income is found as the sum of the PVs of the individual components of the stream. For example, suppose we are trying to find the PV of the stream of payments shown in Table 4-6, discounted at 6 percent. As shown in the table, we multiply each payment by the appropriate $PVIF_{k,n}$, and then sum these products to obtain the PV of the stream, $1,413.24. Figure 4-5 gives a graphic view of the cash flow stream.[11]

The PV of the payments shown in Table 4-6 and Figure 4-5 for Years 2 through 5 can also be found by using the annuity equation; this alternative solution process has the following steps:

Step 1. Find the PV of $100 due in Year 1:

$$\$100(0.9434) = \$94.34.$$

Step 2. Recognize that a $200 annuity will be received during Years 2 through 5. Thus, we could determine the value of a 5-year annuity, subtract from it the value of a 1-year annuity, and have remaining the value of a 4-year annuity whose first payment is due in 2 years. This result is achieved by subtracting the PVIFA for a 1-year, 6 percent annuity from the PVIFA for a 5-year annuity and then multiplying the difference by $200:

---

[11]This general equation may be used to find the PV of an uneven series of payments:

$$PV = \sum_{t=1}^{n} PMT_t \left(\frac{1}{1+k}\right)^t = \sum_{t=1}^{n} PMT_t(PVIF_{k,t}),$$

where PMT_t is the payment in any Year t.

Figure 4-5
Time Line for an Uneven Cash Flow Stream:
Present Value with k = 6%

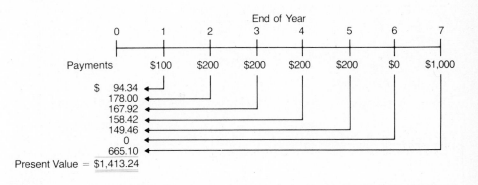

$$\text{PV of the annuity} = \$200(\text{PVIFA}_{6\%,5 \text{ years}}) - \$200(\text{PVIFA}_{6\%,1 \text{ year}})$$
$$= \$200(\text{PVIFA}_{6\%,5 \text{ years}} - \text{PVIFA}_{6\%,1 \text{ year}})$$
$$= \$200(4.2124 - 0.9434)$$
$$= \$200(3.2690) = \$653.80.$$

Thus, the present value of the annuity component of the uneven stream is $653.80.[12]

Step 3. Find the PV of the $1,000 due in Year 7:

$$\$1,000(0.6651) = \$665.10.$$

Step 4. Sum the components:

$$\$94.34 + \$653.80 + \$665.10 = \$1,413.24.$$

Either the Table 4-6 method or the method that utilizes the annuity formula can be used to solve problems of this type. However, the alternative annuity solution is easier if the annuity component runs for many years. For example, the alternative solution would be clearly superior for finding the PV of a stream consisting of $100 in Year 1, $200 in Years 2 through 29, and $1,000 in Year 30.

Notice that *the present value of a stream of future cash flows can always be found by summing the present values of each individual cash flow*. However,

---

[12]An alternative method for finding the present value of the annuity component of the cash flow stream would be (1) to find the value of the annuity at the end of Year 1 = $200(\text{PVIFA}_{6\%,4 \text{ years}}) = \$200(3.4651) = \$693.02$, and (2) discount this lump sum value for one year to the present, $693.02(\text{PVIF}_{6\%,1 \text{ year}}) = \$693.02(0.9434) = \$653.79$. (Note a one cent rounding error.)

cash flow regularities within the stream may allow the use of shortcuts such as finding the present value of several cash flows that comprise an annuity. Also, note that in some instances, we may want to find the value of a stream of payments at some point other than the present (Year 0). In this situation, we proceed as before but compound and discount to some other point in time, say Year 2, rather than Year 0.[13]

Determining Interest Rates

We can use the basic equations that were developed earlier in the chapter to determine the interest rates implicit in financial contracts.

Example 1. A bank offers to lend you $1,000 if you sign a note to repay $1,610.50 at the end of 5 years. What rate of interest is the bank charging you?

1. Recognize that $1,000 is the PV of $1,610.50 due in 5 years:

$$PV = \$1,000 = \$1,610.50(PVIF_{k,5\text{ years}}).$$

2. Solve for $PVIF_{k,5\text{ years}}$:

$$PVIF_{k,5\text{ years}} = \$1,000/\$1,610.50 = 0.6209.$$

3. Now turn to Table 4-3 (or Table A-1). Look across the row for Period 5 until you find the value 0.6209. It is in the 10 percent column, so you would be paying a 10 percent rate of interest if you were to take out the loan.[14]

Example 2. A bank offers to lend you $25,000 to buy a home. You must sign a mortgage calling for payments of $2,545.16 at the end of each of the next 25 years. What interest rate is the bank charging you?

1. Recognize that $25,000 is the PV of a 25-year, $2,545.16 annuity:

$$PV = \$25,000 = \sum_{t=1}^{25} \$2,545.16 \frac{1}{(1+k)^t}$$

$$= \$2,545.16(PVIFA_{k,25\text{ years}}).$$

---

[13]Note that problems involving unequal cash flows can be solved quite easily with a financial calculator. Some of these calculators permit the input of the separate cash flows, plus the interest rate. Then you hit the PV (or NPV) button to obtain the solution. However, this feature is not found on all financial calculators. Also, before closing this section, we should note that the future value of a series of uneven payments, often called the *terminal value*, is found by compounding each payment, and then summing the individual future values:

$$FV_n = \sum_{t=1}^{n} PMT_t(1+k)^{n-t}.$$

[14]Financial calculators are especially useful for finding interest rates in problems such as this one. Merely punch in PV = 1,000, n = 5, and FV = 1,610.5, and then hit the k = i button to obtain the interest rate.

2. Solve for $\text{PVIFA}_{k,25 \text{ years}}$:

$$\text{PVIFA}_{k,25 \text{ years}} = \$25,000/\$2,545.16 = 9.8226.$$

3. Turn to Table A-2. Looking across the row for 25 periods, you find 9.8226 under the column for 9 percent. Therefore, the rate of interest on this mortgage loan is 9 percent.[15]

While the tables can be used to find the interest rate implicit in single payments and annuities, it is more difficult to find the interest rate implicit in an uneven series of payments. One can use a trial-and-error procedure, a financial calculator with an IRR feature (IRRs are discussed in Chapter 8), or a graphic procedure, which is also discussed in Chapter 8. We will defer further discussion of this problem for now, but we will take it up later in our discussion of bond values and again in the capital budgeting chapters.

Semiannual and Other Compounding Periods

In all of our examples thus far, we have assumed that returns are received once a year, or annually. Suppose, however, that you put your $1,000 in a bank which advertises that it pays 6 percent compounded *semiannually*. How much will you have at the end of 1 year? Semiannual compounding means that interest is actually paid each 6 months; the procedures are illustrated in the tabular calculations in Table 4-7. Here the annual interest rate is divided by 2, but twice as many compounding periods are used, because interest is paid twice a year. Comparing the amount on hand at the end of the second six-month period, $1,060.90, with what would have been on hand under annual compounding, $1,060, we see that semiannual compounding is better from your standpoint as a saver. This result occurs because you earn *interest on interest* more frequently.[16]

Throughout the economy, different types of investments use different compounding periods. For example, bank and savings and loan accounts generally pay interest monthly or daily; most bonds pay interest

---

[15]To solve this problem with a financial calculator, punch in PV = 25,000, n = 25, and PMT = 2,545.16, and then hit the k = i button to find the interest rate.

Consider also the situation where the mortgage calls for annual payments of $2,400. Then $\text{PVIFA}_{k,n} = \$25,000/\$2,400 = 0.4167$. This value lies between the $\text{PVIFA}_{k,n}$ for 8 and 9 percent, but closer to 8 percent. The approximate rate for the mortgage could be found by "linear interpolation," a topic discussed in algebra texts, but today, we would use a financial calculator and find the interest rate merely by hitting the i button. The rate in this example is 8.2887 percent.

[16]Semiannual compounding is handled easily with a financial calculator. We merely set i = 3, n = 2, and PV = 1,000, and then hit the FV button to get the solution, FV = $1,060.90.

Table 4-7
Future Value Calculations with
Semiannual Compounding

Period	Beginning Amount, PV	×	(1 + k/2)	=	Ending Amount, FV_n
1	$1,000.00		(1.03)		$1,030.00
2	1,030.00		(1.03)		1,060.90

semiannually; and a few bonds pay annual interest.[17] Thus, if we are to compare securities with different compounding periods, we need to put them on a common basis. This need has led to the development of the terms *nominal*, or *stated, interest rate* versus the *effective annual rate* or *annual percentage rate (APR)*.[18] The stated, or nominal, rate is the quoted rate; thus, in our example, the nominal rate is 6 percent. *The annual percentage rate, or the effective annual rate, is the rate that would have produced the final compound value, $1,060.90, under annual rather than semiannual compounding.* In this case, the effective annual rate is 6.09 percent, found by solving for k in the following equation:

$$\$1,000(1 + k) = \$1,060.90$$

$$k = \frac{\$1,060.90}{\$1,000} - 1 = 0.0609 = 6.09\%.$$

Thus, if one bank offered 6 percent with semiannual compounding, while another offered 6.09 percent with annual compounding, they would both be paying the same effective annual rate of interest. In general, we can determine the effective annual percentage rate given the nominal rate, by solving Equation 4-7:[19]

$$\text{Effective annual rate} = 1 + \left(\frac{k_{Nom}}{m}\right)^m - 1.0. \qquad \textbf{(4-7)}$$

Here k_{Nom} is the nominal, or stated, rate, and m is the number of compounding periods per year. For example, to find the effective annual

---

[17]Many banks and savings and loans are now paying interest compounded continuously. Continuous compounding and discounting is discussed in Appendix 4A.

[18]The term *nominal* as it is used here has a different meaning from the way it was used in Chapter 3. In Chapter 3, *nominal interest rates* meant stated rates as opposed to real (inflation-adjusted) rates. In Chapter 4, the term *nominal rate* means the stated rate as opposed to the effective annual rate.

[19]It should be noted that many banks define the term *APR* simply as the nominal interest rate, that is, APR = k_{Nom}. Although this is a widespread practice, and although it apparently meets the minimum requirements of the "truth in lending" laws, it is somewhat deceptive because the true effective interest rate, which ought to be reported to borrowers, exceeds k_{Nom} except where annual compounding is used.

rate if the nominal rate is 6 percent, compounded semiannually, we make the following calculation:

$$\text{Effective annual rate} = \left[1 + \left(\frac{0.06}{2}\right)\right]^2 - 1.0$$
$$= (1.03)^2 - 1.0$$
$$= 1.0609 - 1.0$$
$$= 0.0609 = 6.09\%.$$

The points made about semiannual compounding can be generalized as follows. When compounding periods are more frequent than once a year, we use a modified version of Equation 4-2 to find the future value of a lump sum:

$$\text{Annual compounding: } FV_n = PV(1 + k)^n. \qquad \text{(4-2)}$$

$$\text{More frequent compounding: } FV_n = PV\left(1 + \frac{k_{Nom}}{m}\right)^{mn}. \qquad \text{(4-2a)}$$

Here m is the number of times per year compounding occurs, and n is the number of years. When banks compute daily interest, the value of m is set at 365, and Equation 4-2a is applied.[20]

The interest tables can be used when compounding occurs more than once a year. Simply divide the nominal, or stated, interest rate by the number of times compounding occurs, and multiply the years by the number of compounding periods per year. For example, to find the amount to which $1,000 will grow after 5 years if semiannual compounding is applied to a stated 4 percent interest rate, divide 4 percent by 2 and multiply the 5 years by 2. Then look in Table A-3 under the 2 percent column and in the row for Period 10. You find an interest factor of 1.2190. Multiplying this by the initial $1,000 gives a value of $1,219, the amount to which $1,000 will grow in 5 years at 4 percent, compounded semiannually. This compares with $1,216.70 for annual compounding.[21] The same procedure is applied in all the cases covered—compounding, discounting, single payments, and annuities.

---

[20]For example, the future value of $1 invested at 6 percent for 1 year under daily compounding is $1.0618:

$$FV_n = \$1\left(1 + \frac{0.06}{365}\right)^{365(1)}$$
$$= \$1(1.0618) = \$1.0618.$$

[21]With a financial calculator, simply press in i = k_{Nom}/m = 2, n = m × n = 10, and then proceed as before. It should be clear that the tables in this book are not complete enough to handle much variability of interest rates. For example, to handle 9 percent, compounded quarterly, we would need a table for 2¼ percent; 10 percent quarterly would require a table for 2½ percent; and so on. Years ago, very complete tables were available, but they were replaced by financial calculators.

One of the most important applications of compound interest involves loans that are to be paid off in installments over time. Examples include automobile loans, home mortgage loans, and most business debt other than very short-term debt. If a loan is to be repaid in equal periodic amounts (monthly, quarterly, or annually), it is said to be an *amortized loan*.[22]

Amortized Loans

To illustrate, suppose a firm borrows $1,000 to be repaid in 3 equal payments at the end of each of the next 3 years. The lender is to receive 6 percent interest on the funds that are outstanding at each point in time. The first task is to determine the amount the firm must repay each year, or the annual payment. To find this amount, recognize that the $1,000 represents the present value of an annuity of PMT dollars per year for 3 years, discounted at 6 percent:

$$\$1,000 = \text{PV of annuity} = \text{PMT}(\text{PVIFA}_{6\%,3 \text{ years}}).$$

The PVIFA is 2.6730, so

$$\$1,000 = \text{PMT}(2.6730).$$

Solving for PMT, we obtain

$$\text{PMT} = \$1,000/2.6730 = \$374.11.$$

If the firm pays the lender $374.11 at the end of each of the next 3 years, the percentage cost to the borrower, and the rate of return to the lender, will be 6 percent.

Each payment consists partly of interest and partly of a repayment of principal. This breakdown is given in the *amortization schedule* shown in Table 4-8. The interest component is largest in the first year, and it de-

Table 4-8
Loan Amortization Schedule

Year	Payment (1)	Interest[a] (2)	Repayment of Principal[b] (3)	Remaining Balance (4)
1	$ 374.11	$ 60.00	$ 314.11	$685.89
2	374.11	41.15	332.96	352.93
3	374.11	21.18	352.93	0
	$1,122.33	$122.33	$1,000.00	

[a]Interest is calculated by multiplying the loan balance at the beginning of the year by the interest rate. Therefore, interest in Year 1 is $1,000(0.06) = $60; in Year 2, $685.89(0.06) = $41.15; and in Year 3, $352.03(0.06) = $21.18.

[b]Repayment of principal is equal to the payment of $374.11 minus the interest charge.

---

[22]The word *amortized* comes from the Latin *mort*, meaning "dead," so an amortized loan is one that is "killed off" over time.

clines as the outstanding balance of the loan goes down. For tax purposes, the borrower reports as a deductible cost each year the interest payments in Column 2, while the lender reports these same amounts as taxable income.

Summary

Financial decisions often involve situations where we pay money at one point in time and receive money at some other time. Dollars paid or received at two different points in time are different, and this difference must be recognized when analyzing financial decisions and transactions.

Several basic equations are used in financial analysis:

Future value:

$$FV_n = PV(1 + k)^n = PV(FVIF_{k,n}).$$

Present value:

$$PV = FV_n\left[\frac{1}{1 + k}\right]^n = FV_n(1 + k)^{-n}$$

$$= FV_n(PVIF_{k,n}).$$

Future value (annuity):

$$S_n = PMT \sum_{t=1}^{n} (1 + k)^{n-t}$$

$$= PMT\left[\frac{(1 + k)^n - 1}{k}\right]$$

$$= PMT(FVIFA_{k,n}).$$

Present value (annuity):

$$A_n = PMT \sum_{t=1}^{n} \left(\frac{1}{1 + k}\right)^t$$

$$= PMT\left[\frac{1 - \frac{1}{(1 + k)^n}}{k}\right]$$

$$= PMT(PVIFA_{k,n}).$$

Present value (perpetuity):

$$PV \text{ (perpetuity)} = \frac{PMT}{k}.$$

These equations may also be applied to find the present or future value of uneven cash flow streams, and to find interest rates in situations where the other values are given but the value of k is unknown. To find the interest rate, one simply inserts the known values into the appropriate formula, solves for the interest factor, and looks up the interest factor in the appropriate table. If fractional rates are involved, one must go through a rather tedious interpolation process or else use a financial calculator.

The chapter also covered situations where compounding occurs more frequently than once a year, for example, semiannually or quarterly.

Here the stated, or nominal, interest rate, k_{Nom}, is divided by m, the number of compounding periods per year; the exponent used is m × n; and the equations given above are used with these modified values. Note that the *effective annual percentage rate* is somewhat greater than k_{Nom} when compounding is more frequent than annual.

The concepts covered in this chapter will be used throughout the remainder of the book. In Chapter 5, we apply present value concepts to the process of valuing stocks and bonds. This discussion is extended in Chapter 6, where we examine the determinants of a stock's required rate of return, and in later chapters, where the same basic concepts are applied to corporate decisions involving expenditures on capital assets as well as to decisions involving the types of capital that should be used to pay for assets.

<table>
<tr><td>4-1</td><td>Define each of the following terms:</td><td rowspan="9">*Questions*</td></tr>
</table>

4-1   Define each of the following terms:

    a. PV; k; I; FV_n; n

    b. $FVIF_{k,n}$; $PVIF_{k,n}$; $FVIFA_{k,n}$; $PVIFA_{k,n}$

    c. Annuity; single sum; uneven payment stream

    d. Deferred annuity; ordinary annuity; annuity due

    e. Perpetuity; consol

    f. Financial calculator versus "regular" calculator

    g. Annual, semiannual, quarterly, monthly, daily, and continuous compounding

    h. Effective annual rate; nominal rate, k_{Nom}

    i. Amortization schedule; principal component versus interest component

4-2   Is it true that for all positive interest rates, the following conditions hold: $FVIF_{k,n} \geq 1.0$; $PVIF_{k,n} \leq 1.0$; $FVIFA_{k,n} \geq$ number of periods the annuity lasts; and $PVIFA_{k,n} \leq$ number of periods the annuity lasts?

4-3   An *annuity* is defined as a series of payments of a fixed amount for a specific number of periods. Thus, $100 a year for 10 years is an annuity, but $100 in Year 1, $200 in Year 2, and $400 in Years 3 through 10 is *not* an annuity. However, the second series *contains* an annuity. Is this statement true or false?

4-4   If a firm's earnings per share grew from $1 to $2 over a 10-year period, the *total growth* was 100 percent, but the *annual growth rate* was *less than* 10 percent. Why is this so?

4-5   Assuming that two banks offer the same stated, or nominal, rate, would you rather have a deposit in a bank that uses annual, semiannual, or quarterly compounding? Explain.

4-6   To find the present value of an uneven series of payments, you can use the $PVIF_{k,n}$ tables; the $PVIFA_{k,n}$ tables can never be of use, even if some of the payments constitute an annuity (for example, $100 each for Years 3, 4, 5, and 6), because the entire series is not an annuity. Is this statement true or false?

4-7   The present value of a perpetual annuity is equal to the payment on the annuity, PMT, divided by the discount rate, k: PV = PMT/k. What is the *sum*, or future value, of a perpetuity?

Self-Test Problems

ST-1   Assume that it is now January 1, 1984. If you were to put $1,000 into a savings account on January 1, 1985, at an 8 percent interest rate, compounded annually, how much would you have in your account on January 1, 1988?

ST-2   Suppose instead that you deposited the $1,000 in 4 payments of $250 each on January 1st of 1985, 1986, 1987, and 1988. How much would you have in your account on January 1, 1988, if you deposited the $1,000 in this fashion?

ST-3   How large would each of your payments in Self-Test Problem ST-2 have to be for you to obtain the same ending balance as you would have obtained by the single $1,000 deposit?

ST-4   Going back to Self-Test Problem ST-1, what would your January 1, 1988, balance be if the bank used quarterly compounding rather than annual compounding?

ST-5   If you needed $1,000 as an ending balance in your account on January 1, 1988, how much would you have to deposit on January 1, 1985? Only one deposit will be made, and the compounding rate is 8 percent annually.

ST-6   If you want to make equal payments on each January 1st from 1985 through 1988 to accumulate the $1,000, how large must each of the 4 payments be? The compounding rate is 8 percent annually.

ST-7   If your father were to offer either to make the payments given in Self-Test Problem ST-6 or to give you a lump sum of $750 on January 1, 1985, which would you choose?

ST-8   If you have only $750 on January 1, 1985, what interest rate, compounded annually, would you have to earn to have the necessary $1,000 on January 1, 1988?

ST-9   Suppose you could only deposit $186.29 each January 1st from 1985 through 1988, but you still need $1,000 on January 1, 1988. What interest rate, with annual compounding, must you seek out to achieve your goal?

ST-10 To help you reach your $1,000 goal, your father offers to give you $400 on January 1, 1985. You will get a part-time job and make six additional payments of equal amounts each six months thereafter. If all of this money is deposited in a bank which pays 8 percent, compounded semiannually, how large must your payments be?

ST-11 What is the effective annual rate being paid by the bank in Self-Test Problem ST-10?

ST-12 Bank A pays 8 percent interest, compounded quarterly, on its money market account. The managers of Bank B want its money market account to equal Bank A's effective annual rate, but compounded on a monthly basis. What nominal, or stated, rate must Bank B set?

4-1 Find the following values *without using tables* and then work the prob-   *Problems*
     lems with tables to check your answers. If you have a financial calcu-
     lator, also use it to check your answers. Disregard rounding errors.
     a. An initial $200 compounded for 1 year at 5 percent.
     b. An initial $200 compounded for 2 years at 5 percent.
     c. The present value of $200 due in 1 year at a discount rate of 5
        percent.
     d. The present value of $200 due in 2 years at a discount rate of 5
        percent.

4-2 Use the tables to find the following values. Check your work with a
     financial calculator if you have one.
     a. An initial $200 compounded for 10 years at 5 percent.
     b. An initial $200 compounded for 10 years at 10 percent.
     c. The present value of $200 due in 10 years at a 5 percent discount
        rate.
     d. The present value of $518.80 due in 10 years at a 10 percent dis-
        count rate.

4-3 To the closest year, how long will it take $200 to double if it is depos-
     ited and earns the following rates?
     a. 10 percent.
     b. 15 percent.
     c. 100 percent.

$$200 = 400 N\left(\frac{1}{1+i}\right)^N$$
$$200 = 400 n\left(\frac{1}{1+.10}\right)^N$$
$$200 = 400\,(.9091)^N$$

4-4 Find the *future value* of the following annuities. The first payment in
     these annuities is made at the *end* of Year 1; that is, they are *ordinary*
     annuities.
     a. $200 per year for 10 years at 10 percent.
     b. $100 per year for 5 years at 5 percent.
     c. $200 per year for 5 years at 0 percent. — *1000*
     d. Now rework Parts a, b, and c assuming that payments are made at
        the *beginning* of each year, that is, they are *annuities due*.

4-5 Find the *present value* of the following *ordinary* annuities.
     a. $200 per year for 10 years at 10 percent.
     b. $100 per year for 5 years at 5 percent.
     c. $200 per year for 5 years at 0 percent.
     d. Now rework Parts a, b, and c assuming that payments are made at
        the *beginning* of each year, that is, that they are *annuities due*.

4-6 a. Find the present values of the following cash flow streams. The
        appropriate discount rate is 10 percent:

Year	Cash Stream A	Cash Stream B
1	$100	$300
2	$200	$200
3	$200	$200
4	$200	$200
5	$300	$100

    b. What is the value of each cash flow stream at a zero percent discount rate?

4-7   Find the present value of the following cash flow stream, discounted at 5 percent: Year 1, $100; Year 2, $200; Years 3 through 20, $300.

4-8   Last year, Spantex Corporation's sales were $4 million. Sales were $2 million 5 years earlier.

    a. To the nearest percentage point, at what rate have sales been growing?

    b. Suppose someone calculated the sales growth for Spantex Corporation in Part a as follows: "Sales doubled in 5 years. This represents a growth of 100 percent in 5 years, so, dividing 100 percent by 5, we find the growth rate to be 20 percent per year." Explain what is wrong with this calculation.

4-9   Find the interest rates, or rates of return, on each of the following:

    a. You borrow $200 and promise to pay back $210 at the end of 1 year.

    b. You lend $200, and you receive a promise of $210 at the end of 1 year.

    c. You borrow $20,000 and promise to pay back $32,578 at the end of 10 years.

    d. You borrow $2,000 and promise to make payments of $514.18 per year for 5 years.

4-10 The Ossenfort Company buys a machine for $20,000 and expects a return of $4,770.42 per year for the next 10 years. What is the expected rate of return on the machine?

4-11 Georgia-Atlantic invests $1 million to clear a tract of land and set out some young pine trees. The trees will mature in 10 years, at which time Georgia-Atlantic plans to sell the forest at an expected price of $3 million. What is Georgia-Atlantic's expected rate of return?

4-12 Your broker offers to sell you a note for $2,395.62 that will pay $600 per year for 5 years. If you buy the note, what rate of interest will you be earning?

4-13 A mortgage company offers to lend you $50,000; the loan calls for payments of $5,477.36 per year for 20 years. What interest rate is the mortgage company charging you?

4-14 To enable you to complete your last year in business school and then go through law school, you will need $7,000 per year for 4 years, starting next year (that is, you need the first payment of $7,000 one year from today). Your rich uncle, who offers to put you through school, deposits in a bank time deposit that pays 8 percent interest a sum of money that is sufficient to cover all expenses. The deposit will be made today.

    a. How large must the deposit be?

    b. How much will be in the account immediately after you make the first withdrawal? After the last withdrawal?

4-15 Find the amount to which $200 will grow under each of the following conditions:

    a. 8 percent compounded annually for 4 years.
    b. 8 percent compounded semiannually for 4 years.
    c. 8 percent compounded quarterly for 4 years.
    d. 12 percent compounded monthly for 1 year.

4-16 Find the present values of $200 due in the future under each of the following conditions:
    a. 8 percent nominal rate, semiannual compounding, discounted back 4 years.
    b. 8 percent nominal rate, quarterly compounding, discounted back 4 years.
    c. 12 percent nominal rate, monthly compounding, discounted back 1 year.

4-17 Find the indicated value of the following regular annuities:
    a. FV of $200 each 6 months for 4 years at a nominal rate of 12 percent, compounded semiannually.
    b. PV of $200 each 3 months for 4 years at a nominal rate of 12 percent, compounded semiannually.
    c. Repeat Parts a and b above, but assume that both rates are annual rates; that is, the compounding period is annually, while the payment period is semiannually and quarterly, respectively.

4-18 The First National Bank pays 13 percent interest compounded annually on time deposits. The Second National Bank pays 12 percent interest compounded quarterly.
    a. In which bank would you prefer to deposit your money?
    b. Could your choice of banks be influenced by the fact that you might want to withdraw your funds during the year as opposed to the end of a year? In answering this question, assume that funds must be left on deposit during the entire compounding period in order to receive any interest.

4-19 What is the present value of a perpetuity of $100 per year if the appropriate discount rate is 5 percent? If interest rates in general were to double, and the appropriate discount rate rise to 10 percent, what would happen to the present value of the perpetuity?

4-20 Set up an amortization schedule for a $20,000 loan to be repaid in equal installments at the end of each of the next 3 years. The interest rate is 10 percent.

4-21 Look back to the introduction of this chapter, where we described the situation facing AT&T's pension fund managers. They had the choice of investing in (1) a bond which costs $519.37 today, pays nothing during its life, and then pays $1,000 after 5 years, or (2) a bond which costs $1,000 today, pays $150 in interest at the end of each of the next 4 years, and pays $1,150 interest and principal at the end of Year 5.
    a. Which alternative provides the higher rate of return?
    b. Assume that the interest rate drops to 10 percent immediately after the bonds were purchased and remains at that level for the next 5 years. What returns would be actually realized on the two bond alternatives?

4-22   Again refer to the introduction. How much would the father have to save each year to send his daughter to college?

4-23   Refer once more to the introduction. Should General Motors invest in electric car production? Assume that the opportunity cost of the funds invested in the project is 10 percent.

Solutions to Self-Test Problems

ST-1

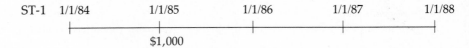

$1,000 is being compounded for 3 years:

$$FV = PV(1 + k)^n$$
$$= \$1,000(1 + 0.08)^3$$
$$= \$1,259.71.$$

ST-2   1/1/84   1/1/85   1/1/86   1/1/87   1/1/88

                 $250 $250 $250 $250

Future value of an annuity:

$$PMT(FVIFA_{k,n}) = \$250(4.5061) = \$1,126.53.$$

ST-3

$$FV = \$1,259.71.$$
$$k = 8\%.$$
$$n = 4.$$

$$PMT(FVIFA_{8\%,4}) = FV$$
$$PMT(4.5061) = \$1,259.71$$
$$PMT = \$1,259.71/4.5061 = \$279.56.$$

ST-4   The effective annual rate for 8 percent, quarterly compounding, is

$$APR = \left(1 + \frac{0.08}{4}\right)^4 - 1.0$$
$$= (1.02)^4 - 1.0 = 0.0824 = 8.24\%.$$

Therefore, $FV = \$1,000(1.0824)^3 = \$1,000(1.2681) = \$1,268.10.$

Alternatively, use FVIF for 2%, $3 \times 4 = 12$ periods:

$$FV = \$1,000(FVIF_{2\%,12})$$
$$= \$1,000(1.2682)$$
$$= \$1,268.20.$$
(Calculator solution = $1,268.24.)

Note that, since the interest factors are carried to only four decimal places, rounding errors occur. Rounding errors also occur between calculator and tabular solutions.

ST-5

$$FV = \$1,000.$$
$$n = 3.$$
$$k = 8\%.$$
$$FV(PVIF_{8\%,3}) = PV$$
$$\$1,000(0.7938) = \$793.80.$$
$$(\text{Calculator solution} = \$793.83)$$

ST-6

$$FV = \$1,000.$$
$$n = 4.$$
$$k = 8\%.$$
$$PMT(FVIFA_{8\%,4}) = FV$$
$$PMT = \frac{FV}{(FVIFA_{8\%,4})}$$
$$= \frac{\$1,000}{4.5061}$$
$$= \$221.92.$$

ST-7

$$PMT = \$221.92.$$
$$k = 8\%.$$
$$n = 4.$$
$$PMT(PVIFA_{8\%,4}) = PV$$
$$\$221.92(3.3121) = \$735.02.$$

This is less than the $750 lump sum offer, so your initial reaction might be to accept the lump sum of $750. However, this would be a mistake. Note that if you were to deposit the $750 on January 1, 1985, at an 8 percent interest rate, to be withdrawn on January 1, 1988, interest would only be compounded for 3 years, from January 1, 1985, to December 31, 1987, and future value would be only

$$PV(FVIF_{8\%,3}) = \$750(1.2597) = \$944.78.$$

The problem is that when you found the $735.02 PV of the annuity, you were finding the value of the annuity *today*, on January 1, 1984. You were comparing $735.02 today with the lump sum $750 one year from now. This is, of course, invalid. What you should have done was take the $735.02 found in Step 1, recognize that this is the PV of an annuity as of January 1, 1984, multiply $735.02 times 1.08 to get $793.82, and compare $793.82 with the lump sum of $750. You would then take your father's offer to pay off the loan rather than the lump sum on January 1, 1985.

ST-8

$$PV = \$750.$$
$$FV = \$1,000.$$
$$n = 3.$$
$$PV(FVIF_{k,3}) = FV$$
$$FVIF_{k,3} = \frac{FV}{PV}$$
$$= \frac{\$1,000}{\$750}$$
$$= 1.3333.$$

Use the Future Value of $1 table (Table A-3 at the end of the book) for 3 periods to find the interest rate corresponding to an FVIF of 1.3333. Look across the Period 3 row of Table A-3 until you come to 1.3333. The closest value is 1.3310 in the 10 percent column. Therefore, you would require an interest rate of approximately 10 percent to achieve your $1,000 goal. The exact rate required, found with a financial calculator, is 10.0642 percent.

ST-9

$$FV = \$1,000.$$
$$PMT = \$186.29.$$
$$n = 4.$$
$$PMT(FVIFA_{k,4}) = FV$$
$$\$186.29(FVIFA_{k,4}) = \$1,000$$
$$FVIFA_{k,4} = \frac{\$1,000}{\$186.29}$$
$$= 5.3680.$$

Using Table A-4 at the end of the book, we find that 5.3680 corresponds to a 20 percent interest rate. You might be able to find a borrower willing to offer you a 20 percent interest rate, but there would be some risk involved, and he might not actually pay you your $1,000! (Calculator solution = 19.9997%.)

ST-10

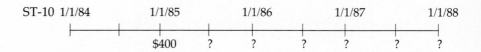

1/1/84		1/1/85		1/1/86		1/1/87		1/1/88
	$400	?	?	?	?	?	?	?

Find the future value of the original $400 deposit:

$$FV = PV(FVIF_{4\%,6}) = \$400(1.2653) = \$506.12.$$

This means that on January 1, 1988, you need an additional sum of $493.88:

$$\$1,000.00 - 505.12 = \$493.88.$$

This will be made in six equal payments:

$$FV = \$493.88.$$
$$n = 6.$$
$$k = 4\%.$$

$$PMT(FVIFA_{4\%,6}) = FV$$
$$PMT = \frac{FV}{(FVIFA_{4\%,6})}$$
$$= \frac{\$493.88}{6.6330}$$
$$= \$74.46.$$

ST-11   Effective annual rate $= \left(1 + \dfrac{k_{Nom}}{m}\right)^m - 1.0$

$$= \left(1 + \frac{0.08}{2}\right)^2 - 1 = (1.04)^2 - 1$$

$$= 1.0816 - 1 = 0.0816 = 8.16\%.$$

ST-12 Bank A's effective annual rate is 8.24 percent:

$$\text{Effective annual rate} = \left(1 + \frac{0.08}{4}\right)^4 - 1.0$$
$$= (1.02)^4 - 1 = 1.0824 - 1$$
$$= 0.0824 = 8.24\%.$$

Now Bank B must have the same effective annual rate:

$$\left(1 + \frac{k}{12}\right)^{12} - 1.0 = 0.0824$$

$$\left(1 + \frac{k}{12}\right)^{12} = 1.0824$$

$$1 + \frac{k}{12} = (1.0824)^{1/12}$$

$$1 + \frac{k}{12} = 1.00662$$

$$\frac{k}{12} = 0.00662$$

$$k = 0.07944 = 7.944\%.$$

Selected
Additional
References

For a more complete discussion of the mathematics of finance, see

Cissell, Robert, Helen Cissell, and David C. Flaspohler, *Mathematics of Finance* (Boston: Houghton Mifflin, 1978).

To learn more about using financial calculators, see the owner's handbook which came with your calculator. For example, see

Hewlett-Packard, HP-I2C, *Owner's Manual and Problem Solving Guide* (1983).

Continuous Compounding and Discounting $\quad$ 4A

In Chapter 4, we implicitly assumed that growth occurs at discrete intervals—annually, semiannually, and so forth. For some purposes, it is better to assume instantaneous, or *continuous*, growth. In this appendix, we develop present value and future value relationships when the interest rate is compounded continuously.

Continuous Compounding

The relationship between discrete and continuous compounding is illustrated in Figure 4A-1. Panel a shows the annual compounding case, where interest is added once a year; in Panel b compounding occurs twice a year; and in Panel c, interest is earned continuously. As the graphs show, the more frequent the compounding period, the larger is the final compound amount, because interest is earned on interest more often.

In Chapter 4, Equation 4-2a was developed to allow for any number of compounding periods per year:

$$FV_n = PV\left(1 + \frac{k_{Nom}}{m}\right)^{mn}. \qquad \textbf{(4-2a)}$$

Here k_{Nom} = the stated interest rate, m = the number of compounding periods per year, and n = the number of years. To illustrate, let PV = $100, k = 10%, and n = 5. At various compounding periods per year, we obtain the following future values at the end of 5 years:

Annual: $FV_5 = \$100\left(1.0 + \frac{0.10}{1}\right)^{1(5)} = \$100(1.10)^5 = \$161.05.$

Semiannual: $FV_5 = \$100\left(1.0 + \frac{0.10}{2}\right)^{2(5)} = \$100(1.05)^{10} = \$162.89.$

Monthly: $FV_5 = \$100\left(1.0 + \frac{0.10}{12}\right)^{12(5)} = \$100(1.0083)^{60} = \$164.53.$

Daily: $FV_5 = \$100\left(1.0 + \frac{0.10}{365}\right)^{365(5)} = \$164.86.$

121

Figure 4A-1
Annual, Semiannual, and Continuous Compounding:
Future Value with k = 25%

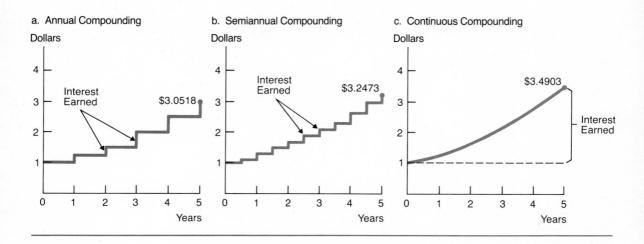

Hourly: $FV_5 = \$100\left(1.0 + \dfrac{0.10}{8{,}760}\right)^{365(24)(5)} = \$164.87.$

We could keep going, compounding every minute, every second, every 1/1,000th of a second, and so on. At the limit, we could compound every instant, or *continuously*. The equation for continuous compounding is

$$FV_n = PVe^{kn}, \tag{4A-1}$$

where e is the value 2.7183⋯.[1] If $100 is invested for 5 years at 10 percent compounded continuously, then FV_5 is computed as follows:

Continuous: $FV_5 = \$100[e^{0.10(5)}] = \$100(2.7183\cdots)^{0.5}$
$= \$164.872.$

Continuous
Discounting

Equation 4A-1 can be transformed into Equation 4A-2 and used to determine present values under continuous compounding:

$$PV = \frac{FV_n}{e^{kn}} = FV_n e^{-kn}. \tag{4A-2}$$

Thus, if $1,649 is due in 10 years, and if the appropriate *continuous* discount rate, k, is 5 percent, then the present value of this future payment is

---

[1]Scientific or financial calculators with antilogarithm, or e^x, functions can be used to evaluate Equation 4A-1.

$$PV = \$1,649\left[\frac{1}{(2.7183\cdots)^{0.5}}\right] = \frac{\$1,649}{1.649} = \$1,000.$$

Equation 4A-3 can be used to determine the effective annual percentage rate under continuous compounding:

Effective Annual Percentage Rate

$$\text{Effective annual rate} = e^k - 1.0. \qquad \text{(4A-3)}$$

Thus, if the nominal rate is 10 percent, compounded continuously, the effective annual rate is 10.52%:

$$\begin{aligned}
\text{Effective annual rate} &= e^{0.10} - 1.0 \\
&= (2.7183\cdots)^{0.10} - 1.0 \\
&= 1.1052 - 1.0 \\
&= 0.1052 = 10.52\%.
\end{aligned}$$

The principles of continuous compounding can also be applied to annuities. If the annuity cash flows occur at discrete intervals, but the interest rate is compounded continuously, then we merely determine the effective annual rate as above and apply the standard annuity valuation techniques developed in Chapter 4.

Annuities

For example, assume that you were to receive a $1,000 ordinary annuity for 3 years with the annual payments to be deposited in an account paying 4 percent compounded continuously. First, find the effective annual rate:

$$\begin{aligned}
\text{Effective annual rate} &= e^{0.04} - 1.0 \\
&= 1.0408 - 1.0 \\
&= 0.0408 = 4.08\%.
\end{aligned}$$

Then find the present value of the annuity using PVIFA = 2.7709, which we found using a calculator:

$$\begin{aligned}
A_n &= PMT(PVIFA_{k,n}) \\
&= \$1,000(2.7709) \\
&= \$2,770.90.
\end{aligned}$$

In theoretical finance, models have been developed which assume that cash flows are received continuously. These models are relatively complex, and they involve the use of integral calculus. A discussion of these models goes beyond the scope of this book.

ST-1 If you were to put $1,000 into a savings account on January 1, 1985, at an 8 percent interest rate, compounded continuously, how much would you have in your account on January 1, 1988?

Self-Test Problems

ST-2 If you needed $1,000 as an ending balance in your account on January 1, 1988, how much would you have to deposit on January 1, 1985? Only one deposit will be made, and the rate is 8 percent, compounded continuously.

ST-3 What is the effective annual percentage rate on an account paying 8 percent, compounded continuously?

Problems

4A-1 You put $500 into a savings account on January 1, 1985; another $500 on January 1, 1986; and a third on January 1, 1987. If the account pays 12 percent, compounded continuously, how much would you have on January 1, 1987?

4A-2 A bank which uses continuous compounding claims that a dollar deposit will grow to $1.822 after 5 years. What is the nominal, or stated, rate of interest?

Solutions to Self-Test Problems

ST-1 $\text{FV} = \text{PVe}^{kn} = \$1{,}000e^{0.08(3)} = \$1{,}000e^{0.24}$
$\quad\quad = \$1{,}000(2.7183\cdots)^{0.24} = \$1{,}000(1.27125) = \$1{,}271.25.$

ST-2 $\text{PV} = \text{FV}_ne^{-kn} = \$1{,}000e^{-0.08(3)}$
$\quad\quad = \$1{,}000e^{-0.24} = \$1{,}000(0.78663) = \$786.63.$

ST-3 Effective annual rate $= e^k - 1.0 = e^{0.08} - 1.0$
$\quad\quad\quad\quad\quad\quad = 1.0833 - 1.0 = 0.0833 = 8.33\%.$

Derivation of Equations

4B

A *perpetuity* is defined as an infinite series of payments of some constant amount, PMT, and its present value may be expressed as follows:

Present Value of a Perpetuity

$$PV = \sum_{t=1}^{\infty} \frac{PMT}{(1 + k)^t}$$

$$= \frac{PMT}{(1 + k)^1} + \frac{PMT}{(1 + k)^2} + \cdots + \frac{PMT}{(1 + k)^{n'}} \tag{4B-1}$$

where $n = \infty$. Equation 4B-1 may be rewritten as follows:

$$PV = PMT \left[\frac{1}{(1 + k)^1} + \frac{1}{(1 + k)^2} + \frac{1}{(1 + k)^n} \right]. \tag{4B-2}$$

Now we multiply both sides of Equation 4B-2 by $(1 + k)$, obtaining

$$PV(1 + k) = PMT \left[1 + \frac{1}{(1 + k)^1} + \frac{1}{(1 + k)^2} + \cdots + \frac{1}{(1 + k)^{n-1}} \right]. \tag{4B-3}$$

Subtract Equation 4B-2 from Equation 4B-3, obtaining this expression:

$$PV(k) = PMT \left[1 - \frac{1}{(1 + k)^n} \right]. \tag{4B-4}$$

As $n \to \infty$, $1/(1 + k)^n \to 0$, Equation 4B-4 approaches $PV(k) = PMT$, and so

$$PV = \frac{PMT}{k}. \tag{4-3}$$

Thus, we have derived Equation 4-3, the present value of a perpetuity.

Figure 4B-1 gives a plot of the present values of a series of payments of $1 per period discounted at a rate of 8 percent; the PVs were obtained from Table A-1 at the back of the book. If we added up all the PV PMT figures,

Figure 4B-1
Graphic View of Perpetuities and Annuities

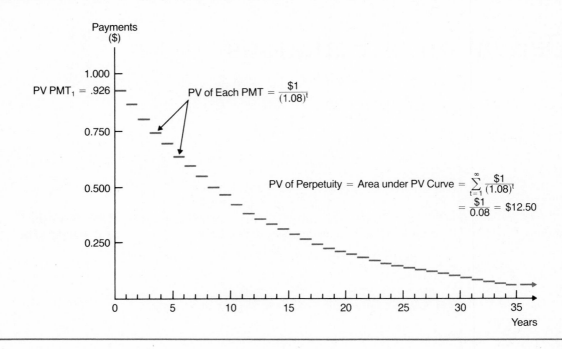

we would have the PV of a perpetuity of $1 per year discounted at an 8 percent rate. Using Equation 4-3 is far more efficient!

Present Value of an Annuity

In Chapter 4, at the top of Table 4-5, we gave this equation for the PV of an annuity:

$$\text{PVIFA}_{k,n} = \sum_{t=1}^{n} \frac{1}{(1 + k)^t} = \frac{1 - \dfrac{1}{(1 + k)^n}}{k}. \qquad \text{(4B-5)}$$

The second expression is not intuitively clear, but it is derived from the perpetuity equation developed above, Equation 4-3.

To better understand Equation 4B-5, consider (1) an *ordinary annuity* of $1 per year for 10 years, (2) an *ordinary perpetuity* of $1 per year forever whose first payment occurs 1 year from today, and (3) a *future perpetuity* of $1 per year whose payments begin 10 years from now. The discount rate is k = 8%.

It is easy to find the present values of the ordinary and the future perpetuities, and the difference between the two.

$$\text{PV of ordinary perpetuity} = \frac{\text{PMT}}{k} = \frac{\$1}{0.08} = \$12.5000$$

$$\text{PV of future perpetuity} = \frac{\text{PMT}}{k}\left[\frac{1}{(1+k)^n}\right]$$

$$= \frac{\$1}{0.08}\left[\frac{1}{(1.08)^{10}}\right]$$

$$= \$12.50(0.4632) = \underline{\$\ 5.7899}$$

$$\text{Difference} = \underline{\underline{\$\ 6.7101}}$$

The difference between these two perpetuities, $6.7101, must be the present value of the 10 payments which the ordinary perpetuity provides but which the deferred perpetuity does not provide. This value, $6.7101, is the PV of a 10-year annuity. You can confirm this by looking up $\text{PVIFA}_{8\%,10}$ years in Table A-2; this PVIFA is 6.7101. In terms of Figure 4B-1, the sum of the PV of the first 10 payments is $6.7101, and the sum of the PVs of the remaining payments is $5.7899.

We can use the knowledge that the PV of an annuity is the difference between the values of a ordinary perpetuity and a deferred perpetuity to derive Equation 4B-5:

$$\text{PV of annuity at } k\% \text{ for } n \text{ years} = \frac{\text{PMT}}{k} - \frac{\text{PMT}}{k}\left[\frac{1}{(1+k)^n}\right].$$

Let PMT = 1, so

$$\text{PV} = \frac{1}{k} - \frac{1}{k}\left[\frac{1}{(1+k)^n}\right],$$

which may be transformed as follows:

$$\text{PV} = \text{PVIFA}_{k,n} = \frac{1 - \dfrac{1}{(1+k)^n}}{k}. \tag{4B-5}$$

Equation 4B-5 is useful when one is calculating PVIFAs for k values not found in the tables, including fractional values, and when fractional years (say 5⅓ years) are involved.

Bond and Stock Valuation Models

5

In the fall of 1979, IBM raised $1 billion of new capital by selling bonds to the public. The issue was in two parts: A $500 million, 7-year issue which pays 9 1/2 percent interest and matures in 1986, and a $500 million, 25-year issue which pays 9 3/8 percent interest and matures in 2004. In each case, the individual bonds have a par value of $1,000 and were sold initially at that price. In 1981, after a sharp increase in interest rates, the IBM 9 1/2s of 1986 were selling for $800, and the 9 3/8s of 2004 were selling for $645. By 1984, however, the 9 1/2s were back up to $970, and the 9 3/8s were up to $830. Thus, in just 5 years, investors first lost 20 percent on the 7-year bonds and over 35 percent on the 25-year bonds of a AAA, super blue chip company, but they later recouped most of the loss on the shorter-term bond and a good part of that on the longer-term bond. How should IBM's financial executives use this information as they make their financial plans for 1985 and beyond? How should investors, both individual savers and institutional investors such as pension plan managers, use this type of information as they plan to put their savings to work?

At the time of its 1979 bond issue, IBM's stock was selling for about $70 per share, and it had fluctuated narrowly around that price since 1968. IBM's earnings per share from 1968 to 1979 had grown from $1.54 to $5.16, or at a rate of 11.6 percent per year; its dividend, which in 1979 was $3.44, had been growing even faster than its earnings. Most security analysts projected a continuation of these growth trends. Although IBM sold bonds rather than common stock to raise the $1 billion, selling stock was an alternative. How could IBM's managers have used the information on its stock price, earnings, and dividends to help reach the decision to finance with bonds rather than with stock? How could investors who were interested in IBM have used the information when deciding whether to buy new IBM bonds or to buy IBM stock on the New York Stock Exchange? What, if anything, could IBM's financial executives have done to increase the stock price and get it to move up and away from the $70 level at which it had been stuck for 11 years?

Providing a method of analysis which will help to answer questions such as these, and others, is the central goal of Chapter 5.

In the last chapter we examined the time value of money. The concepts developed there can be used to analyze the value of any asset whose value is derived from future cash flows, including real estate, factories, machinery, oil wells, coal mines, farmland, stocks, or bonds. In this chapter we use the time value concept to show how investors establish the values of stocks and bonds. The materials covered in the chapter are obviously important to investors and potential investors, and they are also important to corporate decision makers. *All important corporate decisions should be analyzed in terms of how a particular decision will affect the price of the firm's stock, so it is clearly important for management to know what determines a firm's stock price.*

Bond Values

Corporations raise capital in two primary forms—debt and common equity. Our first task in this chapter is to examine the valuation process for bonds, the primary type of long-term debt.

A *bond* is a promissory note issued by a business or governmental unit. For example, on January 1, 1985, the Teletron Electronics Company borrowed $50 million by selling 50,000 individual bonds for $1,000 each. As a first step in explaining how bond values are determined, we need to define some of the terms associated with these securities.

1. **Par value**. This is the stated face value of the bond, and it is usually set as $1,000, although multiples of $1,000 are used on occasion. The par value generally represents the amount of money that the firm borrows and promises to repay at some future date.

2. **Maturity date**. Bonds generally mature at a specified date; the par value is repaid at maturity to each bondholder. Teletron's bonds, which were issued in 1985, will mature in 2000. Thus, they had a 15-year maturity at time of issue. Most bonds have *original maturities* (the maturity at the time the bond is issued) of from 10 to 40 years, but this is not a hard and fast rule.[1] Of course, the maturity of a bond declines each year after it has been issued. Thus, Teletron's bonds had a 15-year original maturity, but in 1986 they will have a 14-year maturity, and so on.

---

[1]Some bonds have a provision whereby the issuer may pay them off prior to maturity. This feature is termed a *call provision*, and it is discussed in detail in Chapter 15. If a bond is callable, and if interest rates on new bonds fall below the coupon rate on the old bond, then the company can sell a new issue of low interest rate bonds and use the proceeds to retire the old high interest rate issue.

3. Coupon interest rate. The bond states that the issuer will pay a specified number of dollars of interest each year (or, more generally, each six months). When this *coupon payment*, as it is called, is divided by the par value, the result is the *coupon interest rate.* For example, Teletron Electronics' bonds have a $1,000 par value and pay $150 in interest each year. The bond's coupon interest is $150, so its coupon interest rate is 15 percent. The $150 is the yearly "rent" on the $1,000 loan. This payment, which is fixed at the time the bond is issued, remains in force, by contract, during the life of the bond. Incidentally, some time ago, each bond literally had small (½-by-2-inch), dated coupons attached to it, and on the interest payment date, the owner clipped the coupon off and either cashed it at his or her bank or mailed it to the company's paying agent, who then mailed back an interest check. Long-term bonds had lots of coupons, while short-term bonds had only a few. However, today virtually all bonds are *registered* bonds, and the interest checks are mailed directly to the owner of the bond.

4. New issues *versus* outstanding bonds. As we shall see, a bond's market price is determined in large part by its coupon interest payment— the higher the coupon, other things held constant, the higher the market price of the bond. At the time a bond is issued, the coupon is generally set at a level that will force the market price of the bond to equal its par value. If a lower coupon were set, investors simply would not be willing to pay $1,000 for the bond, while if a higher coupon were set, investors would clamor for the bond and bid its price up over $1,000. Issuers can judge quite precisely the coupon rate which will cause the bond to sell at its $1,000 par value.

A bond that has just been issued is defined as a *new issue*. (*The Wall Street Journal* classifies a new bond as a new issue for about two weeks after it has first been issued.) Once the bond has been on the market for a while, it is classified as an *outstanding* bond, also called a *seasoned issue*. As we shall see below, although newly issued bonds do generally sell at par, outstanding bonds do not always sell at par. Their coupon interest payments are constant, but economic conditions change, so although a bond with a $150 coupon may sell at par when it is issued, it can sell for more or less than $1,000 thereafter.

As we noted above, bonds call for the payment of a specified amount of interest for a stated number of years, and for the repayment of the par value on the bond's maturity date.[3] Thus, a bond represents an annuity

The Basic Bond Valuation Model[2]

---

[2]In finance, the term *model* refers to an equation or set of equations designed to show how one or more variables affect some other variable. Thus, a bond valuation model shows the mathematical relationship between a bond's price and the set of variables that determines this price.

[3]Actually, most bonds pay interest semiannually, not annually, which makes it necessary that we modify our valuation equation slightly. We abstract from semiannual compounding at this point to avoid unnecessary detail. However, the modification is discussed later in the chapter.

plus a lump sum, and its value is found as the present value of this payment stream.

The following equation is used to find a bond's value:

$$\text{Value} = V = \sum_{t=1}^{n} I\left(\frac{1}{1 + k_d}\right)^t + M\left(\frac{1}{1 + k_d}\right)^n$$

$$= I(\text{PVIFA}_{k_d,n}) + M(\text{PVIF}_{k_d,n}). \qquad \text{(5-1)}$$

Here

I = dollars of interest paid each year = coupon interest rate × par value.

M = par value, or maturity value, which is typically $1,000.

k_d = appropriate rate of interest on the bond.[4]

n = number of years until the bond matures; n declines each year after the bond is issued, so a bond which had a maturity of 30 years when it was issued (original maturity = 30 years) becomes a 29-year bond a year later.

We can use Equation 5-1 to find the value of Teletron's bonds when they were issued. Simply substitute $150 for I, $1,000 for M, and the values of PVIFA and PVIF at 15 percent, 15 periods, as found in Tables A-2 and A-1 at the end of the book:

$$V = \$150(5.8474) + \$1,000(0.1229)$$
$$= \$877.11 + \$122.90$$
$$= \$1,000.01 \approx \$1,000 \text{ when } k_d = 15\%.$$

Figure 5-1 gives a graphic view of the bond valuation process.

If k_d remained constant at 15 percent, what would the value of the bond be one year after it was issued? We can find this value using the same valuation formula, but now the term to maturity is only 14 years; that is n = 14:

$$V = \$150(5.7245) + \$1,000(0.1413)$$
$$= \$999.98 \approx \$1,000.$$

The value of the bond will remain at $1,000 as long as the appropriate interest rate for the bond remains constant at 15 percent.[5]

---

[4]The matter of how the appropriate interest rate is determined was discussed in Chapter 3. The bond's riskiness and years to maturity, as well as supply and demand conditions in the capital markets, all have an influence.

[5]The bond prices quoted by brokers are calculated as described. However, if you bought a bond, you would have to pay this basic price plus accrued interest. Thus, if you purchased a Teletron Electronics bond six months after it was issued, your broker would send you an invoice stating that you must pay $1,000 as the basic price of the bond plus $75 interest, representing one-half the annual interest of $150. The seller of the bond would receive $1,075. If you bought the bond the day before its interest payment date, you would pay $1,000 + 364/365($150) = $1,149.59. Of course, you would receive an interest payment of $150 at the end of the next day.

Note that if you have one of the better financial calculators, you can enter values for n, k = i, PMT, and FV = 1,000, and then press the PV button to find the value of the bond. This provides an exact solution only immediately after the interest payment date, but the same limitation applies to the tabular solution. Not all financial calculators have this feature, but some have built-in calendars which permit the calculation of exact values between interest payment dates.

Figure 5-1
Time Line for Teletron Electronics Bonds

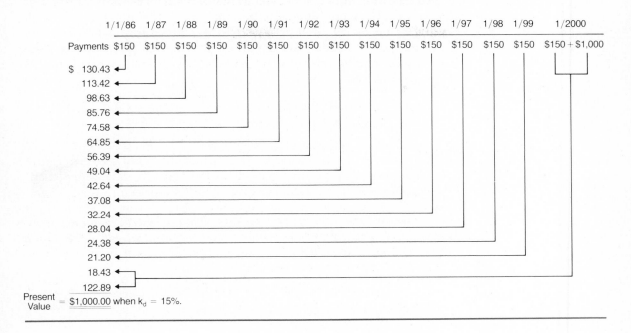

	1/1/86	1/87	1/88	1/89	1/90	1/91	1/92	1/93	1/94	1/95	1/96	1/97	1/98	1/99	1/2000
Payments	$150	$150	$150	$150	$150	$150	$150	$150	$150	$150	$150	$150	$150	$150	$150 + $1,000

$ 130.43
113.42
98.63
85.76
74.58
64.85
56.39
49.04
42.64
37.08
32.24
28.04
24.38
21.20
18.43
122.89

Present Value = $1,000.00 when $k_d = 15\%$.

Now suppose interest rates in the economy fell after the Teletron bonds were issued, and as a result k_d decreased from 15 to 10 percent. Both the coupon interest payments and the maturity value would remain constant, but now 10 percent values for PVIF and PVIFA would have to be used in Equation 5-1. The value of the bond at the end of the first year would be $1,368.31:

$$V = \$150(\text{PVIFA}_{10\%,14 \text{ years}}) + \$1,000(\text{PVIF}_{10\%,14 \text{ years}})$$
$$= \$150(7.3667) + \$1,000(0.2633)$$
$$= \$1,105.01 + \$263.30$$
$$= \$1,368.31.$$

Thus, the bond would sell at a *premium* over its par value.

The arithmetic of the bond price increase should be clear, but what is the logic behind the increase? The reason for it is simple. The fact that k_d has fallen to 10 percent means that, if you had $1,000 to invest, you could buy new bonds like Teletron's (every day some 10 to 12 companies sell new bonds), except that they would pay $100 of interest each year rather than $150. Naturally, you would prefer $150 to $100, so you would be willing to pay more than $1,000 for Teletron's bonds to obtain such a high coupon bond. All investors would recognize these facts, and as a result, the Teletron bonds would be bid up in price to $1,368.31, at which price the Teletron bonds would provide the same rate of return to a potential investor as the new bonds, 10 percent.

Assuming that interest rates remain constant at 10 percent for the next 14 years, what would happen to the value of a Teletron bond? It will fall gradually from $1,368.31 at present to $1,000 at maturity, when Teletron Electronics must redeem each bond for $1,000. This point can be illustrated by calculating the value of the bond 1 year later, when it has 13 years remaining to maturity:

$$V = \$150(\text{PVIFA}_{10\%,13 \text{ years}}) + \$1,000(\text{PVIF}_{10\%,13 \text{ years}})$$
$$= \$150(7.1034) + \$1,000(0.2897) = \$1,355.21.$$

Thus, the value of the bond has fallen from $1,368.31 to $1,355.21, or by $13.10. If you were to calculate the value of the bond at other future dates, the price would continue to fall as the maturity date approached.

Notice also that if you purchased the bond at a price of $1,368.31 and then sold it 1 year later, you would have a capital loss of $13.10, or a total return of $150.00 − $13.10 = $136.90. Your percentage rate of return would consist of an *interest yield* (also called a *current yield*) plus a *capital gains yield* calculated as follows:

Interest, or current, yield =	$150/$1,368.31 =	0.1096 =	10.96%
Capital gains yield =	−$13.10/$1,368.31 =	−0.0096 =	−0.96%
Total rate of return, or yield =	$136.90/$1,368.31 =	0.1001 ≈	10.00%

Had interest rates risen to 20 percent during the first year after issue rather than fallen, the value of Teletron's bonds would have declined to $769.49:

$$V = \$150(\text{PVIFA}_{20\%,14 \text{ years}}) + \$1,000(\text{PVIF}_{20\%,14 \text{ years}})$$
$$= \$150(4.6106) + \$1,000(0.0779)$$
$$= \$691.59 + \$77.90$$
$$= \$769.49.$$

In this case, the bond would sell at a *discount* below its par value.[6] Its total expected future yield would again consist of a current interest yield and a capital gains yield, and the capital gains yield would be *positive*. The total yield would, of course, be 20 percent.

---

[6]The discount or premium on a bond may also be calculated as follows:

$$\text{Discount or premium} = \left[\text{Interest payment on old bond} - \text{Interest payment on new bond}\right](\text{PVIFA}_{k_d,n}),$$

where n = years to maturity on the old bond and k_d = current rate of interest, or yield to maturity, on the new bond. For example, when interest rates rose to 20 percent one year after the bonds were issued, the discount on the Teletron bonds could be calculated as follows:

$$\text{Discount} = (\$150 - \$200)(4.6106) = -\$230.53.$$

Figure 5-2
Time Path of the Value of a 15% Coupon, $1,000 Par Value Bond
When Interest Rates Are 10%, 15%, and 20%

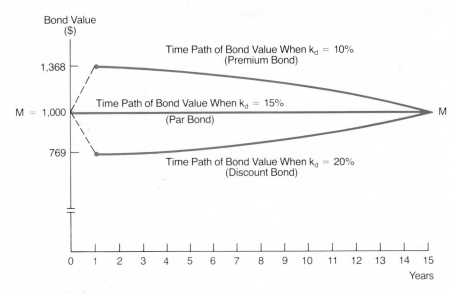

Note: The curves for 10% and 20% have a slight bow.

Figure 5-2 graphs the value of the bond over time, assuming that interest rates in the economy remain constant at 15 percent, fall to 10 percent, or rise to 20 percent. Of course, if interest rates do *not* remain constant, then the price of the bond will fluctuate. However, regardless of what interest rates do, the bond's price will approach $1,000 as the maturity date approaches (barring bankruptcy, in which case the bond's value might drop to zero).

Figure 5-2 illustrates the following key points:

1. Whenever the going rate of interest, k_d, is equal to the coupon rate, a bond will sell at its par value.

(The minus sign indicates discount.) This value agrees (except for a rounding error) with the value calculated above:

$$\text{Discount} = \text{Price} - \text{Par value} = \$769.49 - \$769.49 = -\$230.51.$$

In this form, we see that the discount is equal to the present value of the interest payment one sacrifices to buy a low-coupon old bond rather than a high-coupon new bond. The longer the bond has to run, the greater is the sacrifice, and hence the greater the discount.

2. Whenever the going rate of interest is above the coupon rate, a bond will sell below its par value. Such a bond is called a *discount bond*.

3. Whenever the going rate of interest is below the coupon rate, a bond will sell above its par value. Such a bond is said to sell at a *premium*.

4. An increase in interest rates will cause the price of an outstanding bond to fall, while a decrease in rates will cause the bond's price to rise.

5. The market value of a bond will approach its par value as its maturity date approaches.

These points are very important to investors, for they show that bondholders may suffer capital losses or make capital gains, depending on whether interest rates rise or fall. And, as we saw in Chapter 3, interest rates do indeed change over time.

Finding the Interest Rate on a Bond: Yield to Maturity

Suppose you were offered a 14-year, 15 percent coupon, $1,000 par value bond at a price of $1,368.31. What rate of interest would you earn if you bought the bond and held it to maturity? This rate is defined as the bond's *yield to maturity*, and it is the interest rate discussed by bond traders when they talk about rates of return. To find the yield to maturity, often called the *YTM*, you could solve the following equation for k_d:

$$V = \$1,368.31 = \frac{\$150}{(1 + k_d)^1} + \frac{\$150}{(1 + k_d)^2} + \cdots + \frac{\$150}{(1 + k_d)^{14}} + \frac{\$1,000}{(1 + k_d)^{14}}$$
$$= \$150(PVIFA_{k_d,n}) + \$1,000(PVIF_{k_d,n}).$$

We can substitute values for PVIFA and PVIF until we find a pair that "works" and forces this equality:

$$\$1,368.31 = \$150(PVIFA_{k_d,n}) + \$1,000(PVIF_{k_d,n}).$$

What would be a good interest rate to use as a starting point? First, we know that since the bond is selling at a premium over its par value (1,368.31 versus $1,000), the bond's yield to maturity must be *below* the 15 percent coupon rate. Therefore, we might try a rate of 12 percent. Substituting factors for 12 percent, we obtain

$$\$150(6.6282) + \$1,000(0.2046) = \$1,198.83 \neq \$1,368.31.$$

Our calculated bond value, $1,198.83, is *below* the actual market price, so the YTM is *not* 12 percent. To raise the calculated value, we must *lower* the interest rate used in the process. Inserting factors for 10 percent, we obtain

$$V = \$150(7.3667) + \$1,000(0.2633)$$
$$= \$1,105.01 + \$263.30$$
$$= \$1,368.31.$$

This calculated value is exactly equal to the market price of the bond; thus, 10 percent is the bond's yield to maturity: $k_d = YTM = 10.0\%$.[7]

The yield to maturity is identical to the total rate of return we calculated in the preceding section. The YTM for a bond that sells at par consists entirely of an interest yield, but if the bond sells at a price other then its par value, the YTM consists of the interest yield plus a positive or negative capital gains yield. Note also that a bond's yield to maturity changes whenever interest rates in the economy change, and this is almost daily. One who purchases a bond and holds it until it matures will receive the YTM that existed on the purchase date, but the bond's YTM will change frequently.[8]

As we saw in Chapter 3, interest rates go up and down over time, and as interest rates change, the values of outstanding bonds also fluctuate. Suppose you bought some 15 percent Teletron bonds at a price of $1,000

Interest Rate Risk on a Bond

---

[7]We found the yield to maturity on this bond by trial and error. It should also be noted that some financial calculators can be used to find the YTM on a bond with very little effort. A few years ago, bond traders all had specialized tables called *bond tables* that gave yields on bonds of different maturities selling at different premiums and discounts. Because the calculators are so much more efficient (and accurate), bond tables are rarely used any more.

There is also a formula that can be used to find the *approximate* YTM on a bond:

$$k_d = YTM \approx \frac{I + (M - V)/n}{(M + V)/2}.$$

In our example, I = $150, M = $1,000, V = $1,368.31, and n = 14, so

$$k_d \approx \frac{\$150 + (\$1,000 - \$1,368.31)/14}{(\$1,000 + \$1,368.31)/2} = 0.1045 = 10.45\%.$$

The exact value is 10 percent, so *this formula should only be used to obtain a starting point for the trial-and-error method.*

[8]If you had bought a bond that was callable (see Footnote 1), and the company called it, you would not have the option of holding the bond until it matured, so the yield to maturity would not be applicable. For example, if a firm had callable 15 percent coupon bonds outstanding, and interest rates fell from 15 percent to 10 percent, then the company could call in the 15 percent bonds, replace them with 10 percent bonds, and save $150 − $100 = $50 interest per bond per year. This is beneficial to the company, but not to bondholders.

If current interest rates are well below an outstanding bond's coupon rate, then the bond is likely to be called, and investors should estimate the expected rate of return on the bond as the *yield to call (YTC)* rather than as the yield to maturity (YTM). To calculate the YTC, solve this equation for k_d:

$$\text{Price of bond} = \sum_{t=1}^{N} \frac{I}{(1 + k_d)^t} + \frac{\text{Call price}}{(1 + k_d)^n}.$$

Here N = years until the company can call the bond; call price is the price the company must pay in order to call the bond (it is often set equal to the par value plus one year's interest); and k_d is the YTC. Problem 5-11 at the end of the chapter deals with the YTC calculation.

and interest rates subsequently rose to 20 percent. As we saw above, the price of the bonds would fall to $769.49, so you would have a loss of $230.51 per bond.[9] Interest rates can and do rise, and rising rates will cause a loss of value for bondholders. Thus, people or firms who invest in bonds are exposed to risk from changing interest rates, or *interest rate risk*.

One's exposure to interest rate risk is higher on bonds with long maturities than on those maturing in the near future. This point can be demonstrated by showing how the value of a 1-year, 15 percent coupon bond changes with changes in k_d, and then comparing these changes with those on a 14-year bond as calculated above. The 1-year bond's values at different interest rates are shown here:

Value at $k_d = \$10\%$

$$V = \$150(PVIFA_{10\%,1\ year}) + \$1,000(PVIF_{10\%,1\ year})$$
$$= \$150(0.9091) + \$1,000(0.9091)$$
$$= \$136.37 + \$909.10 = \$1,045.47.$$

Value at $k_d = 15\%$

$$V = \$150(0.8696) + \$1,000(0.8696)$$
$$= \$130.44 + \$869.60 \approx \$1,000.$$

Value at $k_d = 20\%$

$$V = \$150(0.8333) + \$1,000(0.8333)$$
$$= \$125.00 + \$833.30 = \$958.30.$$

The values of the 1-year and 14-year bonds, at different current market interest rates, are summarized and plotted in Figure 5-3. Notice how much more sensitive the price of the long-term bond is to changes in interest rates. At a 15 percent interest rate, both the long- and the short-term bonds are valued at $1,000. When rates rise to 20 percent, the long-term bond falls to $769.49, while the short-term bond falls only to $958.30. A similar situation occurs when rates fall below 15 percent.

For bonds that are selling at par, this differential sensitivity to changes in interest rates always holds true—the longer the maturity of the bond, the greater its price change in response to a given change in interest rates. Thus, even if

---

[9]You would have an *accounting* (and tax) loss only if you sold the bond; if you hold it to maturity, you will not have an accounting loss. However, even if you do not sell, you will have suffered a *real economic loss* in an opportunity cost sense, because you will have lost the opportunity to invest at 20 percent, and you will be stuck with a 15 percent bond in a 20 percent market. So, in finance we regard "paper losses" as being just as real as realized accounting losses.

Figure 5-3
Value of Long- and Short-Term 15% Coupon Rate Bonds
at Different Market Interest Rates

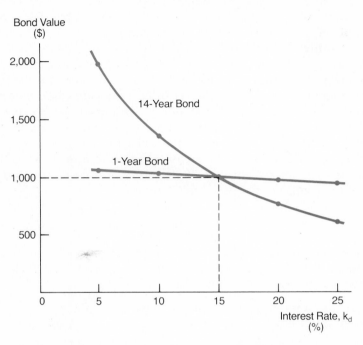

Current Market	Value of	
Interest Rate, k_d	1-Year Bond	14-Year Bond
5%	$1,095.24	$1,989.86
10	1,045.45	1,368.33
15	1,000.00	1,000.00
20	958.33	769.49
25	920.00	617.59

the risk of default on two bonds is exactly the same, the one with the longer maturity is typically exposed to more risk from a rise in interest rates.

The logical explanation for this difference in interest rate risk is simple. Suppose you bought a 14-year bond that yielded 15 percent, or $150 a year. Now suppose interest rates on comparable risk bonds rose to 20 percent. You would be stuck with only $150 interest for the next 14 years. On the other hand, had you bought a 1-year bond, you would only have a low return for one year. At the end of the year, you would get your $1,000 back, and you could then reinvest it and receive 20 percent, or $200 per year, for the next 13 years. Thus, interest rate risk reflects the length of time one is committed to a given investment.[10]

However, buying a 1-year bond instead of a 14-year bond exposes the buyer to *reinvestment rate risk*. Suppose you bought a 1-year bond that yielded 15 percent and then interest rates on comparable risk bonds fell to 10 percent. Now, after 1 year, when you get your $1,000 back, you will have to invest it at only 10 percent, thus losing $150 − $100 = $50 in annual interest. Had you bought the 14-year bond, and interest rates fell, you would continue to receive $150 in annual interest payments. Of course, if you intend to spend the $1,000 after 1 year, then investing in a 1-year bond would guarantee (ignoring default risk) that you would get your $1,000 back (plus interest) after 1 year. The 14-year bond investment, on the other hand, would return less than $1,000 after 1 year if interest rates subsequently increase. The implications of all this for pension fund management, which is of central importance to a firm's financial manager, are discussed in Chapter 27.

Bond Values with Semiannual Compounding

Although some bonds do pay interest annually, most actually pay interest semiannually. To evaluate these bonds, we must modify the valuation model (Equation 5-1) as follows:

1. Divide the annual coupon interest payment by 2 to determine the amount of interest paid each six months.

2. Multiply the years to maturity, n, by 2 to determine the number of periods.

3. Divide the annual interest rate, k_d, by 2 to determine the semiannual interest rate.

---

[10]If a 10-year bond were plotted in Figure 5-3, its curve would lie between those of the 14-year bond and the 1-year bond. The curve of a 1-month bond would be almost horizontal, indicating that its price changes very little in response to an interest rate change.

It should be noted that under certain conditions, a bond with a *shorter* maturity can have more interest rate risk than one with a longer maturity. This situation arises if the longer-maturity bond has much higher coupons than the shorter-maturity bond. For example, if k_d were 12 percent, then a 3 percent coupon, 20-year bond would sell for $328, while a 12 percent coupon, 30-year bond would sell for $1,000 at the same time. Now suppose interest rates rose, and k_d went up to 16 percent. The shorter-maturity, low coupon bond's price would fall from $328 to $229, a drop of 30 percent, while the longer-maturity, high coupon bond's price would fall from $1,000 to $753, a drop of only 25 percent. This situation occurs because, if you were to construct a graph of when the total cash flows (interest each year and final maturity payment) from each bond occur, you would find that a higher percentage of the 30-year bond's cash flows occur in the earlier years.

This situation has led to the concept of *duration*, which is like maturity, except that it gives weight to coupon payments. Duration is a better index of a bond's risk than is maturity, and bonds with longer durations are always subject to more interest rate risk than those with shorter durations. In this case, the 3 percent coupon, 20-year bond has a longer duration than the 12 percent coupon, 30-year bond. See Chapter 27 for a discussion of duration.

By making these changes, we arrive at the following equation for finding the value of a bond that pays interest semiannually:

$$V = \sum_{t=1}^{2n} \frac{I}{2}\left(\frac{1}{1 + \frac{k_d}{2}}\right)^t + M\left(\frac{1}{1 + \frac{k_d}{2}}\right)^{2n}$$

$$= \frac{I}{2}(\text{PVIFA}_{k_d/2, 2n}) + M(\text{PVIF}_{k_d/2, 2n}).$$

(5-1a)

To illustrate, assume now that Teletron Electronics' bonds pay $75 interest each 6 months rather than $150 at the end of each year. Thus, each interest payment is only half as large, but there are twice as many of them. When the going rate of interest is 10 percent, the value of this 15-year bond is found as follows:[11]

$$V = \$75(\text{PVIFA}_{5\%, 30 \text{ periods}}) + \$1,000(\text{PVIF}_{5\%, 30 \text{ periods}})$$
$$= \$75(15.3725) + \$1,000(0.2314)$$
$$= \$1,152.94 + \$231.40$$
$$= \$1,384.34.$$

Students sometimes want to discount the maturity value at 10 percent over 15 years, rather than at 5 percent over 30 six-month periods. This is incorrect—logically, all cash flows in a given contract must be discounted on the same basis, semiannually in this instance. For consistency, bond traders *must* apply semiannual compounding to the maturity value, and they do.

We know from Chapter 3 that interest rates have risen sharply in recent years. We also know that the prices of outstanding bonds fall during periods when interest rates are rising. Therefore, one would expect to find that bond prices in the market have fallen in recent years. Figure 5-4 shows that this is indeed the case. Had you invested $1,000 in a "safe," 30-year AAA bond in 1970, your investment in early 1984 would have been worth only about $690. Had you invested in short-

Bond Prices in Recent Years

---

[11]We should point out a potential problem at this point—it is inaccurate to use Equation 5-1a to evaluate a semiannual payment bond, and Equation 5-1 to evaluate an annual payment bond, without using k_d values that are adjusted to an equivalent effective annual rate. Thus, in the example above, we define the semiannual payment bond's yield to be $k_d = \text{YTM} = 10\%$. This is equivalent to an effective annual return of $(1.05)^2 - 1.0 = 10.25\%$. Now if this bond sold in the market at a price of $1,384.34, what would be the value (and market price) of an equally risky $150 annual coupon bond whose maturity was also 15 years?

$$V = \sum_{t=1}^{15} \frac{\$150}{(1.1025)^2} + \frac{\$1,000}{(1.1025)^{15}} = \$1,356.19.$$

It is tempting to go back to Equation 5-1 and plug in $k_d = 10\%$ and get a value of $1,380.32, but that would be incorrect if the going effective annual rate on bonds of that degree of risk was 10.25%.

Figure 5-4
Bond Price Index, 1970-1984

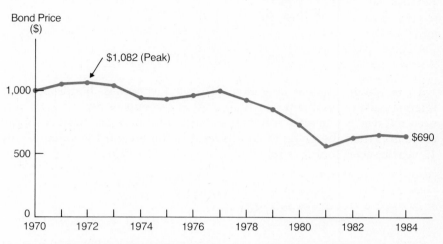

Note: These prices are the average prices during the year of an 8 percent coupon, 20-year, AAA-rated bond.

term bonds (or money market funds), you would still have had your $1,000.[12]

Common Stock Valuation

Common stock represents the ownership of a corporation, but to the typical investor, a share of common stock is simply a piece of paper distinguished by two features:

1. It entitles its owner to dividends, if the company has earnings out of which dividends can be paid and if management chooses to pay dividends rather than retain earnings. Note that whereas a bond contains a promise to pay interest, common stock provides no such promise (in an obligation sense) to pay dividends. If you own a stock, you may *expect* a dividend, but your expectations may not in fact be met. To illustrate, Long Island Lighting Company (Lilco) had paid dividends on its common stock for over 50 years, and people expected these dividends to continue, but when it encountered severe problems in 1984, it stopped paying dividends. However, Lilco continued paying interest on its

---

[12]However, because of inflation, $1,000 in 1984 would only be worth $454 in terms of 1970 purchasing power. Of course, the real value of the long-term bond would be even lower.

bonds, because if it did not, it would have been declared bankrupt and the bondholders could have, in effect, taken over the company.

2. Stock can be sold at some future date, and it is hoped that the sale price will be greater than the purchase price. If the stock is sold at a price above its purchase price, the investor will receive a *capital gain*. Generally, at the time people buy common stocks, they do expect to receive capital gains; otherwise, they would not buy the stocks. However, after the fact, one can end up with capital losses rather than capital gains. Lilco dropped from $17.50 in 1983 to $3.75 in 1984, so expected capital gains can turn out to be actual capital losses.

In Chapter 3, we discussed the markets in which stocks are traded, and in Chapter 14 we shall discuss the rights and privileges of the common stockholders, and the process by which new shares are issued. Our purpose in this chapter, however, is to analyze models that help explain how stock prices are determined.

Common stocks provide an expected future cash flow stream, and stock values are found in the same manner as the values of other financial assets, namely, as the present value of a future cash flow stream. The expected cash flows consist of two elements: (1) the dividend expected in each year and (2) the price investors expect to receive when they sell the stock. The final stock price includes the return of the original investment plus a capital gain (or minus a capital loss).

We saw in Chapter 1 that managers seek to maximize the value of their firms' stocks. Through their actions, managers affect the stream of income to investors and the riskiness of this income stream. Managers need to know how alternative actions will affect stock prices. Therefore, at this point, we develop some models to help show how the value of a share of stock is determined under several different sets of conditions. We begin by defining the following terms:

Definitions of Terms Used in the Stock Valuation Models

D_t = dividend the stockholder *expects* to receive at the end of Year t.[13] D_0 is the most recent dividend, which has already been paid; D_1 is the next dividend expected, which will be paid at the end of this year; D_2 is the dividend expected at the end of 2 years; and so forth. D_1 represents the first cash flow a new purchaser of the stock will receive. Note that D_0, the dividend which has just

---

[13]Stocks generally pay dividends quarterly, so theoretically we ought to evaluate them on a quarterly basis. However, in stock valuation people often work on an annual rather than on a quarterly basis, because the data used in stock valuation are often not precise enough to warrant such refinements for most applications. We discuss a quarterly stock valuation model in Appendix 5C.

been paid, is known with certainty. All future dividends are expected values, so the estimate of D_t may differ among investors.

P_0 = market price of the stock today.

$\hat{P}_t$ = expected price of the stock at the end of each year t, pronounced "P hat t." $\hat{P}_0$ is the intrinsic value of the stock today as seen by the particular investor doing the analysis; $\hat{P}_1$ is the price expected at the end of 1 year; and so on. Note that $\hat{P}_0$ is the intrinsic, or expected, value of the stock today based on the investor's estimate of the stock's expected dividend stream and riskiness. The caret, or "hat," is used to indicate that $\hat{P}_t$ is an estimated value. $\hat{P}_0$, the investor's intrinsic value, could be above or below P_0, the current stock price, but the investor would buy the stock only if $\hat{P}_0$ were equal to or greater than P_0.

g = expected rate of growth in dividends as estimated by the investor. (If we assume that dividends are expected to grow at a constant rate, then g is also equal to the expected rate of growth in the stock's price.)

k_s = minimum acceptable or *required rate of return* on the stock, considering both its riskiness and the returns available on other investments. The determinants of k_s will be discussed in detail in Chapter 6.

$\hat{k}_s$ = *expected rate of return* which the individual who buys the stock actually expects to receive. $\hat{k}_s$ could be above or below k_s, but one would buy the stock only if $\hat{k}_s$ were equal to or greater than k_s.

$\bar{k}_s$ = *actual*, or *realized rate of return*, pronounced "k bar." You may *expect* to obtain a return of $\hat{k}_s$ = 15 percent if you buy Exxon stock today, but if the market goes down, you may end up with an actual, realized return that is much lower, perhaps even negative.

D_1/P_0 = expected *dividend yield* on the stock during the coming year. If the stock is expected to pay a dividend of $1 during the next 12 months, and if its current price is $10, then the expected dividend yield is $1/$10 = 0.10 = 10%.

$\dfrac{\hat{P}_1 - P_0}{P_0}$ = expected *capital gains yield* on the stock during the coming year. If the stock sells for $10 today, and if it is expected to rise to $10.50 at the end of 1 year, then the expected capital gain is $\hat{P}_1 - P_0$ = $10.50 − $10.00 = $0.50, and the expected capital gains yield is $0.50/$10 = 0.05 = 5%.

Expected total return = expected dividend yield plus the expected capital gains yield = $\hat{k}_s$ as defined above. In the example, $\hat{k}_s$ = 10% + 5% = 15%.

In our discussion of bonds, we found the value of a bond as the present value of interest payments over the life of the bond plus the present value of the bond's maturity (or par) value:

Expected Dividends as the Basis for Stock Values

$$V = \frac{I}{(1 + k_d)^1} + \frac{I}{(1 + k_d)^2} + \cdots + \frac{I}{(1 + k_d)^n} + \frac{M}{(1 + k_d)^n}.$$

Stock prices are likewise determined as the present value of a stream of cash flows, and the basic stock valuation equation is similar to the bond value equation. What are the cash flows that corporations provide to their stockholders? First, think of yourself as an investor who buys a stock with the intention of holding it (in your family) forever. In this case, all that you (and your heirs) will receive is a stream of dividends, and the value of the stock today is calculated as the present value of an infinite stream of dividends:

Value of stock $= \hat{P}_0 =$ PV of expected future dividends

$$= \frac{D_1}{(1 + k_s)^1} + \frac{D_2}{(1 + k_s)^2} + \cdots + \frac{D_\infty}{(1 + k_s)^\infty}$$

(5-2)

$$= \sum_{t=1}^{\infty} \frac{D_t}{(1 + k_s)^t}.$$

What about the more typical case, where you expect to hold the stock for a finite period, and then sell it? What will be the value of $\hat{P}_0$ in this case? *The value of the stock is again determined by Equation 5-2.* To see this, recognize that for any individual investor, cash flows consist of dividends plus the sale price of the stock, but the sale price to the current investor will be dependent upon the dividends expected by future investors, so for all present and future investors in total, expected cash flows consist only of future dividends. Unless a firm is liquidated or is sold to another concern, the cash flows it provides to its stockholders consist only of a stream of dividends. Thus, the value of a share of common stock may be established as the present value of its expected stream of dividends.

The general validity of Equation 5-2 can also be seen by asking this question: Suppose I buy a stock expecting to hold it for one year. I will receive dividends during the year, as well as the value $\hat{P}_1$ when I sell the stock at the end of the year. But what will determine the value of $\hat{P}_1$? It will be determined as the present value of the dividends during

Year 2 plus the stock price at the end of Year 2, which, in turn, will be determined as the present value of another set of future dividends and an even more distant stock price. This process can be continued ad infinitum, and the ultimate result is Equation 5-2.[14]

Equation 5-2 is a generalized stock valuation model in the sense that the time pattern of D_t can be anything: D_t can be rising, falling, or constant, or it can even fluctuate randomly, and Equation 5-2 will still hold. For many purposes, however, it is useful to estimate a particular time pattern for D_t and then develop a simplified (that is, easier to evaluate) version of the stock valuation model expressed in Equation 5-2. In the following sections we consider the cases of zero growth, constant growth, and nonconstant growth.

---

[14]Assume that you and all other investors buy a stock expecting to hold it for one year and then sell it at a price $\hat{P}_1$. $\hat{P}_0$ would be found as follows:

$$\hat{P}_0 = \frac{D_1}{1 + k_s} + \frac{\hat{P}_1}{1 + k_s}. \tag{1}$$

The value of $\hat{P}_1$ would be found as the present value of D_2 and $\hat{P}_2$:

$$\hat{P}_1 = \frac{D_2}{1 + k_s} + \frac{\hat{P}_2}{1 + k_s}. \tag{2}$$

We could substitute the Equation 2 value for $\hat{P}_1$ in Equation 1, obtaining Equation 3:

$$\hat{P}_0 = \frac{D_1}{1 + k_s} + \frac{\dfrac{D_2}{1 + k_s} + \dfrac{\hat{P}_2}{1 + k_s}}{1 + k_s}$$

$$= \frac{D_1}{(1 + k_s)} + \frac{D_2}{(1 + k_s)^2} + \frac{\hat{P}_2}{(1 + k_s)^2}. \tag{3}$$

We could continue in similar fashion, finding the values $\hat{P}_2$, $\hat{P}_3$, and so forth, and at the limit, we would have Equation 5-2:

$$\hat{P}_0 = \frac{D_1}{(1 + k_s)} + \frac{D_2}{(1 + k_s)^2} + \cdots + \frac{D_\infty}{(1 + k_s)^\infty}$$

$$= \sum_{t=1}^{\infty} \frac{D_t}{(1 + k_s)^t}. \tag{5-2}$$

Here we developed Equation 5-2 on the assumption that investors have a one-year investment horizon. If they had longer horizons, we would still get to Equation 5-2, but we would simply get there faster because, for example, we could start with Equation 3 if investors had two-year horizons.

We should note that investors periodically lose sight of the long-run nature of stocks as investments and forget that in order to sell a stock at a profit, one must find a buyer who will pay the higher price. If you analyze a stock's value in accordance with Equation 5-2, conclude that the stock's market price exceeds a reasonable value, and then buy the stock anyway, then you are following the "bigger fool" theory of investment. You think that you may be a fool to buy the stock at its excessive price, but you also think that when you get ready to sell it, you can find someone who is an even bigger fool. The bigger fool theory was widely followed in 1929, just before the Great Depression.

Suppose dividends are not expected to grow, but to remain constant. Here we have a *zero growth stock*, where the dividends expected in future years are equal to some constant amount, $D_1 = D_2 = D_3$ and so on. Therefore, we can drop the subscript and rewrite Equation 5-2 as follows:

$$\hat{P}_0 = \frac{D}{(1 + k_s)^1} + \frac{D}{(1 + k_s)^2} + \cdots + \frac{D}{(1 + k_s)^n} + \cdots + \frac{D}{(1 + k_s)^\infty}. \quad \text{(5-2a)}$$

Stock Values with Zero Growth

As we noted in Chapter 4 in connection with the British consol bond, a security that is expected to pay a constant amount each period forever is defined as a perpetuity. Therefore, a zero growth stock may be thought of as a perpetuity. The stock is expected to provide an infinite stream of constant future dividends, but each dividend has a smaller present value than the preceding one, and as n get very large, the present value of the individual future dividends approaches zero. To illustrate, suppose $D = \$1.82$ and $k_s = 16\% = 0.16$. We can rewrite Equation 5-2a as follows:

$$\hat{P}_0 = \frac{\$1.82}{(1.16)^1} + \frac{\$1.82}{(1.16)^2} + \frac{\$1.82}{(1.16)^3} + \cdots + \frac{\$1.82}{(1.16)^{50}} + \cdots + \frac{\$1.82}{(1.16)^{100}} + \cdots$$

$$= \$1.57 + \$1.35 + \$1.17 + \cdots + \$0.001 + \cdots + \$0.000001 + \cdots.$$

We can also show the perpetuity in graph form, as in Figure 5-5. The horizontal line shows the constant dividend stream, $D_t = \$1.82$. The step function curve shows the present value of each future dividend. If we extended the analysis on out to infinity and then summed the present values of all the future dividends, the sum would be equal to the value of the stock.

As we saw in Chapter 4, the value of any perpetuity is simply the cash flow divided by the discount rate, so the value of a zero growth stock reduces to this formula:[15]

$$\hat{P}_0 = \frac{D}{k_s}. \quad \text{(5-3)}$$

Therefore, in our example, the value of the stock is $11.38:

$$\hat{P}_0 = \frac{\$1.82}{0.16} = \$11.38.$$

Thus, if you were to extend Figure 5-5 on out forever and then add up the present value of each individual dividend, you would end up with the intrinsic value of the stock, $11.38.[16] The market value of the stock,

---

[15]The derivation of Equation 5-3 was shown in Appendix 4A.

[16]If you think that having a stock pay dividends forever is unrealistic, then think of it as lasting only for 50 or 100 years. Here we would have an annuity of $1.82 per year for 50 or 100 years. The PV of a 50-year annuity would be $1.82(6.2463) = $11.3683, while the PV of a 100-year annuity would be $11.3750, which is essentially the same as that for the infinite annuity. Thus, the years from 50 to infinity do not contribute much to the value of the stock.

Figure 5-5
Present Values of Dividends of a Zero Growth Stock (Perpetuity)

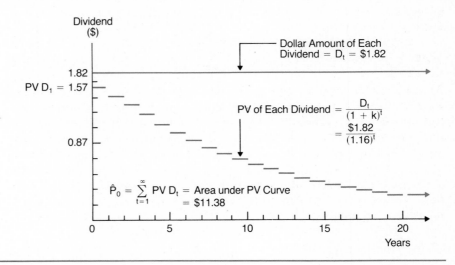

P_0, could be greater than, less than, or equal to $11.38, depending on other investors' perceptions of the dividend pattern and riskiness of the stock. For investors in total, a stock's market price must equal its intrinsic value. This concept, called *market efficiency*, is discussed in Chapter 6. For now, just recognize that the market price can differ from any single investor's estimate of its intrinsic value, and an investor would buy a stock only if its intrinsic value as calculated by him or her equaled or exceeded its market price.

We could transpose the $\hat{P}_0$ and the k_s in Equation 5-3 to solve for k_s. We could then look up the value of the stock and the latest dividend, P_0 and D, in the newspaper, and the value D/P_0 would be the rate of return we would expect to earn if we bought the stock. Since we are dealing with an *expected rate of return*, we put a "hat" on the k value to produce Equation 5-4:

$$\hat{k}_s = \frac{D}{P_0}. \tag{5-4}$$

Thus, if we bought the stock at a price of $11.38 and expected to receive a constant dividend of $1.82, our expected rate of return would be

$$\hat{k}_s = \frac{\$1.82}{\$11.38} = 0.16 = 16\%.$$

Before leaving this section, we should note that Equations 5-3 and 5-4 are also applicable to *preferred stock*, a type of stock that (generally) pays a constant dividend in perpetuity. Preferred stock is discussed in detail in Chapter 15.

"Normal," or
Constant, Growth

Although the zero growth model is applicable to some companies, the earnings and dividends of most companies are expected to increase each year. Although expected growth rates vary from company to company, dividend growth, in general, is expected to continue in the foreseeable future at about the same rate as that of the nominal gross national product (real GNP plus inflation). On this basis, it is expected that an average, or "normal," company will grow at a rate of 8 to 10 percent a year, and this rate will rise if the inflation rate increases. Thus, if such a company's last dividend, which has already been paid, was D_0, its dividend in any future Year t may be forecasted as $D_t = D_0(1 + g)^t$, where g is the constant expected rate of growth. For example, if Teletron Electronics just paid a dividend of $1.82 (that is, $D_0 = \$1.82$), and if investors expect a 10 percent growth rate, then the estimated dividend one year hence will be $D_1 = (\$1.82)(1.10) = \$2.00$; D_2 will be $2.20; and the estimated dividend 5 years hence will be

$$
\begin{aligned}
D_t &= D_0(1 + g)^t \\
&= \$1.82(1.10)^5 \\
&= \$2.93.
\end{aligned}
$$

Using this method of estimating future dividends, the current value, $\hat{P}_0$, is determined by Equation 5-2 as set forth above. In other words, we find the expected future cash flow stream (the dividends), get the present value of each dividend payment, and then sum these present values to find the value of the stock. Thus, the intrinsic value of the stock is equal to the present value of the expected future dividends.

If g is constant, Equation 5-2 may be simplified as follows:[17]

$$
\hat{P}_0 = \frac{D_0(1 + g)}{k_s - g} = \frac{D_1}{k_s - g}. \tag{5-5}
$$

Inserting values into the equation, we find the value of this stock to be $33.33:

$$
\hat{P}_0 = \frac{\$1.82(1.10)}{0.16 - 0.10} = \frac{\$2.00}{0.06} = \$33.33.
$$

The constant growth model expressed in Equation 5-5 is often called the Gordon Model, after Myron J. Gordon, who did much to develop and popularize it.

Note that Equation 5-5 is sufficiently general to encompass the zero growth case described above: If growth is zero, this is simply a special

---

[17]The proof of Equation 5-5 is given in Appendix 5B.

Figure 5-6
Present Values of Dividends of a Constant Growth Stock:
$D_0 = \$1.82$, $g = 10\%$, $k_s = 16\%$

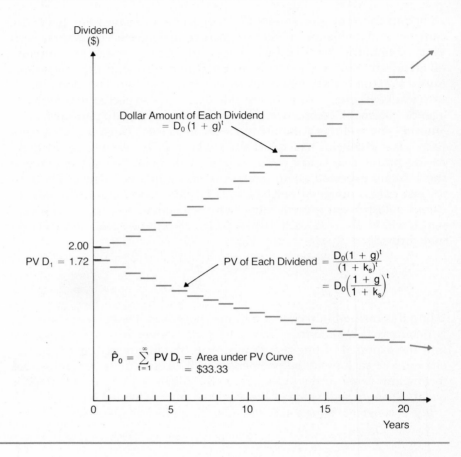

case of constant growth, and Equation 5-5 is equal to Equation 5-3. Note also that a necessary condition for the derivation of Equation 5-5 is that k_s be greater than g. If the equation is used where k_s is not greater than g, the results are meaningless.

The concept underlying the stock valuation process is graphed in Figure 5-6 for the case of a 10 percent growth rate. Dividends grow, but, since $k_s > g$, the present value of each future dividend (the lower step function curve) is declining. For example, the dividend in Year 1 is $D_1 = D_0(1 + g)^1 = \$1.82(1.10) = \$2.00$. The present value of this dividend, discounted at 16 percent, is PV $D_1 = \$2.00/(1.16)^1 = \$2.00/1.16 = \$1.72$. The dividend expected in Year 2 is $\$2.00(1.10) = \$2.20$, and the present value of this dividend is \$1.64. Continuing, $D_3 = \$2.42$ and PV

David

 # Intrinsic value –

$D_3 = \$1.55$. Thus, the expected dividends are growing, but the present values of the successive dividends are declining because $k_s > g$.

If we added up the present values of each future dividend, this summation would be the intrinsic value of the stock, $\hat{P}_0$. And, as we have seen, when g is a constant, this summation is equal to $D_1/(k_s - g)$, the value of Equation 5-5. Therefore, if we extended the lower step-function curve in Figure 5-6 on out to infinity and added up the present values of each future dividend, the summation would be identical to the value given by the formula, $\$33.33$.

Growth in dividends occurs primarily as a result of growth in *earnings per share (EPS)*. Earnings growth, in turn, results from a number of factors, including (1) inflation and (2) the reinvestment of earnings. Regarding inflation, if output (in units) is stable, and if both sales prices and input costs rise at the inflation rate, then EPS will grow. Of course, the purchasing power of EPS will not grow if the firm's costs and prices rise at the same rate as most other products; that is, there will be no "real" growth. However, there is no reason to think that a firm's EPS will necessarily exactly match the rate of general inflation, because some prices rise faster than others.

EPS will also grow as a result of the reinvestment, or plowback, of earnings. If the firm's earnings are not all paid out as dividends (that is, if some fraction of earnings is retained), then the investment behind each share will rise over time, and this rising investment per share should lead to rising earnings and dividends.[18]

We could solve Equation 5-5 for k_s, again using the hat to denote that we are dealing with an expected rate of return:[19]

The Expected Rate of Return on a Constant Growth Stock

$$\begin{matrix} \text{Expected rate} \\ \text{of return} \end{matrix} = \begin{matrix} \text{Expected} \\ \text{dividend} \\ \text{yield} \end{matrix} + \begin{matrix} \text{Expected} \\ \text{capital} \\ \text{gains yield} \end{matrix} \quad (5\text{-}6)$$

$$\hat{k}_s = \frac{D_1}{P_0} + g.$$

---

[18]The specific relationship between reinvestment and growth is discussed in Appendix 7A.

[19]Equation 5-6 is derived from 5-5 as follows:

$$\hat{P}_0 = \frac{D_1}{k_s - g} \quad (5\text{-}5)$$

$$k_s\hat{P}_0 - g\hat{P}_0 = D_1$$
$$k_s\hat{P}_0 = D_1 + g\hat{P}_0$$
$$\hat{k}_s = D_1/P_0 + g. \quad (5\text{-}6)$$

The k_s value of Equation 5-5 is a *required* rate of return, but when we transform to form Equation 5-6, we are finding an *expected* rate of return. Obviously, the transformation requires that $k_s = \hat{k}_s$. This equality holds if the stock market is in equilibrium, a condition discussed at length in Chapter 6.

Thus, if you buy a stock for a price P_0 = \$33.33, and if the stock is expected to pay a dividend D_1 = \$2.00 next year and to grow at a constant rate g = 10% in the future, then your expected rate of return is 16 percent:

$$\hat{k}_s = \frac{\$2.00}{\$33.33} + 10\% = 6\% + 10\% = 16\%.$$

In this form, we see that $\hat{k}_s$ is the *expected total return* and that it consists of an *expected dividend yield*, D_1/P_0 = 6%, and an *expected growth rate or capital gains yield*, g = 10%.

Suppose the analysis described above had been conducted on January 1, 1985, so P_0 = \$33.33 was the January 1, 1985, stock price and D_1 = \$2.00 was the dividend expected during 1985. What should the stock price be at the end of 1985 (or the beginning of 1986)? We would again apply Equation 5-5, but this time, we would use the 1986 dividend, D_2 = $D_1(1 + g)$ = \$2.00(1.10) = \$2.20:

$$\hat{P}_{1/1/1986} = \frac{D_{1986}}{k_s - g} = \frac{\$2.20}{0.16 - 0.10} = \$36.67.$$

Now notice that \$36.67 is 10 percent greater than P_0, the \$33.33 price on January 1, 1985:

$$\$36.67 \approx \$33.33(1.10).$$

Thus, we would expect to make a capital gain of \$36.67 − \$33.33 = \$3.34 during the year, for a capital gains yield of 10 percent:

$$\text{Capital gains yield} = \frac{\$3.34}{\$33.33} = 0.10 = 10\%.$$

We could extend the analysis on out, and in each future year the expected capital gains yield would always equal g, the expected dividend growth rate.

The dividend yield in 1986 can be estimated as follows:

$$\text{Dividend yield}_{1986} = \frac{D_{1986}}{\hat{P}_{1/1/86}} = \frac{\$2.20}{\$36.67} = 0.06 = 6\%.$$

The dividend yield for 1987 could also be calculated, and it would again be 6 percent. Thus, *for a constant growth stock*, these conditions will hold:

1. The dividend is expected to grow at a constant rate, g.

2. The stock price is expected to grow at this same rate.

3. The expected dividend yield is a constant.

4. The expected capital gains yield is also a constant, and it is equal to g.

5. The expected total rate of return, $\hat{k}_s$, is equal to the expected dividend yield plus the expected growth rate.

Figure 5-7
Illustrative Dividend Growth Rates

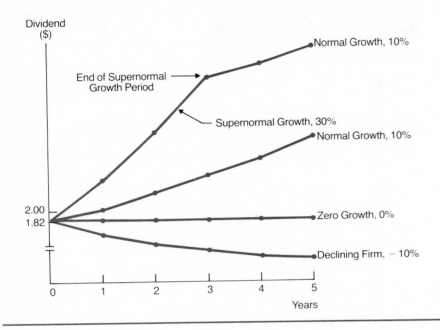

Firms typically go through *life cycles*. During the early part of the cycle, their growth is much faster than that of the economy as a whole, then they match the economy's growth, and finally their growth is slower than that of the economy. Automobile manufacturers in the 1920s, and computer and office equipment manufacturers in the 1980s, are examples of firms in the early part of the cycle, and these firms are called *supernormal* growth firms. Figure 5-7 illustrates such nonconstant (or supernormal) growth and compares it with normal growth, zero growth, and negative growth.[20]

The dividends of the supernormal growth firm are expected to grow at a 30 percent rate for 3 years, after which the growth rate is expected to fall to 10 percent, the assumed norm for the economy. The value of

*Nonconstant
Growth*

---

[20]A negative growth rate indicates a declining company. A mining company whose profits are falling because of a declining ore body is an example. Someone buying such a company would expect its earnings and consequently its dividends and stock price to decline each year, and thus to realize capital losses rather than capital gains. Obviously, a declining company's stock price will be low, and its dividend yield must be high enough to offset the expected capital loss and still produce a competitive total return. Students sometimes argue that they would not be willing to buy a stock whose price was expected to decline. However, if the annual dividends are large enough to *more than offset* the falling stock price, the stock could be a bargain.

this firm, like any other, is the present value of its expected future dividends as determined by Equation 5-2. In the case where D_t is growing at a constant rate, we simplified Equation 5-2 to $\hat{P}_0 = D_1/(k_s - g)$. In the supernormal case, however, the expected growth rate is not a constant—it declines at the end of the period of supernormal growth. To find the value of such stock, or any nonconstant growth stock, we proceed in three steps:

1. Find the PV of the dividends during the period of nonconstant growth.

2. Find the price of the stock at the end of the nonconstant growth period, and then discount this price back to the present.

3. Add these two components to find the intrinsic value of the stock, $\hat{P}_0$.

To illustrate the process of nonconstant growth stock valuation, suppose the following facts exist:

k_s = stockholders' required rate of return = 16%.

N = years of supernormal growth = 3.

g_s = rate of growth in both earnings and dividends during supernormal growth period = 30%.

g_n = rate of growth after supernormal period = 10%.

D_0 = last dividend that the company paid = $1.82.

The valuation process is graphed in Figure 5-8 and explained in the steps set forth below:

Step 1. Find the PV of dividends paid (PV D_t) at the end of Years 1 to 3 using this procedure:

	D_0	$\times$	$FVIF_{30\%,t}$	=	D_t	$\times$	$PVIF_{16\%,t}$	=	PV D_t
D_1:	$1.82	$\times$	1.3000	=	$2.366	$\times$	0.8262	=	$2.040
D_2:	1.82	$\times$	1.6900	=	3.076	$\times$	0.7432	=	2.286
D_3:	1.82	$\times$	2.1970	=	3.999	$\times$	0.6407	=	2.562

Sum of PVs of supernormal period dividends = $6.888

Step 2. Find the PV of the dividends expected in Year 4 and thereafter. This requires that we (a) first find the expected value of the stock at the end of Year 3 and (b) then find the present value of the Year 3 stock price:

a.
$$\hat{P}_3 = \frac{D_4}{k_s - g_n} = \frac{D_0(1 + g_s)^3(1 + g_n)}{k_s - g_n} = \frac{D_3(1 + g_n)}{0.16 - 0.10}$$

$$= \frac{\$3.999(1.10)}{0.06} = \frac{\$4.399}{0.06} = \$73.31.$$

Figure 5-8
Present Values of Dividends of a Supernormal Growth Stock

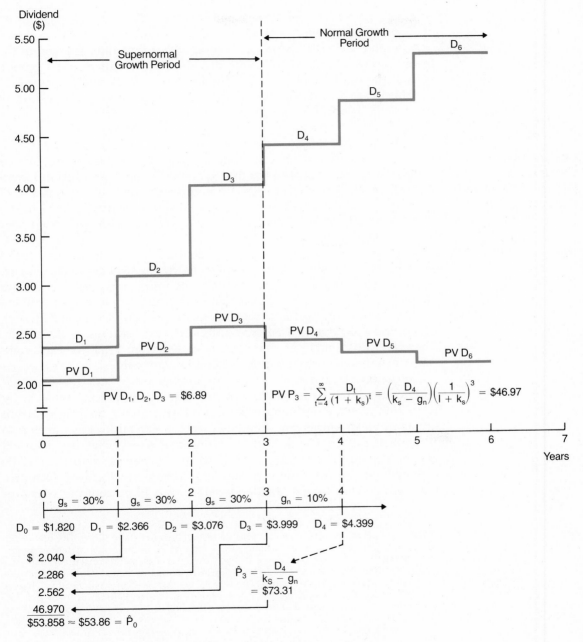

Notes:
a. Recognize that dividends are paid at the end of each year.
b. $\hat{P}_3$, the stock price expected at the end of Year 3, is the sum of the PVs of dividends in Years 4 to infinity, hence $\hat{P}_3 = D_4/(k_s - g_n)$.

b. $PV \hat{P}_3 = \$73.31(PVIF_{16\%, \text{ 3 years}}) = \$73.31(0.6407) = \$46.97.$

Step 3. Find $\hat{P}_0$, the value of the stock today:

$$\hat{P}_0 = \$6.89 + \$46.97 = \$53.86.$$

A graphic view of this process, along with a time line, is given in the lower section of Figure 5-8. Note that during the supernormal growth period, the present values of the dividends are increasing, because $g_s >$ k_s. However, during the normal growth period, the present values of the dividends decrease, because $k_s > g_n$.

Comparing Companies with Different Expected Growth Rates

It is useful to summarize our discussion of stock valuation models by comparing companies with the four growth situations graphed in Figure 5-7. There we have a zero growth company, one with a constant 10 percent expected growth rate, one whose earnings are expected to decline at the rate of 10 percent a year, and one whose growth rate is not a constant.

We can use the valuation equations developed above to determine the stock prices, dividend yields, capital gains yields, total expected returns, and price/earnings ratios (P/E ratios) for the four companies.[21] These are shown in Table 5-1. We assume that each firm had earnings per share (EPS) of $3.41 during the preceding reporting period (that is, $EPS_0 =$ $3.41) and paid out 53.3 percent of its reported earnings as dividends. Therefore, dividends per share last year, D_0, were $1.82 for each company, but the values of D_1 differ among the companies.

The value of each stock equals its market price, and the expected and required return is 16 percent on each of the stocks; thus, $\hat{k}_s =$ $k_s = 16\%$. For the declining firm, this return consists of a high current dividend yield, 26 percent, combined with a capital loss amounting to 10 percent a year. For the zero growth firm, there is neither a capital gain nor a capital loss expectation, so the 16 percent return must be obtained entirely from the dividend yield. The normal growth firm provides a 6 percent current dividend yield plus a 10 percent per year cap-

---

[21]Price/earnings ratios relate a stock's price to its earnings per share (EPS). The higher the P/E ratio, the more investors are willing to pay for a dollar of the firm's current earnings. Other things held constant, investors will pay more for a dollar of current earnings of a rapidly growing firm than for one of a slow growth company; hence, rapid growth companies generally have high P/E ratios. These ratios are discussed in more detail in Chapter 22. The relationships among the P/E ratios, shown in the last column of Table 5-1, are similar to what one would intuitively expect—the higher the expected growth rate (all other things the same), the higher the P/E ratio.

We should note, too, that differences in P/E ratios among firms can also arise from differences in the required rates of return, k_s, which investors use in capitalizing the future dividend streams. If one company has a higher P/E ratio than another, this could be caused by a higher g, a lower k_s, or a combination of these two factors.

Table 5-1
Prices, Dividend Yields, and Price/Earnings Ratios for 16 Percent Returns under Different Growth Assumptions

	Price	Current Dividend Yield (D_1/P_0)	Capital Gains Yield in Year 1 $[(\hat{P}_1 - P_0)/P_0]$	Total Expected Return	P/E Ratio[a]
Declining constant growth (−10%)	$\hat{P}_0 = \dfrac{D_1}{k_s - g} = \dfrac{\$1.64}{0.16 - (-0.10)} = \$6.31$	26%	−10.0%	16%	1.85
Zero growth (0%)	$\hat{P}_0 = \dfrac{D}{k_s} = \dfrac{\$1.82}{0.16} = 11.38$	16	0.0	16	3.34
Normal constant growth (10%)	$\hat{P}_0 = \dfrac{D_1}{k_s - g} = \dfrac{\$2.00}{0.16 - 0.10} = 33.33$	6	10.0	16	9.77
Supernormal growth	$\hat{P}_0 = $ (See Steps 1-3 above) $= 53.86$	4.4	11.6[b]	16	15.79

[a] It was assumed at the beginning of this example that each company is earning $3.41 initially. This $3.41, divided into the various prices, gives the indicated P/E ratios. We might also note that as the supernormal growth rate declines toward the normal rate (or as the time when this decline will occur becomes more imminent), the high P/E ratio must approach the normal P/E ratio; that is, the P/E of 15.79 will decline year by year and equal 9.77, that of the normal growth company, in the third year. Note also that D_1 differs for each firm, being calculated as follows:

$$D_1 = EPS_0(1 + g)(\text{Percentage of earnings paid out}) = \$3.41(1 + g)(0.533).$$
For the declining firm, $D_1 = \$3.41(0.90)(0.533) = \$1.64$.

[b] With $k_s = 16\%$ and $D_1/P_0 = 4.4\%$, then the capital gains yield must be $16.0\% - 4.4\% = 11.6\%$. We could calculate the expected price of the stock at the end of the year, $\hat{P}_1$, using the supernormal growth procedures to confirm that the capital gains yield in Year 1 is indeed 11.6 percent, but this is not necessary.

ital gains expectation. Finally, the supernormal growth firm has a low current dividend yield but a high capital gains expectation.

What is expected to happen to the prices of the four illustrative firms' stocks over time? Three of the four cases are straightforward: the zero growth firm's price is expected to be constant; the declining firm is expected to have a falling stock price; and the constant growth firm's stock is expected to grow at a constant rate, 10 percent. We do not prove it here, but we could show that the supernormal firm's stock price growth rate starts at 11.6 percent per year but declines to 10 percent as the supernormal growth period ends.

Actual Stock Prices and Returns

Our discussion thus far has focused on *expected* stock prices and *expected* rates of return. Anyone who has ever invested in the stock market knows that there can be and generally are large differences between *expected* and *realized* prices and returns. To illustrate, on January 1, 1981, IBM's stock price was $67.875 per share. Its 1980 dividend, D_0, had been $3.44, and the consensus view of security analysts was that IBM would experience a growth rate of about 11 percent in the future. Thus, an average investor who bought IBM at $67.875 would have expected to earn a return of about 16.6 percent:

$$\hat{k}_s = \begin{matrix} \text{Expected} \\ \text{dividend} \\ \text{yield} \end{matrix} + \begin{matrix} \text{Expected growth rate} \\ \text{or expected capital} \\ \text{gains yield} \end{matrix}$$

$$= \frac{D_0(1 + g)}{P_0} + \qquad g$$

$$= \frac{\$3.82}{\$67.875} + \qquad 11\%$$

$$= \quad 5.6\% \quad + \quad 11.0\% = 16.6\%.$$

In fact, things did not work out as expected. The economy in 1981 was weaker than had been predicted, so IBM's earnings did not grow as expected, and its dividend remained at $3.44. Further, interest rates soared during 1981, and capital was attracted out of the stock market and into the bond and money markets to take advantage of the high interest rates. As a result of the two events, IBM's price declined, and it closed on December 31, 1981, at $46.875, down $11 for the year. Thus, on the beginning-of-the-year investment of $67.875, the actual return on IBM for 1981 was -11.1 percent:

$$\bar{k}_s = \begin{matrix} \text{Actual} \\ \text{dividend} \\ \text{yield} \end{matrix} + \begin{matrix} \text{Actual} \\ \text{capital gains} \\ \text{yield} \end{matrix}$$

$$= \frac{\$3.44}{\$67.875} + \frac{-\$11}{\$67.875}$$

$$= \quad 5.1\% - 16.2\% = -11.1\%.$$

Figure 5-9
New York Stock Exchange Prices and Total Returns, 1953-1983

a. Index of NYSE Prices

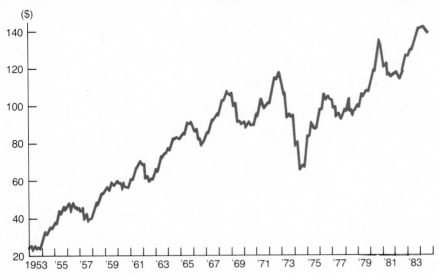

b. Total Returns: Dividend Yield + Capital Gain or Loss

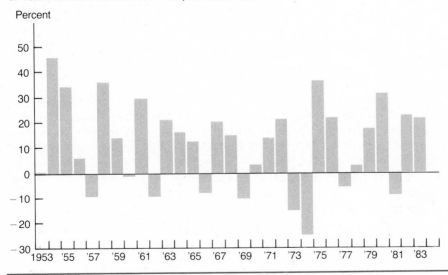

Most other stocks had experiences in 1981 that were similar to that of IBM.

However, the economy improved in 1982 and 1983, and IBM's dividend and stock price improved apace. The total realized return on IBM in 1982 was 77 percent, and in 1983 it was 30 percent. The expected return for 1982 and 1983 was again close to the 16.6 percent expected for 1981, so the realized returns exceeded the expected returns during those years.

Panel a of Figure 5-9 shows how the price of an average share of NYSE stock has varied in recent years, and Panel b shows how total realized returns have varied. The market has gone up in some years and down in others, and the stocks of individual companies have likewise gone up and down. We know from theory that expected returns are always positive, but in some years, as this graph shows, negative returns were realized. Of course, (1) even in bad years some individual companies do well, so the "name of the game" in security analysis is to pick the winners, and (2) financial managers attempt to take actions which will put their companies into the winners' column, but they do not always succeed. In subsequent chapters, we will examine the actions that managers can take to increase the odds of their firms' doing relatively well in the marketplace.

Summary

Corporate decisions should be analyzed in terms of how alternative courses of action are likely to affect the value of the firm's stock. It is necessary to know how stock prices in general are established before attempting to measure how a given decision will affect a specific firm's stock price. Accordingly, this chapter showed how bond and stock values are established, as well as how investors go about estimating the rates of return they expect to receive on these securities if they purchase them at the existing market prices. In all cases, security values were found to be *the present value of the future cash flows expected from the security*. The cash flows from a bond consist of interest payments plus the bond's maturity value, while stocks provide a stream of dividends plus a sale price.

The following equation is used to find the value of an annual coupon bond:

$$V = \sum_{t=1}^{n} \frac{I}{(1 + k_d)^t} + \frac{M}{(1 + k_d)^n}$$
$$= I(PVIFA_{k_d,n}) + M(PVIF_{k_d,n}).$$

Here V is the value of the bond; I is the annual interest payment, or coupon; n is years to maturity; k_d is the appropriate interest rate; and M is the bond's maturity value, generally $1,000. This equation can also be solved for k_d, which is called the *yield to maturity (YTM)*. If the bond pays interest semiannually, as most do, we must divide I and k_d by 2, and multiply n by 2, before applying the formula.

Several different stock valuation formulas were developed; the ones for zero and for constant growth follow:

$$\text{Zero growth stock: } \hat{P}_0 = \frac{D}{k_s}.$$

$$\text{Constant, or normal, growth stock: } \hat{P}_0 = \frac{D_1}{k_s - g}.$$

Here $\hat{P}_0$ is the current intrinsic value of the stock; D is the expected constant dividend; D_1 is the dividend expected during the next year; k_s is the required rate of return on the stock; and g is the expected growth rate. In this equation, g is a constant; if g is not a constant, then the nonconstant growth procedure must be used to find the stock's value.

We can express the equation for the *expected rate of return* on a constant growth stock as follows:

$$\hat{k}_s = \frac{D_1}{P_0} + g.$$

Here P_0 is the stock's current market price. In this form, we see that the total expected return, $\hat{k}_s$, consists of an *expected dividend yield* plus an *expected capital gains yield*. For a constant growth stock, the dividend and capital gains components of total yield are constant over time. For supernormal growth stocks, the dividend yield rises over time, while the capital gains component declines, with the total yield remaining constant.

We saw that differences can and do exist between expected and actual returns in the stock and bond markets—only for short-term, riskless assets do expected and actual, or realized, returns equal one another.

Throughout the chapter we used "appropriate" discount rates, k_d for bonds and k_s for stocks. In Chapter 3, we learned that k_d is composed of a pure rate of interest plus premiums for inflation and risk. In Chapter 6, we shall examine the factors that determine k_s. Then, in the remainder of the book, we consider the types of actions that a firm's financial manager can take to lower the discount rate and to increase the expected growth rate, both of which will increase the value of the firm's stock.

Questions

5-1   Define each of the following terms:
   a. Coupon rate
   b. Par value
   c. Premium; discount
   d. Current yield (on a bond); yield to maturity
   e. Interest rate risk; reinvestment rate risk
   f. Required rate of return, k_s; expected rate of return, $\hat{k}_s$; actual, or realized, rate of return, $\bar{k}_s$
   g. Capital gains yield; dividend yield; expected total return
   h. Nonconstant growth model; supernormal growth stock
   i. Perpetual bond; zero growth stock; preferred stock

5-2   Two investors are evaluating AT&T's stock for possible purchase. They agree on the expected value of D_1 and also on the expected future dividend growth rate. Further, they agree on the riskiness of the stock. However, one investor normally holds stocks for 2 years, while the other holds stocks for 10 years. Based on the type of analysis done in Chapter 5, they should both be willing to pay the same price for AT&T's stock. True or false? Explain.

5-3   A bond that pays interest forever and has no maturity date is a perpetual bond. In what respect is a perpetual bond similar to a no-growth stock and to a share of preferred stock?

5-4   Is it true that the following equation can be used to find the value of an n-year bond that pays interest once a year?

$$\text{Value} = \sum_{t=1}^{n} \frac{\text{Annual interest}}{(1 + k_d)^t} + \frac{\text{Par value}}{(1 + k_d)^n}.$$

5-5   "The values of outstanding bonds change whenever the going rate of interest changes. In general, short-term interest rates are more volatile than long-term interest rates. Therefore, short-term bond prices are more sensitive to interest rate changes than are long-term bond prices." Is this statement true or false? Explain.

5-6   The rate of return you would get if you bought a bond and held it to its maturity date is defined as the bond's yield to maturity. If interest rates in the economy rise after a bond has been issued, what will happen to its YTM? Does the amount of time to maturity affect its YTM?

5-7   If you buy a share of common stock, you would typically expect to receive dividends plus capital gains. Would you expect the distribution between dividend yield and capital gains to be influenced by a firm's decision to pay more dividends rather than to retain and reinvest more of its earnings?

5-8   The next expected dividend, D_1, divided by the current price of a share of stock, P_0, is defined as the stock's expected dividend yield. What is the relationship between the dividend yield, the total yield, and the remaining years of supernormal growth for a supernormal growth firm?

5-9   Is it true that the following expression can be used to find the value of a constant growth stock?

$$\hat{P}_0 = \frac{D_0}{k_s + g}.$$

Self-Test Problems   ST-1 You are considering buying the stock of two very similar companies. Both companies are expected to earn $3 per share this year. However, Company D (for dividend) is expected to pay all of its earnings out as dividends, while Company G (for growth) is expected to pay out only one-third of its earnings, or $1. D's stock price is $20. Which of the following is most likely to be true?

   a. Company G will have a faster growth rate than Company D. Therefore, G's stock price should be greater than $20.

   b. Although G's growth rate should exceed D's, D's current dividend exceeds that of G, and this should cause D's price to exceed G's.

   c. An investor in Stock D will get his or her money back faster because D pays out more of its earnings as dividends. Thus, in a sense, D is like a short-term bond, and G is like a long-term bond. Therefore, if economic shifts cause k_d and k_s to increase, and if the expected streams of dividends from D and G remain constant, then Stocks D and G will both decline, but D's price should decline further.

   d. D's expected and required rate of return is $\hat{k}_s = k_s = 15\%$. G's expected return will be higher because of its higher expected growth rate.

   e. Based on the available information, the best estimate of G's growth rate is 10 percent.

ST-2 A firm issued a new series of bonds on January 1, 1965. The bonds were sold at par ($1,000), have a 12 percent coupon, and mature in 30 years. Coupon payments are made semiannually (on June 30 and December 31).

   a. What was the YTM of the bond on January 1, 1965?

   b. What was the price of the bond on January 1, 1970, 5 years later, assuming that the level of interest rates had fallen to 10 percent?

   c. Find the current yield and capital gains yield on the bond on January 1, 1970, given the price as determined in Part b above.

   d. On July 1, 1985, the bonds sold for $896.64. What was the YTM at that date?

   e. What was the current yield and capital gains yield on July 1, 1985?

   f. Now assume that you purchase an outstanding bond on March 1, 1985. The going rate of interest is 15.5 percent. How large a check must you write to complete the transaction?

ST-3 Karp Company's current stock price and its intrinsic value as seen by the average investor is $24. Karp's last dividend was $1.60. In view of Karp's low risk, its required rate of return is only 12 percent. If dividends are expected to grow at a constant rate, g, in the future, and if k_s is expected to remain at 12 percent, what is Karp Company's expected stock price 5 years from now?

ST-4 Miniscule Computer Chips, Inc., is experiencing a period of rapid growth. Earnings and dividends are expected to grow at a rate of 18 percent during the next 2 years, at 15 percent in the third year, and then at a constant rate of 6 percent thereafter. Miniscule's last dividend was $1.15, and the required rate of return on the stock is 12 percent.

   a. Calculate the value of the stock today.

   b. Calculate $\hat{P}_1$ and $\hat{P}_2$.

   c. Calculate the dividend yield and capital gains yield for Years 1, 2, and 3.

5-1 The Hayes Company's bonds pay $100 annual interest, mature in 15 years, and will pay $1,000 on maturity. *Problems*

   a. What will be the value of these bonds when the going rate of interest is (1) 6 percent, (2) 9 percent, and (3) 12 percent?

b. Now suppose Hayes has some other bonds that pay $100 interest per year, $1,000 at maturity, and mature in one year. What will be the value of these bonds at a going rate of interest of (1) 6 percent, (2) 9 percent, and (3) 12 percent? Assume there is only one more interest payment to be made.

c. Why do the longer-term bonds fluctuate more when interest rates change than do the shorter-term bonds (the one-year bonds)?

5-2   The Coronet Company's bonds have 3 years remaining to maturity. Interest is paid annually, the bonds have a $1,000 par value, and the coupon interest rate is 7 percent.

a. What is the yield to maturity at a current market price of (1) $974 or (2) $1,027?

b. Would you pay $974 for the bond described in Part a if you thought that the appropriate rate of interest for these bonds is 7½ percent; that is, $k_d = 7.5\%$? Explain your answer.

5-3   Suppose Exxon sold an issue of bonds with a 10-year maturity, a $1,000 par value, a 12 percent coupon rate, and semiannual interest payments.

a. Two years after the bonds were issued, the going rate of interest on bonds such as these fell to 8 percent. At what price would the bonds sell?

b. Suppose that, 2 years after the issue, the going interest rate had risen to 14 percent. At what price would the bonds sell?

c. Suppose the conditions in Part a existed; that is, interest rates fell to 8 percent 2 years after the issue date. Suppose, further, that the interest rate remained at 8 percent for the next 8 years. What would happen to the price of the Exxon bonds over time?

5-4   Your broker offers to sell you a share of common stock that paid a dividend of $1 *last year*. You expect the dividend to grow at the rate of 5 percent per year for the next 3 years, and you plan to hold the stock for 3 years, and then to sell it, if you do indeed buy the stock.

a. What is the expected dividend for each of the next 3 years; that is, calculate D_1, D_2, and D_3. Note that $D_0 = \$1$.

b. Given that the appropriate discount rate is 10 percent, and that the first of these dividend payments will occur one year from now, find the present value of the dividend stream; that is, calculate the PV of D_1, D_2, and D_3, and sum these PVs.

c. You expect the price of the stock 3 years from now to be $24.31; that is, you expect $\hat{P}_3$ to equal $24.31. Discounted at a 10 percent rate, what is the present value of this expected future stock price; that is, calculate the PV of $24.31.

d. If you plan to buy the stock, hold it for 3 years, and then sell it for $24.31, what is the most you should pay for it?

e. Use Equation 5-5 to calculate the present value of this stock. Assume that $g = 5\%$, and it is a constant.

f. Is the value of this stock dependent upon how long you plan to hold it? In other words, if your planned holding period were 2 years or 5 years rather than 3 years, would this affect the value of the stock today, $\hat{P}_0$?

5-5   You buy a share of stock for $21.00. You expect the stock to pay dividends of $1.05, $1.1025, and $1.1576 in Years 1, 2, and 3, respectively, and you expect to sell the stock at a price of $24.31 at the end of 3 years.

a. Calculate the growth rate in dividends.

b. Calculate the current dividend yield.

c. Assuming that the calculated growth rate is expected to continue, you can add the dividend yield to the expected growth rate to get the expected total rate of return. What is this expected total rate of return?

5-6   Investors require a 16 percent rate of return on Company X's stock ($k_s = 16\%$).

a. What will be the stock's value if the previous dividend was $D_0 = \$1$ and investors expect dividends to grow at a constant compound annual rate of (1) −5 percent, (2) 0 percent, (3) 5 percent, and (4) 15 percent?

b. In Part a, what is the Gordon (constant growth) model value for Company X's stock if the required rate of return is 16 percent and the expected growth rate is (1) 16 percent or (2) 20 percent? Are these reasonable results? Explain.

c. Is it reasonable to expect that a constant growth stock would have $g > k_s$?

5-7   In February 1956, the Los Angeles Airport authority issued a series of 3.4 percent, 30-year bonds. Interest rates rose substantially in the years following the issue, and as rates rose, the price of the bonds declined. In February 1969, 13 years later, the price of the bonds had dropped from $1,000 to $650. Assume annual interest payments.

a. Each bond originally sold at its $1,000 par value. What was the yield to maturity of these bonds at their time of issue?

b. Calculate the yield to maturity in February 1969.

c. Assume that interest rates stabilized at the 1969 level and remained at this level for the remainder of the life of the bonds. What would have been their price in February 1981, when they had 5 years remaining to maturity?

d. What will the price of the bonds be the day before they mature in 1986?

e. In 1969, the Los Angeles Airport bonds were called "discount bonds." What happens to the price of discount bonds as they approach maturity? Is there a "built-in capital gain" on discount bonds?

f. The coupon interest divided by the market price of a bond is defined as the bond's *current yield*. What would have been the current yield of a Los Angeles Airport bond (1) in February 1969 and (2) in February 1981? What would have been its capital gains yields and total yields (total yield equals yield to maturity) on those same two dates?

5-8   Lehigh Mining Company's ore reserves are being depleted, so its sales are falling. Also, its pit is getting deeper each year, so its costs are rising. As a result, the company's earnings and dividends are declining at the constant rate of 10 percent per year. If $D_0 = \$6$ and $k_s = 15\%$, what is the value of Lehigh Mining's stock?

5-9   It is now January 1, 1985. Overthrust Oil's 1984 dividend, which was paid yesterday, was $2; that is, $D_0 = \$2$. Earnings and dividends are expected to grow at a rate of 15 percent per year for the next 3 years (that is, during 1985, 1986, and 1987) and thereafter to grow indefinitely at the same rate as the national economy, 6 percent. Thus, $g_s = 15\%$ and $g_n = 6\%$, and the period of supernormal growth is 3 years. The required rate of return on the stock, k_s, is 12 percent.

   a. Calculate the expected dividends for 1985, 1986, and 1987.
   b. Calculate the value of the stock today. This is $\hat{P}_0$. Proceed by finding the present value of the dividends expected during 1985, 1986, and 1987, plus the present value of the stock price which should exist at the end of 1987. The year-end 1987 stock price can be found by use of the constant growth equation. Notice that, to find the December 31, 1987, price, you use the dividend expected in 1988, which is 6 percent greater than the 1987 dividend.
   c. Calculate the current dividend yield, D_1/P_0, the capital gains yield expected in 1985, $(\hat{P}_1 - P_0)/P_0$, and the expected total return (dividend yield plus capital gains yield) for 1985. (Assume that $\hat{P}_0 = P_0$.) Also, calculate these same three yields for 1986.
   d. How might an investor's tax situation affect his or her decision to purchase stocks of companies in the early stages of their lives, when they are growing rapidly, versus stocks of older, more mature firms? When does Overthrust Oil's stock become "mature" in this example?

5-10 Overseas Motor Corporation (OMC) has been growing at a rate of 25 percent per year in recent years. This same growth rate is expected to last for another 2 years.

   a. If $D_0 = \$2$, $k = 14\%$, and $g_n = 6\%$, what is OMC's stock worth today? What is its current dividend yield and capital gains yield?
   b. Now assume that OMC's period of supernormal growth is 5 years rather than 2 years. How does this affect its price, dividend yield, and capital gains yield?
   c. What will be OMC's dividend yield and capital gains yield the year after its period of supernormal growth ends? (Hint: These values will be the same regardless of whether you examine the case of 2 or 5 years of supernormal growth.)
   d. Of what interest to investors is the changing relationship between dividend yield and capital gains yield over time?

5-11 It is now January 1, 1985, and you are considering the purchase of an outstanding bond that was issued on January 1, 1983. It has a 10.5 percent annual coupon and a 30-year original maturity (the bond matures in 2013). There is a 5-year call protection (until December 31, 1987), after which time the bond is callable at 110 (that is, at 110 percent of par, or for $1,100). Interest rates have declined since the bond was issued, and the bond is now selling at 115.174 percent, or $1,151.74. You want to determine both the yield to maturity and the yield to call for this bond. (Note: The yield to call considers the impact of a call provision on the actual bond yield. In the calculation, we assume that the bond will be outstanding until the call date, at which time it will be called. Thus, the investor will have received interest payments for the call-protected period and then will receive the call price, in this case, $1,100.)

a. What is the yield to maturity for this bond? What is its yield to call?
b. Which return do you think investors would actually expect? Explain your reasoning.
c. Suppose that the bond had sold at a discount. Would the yield to maturity or the yield to call have been more relevant?

Solutions to Self-Test Problems

ST-1 a. This is not necessarily true. Since G plows back two-thirds of its earnings, its growth rate should exceed that of D, but D pays more dividends ($3 versus $1). We cannot say which stock should have the higher price.

b. Again, we just do not know which price would be higher.

c. This is false. The changes in k_d and k_s would have a greater impact on G—its price would decline more.

d. Once again, we just do not know which expected return would be higher. The total expected return for D is $k_D = D_1/P_0 + g = 15\% + 0\% = 15\%$. The total expected return for G will have D_1/P_0 less than 15 percent and g greater than 0 percent, but $\hat{k}_G$ could be either greater or less than D's total expected return, 15 percent.

e. We have eliminated a, b, c, and d, so e must be correct. Based on the available information, D and G should sell at about the same price, $20. Thus, $\hat{k}_s = \$3/\$20 = 15\%$ for both D and G. G's current dividend yield is $1/$20 = 5%. Therefore, $g = 15\% - 5\% = 10\%$.

ST-2 a. The bonds were sold at par. Therefore, the YTM equals the coupon rate. YTM = 12%.

b.
$$V = \sum_{t=1}^{50} \frac{\$120/2}{\left(1 + \dfrac{0.10}{2}\right)^t} + \frac{\$1,000}{\left(1 + \dfrac{0.10}{2}\right)^{50}}$$

$$= \$60(\text{PVIFA}_{5\%,50}) + \$1,000(\text{PVIF}_{5\%,50})$$

$$= \$60(18.2559) + \$1,000(0.0872)$$

$$= \$1,095.35 + \$87.20 = \$1,182.55.$$

c.
$$\text{Current yield} = \text{Coupon payment/Price}$$
$$= \$120/\$1,182.55$$
$$= 0.1015 = 10.15\%.$$

$$\text{Capital gains yield} = \text{Total yield} - \text{Current yield}$$
$$= 10\% - 10.15\% = -0.15\%.$$

d.
$$\$896.64 = \sum_{t=1}^{19} \frac{\$60}{(1 + k_d/2)^t} + \frac{\$1,000}{(1 + k_d/2)^{19}}.$$

Use the approximate YTM formula to get a starting point:

$$\text{Approximate YTM} = \frac{I + (M - V)/n}{(M + V)/2}$$

$$= \frac{\$60 + (\$1,000 - \$896.64)/19}{(\$1,000 + \$896.64)/2}$$

$$= 6.90\%.$$

Therefore, $k_d \approx 6.9(2) = 13.8\%$.

Try $k_d = 14\%$:

$$V = I(\text{PVIFA}_{7\%,19}) + M(\text{PVIF}_{7\%,19})$$
$$\$896.64 = \$60(10.3356) + \$1,000(0.2765)$$
$$= \$620.14 + \$276.50 = \$896.64.$$

Therefore, the YTM on July 1, 1985, was 14 percent.

e. Current yield = $\$120/\$896.64 = 13.38\%$.

Capital gains yield = $14\% - 13.38\% = 0.62\%$.

f. The following time line illustrates the years to maturity of the bond:

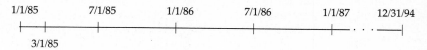

Thus, there are 19⅔ periods left before the bond matures. Bond traders actually use the following procedure to determine the price of the bond:

1. Find the price of the bond on the next coupon date, July 1, 1985.

$$V_{7/1/85} = \$60(\text{PVIFA}_{7.75\%,19}) + \$1,000(\text{PVIF}_{7.75\%,19})$$
$$= \$60(9.7788) + \$1,000(0.2421)$$
$$= \$828.83.$$

Note that we could use a calculator to solve for $V_{7/1/85}$ or could substitute k = 7.75% and n = 19 periods into the equations for PVIFA and PVIF:

$$\text{PVIFA} = \frac{1 - \dfrac{1}{(1 + k)^n}}{k} = \frac{1 - \dfrac{1}{(1 + 0.0775)^{19}}}{0.0775} = 9.7788.$$

$$\text{PVIF} = \frac{1}{(1 + k)^n} = \frac{1}{(1 + 0.0775)^{19}} = 0.2421.$$

2. Add the coupon, $60, to the bond price to get the total value, TV, of the bond on the next payment date: TV = $828.83 + $60.00 = $888.83.

3. Discount this total value back to the purchase date:

$$\begin{array}{l}\text{Value at purchase date} \\ \text{(March 1, 1985)}\end{array} = \$888.83(\text{PVIF}_{7.75\%,4/6})$$

$$= \$888.83(0.9515)$$
$$= \$845.72.$$

Here

$$PVIF_{7.75\%, 2/3} = \frac{1}{(1 + 0.0775)^{2/3}} = \frac{1}{1.0510} = 0.9515.$$

4. Therefore, you would write a check for $845.72 to complete the transaction. Of this amount, $20 = (1/3)($60) represents accrued interest, and $825.72 represents the bond's basic value. This breakdown would affect your taxes and those of the seller.

ST-3 The first step is to solve for g, the unknown variable, in the constant growth equation. Since D_1 is unknown, substitute $D_0(1 + g)$ as follows:

$$\hat{P}_0 = P_0 = \frac{D_0(1 + g)}{k_s - g}$$

$$\$24 = \frac{\$1.60(1 + g)}{0.12 - g}.$$

Solving for g, we find the growth rate to be 5 percent. The next step is to use the growth rate to project the stock price 5 years hence:

$$\hat{P}_5 = \frac{D_0(1 + g)^6}{k_s - g}$$

$$= \frac{\$1.60(1.05)^6}{0.12 - 0.05}$$

$$= \$30.63.$$

(Alternatively, $\hat{P}_5 = \$24(1.05)^5 = \$30.63$.)

Therefore, Karp Company's expected stock price 5 years from now, $\hat{P}_5$, is $30.63.

ST-4 a. **Step 1.** Calculate the PV of the dividends paid during the supernormal growth period:

$$D_1 = \$1.1500(1.18) = \$1.3570.$$
$$D_2 = \$1.3570(1.18) = \$1.6013.$$
$$D_3 = \$1.6013(1.15) = \$1.8415.$$

PV D $= \$1.3570(0.8929) + \$1.6013(0.7972) + \$1.8415(0.7118)$
$= \$1.2117 + \$1.2766 + \$1.3108$
$= \$3.7991 \approx \$3.80.$

Step 2. Find the PV of the stock's price at the end of Year 3:

$$\hat{P}_3 = \frac{D_4}{k_s - g} = \frac{D_3(1 + g)}{k_s - g}$$

$$= \frac{\$1.8415(1.06)}{0.12 - 0.06}$$

$$= \$32.53$$

PV $\hat{P}_3 = \$32.53(0.7118) = \$23.15.$

Step 3. Sum the two components to find the value of the stock today:

$$\hat{P}_0 = \$3.80 + \$23.15 = \$26.95.$$

b. $\hat{P}_1 = \$1.6013(0.8929) + \$1.8415(0.7972) + \$32.53(0.7972)$
$= \$1.4298 + \$1.4680 + \$25.9329$
$= \$28.8307 \approx \$28.83.$

$\hat{P}_2 = \$1.8415(0.8929) + \$32.53(0.8929)$
$= \$1.6443 + \$29.0460$
$= \$30.6903 \approx \$30.69.$

c.

Year	Dividend Yield	Capital Gains Yield	Total Return
1	$\dfrac{\$1.3570}{\$26.95} = 5.04\%$	$\dfrac{\$28.83 - \$26.95}{\$26.95} = 6.98\%$	$\approx 12\%$
2	$\dfrac{\$1.6013}{\$28.83} = 5.55\%$	$\dfrac{\$30.69 - \$28.83}{\$28.83} = 6.45\%$	12%
3	$\dfrac{\$1.8415}{\$30.69} = 6.00\%$	$\dfrac{\$32.53 - \$30.69}{\$30.69} = 6.00\%$	12%

Selected Additional References

Many investments textbooks cover stock and bond valuation models in depth and detail. These are some of the good recent ones:

Francis, Jack C., *Investments: Analysis and Management* (New York: McGraw-Hill, 1980).

Radcliffe, Robert C., *Investment: Concepts, Analysis, and Strategy* (Glenview, Ill.: Scott, Foresman, 1982).

Reilly, Frank K., *Investment Analysis and Portfolio Management* (Hinsdale, Ill.: Dryden, 1985).

Sharpe, William F., *Investments* (Englewood Cliffs, N. J.: Prentice-Hall, 1981).

The classic works on stock valuation models are these:

Gordon, Myron J., and Eli Shapiro, "Capital Equipment Analysis: The Required Rate of Profit," *Management Science*, October 1956, 102-110.

Williams, John B., *The Theory of Investment Value* (Cambridge, Mass.: Harvard University Press, 1938).

Effects of Personal Taxes   5A

All of the calculations in Chapter 5 were based on cash flows to the investor before personal taxes, CF. However, for investors who must pay taxes, the cash flows which they actually get to keep are the after-tax cash flows, ATCF:

$$ATCF = CF - Tax = CF - CF(T) = CF(1 - T).$$

Here T is the investor's effective tax rate applicable to the cash flow. It is these after-tax cash flows which constitute the *relevant* cash flows, and the relevant yield to maturity and expected rate of return are based on these flows. This distinction is quite important: Because different types of income are subject to different tax rates, it is often necessary to compare after-tax returns to make valid choices among alternative investment opportunities. This appendix presents the effects of personal taxes on bond and stock returns.

First, consider the effects on bond returns. If an investor in the 55 percent *Bond Returns* federal plus state tax bracket bought a new 10 percent, 20-year, annual payment Exxon Corporation bond for $1,000, then the before-tax rate of return would be 10 percent, but the after-tax rate of return would be the value of $k_{d(AT)}$ in this equation:

$$\text{Price of bond} = \sum_{t=1}^{n} \frac{I(1 - T)}{(1 + k_{d(AT)})^t} + \frac{\text{Maturity value}}{(1 + k_{d(AT)})^n}$$

$$\$1{,}000 = \sum_{t=1}^{20} \frac{\$100(0.45)}{(1 + k_{d(AT)})^t} + \frac{\$1{,}000}{(1 + k_{d(AT)})^{20}}$$

$$= \$45(PVIFA_{k_{d(AT)},20}) + \$1{,}000(PVIF_{k_{d(AT)},20}).$$

Using interest factors for 4.5 percent, 20 years, obtained with a calculator, we find

$$\$1{,}000 = \$45(13.0079) + \$1{,}000(0.4146) = \$1{,}000,$$

which demonstrates that $k_{d(AT)}$ = 4.5% is the after-tax rate of return on a 10 percent taxable bond sold at par to a 55 percent bracket investor.

If a bond with a 10 percent YTM is bought at a discount, the after-tax return will be higher than that on a bond with a 10 percent YTM bought at par. This result occurs because capital gains are taxed at a lower rate than is interest income, and a discount bond provides some of its return in the form of capital gains. For example, suppose an investor is in the 55 percent federal plus state tax bracket. Recall from Chapter 2 that 60 percent of all long-term capital gains are excluded from income, leaving 40 percent of long-term gains to be taxed. Therefore, the effective tax rate on long-term capital gains for this investor is (Tax rate)(1.0 − Percentage exclusion) = 55%(0.4) = 22%. Now assume that our investor buys an old 6 percent coupon Exxon bond that was issued years ago. This bond now has 20 years remaining to maturity, and its price is $659.42. The annual interest payment is $60, and the YTM on this bond is 10 percent, the same as that on a new 10 percent coupon Exxon bond bought at par. However, the investor's after-tax interest receipt would be $60(1 − T) = $60(0.45) = $27, and the after-tax rate of return on this discount bond would be the value of $k_{d(AT)}$ that solves this equation:

$$\text{Price of bond} = \sum_{t=1}^{20} \frac{\$27}{(1 + k_{d(AT)})^t} + \frac{\$1,000 - 0.22(\$1,000 - \$659.42)}{(1 + k_{d(AT)})^{20}}$$

$$\$659.42 = \$27(\text{PVIFA}_{k_{d(AT)},20}) + \$925.07(\text{PVIF}_{k_{d(AT)},20}).$$

Using a financial calculator, we find $k_{d(AT)}$ = 5.28%.

If you were in the 55 percent tax bracket, and you found that you could buy these two Exxon bonds at the indicated prices, which would you choose? Obviously, the discount bond, because it would offer the higher after-tax return, 5.28 percent versus 4.5 percent on the par bond. Therefore, you (and others) would bid the price of the discount bond up relative to that of the par bond, and this action would continue until the *after-tax* returns on the two bonds were approximately equal.[1]

Now assume that our investor buys an old 14 percent coupon bond that now has 20 years remaining to maturity, at a price of $1,340.54. The annual interest payment is $140, and the YTM on this bond is also 10 percent, the same as that on a new 10 percent coupon Exxon bond bought at par. However, in this case, the investor's annual after-tax interest receipt would be $140(1 − T) = $140(0.45) = $63, and when the bond matured, the investor would receive $1,000 plus a tax credit from the long-term loss of $340.54. The after-tax rate of return on this premium bond would be 4.04 percent:

---

[1]The effect of a deep discount on the likelihood of a call would also have an effect on the bonds' relative prices. A deep discount bond has very good de facto protection against a call. (See Chapter 15 for more on calls.) Another factor which should be noted is the fact that, if the two Exxon bonds were priced so as to provide the same after-tax returns to an investor in the 55 percent bracket, then a zero tax bracket investor, such as a pension fund, would obtain a higher return by buying the bond that is selling close to par. Therefore, the pension funds would tend to bid for these bonds and thus drive their yields down. The final set of equilibrium prices in the economy would reflect the amount of funds available to investors in different tax brackets. In any event, however, one would expect to find (1) investors in high tax brackets buying primarily discount bonds, (2) zero tax rate investors buying par (and premium) bonds, and (3) before-tax YTMs lower on discount than par (and premium) bonds of equivalent risk and maturity.

$$\$1,340.54 = \$63(\text{PVIFA}_{k_{d(AT)},20}) + [\$1,000 + (\$1,340.54 - \$1,000)(0.22)](\text{PVIF}_{k_{d(AT)},20})$$
$$= \$63(\text{PVIFA}_{4.04\%,20}) + \$1,074.92(\text{PVIF}_{4.04\%,20}).$$

Here the investor is incurring a long-term capital loss of $340.54. This loss provides a tax deduction which has a value of $74.92 in Year 20.[2]

Note that, for a given before-tax yield, the after-tax yield to maturity on a bond bought at a premium is lower than that for a bond bought at discount. Our 10 percent before-tax YTM discount bond offered a 5.28 percent after-tax yield, while the 10 percent before-tax YTM premium bond yielded 4.04 percent after-tax. Investors would prefer the bond selling at a discount, or even the bond selling at par, to the premium bond. Therefore, in equilibrium, supply and demand conditions would cause the after-tax yields on all three bonds (assuming equal riskiness) to be the same to the marginal investor. However, investors with exceptionally high or exceptionally low income tax rates would not be indifferent among the bonds: Low-bracket investors would buy premium bonds, while high-bracket investors would be attracted to discount bonds.

Stock Returns

A similar situation holds with common stocks. Recall that a stock's total expected return, $\hat{k}_s$, consists of an expected dividend yield plus an expected capital gains yield. Suppose our 55 percent bracket investor is considering buying some stock of the High-Yield Corporation, with $P_0 = \$30$, $D_1 = \$3.60$, and $g = 3\%$, or alternatively, the stock of High-Growth Company, with $P_0 = \$30$, $D_1 = \$0.90$, and $g = 12\%$. Both companies are constant growth firms. What would the expected before-tax and after-tax rates of return be on the two stocks?

Before-Tax Returns

$$\text{High-Yield: } \hat{k}_s = D_1/P_0 + g = \$3.60/\$30 + 3\% = 15\%.$$
$$\text{High-Growth: } \hat{k}_s = D_1/P_0 + g = \$0.90/\$30 + 12\% = 15\%.$$

After-Tax Returns

High-Yield:

$$\hat{k}_{s_{AT}} = \text{Dividend yield} - \text{T(Dividend yield)}$$
$$+ \text{ Capital gains yield} - \text{T}[0.4(\text{Capital gains yield})]$$
$$= \text{Dividend yield}(1 - \text{T}) + \text{Capital gains yield}(1.0 - 0.4\text{T})$$
$$= 12\%(0.45) + 3\%(0.78)$$
$$= 5.4\% + 2.3\% = 7.7\%.$$

---

[2]Actually, under 1984 tax laws, an investor would have the option of handling the premium bond by following the procedure that we described or by amortizing the premium over the life of the bond and, in effect, using the amortization charge to reduce annual taxable income. The amortization charge would be $340.54/20 = $17.03 per year. This would cause the annual after-tax interest receipt to be CF − Taxes = $140 − ($140 − $17.03)(0.55) = $72.37, and the terminal value would be $1,000 rather than $1,074.92. The resulting $k_{d(AT)}$ would be 4.60 versus 4.04 percent under the first option. Therefore, our investor would choose to amortize the premium and thus obtain a higher effective after-tax yield. Also, note that laws regarding the tax treatment of bonds sold at a discount or premium are changed relatively often. The examples here are meant more to illustrate the various effects of taxes than to perfectly describe the tax code.

High-Growth:

$$\hat{k}_{sAT} = 3\%(0.45) + 12\%(0.78) = 1.3\% + 9.4\% = 10.7\%.$$

This example shows that, to a tax-paying investor, more capital gains income than dividend income flows through to spendable income. This suggests that stockholders might prefer to have corporations retain earnings, plow them back into the business, and provide capital gains instead of paying out dividends. Before accepting this as gospel, however, wait and consider in Chapter 13 some of the other points made in connection with dividend policy. In any event, it is obvious that, at least from the tax standpoint, an investor in a high tax bracket is better off if a high percentage of his or her total return comes as capital gains rather than as dividend income.

Derivation of the Constant Growth Model 5B

The proof for Equation 5-5, the formula for the value of a constant growth stock, $\hat{P}_0 = D_1/(k_s - g)$, is developed as follows. Rewrite Equation 5-2 as follows:

$$\hat{P}_0 = \frac{D_0(1 + g)^1}{(1 + k_s)^1} + \frac{D_0(1 + g)^2}{(1 + k_s)^2} + \frac{D_0(1 + g)^3}{(1 + k_s)^3} + \cdots + \frac{D_0(1 + g)^n}{(1 + k_s)^n}$$

$$= D_0 \left[\frac{(1 + g)}{(1 + k_s)} + \frac{(1 + g)^2}{(1 + k_s)^2} + \frac{(1 + g)^3}{(1 + k_s)^3} + \cdots + \frac{(1 + g)^n}{(1 + k_s)^n} \right]. \quad \textbf{(5B-1)}$$

Multiply both sides of Equation 5B-1 by $(1 + k_s)/(1 + g)$:

$$\left[\frac{(1 + k_s)}{(1 + g)} \right] \hat{P}_0 = D_0 \left[1 + \frac{(1 + g)}{(1 + k_s)} + \frac{(1 + g)^2}{(1 + k_s)^2} + \cdots + \frac{(1 + g)^{n-1}}{(1 + k_s)^{n-1}} \right]. \quad \textbf{(5B-2)}$$

Subtract Equation 5B-1 from Equation 5B-2 to obtain Equation 5B-3:

$$\left[\frac{(1 + k_s)}{(1 + g)} - 1 \right] \hat{P}_0 = D_0 \left[1 - \frac{(1 + g)^n}{(1 + k_s)^n} \right].$$

$$\left[\frac{(1 + k_s) - (1 + g)}{(1 + g)} \right] \hat{P}_0 = D_0 \left[1 - \frac{(1 + g)^n}{(1 + k_s)^n} \right]. \quad \textbf{(5B-3)}$$

Assuming $k_s > g$, as $n \to \infty$, the term in brackets on the right-hand side of Equation 5B-3 approaches 1.0, leaving

$$\left[\frac{(1 + k_s) - (1 + g)}{(1 + g)} \right] \hat{P}_0 = D_0,$$

which simplifies to Equation 5-5:

$$(k_s - g)\hat{P}_0 = D_0(1 + g) = D_1$$

$$\hat{P}_0 = \frac{D_1}{k_s - g}. \quad \textbf{(5-5)} \qquad 175$$

5C

A Quarterly Stock
Valuation Model

Throughout Chapter 5, we discussed stock valuation and rates of return on the assumption that dividends are received once a year. In fact, most companies pay dividends on a quarterly basis, and increase them annually. The top section of Figure 5C-1 shows the annual dividend pattern, while the lower section shows the more typical actual payment pattern. If annual payments occur, and growth is constant, then Equations 5C-1 and 5C-2 are appropriate (since we are dealing only with stocks, we use k to represent k_s):

$$\hat{P}_0 = \frac{D_1}{k - g}. \tag{5C-1}$$

$$\hat{k} = \frac{D_1}{P_0} + g. \tag{5C-2}$$

However, if dividends are paid quarterly, and they grow once a year, then Equations 5C-3 and 5C-4 are appropriate:[1]

$$\hat{P}_0 = \frac{D_{q1}(1 + k)^{0.75} + D_{q2}(1 + k)^{0.50} + D_{q3}(1 + k)^{0.25} + D_{q4}(1 + k)^0}{k - g} \tag{5C-3}$$

$$\hat{k} = \frac{D_{q1}(1 + k)^{0.75} + D_{q2}(1 + k)^{0.50} + D_{q3}(1 + k)^{0.25} + D_{q4}(1 + k)^0}{P_0} + g. \tag{5C-4}$$

Here D_{qt} is the quarterly dividend in Quarter t, k is the expected and required rate of return, and g is the annual dividend growth rate. As is also true with the annual payment model as expressed in Equations 5C-1 and 5C-2, Equations 5C-3 and 5C-4 assume that the analysis is performed on a dividend payment date, so that the next dividend will be received exactly one period hence.

This appendix was coauthored with T. Craig Tapley. It is based on University of Florida, Public Utility Research Center, Working Paper #2-84, October 1984. Our work was stimulated by a paper by Charles M. Linke and J. Kenton Zumwalt, "Estimation Biases in Discounted Cash Flow Analyses of Equity Capital Cost in Rate Regulation," *Financial Management*, Autumn 1984, 15-21.

[1]These equations are derived in Working Paper #2-84, using a procedure that is similar to, but more complicated than, that in Appendix 5B.

Figure 5C-1
Annual versus Quarterly Dividend Payment Patterns

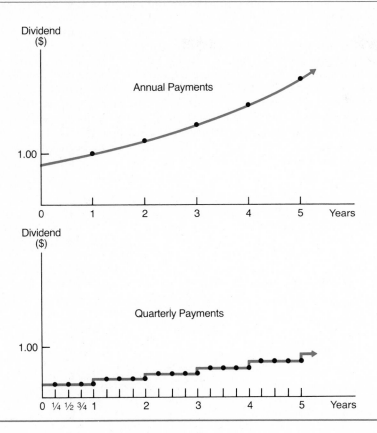

The logic here is similar to that involved in the analysis of a semiannual payment bond: A bond is more valuable if its payments occur every six months, and its effective annual rate of return is higher. Similarly, a stock that pays dividends quarterly is more valuable than an annual payment stock, other things held constant, and its effective annual return is higher.

We can illustrate and compare returns estimated by the two models with data for BellSouth Corporation, the largest of the telephone companies formed when AT&T was broken up. In January 1984, BellSouth sold for $29.25 per share; its dividend was $2.60 per year, payable at the rate of $0.65 per quarter; and the consensus forecast for its dividend growth rate was 7 percent. Using Equation 5C-2, we obtain a 15.89 percent expected return:

$$\hat{k} = \frac{\$2.60}{\$29.25} + 7\% = 15.89\%.$$

However, with the quarterly model, we have this situation:

$$\hat{k} = \frac{\$0.65(1 + k)^{0.75} + \$0.65(1 + k)^{0.50} + \$0.65(1 + k)^{0.25} + \$0.65(1 + k)^{0}}{\$29.25} + 7\%.$$

Thus, we have an equation in one unknown, so we can solve for k. The solution requires a series of iterations, which we perform on a personal computer with a *Lotus 1-2-3* program; the solution value is $k = 16.42\%$. Therefore, assuming annual payments when in fact dividends are paid quarterly results in a $16.42\% - 15.89\% = 0.53$ percentage point understatement of the true expected rate of return on BellSouth's stock.

The quarterly payment model can be adapted (1) to the nonconstant growth situation, (2) to deal with the situation when the first dividend will be received in a relatively few days, and (3) when the dividend is expected to be increased in less than four quarters. For valid comparisons among assets with annual, semiannual, quarterly, and monthly payments, all returns should be put on an equivalent effective annual rate basis. The model set forth in this appendix, modified as need be, can be used to find the effective annual rate for common stocks.

Risk and Rates of Return

6

Common sense tells us that required rates of return on investments increase as the riskiness of the investments increases. However, common sense does not tell us how to measure risk, and, indeed, the proper measurement of risk is rather subtle. To illustrate, consider these two examples:

1. Homestake Mining Company is a leading U.S. gold producer. Gold prices are volatile, and since Homestake's profits vary with the price of gold, its earnings also fluctuate widely from year to year. Moreover, it is one of the few New York Stock Exchange companies which has had to cut its dividend in recent years. All this suggests that Homestake is relatively risky, and hence that the required rate of return on its stock, k_s, should be above those of most other NYSE companies. However, this is not the case; the formula $\hat{k}_s = k_s = D_1/P_0 + g$ indicates that, with any reasonable value for growth, Homestake's k_s in 1984, and all other years, was quite low in relation to other companies. This, in turn, indicates that investors regard Homestake as being a low-risk company in spite of its unstable profits and its unstable dividend stream.

2. Such large, strong, and well-diversified companies as Du Pont and General Electric (GE) have more stable, predictable earnings and dividends than do the 1,600 or so smaller NYSE companies. This suggests that Du Pont, GE, and other giant companies have much less risk and, consequently, should have a much lower required rate of return on their stocks than the smaller companies. However, this is not the case; a careful analysis indicates that Du Pont, GE, and other giant companies are not materially less risky than many smaller, more volatile companies.

The reason for these somewhat counterintuitive facts has to do with diversification and its effects on risk. It so happens that Homestake's

179

stock price rises with inflationary expectations, whereas other stocks tend to decline as inflation heats up. Therefore, holding Homestake in a portfolio of "normal" stocks tends to stabilize returns on the entire portfolio. In the case of Du Pont and GE, it turns out that investors, by forming portfolios of the stocks of smaller companies, can and do diversify away much of the risk that would otherwise be inherent in small companies.

We also know that expectations for inflation, along with risk, have an impact on interest rates and required rates of return generally, and consequently on security prices. Inflationary expectations are worked into security prices in various ways. Sometimes the changes are slow and almost imperceptible, but sometimes they are quite rapid. For example, in the spring of 1984, Henry Kaufman, an economist and senior executive of Salomon Brothers (a major Wall Street investment banking firm), and probably the most listened-to interest rate forecaster in the United States, predicted that in 1985 interest rates would increase sharply. Kaufman's forecast caused the Dow Jones Industrial Average to drop by over 15 points within a few hours.

In this chapter, we take an in-depth look at how investment risk should be measured, and at how both risk and inflation affect security prices and rates of return.

In Chapter 5, we referred frequently to the terms *appropriate interest rate on debt*, k_d, and *appropriate (or required) rate of return on a share of common stock*, k_s. These rates, which we used to help determine the values of bonds and stocks, depend primarily on the level of the riskless rate of interest, R_F, and on the riskiness of the security in question. In this chapter, we define the term *risk* as it relates to securities, examine procedures for measuring it, and then discuss the relationships among risk, returns, and security prices.

Defining and Measuring Risk

Risk is defined in *Webster's* as "a hazard; a peril; exposure to loss or injury." Thus, risk refers to the chance that some unfavorable event will occur. If you engage in skydiving, you take a chance with your life—skydiving is risky. If you bet on the horses, you risk losing your money. If you invest in speculative stocks (or, really, *any* stock), you are taking a risk in the hope of making an appreciable return.

To illustrate the riskiness of financial assets, suppose an investor buys $100,000 of short-term government bonds with an interest rate of 10 percent. In this case, the yield to maturity on the investment, 10 percent, can be estimated quite precisely, and the investment is defined as being risk-free. However, if the $100,000 were invested in the stock of a company just being organized to prospect for oil in the mid-Atlantic, then the investment's return could not be estimated precisely. One might think that the *expected* rate of return, in a statistical sense, is 20 percent, but the *actual* rate of return could range from some extremely large, positive figure to −100 percent, and because there is a significant danger of a return considerably less than the expected return, the stock is described as being relatively risky.

Investment risk, then, is related to the probability of returns less than the expected return—the greater the chance of such low or negative returns, the riskier the investment. However, we can define risk more precisely, and it is useful to do so.

An event's *probability* is defined as the chance that the event will occur. For example, a weather forecaster may state, "There is a 40 percent chance of rain today and a 60 percent chance that it will not rain." If all possible events, or outcomes, are listed, and if a probability is assigned to each event, then the listing is defined as a *probability distribution*. For our weather forecast, we could set up the following probability distribution:

Probability Distributions

Outcome (1)	Probability (2)	
Rain	0.4 =	40%
No rain	0.6 =	60%
	1.0 =	100%

The possible outcomes are listed in Column 1, while the probabilities of these outcomes, expressed both as decimals and as percentages, are given in Column 2. Notice that the probabilities must sum to 1.0, or 100 percent.

In Chapter 5, we defined the expected rate of return on a stock, $\hat{k}_s$, as the sum of the expected dividend yield plus the expected capital gain. We now examine the probability distribution concept as related to rates of return. To begin, consider the possible rates of return (dividend yield plus capital gain or loss) that you might earn next year on a $10,000 investment in the stock of either Kelly Products, Inc., or U.S. Water Company. Kelly manufactures and distributes computer terminals and equipment for the rapidly growing data transmission industry. Its sales are cyclical, so its profits rise and fall with the business cycle. Further, its market is extremely competitive, and some new company could develop better products which could literally bankrupt Kelly. U.S. Water, on the other hand, supplies an essential service, and it has city franchises which make it a monopoly, so its sales and profits are relatively stable and predictable.

The rate of return probability distributions for the two companies are shown in Table 6-1. Here we see that there is a 30 percent chance of a

Table 6-1
Probability Distributions for Kelly Products
and U.S. Water

State of the Economy	Probability of this State Occurring	Rate of Return on Stock under this State	
		Kelly Products	U.S. Water
Boom	0.3	100%	20%
Normal	0.4	15	15
Recession	0.3	− 70	10
	1.0		

boom, in which case both companies will have high earnings, pay high dividends, and enjoy capital gains; a 40 percent probability of a "normal" economy and moderate returns; and a 30 percent probability of a recession, which will mean low earnings and dividends, and also capital losses. Notice, however, that Kelly Products' rate of return could vary far more widely than that of U.S. Water. There is a fairly high probability that the value of the Kelly stock will drop significantly, resulting in a loss of 70 percent, while there is no chance of a loss on U.S. Water.[1]

Expected Rate of Return

If we multiply each possible outcome by its probability of occurrence and then sum these products, we have a *weighted average* of outcomes. The weights are the probabilities, and the weighted average is defined as the *expected rate of return*, k̂. The expected rate of return for Kelly Products is shown in Table 6-2 to be 15 percent, while that of U.S. Water is also 15 percent. This type of table is known as a *payoff matrix*.

The expected rate of return calculation can also be expressed as an equation which does the same thing as the payoff matrix table:

$$\text{Expected rate of return} = \hat{k} = \sum_{i=1}^{n} P_i k_i. \tag{6-1}$$

Here, k_i is the ith possible outcome, P_i is the probability of the ith outcome, and n is the number of possible outcomes. Thus, k̂ is a weighted average of the possible outcomes (the k_i values), with each outcome's

---

[1]It is, of course, completely unrealistic to think that any stock has no chance of a loss. Only in hypothetical instances could this occur. To illustrate, the price of Commonwealth Edison's stock dropped from $27 to $21 on January 16, 1984, a decline of 22 percent in one day. Don't tell people who bought Commonwealth on the 15th that the stock has no chance of a loss!

Table 6-2
Calculation of Expected Rate of Return: Payoff Matrix

State of the Economy (1)	Probability of this State Occurring (2)	Kelly Products		U.S. Water	
		Rate of Return if this State Occurs (3)	Product: (2) × (3) (4)	Rate of Return if this State Occurs (5)	Product: (2) × (5) (6)
Boom	0.3	100%	30%	20%	6%
Normal	0.4	15	6	15	6
Recession	0.3	−70	−21	10	3
	1.0		$\hat{k} = $ 15%		$\hat{k} = $ 15%

weight being equal to its probability of occurrence.[2] Using the data for Kelly Products, we obtain its expected rate of return as follows:

$$\hat{k} = P_1(k_1) + P_2(k_2) + P_3(k_3)$$
$$= 0.3(100\%) + 0.4(15\%) + 0.3(-70\%) = 15\%.$$

U.S. Water's expected rate of return is also 15 percent:

$$\hat{k} = 0.3(20\%) + 0.4(15\%) + 0.3(10\%) = 15\%.$$

We can graph the rates of return to obtain a picture of the variability of possible outcomes; this is shown in the bar charts in Figure 6-1. The height of each bar signifies the probability that a given outcome will occur. The range of probable returns for Kelly Products is from 100 to −70 percent, with an expected return of 15 percent. The expected return for U.S. Water is also 15 percent, but its range is much narrower.

Continuous Probability Distributions

Thus far, we have assumed that only three states of the economy can exist: recession, normal, and boom. Actually, of course, the state of the economy could range from a deep depression to a fantastic boom, and there are an unlimited number of possibilities in between. Suppose we had the time and patience to assign a probability to each possible state

---

[2]In this section, we discuss only returns on stock. Thus, the subscript s is unnecessary, and we use the term $\hat{k}$ rather than $\hat{k}_s$. Also, keep in mind that $\hat{k} = D_1/P_0 + g$ for a constant growth stock:

$$\hat{k} = \frac{D_1}{P_0} + g = \sum_{i=1}^{n} P_i k_i.$$

Further, note that the uncertainty about $\hat{k}$, the expected *total* return, reflects uncertainty about the two return components, D_1/P_0 and g. There is more uncertainty regarding g than there is regarding the dividend yield. Thus, companies with high growth and low current dividend yields are often regarded as being riskier than low-growth companies. This point is discussed further in Chapter 13.

Figure 6-1
Probability Distributions of Kelly Products' and
U.S. Water's Rates of Return

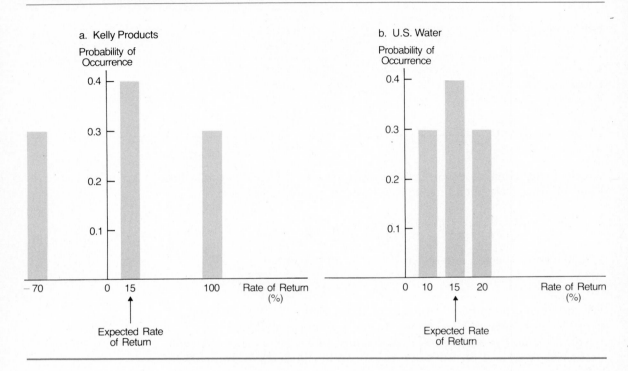

of the economy (with the sum of the probabilities still equaling 1.0), and to assign a rate of return to each stock for each state of the economy. We would have a table similar to Table 6-2, except that it would have many more entries in each column. This table could be used to calculate expected rates of return as shown above, and the probabilities and outcomes could be approximated by continuous curves such as those presented in Figure 6-2. Here we have changed the assumptions so that there is essentially a zero probability that the return of Kelly Products will be less than −70 percent or more than 100 percent, or that U.S. Water will return less than 10 percent or more than 20 percent, but virtually any return within these limits is possible.

The tighter the probability distribution, the more likely it is that the actual outcome will be close to the expected value, and the less likely it is that the actual return will be far below the expected return. Thus, the tighter the probability distribution, the lower is the risk assigned to a stock. Since U.S. Water has a relatively tight probability distribution, its *actual return* is likely to be closer to its 15 percent *expected return* than is that of Kelly Products.

Figure 6-2
Continuous Probability Distributions of Kelly Products'
and U.S. Water's Rates of Return

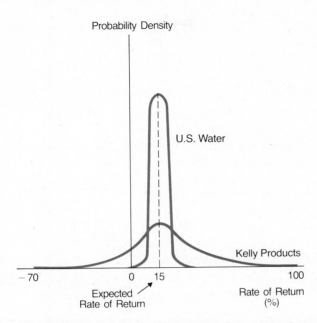

Note: The assumptions regarding the probabilities of various outcomes have been changed from those in Figure 6-1. The probability of obtaining exactly 15 percent was 40 percent in Figure 6-1; in Figure 6-2 it is *much smaller*, because here there are many possible outcomes instead of just three. With continuous distributions such as in Figure 6-2, it is more appropriate to ask what the probability is of obtaining *at least* some specified rate of return than to ask what the probability is of obtaining exactly that rate of return. This cumulative probability is equal to the area under the probability distribution curve to the right of the point of interest, or 1 minus the area under the curve up to the point of interest. This topic is covered in detail in statistics courses.

Risk is a difficult concept to grasp, and a great deal of controversy has surrounded attempts to define and measure it. However, a common definition, and one that is satisfactory for many purposes, is stated in terms of probability distributions such as those presented in Figure 6-2: *The tighter the probability distribution of expected future returns, the smaller is the risk of a given investment.* According to this definition, U.S. Water is less risky than Kelly Products *because the chances of returns that are far below the expected level are smaller for U.S. Water than for Kelly Products.*

To be most useful, any measure of risk should have a definite value— we need a measure of the tightness of the probability distribution. One such measure is the *standard deviation*, the symbol for which is σ, pronounced "sigma." The smaller the standard deviation, the tighter is the probability distribution and, accordingly, the lower is the riskiness of the

Measuring Risk:
The Standard
Deviation

Table 6-3
Calculating Kelly Products' Standard Deviation

$k_i - \hat{k}$ (1)	$(k_i - \hat{k})^2$ (2)	$(k_i - \hat{k})^2 P_i$ (3)
$100 - 15 = 85$	7,225	$(7,225)(0.3) = 2,167.5$
$15 - 15 = 0$	0	$(0)(0.4) = 0$
$-70 - 15 = -85$	7,225	$(7,225)(0.3) = \underline{2,167.5}$
		Variance $= \sigma^2 = \underline{\underline{4,335.0}}$

Standard deviation $= \sigma = \sqrt{\sigma^2} = \sqrt{4,335} = 65.84\%$.

stock.[3] To calculate the standard deviation, we proceed as shown in Table 6-3, which is explained below:

1. Calculate the expected rate of return:

$$\text{Expected rate of return} = \hat{k} = \sum_{i=1}^{n} P_i k_i. \qquad (6\text{-}1)$$

For Kelly, we previously found $\hat{k} = 15\%$.

2. Subtract the expected rate of return from each possible outcome to obtain a set of deviations about the expected rate of return:

$$\text{Deviation}_i = k_i - \hat{k}.$$

The deviations for Kelly Products are shown in Column 1 of Table 6-3.

3. Square each deviation, multiply the squared deviation by the probability of occurrence for its related outcome, and sum these products to obtain the *variance* of the probability distribution:

$$\text{Variance} = \sigma^2 = \sum_{i=1}^{n} (k_i - \hat{k})^2 P_i. \qquad (6\text{-}2)$$

This is done in Columns 2 and 3 of the table.

---

[3] Since we define risk in terms of the chances of returns being less than expected, it would seem logical to measure risk in terms of the probability of returns below the expected return, rather than by the entire distribution. Measures of below-expected returns, which are known as *semivariance measures*, have been developed, but they are difficult to analyze. Additionally, if the distribution is approximately symmetric, which is often the case in security returns, then the standard deviation is about as good a risk measure as the semi-variance.

Note also that it is sometimes useful to calculate the *coefficient of variation*, which is the standard deviation divided by the expected value. The advantage of the coefficient of variation is that it permits better comparisons when the expected values of two alternatives are not the same. We will use the coefficient of variation when we discuss project risk in Chapter 10.

4. Now take the square root of the variance to obtain the standard deviation:

$$\text{Standard deviation} = \sigma = \sqrt{\sum_{i=1}^{n} (k_i - \hat{k})^2 P_i}. \tag{6-3}$$

Using these same procedures, we find U.S. Water's standard deviation to be 3.87 percent. Since Kelly's standard deviation is larger, it is the riskier stock according to this measure of risk.

If a probability distribution is normal, the *actual* return will be within ±1 standard deviation of the *expected* return about 68 percent of the time. Figure 6-3 illustrates this point and also shows the situation for ±2σ and ±3σ. For Kelly Products, $\hat{k}$ = 15% and σ = 65.84%. Thus, there is a 68.26 percent probability that the actual return will be in the range of 15 to ±65.84 percent, or from −50.84 to 80.84 percent. For U.S. Water, the 68.26 percent range is 15 to ±3.87 percent, or from 11.13 to 18.87 percent. With such a small σ, there is only a small probability that U.S. Water's return will be significantly less than expected, so the stock is not very risky. For the average firm listed on the New York Stock Exchange, σ has been close to 30 percent in recent years.[4]

---

[4]In this section, we have described the procedure for finding the mean and standard deviation where the data are in the form of a known probability distribution. If only sample returns data over some past period are available, then the standard deviation of returns can be estimated using this formula:

$$\text{Estimated } \sigma = S = \sqrt{\frac{\sum_{t=1}^{n} (\bar{k}_t - \bar{k}_{Avg})^2}{n - 1}}, \tag{6-3a}$$

where $\bar{k}_t$ ("k bar") denotes the past realized rate of return in period t. Here is an example:

Year	$\bar{k}_t$
1982	15%
1983	−5
1984	20

$$\bar{k}_{Avg} = \frac{(15 - 5 + 20)}{3} = 10.0\%.$$

$$\text{Estimated } \sigma \text{ (or S)} = \sqrt{\frac{(15 - 10)^2 + (-5 - 10)^2 + (20 - 10)^2}{3 - 1}}$$

$$= \sqrt{\frac{350}{2}} = 13.2\%.$$

Often, the historical σ is used as an estimate of the future σ. Much less often, and generally incorrectly, $\bar{k}_{Average}$ is used as an estimate of $\hat{k}$.

Figure 6-3
Probability Ranges for a Normal Distribution

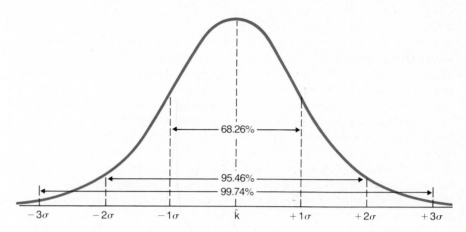

Notes:

a. The area under the normal curve equals 1.0, or 100 percent. *Thus, the areas under any pair of normal curves drawn on the same scale, whether they are peaked or flat, must be equal.*

b. Half of the area under a normal curve is to the left of the mean, indicating that there is a 50 percent probability that the actual outcome will be less than the mean and a 50 percent probability that it will be greater than the mean, or to the right of $\hat{k}$.

c. Of the area under the curve, 68.26 percent is within $\pm 1\sigma$ of the mean, indicating that the probability is 68.26 percent that the actual outcome will be within the range $\hat{k} - 1\sigma$ to $\hat{k} + 1\sigma$.

d. Procedures exist for finding the probability of other earnings ranges. These procedures are covered in statistics courses.

e. For a normal distribution, the larger the value of σ, the greater the probability that the actual outcome will vary widely from, and hence perhaps be far below, the expected, or most likely, outcome. *Since the probability of having the actual result turn out to be far below the expected result is our definition of risk, and since σ measures this probability, we can use σ as a measure of risk.* This definition may not be a good one, however, if we are dealing with an asset held in a diversified portfolio. This point is covered later in the chapter.

Risk Aversion and Required Returns

Suppose you had worked hard and saved $1 million, which you now plan to invest. You can buy a 10 percent Treasury note, and at the end of 1 year you will have a sure $1,100,000, which is your original investment plus $100,000 in interest. Alternatively, you can buy stock in R&D Enterprises. If R&D's research programs are successful, your stock will increase in value to $2.2 million; however, if the research is a failure, the value of your stock will go to zero, and you will be penniless. You regard R&D's chances of success or failure as being 50-50, so the expected value of the stock investment is 0.5($0) + 0.5($2.2 million) = $1,100,000. Subtracting the $1 million cost of the stock leaves an expected profit of $100,000, or an expected (but risky) 10 percent rate of return.

Thus, you have a choice between a sure $100,000 profit (a 10 percent rate of return) on the Treasury note, or a risky expected $100,000 profit (also a 10 percent expected rate of return) on the R&D Enterprises stock.[5] Which one would you choose? *If you choose the less risky invest-ment, you are risk averse. Most investors are indeed risk averse, and certainly the average investor is risk averse, at least with regard to his or her "serious money." Since this is a well-documented fact, we shall assume risk aversion throughout the remainder of the book.*

What are the implications of risk aversion for security prices and rates of return? The answer is that, other things held constant, the higher a security's risk, (1) the lower its price and (2) the higher its expected return. To see how this works, we can analyze the situation with U.S. Water and Kelly Products stocks. Suppose each stock sold for $100 per share, and each had an expected rate of return of 15 percent. Investors are averse to risk, so there would be a general preference for U.S. Water. People with money to invest would bid for Water rather than Kelly stock, and Kelly stockholders would start selling it and using the money to buy Water stock. The buying pressure would tend to drive up the price of Water stock, and the selling pressure would cause Kelly's price to decline.

These price changes, in turn, would cause changes in the expected rates of return on the two securities. Suppose, for example, the price of Water stock was bid up from $100 to $150, while the price of Kelly stock declined from $100 to $75. Further, suppose this caused Water's ex-pected return to fall to 10 percent, while Kelly's expected return rose to 20 percent. The difference in returns, 20% − 10% = 10%, is a *risk pre-mium*, which represents the compensation investors require for assum-ing the additional risk of Kelly stock.

This example demonstrates a very important principle: *In a market dominated by risk-averse investors, riskier securities must have higher expected returns than less risky ones, for if this situation does not hold, then actions will occur in the market to force it to occur.* We will consider the question of *how much* higher the returns on risky securities must be later in the chapter, after we examine in more depth how risk should be measured.

In the preceding section, we considered the riskiness of a stock held in isolation. Now we analyze the riskiness of stocks held in portfolios.[6] As we shall see, a stock held as part of a portfolio is less risky than the same stock held in isolation. This fact has been incorporated into a gen-eralized framework for analyzing the relationship between risk and rates

Portfolio Risk and the Capital Asset Pricing Model

---

[5]Actually, the Treasury note investment is riskless only in the nominal as opposed to the real return sense. Since the inflation rate over the next year could be more than expected, the real return realized after the year is up could be less than expected even though the nominal rate of return is a sure 10 percent.

[6]A *portfolio* is a collection of investment securities. If you owned some General Motors stock, some Exxon stock, and some IBM stock, you would be holding a three-stock port-folio. For reasons set forth in this section, the vast majority of all stocks are held as parts of portfolios.

of return; this framework is called the *Capital Asset Pricing Model*, or *CAPM*. The CAPM framework is, as we shall see, an extremely important analytical tool in both financial management and investment analysis. In the following sections, we discuss the basic CAPM concepts and results. Appendix 6B contains a more rigorous discussion of portfolio theory and the CAPM.

Portfolio Risk and Return

Most financial assets are not held in isolation; rather, they are held as parts of portfolios. Banks, pension funds, insurance companies, mutual funds, and other financial institutions are required by law to hold diversified portfolios. Even individual investors—at least those individuals whose security holdings constitute a significant part of their total wealth—generally hold stock portfolios, not just the stock of one firm. This being the case, from an investor's standpoint the fact that a particular stock goes up or down is not very important; *what is important is the return on his or her portfolio, and the portfolio's risk. Logically, then, the risk and return of an individual security should be analyzed in terms of how the security affects the risk and return of the portfolio in which it is included.*

Portfolio Returns. The expected return on a portfolio, $\hat{k}_p$, is simply the weighted average expected return of the individual stocks in the portfolio, with the weights being the fraction of the total portfolio invested in each stock:

$$\hat{k}_p = w_1\hat{k}_1 + w_2\hat{k}_2 + \cdots w_n\hat{k}_n \qquad \text{(6-4)}$$
$$= \sum_{i=1}^{n} w_i\hat{k}_i.$$

Here the $\hat{k}_i$'s are the expected returns on the individual stocks, the w_i's are the weights, and there are n stocks in the portfolio. Note (1) that w_i is the proportion of the portfolio's dollar value invested in Stock i, that is, the value of the investment in Stock i divided by the total value of the portfolio, and (2) that the w_i's must sum to 1.0. To illustrate, given the following w_i's and $\hat{k}_i$'s, the expected return on a hypothetical four-stock portfolio is 11.8 percent:

$$\hat{k}_p = w_1\hat{k}_1 + w_2\hat{k}_2 + w_3\hat{k}_3 + w_4\hat{k}_4$$
$$= 0.20(10\%) + 0.25(12\%) + 0.30(11\%) + 0.25(14\%)$$
$$= 2.0\% + 3.0\% + 3.3\% + 3.5\% = 11.8\%.$$

Of course, after the fact and a year later, the actual *realized* rates of return on the individual stocks, the $\bar{k}_i$ values, will probably be different from their expected values, so $\bar{k}_p$ will be somewhat different from $\hat{k}_p = 11.8\%$.

Portfolio Risk. As we just saw, the expected return on a portfolio is simply a weighted average of the expected returns on the individual stocks in the portfolio, and each stock's contribution to the expected portfolio return is $w_i\hat{k}_i$. However, unlike returns, the riskiness of a portfolio, σ_p, is generally *not* a weighted average of the standard deviations of the individual securities in the portfolio, and each stock's contribution to the portfolio's risk is *not* $w_i\sigma_i$. It is theoretically possible to combine two stocks which are, individually, quite risky as measured by their standard deviations, and to form a portfolio which is completely riskless, with $\sigma_p = 0$. To illustrate, consider the situation in Figure 6-4. The bottom section gives data on rates of return for Stocks W and M, and for a portfolio invested 50 percent in each stock. Panel a plots the data in a time series format, and Panel b shows the probability distributions of returns, assuming the future is expected to be like the past. The two stocks would be quite risky if they were held in isolation, but, when they are combined to form Portfolio WM, they are not risky at all. (Note: These stocks are called W and M because their returns graphs in Figure 6-4 resemble a W and an M.)

The reason Stocks W and M can be combined to form a riskless portfolio is that their returns move countercyclically to one another—when W's returns fall, those of M rise, and vice versa. In statistical terms, we say that the returns on Stocks W and M are *perfectly negatively correlated*, with r = correlation coefficient = -1.0.[7]

The opposite of perfect negative correlation, with r = -1.0, is perfect positive correlation, with r = $+1.0$. Returns on two perfectly positively correlated stocks would move up and down together, and a portfolio consisting of two such stocks would be just as risky as the individual stocks. This point is illustrated in Figure 6-5, where we see that the portfolio's standard deviation is equal to that of the individual stocks, indicating that diversification does nothing to reduce risk if the portfolio consists of perfectly positively correlated stocks.

Figure 6-4 and 6-5 demonstrate (1) that when stocks are perfectly negatively correlated (r = -1.0), all risk can be diversified away, but (2) that when stocks are perfectly positively correlated (r = $+1.0$), diversification does no good whatever in terms of reducing risk. In reality, most stocks are positively correlated, but not perfectly so. On average, the correlation coefficient for the returns on two randomly selected stocks would be about $+0.6$, and for most pairs of stocks, r would lie in the range of $+0.5$ to $+0.7$. *Under such conditions, combining stocks into portfolios reduces risk but does not eliminate it completely.* Figure 6-6 illustrates this point with two stocks whose correlation coefficient is r =

---

[7]*Correlation* is defined as the tendency of two variables to move together. The *correlation coefficient*, r, measures this tendency, and it can range from $+1.0$, denoting that the two variables move up and down in perfect synchronization, to -1.0, denoting that the variables always move in exactly opposite directions. A correlation coefficient of zero suggests that the two variables are not related to one another, that is, changes in one variable are *independent* of changes in the other. If you have a financial calculator, you can use it to confirm that $r_{WM} = -1.0$.

Figure 6-4
Rate of Return Distributions for Two Perfectly Negatively
Correlated Stocks (r = −1.0), and Portfolio WM

a. Rate of Return

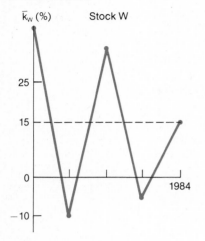

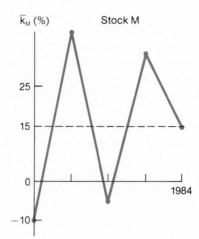

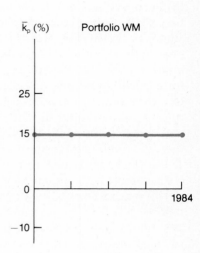

b. Probability Distribution of Returns

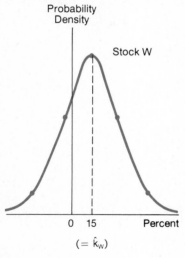

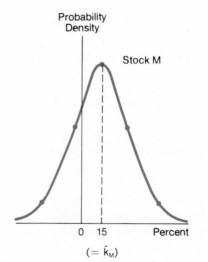

Year	Stock W $\bar{k}_W$	Stock M $\bar{k}_M$	Portfolio WM $\bar{k}_p$
1980	40%	−10%	15%
1981	−10	40	15
1982	35	−5	15
1983	−5	35	15
1984	15	15	15
Average return	15%	15%	15%
Standard deviation	22.6%	22.6%	0.0%

Figure 6-5
Rate of Return Distributions for Two Perfectly Positively
Correlated Stocks (r = +1.0), and for Portfolio MM

a. Rate of Return

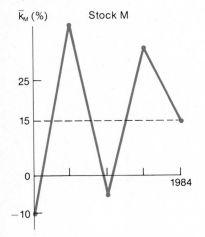

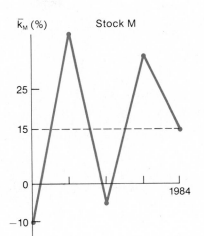

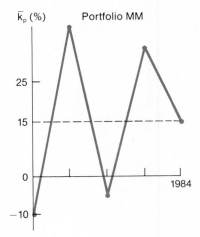

b. Probability Distribution of Returns

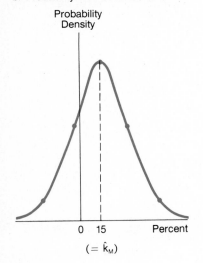

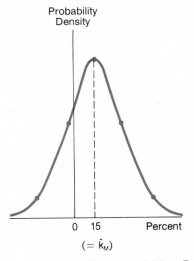

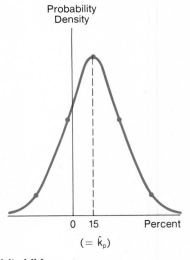

Year	Stock M $\bar{k}_M$	Stock M $\bar{k}_M$	Portfolio MM $\bar{k}_P$
1980	−10%	−10%	−10%
1981	40	40	40
1982	− 5	− 5	− 5
1983	35	35	35
1984	15	15	15
Average return	15%	15%	15%
Standard deviation	22.6%	22.6%	22.6%

Figure 6-6
Rate of Return Distributions for Two Partially Correlated
Stocks (r = +0.65), and for Portfolio WY

a. Rate of Return

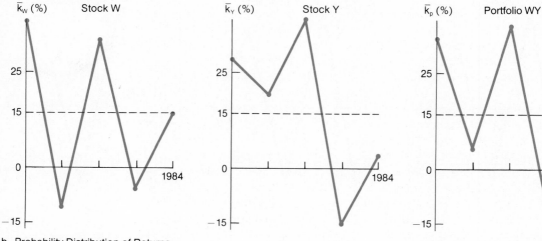

b. Probability Distribution of Returns

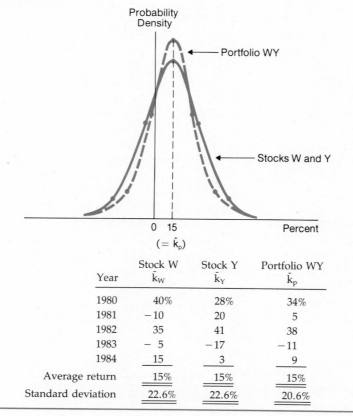

Year	Stock W $\bar{k}_W$	Stock Y $\bar{k}_Y$	Portfolio WY $\bar{k}_p$
1980	40%	28%	34%
1981	−10	20	5
1982	35	41	38
1983	−5	−17	−11
1984	15	3	9
Average return	15%	15%	15%
Standard deviation	22.6%	22.6%	20.6%

+0.65. The portfolio's average return is 15.0 percent, which is exactly the same as the average return for each of the two stocks, but the portfolio's standard deviation is 20.6 percent, which is less than the standard deviation of either stock. Thus, the portfolio's risk is *not* an average of the risks of its individual stocks—diversification has reduced, but not eliminated, risk.

From these two-stock portfolio examples, we have seen that in one extreme case (r = −1.0), risk can be completely eliminated, while in the other extreme case (r = +1.0), diversification does no good whatever. In between these extremes, combining two stocks into a portfolio reduces but does not eliminate the riskiness inherent in the individual stocks.

What would happen if we included more than two stocks in the portfolio? *As a rule, the riskiness of a portfolio will be reduced as the number of stocks in the portfolio increases.* If we added enough partially correlated stocks, could we completely eliminate risk? In general, the answer is no, but the extent to which adding stocks to a portfolio reduces the portfolio's risk depends on the *degree of correlation* among the stocks. The smaller the correlation coefficient, the lower is the remaining risk in a large portfolio. If we could find a set of stocks whose correlation coefficients were zero or negative, all risk could be eliminated. *In the typical case, where the correlations among the individual stocks are positive but less than +1.0, some but not all risk can be eliminated.*

As noted earlier, it is very difficult, if not impossible, to find stocks whose expected returns are not positively correlated—most stocks tend to do well when the economy is strong, and badly when the national economy is weak.[8] Thus, even very large portfolios end up with a material amount of risk. For example, in Figure 5-9 in Chapter 5, we saw that actual returns varied quite a bit from year to year on a portfolio consisting of all New York Stock Exchange (NYSE) stocks. To see more precisely how portfolio size affects portfolio risk, consider Figure 6-7, which shows how portfolio risk is affected by forming larger and larger portfolios of NYSE stocks. Standard deviations are plotted for an average 1-stock portfolio, 2-stock portfolio, and so on, up to a portfolio consisting of all 1,500+ common stocks that were listed on the NYSE at the time the data were graphed. The graph illustrates that, in general, the riskiness of a portfolio consisting of average NYSE stocks tends to decline and to asymptotically approach a limit as the size of the portfolio increases. According to data accumulated in recent years, σ_1, the standard deviation of a one-stock portfolio (or an average stock), is approximately 28 percent. A portfolio consisting of all stocks, which is called "the market portfolio," would have a standard deviation of about 15.1

---

[8]It is not too hard to find a few stocks that happened to decline because of a particular set of circumstances in the past while most other stocks were advancing; it is much harder to find stocks that could logically be *expected* to decline in the future when other stocks are rising.

Figure 6-7
Effects of Portfolio Size on Portfolio Risk for Average Stocks

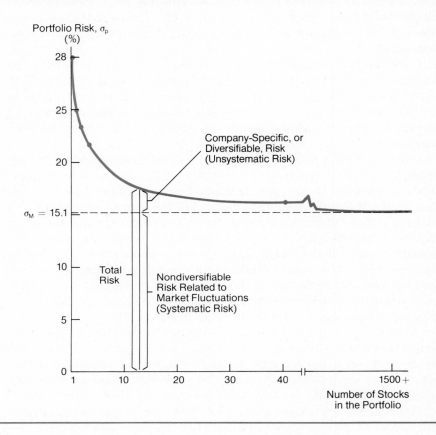

percent. The market portfolio's standard deviation is given the symbol σ_M, so $\sigma_M = 15.1\%$.

Thus, a great deal of the riskiness inherent in an average individual stock can be eliminated if the stock is held in a reasonably well-diversified portfolio, one containing about 40 stocks. Some risk always remains, however, so it is virtually impossible to diversify away the effects of broad stock market declines that affect almost all stocks.

That part of the risk of a stock which can be eliminated is called *diversifiable*, or *company-specific, risk*. That part which cannot be eliminated is called *nondiversifiable*, or *market, risk*. The name is not especially important, but the fact that part of the riskiness of any individual stock can be eliminated is vitally important.[9]

Company-specific risk is caused by such things as lawsuits, strikes, suc-

---

[9]Company-specific risk is also known as *unsystematic risk*, while market risk is sometimes called *systematic risk*.

cessful and unsuccessful marketing programs, winning and losing major contracts, and other events that are unique to a particular firm. Since these events are essentially random, their effects on a portfolio can be eliminated by diversification—bad events in one firm will be offset by good events in another. *Market risk*, on the other hand, stems from factors which affect all firms simultaneously, such as war, inflation, recessions, and high interest rates. Since all firms are affected simultaneously by these factors, this type of risk cannot be eliminated by diversification.

We know that investors demand a premium for bearing risk; that is, the higher the riskiness of a security, the higher its expected return must be to induce investors to buy (or to hold) it. But if investors are primarily concerned with *portfolio risk* rather than the risk of the individual securities in the portfolio, how should the riskiness of an individual stock be measured? The answer is this: *The relevant riskiness of an individual stock is its contribution to the riskiness of a well-diversified portfolio.* In other words, the riskiness of Stock X to a doctor who has a portfolio of 40 stocks, or to a trust officer managing a 150-stock portfolio, is the contribution that Stock X makes to the portfolio's riskiness. The stock might be quite risky if held by itself, but if most of its risk can be eliminated by diversification, the stock's *relevant risk*, which is its *contribution to the portfolio's risk*, may be small.

A simple example will help make this point clear. Suppose you can flip a coin once. If a head comes up, you win $10,000, but you lose $8,000 if it comes up tails. Although this may be considered to be a good bet—the expected return is 0.5($10,000) + 0.5(−$8,000) = $1,000—it is a highly risky proposition, because you have a 50 percent chance of losing $8,000. Alternatively, suppose you can flip a coin 100 times and win $100 for each head but lose $80 for each tail. It is possible that you would hit all heads and win $10,000, and it is also possible that you would flip all tails and lose $8,000, but the chances are very high that you would actually flip about 50 heads and about 50 tails, winning a net $1,000. Although each individual flip is a risky bet, collectively you have a very low-risk proposition because you have diversified away most of the risk. This is the idea behind holding portfolios of stocks rather than just one stock, except that with stocks, all of the risk cannot be eliminated by diversification—those risks related to broad changes in the stock market will remain.

Are all stocks equally risky in the sense that adding them to a well-diversified portfolio would have the same effect on the portfolio's riskiness? The answer is no—different stocks will affect the portfolio differently; hence, different securities have different degrees of relevant risk. How can the relevant risk of an individual stock be measured? As we have seen, all risk except that related to broad market movements can, and presumably will, be diversified away. After all, why accept risk that can easily be eliminated? *The risk that remains after diversifying is market risk, or risk that is inherent in the market, and this risk can be measured by the degree to which a given stock tends to move up and down with the market.*

The Concept of Beta

The tendency of a stock to move with the market is reflected in its *beta coefficient, b,* which is a measure of the stock's volatility relative to an average stock.

An *average risk stock* is defined as one which tends to move up and down in step with the general market as measured by some index such as the Dow Jones Industrials, the S&P 500, or the New York Stock Exchange Index. Such a stock will, by definition, have a beta, b, of 1.0, which indicates that, in general, if the market moves up by 10 percent, the stock will also move up by 10 percent, while if the market falls by 10 percent, the stock will likewise fall by 10 percent. A portfolio of such b = 1.0 stocks will move up and down with the broad market averages and will be just as risky as the averages. If b = 0.5, the stock is only half as volatile as the market—it will rise and fall only half as much— and a portfolio of such stocks is half as risky as a portfolio of b = 1.0 stocks. On the other hand, if b = 2.0, the stock is twice as volatile as an average stock, so a portfolio of such stocks will be twice as risky as an average portfolio.

Figure 6-8 shows betas in a graphic sense. Assume that in 1982, the "market," or a portfolio consisting of all stocks, had a total return (dividend yield plus capital gains yield) of 10 percent. Stocks H, A, and L also had returns of 10 percent in 1982. Now assume that in 1983 the market went up sharply, and the return on the market portfolio was $\bar{k}_M = 20\%$. Returns on our three stocks also went up: H soared to 30 percent; A went up to 20 percent, the same as the market; and L went up only to 15 percent. Now suppose that the market dropped in 1984, and the market return was $\bar{k}_M = -10\%$. Our three stocks' returns also fell, H plunging to -30 percent, A falling to -10 percent, and L going down only to $\bar{k}_L = 0\%$.

Our three stocks all move in the same direction as the market, but H, the high-beta stock, is by far the most volatile; A is just as volatile as the market; and L is less volatile than average. Betas are actually calculated by plotting graphs such as Figure 6-8. The slopes of the lines show how each stock moves in response to a movement in the general market. *Indeed, the slope coefficient of such "regression lines" is the beta coefficient.*

Procedures for actually calculating betas are described in Appendix 6A, while Appendix 6B provides a stronger theoretical basis for the use of betas. Betas for literally thousands of companies are calculated and published by Merrill Lynch, Value Line, and numerous other organizations. The beta coefficients of some well-known companies are shown in Table 6-4. Most stocks have betas in the range of 0.50 to 1.50. The average for all stocks is 1.0 by definition.[10]

---

[10]The betas we have been discussing are called *historic,* or *ex post,* betas because they are based strictly on historic, or past, data. Another type of beta, the *fundamental beta,* which is based partly on past actions and partly on expected future conditions not yet reflected in historic data, is also in wide use today. Appendix 7A provides additional information on various types of beta, their determination, and their use.

Figure 6-8
Beta Graph

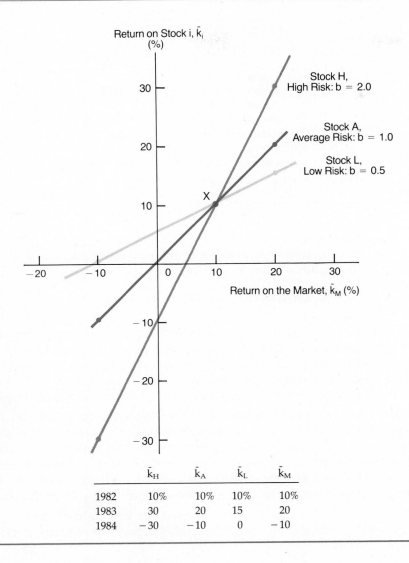

Return on Stock i, $\bar{k}_i$ (%)

Stock H,
High Risk: b = 2.0

Stock A,
Average Risk: b = 1.0

Stock L,
Low Risk: b = 0.5

Return on the Market, $\bar{k}_M$ (%)

	$\bar{k}_H$	$\bar{k}_A$	$\bar{k}_L$	$\bar{k}_M$
1982	10%	10%	10%	10%
1983	30	20	15	20
1984	−30	−10	0	−10

If a higher-than-average-beta stock (one whose beta is greater than 1.0) is added to an average-risk (b = 1.0) portfolio, then the beta, and consequently the riskiness of the portfolio, will increase. Conversely, if a lower-than-average-beta stock (one whose beta is less than 1.0) is added to an average-risk portfolio, the portfolio's beta and risk will decline. *Thus, since a stock's beta measures its contribution to the riskiness of a portfolio, beta is the appropriate measure of the stock's riskiness.*

Table 6-4
Illustrative List of Beta Coefficients

Stock	Beta
Apple Computer	2.74
Mesa Petroleum	1.86
Polaroid	1.15
Caterpillar Tractor	1.11
General Electric	0.92
Eastman Kodak	0.73
General Motors	0.68
Anheuser-Busch	0.61
Safeway Stores	0.58
Campbell Soup Company	0.33

Source: Merrill Lynch, April 1983.

We can summarize our analysis of the Capital Asset Pricing Model's logic to this point as follows:

1. A stock's risk consists of two components, market risk and company-specific risk.

2. Company-specific risk can be eliminated by diversification, and most investors do indeed diversify. We are left, then, with market risk, which is caused by general movements in the stock market and reflects the fact that all stocks are affected by certain overall economic events. This market risk is the only relevant risk to a rational, diversified investor.

3. Investors must be compensated for bearing risk—the greater the riskiness of a stock, the higher is its required return. However, compensation is required only for risk which cannot be eliminated by diversification. If risk premiums existed for diversifiable risk, well-diversified investors would buy these securities and bid up their prices, and their final expected returns would reflect only nondiversifiable market risk.

4. The market risk of a stock is measured by its beta coefficient, which is an index of the stock's relative volatility. Some benchmark betas follow:

$b = 0.5$: Stock is only half as volatile, or risky, as the average stock.
$b = 1.0$: Stock is of average risk.
$b = 2.0$: Stock is twice as risky as the average stock.

5. *Since a stock's beta coefficient determines how it affects the riskiness of a diversified portfolio, beta is the most relevant measure of a stock's risk.*

A portfolio consisting of low-beta securities will itself have a low beta, *Portfolio Beta* since the beta of any set of securities is a weighted average of the indi- *Coefficients* vidual securities' betas:

$$b_p = \sum_{i=1}^{n} w_i b_i. \tag{6-5}$$

Here b_p is the beta of the portfolio, which reflects how volatile the port-folio is in relation to the market index; w_i is the fraction of the portfolio invested in the ith stock; and b_i is the beta coefficient of the ith stock.

If an investor holds a $100,000 portfolio consisting of $10,000 invested in each of 10 stocks, and if each stock has a beta of 0.8, then the portfolio will have $b_p = 0.8$. Thus, the portfolio is less risky than the market, and it should experience relatively narrow price swings and have small rate of return fluctuations.

Now suppose one of the existing stocks is sold and replaced by a stock with $b_i = 2.0$. This action will increase the riskiness of the portfolio from $b_{p1} = 0.8$ to $b_{p2} = 0.92$:

$$b_{p2} = \sum_{i=1}^{n} w_i b_i = 0.9(0.8) + 0.1(2.0) = 0.92.$$

Had a stock with $b_i = 0.2$ been added, the portfolio beta would have declined from 0.8 to 0.74. Adding this stock would, therefore, reduce the riskiness of the portfolio.

The Relationship between Risk and Rates of Return

In the preceding section, we saw that under the CAPM framework, beta is the appropriate measure of a stock's relevant risk. Now we must spec-ify the relationship between risk and return—if beta rises by some spe-cific amount, by how much must the stock's expected return increase to compensate for the increase in risk? To begin, let us define the following terms:

$\hat{k}_i$ = expected rate of return on the ith stock.

k_i = required rate of return on the ith stock. If $\hat{k}_i$ is less than k_i, then you would not purchase this stock, or you would sell it if you owned it.

R_F = riskless rate of return, generally measured by the rate of return on U.S. Treasury securities.

b_i = beta coefficient of the ith stock.

k_M = required rate of return on an average (b = 1.0) stock. k_M is also the required rate of return on a portfolio consisting of all stocks, or the market portfolio.

$RP_M = (k_M - R_F)$ = market risk premium. It is the additional return over the riskless rate required to compensate investors for assuming an "average" amount of risk.

$RP_i = b_i(k_M - R_F)$ = risk premium on the ith stock. The stock's risk premium is less than, equal to, or greater than the premium on an average stock, depending on whether its beta is less than, equal to, or greater than 1.0. If $b_i = 1.0$, then $RP_i = RP_M$.

The market risk premium, RP_M, depends on the degree of aversion that investors, in the aggregate, have to risk.[11] Let us assume that at the current time Treasury bonds yield $R_F = 8\%$, and an average share of stock has a required return of $k_M = 12\%$. Therefore, the market risk premium is 4 percent:

$$RP_M = k_M - R_F = 12\% - 8\% = 4\%.$$

It follows that, if one stock were twice as risky as some other, its risk premium would be twice as high, and, conversely, if its risk were only half as high, its risk premium would be half as high. Further, we can measure a stock's relative riskiness by its beta coefficient. Therefore, if we know the market risk premium, RP_M, and the stock's beta coefficient, b_i, we can find its risk premium as the product $b_i(RP_M)$. For example, if $b_i = 0.5$ and $RP_M = 4\%$, then RP_i is 2 percent:

$$\text{Risk premium for Stock i} = RP_i = b_i(RP_M) = 0.5(4\%) = 2.0\%. \quad \textbf{(6-6)}$$

To summarize, given estimates of R_F, k_M, and b_i, we can find the required rate of return on Stock i:

$$k_i = R_F + b_i(k_M - R_F) = R_F + b_i(RP_M) \quad \textbf{(6-7)}$$
$$= 8\% + 0.5(12\% - 8\%) = 8\% + 0.5(4\%) = 10\%.$$

If some other stock, j, were more risky than Stock i and had $b_j = 2.0$, then its required rate of return would be 16 percent:

$$k_j = 8\% + 2.0(4\%) = 16\%.$$

An average stock, with $b = 1.0$, would have a required return of 12 percent, the same as the market return:

$$k_{\text{Average}} = 8\% + 1.0(4\%) = 12\% = k_M.$$

Equation 6-7 is often expressed as a graph called the *Security Market Line (SML)*; Figure 6-9 shows the SML when $R_F = 8\%$ and $k_M = 12\%$. Note the following points:

---

[11]This concept is discussed in some detail in Appendix 6B. It should be noted that the risk premium of an average stock, $k_M - R_F$, cannot be measured with great precision because it is impossible to obtain precise values for k_M. However, empirical studies suggest that, where long-term U.S. Treasury bonds are used to measure R_F and where k_M is the expected return on the S&P 400 Industrial Stocks, the market risk premium varies somewhat from year to year, and it has generally ranged from 3 to 6 percent during the last 20 years.

Figure 6-9
The Security Market Line (SML)

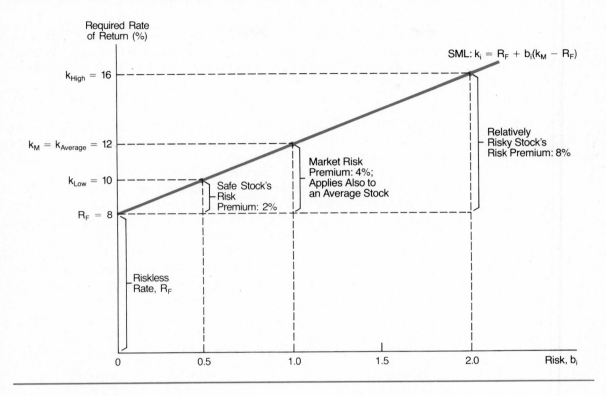

1. Required rates of return are shown on the vertical axis, while risk as measured by beta is shown on the horizontal axis.

2. Riskless securities have $b_i = 0$; therefore, R_F appears as the vertical axis intercept.

3. The slope of the SML reflects the degree of risk aversion in the economy—the greater the average investor's aversion to risk, then (1) the steeper is the slope of the line, (2) the greater is the risk premium for any risky asset, and (3) the higher is the required rate of return on risky assets.[12] These points are discussed further in a later section.

---

[12]Students sometimes confuse beta with the slope of the SML. This is a mistake. As we saw earlier in connection with Figure 6-8, and as is developed further in Appendix 6A, beta does represent the slope of a line, but *not* the Security Market Line. This confusion arises partly because the SML equation is generally written, in this book and throughout the finance literature, as $k_i = R_F + b_i(k_M - R_F)$, and in this form b_i looks like the slope coefficient and $(k_M - R_F)$ the variable. It would perhaps be less confusing if the second term were written $(k_M - R_F)b_i$, but this is not generally done.

4. The values we worked out for stocks with $b_i = 0.5$, $b_i = 1.0$, and $b_i = 2.0$ agree with the values shown on the graph for k_{Low}, $k_{Average}$, and k_{High}.

The Security Market Line, and a company's position on the line, change over time as interest rates, investors' risk aversion, and individual companies' betas change. Such changes are discussed in the following sections.

The Impact of Inflation

As we saw in Chapter 3, interest amounts to "rent" on borrowed money, or the "price" of money. Thus, R_F is the price of money to a riskless borrower. The existing market risk-free rate is called the *nominal rate*, and it consists of two elements: (1) a *real*, or *inflation-free*, *rate of return*, k^*, and (2) an *inflation premium*, IP, equal to the anticipated rate of inflation. Thus, $R_F = k^* + IP$. The real rate on risk-free government securities has, historically, ranged from 2 to 4 percent, with a mean of about 3 percent. Thus, if no inflation were expected, risk-free government securities would tend to yield about 3 percent. However, as the expected rate of inflation increases, a premium must be added to the real rate of return to compensate investors for the loss of purchasing

Figure 6-10
Shift in the SML Caused by an Increase in Inflation

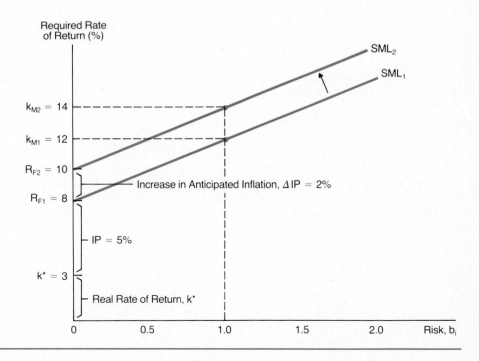

power that results from inflation. Thus, the 8 percent R_F shown in Figure 6-9 may be thought of as consisting of a 3 percent real rate of return plus a 5 percent inflation premium: $R_F = k^* + IP = 3\% + 5\% = 8\%$.

If the expected rate of inflation rose to 7 percent, this would cause R_F to rise to 10 percent. Such a change is shown in Figure 6-10. Notice that the increase in R_F also causes an *equal* increase in the rate of return on all risky assets, since the inflation premium is built into the required rate of return of both riskless and risky assets. For example, the rate of return on an average stock, k_M, increases from 12 to 14 percent. Other risky securities' returns also rise by 2 percentage points.

Changes in Risk Aversion

The slope of the Security Market Line (SML) reflects the extent to which investors are averse to risk—the steeper the slope of the line, the greater is the average investor's risk aversion. If investors were not at all averse to risk, and if R_F were 8 percent, then risky assets would also sell to provide an expected return of 8 percent—with no risk aversion, there would be no risk premium, and the SML would be horizontal. As risk aversion increases, so does the risk premium and, thus, the slope of the SML.

Figure 6-11 illustrates an increase in risk aversion. The market risk premium rises from 4 to 6 percent, and k_M rises from 12 to 14 percent. The returns on other risky assets also rise, with the impact of this shift in risk aversion being more pronounced on riskier securities. For example, the required return on a stock with $b_i = 0.5$ increases by only 1 percentage point, from 10 to 11 percent, while the required return on a stock with $b_i = 1.5$ increases by 3 percentage points, from 14 to 17 percent.

Changes in a Stock's Beta Coefficient

As we shall see later in the book, a firm can affect its market, or beta, risk through changes in the nature and composition of its assets, and also through its use of debt financing. A company's beta can also change as a result of increased competition in its industry, the expiration of basic patents, a change in management, and the like. When such changes occur, the demanded or required rate of return also changes, and this will affect the price of the firm's stock. For example, consider Teletron Electronics Corporation, a constant growth firm with $b = 1.0$, $D_1 = \$2.00$, and $g = 5\%$. Now, suppose some action occurred that caused Teletron Electronics' beta to increase from 1.0 to 1.5. If the conditions depicted in Figure 6-9 held, Teletron's required rate of return would increase from

$$k_1 = R_F + b_i(k_M - R_F) = 8\% + 1.0(12\% - 8\%) = 12\%$$

to

$$k_2 = 8\% + 1.5(12\% - 8\%) = 14\%.$$

Figure 6-11
Shift in the SML Caused by Increased Risk Aversion

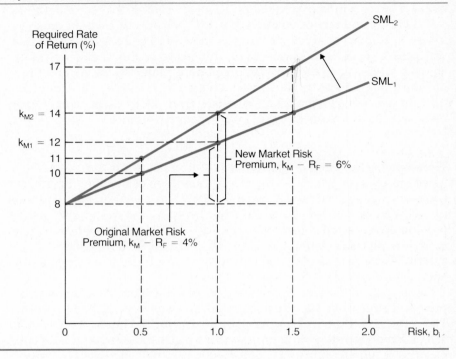

This change in k would cause Teletron's equilibrium stock price, assuming no change in its expected dividend and its expected growth rate, to fall from $28.57 to $22.22:[13]

$$\text{Old price} = \hat{P}_0 = \frac{D_1}{k_1 - g} = \frac{\$2.00}{0.12 - 0.05} = \$28.57.$$

$$\text{New price} = \hat{P}_0 = \frac{D_1}{k_2 - g} = \frac{\$2.00}{0.14 - 0.05} = \$22.22.$$

Notice that at its new equilibrium price of $22.22, Teletron's new expected rate of return is exactly equal to its new 14 percent required rate of return:

$$\hat{k}_2 = D_1/P_0 + g = \$2.00/\$22.22 + 5\% = 14.0\%.$$
$$k_2 = R_F + b_i(k_M - R_F) = 8\% + 1.5(12\% - 8\%) = 14.0\%.$$

---

[13]Companies do sometimes deliberately increase their risk, but only if the action that raises risk also raises the expected earnings and the expected growth rate. Trying to determine the effects of a given action on risk and profitability, which affects growth, is one of the financial manager's central tasks.

Since the expected rate of return is equal to the required return, we know that $22.22 is Teletron's new equilibrium stock price.

Suppose a "typical" investor's required rate of return on Stock X, with $b_X = 2$, is 16 percent, determined as follows:

Security Market Equilibrium

$$k_X = R_F + b_X(k_M - R_F)$$
$$= 8\% + 2.0(12\% - 8\%)$$
$$= 16\%.$$

This 16 percent required return is indicated in Figure 6-12.

Our typical investor will want to buy Stock X if the expected rate of return is more than 16 percent, will want to sell it if the expected rate of return is less than 16 percent, and will be indifferent if the expected rate of return is exactly 16 percent. Now suppose the investor, whose portfolio contains X, analyzes the stock's prospects and concludes that its earnings, dividends, and price can be expected to grow at a constant rate of 5 percent per year. The last dividend was $D_0 = \$2.8571$, so the next expected dividend is

$$D_1 = \$2.8571(1.05) = \$3.$$

The investor observes that the present price of the stock, P_0, is $30. Should more of Stock X be purchased, should the present holdings be sold, or should the present position be maintained?

Figure 6-12
Expected and Required Returns on Stock X

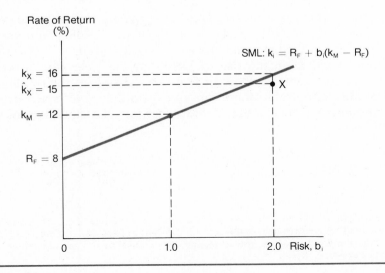

The investor can calculate Stock X's expected rate of return as follows:

$$\hat{k}_X = \frac{D_1}{P_0} + g = \frac{\$3}{\$30} + 5\% = 15\%.$$

This value is plotted on Figure 6-12 as Point X, which is below the SML. Since the expected rate of return is less than the required return, this typical investor will want to sell the stock, as will other holders. However, few people will want to buy at the $30 price, so present owners will only be able to find buyers if they cut the price of the stock. Thus, the price will decline until it reaches $27.27, at which point the expected rate of return, 16 percent, is equal to the required rate of return:

$$\hat{k}_X = \frac{\$3}{\$27.27} + 5\% = 16\% = k_X.$$

Had the stock initially sold for less than $27.27, then events would have been reversed. Investors would have wanted to buy the stock, because its expected rate of return would have exceeded its required rate of return. These buy orders would have driven the stock's price up to $27.27.

To summarize, in equilibrium (1) the expected rate of return as seen by the average investor must equal this investor's required rate of return, or $\hat{k}_i = k_i$, and (2) the market price must equal the stock's intrinsic value, or $P_0 = \hat{P}_0$. Of course, some investors will estimate $\hat{k}_i > k$ and $\hat{P}_0 > P_0$, and hence will invest most of their funds in the stock, and other investors will have an opposite view and will sell all of their shares. However, the average investor, trading at the margin, establishes the market price, and for this investor, $\hat{k}_i = k_i$ and $P_0 = \hat{P}_0$.

Changes in Equilibrium Stock Prices

Stock market prices are *not* constant—they undergo violent changes at times. Let us assume that Stock X is in equilibrium, selling at a price of $27.27 per share. If all expectations were exactly met, over the next year the price would gradually rise to $28.63, or by 5 percent. However, many different events could occur to cause a change in the equilibrium price of the stock. To illustrate, consider again the set of inputs used to develop Stock X's price of $27.27, and a new set of assumed input variables:

	Variable Value	
	Original	New
Riskless rate, R_F	8%	7%
Market risk premium, $k_M - R_F$	4%	3%
Stock X's beta coefficient, b_X	2.0	1.0
Stock X's expected growth rate, g_X	5%	6%

The first three variables influence k_X, which declines from 16 to 10 percent as a result of the new set of variables:

$$\text{Original } k_X = 8\% + 2.0(4\%) = 16\%.$$
$$\text{New } k_X = 7\% + 1.0(3\%) = 10\%.$$

Using these values, together with the new g value, we find that $\hat{P}_0$, and presumably P_0, rises from \$27.27 to \$75.71.[14]

$$\text{Original } \hat{P}_0 = \frac{\$2.8571(1.05)}{0.16 - 0.05} = \frac{\$3}{0.11} = \$27.27.$$

$$\text{New } \hat{P}_0 = \frac{\$2.8571(1.06)}{0.10 - 0.06} = \frac{\$3.0285}{0.04} = \$75.71.$$

At the new price, the expected and required rates of return will be equal:[15]

$$\hat{k}_X = \frac{\$3.0285}{\$75.71} + 6\% = 10\% = k_X.$$

Evidence suggests that stocks, and especially those of large NYSE companies, adjust quite rapidly to disequilibrium situations. Consequently, equilibrium ordinarily exists for any given stock, and, in general, required and expected returns are equal. Stock prices certainly change, sometimes violently and rapidly, but this simply reflects changing conditions and expectations. There are, of course, times when a stock continues to react for several months to a favorable or unfavorable development, but this does not signify a long adjustment period; rather, it simply illustrates that as more new bits of information about the situation become available, the market adjusts to them. The ability of the market to adjust to new information is discussed in the next section.

The Efficient Markets Hypothesis

A body of theory called the *Efficient Markets Hypothesis (EMH)* holds (1) that stocks are always in equilibrium and (2) that it is impossible for an investor to consistently "beat the market." Essentially, the EMH states that there are some 100,000 or so full-time, highly trained, professional analysts and traders operating in the market and following some 3,000

---

[14]A price change of this magnitude is by no means rare. The prices of *many* NYSE stocks double or halve during a year. For example, during 1983, International Harvester increased in value by 333 percent. On the other hand, Baldwin-United fell from 37¾ to 2½, a 91 percent loss.

[15]It should be obvious by now that actual realized rates of return are not necessarily equal to expected and required returns. Thus, an investor might have *expected* to receive a return of 15 percent if he or she had bought International Harvester or Baldwin-United stock in 1983, but after the fact, the realized return on International Harvester was far above 15 percent but that on Baldwin-United was far below.

major stocks. If each analyst followed only 30 stocks, there would still be 1,000 analysts following each stock. Further, these analysts work for organizations such as Merrill Lynch and Prudential Insurance, which have billions of dollars available to take advantage of bargains. As new information about a stock became available, these 1,000 analysts all would receive and evaluate it at approximately the same time, and the price of the stock would adjust almost immediately to reflect the new information.

Financial theorists generally define three forms, or levels, of market efficiency:

1. *Weak-form* efficiency implies that all information contained in past price movements is fully reflected in current market prices. Therefore, information about recent trends in a stock's price is of no use in selecting stock—the fact that a stock has risen for the past three days, for example, gives us no useful clues as to what it will do today or tomorrow. People who believe that weak form efficiency exists also believe that "tape watchers" and "chartists" are wasting their time.[16]

2. *Semistrong-form* efficiency implies that current market prices reflect all *publicly available* information. If this is true, no abnormal returns can be gained by acting on publicly available information.[17] Thus, if semistrong efficiency exists, it would do no good to pore over annual reports or other published data, because market prices would have adjusted to any good or bad news contained in such reports as soon as they came out. However, insiders (say the president of a company) could, even under semistrong efficiency, still make abnormal returns on their own companies' stocks.

3. *Strong-form* efficiency implies that current market prices reflect all pertinent information, whether publicly available or privately held. If this form holds, then even insiders would find it impossible to earn abnormal returns in the stock market.[18]

Many empirical studies have been conducted to test for the three forms of market efficiency. Most studies suggest that the stock market, indeed all well-developed capital markets, are highly efficient in the weak form, and reasonably efficient in the semistrong form, at least for the larger and more widely followed stocks. However, capital markets

---

[16]Tape watchers are people who watch the NYSE tape, while chartists plot past patterns of stock price movements. Both believe that they can see if something is happening to the stock that will cause its price to move up or down in the near future.

[17]An abnormal return exceeds that return which is justified by the riskiness of the investment, that is, a return which plots above the SML.

[18]As we were writing this chapter, in the spring of 1984, it was reported in the press that the assistant to a New York lawyer who worked on takeover deals had made $2 million in the stock market in less than a year. He went to jail, but he did help to disprove strong-form EMH.

are not strong-form efficient, so abnormal profits can be gained by those who possess insider information.

What effect does the EMH have on financial decisions? Since stock prices do reflect public information, most stocks do seem to be fairly valued. This does not mean that new information could not cause a stock's price to soar or to plummet, but it does mean that stocks, in general, are neither overvalued nor undervalued—they are fairly priced, and in equilibrium. Certainly there are cases where financial managers do have some special information not known to outsiders, but for the larger, actively traded firms, which are followed by literally hundreds of full-time security analysts backed by billions of dollars of capital, the market quickly reacts to all new developments.

If the EMH is correct, then it would be a waste of time to analyze stocks to find some that are undervalued—if stock prices already reflect all available information, and hence are fairly priced, one could "beat the market" only by luck, and it would be difficult if not impossible for anyone to consistently outperform the market averages. Empirical tests have shown that the EMH is, to a very large extent, valid. People such as corporate officers who have insider information can do better than the averages, and individuals and organizations that are especially good at digging out information on small, new companies also seem to do consistently well. However, the market for large firms such as those traded on the NYSE is highly efficient. Therefore, for NYSE companies, it is generally safe to assume that $\hat{k} = k$, $\hat{P}_0 = P_0$, and that stocks plot on the SML.[19]

Physical Assets' Risk versus Securities' Risk

In a book on the financial management of business firms, why do we develop the basic risk concepts in a context of security investments? Why not begin by looking at the riskiness of such business assets as plant, equipment, or inventories? *The reason is that, for a management whose goal is stock price maximization, the overriding consideration is the riskiness of the firm's stock, and the relevant risk of any physical asset must be measured in terms of its effect on the stock's risk.* For example, suppose General Motors were to go into a new operation, say electric cars, whose sales and earnings were highly uncertain. This would seem to be a very risky investment. However, suppose the returns of this particular operation were not highly correlated with returns on GM's other operations, or with returns on GM's stockholders' other investments. Perhaps electric cars could be expected to sell best if gasoline prices rose sharply,

---

[19]Market efficiency also has significant implications for managerial decisions, especially those pertaining to common stock issues, stock repurchases, and tender offers. Financial assets appear to be fairly valued, and decisions based on a stock being undervalued or overvalued must be approached with caution.

pulling down sales of both regular cars and corporate profits in general. In this case, most of the new plant's risk would not be relevant, because it would be offset in a diversification sense within GM's overall operations and also within stockholders' portfolios. Thus, the riskiness of a corporate asset investment should be considered within the context of security risk: What does the investment in a particular physical asset do to the riskiness of the firm as viewed by stockholders?

A Word of Caution

A word of caution about betas and the Security Market Line is in order. Although these concepts are very logical, the entire theory is based on *ex ante*, or expected, conditions, yet we have available only *ex post*, or past, data. Thus, the betas we calculate show how volatile a stock has been in the *past*, but conditions may change and alter its *future volatility*, which is the item of real concern to investors. Additionally, the Security Market Line is but one part of the overall Capital Asset Pricing Model. Although the CAPM is a significant step forward in security pricing theory, it does have some potentially serious deficiencies, both in theory and use, and estimates of k_i found through use of the SML are clearly subject to considerable errors.[20] Appendix 6B provides a more complete discussion of the development and deficiencies of the CAPM, while Appendix 7A points out some of the problems involved in using the CAPM.

Summary

The primary goals of this chapter were (1) to show how risk is measured in financial analysis and (2) to explain how risk affects security prices and rates of return. We began by showing that risk is related to variability of expected future returns. However, we soon saw that most rational investors hold *portfolios of stocks*, and that such investors are more concerned with the risks of their portfolios than with the risks of individual stocks.

Next, we saw that the riskiness of a given stock can be split into two components—*market risk*, which is caused by changes in the broad stock

---

[20]The concept of beta was discovered and developed by academicians, and then seized upon and used by business practitioners. To some extent, betas seem to have been oversold—the beauty of the concept has been overemphasized, and the difficulties with actually implementing the theory in practice have not been pointed out sufficiently. In a recent article, Anise Wallace ("Is Beta Dead?" *Institutional Investor*, July 1980, 23-30) reached this conclusion: "It took nearly a decade for money managers to learn to love beta. Now it looks as if they were sold a bill of goods—and the whole MPT [Modern Portfolio Theory] house of cards could come tumbling down." This judgment is, in the minds of most observers, far too harsh. The concept of beta obviously reflects the way sophisticated investors should and do look at the risk inherent in a security. Problems do arise when one attempts to measure *future* events on the basis of *past* data, but abandoning the beta concept because of these difficulties would be like throwing out the baby with the bath water!

market and which cannot be eliminated by diversification, and *company-specific risk*, which can be eliminated by holding a diversified portfolio. Since investors can and do diversify and thus eliminate company risk, the most *relevant risk* inherent in stocks is their market risk, which is measured by the *beta coefficient, b.*

Betas measure the tendency of stocks to move up and down with the market—a high-beta stock is more volatile than the market, while a low-beta stock is less volatile than average. An average stock has b = 1.0 by definition.

The required rate of return on a stock consists of the rate of return on riskless bonds, R_F, plus a risk premium that depends on the stock's beta coefficient:

$$k_i = R_F + b_i(k_M - R_F).$$

This formula is called the *Security Market Line (SML) equation* or, sometimes, the *Capital Asset Pricing Model (CAPM) equation*, and it is of fundamental importance in finance.

We also saw that stocks are typically in equilibrium, with their expected and required rates of return as seen by the average investor equal to one another. This is because the capital markets in the United States are, in general, *efficient*. However, even though stocks are generally in equilibrium, a number of things can happen to cause prices to change: The riskless rate can change because of changes in anticipated inflation; a stock's beta can change; or its rate of expected growth can increase or decrease. In the remainder of this book, we will examine the ways a firm's management can influence its stock's riskiness and expected growth rate, and hence its price.

Questions

6-1   Define the following terms, using graphs or equations to illustrate your answers wherever feasible:
   a. Uncertainty
   b. Probability distribution
   c. *Expected* rate of return, $\hat{k}$, versus *required* rate of return, k, versus *past realized* rate of return, $\bar{k}$
   d. Standard deviation, σ
   e. Security Market Line (SML)
   f. Market risk
   g. Company-specific risk
   h. Beta coefficient, b
   i. Relevant risk
   j. Capital Asset Pricing Model (CAPM)
   k. Risk premium (RP_i, RP_M)
   l. Inflation premium (IP)
   m. Risk aversion and relation to RP_M
   n. Market equilibrium
   o. Efficient Markets Hypothesis (EMH)
   p. Correlation coefficient, r

6-2   The probability distribution of a less risky expected return is more peaked than that of a more risky return. What shape would the probability distribution have (a) for completely certain returns and (b) for completely uncertain returns?

6-3   Security A has an expected return of 6 percent, a standard deviation of expected returns of 30 percent, a correlation coefficient with the market of −0.25, and a beta coefficient of −0.5. Security B has an expected return of 11 percent, a standard deviation of returns of 10 percent, a correlation with the market of 0.75, and a beta coefficient of 1.0. Which security is more risky? Why?

6-4   Suppose you owned a portfolio consisting of $500,000 worth of long-term U.S. government bonds.
   a. Would your portfolio be riskless?
   b. Now suppose you held a portfolio consisting of $500,000 worth of 30-day Treasury bills. Every 30 days your bills mature and you reinvest the principal ($500,000) in a new batch of bills. Would your portfolio be truly riskless? (Hint: Assume that you live on the investment income from your portfolio, and that you want to maintain a constant standard of living.)
   c. You should have concluded that both long-term and short-term portfolios of government securities have some element of risk. Can you think of any asset that would be completely riskless?

6-5   An insurance policy is a financial asset. The investment cost is the premium paid.
   a. How would you calculate the expected return on a life insurance policy?
   b. Suppose the owner of the life insurance policy has no other financial assets—the person's only other asset is "human capital" or lifetime earnings capacity. What is the correlation coefficient between returns on the insurance policy and returns on the policyholder's human capital?
   c. Life insurance companies have administrative costs and sales representatives' commissions; hence, the expected rate of return on insurance premiums is low or even negative. Use the portfolio concept to explain why people buy life insurance in spite of negative expected returns.

6-6   If investors' aversion to risk increases, would the risk premium on a high-beta stock increase more or less than that on a low-beta stock? Explain.

Self-Test Problem   ST-1 Stocks A and B have the following historical dividend and price data:

	Stock A		Stock B	
Year	Dividend	Year-End Price	Dividend	Year-End Price
1979	—	$22.50	—	$43.75
1980	$2.00	16.00	$3.40	35.50
1981	2.20	17.00	3.65	38.75
1982	2.40	20.25	3.90	51.75
1983	2.60	17.25	4.05	44.50
1984	2.95	18.75	4.25	45.25

a. Calculate the realized rate of return (or holding period return) for each stock in each year. Then assume that someone had held a portfolio consisting of 50 percent of A and 50 percent of B. (The portfolio is rebalanced every year so as to maintain these percentages.) What would the realized rate of return on the portfolio have been in each year from 1980 through 1984? What would the average returns have been for each stock and for the portfolio?

b. Now calculate the standard deviation of returns for each stock and for the portfolio.

c. Based on the extent to which the portfolio has a lower risk than the stocks held individually, would you guess that the correlation coefficient between returns on the two stocks is closer to 0.9 or to -0.9?

d. If you added more stocks at random to the portfolio, what is the most accurate statement of what would happen to σ_p?

   1. σ_p would remain constant.

   2. σ_p would decline to somewhere in the vicinity of 15 percent.

   3. σ_p would decline to zero if enough stocks were included.

6-1   Stocks A and B have the following probability distributions of expected   *Problems*
future returns:

Probability	A	B
0.1	-10%	-30%
0.2	5	0
0.4	15	17
0.2	25	34
0.1	40	64

a. Calculate the expected rate of return, $\hat{k}$, for Stock B. $\hat{k}_A = 15\%$.

b. Calculate the standard deviation of expected returns for Stock A. That for Stock B is 23.6 percent. Is it possible that most investors might regard Stock B as being *less* risky than Stock A? Explain.

6-2   Suppose $R_F = 10\%$, $k_M = 14\%$, and $b_A = 1.4$.

a. What is k_A, the required rate of return on Stock A?

b. Now suppose R_F (1) increases to 11 percent, or (2) decreases to 9 percent. The slope of the SML remains constant. How will this affect k_M and k_A?

c. Now assume R_F remains at 10 percent, but k_M (1) increases to 15 percent, or (2) falls to 12 percent. The slope of the SML does not remain constant. How will this affect k_A?

6-3   Suppose you are offered (a) $1 million or (b) a gamble where you get $2 million if a head is flipped but zero if a tail comes up.

a. What is the expected value of the gamble?

b. Would you take the sure $1 million or the gamble?

c. If you take the sure $1 million, are you a risk averter or a risk seeker?

d. Suppose you actually take the sure $1 million. You can invest it in either a U.S. Treasury bond that will return $1,075,000 at the end of a year or a common stock that has a 50-50 chance of being either worthless or worth $2,300,000 at the end of the year.

1. What is the expected profit on the stock investment? The expected profit on the T-bond investment is $75,000.

2. What is the expected rate of return on the stock investment? The expected rate of return on the T-bond investment is 7.5 percent.

3. Would you invest in the bond or the stock?

4. Just how large would the expected profit and the expected rate of return have to be on the stock investment to make you invest in the stock?

5. How might your decision be affected if, rather than buying one stock for $1 million, you could construct a portfolio consisting of 100 stocks with $10,000 in each? Each of these stocks has the same return characteristics as the one stock, that is, a 50-50 chance of being worth either zero or $23,000 at year-end. Would the correlation between returns on these stocks matter?

6-4 The risk-free rate of return, R_F, is 10 percent; the required rate of return on the market, k_M, is 15 percent; and Stock X has a beta coefficient of 1.4.

a. If the dividend expected during the coming year, D_1, is $2.50, and g = a constant 5%, at what price should Stock X sell?

b. Now suppose the Federal Reserve Board increases the money supply, causing the riskless rate to drop to 9 percent. What would this do to the price of the stock?

c. In addition to the change in Part b, suppose investors' risk aversion declines; this fact, combined with the decline in R_F, causes k_M to fall to 13 percent. At what price would Stock X sell?

d. Now suppose Firm X has a change in management. The new group institutes policies that increase the constant growth rate to 6 percent. Also, the new management stabilizes sales and profits, and thus causes the beta coefficient to decline from 1.4 to 1.1. After all these changes, what is Stock X's new equilibrium price? (Note: D_1 goes to $2.52.)

6-5 Suppose Regal Chemical Company's management conducts a study and concludes that, if Regal expands its consumer products division (which is less risky than its primary business, industrial chemicals), the firm's beta would decline from 1.2 to 0.9. However, consumer products have a somewhat lower profit margin, and this would cause Regal's constant growth rate in earnings and dividends to fall from 7 to 5 percent.

a. Should management make the change? Assume the following: $k_M = 11\%$; $R_F = 7.5\%$; $D_0 = \$2$.

b. Assume all the facts as given above except the change in the beta coefficient. By how much would the beta have to decline to cause the expansion to be a good one? (Hint: Set $\hat{P}_0$ under the new policy equal to $\hat{P}_0$ under the old one, and find the new beta that produces this equality.)

6-6 The beta coefficient for Stock C is $b_C = 0.4$, while that for Stock D is $b_D = -0.5$. (Stock D's beta is negative, indicating that its rate of return rises whenever returns on most other stocks fall. There are very few negative beta stocks, although gold mining stocks are often cited as an example.)

a. If the risk-free rate is 9 percent, and the expected rate of return on an average stock is 13 percent, what are the required rates of return on Stocks C and D?

b. For Stock C, suppose the current price, P_0, is $25; the next expected dividend, D_1, is $1.50; and the stock's expected constant growth rate is 4 percent. Is the stock in equilibrium? Explain, and describe what will happen if the stock is not in equilibrium.

6-7 The T. Lowe Brice Investment Fund has a total investment of $400 million in five stocks:

Stock	Investment	Stock's Beta Coefficient
A	$120 million	0.5
B	100 million	2.0
C	60 million	4.0
D	80 million	1.0
E	40 million	3.0

The beta coefficient for a fund such as this can be found as a weighted average of the fund's investments. The current risk-free rate is 7 percent, while expected market returns have the following estimated probability distribution for next period:

Probability	Market Return
0.1	8%
0.2	10
0.4	12
0.2	14
0.1	16

a. What is the estimated equation for the Security Market Line (SML)?

b. Compute the required rate of return on the Brice Fund for the next period.

c. Suppose management receives a proposal for a new stock. The investment needed to take a position in the stock is $50 million; it will have an expected return of 16 percent; and its estimated beta coefficient is 2.5. Should the new stock be purchased? At what expected rate of return would management be indifferent to purchasing the stock?

ST-1 a. The realized return in Period t is estimated as follows:

$$\bar{k}_t = \frac{D_t + P_t - P_{t-1}}{P_{t-1}}.$$

Solution to Self-Test Problem

For example, the realized return for Stock A in 1980 was -20.0 percent:

$$\bar{k}_{80} = \frac{D_{80} + P_{80} - P_{79}}{P_{79}}$$

$$= \frac{\$2.00 + \$16.00 - \$22.50}{\$22.50}$$

$$= -0.200 = -20.0\%.$$

The table that follows shows the realized returns for each stock in each year, the averages for the five years, and the same data for the portfolio:

Year	Stock A's Return, $\bar{k}_a$	Stock B's Return, $\bar{k}_B$	Portfolio AB's Return, $\bar{k}_{AB}$
1980	-20.0%	-11.1%	-15.6%
1981	20.0	19.4	19.7
1982	33.2	43.6	28.4
1983	-2.0	-6.2	-4.1
1984	25.8	11.2	18.5
$\bar{k}_{Average}$	11.4%	11.4%	11.4%

b. The standard deviation of returns is estimated, using Equation 6-3a, as follows:

$$\text{Estimated } \sigma = \sqrt{\frac{\sum\limits_{t=1}^{n} (\bar{k}_t - \bar{k}_{Avg})^2}{n - 1}}. \tag{6-3a}$$

For Stock A, the estimated σ is 21.9 percent:

$$\sigma_A = \sqrt{\frac{(-20.0 - 11.4)^2 + (20.0 - 11.4)^2 + \cdots + (25.8 - 11.4)^2}{5 - 1}}$$

$$= \sqrt{\frac{1,922.08}{4}} = 21.9\%.$$

The standard deviation of returns for Stock B and for the portfolio are similarly determined, and they are shown here:

	Stock A	Stock B	Portfolio AB
Average return, $\bar{k}_{Avg}$	11.4%	11.4%	11.4%
Standard deviation	21.9	21.9	21.3

c. Since the risk reduction from diversification is small (σ_{AB} falls only from 21.9 to 21.3 percent), the most likely value of the correlation coefficient is 0.9. If the correlation coefficient were -0.9, the risk reduction would have been much larger. In fact, the correlation coefficient between Stocks A and B is 0.9.

d. If more randomly selected stocks were added to the portfolio, σ_p would decline to somewhere in the vicinity of 15 percent. σ_p would have remained constant only if the correlation coefficient were $+1.0$, which is most unlikely. σ_p would decline to zero only if the correlation coefficient, r, were equal to zero, and a large number of stocks were added to the portfolio, or if the proper proportions were held in a two-stock portfolio with $r = -1.0$.

Selected Additional References

Probably the best place to find an extension of the basic contents of Chapter 6 is one of the investments textbooks listed in the Chapter 5 references. Those who want to start at the beginning in studying the CAPM in depth should see

Markowitz, Harry H., "Portfolio Selection," *Journal of Finance*, March 1952, 77-91.

Sharpe, William F., "Capital Asset Prices: A Theory of Market Equilibrium under Conditions of Risk," *Journal of Finance*, September 1964, 425-442.

Literally thousands of articles providing theoretical extensions and tests of the CAPM theory have appeared in the last 20 years. Some of the more important earlier papers appeared in a book compiled by Jensen:

Jensen, Michael C., ed., *Studies in the Theory of Capital Markets* (New York: Praeger, 1972).

However, the validity of the empirical tests has been questioned; see

Roll, Richard, "A Critique of the Asset Pricing Theory's Tests," *Journal of Financial Economics*, March 1977, 129-176.

Wallace, Anise, "Is Beta Dead?" *Institutional Investor*, July 1980, 23-30.

The following articles provide some valuable general insights into the use of the CAPM in financial management:

Beaver, William H., Paul Kettler, and Myron Scholes, "The Association between Market Determined and Accounting Determined Risk Measures," *Accounting Review*, October 1970, 654.

Blume, Marshall E., "Betas and Their Regression Tendencies," *Journal of Finance*, June 1975, 785-795.

Bowman, Robert G., "The Theoretical Relationship between Systematic Risk and Financial (Accounting) Variables," *Journal of Finance*, June 1979, 617-630.

Rosenberg, Barr, and James Guy, "Beta and Investment Fundamentals," *Financial Analysts' Journal*, May-June 1976, 60-72.

Additional references for the CAPM are given in Chapters 7 and 10.

6A

Calculating Beta Coefficients

The CAPM is an *ex ante* model, which means that all of the variables represent before-the-fact, expected values. In particular, the beta coefficient used in the SML equation should reflect volatility of a given stock versus the market expected during some *future* period. However, people generally calculate betas during some *past* period and then assume that the stocks' relative volatility will remain constant in the future.

To illustrate how betas are calculated, consider Figure 6A-1. The data at the bottom of the figure show the historic realized returns for Stock J and the market for the last five years. The data points were then plotted on the scatter diagram, and a regression line drawn. If all the data points fell on a straight line, as they did in Figure 6-8 in Chapter 6, it would be easy to draw an accurate line. If they do not, then you can fit the line "by eye" as an approximation.

Recall what the term *regression line* or *regression equation* means: The equation $Y = a + bX + e$ is the standard form of a simple linear regression. It states that the dependent variable, Y, is equal to a constant, a, plus b times X, where b is the slope coefficient (or parameter) and X is the "independent" variable, plus an error term, e. Thus, the rate of return on the stock during a given time period depends on what happens to the general stock market, which is measured by $X = \bar{k}_M$.

Once the line has been drawn on the graph paper, we can estimate its intercept and slope, the a and b values in $Y = a + bX$. The intercept, a, is simply the point where the line cuts the vertical axis. The slope coefficient, b, can be estimated by the "rise over run" method. This involves calculating the amount by which $\bar{k}_J$ increases for a given increase in $\bar{k}_M$. For example, we observe (in Figure 6A-1) that $\bar{k}_J$ increases from -8.9 to $+7.1$ percent (the rise) when $\bar{k}_M$ increases from 0 to 10.00 percent (the run). Thus, the b, the beta coefficient, can be measured as follows:

$$b = \text{Beta} = \frac{\text{Rise}}{\text{Run}} = \frac{\Delta Y}{\Delta X} = \frac{7.1 - (-8.9)}{10.00 - 0.00} = \frac{16.0}{10.00} = 1.6.$$

Note that rise over run is a ratio, and it would be the same if measured using any two arbitrarily selected points on the line.

Figure 6A-1
Calculating Beta Coefficients

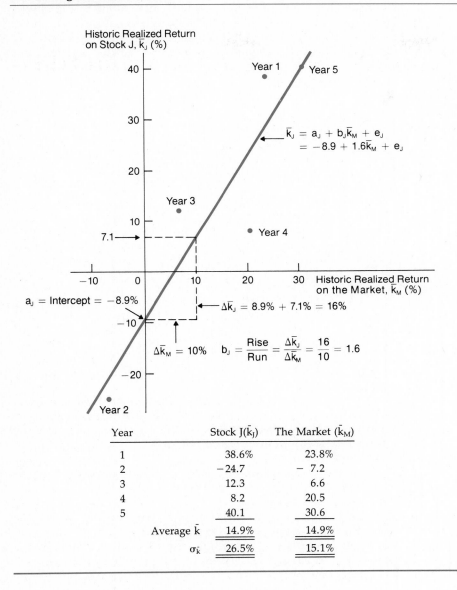

Year	Stock J($\bar{k}_J$)	The Market ($\bar{k}_M$)
1	38.6%	23.8%
2	−24.7	− 7.2
3	12.3	6.6
4	8.2	20.5
5	40.1	30.6
Average $\bar{k}$	14.9%	14.9%
$\sigma_{\bar{k}}$	26.5%	15.1%

The regression line, or equation, enables us to predict a rate of return for Stock J, given a value of $\bar{k}_M$. For example, if $\bar{k}_M = 15\%$, we would predict $\hat{k}_J = -8.9\% + 1.6(15\%) = 15.1\%$. The actual return would probably differ from the predicted return. This deviation is the error term, e_J, for the year, and it varies randomly from year to year depending on company-specific factors.

In actual practice, monthly rather than annual returns are generally used for $\bar{k}_J$ and $\bar{k}_M$, and five years of data are employed. Thus, there would be 5 × 12 = 60 dots on the scatter diagram. Also, in practice one would always use the *least squares method* for finding the regression coefficients a and b; the least squares procedure minimizes the squared values of the error terms, and it is discussed in statistics courses. Note also that the least squares value of beta can be obtained quite easily by computer or even with a calculator that has statistical functions.

Problems   6A-1 You are given the following set of data:

Year	Historic Rates of Return ($\bar{k}$)	
	NYSE ($\bar{k}_M$)	Stock Y ($\bar{k}_Y$)
1	4.0%	3.0%
2	14.3	18.2
3	19.0	9.1
4	−14.7	−6.0
5	−26.5	−15.3
6	37.2	33.1
7	23.8	6.1
8	−7.2	3.2
9	6.6	14.8
10	20.5	24.1
11	30.6	18.0
Mean	9.8%	9.8%
σ	18.7%	13.1%

a. Construct a "standard" graph showing the relationship between returns on Stock Y and the market; then draw a freehand approximation of the regression line. What is the approximate value of the beta coefficient? (If you have a calculator with statistical functions, use it to calculate beta.)

b. Give a verbal interpretation of what the regression line and the beta coefficient show about Stock Y's volatility and relative riskiness as compared with other stocks.

c. Suppose the scatter of points had been more spread out, but the regression line was exactly where your present graph shows it. How would this affect (1) the firm's risk if the stock were held in a one-asset portfolio and (2) the actual risk premium on the stock if the CAPM held exactly? How would the degree of scatter (or the correlation coefficient) affect your confidence in the likelihood that the calculated beta will hold true in the years ahead?

d. Suppose the regression line had been downward sloping, and the beta coefficient had been negative. What would this imply about (1) Stock Y's relative riskiness and (2) its probable risk premium?

e. Construct an illustrative probability distribution graph of returns on portfolios consisting of (1) only Stock Y, (2) 1 percent each of 100 stocks with beta coefficients similar to that of Stock Y, and (3) all stocks (that is, the distribution of returns on the market). Use as the expected rate of return the arithmetic mean as given above for both Stock Y and the market, and assume that the distributions are normal. Are the expected returns "reasonable"; that is, is it reasonable that $\hat{k}_Y = \hat{k}_M = 9.8\%$?

f. Now suppose that in the next year, Year 12, the market return were 27 percent, but Stock Y increased its use of debt, which raised its perceived risk to investors. Further, this risk increase is expected to have no effect on Firm Y's dividend stream. What would happen to its stock price? Do you think that the return in Year 12 could be approximated by the following historic characteristic line?

$$\bar{k}_Y = 3.8\% + 0.62(\bar{k}_M) = 3.8\% + 0.62(27\%) = 20.5\%.$$

g. Suppose $\bar{k}_Y$ in Year 12 were actually 0 percent, with the stock price decline exactly offsetting its dividend yield. What would the new beta be based on the past 11 years data, that is, Years 2 through 12? Does this beta make sense?

6A-2 You are given the following historic data on market returns, $\bar{k}_M$, and the returns on Stocks A and B, $\bar{k}_A$ and $\bar{k}_B$:

Year	$\bar{k}_M$	$\bar{k}_A$	$\bar{k}_B$
1	37.2%	37.2%	26.1%
2	23.8	23.8	19.4
3	-7.2	-7.2	3.9
4	6.6	6.6	10.8
5	20.5	20.5	17.7
6	30.6	30.6	22.8

R_F, the riskless rate, is 10 percent. Your probability distribution for k_M for next year is as follows:

Probability	k_M
0.1	-15%
0.2	0
0.4	15
0.2	30
0.1	45

a. Determine graphically the beta coefficients for Stocks A and B.
b. Graph the Security Market Line and give its equation.
c. Calculate the required rates of return on Stocks A and B.
d. Suppose Stock C has $b_C = 2$, $D_1/P_0 = 8\%$, and an expected growth rate of 8 percent. Is the stock in equilibrium? Explain, and if the stock is not in equilibrium, explain how equilibrium will be restored.

6B

Risk Aversion, Portfolio Theory, and the Capital Asset Pricing Model

Chapter 6 dealt with the relationship between risk and rates of return in an intuitive, informal manner. This appendix examines the relationship more systematically. First, we set forth the basic elements of portfolio theory. Second, we show how portfolio theory has been extended to relate assets' risks to their rates of return through the Capital Asset Pricing Model (CAPM). Finally, we discuss some of the empirical studies that have been undertaken (1) to test the validity of the CAPM and (2) to measure the specific relationship between risk and return.

Portfolio Theory

A *portfolio* is defined as a combination of assets, and *portfolio theory* deals with the selection of *efficient* portfolios, or portfolios that provide either (1) the highest possible expected return for any specified degree of risk or (2) the lowest possible risk for any specified rate of return.

Expected Return on a Portfolio

The expected rate of return on a portfolio is always a linear function—it is simply a weighted average of the expected returns of the individual securities in the portfolio. For example, if 50 percent of the portfolio is invested in a security with a 6 percent expected return (Security A), and 50 percent in one with a 10 percent expected return (Security B), the expected rate of return on the portfolio is

$$\hat{k}_p = \sum_{i=1}^{n} w_i\hat{k}_i = w_A\hat{k}_A + w_B\hat{k}_B \qquad \text{(6B-1)}$$
$$= 0.5(6\%) + 0.5(10\%) = 8\%.$$

If all of the portfolio were invested in A, the expected return would be 6 percent, and if all were invested in B, the expected return would be 10 percent. Since our portfolio contained some of each, the expected portfolio return is a linear combination of the two securities' expected returns—it is 8 percent. In general, given the expected returns on the individual securities,

Figure 6B-1
Expected Rate of Return on a Two-Asset Portfolio

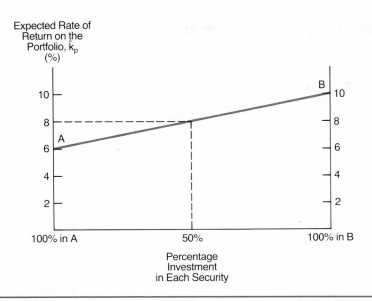

the expected return on the portfolio depends on the percentage of the total funds invested in each security.

Figure 6B-1 illustrates the set of expected returns for our two-asset portfolio. The line AB represents all possible expected returns when Securities A and B are combined in different proportions.

The riskiness of a portfolio is measured by the standard deviation of expected returns. Equation 6B-2 is used to calculate the standard deviation of any portfolio:

Riskiness of a Portfolio

$$\sigma_p = \sqrt{\sum_{i=1}^{n} (k_{pi} - \hat{k}_p)^2 P_i}. \qquad \textbf{(6B-2)}$$

Here σ_p is the standard deviation of the portfolio's expected returns; k_{pi} is the estimated return on the portfolio given the ith state of the economy; $\hat{k}_p$ is the expected return on the portfolio over all n states of the economy; and P_i is the probability of occurrence of the ith state of the economy.

Figure 6B-2 illustrates two possible distributions of estimated portfolio returns for two portfolios. Portfolio X has more variability than Portfolio Y; consequently, investors view Portfolio X as being riskier than Y. Incidentally, the graph shows the expected returns on the two portfolios as being equal. Typically, in equilibrium, this equality would not hold—the expected

Figure 6B-2
Distributions of Portfolio Returns

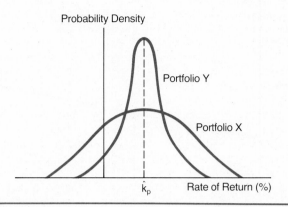

return on the riskier portfolio, X, would be higher, so the entire distribution for Portfolio X in Figure 6B-2 would be shifted to the right.

A fundamental aspect of portfolio theory is the idea that the riskiness inherent in any single asset held in a portfolio is different from the riskiness of that asset held in isolation. As we shall see, it is possible for a given asset to be quite risky when held in isolation, but to be relatively safe if held in a portfolio.

Measuring the Riskiness of a Portfolio: The Two-Asset Case

Equation 6B-2 could be used to calculate the riskiness of a portfolio, but, under the assumption that the distributions of returns on the individual securities are normal, a complicated looking but operationally simple equation can be derived from Equation 6B-2 to determine the risk of a two-asset portfolio:[1]

$$\sigma_p = \sqrt{w_A^2\sigma_A^2 + (1 - w_A)^2\sigma_B^2 + 2w_A(1 - w_A)r_{AB}\sigma_A\sigma_B}. \quad \text{(6B-3)}$$

Here σ_p is the standard deviation of the portfolio; w_A is the fraction of the portfolio invested in Security A; $(1 - w_A)$ is the fraction invested in Security B; σ_A and σ_B are the standard deviations of returns on Securities A and B; and r_{AB} is the correlation between the two securities. Note that the term $r_{AB}\sigma_A\sigma_B$ is called the *covariance (cov)* between Securities A and B.

---

[1]The derivation of Equation 6B-3 appears in standard statistics books. Notice that if $w_A = 1$, all of the portfolio is invested in Security A, and Equation 6B-3 reduces to

$$\sigma_p = \sqrt{\sigma_A^2} = \sigma_A.$$

The portfolio contains but a single asset, so the risk of the portfolio and that of Asset A are identical. Equation 6B-3 can be expanded to include any number of assets by adding additional terms, but we shall not do so here.

As was indicated at the beginning of the appendix, portfolio theory is used to select *efficient* portfolios—those portfolios which provide either the highest expected return for any degree of risk, or the lowest degree of risk for any given expected return. To illustrate the concept, assume that two investment securities, A and B, are available, and that we have a specific amount of money to invest in these securities. We can allocate our funds between the securities in any proportion. Security A has an expected rate of return of $\hat{k}_A = 5\%$ and a standard deviation of returns $\sigma_A = 4\%$; for Security B the expected return is $\hat{k}_B = 8\%$ and the standard deviation is $\sigma_B = 10\%$. Our first task is to determine the set of *attainable* portfolios, and then we must select the subset of *efficient* portfolios.

We need data on the degree of correlation between the two securities' expected returns, r_{AB}, in order to construct the attainable and efficient sets of portfolios. Let us develop the portfolios' expected returns, $\hat{k}_p$, and standard deviation of returns, σ_p, using three assumed degrees of correlation: $r_{AB} = +1.0$, $r_{AB} = 0$, and $r_{AB} = -1.0$. (Of course, only one correlation can exist; our example simply shows three alternative situations.)

To calculate $\hat{k}_p$ and σ_p, we use Equations 6B-1, modified for a two-asset portfolio, and 6B-3:

$$\hat{k}_p = w_A\hat{k}_A + (1 - w_A)\hat{k}_B, \tag{6B-1}$$

and

$$\sigma_p = \sqrt{w_A^2\sigma_A^2 + (1 - w_A)^2\sigma_B^2 + 2w_A(1 - w_A)r_{AB}\sigma_A\sigma_B}. \tag{6B-3}$$

We now substitute the given values for $\hat{k}_A$ and $\hat{k}_B$, and then solve Equation 6B-1 for $\hat{k}_p$ at different values of w_A. For example, when w_A equals 0.75, then

$$\hat{k}_p = 0.75(5\%) + 0.25(8\%) = 5.75\%.$$

Similarly, we can substitute in the given values for σ_A, σ_B, and r_{AB} and then solve Equation 6B-3 for σ_p at different values of w_A. For example, when $r_{AB} = 0$ and $w_A = 75\%$, then

$$\sigma_p = \sqrt{0.5625(16) + 0.0625(100) + 2(0.75)(0.25)(0)(4)(10)}$$
$$= \sqrt{9 + 6.25} = \sqrt{15.25} = 3.9\%.$$

The equations can be solved for other values of w_A and for the three cases, $r_{AB} = +1.0$, 0, and -1.0. Table 6B-1 gives the solution values for $w_A = 100\%$, 75%, 50%, 25%, and 0%, and Figure 6B-3 gives plots of $\hat{k}_p$, σ_p, and the attainable set of portfolios for each case. In both the table and the graphs, note the following points:

1. The three graphs across the top row of Figure 6B-3 apply to Case I, where the two assets are perfectly positively correlated; that is, $r_{AB} = +1.0$. The middle row of graphs is for the zero correlation case, and the bottom row is for perfect negative correlation.

2. All three cases are theoretical in the sense that we would rarely encounter $r_{AB} = -1.0$, 0.0, or $+1.0$. Case II (zero correlation) produces graphs which

Table 6B-1
$\hat{k}_p$ and σ_p under Various Assumptions

Percent of Portfolio in Security A (Value of w_A)	Percent of Portfolio in Security B (Value of $1 - w_A$)	$r_{AB} = +1.0$		$r_{AB} = 0$		$r_{AB} = -1.0$	
		$\hat{k}_p$	σ_p	$\hat{k}_p$	σ_p	$\hat{k}_p$	σ_p
100	0	5.00%	4.0%	5.00%	4.0%	5.00%	4.0%
75	25	5.75	5.5	5.75	3.9	5.75	0.5
50	50	6.50	7.0	6.50	5.4	6.50	3.0
25	75	7.25	8.5	7.25	7.6	7.25	6.5
0	100	8.00	10.0	8.00	10.0	8.00	10.0

Figure 6B-3
Illustrations of Portfolio Returns, Risk, and the Attainable Set of Portfolios

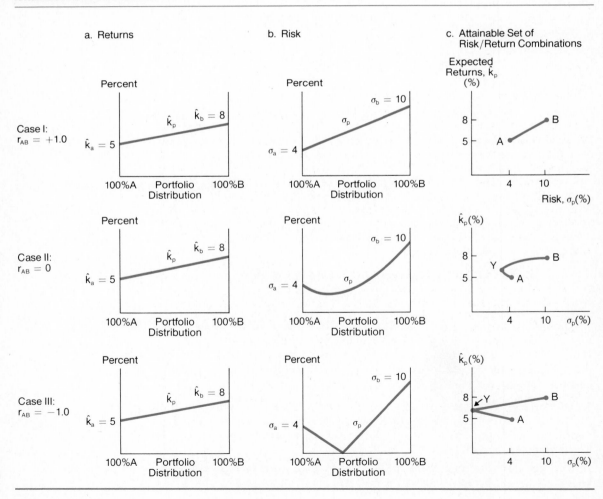

would most closely resemble those of a real world example, where the correlation would probably be in the range of $+0.5$ to $+0.7$.

3. The left column of graphs shows the expected returns with different combinations of A and B; the middle column shows risk in the three cases; and the right column shows the attainable set of risk/return combinations.

4. In the left column of graphs, since $\hat{k}_p$ is a linear function of w_A, the graphs are identical in each of the three cases. Thus, we see that $\hat{k}_p$ does not depend on correlation; it only depends on the weights.

5. In the middle column of graphs we see that σ_p is linear in Case I, where $r_{AB} = +1.0$; it is nonlinear in Case II; and in Case III, we see that σ_p consists of two linear segments and that risk can be completely diversified away when $r_{AB} = -1.0$. Thus σ_p does depend on correlation, although $\hat{k}_p$ does not.

6. The right column of graphs shows the *attainable*, or *feasible*, *set* of portfolios consisting of Securities A and B. With only two securities, the attainable set is a curve or line.[2]

7. That part of the attainable set from Y to B in Cases II and III is defined to be efficient; the part from Y to A is inefficient. That is, for any degree of risk on the line segment YA, a higher return can be found on segment YB.

With only two assets, the feasible set of portfolios is a line (or curve) as shown in the third column of graphs in Figure 6B-3. However, if we were to increase the number of assets, we would obtain a space, or area, such as the shaded area in Figure 6B-4. The points A, H, G, and F represent single securities (or portfolios containing only one security). All the other points in the shaded area, including its boundaries, represent portfolios of two or more securities. The space itself is called the *feasible* (or attainable) region. Each point in this area represents a particular portfolio with a risk of σ_p and an expected return of $\hat{k}_p$. For example, Point X represents one such portfolio's risk and expected return, as do B, C, D, and E.

Given the full set of potential portfolios that could be constructed from the available assets, which portfolio should *actually* be constructed? This choice involves two separate decisions: (1) determining the efficient set of portfolios, and (2) choosing from the efficient set the single portfolio that is best for the individual investor.

The Efficient Frontier

---

[2]If we differentiate Equation 6B-3, set the derivative equal to zero, and then solve for w_A, we obtain the fraction of the portfolio which should be invested in Security A if we wish to have the least-risk portfolio. Here is the equation:

$$w_A = \frac{\sigma_B(\sigma_B - r_{AB}\sigma_A)}{\sigma_A^2 + \sigma_B^2 - 2r_{AB}\sigma_A\sigma_B}. \tag{6B-4}$$

As a rule, we limit w_A to the range 0 to $+1.0$, that is, if the solution value is $w_A > 1.0$, set $w_A = 1.0$, while if w_A is negative, set $w_A = 0$. A negative w_A would imply short sales, while $w_A > 1.0$ would imply borrowing.

Figure 6B-4
The Efficient Set of Investments

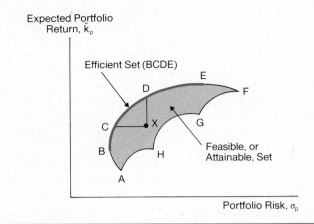

As we noted earlier, an *efficient portfolio* is defined as a portfolio that provides either the highest possible expected return for any degree of risk, or the lowest possible degree of risk for any expected return. In Figure 6B-4, the boundary line BCDE defines the *efficient set of portfolios.*[3] Portfolios to the left of the efficient set are not possible because they lie outside of the attainable set. In other words, there is no set of w_i values that will produce a portfolio with an expected rate of return, $\hat{k}_p$, and risk, σ_p, represented by a point to the left of BCDE. Portfolios to the right of the boundary line are inefficient because some other portfolio would provide either a higher return with the same degree of risk or a lower risk for the same rate of return. To illustrate, consider Point X. Portfolio C provides the same expected rate of return as does Portfolio X, but C is less risky. At the same time, Portfolio D is as risky as Portfolio X, but D provides a higher expected rate of return. Points C and D (and other points on the boundary of the efficient set between C and D) are said to *dominate* Point X. Similarly, points on the curve from B to A and from E to F are dominated by points on the efficient set BCDE.

Risk/Return   Given the efficient set of portfolio combinations, which specific portfolio
Indifference Curves   should an investor choose? To determine the optimal portfolio for a particular investor, we must know the investor's attitude toward risk as reflected in his or her risk/return tradeoff function.

---

[3]A computational procedure for determining the efficient set of portfolios was developed by Harry Markowitz and first reported in his article, "Portfolio Selection," *Journal of Finance*, March 1952, 77-91. In this article, Markowitz developed the basic concepts of portfolio theory.

Figure 6B-5
Indifference Curves for Risk and Expected Rate of Return

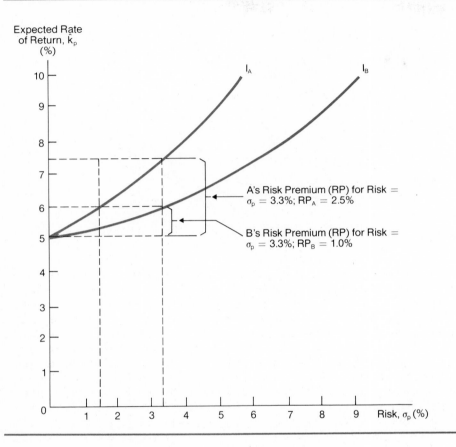

An investor's risk/return preference function is based on the standard economic concept of *indifference curves* as illustrated in Figure 6B-5. The curves labeled I_A and I_B represent the indifference curves of Individuals A and B. Ms. A is indifferent with regard to the riskless 5 percent portfolio, a portfolio with an expected return of 6 percent but with a risk of $\sigma_p = 1.4\%$, and so on. Mr. B is equally well satisfied with a riskless 5 percent return, an expected 6 percent return with risk of $\sigma_p = 3.3\%$, and so on.

Notice that Ms. A requires a higher expected rate of return to compensate her for a given amount of risk than does Mr. B; thus, Ms. A is said to be more *risk averse* than Mr. B. Her higher risk aversion causes Ms. A to require a higher *risk premium*—defined as the difference between the 5 percent riskless return and the required return associated with any specific amount of risk—than does Mr. B. Thus, Ms. A requires a premium of 7.5% − 5.0% = 2.5% to compensate for a risk $\sigma_p = 3.3\%$, while Mr. B's risk premium for this degree of risk is only 1 percent. *As a generalization, the steeper the slope of*

Figure 6B-6
Selecting the Optimal Portfolio of Risky Assets

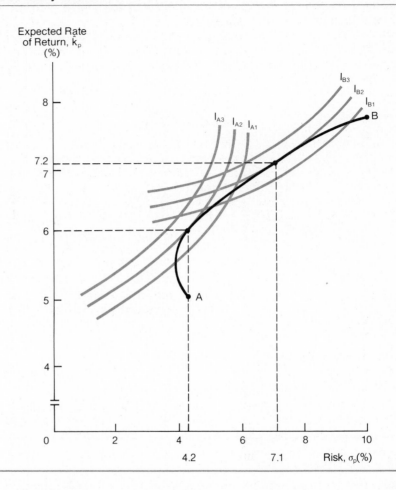

the indifference curve, the more risk averse is the investor. Thus, it is clear that Ms. A is more averse to risk than is Mr. B.

Each individual has a "map" of indifference curves; the indifference maps for Ms. A and Mr. B, along with a two-asset feasible set, are shown in Figure 6B-6. The higher curves denote a greater level of satisfaction (or utility). Thus, I_{B2} is better than I_{B1} because, for any level of risk such as $\sigma_p = 6\%$, Mr. B has a higher expected return, and hence greater utility. An infinite number of utility curves could be drawn for each individual, and different individuals are likely to have somewhat different sets of curves.

The Optimal Portfolio for an Investor

Figure 6B-6 combines the feasible set of portfolios for the two-asset case with $r_{AB} = 0$ as it was developed in Figure 6B-3 with the indifference curves for Ms. A and Mr. B. The optimal portfolio for each investor is found at the tangency point between the efficient set of portfolios and one of the investor's indifference curves. This tangency point marks the highest level of satisfaction the investor can attain. Ms. A, who is more risk averse than Mr. B, chooses a portfolio with a lower expected return (about 6 percent) but a riskiness of only $\sigma_p = 4.2\%$. Mr. B picks a combination of securities (a portfolio) that provides an expected return of about 7.2 percent with a riskiness of about $\sigma_p = 7.1\%$. Ms. A selects a portfolio more heavily weighted with the low-risk security, while Mr. B's portfolio contains a larger proportion of the more risky security.[4]

The Capital Asset Pricing Model (CAPM)

As we have now seen, the riskiness of a portfolio of assets as measured by its standard deviation of returns is generally less than the average of the risks of the individual assets as measured by their standard deviations. This phenomenon, in turn, has direct implications for the required rate of return on a given security: Since investors generally hold portfolios of securities, not just one security, it is reasonable to consider the riskiness of a security in terms of its contribution to the riskiness of the portfolio rather than in terms of its riskiness if held in isolation. The *Capital Asset Pricing Model (CAPM)* was developed to analyze the riskiness and the required rates of return on assets when they are held in portfolios.

Basic Assumptions of the CAPM

As in all financial theories, a number of assumptions were made in the development of the CAPM; they are listed below:[5]

1. All investors are single-period expected utility of terminal wealth maximizers who choose among alternative portfolios on the basis of means and standard deviations of portfolio returns.

2. All investors can borrow or lend an unlimited amount at a given risk-free rate of interest, R_F, and there are no restrictions on short sales of any asset.

3. All investors have identical subjective estimates of the means, variances, and covariances of return among all assets; that is, investors have homogeneous expectations.

4. All assets are perfectly divisible and perfectly liquid (that is, marketable at the going price), and there are no transactions costs.

5. There are no taxes.

6. All investors are price takers (that is, all investors assume that their own buying and selling activity will not affect stock prices).

7. The quantities of all assets are given and fixed.

---

[4]Ms. A's portfolio contains 67 percent of Security A and 33 percent Security B, while Mr. B's portfolio consists of 27 percent Security A and 73 percent Security B. These percentages can be determined from Panel a in Figure 6B-3 or by Equation 6B-1 by simply seeing what percentage of the two securities is consistent with $\hat{k}_p = 6.0\%$ and 7.2%. For example, $w_A(5\%) + (1 - w_A)(8\%) = 7.2\%$; solving for w_A, we obtain $w_A = 0.27$ and $(1 - w_A) = 0.73$.

[5]See Michael C. Jensen, "Capital Markets: Theory and Evidence," *Bell Journal*, Autumn 1972, 357-398.

Theoretical extensions in the literature, attempting to relax the basic CAPM assumptions, have yielded results that are generally consistent with the basic theory. However, the assumptions which underlie the model are both strong and unrealistic. Therefore, the validity of the model can only be established through empirical tests. More will be said later in this appendix about the empirical validity of the CAPM.

The Capital Market Line (CML)

In Figure 6B-6 we graphed a set of portfolio opportunities for the two-asset case and illustrated a method of selecting the optimal portfolio. In Figure 6B-7 we show a similar diagram for the multi-asset case, but here we also include a risk-free asset with a return R_F. The riskless asset has zero risk, so it is plotted on the vertical axis.

Figure 6B-7 shows the feasible set of portfolios of risky assets (the shaded area) and a set of indifference curves (I_1, I_2, I_3), which represent the trade-off between risk and return for a particular investor. Point N, where the indifference curve is tangent to the efficient set ANMB, represents a possible equilibrium; it is the point on the efficient set where the investor obtains the highest return for a given amount of risk, σ_p, or the smallest risk for a given expected return, $\hat{k}_p$. Indeed, if no riskless asset were available, our investor would choose Portfolio N.

Figure 6B-7
Investor Equilibrium: Combining the Risk-Free Asset
with the Market Portfolio

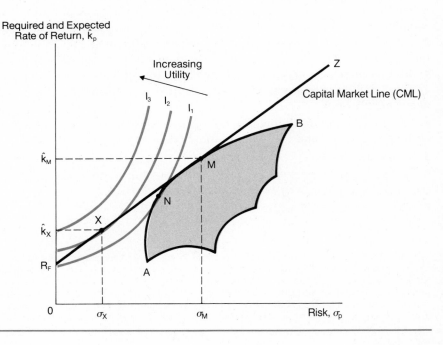

However, with the riskless asset the investor can do better than Portfolio N; it is possible to reach a higher indifference curve. In addition to the risky securities represented in the feasible set of portfolios, we now have a risk-free asset that yields R_F. With the additional alternative of investing in the risk-free asset, the investor can create a new portfolio that combines the risk-free asset with a portfolio of risky assets. This enables us to achieve any combination of risk and return lying along a straight line connecting R_F and the point of tangency of that straight line at M on the portfolio opportunities curve.[6] All portfolios on the line R_FMZ are preferred to the other risky portfolio opportunities on curve ANMB; the points on the line R_FMZ represent the best attainable combinations of risk and return.

Given the new opportunity set R_FMZ, our investor will move from Point N to Point X, which is on the highest attainable risk/return indifference curve. Note that line R_FMZ *dominates* the opportunities that could have been achieved from the portfolio opportunities curve ANMB alone. In general, since investors can include both the risk-free security and a fraction of the risky portfolio, M, in a portfolio, it will be possible to move to a point such as X. In addition, if the investor can borrow as well as lend (lending is equivalent to buying risk-free securities) at the riskless rate R_F, it is possible to move out the line segment MZ, and one would do so if his or her utility indifference curve were tangent to R_FMZ in that section.[7]

---

[6]The risk/return combinations of a risk-free asset and a risky asset (a single stock or a portfolio of stocks) will always be linear. To see this, consider the equations for return, $\hat{k}_p$, and risk, σ_p, for any combination w and $(1 - w)$, where w is the fraction of the portfolio invested in the riskless asset:

$$\hat{k}_p = wR_F + (1 - w)\hat{k}_M, \qquad \textbf{(6B-1)}$$

and

$$\sigma_p = \sqrt{w^2\sigma_{R_F}^2 + (1 - w)^2\sigma_M^2 + 2w(1 - w)r_{R_FM}\sigma_{R_F}\sigma_M}. \qquad \textbf{(6B-3)}$$

Equation 6B-1 is obviously linear. For Equation 6B-3 we know that R_F is the risk-free asset, so $\sigma_{R_F} = 0$; hence, $\sigma_{R_F}^2$ is also zero. Using this information, we can simplify Equation 6B-3 as follows:

$$\sigma_p = \sqrt{(1 - w)^2\sigma_M^2} = (1 - w)\sigma_M.$$

Thus, σ_p is also linear when a riskless asset is combined with a portfolio of risky assets.

We see, then, that a portfolio with w percent invested in the riskless asset and $(1 - w)$ invested in the market portfolio of risky assets will have a linear risk/return relationship. For example, if 100 percent of the portfolio is invested in $R_F = 8\%$, the portfolio return will be 8 percent with $\sigma_p = 0$. If 100 percent is invested in M, with $\hat{k}_M = 12\%$ and $\sigma_M = 10\%$, then $\sigma_p = 1.0(10\%) = 10\%$, and $\hat{k}_p = 0(8\%) + 1.0(12\%) = 12\%$. If 50 percent of the portfolio is invested in M and 50 percent in the risk-free asset, than $\sigma_p = 0.5(10\%) = 5\%$, and $\hat{k}_p = 0.5(8\%) + 0.5(12\%) = 10\%$. Plotting these points will reveal the linear relationship given as R_FMZ in Figure 6B-7.

[7]An investor who is relatively averse to risk will go to a point such as X, holding some of the risky market portfolio and some of the riskless asset. An investor who is less averse to risk could move out beyond M toward Z, borrowing to do so. Such an investor might be buying stocks on margin. If the borrowing rate is higher than R_F, then the line R_FMZ will tilt down (that is, be less steep) beyond M. This condition would invalidate the basic CAPM equation. Therefore, the assumption of equal lending and borrowing rates is crucial to the CAPM theory.

Under the conditions set forth in Figure 6B-7, all investors would hold portfolios lying on the line $R_F MZ$; this implies that they would hold only efficient portfolios that are linear combinations of the risk-free security and the risky portfolio M. For the capital market to be in equilibrium, M must be a portfolio that contains every asset in exact proportion to that asset's fraction of the total market value of all assets; that is, if Security i is w_i percent of the total market value of all securities, w_i percent of the market portfolio M will consist of Security i. In effect, M represents "the market." Thus, in equilibrium, all investors will hold efficient portfolios with standard deviation and return combinations along the line $R_F MZ$. The particular location of a given individual on the line will be determined by the point at which his or her indifference curve is tangent to the line, and this in turn reflects the investor's attitude toward risk, or degree of risk aversion.

The line $R_F MZ$ in Figure 6B-7 is defined as the *Capital Market Line (CML)*. It has an intercept of R_F and a slope (using the "rise over run" concept) of $(\hat{k}_M - R_F)/\sigma_M$. Thus,

$$\text{CML: } \hat{k}_p = R_F + \left[\frac{\hat{k}_M - R_F}{\sigma_M} \right] \sigma_p. \tag{6B-5}$$

In words, the expected return on any efficient portfolio is equal to the riskless rate plus a risk premium equal to $(\hat{k}_M - R_F)/\sigma_M$ times the portfolio's standard deviation. Therefore, the CML for efficient portfolios shows a linear relationship between expected return and risk, and it can be rewritten as follows:

$$\text{CML: } \hat{k}_p = R_F + \lambda \sigma_p. \tag{6B-6}$$

Here

$\hat{k}_p$ = expected return on an efficient portfolio.

R_F = risk-free interest rate.

λ = market price of risk (pronounced "lambda"), with $\lambda = (\hat{k}_M - R_F)/\sigma_M$ = the slope of the CML.

σ_p = standard deviation of returns on an efficient portfolio.

$\hat{k}_M$ = expected return on the market portfolio.

σ_M = standard deviation of returns on the market portfolio.

All efficient portfolios, including the market portfolio, lie on the CML. Hence,

$$\hat{k}_M = R_F + \lambda \sigma_M. \tag{6B-6a}$$

Both Equations 6B-6 and 6B-6a state that the expected return on an efficient portfolio in equilibrium is equal to a risk-free return plus the market price of risk multiplied by the standard deviation of the portfolio's returns. This re-

Figure 6B-8
Expected Return on an Efficient Portfolio

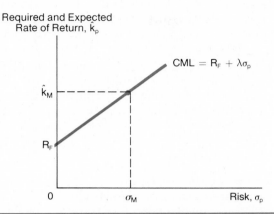

lationship is graphed in Figure 6B-8. The CML is drawn as a straight line with an intercept at R_F, the risk-free return, and a slope equal to the market price of risk (λ), which is the market risk premium ($\hat{k}_M - R_F$) divided by σ_M. The market price of risk, or the slope of the CML, reflects the attitudes of individuals in the aggregate (that is, the average of all individuals) toward risk.

The Security Market Line

The next step in the development of the CAPM calls for going from risk and returns on *portfolios* to risk and returns on *individual securities*. We stated in Chapter 6 that, under the CAPM theory, the riskiness of a security is measured by its beta coefficient, b_i, and that the required return (and, in equilibrium, the expected return also) is found by this equation:

$$\hat{k}_i = k_i = R_F + b_i(k_M - R_F). \qquad \textbf{(6B-7)}$$

Equation 6B-7 is actually derived from Equation 6B-6. However, the derivation is somewhat lengthy, so it is not presented in detail here.[8] Essentially, the proof involves first showing how, given a security's covariance with the market ($\sigma_i\sigma_M r_{iM}$), the security affects the market portfolio's risk. The following equation results:

$$\hat{k}_i = R_F + \left[\frac{\hat{k}_M - R_F}{\sigma_M^2}\right]\sigma_i\sigma_M r_{iM}. \qquad \textbf{(6B-8)}$$

---

[8]The interested reader is referred to Eugene F. Fama and Merton H. Miller, *The Theory of Finance* (New York: Holt, Rinehart & Winston, 1972), for a complete derivation of Equation 6B-7.

Then, it is demonstrated that the beta coefficient, which we found in Chapter 6 by regressing a stock's return on the market return, is equal to

$$b_i = \frac{\sigma_i r_{iM}}{\sigma_M}. \tag{6B-9}$$

Thus, a stock's CAPM risk index, which is its beta coefficient, is dependent on (1) its own standard deviation, (2) its correlation with other stocks (the market), and (3) the standard deviation of returns on the market portfolio. An individual firm's management cannot significantly affect the market's variability, σ_M, but it can take actions that will raise or lower the firm's variability, σ_i, and the firm's correlation with the market, r_{iM}. Such actions will affect the firm's beta, its required rate of return, and consequently its stock price.

Some Observations about Betas

In Appendix 6A, we calculated Stock J's beta coefficient by regressing Stock J's historic returns against historic market returns. With this in mind, we can note the following points: First, the *future* returns on Stock J are presumed to bear a linear relationship of the following form to those of the market:

$$\hat{k}_J = a_J + b_J \hat{k}_M + e_J.$$

In other words, the historic relationship between Stock J and the market as a whole is assumed to continue on into the future.

Second, in addition to general market movements, each firm also faces events that are peculiar to it and independent of the general economic climate. Such events tend to cause the returns on any Firm J's stock to move at least somewhat independently of those for the market as a whole, and these random events are accounted for by the random error term e_J. Before the fact, the expected value of the error term is zero; after the fact, it generally will be either positive or negative.

Third, the regression coefficient, b_J (the beta coefficient), is a market sensitivity index; it measures the relative volatility of a given stock (J) versus the average stock, or the "market." This tendency of an individual stock to move with the market constitutes a risk, because the market does fluctuate, and these fluctuations cannot be diversified away. This component of total risk is the stock's *market, or nondiversifiable, risk.*

Finally, the relationship between a stock's total risk, market risk, and diversifiable risk can be expressed as follows:

$$\text{Total risk} = \text{Variance} = \text{Market risk} + \text{Diversifiable risk}$$
$$\sigma_J^2 \quad = \quad b_J^2 \sigma_M^2 \quad + \quad \sigma_{e_J}^2.$$

Here σ_J^2 is the variance or total risk of Stock J, σ_M^2 is the variance of the market, b_J is Stock J's beta coefficient, and $\sigma_{e_J}^2$ is the variance of Stock J's regression error term.

Several points about total and relevant risk are significant:

1. If, in a graph such as the one presented in Appendix 6A, all the points plotted exactly on the regression line, then the error term would be zero and all of the stock's risk would be market related. On the other hand, if the points were widely scattered about the regression line, much of the stock's risk would be diversifiable. The shares of a large, well-diversified mutual fund would plot very close to the regression line, as would those of a broadly diversified conglomerate corporation.

2. If the stock market never fluctuated, then stocks would have no market risk. Of course, the market does fluctuate, so market risk is present—even if you hold an extremely well-diversified portfolio, you will still suffer losses if the market falls. In recent years, the standard deviation of market returns, σ_M, has generally run about 15 percent. Back in the "wild" days of the 1920s, before regulation and other forces helped stabilize the market, fluctuations were even greater.

3. Beta is a measure of a stock's relative market risk, and the actual market risk of Stock J is $b_J^2\sigma_M^2$. It can also be expressed in standard deviation form as $b_J\sigma_M$. Therefore, for any given level of market volatility as measured by the market's standard deviation, σ_M, the higher a stock's beta, the higher is its market risk. If beta were zero, the stock would have no market risk, while if beta were 1.0, the stock would be exactly as risky as the market— assuming the stock is held in a diversified portfolio—and the stock's market risk would be σ_M.

4. The diversifiable risk can be eliminated by diversification, so the *relevant* risk is not total risk, but market risk. If a given stock has $b_J = 0.5$, and if $\sigma_M = 15$ percent, then the stock's relevant risk equals $b_J\sigma_M = 0.5(15\%) = 7.5\%$. A portfolio of such low-beta stocks would have a standard deviation of expected returns of $\sigma_p = 7.5\%$, or one-half the standard deviation of expected returns of a portfolio of average ($b = 1.0$) stocks. Had Stock J been a high-beta stock ($b = 2.0$), then its relevant risk would have been $b_J\sigma_M = 2.0(15\%) = 30\%$. A portfolio of $b = 2.0$ stocks would have $\sigma_p = 30\%$, so such a portfolio would be twice as risky as a portfolio of average stocks.

5. A stock's risk premium depends only on its market risk, not its total risk: $RP_J = b_J(k_M - R_F)$. Mr. S might have only one stock, and hence be concerned with total risk and seek a return based on that risk. However, if Ms. D has a well-diversified portfolio, she would face less risk from Stock J. Therefore, if Stock J offered a return high enough to satisfy Mr. S, it would represent a bargain for Ms. D. She would then buy it, pushing its price up and its yield down in the process. Since most financial assets are held by diversified investors, and since any given security can have only one price and hence only one rate of return, market action drives each stock's risk premiums to the level specified by its relevant, or market, risk.

Empirical Tests of the CAPM

The idea that risk should be associated with portfolios, and that the relevant risk of an individual security depends upon the security's effect on portfolio's risk, is quite logical. Thus, the conclusions of the CAPM are intuitively appealing. As we noted earlier, however, the precise form of the model was developed on the basis of a set of assumptions that are most unrealistic. Therefore, while the basic CAPM equation, $k_i = R_F + b_i(k_M - R_F)$, *might* represent an accurate description of how rates of return are established in the marketplace, the model could actually be invalid if investors do not behave as the model assumes they do. For example, if many investors are not fully diversified, and hence have not eliminated all nonmarket (or nonsystematic) risk from their portfolios, then beta would not be an adequate measure of risk, and Equation 6B-7 would not explain how required returns are really set. Also, if the rate investors must pay to borrow money is greater than the risk-free rate (in other words, if the borrowing rate is greater than the lending rate), then the CML will not be a straight line beyond Point M in Figure 6B-7, and this will produce a "bend" in the CML in Figure 6B-8 and also invalidate the basic CAPM equation, Equation 6B-7. Thus, like all theories, the CAPM must be tested empirically and validated before it can be used with any real confidence. The literature dealing with empirical tests of the CAPM is quite extensive. We give here a brief synopsis of some of the empirical tests.

Tests of the Stability of Beta Coefficients

According to the CAPM, the beta that should be used to estimate a stock's market risk reflects investors' estimates of the stock's *future* volatility in relation to that of the market. Obviously, we do not know now how a stock will be related to the market in the future, nor do we know how the average investor views this expected future relative volatility. All we have are data on past volatility. We can use these data to calculate *historic betas*. If the historic betas are stable over time, then there would seem to be reason for investors to use past betas as estimators of future volatility. In other words, if Stock J's beta had been stable in the past, then the historic b_J would probably be a good proxy for the ex ante, or expected, b_J. By "stable," we mean that if b_J is calculated using data from the period of, say, 1980 to 1984, then this same beta (approximately) should be found from 1985 to 1989.

Robert A. Levy, Marshall E. Blume, and others have studied the question of stability of betas in depth.[9] Levy calculated betas for individual securities, as well as for portfolios of securities, over a range of time intervals. He concluded (1) that the betas of individual stocks are unstable, and hence that past betas for *individual securities* are *not* good estimators of future risk, but (2) that betas of portfolios of ten or more randomly selected stocks are quite stable, and hence that past *portfolio* betas are good estimators of future volatility. In effect, in a portfolio the errors in estimating individual securities' betas tend to offset one another. This means that the CAPM is better for selecting portfolios than it is for estimating the required rate of return on an individual stock. The work of Blume and others supports Levy's position.

The conclusion that follows from the beta stability studies is that the CAPM is a better concept for structuring investment portfolios than it is for purposes of estimating the cost of equity for individual securities. We will address this issue in Chapter 7, where we discuss cost of capital estimation procedures.

---

[9]See Robert A. Levy, "On the Short-Term Stationarity of Beta Coefficients," *Financial Analysts' Journal*, November-December 1971, 55-62; and Marshall E. Blume, "Betas and Their Regression Tendencies," *Journal of Finance*, June 1975, 785-796.

As we have seen, the CAPM states that a linear relationship should exist between a security's required rate of return and its beta. Further, when the SML is graphed, the vertical axis intercept should be R_F, and the required rate of return for a stock (or portfolio) with b = 1.0 should be k_M, the rate of return on the market. Various researchers have attempted to test the validity of the model by calculating betas and rates of return, plotting these values in graphs such as Figure 6B-9, and observing whether or not (1) the intercept is equal to R_F, (2) the regression line is linear, and (3) the line passes through the point b = 1.0, k_M. Monthly historic rates of return are generally used for the stocks, and both 30-day Treasury bill rates and long-term Treasury bond rates have been used to estimate the value of R_F. Also, most of the studies actually analyze portfolios rather than individual securities because security betas are so unstable.

Estimating the Slope of the SML

Before discussing the actual results of the tests, it is critical to recognize that although the CAPM is an ex ante, or forward-looking, model, the data used to test it are entirely historical. There is no reason to believe that realized rates of return over past holding periods necessarily reflect expected rates of return such as the model deals with. Also, historical betas may or may not reflect either current or expected future risk. This lack of ex ante data makes it extremely difficult to test the true CAPM. Still, for what it is worth, here is a summary of the key empirical tests:

1. The evidence generally shows a significant positive relationship between realized returns and systematic risk. However, the slope of the relationship is usually less than that predicted by the CAPM.

Figure 6B-9
Tests of the CAPM

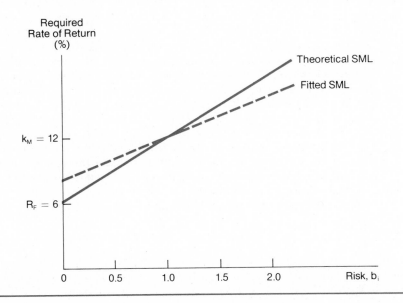

2. The relationship between risk and return appears to be linear. Empirical studies give no evidence of significant curvature in the risk/return relationship.

3. Tests that attempt to discriminate between the effects of market and company specific risk do not yield definitive results. Both kinds of risk appear to be positively related to security returns; that is, higher returns are required to compensate for both diversifiable and market risk. However, it may be that the relationship between return and diversifiable risk is at least partly spurious; that is, it may reflect statistical problems rather than the true nature of capital markets.

4. In a very important paper, Richard Roll has questioned whether it is even conceptually possible to test the CAPM.[10] Also, Roll showed that the linear relationship which prior researchers had observed in graphs like Figure 6B-9 resulted from the mathematical properties of the models being tested, hence that a finding of linearity proved nothing whatever. Roll's work does not disprove the CAPM theory, but he does show that it is *impossible* to prove that investors behave in accordance with the theory.

5. If the CAPM were completely valid, it should apply to all financial assets, including bonds. In fact, when bonds are introduced into the analysis, they *do not* plot on the SML. This is worrisome, to say the least.

6. The stocks of certain industries may not conform to the CAPM postulates; the public utilities are an example. In effect, profit regulation by utility commissions puts an upper bound on utilities' returns. As a result, their distributions of expected future returns are skewed to the left rather than being symmetric. This makes their nonmarket risk important; and this, in turn, may invalidate the CAPM for this group of stocks.[11]

We shall return to the CAPM in Chapter 7 and Appendix 7A, where we employ the CAPM framework to help estimate the cost of equity capital for a firm.

Problems

6B-1 An investor plans to invest in Stock A, Stock B, or some combination of the two stocks. The expected return for A is 9 percent and $\sigma_A = 4\%$; the expected return for B is 10 percent and $\sigma_B = 5\%$. $r_{AB} = 0.5$.

    a. Construct a table similar to Table 6B-1 giving $\hat{k}_p$ and σ_p for 100 percent, 75 percent, 50 percent, 25 percent, and 0 percent investment in Stock A. (Hint: For $w_A = 75\%$, $\hat{k}_p = 9.25\%$ and $\sigma_p = 3.78\%$, while for $w_A = 50\%$, $\hat{k}_p = 9.5\%$, and $\sigma_p = 3.9\%$.)

    b. Use your calculated $\hat{k}_p$ and σ_p values to graph the attainable set of portfolios, and indicate which part of the attainable set is efficient.

    c. Using hypothetical indifference curves, show how an investor might choose a portfolio consisting of Stocks A and B.

---

[10]See Richard Roll, "A Critique of the Asset Pricing Theory's Tests," *Journal of Financial Economics*, March 1977, 129-176.

[11]See the set of articles by Eugene F. Brigham and Roy L. Crum, William F. Sharpe, and others in the Fall 1978 issue of *Financial Management* for more on the use of the CAPM to estimate required returns on utility stocks.

6B-2 You are planning to invest $200,000. Two securities, A and B, are available, and you can invest in either of them or in a portfolio with some of each. Returns on A and B have a correlation coefficient of r_{AB} = −0.5. You estimate that the following probability distributions of returns are applicable for A and B:

Security A			Security B	
P_A	k_A		P_B	k_B
0.1	− 10%		0.1	− 30%
0.2	5		0.2	0
0.4	15		0.4	20
0.2	25		0.2	40
0.1	40		0.1	70
	$\hat{k}_A$ = ?			$\hat{k}_B$ = 20.0%
	σ_A = ?			σ_B = 25.7%

a. The expected return for Security B is $\hat{k}_B$ = 20%, and σ_B = 25.7%. Find $\hat{k}_A$ and σ_A.

b. Use Equation 6B-4 to find the value of w_A that produces the minimum risk portfolio. Assume r_{AB} = −0.5.

c. Construct a table giving $\hat{k}_p$ and σ_p for portfolios with w_A = 1.00, 0.75, 0.50, 0.25, 0.0, and the minimum risk value of w_A. (Hint: For w_A = 0.75, $\hat{k}_p$ = 16.25% and σ_p = 8.5%; for w_A = 0.5, $\hat{k}_p$ = 17.5% and σ_p = 11.1%; for w_A = 0.25, $\hat{k}_p$ = 18.75% and σ_p = 17.9%.)

d. Graph the feasible set of portfolios and identify the efficient frontier of the feasible set.

e. Suppose your risk/return trade-off function, or indifference curve, is tangent to the efficient set at the point where $\hat{k}_p$ = 18%. Use this information, plus the graph constructed in Part d above, to locate (approximately) your optimal portfolio. Draw in a reasonable indifference curve, indicate the percentage of your funds invested in each security, and determine the optimal portfolio's σ_p and $\hat{k}_p$. (Hint: Estimate σ_p and $\hat{k}_p$ graphically and then use the equation for $\hat{k}_p$ to determine w_A.)

f. Now suppose a riskless asset with a return R_F = 10% becomes available. How would this change the investment opportunity set? Explain why the investment opportunity set becomes linear.

g. Given the indifference curve in Part e above, would you change your portfolio? If so, how? (Hint: Assume the indifference curves are parallel.)

h. What are the beta coefficients of Stocks A and B? [Hints: (1) Recognize that k_i = R_F + $b_i(k_M$ − $R_F)$ and solve for b_i and (2) assume that your preferences match those of most other investors.]

6B-3 Stock A has an expected return $\hat{k}_A$ = 10% and σ_A = 10%. Stock B has $\hat{k}_B$ = 14% and σ_B = 15%. r_{AB} = 0. The rate of return on riskless assets is 6 percent.

a. Construct a graph that shows the feasible and efficient sets, giving consideration to the existence of the riskless asset.

b. Explain what would happen to the CML if the two stocks had (1) a positive correlation coefficient or (2) a negative correlation coefficient. Assume everything else is held constant.

c. Suppose these were the only three securities (A, B, and riskless) in the economy, and everyone's indifference curves were such that they were tangent to the CML to the right of the point where the CML was tangent to the efficient set of risky assets. Would this represent a stable equilibrium? If not, how would an equilibrium be produced? Do *not* assume that everything else is held constant.

Arbitrage Pricing Theory

6C

As noted in Chapter 6 and Appendix 6B, the CAPM has several weaknesses, including (1) the fact that it is based on some unrealistic assumptions, (2) the argument raised by Roll that it cannot be tested empirically, and (3) the fact that the CAPM assumes that a stock's required return is based on one factor (the general stock market) whereas other factors such as relative sensitivity to inflation, dividend payout, and the like may also influence a stock's returns relative to those of other stocks. The *Arbitrage Pricing Theory (APT)* is designed to help overcome these weaknesses.[1] We should note at the outset that the APT is based on complex mathematical and statistical theory which goes far beyond the scope of this text. However, the APT model is widely discussed in the current academic literature, and it is being recommended in practitioner-oriented journals for such uses as measuring the cost of equity. Actual usage to date is extremely limited, but it may increase, so students of finance should at least have an intuitive idea of what APT is all about.

The CAPM assumes that each stock's expected return is equal to the risk-free rate plus its beta coefficient times the market risk premium:

$$\hat{k}_i = R_F + b_i(\hat{k}_M - R_F). \tag{6C-1}$$

The realized return, $\bar{k}_i$, will be

$$\bar{k}_i = \hat{k}_i + b_i(\bar{k}_M - \hat{k}_M) + e_i, \tag{6C-2}$$

that is, the realized return, $\bar{k}_i$, will be equal to the expected return, $\hat{k}_i$, plus an increment or decrement, $b_i(\bar{k}_M - \hat{k}_M)$, whose magnitude depends on the stock's sensitivity to market returns, b_i, and the realized excess or shortfall in the market return, plus a random error term, e_i.

The market return, $\bar{k}_M$, is actually determined by a number of factors, including economic activity as measured by GNP, the strength of the world

---

[1]See Stephen A. Ross, "The Arbitrage Theory of Capital Asset Pricing," *Journal of Economic Theory*, December 1976, 341-360.

economy, the level of inflation, changes in tax laws, and so forth. Further, different groups of stocks are affected in different ways by these fundamental factors. Thus, rather than specifying the stock's returns as a function of one factor (returns on the market), one could specify required and realized returns of individual stocks to be a function of various fundamental economic factors. If this were done, we would transform Equation 6C-2 into 6C-3:

$$\bar{k}_i = \hat{k}_i + b_{il}(\bar{F}_l - \hat{F}_l) + \cdots + b_{ij}(\bar{F}_j - \hat{F}_j) + e_i, \tag{6C-3}$$

where

$\bar{k}_i$ = realized rate of return on Stock i.

$\hat{k}_i$ = expected rate of return on Stock i.

b_{ij} = sensitivity of Stock i to economic Factor j.

$\bar{F}_j$ = realized value of economic Factor j.

$\hat{F}_j$ = expected value of Factor j.

e_i = effect of unique factors on the realized return of Stock i.

Equation 6C-3 shows that the realized return on any stock is equal to the stock's expected return plus increments or decrements which depend on (1) changes in fundamental economic factors, (2) the sensitivity of the stock to these changes, b_{ij}, plus (3) a random term which reflects changes in those factors unique to the firm or industry.

Certain stocks or groups of stocks are most sensitive to Factor 1, others to Factor 2, and so forth, and every portfolio's returns would depend on what happened to the different fundamental factors. Theoretically, one could construct a portfolio such that (1) the portfolio was riskless and (2) its net investment was zero (some stocks were sold short, with the proceeds from the short sales being used to buy the stocks held long). Such a portfolio would have to have a zero expected return, or else arbitrage operations would occur, which in turn would cause the prices of the underlying assets to change until the portfolio's expected return was zero. Using some complex mathematics and assumptions similar to those used to derive the CAPM relationships, plus the short sales assumption, the APT equivalent of the CAPM's Security Market Line can be developed from Equation 6C-3:[2]

$$\hat{k}_i = k_i = R_F + b_{il}(\lambda_l - R_F) + \cdots + b_{ij}(\lambda_j - R_F). \tag{6C-4}$$

---

[2]See Thomas E. Copeland and J. Fred Weston, *Financial Theory and Corporate Policy* (Reading, Mass.: Addison-Wesley, 1983).

Here λ_j is the required rate of return on a portfolio with unit sensitivity to the jth economic factor ($b_j = 1.0$) and zero sensitivity to all other factors. Thus, for example, ($\lambda_2 - R_F$) is the risk premium on a portfolio with $b_2 = 1.0$ and all other $b_j = 0.0$. Note that Equation 6C-4 is identical in form to the SML, but it permits a stock's required return to be a function of multiple factors.

The APT has several advantages over the CAPM:

1. It requires fewer and less restrictive assumptions about the distribution of returns on stocks. (CAPM assumes that expected returns on stocks are normally distributed; APT permits any returns distribution.)

2. APT does not require strong assumptions about investor's utility functions.

3. It is not necessary to measure the return on the market portfolio (which gets around Roll's argument that the CAPM is untestable because the market portfolio is not measurable).

However, the APT also has some disadvantages:

1. In addition to many of the CAPM's assumptions about perfect markets, APT also assumes the possibility of unlimited short sales and the ability to net short sale proceeds against long purchases of stocks.

2. The fundamental factors are not actually specified. People use a complex statistical procedure (factor analysis) to categorize stocks into groups whose returns (1) move up and down together but (2) are uncorrelated with returns movements in other stock groups. Presumably, the stocks in each group are affected by some "factor," but this factor cannot be identified with real precision.

3. The CAPM has been around a long time, and its implementation problems (for example, difficulties in measuring ex ante betas and in testing the model for empirical validity) are well known. The APT is new, and hence has not been examined as closely, but when it is, the same kinds of implementation problems are likely to surface.

4. Finally, the CAPM is intuitively appealing, but the APT is not intuitively clear, and no one (to our knowledge) has figured out a way to explain it to practitioners. Until a clear explanation is forthcoming, the APT is not likely to be used by real-world decision makers.

The Cost of Capital

7

In the fall of 1983, Shell Oil Company and the Newport News Ship-building and Drydock division of Tenneco, Inc., were involved in a lawsuit regarding two large tankers which Newport News was building for Shell at a cost of about $100 million. Shell paid in advance for the ships, and was to take delivery on a specified date. The contract stated that if the ships were not completed on time, Shell could sue for damages based on the cost of the capital which Shell had invested. Newport News did fail to complete the ships on time (they were about a year late), so Shell sued.

The theory behind the contract clause, and hence the lawsuit, was (1) that Shell was investing money, (2) that this money had a cost, (3) that Shell expected to earn a return on the ships which would cover the cost of the money invested, (4) that if Shell did not get the ships, then it could not earn the cost of the capital it had invested in them, and (5) that it should be entitled to recover its capital costs from Newport News. The principal issue in the suit was this: What was the cost of the approximately $100 million which Shell had invested in the tankers? That determination required an assessment of how Shell had actually raised the $100 million (it was raised partly as debt and partly as equity), and how much funds from each source cost. The techniques discussed in this chapter were used to help ascertain the proper amount of the damages. Exactly the same procedures are (or should be) used by Shell and other companies for many other purposes.

The cost of capital is critically important in finance for three reasons: (1) Maximizing the value of a firm requires that the costs of all inputs, including capital, be minimized, and to minimize the cost of capital we must be able to estimate it. (2) Proper capital budgeting decisions require an estimate of the cost of capital. (3) Many other types of decisions,

249

including those related to leasing, bond refunding, and working capital policy, require estimates of the cost of capital.[1]

Our first topic in this chapter is the logic of the weighted average cost of capital. Next, we consider the costs of the major capital structure components. Then, we will see how the individual component costs are brought together to form a weighted average cost of capital. Finally, we examine a number of items that affect the cost of capital.

The Logic of the Weighted Average Cost of Capital

Suppose a particular firm's cost of debt is estimated to be 13 percent, its cost of equity is estimated to be 18 percent, and the decision has been made to finance next year's projects by selling debt. The argument is sometimes made that the cost of capital for these projects is 13 percent, because debt will be used to finance them. However, this position is incorrect. To finance a particular set of projects with debt implies that the firm is also using up some of its potential for obtaining new debt in the future. As expansion occurs in subsequent years, at some point the firm will find it necessary to use additional equity financing to prevent an excessive use of debt. To illustrate, suppose a firm borrows heavily at 13 percent during 1984, using up its debt capacity in the process, to finance projects yielding 15 percent. In 1985 it has projects available that yield 17 percent, well above the return on 1984 projects, but it cannot accept these new projects because they would have to be financed with 18 percent equity money. To avoid this problem, the firm should be viewed as an ongoing concern, and the cost of capital should be calculated as a weighted average, or composite, of the various types of funds it uses *regardless of the specific financing used to fund a particular project.*

Basic Definitions

The items on the right-hand side of a firm's balance sheet—various types of debt, preferred stock, and common equity—are defined as its *capital components.* Any net increase in assets must be financed by an increase in one or more capital components.

Capital is a necessary factor of production, and like any other factor, it has a cost. The cost of each component is defined as the *component cost* of that particular type of capital. For example, if the firm can borrow money at 13 percent, the component cost of debt is defined to be 13 percent. Throughout most of this chapter, we concentrate on debt, pre-

---

[1]The cost of capital is also vitally important in regulated industries, including electric, gas, telephone, and water companies. In essence, regulatory commissions first measure a utility's cost of capital and then set prices so that the company will just earn this rate of return. If the cost of capital estimate is too low, then the company will not be able to attract sufficient capital to meet long-run demands for service, and the public will suffer. If the estimate of capital costs is too high, customers will pay too much for service.

ferred stock, retained earnings, and new issues of common stock. These are the major capital structure components, and their component costs are identified by the following symbols:

k_d = interest rate on the firm's new debt = before-tax component cost of debt.

$k_d(1 - T)$ = after-tax component cost of debt, where T is the firm's marginal tax rate. $k_d(1 - T)$ is the debt cost used to calculate the weighted average cost of capital.

k_p = component cost of preferred stock.

k_s = component cost of retained earnings (or internal equity). This k_s is identical to the k_s developed in Chapter 6 and defined there as the required rate of return on common stock.

k_e = component cost of equity capital obtained by issuing new common stock, or external equity as opposed to internal equity. As we shall see, it is necessary to distinguish between equity raised by retaining earnings versus that raised by selling new stock. This is why we distinguish between k_s and k_e.

k_a = weighted average, or composite, cost of capital. k_a is also called the weighted average cost of capital, WACC, so k_a = WACC. If a firm raises $1 of new capital to finance asset expansion, and if it is to keep its capital structure in balance (that is, if it is to keep the same percentage of debt, preferred stock, and common equity), then it will raise part of the $1 as debt, part as preferred stock, and part as common equity (with equity coming either as retained earnings or from the sale of new common stock).[2]

These definitions and concepts are explained in detail in the remainder of this chapter.

Cost of Debt

The *after-tax component cost of debt* is the interest rate on debt, k_d, multiplied by $(1 - T)$, where T is the firm's marginal tax rate:[3]

$$\text{Component cost of debt} = k_d(1 - T). \qquad (7\text{-}1)$$

---

[2]Firms try to keep their debt, preferred, and common equity in optimal proportions. We will see why they do this, and how they establish the optimal proportions, in Chapters 11 and 12. However, firms do not try to maintain any proportional relationship between the common stock and retained earnings accounts as shown on the balance sheet. Common equity is common equity, whether it is represented by common stock or by retained earnings.

[3]Note that the cost of debt is considered in isolation. The impact of debt on the cost of equity, as well as on future increments of debt, is treated when the weighted cost of a combination of debt and equity is derived. Also, *flotation costs,* or the costs of selling the debt, are ignored. Flotation costs for debt issues are generally quite low; in fact, most debt is placed directly with banks, insurance companies, pension funds, and the like, and involves only administrative costs. Debt and stock flotation costs are discussed in detail in Chapters 14 and 15.

For example, if a firm can borrow at an interest rate of 10 percent, and if it has a marginal tax rate of 40 percent, then its after-tax cost of debt is 6 percent:

$$k_d(1 - T) = 10\%(0.6) = 6.0\%.$$

The reason for making the tax adjustment is as follows. The value of the firm's stock, which we want to maximize, depends on *after-tax* income. Interest is a deductible expense. The effect of this is that the federal government pays part of the interest charges. Therefore, to put the costs of debt and equity on a comparable basis, we adjust the interest rate downward to take account of the preferential tax treatment of debt.[4]

Note that the cost of debt is the interest rate on *new* debt, not the interest rate on any old, previously outstanding debt. In other words, we are interested in the cost of new debt, or the *marginal* cost of debt. Our primary concern with the cost of capital is to use it in a decision-making process—for example, the decision whether to obtain capital to buy plant and equipment. Whether the firm borrowed at high or low rates in the past is irrelevant for this purpose.

Cost of Preferred Stock

The component cost of preferred stock, k_p, that is used to calculate the weighted average cost of capital is the preferred dividend, D_p, divided by the net issuing price, P_n, or the price the firm receives after deducting flotation costs:

$$\text{Component cost of preferred stock} = k_p = \frac{D_p}{P_n}. \tag{7-2}$$

For example, suppose a firm has perpetual preferred stock that pays an $11.70 dividend per share and sells for $100 per share in the market. If it issues new shares of preferred, it would incur an underwriting (or flotation) cost of 2.5 percent, or $2.50 per share, so it would net $97.50 per share. Therefore, the cost of preferred stock would be 12.00 percent:

$$k_p = \$11.70/\$97.50 = 12.00\%.$$

Note that no tax adjustments are made when calculating k_p because unlike interest expense on debt, dividend payments on preferred stock are *not* tax deductible.

---

[4]It should also be noted that the tax rate is *zero* for a firm with losses. Therefore, for a company that does not pay taxes, the cost of debt is not reduced; that is, in Equation 7-1 the tax rate equals zero, so the after-tax cost of debt is equal to the interest rate.

The costs of debt and preferred stock are based on the returns investors require on these securities. The cost of equity obtained by retaining earnings can be defined similarly; it is k_s, the rate of return stockholders require on the firm's common stock.[5]

Cost of Retained Earnings, k_s

The reason why we must assign a cost of capital to retained earnings involves the *opportunity cost principle*. The firm's after-tax earnings literally belong to the stockholders. Bondholders are compensated by interest payments, while earnings belong to the common stockholders and serve to "pay the rent" on stockholders' capital. Management may either pay out earnings in the form of dividends or retain and reinvest earnings in the business. If management decides to retain earnings, there is an opportunity cost involved—stockholders could have received the earnings as dividends and invested this money in other stocks, in bonds, in real estate, or in anything else. Thus, the firm should earn on the retained earnings at least as much as stockholders themselves could earn in alternative investments of comparable risk.

What rate of return can stockholders expect to earn on equivalent risk investments? The answer is k_s. *Therefore, if the firm cannot invest retained earnings and earn at least k_s, then it should pay these funds to its stockholders and let them invest directly in other assets that do provide this return.*[6]

Whereas debt and preferred stock are contractual obligations which have easily determined costs, it is not at all easy to measure k_s. However, we can employ the principles developed in Chapters 5 and 6 to produce reasonably good cost of equity estimates. To begin, recall that for stocks in equilibrium (which is the typical situation), the required rate of return, k_s, is also equal to the expected rate of return, $\hat{k}_s$. Further, the required return is equal to a riskless rate, R_F, plus a risk premium, RP, while the expected return on a constant growth stock is equal to a dividend yield, D_1/P_0, plus an expected growth rate, g:

$$\text{Required rate of return} = \text{Expected rate of return}$$
$$k_s = R_F + RP = D_1/P_0 + g = \hat{k}_s. \qquad \text{(7-3)}$$

Therefore, we can estimate k_s either directly as $k_s = R_F + RP$, or indirectly as $k_s = \hat{k}_s = D_1/P_0 + g$. Actually, we will present three methods for finding the cost of retained earnings: (1) the CAPM approach, (2) the

---

[5]The term *retained earnings* can be interpreted to mean the balance sheet item retained earnings, consisting of all the earnings retained in the business throughout its history, or it can mean the income statement item *additions to retained earnings*. The income statement definition is used in the present chapter. Retained earnings for our purpose here refers to that part of current earnings which is not paid out in dividends but, rather, is retained and reinvested in the business.

[6]One complexity in estimating the cost of retained earnings deals with the fact that dividends and capital gains are taxed differently. Retaining earnings rather than paying them out as dividends can convert ordinary income to capital gains. This point is discussed later in the chapter.

bond yield plus risk premium approach, and (3) the Discounted Cash Flow (DCF) approach.

The CAPM Approach

To use the Capital Asset Pricing Model (CAPM) as developed in Chapter 6 to estimate the cost of equity, we proceed as follows.

Step 1. Estimate the riskless rate, R_F, generally taken to be either the U.S. Treasury bond rate or the short-term Treasury bill rate.

Step 2. Estimate the stock's beta coefficient, b_i, and use this as an index of the stock's market risk.

Step 3. Estimate the rate of return on the "market," or on an "average" stock, k_M.

Step 4. Estimate the required rate of return on the firm's stock as follows:

$$k_s = R_F + b_i(k_M - R_F). \tag{7-4}$$

The value $(k_M - R_F)$ is the risk premium on the average stock, while b_i is an index of the particular stock's own risk.

To illustrate the CAPM approach, assume that $R_F = 10\%$, $k_M = 16\%$, and $b_i = 0.7$ for a given stock. The stock's k_s is calculated as follows:

$$k_s = 10\% + 0.7(16\% - 10\%) = 10\% + 4.2\% = 14.2\%.$$

Had b_i been 1.8, indicating that the stock was riskier than average, k_s would have been

$$k_s = 10\% + 1.8(6\%) = 10\% + 10.8\% = 20.8\%.$$

It should be noted that while the CAPM approach appears to yield accurate, precise estimates of k_s, we saw in Chapter 6 that there are several problems with it. First, if a firm's stockholders are not well diversified, then they may be concerned about *total risk* rather than market risk only; in this case, the firm's true investment risk will not be measured by beta, and the CAPM procedure will understate the correct value of k_s. Further, even if the CAPM method is valid, it is hard to get correct estimates of the inputs required to make it operational: There is uncertainty over whether to use long-term or short-term Treasury securities for R_F; it is hard to estimate the beta that investors expect the company to have in the future; and it is hard to estimate the market risk premium. This latter problem has been especially vexing in the 1980s, because the riskiness of stocks versus bonds has been changing, making the market risk premium unstable. Appendix 7A takes a closer look at the difficulties involved in finding k_s in practice.

Although it is essentially an *ad hoc*, subjective procedure, analysts often estimate a firm's cost of retained earnings by adding a risk premium to the interest rate on the firm's own long-term debt. It is logical to think that firms with risky, low-rated, and consequently high-interest rate debt will also have risky, higher-cost equity, and the procedure of basing the cost of equity on a readily observable debt cost utilizes this precept. For example, if an Aaa-rated firm's bonds yield 11 percent, then its cost of equity might be estimated as follows:

Bond Yield plus Risk Premium Approach

$$k_s = \text{Bond rate} + \text{Risk premium} = 11\% + 3\% = 14\%.$$

A Baa firm's debt might carry a yield of 13 percent, making its estimated cost of equity 16 percent:

$$k_s = 13\% + 3\% = 16\%.$$

Note that the 3 percent risk premium is a judgmental estimate, so the estimated value of k_s is also judgmental. In recent years, our work suggests that the over-own-debt risk premium has ranged from about 1.0 to about 4.5 percentage points. The low premium occurred when interest rates were quite high and people were reluctant to invest in long-term bonds because of a fear of run-away inflation, further increases in interest rates, and losses on investments in bonds.

In Chapter 5, we saw that the expected rate of return on a share of common stock depends, ultimately, on the dividends paid on the stock:

Discounted Cash Flow (DCF) Approach

$$P_0 = \frac{D_1}{(1 + \hat{k}_s)^1} + \frac{D_2}{(1 + \hat{k}_s)^2} + \cdots \qquad \text{(7-5)}$$

Here P_0 is the current price of the stock; D_t is the dividend expected to be paid at the end of Year t; and $\hat{k}_s$ is the expected rate of return. If dividends are expected to grow at a constant rate, then, as we saw in Chapter 5, Equation 7-5 reduces to the following expression:

$$P_0 = \frac{D_1}{\hat{k}_s - g}. \qquad \text{(7-6)}$$

We can solve for $\hat{k}_s$ to obtain the expected rate of return on common equity, which in equilibrium is also equal to the required rate of return:[7]

$$\hat{k}_s = k_s = \frac{D_1}{P_0} + g. \qquad \text{(7-7)}$$

---

[7]Note that dividends are actually paid quarterly, and D_1 is generally taken to be the total dividend expected to be paid during the next four quarters. The model could be worked out on a quarterly basis, as we explain in Appendix 5C.

Again, note that this estimate of $\hat{k}_s$ is based upon the assumption that g is expected to remain constant in the future. If this assumption is not correct, then it will be necessary to solve for $\hat{k}_s$ using Equation 7-5.[8]

To illustrate the DCF approach, suppose a firm's stock sells for $18.82; its next expected dividend is $1.43; and its expected growth rate is a constant 6.6 percent. The firm's expected and required rate of return, and hence its cost of retained earnings, is 14.2 percent:

$$\hat{k}_s = k_s = \frac{\$1.43}{\$18.82} + 6.6\% = 7.6\% + 6.6\% = 14.2\%.$$

This 14.2 percent is the minimum rate of return that management must expect to earn on equity capital to justify retaining earnings and plowing them back into the business rather than paying them out to stockholders as dividends. Henceforth, in this chapter we assume that equilibrium exists, so we use the terms k_s and $\hat{k}_s$ interchangeably.

In practical work, *it is often best to use all three methods*—CAPM, bond yield plus risk premium, and DCF—and then apply judgment when the methods produce different results. People experienced in estimating equity capital costs recognize that both careful analysis and some very fine judgments are required. It would be nice to pretend that these judgments are unnecessary and to specify an easy, precise way of determining the exact cost of equity capital. Unfortunately, this is not possible. Finance is in large part a matter of judgment, and we simply must face this fact.

Cost of Newly Issued Common Stock, or External Equity, k_e

The cost of new common stock, or external equity capital, k_e, is higher than the cost of retained earnings, k_s, because of flotation costs involved in selling new common stock. What rate of return must be earned on funds raised by selling stock in order to make issuing new stock worthwhile? To put it another way, what is the cost of *new common stock*?

For a firm with a constant growth rate, the answer is found by applying the following formula:

---

[8]When the DCF method is used, we are implicitly assuming that the stock's price is in equilibrium, with $\hat{k}_s = D_1/P_0 + g = R_F + \text{Risk premium} = k_s$. Thus, the DCF and the CAPM methods will, if all inputs are estimated correctly, produce similar cost of capital estimates. Also, growth rates may be estimated (1) by projecting past trends if there is reason to think these trends will continue, (2) by asking security analysts what growth rates they are projecting (or, alternatively, by looking up projected growth rates in such publications as *Value Line*, a financial service subscribed to by many investors), and (3) by projecting the firm's dividend payout ratio and the complement of this ratio, the *retention rate*, and then multiplying the retention rate by the company's projected rate of return on equity (ROE):

$$g = (\text{Retention rate})(\text{ROE}) = (1.0 - \text{Payout rate})(\text{ROE}).$$

These methods of estimating dividend growth are discussed in more detail in Appendix 7A.

$$k_e = \frac{D_1}{P_0(1 - F)} + g. \qquad (7\text{-}8)$$

Here F is the percentage flotation cost incurred in selling the issue, so $P_0(1 - F)$ is the net price per share received by the company when it sells a new stock issue.[9]

Assuming that the illustrative firm previously discussed has a flotation cost of 10 percent, its cost of new outside equity is computed as follows:

$$k_e = \frac{\$1.43}{\$18.82(1 - 0.10)} + 6.6\% = \frac{\$1.43}{\$16.94} + 6.6\%$$
$$= 8.4\% + 6.6\% = 15.0\%.$$

Investors require a return of $k_s = 14.2\%$ on the stock. However, because of flotation costs, the company must earn *more* than 14.2 percent on funds obtained by selling stock in order to provide this 14.2 percent. Specifically, if the firm earns 15.0 percent on funds obtained from new common stock issues, then earnings per share will not fall below previously expected earnings; its expected dividend can be maintained; and as a result of all this, the price per share will not decline. If the firm earns less than 15.0 percent, then earnings, dividends, and growth will fall below expectations, causing the price of the stock to decline. If it earns more, the price of the stock will rise.[10]

---

[9]Equation 7-8 is derived as follows:

Step 1. The old stockholders expect the firm to pay a stream of dividends, D_t. New investors will likewise expect to receive the same stream of dividends, D_t. For new investors to obtain this stream *without impairing the D_t stream of the old investors*, the new funds obtained from the sale of stock must be invested at a return high enough to provide a dividend stream whose present value is equal to the price the firm receives:

$$P_n = \sum_{t=1}^{\infty} \frac{D_t}{(1 + k_e)^t}. \qquad (7\text{-}9)$$

Here P_n is the net price to the firm, and $P_n = P_0(1 - F)$; D_t is the dividend stream to new stockholders; and k_e is the cost of new outside equity.

Step 2. When growth is a constant, Equation 7-9 reduces to

$$P_n = P_0(1 - F) = \frac{D_1}{k_e - g}. \qquad (7\text{-}9a)$$

Step 3. Equation 7-9a may be solved for k_e.

$$k_e = \frac{D_1}{P_0(1 - F)} + g. \qquad (7\text{-}8)$$

[10]On occasion, it may be useful to use another equation to calculate the cost of external equity:

$$k_e = \frac{\text{Dividend yield}}{(1 - F)} + g = \frac{D_1/P_0}{(1 - F)} + g. \qquad (7\text{-}8a)$$

Equation 7-8a is derived algebraically from Equation 7-8, and it is useful when information on dividend yields, but not on dollar dividends and stock prices, is available.

Finally, note that we are really determining the difference between k_e and k_s as indicated by the DCF method. In this case, the difference is $15.0\% - 14.2\% = 0.8$ percentage points. If all three methods of finding k_s agree, and we assign a value of $k_s = 14.2\%$, then $k_e = 15.0\%$. But, if the three methods are not in agreement, and we consequently exercise judgment and assign k_s a value of, say, 14.5 percent, then $k_e = k_s +$ Flotation premium $= 14.5\% + 0.8 = 15.3\%$.

The Weighted Average Cost of Capital, WACC = k_a

As we shall see in Chapters 11 and 12, each firm has an optimal capital structure, which is the mix of debt, preferred, and common equity that causes its stock price to be maximized. Therefore, a rational, value-maximizing firm will establish its *optimal*, or *target, capital structure* and raise new capital in a manner that will keep the actual capital structure on target over time. In the remainder of this chapter we will assume that the firm has identified its optimal capital structure, uses this optimum as the target, and finances so as to remain constantly on target. How the target is established will be examined in Chapter 12.

The target proportions of debt, preferred, and common equity, along with the component costs of capital, are used to calculate the firm's overall, or weighted average, cost of capital, WACC = k_a. To illustrate, suppose Firm M has a target capital structure calling for 30 percent debt, 10 percent preferred stock, and 60 percent common equity. Its before-tax cost of debt, k_d, is 10.0 percent; its cost of preferred stock, k_p, is 12.0 percent; its cost of common equity from retained earnings, k_s, is 14.2 percent; and its marginal tax rate is 40 percent. Note that Firm M's after-tax, or component, cost of debt = $k_d(1 - T) = 10\%(0.6) = 6.0\%$.

Now suppose the firm needs to raise $100. In order to keep its capital structure on target, it must obtain $30 as debt, $10 as preferred, and $60 as common equity. (Common equity can come either from retained earnings or from the sale of new stock.) The weighted average cost of the $100, assuming the equity portion is from retained earnings, is calculated as follows:

Component	Weight	Component Cost	Product
Debt	0.30	6.0%	1.8%
Preferred	0.10	12.0	1.2
Common equity	0.60	14.2	8.5

Weighted average cost of capital = WACC = k_a = 11.5%

In equation format, we would have

$$WACC = k_a = w_d k_d (1 - T) + w_p k_p + w_s k_s \tag{7-10}$$
$$= 0.3(10\%)(0.6) + 0.1(12\%) + 0.6(14.2\%) = 11.5\%.$$

Here, w_d, w_p, and w_s are the weights used for debt, preferred stock, and common equity.

Every dollar of new capital that Firm M obtains consists of 30 cents of debt with an after-tax cost of 6 percent, 10 cents of preferred with a cost of 12 percent, and 60 cents of common equity with a cost of 15 percent. The average cost of each whole dollar is 11.5 percent.

The weights could be based either on the accounting values shown on the firm's balance sheet (book values) or on the market values of the different securities. Theoretically, the weights should be based on market values, but if a firm's book value weights are reasonably close to its market value weights, book value weights can be used as a proxy for market value weights. This point is discussed further in Chapters 11 and 12, but in the remainder of Chapter 7 we shall assume that the firm's market values are approximately equal to its book values, and on this basis we can use book value capital structure weights.

The *marginal cost* of any item is the cost of another unit of that item; for example, the marginal cost of labor is defined as the cost of adding one additional worker. The marginal cost of labor might be $25 per person if 10 workers are added, but $35 per person if the firm tries to hire 100 new workers, because it would be harder to find that many people willing and able to do the work. The same concept applies to capital. As the firm tries to attract more new dollars, the cost of each dollar will, at some point, rise. *Thus, the marginal cost of capital is defined as the cost of obtaining another dollar of new capital, and the marginal cost rises as more and more capital is raised.*

We can use Firm M to illustrate the marginal cost of capital concept. Firm M's target capital structure and other data follow:[11]

The Marginal Cost of Capital

Debt	$ 3,000,000	30%
Preferred	1,000,000	10
Common equity	6,000,000	60
Total value	$10,000,000	100%

---

[11]Firm M has only a negligible amount of payables and accruals, so these items were ignored. However, suppose the company had had $2 million of payables/accruals in addition to $3 million of interest-bearing debt. Payables/accruals could be handled in one of two ways:

1. We could simply ignore these items on the grounds that, in the fixed asset acquisition process (capital budgeting), these spontaneously generated funds are netted out against the required investment outlay and then ignored in the cost of capital calculation. This treatment of payable/accruals will be used in Chapter 9 when we consider capital budgeting cash flow estimation.

2. Alternatively, we could bring payables/accruals into the calculation directly. Accruals virtually always have a zero cost, as do payables for firms that take all discounts offered. If a firm has discounts available but does not take them, then it would be necessary to separate payables into "free" and "costly" components, and to determine an interest cost on the costly trade credit. See Chapter 21 for a discussion of trade credit.

$P_0 = \$18.82$.

$D_1 = \$1.43$.

$g = 6.6\%$, and it is expected to remain constant.

$k_s = \dfrac{D_1}{P_0} + g = \dfrac{\$1.43}{\$18.82} + 6.6\% = 7.6\% + 6.6\% = 14.2\%$.

$k_d = 10\%$.

$k_p = 12\%$.

$T = 40\%$.

Based on these data, the weighted average cost of capital, k_a, is 11.5 percent:

$$k_a = w_d k_d (1 - T) + w_p k_p + w_s k_s$$
$$= 0.3(10\%)(0.6) + 0.1(12\%) + 0.6(14.2\%)$$
$$= 1.8\% + 1.2\% + 8.5\% = 11.5\%.$$

Since Firm M's optimal capital structure calls for 30 percent debt, 10 percent preferred, and 60 percent equity, each new (or marginal) dollar will be raised as 30 cents of debt, 10 cents of preferred, and 60 cents of common equity. Otherwise, the capital structure would not stay on target. As long as Firm M's debt has an after-tax cost of 6 percent, its preferred has a cost of 12 percent, and its common equity has a cost of 14.2 percent, then its weighted average cost of capital will be 11.5 percent. Thus, each new dollar will be raised as 30 cents of debt, 10 cents of preferred, and 60 cents of equity, and each new (or marginal) dollar will have a weighted average cost of 11.5 percent.

The graph shown in Figure 7-1 is defined as Firm M's *marginal cost of capital schedule*. Here the dots represent dollars raised. Since each dollar of new capital has a cost of 11.5 percent, the marginal cost of capital (MCC) for Firm M is constant at 11.5 percent under the assumptions we have used thus far.[12]

Breaks, or Jumps, in the MCC Schedule

Could Firm M raise an unlimited amount of new capital at the 11.5 percent cost? The answer is *no*. As companies raise larger and larger sums during a given time period, the costs of both the debt and the equity components begin to rise, and as this occurs, the weighted average cost

---

[12]Firm M's MCC schedule in Figure 7-1 would be different (higher) if the company used any capital structure other than 30 percent debt, 10 percent preferred, and 60 percent equity. This point will be developed in Chapters 11 and 12, but as a general rule, a different MCC schedule would exist for every possible capital structure, and the optimal structure is the one that produces the lowest MCC schedule.

Figure 7-1
Marginal Cost of Capital (MCC) Schedule for Firm M
Using Retained Earnings

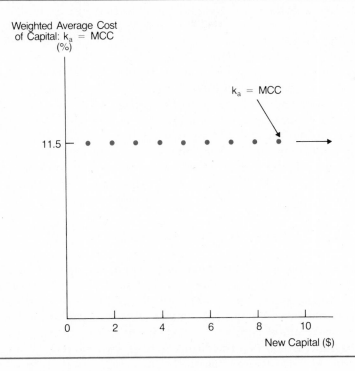

of new dollars also rises. Thus, just as corporations cannot hire unlimited numbers of workers at a constant wage, neither can they raise unlimited amounts of capital at a constant cost. At some point, the cost of each new dollar will increase above 11.5 percent.

Where will this point occur for Firm M? As a first step to determining the point of increasing costs, recognize that, although the company has total capital of $10 million, all of this capital was raised in the past, and all of it is invested in assets which are used in operations. Now suppose Firm M's capital budget calls for net expenditures of $1 million during 1986. This new (or marginal) capital will presumably be raised so as to maintain the 30/10/60 debt/preferred/common equity relationship. Therefore, the company will obtain $300,000 of debt, $100,000 of preferred, and $600,000 of common equity.[13] The new common equity could come

---

[13]In reality, Firm M might raise the entire $1 million by issuing new debt, or perhaps by issuing new common equity. By issuing large blocks of securities, Firm M saves on flotation costs. However, over the long haul the firm will stick to its target capital structure. Thus, any financing deviation in one year will be offset by other financing deviations in future years. The cost of capital remains a function of the target capital structure regardless of year-to-year financing decisions.

from two sources: (1) that part of this year's profits which management decides to retain in the business rather than use for dividends (but not from earnings retained in the past) or (2) the sale of new common stock.

The debt will have an interest rate of 10 percent, or an after-tax cost of 6 percent. The preferred stock will have a cost of 12 percent. The cost of common equity will be k_s if the equity is obtained by retained earnings, but it will be k_e if the company must sell new common stock. Consider first the case where the new equity comes from retained earnings. As we have seen, Firm M's cost of retained earnings is 14.2 percent, and its weighted average cost of capital when using retained earnings as the common equity component is 11.5 percent.

Now consider the case where the company expands so rapidly that its retained earnings for the year are not sufficient to meet its needs for new equity, forcing it to sell new common stock. If the flotation cost of new stock is $F = 10\%$, then Firm M's cost of equity will, after it exhausts its retained earnings, rise from 14.2 to 15.0 percent:

$$k_e = \frac{P_1}{P_0(1 - F)} + g = \frac{\$1.43}{\$18.82(0.9)} + 6.6\% = 15.0\%.$$

Firm M's weighted average cost of capital, using first new retained earnings (earnings retained this year, and not in the past) and then new common stock, is shown in Table 7-1. We see that the weighted average cost of each dollar, which is the marginal cost of capital, is 11.5 percent so long as retained earnings are used; but the marginal cost jumps to 12.0 percent as soon as the firm exhausts its retained earnings and is forced to sell new common stock.[14]

How much new capital can Firm M raise before it exhausts its retained earnings and is forced to sell new common stock? Assume that the company expects to have total earnings of $840,000 for the year, and that it has a policy of paying out half of its earnings as dividends. Thus, its *payout ratio*, which is the proportion of net income paid out as dividends, is 0.50. (Firm M's *retention ratio*, which is the proportion of net income retained within the firm, is also 0.50. Note that the retention ratio is 1.0 minus the payout ratio.) Therefore, the addition to retained earnings will be $420,000 during the year. How much *total financing*, debt and preferred plus this $420,000 of retained earnings, can be done before the retained earnings are exhausted and the firm is forced to sell new common stock? In effect, we are seeking some amount of capital, X, which is defined as a *break point* and which represents the total financing that can be done before Firm M is forced to sell new common

---

[14]At relatively low growth rates, expansion can be financed by debt and retained earnings, but at higher growth rates, external equity capital is needed. If Firm M needs no external equity, then its marginal cost of capital would be 11.5 percent. However, if its growth rate were rapid enough to require it to sell new common stock, then its marginal cost of capital would rise to 12.0 percent.

Table 7-1
Firm M's Marginal Cost of Capital Using (a) New
Retained Earnings and (b) New Common Stock

a. MCC when equity is from new retained earnings

Component	Weight	Component Cost	Product
Debt	0.3	6.0%	1.8%
Preferred	0.1	12.0	1.2
Common equity	0.6	14.2	8.5
	1.0	MCC = k_a =	11.5%

b. MCC when equity is from sale of new common stock

Component	Weight	Component Cost	Product
Debt	0.3	6.0%	1.8%
Preferred	0.1	12.0	1.2
Common equity	0.6	15.0	9.0
	1.0	MCC = k_a =	12.0%

stock. We know that 60 percent of X will be the new retained earnings, while 40 percent will be debt plus preferred. We also know that retained earnings will amount to $420,000. Therefore,

$$0.6X = \text{Retained earnings} = \$420,000.$$

Solving for X, which is the *retained earnings break point*, we obtain

$$\text{Break point} = X = \frac{\text{Retained earnings}}{\text{Equity fraction}} = \frac{\$420,000}{0.6} = \$700,000.$$

Thus, Firm M can raise a total of $700,000, consisting of $420,000 of retained earnings and $700,000 − $420,000 = $280,000 of new debt and preferred stock supported by these new retained earnings, without altering its capital structure:

New debt supported by retained earnings	$210,000	30%
Preferred stock supported by retained earnings	70,000	10
Retained earnings	420,000	60
Total expansion supported by retained earnings (that is, break point for retained earnings)	$700,000	100%

Figure 7-2 graphs Firm M's marginal cost of capital schedule. Each dollar has a weighted average cost of 11.5 percent until the company has raised a total of $700,000. This $700,000 will consist of $210,000 of new debt with an after-tax cost of 6 percent, $70,000 of preferred stock with a cost of 12 percent, and $420,000 of retained earnings with a cost of 14.2 percent. However, if Firm M raises $700,001, the last dollar will contain 60 cents of equity *obtained by selling new common equity at a cost of*

Figure 7-2
Marginal Cost of Capital Schedule for Firm M
Using Both Retained Earnings and New Common Equity

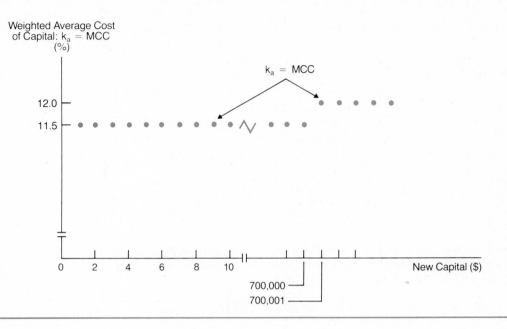

15.0 percent, so MCC = k_a rises from 11.5 to 12.0 percent, as calculated in Table 7-1.

The MCC Schedule beyond the Retained Earnings Break Point

There is a jump, or break, in Firm M's MCC schedule at $700,000 of new capital. Could there be other breaks in the schedule? Yes, there could be. The cost of capital could also rise due to increases in the cost of debt or the cost of preferred stock, or due to further increases in the cost of new common stock, as the firm issues more and more securities. Some people have argued that the costs of capital components other than common stock should not rise. Their argument is that as long as the capital structure does not change, and presuming that the firm uses new capital to invest in projects with the same degree of risk as its existing projects, investors should be willing to invest additional capital at the same rate. However, this argument assumes an infinitely elastic demand for a firm's securities. For many firms, the demand curve of investors for its securities seems to be downward sloping, so the more securities sold during a given period, the lower the price received for the securities and the higher the required rate of return. Thus, the more new financing required, the higher the firm's marginal cost of capital.

Here are some other points to consider concerning the shape of the MCC schedule:

1. Firms often have lines of credit established with lenders, and even if formal lines of credit are not established, a firm will usually have business relationships with certain lenders. These lenders will have already conducted credit checks and risk analyses of the company, and thus they can lend additional funds without incurring significant fixed costs. Once a firm reaches its lending limit, however, it will be forced to borrow from other creditors that will have to incur investigation costs.[15] Thus, as the firm borrows more and more and is forced to turn to additional loan sources, it may find that its debt costs increase.

2. There may exist a "clientele," or group of investors, that is particularly attracted to a firm's common stock. This could be the firm's existing stockholders, people in its operating area, or others who know and respect its managers. At any rate, as more and more new common stock is sold in any period, some current investors may be able and willing to buy additional shares, but at some point new investors will surely have to be brought in. If these new investors did not view the firm's stock as being attractive at its original price, then additional sales could only occur if the stock price is lowered, and this action would have the effect of increasing the firm's cost of equity.

3. Both debt and equity investors base their required rates of return on the perceived riskiness of the firm. That perceived risk embodies a number of factors, one of which is the rate at which the firm expands its operations. At low expansion rates, proven managers can continue to control things, finances will not be strained, and so on. However, if the expansion rate exceeds the expected level, investors could begin to worry that the firm's risk may be increasing. Such perceptions of increasing risk, whether justified or not, would cause the costs of both debt and equity to increase as more and more funds are required.

For these reasons, we believe that firms do face increasing MCC schedules such as the one shown for Firm M in Figure 7-3. Here we have identified a specific retained earnings break point, but because of estimation difficulties, we have not attempted to identify precisely any additional break points. However, we have (1) shown the MCC schedule to be upward sloping, reflecting a positive relationship between capital raised and capital costs, and (2) indicated our inability to measure these costs precisely by using a band of costs rather than a line. Note that this band exists even at the first dollar of capital raised, since our component costs are only estimates, and these estimates become more uncertain as

---

[15]For safety, lenders desire to hold a diversified portfolio of loans. Thus, they are reluctant to lend a significant percentage of their funds, say more than 2 percent, to any one borrower.

Figure 7-3
Marginal Cost of Capital Schedule for Firm M
Using Retained Earnings, New Common Stock, and
Higher-Cost Debt

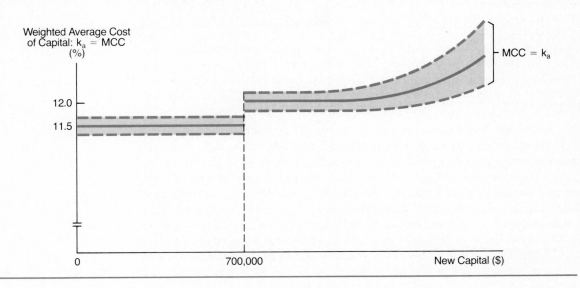

the firm requires more and more capital, and thus the band widens as new capital increases.

Appendix 7B provides a more detailed look at the MCC schedule, while in Chapter 10 we use the MCC schedule to help determine the optimal level of new investment.

Other Issues in the Cost of Capital

Thus far in the chapter, we have abstracted from several factors which affect the cost of capital. The most important of these—the riskiness inherent in the new assets which will be acquired with the new capital—will be discussed in Chapter 10. The other factors are discussed in the following sections. Some of the issues are complex and controversial, and we raise more questions than we answer. Still, the material does have important practical implications, so anyone concerned with financial management should be aware of the issues and understand how they impact the practical, rule-of-thumb procedures that financial managers are necessarily forced to follow.

The Effects of Personal Taxes

As we previously discussed, whenever a firm retains a portion of its net income rather than pays it out in dividends, there is an "opportunity cost" to the stockholders. If the firm in question has a required rate of return of 12 percent on its stock (that is, $k_s = 12\%$), then presumably its shareholders could have invested the retained earnings, had they been paid out in dividends, in other firms of similar risk and received a 12 percent return. Assuming that two conditions exist, this 12 percent is the opportunity cost of retained earnings. The two conditions are (1) that the stockholders pay no income tax on dividends, and (2) that they incur no brokerage costs when they reinvest dividends. However, to the extent that these assumptions are not met, the opportunity cost of retained earnings, and hence the cost of capital from retained earnings, might be lower than the required rate of return, k_s. The following example illustrates this point.

The ABC Company has net earnings of $1 million; all of its stockholders are in the 30 percent marginal tax bracket; and all of them are net savers as opposed to people who are living on investment income. Management estimates that under present conditions, the stockholders' required rate of return is $k_s = 12\%$; that is, stockholders could invest in firms of similar risk and receive a return of 12 percent. On earnings paid out as dividends, the recipients will pay income taxes, then reinvest the proceeds in the stock of the same or similar firms, and obtain a 12 percent return on these stocks. Brokerage costs incurred to reinvest dividends will average 3 percent of the newly purchased stocks. What rate of return must be earned *internally* to provide ABC's stockholders with incremental earnings equal to what they would receive *externally*?

1. $\dfrac{\text{After-tax proceeds}}{\text{of dividend payment}}$ = $1,000,000 − Personal taxes

   = $1,000,000 − $300,000
   = $700,000.

2. $\dfrac{\text{Net investment}}{\text{after brokerage costs}}$ = $700,000 − Brokerage costs

   = $700,000 − $21,000
   = $679,000.

3. Earnings on new investment = $(679,000)(0.12) = \$81,480$.

4. Internal rate of return, k_r, necessary to provide stockholders with incremental income of $81,480:

$$\$81,480 = (\$1,000,000)(k_r)$$
$$k_r = 0.08148 = 8.148\%.$$

Therefore, if the firm were able to earn 8.148 percent on retained earnings, its stockholders would be as well off as they would be if all earnings were paid out and then reinvested to yield 12 percent. Thus, the internal opportunity cost, or the required rate of return on retention-financed investments, k_r, is less than the stockholders' required rate of return, k_s. We may calculate k_r as follows:

$$k_r = k_s(1 − T)(1 − B). \qquad \text{(7-11)}$$

Here k_r is the required return on retention-financed investments, k_s is the stockholders' required rate of return, T is the stockholders' marginal tax rate, and B represents brokerage cost in decimal form. In the example being considered,

$$k_r = (0.12)(0.7)(0.97) = 0.08148, \text{ or } 8.148\%.$$

Thus, Equation 7-11 gives the same value for k_r that we developed earlier.

This procedure, while it appears reasonable at first glance, actually understates to some extent the true cost of retained earnings. This point is developed in the two following subsections.

Publicly Held Companies. Publicly owned firms can invest in their own shares by buying them in the open market. (This process is discussed in detail in Chapter 13.) If the firm does repurchase its shares in the marketplace, it would presumably earn a return of $k_s = 12\%$ on funds so invested. Thus, assuming it can buy back its shares at the current market price, the firm should not make a physical asset investment that has a risk-adjusted expected equity return of less than k_s.

Most firms do have the opportunity to invest in their own shares. As we shall see in Chapter 13, open market stock repurchases are fairly common for firms whose internal investment opportunities are limited. Indeed, the only type of company that might not have the opportunity to invest in its stock, and hence the only type of company for which Equation 7-11 would be applicable, is a *closely held firm*. For such firms, a major repurchase could be deemed by the IRS to be an attempt on the part of the controlling stockholders to avoid personal income taxes, and hence the firm could be subject to severe penalties. Thus, our major conclusion is this: *Equation 7-11 is not applicable for any publicly owned firm. Such firms should never invest internally to earn risk-adjusted equity returns of less than k_s, because they have the opportunity to earn k_s on stock repurchases.*

Closely Held Companies. The procedure set forth in Equation 7-11 is approximately correct for closely held firms which do not, for tax reasons, have an opportunity to repurchase their stock. However, Equation 7-11 still understates the correct rate of return to some extent. Note that retaining earnings will give rise to an increase in the value of the firm's stock, and if investors sell it, their profits will be subject to a capital gains tax. The capital gains tax rate is lower than the rate applicable to dividends, and since this tax is deferred, it has a lower present value. Nevertheless, some capital gains tax will generally be paid on retained earnings at some future point, and this fact is not reflected in Equation 7-11. Therefore, Equation 7-11 understates to some extent the correct cost of retained earnings.

Two limiting cases can be developed. First, it can be assumed that the stockholders never sell the stock, passing it on to their heirs, who do the same, *ad infinitum*. In this case—which might be appropriate for a closely held firm—the procedures outlined in Equation 7-11 would be correct. Alternatively, we could assume that investors will hold the stock for the minimum holding period (6 months) to receive long-term capital gains tax treatment, then sell the stock (in a privately arranged transaction, because the stock is not publicly traded), and pay a tax at 40 percent of their normal tax rate. In this case, the value of T for the example would be $0.4(30\%) = 12\%$, and the resultant cost of retained earnings would be computed to be

$$k_r = k_s(1 - T)(1 - B) = 0.12(0.88)(0.97) = 0.102, \text{ or } 10.2\%.$$

The correct figure probably lies somewhere between the 8.1 and the 10.2 percent, but there is no way of knowing exactly where without having information on the stockholders' tax brackets, time horizons, and needs for cash income.[16]

Cost of Depreciation-Generated Funds

The very first increment of internal funds used to finance any year's new asset investment, or capital budget, is depreciation-generated funds. In their statements of sources and uses of funds, corporations generally show depreciation charges to be one of the most important, if not the most important, source of funds.[17] Of course, depreciation is an allow-

---

[16]The following equation for determining a tax-and-brokerage adjusted cost of retained earnings which does take account of the capital gains tax was developed by Wilbur Lewellen:

$$k_r = k_s \left[\frac{(1 - B)(1 - T_d)}{(1 - T_g)} \right]. \tag{7-11a}$$

Here T_d is the personal tax on dividend income and T_g is the tax on capital gains. Using our illustrative values, we find k_r as follows:

$$k_r = 12\% \left[\frac{(0.97)(0.7)}{0.88} \right] = 12\%(0.7716) = 9.3\%.$$

Thus, this estimate of k_r lies between our extreme cases, 8.1 and 10.2 percent.

[17]Depreciation is a noncash charge. To illustrate, suppose a company reports the following income statement:

Sales		$100
Costs:	Operating	60
	Depreciation	20
Taxable income		20
Taxes (50%)		10
Net income		$ 10

If sales are all collected during the year, and all costs except depreciation must be paid in cash during the year, then cash flow from operations available for dividends or reinvestment will be $30:

$$\text{Cash flow} = \text{Net income} + \text{Depreciation} = \$10 + \$20 = \$30.$$

This point is discussed in greater depth in Chapter 9.

ance for the annual reduction in value of a firm's fixed assets. Thus, for an on-going firm, depreciation-generated funds should be used to replace worn-out and obsolete assets.

For capital budgeting purposes, should depreciation be considered "free" capital; should it be ignored completely; or should a charge be assessed against it? *The answer is that a charge should indeed be assessed against these funds, and this cost is approximately equal to the average cost of capital before outside equity is used.* The reasoning here is that the firm could, if it so desired, distribute the depreciation-generated funds to its stockholders and creditors, the parties who financed the assets in the first place, so these funds definitely have an opportunity cost. For example, suppose a firm has $10 million of depreciation-generated funds available. Its equity has a cost of $k_s = 15\%$, and its debt has an after-tax cost of $k_d(1 - T) = 12\%(1 - T) = 12\%(0.54) = 6.48\%$. If it has a 50-50 capital structure, then its weighted average cost of capital is $k_a = 0.5(6.48\%) + 0.5(15\%) = 10.74\%$.

Now suppose the firm has no projects available to it, not even projects which replace worn-out equipment, that return 10.74 percent or more. It obviously should not raise new capital, and it should not even retain any earnings for internal investment, because stockholders would be better off receiving the earnings as dividends and investing them themselves at $k_s = 15\%$, or having the company repurchase its stock. Going on, this firm should not even invest its depreciation-generated $10 million. If it did keep and invest this money, it would receive a return of less than 10.74 percent. If it distributed the $10 million to its investors, with $5 million going to stockholders and $5 million to bondholders so as to maintain the target capital structure, then the stockholders could buy the stock of similar-risk companies and earn 15 percent on their money. (Such a distribution would, under certain conditions, be a return of capital, and hence not taxable. If the distribution were taxable, then the company could repurchase its shares rather than make a direct distribution to stockholders.) *The conclusion from all this is that depreciation has a cost which is approximately equal to the weighted average cost of capital before external equity is used.* This cost is based on the opportunity cost to existing investors rather than the required rate of return of new investors, but opportunity costs are just as real as other costs.

Depreciation also affects the marginal cost of capital schedule, and in a very significant way. The marginal cost of capital increases when retained earnings are exhausted and the firm must begin to use new equity financing. In our earlier Firm M example, we saw that this would occur when $700,000 of new capital is raised. However, if depreciation is considered to be a source of funds available for capital budgeting purposes, as it should be, then the retention-based marginal cost of capital of 11.5 percent would be extended out by the amount of the depreciation. Assume that Firm M's depreciation expense is expected to be $500,000. As we just saw, the cost of this $500,000 is the weighted average cost of capital. Therefore, Firm M's marginal cost of capital would be 11.5 percent until $700,000 + $500,000 = $1.2 million of capital had been raised (depreciation and retained earnings plus some external debt and preferred stock). After $1.2 million, the MCC would increase from 11.5 to 12.0 percent.

What difference does all this make, and should we be concerned with a cost of capital schedule that includes or excludes depreciation? If we were concerned with the effects of *net increases* in assets, then the schedule without depreciation would be appropriate. *However, we are normally concerned with gross capital expenditures—replacement as well as expansion investments—so the schedule that includes depreciation is the relevant one.*

Thus far, we have discussed the major sources of funds for most firms. However, we have not been exhaustive. In addition to the sources mentioned, some firms finance a significant portion of their assets through leasing arrangements, or by selling securities with warrants or that are convertible into common stock. The cost of these sources will be discussed later in the book. If a company uses any of these sources to a significant extent and on a permanent basis, they should be incorporated into its weighted average cost of capital.

Cost of Other Sources

Throughout this chapter, we incorporated flotation costs in the component costs of capital. We ignored debt flotation costs on the grounds that they were relatively small, but we explicitly included flotation costs when we estimated the costs of preferred stock and new common stock. The inclusion of flotation costs raises component costs, and hence increases the firm's weighted average cost of capital, MCC = k_a.

An alternate approach to handling flotation costs is to ignore such costs when estimating the firm's MCC = k_a. Then, in the capital budgeting process, the dollar flotation costs are allocated to the firm's new projects, and hence increase project costs rather than capital costs. Although the alternative approach has some theoretical superiority, it is very difficult to implement in practice, and hence not generally used by firms today.[18]

Alternative Approach to Handling Flotation Costs

This chapter showed how a firm's *weighted average cost of capital* is developed. We began by discussing the process of estimating the cost of each capital structure component. The *cost of debt* is simply $k_d(1 - T)$. The *cost of preferred stock* is $k_p = D_p/P_n$. The first increment of *common equity* is raised by *retaining*

Summary

---

[18]For a more complete discussion of the alternative approach, see Carl M. Hubbard, "Flotation Costs in Capital Budgeting: A Note on the Tax Effect," *Financial Management*, Summer 1984, 38-40; and John P. Ezzell and R. Burr Porter, "Flotation Costs and the Weighted Average Cost of Capital," *Journal of Financial and Quantitative Analysis*, September 1976, 403-413.

earnings whose cost, k_s, may be estimated in one of three ways: (1) the CAPM equation, $k_s = R_F + b(k_M - R_F)$; (2) the dividend growth model, $k_s = D_1/P_0 + g$ for a constant growth stock; or (3) the addition of a risk premium of 1.0 to 4.5 percentage points to the firm's cost of long-term debt. Once retained earnings have been exhausted, the firm must sell new common stock, or *external equity*, whose cost is $k_e = D_1/[P_0(1 - F)] + g$ in the case of a constant growth stock.

The next task is to combine the component costs to form a *weighted average cost of capital, k_a*. The weights used to develop k_a should be based on the firm's target capital structure. If these weights are used, the stock price will be maximized and the cost of capital will simultaneously be minimized.

Capital typically has a higher cost if the firm expands beyond certain limits. This means that the *marginal cost of capital (MCC)* curve turns up beyond some point. In this chapter, we noted that the firm's cost of capital increases when the firm exhausts its retained earnings and must issue new common stock. Further, the cost of capital for most firms continues to rise as additional capital is required.

Finally, we discussed the implications of personal income taxes and depreciation. We concluded that personal income taxes may be ignored with regard to estimating the cost of capital for publicly owned firms, although these taxes lower somewhat the cost of retained earnings, k_s, for privately held companies whose owners are in positive tax brackets. We also concluded (1) that depreciation has a cost—an opportunity cost—which is equal to the weighted average cost of capital based on retained earnings (rather than external equity), and (2) that the MCC schedule should be shifted out, or to the right, in Figure 7-3, by the amount of depreciation reported for the year.

Questions

7-1   Define each of the following terms:
   a. Weighted average cost of capital, k_a
   b. After-tax cost of debt, $k_d(1 - T)$
   c. Cost of preferred stock, k_p
   d. Cost of retained earnings, k_s
   e. Cost of new common equity, k_e
   f. Flotation cost, F
   g. Target capital structure
   h. Marginal cost of capital, MCC = k_a
   i. MCC schedule; break, or jump, in the MCC schedule; break point
   j. Cost of depreciation-generated funds

7-2   In what sense is the marginal cost of capital an average cost?

7-3   How would each of the following affect a firm's cost of debt, $k_d(1 - T)$; its cost of equity, k_s; and its average cost of capital, WACC = k_a? Indicate by a plus (+), a minus (−), or a zero (0) if the factor would raise, lower, or have an indeterminate effect on the items in question. Assume other things are held constant. Be prepared to justify your answer, but recognize that several of the parts probably have no single correct answer; these questions are designed to stimulate thought and discussion.

	Effect on		
	$k_d(1 - T)$	k_s	k_a
a. The corporate tax rate is lowered.	_____	_____	_____
b. The Federal Reserve tightens credit.	_____	_____	_____
c. The firm uses more debt.	_____	_____	_____
d. The dividend payout ratio is increased.	_____	_____	_____
e. The firm doubles the amount of capital it raises during the year.	_____	_____	_____
f. The firm expands into a risky new area.	_____	_____	_____
g. The firm merges with another firm whose earnings are countercyclical to those of the first firm and to the stock market.	_____	_____	_____
h. The stock market falls drastically, and our firm's stock price falls along with the rest.	_____	_____	_____
i. Investors become more risk averse.	_____	_____	_____
j. The firm is an electric utility with a large investment in nuclear plants. Several states propose a ban on nuclear power generation.	_____	_____	_____

Self-Test Problem

ST-1 Laser Communications, Inc. (LCI), has the following capital structure, which it considers to be optimal:

Debt	25%
Preferred stock	15
Common stock	60
Total capital	100%

LCI's net income expected this year is $17,142.86; its established dividend payout ratio is 30 percent; its tax rate is 40 percent; and investors expect earnings and dividends to grow at a constant rate of 9 percent in the future. LCI paid a dividend of $3.60 per share last year (D_0), and its stock currently sells at a price of $60 per share. Treasury bonds yield 11 percent; an average stock has a 14 percent expected rate of return; and LCI's beta is 1.51. These terms would apply to new security offerings:

Common: New common stock would have a flotation cost of 10 percent.

Preferred: New preferred could be sold to the public at a price of $100 per share, with a dividend of $11. Flotation costs of $5 per share would be incurred.

Debt: Debt could be sold at an interest rate of 12 percent.

a. Find the component cost of debt, preferred stock, retained earnings, and new common stock.

b. How much new capital can be raised before LCI must sell new equity? (In other words, find the retained earnings break point.)
c. What is the MCC when LCI meets its equity requirement with retained earnings? With new common stock?
d. Construct a graph showing LCI's MCC schedule.

Problems   7-1   Calculate the after-tax cost of debt under each of the following conditions:
a. Interest rate, 10 percent; tax rate, 0 percent.
b. Interest rate, 10 percent; tax rate, 40 percent.
c. Interest rate, 10 percent; tax rate, 60 percent.

7-2   XYZ Company's last dividend per share was $1; that is, $D_0 = \$1$. The stock sells for $20 per share. The expected growth rate is a constant 5 percent. Calculate XYZ's cost of retained earnings.

7-3   On January 1, the total market value of the Garrett Company was $60 million. During the year, the company plans to raise and invest $30 million in net new projects. The firm's present market value capital structure, shown below, is considered to be optimal. Assume that there is no short-term debt.

Debt	$30,000,000
Common equity	30,000,000
Total capital	$60,000,000

New bonds will have an 8 percent coupon rate, and they will be sold at par. Common stock, currently selling at $30 a share, can be sold to net the company $27 a share. Stockholders' required rate of return is estimated to be 12 percent, consisting of a dividend yield of 4 percent and an expected constant growth rate of 8 percent. (The next expected dividend is $1.20, so $1.20/$30 = 4%.) Retained earnings for the year are estimated to be $3 million. The marginal corporate tax rate is 40 percent.
a. To maintain the present capital structure, how much of the new investment must be financed by common equity?
b. How much of the new common equity funds needed must be generated internally? Externally?
c. Calculate the cost of each of the common equity components.
d. At what level of capital expenditures will k_a = WACC increase?
e. Calculate k_a using (1) the cost of retained earnings, and (2) the cost of new equity.

7-4   The following tabulation gives earnings per share figures for Dayton Manufacturing during the preceding 10 years. The firm's common stock, 140,000 shares outstanding, is now selling for $50 a share, and the expected dividend for the current year (1985) is 50 percent of EPS for the year. Investors expect past trends to continue, so g may be based on the historic earnings growth rate.

Year	EPS
1975	$2.00
1976	2.16
1977	2.33
1978	2.52
1979	2.72
1980	2.94
1981	3.18
1982	3.43
1983	3.70
1984	4.00

The current interest rate on new debt is 8 percent. The firm's marginal tax rate is 40 percent. The firm's market value capital structure, considered to be optimal, is as follows:

Debt	$ 3,000,000
Common equity	7,000,000
Total capital	$10,000,000

a. Calculate the after-tax cost of new debt and of common equity, assuming new equity comes only from retained earnings. Calculate the cost of equity assuming constant growth; that is, $k_s = D_1/P_0 + g = k_s$.
b. Find the marginal cost of capital, again assuming no new common stock is sold.
c. How much can be spent for net new capital investments before external equity must be sold?
d. What is the marginal cost of capital beyond the retained earnings break point if new common stock can be sold to the public at $50 a share to net the firm $45 a share? The cost of debt is constant.

7-5   Suppose the Cromwell Company has this *book value* balance sheet:

Current assets	$30,000,000	Current liabilities	$10,000,000
Fixed assets	50,000,000	Long-term debt	30,000,000
		Common equity:	
		Common stock	
		(1 million shares)	1,000,000
		Retained earnings	39,000,000
Total assets	$80,000,000	Total claims	$80,000,000

The current liabilities consist entirely of notes payable to banks, and the interest rate on this debt is 10 percent, the same as the rate on new bank loans. The long-term debt consists of 30,000 bonds, each of which has a par value of $1,000, carries a coupon interest rate of 6 percent, and matures in 20 years. The going rate of interest on new long-term debt, k_d, is 10 percent, and this is the present yield-to-maturity on the bonds. The common stock sells at a price of $60 per share. Calculate Cromwell's market value capital structure.

7-6   The Brown Tractor Company's EPS in 1984 was $2.00. EPS in 1979 was $1.3612. The company pays out 40 percent of its earnings as dividends, and the stock currently sells for $21.60. The company expects earnings of $10 million in 1985. Its optimal market value debt/assets ratio is 60 percent, and the firm has no preferred stock outstanding.
   a. Calculate the growth rate in earnings.
   b. Calculate the dividend per share expected in 1985. Assume that the growth rate calculated in Part a will continue.
   c. What is the cost of retained earnings, k_s?
   d. What amount of retained earnings is expected in 1985?
   e. At what amount of total financing will the cost of equity increase?
   f. The sale of new stock would net the company $18.36 per share. What is Brown's percentage flotation cost, F? What is the cost of new common stock, k_e?

Solution to Self-Test Problem   ST-1

   a. *Cost of debt*:

$$k_d(1 - T) = 12\%(1 - 0.40) = 12\%(0.60) = 7.20\%.$$

   Cost of preferred stock:

$$k_p = \frac{D}{P_n} = \frac{\$11}{\$100 - \$5} = \frac{\$11}{\$95} = 11.58\%.$$

   Cost of retained earnings:

$$k_s = \frac{D_1}{P_0} + g = \frac{D_0(1 + g)}{P_0} + g$$

$$= \frac{\$3.60(1.09)}{\$60} + 0.09$$

$$= 0.0654 + 0.09 = 0.1554 = 15.54\%.$$

   Cost of new common stock:

$$k_e = \frac{D_1}{P_0(1.0 - F)} + g = \frac{\$3.924}{\$60(0.9)} + 9\% = 16.27\%.$$

   b. LCI's forecasted retained earnings are $17,142.86(1 - 0.30) = $12,000. Thus, the retained earnings break point, BP_{RE}, is $20,000:

$$BP_{RE} = \frac{RE}{\text{Equity fraction}} = \frac{\$12,000}{0.60} = \$20,000.$$

   c. *MCC using retained earnings*:

$$\begin{aligned}
MCC_1 = k_a &= w_d k_d (1 - T) + w_p k_p + w_s k_s \\
&= 0.25(7.2\%) + 0.15(11.58\%) + 0.60(15.54\%) \\
&= 1.80\% + 1.74\% + 9.32\% = 12.86\%.
\end{aligned}$$

MCC using new common stock:

$$MCC_2 = k_a = 1.80\% + 1.74\% + 0.60(16.27\%) = 13.30\%.$$

d. See the following graph:

MCC Schedule for LCI

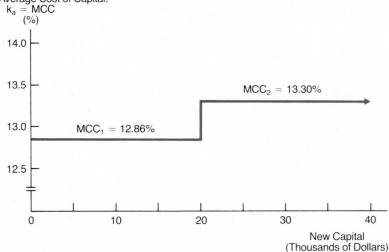

The following articles provide some valuable insights into the CAPM approach to estimating the cost of equity:

Beaver, William H., Paul Kettler, and Myron Scholes, "The Association between Market Determined and Accounting Determined Risk Measures," *Accounting Review*, October 1970, 654-682.

Bowman, Robert G., "The Theoretical Relationship between Systematic Risk and Financial (Accounting) Variables," *Journal of Finance*, June 1979, 617-630.

Chen, Carl R., "Time-Series Analysis of Beta Stationarity and Its Determinants: A Case of Public Utilities," *Financial Management*, Autumn 1982, 64-70.

Cooley, Philip L., "A Review of the Use of Beta in Regulatory Proceedings," *Financial Management*, Winter 1981, 75-81.

The weighted average cost of capital as described in this chapter is widely used in both industry and academic circles. It has been criticized on several counts, but to date it has withstood the challenges. See the following articles:

Arditti, Fred D., and Haim Levy, "The Weighted Average Cost of Capital as a Cutoff Rate: A Critical Examination of the Classical Textbook Weighted Average," *Financial Management*, Fall 1977, 24-34.

Selected Additional References and Cases

Beranek, William, "The Weighted Average Cost of Capital and Shareholder Wealth Maximization," *Journal of Financial and Quantitative Analysis*, March 1977, 17-32.

Boudreaux, Kenneth J., and Hugh W. Long; John R. Ezzell and R. Burr Porter; Moshe Ben Horim; and Alan C. Shapiro, "The Weighted Average Cost of Capital: A Discussion," *Financial Management*, Summer 1979, 7-23.

Reilly, Raymond R., and William E. Wacker, "On the Weighted Average Cost of Capital," *Journal of Financial and Quantitative Analysis*, January 1973, 123-126.

Some other works that are relevant include the following:

Alberts, W. W., and Stephen H. Archer, "Some Evidence on the Effect of Company Size on the Cost of Equity Capital," *Journal of Financial and Quantitative Analysis*, March 1973, 229-242.

Chen, Andrew, "Recent Developments in the Cost of Debt Capital," *Journal of Finance*, June 1978, 863-883.

Myers, Stewart C., "Interactions of Corporate Financing and Investments Decisions—Implications for Capital Budgeting," *Journal of Finance*, March 1974, 1-25.

Nantell, Timothy J., and C. Robert Carlson, "The Cost of Capital as a Weighted Average," *Journal of Finance*, December 1975, 1343-1355.

For some insights into the cost of capital techniques used by major firms, see

Gitman, Lawrence J., and Vincent A. Mercurio, "Cost of Capital Techniques Used by Major U.S. Firms: Survey and Analysis of Fortune's 1000," *Financial Management*, Winter 1982, 21-29.

The following cases focus on the estimation of a firm's cost of capital:

"American Telephone & Telegraph," which illustrates the estimation of AT&T's cost of capital in the summer of 1983. Harrington, Diana, *Case Studies in Financial Decision Making* (Hinsdale, Ill.: Dryden, 1985).

"Communications Satellite Corporation," which examines the problems in estimating equity costs when new technology is involved. Available from HBS Case Services, Cambridge, Mass.

Estimating the Cost of
Equity in Practice

In Chapter 7, we presented three methods which can be used to estimate the cost of retained earnings, k_s: (1) the Capital Asset Pricing Model (CAPM) approach, (2) the Discounted Cash Flow (DCF) approach, and (3) the bond yield plus risk premium approach. Each of these methods requires the estimation of model parameters. The CAPM approach requires the estimation of R_F, k_M, and beta; the DCF approach requires that g be estimated; and the risk premium plus bond yield approach requires that the risk premium be estimated.

Unfortunately, none of these parameters can be easily estimated. In this appendix, we first discuss the difficulties involved in using the three approaches to estimate k_s and then suggest some guidelines for estimating k_s in practice.

Under the CAPM, we assume that common stockholders view only market risk as being relevant. Thus, the risk premium that investors demand is assumed to be based solely on the stock's beta coefficient as set forth in the Security Market Line (SML) equation:

The CAPM Approach

$$k_s = R_F + b_i(k_M - R_F).$$

Given an estimate of (1) the risk-free rate, R_F, (2) the beta of the firm's stock, b_i, and (3) the required rate of return on the market, k_M, we could estimate the required rate of return on the firm's stock, k_s. This required return would then be used as an estimate of the cost of retained earnings to the firm.

The starting point for the CAPM cost of equity estimate is R_F, the risk-free rate. There is really no such thing in the U.S. economy as a riskless asset. Treasury securities are essentially free of default risk, but long-term T-bonds are subject to capital losses if interest rates rise, while short-term T-bills are

Estimating the Risk-Free Rate

not riskless to an investor with a long time horizon because the rate paid on T-bills varies over time. Thus, the only riskless asset to a long-term investor would be a long-term Treasury security that is indexed to the inflation rate, but no such security exists in the United States.

Since we cannot in practice find a truly riskless rate upon which to base the CAPM, what rate should we use? Our preference—and this preference is shared by most practitioners—is to use the rate on long-term Treasury bonds. Our reasons follow:

1. Capital market rates include a pure rate (generally thought to vary from 2 to 4 percent) plus a premium for expected inflation. This premium reflects the inflation rate expected over the life of the asset, be it 30 days or 30 years. The rate of inflation is likely to be relatively high during booms and low during recessions. Therefore, during booms T-bill rates tend to be high to reflect the high current inflation rate, while in recessions T-bill rates are generally low. T-bond rates, on the other hand, reflect expected inflation rates over a long period. Therefore, during the recession of early 1983, when the current inflation rate was only about 4 percent, T-bills yielded about 7 percent (a 3 percent real rate plus a 4 percent premium for current year inflation), but T-bond yields, which reflected the expectation of a return to an inflation rate of 7 to 8 percent once the recession ended, yielded about 11 percent.

2. Common stocks are long-term securities, and while a particular stockholder may not have a long investment horizon, the majority of stockholders do invest on a long-term basis. Therefore, it seems more reasonable to think that stocks would embody long-term inflation expectations similar to those embodied in bonds rather than the short-term inflation expectations in bills. On this account, the cost of equity should be more highly correlated with T-bond rates than with T-bill rates.

3. Treasury bill rates are subject to more random disturbances than are Treasury bonds rates. For example, bills are used by the Federal Reserve System to control the money supply, and bills are also used by foreign governments, firms, and individuals as a temporary safe-house for money. Thus, if the Fed decides to stimulate the economy, it drives down the bill rate, and the same thing happens if trouble erupts somewhere in the world and money flows into the United States seeking a temporary haven. T-bond rates are also influenced by Fed actions and by international money flows, but not to the same extent as T-bill rates. Therefore, T-bill rates are more volatile than T-bond rates and, we think, more volatile than k_s.

4. We have seen the CAPM used to estimate a particular firm's cost of equity over time. When T-bill rates were low, as in 1977 (see Figure 3-3), the CAPM cost of equity estimate was about 11 percent. When T-bill rates shot up in 1979 and 1980, the CAPM estimate more than doubled, to 23 percent. The company's bond yields, meanwhile, only rose from 8 to 10 percent. Neither we nor the company's management believed that the cost of equity rose by 12 full percentage points while the cost of long-term debt was only rising by 2 percentage points. CAPM estimates based on T-bond yields produced much more reasonable results.

In view of the preceding discussion, it is our view that common equity costs are more logically related to Treasury bond rates than to T-bill rates. This

Table 7A-1
I&S Risk Premiums

Risk Premium	Arithmetic Mean	Standard Deviation
Stocks over T-bills	8.3%	22.0%
Stocks over T-bonds	8.3	a
Stocks over corporate bonds	7.7	a

[a]I&S did not report a standard deviation for risk premiums of stocks over T-bonds and corporate bonds. However, we made several estimates and concluded that its magnitude is comparable to that of the stocks-over-T-bills risk premium.

leads us to favor T-bonds as the base rate, or R_F, in a CAPM cost of equity analysis. T-bond rates can be found in *The Wall Street Journal* or the *Federal Reserve Bulletin*. Generally, we use the yield on a 20-year T-bond as the proxy for the risk-free rate. In May 1983, this rate was 10.7 percent. Thus, we would use this as our estimate for R_F in May 1983 CAPM cost of equity estimates.

Estimating the Market Risk Premium, RP_M

Several methodologies are available for estimating the market risk premium, $RP_M = k_M - R_F$. None of them is obviously best, so choosing the proper value for RP_M is a problem. The methodologies break down into two major subgroups: (1) those based on *ex post*, or historic, returns and (2) those based on *ex ante*, or forward-looking, returns.

Ex Post Risk Premiums. The most thorough and widely publicized ex post risk premium study is one by Ibbotson and Sinquefield (I&S), who examined data on the stocks of most of the larger companies over the period 1926-1981.[1] I&S found the average annual rates of return on stocks, T-bills, T-bonds, and a set of high-grade corporate bonds; Table 7A-1 summarizes their study. By subtracting the historic, or realized, returns on the various debt securities from the historic realized return on stocks, I&S developed historic risk premiums of stocks over T-bills, T-bonds, and corporate bonds.

I&S found the average risk premium of both stocks over T-bills and stocks over T-bonds to be 8.3 percent.[2] However, these premiums have large standard deviations, so one must use them with caution. Also, it should be noted that the choice of the beginning and ending periods can have a major impact on the calculated risk premiums. I&S used the longest period available to them, but had their data began a few years earlier or later, or ended earlier, their results would have been seriously affected. Indeed, over many periods their data would indicate *negative* risk premiums, which would lead to the conclusion that Treasury securities have a higher required return than common stocks. Again, this suggests that historic risk premiums should be

[1]See Roger G. Ibbotson and Rex A. Sinquefield, *Stocks, Bonds, Bills, and Inflation: The Past and the Future* (Charlottesville, Va.: Financial Analysts Research Foundation, 1982).

[2]I&S report both arithmetic and geometric average risk premiums. Since the CAPM assumes that investors operate on a one-period time horizon, the arithmetic average, which is an average of single-period returns, should logically be used in cost of equity studies.

approached with caution. As one businessman muttered after listening to a professor give a lecture on the CAPM, "Beware of academicians bearing gifts!"

Ex Ante Risk Premiums. Ibbotson and Sinquefield's ex post approach to risk premiums assumes that investors expect future results, on average, to equal past results. However, results vary depending on the period selected, and, in any event, investors in the 1980s probably expect results in the future to be different from those achieved during the Great Depression of the 1930s, the World War II of the 1940s, and the peaceful years of the 1950s, all of which had relatively little inflation. The highly questionable assumption that future expectations are equal to past realizations, together with the sometimes nonsensical results obtained in historic risk premium studies, have led to a search for ex ante risk premiums.

The most fruitful approach to ex ante premiums uses the discounted cash flow (DCF) model to determine the expected market rate of return. In other words, use DCF to develop a current estimate of $\hat{k}_M = k_M$; then find $RP_M = k_M - R_F$; and finally use this estimate of RP_M in the CAPM model. Recognize that, in equilibrium, the expected rate of return on the market is also its required rate of return. Thus, if we can estimate $\hat{k}_M$, we also have an estimate of k_M:

$$\hat{k}_M = \frac{D_1}{P_0} + g = R_F + RP_M = k_M.$$

Since D_1 for the market, say the S&P 500, can be predicted quite accurately, and since the current market value of the index is known, the major task is to estimate g, the average long-term growth rate of the market index. Even here, however, the estimation task is simplified, because one can reasonably assume a constant long-term growth rate for a market proxy such as the S&P 500, whereas the constant growth assumption is often not appropriate for a single stock.

Financial services companies such as Merrill Lynch publish, on a regular basis, a forecast based on DCF methodology for the expected rate of return on the market, $\hat{k}_M$. For example, Merrill Lynch puts out such a forecast in its bimonthly publication *Quantitative Analysis*. One can subtract the current T-bond rate from such a market forecast to obtain an estimate of the current market risk premium, RP_M. To illustrate, Merrill Lynch's reported expected return on the market in May 1983 was 14.7 percent. The T-bond rate at the time was 10.7 percent. Thus, Merrill Lynch's implied market risk premium over T-bonds was 4.0 percent.

Two potential problems arise when we attempt to use data from organizations such as Merrill Lynch. First, what we really want is *investors'* expectations, and not those of security analysts. However, this is probably not a major problem, since several studies have proved beyond much doubt that investors, on average, do form their own expectations on the basis of professional analysts' forecasts. The second problem is that there are a number of investments organizations besides Merrill Lynch, and at any given time their forecasts of future market returns are generally somewhat different. This suggests that it would be most appropriate to obtain a number of forecasts of $\hat{k}_M$, to develop estimates of the market risk premium on the basis of each of them, and then to average these RP_M values to obtain an average RP_M for use in the CAPM. A service (Institutional Brokers Estimate Service, or IBES) now exists which publishes data on the forecasts of essentially all widely followed analysts, so one can use the IBES growth rate forecasts to avoid potential bias from the use of only one organization's analysts. However, we have followed the forecasts of several of the larger organizations over a period of several years, and we have rarely found them to differ by more than ±0.3 percentage points from one another. Therefore, for present purposes, the Merrill Lynch $k_M = 14.7\%$ and $RP_M = 4.0\%$ may be considered "reasonable."

Risk premiums are not stable, so in CAPM estimates of the cost of equity it is essential to use current estimates of RP_M. Further, neither logic nor empirical data support the use of historic, or ex post, premia. Therefore, when we do cost of capital studies, we obtain estimates of $\hat{k}_M$ as published by a number of brokerage houses and then use the average $\hat{k}_M$ as the basis for $RP_M = k_M - R_F$.

Estimating Beta

The last parameter needed for a CAPM cost of equity estimate is the beta coefficient. Recall from Chapter 6 that a stock's beta is a measure of its volatility relative to that of an average stock, and that betas are generally calculated by running a linear regression between past returns on the stock in question and past returns on some market index. We will define betas developed in this manner as *historic betas*. A stock is then judged to have more, less, or the same market risk as an average stock depending on whether its historic beta is greater than, less than, or equal to 1.0.

Note, however, that historic betas show how risky a stock was *in the past*, whereas investors are interested in *future* risk. It may be that a given company appeared to be quite safe in the past, but that things have changed, and its future risk is judged to be higher than its past risk, or vice versa. AT&T is a good example. Historically, AT&T has been among the bluest of the blue chips, but in 1984 investors recognized that on January 1, 1984, the Bell System was broken up and simultaneously subjected to far more intense competition than it had ever faced in the past. Chrysler, on the other hand, was practically bankrupt during the late 1970s and early 1980s, but by 1984 it was earning record profits, and it appeared to be quite healthy. Therefore, one would think that Chrysler's risk had declined while AT&T's had increased.

Now consider the use of beta as a measure of a company's risk. If we use an historic beta in a CAPM framework to measure the firm's cost of equity, we are implicitly assuming that its future risk is the same as its past risk. This would be a troublesome assumption for a company like Chrysler or AT&T in 1984. But what about most companies in most years—as a general rule, is future risk sufficiently similar to past risk to warrant the use of historic betas in a CAPM framework? For individual firms, past risk is *not* a good predictor of future risk, and historic betas of individual firms are not very stable.

Since historic betas are not very good predictors of future risk, researchers have sought ways to improve them. This has led to the development of two different types of betas: (1) *adjusted historic betas* and (2) *fundamental betas*. Adjusted betas grew largely out of the work of Marshall E. Blume, who showed that true betas tend to move toward 1.0 over time.[3] One begins with a firm's pure historic statistical beta, makes an adjustment for the expected future movement toward 1.0, and produces an adjusted beta which will, on average, be a better predictor of the future beta than would the unadjusted historic beta. The adjustment process involves some complex statistics, so we shall not cover it here.

Other researchers have extended the adjustment process to include such fundamental risk variables as financial leverage, sales volatility, and the like. The end product here is a *fundamental beta*.[4] These betas are constantly adjusted to reflect changes in a firm's operations and capital structure, whereas with historic betas (including adjusted ones) such changes might not be reflected until several years after the company's "true" beta had changed.

Adjusted historic betas are obviously heavily dependent on unadjusted betas, and so are fundamental betas as they are actually calculated. Therefore, the plain old historic beta is important even if one goes on to develop a more exotic version. With this in mind, it should be noted that there are several different ways to calculate historic betas, and the different methods produce different results. Here are some points to note:

1. Betas can be based on historic periods of different lengths. For example, data for the past one, two, three, and so on years may be used. Most people who calculate betas today use five years of data, but this choice is arbitrary, and different lengths of time usually alter significantly the calculated beta for a given company.[5]

2. Returns may be calculated on holding periods of different lengths—a day, a week, a month, a quarter, a year, and so on. For example, if it has been decided to analyze data on NYSE stocks over a 5-year period, then we might obtain 52 x 5 = 260 weekly returns on each stock and on the market index, or 12 x 5 = 60 monthly returns, or 1 x 5 = 5 annual returns, and so on. The set of returns on each stock, however large it turns out to be, would then be regressed on the corresponding market returns to obtain the stock's beta. In statistical analysis, it is generally better to have more rather than fewer observations, because more observations generally lead to greater statistical confidence. This suggests the use of weekly returns, and say five years of data, for a sample size of 260. However, the shorter the holding period, the more likely the data are to exhibit random "noise," and the greater the number of years of data, the more likely it is that the company's basic risk position will have changed (for example, see the comments above

---

[3]See Marshall E. Blume, "Betas and Their Regression Tendencies," *Journal of Finance*, June 1973, 785-796.

[4]See Barr Rosenberg and James Guy, "Beta and Investment Fundamentals," *Financial Analysts' Journal*, May-June 1976, 60-72. Rosenberg, a professor at the University of California at Berkeley, later set up a company which calculated fundamental betas by a proprietary procedure and then sold them to institutional investors.

[5]A commercial provider of betas once told the author that his firm, and others, did not know the right period to use, but they decided to use a 5-year period in order to reduce the apparent differences among various services' betas, because these differences reduced everyone's credibility!

Table 7A-2
Beta Coefficients for Three Companies, May 1983

	Merrill Lynch		Value Line
	Unadjusted	Adjusted	
General Foods	0.57	0.70	0.80
Du Pont	0.97	0.99	1.15
Texas Instruments	1.45	1.25	1.10

on Chrysler and AT&T). Thus, the choice of both number of years of data and length of the holding period for calculating rates of return involves trade-offs between a desire to have a lot of observations versus a desire to have internally consistent data.

3. The value used to represent "the market" is also an important consideration, and one that can have a significant effect on the calculated beta. Most beta calculators today use the New York Stock Exchange Composite Index (based on about 1,700 stocks), but others use the S&P 500 Index or other groups, up to one (the Wilshire Index) with over 5,000 stocks. In theory, the broader the index, the better the beta—indeed, the index should really include returns on all stocks, bonds, leases, private businesses, real estate, and even "human capital." As a practical matter, however, we cannot get accurate returns data on most types of assets, so measurement problems largely restrict us to stock indices.

The bottom line of all this is that one can calculate betas in many different ways, and depending on the method used, different betas, and hence different costs of capital, will result. To illustrate this point, consider Table 7A-2, which contains the May 1983 beta coefficients for three well-known companies as reported by Merrill Lynch and Value Line. Merrill Lynch uses the S&P 500 as the market index, while Value Line uses the New York Stock Exchange Composite Index. Further, Value Line betas are adjusted, while Merrill Lynch reports both pure historic betas and adjusted ones. Merrill Lynch uses five years of monthly returns, or 60 observations; Value Line uses 260 weekly observations.

Where does this leave financial managers regarding the proper beta? They must "pay their money and take their choice." Some managers will calculate their own betas, using whichever procedure seems most appropriate under the circumstances. Others will use betas calculated by organizations such as Merrill Lynch or Value Line, perhaps using one service or perhaps averaging the betas of several services. The choice is a matter of judgment and data availability, for there is no "right" beta. With luck, the betas derived from different sources will, for a given company, be close together. If they are not, then our confidence in the CAPM cost of capital estimate will be diminished.

We are now in a position to estimate the cost of equity from retained earnings by the CAPM method. We use as the risk-free rate the T-bond rate in May 1983, which was 10.7 percent, and Merrill Lynch's estimate of the cur-

Illustration of the CAPM Approach

rent expected return on the market, $\hat{k}_M = k_M = 14.7\%$. Thus, we can write the SML equation for May 1983 as follows:

$$
\begin{aligned}
k_i &= R_F + b_i(k_M - R_F) \\
&= 10.7\% + b_i(14.7\% - 10.7\%) \\
&= 10.7\% + b_i(4.0\%).
\end{aligned}
$$

Therefore, if we know a company's beta, we can insert it into the SML equation and estimate the company's cost of retained earnings, k_i. For General Foods, using the Value Line beta, we obtain $k_{GF} = 13.9\%$:

$$
k_{GF} = 10.7\% + 0.80(4.0\%) = 13.9\%.
$$

Using Merrill Lynch's unadjusted beta, we obtain an estimate of 13.0 percent. Therefore, based on this CAPM analysis, General Foods' cost of retained earnings is within a range of 13.0 to 13.9 percent.

Rather than picking single values, we could have developed high and low estimates for both the risk-free rate and the market risk premium. Then, by combining all of the low estimators, and all of the high estimators, we could have estimated the extreme low and high values of General Foods' cost of retained earnings. Obviously, this expected range would have been greater than 13.0 to 13.9 percent.

The DCF Approach

The second major procedure for estimating the cost of retained earnings is the Discounted Cash Flow (DCF) approach. We know that if a stock is expected to grow at a constant rate, and if the stock is in equilibrium, we can use the Gordon model to estimate $k_s = \hat{k}_s$:

$$
k_s = \hat{k}_s = \frac{D_1}{P_0} + g.
$$

Here P_0 is read from *The Wall Street Journal*, and next year's annual dividend, D_1, can be estimated relatively easily. Unfortunately, it is not easy to estimate g, the growth rate expected by the marginal investor. There are several ways to estimate the growth rate; we will examine three.

Historic Growth Rates

First, if earnings and dividend growth rates have been relatively stable in the past, and if investors expect these trends to continue, then the past realized growth rate may be used as an estimate of the expected future growth rate. To illustrate the use of historic data, consider Figure 7A-1, which gives EPS and DPS data from 1968 to 1982 for General Foods, along with a plot of these data on a semilog scale. Note these points:

1. Time period. We show 15 years of data in Figure 7A-1. However, we could have used 25 years, 5 years, or 10 years. There is no rule as to the appropriate number of years to analyze when calculating historic growth rates.

Figure 7A-1
Semi-Log Plot of EPS and DPS for General Foods, 1968-1982

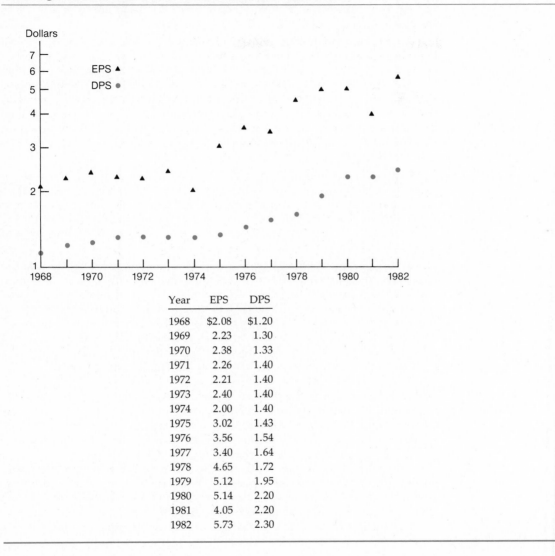

Year	EPS	DPS
1968	$2.08	$1.20
1969	2.23	1.30
1970	2.38	1.33
1971	2.26	1.40
1972	2.21	1.40
1973	2.40	1.40
1974	2.00	1.40
1975	3.02	1.43
1976	3.56	1.54
1977	3.40	1.64
1978	4.65	1.72
1979	5.12	1.95
1980	5.14	2.20
1981	4.05	2.20
1982	5.73	2.30

2. Compound growth rate, point-to-point. The easiest historic growth rate to calculate is the compound rate between two dates. For example, EPS grew at an annual rate of 7.51 percent from 1968 to 1982, while DPS grew at a 4.76 percent rate during this same period.[6] Note that the point-to-point growth rate could change radically if we used two other points. For exam-

---

[6]However, dividends are received quarterly, not annually, and that fact leads to an error. See Appendix 5C.

ple, if we calculated the 5-year EPS growth rate from 1976 to 1981, we would obtain 2.6 percent, but the 5-year rate one year later, from 1977 to 1982 is 11.0 percent. This radical change occurs because the point-to-point rate is extremely sensitive to the base and terminal years.[7]

3. Compound growth rate, average-to-average. To alleviate the problem of base and terminal year sensitivity, some analysts use an average-to-average calculation. For example, to calculate General Foods' EPS growth rate over the period 1976 to 1981, the Value Line analysts would (1) get the average EPS over the years 1975 to 1977 and use this value ($3.33) as the base year, (2) get the average EPS over the years 1980 to 1982 and use this value ($4.97) as the terminal year, and (3) calculate a growth rate of 8.3 percent based on these data. This procedure is superior to the simple point-to-point calculation for purposes of a DCF analysis.

4. Least squares regression. A third way, and in our view the best way, to estimate historic growth rates is by log-linear least squares regression.[8] The regression method gives consideration to all data points in the series, and hence it is the least likely to be biased by a randomly high or low beginning or ending year. The only practical way to estimate a least squares growth rate is with a computer or a financial calculator.

5. Earnings versus dividends. If earnings and dividends are growing at the same rate, there is no problem, but if these two growth rates are unequal, we do have a problem. First, the DCF model calls for the expected *dividend* growth rate. However, if EPS and DPS are growing at different rates, something is going to have to change—these two series cannot grow at two different rates indefinitely. There is no rule for handling differences in g_{EPS} and g_{DPS}; we often average the two for want of a better way of dealing with the problem. Like many aspects of finance, judgment is required here.

Table 7A-3 summarizes the historic growth rates we have just discussed. It is obvious that one can take a given set of historic data and, depending on the years and calculation method used, obtain a large number of quite different growth rates. We deliberately selected General Foods as our illustrative company because its operations are more stable than most. Nevertheless, we still find major differences in historic growth rates. Now recall our purpose in making these calculations: We are seeking the future dividend growth rate that investors expect, and we reasoned that, if past growth rates have been stable, then investors might base future expectations on past trends. This is a reasonable proposition, but, unfortunately, one never finds

---

[7]To obtain g_{EPS} using a financial calculator, say from 1968 to 1982, enter 2.08 as PV, 5.73 as FV, 14 as n (because, with 15 data points, we have 14 growth periods), and then press i to obtain the growth rate, 7.51 percent. Using tables, proceed as follows:

1. Obtain this factor: $EPS_{1968}/EPS_{1982} = 2.08/5.73 = 0.3630$. The factor is the PVIF for 14 years.

2. Turn to Table A-1, the one for the PV of $1. Look down to Period 14. Then go across the Period 14 row, looking for 0.3630, which is seen to lie about halfway between the factors for 7 and 8 percent, or at about 7.5 percent.

[8]For a short discussion of log-linear regressions, see Eugene F. Brigham and Louis C. Gapenski, *Intermediate Financial Management* (Hinsdale, Ill.: Dryden, 1985, Appendix 4A).

Table 7A-3
Historic Growth Rates for General Foods

	EPS	DPS
Point-to-point (1977-1982)	11.0%	7.0%
Point-to-point (1968-1982)	7.5	4.8
Average-to-average (1976-1981)	8.3	7.7
Average-to-average (1969-1981)	8.2	5.0
Least squares regression (1977-1982)	6.6	7.6
Least squares regression (1968-1982)	7.9	4.6

very much historic stability, even with a company such as General Foods. Therefore, the use of historic growth rates in a DCF analysis must be applied with judgment, and also used in conjunction with other growth estimation methods as discussed below.

Retention Growth

Another method for estimating the growth rate is to use Equation 7A-1:

$$g = b(r). \qquad (7A-1)$$

Here r is the expected future return on equity, and b is the fraction of its earnings that a firm is expected to retain.[9] Equation 7A-1 produces a constant growth rate, and when we use it we are, by implication, making four important assumptions: (1) that the retention ratio, b, will remain constant; (2) that the return on equity on new investment, r, will equal the firm's current ROE, which implies that the return on equity will remain constant; (3) that the firm will not issue new common stock or, if it does, that this new stock will be sold at a price equal to its book value; and (4) that future projects will have the same degree of risk as the firm's existing assets.

General Foods has had an average return on equity of about 15 percent over the past 10 years. The ROE has been relatively steady, ranging from a low of 11.0 percent to a high of 17.6 percent during this period. In addition, General Foods' dividend payout ratio has averaged 0.42 over the past 10 years, so its retention rate, b, has averaged 1.0 − 0.42 = 0.58. Using Equation 7A-1, we estimate g to be 8.7 percent:

$$g = 0.58(15\%) = 8.7\%.$$

This figure, together with the historic EPS growth rates examined earlier, might lead us to conclude that General Foods' expected growth rate is in the range of 8 to 9 percent. Therefore, if we forecasted General Foods' next

[9]Since there are more terms for which symbols are needed than there are letters in the alphabet, some letters are used to denote several different things. This is one of those instances, and "b" is standard notation for both the beta coefficient and the retention rate. Also, return on equity, ROE = r, is defined as net income divided by the book value of total equity.

annual dividend to be $2.40, and determined that its current stock price is $41, then its dividend yield is $D_1/P_0 = \$2.40/\$41 = 0.059$ or 5.9% and its DCF cost of capital range is in the range of 13.9 to 14.9 percent:

$$\text{Lower end: } \hat{k}_{GF} = k_{GF} = 5.9\% + 7\% = 13.9\%.$$
$$\text{Upper end: } \hat{k}_{GF} = k_{GF} = 5.9\% + 8\% = 14.9\%.$$

This is a little higher than the 13.0 to 13.9 percent estimate obtained by the CAPM method.

Analysts'
Forecasts

A final method of estimating g is to use analysts' forecasts. However, these forecasts seldom assume constant growth. For example, in May 1983, Merrill Lynch's analysts were forecasting that General Foods would have a 10.4 percent annual growth rate in earnings and dividends over the next 5 years, or from 1983 to 1988. Additionally, they were forecasting a steady-state growth rate beyond 1988 of 7.5 percent. Based on the current $41 market price and a D_1 of $2.40, we can use the nonconstant growth stock valuation equation developed in Chapter 5 to find the expected rate of return:

$$P_0 = \sum_{t=1}^{5} \frac{D_1(1 + g_s)^{t-1}}{(1 + \hat{k}_s)^t} + \left(\frac{D_6}{\hat{k}_s - g_n}\right)\left(\frac{1}{1 + \hat{k}_s}\right)^5.$$

$$\$41 = \sum_{t=1}^{5} \frac{\$2.40(1.104)^{t-1}}{(1 + \hat{k}_s)^t} + \left(\frac{\$3.83}{\hat{k}_s - 0.075}\right)\left(\frac{1}{1 + \hat{k}_s}\right)^5.$$

Solving for $\hat{k}_s$ is no trivial matter—we used a financial calculator, but the solution process still involved a trial and error procedure. We found $\hat{k}_s = k_s$ to be about 13.9 percent.

As an alternative, the nonconstant growth forecasts could be used to develop a proxy constant growth rate. For example, since dividends beyond Year 50 contribute virtually zero to today's stock price, we can obtain a weighted average constant growth rate by assuming a growth rate of 10.4 percent for 5 years followed by a growth rate of 7.5 percent for 45 years, or $0.10(10.4\%) + 0.90(7.5\%) = 7.8\%$. This constant growth rate proxy results in $k_s = \hat{k}_s = 13.7\%$:

$$k_s = \hat{k}_s = \frac{\$2.40}{\$41} + 7.8\%$$
$$= 5.9\% + 7.8\% = 13.7\%.$$

These calculations suggest a range for k_s of perhaps 13.4 to 14.0 percent.

Bond Yield plus Risk Premium Approach

The last method we will discuss for estimating the required rate of return on retained earnings is the company's own bond yield plus risk premium approach:

$$k_s = \text{Bond yield} + \text{Risk premium}.$$

A corporate treasurer can easily look up his or her own firm's bond yield if it is publicly traded, or ask an investment banker for k_d if the bonds are not traded. The real problem occurs when trying to estimate the appropriate risk premium for the firm.

Table 7A-1 presented historic risk premiums as reported by Ibbotson and Sinquefield. If risk premiums were stable over time, or if they fluctuated randomly about a stable mean, then the average historic premium could be used as an estimate of the current and prospective future risk premium. However, risk premiums are not stable, so it is necessary to estimate risk premiums on a current basis, and more reliance should be placed on the current level of the risk premium than on its historic average. Studies suggest that risk premiums are reasonably stable during "normal" periods, but that they become volatile during periods in which interest rates are volatile.

There are two common methods of estimating current risk premiums: A survey approach and a DCF-based approach, similar to the method we discussed earlier in connection with the CAPM. One example of the survey approach is the work of Charles Benore, a security analyst with Paine Webber. Benore surveys a large number of institutional investors, asking them what expected return on a company's common stock, over and above the return on the company's bonds, would make them indifferent to the choice of investing in the stock or the bonds. Benore's May 1983 survey found that most investors required a premium of from 2 to 4 percentage points on stock over the company's bond yield, with a mean value of 3.6 percentage points which can be used as an estimate of the risk premium. Benore's survey analyzes only public utility companies, but the approach is applicable to any company or industry.

The second method for estimating risk premiums is based on the DCF model. To illustrate, we stated earlier that in May 1983 Merrill Lynch, using the DCF approach, estimated that the required rate of return on the market, as measured by the S&P 500, was 14.7 percent. At the same time, the *Federal Reserve Bulletin* reported that the yield on an average corporate long-term bond was 12.3 percent. Using these data, we estimate the market risk premium of an average stock over an average bond to be $14.7 - 12.3 = 2.4$ percentage points, or 240 basis points. However, recognizing that this figure of 2.4 percentage points is imprecise, we would conclude that the risk premium of an average company's stock over its own bonds, in the spring of 1983, was somewhere between 2.0 and 3.0 percentage points.

We can apply this approach to estimate the required rate of return on General Foods' equity. General Foods is a relatively strong company, and its bonds are rated Aa, which is just one notch below the top Aaa rating. Therefore, whereas the *Federal Reserve Bulletin* reported that an average corporate bond yielded 12.3 percent in May 1983, General Foods' bonds yielded only 12.1 percent. Assuming that every company's required equity return exceeds its cost of debt by the amounts estimated above, we would determine the high and low values of General Foods' cost of equity as follows:

High: $k_{GF} = 12.1\% + 3.0\% = 15.1\%$.
Low: $k_{GF} = 12.1\% + 2.0\% = 14.1\%$.

Table 7A-4
Estimated Required Rates of Return for General Foods

Method	Estimate Low	Estimate High
CAPM	13.0%	13.9%
DCF (constant growth)	13.9	14.9
DCF (nonconstant growth)	13.4	14.0
Over-own-bonds risk premium	14.1	15.1
Average	13.6%	14.5%
Overall average		14.0%

Had General Foods had a lower bond rating and a higher cost of debt, its estimated cost of equity would have been higher, and vice versa had its bonds been rated triple A.[10]

Note, however, that risk premiums have not been stable over time, so it is not appropriate as a general rule to add 2.0 to 3.0 percentage points to a company's bond yield to indicate its cost of equity. In recent years, our work suggest that the over-own-debt risk premium has ranged from about 1.5 to about 4.5 percentage points. (The low premium occurred when interest rates were quite high and people were reluctant to invest in long-term bonds because of a fear of run-away inflation, further increases in interest rates, and losses on investments in bonds.) Therefore, we repeat our earlier warning—use a current risk premium when estimating equity capital costs by the over-own-bonds risk premium method.

Comparison of the CAPM, DCF, and Risk Premium Methods

We have discussed three methods for estimating the required rate of return on retained earnings—CAPM, DCF, and generalized risk premiums. Table 7A-4 summarizes the results for General Foods. We see that the estimates range from 13.0 to 15.1 percent, that the average highs and average lows produce a range of 13.6 to 14.5 percent, and that the overall average is 14.0 percent. In our view, there is sufficient consistency in the results to warrant the use of 14.0 percent as an estimate of the cost of retained earnings for General Foods. If the methods had produced widely varied estimates, then the financial manager would have to use his or her judgment as to the relative merits of each estimate, and then choose the estimate which seemed most reasonable under the circumstances.

---

[10]Other variations on this theme could be employed. We could, for example, develop DCF cost of equity estimates for different industries, for firms with similar bond ratings, and so on. Also, note that if you know a company's bond rating, or can estimate from an analysis of its financial statements what rating it would have if its debt were rated, then you could look up in Moody's or Standard & Poor's bond yield publications the company's approximate k_d. This procedure is useful for outsiders who analyze companies that have no publicly traded debt. The company's own treasurer would always know, or could quickly find out, the value of k_d from the firm's investment bankers.

7A-1 A summary of the balance sheet of Travellers Inn, Inc. (TII), a company which was formed by merging a number of regional motel chains and which hopes someday to rival Holiday Inn on the national scene, is shown below:

Problem

Travellers Inn
December 31, 1984
(Millions of Dollars)

Cash	$ 10	Accounts payable	$ 10
Accounts receivable	20	Accruals	10
Inventories	20	Short-term debt	5
Current assets	$ 50	Current liabilities	$ 25
Net fixed assets	50	Long-term debt	30
		Preferred stock	5
		Common equity:	
		Common stock $10	
		Retained earnings 30	
		Total common equity	40
Total assets	$100	Total claims	$100

These facts are also given for TII:

1. Short-term debt consists of bank loans which currently cost 10 percent, with interest payable quarterly. These loans are used to finance receivables and inventories on a seasonal basis, so in the off-season bank loans are zero.

2. The long-term debt consists of 20-year, semiannual payment mortgage bonds with a coupon rate of 8 percent. Currently, these bonds provide a yield to investors of $k_d = 12\%$. If new bonds were sold, they would also yield investors 12 percent, but a flotation cost of 5 percent would be required to sell new bonds.

3. TII's perpetual preferred stock has a $100 par value; it pays a quarterly dividend of $2; and it has a yield to investors of 11 percent. New preferred would have to provide the same yield to investors, but the company would incur a 5 percent flotation cost to sell it.

4. The company has 4 million shares of common stock outstanding. $P_0 = \$20$, and the stock has recently traded in a range of $17 to $23. $D_0 = \$1$, and $EPS_0 = \$2$. ROE based on average equity was 24 percent in 1984, and management expects to increase this return on equity to 30 percent; however, security analysts are not aware of management's optimism in this regard, so analysts are generally forecasting ROE = 24%.

5. Betas as reported by security analysts range from 1.3 to 1.7; the T-bond rate is 10 percent; and k_M is estimated by various brokerage houses to be in the range of 14.5 to 15.5 percent. Brokerage house reports forecast growth rates in the range of 10 to 15 percent over the foreseeable future. Some analysts do not explicitly forecast growth rates, but they indicate to their clients that they expect TII's historic trends as shown below to continue.

6. TII's financial vice-president, at a recent conference, polled some pension fund investment managers as to the minimum rate of return they would have to expect on TII's common to make them willing to buy the common rather than TII bonds, assuming the bonds yield 12 percent. The responses suggested a risk premium over TII bonds of 4 to 6 percent.

7. Depreciation for the coming year, 1985, is estimated to be $5 million. Net income for the same period is projected to be $12 million.

8. If the capital budget is $5 million or less, all funds to support this budget will come from depreciation cash flows. If the capital budget exceeds $5 million, additional funds will be obtained as retained earnings, from sale of debt and preferred stock, and possibly from sale of new common stock. Note also that if the capital budget is less than $5 million, TII will not be replacing all of its depreciated assets, and hence net assets will actually decline.

9. TII is in the 40 percent corporate tax bracket. Its dominant stockholders are in the 50 percent bracket.

10. New common stock would have a 10 percent flotation cost.

11. TII's principal investment banker, Henry, Kaufman & Company, predicts a decline in interest rates, with k_d falling to 10 percent and the T-bond rate to 8 percent, although Henry, Kaufman & Company acknowledges that an increase in the expected inflation rate could lead to an increase rather than a decrease in rates.

12. Here is TII's historic record of EPS and DPS:

Year	EPS*	DPS*
1970	$0.09	$0.00
1971	−0.20	0.00
1972	0.40	0.00
1973	0.52	0.00
1974	0.10	0.00
1975	0.57	0.00
1976	0.61	0.00
1977	0.70	0.00
1978	0.78	0.00
1979	0.80	0.00
1980	1.20	0.20
1981	0.95	0.40
1982	1.30	0.60
1983	1.60	0.80
1984	2.00	1.00

*Adjusted for a 2:1 stock split in 1975, a 3:1 split in 1983, and 10 percent stock dividends in 1972 and 1980.

Assume that you are a recently hired financial analyst, and your boss, the treasurer, has asked you to estimate the company's cost of capital, assuming that it must support a capital budget of (a) $3 million, (b) $6 million, (c) $10 million, and (d) $20 million. Your cost of capital figures at each level, k_a = MCC, should be appropriate for use in evaluating projects which are in the same risk class as the firm's average assets now on the books.

The MCC Schedule

In Chapter 7, we introduced the concept of the marginal cost of capital (MCC) schedule. We also noted that the marginal cost of capital will, after some point, rise as more and more capital is raised during a given year. This tendency to increase occurs because (1) flotation costs cause the cost of new equity to be higher than the cost of retained earnings, and (2) higher rates of return on debt, preferred stock, and common stock may be required to induce more and more new investors to supply capital to the firm.

In this appendix, we extend the MCC schedule beyond the retained earnings break point to see what the schedule might look like as more and more capital is required. Because of the difficulties in estimating the effects of capital requirements on k_d, k_p, and k_e, firms do not, in general, attempt to precisely define the MCC schedule beyond the retained earnings break point as we do in this appendix. Thus, the following discussion is intended more to provide a conceptual view of the complete MCC schedule rather than to serve as a prescription for use in practice.

The Retained Earnings Break Point

Figure 7-2 graphed Firm M's marginal cost of capital schedule as developed in Chapter 7. We concluded that, based on the firm's target capital structure and 40 percent tax rate, and its capital costs of $k_d = 10\%$, $k_p = 12\%$, and $k_s = 14.2\%$, its marginal cost of capital is 11.5%:

$$k_a = w_d k_d (1 - T) + w_p k_p + w_s k_s$$
$$= 0.3(10\%)(0.6) + 0.1(12\%) + 0.6(14.2\%)$$
$$= 11.5\%.$$

However, after Firm M has used up its $420,000 in retained earnings, then it will have to sell new common equity at a cost of 15.0 percent. This will cause the marginal cost of capital to increase to 12 percent:

$$k_a = 0.3(10\%)(0.6) + 0.1(12\%) + 0.6(15.0\%)$$
$$= 12.0\%.$$

This increase in the MCC schedule, called the *retained earnings break point*, occurs when $700,000 of new capital has been raised:

$$\text{Retained earnings break point} = X = \frac{\text{Retained earnings}}{\text{Equity fraction}}$$

$$= \frac{\$420,000}{0.6} = \$700,000.$$

There is a jump, or break, in Firm M's MCC schedule at $700,000 of new capital. Could there be other breaks in the schedule? Yes, there could be. For example, suppose Firm M could obtain only $300,000 of debt at a 10 percent interest rate, with additional debt costing 12 percent. This would result in a second break point in the MCC schedule at the point where the $300,000 of 10 percent debt is exhausted. At what amount of *total financing* would the 10 percent debt be used up? If we let Y represent the total financing at this second break point, then

Other Breaks in the MCC Schedule

$$0.3Y = \$300,000,$$

and, solving for Y, we obtain

$$Y = \frac{\text{Dollars of } 10\% \text{ debt}}{\text{Debt fraction}} = \frac{\$300,000}{0.3} = \$1,000,000 = \text{Break point for debt.}$$

Thus, there will be a second break in the MCC schedule after Firm M has raised a total of $1 million: Beyond $1 million, the MCC rises from 12.0 to 12.4 percent as a result of the increase in k_d from 10 to 12 percent:

$$k_a = 0.3(12\%)(0.6) + 0.1(12\%) + 0.6(15.0\%) = 12.4\%.$$

In other words, the next dollar beyond $1 million will consist of 30 cents of 12 percent debt (7.2 percent after taxes), 10 cents of 12 percent preferred, and 60 cents of new common stock (retained earnings were used up back at $700,000 of capital), and this marginal dollar will have an average cost of 12.4 percent.

The effect of this new MCC increase is shown in Figure 7B-1. We now have two breaks, one caused by using up all the retained earnings and the other caused by using up all the 10 percent debt. With the two breaks, we have three different MCCs: $MCC_1 = 11.5\%$ for the first $700,000 of new capital; $MCC_2 = 12.0\%$ in the interval between $700,000 and $1 million; and $MCC_3 = 12.4\%$ for all new capital beyond $1 million.[1]

---

[1]When we use the term *weighted average cost of capital*, we are referring to k_a, which is the cost of $1 raised partly as debt, partly as preferred, and partly as equity. One could also calculate the average cost of *all* capital the firm raises during a given year. For example, if Firm M raised $2 million, then the first $700,000 would have a cost of 11.5 percent, the next $300,000 would have a cost of 12.0 percent, and the last $1 million would have a cost of 12.4 percent. The entire $2 million would have an average cost of 12.03 percent:

$$(0.7/2)(11.5\%) + (0.3/2)(12.0\%) + (1.0/2)(12.4\%) = 12.03\%.$$

This particular cost of capital should *not* be used for financial decisions; *it generally has no relevance in finance.*

Figure 7B-1
Marginal Cost of Capital Schedule for Firm M
Using Retained Earnings, New Common Stock, and
Higher-Cost Debt

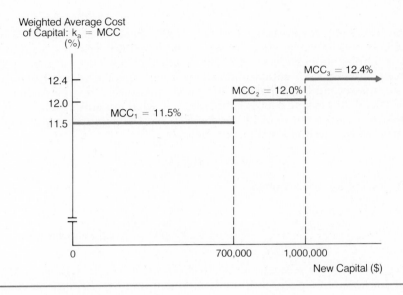

There could, of course, be still more break points. For example, the interest rate on debt might rise again, from 12 to 14 percent, after the firm had used $200,000 of the 12 percent debt. In this case, the 14 percent debt would be used after a total of $500,000 of lower-cost debt had been used—$300,000 of 10 percent debt plus $200,000 of 12 percent debt. Therefore, a new break would occur at $1,666,667:

$$\frac{\text{Break point}}{\text{for 14\% debt}} = \frac{\$300,000 + \$200,000}{0.3} = \frac{\$500,000}{0.3} = \$1,666,667.$$

Other break points would occur if the interest rate continued to rise, if the cost of preferred stock rose, or if, as larger amounts of common stock were sold, market pressure lowered the offering price of the stock and, consequently, raised the cost of common equity. *In general, a break point will occur whenever the cost of one of the capital components rises, and the break point can be determined by this equation:*

$$\text{Break point} = \frac{\begin{array}{c}\text{Total amount of lower cost}\\\text{capital of a given type}\end{array}}{\begin{array}{c}\text{Fraction of this type of capital}\\\text{in the capital structure}\end{array}}. \qquad \text{(7B-1)}$$

The break point for the 14 percent debt was found by application of this formula.

We see, then, that numerous break points can occur. At the limit, we can even think of an MCC with so many break points that it rises almost continuously beyond some given level of new financing. Such an MCC schedule was shown in Figure 7-3 in Chapter 7.[2]

ST-1 (This problem extends the self-test problem at the end of Chapter 7.) *Self-Test Problem*
Laser Communications, Inc. (LCI), has the following capital structure, which it considers to be optimal:

Debt	25%
Preferred stock	15
Common equity	60
Total capital	100%

LCI's net income expected this year is $17,142.86; its established dividend payout ratio is 30 percent; its tax rate is 40 percent; and investors expect earnings and dividends to grow at a constant rate of 9 percent in the future. LCI paid a dividend of $3.60 per share last year, and its stock currently sells at a price of $60 per share. Treasury bonds yield 11 percent; an average stock has a 14 percent expected rate of return; and LCI's beta is 1.51.

LCI can obtain new capital in the following ways:

Common: New common stock would have a flotation cost of 10 percent for up to $6,000 of new stock and 20 percent for all common over $6,000.

Preferred: New preferred could be sold to the public at a price of $100 per share, with a dividend of $11. Flotation costs of $5 per share would be incurred for up to $3,750 of preferred, while these costs would rise to $10, or 10 percent, on all preferred over $3,750.

Debt: Up to $2,500 of debt could be sold at an interest rate of 12 percent; debt in the range of $2,501 to $5,000 would carry an interest rate of 14 percent; and all debt over $5,000 would have an interest rate of 16 percent.

a. Find the break points in the MCC schedule.
b. Determine the component costs of capital for each capital structure component.

---

[2]The first break point is not necessarily the point where retained earnings are used up—it is possible that low-cost debt could be exhausted *before* retained earnings have been used up. For example, if Firm M had available only $150,000 of 10 percent debt, then Point Y would have occurred at $500,000:

$$Y = \frac{\$150,000}{0.3} = \$500,000.$$

This is well before the break for retained earnings, which occurs at $700,000.

c. Calculate the weighted average cost of capital (or the MCC) in the interval between each break in the MCC schedule.
d. Construct a graph showing LCI's MCC schedule.

Solution to Self-Test Problem   **ST-1**

a. *Determination of break points:*

A break point will occur each time a low-cost type of capital is used up. We establish the break points as follows, after first noting that LCI has $12,000 of retained earnings:

$$\text{Retained earnings} = (\text{Total earnings})(1.0 - \text{Payout})$$
$$= (\$17,142.86)(0.7)$$
$$= \$12,000.$$

Capital Used Up	Break Point Calculation	Break No.
Retained earnings	$BP_{RE} = \dfrac{RE}{\text{Equity fraction}}$ $= \$12,000/0.60 = \$20,000.$	②
10% flotation common	$BP_{10\%E} = \dfrac{RE + \begin{matrix}\text{Equity at 10\%}\\\text{flotation}\end{matrix}}{\text{Equity fraction}}$ $= \dfrac{\$12,000 + \$6,000}{0.60} = \$30,000.$	④
5% flotation preferred	$BP_{5\%P} = \dfrac{\text{Preferred at 5\% flotation}}{\text{Preferred fraction}}$ $= \$3,750/0.15 = \$25,000.$	③
12% debt	$BP_{12\%D} = \dfrac{12\% \text{ debt}}{\text{Debt fraction}}$ $= \$2,500/0.25 = \$10,000.$	①
14% debt	$BP_{14\%D} = \dfrac{12\% \text{ debt} + 14\% \text{ debt}}{\text{Debt fraction}}$ $= \dfrac{\$2,500 + \$2,500}{0.25} = \$20,000.$	②

Summary of Break Points:

1. There are three common equity costs, and hence two changes and two equity-induced breaks in the MCC. There are two preferred costs, and hence one preferred break. There are three debt costs, and hence two debt breaks.

2. The circled numbers in the right column of the table above designate the sequential order of the breaks. They were determined by inspection after the break points were calculated. Note that the second debt break and the break for retained earnings both occur at $20,000.

3. The breaks themselves are summarized here:

Break Number	Total Dollars of Capital Raised	Cause of Break
1	$10,000	Used up 12% debt and therefore had to go to 14% debt
2	$20,000	(1) Used up retained earnings and (2) used up 14% debt
3	$25,000	Used up preferred with F = 5%
4	$30,000	Used up common with F = 10%

b. Component costs within indicated total capital intervals:

Retained earnings (used in Interval $0 to $20,000):

$$k_s = \frac{D_1}{P_0} + g = \frac{D_0(1 + g)}{P_0} + g$$

$$= \frac{\$3.60(1.09)}{\$60} + 0.09$$

$$= 0.0654 + 0.09 = 15.54\%.$$

We could also calculate k_s by the CAPM method:

$$k_s = R_F + b(k_M - R_F) = 11\% + 1.51(14\% - 11\%) = 15.53\%.$$

If the DCF model and the CAPM had not given consistent results, further analysis would have been necessary to determine which k_s estimate was better. Here we will use 15.54 percent.

Common with F = 10% ($20,000 to $30,000):

$$k_e = \frac{D_1}{P_0(1.0 - F)} + g = \frac{\$3.924}{\$60(0.9)} + 9\% = 16.27\%.$$

Common with F = 20% (Over $30,000):

$$k_e = \frac{\$3.924}{\$60(0.8)} + 9\% = 17.18\%.$$

Preferred with F = 5% ($0 to $25,000):

$$k_p = \frac{\text{Preferred dividend}}{P_n} = \frac{\$11}{\$100(0.95)} = 11.58\%.$$

Preferred with F = 10% (Over $25,000):

$$k_p = \frac{\$11}{\$100(0.9)} = 12.22\%.$$

Debt at $k_d = 12\%$ ($0 to $10,000):

$$k_d(1 - T) = 12\%(0.6) = 7.20\%.$$

Debt at $k_d = 14\%$ ($10,000 to $20,000):

$$k_d(1 - T) = 14\%(0.6) = 8.40\%.$$

Debt at $k_d = 16\%$ (Over $20,000):

$$k_d(1 - T) = 16\%(0.6) = 9.60\%.$$

c. MCC calculations within indicated total capital intervals:

(1) $0 to $10,000 (Debt = 7.2%; Preferred = 11.58%; and RE = 15.54%):

$$\begin{aligned} MCC_1 = k_a &= w_d k_d(1 - T) + w_p k_p + w_s k_s \\ &= 0.25(7.2\%) + 0.15(11.58\%) + 0.60(15.54\%) \\ &= 12.86\%. \end{aligned}$$

(2) $10,001 to $20,000 (Debt = 8.4%; Preferred = 11.58%; and RE = 15.54%):

$$\begin{aligned} MCC_2 = k_a &= 0.25(8.4\%) + 0.15(11.58\%) + 0.60(15.54\%) \\ &= 13.16\%. \end{aligned}$$

(3) $20,001 to $25,000 (Debt = 9.6%; Preferred = 11.58%; and Equity = 16.27%):

$$\begin{aligned} MCC_3 = k_a &= 0.25(9.6\%) + 0.15(11.58\%) + 0.60(16.27\%) \\ &= 13.90\%. \end{aligned}$$

(4) $25,001 to $30,000 (Debt = 9.6%; Preferred = 12.22%; and Equity = 16.27%):

$$\begin{aligned} MCC_4 = k_a &= 0.25(9.6\%) + 0.15(12.22\%) + 0.60(16.27\%) \\ &= 14.00\%. \end{aligned}$$

(5) Over $30,000 (Debt = 9.6%; Preferred = 12.22%; and Equity = 17.18%):

$$\begin{aligned} MCC_5 = k_a &= 0.25(9.6\%) + 0.15(12.22\%) + 0.60(17.18\%) \\ &= 14.54\%. \end{aligned}$$

d. See the following graph:

MCC Schedule for LCI

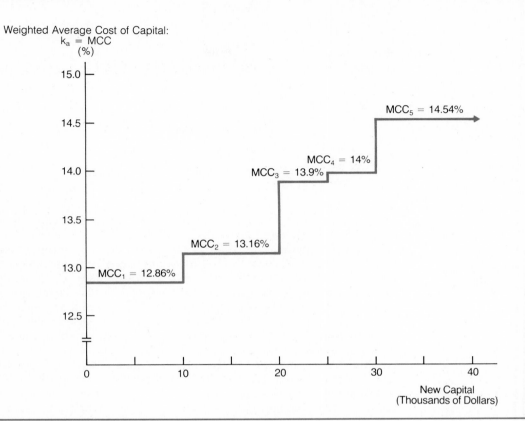

7C   The Cost of Deferred Taxes

Most companies show on their balance sheets, as a liability, an item called deferred taxes. Deferred taxes arise principally from accelerated tax depreciation, which permits delays in payments of corporate income taxes, and these deferred taxes constitute an important source of funds for many companies. For example, suppose the XYZ Company uses ACRS depreciation for tax purposes but straight line for book (or stockholder reporting) purposes.[1] Its ACRS depreciation for 1984 might be $20 million versus $10 million had it used straight line. XYZ's tax and book income statements are given in Table 7C-1. As a result of using ACRS depreciation, the company writes off assets for tax purposes over a period which is shorter than their economic lives. Therefore, in the early years of an asset's life, tax depreciation is high, so actual taxes are low. Later on, tax depreciation will be low, so actual taxes will be high. The deferred taxes represent the taxes that do not have to be paid currently, but which will have to be paid at some future date.

Companies keep a "running total" of the accumulated deferred taxes that have accrued over time, and the net balance is reported on the balance sheet as accumulated deferred income taxes. Thus, XYZ Company would add $4.6 million to the accumulated deferred tax figure reported on its balance sheet. In later years, when tax depreciation falls below straight line depreciation, the accumulated deferred income taxes account will be drawn down, and a credit will appear on the income statement seen by investors.

Deferred taxes represent a noncash charge, and hence they constitute a source of funds in a cash flow sense. In effect, deferred taxes represent a tax-free loan from the federal government, so they represent zero cost capital. From a theoretical standpoint, deferred taxes should be assigned a zero cost and included in the weighted average cost of capital. If deferred taxes are material for a given company, this approach should be taken.[2]

---

[1] ACRS depreciation was discussed in detail in Chapter 2.

[2] When we were working on this section, we looked at several companies' financial statements to see how they reported taxes. Three cases were noted. (1) Most industrial companies reported income to stockholders in their annual reports as we show in Column 2

Table 7C-1
Illustration of XYZ Company's Deferred Taxes
(Millions of Dollars)

	Tax Books (1)	Stockholder Books (2)
Income Statement		
Sales	$100.0	$100.0
Costs except depreciation	60.0	60.0
Depreciation (noncash charge)	20.0	10.0
Operating income	$ 20.0	$ 30.0
Taxes: Current (46%)	9.2	9.2[a]
Deferred (noncash charge)		4.6[b]
Net income	$ 10.8	$ 16.2
Cash flow[c]	$ 30.8	$ 30.8

[a]Taken from tax books.

[b]Represents the difference between taxes paid and taxes that would have been paid had straight line been used for tax purposes:

$$\text{Deferred taxes} = \$30(0.46) - \$9.2 = \$4.6.$$

[c]Cash flow = Net income + Noncash expenses
= Net income + Depreciation + Deferred taxes.

Balance Sheet

If the firm had started the year with fixed assets of $100 million in both the tax and book accounts, and if it acquired no additional assets during the year, on its end-of-year tax books fixed assets would be $100 − $20 = $80 million, while its stockholder record books would show assets of $100 − $10 = $90 million. However, it would also show a liability, called deferred taxes or reserve for deferred taxes, of $4.6 million.

of Table 7C-1. (2) IBM and several other extremely strong firms used accelerated (ACRS) depreciation for book and tax purposes. Thus, in effect, IBM would show Column 1, reporting a net income of $10.8 million versus $16.2 million if it chose to report as a cost straight line depreciation. This is a very conservative accounting practice, and it lowers reported earnings substantially. (3) At the other extreme, some public utilities would report income as shown in Column 2 but *without subtracting the deferred taxes*. In this case, reported income would be $30.0 − $9.2 = $20.8 million. This treatment is very unconservative, since it disregards the fact that future taxes will rise as tax depreciation falls. Utilities report profits this way because their regulatory commissions force them to do so to make their profits look higher and thus to postpone the need for rate increases.

The main point of this footnote is to illustrate one situation where similar companies can report very different levels of earnings. Security analysts and investors generally need to be aware of the accounting treatment that different companies use. A rose is a rose is a rose, but a dollar of reported profits for one company is not necessarily equal to a dollar reported by another.

Capital Budgeting

The Basics of Capital Budgeting

8

Each year, businesses invest hundreds of billions of dollars in fixed assets. By their very nature, such investments affect a firm's fortunes for many years. A good decision can boost earnings sharply and increase dramatically the price of a firm's stock. A bad decision can lead to bankruptcy.

A classic example of a bad capital budgeting decision which could have easily been avoided involved Lockheed's production of the L-1011 Tri-Star commercial jet. At the time Lockheed made the final decision to go forward with Tri-Star production, it estimated the breakeven volume at about 200 planes. The company had orders for about 180 planes, and it was sure of getting at least 20 more orders. Consequently, it decided to commit $1 billion and to commence production.

However, Lockheed's analysis was flawed—it failed to account properly for the cost of the capital tied up in the project. Had its analysts appraised the project correctly, they would have found that the breakeven point was far above 200 planes—so far above that the Tri-Star program was almost certainly doomed to financial failure. This mistake contributed to a decline in Lockheed's stock from $73 per share to $3. Had Lockheed's managers read Chapter 8 and heeded its advice, at least some of that loss might have been avoided.

In previous chapters we have seen (1) how investors value corporate securities and (2) how the firm estimates its cost of capital based on investors' required rates of return. Now we turn to investment decisions involving fixed assets, or *capital budgeting*. The term *capital* refers to fixed assets used in production, while a *budget* is a plan which details projected inflows and outflows during some future period. Thus, the *capital budget* outlines the planned expenditures on fixed assets, and *capital budgeting* is the whole process of analyzing projects and deciding whether they should be included in the capital budget. This process is of fundamental importance to the success or failure of the firm, for its fixed asset investment decisions chart the course of a company for many years into the future. Indeed, these decisions *determine* the future.

Our treatment of capital budgeting is divided into three parts. First, Chapter 8 gives an overview and explains the basic techniques used in capital budgeting analysis. Then, in Chapter 9, we go on to consider how cash flows are estimated. Finally, in Chapter 10, we discuss risk analysis in capital budgeting and explain how the optimal capital budget is established.

Project Proposals and Classifications

The same general concepts are involved in both capital budgeting and security analysis. However, whereas a set of stocks and bonds exists in the securities market, and investors select a portfolio from this set, *capital projects are created by the firm*. For example, a sales representative may report that customers are asking for a particular product that the company does not now produce. The sales manager then discusses the idea with the marketing research group to determine the size of the market for the proposed product. If it appears likely that a significant market does exist, cost accountants and engineers will be asked to estimate production costs. If the whole analysis suggests that the product can be produced and sold to yield a sufficient profit, then the project will be undertaken.

A firm's growth and development, even its ability to remain competitive and to survive, depend upon a constant flow of new investment ideas. Accordingly, a well-managed firm will go to great lengths to develop good capital budgeting proposals. For example, the executive vice-president of a very successful corporation indicated that his company takes the following steps to generate projects:

> Our R&D department is constantly searching for new products or for ways to improve existing products. In addition, our executive committee, which consists of senior executives in marketing, production, and finance, identifies the products and markets in which our company will compete, and the committee sets long-run targets for each division. These targets, which are formalized in the corporation's strategic business plan, provide a general guide to the operating executives who must meet them. These executives then seek new products, set expansion plans for existing products, and look for ways to reduce production and distribution costs. Since bonuses and promotions are based in large part on each unit's ability to meet or exceed its targets, these economic incentives encourage our operating executives to seek out profitable investment opportunities.
>
> While our senior executives are judged and rewarded on the basis of how well their units perform, people further down the line are given bonuses for specific suggestions, including ideas that lead to profitable investments. Additionally, a percentage of our corporate profit is set aside for distribution to nonexecutive employees. Our objective is to encourage lower-level workers

to keep on the lookout for good ideas, including those that lead to capital investments.

If a firm has capable and imaginative executives and employees, and if its incentive system is working properly, many ideas for capital investment will be advanced. Since some ideas will be good ones while others will not, procedures must be established for screening projects.

Analyzing capital expenditure proposals is not a costless operation—benefits can be gained from a careful analysis, but such an investigation does have a cost. For certain types of projects, a relatively detailed analysis may be warranted; for others, cost/benefit studies may suggest that a simpler procedure should be used. Accordingly, firms generally classify projects into the following categories:

1. **Replacement: maintenance of business.** Expenditures necessary to replace worn-out or damaged equipment used to produce profitable products are in this group.

2. **Replacement: cost reduction.** Expenditures to replace serviceable but obsolete equipment fall into this category. The purpose of these expenditures is to lower the cost of labor, materials, or other items such as electricity.

3. **Expansion of existing products or markets.** Expenditures to increase output of existing products or to expand outlets or distribution facilities in markets now being served are included here.

4. **Expansion into new products or markets.** These are expenditures necessary to produce a new product, or to expand into a geographic area not currently being served.

5. **Safety and/or environmental projects.** Expenditures necessary to comply with government orders, labor agreements, or insurance policy terms are listed here. These expenditures are often called *mandatory investments*, or *nonrevenue-producing projects*.

6. **Other.** This catch-all includes office buildings, parking lots, and so on.

In general, relatively simple calculations and only a few supporting documents are required for replacement decisions, especially maintenance-type investments in profitable plants. More detailed analysis is required for cost reduction replacements, for expansion of existing product lines, and especially for investments in new products or areas. Also, within each category, projects are broken down by their dollar costs: The larger the required investment, the more detailed is the analysis and the higher is the level of the officer who must authorize the expenditure. Thus, while a plant manager may be authorized to approve maintenance expenditures up to $10,000 on the basis of a relatively unsophisticated analysis, the full board of directors may have to approve decisions which involve either amounts over $1 million or expansions into new products or markets, and a very detailed, refined analysis will be required to support these decisions.

Similarities between Capital Budgeting and Security Valuation

The capital budgeting process involves exactly the same five conceptual steps that are used in security analysis as described in Chapters 5 and 6:

1. First, management estimates the expected cash flows from a given project, including the value of the asset at a specified terminal date. This is similar to estimating the future dividend or interest payment stream in security analysis.

2. Next, the riskiness of the projected cash flows must be estimated. To do this, management needs information about the probability distributions of the cash flows.

3. Then, given the riskiness of the projected cash flows and the general level of money costs in the economy as reflected in the riskless rate, R_F, the firm determines the appropriate discount rate, or cost of capital, at which the project's cash flows are to be discounted. This is equivalent to finding the required rate of return on a stock as we did in Chapter 6.

4. Next, the expected cash flows are put on a present value basis to obtain an estimate of the asset's value to the firm. This is equivalent to finding the present value of expected future dividends.

5. Finally, the present value of the expected cash inflows is compared with the required outlay, or cost, of the project; if the asset's present value exceeds its cost, the project should be accepted. Otherwise, the project should be rejected.

If an individual investor identifies and invests in a stock or bond whose market price is less than its true value, then the value of the investor's portfolio will increase. Similarly, if the firm identifies (or creates) an investment opportunity with a present value greater than its cost, the value of the firm will increase. This increase in firm value from capital budgeting will be reflected in the growth factor, g, that we discussed in Chapters 5 and 6. Thus, there is a very direct link between capital budgeting and stock values: The more effective the firm's capital budgeting procedures, the higher is its growth rate, and hence the higher the price of its stock.

Capital Budgeting Decision Rules

A number of different methods are used to rank projects and to decide whether or not they should be accepted for inclusion in the capital budget. In this section we will discuss five different methods that are used by firms today: payback, accounting rate of return (ARR), net present value (NPV), internal rate of return (IRR), and profitability index (PI). Then, in the next section, we will evaluate the methods with respect to how well they help achieve our goal of value maximization.

We will use the cash flow data shown in Table 8-1 for Projects S and L to illustrate each method. We assume that the projects are equally risky. Note that the cash flows, CF_t, are expected values, and that they

Table 8-1
Cash Flows for Projects S and L

Year (t)	Expected After-Tax Net Cash Flow, CF_t	
	Project S	Project L
0	($1,000)[a]	($1,000)[a]
1	500	100
2	400	300
3	300	400
4	100	600

[a]Represents the net investment outlay, or initial cost. The parentheses indicate a negative number, or cash outflow.

are adjusted for tax, depreciation, and salvage value effects. Also, since many projects require both fixed assets plus an addition to net working capital, the investment outlays shown as CF_0 include any necessary changes in net working capital.[1] Finally, we assume that all cash flows occur at the end of the designated year. Incidentally, the S stands for *short* and the L for *long*: Project S is a short-term project and L is a long-term one in the sense that S's cash inflows tend to come in sooner than L's.

Payback Period

The *payback period*, defined as the number of years a firm expects it will take to recover its original investment from net cash flows, was the first formal method developed for use in evaluating capital budgeting projects. When applied to Projects S and L, the payback period is 2⅓ years for S and 3⅓ years for L:[2]

---

[1]Perhaps the most difficult part of the capital budgeting process is the estimation of the relevant cash flows. For simplicity, the net cash flows are treated as a given in this chapter, since this will allow us to focus on our main area of concern, the capital budgeting decision rules. Then, in Chapter 9, we will discuss cash flow estimation in detail. Also, note that *working capital* is defined as the firm's current assets, while *net working capital* is current assets minus current liabilities.

[2]The easiest way to calculate the payback period is to accumulate the project's net cash flows and see when they sum to zero. For example, the *cumulative* net cash flows of Project S are listed below:

Year 0	($1,000)
Year 1	(500)
Year 2	(100)
Year 3	200
Year 4	300

Thus, the investment is recovered in Year 3. Assuming that cash flows occur evenly during the year, the recovery actually occurs one-third of the way into Year 3: $100 remains to be recovered at the end of Year 2, and since Year 3 produces $300 in net cash flow, the payback period for Project S is 2⅓ years.

$$\text{Payback}_S: 2^1/_3 \text{ years.}$$
$$\text{Payback}_L: 3^1/_3 \text{ years.}$$

If the firm required a payback of three years or less, Project S would be accepted, but Project L would be rejected. If the projects were *mutually exclusive*, S would be accepted over L because S has the shorter payback.[3] Thus, the payback method ranks S over L.

The *discounted payback period* is similar to the regular payback period except that the expected cash flows are discounted by the project's cost of capital.[4] Thus, the discounted payback period is defined as the number of years a firm expects to take to recover its original investment from *discounted* net cash flows. Table 8-2 contains the discounted net cash flows for Projects S and L, assuming a project cost of capital of 10 percent. To construct Table 8-2, each cash inflow in Table 8-1 is divided by $(1 + k)^t = (1.10)^t$, where t is the year in which the cash flow occurs and k is the project's cost of capital. After 3 years, Project S should have generated $1,011 in discounted cash inflows. Since the cost is $1,000, the discounted payback is just under 3 years or, to be precise, 2 + ($214/ $225) = 2.95 years. Project L's discounted payback is 3.88 years:

$$\text{Discounted payback}_S = 2.95 \text{ years.}$$
$$\text{Discounted payback}_L = 3.88 \text{ years.}$$

For Projects S and L, the rankings are the same regardless of which payback method is used; that is, Project S is preferred to Project L, and Project S would still be selected if the firm were to require a payback of three years or less. Often, however, the regular and the discounted paybacks produce conflicting rankings.

The advantage of the discounted payback is that it gives consideration to the project's cost of capital. For example, if a project's regular payback were three years, this would suggest that if the project did produce the forecasted cash flows for three years, then it would at least be a break-even proposition. However, this is not really true, since no consideration has been given to the cost of the funds used to finance it. The discounted payback avoids this difficulty. However, as we shall see, both payback methods have some serious deficiencies, and other procedures are better from the standpoint of stock price maximization.

It should be noted that the payback period does provide information on how long funds will be tied up in a project. Thus, the shorter the

---

[3]*Mutually exclusive* means that if one project is taken on, the other must be rejected. For example, the installation of a conveyor-belt system in a warehouse and the purchase of a fleet of forklift trucks for the same warehouse would be mutually exclusive projects— accepting one implies rejection of the other. *Independent* projects are projects whose costs and revenues are independent of one another.

[4]The project's cost of capital reflects (1) the marginal cost of capital to the firm and (2) the differential risk between the firm's existing projects and the project being evaluated. This concept will be discussed in detail in Chapter 10.

Table 8-2
Discounted Cash Flows for Projects S and L

Year (t)	Discounted Net Cash Flow			
	Project S		Project L	
	Annual	Cumulative	Annual	Cumulative
0	($1,000)	($1,000)	($1,000)	($1,000)
1	455	(545)	91	(909)
2	331	(241)	248	(661)
3	225	11	301	(360)
4	68	79	410	50

payback period, other things held constant, the greater is the project's liquidity. Also, since cash flows expected in the far future are often regarded as being riskier than near-term cash flows, the payback is often used as a rough measure of project riskiness.

The *accounting rate of return (ARR)*, which looks at a project's contribution to net income rather than its cash flow, is the second oldest evaluation technique. In its most commonly used form, the ARR is measured as the ratio of the project's average annual expected net income to its average investment. If we assume that both Projects S and L will be depreciated by the straight line method to a book value of zero, then each will have a total depreciation expense of $1,000, or $1,000/4 = $250 per year. The average cash flow minus the average depreciation charge is the average annual income. For Project S, average annual income is $75:

Accounting Rate of Return (ARR)

$$\text{Average annual income} = \text{Average cash flow} - \text{Annual depreciation}$$
$$= (\$1,300/4) - \$250 = \$75.$$

The average investment is the beginning investment minus one-half the total depreciation, or $500:

$$\text{Average investment} = \text{Cost} - 0.5(\text{Depreciation})$$
$$= \$1,000 - \$500 = \$500.$$

This $500 is also the undepreciated value of the asset halfway through its life.

Combining the average annual income with the average investment, we obtain an ARR for Project S of 15 percent:

$$\text{ARR}_\text{S} = \frac{\text{Average annual income}}{\text{Average investment}} = \frac{\$75}{\$500} = 15\%.$$

By a similar calculation, we determine ARR_L to be 20 percent. Thus, the ARR method ranks Project L over Project S. If the firm required an ARR of 16 percent or more, Project L would be accepted, but Project S would be rejected. Note also that in this case, the project rankings under the ARR method are the opposite of the project rankings using either payback period method. One could argue about which method is better, and hence which set of rankings should be used, but this would really be a hollow argument, because all three methods are badly flawed. The regular payback and the ARR both ignore the time value of money, and the discounted payback ignores cash flows that are expected after the payback year.[5] Therefore, all three procedures could lead to errors in capital budgeting.

Net Present Value (NPV)

As the flaws in the payback and the ARR methods were recognized, people began to search for methods to improve the effectiveness of project evaluations. One such method is the *net present value (NPV)* method. To implement this approach, one proceeds as follows:

1. Find the present value of each cash flow, discounted at the project's cost of capital.

2. Add up these discounted cash flows; their sum is defined as the project's NPV.

3. If the NPV is positive, the project should be accepted; if the NPV is negative, it should be rejected; and if two projects are mutually exclusive, the one with the higher positive NPV should be chosen.

The NPV can be expressed as follows:

$$\text{NPV} = \sum_{t=0}^{n} \frac{\text{CF}_t}{(1 + k)^t}. \tag{8-1}$$

Here CF_t is the expected net cash flow at Period t, and k is the project's cost of capital. Cash outflows (expenditures on the project, such as the cost of buying equipment or building factories) are treated as *negative* cash flows. In evaluating Projects S and L, only CF_0 is negative, but for many large projects such as the Alaska Pipeline, an electric generating plant, or a new generation of computers, outflows occur for several years before operations begin and the cash flows become positive. Also, note that Equation 8-1 is quite general, so inflows and outflows could occur on any basis (say quarterly), and t could represent quarters or months rather than years.

At a 10 percent cost of capital, the NPV of Project S is $78.82:

$$\text{NPV}_S = \frac{-\$1,000}{(1.10)^0} + \frac{\$500}{(1.10)^1} + \frac{\$400}{(1.10)^2} + \frac{\$300}{(1.10)^3} + \frac{\$100}{(1.10)^4}$$

$$= -\$1,000 + \$454.55 + \$330.58 + \$225.39 + \$68.30$$

$$= \$78.82.$$

[5]Actually, there are many ways to calculate ARRs. Since all of them have major deficiencies, we see no point in extending the discussion.

By a similar process, we find NPV_L = \$49.18. On this basis, both projects should be accepted if they are independent, but S should be the one chosen if they are mutually exclusive.[6]

The rationale for the NPV method is straightforward. The value of a firm is the sum of the values of its parts. If a firm takes on a zero-NPV project, the position of the original investors remains constant—the firm becomes larger, but the price of its stock remains unchanged. However, if the firm takes on a project with a positive NPV, the position of the original investors is improved. In our example, the original shareholders' wealth would increase by \$78.82 if the firm takes on Project S, but by only \$49.18 if it takes on Project L. Viewed in this manner, it is easy to see why S is preferred to L, and it is also easy to see the logic of the NPV approach.[7]

In Chapter 5, we examined procedures for finding the yield to maturity, or rate of return, on a bond. Exactly the same concepts are employed in capital budgeting when the IRR method is used. The IRR is defined as that discount rate, r, which equates the present value of a project's expected cash inflows to the present value of the project's expected costs: *Internal Rate of Return (IRR)*

$$PV(\text{Inflows}) = PV(\text{Investment costs}),$$

or, equivalently,

$$\sum_{t=0}^{n} \frac{CF_t}{(1 + r)^t} = 0. \qquad (8\text{-}2)$$

For our Project S, here is the set-up:

$$\frac{-\$1,000}{(1 + r)^0} + \frac{\$500}{(1 + r)^1} + \frac{\$400}{(1 + r)^2} + \frac{\$300}{(1 + r)^3} + \frac{\$100}{(1 + r)^4} = 0.$$

Here we know the value of CF_t for all t, but we do not know the value of r. Thus, we have an equation with one unknown, and we can solve for the value of r. *This value of r is defined as the IRR.*

Notice that the internal rate of return formula, Equation 8-2, is simply the NPV formula, Equation 8-1, solved for the particular discount rate that causes the NPV to equal zero. Thus, the same basic equation is used for both methods, but in the NPV method the discount rate, k, is specified and the NPV is found, while in the IRR method the NPV is specified to equal zero and the value of r = IRR that forces this equality is determined.

---

[6] If you have one of the better financial calculators, you can input the cash flows and the cost of capital, and then hit a button marked "NPV" to find a project's NPV.

[7] Of course, this description of the process is oversimplified. Both analysts and investors anticipate that firms will identify and accept positive NPV projects, and stock prices reflect these expectations. Thus, stock prices react to announcements of new capital projects only to the extent that such projects were not already expected.

The internal rate of return may be found by several procedures. We will discuss three here.

Procedure 1: Trial and Error. In the trial and error method, we first compute the present value of cash inflows from an investment using a somewhat arbitrarily selected discount rate. Since the cost of capital for most firms is in the range of 10 to 20 percent, it is to be hoped that projects will promise a return of at least 10 percent. Therefore, 10 percent is a good starting point for most problems. Then we compare the present value at a 10 percent cost of capital with the present value of the investment's cost. Suppose the present value of the inflows is *smaller* than the present value of the project's cost. What do we do now? We must *raise* the present value of the inflows, and to do this we must *lower* the discount rate, say from 10 percent to 8 percent, and go through the process again. Conversely, if the inflow present value is higher than the cost present value, we raise the discount rate and repeat the process. We continue until Equation 8-2 is approximately equal to zero. *The discount rate that forces this solution is defined as the internal rate of return.*

This calculation process is illustrated in Table 8-3 for the same Projects S and L that we analyzed earlier. First, the present value interest factors are obtained from Table A-1 in Appendix A, at the end of the text; note that for t = 0, PVIF is always equal to 1.0. These factors are then multiplied by the cash flows for the corresponding years, and the present

Table 8-3
Finding the Internal Rate of Return for Projects S and L

Year	Cash Flow (CF_t Values) S	L
0	($1,000)	($1,000)
1	500	100
2	400	300
3	300	400
4	100	600

		NPV at 10%			NPV at 15%	
		Present Value			Present Value	
Year	PVIF	PV_S	PV_L	PVIF	PV_S	PV_L
0	1.0000	($1,000.00)	($1,000.00)	1.0000	($1,000.00)	($1,000.00)
1	0.9091	454.55	90.91	0.8696	434.80	86.96
2	0.8264	330.56	247.92	0.7561	302.44	226.83
3	0.7513	225.39	300.52	0.6575	197.25	263.00
4	0.6830	68.30	409.80	0.5718	57.18	343.08
NPV		$ 78.80	$ 49.15		($ 8.33)	($ 80.13)

values of the annual cash flows are placed in the appropriate columns. Finally, we sum the present values of the yearly cash flows to obtain the investment's net present value. Because the net present value of both investments is positive at the 10 percent rate, we increase the rate to 15 percent and try again. At this point, the net present value of S is just below zero, which indicates that its IRR is slightly less than 15 percent. L's net present value at 15 percent is well below zero, so its IRR is quite a bit less than 15 percent. These trials could be continued to obtain closer and closer approximations to the exact IRR, but as noted below, procedures are available to speed up the process.

Procedure 2: Graphic Solution. The graphic method for finding IRRs involves plotting curves that show the relationship between a project's NPV and the discount rate used to calculate the NPV. Such a curve is defined as the project's *net present value profile*; profiles for Projects L and S are shown in Figure 8-1. To construct the profiles, we first note that at a zero discount rate, the NPV is simply the total of the undiscounted cash flows of the project; thus, at a zero discount rate NPV_S = \$300, while NPV_L = \$400. These values are plotted as the vertical axis intercepts in Figure 8-1. Next, we calculate the projects' NPVs at three discount rates, say 5, 10, and 15 percent and plot these values. The four points plotted on our graph are shown at the bottom of the figure. When we connect the plot points, we have the net present value profiles.[8]

Since the IRR is defined as the discount rate at which a project's NPV equals zero, *the point where its net present value profile crosses the horizontal axis indicates the project's internal rate of return.* Figure 8-1 shows that IRR_S is 14.5 percent, while IRR_L is 11.8 percent. With graph paper and a sharp pencil, the graphic method yields reasonably accurate results.[9]

Procedure 3: Financial Calculator and Computer Solutions. Internal rates of return can be calculated very easily by computers, and many firms have now computerized their capital budgeting processes and automatically generate IRRs, NPVs, and paybacks for all projects. Even many hand-held calculators have built-in functions for calculating IRRs. Thus, business firms have no difficulty whatever with the mechanical side of capital budgeting, and a serious business student should have a

---

[8]Notice that the present value profiles are curved—they are *not* straight lines. Also, the NPVs approach the t = 0 cash flow (the cost of the project) as the discount rate increases without limit. The reason is that, at an infinitely high discount rate, the PV of the inflows would be zero, and NPV = CF_0, which in our example is −\$1,000. We should also note that under certain conditions the NPV profiles can cross the horizontal axis several times, or never cross it. This point is discussed in Appendix 8A.

[9]For all practical purposes, an IRR that is accurate to within about one-half percent is sufficient, given the inaccuracy inherent in the cash flow estimates. The calculations may be carried out to several decimal places, but for most projects this is spurious accuracy.

Figure 8-1
Net Present Value Profiles:
NPVs of Projects S and L at Different Discount Rates

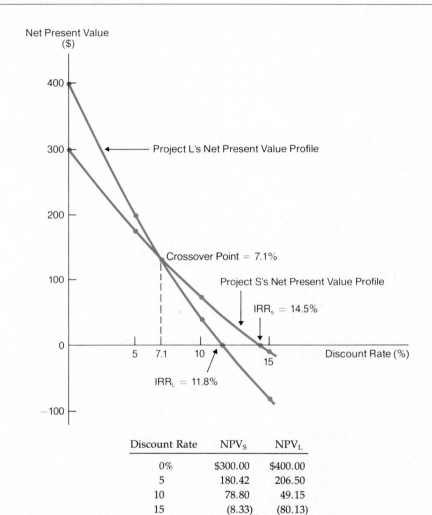

Discount Rate	NPV$_S$	NPV$_L$
0%	$300.00	$400.00
5	180.42	206.50
10	78.80	49.15
15	(8.33)	(80.13)

financial calculator capable of finding IRRs. All IRRs reported hereafter in this and the following chapters were obtained using a computer or a financial calculator. By keying in the cash flows and then hitting the IRR button, we find that Project S has IRR$_S$ = 14.5%, while IRR$_L$ = 11.8%.

Rationale and Use
of the IRR Method

What is so special about the particular discount rate that equates a project's cost with the present value of its receipts (the IRR)? To answer this question, let us first assume that our illustrative firm obtains the $1,000

Table 8-4
Analysis of Project S's IRR as a Loan Rate

Investment (1)	Cash Flow (2)	Interest on the Loan at 14.5% $0.145 \times (1) = (3)$	Repayment of Principal $(2) - (3) = (4)$	Ending Loan Balance $(1) - (4) = (5)$
$1,000.00	$500	$145.00	$355.00	$645.00
645.00	400	93.53	306.47	338.53
338.53	300	49.09	250.91	87.62
87.62	100	12.70	87.30	0.32

needed to take on Project S by borrowing from a bank at an interest rate of 14.5 percent. Since the internal rate of return on this particular project was calculated to be 14.5 percent, the same as the cost of the bank loan, the firm can invest in the project, use the cash flows generated by the investment to pay off the principal and interest on the loan, and come out exactly even on the transaction. This point is demonstrated in Table 8-4, which shows that Project S provides cash flows that are just sufficient to pay 14.5 percent interest on the unpaid balance of a bank loan, retire the loan over the life of the project, and end up with a balance that differs from zero only by a rounding error of 32 cents.

If the internal rate of return exceeds the cost of the funds used to finance a project, a surplus remains after paying for the capital. This surplus accrues to the firm's stockholders, so taking on the project increases the value of the firm's stock. If the internal rate of return is less than the cost of capital, taking on the project imposes a cost on existing stockholders, so in this case accepting the project would result in a reduction of value. It is this "breakeven" characteristic that makes us interested in the internal rate of return.[10]

Continuing with our example of Projects S and L, if both projects have a cost of capital of 10 percent, the internal rate of return rule indicates that if the projects are independent, both should be accepted—they both do better than "break even." If they are mutually exclusive, S ranks higher and should be accepted, while L should be rejected. If the cost of capital is 15 percent, both projects should be rejected.

Another method that is used to evaluate projects is the *profitability index* (PI), or the *benefit/cost ratio*, as it is sometimes called:

Profitability Index (PI)

$$PI = \frac{PV \text{ benefits}}{PV \text{ costs}} = \frac{\sum_{t=0}^{n} \dfrac{CIF_t}{(1 + k)^t}}{\sum_{t=0}^{n} \dfrac{COF_t}{(1 + k)^t}}. \tag{8-3}$$

[10]This example illustrates the logic of the IRR method, but for technical correctness, the capital used to finance the project should be assumed to come from both debt and equity, and not from debt alone.

Here, CIF_t represents the expected cash inflows, or benefits, and COF_t represents the expected cash outflows, or costs. The PI shows the *relative* profitability of any project, or the present value of benefits per dollar of costs. The PI for Project S, based on a 10 percent cost of capital, is 1.079:

$$PI_S = \frac{\$1,078.82}{\$1,000} = 1.079.$$

Similarly, $PI_L = 1.049$.

A project is acceptable if its PI is greater than 1.0, and the higher the PI, the higher is the project's ranking. Mathematically, the NPV, the IRR, and the PI methods must always reach the same accept/reject decisions for independent projects: If a project's NPV is positive, its IRR must exceed k and its PI must be greater than 1.0. However, NPV, IRR, and PI can give different rankings for pairs of projects, which can lead to conflicts between the three methods when mutually exclusive projects are being compared.

Evaluation of the Decision Rules

We have presented five possible capital budgeting rules, all of which are used to a greater or lesser extent in practice. However, the methods can lead to quite different accept/reject decisions, so we need to answer this question: Which of the methods is best? Obviously, the best method is the one which selects the set of projects that maximizes shareholder wealth. If more than one method does this, then the best method would be the method that is easiest to use in practice.

Here are three properties that must be exhibited by a selection method if it is to lead to consistently correct capital budgeting decisions:

1. The method must consider all cash flows throughout the entire life of a project.

2. The method must consider the time value of money; that is, it must reflect the fact that dollars which come in sooner are more valuable than distant dollars.

3. When the method is used to select from a set of mutually exclusive projects, it must choose that project which maximizes the firm's stock value.

Now, how do the five decision criteria stand in regard to the required properties? Both the regular and the discounted paybacks violate Property 1. They do not consider all cash flows. Additionally, the undiscounted payback also violates Property 2. The accounting rate of return also violates Property 2: It uses accounting income rather than cash flow, and it does not differentiate between early and late dollars. The NPV, IRR, and PI methods all satisfy Properties 1 and 2, and all three lead to identical and correct accept/reject decisions for independent projects. However, only the NPV method satisfies Property 3 under all conditions: There are certain conditions under which the IRR and the PI methods fail to identify correctly that project, in a set of mutually exclusive projects, which maximizes the firm's stock price. This point is explored in depth in the following sections.

We noted above that the NPV method exhibits all the desired decision rule properties and, as such, it is the best method for evaluating projects. Because the NPV method is better than IRR and PI, we were tempted to explain NPV only, state that it should be used as the acceptance criterion, and go on to the next topic. However, the IRR and PI methods are familiar to many corporate executives, and they are widely entrenched in industry. Therefore, it is important that finance students thoroughly understand the IRR and PI methods and be prepared to explain why, at times, a project with a lower IRR or PI may be preferable to one with a higher IRR or PI. Also, it is at times useful to compare alternatives in terms of their IRRs or PIs. However, when such comparisons are made, it is essential that the analyst be fully aware of how the IRR and the PI are developed, and when they can be used in a rational manner.

Comparison of the NPV and IRR Methods

NPV Rankings Depend on the Discount Rate

We saw in Figure 8-1 that each project's NPV declines as the discount rate increases. Notice in the figure that Project L has the higher NPV at low discount rates, while NPV_S exceeds NPV_L if the discount rate is above 7.1 percent. Notice also that Project L's NPV is "more sensitive" to changes in the discount rate than is NPV_S; that is, Project L's net present value profile has the steeper slope, indicating that a small change in k has a larger effect on NPV_L than on NPV_S.

To see why L has the greater sensitivity, recall first that the cash flows from S are received faster than those from L; in a payback sense, S is a short-term project, while L is a long-term project. Next, recall the equation for the NPV:

$$NPV = \frac{CF_0}{(1 + k)^0} + \frac{CF_1}{(1 + k)^1} + \frac{CF_2}{(1 + k)^2} + \frac{CF_3}{(1 + k)^3} + \frac{CF_4}{(1 + k)^4}.$$

Now notice that the denominators of the terms in this equation increase as k and t increase, and the increase is exponential; that is, the effect of a higher k is more pronounced if t is larger. To understand this point more clearly, consider the following data:

PV of $100 due in 1 year, discounted at 5%	$95.24
PV of $100 due in 1 year, discounted at 10%	$90.91
Percentage decline in PV resulting from a 5% increase in k when t = 1	−4.5%
PV of $100 due in 10 years, discounted at 5%	$61.39
PV of $100 due in 10 years, discounted at 10%	$38.55
Percentage decline in PV resulting from a 5% increase in k when t = 10	−37.2%

A doubling of the discount rate causes only a slight decline in the PV of a Year 1 cash flow, but the same discount rate increase causes the PV of a Year 10 cash flow to fall by 37 percent. Thus, if a project has most of its cash flows coming in the early years, its NPV will not be lowered very much if the discount rate increases, but a project whose cash flows come later will be severely penalized by high discount rates. Accordingly, Project L, which has its largest cash flows in the later years, is hurt badly when the discount rate is high, while Project S, which has relatively rapid cash flows, is affected less by high discount rates.

Independent Projects

If two projects are *independent*, then the NPV and IRR criteria always lead to the same accept/reject decision—if NPV says accept, IRR also says accept. To see why this is so, look back at Figure 8-1 and notice (1) that the IRR criterion for acceptance is that the project's cost of capital is less than (or to the left of) the IRR, and (2) that whenever the project's cost of capital is less than the IRR, its NPV is positive. Thus, for any cost of capital less than 11.8 percent, Project L is acceptable by both the NPV and the IRR criteria, while both methods reject the project if the cost of capital is greater than 11.8 percent. Project S—and all other independent projects under consideration—could be analyzed similarly.

Mutually Exclusive Projects

Now assume that Projects S and L are *mutually exclusive*, and not independent. That is, we can choose either Project S or Project L, or we can reject both, but we cannot accept both projects. Notice in Figure 8-1 that, as long as the cost of capital is *greater than* the crossover rate of 7.1 percent, NPV_S is greater than NPV_L, and also that IRR_S is greater than IRR_L. Therefore, for k greater than the crossover rate of 7.1 percent, the two methods lead to the selection of the same project. However, if the cost of capital is *less than* the crossover rate, the NPV method ranks Project L higher, but the IRR method indicates that Project S is better. Thus, a conflict exists. NPV says choose mutually exclusive L, while IRR says take S. Which answer is correct? Logic suggests that the NPV method is best, since it selects the project which adds the most to share-holder wealth.

There are two basic conditions which cause NPV profiles to cross, and thus which lead to potential conflicts between NPV and IRR: (1) when *project size (or scale) differences* exist, meaning that the cost of one project is larger than that of the other, or (2) when *timing differences* exist, meaning that the timing of cash flows from the two projects differs, with most of the cash flows from one project coming in the early years and most of the cash flows from the other project coming in the later years, as occurred with Projects L and S.[11]

When either size or timing differences occur, the firm will have different amounts of funds to invest in the various years, depending on which of the two mutually exclusive projects it chooses. For example, if one project costs more than the other, then the firm will have more money at t = 0 to invest elsewhere if it selects the smaller project, while for projects of equal size, the one with the large early cash flows provides more funds for reinvestment in the early years. Thus, the assumed rate of return at which differential cash flows can be invested is an important consideration. This point is illustrated in the following sections.

Project Scale. Mutually exclusive projects often differ in size. For example, suppose a firm has the opportunity to buy a copper mine for $600,000. If it buys the mine, the company can get the ore to its smelter in two different ways. Plan S (the smaller project) calls for buying a fleet of trucks for $400,000, resulting in a total cost of the project of $600,000 + $400,000 = $1,000,000. Plan L (the larger project) calls for spending $4.4 million to install a conveyor-belt system for moving the ore, making the total cost $600,000 + $4,400,000 = $5,000,000. If trucks are used, then fuel, labor, and other operating costs will be much higher than with the conveyor system. For simplicity, assume that the project will operate for only one year, after which the ore body will be exhausted. Assume also that after-tax expected net cash inflows, which occur at the end of the year, will be $1.28 million under Plan S but $6.0 million under Plan L.

Assuming that both projects' cost of capital is 10 percent, we can find each project's NPV as follows:

$$\text{NPV}_\text{S} = -\$1,000,000 + \$1,280,000/(1.10) = \$163,636.$$
$$\text{NPV}_\text{L} = -\$5,000,000 + \$6,000,000/(1.10) = \$454,545.$$

---

[11]Of course, it is possible for mutually exclusive projects to differ with respect to both scale and timing. Also, if mutually exclusive projects have different lives (as opposed to different cash flow patterns over a common life), this introduces further complications, and for meaningful comparisons, mutually exclusive projects must be evaluated over a common life. This point will be discussed in detail in the next chapter.

We can also find each project's IRR:

$$\text{IRR}_\text{S}: \quad -\$1,000,000 + \$1,280,000/(1 + r) = 0$$
$$\$1,280,000/(1 + r) = \$1,000,000$$
$$1 + r = \$1,280,000/\$1,000,000 = 1.28$$
$$\text{IRR}_\text{S} = r = 0.28 = 28\%.$$

$$\text{IRR}_\text{L}: \quad -\$5,000,000 + \$6,000,000/(1 + r) = 0$$
$$\$6,000,000/(1 + r) = \$5,000,000$$
$$1 + r = \$6,000,000/\$5,000,000 = 1.20$$
$$\text{IRR}_\text{L} = r = 0.20 = 20\%.$$

Thus, there is a conflict, with $\text{NPV}_\text{L} > \text{NPV}_\text{S}$, but $\text{IRR}_\text{S} > \text{IRR}_\text{L}$.

Given this conflict, which project should be accepted? If we assume that the cost of capital is constant, meaning that the firm can raise all the capital it wants at a cost of 10 percent, then the answer is L, the project with the higher NPV. The differential between the initial outlays on the two projects ($4 million) can be looked upon as an investment itself, Project Δ. That is, Project L can be broken down into two components, one equal to Project S and the other a "residual project" equal to a hypothetical Project Δ. The hypothetical investment has a "cost" of $4 million and a net present value equal to the differential between the NPVs of the first two projects, or $290,909. This is shown below:

Project	Cost	NPV
L	$5,000,000	$454,545
S	1,000,000	163,636
Δ	$4,000,000	$290,909

Since the hypothetical Project Δ has a positive net present value, it should be accepted. This amounts to accepting Project L.

To put it another way, Project L can be split into two components, one costing $1 million and having a net present value of $163,636 and the other costing $4 million and having a net present value of $290,909. Since each of the two components has a positive net present value, both should be accepted. But if Project S is accepted, the second component of Project L, the hypothetical Project Δ, is rejected. Since the IRR method selects Project S, while the NPV method selects Project L, we conclude that the NPV method is better.[12]

---

[12]The matter of project size can be considered in more dramatic terms: Would a business that is able to raise all the capital it wants at a cost of 10 percent rather have a 20 percent rate of return on a 10 cent investment or a 15 percent return on a $1 million investment? The answer is obvious here, and the same principle applies in more realistic situations. Notice also that, under the assumption of unlimited capital at a constant cost, the existence of other projects is irrelevant to the choice between L and S. Any other projects that are "good" can be accepted and financed regardless of whether or not L or S is selected.

NPV profiles for these two projects are shown in Panel a of Figure 8-2. The crossover point for the two profiles is 18 percent, indicating that no NPV/IRR conflict occurs unless the cost of capital is less than 18 percent. In our example, k = 10%, and this is why the conflict occurred.[13]

Timing of Cash Flows. Conflicts between NPV and IRR can also arise due to differences in the timing of projects' cash flows, even when the two projects have exactly the same initial investment cost. To illustrate, suppose we were considering the purchase of timber rights in a forest for $1 million. If we were to log the property immediately according to Plan S (which is thus a short-term project), our expected cash flow would be $1.28 million at the end of Year 1. Alternatively, if we were to delay logging the property for 10 years according to Plan L (which is a long-term project), the larger trees would produce a net cash inflow of $4,046,000 at the end of Year 10.

Assuming that each project's cost of capital is 10 percent, we can find each project's NPV as follows:

$$NPV_S = -\$1,000,000 + \$1,280,000/(1.10)^1 = \$163,636.$$
$$NPV_L = -\$1,000,000 + \$4,046,000/(1.10)^{10} = \$559,908.$$

We can also find each project's IRR:

$$IRR_S: -\$1,000,000 + \$1,280,000/(1 + r)^1 = 0$$
$$r = IRR_S = 0.28 = 28\%.$$
$$IRR_L: -\$1,000,000 + \$4,046,000(1 + r)^{10} = 0$$
$$r = IRR_L = 0.15 = 15\%.$$

---

[13]The exact crossover point between the NPV profiles of Projects S and L can be calculated by finding Project Δ's IRR. First, note that Δ's cash flows are as follows:

	t = 0	t = 1
CF_L	($5,000,000)	$6,000,000
$-CF_S$	− (1,000,000)	− 1,280,000
CF_Δ	($4,000,000)	$4,720,000

Then, find Project Δ's IRR:

$$-\$4,000,000 + \$4,720,000/(1 + r) = 0$$
$$IRR_\Delta = r = 0.18 = 18\%.$$

If we developed an NPV profile for Project Δ and plotted it on Panel a of Figure 8-2, its vertical axis intercept would be at +$720,000, and it would decline and cross the horizontal axis at 18 percent, immediately below the crossover point.

As we shall see later in the chapter, k is the proper reinvestment rate. If k, and hence reinvestment rates, are low, then Project Δ has a positive NPV. However, as k rises, then Project Δ becomes less attractive. At a rate of 18 percent, Δ's NPV = 0, and NPV_Δ becomes negative as the assumed reinvestment rate rises above 18 percent.

Figure 8-2
NPV Profiles of Mutually Exclusive Projects
That Differ in Size and Timing

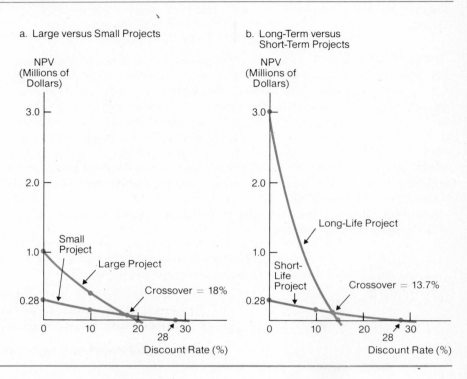

a. Large versus Small Projects

b. Long-Term versus
    Short-Term Projects

Again, we have a conflict: Because of timing differences, $NPV_L > NPV_S$, but $IRR_S > IRR_L$.

We know that high discount rates impose a greater penalty on distant cash flows than on near-term cash flows. Therefore, long-term projects such as Project L have NPV profiles which decline quite steeply relative to the NPV profiles of projects such as S. Panel b of Figure 8-2 illustrates this point for the two projects under consideration here. If the cost of capital is to the left of the crossover point, 13.7 percent, then a conflict occurs between NPV and IRR. In this case, $k = 10\%$, so a conflict does exist.

Earlier, where our two projects differed in scale but had no difference in the timing of cash flows, we set up a hypothetical Project Δ, which had a positive NPV, to show why the project with the larger basic NPV should be accepted. We can illustrate timing differences similarly. Project S provides a cash flow of $1,280,000 at the end of Year 1, while Project L has a cash flow of $4,046,000 at the end of Year 10. If we accept Project S, we get a cash flow of $1,280,000 at $t = 1$. If we accept Project L, we give up this Year 1 cash flow, which amounts to making an investment, in order to get $4,046,000 at t = 10. Thus, our "timing differ-ence" Project Δ has a cost of $1,280,000 at the end of Year 1 and a cash inflow of $4,046,000 at the end of Year 10, and its NPV is $396,272:

$$NPV_\Delta = -\$1,280,000/(1.10)^1 + \$4,046,000/(1.10)^{10}$$
$$= -\$1,163,636 + \$1,559,908 = \$396,272.$$

If we accept Project S, we are rejecting Project Δ, with its positive NPV of $396,272. Since we would be foregoing a $396,272 increase in the value of the firm if we accepted S, we should reject it and accept Project L.

The Reinvestment Rate Assumption

In both our differential size and differential timing examples, we found that *cash flow differentials* existed. In the size example, we would have had an extra $4 million at t = 0 if we had taken the smaller project, but our cash flow at t = 1 would have been smaller by $4.72 million. In the timing example, we would have had an extra $1.28 million in Year 1 if we had taken the shorter-term project, but $4.046 million less at t = 10. The critical issue in resolving conflicts between mutually exclusive proj-ects is this: What can we do with cash flows generated earlier rather than later, or to put it another way, at what rate can we reinvest differ-ential early years' cash flows? *The use of the NPV method to compare projects implicitly assumes that the rate at which cash flows generated by a project can be reinvested is the cost of capital, while use of the IRR method implies that the firm has the opportunity to reinvest at the IRR.* Thus, the NPV method eval-uates the cash flows at the cost of capital, while the IRR method evalu-àtes them at the project's IRR. The cash flows may actually be with-drawn as dividends by the stockholders and spent on beer and pizza, but the assumption of a reinvestment opportunity is still implicit in the calculations. To demonstrate this, consider the following steps:

Step 1. Notice that both the NPV and IRR methods involve the use of present value interest factors (PVIFs) in the solution process; for exam-ple, to determine the NPV, we multiply a series of cash flows by appro-priate PVIFs, sum these products, subtract the initial cost, and the result is the NPV. Thus, the NPV method involves using present value tables, and the same thing holds for finding the IRR.

Step 2. Refer back to Chapter 4, Table 4-1 and Equation 4-2, and notice how present value tables are constructed. *The present value of any future sum is defined as the beginning amount which, when compounded at a specified constant interest rate, will grow to equal the future amount over the stated time period.* From Table 4-1, we can see that the present value of $127.63 due in 5 years, when discounted at 5 percent, is $100 because when interest is earned on $100 and reinvested at a 5 percent rate for 5 years, it will grow to \$127.63. Thus, compounding and discounting are reciprocal relationships, and the *very construction of PV tables implies a reinvestment process*.

Step 3. Since both the NPV and IRR methods involve the use of compound interest tables, and since the very construction of these tables involves an assumed reinvestment process, the concept of reinvestment opportunities underlies both methods.

Step 4. The implicitly assumed reinvestment rate used in the NPV method is the cost of capital, k; that used in the IRR method is r, which is the IRR in the solution process. These are the rates built into the PVIFs. *Thus, the NPV method implicitly assumes that cash flows can be reinvested at the cost of capital, while the IRR method assumes reinvestment at the IRR itself.*

Suppose the cash flows from a project are not reinvested but are used to pay dividends. No reinvestment is involved, yet an IRR for the project could still be calculated—does this show that the reinvestment assumption is not *always* implied in the IRR calculation? The answer is *no*; reinvestment itself is not necessarily assumed, but the *opportunity for reinvestment* is *assumed*. Because that assumption is made in the very construction of the PV tables, we simply could not define or interpret the concepts of NPV or IRR without it.

Which is the better assumption, reinvestment at the cost of capital or reinvestment of each project's cash flows at that project's IRR? We can answer the question as follows:

1. Assume that the firm's cost of capital is 10 percent. Management can obtain all the funds it wants at this rate. This condition is expected to hold in the foreseeable future. Further, assume that all potential projects have the same risk as the firm's current projects.

2. The capital budgeting process calls for all potential projects to be evaluated at k = 10%. All projects with NPV > 0 are accepted. Plenty of capital is available to finance these projects, both now and in the future.

3. As cash flows come in from past investments, what will be done with them? These cash flows can either (1) be paid out to investors who, on average, require a 10 percent rate of return, or (2) be used as a substitute for outside capital that costs 10 percent. Thus, since the cash flows are expected to save the firm 10 percent, this is their value to the firm, and hence their opportunity cost reinvestment rate.

4. The IRR method implicitly assumes reinvestment at the internal rate of return itself. Under the assumptions of our example—which is generally very close to true for most firms during most time periods—reinvestment would not occur at the IRR rate. Given (1) ready access to capital markets and (2) a constant expected future cost of capital, the appropriate reinvestment rate is the opportunity cost of capital, or 10 percent. Even if the firm takes on projects in the future whose IRRs average some high rate, say 30 percent, this is irrelevant—those projects could be financed with new external capital anyway, so cash flows from past projects have an opportunity cost reinvestment rate which is only equal to the cost of capital.

Therefore, we simply must come to the conclusion that *the correct reinvestment rate assumption is the cost of capital, which is implicit in the NPV method*. This, in turn, leads to a preference for the NPV method, at least for firms willing and able to obtain capital at a cost reasonably close to their current cost of capital. In Chapter 10, when we get into capital rationing, we will see that under certain conditions the NPV rule may be questionable, but for most firms at most times, NPV is without a doubt conceptually better than IRR.

We should reiterate that, when projects are independent, the NPV and IRR methods both make exactly the same accept/reject decision. However, *when evaluating mutually exclusive projects, the NPV method should be used*. We should also note that there is one other situation in which the IRR approach cannot be used—this is when evaluating *nonnormal* projects. A *normal* capital project is one that has one or more cash outflows (costs) followed by a series of positive cash inflows. If, however, a project calls for a large cash outflow either sometime during or at the end of its life, then it is a nonnormal project. Nonnormal projects, which present unique difficulties when evaluated by the IRR method, are discussed in Appendix 8A.

Comparison of the NPV and PI Methods

We can use our earlier example of differing project size to illustrate the conflict between NPV and PI. In that example, we compared Project L (for large), which called for investing $5 million in a mine equipped with a conveyor-belt system for handling ore, with Project S (for small), which called for an expenditure of only $1 million to do the same thing by employing a fleet of trucks. However, the conveyor-belt system had lower operating costs, so its cash flows were larger, and the net present values were found to be $454,545 for L and $163,636 for S. Using the NPV criterion, on the one hand, we would select Project L. On the other hand, if we compute the ratio of the present value of the returns (or benefits) of each project to its cost, we find S's ratio to be $PI_S = \$1,163,636/\$1,000,000 = 1.16$, and L's ratio to be $PI_L = \$5,454,545/\$5,000,000 = 1.09$. Thus, the NPV method suggests that we should accept Project L because $NPV_L > NPV_S$, but the PI method suggests acceptance of Project S, because $PI_S > PI_L$.

Given this conflict, which project should be accepted? Alternatively stated: Is it better to use the net present value approach on an absolute basis (NPV) or on a relative basis (PI)? *For a firm that seeks to maximize stockholders' wealth, the NPV method is better.* Recall that the differential between the initial outlays of the two projects ($4,000,000) can itself be looked upon as an investment, Project Δ, with an NPV equal to the differential in the NPVs of the two projects ($290,909). Thus, Project L can be broken down into two projects, one equal to Project S and one a residual project equal to the hypothetical Project Δ. Since both Project S and Project Δ contribute positively to the value of the firm, they should both be accepted. This amounts to accepting Project L, the one chosen by the NPV method. Thus, we conclude that the NPV method leads to better decisions than does the PI method.

The Post-Audit

An important aspect of the capital budgeting process is the *post-audit*, which involves (1) a comparison of actual results to those predicted in the request for funds, and (2) an explanation of observed differences. For example, many firms require that the operating divisions send a monthly report for the first six months after a project goes into operation, and a quarterly report thereafter until the project's results are up to expectations. From then on, reports on the project are handled like those of other operations.

The post-audit has several purposes, including the following:

1. Improve forecasts. When decision makers systematically compare their projections to actual outcomes, there is a tendency for estimates to improve. Conscious or unconscious biases are observed and eliminated; new forecasting methods are sought as the need for them becomes apparent; and people simply tend to do everything better, including forecasting, if they know that their actions are being monitored.

2. Improve operations. Businesses are run by people, and people can perform at higher or lower levels of efficiency. When a divisional team has made a forecast about a new installation, its members are, in a sense, putting their reputations on the line. If costs are above predicted levels, sales below expectations, and so on, then executives in production, sales, and other areas will strive to improve operations and to bring results into line with forecasts.

The post-audit is not a simple process. There are a number of factors that can cause complications. First, we must recognize that each element of the cash flow forecast is subject to uncertainty, so a percentage of all projects undertaken by any reasonably venturesome firm will necessarily go awry. This fact must be considered when appraising the performances of the operating executives who submit capital expenditure requests. Second, projects sometimes fail to meet expectations for reasons beyond the control of the operating executives and for reasons that no one could realistically be expected to anticipate.[14] For example, the imposition of price controls in the 1970s adversely affected many projects for which price increases had been projected, and the unexpected quadrupling of oil prices in the mid-1970s hurt others. Third, it is often difficult to separate the operating results of one investment from those of a larger system. While some projects stand alone and permit ready identification of costs and revenues, the actual cost savings that result from a replacement project may be very hard to measure. Fourth, if the postaudit process is not used with care, executives may be reluctant to suggest potentially profitable but risky projects. And fifth, the executives who were actually responsible for a given decision may have moved on by the time the results of the decision are known.

Because of these difficulties, some firms tend to play down the importance of the post-audit. However, observations of both businesses and governmental units suggest that the best-run and most successful organizations are the ones that put the greatest stress on post-audits. Accordingly, the post-audit is one of the most important elements in a good capital budgeting system.

Summary

Capital budgeting is similar in principle to security valuation—future cash flows are estimated, risks are appraised and reflected in a project's cost of capital discount rate, all cash flows are put on a present value basis, and if a project's *net present value (NPV)* is positive, it is accepted. Alternatively, if a project's *internal rate of return (IRR)* is greater than its cost of capital, it is accepted. Because of differing reinvestment rate assumptions, the NPV and IRR methods can lead to conflicts when evaluating *mutually exclusive* projects. When conflicts exist, they should, in general, be resolved in favor of the project with the higher NPV.

In outline form, the capital budgeting process centers around the following steps:

1. Ideas for projects are developed.

2. Projects are classified by type of investment: replacement, expansion of existing product lines, expansion into new markets, and "other."

3. The expected future cash flows from a project are estimated. This involves estimating (a) the investment outlay required for the project and (b) the cash inflows over the project's projected life. Cash flow estimation is the most important, yet the most difficult, step in the capital budgeting process. It will be discussed in detail in the next chapter.

4. The riskiness inherent in the project is appraised. This important subject is taken up in Chapter 10.

---

[14]Because of such uncertainties, many firms include in their "request for expenditure" package a list of key assumptions. Top managers often have more information on national political and economic trends than do division managers, engineers, and lower-level people, and highlighting the key assumptions in a separate exhibit helps to better utilize top management's unique expertise.

5. The next step is to rank projects by their NPVs or IRRs, accepting those with NPV > 0 or IRR > the cost of capital. Conflicts between NPV and IRR rankings should be resolved in favor of the NPV. Some firms also calculate projects' *payback periods, accounting rates of return (ARRs),* and *profitability indices (PIs).* The payback does provide an indication of a project's risk and liquidity, because it shows how long the original capital will be "at risk." Therefore, firms often calculate projects' NPVs, IRRs, and PIs as measures of profitability, and paybacks as a risk/liquidity indicator. We will discuss the use of these methods in actual capital budgeting decisions in the next two chapters.

6. The final step in a good capital budgeting system is the *post-audit*, which involves comparing actual to predicted results. Post-audits help get the best results from every accepted project; they also lead to improvements in the forecasting process, and hence to better future capital budgeting decisions.

While this chapter has presented the basic elements of the capital budgeting process, there are many other aspects of this crucial topic. Some of the more important ones are discussed in the following two chapters.

Questions

8-1   Define each of the following terms:
  a. The capital budget
  b. Regular payback; discounted payback
  c. Accounting rate of return (ARR)
  d. Net present value (NPV)
  e. Internal rate of return (IRR)
  f. Profitability index (PI)
  g. NPV profile; crossover point
  h. Independent projects; mutually exclusive projects
  i. Project cost of capital, or discount rate
  j. Post-audit
  k. Reinvestment rate assumption

8-2   How is a project classification scheme (for example, replacement, expansion into new markets, and so forth) used in the capital budgeting process?

8-3   Explain why the NPV of a relatively long-term project, defined as one where a high percentage of its cash flows is expected in the distant future, is more sensitive to changes in the cost of capital than is the NPV of a short-term project.

8-4   Explain why, if two mutually exclusive projects are being compared, the short-term project might have the higher ranking under the NPV criterion if the cost of capital is high, but the long-term project might be deemed better if the cost of capital is low. Would changes in the cost of capital ever cause a change in the IRR ranking of two such projects?

8-5   For independent projects, is it true that if PI > 1.0, then NPV > 0 and IRR > k? Prove it.

8-6   In what sense is a reinvestment rate assumption embodied in the NPV and IRR methods? What is the implicitly assumed reinvestment rate of each method?

8-7   "Assume that a firm has no mutually exclusive projects but only independent ones, that its cost of capital is constant, and that all of its
projects are normal in the sense of having one or more outflows followed by a stream of inflows. Under these conditions, the NPV and
IRR methods will always result in identical capital budgets." Discuss
the statement. What does the statement imply about using the IRR
method in lieu of the NPV method?

ST-1 You are a financial analyst for Porter Electronics Company. The direc-   *Self-Test Problem*
tor of capital budgeting has asked you to analyze two proposed capital
investments, Projects X and Y. Each project has a cost of $10,000, and
the cost of capital for both projects is 12 percent. The projects' expected net cash flows are:

| Year | Net Cash Flow | |
	Project X	Project Y
0	($10,000)	($10,000)
1	6,500	3,500
2	3,000	3,500
3	3,000	3,500
4	1,000	3,500

a. Calculate each project's payback, accounting rate of return (ARR),
   net present value (NPV), internal rate of return (IRR), and profitability index (PI). (To determine the accounting rate of return, assume that the depreciation expense is $500 per year for both pro-
   jects.)
b. Which project, or projects, should be accepted if they are independent?
c. Which project should be accepted if they are mutually exclusive?
d. How might a change in the cost of capital produce a conflict between the NPV and IRR rankings of these two projects? At what
   values of k would this conflict exist?
e. Why does the conflict exist?

8-1   Two projects each involve an investment of $4,500. Expected annual   *Problems*
net cash flows are $3,000 for 2 years for Project S and $1,200 for 6 years
for Project L.
a. Compute the net present value of each project if the firm's cost of
   capital is 0 percent and if it is 6 percent. NPVs for S at 10 and 20
   percent, respectively, are $706.50 and $83.40, while NPVs for L at
   10 and 20 percent are $726.36 and −$509.40.
b. Graph the net present value profiles of the two projects, and use
   the graph to estimate each project's IRR.
c. Use a calculator to find the internal rate of return for each project.
d. If these projects were mutually exclusive, which one would you
   select, assuming a cost of capital of (1) 8 percent, (2) 10.3 percent,
   or (3) 12 percent? Explain. (Note: In Chapter 9, we shall discuss
   replacement chains, where projects such as these are extended out to

a common life. For this problem, assume that the operation will terminate at the end of the project's life, making replacement chain analysis unnecessary.)

8-2   Western States Chemical Company (WSC) is considering two mutually exclusive investments. The projects' expected net cash flows follow:

| | Expected Net Cash Flow | |
Year	Project A	Project B
0	($300)	($405)
1	(387)	134
2	(193)	134
3	(100)	134
4	600	134
5	600	134
6	850	134
7	(180)	0

a. Construct NPV profiles for Projects A and B.
b. What is each project's IRR?
c. If you were told that each project's cost of capital is 10 percent, which project should be selected? What if the cost of capital were 17 percent?
d. What is the crossover rate?

8-3   Project S has a cost of $10,000 and is expected to produce benefits (cash flows) of $3,000 per year for 5 years. Project L costs $25,000 and is expected to produce cash flows of $7,400 per year for 5 years. Calculate the two projects' NPVs, IRRs, and PIs, assuming a cost of capital of 12 percent. Which project would be selected, assuming they are mutually exclusive, using each ranking method? Which should actually be selected? Assume that the projects are equally risky.

8-4   P. Hunt & Company is considering two mutually exclusive plans for extracting oil on property for which it has mineral rights. Both plans call for the expenditure of $10 million to drill development wells, but under Plan A all the oil will be extracted in one year, producing a cash flow at t = 1 of $12 million, while under Plan B cash flows will be $1,750,000 per year for 20 years.

a. What are the annual cash flows that will be available to P. Hunt if it undertakes Plan B rather than Plan A?
b. If P. Hunt accepts Plan A and then invests the extra cash generated at the end of Year 1, what rate of return (reinvestment rate) would cause the cash flows from reinvestment to equal the cash flows from Plan B?
c. Suppose a company has a cost of capital of 10 percent. Is it logical to assume that it would take on all available independent projects (of average risk) with returns greater than 10 percent? Further, if all available projects with returns greater than 10 percent have been taken, would this mean that cash flows from past investments would have an opportunity cost of only 10 percent, because all the firm could do with these cash flows would be to replace money that has a cost of 10 percent? Finally, does this imply that the cost of

capital is the correct rate to assume for the reinvestment of a project's cash flows?

   d. Construct NPV profiles for Plans A and B, identify each project's IRR, and indicate the crossover rate of return.

8-5 The Schatz Brewing Company is considering two mutually exclusive expansion plans. Plan A calls for the expenditure of $50 million on a large-scale, integrated brewery which will provide an expected cash flow stream of $8 million per year for 20 years. Plan B calls for the expenditure of $15 million to build a somewhat less efficient, more labor intensive plant which has an expected cash flow stream of $3.4 million per year for 20 years. Schatz's cost of capital is 10 percent.

   a. Calculate each project's NPV and IRR.

   b. Set up a Project Δ by showing the cash flows that will exist if Schatz goes with the large plant rather than the smaller plant. What is the NPV and the IRR for this Project Δ?

   c. Graph the NPV profiles for Project A, Project B, and Project Δ.

   d. Give a logical explanation, based on reinvestment rates and opportunity costs, as to why the NPV method is better than the IRR method when the firm's cost of capital is constant at some value such as 10 percent.

ST-1 a. *Payback:*

Solution to Self-Test Problem

To determine the payback, construct the cumulative cash flows for each project:

	Cumulative Cash Flow	
Year	Project X	Project Y
0	($10,000)	($10,000)
1	(3,500)	(6,500)
2	(500)	(3,000)
3	2,500	500
4	3,500	4,000

$$\text{Payback}_X = 2 + \frac{\$500}{\$3,000} = 2.17 \text{ years.}$$

$$\text{Payback}_Y = 2 + \frac{\$3,000}{\$3,500} = 2.86 \text{ years.}$$

Accounting Rate of Return (ARR):

First, subtract the annual depreciation expense of $500 to develop the projects' net income stream:

	Net Income	
Year	Project X	Project Y
1	$ 6,000	$ 3,000
2	2,500	3,000
3	2,500	3,000
4	500	3,000
Total	$11,500	$12,000

Now, the average annual net incomes (AAI) are

$$AAI_X = \frac{\$11,500}{4} = \$2,875,$$

and

$$AAI_Y = \frac{\$12,000}{4} = \$3,000.$$

Next, determine each project's average investment (AI), which is the beginning investment minus one-half the total depreciation. Since both projects have an investment of $10,000 and a total depreciation expense of 4($500) = $2,000, the AI for both projects is $10,000 − $1,000 = $9,000.

Finally, the accounting rate of return (ARR) is

$$ARR = \frac{AAI}{AI}, \text{ or}$$

$$ARR_X = \frac{\$2,875}{\$9,000} = 31.9\%.$$

$$ARR_Y = \frac{\$3,000}{\$9,000} = 33.3\%.$$

Net Present Value (NPV):

$$NPV_X = -\$10,000 + \frac{\$6,500}{(1.12)^1} + \frac{\$3,000}{(1.12)^2} + \frac{\$3,000}{(1.12)^3} + \frac{\$1,000}{(1.12)^4}$$

$$= \$966.01.$$

$$NPV_Y = -\$10,000 + \frac{\$3,500}{(1.12)^1} + \frac{\$3,500}{(1.12)^2} + \frac{\$3,500}{(1.12)^3} + \frac{\$3,500}{(1.12)^4}$$

$$= \$630.72.$$

Internal Rate of Return (IRR):
To solve for the IRR, find the discount rates which equate each NPV to zero:

$$IRR_X = 18.0\%.$$
$$IRR_Y = 15.0\%.$$

Profitability Index (PI):

$$PI_X = \frac{PV \text{ benefits}}{PV \text{ costs}} = \frac{\$10,966.01}{\$10,000} = 1.10.$$

$$PI_Y = \frac{\$10,630.72}{\$10,000} = 1.06.$$

b. The following table summarizes the project rankings by each method:

	Ranks Higher
Payback	X
ARR	Y
NPV	X
IRR	X
PI	X

Note that all methods except ARR rank Project X over Project Y. Additionally, both projects are acceptable under the NPV, IRR, and PI criteria. Thus, both projects should be accepted if they are independent.

c. Choose the project with the highest NPV, or Project X. Note that both projects have 4-year lives, so the NPV comparison is appropriate. If Project X and Project Y had different lives and were repeatable, a different procedure would be required. This is discussed in Chapter 9.

d. To determine the effects of changing the cost of capital, plot the NPV profiles of each project:

NPV Profiles for Projects X and Y

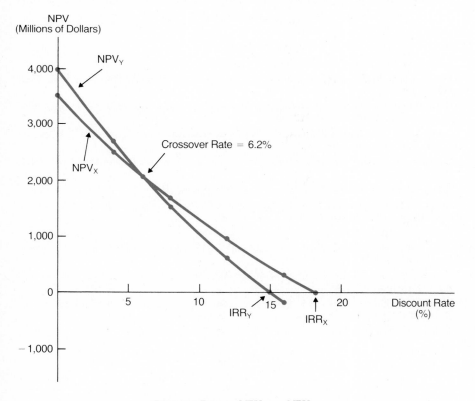

Discount Rate	NPV$_X$	NPV$_Y$
0%	$3,500	$4,000
4	2,546	2,705
8	1,707	1,592
12	966	630
16	307	(206)

The crossover point occurs at about 6-7 percent. To find this rate exactly, create a Project Δ, which is the difference in cash flows between Projects X and Y:

Year	Project X − Project Y = Project Δ Net Cash Flow
0	$ 0
1	3,000
2	(500)
3	(500)
4	(2,500)

Then find the IRR of Project Δ:

$$IRR_\Delta = \text{Crossover rate} = 6.2\%.$$

Thus, if the firm's cost of capital is less than 6.2 percent, a conflict exists since $NPV_Y > NPV_X$, but $IRR_X > IRR_Y$.

Selected Additional References

For an in-depth treatment of capital budgeting techniques, see

Bierman, Harold, Jr., and Seymour Smidt, *The Capital Budgeting Decision* (New York: Macmillan, 1984).

Grant, Eugene L., William G. Ireson, and Richard S. Leavenworth, *Principles of Engineering Economy* (New York: Ronald, 1976).

Levy, Haim, and Marshall Sarnat, *Capital Investment and Financial Decisions* (Englewood Cliffs, N. J.: Prentice-Hall, 1982).

Osteryoung, Jerome, *Capital Budgeting: Long-Term Asset Selection* (Columbus, Ohio: Grid, 1974).

For a discussion of strategic considerations in capital budgeting, see

Crum, Roy, and Frans D. J. Derkinderen, eds., *Readings in Strategies for Corporate Investments* (New York: Pitman, 1980).

Three articles related to the topics covered in Chapter 8 are

Bacon, Peter W., "The Evaluation of Mutually Exclusive Investments," *Financial Management*, Summer 1977, 55-58.

Kim, Suk H., and Edward J. Farragher, "Current Capital Budgeting Practices," *Management Accounting*, June 1981, 26-30.

Lewellen, Wilbur G., Howard P. Lanser, and John J. McConnell, "Payback Substitutes for Discounted Cash Flow," *Financial Management*, Summer 1973, 17-23.

Additional capital budgeting references are provided in Chapters 9 and 10.

Nonnormal Capital Projects: Multiple Internal Rates of Return

8A

A *normal* capital project is one that has one or more cash outflows (costs) followed by a series of cash inflows. If, however, a project calls for a large cash outflow either sometime during or at the end of its life, then it is a *nonnormal* project. A coal strip mine, where the company must spend a large amount of money to put the land back into good shape when the ore body has been exhausted, is an example of a nonnormal project. These projects can present three unique difficulties when evaluated by the IRR criterion: (1) The IRR criterion can lead to an improper decision. (2) The project may have no real IRR. (3) The project may have multiple IRRs. These unique problems are discussed in the following sections.

Suppose a firm is evaluating the following two projects, L and B:

Improper Decisions

Project	Expected Net Cash Flow		
	Year 0	End of Year 1	IRR
L	($100,000)	$120,000	20%
B	83,333	(100,000)	20

Both projects have the same IRR, 20 percent. If the projects each have a project cost of capital of 10 percent, then both projects are acceptable according to the IRR decision rule.

But what are the projects' NPVs?

$$NPV_L = -\$100,000 + \frac{\$120,000}{(1.10)^1} = \$9,091.$$

$$NPV_B = \$83,333 + \frac{-\$100,000}{(1.10)^1} = -\$7,576.$$

According to the NPV criterion, Project L is acceptable, but Project B is not—it has a negative NPV. In this situation, the IRR criterion would result in an improper accept/reject decision. Project L can be thought of as a loan. The firm is "lending" $100,000 today (or investing $100,000 at t = 0), ex-

341

Figure 8A-1
NPV Profiles for Project L and Project B

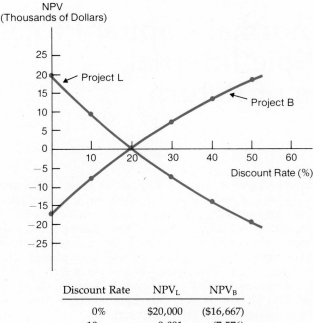

Discount Rate	NPV$_L$	NPV$_B$
0%	$20,000	($16,667)
10	9,091	(7,576)
20	0	0
30	(7,692)	6,410
40	(14,286)	11,904
50	(20,000)	16,666

pecting to receive $120,000 in one year. When "lending" funds, the expected return should be higher than the opportunity cost of those funds; thus, the firm should require an IRR greater than the project's cost of capital.

Conversely, Project B represents "borrowing"; an example would be a financial or real estate transaction where the investor gets tax shelter cash flows during the first year and then has cash outflows thereafter. So, in effect, in our example the firm "borrows" $83,333 today, but must pay back $100,000 at the end of one year. The firm would accept a "borrowing" project only if the borrowing rate were less than the alternative opportunity cost of capital. Thus, Project B is acceptable only if its IRR is less than its cost of capital.

Figure 8A-1 contains the NPV profiles for Projects L and B. Notice that Project L has a "typical" profile, but Project B's NPV profile increases as the cost of capital increases. Thus, Project B has a positive NPV only if the project's cost of capital is greater than its IRR.

Figure 8A-2
NPV Profile for Project Z
(Millions of Dollars)

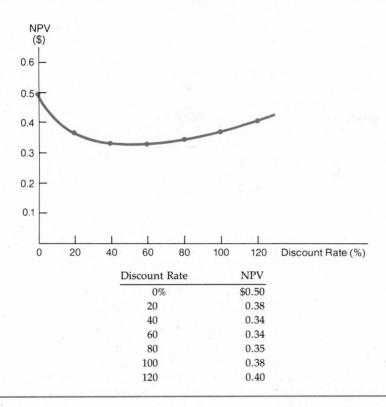

Discount Rate	NPV
0%	$0.50
20	0.38
40	0.34
60	0.34
80	0.35
100	0.38
120	0.40

It is possible that a nonnormal project might have no real IRR. To illustrate, *No Real IRR* consider Project Z, which has the following expected net cash flows:

Year end:	0	1	2
Cash flow:	$1.0 million	−$2.0 million	$1.5 million

Should Project Z be accepted if its cost of capital is 10 percent? To answer this question, we might begin by plotting the project's NPV profile as in Figure 8A-2. Notice that the NPV profile does not cross the horizontal axis—there is no real value of k which causes NPV = 0. Thus, the IRR criterion cannot be used in evaluating this project. However, the NPV criterion can be easily applied. From Figure 8A-2, we see that the project has a positive NPV at a 10 percent cost of capital; specifically, $NPV_Z = \$0.42$ million:

$$NPV_Z = \$1.0 \text{ million} + \frac{-\$2.0 \text{ million}}{(1.10)^1} + \frac{\$1.5 \text{ million}}{(1.10)^2}$$
$$= \$0.42 \text{ million}.$$

Multiple Internal Rates of Return

A third problem that can arise with the IRR method is that in solving Equation 8-2,

$$\sum_{t=0}^{n} \frac{CF_t}{(1 + r)^t} = 0, \tag{8-2}$$

it is possible to obtain more than one positive value of r. Notice that this equation is a polynomial of degree n. Therefore, there are n different roots, or solutions, to the equation. All except one of the roots either are imaginary numbers or are negative when investments are normal, so in the normal case only one positive value of r appears. However, the possibility of multiple real roots arises when the project is nonnormal.

To illustrate this problem, suppose a firm is considering the expenditure of $1.6 million to develop a strip mine. The mine will produce a cash flow of $10 million at the end of Year 1. Then, at the end of Year 2, $10 million must be expended to restore the land to its original condition. Therefore, the project's expected net cash flows are as follows:

Year end:	0	1	2
Cash flow:	−$1.6 million	$10 million	−$10 million

These values can be substituted into Equation 8-2 to derive the IRR for the investment:

$$\frac{-\$1.6 \text{ million}}{(1 + r)^0} + \frac{\$10 \text{ million}}{(1 + r)^1} - \frac{\$10 \text{ million}}{(1 + r)^2} = 0,$$

which has NPV = 0 when r = 25% and also when r = 400%. Therefore, the IRR of the investment is both 25 and 400 percent. This relationship is depicted graphically in Figure 8A-3. Note that no dilemma would arise if the NPV method were used; we would simply use Equation 8-1, find the NPV, and use this for ranking.[1]

The authors encountered another example of multiple internal rates of return when a major California bank *borrowed* funds from an insurance company and then used these funds (plus an initial investment of its own) to buy a number of jet engines, which it then leased to a major airline. The bank expected to receive positive net cash flows (lease payments plus tax credits minus interest on the insurance company loan) for a number of years, then several large negative cash flows as it repaid the insurance company loan, and, finally, a large inflow from the sale of the engines when the lease expired.[2]

---

[1]Does Figure 8A-3 suggest that the firm should try to *raise* its cost of capital to about 100 percent in order to maximize the NPV of the project? Certainly not. The firm should seek to *minimize* its cost of capital—this will maximize the price of its stock. Taking actions to raise the cost of capital might make this particular project look good, but these actions would be terribly harmful to the firm's more numerous normal projects. Only if the firm's cost of capital is high, in spite of efforts to keep it down, will the illustrative project have a high NPV.

[2]The situation described here is a *leveraged lease*. See Chapter 16 for more on leveraged leases.

Figure 8A-3
NPV Profile for Strip Mine Project

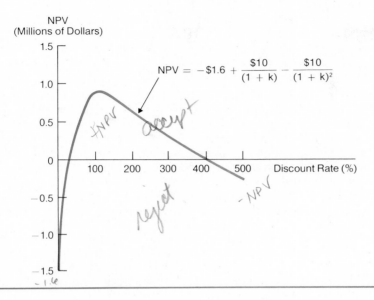

NPV
(Millions of Dollars)

$$NPV = -\$1.6 + \frac{\$10}{(1 + k)} - \frac{\$10}{(1 + k)^2}$$

The bank discovered two IRRs and wondered which was correct. It could not ignore the IRR and use the NPV method, since the lease was already on the books, and the bank's senior loan committee as well as the Federal Reserve Bank's examiners wanted to know the return on the lease. The bank's solution called for compounding the cash flows—both positive and negative—at an assumed reinvestment rate of 9 percent, its average return on loans, to arrive at a compounded terminal value for the operation. Then the interest rate that equated this terminal sum to the bank's initial cost was called the IRR, or the rate of return on the lease. This procedure satisfied both the loan committee and the bank examiners.[3]

All the examples just presented illustrate some problems that can arise when the IRR criterion is used with a project that has nonnormal cash flows. However, in all cases, the NPV criterion can be easily applied, and this criterion leads to conceptually correct capital budgeting decisions.

Problems

8A-1 The Colorado Coal Company is considering opening a strip mine, the net cost of which is $4.4 million. Net cash inflows are expected to be $27.7 million, all coming at the end of Year 1. The land must then be returned to its natural state at a cost of $25 million, payable at the end of Year 2.

---

[3]For additional insights into the multiple root problem, see William H. Jean, "On Multiple Rates of Return," *Journal of Finance*, March 1968, 187-192.

a. Plot the project's NPV profile.
b. Should the project be accepted (1) if k = 8%, or (2) if k = 14%? Explain your reasoning.
c. Can you think of some other capital budgeting situations where negative cash flows during or at the end of the project's life might lead to multiple IRRs?

8A-2 The Sacramento Development Company (SDC) has many excellent investment opportunities, but it has insufficient cash to undertake them all. Now SDC is offered the chance to borrow $2 million from the Pacific City Retirement Fund at 10 percent, the loan to be repaid at the end of one year. Also, a "consulting fee" of $700,000 will be paid to Pacific City's mayor at the end of one year for helping to arrange the credit. Of the $2 million received, $1 million will be used immediately to buy a city-owned hotel and convert it to a gambling casino. The other $1 million will be invested in other lucrative SDC projects that otherwise would have to be foregone because of a lack of capital. For two years, all cash generated by the casino will be plowed back into the casino project. At the end of the 2 years the casino will be sold for $2 million.

Assuming (1) the facts as given, (2) that the deal has been worked out in the sunshine and is completely legal, and (3) that cash from other SDC operations will be available to make the required payments at the end of Year 1, under what rate of return conditions should SDC accept the offer? Disregard taxes.

Cash Flow Estimation and Other Topics in Capital Budgeting

9

When Edwin Land invented instant photography, there was simply no question as to whether or not his Polaroid Corporation should build plants to manufacture the cameras—the projected cash flows were so large that any type of capital budgeting analysis would have given the "go" signal. However, most capital expenditure decisions are not so clear-cut. Often, firms must make fairly close decisions regarding starting a new product line, replacing existing machinery versus continuing to use the old equipment, and so on. Similarly, hard choices must be made between expensive, long-lived equipment versus equipment that will wear out sooner but will have a lower initial cost. These "bread and butter" decisions have a major effect on the long-run success or failure of a company.

Postmortems on failed companies often reveal technical weaknesses in their capital budgeting systems. These firms did not analyze and compare properly projects with different lives; they did not take account of inflation in their capital budgeting analysis; and most important, they did not estimate projects' cash flows properly. Such technical, but frequently encountered, problems in capital budgeting are discussed in this chapter.

The basic principles of capital budgeting were covered in Chapter 8. Now we examine some additional issues, including (1) cash flow estimation, (2) replacement decisions, (3) mutually exclusive projects with unequal lives, and (4) the effects of inflation on capital budgeting analysis.[1]

---

[1]If time pressures do not permit coverage of the entire chapter, we suggest that cash flow estimation be covered; the remainder of the chapter can be omitted without loss of continuity.

Cash Flow Estimation

The most important, but also the most difficult, step in the analysis of a capital project is estimating its cash flows—the investment outlays that will be required and the annual net cash inflows the project will produce after it goes into operation. A great many variables are involved in cash flow forecasting, and many individuals and departments participate in the process. For example, the forecasts of unit sales and sales prices are normally made by the marketing department, based on its knowledge of price elasticity, advertising effects, the state of the economy, competitors' reactions, and trends in consumers' tastes. Similarly, the capital outlays associated with a new product are generally obtained from the engineering and product development staffs, while operating costs are estimated by cost accountants, production experts, personnel specialists, purchasing agents, and so forth.

Obtaining accurate estimates of the costs and revenues associated with a large, complex project can be exceedingly difficult, and forecast errors can be quite large. For example, when several large oil companies decided to build the Alaska Pipeline, the original cost forecasts were in the neighborhood of $700 million. The final cost was closer to $7 billion. Similar, or even worse, miscalculations are common in product design cost estimates, such as the costs to develop a new personal computer. Further, as difficult as plant and equipment costs are to estimate, sales revenues and operating costs over the life of the project are generally even harder to forecast. For example, when AT&T developed the Picturephone, it envisaged large sales in both the residential and business markets, yet it turned out that virtually no one was willing to pay the price required to cover the project's costs. Because of its financial strength, AT&T was able to absorb losses on the project with no problem, but the Picturephone venture would surely have forced a weaker firm into bankruptcy.

The major roles of the financial staff in the forecasting process are (1) to coordinate the efforts of the other departments, such as engineering and marketing, (2) to insure that everyone involved with the forecast uses a consistent set of economic assumptions, and (3) to make sure that no biases are inherent in the forecasts. This last point is extremely important, because division managers often become emotionally involved with pet projects and/or develop empire-building complexes, possibly leading to cash flow forecasting biases which make bad projects look good on paper. The AT&T Picturephone project is an example of this problem.

It is not sufficient that the financial staff have unbiased point estimates of the key variables—as we shall see in detail in the next chapter, data on probability distributions or other indications of the likely ranges of error are also essential. Moreover, it is useful to have an idea of the relationship between each input variable and some basic economic variable such as gross national product, for if all production and sales variables are related to such a variable, then the financial manager will have an idea of how the project will do under different economic conditions.

It is impossible to overstate either the difficulties that are encountered in cash flow forecasts or the importance of these forecasts. It is also impossible to cover the subject adequately in a text such as this. Still, there are certain principles which, if observed, will help to minimize errors.

One important element in cash flow estimation is the identification of the *relevant cash flows*, that is, those cash flows within the firm which should be considered in the decision at hand. Errors are often made here, but there are two cardinal rules which can help financial analysts avoid mistakes: (1) Capital budgeting decisions must be based on *cash flows* rather than accounting income, and (2) only *incremental cash flows* are relevant to the accept/reject decision. These two rules are discussed in detail in the following sections.

Identifying the Relevant Cash Flows

1) Cash flows, Not accounting income

2.) Incremental cash flows

Cash Flow versus Accounting Income

Accounting statements are, in some respects, a mix of apples and oranges. For instance, we deduct labor costs, which are cash outflows, from revenues, which may or may not be entirely cash (some sales may be on credit). At the same time, we do not deduct capital outlays, which are cash outflows, but we do deduct depreciation expenses, which are not cash outflows. Nevertheless, in capital budgeting, it is critical that we base decisions strictly on cash flows, the actual dollars that flow into and out of the company during each time period.

For most new projects, we can approximate the operating cash flows by merely adding all noncash expenses to the project's net income. Often, the only noncash expense is depreciation, so the net cash flow in period t, NCF_t, is the project's net income plus depreciation:

$$NCF_t = \text{Project net income} + \text{Depreciation.} \qquad (9\text{-}1)$$

Note that the project's net income is determined in the same manner as the firm's net income, except that interest expense is *not* deducted to obtain project net income. Also, note that the net cash flow is on an after-tax basis, since project net income is an after-tax amount.

We can use a shortcut method to determine NCF_t without creating the entire income statement. We begin with a basic algebraic project income statement:

$$PNI = (R - C - D)(1 - T), \qquad (9\text{-}2)$$

where

PNI = project net income,

  R = revenues, assumed to be all cash,

C = cash costs,

D = depreciation expense, a noncash charge, and

T = marginal corporate tax rate.

Rearranging terms, we obtain this statement:

$$PNI = (R - C)(1 - T) - D(1 - T)$$
$$PNI = (R - C)(1 - T) - D + TD$$
$$PNI + D = (R - C)(1 - T) + TD,$$

or, since $NCF_t = PNI + D$,

$$NCF_t = (R - C)(1 - T) + TD. \tag{9-3}$$

Equation 9-3 states that the net operating cash flow, NCF_t, during a given period consists of two terms: (1) an after-tax net cash revenue component and (2) a depreciation cash flow equal to the amount of depreciation taken during the period times the tax rate. In this form, it is clear that the basic effect of depreciation on cash flows is the reduction in taxes caused by the depreciation expense. Equations 9-1 and 9-3 are equivalent methods for calculating net operating cash flows, and either method can be used in capital budgeting analysis, depending on the form in which data are available.

In financial analysis, we must be careful to account properly for the timing of cash flows. Accounting income statements are for a period such as a year; hence, they do not reflect revenues or expenses as they occur. However, because of the time value of money, capital budgeting cash flows should be analyzed as they actually occur. Of course, there must be a compromise between accuracy and simplicity. A time line with daily cash flows would in theory provide the most accuracy, but daily cash flow estimates would be time consuming to produce, unwieldy to use, and probably no more accurate than annual cash flows because our ability to forecast is simply not good enough to warrant this degree of detail. Therefore, in most cases, we simply assume that all cash flows occur at the end of every year. However, for some projects, it may be useful to assume that cash flows occur at mid-year, or even to forecast quarterly or monthly cash flows. In any event, it is important to specify the exact timing of cash flows on some reasonable basis.

Incremental Cash Flows

In evaluating a capital project, we are concerned only with those cash flows that result directly from the project. These cash flows, called *incremental cash flows*, represent the change in the firm's total cash flows that occurs as a direct result of the accept/reject decision on the project. Three special problems in determining incremental cash flows are discussed next.

Sunk Costs. Sunk costs are not incremental costs, and they should not be included in the analysis.[2] A *sunk cost* refers to an outlay that has already been committed or that has already occurred, and hence an outlay that is not affected by the accept/reject decision under consideration. Suppose, for example, that in 1985 Northeast BankCorp was evaluating the establishment of a branch office in a newly developed section of Boston. To help perform the analysis, Northeast had, back in 1984, hired a consulting firm to perform a site analysis at a cost of $100,000; this $100,000 was expensed for tax purposes in 1984. Is this 1984 expenditure a relevant cost with respect to the 1985 capital budgeting decision? The answer is "no." The $100,000 is a sunk cost; Northeast cannot recover it regardless of whether or not the new branch is built. It often turns out that a particular project looks bad (it has a negative NPV, or an IRR less than the cost of capital) when all the associated costs, including sunk costs, are considered. However, on an incremental basis, the project may be a good one, because the incremental cash flows are large enough to produce a positive NPV on the incremental investment. Thus, the correct treatment of sunk costs is critical to a proper capital budgeting analysis.

Opportunity Costs. The second potential problem relates to *opportunity costs*: All relevant opportunity costs must be included in a correct capital budgeting analysis. For example, suppose Northeast BankCorp already owns a piece of land that is suitable for the branch location. When evaluating the prospective branch, should the cost of the land be disregarded because no additional cash outlay would be required? No, because there is an opportunity cost inherent in the use of the property. For example, suppose the land could be sold to yield $150,000 after taxes. Use of the site for the branch would require foregoing this inflow, so the $150,000 must be charged as an opportunity cost against the project. Note, though, that the proper land cost in this example would be the $150,000 market-determined value, irrespective of whether Northeast had paid $50,000 or $500,000 for the property when it was acquired.

Effects on Other Parts of the Firm. The third potential problem involves the effects of a project on other parts of the firm. For example, suppose some of Northeast's customers that would use the new branch are already banking with Northeast's downtown office. The loans and deposits, and hence profits, generated by these customers would not be new to the bank, but rather they would represent a transfer from the main office to the branch. Thus, the net revenues produced by these customers should not be treated as incremental income in the capital budgeting

---

[2]For an excellent example of the improper treatment of sunk costs by a major corporation, see U. E. Reinhardt, "Break-Even Analysis for Lockheed's TriStar: An Application of Financial Theory," *Journal of Finance*, September 1973, 821-838.

decision. On the other hand, having a suburban branch might actually attract new business to the downtown office, because some potential customers would want to make transactions both from home and from work. In this case, the additional revenues that would flow to the downtown office should be attributed to the branch.

Although often difficult to quantify, "externalities" such as these must be considered. They should, if possible, be quantified, or at least noted, so the final decision-maker will be aware of their existence.

Tax Effects

Tax effects can have a major impact on cash flows, and many times, the improper treatment of taxes could completely reverse the accept/reject decision. Therefore, it is critical that taxes be dealt with correctly in capital budgeting decisions. However, as financial analysts, we encounter two problems: (1) the tax laws are extremely complex, and (2) these laws are subject to interpretation and to change. Fortunately, the financial staff can get assistance from the firm's internal or external accountants and tax lawyers. Even so, it is necessary for financial managers to have a fairly good working knowledge of the current tax laws and their effects on cash flows.

Corporate taxes, including the tax implications of fixed asset investments, were discussed in Chapter 2. Later in this chapter, in the illustrative cash flow analysis, we apply the tax laws as discussed in Chapter 2 to a particular capital budgeting example. At that point, it might be a good idea to review Chapter 2 if your understanding of corporate taxes is hazy.

Changes in Net Working Capital

Normally, additional inventories are required to support a new operation, and expanded sales also produce additional accounts receivable, both of which must be financed. On the other hand, accounts payable and accruals will also increase spontaneously as a result of the expansion, and this reduces the need to finance inventories and receivables. The difference between the increased current assets and the projected increase in current liabilities is defined as a *change in net working capital*. If this change is positive, as it generally is for expansion projects, this indicates that additional financing, over and above the cost of the fixed assets, is needed to fund the change in current assets. Conversely, if the change in net working capital is negative, the project is generating a cash inflow from changes in net working capital.

Net working capital changes may occur over several periods, so the increase (or decrease) could be reflected in the cash flows of several periods. However, once the operation has stabilized, working capital should also stabilize at the new level, and beyond this time no changes will occur until the project is terminated. At termination, we generally assume that the firm's total working capital requirements revert back to prior levels. Thus, the firm will experience an end-of-project cash flow that is equal, but opposite in sign, to the total net working capital change that occurred in the project's early years. This point is illustrated in the next section.

Up to this point, we have discussed several important aspects of cash flow analysis, but we have not shown how they relate to one another and affect the capital budgeting decision. In this section, we illustrate all this by examining a capital budgeting decision that faces Robotics International, Inc. (RII). RII, a world leader in the robotics industry, produces a line of industrial robots and peripheral equipment which perform many routine assembly line tasks. The company enjoyed much success, in terms of profit and sales growth, in the late 1970s and early 1980s, when automobile manufacturers and other durable goods producers sought to cut costs by automating the production process. However, by 1984 increased competition, particularly from Japanese firms, had caused RII's management to be concerned about the company's growth potential. RII's research and development department had been applying industrial robot technology to develop a line of office maintenance robots. (The maintenance robot is designed to function as a janitor, performing such tasks as vacuuming, dusting, and emptying trash cans. A floor plan of the office is programmed into the robot to enable it to move freely about the facility.) This effort has now reached the stage where a decision on whether or not to go forward with production must be made.

Cash Flow Analysis Example

RII's marketing department has plans to target sales of the robots to the larger office complexes, and if they are successful there, then the robots could be marketed to a wide variety of businesses, including schools, hospitals, and eventually even to households. The marketing vice-president believes that annual sales would be 25,000 units if the robots were priced at $2,200 each. The engineering department has estimated that the firm would need a new manufacturing plant; this plant could be built and made ready for production in 2 years, once the "go" decision is made. The plant would require a 25-acre site, and RII currently has an option to purchase a suitable tract of land for $1.2 million. Building construction would begin in early 1986 and continue through 1987. The building is expected to cost $8 million, with a $4 million payment due to the contractor on December 31, 1986, and another $4 million payable on December 31, 1987. Neither the building nor the land qualifies for an investment tax credit, since they are real rather than personal property, and the building falls into the 15-year ACRS class. (This analysis was conducted in early 1984. Subsequent tax law changes would now place the building into the 18-year class.)

The necessary manufacturing equipment would be installed late in 1987 and would be paid for on December 31, 1987. The equipment has a cost of $9.5 million, including transportation, plus another $500,000 for installation. The equipment qualifies for an ITC and falls into the 5-year ACRS class.[3] RII will not expense any portion of this project under Section 179. To date, RII has spent $10 million on research and development of the office robot. The company has expensed $2.5 million of the R&D costs, and the remaining $7.5 million has been capitalized and will be amortized over the life of the project. However, if RII decides not to go forward with the project, the capitalized R&D expenditures could be written off on December 31, 1985.

The project would also require an initial investment in net working capital equal to 12 percent of the estimated sales in the first year. The initial working capital investment would be made on December 31, 1987, and on December 31 of each following year, net working capital would be increased by an amount equal to 12 percent of the sales increase expected for the coming year. The project has an estimated economic life of 6 years. At that time, the expected market value of the land is $1.7 million, the expected market value of the building is $1.0 million, and the expected market value of the equipment is $2 million. The production department has estimated that variable manufacturing costs would total 65 percent of dollar sales, and that fixed overhead costs, excluding depreciation, would be $8 million for the first year of operations. Sales prices and fixed overhead costs, other than depreciation, are projected to increase with inflation, which is expected to average 6 percent per year over the 6-year life of the project.

RII's marginal tax rate is 46 percent on ordinary income and 28 percent on long-term capital gains; its weighted average cost of capital is 10 percent; and it is RII's policy, for capital budgeting purposes, to assume that net operating cash inflows occur at the end of each year. Since the plant would begin operations on January 1, 1988, the first operating cash flows would thus occur on December 31, 1988.

As an RII financial analyst, you have been directed to conduct the initial capital budgeting analysis. For now, you are to assume that the project has the same risk as the firm's current average project. Thus, the project's cost of capital is 10 percent. (However, the departments that have provided input to the analysis have been directed to provide additional information concerning the distributions of their estimates for use in a second-stage analysis. These probability distribution estimates will be used in Chapter 10, where we assess the riskiness of the project.) At this point, you should simply recognize that all of the cash flow estimates are expected values based on assumed probability distributions.

---

[3]The ITC is generally taken in the year the equipment is placed in service. However, for projects which have investment outflows over a number of years, the ITC can often be taken in the year the investment is made. In RII's case, the ITC on the total $10,000,000 equipment cost could be taken in 1987.

The first step in the analysis is to summarize the investment outlays required for the project; this is done in Table 9-1. Note that neither the land nor the building qualifies for an investment tax credit and that the land does not qualify for depreciation. The equipment does qualify for the investment tax credit; thus, the depreciable basis to which the ACRS depreciation applies is reduced by one-half of the investment tax credit. Also, since the project requires an increase in net working capital, this is shown as an investment requirement. The $2,500,000 of already ex-pensed R&D costs are not relevant to the analysis, since these are sunk costs. If the project is not undertaken, the entire $7.5 million in capital-ized R&D expenses can be written off in 1985. However, if RII accepts the project, this immediate write-off is not available, and hence its 1985 value as a tax shelter ($7.5 million x 0.46 = $3,450,000) must be included as an investment opportunity cost.

Next, we must determine the cash flows (operating revenues and net working capital outlays) which occur once production begins; see Table 9-2. These cash flows are based on the information received from RII's various departments. Note that the sales price and fixed costs are projected to increase each year by the 6 percent inflation rate, and since variable costs are 65 percent of sales, they too rise by 6 percent per year. R&D expenses represent the amortization of the $7.5 million of capital-ized R&D costs; since this is a noncash charge, it is added to deprecia-tion and net income to develop the cash flow from operations. The change in net working capital (NWC) represents the additional invest-ment required by sales increases (12 percent of the next year's increase,

Analysis of the Cash Flows

Table 9-1
RII: Investment Requirements, 1985-1987

Fixed Assets	1985	1986	1987	Total Costs, 1985-1987	Depreciable Basis
Land	$1,200,000	$ 0	$ 0	$ 1,200,000	$ 0
Building	0	4,000,000	4,000,000	8,000,000	8,000,000
Equipment	0	0	10,000,000	10,000,000	9,500,000[b]
Equipment ITC[a]	0	0	(1,000,000)	(1,000,000)	
Total fixed assets	$1,200,000	$4,000,000	$13,000,000	$18,200,000	
Net working capital[c]	0	0	6,600,000	6,600,000	
R&D opportunity cost[d]	3,450,000	0	0	3,450,000	
Total investment	$4,650,000	$4,000,000	$19,600,000	$28,250,000	

[a]See Footnote 3.

[b]Equipment cost less one-half of the ITC.

[c]12 percent of first year's sales, or 0.12($55,000,000) = $6,600,000.

[d]R&D expenditures of $10 million were made prior to 1985; $2.5 million of these costs have been expensed, and $7.5 million were capitalized. If the project is abandoned, then the $7.5 million of capitalized R&D costs can be expensed immediately, producing a tax saving of 0.46($7,500,000) = $3,450,000. If the project is accepted, the company will not get this immediate tax saving (it would, in that case, amortize the R&D costs and receive the associated tax savings over the life of the project). Thus, the $3,450,000 is an opportunity cost which must be charged to the project at t = 0.

Table 9-2
RII: Operating and Net Working Capital
Cash Flows, 1988-1993

	1988	1989	1990	1991	1992	1993
Unit sales	25,000	25,000	25,000	25,000	25,000	25,000
Sale price[a]	$ 2,200	$ 2,332	$ 2,472	$ 2,620	$ 2,777	$ 2,944
Net sales[a]	$55,000,000	$58,300,000	$61,800,000	$65,500,000	$69,425,000	$73,600,000
Variable costs[b]	35,750,000	37,895,000	40,170,000	42,575,000	45,126,250	47,840,000
Fixed costs (overhead)[a]	8,000,000	8,480,000	8,988,800	9,528,128	10,099,816	10,705,805
R&D expense[c]	1,250,000	1,250,000	1,250,000	1,250,000	1,250,000	1,250,000
Depreciation (building)[d]	400,000	800,000	720,000	640,000	560,000	560,000
Depreciation (equipment)[d]	1,425,000	2,090,000	1,995,000	1,995,000	1,995,000	0
Earnings before taxes	$ 8,175,000	$ 7,785,000	$ 8,676,200	$ 9,511,872	$10,393,934	$13,244,195
Taxes (46%)	3,760,500	3,581,100	3,991,052	4,375,461	4,781,210	6,092,330
Project net income	$ 4,414,500	$ 4,203,900	$ 4,685,148	$ 5,136,411	$ 5,612,724	$ 7,151,865
Noncash expenses[e]	3,075,000	4,140,000	3,965,000	3,885,000	3,805,000	1,810,000
Cash flow from operations[f]	$ 7,489,500	$ 8,343,900	$ 8,650,148	$ 9,021,411	$ 9,417,724	$ 8,961,865
Addition to NWC[g]	(396,000)	(420,000)	(444,000)	(471,000)	(501,000)	8,832,000
Net operating and NWC cash flows	$ 7,093,500	$ 7,923,900	$ 8,206,148	$ 8,550,411	$ 8,916,724	$17,793,865

[a]1988 estimate increased by an assumed 6 percent inflation rate.

[b]65 percent of net sales.

[c]If the project is accepted, RII will amortize the $7.5 million of capitalized R&D costs over 6 years, so it will have a noncash, deductible expense of $7,500,000/6 = $1,250,000 per year.

[d]ACRS depreciation rates (see Chapter 2) are as follows:

Year	1	2	3	4	5	6
Building	5%	10%	9%	8%	7%	7%
Equipment	15%	22%	21%	21%	21%	—

These percentages are multiplied by the depreciable basis to obtain the depreciation expense for the year.

[e]Sum of R&D expense and depreciation on building and equipment.

[f]Net income plus noncash expenses.

[g]12 percent of next year's increase in sales. For example, 1989 sales are $3.3 million over 1988 sales, so the addition to NWC in 1988 to prepare for the 1989 sales increase is (0.12)($3,300,000) = $396,000. The cumulative working capital investment is recovered in 1993.

all of which results from inflation) during 1988-1992 and the recovery of the cumulative net working capital investment in 1993. The depreciation amounts are obtained by multiplying the depreciable basis by the appropriate ACRS allowance rate.

Now, the financial analyst must determine the cash flows generated by salvage values; Table 9-3 summarizes this analysis. Here, we compare the projected 1993 market values against the 1993 book values and initial costs. The land cannot be depreciated, and it has an estimated 1993 salvage value greater than the initial purchase price. Thus, RII

Table 9-3
RII: Projected Net Salvage Values, 1993

	Land	Building	Equipment
Salvage (ending market) value	$1,700,000	$1,000,000	$ 2,000,000
Initial cost	$1,200,000	$8,000,000	$10,000,000
Depreciable basis	0	8,000,000	9,500,000
Book value (1993)[a]	1,200,000	4,320,000	0
Capital gains income	$ 500,000	0	0
Ordinary income (loss)[b]	0	($3,320,000)	$ 2,000,000
Taxes[c]	(140,000)	1,527,200	(920,000)
Net salvage value	$1,560,000	$2,527,200	$ 1,080,000

Total CF from salvage value = $1,560,000 + $2,527,200 + $1,080,000 = $5,167,200.

[a]Book value for building in 1993 equals depreciable basis minus accumulated ACRS depreciation of $3,680,000.

[b]Building: $4,320,000 book value − $1,000,000 market value = $3,320,000 depreciation shortfall treated as an operating expense in 1993.

Equipment: $0 book value − $2,000,000 market value = $2,000,000 depreciation recapture treated as ordinary income in 1993.

[c]The capital gains tax on the land assumes a corporate long-term capital gains tax of 28 percent. The loss on the building produces a 1993 tax credit based on the 46 percent tax rate on ordinary income, while the recapture of depreciation on equipment is taxed at the 46 percent rate.

would have to pay a capital gains tax on the profit. The building has an estimated salvage value less than the book value—it will be sold at a loss for tax purposes. The loss reduces ordinary income and thus generates a tax savings; in effect, the company has been depreciating the building too slowly, so it writes off the loss against ordinary income just as if it had been depreciated. Conversely, the equipment will be sold for more than book value, but for less than its original depreciable basis, so RII will have to pay ordinary taxes on the $2 million profit.[4] In all cases, the book value is the depreciable basis less accumulated depreciation. The total cash flow from salvage is merely the sum of the land, building, and equipment components.

---

[4]In this case, the tax depreciation charges exceeded "true" depreciation, and the excess depreciation is "recaptured." Since the depreciation reduced ordinary income, the recapture is treated as ordinary income rather than as capital gains income. In some instances, the salvage value of personal property could be greater than the original depreciable basis of the property. In this case, the total difference between market value and book value would be split into two components: (1) the difference between the ending book value and the original depreciable basis, which would be defined as a "recapture of depreciation" and taxed at the ordinary income rate, and (2) the difference between the original depreciable basis and the actual sale price, which would be classified as a long-term capital gain and taxed at the capital gains rate. Also, note that the ending book value is the original depreciable basis less the depreciation accumulated up to that point in time. The corporate capital gains tax, unlike the personal capital gains tax, is based on several factors and can quickly become quite complex. In this text, we will assume that the corporate long-term capital gains tax is 28 percent.

Table 9-4
RII: Time Line of Consolidated Cash Flows

			End-of-Year Net Cash Flows					
1985	1986	1987	1988	1989	1990	1991	1992	1993
($4,650,000)	($4,000,000)	($19,600,000)	$7,093,500	$7,923,900	$8,206,148	$8,550,411	$8,916,724	$22,961,065

Payback period: 5.6 years from first outflow.
IRR: 20.4% versus a 10% cost of capital.
NPV: $11,465,923.
PI: 1.5.

Finally, it is useful to combine all of the net cash flows on a time line such as the one in Table 9-4. Here we also show the payback period, IRR, NPV (at the 10 percent cost of capital), and the PI. Obviously, the project is acceptable using the IRR, NPV, or PI, methods and it would also be acceptable for a required payback of six years or less. Note, however, that the analysis thus far has been based on the assumption that the project is as risky as RII's current average project. If the project is riskier than RII's average project, then it would be necessary to increase the cost of capital, which in turn could cause the NPV to become negative, the IRR to fall below k, and the PI to be less than 1.0. In Chapter 10, we will extend the evaluation of this project to include the necessary risk analysis. In particular, we will examine how the NPV would change if sales and/or costs turn out to be different from the forecasted levels (sensitivity analysis), and we will consider how this project fits into RII's "portfolio of projects" and how it affects the company's beta coefficient.

At this point in the analysis, it is often prudent to stand back and take a hard look at the estimated cash flows and the resulting IRR. Suppose the project had a relatively long life and an IRR which was significantly above the firm's cost of capital. The very fact that the project is attractive to one firm could make it attractive to other firms. Its high profitability could be recognized by potential competitors who could enter the market and cause the actual cash flows to fall far below those originally estimated. Thus, the financial analyst should view long-term, high profitability projects with some skepticism. In evaluating RII's office robot project, it is not likely that competitors would be able to develop and produce office robots within the next eight years. Additionally, the 20 percent IRR, along with the project's above-average risk (as determined in Chapter 10), is not likely to cause a competitor to embark on a crash program.

Replacement Analysis

RII's office robot project was used to show how an expansion project is analyzed. RII and other companies also make *replacement decisions*, and the analysis relating to replacements is somewhat different from that for expansion projects because the cash flows from the old asset must be considered. Replacement analysis is illustrated with another RII example, this time from the company's plastics division.

A lathe for trimming molded plastics was purchased 10 years ago at a cost of $7,500. The machine had an expected life of 15 years at the time it was purchased, and management originally estimated, and still believes, that the salvage value will be zero at the end of the 15-year life. The machine is being depreciated on a straight line basis; therefore, its annual depreciation charge is $500, and its present book value is $2,500.[5]

The division manager reports that a new machine can be purchased for $12,000 (including freight and installation), which over its 5-year life will reduce labor and raw materials usage sufficiently to cut operating costs from $7,000 to $4,000. This reduction in costs will cause before-tax profits to rise by $7,000 − $4,000 = $3,000 per year.

It is estimated that the new machine can be sold for $2,000 at the end of 5 years; this is its estimated salvage value. The old machine's actual current market value is $1,000, which is below its $2,500 book value. If the new machine were acquired, the old lathe would be sold to another company rather than exchanged for the new machine. Taxes are at a 46 percent rate, and the replacement project is of average risk. An investment tax credit (ITC) of 10 percent of the purchase price can be used if the new machine is acquired. Net working capital requirements will also increase by $1,000 at the time of replacement. The new machine falls into the 5-year ACRS class, and RII's cost of capital is 10 percent. Should the replacement be made?

Table 9-5 shows the worksheet format that RII uses to analyze replacement projects. A line-by-line description of the table follows.

Line 1. The top section of the table, Lines 1 through 6, relates to cash flows which occur at (approximately) t = 0, the time the investment is made. Line 1 shows the purchase price of the new machine, including any installation and freight charges.

Line 2. The ITC on the new machine is equal to 10 percent of the purchase price.[6] The parentheses denote that this amount is deducted when finding the net cash outflow at t = 0.

Line 3. Here we show the price received from the sale of old equipment.

---

[5]This machine was purchased prior to the Economic Recovery Tax Act of 1981, so the Accelerated Cost Recovery System was not in place at the time. RII chose to depreciate the lathe on a straight line basis.

[6]If RII had taken an ITC on the old machine, and then sold it before the end of the ITC qualifying period, then a portion of that ITC would have to be repaid, and this recapture of ITC would be included in the replacement analysis as an outflow. However, in the case at hand, the old machine was in use for 10 years, so no ITC recapture is involved.

Table 9-5
Replacement Analysis Worksheet

Net Outflows at the Time the Investment Is Made	t = 0
1. Cost of new equipment	$12,000
2. Investment tax credit	(1,200)
3. Market value of old equipment	(1,000)
4. Tax effect of sale of old equipment (T)	(690)
5. Increase in net working capital	1,000
6. Total initial outflow	$10,110

Net Inflows over the Project's Life	t = 1	t = 2	t = 3	t = 4	t = 5
7. After-tax decrease in costs $(1-T)$	$1,620	$1,620	$1,620	$1,620	$1,620
8. Depreciation on new machine	1,710	2,508	2,394	2,394	2,394
9. Depreciation on old machine	500	500	500	500	500
10. Change in depreciation	1,210	2,008	1,894	1,894	1,894
11. Depreciation tax savings (T)	557	924	871	871	871
12. Estimated salvage value of new machine $(1-T)$					1,080
13. Return of working capital					1,000
14. Total net inflow	$2,177	$2,544	$2,491	$2,491	$4,571

Results

Payback period: 4.1 years.
IRR: 11.3% versus a 10% cost of capital.
NPV: $382.71.
PI: 1.04.

Line 4. Since the old equipment would be sold at less than book value, this creates a loss which reduces RII's taxable income, and hence its next quarterly income tax payment. The tax saving is equal to (Loss)(T) = ($1,500)(0.46) = $690, where T is the marginal corporate tax rate. The Tax Code defines this loss as an operating, not a capital, loss, because it reflects the fact that inadequate depreciation was taken on the old asset. If there had been a profit on the sale (that is, if the sales price had exceeded book value), Line 3 would have shown taxes paid, a positive cash outflow. In the actual case, the equipment would be sold at a loss, so no taxes would be paid, and RII would realize a tax savings of $690.[7]

---

[7]If the old asset were being exchanged for the new asset, rather than being sold to a third party, the tax consequences would be different. In an exchange of similar assets, no gain or loss is recognized. If the market value of the old asset is greater than its book value, the depreciable basis of the new asset is decreased by the excess amount. Conversely, if the market value of the old asset is less than its book value, the depreciable basis is increased by the shortfall.

Line 5. The investment in additional net working capital (new current asset requirements less increases in accounts payable and accruals) is shown here. This investment will be recovered at the end of the project's life. No taxes are involved.

Line 6. Here we show the total net cash outflow at the time the replacement is made. RII writes a check for $12,000 to pay for the machine, and another $1,000 is invested in net working capital. However, these outlays are partially offset by the items on Lines 2, 3, and 4.

Line 7. The center section of the table shows the *incremental future* cash flows, or benefits, that are expected if the replacement is made. The first of these benefits is the reduction in operating costs shown on Line 7, which (1) increases cash flows because operating costs are reduced by $3,000, but (2) also raises taxable income, and hence income taxes payable. Therefore, the after-tax benefit is $3,000(1 − T) = $3,000(1 − 0.46) = $3,000(0.54) = $1,620. Note that had the replacement resulted in an increase in sales in addition to the reduction in costs (if the new machine had been both larger and more efficient), then this amount would also be reported on Line 7. Alternatively, a separate line could be added. Finally, note that the $3,000 cost savings occur in Years 1-5, and that had the annual savings been expected to change over time, this fact would have to be built into the analysis.

Line 8. The depreciable basis of the new machine, $12,000 − 0.5($1,200) = $11,400, is multiplied by the appropriate ACRS recovery allowance for 5-year class property to obtain the data shown on Line 8.

Line 9. Line 9 shows the $500 straight line depreciation on the old machine.

Line 10. The depreciation expense on the old machine as shown on Line 9 will not be available if the replacement is made. Therefore, the $500 is subtracted from the depreciation expense on the new machine to show the net change in annual depreciation. Since the result is positive, purchase of the new machine creates a tax benefit. Of course, a reduction in net depreciation expense would have resulted in a reduction of tax benefits.

Line 11. The net increase in depreciation results in a depreciation tax savings. The annual savings are determined by multiplying the change in depreciation by the tax rate, 0.46: Depreciation savings = T (Change in depreciation). Note that the relevant cash flow is the tax savings on the *net change* in depreciation, and not the depreciation on the new equipment. Capital budgeting decisions are based on *incremental* cash flows. Since we lose $500 of depreciation if we replace the old machine, the incremental or additional depreciation in Year 1 that occurs as a result of the replacement is only $1,710 − $500 = $1,210, so the incremental cash flow from taxes saved is 0.46($1,210) = $557.

Line 12. The estimated salvage value of the new machine at the end of its 5-year life is $2,000. Since the book value of the new machine at the end of 5 years is zero, RII will have to pay ordinary taxes on the sale. The after-tax salvage value cash flow is $2,000(1 − 0.46) = $2,000(0.54) = $1,080.[8]

Line 13. An investment of $1,000 in net working capital was shown as an outflow at t = 0. This investment, like the salvage value, will be recovered when the project is terminated at the end of Year 5. Accounts receivable will be collected, and inventories will be drawn down and not replaced. So, RII will have a $1,000 inflow at t = 5.

Line 14. The total net inflows shown on Line 14 are the sums of Lines 7 plus 11 through 13.

The lower section of the table, "Results," shows the replacement project's payback, IRR, NPV, and PI. The project is assumed to be of similar risk to the old project, and the old project is assumed to be about as risky as RII's average project. Therefore, a 10 percent project cost of capital is appropriate. At this cost of capital, the project is acceptable, and hence the old lathe should be replaced.

Evaluating Projects with Unequal Lives

Note that a replacement decision involves two mutually exclusive projects: The firm can either retain the old asset or replace it with a new asset. To simplify matters, in our replacement example we assumed that the new machine had a life equal to the remaining life of the old machine. If, however, we were choosing between two mutually exclusive alternatives that had *different* lives, it would be necessary to put the alternatives on a common life basis, using one of two methods: (1) the *replacement chain* approach or (2) the *equivalent annual annuity* approach. We will illustrate both approaches in the following example.

Suppose RII is planning to modernize its production facilities, and as a part of the process, it is considering either a conveyor system (Project C) or a forklift truck (Project F) for moving industrial robot components from the parts department to the main assembly line. Table 9-6 shows

[8]In this analysis, the salvage value of the old machine is zero. However, if the old machine could be sold at the end of five years, then replacing the old machine deprives the firm of this cash flow. Thus, the after-tax salvage value of the old machine represents an opportunity cost to the firm, and it would be included as a Year 5 cash outflow in the middle part of the worksheet.

Table 9-6
Expected Net Cash Flows for Projects C and F

Year	Project C	Project F
0	($40,000)	($20,000)
1	8,000	7,000
2	14,000	13,000
3	13,000	12,000
4	12,000	—
5	11,000	—
6	10,000	—
NPV	$9,281	$6,123

the expected net cash flows and the NPV for each of these mutually exclusive alternatives. We see that Project C, when discounted at a cost of capital of 10 percent, has the higher NPV and hence appears to be the better project.

Replacement Chain (Common Life) Approach

Although the analysis in Table 9-6 suggests that Project C should be selected, this analysis is incomplete, and the decision to choose Project C is actually incorrect. If we choose Project F, we will have an opportunity to make a similar investment after 3 years, and presumably this second investment will also be profitable. However, if we choose Project C, we will not have this second investment opportunity. Therefore, to make a proper comparison of Projects C and F, we must find the net present value of Project F over a 6-year period and then compare this extended NPV with the net present value of Project C over the same 6 years.

The NPV for Project C, as calculated in Table 9-6, is over a 6-year life. For Project F, however, we must take three additional steps: (1) determine the NPV of a second Project F three years hence, (2) bring this NPV back to the present, and (3) sum these two component NPVs:

1. If we make the assumption that Project F's cost and annual cash flows will not change if the project were repeated in three years, and that RII's cost of capital will remain at 10 percent, then Project F's second-stage NPV would remain the same as its first-stage NPV, $6,123. However, the second NPV would not accrue for three years, and hence it would represent a present value at $t = 3$.

2. The present value (at $t = 0$) of the repeated Project F is determined by discounting the second NPV (at $t = 3$) back three years at 10 percent to determine its value at $t = 0$: $6,123/(1.10)^3 = $4,600$.

3. The "true" NPV of Project F is $6,123 + $4,600 = $10,723$. This is the value which should be compared with the NPV of Project C, $9,281.

Since the "true" NPV of Project F is greater than the NPV of Project C, Project F should be selected.

Equivalent Annual Annuity Approach

Although the example illustrates why a chain analysis is necessary if mutually exclusive projects have different lives, the arithmetic is generally more complex in practice. For example, one project might have an 8-year life versus an 11-year life for the other. This would require an analysis over 88 years, the lowest common denominator of the two lives. In such a situation, it is often simpler to use a second procedure, the equivalent annual annuity method, which involves three steps:

1. Find each project's NPV over its original life. In the previous example, we found $NPV_C = \$9,281$ and $NPV_F = \$6,123$.

2. Divide the original NPV of each project by the present value annuity factor, PVIFA, for the project's original life to obtain the annual annuity which would be equivalent in value to this NPV:

$$\text{Equivalent annual annuity, Project C} = NPV_C/PVIFA_{10\%,6\text{ yrs}}$$
$$= \$9,281/4.3553$$
$$= \$2,131.$$
$$\text{Equivalent annual annuity, Project F} = \$6,123/2.4869$$
$$= \$2,462.$$

Project C has an NPV which is equivalent to an annuity of $2,131 per year for 6 years—such an annuity would be worth exactly 4.3553($2,131) = $9,281—while Project F's NPV is equivalent to an annuity of $2,462 for 3 years.

3. Assuming continuous replacements are made when each project's life ends, these equivalent annual annuities will continue on out to infinity; that is, they will constitute perpetuities. Recognizing that the value of a perpetuity is V = Annual receipt/k, we can find the net present values of the infinite annuities of Projects C and F as follows:

$$\text{Infinite horizon } NPV_C = \$2,131/0.10 = \$21,310.$$
$$\text{Infinite horizon } NPV_F = \$2,462/0.10 = \$24,620.$$

Since the infinite horizon NPV of F exceeds that of C, Project F should be accepted. Therefore, the equivalent annual annuity method leads to the same decision rule as the simple chain method—accept Project F.

Computationally, the equivalent annual annuity method is often easier to apply than the chain method. However, the chain method is often easier to explain to decision makers, and it does not require the assumption of an infinite time horizon. Also, note that Step 3 above is not really necessary to make the decision—we could have stopped after Step 2. However, Step 3 does point out by how much each project will increase the value of the firm, assuming continuous replacement forever.

Once students become aware of the replacement chain problem, they often ask this question: "Shouldn't replacement chains, or common life analysis, be used for *all* capital budgeting analysis? For example, if we were analyzing one project with an 8-year life and another with a 10-year life, shouldn't we put them on a common time basis?" The answer is, "Not necessarily." As a general rule, the replacement chain issue (1) does not arise for independent projects but (2) can arise if mutually exclusive projects with different lives are being evaluated. However, even for mutually exclusive projects, it is not always appropriate to extend the analysis to a common denominator year: Only if the operation is likely to be continued should the extension be made.

We should also note a potentially serious weakness of our replacement analysis: If inflation is expected to continue, then replacement equipment will have a higher price, and revenues will likely increase, and this should be incorporated into the analysis. However, there may be an offset to inflation—future generations of equipment may have better performance characteristics and therefore may provide additional cost reductions. Also, some types of equipment—computers, for example—have had declining costs. The best way of handling these complications is to build expected inflation and/or possible efficiency gains directly into the cash flow estimates, and then use the replacement chain approach (but not the equivalent annual annuity method). The arithmetic is more complicated, but the concepts are exactly the same as in our example.

Adjusting for Inflation

Inflation is a fact of life in the United States and most other nations, so it must be considered in any sound capital budgeting analysis. Several procedures are available for dealing with inflation.[9] To see how inflation enters the picture, suppose an investor lends $100 for one year at a rate of 5 percent. At the end of the year, the investor would have $100(1.05) = $105. However, if prices rose by 6 percent during the year, the ending $105 would have a purchasing power, in terms of beginning-of-year values, of only $105/1.06 = $99. Thus, the investor would have lost about 1 percent of his or her original purchasing power, in spite of having earned 5 percent interest: $105 at the end of the year will buy only as much as $99 would have bought at the beginning of the year.

As we discussed in Chapter 3, investors recognize this problem, so they incorporate expectations about inflation into the required rate of return. For example, suppose investors seek a *real rate of return*, k_r, of 8

---

[9]For a formal discussion of this subject, see James C. Van Horne, "A Note on Biases in Capital Budgeting Introduced by Inflation," *Journal of Financial and Quantitative Analysis*, January 1971, 653-658; Philip L. Cooley, Rodney L. Roenfeldt, and It-Keong Chew, "Capital Budgeting Procedures under Inflation," *Financial Management*, Winter 1975, 18-27; and "Cooley, Roenfeldt, and Chew vs. M. C. Findlay and A. W. Frankle," *Financial Management*, Autumn 1976, 83-90.

percent on an investment with a given degree of risk. Suppose, further, that they anticipate an *annual rate of inflation*, i, of 6 percent. Then, in order to end up with the 8 percent real rate of return, the *nominal rate of return*, k_n, must be a value such that

$$1 + k_n = (1 + k_r)(1 + i),$$

or

$$
\begin{aligned}
k_n &= (1 + k_r)(1 + i) - 1 \\
&= 1 + k_r + i + k_r i - 1 \\
&= k_r + i + k_r i.
\end{aligned}
\tag{9-4}
$$

In words, the nominal interest rate, k_n, must be set equal to the real rate, k_r, plus the expected inflation rate, i, plus a cross-product term, $k_r i$. In our example,

$$
\begin{aligned}
k_n &= 0.08 + 0.06 + (0.08)(0.06) \\
&= 0.08 + 0.06 + 0.0048 \\
&= 0.1448 = 14.48\%.
\end{aligned}
$$

Thus, if the investor earns a nominal return of 14.48 percent on a \$100 investment, the ending value, in real terms, will be

$$\frac{\$100(1.1448)}{1.06} = \frac{\$114.48}{1.06} = \$108,$$

producing the required 8 percent real rate of return. This example demonstrates the fact that Equation 9-4 "works."[10]

The Cost of Capital under Inflation

We can use these concepts to analyze capital budgeting under inflation. First, note that *in the absence of inflation*, where the real rate, k_r, and the nominal rate, k_n, are equal (as are the real and nominal expected cash flows—RCF_t and CF_t respectively), a project's NPV is calculated as follows:

$$\text{NPV (no inflation)} = \sum_{t=0}^{n} \frac{RCF_t}{(1 + k_r)^t}.
\tag{9-5}$$

Now suppose the expected rate of inflation becomes positive, and we expect both sales prices and input costs to rise at the rate i. Further, this same inflation rate, i, is built into the market cost of capital as developed

---

[10]Notice that if the cross-product term in Equation 9-4, $k_r i$, is disregarded on the grounds that it is typically small, we are left with this equation for nominal interest rates:

$$k_n = k_r + i.$$

This is the well-known "Fisher Equation," named after the great economist Irving Fisher, who studied the relationship between inflation and the cost of capital in the early 20th century.

in Equation 9-4. In this event, the nominal cash flow, CF_t, will increase annually at the rate i percent, producing this situation:

$$CF_t = RCF_t(1 + i)^t.$$

For example, if we expected a net cash flow of \$100 in Year 5 in the absence of inflation, then with a 5 percent rate of inflation, $CF_5 = \$100(1.05)^5 = \$127.63$.

Now if net cash flows increase at the rate i percent per year, and if this same inflation factor is built into the firm's cost of capital, then the NPV is calculated as follows:

$$\text{NPV (with inflation)} = \sum_{t=0}^{n} \frac{RCF_t(1 + i)^t}{(1 + k_r)^t(1 + i)^t}. \qquad \textbf{(9-6)}$$

Since the $(1 + i)^t$ terms in the numerator and denominator cancel, we are left with Equation 9-5:

$$\text{NPV} = \sum_{t=0}^{n} \frac{RCF_t}{(1 + k_r)^t}.$$

Thus, whenever both costs and sales prices, and hence annual cash flows, are expected to rise at the same inflation rate that investors have built into the cost of capital, then the inflation-adjusted NPV determined using Equation 9-6 is identical to the inflation-free NPV found using Equation 9-5.[11]

However, firms occasionally use base year dollars throughout the analysis—say 1985 dollars if the analysis is done in 1985—along with a cost of capital as determined in the marketplace. This is wrong: *If the cost of capital includes an inflation premium, as it typically does, but the cash flows are all stated in current dollars, then the calculated NPV will be downward biased.* The denominator will reflect inflation, but the numerator will not, producing a downward bias in NPV. If sales prices and all costs are expected to rise at exactly the same rate, then the bias can be corrected by (1) increasing cash flows in the numerator at the inflation rate and (2) using the nominal cost of capital, k_n, as the discount rate. Alternatively, we could leave RCF_t in the numerator but use k_r rather than k_n in the denominator. Either procedure will insure consistency and thus eliminate the bias.

Adjusting for Nonneutral Inflation

With nonneutral inflation (which means a situation where input costs, output prices, and/or the cost of capital have different inflation rates), it is necessary to develop annual cash flows, CF_t, which specifically account for inflation. This is what we did earlier in our RII example as

---

[11]We could make the NPV expression even more complicated by incorporating differing inflation rates over time. Then, the inflation rates would not be constant across time periods but would vary from period to period.

summarized in Table 9-4. There we assumed that sales prices, variable costs, and fixed overheard costs would all increase at a rate of 6 percent per year, but that depreciation charges would not be affected by inflation. Of course, we could have assumed different rates of inflation for sales prices, for variable costs, and for fixed overheads. For example, RII might have long-term labor contracts which cause wage rates to rise with the Consumer Price Index (CPI), but its raw materials might be purchased under a fixed price contract, with the net result that variable costs are expected to rise by a smaller percentage than sales prices. In any event, one should build inflation into the capital budgeting analysis, with the specific adjustment reflecting as accurately as possible the most likely set of circumstances.

Our conclusions about inflation may be summarized as follows. First, inflation is critically important, for it can and does have major effects on businesses. Therefore, it must be recognized and dealt with. Second, there is really no simple, easy way to bring inflation into the decision process. The only effective way of getting a handle on inflation and its effects is to build inflation estimates into each cash flow element, using the best available information on how each element will be affected. Third, since we cannot estimate future inflation rates with precision, errors are bound to be made. Thus, inflation adds to the uncertainty, or riskiness, of capital budgeting as well as to its complexity. Fortunately, computers are available to help with inflation analysis, but an awareness of the nature of the problem is essential for financial analysis.

Summary

This chapter has dealt with four issues in capital budgeting: cash flow estimation, replacement decisions, unequal life adjustments, and inflation adjustments.

The most important, yet most difficult, step in capital budgeting analysis is *cash flow estimation*. The key to cash flow estimation is to consider only *incremental* after-tax cash flows. *Replacement analysis* is conceptually similar to new project analysis, except that replacement cash flow estimation requires consideration of the fact that the old asset could continue to generate additional cash flows. Additionally, if the replacement asset has a life different from that remaining on the old asset, it may be necessary to adjust to a common life. This adjustment can be made either by *replacement chains* or by *equivalent annual annuities*. Adjusting for unequal lives may actually be necessary for analyzing any set of mutually exclusive projects when (1) different lives are involved and (2) the projects are expected to continue beyond the assets' initial lives.

Inflation exists in the United States and most other economies, and it must be dealt with in capital budgeting analysis. If inflation is ignored, then (1) the cash flows in the numerator of the NPV equation are not adjusted for expected inflation, but (2) an adjustment is automatically (and generally unconsciously) made in the denominator because market forces build inflation into the cost of capital. Thus, the net result is to create a downward bias in evaluating projects. The best way of correcting for this bias is to build price increases based on expected inflation rates directly into the expected cash flows.

This chapter has considered a number of important issues which financial managers must deal with in their capital budgeting procedures. In Chapter 10, we will conclude the discussion of capital budgeting with risk analysis and the optimal capital budget.

Questions

9-1   Define each of the following terms:
    a. Cash flow; accounting income
    b. Incremental cash flow; sunk cost; opportunity cost
    c. Net working capital changes
    d. Salvage value
    e. Replacement decision
    f. Replacement chain
    g. Equivalent annual annuity
    h. Real rate of return, k_r, versus nominal rate of return, k_n

9-2   Operating cash flows rather than accounting profits are listed in Table 9-2. What is the basis for this emphasis on cash flows as opposed to net income?

9-3   Why is it true, in general, that a failure to adjust expected cash flows for expected inflation biases the calculated NPV downward?

9-4   Suppose a firm is considering two mutually exclusive projects. One has a life of 6 years and the other a life of 10 years. Would the failure to employ some type of replacement chain analysis bias an NPV analysis against one of the projects? Explain.

9-5   Look at Table 9-5 and answer these questions:
    a. Why is the salvage value shown on Line 12 reduced for taxes?
    b. Why is depreciation on the old machine deducted on Line 9?
    c. What would happen if the new machine permitted a *reduction* in working capital?
    d. Why are the cost savings on Line 7 reduced by multiplying the before-tax figure by $(1 - T)$, whereas the net depreciation figure on Line 10 is multiplied by T?

Self-Test Problems

ST-1 You have been asked by the president of your company to evaluate the proposed acquisition of a new earthmover. The mover's basic price is $50,000, and it would cost another $10,000 to modify it for special use by your firm. The mover falls into the ACRS 3-year class, and it qualifies for an investment tax credit. The mover would be sold after 3 years for $20,000. Use of the mover would require an increase in net working capital (spare parts inventory) of $2,000. The earthmover would have no effect on revenues, but it is expected to save the firm $20,000 per year in before-tax operating costs, mainly labor. The firm's marginal tax rate is 40 percent. Section 179 expensing would *not* be used on this project.

   a. What is the net cost of the earthmover? (That is, what are the Year 0 cash flows?)

   b. What are the operating cash flows in Years 1, 2, and 3?

   c. What are the additional (nonoperating) cash flows in Year 3?

   d. If the project's cost of capital is 10 percent, should the earthmover be purchased?

ST-2 The Boston Toy Corporation (BTC) currently uses an injection molding machine that was purchased 2 years ago. This machine is being depreciated on a straight line basis toward a $500 salvage value, and it has 6 years of remaining life. Its current book value is $2,600, and it can be sold for $3,000 at this time. Thus, the annual depreciation expense is ($2,600 − $500)/6 = $350 per year. No ITC was taken on the old machine.

   BTC is offered a replacement machine which has a cost of $8,000, an estimated useful life of 6 years, and an estimated salvage value of $800. This machine falls into the ACRS 5-year class, and thus qualifies for a 10 percent investment tax credit. The replacement machine would permit an output expansion, so sales would rise by $1,000 per year; even so, the new machine's much greater efficiency would still cause operating expenses to decline by $1,500 per year. The new machine would require that inventories be increased by $2,000, but accounts payable would simultaneously increase by $500. No Section 179 expense would be applied to this project.

   BTC's effective tax rate is 46 percent, and its cost of capital is 15 percent. Should it replace the old machine?

Problems

9-1 (Depreciation effects.) Sylvestor Cabot-Lodge, great grandson of the founder of Cabot-Lodge Textiles and current president of the company, believes in simple, conservative accounting. In keeping with his philosophy, he has decreed that the company shall use straight-line depreciation, based on the ACRS class lives, for all newly acquired assets. Your boss, the financial vice-president and the only nonfamily officer, has asked you to develop an exhibit which shows how much this policy costs the company in terms of market value. Mr. Cabot-Lodge is interested in increasing the value of the firm's stock because he fears a family stockholder revolt which might remove him from office. For your exhibit, assume that the company spends $50 million each year on new capital projects, that the projects have, on average, a 10-year class life, that the company has a 15 percent cost of capital, and that its tax rate is 46 percent. Ignore the investment tax credit. (Hints: (1) Review the section in Chapter 2 on ACRS depreciation. (2) Show how much the NPV of projects in an average year would increase if Cabot-Lodge used the maximum ACRS depreciation.)

9-2 (New project.) You have been asked by the president of your company to evaluate the proposed acquisition of a new milling machine. The machine's basic price is $100,000, and it would cost another $20,000 to modify it for special use by your firm. The machine falls into the ACRS 3-year class, and it qualifies for an investment tax credit. The machine would be sold after 3 years for $50,000. Use of the machine would require an increase in net working capital (milling blanks) of $5,000. The machine would have no effect on revenues, but it is expected to save the firm $40,000 per year in before-tax operating costs, mainly labor. The firm's marginal tax rate is 46 percent, and no Section 179 expensing would be applied.

a. What is the net cost of the machine? (That is, what is the Year 0 net cash flow?)
b. What are the operating cash flows in Years 1, 2, and 3?
c. What are the additional (nonoperating) cash flows in Year 3?
d. If the project's cost of capital is 10 percent, should the machine be purchased?

9-3   (Inflation adjustments.) The Fischer Corporation is considering an average risk investment in a mineral water spring project that has a cost of $150,000. The project will produce 1,000 cases of mineral water per year indefinitely. The current sales price is $138 per case, and the current cost per case (all variable) is $105. Fischer is taxed at a rate of 46 percent. Both prices and costs are expected to rise at a rate of 6 percent per year. Fischer uses only equity, and it has a cost of capital of 15 percent ($k = D_1/P_0 + g = 15\%$). Assume that cash flows consist only of after-tax profits, since the spring has an indefinite life and will not be depreciated.

a. Should Fischer accept the project? (Hint: The project is a perpetuity, so you must use the formula for a perpetuity to find the NPV.)
b. If total costs consisted of a fixed cost of $10,000 per year and variable costs of $95 per unit, and if only the variable costs were expected to increase with inflation, would this make the project better or worse? Continue with the assumption that the output price will rise with inflation.

9-4   (Replacement project.) Molded Plastics, Inc., has an opportunity to purchase a new, more efficient press, Model L, to replace an old press, Model S, now in use. MPI's vice-president in charge of purchasing has reported that the new press, Model L, will cost $69,500. It has an expected 10-year useful life; it will be depreciated over this life using the ACRS method; and it will have no salvage value at the end of 10 years.

From an examination of the company's books, you have determined that Model S, which was purchased 3 years ago (in 1982) for $56,000, is being depreciated on a straight line basis over an original 8-year period. It too is expected to have a zero salvage value at the end of its 8-year life. The demand in the market for older presses is such that Model S could be sold today for $23,000.

If Model S is not replaced now, it will be replaced in 5 years by Model L, but the cost of Model L will increase at the same rate as inflation, 5 percent. The plant in which Model S operates is to be shut down in 10 years. Therefore, if the new press is purchased in 5 years, it will be sold after 5 years of use, and its expected abandonment value is $49,000.

MPI will be able to *decrease* inventories by $7,000, and accounts payable will also decline by $4,000, during the time that the Model L press is in use.

If Model L is purchased now, the company will be able to reduce operating costs by $10,800 in the first year of Model L's service. Operating costs are expected to increase by 5 percent per year over the life of the plant; therefore, the cost savings would also increase by 5 pecent per year during the next 5 years.

MPI's income tax rate is 40 percent; its long-term capital gains tax rate is 30 percent; and Model L is eligible for a 10 percent investment tax credit. The company's cost of capital is 14 percent. Should MPI replace Model S with Model L now, or should it wait and replace Model S in 5 years?

9-5   (Unequal lives.) The Sweater Mill, Inc., is considering the replacement of its old, fully depreciated knitting machine. Two new models are available: Machine 190-3, which has a cost of $190,000, a 3-year expected life, and after-tax cash flows (labor savings and depreciation) of $87,000 per year; and Machine 360-6, which has a cost of $360,000, a 6-year life, and after-tax cash flows of $98,300 per year. Knitting machine prices are not expected to rise, because inflation will be offset by cheaper components (microprocessors) used in the machines. Assume that The Sweater Mill's cost of capital is 14 percent.
   a. Should The Sweater Mill replace its old knitting machine, and, if so, which new machine should it use?
   b. Suppose The Sweater Mill's basic patents will expire in 9 years, and the company expects to go out of business at that time. Assume further that The Sweater Mill depreciates its assets using the straight-line method, that its marginal tax rate is 40 percent, and that the used machines can be sold at their book values. Under these circumstances, should the company replace the old machine, and, if so, which new model should the company purchase?

9-6   (Inflation adjustments.) The A. C. Baldwin Company is evaluating an average-risk capital project that has both a 3-year economic and ACRS class life. The net investment outlay at Year 0 is $18,800. The expected end-of-year cash flows, expressed in Year 0 dollars, are listed below:

	Year 1	Year 2	Year 3
Revenues	$30,000	$30,000	$30,000
Variable costs	15,000	15,000	15,000
Fixed costs	6,500	6,500	6,500
Depreciation	4,850	7,372	7,178

The firm has a marginal tax rate of 40 percent. Baldwin's current cost of debt is 12 percent, and its cost of equity is 16 percent. These costs include an estimated inflation premium of 6 percent. The firm's target capital structure is 50 percent debt and 50 percent equity.
   a. What is Baldwin's nominal cost of capital? Its real cost of capital?
   b. What are the project's relevant real cash flows? What is the project's NPV based on the nominal cost of capital?
   c. Is the nominal cost of capital the correct discount rate? Why? What is the project's NPV based on the real cost of capital? Should the project be accepted?

   d. Now assume that all revenues and costs, except depreciation, are expected to increase at the inflation rate of 6 percent. What are the project's nominal cash flows and NPV based on these flows? Why is this NPV different from the NPV calculated in Part c?

   e. If a company, in its capital budgeting process, bases its cash flows on sales prices and unit costs as of the time it analyzes the project, (1) would this tend to produce systematic errors in its capital budgeting evaluations, (2) would any such error be more serious for long-term or short-term projects, and (3) if you do think that systematic errors are likely to occur, how could they be corrected?

Solutions to Self-Test Problems

ST-1 a. *Estimated investment requirements:*

Price	($50,000)
Modification	(10,000)
Investment tax credit*	3,600
Net working capital	(2,000)
Total investment	($58,400)

*ITC = 6% of capitalized cost
    = 0.06 ($50,000 + $10,000) = $3,600.

b. *Operating cash flows:*

	Year 1	Year 2	Year 3
1. After-tax cost savings	$12,000	$12,000	$12,000
2. Depreciation*	14,550	22,116	21,534
3. Depreciation tax savings**	5,820	8,846	8,614
Net Cash Flow (1 + 3)	$17,820	$20,846	$20,614

*Depreciable basis = $60,000 − 0.5($3,600) = $58,200; allowances = 0.25, 0.38, and 0.37; depreciation in Year 1 = 0.25($58,200) = $14,550, and so on.
**T(Depreciation) = tax savings.

c. *End of project cash flows:*

Salvage value	$20,000
Tax on salvage value*	(8,000)
Net working capital recovery	2,000
	$14,000

*Sale price	$20,000	
− Book value	0	
Taxable income	$20,000	
Tax at 40%	8,000	

d. *Project NPV:*

$$NPV = -\$58,400 + \frac{\$17,820}{(1.10)^1} + \frac{\$20,846}{(1.10)^2} + \frac{\$34,614}{(1.10)^3}$$

$$= \$1,034.$$

Since the project has a positive NPV, the earthmover should be purchased.

ST-2 *First determine the net cash outflow at t = 0:*

Purchase price	$8,000
Investment tax credit	(800)
Sale of old machine	(3,000)
Tax on sale of old machine	184*
Net working capital	1,500**
Total investment	$ 5,884

*The market value is $3,000 − $2,600 = $400 above the book value. Thus, there is a $400 recapture of depreciation, and BTC would have to pay 0.46($400) = $184 in taxes.

**The change in net working capital is a $2,000 increase in current assets less a $500 increase in current liabilities, or $1,500.

Now, examine the operating cash inflows:

Sales increase	$1,000
Cost decrease	1,500
Pre-tax operating revenue increase	$2,500

After-tax operating revenue increase = $2,500(1 − T) = $2,500(0.54) = $1,350.

Depreciation:

	1	2	3	4	5	6
New*	$1,140	$1,672	$1,596	$1,596	$1,596	$ 0
Old	350	350	350	350	350	350
ΔDepreciation	790	1,322	1,246	1,246	1,246	(350)
Depreciation tax savings**	$ 363	$ 608	$ 573	$ 573	$ 573	($ 161)

*Depreciable basis = Cost − 0.5(ITC) = $8,000 − $400 = $7,600.

Depreciation expense each year equals depreciable basis times the ACRS factor of 0.15 for Year 1, 0.22 for Year 2, and 0.21 for Years 3-5.

**Depreciation tax-savings = ΔDepreciation(T).

Now recognize that at the end of Year 6 BTC will recover its working
capital investment of $1,500, and it will also receive $800 from the sale
of the replacement machine. However, the firm must pay 0.46($800)
= $363 in taxes on the sale of the machine. Note also that by under-
taking the replacement now, the firm forgoes the right to sell the old
machine for $500 in Year 6; thus, this $500 in Year 6 must be considered as an opportunity cost in that year. There is no tax effect here
since the $500 salvage value would equal the old machine's Year 6
book value.

Finally, place all the cash flows on a time line:

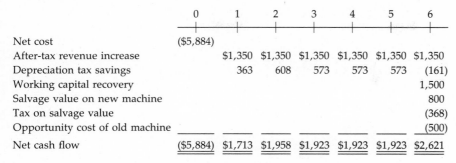

	0	1	2	3	4	5	6
Net cost	($5,884)						
After-tax revenue increase		$1,350	$1,350	$1,350	$1,350	$1,350	$1,350
Depreciation tax savings		363	608	573	573	573	(161)
Working capital recovery							1,500
Salvage value on new machine							800
Tax on salvage value							(368)
Opportunity cost of old machine							(500)
Net cash flow	($5,884)	$1,713	$1,958	$1,923	$1,923	$1,923	$2,621

The net present value of this incremental cash flow stream, when discounted at 15 percent, is $1,539. Thus, the replacement should be made.

Several articles have been written regarding the capital budgeting implications of the Accelerated Cost Recovery System (ACRS). Among them are the following:

Angell, Robert J., and Tony R. Wingler, "A Note on Expensing versus Depreciating under the Accelerated Cost Recovery System," *Financial Management*, Winter 1982, 34-35.

McCarty, Daniel E., and William R. McDaniel, "A Note on Expensing versus Depreciating under the Accelerated Cost Recovery System: Comment," *Financial Management*, Summer 1983, 37-39.

For further information on replacement analysis, as well as other aspects of capital budgeting, see the texts by Bierman and Smidt, by Grant, Ireson, and Leavenworth, and by Levy and Sarnat as referenced in Chapter 8.

Two additional papers on the impact of inflation on capital budgeting are the following:

Bailey, Andrew D., and Daniel L. Jensen, "General Price Level Adjustments in the Capital Budgeting Decision," *Financial Management*, Spring 1977, 26-32.

Rappaport, Alfred, and Robert A. Taggart, Jr., "Evaluation of Capital Expenditure Proposals under Inflation," *Financial Management*, Spring 1982, 5-13.

For additional insights into unequal life analysis, see

Emery, Gary W., "Some Guidelines for Evaluating Capital Investment Alternatives with Unequal Lives," *Financial Management*, Spring 1982, 15-19.

The Brigham-Crum casebook contains the following cases that focus on Chapters 7 and 8 material:

Case 10, "Precision Control and Engineering, Inc.," which focuses on the replacement decision.

Case 11, "Lastinger Implement Company," which emphasizes the determination of relevant costs.

Case 12, "Fibertech Labs, Inc.," which illustrates the need to use replacement chains when alternatives with unequal lives are being compared.

Case 14, "American Business Machines, Inc.," which provides an overview of the problem of determining relevant costs and comparing mutually exclusive projects.

The Harrington casebook contains the following relevant cases:

"Federal Reserve Bank of Richmond", which analyzes the choice among three mutually exclusive methods of automating savings bond operations.

"Ing. C. Olivetti & Co.: The Pozzuoli Project," which describes alternative plant investments.

Selected Additional References and Cases

9A   Optimal Project Life

In Chapters 8 and 9, all of our capital budgeting examples were based on a specific estimated economic life for each project, and our accept/reject decisions were based on cash flows occurring over these estimated lives. In this appendix, we will see that a project's economic, or optimal, life is not always easy to estimate, and it may be quite different from the project's engineering life. Indeed, for many projects, determining the optimal project life is a key part of the capital budgeting analysis.

Abandonment Value

Customarily, projects are analyzed as though the firm were committed to each project over some specific useful life. However, it occasionally turns out best to abandon a project prior to its potential life, and this possibility can materially affect the project's calculated NPV and IRR.[1] The easiest way to illustrate the abandonment value concept and its effects on capital budgeting is by illustration. Table 9A-1 contains the expected net cash flows and expected net abandonment values for Project A. The abandonment values are equivalent to salvage values, except that they have been estimated for each year of Project A's life.

Using a cost of capital of 10 percent, the expected NPV over the three-year economic life is $-\$117$:

$$NPV = -\$4,800 + \$2,000/(1.10)^1 + \$1,875/(1.10)^2 + \$1,750/(1.10)^3$$
$$= -\$117.$$

Thus, Project A would not be accepted if we viewed the single alternative of a 3-year life with a zero salvage (abandonment) value. However, what would be the NPV of Project A if it were abandoned after 2 years? Here, we would receive operating cash flows in Years 1 and 2, plus the abandonment value at the end of Year 2, and the NPV would be $138:

---

[1]See Alexander A. Robichek and James C. Van Horne, "Abandonment Value and Capital Budgeting," *Journal of Finance*, December 1967, 577-589.

Table 9A-1
Net Operating and Abandonment Cash Flows
for Project A

Year	Operating Cash Flows	Abandonment Cash Flows
0	($4,800)	$4,800
1	2,000	3,000
2	1,875	1,900
3	1,750	0

$$\text{NPV} = -\$4,800 + \$2,000/(1.10)^1 + \$1,875/(1.10)^2 + \$1,900/(1.10)^2$$
$$= \$138.$$

Thus, Project A becomes acceptable if we plan to operate it for 2 years and then abandon it. To complete the analysis, we note that if the project were abandoned after 1 year, its NPV would be $-\$255$. Thus, the optimal project life is 2 years. In fact, this is the only life which gives a positive NPV, and hence an accept decision.

As a general rule, any project should be abandoned when the abandonment value is greater than the present value of all cash flows beyond the abandonment year, discounted to the abandonment decision point. For example, if we accept Project A and operate it for one year, then the abandonment value is $3,000, but the present value at Year 1 of cash flows beyond Year 1 is $1,875/(1.10)^1 + \$1,750/(1.10)^2 = \$3,151$, assuming the project continues through Year 3, and $1,875/(1.10)^1 + \$1,900/(1.10)^1 = \$3,432$, assuming abandonment at the end of Year 2. Thus, the Year 1 abandonment value is less than the Year 1 present values of the expected future cash flows under either of the two alternative longer lives, so the project should not be abandoned at this point. However, a similar analysis at Year 2 would show that the abandonment value of $1,900 is greater than the discounted value of future cash flows of $1,750/(1.10)^1 = \$1,591$, so our decision rule would tell us to abandon the project in Year 2. This is, of course, the same conclusion that we reached from the NPV calculations.

Abandonment value should be considered in the capital budgeting process because, as our example illustrates, there are cases where recognition of abandonment can make an otherwise unacceptable project acceptable. Indeed, this type of analysis is required to determine a project's economic life. For Project A, the economic life is actually two years rather than the three years originally estimated, the economic life being that project life which maximizes the project's NPV, and thus maximizes shareholder wealth.

Finding the Optimal Project Life

Some projects do not have well-defined economic lives; two common examples are the growing of trees for timber and the aging of wines. In each case, the value of the product increases with time, at least up to some point, but costs are involved in carrying the initial capital investment and in maintaining the forest or storing the wine. Thus, we have a trade-off, and the problem of finding the optimal project life can be very complex. In this section, we present a simple example to illustrate the general approach.

Assume that the manager of a winery estimates that the net after-tax dollar profit on a bottle of red wine can be approximated by the following formula:

$$\text{Profit} = (3t)^{1/2},$$

where t is the number of years held for aging prior to sale. For example, wine aged for one year can be sold at a profit of $[3(1)]^{1/2} = \$1.73$ per bottle; wine aged for 2 years can be sold to yield $[3(2)]^{1/2} = \$2.45$ per bottle; 10-year-old wine will yield $5.48; and so on. Further, assume that the investment outlay for each bottle of wine is $1.00, and the company's cost of capital, k, is 10 percent. Thus, the NPV for each bottle is found as follows:

$$
\begin{aligned}
\text{NPV} &= -\text{Cost} + \frac{(3t)^{1/2}}{(1 + k)^t} \\
&= -\text{Cost} + (3t)^{1/2}(1 + k)^{-t} \\
&= -\$1.00 + (3t)^{1/2}(1.10)^{-t}.
\end{aligned}
\qquad \text{(9A-1)}
$$

Aging the wine longer increases the net revenue, but it also increases the capital, or carrying, costs. We want to choose t, the number of years the wine is aged, to maximize net present value.

One method of optimizing NPV is to take the first derivative of Equation 9A-1 with respect to time, t, set this derivative equal to zero, and end up with Equation 9A-2:[2]

$$
t^* = \frac{1}{2 \ln(1 + k)},
\qquad \text{(9A-2)}
$$

where t^* is the optimal project life. If the cost of capital is 10 percent, then the optimal project life is 5.2 years:

$$
\begin{aligned}
t^* &= \frac{1}{2 \ln(1.10)} = \frac{1}{2(0.0953)} \\
&= \frac{1}{0.1906} = 5.2 \text{ years.}
\end{aligned}
$$

---

[2]The derivation of Equation 9A-2 is as follows:

$$\text{NPV} = -\text{Cost} + (3t)^{1/2}(1 + k)^{-t}.$$

The cost is a constant, so it falls out, and

$$
\frac{d(\text{NPV})}{dt} = (1/2)(3t)^{-1/2}(3)(1 + k)^{-t} - (3t)^{1/2}(1 + k)^{-t} \ln(1 + k) = 0
$$

$$
(3/2)(3t)^{-1/2} = (3t)^{1/2}\ln(1 + k)
$$

$$
3t = \frac{3}{2 \ln(1 + k)}
$$

$$
t^* = \frac{1}{2 \ln(1 + k)}.
$$

Note that Equation 9A-2 is not a general equation for finding the optimal life of projects—it applies only to the specific function used in this illustrative problem. Note also that the more complicated the function, and consequently the harder it is to differentiate, the greater is the advantage to an evaluation such as that given in Table 9A-2. Finally, recognize that for ease of illustration, we have assumed that inventory storage costs can be built into the profit function.

Table 9A-2
NPV versus Project Life

Year	Price/Bottle	PV of Price/Bottle	NPV
1	$1.73	$1.57	$0.57
2	2.45	2.02	1.02
3	3.00	2.25	1.25
4	3.46	2.36	1.36
5	3.87	2.40	1.40
6	4.24	2.39	1.39

This result can be verified by calculating the NPV at various project lives as shown in Table 9A-2. Here we see that the highest NPV occurs at about the fifth year.

This example was intended merely to introduce the topic of optimal project life—this type of analysis can get much more complicated.[3] Also, note that a conventional NPV analysis can be used to determine the optimal project life, as in Table 9A-2. The equation format is a more efficient way of solving such problems, provided the equation is simple enough to differentiate, but it is often easier to set up a simple computer model and use it to find the optimal life than it is to obtain an analytical solution.

Problem

9A-1 The Clayton Machine Company recently purchased a new delivery truck. The new truck cost $22,500, and it is expected to generate net after-tax cash flows, including depreciation, of $6,250 per year. The truck has a 5-year expected life. The expected abandonment values (in this case, salvage values after tax adjustments) for the truck are given below. The company's cost of capital is 10 percent.

Year	Annual Cash Flow	Abandonment Value
0	($22,500)	$22,500
1	6,250	17,500
2	6,250	14,000
3	6,250	11,000
4	6,250	5,000
5	6,250	0

a. Should Clayton operate the truck until the end of its 5-year life, or, if not, what is its optimal (economic) life?

b. Would the introduction of abandonment values, in addition to operating cash flows, ever *reduce* the expected NPV and/or the IRR of a project?

---

[3]For a further discussion of optimal project life, see Thomas E. Copeland and J. Fred Weston, *Financial Theory and Corporate Policy* (Reading, Mass.: Addison-Wesley, 1983).

9B Sequential Decisions

Many capital budgeting decisions are not made at a single point in time. Rather, they consist of two or more sequential decisions, which are made as the project progresses through stages. For example, suppose Robotics International, Inc. (RII) is considering the production of industrial robots for the television manufacturing industry. The capital budgeting decision for this project will be broken down into three stages:

Stage 1. At t = 0, conduct a $500,000 study of the market potential for robot use in the television assembly-line process.

Stage 2. If it appears that a sizable market for robotics does exist, then at t = 1, spend $1 million to design and fabricate several prototype robots. These robots would then be evaluated by television industry engineers, and their reactions would determine whether RII proceeds with the project.

Stage 3. If reaction to the prototype robots is good, then at t = 2, build a production plant with a net cost of $10 million. If this stage were reached, the net payoff one year later is expected to be either $13 million or $16 million, depending on the state of the economy, competition, and so forth.

The diagram in Figure 9B-1 is called a *decision tree*, a procedure often used to analyze multi-stage, or sequential, decisions. A decision tree lays out the analysis like the branches of a tree. In Figure 9B-1, we assume that one year goes by between decisions and that a single net cash inflow from the project would occur one year after the final decision to go into production. Each circle represents a decision point, or stage. The dollar value to the left of each decision point represents the investment required if the decision is "go" at that point. Each diagonal line represents a branch of the decision tree, and each branch has an estimated probability. For example, if RII decides to "go" with the project at Decision Point 1, it will have to spend $500,000 on a marketing study. Management estimates that there is a probability of 0.8 that the study will produce favorable results leading to the decision to move on to Stage 2, and a 0.2 probability that the marketing

Figure 9B-1
RII Decision Tree (Thousands of Dollars)

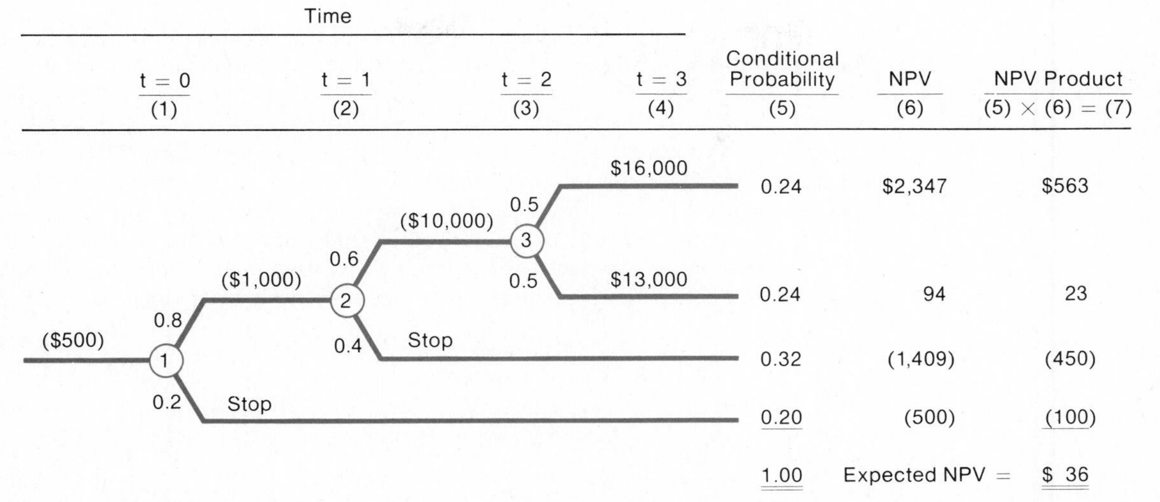

	Time				Conditional Probability	NPV	NPV Product
t = 0 (1)	t = 1 (2)	t = 2 (3)	t = 3 (4)		(5)	(6)	(5) × (6) = (7)

	Conditional Probability (5)	NPV (6)	NPV Product (5) × (6) = (7)
$16,000	0.24	$2,347	$563
$13,000	0.24	94	23
Stop	0.32	(1,409)	(450)
Stop	0.20	(500)	(100)
	1.00	Expected NPV =	$ 36

Tree branches: ($500) node 1; 0.8 to ($1,000) node 2; 0.2 Stop. From node 2: 0.6 to ($10,000) node 3; 0.4 Stop. From node 3: 0.5 to $16,000; 0.5 to $13,000.

study will produce negative results, indicating that the project should be canceled after Stage 1. If the project is stopped here, the cost to RII will be $500,000 for the initial marketing study.

If the marketing study is undertaken, and if it does yield positive results, then RII will go on to Decision Point 2 and spend $1 million on the prototype robot. Management estimates before even making the initial $500,000 investment that there is a 60 percent probability that the television engineers will find the robot useful and a 40 percent probability that they will not like it. If the engineers accept the robot, RII would then spend the final $10 million, while if the engineers do not like it, the project would be dropped. Finally, if RII does go into production, the payoff is assumed to be either $16 million or $13 million, with each outcome having a 50 percent probability. (Although we used only two production outcomes for simplicity, we could have used any number of outcomes or even a continuous distribution of outcomes.)

Column 5 of Figure 9B-1 gives the conditional probability of occurrence of each final outcome. Each conditional probability is obtained by multiplying together all probabilities on a particular branch. For example, the probability that RII will, if Stage 1 is undertaken, move through Stages 2 and 3, and that a strong economy will produce a $16 million net cash inflow, is $(0.8)(0.6)(0.5) = 0.24$.

Column 6 of Figure 9B-1 gives the NPV of each final outcome. RII has a cost of capital of 10 percent, and management assumes initially that all projects have average risk. The NPV of the top (most favorable) outcome is about $2,347,000:

$$\text{NPV} = \frac{\$16,000,000}{(1.10)^3} - \frac{\$10,000,000}{(1.10)^2} - \frac{\$1,000,000}{(1.10)^1} - \$5,000,000 = \$2,347,483.$$

Other NPVs were calculated similarly.

Column 7 of Figure 9B-1 gives the product of the NPVs in Column 6 times the probabilities in Column 5. The sum of the NPV products is the expected NPV of the project. Based on the expectations set forth in Figure 9B-1, and a cost of capital of 10 percent, the expected NPV is approximately $36,000.

Since the expected NPV is positive, should RII initiate Stage 1? Not necessarily, since management only assumed that the project is of average risk, and hence used the unadjusted cost of capital to evaluate it. However, RII must now reconsider and decide whether this project is more, less, or as risky as an average project. The company would need to conduct a risk analysis as described in Chapter 10 before making a final decision on the project.

Problem

9B-1 The Horgan Yacht Company (HYC), a prominent sailboat builder in Florida, may design a new 30-foot sailboat based on the "winged" keel used by Australia II that won the America's Cup after 132 years of dominance by the United States.

First, HYC would have to invest $10,000 (t = 0) for the design and model tank testing of the new boat. HYC's managers believe that there is a 60 percent probability that this phase will be successful and hence the project will continue. If Stage 1 is not successful, the project will be abandoned with zero salvage value.

The next stage, if undertaken, would consist of making the molds and producing two prototype boats. This would cost $500,000 at t = 1. If the boats test well, HYC would go into production. If they do not, the molds and prototypes could be sold for $100,000. The managers estimate that the probability is 80 percent that the boats will pass testing and hence Stage 3 will be undertaken.

Stage 3 consists of changing over one current production line to produce the new design. This would cost $1 million at t = 2. If the economy is strong at this point, the net value of sales would be $3 million, while if the economy is weak, the net value would be $1.5 million. Both net values occur at t = 3, and each state of the economy has a probability of 0.5. HYC's cost of capital is 12 percent. Assume that this project has average risk. Construct a decision tree and determine the project's expected NPV.

Risk Analysis and the Optimal Capital Budget

10

Capital budgeting is, in theory, a relatively straightforward, mechanical exercise—we simply estimate the cost of a project and its future cash flows, find the PV of the cash flows, and, if this PV exceeds the cost of the project, accept it. This is fine if we know the project's costs and its cash flows with relative certainty. However, if our estimates are wrong, what initially looked like a good project can turn out to be a disaster.

To illustrate, Long Island Lighting Company (LILCO) contracted to build the Shoreham nuclear power plant in the 1970s. At the time, the demand for electricity was growing at a rate of 7 percent per year, so it looked as though LILCO's capacity would have to be doubled every 10 years in order to serve the electrical needs of its area. Thus, LILCO began the construction of Shoreham at a forecasted cost of $500 million.

The project turned out to be a fiasco. First, the demand for power began to fall in the late 1970s, causing the original power usage estimates to be about twice as high as they should have been, but LILCO failed to make adequate adjustments to its demand forecast. Second, the cost of building the plant had been drastically underestimated—in 1984 it was learned that construction costs would actually be about $5 billion rather than the originally forecasted $0.5 billion!

With lower revenues and a higher initial cost, the project's large positive NPV turned out to be a huge negative one. As this book goes to press, the future of Shoreham is uncertain—the completion cost is uncertain, as is demand for the plant's output. LILCO is no longer able to pay dividends. If the plant is abandoned, and if LILCO has to write it off, the company will have to declare bankruptcy, its stockholders will be wiped out, and the bondholders will also suffer losses in spite of their senior position. The company's top executives have lost their jobs, and the remaining employees have been forced to take salary cuts. Finally, LILCO's customers, who already have close to the highest costs in the nation for electricity, will probably see rates rise by another 50 percent as a direct result of the Shoreham project.

About the same time LILCO was giving the green light to the Shoreham project, Florida Power Corporation was deciding whether to use coal or nuclear to meet future needs. Several University of Florida finance professors met with the FPC planners and discussed with them the topics contained in this chapter as applied to the coal versus nuclear decision. FPC chose coal, and it is today in good shape whereas LILCO is threatened by bankruptcy.

Risk Analysis

Risk analysis is important in all financial decisions, especially those relating to capital budgeting. As we saw in Chapter 6, the higher the risk associated with an investment, the higher is the rate of return needed to compensate investors for assuming the risk. The same concept holds true for capital projects. Procedures for both measuring project risk and incorporating it into the accept/reject decision are covered in the following sections.

Corporate Risk versus Beta Risk

Two separate and distinct types of risk have been identified in capital budgeting: (1) *market*, or *beta*, *risk*, which measures risk from the standpoint of an investor who holds a highly diversified portfolio, and (2) *total*, or *corporate*, *risk*, which looks at a firm's risk without considering the effects of its stockholders' own personal diversification. A particular project might have highly uncertain returns, yet taking it on might not affect the firm's beta coefficient at all. Recall that the beta coefficient reflects only that part of an investor's risk which cannot be eliminated by forming a large portfolio of stocks.

To illustrate, suppose 100 firms in the oil business each drill one wildcat well. Each company has $1 million of capital which it will invest in one well. If a firm strikes oil, then it will get a return of $2.4 million, and hence earn a profit of $1.4 million, while if it hits a dry hole, it will lose its $1 million investment and go bankrupt. The probability of striking oil is 50 percent. From the standpoint of the 100 individual firms, this is a very risky business. Their expected rate of return is 20 percent, calculated as follows:

$$\begin{aligned} \text{Expected rate} \atop \text{of return} &= \frac{\text{Expected profit}}{\text{Investment}} \\ &= \frac{0.5(-\$1,000,000) + 0.5(+\$1,400,000)}{\$1 \text{ million}} \\ &= \frac{-\$500,000 + \$700,000}{\$1,000,000} = 20\%. \end{aligned}$$

Note, however, that even though the expected return is 20 percent, there is a 50 percent probability of each firm being wiped out.

Although the riskiness of each firm is high, if a stockholder constructs a portfolio consisting of one share of each of the 100 companies' stock, the riskiness of this portfolio is not high at all. Some of the companies will hit oil and do well, while others will miss and go out of business, but the portfolio's return will be very close to the expected 20 percent. Therefore, since investors can diversify away the risks inherent in each of the individual companies, these risks are *not market-related* and so do not affect the companies' beta coefficients.[1] However, the firms remain quite risky from the standpoint of the firms' managers and employees who, essentially, bear risk similar to that borne by undiversified shareholders.

With this background, *we may define the corporate risk of a capital budgeting project as the probability that the project will incur losses which will, at a minimum, destabilize the corporation's earnings and, at the extreme, cause it to go bankrupt.* Taking on a project with a high degree of corporate risk will not necessarily affect the firm's beta to any great extent; our oil drilling example demonstrates this point. On the other hand, if a project has highly uncertain returns, and if those returns are highly correlated with those of most other assets in the economy, then the project may have a high degree of both corporate and beta risk. For example, suppose a firm decides to undertake a major expansion to build solar-powered autos. The firm is not sure if its technology will work on a mass production basis, so there are great risks in the venture. Management also estimates that the project will have a higher probability of success if the economy is strong, for then people will have money to spend on the new autos. This means that the project will tend to do well if other companies are also doing well, and to do poorly if others do poorly; hence, the project's beta coefficient will be high. A project like this would have a high degree of both corporate risk and beta risk.

Beta risk is obviously important because of beta's effect on the firm's cost of capital and the value of its stock. At the same time, corporate risk is also important for three primary reasons:

1. Undiversified stockholders, including the owners of small businesses, are more concerned about total risk than about beta risk.

2. Many financial theorists argue that investors, even those who are well diversified, consider factors other than market risk when setting re-

---

[1]Note also that if the 100 separate companies were merged, the combined company would not be very risky—it would drill lots of wells, losing on some and hitting on others, but it would earn a relatively steady profit. This helps explain why large oil (and other) companies are less risky than smaller companies, but it also explains why an investor who holds the stocks of many small companies may not have a riskier portfolio than someone who invests only in large companies. The value of firm diversification will be discussed in detail in Chapter 24.

quired returns. Empirical studies of the determinants of required rates of return generally find both beta and total risk to be important.

3. The firm's stability is important to its managers, workers, customers, suppliers, and creditors, and also to the community in which it operates. Firms that are in serious danger of bankruptcy, or even of suffering low profits and reduced output, have difficulty attracting and retaining good managers and workers. Also, both suppliers and customers are reluctant to depend on weak firms, and such firms have difficulty borrowing money except at high interest rates. These factors will tend to reduce risky firms' profitability, and hence the price of their stock.

We see, then, that corporate risk is also important even to well-diversified stockholders.

Techniques for Measuring Corporate Risk

The starting point for analyzing corporate risk involves determining the uncertainty inherent in a project's cash flows. This analysis can be handled in a number of ways, ranging from informal judgments to complex economic and statistical analyses involving large-scale computer models. To illustrate what is involved here, refer back to Robotics International's office robot project as described in Chapter 9. Most of the elements in Tables 9-1, 9-2, and 9-3, which gave the expected cash flows for the project as set forth in Table 9-4, are subject to uncertainty. For example, sales for 1988 were projected at 25,000 units to be sold at a net price of $2,200 per unit, or $55 million in total. However, unit sales would almost certainly be somewhat higher or lower than 25,000, and the sales price would probably be different from $2,200 per unit. In effect, the sales volume and price estimates were really expected values taken from probability distributions, as were many of the other values listed in Tables 9-1 through 9-3. The distributions could be relatively "tight," reflecting small standard deviations and low risk, or they could be "flat," denoting a great deal of uncertainty about the variable in question, and hence a high risk.

Sensitivity Analysis

Intuitively, we know that most of the variables which determine a project's cash flows are based on some type of probability distribution rather than known with certainty. We also know that if a key input variable, such as units sold, changes, so will the project's NPV. *Sensitivity analysis indicates exactly how much NPV will change in response to a given change in an input variable, other things held constant.* Sensitivity analysis is sometimes called "what if" analysis because it answers questions such as this: "What if sales are only 20,000 units rather than 25,000? Then what will the NPV be?"

Sensitivity analysis begins with a *base case* situation based on expected input values. To illustrate the procedure, we shall consider the data given in Table 9-2 in Chapter 9, where projected income statements for RII's office robot project were shown. The values for unit sales, sales price, fixed costs, and variable costs are the *expected*, or *base case*, values, and the resulting $11,465,923 NPV shown in Table 9-4 is called the *base case NPV*. Now we ask a series of "what if" questions: "What if sales quantity is 20 percent below the expected level?" "What if sales prices fall?" "What if variable costs are 70 percent of dollar sales rather than the expected 65 percent?" *Sensitivity analysis is designed to provide the decision maker with answers to questions such as these.*

In a sensitivity analysis, we change each variable by specific percentages above and below the base case value, calculate new NPVs, holding other things constant, and then plot the derived NPVs against the variable in question. Figure 10-1 shows the office robot project's sensitivity

Figure 10-1
Sensitivity Analysis for RII (Thousands of Dollars)

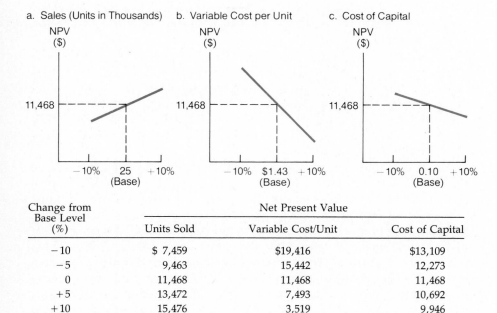

Change from Base Level (%)	Net Present Value		
	Units Sold	Variable Cost/Unit	Cost of Capital
−10	$ 7,459	$19,416	$13,109
−5	9,463	15,442	12,273
0	11,468	11,468	11,468
+5	13,472	7,493	10,692
+10	15,476	3,519	9,946

Note: This analysis was performed using *VisiCalc*, so the values are slightly different than those that would be obtained using a hand-held calculator due to rounding differences.

graphs for three of the key input variables. The table below the graphs gives the NPVs that were used to construct the graphs. The slopes of the lines in the graphs show how sensitive NPV is to changes in each of the inputs: the steeper the slope, the more sensitive the NPV is to a change in the particular variable. Here we see that the project's NPV is very sensitive to changes in variable costs, fairly sensitive to changes in sales volume, and relatively insensitive to changes in the cost of capital.

If we were comparing two projects, then, other things held constant, the one with the steeper sensitivity lines would be regarded as riskier— a relatively small error in estimating variables such as the variable cost per unit or demand for the product would produce a large error in the project's projected NPV. Thus, sensitivity analysis provides useful insights into the relative riskiness of different projects.

Scenario Analysis   Although sensitivity analysis is widely used in industry, it does have limitations. Consider, for example, a proposed coal mine whose NPV is highly sensitive to changes in both output and sales prices. However, if a utility company has contracted to buy most of the mine's output at a fixed price per ton, plus inflation adjustments, then the mining venture may not be very risky in spite of the steep sensitivity lines. *In general, a project's risk depends on both (1) its sensitivity to changes in key variables and (2) the range of likely values of these variables as reflected in their probability distributions.* Because sensitivity analysis considers only the first factor, it is incomplete.

A risk analysis technique which considers the sensitivity of NPV both to changes in key variables and also to the range of likely variable values is *scenario analysis*. Here the operating executives pick a "bad" set of circumstances (low unit sales, low sales price, high variable cost per unit, high construction cost, and so on) and a "good" set. The NPV under the "bad" and "good" conditions would be calculated and compared to the expected, or base case, NPV.

As an example, consider again the RII office robot project. Assume that RII's executives are fairly confident in their estimates of all the project's cash flow variables except price and unit sales. Further, assume they regard a drop in unit sales below 5,000, or a rise above 40,000 units, as being extremely unlikely. Similarly, they expect the sales price as set in the marketplace to fall within the range of $1,700 to $2,700. Thus, 5,000 units at a price of $1,700 defines the lower bound or the worst case scenario, while 40,000 units at a price of $2,700 defines the upper bound or the best case scenario. Remember that the expected, or base case, values are 25,000 units at a price of $2,200. Also, note that the indicated sales prices are for 1988, with future years' prices expected to rise because of inflation.

To carry out the scenario analysis, we use the worst case variable values to obtain the worst case NPV and the best case variable values to

Table 10-1
Scenario Analysis Results Summary

Scenario	Sales Volume (Units)	Sales Price	NPV (Thousands)
Worst case	5,000	$1,700	($22,421)
Base case	25,000	2,200	11,468
Best case	40,000	2,700	50,093

Notes:

a. NPVs were developed using *VisiCalc*.

b. Variables other than unit sales and sales prices were set at their expected values.

obtain the best case NPV.[2] We actually performed the analysis using *VisiCalc*, a popular spread sheet program which is described in Appendix 10A, and Table 10-1 summarizes the results of our analysis. We see that the base case forecasts a positive NPV; the worst case, a negative NPV; and the best case, a very large positive NPV. However, it is not easy to interpret this scenario analysis, or to make a decision based on it. In our example, we can say that there is a chance of losing on the project, but we cannot easily attach a specific probability to this loss. Clearly, what we need is some idea about the *probability of occurrence* of the worst case, the best case, the most likely case, and all the other cases that might arise. This leads us directly to Monte Carlo simulation, which is described in the next section.

Monte Carlo simulation, so named because this type of analysis grew out of work on the mathematics of casino gambling, ties together sensitivities and input variable probability distributions.[3] However, simulation requires a relatively sophisticated computer, coupled with an efficient financial planning software package, while scenario analysis can be done with a hand-held calculator.

Monte Carlo Simulation

The first step in a computer simulation is to specify a probability distribution for each of the key variables in the analysis. To illustrate, suppose we have estimated the probability distribution of the RII office ro-

---

[2]We could have included worst and best case values for fixed and variable costs, the inflation rate, salvage values, and so on. For illustrative purposes, we limit the changes to only two variables. Also, note that we are treating sales price and quantity as independent variables, that is, a low sales price could occur when unit sales were low, and a high sales price could be coupled with high unit sales, or vice versa. As we discuss in the next section, it is relatively easy to vary these assumptions if the facts of the situation suggest a different set of assumptions.

[3]The concept of simulation analysis in capital budgeting was first reported by David B. Hertz, "Risk Analysis in Capital Investments," *Harvard Business Review*, January-February 1964, 95-106.

Table 10-2
Probability Distribution for Robot Sales Price

Sales Price (1)	Probability (2)	Associated Random Numbers (3)
$1,700	0.05	00-04
2,000	0.20	05-24
2,200	0.50	25-74
2,400	0.20	75-94
2,700	0.05	95-99

bot's sales price as represented by Columns 1 and 2 of Table 10-2.[4] The expected sales price is $2,200, but the price can range from $1,700 to $2,700. The third column gives a set of random numbers associated with each price estimate. Notice that in Column 2, there is a 5 percent probability that sales price will be $1,700; therefore, 5 digits (0, 1, 2, 3, and 4) are assigned to this price. Twenty digits are assigned to a price of $2,000, and so on for the other possible prices. Once the distributions and associated random numbers have been specified for all the key variables—in other words, once a table such as 10-2 has been set up for sales quantity, unit variable costs, construction costs, and so on—the computer simulation can begin. These are the steps involved:

1. Computers have stored in them, or they can generate, random numbers. First, on Trial Run 1, the computer will select a different random number for each uncertain variable. For example, it might select 44 for units sold, 17 for the sales price, and 16 for labor costs.

2. Depending on the random number selected, a value is determined for each variable. The 17 associated with the sales price indicates (in Table 10-2) that the appropriate sales price for use in the first run is $2,000. Values for all the other variables are set in like manner.[5]

3. Once a value has been established for each of the variables, the computer generates a set of income statements and cash flows. These cash

---

[4]Here we assume that sales price is a discrete variable which can take on only five values. This simplification is purely for illustrative purposes; actual simulation models need have no such restrictions. In fact, the simulation model which we will use shortly allows the variable values to be specified either by continuous distribution parameters or by discrete values.

[5]Simulation models can handle either independence or dependence among variables. In this simple example, we assume independence; however, in many simulations it is more realistic to assume dependence. Thus, it might be assumed that if demand is weak and the figure for units sold is relatively low, then prices will also be weak. Similarly, the sales price in one year can be completely independent of or dependent on the price in the preceding year, or it can be somewhat correlated with the previous year's price. Simulation programs can handle these issues, although decision makers often have trouble specifying exactly how the different variables are related to one another.

flows are then discounted at the cost of capital (which may also be treated as a random variable), and the result is the net present value of the project on the computer's first run.[6]

4. The NPV generated on Run 1 is stored in memory, and the computer then goes on to Run 2. Here a different set of random numbers, and hence cash flows, is used. The NPV generated in Run 2 is again stored, and the model proceeds on for perhaps 500 runs. Modern computers can complete this operation almost instantaneously for a cost of less than two dollars.

5. The stored NPVs (all 500 of them) are then printed out in the form of a frequency distribution, together with the expected NPV and the standard deviation of this NPV.

Using this procedure, we can perform a simulation analysis on RII's office robot project. As in our scenario analysis, we have simplified the illustration by specifying the distributions for only two key variables, sales quantity and sales price. For all the other variables, we merely specify their expected values.

In our simulation analysis, we assume that sales prices can be represented by a continuous normal distribution.[7] Further, suppose that the expected value is $2,200 and that the actual sales price is very unlikely to vary by more than $500 from the expected value, that is, fall below $1,700 or rise above $2,700. We know that in a normal distribution, the expected value plus or minus three standard deviations will encompass virtually the entire distribution. Thus, for sales price, three standard deviations should equal $500, so as a reasonable approximation, we assume that $\sigma_{Sales\ price} = \$500/3 = \$166.67 \approx \$167$. Therefore, we tell the computer that the sales prices are normally distributed with an expected value of $2,200 and a standard deviation of $167.

Next, we assume that the estimated distribution of unit sales has an expected value of 25,000 units, but sales could be as high as 40,000 units, given our production capacity, or, if public acceptance is poor, as low as

---

[6]An alternative procedure is to use as the discount rate in simulation analysis the risk-free rate rather than the cost of capital. The logic behind this approach is the fact that, in simulation analysis, we are trying to assess a project's risk as reflected by the uncertainty inherent in its cash flows, and then to use this observed uncertainty as a basis for establishing a risk-adjusted discount rate. Thus, under the alternative procedure, one finds the NPV distribution based on R_F, which reflects only the time value of money. The variability inherent in the NPV distribution is then used as the basis for setting the project's cost of capital. Finally, the project's NPV is calculated using the project's own risk-adjusted cost of capital to determine if the project should be accepted or rejected.

One can certainly argue that the approach based on R_F is more logical than the one based on the average cost of capital. However, as we discuss later in the chapter, both procedures—and indeed the entire simulation approach—are only aids to informed judgmental decisions, so one discount rate is probably as good as another as long as one maintains consistency among the projects being analyzed.

[7]See Chapter 6 for a discussion of the normal distribution.

Table 10-3
Summary of Simulation Results

	Probability of NPV Being Greater than the Indicated Value (Thousands of Dollars)								
	0.90	0.80	0.70	0.60	0.50	0.40	0.30	0.20	0.10
NPV	−$1,860	$1,825	$5,144	$8,397	$11,393	$13,683	$16,516	$19,639	$25,286

Expected NPV = $11,228.
σ_{NPV} = $10,124.
Skewness$_{NPV}$ = +0.1.

10,000 units. Again, we could have specified a normal distribution, but in this case management feels that a triangular distribution, with an expected value of 25,000, a lower limit of 10,000, and an upper limit of 40,000, is most appropriate.[8]

We used the *Interactive Financial Planning System (IFPS)*, which is also described in Appendix 10A, to conduct a simulation analysis on the office robot project. Most large corporations have *IFPS* or a similar model either on their own computer or available through a time sharing system, and the same is true of many universities. The key results of our simulation are presented in Table 10-3. The top line of the table shows the cumulative probability distribution for NPV. Suppose someone asks, "What is the probability that the project will have an NPV greater than $5,000,000?" The answer is, "About 70 percent," because NPV = $5,000,000 lies between 70 and 80 percent, but much closer to 70 percent.

Notice that the mean, or expected, NPV is $11,228,000. This value is slightly smaller than the NPV we calculated in Chapter 9. This is because we used 500 iterations in the simulation analysis, and this number is not enough to produce an NPV distribution with an exactly matching expected value. Also, note that even though both input distributions (price and quantity) are symmetric, the distribution of NPV is not symmetric—it is skewed slightly to the right as indicated by a skewness coefficient of +0.1. This is because our two random variables, sales price and quantity, are multiplied together to get dollar sales in figuring NPV. The multiplication process skews the resulting dollar sales distribution to the right, and this skewness is reflected in the NPV distribution.

The primary advantage of simulation is that it shows us the range of possible outcomes, with attached probabilities, and not just a point estimate of the NPV. The expected NPV can be used as a measure of the

---

[8]A triangular distribution is, not surprisingly, shaped like a triangle, and it is specified by defining its most likely value along with its upper and lower limits. If the distribution is symmetric, as it is in this case, its most likely value is also its expected value.

project's profitability, while the variability of this NPV as measured by σ_{NPV} can be used to measure risk. To illustrate, the office robot project's expected NPV is $11,288,000, and the standard deviation of this NPV, as calculated by the computer in the simulation, is $\sigma_{NPV} = \$10,124,000$.[9] If we assume that RII's average project has an expected NPV of $975,000 and $\sigma_{NPV} = \$370,000$, then we can calculate the *coefficient of variation (CV)* for the office robot project and compare it with the CV of the average project as follows:

$$\text{Coefficient of variation} = \text{CV} = \frac{\text{Standard deviation}}{\text{Expected value}} = \frac{\sigma_{NPV}}{\text{Expected NPV}}.$$

$$\text{CV}_{\text{Office robot}} = \frac{\$10,124,000}{\$11,228,000} = 0.90.$$

$$\text{CV}_{\text{Average project}} = \frac{\$370,000}{\$975,000} = 0.38.$$

Since the coefficient of variation is a standardized risk measure, it can be used to compare the relative riskiness of projects which differ in size. We see that the CV of the office robot project is much larger than the CV of RII's average project. To account for risk, RII adds 2 percentage points to the cost of capital of such high-risk projects as the office robot. Our analysis thus far was based on RII's average cost of capital, 10 percent. Therefore, we must now reevaluate the project with a project cost of capital of 12 percent. When evaluated at a cost of capital of 12 percent, the NPV of the office robot project, using expected values of all variables, is $8,533,722. Thus, even at the high-risk cost of capital, the office robot project has a positive NPV. Thus, it appears to be acceptable.

In spite of its obvious appeal, simulation analysis has not been as widely used in industry as one might think. Five major reasons for this lack of general acceptance have been advanced.

Limitations of Simulation Analysis

1. Cost versus benefits. One reason that simulation is not more widely used has to do with its cost in relation to the benefits of its use. Until quite recently, developing a simulation model was a major undertaking that required a good deal of high-powered programming talent and a lot of expensive computer time. This is no longer true. Simulation software such as *IFPS* and computer hardware have both been developed to the point where cost is not a major consideration, at least for the larger firms. This suggests that we may see more simulation analysis in the future.

---

[9]Since the distribution is not normal, the standard deviation cannot be used to make precise statements about risk, as it could be were the distribution of NPV normal. Nevertheless, the distribution is not badly skewed, and thus the standard deviation and coefficient of variation can still be used to gain insights into the relative total riskiness of the project.

2. Implementation lag. It generally takes a while for any new manage-rial technology to become widely accepted, and simulation analysis may be in this position. This point was made by several executives who reviewed this book. Again, this suggests that the use of simulation may increase in the future.

3. Interdependencies among the variables. The simulation process described above assumes that the variables are independent of one another. However, it may be that such variables as unit sales and sales prices are correlated. For example, if demand is weak, sales prices may also be depressed. This suggests that if units sold is low, then a low sales price should also be used.[10] Similarly, the simulation process described above assumes that the values of each variable, and hence the bottom line cash flows, are independent over time. However, in many situations, it seems more reasonable to assume that high sales in the early years imply market acceptance, and hence high sales in future years, rather than to assume that sales in one year are not correlated with sales levels in other years.

It is easy enough to incorporate any type of correlation among variables into a simulation analysis; for example, *IFPS* permits us to specify both intervariable and intertemporal correlations. However, it is *not* easy to specify what the correlations should be. Indeed, people who have tried to obtain such relationships from the operating executives who must estimate them have eloquently emphasized the difficulties involved.[11] Clearly, the problem is not insurmountable, as the use of simulation is growing rapidly. Still, it is important not to underestimate the difficulty of obtaining valid estimates of both probability distributions and correlations among the variables.

4. No specific decision rule. A fourth problem with simulation analysis is that, even when a simulation analysis has been completed, no clear-cut decision rule emerges. We end up with an expected NPV and a distribution about this expected value, which we can use to judge the project's risk. However, the analysis has no mechanism to indicate whether the profitability as measured by the expected NPV is sufficient to compensate for the risk as indicated by σ_{NPV} or CV_{NPV}. This is in sharp contrast to the beta approach discussed later in the chapter, where a project is defined to be acceptable if its expected rate of return exceeds its beta-determined required rate of return.

---

[10]This statement implies a *downward (or left) shift* in the demand curve for the product. One can also visualize *movement along the demand curve*, which would imply that low sales prices would be associated with high demand. This relationship would be built into the simulation by the analyst. For example, if RII decided to price office robots at a base price of $2,000 rather than $2,200, then the base case expected sales level would probably be set somewhat above 25,000 units.

[11]For an excellent discussion of this problem, see K. Larry Hastie, "One Businessman's View of Capital Budgeting," *Financial Management*, Winter 1974, 36-43.

5. Ignores diversification. The fifth problem with simulation is that it ignores the effects of diversification, both among projects within the firm and by investors in their personal investment portfolios. Thus, an individual project may have highly uncertain returns, but if those returns are not correlated with the returns on the firm's other assets, then the project may not be risky in the sense of destabilizing the firm as a whole. Indeed, if the project's returns are negatively correlated with the firm's other assets, it may stabilize earnings. Similarly, if a project's returns are not correlated with the stock market, then even a project with highly variable returns might not be regarded as risky by well-diversified stockholders, who are probably more concerned with market risk than with total risk.

The types of corporate risk analysis discussed thus far in the chapter provide insights into projects' risk, and thus help us make better accept/reject decisions. However, as we noted above, they do not take account of portfolio risk, and they are subjective rather than objective in that they do not state specifically which projects should be accepted and which rejected. In this section, we show how the CAPM can be used to help overcome those shortcomings. Of course, the CAPM has shortcomings of its own, but it does nevertheless offer additional insights into risk analysis in capital budgeting.

Beta Risk

To begin, recall that the Security Market Line equation expresses the risk/return relationship as follows:

$$k_s = R_F + b_i(k_M - R_F).$$

For example, if RII stock's beta = 1.6, R_F = 8%, and k_M = 13%, then RII's cost of equity is 16 percent:

$$k_s = 8\% + 1.6(13\% - 8\%)$$
$$= 8\% + 1.6(5\%) = 16.0\%.$$

Further, if RII's cost of debt is 12 percent, its marginal tax rate is 46 percent, and its target capital structure calls for 63 percent debt and 37 percent common equity, then its weighted average cost of capital is 10 percent:

$$k_a = w_d k_d(1 - T) + w_s k_s$$
$$= 0.63(12\%)(0.54) + 0.37(16\%)$$
$$= 4.1\% + 5.9\% = 10.0\%.$$

This suggests that investors would be willing to give RII money to invest in average-risk projects if the company could earn 10 percent or more on this money. Here again, by average risk we mean projects having risk similar to the firm's existing assets.

Suppose, however, that taking on a particular project will cause a change in RII's 1.60 beta coefficient, and hence change the company's cost of equity. For example, the office robot project might have a beta, after adjusting for leverage, of 2.0. Since the firm itself may be regarded as a "portfolio of assets," and since the beta of any portfolio is a weighted average of the betas of its individual assets, taking on the office robot project would cause the overall corporate beta to rise and to end up somewhere between the original beta of 1.6 and the office robot project's beta of 2.0. The exact value would depend on the relative size of the investment in office robots versus RII's other assets. If 80 percent of RII's total funds would end up in commercial robotics with a beta of 1.6, and 20 percent in office robotics with a beta of 2.0, then the new corporate beta would be 1.68:

$$\text{New } b_i = 0.8(1.6) + 0.2(2.0) = 1.68.$$

This increase in RII's beta coefficient would cause the stock price to decline *unless the increased beta were offset by a higher expected rate of return*. Specifically, taking on the new project would cause the required rate of return on equity to rise to 16.4 percent,

$$k_s = 8\% + 1.68(5\%) = 16.4\%,$$

and the overall corporate cost of capital would rise to 10.15 percent:

$$k_a = 0.63(12\%)(0.54) + 0.37(16.4\%)$$
$$= 10.15\%.$$

Therefore, to keep the office robot investment from lowering the value of the firm, RII's overall expected rate of return would have to rise from 10.00 to 10.15 percent.

If investments in commercial robotics must earn 10.0 percent, how much must the office robot investment earn in order for the new overall rate of return to equal 10.15 percent? We know that, if it completes the office robot investment, RII would have 80 percent of its assets invested in commercial robotics earning 10.0 percent, that 20 percent of its assets would be in office robots earning X percent, and that the average required rate of return would be 10.15 percent. Therefore,

$$0.8(10.0\%) + 0.2X = 10.15\%.$$

Solving for X, we find that the office robot project must have an overall expected return of 10.75 percent if the corporation is to earn its new cost of capital.

In summary, if RII takes on the office robot project, the corporate beta would rise from 1.6 to 1.68; the cost of equity would increase from 16.0 to 16.4 percent; the overall cost of capital would rise from 10.0 to 10.15 percent; and the office robot investment would have to earn at least 10.75 percent in order for RII to earn its overall cost of capital.

This line of reasoning leads to the conclusion that if the beta coefficient for each project, b_p, could be determined, then individual projects' costs of capital, k_{ap}, could be found as follows:

1. Find the project's required rate of return on equity, k_{sp}:

$$k_{sp} = R_F + b_p(k_M - R_F).$$

2. Use k_{sp} to find the project's overall required rate of return, k_{ap}:

$$k_{ap} = w_d(k_d)(1 - T) + w_s k_{sp}.$$

Applying these two steps to RII's office robot decision gives this result:

$$k_{sp} = 8\% + 2.0(5\%) = 18.0\%.$$
$$k_{ap} = 0.63(12\%)(0.54) + 0.37(18.0\%) = 10.74\%.$$

We see that, except for a rounding error, the required rate of return on the office robot project is the same using this "short-cut" method as it was when we developed the project's cost of capital by solving for X in the equation $10.15\% = 0.8(10\%) + 0.2X$. Note, however, that both solutions disregard any effects of the new project on the firm's capital structure and cost of debt; implicitly, we assumed that the new project's debt cost and capital structure would be the same as the firm's old values. Potential effects of projects on the firm's debt capacity and cost of debt are taken up next.

Relationship between Firm Betas, Asset Betas, and Capital Structure

Betas, as we developed them in Chapter 6, show how returns on a firm's stock covary with returns on the market. Moreover, the beta of the firm is based on the betas of its individual assets. Therefore, we can think of each project, or asset, as a "mini-firm," and of the firm itself as a portfolio of mini-firms. Now *if a firm were financed only with common equity, and if it consisted of only one asset, then the beta of the firm and that of the asset (or project) would be identical*. Thus, we can regard a *project beta* as being equal to the beta of an unleveraged, single-asset mini-firm.

The beta of a firm with an all-equity capital structure (or a firm with zero financial leverage) is defined as an *unlevered beta*. If the firm then begins to use debt, the riskiness inherent in its equity, and consequently its *levered beta*, will begin to rise. In Appendix 12B, we will present the results of Robert Hamada's important work on the relationship between capital structure and betas. Basically, he develops this formula for the relationship between levered and unlevered betas:

$$\text{Hamada formula: } b_L = b_U[1 + (1 - T)(D/S)]. \qquad \text{(10-1)}$$

Here b_U = the beta of a firm (or asset) which uses no debt financing; b_L = the beta of the same firm (or asset) when debt financing is used; D = the market value of the firm's (or asset's) debt; and S = the market value of the firm's (or asset's) equity. If we were dealing with an unlevered, single-project firm, then its beta, b_U, would also be the beta of the firm's single asset. Thus, b_U can be thought of as an unlevered asset's beta.

The beta of the equity of a single-asset firm is a function of both the asset's business risk, b_U, and how the asset is financed, and b_L can be approximated by the Hamada equation. We stated earlier that the beta on RII's stock before it takes on the office robot project (its levered beta) is 1.6. This value was determined by regressing historic returns of the company on those of the market. RII's debt financing, that is, its capital structure, is already embedded in its calculated beta. However, what is the average underlying beta of RII's existing assets, that is, the beta the company would have if it used no debt? To find this average asset beta, we must remove the financing effect; this can be approximated by solving Equation 10-1, the Hamada formula, for b_U:

$$b_U = \frac{b_L}{1 + (1 - T)(D/S)}. \tag{10-1a}$$

For RII, with a debt/equity ratio of 0.63/0.37, we obtain an asset beta of 0.83:

$$b_U = \frac{1.6}{1 + (0.54)(0.63/0.37)} = \frac{1.6}{1.92} = 0.83.$$

Thus, the beta of RII's existing corporate assets (which are invested in equipment to produce commercial robots) is approximately equal to the beta the company would have if it used no debt, 0.83. Financial leverage has pushed its stock beta up from 0.83 to 1.60.

Equations 10-1 and 10-1a enable us to convert between asset betas and firm betas, and vice versa, which is to say between unlevered betas and levered betas. We will use these equations in the next section, where we discuss the "pure play" method to estimate project betas. However, as we discuss in Appendix 12A, Equations 10-1 and 10-1a were derived under some very restrictive assumptions, so our results must be viewed as rough approximations.

Techniques for Measuring Beta Risk

In Chapters 6 and 7, where we discussed the estimation of firms' betas, we indicated that it is difficult to estimate "true future betas." The estimation of project betas is even more difficult and more fraught with uncertainty—because individual assets pay no dividends and have no quoted market prices, we cannot calculate historic betas to use as a starting point. However, there are two approaches available for the estimation of individual assets' betas: (1) the "pure play" method and (2) the accounting beta method.

In the *pure play* approach, the company tries to find one or more non-integrated, single-product companies in the same line of business as the project being evaluated.[12] For example, suppose RII could find several existing single-product firms that manufacture office robots. Further, suppose it believes that its office robot project would be subject to the same risks as these existing firms. Then it could determine betas of these firms by the regular regression process, average them, and use this beta as a proxy for the office robot project's beta.

To illustrate, assume that RII's analysts have identified three publicly owned companies which produce and distribute only office robots. Further, assume that the average beta of these firms is 1.667, that their average debt-to-equity ratio, D/S, is 0.5/0.5 = 1.0, and that their average tax rate is 40 percent. We cannot, however, conclude that the office robot project's appropriate leverage-adjusted beta is 1.667, because RII has a different capital structure and tax rate than the proxy firms.

To adjust for the difference in financial leverage and tax rates, we can employ Equations 10-1 and 10-1a.

Step 1. Note that the proxy firms' average beta of 1.667 reflects their average D/S ratio of 1.0 and their average tax rate of 40 percent.

Step 2. Use these values, and Equation 10-1a, to determine the proxy firms' underlying asset beta:

$$b_U = \frac{1.667}{1 + (0.60)(1.0)} = 1.042.$$

Step 3. Use Equation 10-1 to find what the proxy firms' asset betas would have been had they had the same capital structure and tax rate as RII:

$$b_L = 1.042[1 + (0.54)(0.63/0.37)] = 2.0.$$

Step 4. Determine the office robot project's cost of equity and its weighted average cost of capital, using RII's capital structure:

$$k_{sp} = 8\% + 2.0(13\% - 8\%) = 18\%.$$
$$k_{ap} = 0.63(12\%)(0.54) + 0.37(18\%) = 10.74\%.$$

These values are consistent with those we calculated earlier.

The pure play approach is difficult to implement because it is often impossible to find pure play proxy firms. For our illustration, we as-

---

[12]See Russell Fuller and Halbert S. Kerr, "Estimating the Divisional Cost of Capital: An Analysis of the Pure-Play Technique," *Journal of Finance*, December 1981, 997-1009, for a more thorough discussion of the pure play method. Fuller and Kerr use the method to estimate divisional betas, and then they test the results empirically. They conclude that the pure play method is a valid technique for estimating the betas of subparts of a firm.

sumed the existence of three pure play proxies. In reality, there is no pure play office robot manufacturer. In fact, most robots are made by IBM, GE, Westinghouse, and other large, multidivisional firms, and their robot operations are blended in with their other operations in a manner that makes it impossible to ascertain market betas for their robots. However, when IBM was considering going into personal computers, it was able to get data on Apple Computers and several other essentially pure play personal computer companies, and this is often the case when firms consider major investments outside their primary fields. More will be said about all this in the section on divisional costs of capital.

The Accounting Beta Method

As noted previously, it is generally not possible to find single-product, publicly traded firms suitable for the pure play approach. In this case, we may be able to use the *accounting beta method*. Normally, betas are found by regressing the returns of a particular company's stock against returns on a stock market index. However, one could run a regression of the company's rate of return on assets (EBIT/Total assets) over time against the average return on assets of a large sample of stocks such as the NYSE or the S&P 500. Betas determined in this way, that is, by using accounting data rather than stock market data, are called *accounting betas*.

Historic accounting betas can be calculated for all types of companies (publicly owned or privately held), for divisions, or even for single projects. How good are accounting betas as proxies for market betas? Many studies have addressed this issue.[13] While the results vary, most studies do support the conclusion that firms with high accounting betas tend to have high market betas, and firms with low accounting betas tend to have low market betas. However, the correlations are generally only in the 0.5 to 0.6 range, so accounting-determined betas are only approximations for market-determined betas. Therefore, accounting betas can provide only a rough estimate of projects' systematic risk and consequently their cost of capital. Further, accounting betas for projects can only be calculated *after* the project has been accepted, placed in operation, and begins to generate output and accounting results.

To illustrate, suppose RII went forward with the office robot project, and, several years later, the results of this decision were embedded in the corporation's operating results. Now, suppose RII was considering a major expansion in either office robotics or in its other divisions, and it wanted an update on the cost of capital in the office robot division versus that in the other segments of the firm. It could, now that historic operating data have become available, use these data to calculate ac-

---

[13]For example, see William Beaver and James Manegold, "The Association between Market-Determined Measures of Systematic Risk: Some Further Evidence," *Journal of Financial and Qualitative Analysis*, June 1975, 231-284. Additionally, many of the accounting versus market beta studies are summarized in George Foster, *Financial Statement Analysis* (Englewood Cliffs, N. J.: Prentice-Hall, 1984).

counting betas for office robots and other product lines, and then use these betas to establish risk-adjusted costs of capital for use in the capital budgeting decision process. This point will be explored in more detail later in the chapter.

Portfolio Effects within the Firm

As we noted in Chapter 6, a security might be quite risky if held in isolation but not very risky if held as part of a well-diversified portfolio. The same thing is true of capital budgeting—the returns on an individual project might be highly uncertain, but if the project is small relative to the total firm, or if its returns are not highly correlated with the firm's other assets, then the project may not be very risky in either the corporate or the beta sense.

Many firms do make serious efforts to diversify; often, this is a specific objective of the long-run strategic plan. For example, the oil companies have diversified into both coal and other forms of energy to broaden their operating bases, while real estate developers have diversified geographically to lessen the impact of a slowdown in one region. The major objective of many such moves is to stabilize earnings, reduce corporate risk, and thereby raise the value of the firm's stock.

The wisdom of corporate diversification designed to reduce risk has been questioned—why should a firm diversify when stockholders can so easily diversify on their own? In other words, it may be true that, if the returns on DuPont and on Conoco are not perfectly positively correlated, then merging the companies (as happened in 1982) will reduce their risks somewhat, but would it not be just as easy for investors to carry out this risk-reducing diversification directly without all the trouble and expense of a merger?

As you might suspect, the answer is not so simple. While stockholders could accomplish directly some of the risk-reduction benefits from corporate diversification, other benefits can only be gained by diversification at the corporate level. A relatively stable corporation may be able to attract a better work force, and also to use more low-cost debt, than could two less stable firms. And, of course, there may also be spillover effects from diversification: For example, DuPont could provide Conoco with a more stable market for its oil; Conoco could provide DuPont with a stable supply of raw materials; and the two companies' research departments might be able to gain economies of scale from combined operations. More will be said about all this in Chapter 24.

Project Risk Conclusions

We have discussed two types of risk in capital budgeting analyses—corporate risk and beta risk—and we have looked at ways of assessing each. However, two important questions remain: (1) Should a firm consider both corporate risk and beta risk in its capital budgeting decisions?

(2) What do we do when our beta and corporate risk assessments lead to different conclusions?

These questions do not have easy answers. From a theoretical standpoint, well-diversified investors should be concerned primarily with beta risk, managers should be concerned with stock price maximization, and these two factors lead to the conclusion that market (or beta) risk should be given the most weight in capital budgeting decisions. However, if investors are not well diversified, if market imperfections prevent the CAPM from functioning as theory says it should, or if measurement problems keep us from implementing the CAPM approach in capital budgeting, then total risk may be given more weight than theory would suggest. An important part of all this is the fact that the CAPM does not consider bankruptcy costs, even though such costs are in reality often very significant, and the probability of bankruptcy depends on a firm's total risk, not just on its beta risk. Therefore, one could easily conclude that even well-diversified investors should want a firm's management to give at least some consideration to total risk rather than concentrating exclusively on beta risk.

Although it would be desirable to measure project risk on some absolute scale, the best we can do in practice is to determine project risk in a somewhat nebulous, relative sense. For example, we might be able to say, with a fair degree of confidence, that Project A has less total risk than the firm's average project. Then, if beta risk and corporate risk are highly correlated (as studies suggest), a project with more total risk than average is also likely to have more beta risk.[14]

What does all this mean to the financial manager? He or she should make as good an assessment as possible of projects' relative total risk and beta risk. If each type of risk is higher than average for a given project, then that project's cost of capital should be increased relative to the firm's overall cost of capital. If both relative risks are below average, then the adjustment is reversed. Unfortunately, it is impossible to specify exactly how large the adjustments should be. This topic is pursued in the following sections.

Divisional Costs of Capital

Thus far, we have seen that capital budgeting can affect a firm's beta risk, its corporate risk, or both. We have also seen that it is exceedingly difficult to quantify either effect. In other words, it may be possible to reach the general conclusion that one project is riskier than another (in either the beta or the corporate sense), but it is difficult to develop a really good *measure* of project risk. Further, this lack of precision in mea-

---

[14]For example, see M. Chapman Findlay, Arthur E. Gooding, and Wallace Q. Weaver, Jr., "On the Relevant Risk for Determining Capital Expenditure Hurdle Rates," *Financial Management*, Winter 1976, 9-16.

suring project risk makes it difficult to specify risk-adjusted rates of return, or project costs of capital, with which to evaluate individual projects. As we saw in Chapter 7, it is possible to estimate a firm's overall cost of capital reasonably well. Moreover, it is generally agreed that riskier projects should be evaluated with a higher cost of capital than the overall corporate cost, while a lower discount rate should be used for lower-risk projects. Unfortunately, there is no good way of specifying exactly *how much* higher or lower these discount rates should be; given the present state of the art, risk adjustments are necessarily judgmental and somewhat arbitrary.

Debt effects must also be taken into account. For example, one division might have a lot of assets such as real estate, which are well suited as collateral for loans, whereas some other division might have most of its capital tied up in special purpose machinery, which is not good collateral. As a result, the division with the real estate might have a higher *debt capacity* than the machinery division. In this case, the first division might calculate its cost of capital using a higher debt ratio than the second division.

Although the process is not exact, RII (and many other companies) develops risk-adjusted discount rates for use in capital budgeting in a two-step process: (1) Divisional costs of capital are established for each of the major operating divisions on the basis of the divisions' estimated risk and capital structures, and (2) within each division, all projects are classified into three categories—high risk, average risk, and low risk. Each of RII's divisions then uses its basic divisional cost of capital as the discount rate for average-risk projects, reduces the divisional cost of capital by one percentage point when evaluating low-risk projects, and raises the discount rate by two percentage points for high-risk projects. For example, if a division's basic cost of capital is estimated to be 10 percent, then a 12 percent discount rate would be used for high-risk projects and a 9 percent rate for low-risk projects. Average-risk projects, which constitute about 80 percent of most of its divisions' capital budgets, would be evaluated at the 10 percent divisional cost of capital. This procedure is not very elegant, but it does at least recognize that different divisions have different characteristics, and hence different costs of capital, and it also acknowledges differential project riskiness within divisions. RII's financial staff feels that these adjustments are in the right direction, and that they result in better decisions than would be obtained if no adjustments at all were made.

Risky Cash Outflows

Firms must make accept/reject decisions for some projects on the basis of minimizing the present value of future costs, or cash outflows, rather than on the basis of the projects' NPVs. This is done because (1) it is often impossible to allocate revenues to a particular project and (2) it is easier to focus on costs when two projects will generate identical incremental revenues. For example, suppose Midwest Electric Company must build a new power plant to provide electricity to a city. Several alternative types of plants are available, and they have different initial costs, different lives, and different operating and fuel costs. There is no question about building some type of plant, because the utility's franchise agreement with the state requires it to supply power to the city. In this case, the decision will be based on the *minimization of the PV of expected future costs*.

Some projects also have large cash outflows which occur at the end of the project's life. For example, if the utility decides to build a nuclear plant, it will incur a cost to decommission the radioactive plant at the end of its operating life. In this situation, the decision maker must apply risk adjustments to cash outflows, and *the risk adjustment for a risky cash outflow is the exact opposite of that for an inflow, or the "normal" risk adjustment*.

We can illustrate the nature of the outflow adjustment problem with the Midwest Electric generating plant example. Suppose Midwest is choosing between a coal-fired plant and a nuclear plant. The coal plant has a lower initial cost but much higher operating costs during the plant's life. Also, the coal plant has a zero salvage value—removal costs equal the scrap value of the plant—but the costs of disassembling and disposing of the radioactive nuclear plant are quite high, and uncertain. Further, nuclear plants are less reliable than coal plants, and hence costly repairs may be necessary. There is also more uncertainty about the construction cost, the in-service timing, and the life of a nuclear plant. For all these reasons, there is good reason to regard the nuclear plant as being riskier than the coal plant. Both nuclear and coal plants generally take several years to build, and they have expected lives of about 30 years. However, for simplicity, we shall assume that both plants have a 1-year construction period and a 5-year operating life. Further, we shall disregard inflation, and we also assume that the two plants have an equal capacity and that the outputs of both plants would be sold at the same price per unit.

Table 10-4 gives the projected costs associated with the two power plants: The investment costs at t = 0 and the operating cost plus decomissioning costs during t = 1 to t = 5. Midwest Electric's overall cost of capital, before it announces plans for a new generating plant, is 10 percent. If this cost rate were used to find the PV of future costs, the plants would be judged equal. However, if Midwest recognizes that the nuclear plant is more risky, and it therefore evaluates this project with a 12 percent cost of capital, then the nuclear plant's PV of future costs declines to $2,973 million, while at a still higher cost of 15 percent, the nuclear plant's costs drop to only $2,916 million. Thus, the riskier the nuclear plant is judged to be, the better it looks!

Table 10-4
Expected Costs: Coal versus Nuclear Power Plants
(Millions of Dollars)

Year (t)	Coal Plant	Nuclear Plant
0	($1,500)	($2,500)
1	(400)	(10)
2	(400)	(10)
3	(400)	(10)
4	(400)	(10)
5	(400)	(10) + (770) = (780)
PV of costs at: 10%	($3,016)	($3,016)
12%	—	($2,973)
15%	—	($2,916)

Correct analysis: PV_{Coal} (at 10%) = ($3,016).

$PV_{Nuclear}$ (at 7%) = ($3,090).

Something is obviously wrong. Clearly, if two alternative investments have the same expected value, then a risk-averse decision maker would favor the less-risky alternative. Therefore, if we want to penalize a cash outflow for higher-than-average risk, then we want that outflow to have a *higher* absolute present value, and not a *lower* value. *Therefore, a stream of cash outflows that has higher-than-average risk must be evaluated with a lower-than-average cost of capital.*

Recognizing this situation, Midwest Electric might discount the nuclear plant's costs at a 7 percent rate versus a 10 percent rate for the coal plant. In this case, the coal plant, with a PV cost of $3,016 million versus $3,090 million for the nuclear plant, would be chosen. Of course, this example is not representative of the true relative costs of nuclear and coal power plants, but it does illustrate the problem that negative outflows cause and an approach for dealing with the problem.[15]

---

[15]An obvious question, but one we have no answer for, is "Where did you get the 7 percent?" The 10 percent was found as the company's cost of capital; the cost of capital rises as the firm takes on riskier projects; but things do not work out as they should if large, but risky, cash outflows are expected during or at the end of the project's life. We wish we had a good answer to this dilemma, but we don't!

The negative outflow problem could also arise in a conventional NPV analysis as well as a PV of future cost analysis. For example, we could have included estimated revenues in the power plant analysis and developed NPVs for the two projects. The nuclear plant would have had a large, but highly uncertain, negative salvage value. If that value were discounted at a high risk-adjusted discount rate, it would incorrectly bias the evaluation toward the nuclear option.

For more on the effects of negative cash flows, see Wilbur G. Lewellen, "Some Observations on Risk-Adjusted Discount Rates," *Journal of Finance*, September 1977, 1331-1337; and a comment on that paper by Stephen E. Celec and Richard H. Pettway plus a reply by Lewellen in *Journal of Finance*, September 1979, 1061-1066.

The Optimal Capital Budget

In Chapter 7, we developed the concepts of the marginal cost of capital (MCC) and the MCC schedule. Then, in Chapters 8 and 9, we saw how capital projects are evaluated. However, capital budgeting and the cost of capital are actually interrelated—we cannot determine the cost of capital unless we know how large the capital budget will be, and we cannot determine the size of the capital budget unless we know the cost of capital. Therefore, the cost of capital and the size of the capital budget must be determined simultaneously. In this section, we bring together these two concepts and show how both the optimal capital budget and its related cost of capital are established.

The Investment Opportunity Schedule (IOS)

Carson Foods Company, a relatively small Midwestern wholesaler, is used to illustrate the concepts involved. Consider first Figure 10-2, which gives some information on Carson's potential capital projects for next year. The tabular data show each project's cash flows, IRR, and payback. The graph is defined as the firm's *Investment Opportunity Schedule (IOS)*, which is a plot of each project's IRR, in descending order, versus the dollars of new capital required to finance it. Notice that Projects A and B are mutually exclusive. Thus, Carson Foods has two possible IOS schedules: the one defined by the dots contains Project A, plus C, D, E, and F, while the one defined by the solid line contains Project B, plus C, D, E, and F. Beyond $600,000, the two IOS schedules are identical. For now, we assume that all six projects have the same risk as Carson's "average" project.

Note that we will be using the IRR rule rather than the NPV rule to determine if a project is acceptable. This causes no problems as long as we are evaluating independent projects, because with independent projects, the IRR rule leads to the same conclusions as the NPV rule. Thus, we are really using the IRR rule as a proxy for the NPV rule. However, later on, we will use the NPV rule to evaluate the mutually exclusive projects, A and B.

The Marginal Cost of Capital (MCC) Schedule

In Chapter 7, we introduced the concept of the marginal cost of capital, defined as the cost of obtaining another dollar of new capital. We also noted that the marginal cost of capital will, at some point, rise as more and more capital is raised during a given year. This increase occurs because (1) flotation costs cause the cost of new equity to be higher than the cost of retained earnings, and (2) higher rates of return on debt, preferred stock, and common stock may be required to induce additional investors to supply capital to the firm. Carson's market value target capital structure and estimated investor-required rates of return are given in Table 10-5.

Figure 10-2
Carson Foods: IOS Schedules

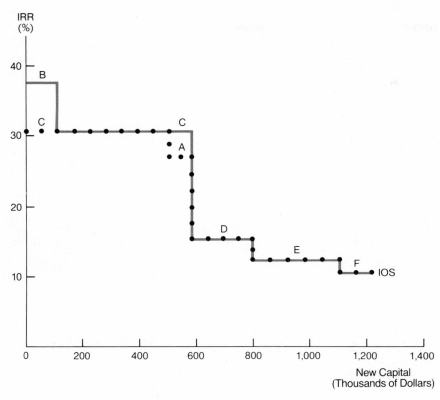

Year	Aᵃ	Bᵃ	C	D	E	F
0	($100,000)	($100,000)	($500,000)	($200,000)	($300,000)	($100,000)
1	10,000	90,000	190,000	52,800	98,800	58,781
2	70,000	60,000	190,000	52,800	98,800	58,781
3	100,000	10,000	190,000	52,800	98,800	—
4	—	—	190,000	52,800	98,800	—
5	—	—	190,000	52,800	—	—
6	—	—	190,000	52,800	—	—
IRR	27.0%	38.5%	30.2%	15.2%	12.0%	11.5%
Payback	2.2	1.2	2.6	3.8	3.0	1.7

ᵃProjects A and B are mutually exclusive.

Table 10-5
Carson Foods: Cost of Capital Data

Market Value Capital Structure

Debt	$3,000,000	30%
Preferred stock	1,000,000	10
Common stock (300,000 shares)	6,000,000	60
Total market value	$10,000,000	100%

Other Data
Stock price = P_0 = $20.
Next expected dividend = D_1 = $1.60.
Expected constant growth rate = g = 7%.
Current interest rate on debt = k_d = 10%.
Current cost of preferred stock = k_p = 12%.
Tax rate = T = 40%.
Flotation cost for equity = F = 10%.

Carson has been growing at a constant 7 percent rate, a growth rate that is expected to remain stable into the future. Thus, we can use the constant growth model to estimate the cost of retained earnings:

$$k_s = \hat{k}_s = \frac{D_1}{P_0} + g = \frac{\$1.60}{\$20} + 0.070$$
$$= 0.080 + 0.070 = 0.150 = 15.0\%.$$

Also, Carson's weighted average cost of capital, k_a, is 12 percent:

$$k_a = w_d(k_d)(1 - T) + w_p k_p + w_s k_s$$
$$= 0.3(10\%)(1 - 0.40) + 0.1(12\%) + 0.6(15\%)$$
$$= 1.8\% + 1.2\% + 9.0\% = 12.0\%.$$

Since the firm's optimal capital structure calls for 30 percent debt, 10 percent preferred, and 60 percent equity, each new (or marginal) dollar will be raised as 30 cents of debt, 10 cents of preferred, and 60 cents of common equity; otherwise, the capital structure would not stay on target. As long as Carson's after-tax cost of debt remains at 6 percent, its preferred cost remains at 12 percent, and its common equity cost remains at 15 percent, then its weighted average cost of capital will hold constant at 12 percent. Thus, each new dollar will be raised as 30 cents of debt, 10 cents of preferred, and 60 cents of equity, and each new (or marginal) dollar will have a weighted average cost of 12 percent.[16]

---

[16]Of course, Carson Foods does not really sell 30 cents of debt, 10 cents of preferred, and 60 cents of common equity for every $1 of capital raised. In fact, most of the financing for a year, or even for two years, might be done using a single source of funds, say a large stock offering. Still, over the long run, Carson does plan to raise capital using a mix of all three sources, and, on average, its capital will be raised in proportion to the target capital structure.

Now suppose the company expands so rapidly that its retained earnings for the year are not sufficient to meet its needs for new equity, forcing it to sell new common stock in order to keep the capital structure in balance. According to Table 10-5, the flotation cost on new stock is 10 percent, so we can use Equation 7-8 from Chapter 7 to find Carson's cost of external equity:

The Retained Earnings Break Point

$$k_e = \frac{D_1}{P_0(1 - F)} + g = \frac{\$1.60}{\$20(0.9)} + 7\% = 15.9\%.$$

Thus, Carson's cost of external equity is 15.9 percent, up from the 15 percent cost of retained earnings, and this increase in the cost of equity causes Carson's MCC to increase from 12.0 to 12.5 percent:

$$k_a = w_d(k_d)(1 - T) + w_p k_p + w_s k_e$$
$$= 0.3(10\%)(0.60) + 0.1(12\%) + 0.6(15.9\%)$$
$$= 1.8\% + 1.2\% + 9.5\% = 12.5\%.$$

How much new capital can Carson raise before it exhausts its retained earnings and is forced to sell new common stock; that is, where will the break point in the MCC occur? Assume that the company expects to have total earnings of $1 million for the year, and that it has a policy of paying out 58 percent of its earnings as dividends. Thus, the addition to retained earnings will be $(1 - 0.58)\$1,000,000 = \$420,000$ during the year. How much total financing—debt, preferred, and this $420,000 of retained earnings—can be done before the retained earnings are exhausted and the firm is forced to sell new common stock? In effect, we are seeking some amount, X, which is defined as a *break point*, representing the total financing that can be done alone before Carson is forced to sell new common stock.

We know that 60 percent of X will be the new retained earnings, which will amount to $420,000. Therefore,

$$\text{Retained earnings} = 0.6X = \$420,000.$$

Solving for X, which is the *retained earnings break point*, we obtain

$$\text{Break point} = X = \frac{\text{Retained earnings}}{0.6} = \frac{\$420,000}{0.6} = \$700,000.$$

Thus, Carson Foods can raise a total of $700,000, consisting of $420,000 of retained earnings and $700,000 - \$420,000 = \$280,000$ of new debt and preferred stock supported by the $420,000 of retained earnings, without altering its capital structure.

Figure 10-3 graphs Carson Foods' marginal cost of capital schedule. Each dollar has a weighted average cost of 12 percent until the company has raised a total of $700,000. This $700,000 will consist of $210,000 of new debt with an after-tax cost of 6 percent, $70,000 of preferred stock with a cost of 12 percent, and $420,000 of retained earnings with a cost

Figure 10-3
Carson Foods: Marginal Cost of Capital Schedule
Using Both Retained Earnings and New Common Equity

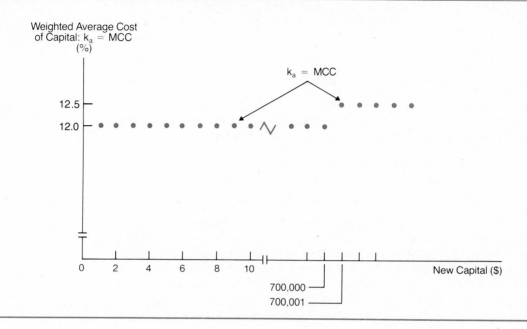

of 15 percent. However, if Carson's raises $700,001 or more, each additional dollar will contain 60 cents of equity obtained by selling new common equity at a cost of 15.9 percent, so k_a = MCC rises from 12.0 to 12.5 percent.

*Beyond the
Retained Earnings
Break Point*

Carson Foods' management believes that the firm's component costs of capital are an increasing function of the amount of new capital required. Thus, Carson's MCC schedule will continue to rise as the capital budget exceeds $700,000 by larger and larger amounts. However, the precise data required to calculate additional break points are difficult to obtain. Moreover, as we will see in the next section, this year's capital budget is not unusually large, so management concludes that an additional adjustment is not required. Thus, the MCC schedule as set forth in Figure 10-3 will be used in the analysis.

**Combining the
MCC and IOS
Schedules**

Now that we have estimated the MCC schedule, we can use it to determine the discount rate for the capital budgeting process; *that is, we can use the MCC schedule to find the cost of capital for use in determining projects' net present values (NPVs) as discussed in Chapter 8.* To do this, we combine

Figure 10-4
Carson Foods: Combined IOS and MCC Schedules

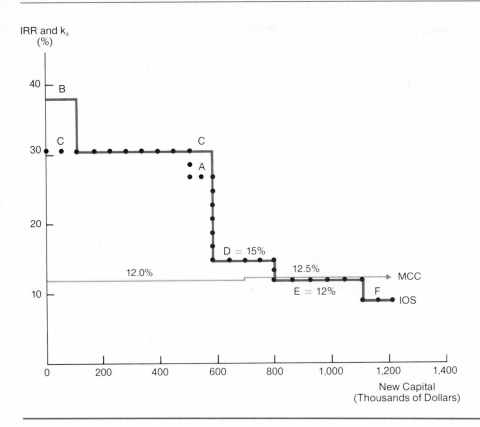

the IOS and MCC schedules on the same graph, as shown in Figure 10-4, and then we analyze this consolidated figure.

Finding the Marginal Cost of Capital

Just how far down its IOS curve should Carson go? That is, which of its available projects should it accept? *First, Carson Foods should accept all independent projects which have rates of return in excess of the cost of the capital that would be used to finance them.* Projects E and F should be rejected, because they would have to be financed with capital that has a cost of 12.5 percent, and, at that cost of capital, both projects have negative NPVs since their IRRs are below their costs of capital. Therefore, Carson's capital budget should consist of either Project A or B, plus C and D, and the firm should thus raise a total of $800,000.

The above analysis, as summarized in Figure 10-4, reveals a very important point: *The cost of capital used in the capital budgeting process is actually determined at the intersection of the IOS and MCC schedules. If this intersection rate is used, then the firm will make correct accept/reject decisions, and its level of financing and investment will be optimal. If it uses any other rate, its capital budget will not be optimal.*

If Carson had fewer good investment opportunities, then its IOS schedule would be shifted to the left, possibly causing the intersection to occur at the lower level on the MCC curve. Conversely, if it had a great many good projects, the IOS would be shifted far to the right, and it might be necessary to adjust the MCC upward, in which case, the MCC at the intersection would be above 12.5 percent. Thus, we see that the discount rate used in capital budgeting is influenced by the set of projects that is available. We have, of course, abstracted from differential project riskiness in this section, because we assumed that all of Carson's projects are equally risky. We will discuss the impact of differential risk on the optimal capital budget in a later section.

Choosing between Mutually Exclusive Projects

We have not, at this point, actually determined Carson's optimal capital budget. We know that it should total $800,000 and that Projects C and D should be included, but we do not know which of the mutually exclusive projects, A or B, should be included in the final budget. How can we choose between A and B? We know that the final set of projects should be the one which has the highest total NPV, as this set will increase the value of the firm by the larger amount. We also know that Projects C and D should be included in the final set, so their contributions to the total NPV will be the same regardless of whether we choose Project A or B. This narrows our analysis to the NPVs of A and B. The project with the higher NPV should be chosen.

Notice that Figure 10-2 contained the projects' paybacks and IRRs, but no NPVs: We were not able to determine the NPVs at that point because we did not know the correct marginal cost of capital. Now, in Figure 10-4, we see that the last dollar raised will cost 12.5 percent, so MCC = k_a = 12.5%. Therefore, assuming the projects are equally risky, we can use 12.5 percent to find NPV_A = $34,431 and NPV_B = $34,431. Therefore, in our example, Carson should be indifferent to the choice between the two mutually exclusive projects, according to the NPV criterion. Assume for the sake of argument that B is selected because of its faster payback and higher IRR.

Evaluating the Marginal Project

With the MCC and IOS schedules contained in Figure 10-4, it is easy to decide where to stop accepting projects. With that particular set of data, Project D is clearly acceptable, Projects E and F should clearly be rejected, and the firm's marginal cost of capital is clearly 12.5 percent. Now consider another situation, where the analysis is not so clear-cut. Figure 10-5 contains the same IOS schedules as before, but here we assume that Carson's treasurer found an error in the original cost of capital

Figure 10-5
Carson Foods: Revised Combined IOS and MCC Schedules

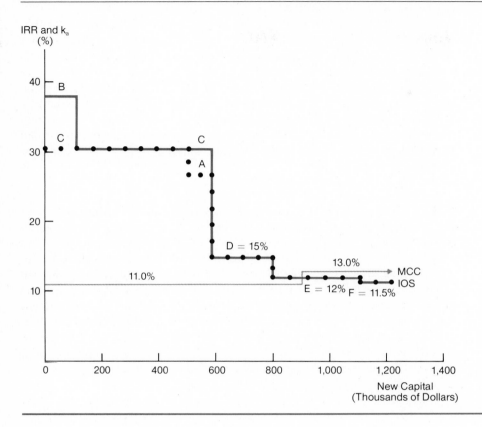

data and has developed a new MCC schedule. Under these revised cost conditions, the marginal cost of capital is 11.0 percent for the first $900,000 of new capital and 13.0 percent beyond $900,000.

Clearly, Project F remains unacceptable, but the revised MCC schedule now cuts through Project E. Should Carson accept or reject Project E? First, note that if Project E could be accepted in part, then Carson would take on only part of it. That is, if Project E were completely divisible, then Carson should invest only $100,000 in the project, since this level of investment would have a marginal cost of capital of 11.0 percent but a 12.0 percent rate of return.

Most projects, however, are not infinitely divisible. If Project E were completely indivisible, meaning that Carson would have to accept it in its entirety or else reject it, should it be accepted? To answer this question, we must determine Project E's average cost of capital, proceeding as follows. First, note that Project E requires an initial investment of $300,000. Next, we see in Figure 10-5 that the first $100,000 of capital raised for Project E has a cost of 11.0 percent and that the remaining $200,000 has a cost of 13.0 percent. Thus, one-third of the capital required has a cost of 11.0 percent, and two-thirds has a cost of 13.0 percent. Therefore, the average cost of capital for Project E is 12.3 percent:

$$k_{aE} = \left(\frac{\$100,000}{\$300,000}\right)(11.0\%) + \left(\frac{\$200,000}{\$300,000}\right)(13.0\%) = 12.3\%.$$

Now recall that $IRR_E = 12.0\%$. Since Project E's average cost of capital exceeds its IRR, NPV_E will be negative, and, hence, Project E should be rejected. Therefore, with the revised MCC schedule, Carson's optimal capital budget appears to be $800,000, and its marginal cost of capital appears to be 11.0 percent. However, we may have to revise these conclusions.

Effect of Rejecting the Marginal Project

In the preceding section, we discussed the effect of accepting or rejecting a marginal project on the MCC. However, rejection of the marginal project could also lead to a reevaluation of low IRR projects that were previously rejected, and also the mutually exclusive projects. Note that the IOS and MCC schedules that were shown in Figure 10-5 resulted in Project E being rejected. It would appear at first glance that the optimal capital budget would include either A or B, plus both C and D. However, rejection of Project E produces a major change in the IOS schedules. With E gone, the IOS shifts to the left, and Project F, which has an IRR of 11.5 percent, can now be financed at a cost of capital of 11.0 percent. Therefore, at 11 percent, F becomes acceptable.

Note also that with the original MCC schedule, Projects A and B had identical NPVs, but B was selected because of its faster payback and higher IRR. However, with the new MCC of 11 percent, A's NPV exceeds that of B:

$$NPV_A = \$38,942 > NPV_B = \$37,090.$$

Thus, A should be chosen over B because it adds the most to the value of the firm. In summary, under the revised MCC conditions Carson's optimal capital budget consists of A, C, D, and F, for a total of $900,000.

Establishing the Capital Budget in Practice

Carson Foods, and many other companies, actually uses a more judgmental, less "quantitative" four-step process for establishing its final capital budget.

Step 1. The financial vice-president obtains a reasonably good fix on the firm's IOS from the director of capital budgeting, and a reasonably good estimate of the MCC schedule from the treasurer. These two schedules are then combined, as in Figures 10-4 and 10-5, to get a reasonably good approximation of the corporation's marginal cost of capital.

Step 2. The corporate MCC is scaled up or down by each division to reflect the division's capital structure and risk characteristics. Carson Foods, for example, assigns a factor of 0.9 to its low-risk canned vegetables division and a factor of 1.1 to its more risky frozen foods group. Therefore, if the corporate cost of capital is determined to be 12 percent, the cost for canned vegetables is 0.9(12%) = 10.8%, while that for frozen foods is 1.1(12%) = 13.2%.

Step 3. Each project within each division is classified into one of three groups—high-risk, average-risk, and low-risk, and the same 0.9 and 1.1 factors are used to adjust the divisional costs. For example, a low-risk project in the canned vegetables division would have a cost of capital of 0.9(10.8%) = 9.7% if the corporate cost of capital were 12 percent, while a high-risk project in the frozen foods division would have a cost of 1.1(13.2%) = 14.5%.

Step 4. Each project's NPV is then determined using the risk-adjusted project cost of capital. The optimal capital budget consists of all independent projects with positive risk-adjusted NPVs plus those mutually exclusive projects with the highest positive NPVs.

The steps described above implicitly assume that, on average, the projects taken on have about the same risk characteristics and consequently the same average cost of capital as the firm's existing assets. If this is not true, then the corporate MCC determined in Step 1 will not be correct, and it will have to be adjusted. However, given all the measurement errors and uncertainties inherent in the entire cost of capital/capital budgeting process, it does not pay to push the adjustment process very far.

All of this may seem rather arbitrary, and we agree. Nevertheless, the procedure does force the firm to think carefully about relative risk for different divisions and projects, and about the relationship between the amount of capital required and the cost of that capital. Furthermore, the procedure forces the firm to adjust its capital budget to conditions in the capital markets—if the costs of debt and equity rise, this fact will be reflected in the cost of capital used to evaluate projects, and projects that would be marginally acceptable when capital costs were low would be ruled unacceptable when capital costs were high.

Summary

Our analysis of risk has focused on two issues: (1) the effect of a given project on the firm's beta coefficient (*beta risk*) and (2) the project's effect on the probability of bankruptcy (*corporate risk*). Both types of risk are important. Beta risk directly affects the value of the stock. Corporate risk affects the financial strength of the firm, and this, in turn, influences its ability to use debt, to maintain smooth operations over time, and to avoid crises that might consume the energy of the firm's managers and disrupt its employees, customers, suppliers, and community.

There are several analytical techniques available to help measure a project's corporate risk. Among these are (1) *sensitivity analysis,* (2) *scenario analysis,* and (3) *Monte Carlo simulation.* However, the final decision regarding a project's corporate risk remains judgmental.

The major difficulty in determining the beta risk of a given project is to establish the project's beta coefficient. It is not really meaningful to think about the beta of a particular asset such as a truck or a machine, but it is meaningful to think of betas for divisions that are large enough to be operated as independent firms. Therefore, in practice, beta risk can be estimated for large divisions of firms and then used to establish divisional costs of capital, which are then scaled up or down in a subjective manner to reflect a given project's own risk. There are two approaches to measuring beta risk: (1) the *pure play method* and (2) the *accounting beta method.*

This chapter also showed how the MCC and IOS schedules are developed and then used to determine the optimal capital budget. Capital typically has a higher cost if the firm expands beyond certain limits. This means that the MCC schedule turns up beyond some point. We used the *break point concept* to develop a single step-function MCC schedule, which we then combined with the IOS schedule to determine both the optimal capital budget and the cost of capital that should be used in capital budgeting. If the requirement for new capital were exceptionally large (that is, the firm had an abundance of costly high-IRR projects), then a further upward adjustment could be made to the cost of capital schedule. This judgmental increase would reflect the fact that the component costs of capital rise further as more and more new capital is required.

Questions

10-1 Define each of the following terms:
   a. Beta risk
   b. Project beta versus corporate beta
   c. Accounting beta versus stock market beta
   d. "Pure play" method of estimating divisional betas
   e. Corporate risk
   f. Sensitivity analysis
   g. Simulation analysis
   h. Scenario analysis
   i. Coefficient of variation versus standard deviation
   j. Corporate diversification versus stockholder diversification
   k. Risk-adjusted discount rate; project cost of capital
   l. IOS schedule; intersection of the IOS and MCC schedules
   m. Levered beta versus unlevered beta

10-2 Differentiate between (a) simulation analysis, (b) optimistic-pessimistic-most likely analysis, and (c) sensitivity analysis. If AT&T were considering two investments, one calling for the expenditure of $100 million to develop a satellite communications system and the other involving the expenditure of $5,000 for a new truck, on which one would the company be more likely to use simulation?

10-3 Distinguish between the beta risk and the corporate risk of a project being considered for inclusion in the capital budget. Which type do you feel should be given the greater weight in capital budgeting decisions?

10-4 Suppose Lima Locomotive Company, which has a high beta and also a great deal of corporate risk, merged with Homestake Mining, which has a low beta but relatively high corporate risk. What would the merger do to the cost of capital in the consolidated company's locomotive division and its gold mining division?

10-5 Suppose a firm estimates its MCC and IOS schedules for the coming year and finds that they intersect at the point 10%, $10 million. What cost of capital should be used to evaluate average-risk projects, high-risk projects, and low-risk projects?

10-6 The MCC and IOS schedules can be thought of as "bands" rather than as lines to show that they are not known with certainty but, rather, are merely estimates of the true MCC and IOS schedules.
   a. Do you think that the bands would be wider for the MCC or for the IOS schedule? In answering this question, visualize each point on the MCC and IOS schedules as being the expected value of a probability distribution.
   b. For the IOS schedule, would the band, or confidence interval, associated with each project be identical? If not, what would this imply, and how might it affect the firm's capital budgeting analysis?

ST-1 (Corporate risk.) The staff of Gordon Manufacturing has estimated the following net cash flows and probabilities for a new manufacturing process:

Self-Test Problems

	Net Cash Flow		
Year	P = 0.2	P = 0.6	P = 0.2
0	($100,000)	($100,000)	($100,000)
1	20,000	30,000	40,000
2	20,000	30,000	40,000
3	20,000	30,000	40,000
4	20,000	30,000	40,000
5	20,000	30,000	40,000
5*	0	20,000	30,000

Line 0 is the cost of the process, Lines 1-5 are operating cash flows, and Line 5* contains the estimated salvage values. Gordon's cost of capital for an average risk project is 10 percent.
   a. Assume that the project has average risk. Find the project's expected NPV.
   b. Perform a scenario analysis on the project. Assume that the cash flows are uncorrelated so that all worst case values, or all best case values, could arise. What are the probabilities of occurrence of the worst and best cases?

c. Assume that all the cash flows are perfectly positively correlated; that is, there are only three possible cash flow streams over time: (1) the worst case, (2) the base case, and (3) the best case, with probabilities of 0.2, 0.6, and 0.2 respectively. Find the expected NPV, its standard deviation, and its coefficient of variation.

d. The coefficient of variation of Gordon's average project is in the range 0.8 to 1.0. If the coefficient of variation of a project being evaluated is greater than 1.0, 2 percentage points are added to the firm's cost of capital. Similarly, if the coefficient of variation is less than 0.8, 1 percentage point is deducted from the cost of capital. What is the project's cost of capital? Should Gordon accept or reject the project?

ST-2 (Beta risk.) Minute Man Company (MMC) has a target capital structure of 40 percent debt and 60 percent equity. Its beta, which is an average of 5 estimates by financial service firms, is 1.5. MMC is evaluating a new project which is totally unrelated to its existing line of business. However, it has identified two proxy firms exclusively engaged in this business line. They, on average, have a beta of 1.2 and a debt ratio of 50 percent. MMC's new project has an estimated IRR of 13.5 percent. The risk-free rate is 10 percent, and the market risk premium is 5 percent. All firms have a marginal tax rate of 46 percent. MMC's before-tax cost of debt is 14 percent.

a. What is the unlevered project beta, b_U?

b. What is the beta of the project if undertaken by MMC?

c. Should MMC accept the project?

ST-3 (Optimal capital budget.) Haslem Enterprises has the following capital structure, which it considers to be optimal under the present and forecasted conditions:

Debt	30%
Common equity	70
Total capital	100%

For the coming year, management expects to realize net earnings of $105,000. The past dividend policy of paying out 50 percent of earnings will continue. Present commitments from its banker will allow Haslem to borrow at a rate of 8 percent.

The company's tax rate is 40 percent, the current market price of its stock is $50 per share, its *last* dividend was $1.85 per share, and the expected constant growth rate is 8 percent. External equity (new common) can be sold at a flotation cost of 15 percent.

The firm has the following investment opportunities for the next period:

Project	Cost	IRR
A	$50,000	12%
B	15,000	11
C	20,000	10
D	50,000	9

Management asks you to help them determine what projects (if any) should be undertaken. You proceed with this analysis by answering the following questions:

a. Calculate the marginal cost of capital using both retained earnings and new common stock.

b. Graph the IOS and MCC schedules.

c. Which projects should Haslem's management accept?

d. What implicit assumptions about project risk are embodied in this problem? If you learned that Projects A and B were of above-average risk, yet Haslem chose the projects which you indicated in Part c, how would this affect the situation?

e. The problem stated that Haslem pays out 50 percent of its earnings as dividends. How would the analysis change if the payout ratio were changed to 0 percent? To 100 percent?

Problems

10-1 (CAPM approach to risk adjustments.) Goodtread Rubber Company has two divisions: (1) the tire division, which manufactures tires for new autos, and (2) the recap division, which manufactures recapping materials that are sold to independent tire recapping shops throughout the United States. Since auto manufacturing moves up and down with the general economy, the tire division's earnings contribution to Goodtread's stock price is highly correlated with returns on most other stocks. If the tire division were operated as a separate company, its beta coefficient would be about 1.60. The sales and profits of the recap division, on the other hand, tend to be counter-cyclical—recap sales boom when people cannot afford to buy new tires, so Recap's beta is estimated to be 0.40. Approximately 75 percent of Goodtread's corporate assets are invested in the tire division and 25 percent are in the recap division.

Currently, the rate of interest on Treasury securities is 10 percent, and the expected rate of return on an average share of stock is 15 percent. Goodtread uses only common equity capital; it has no debt outstanding.

a. What is the required rate of return on Goodtread's stock?

b. What discount rate should be used to evaluate capital budgeting projects? Explain your answer fully, and in the process, illustrate your answer with a project which costs $100,000, has a 10-year life, and provides expected after-tax net cash flows of $20,000 per year.

10-2 (Risky cash outflows.) Far West Utilities is making a decision as to whether to build an oil or a coal generating plant. The company's MCC is 8 percent for low-risk projects, 10 percent for projects of average risk, and 12 percent for high-risk projects. Management believes that an oil-burning plant is of average risk, but that a coal plant is of high risk due to problems associated with acid rain. The cash *outflows* required to construct each plant are listed below. The fuel costs and other operating costs are expected to be the same under both plans over the 30-year operating life of the project. Which type plant should be constructed?

	Construction Cost (Thousands of Dollars)	
Year	Coal Plant	Oil Plant
0	($ 100)	($ 400)
1	(500)	(1,000)
2	(1,500)	(1,000)
3	(1,500)	(1,000)
4	(1,500)	(1,500)
5	(1,000)	(1,000)
6	(500)	(200)

10-3 (Simulation.) Hospital Supplies Corporation (HSC) manufactures medical products for hospitals, clinics, and nursing homes. HSC is considering introducing a new type of X-ray scanner designed to identify certain types of cancers in their early stages. There are a number of uncertainties about the proposed project, but the following data are believed to be reasonably accurate.

	Probability	Value	Random Numbers
Developmental cost	0.3	$2,000,000	00-29
	0.4	4,000,000	30-69
	0.3	6,000,000	70-99
Project life	0.2	3 years	00-19
	0.6	8 years	20-79
	0.2	13 years	80-99
Sales in units	0.2	100	00-19
	0.6	200	20-79
	0.2	300	80-99
Sales price	0.1	$13,000	00-09
	0.8	13,500	10-89
	0.1	14,000	90-99
Cost per unit	0.3	$5,000	00-29
(excluding develop-	0.4	6,000	30-69
mental costs)	0.3	7,000	70-99

HSC uses a cost of capital of 15 percent to analyze average-risk projects, 12 percent for low-risk projects, and 18 percent for high-risk projects. These risk adjustments reflect primarily the uncertainty about each project's NPV and IRR as measured by the coefficients of variation of NPV and IRR. HSC is in the 40 percent income tax bracket.

a. What is the expected IRR for the X-ray scanner project? Base your answer on the expected values of the variables. Also, assume the after-tax "profits" figure you develop is equal to annual cash flows. All facilities are leased, so depreciation may be disregarded. Can you determine the value of σ_{IRR} short of actual simulation or a fairly complex statistical analysis?

b. Assume that HSC uses a 15 percent cost of capital for this project. What is the project's NPV? Could you estimate σ_{NPV} without either simulation or a complex statistical analysis?

c. Show the process by which a computer would perform a simulation analysis for this project. Use the random numbers 44, 17, 16, 58, 1; 79, 83, 86; and 19, 62, 6 to illustrate the process with the first computer run. Actually, calculate the first-run NPV and IRR. Assume that the cash flows for each year are independent of cash flows in other years. Also, assume that the computer operates as follows: (1) A developmental cost and a project life are estimated for the first run. (2) Next, sales volume, sales price, and cost per unit are estimated and used to derive a first-year cash flow. (3) Then, the next three random numbers are used to estimate sales volume, sales price, and cost per unit for the second year, and hence the second year's cash flow. (4) Cash flows for other years are developed similarly, on out to the end of the first run's estimated life. (5) With the developmental cost and the cash flow stream established, NPV and IRR for the first run are derived and stored in the computer's memory. (6) The process is repeated to generate perhaps 500 other NPVs and IRRs. (7) Frequency distributions for NPV and IRR are plotted by the computer, and the distributions' means and standard deviations are calculated.

d. Does it seem a little strange to conduct a risk analysis such as the one done here *after* having already established a cost of capital for use in the analysis? What might be done to improve this situation?

e. In this problem, we assumed that the probability distributions were all independent of one another. It would have been possible to use conditional probabilities where, for example, the probability distribution for cost per unit would vary from trial to trial, depending on the unit sales for the trial. Also, it would be possible to construct the simulation model such that the sales distribution in Year t would depend on the sales level attained in Year $t - 1$. Had these modifications been made in this problem, do you think the standard deviation of the NPV distribution would have been larger (riskier) or smaller (less risky) than where complete independence is assumed?

f. Name two *major* difficulties not mentioned above that occur with the kind of analysis discussed in this problem.

10-4 (Optimal capital budget.) Midterm Corporation's present capital structure, which is also its target capital structure, calls for 50 percent debt and 50 percent common equity. The firm has only one potential project, an expansion program with a 10.2 percent IRR and a cost of $20 million. However, the project is completely divisible; that is, Midterm can invest any amount up to $20 million. Midterm expects to retain $3 million of earnings next year. It can raise debt at a before-tax cost of 10 percent. The cost of retained earnings is 12 percent; Midterm can sell new common stock at a constant cost of new equity of 15 percent. The firm's marginal tax rate is 40 percent. What is Midterm's optimal capital budget?

10-5 (Optimal capital budget.) The management of Florida Phosphate Industries is planning next year's capital budget. FPI projects its net income at $10,500, and its payout ratio is 40 percent. The company's earnings and dividends are growing at a constant rate of 5 percent; the last dividend, D_0, was $0.90; and the current stock price is $8.59. FPI's new debt will cost 14 percent. If FPI issues new common stock, flotation costs will be 20 percent. FPI is at its optimal capital structure, which is 40 percent debt and 60 percent equity, and the firm's marginal tax rate is 40 percent. FPI has the following independent, indivisible, and equally risky investment opportunities:

Project	Cost	IRR
A	$15,000	17%
B	20,000	14
C	15,000	16
D	12,000	15

What is FPI's optimal capital budget?

10-6 (Risk-adjusted optimal capital budget.) Refer to Problem 10-5. Management neglected to incorporate project risk differentials into the analysis. FPI's policy is to add 2 percentage points to the cost of capital of those projects significantly more risky than average and to subtract 2 percentage points from the cost of capital of those which are substantially less risky than average. Management judges Project A to be of high risk, Projects C and D to be of average risk, and Project B to be of low risk. No projects are divisible. What is the optimal capital budget after adjustment for project risk?

Solutions to Self-Test Problems

ST-1 a. First, find the expected cash flows:

Year		Expected Cash Flow	
0	$0.2(-\$100,000) + 0.6(-\$100,000) + 0.2(-\$100,000)$	= ($100,000)
1	$0.2(\$20,000) + 0.6(\$30,000) + 0.2(\$40,000)$	= $30,000
2		$30,000
3		$30,000
4		$30,000
5		$30,000
5*	$0.2(\$0) + 0.6(\$20,000) + 0.2(\$30,000)$	= $18,000

Next, determine the NPV based on the expected cash flows:

$$NPV = -\$100,000 + \frac{\$30,000}{(1.10)^1} + \frac{\$30,000}{(1.10)^2} + \frac{\$30,000}{(1.10)^3} + \frac{\$30,000}{(1.10)^4} + \frac{\$30,000 + \$18,000}{(1.10)^5}$$
$$= \$24,900$$

b. For the worst case, the cash flow values from the left-most cash flow column are used to calculate NPV:

$$NPV = -\$100,000 + \frac{\$20,000}{(1.10)^1} + \frac{\$20,000}{(1.10)^2} + \frac{\$20,000}{(1.10)^3} + \frac{\$20,000}{(1.10)^4} + \frac{\$20,000 + \$0}{(1.10)^5}$$
$$= -\$24,184.$$

Similarly, for the best case, use the values from the right-most column. Here the NPV is $70,259.

Thus, our results are

Scenario	NPV
Worst case	($24,184)
Base case	24,900
Best case	70,259

Here the worst case is negative. If management were very risk averse, they might not be willing to accept any probability of a negative NPV; therefore, they might reject the project. But, what is the probability of the worst case occurring? If the cash flows in each year are totally *uncorrelated*, then the probability of the worst case occurring in every year over the 5-year period is

$$(0.2)(0.2)(0.2)(0.2)(0.2) = 0.0003,$$

or 3 in 10,000.

c. Under these conditions, the NPV distribution is

P	NPV
0.2	($24,184)
0.6	24,900
0.2	70,259

Thus, the expected NPV is $0.2(-\$24,184) + 0.6(\$24,900) + 0.2(\$70,259) = \$24,155$. Note that this is less than the base case NPV because the salvage value distribution, thus the resulting NPV distribution, is skewed left. The standard deviation is $29,879:

$$\sigma_{NPV}^2 = 0.2(-\$24,184 - \$24,155)^2 + 0.6(\$24,900 - \$24,155)^2$$
$$+ 0.2(\$70,259 - \$24,155)^2$$
$$= \$892,780,562.$$
$$\sigma_{NPV} = \sqrt{\$892,780,562} = \$29,879.$$

The coefficient of variation, CV, is $29,879/$24,155 = 1.24.

d. Since the project's coefficient of variation is 1.24, the project cost of capital is 10% + 2% = 12%. Now the project should be evaluated by finding the NPV of the expected cash flows as in Part a, but using a 12 percent discount rate. The risk-adjusted NPV is $18,357, and thus the project should be accepted.

ST-2 a. Equation 10-6a can be used to estimate the project, or unlevered, beta:

$$b_U = \frac{b_L}{1 + (1 - T)(D/S)}$$
$$= \frac{1.2}{1 + (1 - 0.46)(0.5/0.5)}$$
$$= 1.2/1.54 = 0.78.$$

b. Equation 10-6 is then used to adjust for MMC's leverage:

$$b_L = b_U[1 + (1 - T)(D/S)]$$
$$= 0.78[1 + 0.54(0.4/0.6)]$$
$$= 0.78(1.36) = 1.06.$$

c. The required rate of return on the project is found as follows:

$$k_{sp} = R_F + b_p(k_M - R_F)$$
$$= 10\% + 1.06(5\%) = 15.3\%.$$
$$k_{ap} = w_d(k_d)(1 - T) + w_s k_{sp}$$
$$= 0.4(14\%)(0.54) + 0.6(15.3\%)$$
$$= 3.02\% + 9.18\% = 12.2\%.$$

Since the project's IRR is 13.5 percent, IRR $>$ k_{ap}, and the project should be accepted.

ST-3 a. (1) Cost using retained earnings:

Component	% Capital Structure	×	After-tax Cost	= Product
Debt [8%(0.6)]	0.30		4.80%	1.44%
Retained earnings*	0.70		12.00	8.40
			MCC₁ =	9.84%

(2) Cost using new common stock:

Component	% Capital Structure	×	After-tax Cost	= Product
Debt [8%(0.6)]	0.30		4.80%	1.44%
External equity**	0.70		12.70	8.89
			MCC₂ =	10.33%

*Cost of retained earnings:

$$k_s = \frac{D_1}{P_0} + g = \frac{(\$1.85)(1.08)}{(\$50)} + 0.08 = 12.00\%.$$

**Cost of external equity:

$$k_e = \frac{D_1}{P_0(1 - F)} + g = \frac{(\$1.85)(1.08)}{(\$50)(0.85)} + 0.08 = 12.70\%.$$

(3) Break point:

$$\text{Break point} = \frac{\$52,500}{0.7} = \$75,000.$$

b. The MCC and IOS schedules are shown below:

MCC and IOS Schedule for Haslem

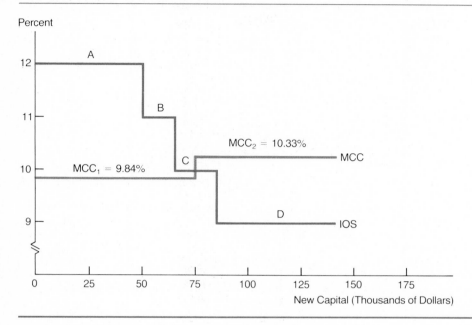

c. From the above graph, we conclude that Haslem's management should definitely undertake Projects A and B, assuming that these projects are of about "average risk" in relation to the rest of the firm. Now, to evaluate Project C, recognize that one-half of its capital would cost 9.84 percent, while the other half would cost 10.33 percent. Thus, the cost of capital required for Project C is 10.09 percent:

$$0.5(9.84\%) + 0.5(10.33\%) = 10.09\%.$$

Since the cost is greater than Project C's return of 10 percent, Haslem should not accept Project C.

d. The solution implicitly assumes (1) that all of the projects are equally risky and (2) that these projects are as risky as the firm's existing assets. If the accepted projects (A and B) were of above average risk, this could raise the company's overall risk, and hence its cost of capital. Taking on these projects could result in a decline in the company's value.

e. If the payout ratio were lowered to zero, this would shift the break point to the right, from $75,000 to $150,000. As the problem is set up, this would make Project C acceptable. If the payout were changed to 100 percent, there would be no retained earnings, and hence no break point, and the optimal capital budget would not change. This assumes that the change in payout would not affect k_s or k_d; as we shall see in Chapter 13, this assumption may not be correct.

Selected Additional References and Cases

The literature on risk analysis in capital budgeting is vast; here is a small but useful selection of additional references that bear directly on the topics covered in this chapter:

Ang, James S., and Wilbur G. Lewellen, "Risk Adjustment in Capital Investment Project Evaluations," *Financial Management*, Summer 1982, 5-14.

Bower, Richard S., and Jeffrey M. Jenks, "Divisional Screening Rates," *Financial Management*, Autumn 1975, 42-49.

Fama, Eugene F., "Risk-Adjusted Discount Rates and Capital Budgeting under Uncertainty," *Journal of Financial Economics*, August 1977, 3-24.

Gehr, Adam K., Jr., "Risk-Adjusted Capital Budgeting Using Arbitrage," *Financial Management*, Winter 1981, 14-19.

Gup, Benton E., and S. W. Norwood III, "Divisional Cost of Capital: A Practical Approach," *Financial Management*, Spring 1982, 20-24.

Lessard, Donald R., and Richard S. Bower, "An Operational Approach to Risk Screening," *Journal of Finance*, May 1973, 321-338.

Myers, Stewart C., and Samuel M. Turnbull, "Capital Budgeting and the Capital Asset Pricing Model: Good News and Bad News," *Journal of Finance*, May 1977, 321-333.

Robichek, Alexander A., "Interpreting the Results of Risk Analysis," *Journal of Finance*, December 1975, 1384-1386.

NPV criterion superiority rests on the assumption that the cost of capital is the appropriate opportunity cost of future project cash flows. For a discussion of this issue, see

Bacon, Peter W., "The Evaluation of Mutually Exclusive Projects," *Financial Management*, Summer 1977, 55-58.

The Brigham-Crum casebook contains the following cases which focus on capital budgeting under uncertainty:

Case 13, "Tarheel Forwarding, Inc.," which focuses primarily on the optimal capital budget.

Case 32, "Nature's Bounty, Inc.," which illustrates many of the techniques used in marginal cost of capital calculations.

Case 33, "National Telecommunications Corporation," which is a two-part integrated case on capital budgeting and cost of capital.

The Harrington casebook contains these applicable cases:

"Interchemical Consumer Products Division," which focuses on simulation analysis.

"Alaska Interstate," which illustrates a variety of ways to measure the riskiness of a conglomerate's subsidiaries.

The Use of Computers in the Capital Budgeting Process

In Chapter 10, we presented three methods of assessing a project's corporate risk: (1) sensitivity analysis, (2) scenario analysis, and (3) Monte Carlo simulation. While sensitivity and scenario analyses require only paper, pencil, and a calculator, simulation analysis cannot be performed without the aid of a computer. Additionally, sensitivity and scenario analysis can be performed much more efficiently using a computer rather than a calculator. Thus, for corporations of any size, virtually all capital budgeting analyses are done with the aid of computer models. Indeed, virtually all financial decisions are made on the basis of computerized financial analyses. These models vary greatly in complexity, ranging from simple electronic spreadsheets that can be run on personal home computers to very complex models which require mainframe computers. This appendix begins with a general discussion of computerized financial models, and then goes on to illustrate the use of an electronic spreadsheet model to analyze a capital budgeting proposal.

Spreadsheet Models

The most straightforward computerized financial models are based on electronic spreadsheets, which are ideally suited for forecasting future cash flows. The user first inputs various cash flow data such as costs, unit sales, and sales price and then specifies the relationships required to calculate each year's net cash flow. Finally, the computer performs the same calculations the analyst would have made using a calculator.

The spreadsheet has two major advantages over pencil and paper calculations: (1) It is much faster to use a spreadsheet if the forecast extends beyond two or three years, and (2) the spreadsheet automatically recomputes all net cash flows, and the NPVs, if one of the input variables is changed. Electronic spreadsheets, which are available for most personal computers, are simply computer programs which (1) set up cash flows as a series of rows and columns, that is, like a sheet of accounting paper, and then (2) do arithmetic on the rows and columns automatically. For example, Column 1 can be set up to determine the project's net investment, and then Columns 2, 3, and so forth can be used to develop the operating income for

427

Years 1, 2, and so forth. Finally, the cash flow relationships are specified so that the spreadsheet will automatically calculate the net cash flow in each year and then use these cash flows, plus an inputted cost of capital, to calculate the project's NPV. Some of the more popular spreadsheets are *VisiCalc, Lotus 1-2-3, Multiplan,* and *SuperCalc.*

Interactive Models

Interactive financial models operate much like the spreadsheets, but they are far more powerful. Some interactive models are available for use on large-memory personal computers, but most require a mainframe computer. The most widely used interactive model is *Interactive Financial Planning System, or IFPS,* for which both mainframe and personal computer versions are available. A model like *IFPS* allows the forecaster to "work backwards" to find the value of a particular variable which will produce a desired outcome. For example, instead of determining the expected NPV which will result if a new project's sales grow at a specified rate, the model can determine the level of sales growth required to produce a target NPV. Interactive systems can also be linked with other personal and mainframe computers within a firm, allowing many users to share data and programs.

Models such as *IFPS* also allow the user to specify variables as probability distributions rather than as discrete values. Then the model simulates real-world situations as we discussed in Chapter 10.

Integrated Systems

Among the most complex computerized financial models are integrated financial planning systems. These systems link all areas of a corporation's operations in order to plan for the most efficient utilization of its financial and physical resources. Further, these models can use the firm's data base of historic information to form probability distributions for use in the forecasting models. Oil companies, for example, use integrated planning models to forecast regional and worldwide demands for different types of petroleum products, to plan the best way to utilize their resources to meet these demands, and finally to forecast the financial conditions that will result under different operating plans. These models analyze a number of variables, including the company's own oil production, the cost of purchased crude oil, the capacity and operating costs of its plants, and the type of fuel used by each. These input-costs and output-prices are then worked into financial statements and used to forecast the firm's future financial condition, need for outside capital, and so forth.

Even small firms such as retail stores and auto repair shops are finding that they simply cannot compete effectively if they do not use computers for planning and control purposes. Indeed, now that hardware and software costs have fallen so drastically, most businesses larger than shoeshine stands can use computers in a cost-effective way, and competing in business without a computer is about like competing on a finance exam without a calculator. So, our advice is this—if you want to be a success (or even a nonfailure) in the business world, learn something about computers!

We can best demonstrate the usefulness of computer capital budgeting models by discussing one. In Table 10A-1, we show a simplified electronic spreadsheet model which was developed to analyze a 3-year capital budgeting project. The model, which analyzes Project F as given in Table 9-6 of Chapter 9, was constructed under the following assumptions: (1) The cost of the new equipment is $21,277; (2) sales attributable to the project will be $16,000 in Year 1, $31,400 in Year 2, and $27,700 in Year 3; (3) variable costs will total 60 percent of the project's sales; (4) fixed costs will total $3,000 annually; (5) the firm's marginal cost of capital, k, is 10 percent; (6) the equipment will be depreciated using the ACRS method; (7) no increase in working capital is required; and (8) the equipment has a zero salvage value. The model calculates depreciation, net income, and annual net cash flows, and then it computes the project's net present value.

The spreadsheet is set up as a matrix, with the columns designated A, B, C, ..., and the rows 1, 2, 3. Thus, each cell in the matrix has a designation such as A1, A2, B1, and B2. In Table 10A-1, we use Column A for headings, Column B to show the formulas, and Columns C, D, E, and F to calculate the cash flows in Years 0 through 3. The years are shown in Row 1; the equipment cost is in Row 2; dollar sales are in Row 8; fixed costs are in Row

A Simplified Capital Budgeting Spreadsheet Model

Table 10A-1
Simplified Capital Budgeting Model for Project F

(A)	(B)	(C)	(D)	(E)	(F)
1. YEAR		0	1	2	3
2. COST		21277			
3. ITC RATE		.06			
4. ITC	+C2*C3	1277			
5. NET EQUIPMT	+C2−C4	20000			
6. DEP RATE			.25	.38	.37
7. DEPRECIATION	+D6*(C2−(.5*C4))		5160	7843	7636
8. SALES			16000	31400	27700
9. VC%			.6	.6	.6
10. VC	+D8*D9		9600	18840	16620
11. FC			3000	3000	3000
12. TAX INCOME	+D8−D10−D11		3400	9560	8080
13. TAX RATE			.46	.46	.46
14. TAXES	+D12*D13		1564	4397	3716
15. NET INCOME	+D12−D14		1836	5162	4363
16. CASH FLOWS	+D15+D7		6996	13005	12000
17. k					.1
18. PV CASHFLOWS	@NPV(F17,D16...F16)				26123
19. NPV	−C5+F18				6123

Note: The formulas in Column B would not appear on the printout of an actual spreadsheet model; rather, they appear at the top of the screen when the cursor is set on a particular cell. For example, if you put the cursor on Cell D14, the equation "+D12*D13" would appear at the top of the screen, and the value 1564 would appear in the cell block itself. We show the formulas in Column B to aid in the explanation. If no formula is shown in Column B, the data are entered directly.

11; and so forth. Thus, Cell D7 gives the Year 1 value for depreciation, Cell D8 gives the Year 1 value for sales, and so on.

The Year 1 value for variable cost is 60 percent of Year 1 sales, and the electronic spreadsheet automatically makes this calculation, using the formula D10 = D8*D9. An asterisk indicates "multiply." The depreciation allowance in each year is equal to the year's depreciation rate times the depreciable basis of the equipment, which is the cost of the equipment reduced by one-half the ITC. The model computes Year 1 depreciation using the formula D6*(C2 − (.5*C4)), and then it automatically substitutes in the depreciation rates for Years 2 and 3 to complete the depreciation calculation for those years. Going on, the model computes the net cash flows for each year and then calculates the NPV of the project.

We can see from Table 10A-1 that Project F has an NPV of $6,123, which is the same as the NPV calculated in Chapter 9. Although this particular problem could be solved quite easily with a calculator, the spreadsheet model is vastly better for most real world problems. The spreadsheet model (1) requires us to input only the data and formulas for Years 0 and 1, and it then automatically repeats (replicates) the calculations for succeeding years (a significant advantage for long-lived projects) and (2) allows us to analyze the sensitivity of the NPV to changes in such variables as the firm's sales, variable costs, or cost of capital. For example, in a matter of seconds, the model can recalculate the NPV to show the impact of a 10 percent decrease in sales, an increase in the variable cost ratio to 70 percent, or any other change. The model also can be extended to deal with more complex analyses, such as those involving outflows in more than one year, with inflation, and so on.

It should be noted that, in practice, computerized models are used to analyze many of the financial decisions covered in this book, including cash budgeting, financial forecasting, establishing a target capital structure, lease analysis, and bond refunding. We have written "template models" similar to the one in Table 10A-1 programmed in *VisiCalc*, *Lotus 1-2-3*, and *IFPS* for each of the above-listed financial decisions.[1] Information on these models is available to instructors (only) who have adopted this book for class use.

---

[1] A template model is one that sets forth the basic format of a specific type of decision. These models can be used to solve similar problems or modified to solve slightly different ones.

Capital Rationing

10B

Under ordinary circumstances, capital budgeting is, in essence, an application of a classic economic principle: A firm should expand to the point where its marginal revenue is just equal to its marginal cost. When this rule is applied to the capital budgeting decision, marginal revenue is taken to be the rate of return on projects, while marginal cost is the project's marginal risk-adjusted cost of capital. A simplified view of the concept is shown in Figure 10B-1. Here we assume that the firm has five equally risky and independent investment opportunities which would cost in total $23 million. Its cost of capital is assumed to be constant at 10 percent, implying that the firm can raise all the money it wants at a cost of 10 percent. Under these conditions, the firm would accept Projects V, W, and X, since they all have IRRs greater than the cost of capital, and hence NPVs greater than zero. It would reject Y and Z because they have IRRs less than k, indicating negative NPVs. This decision would maximize the value of the firm and the wealth of its stockholders.

Firms ordinarily operate in the manner depicted in the graph—they accept all independent projects having positive NPVs, reject those with negative NPVs, and choose between mutually exclusive investments on the basis of the higher NPV. However, some firms set an absolute limit on the size of their capital budgets such that the size of the budget is less than the level of investment called for by the NPV (or IRR) criterion. This is called *capital rationing*, and it is the topic of this appendix.

The principal reason for capital rationing is that some firms are reluctant to engage in external financing (either borrowing or selling stock). One management, recalling the plight of firms with substantial amounts of debt during recent credit crunches, may simply refuse to use debt. Another management, which has no objection to selling debt, may not want to sell equity capital for fear of losing some measure of voting control. Still others may refuse to use any form of outside financing, considering safety and control to be more important than additional profits. These are all cases of capital rationing, and they result in limiting the rate of expansion to a slower pace than would be dictated by "purely rational wealth-maximizing behavior."

Reasons for Capital Rationing

Figure 10B-1
The Typical Capital Budgeting Situation

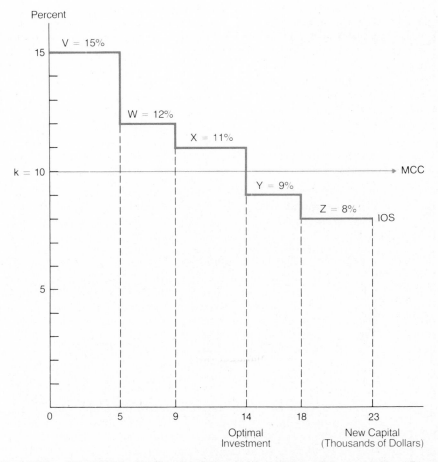

Note: If IRR > 10%, NPV is positive. Therefore, Projects V, W, and X have NPV > 0, while Y and Z have NPV < 0.

We should make three points here. First, a decision to hold back on expansion is not necessarily irrational. If the owners/managers of a privately held firm have what they consider to be plenty of income and wealth, then it might be quite rational for them to "trim their sails," relax, and concentrate on enjoying what they have already earned rather than on earning still more. Such behavior would not, however, be appropriate for a publicly owned firm.

Second, it is not correct to interpret as capital rationing a situation where the firm is willing to sell additional securities at the going market price but finds that it cannot because the market simply will not absorb more of its issues. Rather, such a situation indicates that the marginal cost of capital is rising. If more acceptable investments are indicated than can be financed, then the cost of capital being used is too low and should be raised.

Third, firms sometimes set a limit on capital expenditures, not because of a shortage of funds, but because of limitations on other resources, especially managerial talent. A firm might, for example, feel that its personnel development program is sufficient to handle an expansion of no more than 10 percent a year, and then set a limit on the capital budget to insure that expansion is held to that rate. This is not capital rationing—rather, it involves a downward reevaluation of project returns if growth exceeds some limit; that is, expected rates of return are, after some point, a decreasing function of the level of expenditures.

How should projects be selected under conditions of true capital rationing? First, note that if a firm truly rations capital, its value is not being maximized: If management were maximizing, then they would move to the point where the marginal project's NPV was zero, and capital rationing as defined would not exist. So, if a firm uses capital rationing, it has ruled out value maximization. The firm may, however, want to maximize value *subject to the constraint that the capital ceiling not be exceeded.* Constrained maximization behavior will, in general, result in a lower value than following unconstrained maximization, but some type of constrained maximization may produce reasonably satisfactory results. *Linear programming* is one method of constrained maximization that has been applied to capital rationing. Much work has been done in this area, and linear programming may, in the future, be widely applied in capital budgeting.[1]

If the firm does face capital rationing, and if the constraint cannot be lifted, what can the financial manager do? The objective should be to select projects, subject to the capital rationing constraint, such that the sum of the projects' NPVs is maximized. Linear programming can be used, or if there are not too many projects involved, the financial manager can simply enumerate all the sets of projects that meet the budget constraint and then select the set with the largest total NPV.

The complexities involved in a capital rationing situation are indicated in Table 10B-1. Here we assume that the firm is considering a total of eight potential projects; all are independent and have average risk. The firm has a 10 percent cost of capital, but management has decided to limit capital expenditures during the year to the amount of money that can be generated internally, $500,000. In the table, the projects are listed in the order of their NPVs, but their IRRs and profitability indices (PIs) are also shown.

If it is to maximize the value of the firm, management must choose that set of projects with the greatest total NPV, subject to the constraint that total

Project Selection under Capital Rationing

[1]For further information on mathematical programming solutions to capital rationing, and for a review and analysis of the literature on this issue, see H. Martin Weingarten, "Capital Rationing: n Authors in Search of a Plot," *Journal of Finance*, December 1977, 1403-1431; and Stephen P. Bradley and Sherwood C. Frey, Jr., "Equivalent Mathematical Programming Models of Pure Capital Rationing," *Journal of Financial and Quantitative Analysis*, June 1978, 345-361.

Table 10B-1
Illustration of Capital Rationing

Project Number	Project Cost, or Outlay, at t = 0	Project Life (Years)	Cash Flow per Year	NPV at the 10% Cost of Capital	IRR	Profit-ability Index
1	$400,000	20	$58,600	$98,894	13.5%	1.25
2	250,000	10	55,000	87,951	17.7	1.35
3	100,000	8	24,000	28,038	17.3	1.28
4	75,000	15	12,000	16,273	13.7	1.22
5	75,000	6	18,000	3,395	11.5	1.05
6	50,000	5	14,000	3,071	12.4	1.06
7	250,000	10	41,000	1,927	10.2	1.01
8	250,000	3	99,000	−3,802	9.1	0.98

expenditures must not exceed $500,000. With only eight projects in total, we can try all different combinations and, by "brute force," determine the set which maximizes NPV. This set is optimal:

Project	Cost	NPV
2	$250,000	$ 87,951
3	100,000	28,038
4	75,000	16,273
5	75,000	3,395
	$500,000	$135,657

This analysis seems simple enough, but there are three factors which complicate it greatly in realistic situations:

1. Number of projects. In the example, we have only eight projects, so it is easy to simply list all the combinations whose costs do not exceed $500,000 and then see which combination provides the greatest total NPV. For a large firm with thousands of projects, this would be a tedious process, although computer programs are available to solve such problems. However, the other problems listed below are more serious.

2. Project risk. In our example, we assumed that the eight projects are equally risky, and hence have the same cost of capital. If this were not the case, and if the number of projects were so large as to preclude hand analysis, then it would be difficult, if not impossible, to reach an optimal solution, because the computer programs currently available cannot deal efficiently with projects having differential risks.

3. Multiple time constraints. Our example also assumed a single-time-period capital constraint. Yet, realistically, when capital rationing is practiced, the constraints usually extend for several years. However, the funds available in future years depend on cash throw-offs from investments made in earlier years. Thus, the constraint in Year 2 depends on the investments made in Year 1, and so on. For example, we might have investment funds of $500,000 per year available from external sources for 1985 through 1989 plus the cash flows from investments made in previous years. To solve this type of multiperiod problem, we need information on both investment opportunities and funds availability in future years, and not just on the situation in the current year. Also, the NPV we seek to maximize is the sum of the present values of the NPVs in each year over the time horizon being analyzed, say 1985 to 1989. In such a situation, we might even choose Project 8 in Table 10B-1, in spite of its negative NPV, because it has rapid cash throw-offs. In fact, if excellent investment opportunities are expected to be available in 1986, 1987, and 1988, taking Project 8 might be part of the best long-run strategy.

Our main conclusion thus far about capital rationing—which means deliberately foregoing projects with positive NPVs—is that practicing it is irrational for any firm which seeks to maximize its stockholders' wealth. Also, while mathematical programming methods are available to help solve the simpler cases of capital rationing so that management can make the best of a bad situation, programming methods are really not capable of dealing with all the complexities encountered in the real world.

A Better Approach to Capital Rationing

Fortunately, there is a better method for handling the types of situations that give rise to capital rationing. Usually, capital rationing occurs when the firm believes that it will encounter severe problems if it attempts to raise capital beyond some specified amount. For example, the interest rate it would have to pay would rise sharply if it attempted to increase its existing lines of credit. Such situations can be rationally handled by increasing the assigned cost of capital as the amount of capital raised increases. In effect, in terms of Figure 10B-1, the marginal cost of capital (MCC) would begin to rise beyond some amount of capital, and this higher MCC should be used as the discount rate when determining a project's NPV.

10C   Certainty Equivalents

There are two basic approaches to risk adjustment. First, there is the *risk-adjusted discount rate (RADR)* method, which involves adjusting the denominator of the present value equation—the higher the riskiness of the cash flows, the higher is the discount rate and consequently the lower is the present value of the asset. This is the approach we took in Chapter 10. Alternatively, we could adjust for risk by altering the numerator of the present value equation. Here, we reduce the value of expected cash inflows to adjust for risk—the riskier the cash flow, the more it is reduced and consequently the lower the present value of the asset. This method of risk adjustment is called the *certainty equivalent (CE)* method. Although the risk-adjusted discount rate method is most commonly used, and the one most people are familiar with, the CE method does have some advantages. Also, a study of the CE method will teach us more about the nature of risk-adjusted discount rates.

The Certainty Equivalent Concept

The *certainty equivalent (CE)* concept follows directly from the concept of utility theory. Under the certainty equivalent approach, the decision maker must first evaluate a cash flow's risk and then specify how much money he or she would require, with certainty, to produce an equivalency between this riskless sum and the risky cash flow's expected value. To illustrate, suppose a rich eccentric offered you the following two choices:

1. Flip a fair coin. If a head comes up, you receive $1 million, but if a tail comes up, you get nothing. The expected value of the gamble is (0.5 × $1,000,000) + (0.5 × $0) = $500,000.

2. Do not flip the coin and simply pocket $300,000 cash.

If you find yourself indifferent to the two alternatives, then $300,000 is defined to be your certainty equivalent for this particular risky $500,000 expected return. In other words, the certain (or riskless) $300,000 amount provides you with exactly the same utility as the risky $500,000 expected value.

Now ask *yourself* this question: In the example, exactly how much cash-in-hand would it take to make *you* indifferent to the choices of the certain

Figure 10C-1
Certainty Equivalent Returns

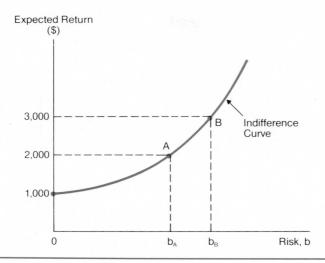

Expected Return
($)

3,000 ---------------------- B   Indifference
                                    Curve
              A
2,000 ----------

1,000

0   b_A b_B Risk, b

sum and the risky $500,000 expected value of the coin flip? If you are like
most people, your certainty equivalent would be significantly less than
$500,000, indicating that you are *risk averse*. In general, if the certainty equiv-
alent is less than the expected value of an investment, risk aversion is present, and the lower the certainty equivalent, the greater the risk aversion.

The certainty equivalent concept is illustrated in Figure 10C-1. The curve
shows a series of risk/return combinations to which this particular individual
is indifferent. For example, Point A represents an investment with a perceived degree of risk as measured by the risk coefficient, b_A, and with an
expected dollar return of $2,000. The individual with the risk/return trade-
off function, or indifference curve, shown here is indifferent to the choices
of a sure $1,000, an expected $2,000 with risk b_A, and an expected $3,000
with risk b_B.[1]

The certainty equivalent concept can be applied to the capital budgeting
decision as an alternative to the use of risk-adjusted discount rates. We proceed as follows:

1. Divide the certainty equivalent of the risky cash flow in each year t by
the expected value of the cash flow, CF_t, to obtain a *certainty equivalent adjustment factor*, a_t. For the cash flows in Figure 10C-1, we would have

---

[1]If the investor were *risk-neutral*, his or her indifference curve would be a horizontal line.
A *risk-seeker*'s indifference curve would slope downward. The curve shown in Figure 10C-
1 shows risk aversion, and, specifically, *increasing risk aversion*; an upward sloping *straight*
line would show *constant risk aversion*.

$$a_t = \frac{\text{Certainty equivalent}}{CF_t} = \frac{\$1,000}{\$2,000} = 0.50 \text{ for risk } b_A, \text{ and}$$

$$a_t = \frac{\$1,000}{\$3,000} = 0.33 \text{ for risk } b_B.$$

2. Conceptually, a_t values could be developed for all possible values of b. The range of a_t would be from 1.0 for b = 0 to a value close to zero for large values of b, assuming the investor is averse to risk.

3. The risk-aversion functions of all individuals could, conceptually, be averaged to form a "market risk-aversion function." An example of such a function is shown in Figure 10C-2.

4. Given the market risk-aversion function and the degree of risk inherent in any expected cash flow, CF_t, the risky cash flow in Year t could be replaced by its certainty equivalent:

$$\text{Certainty equivalent of } CF_t = a_t CF_t.$$

5. Once we have expressed the risky cash flow for each Year t as a certainty equivalent, $a_t CF_t$, we can discount by the risk-free rate to obtain the project's NPV:

$$NPV = \sum_{t=0}^{n} \frac{a_t CF_t}{(1 + R_F)^t}. \tag{10C-1}$$

To illustrate, suppose Project C, whose expected net cash flows are shown in Table 10C-1, is to be evaluated using the certainty equivalent method. Further, suppose the capital budgeting analyst estimates that the cash inflows in Years 1-4 all have the same risk, b_c, and that the appropriate adjustment factor, a_t, as determined in Figure 10C-2, is 0.7 for each of the four

---

Figure 10C-2
Hypothetical Market Risk-Aversion Function

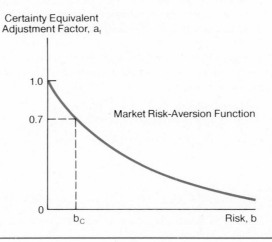

Table 10C-1
Project C's Certainty Equivalent Analysis

Year	Expected but Risky Net Cash Flow	Adjustment Factor	Certainty Equivalent
0	($2,000)	0.0	($2,000)
1	1,000	0.7	700
2	1,000	0.7	700
3	1,000	0.7	700
4	1,000	0.7	700

years. The cost of the project, $2,000, is known with certainty, so $a_0 = 1.0$, and the certainty equivalent of this cost is $2,000. However, each of the $1,000 cash inflows has a certainty equivalent of $0.7(\$1,000) = \$700$, and the project's NPV, found with an after-tax risk-free discount rate of 5 percent, is approximately $482:

$$NPV_c = -\$2,000 + \frac{\$700}{(1.05)^1} + \frac{\$700}{(1.05)^2} + \frac{\$700}{(1.05)^3} + \frac{\$700}{(1.05)^4}$$
$$= \$482.17.$$

The risk-adjusted NPV is positive, so the project should be accepted.

Certainty Equivalents versus Risk-Adjusted Discount Rates

As noted above, investment risk can be handled by making adjustments to the numerator of the present value equation (the certainty equivalent, or CE, method) or to the denominator of the equation (the risk-adjusted discount rate, RADR, method). The RADR method is most frequently used in practice, probably because it is easier to estimate suitable discount rates using current market data than it is to derive certainty equivalent adjustment factors. However, some financial theorists have advocated the certainty equivalent approach as being theoretically superior.[2] Still, other theorists have shown that if risk is perceived to be an increasing function of time, then using a risk-adjusted discount rate is a valid procedure.[3]

Risk-adjusted rates lump together the pure time value of money as represented by the risk-free rate and risk as represented by the risk premium, while the certainty equivalent approach keeps risk and the time value of money separate. This separation gives an advantage to certainty equivalents. To see why, suppose we are comparing two investments, A and B. Our analysis of these projects' risk suggests that their required rates of return are 5 percent for A because it is riskless ($R_F = 5\%$), and 10 percent for B. To estimate the value of each project, we discount its expected cash flows

[2]See Alexander A. Robichek and Stewart C. Myers, "Conceptual Problems in the Use of Risk-Adjusted Discount Rates," *Journal of Finance*, December 1966, 727-730.

[3]See Houng-Yhi Chen, "Valuation under Uncertainty," *Journal of Financial and Quantitative Analysis*, September 1967, 313-326.

by its risk-adjusted discount rate. Since the after-tax riskless rate is 5 percent, the risk premium for project A is zero and for B it is 5 percent. Does B's constant risk premium imply that the relative riskiness of its cash flows over time is also perceived to be constant, that is, that the riskiness of CF_1 is the same as that of CF_{10}? The answer is no, but to see why, we must first look at the assumptions inherent in the risk-adjusted discount rate.

By its nature, the risk-adjusted discount rate serves both to account for the time value of money and to provide an allowance for the relative riskiness of an investment's returns. In other words, both time and risk are accounted for by one adjustment process. Since time and risk are really separate variables, when we use one term to account for both elements, this term must be carefully chosen if it is to be appropriate for its intended purpose.

Consider the particular assumptions that are implicit in the choice of a constant discount rate over time. The present value of a cash flow in Year t, using the CE approach, is

$$PV\ CF_t = \frac{a_t CF_t}{(1 + R_F)^t}.$$

The present value of a Year t cash flow, using the RADR approach, is

$$PV\ CF_t = \frac{CF_t}{(1 + k)^t}.$$

Now, for the two methods to be equivalent, the present values must be equal. Therefore, we must have

$$\frac{a_t CF_t}{(1 + R_F)^t} = \frac{CF_t}{(1 + k)^t}.$$

We can divide both sides by CF_t and then solve for the adjustment factor, a_t:

$$a_t = \frac{(1 + R_F)^t}{(1 + k)^t}. \tag{10C-2}$$

To illustrate, suppose we are calculating a_{10}, the CE adjustment factor for a cash flow expected after 10 years when the riskless rate is 5 percent and the risky rate is 10 percent. Substituting these values into Equation 10C-2, the certainty equivalent adjustment factor is found as follows:

$$a_{10} = \frac{(1 + R_F)^{10}}{(1 + k)^{10}} = \frac{(1.05)^{10}}{(1.10)^{10}}$$

$$= \frac{0.3855}{0.6139} = 0.6280.$$

This is the only certainty equivalent adjustment factor value that is consistent with $R_F = 5\%$, $RP = 5\%$, and $t = 10$.

Equation 10C-2 has some interesting implications that can be seen in Figure 10C-3, which works out the a_t values for a pair of interest rates over time and then plots these values. Note first that a_t is a direct measure of the perceived risk of CF_t—the smaller the value of a_t, the greater the perceived risk. Second, with constant R_F, RP, and k values, risk, as measured by a_t, is

Figure 10C-3
Changes in Perceived Risk over Time

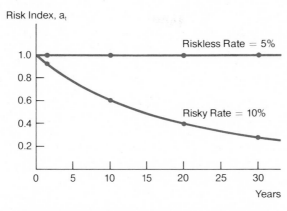

Illustrative Calculations of CE Adjustment Factors, a_t

Years	Riskless Investment, $(1.05)^t$	Risky Investment, $(1.10)^t$	Certainty Equivalent Adjustment Factor, a_t
0	1.0000	1.0000	1.0000
1	0.9524	0.9091	0.9545
10	0.6139	0.3855	0.6280
20	0.3769	0.1486	0.3943
30	0.2314	0.0573	0.2476

Notes:
a. The value of a_t reflects risk, and the smaller the value of a_t, the certainty equivalent factor used as an index of risk, the greater the perceived risk.
b. For a given riskless rate and risky rate, the calculated value of a_t declines over time; that is, with a constant risk premium (RP = 5% = 10% − 5%), the declining a_t values indicate that perceived risk increases with time. Therefore, a constant risk premium (and consequently a constant risk-adjusted discount rate) implies that the risk of an individual cash flow is perceived to be higher and higher the further into the future the cash flow is due.
c. If we plotted a_t values for other k values, we would see that the higher the value of k, and consequently the higher the risk premium, the faster the decline in a_t as t increases.
d. $a_0 = 1.0$ because

$$\frac{(1 + R_F)^0}{(1 + k)^0} = \frac{1}{1} = 1.0.$$

an increasing function of both *time* and the *risk premium*. In other words, a given risk premium has a larger and larger impact on the CE adjustment factor as the time horizon is lengthened. This phenomenon occurs because the risk premium itself is compounded.

To see the compounding effect, let us express the CE adjustment factor for Year t as follows:

$$a_t = \frac{(1 + R_F)^t}{(1 + R_F + RP)^t} = \frac{(1 + R_F)^t}{(1 + k)^t}.$$

Figure 10C-4
Relationship between Risk and Time

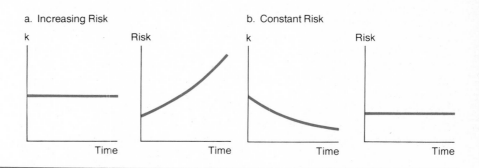

Here R_F is the after-tax riskless rate and RP is the risk premium. Now notice that for a longer period of $t + 1$ years, and holding constant both R_F and k, and hence RP, we obtain this CE factor:

$$a_{t+1} = \frac{(1 + R_F)^{t+1}}{(1 + k)^{t+1}} = \frac{(1 + R_F)^t}{(1 + k)^t} \left[\frac{(1 + R_F)}{(1 + k)} \right]$$

$$= a_t \left[\frac{(1 + R_F)}{(1 + k)} \right].$$

Now note these points:

1. a_{t+1} is smaller than a_t whenever $k > R_F$, as would be true for all risky projects.

2. A smaller value of a_t signifies greater risk. Thus the fact that $a_t > a_{t+1}$ implies that risk is increasing over time.

3. Therefore, since the use of a constant value of k leads to a condition of $a_t > a_{t+1}$, it follows that the use of a constant k in capital budgeting analysis (or any other discounted cash flow analysis) implies that risk is increasing over time. So, if risk is constant, then a constant k is *not* appropriate.

The relationship between k, risk, and time is graphed in Figure 10C-4. A constant value of k implies increasing risk; this condition is shown in Panel a. However, if the riskiness of returns is no higher for distant than for close-at-hand returns, then distant returns should be discounted at a lower k than are close returns; this condition is shown in Panel b. Note again that the reason behind this result is the fact that the risk premium component of k is being compounded.

Implications

A firm using the risk-adjusted discount rate approach for its capital budgeting decisions will have an overall cost of capital that reflects its overall market-determined riskiness. This rate will normally be used for "average" projects, that is, projects having the same risk as the firm's existing projects. Lower rates will be used for less risky projects, and higher rates will be used for riskier projects. To facilitate the decision process, corporate headquarters generally prescribes rates for different classes of investments (for example, replacement, expansion of existing lines, and expansion into new lines). Then, investments of a given class within a given division are analyzed in terms of the prescribed rate. For example, replacement decisions in the retailing division of an oil company might all be evaluated with a constant 10 percent discount rate.

Such a procedure implicitly assumes that risk increases with time, and it therefore imposes a relatively severe burden on long-term projects. This means that short-payoff alternatives will tend to be selected over those with longer payoffs when, for example, there are alternative ways of performing a given task.

However, there may be a substantial number of projects for which distant returns are *not* more risky than near-term returns. For example, the estimated returns on a water pipeline serving a developing community may be quite uncertain in the short run, because the rate of growth of the community is uncertain. However, the water company may be quite sure that in time the community will be fully developed and will utilize the full capacity of the pipeline. Similar situations could exist in many public projects—water projects, highway programs, schools, and so forth; in public utility investment decisions; and when industrial firms are building plants or retailers stores to serve growing geographic markets.

To the extent that the implicit assumption of rising risk over time reflects the facts, then a constant discount rate, k, may be appropriate. Indeed, in the vast majority of business situations, risk actually is an increasing function of time, so a constant risk-adjusted discount rate is generally reasonable. However, there are situations for which this is not true, so one should be aware of the relationships described in this section and avoid the pitfall of unwittingly penalizing long-term projects when they are not, in fact, more risky than short-term projects.

10C-1 You are the director of capital budgeting for Minute Man Company (MMC), a producer of frozen cranberry juice. MMC uses the certainty equivalent approach to capital budgeting decisions. You are evaluating the acquisition of a new juice press with the following *expected* net cash flows. Further, you estimate the certainty equivalent adjustment factors, a_t, as listed:

Problem

Year	Cash Flow	a_t
0	($20,000)	1.0
1	5,000	0.9
2	5,000	0.9
3	5,000	0.9
4	15,000	0.7

You view the Year 4 cash flow as being more risky than Years 1-3 because a large proportion of the Year 4 cash flow is salvage value, and MMC's engineering estimates of salvage value are especially uncertain. Conversely, you know the cost of the machine with certainty because its manufacturer has given MMC a fixed bid for a 90-day period. If the after-tax risk-free rate is 8 percent, and MMC's cost of capital is 12 percent, should the project be accepted?

Capital Structure and Dividend Policy

IV

Capital Structure Theory 11

At the end of 1983, AT&T and its subsidiaries had $148 billion of assets. These assets were financed with $84 billion of debt and $64 billion of common and preferred equity. Thus, from a total financing perspective, AT&T had a debt-to-assets ratio of $84/$148 = 57%. This ratio was comparatively high, and it reflected primarily the earnings stability that had been associated with regulation.

However, on January 1, 1984, AT&T was forced to divest its local operating subsidiaries. They took with them $100 billion of assets, leaving the "new" AT&T with $48 billion. One key issue in the breakup was this—how much of the consolidated debt, and how much equity, should be transferred to the newly spun-off operating companies, and how much debt and equity should AT&T keep? In other words, how should the debt be allocated, and what capital structures should the various entities have after the breakup? This issue was addressed in the court, where it was noted that the Bell operating companies will continue to be regulated monopolies (to a large extent) whereas the surviving AT&T (to a large extent) will no longer be operated in a regulatory environment but must compete against such information services giants as IBM, MCI, ITT, and Hewlett-Packard. All of this brought up these questions: Why do firms use debt financing at all, and why do different firms use different proportions of debt? Further, should AT&T and its subsidiaries' use of debt change as a result of their change in economic environment from a regulated monopoly to one in which they face different degrees of competition?

The materials covered in Chapters 11 and 12 are useful in addressing the issues posed by the AT&T breakup. Financial theorists have grappled with these questions for years, and many theories have been proposed to explain why firms use debt financing. We begin our discus-

---

This chapter was coauthored with Dilip K. Shome.

sion of financing mix by examining capital structure theory as it has developed in recent years. Then, in Chapter 12, we discuss the ways in which firms actually go about setting their optimal capital structure in view of the data limitations which make strict application of the theoretical rules impossible.

One of the most perplexing questions facing financial managers is the relationship between capital structure and firm value. Several theories of capital structure have been proposed. We begin by presenting some key terms and equations. Then, we discuss briefly three early (pre-1958) theories: the net income (NI) approach, the net operating income (NOI) approach, and the traditional approach. Next, we consider the classic 1958 Modigliani and Miller (MM) analysis of capital structure theory, which marked the beginning of "modern financial theory." Finally, we go on to expand the basic MM analysis to include the effects of personal taxes, bankruptcy, and agency costs. Our conclusions are as follows: (1) There does exist an optimal capital structure, or at least an optimal range of structures, for every firm. (2) However, financial theory is not powerful enough at this point to enable us to locate the optimal structure with any degree of precision. (3) Still, financial theory does help us identify the key factors which influence the value-maximizing structure, so an understanding of the material in this chapter will aid a firm that is attempting to establish its target capital structure.

Key Terms and Equations

A number of theories have been set forth regarding how *leverage*, or the use of debt, affects the value of a firm and its cost of capital. These theories address two basic questions: Can a firm increase the wealth of its stockholders by replacing some of its equity with debt, and, if so, exactly how much debt should it use? As we explore these two questions, we will utilize several valuation equations; the key terms used in these equations are as follows:

S = market value of all the firm's common stock (price per share times number of shares outstanding).

D = market value of its debt. For simplicity, we shall ignore preferred stock and assume that the firm uses only one class of debt, which is a perpetuity. (Assuming perpetual debt simplifies the analysis.)

$V = D + S$ = total market value of the firm.

EBIT = earnings before interest and taxes, also called net operating income (NOI). Again for simplicity, we shall assume that the expected value of EBIT is a constant over time. EBIT could rise or fall, but the best guess for the EBIT in any future year is the same as that for any other year.

k_d = interest rate on the firm's single class of perpetual debt.

k_s = cost of equity, or required rate of return on the firm's common stock.

k_a = weighted average cost of capital.

T = corporate tax rate.

We assume that the firm is in a zero-growth situation, that is, EBIT is expected to remain constant and all earnings are to be paid out as dividends. Therefore, the total market value of its common stock, S, is a perpetuity whose value is found as follows:

$$S = \frac{\text{Dividends}}{k_s} = \frac{\text{Net income}}{k_s}$$
$$= \frac{(\text{EBIT} - k_d D)(1 - T)}{k_s}. \tag{11-1}$$

Equation 11-1 is a perpetuity whose numerator gives the net income available to common stockholders, which we assume is all paid out as dividends, while the denominator is the cost of common equity. We shall use Equation 11-1 to show how changes in the amount of debt financing would affect the value of the firm's stock under the different capital structure theories. Also, note that, by transposition, we can solve for k_s, the cost of equity:

$$k_s = \frac{(\text{EBIT} - k_d D)(1 - T)}{S}. \tag{11-1a}$$

Another basic required equation is that for the weighted average cost of capital as developed in Chapter 7:

$$k_a = w_d k_d (1 - T) + w_s k_s$$

$$= \left(\frac{D}{V}\right) k_d (1 - T) + \left(\frac{S}{V}\right) k_s. \tag{11-2}$$

We will use Equation 11-2 to examine how changes in the debt ratio affect the firm's average cost of capital.

A third basic equation is that for the total market value of the firm, V. Note that we could find V by first using Equation 11-1 to find the value of the equity and then adding the value of the debt: $V = S + D$. However, another expression for the value of the firm is required in our analysis. We develop this alternative expression for V as follows:

Step 1. Solve Equation 11-2 for V:

$$V = \frac{(D)k_d(1 - T) + (S)k_s}{k_a}.$$

Step 2. Substitute Equation 11-1 for S in the Step 1 equation:

$$V = \frac{(D)k_d(1 - T) + \left[\dfrac{(EBIT - k_dD)(1 - T)}{k_s}\right]k_s}{k_a}.$$

Step 3. Cancel the k_s values in the numerator and then modify the equation to produce this expression:

$$V = \frac{k_dD(1 - T) + EBIT(1 - T) - k_dD(1 - T)}{k_a}.$$

Step 4. Cancel the $k_dD(1 - T)$ terms, producing this important new equation:

$$V = \frac{EBIT(1 - T)}{k_a}. \qquad (11\text{-}3)$$

Equation 11-3 shows that V can be found as the value of a perpetuity which capitalizes the constant after-tax operating income, $EBIT(1 - T)$, at the firm's weighted average cost of capital, k_a. Note that Equation 11-1 capitalizes the earnings available to common stockholders, while Equation 11-3 capitalizes the cash flows accruing to both debtholders and stockholders. Note also that we could solve Equation 11-3 for k_a to obtain an alternative expression for the average cost of capital:

$$k_a = \frac{EBIT(1 - T)}{V}. \qquad (11\text{-}3a)$$

We will use Equations 11-1, 11-1a, 11-2, 11-3, and 11-3a to examine the way changes in capital structure affect the firm's value and cost of capital under each of the capital structure theories. This is our task in the remainder of the chapter.

Early Theories of Capital Structure

One of the earliest formal works on the theory of capital structure was the 1952 study of David Durand, who identified the three positions that had been taken by writers up to that time:[1] (1) the *net income (NI) approach*, (2) the *net operating income (NOI) approach*, and (3) a middle-ground position called the *traditional approach*. The differences among the three approaches result solely from differing assumptions about how

---

[1]See David Durand, "Costs of Debt and Equity Funds for Business: Trends and Problems of Measurement," *Conference on Research in Business Finance*, National Bureau of Economic Research, New York, 1952. Although Durand's work is dated, we include it in the text to provide historical perspective.

investors value a firm's debt and equity. For convenience, we examine these positions under the assumption of a zero tax rate.

The *NI approach* assumes (1) that investors capitalize, or value, the firm's net income at a constant rate (k_s = constant) and (2) that firms can raise all the debt they want at a constant rate (k_d = constant). With both k_s and k_d constant, as the firm uses more and more debt, the average cost of capital, k_a, as given by Equation 11-2, declines, because debt is cheaper than equity. Further, if k_a declines as debt is increased, then, because of the Equation 11-3 relationship, a firm's value must be directly related to its use of debt. Thus, as shown in the two left graphs of Figure 11-1, as the firm moves from zero to 100 percent debt, its overall cost of capital decreases continuously, and its value increases continuously. We

The Net Income (NI) Approach

Ka related to Value)

Figure 11-1
Effects of Leverage:
NI, NOI, and Traditional Approaches

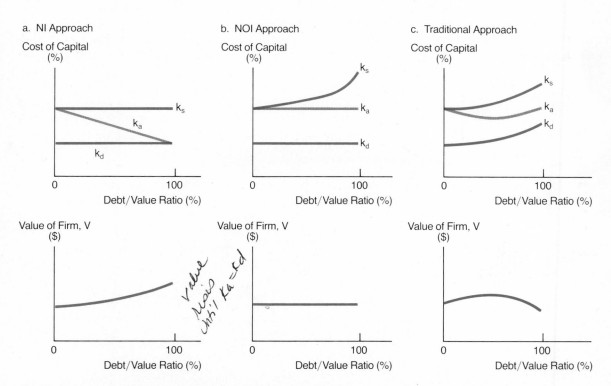

a. NI Approach

b. NOI Approach

c. Traditional Approach

Note: Under the NI approach, the plot of value versus D/V is slightly bowed. A plot of value versus dollars of debt would be linear.

see that if the NI assumptions are correct, firms should use (almost) 100 percent debt to maximize value.

The Net Operating Income (NOI) Approach

The *NOI approach* assumes that investors have an entirely different reaction to corporate debt. Specifically, the NOI approach assumes that investors value NOI (or EBIT) at a constant rate (k_a = constant). As in the NI approach, the NOI advocates assume that k_d is a constant. Notice (1) that a constant k_a results in a constant value for the firm regardless of its use of debt (Equation 11-3), and (2) that a constant k_a implies that k_s increases with leverage (Equation 11-2), and hence that stockholders believe the use of leverage increases the riskiness of their cash flows. Working through the equations under the NOI assumptions leads to the relationships shown in the middle two graphs of Figure 11-1. Thus, if the NOI assumptions are true, then capital structure decisions would be unimportant—one capital structure would be as good as any other.[2]

The Traditional Approach

Most academicians and practitioners at the time of Durand's work took a middle-of-the-road approach, somewhere between NI and NOI, which Durand called the *traditional approach*. The graphs on the right side of Figure 11-1 illustrate the traditionalists' view, which suggests that "moderate" amounts of leverage do not noticeably increase the risks to either the debt or the equity holders, so k_d and k_s are both relatively constant out to some point. However, beyond that critical debt percentage, both debt and equity costs begin to rise, and these increases offset the advantages of cheaper debt, resulting in (1) a U-shaped average cost of capital curve and (2) a value of the firm which first rises, then hits a peak, and finally declines as the debt ratio increases. Thus, according to the traditionalists, there is some capital structure, other than almost all debt, which maximizes the value of the firm.

Whereas the NI and NOI theories as set forth by Durand are quite specific, the traditional approach was more judgmental than quantitative in nature. Moreover, a review of the literature of the time offers little in the way of explanation for the assumed shape of the traditional curves. We will return to a discussion of the traditional view later in the chapter, but first we must examine the Modigliani-Miller model and its extensions.

---

[2]The NI and NOI theories, as they were typically set forth, assumed away corporate income taxes. However, Durand did examine the two approaches including corporate income taxes. Here, under the NOI approach, the firm's value does increase with leverage due to the tax deductibility of interest even though the capitalization rate, k_a, remains constant. However, the firm's value under the NI approach increases at an even faster rate. Thus, in a world with corporate taxes, both approaches would indicate that the optimal capital structure calls for virtually 100 percent debt.

The capital structure theories presented thus far are based on assertions about investor behavior rather than a carefully constructed formal proof. In what has been called the most important paper on financial research ever published, Franco Modigliani and Merton Miller (MM) addressed the capital structure issue in a rigorous, scientific fashion, and they set off a chain of research that continues to this day.[3]

The Modigliani-Miller Models

To begin, MM made the following assumptions, some of which were later relaxed:

Assumptions

1. Firms' business risk can be measured (by σ_{EBIT}), and firms with the same degree of business risk are said to be in a *homogeneous risk class*.

2. All present and prospective investors have identical estimates of each firm's future EBIT; that is, investors have *homogeneous expectations* about expected future corporate earnings and the riskiness of these earnings. This assumption is comparable to our use of a "representative investor" in earlier chapters when we discussed the DCF model and market equilibrium ($\hat{k}_s = k_s$).

3. Stocks and bonds are traded in *perfect capital markets*. This assumption implies, among other things, (1) that there are no brokerage costs and (2) that investors (both individuals and institutions) can borrow at the same rate as corporations.

4. The debt of firms and individuals is riskless, so the interest rate on debt is the risk-free rate. Further, this situation holds regardless of how much debt a firm (or an individual) issues.

5. All cash flows are perpetuities; that is, the firm is a zero-growth firm with an "expectationally constant" EBIT, and its bonds are perpetuities. "Expectationally constant" means that we expect EBIT to attain some constant level each year, but the actual level could be different from the expected level, i.e., some risk is present.

MM first performed their analysis under the assumption that there are no corporate income taxes. Based on the preceding assumptions, and in the absence of corporate taxes, MM stated and then proved two propositions:

MM without Corporate Taxes

---

[3]See Franco Modigliani and Merton H. Miller, "The Cost of Capital, Corporation Finance and the Theory of Investment," *American Economic Review*, June 1958, 261-297; "The Cost of Capital, Corporation Finance and the Theory of Investment: Reply," *American Economic Review*, September 1958, 655-669; "Taxes and the Cost of Capital: A Correction," *American Economic Review*, June 1963, 433-443; and "Reply," *American Economic Review*, June 1965, 524-527. In a 1979 survey of Financial Management Association members, the original MM article was judged to have had the greatest impact on the field of finance of any work ever published. See Philip L. Cooley and J. Louis Heck, "Significant Contributions to Finance Literature," *Financial Management*, Tenth Anniversary Issue 1981, 23-33.

Proposition I. The value of the firm is established by capitalizing the expected net operating income (NOI = EBIT) at a rate appropriate for the firm's risk class:

$$V = \frac{\text{EBIT}}{k_a} = \frac{\text{EBIT}}{k_{sU}}.$$

Here k_{sU} is the required rate of return for an unlevered, or all-equity, firm in a given risk class.

Since V is established by the Proposition I equation, *under the MM theory, the value of the firm is independent of its leverage.* This also implies that the average cost of capital to any firm, leveraged or not, is (1) completely independent of its capital structure and (2) equal to the capitalization rate of an unlevered firm in the same risk class. Thus, MM's Proposition I is identical to the NOI hypothesis as expressed in Figure 11-1.

Proposition II. The cost of equity to a levered firm is equal to the cost of equity to an unlevered firm plus a risk premium which depends in the following way on the degree of financial leverage the firm uses:

$$k_{sL} = k_{sU} + \text{Risk premium}$$
$$= k_{sU} + (k_{sU} - k_d)(D/S).$$

Here the subscripts L and U designate levered and unlevered firms in a given risk class, and Proposition II states that as the firm's use of debt increases, its cost of equity also rises, and in an exactly specified manner.

Taken together, the two MM propositions imply that the inclusion of more debt in the capital structure will not increase the value of the firm because the benefits of cheaper debt will be exactly offset by an increase in the cost of equity. *Thus, the basic MM theory states that in a world without taxes, both the value of a firm and its cost of capital are completely unaffected by its capital structure.*

Proof of the MM Propositions without Corporate Taxes

Proof of Proposition I. MM use an *arbitrage proof* to support their propositions. They show that, under their assumptions, if two companies differ only (1) in the way they are financed and (2) in their total market values, then investors will sell shares of the overvalued firm, buy those of the undervalued firm, and continue this process until the companies have exactly the same market value. To illustrate, assume that two firms, Firm L (for levered) and Firm U (for unlevered), are identical in all important respects except financial structure. Firm L has $4,000,000 of 7.5 percent debt, while Firm U is all equity financed. Both firms have EBIT = $900,000, and σ_{EBIT} is the same for both firms, so they are in the same risk class.

In the initial situation, before any arbitrage occurs, assume that both firms have an equity capitalization rate of $k_{sU} = k_{sL} = 10\%$. Under this condition, according to Equation 11-1, the following situation would exist:

Firm U:

$$\begin{array}{l}\text{Value of} \\ \text{Firm U's} = S_U = \dfrac{\text{EBIT} - k_dD}{k_{sU}} = \dfrac{\$900,000 - 0}{0.10} = \$9,000,000. \\ \text{stock}\end{array}$$

$$\begin{array}{l}\text{Total market} \\ \text{value of} \quad = V_U = D_U + S_U = \$0 + \$9,000,000 = \$9,000,000. \\ \text{Firm U}\end{array}$$

Firm L:

$$\begin{array}{l}\text{Value of} \\ \text{Firm L's} = S_L = \dfrac{\text{EBIT} - k_dD}{k_{sU}} \\ \text{stock}\end{array}$$

$$= \dfrac{\$900,000 - 0.075(\$4,000,000)}{0.10} = \$6,000,000.$$

$$\begin{array}{l}\text{Total market} \\ \text{value of} \quad = V_L = D_L + S_L = \$4,000,000 + \$6,000,000 = \$10,000,000. \\ \text{Firm L}\end{array}$$

Thus, before arbitrage, the value of the levered company, Firm L, exceeds that of unlevered Firm U.

MM argue that this is a disequilibrium situation which cannot persist. To see why, suppose you owned 10 percent of L's stock, so the market value of your investment is $600,000. According to MM, you could increase your total investment income, without increasing your financial risk, by (1) selling your stock in L for $600,000, (2) borrowing an amount equal to 10 percent of L's debt ($400,000), and then (3) buying 10 percent of U's stock for $900,000. Notice that you would receive $1 million from the sale of your 10 percent of L's stock plus your borrowing, and you would be spending only $900,000 on U's stock, so you would have $100,000 which could be invested in riskless debt to yield 7.5 percent, or $7,500 annually.

Now consider your income position:

Old Income:	10% of L's $600,000 equity income		$60,000
New Income:	10% of U's $900,000 equity income	$90,000	
	Less 7.5% interest on $400,000 loan	(30,000)	60,000
	Plus 7.5% interest on extra $100,000		7,500
	New net income		$67,500

Thus, your net investment income from common stock would be exactly the same as before, $60,000, but you would have $100,000 left over for investment in riskless debt, which would increase your income by $7,500. Therefore, the total return on your $600,000 net worth would rise. Further, your risk, according to MM, would be the same as before—you would have simply substituted $400,000 of "homemade" leverage for your 10 percent share of Firm L's $4 million of corporate leverage, and hence neither your "effective" debt nor your risk would have changed.

MM argue that this arbitrage process would actually occur, with sales of L's stock driving its price down, and purchases of U's stock driving its price up, until the market values of the two firms were equal. Until this equality was established, there would be gains to be had from switching from one stock to the other, so the profit motive would force the equality to be reached. When equilibrium was established, the NOI conditions would be fulfilled, and the values of Firms L and U, and their average costs of capital, would be equal. Thus, according to Modigliani and Miller, V and k_a must be independent of capital structure under equilibrium conditions.

Proof of Proposition II. Earlier in the chapter, we noted that Equation 11-1a could be used to find the cost of equity for a zero-growth company. Here is Equation 11-1a with $T = 0$, and substituting k_{sL} for k_s to denote the use of leverage:

$$k_{sL} = \frac{(EBIT - k_dD)}{S}. \tag{11-1a}$$

From the Proposition I equation, plus the fact that $V = S + D$, we can write

$$V = S + D = \frac{EBIT}{k_{sU}}.$$

This equation can be rearranged as follows:

$$EBIT = k_{sU}(S + D).$$

Now, substitute this expression for EBIT in Equation 11-1a:

$$k_{sL} = \frac{k_{sU}(S + D) - k_dD}{S}$$

$$= \frac{k_{sU}S}{S} + \frac{k_{sU}D}{S} - \frac{k_dD}{S}.$$

Simplifying, we obtain this expression:

$$k_{sL} = k_{sU} + (k_{sU} - k_d)(D/S).$$

This is the Proposition II equation we sought to prove.

When taxes are introduced, MM derive a new set of propositions. With corporate income taxes, they conclude that leverage will increase a firm's value because interest on debt is a deductible expense, and hence more of the operating income flows through to investors. Here are the MM propositions for corporations subject to income taxes.

MM with
Corporate Taxes

Proposition I. The value of an unlevered firm is the firm's after-tax operating income divided by its cost of equity,

$$V_U = \frac{EBIT(1 - T)}{k_{sU}},\qquad\text{(11-4)}$$

while the value of a levered firm is equal to the value of an unlevered firm of the same risk class plus the value of the tax savings:

$$V_L = V_U + TD.\qquad\text{(11-5)}$$

Here T is the corporate tax rate. The important point here is that when corporate taxes are introduced, the value of the levered firm exceeds that of the unlevered firm. Additionally, the differential increases as the use of debt increases, so a firm's value is maximized at virtually 100 percent debt financing.

Proposition II. The cost of equity to a levered firm is equal to the cost of equity to an unlevered firm in the same risk class plus a risk premium which depends on both the degree of financial leverage and the corporate tax rate:

$$k_{sL} = k_{sU} + (k_{sU} - k_d)(1 - T)(D/S).\qquad\text{(11-6)}$$

Thus, according to Proposition II with taxes, as the firm's use of debt increases, its cost of equity also rises, and in an exactly specified manner. However, in the tax situation, the cost of equity rises at a slower rate than it did in the absence of taxes. It is this characteristic that produces the increase in firm value as leverage increases as shown in Proposition I. The proofs of Propositions I and II with taxes are given in Appendix 11A.

To illustrate the MM model, we assume that the following data and conditions hold for Mid-State Water Company, an old, established firm that supplies water to business and residential customers in several low-growth midwestern metropolitan areas.

Illustration of the
MM Model with
Corporate Taxes

1. Mid-State currently has no debt; it is an all equity company.
2. Expected EBIT = $4,000,000. EBIT is not expected to increase over time, so Mid-State is in a no-growth situation.

3. Mid-State has a 40 percent tax rate, so T = 40%.

4. Mid-State pays out all of its income as dividends.

5. If Mid-State begins to use debt, it can borrow at a rate k_d = 8%. This borrowing rate is constant, and it is independent of the amount of debt used. Any money raised by selling debt would be used to retire common stock, so Mid-State's assets would remain constant.

6. The risk of Mid-State's assets, and thus its EBIT, is such that its shareholders require a rate of return, k_{sU}, of 12 percent if no debt is used.

When Mid-State has zero debt, its value is found, by applying Equation 11-4, to be $20 million:

$$V_U = \frac{EBIT(1 - T)}{k_{sU}} = \frac{\$4 \text{ million}(0.6)}{0.12} = \$20.0 \text{ million}.$$

With $10 million of debt, we see by Equation 11-5 that total market value rises to $24 million:

$$V_L = V_U + TD = \$20 \text{ million} + 0.4(\$10 \text{ million}) = \$24 \text{ million}.$$

Therefore, the value of Mid-State's stock must be $14 million:

$$S = V - D = \$24 \text{ million} - \$10 \text{ million} = \$14 \text{ million}.$$

We can also find Mid-State's cost of equity, k_{sL}, and its weighted average cost of capital, k_a, at a debt level of $10 million. First, we use Equation 11-6 to find k_{sL}, Mid-State's leveraged cost of equity:

$$
\begin{aligned}
k_{sL} &= k_{sU} + (k_{sU} - k_d)(1 - T)(D/S) \\
&= 12\% + (12\% - 8\%)(0.6)(\$10 \text{ million}/\$14 \text{ million}) \\
&= 12\% + 1.71\% = 13.71\%.
\end{aligned}
$$

Now we can find the company's weighted average cost of capital, k_a:

$$
\begin{aligned}
k_a &= (D/V)(k_d)(1 - T) + (S/V)k_s \\
&= (\$10/\$24)(8\%)(0.6) + (\$14/\$24)(13.71\%) = 10\%.
\end{aligned}
$$

Alternatively, we could have found k_a as follows:

$$
\begin{aligned}
k_a &= \frac{EBIT(1 - T)}{V} = \frac{\$4 \text{ million}(0.6)}{\$24 \text{ million}} \\
&= 0.10 = 10\%.
\end{aligned}
$$

Mid-State's value and cost of capital at other debt levels are shown in Figure 11-2. Here we see that in an MM world with taxes, financial le-

Figure 11-2
Effects of Leverage:
MM with Taxes (Millions of Dollars)

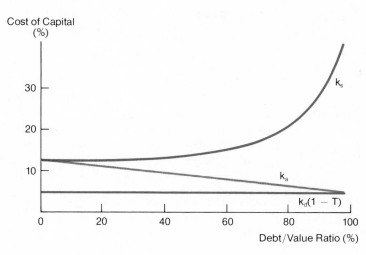

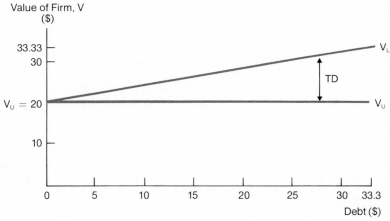

D (1)	V (2)	S (3)	D/V (4)	k_d (5)	k_s (6)	k_a (7)
$ 0	$20.00	$20.00	0.00%	8.0%	12.00%	12.00%
5	22.00	17.00	22.73	8.0	12.71	10.91
10	24.00	14.00	41.67	8.0	13.71	10.00
15	26.00	11.00	57.69	8.0	15.27	9.23
20	28.00	8.00	71.43	8.0	18.00	8.57
25	30.00	5.00	83.33	8.0	24.00	8.00
30	32.00	2.00	93.75	8.0	48.00	7.50
33.33[a]	33.33	0.00	100.00	12.0	—	12.00

[a]The case of 100 percent debt is the theoretically limiting case. See Footnote 4 for a discussion.

verage does matter—the value of the firm is maximized, and its cost of capital is minimized, if it uses virtually 100 percent debt financing.[4]

Criticisms of the MM Model

MM's conclusions follow logically from their initial assumptions—if their assumptions are correct, then their conclusions must be reached. However, academicians and financial executives have voiced concern over the validity of the MM propositions because of the fact that virtually no firms follow their recommendations. MM's theory leads to the conclusion that to maximize value, firms should use 100 percent debt. If MM's theory were correct, then competition would force firms to act as the theory suggests. However, firms clearly do not use 100 percent debt. Therefore, people who disagree with the MM theory and its suggestions for financial policy generally attack them on the grounds that their assumptions are unrealistic. Some of the main objections are listed below:

1. The MM analysis implies that personal and corporate leverage are perfect substitutes. However, an individual investing in a levered firm has less loss exposure, which means a more *limited liability*, than if he or she used "homemade" leverage. In our earlier illustration of the MM arbitrage argument, it should be noted that only the $600,000 our investor had in Firm L would be lost if that firm were to go bankrupt. However, if the investor engaged in arbitrage transactions and employed "homemade" leverage to invest in Firm U, then he or she could lose $900,000—the original $600,000 investment plus the $400,000 loan less the $100,000 investment in riskless bonds. This increased personal risk

---

[4]In the limiting case, where the firm used 100 percent debt financing, the bondholders would own the entire company, and hence they would have all the business risk. (Up until this point, MM assume that the stockholders have all of the risk.) If the bondholders have all of the risk, then the capitalization rate on the debt should be equal to the equity capitalization rate at zero debt, $k_d = k_{sU} = 12\%$.

The income stream to the stockholders in the all-equity case was $CF_U = \$4,000,000 (1 - T) = \$2,400,000$, and the value of the firm was

$$V_U = \frac{\$2,400,000}{0.12} = \$20,000,000.$$

With all debt, the entire $4,000,000 of EBIT would be used to pay interest charges. k_d would be 12%, so $I = 0.12(\text{Debt}) = \$4,000,000$. Taxes would be zero, and investors (bondholders) would get the entire $4,000,000 of operating income; they would not have to share it with the government. Thus, at 100 percent debt, the value of the firm would be

$$V_L = \frac{\$4,000,000}{0.12} = \$33,333,333 = D.$$

There is, of course, a transition problem in all this—MM assume that $k_d = 8\%$ regardless of how much debt the firm has until debt reaches 100 percent, at which point k_d jumps to 12 percent, the cost of equity. As we shall see later in the chapter, k_d realistically rises more or less continuously as the use of financial leverage increases.

exposure would tend to restrain investors from engaging in arbitrage, and that could cause the equilibrium values of V_L, V_U, k_{sL}, and k_{sU} to be different from those specified by the MM equations.

2. In the MM analysis, brokerage costs were assumed away, making the switch from L to U costless. However, brokerage and other transactions costs do exist, and they too impede the arbitrage process.

3. Restrictions on institutional investors may also retard the arbitrage process. Institutional investors dominate the stock markets today, but most institutional investors cannot legally borrow to buy stocks, and hence they are prohibited from engaging in homemade leverage.

4. MM assume that both corporations and investors can borrow at the risk-free rate. Although, as noted in the next section, risky debt has been introduced into the analysis, it is still necessary to assume that both corporations and investors can borrow at the same rate. Although major institutional investors could probably borrow at the corporate rate, many institutions are not allowed to borrow to buy securities. Further, most individual investors probably must borrow at higher rates than those paid by large corporations. Therefore, lower interest rates on corporate borrowings could prevent the arbitrage solution from working out to the exact MM solution.

5. A corporation with debt outstanding will use all available cash flows to service its debt and thus avoid bankruptcy. However, if an investor has used homemade leverage to take a position in an unlevered firm, and then the firm's cash flows decline, the investor may experience serious cash flow problems. The firm would probably reduce its dividends below the level the investor needs to service his or her debt, which could force the investor into bankruptcy even though the corporation's problem might be a short-term one. This too increases the relative riskiness of homemade leverage.

6. MM do not take account of personal income taxes, which amounts to implicitly assuming a zero personal tax rate. However, as noted later in the chapter, Miller addressed this issue in his later work.

7. MM assume that the cost of debt does not increase as the use of debt increases. Obviously, this is not a valid assumption, and relaxing it leads to some major alterations to the MM conclusions.

8. MM also assume that EBIT is a constant which is independent of the amount of debt a firm has outstanding. As we shall see, this assumption is invalid if the amount of debt exceeds certain limits.

It seems reasonable, in our search for a better capital structure theory, to begin by relaxing some of the MM assumptions. The assumption of risk-free debt is, perhaps, the most unrealistic of the MM assumptions.

Relaxing the MM Assumptions

Several authors have extended the MM analysis to include risky debt.[5] The introduction of risky debt, without bankruptcy costs, does not alter the basic MM propositions, and their conclusion that 100 percent debt is optimal still stands. However, as we explain below, when bankruptcy and agency costs are introduced along with risky debt, this does have a profound effect on the MM model, and the conclusion that 100 percent debt is optimal no longer holds.

Bankruptcy, Agency, and Related Costs

As we shall see in Chapter 25, quite a few firms go bankrupt each year, and the operations of many more businesses are affected by efforts to ward off bankruptcy. When bankruptcy occurs, several things happen:

1. Bankrupt firms are generally forced to sell assets at abnormally low prices. For example, we often hear of someone buying assets in a bankruptcy sale for say $1 million and then, a few months later, reselling them for $2 or $3 million.

2. Arguments between claimants may delay the liquidation of assets, thus leading to physical deterioration and/or obsolescence of inventories and fixed assets. Bankruptcy cases can take many years to settle, and during this time machinery rusts, buildings are vandalized, inventories become obsolete, and the like.

3. Lawyer's fees, court costs, and administrative expenses can absorb a large part of the firm's value. These costs are significant, but they are not as large as the first two cost elements.

4. Managers and other employees generally lose their jobs when a firm fails. Knowing this, the management of a firm that is in trouble may take actions which keep it alive in the short run but dilute long-run value. For example, the firm may defer maintenance of machinery, sell off valuable assets at bargain prices to raise cash, or cut costs so much that the quality of its products is impaired and the firm's long-run position is eroded.

5. Both customers and suppliers of companies that appear to be on the verge of bankruptcy are aware of the problems that can arise, and they often take "evasive action" that further damages the troubled firm. For example, Air Florida, as it struggled to avoid bankruptcy in 1984, was reported to be having trouble making sales because potential customers

---

[5]See Robert A. Haugen and James L. Pappas, "Equilibrium in the Pricing of Capital Assets, Risk-Bearing Debt Instruments, and the Question of Optimal Capital Structure," *Journal of Financial and Quantitative Analysis*, June 1971, 943-954; Joseph Stiglitz, "A Re-Examination of the Modigliani-Miller Theorem," *American Economic Review*, December 1969, 784-793; and Mark E. Rubenstein, "A Mean-Variance Synthesis of Corporate Financial Theory," *Journal of Finance*, March 1973, 167-181.

were worried about buying a seat for a future flight and then have the company fail before they could take the trip. Potential customers were also worried that the company did not have enough money to maintain its planes properly, and its suppliers were reluctant to grant normal credit terms, or to gear up to supply Air Florida with parts and other materials on a long-term basis. Further, Air Florida was having great difficulty obtaining capital. Finally, Air Florida had trouble attracting and retaining the highest quality workers; most workers prefer employment with a more stable airline to one that could go bankrupt any day. Indeed, Air Florida subsequently suspended operations and filed for bankruptcy under Chapter 11 of the Bankruptcy Act.

All things considered, the costs associated with both actual and potential bankruptcy are high.[6] Further, bankruptcy problems occur only if a firm has debts—debt-free firms just don't go bankrupt. *Therefore, the greater the use of debt financing, and the larger the fixed interest charges, the greater the probability that a decline in earnings will lead to bankruptcy, and hence the higher the probability of a bankruptcy-related loss of value.*

An increase in the probability of bankruptcy lowers the current value of a firm and raises its cost of capital. To see why, suppose we estimated that Mid-State Water would incur bankruptcy costs of $7 million if it failed at some future date, and that the *present value* of this possible future cost is $5 million. Suppose, further, that the probability of bankruptcy increases with leverage, causing the expected present value cost of bankruptcy to rise from zero at zero debt to $4.75 million at $30 million of debt as shown below:

		Amount of Debt		
	$0	$5 Million	$10 Million	$20 Million	$30 Million
Probability of bankruptcy	0.0	0.05	0.15	0.50	0.95
PV of expected costs of bankruptcy ($5 million times the indicated probability)	$0	$250,000	$750,000	$2,500,000	$4,750,000

These expected bankruptcy costs must be subtracted from the values we previously calculated in the lower section of Figure 11-2 to find the firm's value at various degrees of leverage—they would reduce the values of V and S in Columns 2 and 3, and, as a result, would raise k_s and k_a in Columns 6 and 7. For example, at $20 million of debt, we would

---

[6]See Edward I. Altman, "A Further Empirical Investigation of the Bankruptcy Cost Question," *Journal of Finance*, September 1984, 1067-1089. Based on a recent sample of 26 bankrupt companies, Altman found that bankruptcy costs often exceeded 20 percent of firm value.

Table 11-1
Effects of Bankruptcy
(Millions of Dollars)

	Figure 11-2 Values at D = $20 Million with Bankruptcy Effects Ignored: Pure MM	Figure 11-2 Values at D = $20 Million with Bankruptcy Effects Considered: Modified MM
V	$28.00	$28.00 − $2.5 = $25.5
S	$8.00	$8.00 − $2.5 = $5.5
k_s	18.00%	26.18%
k_a	8.57%	9.41%

obtain the values in Table 11-1.[7] These changes would, of course, then have carry-through effects on the graphs in Figure 11-2—most important, they would (1) reduce the decline of the k_a line and (2) reduce the slope of the V_L line. We shall modify Figure 11-2 for bankruptcy costs shortly, but it is useful to first look at other factors which also affect the graph.

Interest Rates

MM assume that k_d is a constant irrespective of how much debt a firm uses. This is not realistic—beyond some moderate amount of debt, as the debt ratio rises, so will the interest rate on that debt. This will not affect EBIT, but it will cause a reduction in both S and V, and this in turn will cause k_s and k_a to rise. Thus, recognizing that k_d increases with leverage causes several elements in Figure 11-2 to change.

Effects of Leverage on Expected EBIT

Modigliani and Miller assumed that EBIT is a constant and is independent of the degree of financial leverage. This assumption is correct if the firm uses only a moderate amount of debt, but as we discussed above in connection with Air Florida, if debt becomes excessive, expected EBIT will fall for a number of reasons. First, firms with high debt ratios find it difficult to obtain operating capital when money gets tight or when the economy is weak. Such firms may have to pass up favorable investment opportunities or even curtail normal operations because of financial problems. Second, the management of firms with excessive leverage

---

[7]To find k_s and k_a in Table 11-1, apply Equations 11-1a and 11-2, respectively:

$$k_s = \frac{(EBIT - k_dD)(1 - T)}{S} = \frac{[\$4 - 0.08(\$20)](1 - 0.4)}{\$5.5} = 26.18\%.$$

$$k_a = (D/V)(k_d)(1 - T) + (S/V)(k_s)$$
$$= (20/25.5)(8\%)(0.6) + (5.5/25.5)(26.18\%)$$
$$= 3.76\% + 5.65\% = 9.41\%.$$

have to devote most of their time and energy to raising the capital needed for survival rather than to running the company. Finally, firms whose excessive debt places them in danger of bankruptcy have a problem retaining good managers, employees, and customers.

Agency Costs

We introduced agency problems and agency costs in Chapter 1. One type of agency cost is associated with the use of debt, and the relationship between a firm's stockholders and its bondholders. In the absence of any restrictions, a firm's management might take actions that would benefit stockholders at the expense of bondholders. For example, if Mid-State Water were to sell only a small amount of debt, then this debt would have relatively little risk, and hence a high bond rating and a low interest rate. Yet, having sold the low-risk debt, Mid-State could then issue more debt secured by the same assets as the original debt. This would raise the risks faced by *all bondholders*, cause k_d to rise, and consequently cause the original bondholders to suffer capital losses. Or suppose, after issuing a substantial amount of debt, Mid-State decided to restructure its assets, selling off assets with low business risk and acquiring assets that were more risky but which had higher expected rates of return. If things worked out well, the stockholders would benefit. If things went sour, most of the loss in a highly leveraged firm would fall on the bondholders. In other words, the stockholders would be playing a game of "heads, I win; tails, you lose" with the bondholders.

Because of the possibility that stockholders would try to take advantage of bondholders in these and other ways, bonds are protected by restrictive covenants. These covenants hamper the corporation's legitimate operations to some extent, and further, the company must be monitored to insure that the covenants are being obeyed. The costs of lost efficiency plus monitoring are what we mean here by the term *agency costs,* and the existence of these costs reduces the advantage of debt.[8]

Value and the Cost of Capital with Bankruptcy and Related Costs

Under the MM assumptions with corporate taxes, a firm's value would rise continuously as it moved from zero debt toward 100 percent debt: the equation $V_L = V_U + TD$ shows that TD, and hence V_L, is maximized if D is at a maximum. Recall that the rising component of value, TD, results directly from the shelter provided by the debt interest. However, the following factors, which were ignored by MM, could all cause

---

[8]Jensen and Meckling point out that there are also agency costs between outside equity holders and management, just as there are between bondholders and equity holders. See "Theory of the Firm: Managerial Behavior, Agency Costs, and Ownership Structure," *Journal of Financial Economics,* October 1976, 305-360. Their study further suggests that (1) bondholder agency costs increase as the debt ratio increases, but (2) outside stockholder agency costs move in reverse fashion, falling with increased use of debt.

V_L to decline with increases in debt: (1) the present value of potential future bankruptcy, (2) the effects of high leverage and a weak balance sheet on expected future EBIT, (3) agency costs, and (4) a higher corporate interest rate at high debt levels. Therefore, the true relationship between a firm's value and its use of leverage looks like this:

$$V_L = V_U + TD - \begin{pmatrix} PV\ of \\ expected \\ bankruptcy \\ costs \end{pmatrix} - \begin{pmatrix} Reduction \\ in\ value \\ from\ lower \\ EBIT \end{pmatrix}$$

$$- \begin{pmatrix} Reduction \\ in\ value \\ from\ agency \\ costs \end{pmatrix} - \begin{pmatrix} Reduction\ in \\ value\ from \\ increased \\ cost\ of\ debt \end{pmatrix}. \quad (11\text{-}7)$$

The relationship expressed in Equation 11-7 is graphed in Figure 11-3. The tax shelter effect totally dominates until the debt ratio reaches Point A. After Point A, bankruptcy and related costs become increasingly important, offsetting some of the tax advantages. At Point B, the marginal tax shelter benefits of additional debt are exactly offset by the

Figure 11-3
Net Effects of Leverage
on the Value of the Firm

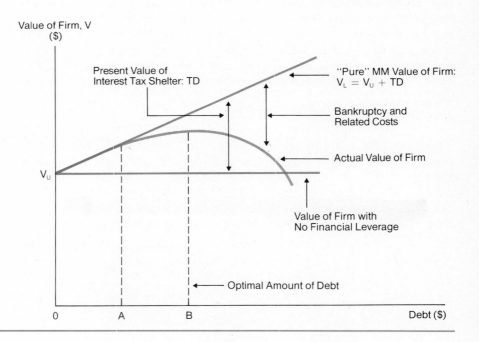

disadvantages of debt, and beyond Point B, the disadvantages outweigh the tax benefits.

The tax benefits, TD, can be estimated relatively precisely, but the value reduction resulting from potential bankruptcy, lower expected EBIT, agency costs, and higher interest expenses cannot be measured with much precision at all.[9] We know these costs must increase as leverage rises, but we do not know the exact functional relationship. Further, the functional relationship almost certainly varies among firms and industries, and even for a given firm over time. For example, if Mid-State Water had less business risk than most other firms, then Mid-State could carry more debt before the threat of bankruptcy and/or reduced expected EBIT became serious problems. Thus, Mid-State could afford to use more debt and to take advantage of more interest tax shelter than could the average firm. In terms of Figure 11-3, its Point B would be further to the right, and its optimal debt/value would be higher.

Similarly, if one firm uses assets which make good collateral for mortgage bonds, it can have a higher debt ratio without having to worry too much about agency costs, while another firm which uses most of its funds for research and development, and hence has fewer mortgageable assets, would have a lower optimal debt ratio.[10] Mortgageable assets are

---

[9]Even the tax benefits may be different from TD. If brokerage and other transactions costs, a higher interest rate on personal versus corporate debt, concerns about limited liability, and so on impede arbitrage, then (1) corporate leverage would be better than "homemade" leverage, (2) this would cause the slope of the line labeled "Pure MM Value" in Figure 11-3 to increase, and (3) this in turn would increase the optimal debt ratio for the firm. However, as we shall see in the next section, personal income taxes offset these factors to some extent, and thus decrease the optimal capital structure somewhat.

[10]In 1983, the Washington Public Power Supply System, generally known as WHOOPS, went into default on $2.25 billion of bonds that had been sold to finance two nuclear power plants. The system consisted primarily of a consortium of local governmental units (essentially, small cities), which had guaranteed the bonds. Major construction cost overruns occurred, and the demand for power dropped below demand forecasts that had been made in the 1970s, when the consortium was organized and the plants were begun. These changed conditions combined to make the plants a bad deal for the cities that had contracted to build them.

At this point, the cities that had set up WHOOPS decided to back out of the deal. They argued that their elected representatives did not actually have the authority to sign the agreements they had earlier signed, and on this basis, the city governments simply reneged on their promise to pay interest and principal on the bonds, forcing the bonds into default. The cities' position was upheld by the State of Washington's courts, and at this time (Summer 1984), it appears that the bondholders will end up with a $2.25 billion loss. (The bonds have declined in value from $1,000 to about $120, with the $120 based mainly on the hope of a federal bailout or a reversal of the last court decision.)

Now that cities in Washington State have demonstrated both a willingness and the ability to renege on contracts, their costs of borrowing have gone up substantially. For example, in August 1983, the city of Seattle, which was not even one of the WHOOPS partners, had to pay three-quarters of a percentage point more on a new debt issue than similarly rated cities outside the region were paying. Further, there have been ripple effects all across the country. For example, a North Carolina consortium set up similarly to the Washington Power Supply System had to withdraw a bond offering because of a lack of bidders. The WHOOPS experience is an excellent example of agency problems, and it has led to a sharp increase in agency costs associated with all state and local government borrowings.

said to have a greater "debt-carrying capacity" than assets such as capitalized R&D costs. As we noted in Chapter 10, some consideration should be given to debt capacity in the capital budgeting process, if it is important in individual cases.

The Miller Model

Although MM included *corporate* taxes in the second version of their model, they did not extend the model to include *personal* tax effects. However, in his 1976 presidential address to the American Finance Association, Merton Miller did introduce a model designed to show how leverage affects firm value when both personal and corporate taxes are taken into account.[11] To explain Miller's model, let us begin by defining T_c as the corporate tax rate, T_s as the personal tax rate on stock income, and T_d as the personal tax rate on debt income. Note that stock returns come partly as dividends and partly as capital gains, so T_s is a weighted average of the tax rates on dividends and capital gains, while essentially all debt income comes from interest, which is all taxed at the top rates.

With personal taxes included, the value of an unlevered firm with a constant cash flow is found as follows:

$$V_U = \frac{\text{EBIT}(1 - T_c)(1 - T_s)}{k_{sU}}. \tag{11-8}$$

The $(1 - T_s)$ term adjusts for personal taxes. Therefore, the numerator shows how much of the firm's operating income is left after the firm itself pays corporate income taxes and the investors subsequently pay personal taxes on dividend and capital gains. Since the introduction of personal taxes lowers the numerator, these taxes are seen to reduce the value of the unlevered firm.

Moving on to the levered firm, we first partition its annual cash flows, CF_L, into those going to the stockholders and to the bondholders as follows:

$$CF_L = \text{Net CF to stockholders} \quad + \quad \begin{array}{c}\text{Net CF to}\\ \text{bondholders}\end{array} \tag{11-9}$$
$$= (\text{EBIT} - I)(1 - T_c)(1 - T_s) + I(1 - T_d).$$

Here I is the annual interest payment.

Equation 11-9 can be rearranged as follows:

$$CF_L = \text{EBIT}(1 - T_c)(1 - T_s) - I(1 - T_c)(1 - T_s) + I(1 - T_d). \tag{11-9a}$$

The first term in Equation 11-9a is merely the after-tax cash flow of an unlevered term, and the present value of this term is found by discounting the perpetual cash flow by k_{sU}. The second and third terms, which

---

[11]See Merton H. Miller, "Debt and Taxes," *Journal of Finance*, May 1977, 261–275.

reflect leverage, result from the cash flows produced by interest payments. These two cash flows are assumed to be of equal risk as the basic interest rate stream, and hence their present values are obtained by dividing by the cost of debt, k_d. Combining the present values of the three terms, we obtain this value for the levered firm:

$$V_L = \frac{EBIT(1 - T_c)(1 - T_s)}{k_{sU}} - \frac{I(1 - T_c)(1 - T_s)}{k_d} + \frac{I(1 - T_d)}{k_d}. \qquad \textbf{(11-10)}$$

The first term in Equation 11-10 is equal to V_U as set forth in Equation 11-8, and we can consolidate the second two terms:

$$V_L = V_U + \frac{I(1 - T_d)}{k_d}\left[1 - \frac{(1 - T_c)(1 - T_s)}{(1 - T_d)}\right]. \qquad \textbf{(11-10a)}$$

Now recognize that the after-tax perpetual interest payment divided by the required rate of return on debt, $I(1 - T_d)/k_d$, equals the market value of the debt, D. Substituting D into the preceding equation, and putting it at the end, we obtain this expression:

$$V_L = V_U + \left[1 - \frac{(1 - T_c)(1 - T_s)}{(1 - T_d)}\right]D. \qquad \textbf{(11-10b)}$$

Equation 11-10b is the very important Miller Model.

The Miller Model has several significant implications:

1. The term in brackets,

$$\left[1 - \frac{(1 - T_c)(1 - T_s)}{(1 - T_d)}\right],$$

multiplied by D is the gain from leverage. The bracketed term replaces the factor $T = T_c$ in the earlier MM model with corporate taxes.

2. If we ignore all taxes, that is, if $T_c = T_s = T_d = 0$, then the bracketed term reduces to zero, which is the same as the original MM model without corporate taxes.

3. If we ignore personal taxes, that is, if $T_s = T_d = 0$, then the bracketed term reduces to $[1 - (1 - T_c)] = T_c$, which is the same as in the MM model with corporate taxes.

4. If the personal tax rates on stock and bond incomes were equal, that is, if $T_s = T_d$, then the bracketed term would again reduce to T_c.

5. However, under U.S. tax laws, the personal tax rate on stock is less than the personal tax rate on bonds due to the favorable treatment of capital gains. Thus, $T_s < T_d$. Under this condition, the bracketed term is less than T_c, and the value of debt is less than would be true in the absence of personal taxes.

6. If $(1 - T_c)(1 - T_s) = (1 - T_d)$, then the value of debt to the firm would be reduced to zero. Here, the tax advantage of debt to the firm

would be exactly offset by the personal tax advantage of equity. Miller himself took this position, which implies that there is no advantage to a firm's use of debt. Thus, Miller's 1977 paper leads to the same conclusion as his and Modigliani's 1958 no-tax position, namely, that capital structure has no effect on a firm's value or its cost of capital.

7. Miller did go on to argue that there is an optimal level of corporate debt in the aggregate and that aggregate corporate debt will somehow reach the optimal level. Still, for any individual firm, one capital structure should, according to Miller, be as good as any other.

Others have extended and tested Miller's 1977 analysis. Generally, these extensions disagree with Miller's earlier conclusion that there is no advantage whatever from the use of corporate debt. In all probability, based on the most recently available empirical evidence, the product $(1 - T_c)(1 - T_s)$ is less than $(1 - T_d)$, and this condition gives rise to some tax advantage to the use of corporate debt. However, Miller's 1977 work does show that the tax advantages of debt are clearly less than were implied in the original MM with-tax article.

The Current View of Financial Leverage

The great contribution of MM and their followers was that they specifically identified the benefits and costs of using debt—the tax effects, bankruptcy costs, EBIT effects, agency costs, and interest rate effects. Prior to MM, no good capital structure theory existed, so we had no way of rationally considering just how much debt a firm should use.

The current view of most authorities is captured in Figure 11-4. The top graph shows the relationship between the debt ratio and the costs of debt, equity, and the average cost of capital. Both k_s and $k_d(1 - T)$ rise steadily with increases in leverage, but the rate of increase accelerates at higher debt levels, reflecting the increased likelihood of bankruptcy and its related costs and effects on EBIT. The weighted average cost first declines, then hits a minimum at D/V*, and then begins to rise. Note, however, that the k_a curve is shaped more like a shallow bowl than like a sharp V, indicating that over a fairly wide range the debt ratio does not have a pronounced effect on the average cost of capital.

The bottom graph in Figure 11-4 shows the general relationship between the value of the firm and its debt ratio. This graph is similar to the "actual value" line in Figure 11-3. Notice that the same debt ratio which minimizes the weighted average cost of capital also maximizes the firm's value. Thus, the optimal capital structure can be defined in terms of cost minimization or value maximization, for the same capital structure does both.

It is interesting to note that Figure 11-4 looks very much like the graphs on the right side of Figure 11-1, which represent the traditional position. Although the traditionalists did not state very clearly why they

Therefore, establishing the target capital structure remains a matter of informed judgment. However, as we shall see in the next chapter, the theory as set forth in this chapter can help when we attempt to set the target capital structure.

11-1 Define each of the following terms:

    a. Leverage
    b. Net income (NI) theory
    c. Net operating income (NOI) theory
    d. Traditional theory
    e. MM Proposition I without corporate taxes; with corporate taxes
    f. MM Proposition II without corporate taxes; with corporate taxes
    g. MM with taxes plus bankruptcy, agency, and related costs
    h. Miller model

Questions

11-2 Explain why agency costs would probably be more of a problem for a large, publicly owned firm that uses both debt and equity capital than for a small, unleveraged, owner-managed firm.

11-3 Use Equation 11-3 to explain why the capital structure which maximizes a firm's value must also minimize its weighted average cost of capital.

11-4 The stock of Gentech Company is currently selling at its low for the year, but management feels that the stock price is only temporarily depressed because of investor pessimism. The firm's capital budget this year is so large that the use of new outside equity is contemplated. However, management does not want to sell new stock at the current low price and is therefore considering a temporary departure from its "optimal" capital structure by borrowing the funds it would otherwise have raised in the equity markets. Does this seem to be a wise move?

11-5 Explain, in words, how MM use the arbitrage process to prove the validity of Proposition I. Also, list the major MM assumptions and explain why each of these assumptions is necessary in the arbitrage proof.

11-6 A utility company is supposed to be allowed to charge prices high enough to cover all costs, including its cost of capital. Public service commissions are supposed to take actions to stimulate companies to operate as efficiently as possible in order to keep costs, and hence prices, as low as possible. In the mid-1960s, AT&T's debt ratio was about 33 percent. Some people (Myron J. Gordon in particular) argued that a higher debt ratio would lower AT&T's cost of capital and permit it to charge lower rates for telephone service. Gordon thought an optimal debt ratio for AT&T was about 50 percent. How would people who believe in the NI, NOI, MM, and MM with bankruptcy cost theories react to this controversy?

ST-1 Nadir, Inc., is an unlevered firm, and it has constant expected operating earnings (EBIT) of $2 million per year. Nadir's tax rate is 40 percent, and its market value is $V = S = \$12$ million. Management is considering the use of debt. (Debt would be issued and used to buy

Self-Test Problem

back stock, so the size of the firm would remain constant.) Since interest expense is tax deductible, the value of the firm would tend to increase as debt is added to the capital structure, but there would be an offset in the form of a rising risk of bankruptcy. The firm's analysts have estimated, as an approximation, that the present value of any future bankruptcy cost is $8 million, and that the probability of bankruptcy would increase with leverage according to the following schedule:

Value of Debt	Probability of Failure
$ 2,500,000	0.00%
5,000,000	1.25
7,500,000	2.50
10,000,000	6.25
12,500,000	12.50
15,000,000	31.25
20,000,000	75.00

a. What is Nadir's cost of equity and average cost of capital at this time?
b. According to the "pure" MM after-tax valuation model, what is the optimal level of debt?
c. What is the optimal capital structure when bankruptcy costs are included?
d. Plot the value of the firm, with and without bankruptcy costs, as a function of the level of debt.

Problems

11-1 The three early approaches to capital structure theory are (1) the net income (NI) approach, (2) the net operating income (NOI) approach, and (3) the traditional approach. Assuming no taxes, answer the following questions.
a. What assumptions must be made to support each theory?
b. Draw graphs which show the relationships among a firm's capital costs, its value, and its use of leverage.
c. What do these graphs suggest about the optimal capital structure?
d. Which theory do MM support?

11-2 Companies U and L are identical in every respect except that U is unlevered while L has $10 million of 5 percent bonds outstanding. Assume (1) that all of the MM assumptions are met, (2) that the tax rate is 40 percent, (3) that EBIT is $2 million, and (4) that the equity capitalization rate for Company U is 10 percent.
a. What value would MM estimate for each firm?
b. Suppose V_U = $8 million and V_L = $18 million. According to MM, do these values represent an equilibrium? If not, explain the process by which equilibrium will be restored. No calculations are necessary.
c. What is k_s for Firm U? For Firm L?
d. What is k_a for Firm U? For Firm L?

11-3 MM, in their article, prove that a firm should accept new capital projects only if the project's IRR is greater than $k_{sU}[1 - T(D/V)]$. This expression is called the firm's *cut-off rate.*

    a. What is the cut-off rate for Firm U? For Firm L? (Refer to Problem 11-2 above.)

    b. How does this cut-off rate compare with the conventional IRR rule of accepting a project if its IRR is greater than the project's cost of capital? Assume that all projects have "average" risk. (Hint: Compare each firm's MM cut-off rate with its weighted average cost of capital, k_a.)

11-4 Overseas Enterprises, Inc., is just about to commence operations as an international trading company. The firm will have book assets of $10 million, and it expects to earn a 20 percent return on these assets before taxes. However, because of certain tax arrangements with foreign governments, OEI will not pay any taxes; that is, its tax rate will be zero. Management is trying to decide how to raise the required $10 million. It is known that the capitalization rate for an all-equity firm in this business is 10 percent; that is, $k_{sU} = 10\%$. Further, OEI can borrow at a rate $k_d = 6\%$. Part of the management team believes the NI theory of valuation is the correct one, while others are convinced that the NOI theory is valid.

    a. According to MM, what will be the value of OEI if it uses no debt and it uses $6 million of 6 percent debt?

    b. What are the values of k_a and k_s at debt levels of D = $0, D = $6 million, D = $10 million, and D = $20 million? Plot the relationships between the value of the firm and the debt ratio, and between the cost of capital and the debt ratio.

    c. Assume the initial facts of the problem ($k_d = 6\%$, EBIT = $2 million, $k_{sU} = 10\%$), but now assume that a 40 percent corporate tax rate exists. Find the new values for OEI with zero debt and with $6 million of debt, using the MM formulas.

    d. What are the values of k_a and k_s at debt levels of D = $0, D = $6 million, D = $10 million, and D = $20 million, assuming a 40 percent corporate tax rate? Plot the relationships between the value of the firm and the debt ratio, and between the cost of capital and the debt ratio.

    e. How would each of the following factors tend to change the values you plotted in your graph?

        (1) The interest rate on debt increases as the debt ratio rises.

        (2) At higher levels of debt, the probability of bankruptcy rises. This causes a reduction in expected EBIT.

11-5 Until recently, the Warren Company carried a triple-A bond rating and was strong in every respect. However, a series of problems has afflicted the firm: It is currently in severe financial distress, and its ability to make future payments on outstanding debt is questionable. If the firm were forced into bankruptcy at this time, the common stockholders would almost certainly be wiped out. Although Warren has limited financial resources, its cash flows (primarily from depreciation) are sufficient to support one of two mutually exclusive investments, each

costing $150 million and having a 10-year expected life. These projects
have the same market (or systematic) risk, but different total risk as
measured by the variance of returns. Each project has the following
after-tax cash flows for 10 years:

	Annual Cash Inflows	
Probability	Project A	Project B
0.5	$30,000,000	$10,000,000
0.5	35,000,000	50,000,000

Warren's weighted average cost of capital is 15 percent regardless of
which project it chooses.

a. What is the expected annual cash inflow from each project?

b. Which project has the greater total risk?

c. Which project would you choose if you were a Warren stockholder?
Why?

d. Which project would the bondholders prefer to see management
select? Why?

e. If the choices conflict, what "protection" do the bondholders have
against the firm's making a decision that is contrary to their interests?

f. Who bears the cost of this "protection"? How is this cost related to
leverage and the optimal capital structure?

11-6 Baxter, Inc., currently has no debt. An in-house research group has
just been assigned the job of determining whether the firm should
change its capital structure. Because of the importance of the decision,
management has also hired the investment banking firm of Stanley
Morgan & Company to conduct a parallel analysis of the situation. Mr.
Smith, the in-house analyst, who is well versed in modern finance
theory, has decided to carry out the analysis using the MM framework. Mr. Jones, the Stanley Morgan consultant, who has a good
knowledge of capital market conditions and is confident of his ability
to predict the firm's debt and equity costs at various levels of debt, has
decided to estimate the optimal capital structure as that structure
which minimizes the firm's weighted average cost of capital. The following data are relevant to both analyses:

EBIT = $4 million per year, in perpetuity.

Tax rate = 40%.

Dividend payout ratio = 100%.

Current required rate of return on equity = 12%.

The cost of capital schedule predicted by Mr. Jones follows:

	At a Debt Level of (Millions of Dollars)							
	$0	$2	$4	$6	$8	$10	$12	$14
Interest rate	8.0%	8.0	8.3	9.0	10.0	11.0	13.0	16.0
Cost of equity	12.0	12.25	12.75	13.0	13.15	13.4	14.65	17.0

Mr. Smith estimated the present value of bankruptcy-related costs at
$8 million. Additionally, he estimated the following probabilities of
bankruptcy:

	At a Debt Level of (Millions of Dollars)							
	$0	$2	$4	$6	$8	$10	$12	$14
Probability of bankruptcy	0	0	0.05	0.07	0.10	0.17	0.47	0.90

a. What level of debt would Mr. Jones and Mr. Smith recommend as optimal?

b. Comment on the similarities and differences in their recommendations.

11-7 The Charles Corporation (CC), which uses no debt financing, has a firm value of $20 million. Its corporate tax rate is 46 percent. The firm's investors are estimated to have a marginal tax rate of 50 percent on interest income and a weighted average tax rate of 30 percent on dividend and capital gains income. The firm is planning to alter its current capital structure by issuing $10 million in perpetual debt and using these funds to repurchase $10 million of common stock.

a. According to the MM view with corporate taxes, what would be the value of CC after the capital structure change?

b. What would CC's value be according to Miller?

c. Discuss the reasons for the difference between your Part a and Part b answers.

d. How would your answers to Parts a and b be affected by the addition of bankruptcy-related costs?

Solution to Self-Test Problem

ST-1 a. Value of unlevered firm, $V_U = EBIT(1 - T)/k_{sU}$:

$$\$12 = \$2(1 - 0.4)/k_{sU}$$
$$\$12 = \$1.2/k_{sU}$$
$$k_{sU} = \$1.2/\$12 = 10.0\%.$$

Therefore, $k_{sU} = k_a = 10.0\%$.

b. Value of levered firm according to MM model with taxes:

$$V_L = V_U + TD.$$

As shown in the table below, value increases continuously with debt, and the optimal capital structure consists of 100 percent debt. Note: The table is not necessary to answer this question, but the data (in millions of dollars) are necessary for Part c of this problem.

Debt, D	V_U	TD	$V_L = V_U + TD$
$ 0	$12.0	$ 0	$12.0
2.5	12.0	1.0	13.0
5.0	12.0	2.0	14.0
7.5	12.0	3.0	15.0
10.0	12.0	4.0	16.0
12.5	12.0	5.0	17.0
15.0	12.0	6.0	18.0
20.0	12.0	8.0	20.0

c. With bankruptcy costs included in the analysis, the value of the levered firm is

$$V_B = V_U + TD - PC,$$

where

$$V_U + TD = \text{value according to MM after-tax model.}$$
$$P = \text{probability of bankruptcy.}$$
$$C = \text{present value of bankruptcy cost.}$$

D	$V_U + TD$	P	$PC = (P)\$8$	$V_B = V_U + TD - PC$
$ 0	$12.0	0	$ 0	$12.0
2.5	13.0	0	0	13.0
5.0	14.0	0.0125	0.10	13.9
7.5	15.0	0.0250	0.20	14.8
10.0	16.0	0.0625	0.50	15.5
12.5	17.0	0.1250	1.00	16.0
15.0	18.0	0.3125	2.50	15.5
20.0	20.0	0.7500	6.00	14.0

Optimal debt level: D = \$12.5 million.
Maximum value of firm: V = \$16.0 million.
Optimal debt/value ratio: D/V_L = \$12.5/\$16 = 78%.

d. Value of firm versus value of debt (millions of dollars):

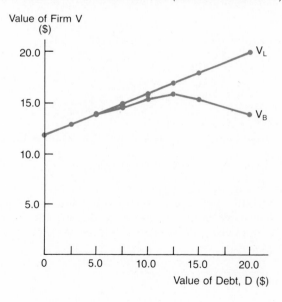

Selected
Additional
References

The body of literature on capital structure—and the number of potential references—is huge. There-fore, only a sampling can be given here. For an extensive review of the recent literature, as well as a detailed bibliography, see

Beranek, William, "Research Directions in Finance," *Quarterly Review of Business and Economics*, Spring 1981, 6-24.

The major theoretical works on capital structure theory, in the order of their appearance, include the following:

Durand, David, "Costs of Debt and Equity Funds for Business: Trends and Problems of Measurement," *Conference on Research in Business Finance*, National Bureau of Economic Research, New York, 1952.

Modigliani, Franco, and Merton H. Miller, "The Cost of Capital, Corporation Finance and the Theory of Investment," *American Economic Review*, June 1958, 261-297.

————, "The Cost of Capital, Corporation Finance and the Theory of Investment: Reply," *American Economic Review*, September 1958, 655-669; "Taxes and the Cost of Capital: A Correction," *American Economic Review*, June 1963, 433-443; "Reply," *American Economic Review*, June 1965, 524-527.

Miller, Merton H., "Debt and Taxes," *Journal of Finance*, May 1977, 261-275.

These works, and others, are discussed in an integrated framework in

Fama, Eugene F., and Merton H. Miller, *The Theory of Finance* (New York: Holt, Rinehart and Winston, 1972).

In addition to Miller's work, the effect of personal taxes on capital structure decisions has been addressed by

Gordon, Myron J., and Lawrence I. Gould, "The Cost of Equity Capital with Personal Income Taxes and Flotation Costs," *Journal of Finance*, September 1978, 1201-1212.

Some other references of note include the following:

Conine, Thomas E., Jr., "Debt Capacity and the Capital Budgeting Decision: Comment," *Financial Management*, Spring 1980, 20-22.

Ferri, Michael, and Wesley H. Jones, "Determinants of Financial Structure: A New Methodological Approach," *Journal of Finance*, June 1979, 631-644.

Flath, David, and Charles R. Knoeber, "Taxes, Failure Costs, and Optimal Industry Capital Structure," *Journal of Finance*, March 1980, 89-117.

Lee, Wayne Y., and Henry H. Barker, "Bankruptcy Costs and the Firm's Optimal Debt Capacity: A Positive Theory of Capital Structure," *Southern Economic Journal*, April 1977, 1453-1465.

Martin, John D., and David F. Scott, "Debt Capacity and the Capital Budgeting Decision: A Revisitation," *Financial Management*, Spring 1980, 23-26.

Schneller, Meir I., "Taxes and the Optimal Capital Structure of the Firm," *Journal of Finance*, March 1980, 119-127.

Taggart, Robert A., Jr., "Taxes and Corporate Capital Structure in an Incomplete Market," *Journal of Finance*, June 1980, 645-659.

Warner, Jerold B., "Bankruptcy Costs: Some Evidence," *Journal of Finance*, May 1977, 337-348.

There has been considerable discussion in the literature concerning a financial leverage clientele effect. Many theorists postulate that firms with low leverage are favored by high-tax bracket investors and vice versa. Two recent articles on this subject are

Harris, John M., Jr., Rodney L. Roenfeldt, and Philip L. Cooley, "Evidence of Financial Leverage Clienteles," *Journal of Finance*, September 1983, 1125-1132.

Kim, E. Han, "Miller's Equilibrium, Shareholder Leverage Clienteles, and Optimal Capital Leverage," *Journal of Finance*, May 1982, 301-319.

11A

Proof of the MM Propositions with Corporate Taxes

In Chapter 11, we presented proofs for the MM propositions under the assumption of no corporate taxes. However, the MM propositions with corporate taxes were presented without proofs. We present proofs of the MM propositions with corporate taxes in this appendix.

Proof of Proposition I

MM originally used an arbitrage proof similar to the one we gave in Chapter 11 to prove Proposition I without corporate taxes, but their points can be confirmed with a simpler alternate proof. First, assume that two firms are identical in all respects except capital structure. Firm U has no debt in its capital structure, while L uses debt. Expected EBIT and σ_{EBIT} are identical for each firm.

Under these assumptions, the operating cash flows available to Firm U's investors, CF_U, are

$$CF_U = EBIT(1 - T), \tag{11A-1}$$

while the cash flows to Firm L's investors (stockholders and bondholders) are

$$CF_L = (EBIT - k_dD)(1 - T) + k_dD. \tag{11A-2}$$

Equation 11A-2 can be rearranged as follows:

$$
\begin{aligned}
CF_L &= EBIT(1 - T) - k_dD + Tk_dD + k_dD \\
&= EBIT(1 - T) + Tk_dD.
\end{aligned} \tag{11A-2a}
$$

The first term in Equation 11A-2a, $EBIT(1 - T)$, is identical to Firm U's income, while the second term, Tk_dD, represents the tax savings, and hence the additional operating income that is available to Firm L's investors because of the fact that interest is deductible.

The value of the unlevered firm, V_U, may be determined by capitalizing its annual net income after corporate taxes, $CF_U = EBIT(1 - T)$, at its cost of equity:

$$V_U = \frac{CF_U}{k_{sU}} = \frac{EBIT(1 - T)}{k_{sU}}. \qquad \textbf{(11A-3)}$$

The value of the levered firm, on the other hand, is found by capitalizing both parts of its after-tax cash flows as expressed in Equation 11A-2a above. MM argue that because L's "regular" earnings stream is precisely as risky as the income of Firm U, it should be capitalized at the same rate, k_{sU}. However, they argue that the tax savings are more certain—these savings will occur as long as interest on the debt is paid, so the tax savings are exactly as risky as the firm's debt, which MM assume to be riskless. Therefore, the cash flows represented by the tax savings should be discounted at the risk-free rate, k_d. Thus, we obtain Equation 11A-4 for Firm L's value:

$$
\begin{aligned}
V_L &= \frac{EBIT(1 - T)}{k_{sU}} + \frac{Tk_dD}{k_d} \\
&= \frac{EBIT(1 - T)}{k_{sU}} + TD.
\end{aligned}
\qquad \textbf{(11A-4)}
$$

Since the first term in Equation 11A-4, $EBIT(1 - T)/k_{sU}$, is identical to V_U in Equation 11A-3, we may also express V_L as follows:

$$V_L = V_U + TD. \qquad \textbf{(11A-4a)}$$

Equation 11A-4a is MM's Proposition I with taxes. Thus, we see that the value of the levered firm exceeds that of the unlevered company, and the differential increases as the use of debt, D, goes up.

The value of a levered firm's equity may be found by use of Equation 11-1 in Chapter 11 as follows:

Proof of Proposition II

$$S_L = \frac{(EBIT - k_dD)(1 - T)}{k_{sL}}. \qquad \textbf{(11-1)}$$

Solving for k_{sL}, we obtain

$$k_{sL} = \frac{(EBIT - k_dD)(1 - T)}{S_L}, \qquad \textbf{(11-1a)}$$

which can be rewritten as

$$k_{sL} = \frac{EBIT(1 - T) - k_dD(1 - T)}{S_L}. \qquad \textbf{(11A-5)}$$

From Proposition I, Equation 11A-4, we know that

$$V_L = \frac{EBIT(1 - T)}{k_{sU}} + TD,$$

which can be rewritten as

$$V_L k_{sU} = EBIT(1 - T) + k_{sU}TD,$$

and hence as

$$EBIT(1 - T) = (V_L - TD)k_{sU}.$$

Now substitute this expression for $EBIT(1 - T)$ in Equation 11A-5:

$$k_{sL} = \frac{(V_L - TD)k_{sU} - k_dD(1 - T)}{S_L}$$

$$= \frac{V_Lk_{sU} - TDk_{sU} - k_dD + TDK_d}{S_L}.$$

Now recognize that $V_L = S_L + D$, and substitute for V_L in the preceding equation:

$$k_{sL} = \frac{(S_L + D)k_{sU} - TDk_{sU} - k_dD + TDk_d}{S_L}$$

$$= \frac{S_Lk_{sU} + Dk_{sU} - TDk_{sU} - k_dD + TDk_d}{S_L}$$

$$= \frac{S_Lk_{sU}}{S_L} + \frac{Dk_{sU} - TDk_{sU} - k_dD + TDk_d}{S_L}$$

$$= k_{sU} + (k_{sU} - Tk_{sU} - k_d + Tk_d)\frac{D}{S_L},$$

or

$$k_{sL} = k_{sU} + (k_{sU} - k_d)(1 - T)(D/S).$$

This last expression is the equation set forth in MM's Proposition II, and hence we have proved the proposition.

Capital Structure Policy

12

Several years ago, analysts at Chrysler Corporation reported that future earnings per share could be expected to double if the company financed its expansion program with debt rather than common equity. General Motors' analysts reached similar conclusions at about the same time. In each case, there were two principal reasons for the apparent advantage of debt: (1) The company's tax bill would be lower if it used debt, so more of its operating income would flow through to investors, and (2) the interest rate on debt (about 8 percent) was lower than the expected rate of return on new assets (about 15 percent), and stockholders would capture this differential if debt financing were used.

However, the Chrysler and GM analysts also reported that, while they *expected* EPS to be higher if more debt financing were used, the *actual* EPS would be lower if the targeted level of sales and operating profits were not attained. Thus, increasing the use of debt would increase the firms' risk as well as their expected profitability. Chrysler's management decided to take the gamble, and to "reach out for speculative profits," while GM's managers took a more conservative stance and financed primarily with equity.

In this particular case, GM was right and Chrysler was wrong, but there are many examples of success stories in which debt financing paid off fantastically well. To be perfectly honest, it is simply not possible to state unequivocally what the proper debt/equity mix is for a given firm. We can, however, make estimates of what is likely to happen under different circumstances, and then provide this information to top management for its use in setting financial policy. Procedures for analyzing the capital structure decision are addressed in this chapter.

In Chapter 11, we saw that each firm has an optimal, or value-maximizing, capital structure which exactly balances the costs and the benefits of debt financing. Using more debt increases the riskiness of the firm's earnings stream, which tends to lower the stock's value, but the expected rate of return on equity generally rises with the use of debt, which tends to increase stock prices. *The optimal capital structure strikes a balance between these risks and returns and thus maximizes the price of the firm's stock.*

As we also noted in Chapter 11, it is very difficult to pinpoint the optimal capital structure. Still, it is possible to identify the factors that influence it, and then to establish a *target capital structure*. This target may change over time as conditions vary, but at any given moment, the firm's management does have a specific capital structure in mind, and financing decisions should be consistent with this target. If the actual debt ratio is below the prescribed ratio, expansion capital should be raised by issuing debt, while stock should be sold if the debt ratio is above the target level.

Some of the factors which affect the optimal capital structure are related to the industry, while other factors are unique to individual firms. Since some factors are common to all firms in an industry, we should expect to find similarities in capital structures within industries but differences among industries. We will look at the empirical evidence to see to what extent industry patterns do exist. As we shall see, the evidence reinforces our conclusion that an optimal capital structure does exist for each firm, but that actually establishing the proper target structure is an imprecise process which involves a combination of quantitative analysis and informed judgment.

Business and Financial Risk

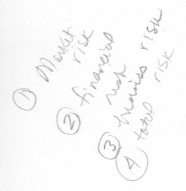

In Chapter 6, when we examined risk from the viewpoint of the individual investor, we distinguished between *market risk*, which is measured by the firm's beta coefficient, and *total risk*, which includes both market risk and an element of risk which can be eliminated by diversification. Now we introduce two new dimensions of risk: (1) *business risk*, or the riskiness of the firm's assets if it used no debt, and (2) *financial risk*, the additional risk placed on the common stockholders as a result of the firm's decision to use debt.[1] Conceptually, the firm has a certain amount of risk inherent in its operations—this is its business risk. If it uses debt, then it in effect partitions this risk and concentrates most of it on one class of investors—the common stockholders. However, the common stockholders are compensated for their higher risk by a higher expected return.

---

[1]Using preferred stock also adds to financial risk. To simplify matters somewhat, we shall consider only debt and common equity in this chapter.

Business risk, which is defined as the uncertainty inherent in projections of future *operating income,* or *earnings before interest and taxes (EBIT),* is the single most important determinant of a firm's capital structure. Figure 12-1 gives some clues about Porter Electronics Company's business risk. The top graph shows the trend in EBIT over the past 11 years; this graph gives both security analysts and Porter's management an idea of the degree to which EBIT has varied in the past and might vary in the future. The bottom graph shows a subjectively estimated probability distribution of Porter's EBIT for 1984. The estimate was made at the beginning of 1984, and the expected value of $275 million was read from the

Business Risk

Figure 12-1
Porter Electronics Company: Trend in EBIT, 1974-1984,
and Subjective Probability Distribution of EBIT, 1984

a. Trend in Earnings before Interest and Taxes (EBIT)

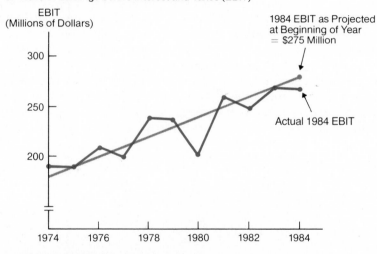

b. Subjective Probability Distribution of EBIT

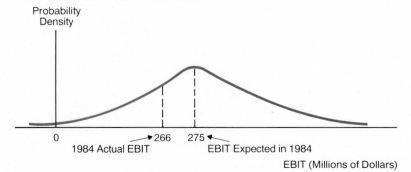

trend line in the top section of Figure 12-1. As the graphs indicate, actual EBIT in 1984 fell below the expected value.

Porter's past fluctuations in EBIT were caused by many factors—booms and recessions in the national economy, successful new products introduced both by Porter and by its competitors, labor strikes, price controls, fires in Porter's major plants, and so on. Similar events will doubtless occur in the future, and when they do, EBIT will rise or fall. Further, there is always the possibility that a long-term disaster might strike, permanently depressing the company's earning power; for example, a competitor could introduce a new product that might permanently lower Porter's earnings.[2] This element of uncertainty regarding Porter's future operating income is defined as the company's *basic business risk*.

Business risk varies not only from industry to industry but also among firms in a given industry. Further, business risk can change over time. For example, the electric utilities were regarded for years as having little business risk, but a combination of events in the 1970s and 1980s altered the utilities' situation, producing sharp declines in their operating income, and greatly increasing the industry's business risk. Now, food processors and grocery retailers are frequently given as examples of industries with low business risk, while cyclical manufacturing industries such as steel are regarded as having especially high business risk. Also, smaller companies, and those that are dependent on a single product, are often regarded as having a high degree of business risk.[3]

Business risk depends on a number of factors, the more important of which include the following:

1. **Demand variability.** The more stable the demand for a firm's products, other things held constant, the lower is its business risk.

2. **Sales price variability.** Firms whose products are sold in highly volatile markets are exposed to more business risk than similar firms whose output prices are more stable.

3. **Input price variability.** Firms whose input prices are highly uncertain are exposed to a high degree of business risk.

4. **Ability to adjust output prices for changes in input prices.** Some firms are better able to raise their own output prices when input costs rise than are others. The greater the ability to adjust output prices, the

---

[2]Two examples of "safe" industries that turned out to be risky are the railroads just before automobiles, airplanes, and trucks took away most of their business, and Western Union just before telephones came on the scene. Numerous individual companies have also been hurt, if not destroyed, by antitrust actions, fraud, or plain old bad management.

[3]We have avoided any discussion of market versus company-specific risk in this section. We note now (1) that any action which increases business risk will generally increase a firm's beta coefficient but (2) that a part of business risk as we define it will generally be company-specific, and hence subject to elimination by diversification by the firm's stockholders. This point is discussed at some length later in the chapter.

lower is the degree of business risk, other things held constant. This factor became increasingly important during the 1980s because of inflation.

5. The extent to which costs are fixed: operating leverage. If a high percentage of a firm's costs are fixed, and hence do not decline when demand falls off, then it is exposed to a relatively high degree of business risk. This factor is called *operating leverage*, and it is discussed at length in the next section.

Each of these factors is determined partly by the firm's industry characteristics, but each of them is also controllable to some extent. For example, most firms can, through their marketing policies, take actions to stabilize both unit sales and sales prices. However, this stabilization may require firms to spend a great deal on advertising and/or price concessions in order to get commitments from their customers to purchase fixed quantities at fixed prices in the future. Similarly, firms such as Porter Electronics may reduce the volatility of future input costs by negotiating long-term labor and materials supply contracts, but it may have to agree to pay prices above the current spot price level to obtain these contracts.[4]

Operating Leverage

As was noted above, business risk depends in part on the extent to which a firm builds fixed costs into its operations—if fixed costs are high, even a small decline in sales can lead to a large decline in EBIT, so, other things held constant, the higher a firm's fixed costs, the greater is its business risk. Higher fixed costs are generally associated with more highly automated, capital-intensive firms and industries. Also, businesses that employ highly skilled workers who must be retained and paid even during recessions have relatively high fixed costs.

If a high percentage of a firm's total costs are fixed, then the firm is said to have a high degree of operating leverage. In physics, leverage implies the use of a lever to raise a heavy object with a small force. In politics, if people have leverage, their smallest word or action can accomplish a lot. *In business terminology, a high degree of operating leverage, other things held constant, implies that a relatively small change in sales results in a large change in operating income.*

Figure 12-2 illustrates the concept of operating leverage by comparing the results that a new firm can expect if it uses different degrees of operating leverage. Plan A calls for a relatively small amount of fixed charges—here the firm would not have much automated equipment, so its depreciation, maintenance, property taxes, and so on would be low. Note, however, that under Plan A the total cost line has a relatively

---

[4]For example, in 1983 utilities could buy coal in the spot market for about $30 per ton. Under a 5-year contract, coal costs about $50 per ton. Clearly, the price for reducing uncertainty was high!

Figure 12-2
Illustration of Operating Leverage

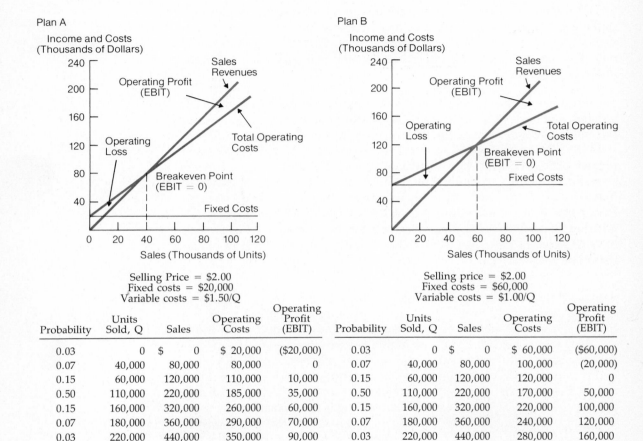

Plan A

Income and Costs
(Thousands of Dollars)

Selling Price = $2.00
Fixed costs = $20,000
Variable costs = $1.50/Q

Plan B

Income and Costs
(Thousands of Dollars)

Selling price = $2.00
Fixed costs = $60,000
Variable costs = $1.00/Q

Probability	Units Sold, Q	Sales	Operating Costs	Operating Profit (EBIT)	Probability	Units Sold, Q	Sales	Operating Costs	Operating Profit (EBIT)
0.03	0	$ 0	$ 20,000	($20,000)	0.03	0	$ 0	$ 60,000	($60,000)
0.07	40,000	80,000	80,000	0	0.07	40,000	80,000	100,000	(20,000)
0.15	60,000	120,000	110,000	10,000	0.15	60,000	120,000	120,000	0
0.50	110,000	220,000	185,000	35,000	0.50	110,000	220,000	170,000	50,000
0.15	160,000	320,000	260,000	60,000	0.15	160,000	320,000	220,000	100,000
0.07	180,000	360,000	290,000	70,000	0.07	180,000	360,000	240,000	120,000
0.03	220,000	440,000	350,000	90,000	0.03	220,000	440,000	280,000	160,000

steep slope, indicating that variable costs per unit are higher than they would be if the firm used more leverage. Plan B calls for a higher level of fixed costs. Here the firm uses automated equipment (with which one operator can turn out a few or many units at the same labor cost) to a much larger extent. The breakeven point is higher under Plan B: Breakeven occurs at 40,000 units under Plan A versus 60,000 units under Plan B.

We can calculate the breakeven quantity by recognizing that breakeven occurs when EBIT = 0:

$$EBIT = 0 = PQ - VQ - F. \qquad \text{(12-1)}$$

Here P is average sales price per unit of output, Q is units of output, V is variable cost per unit, and F is fixed operating costs.[5] We can solve Equation 12-1 for the breakeven quantity, Q_{BE}:

$$Q_{BE} = \frac{F}{P - V}$$ (12-1a)

Thus, for Plan A,

$$Q_{BE} = \frac{\$20{,}000}{\$2.00 - \$1.50} = 40{,}000 \text{ units,}$$

and for Plan B,

$$Q_{BE} = \frac{\$60{,}000}{\$2.00 - \$1.00} = 60{,}000 \text{ units.}$$

How does operating leverage affect business risk? *Other things held constant, the higher a firm's operating leverage, the higher is its business risk.* This point is demonstrated in Figure 12-3, where we show how probability distributions for EBIT under Plans A and B are developed.

The top section of Figure 12-3 gives the probability distribution of sales. This distribution depends on how demand for the product varies, and not on whether the product is manufactured by Plan A or by Plan B. Therefore, the same sales probability distribution applies to both production plans, and expected sales are $220,000, but with a range from zero to about $450,000, under either plan.

We can use the information on the sales probability distribution, together with the operating profit (EBIT) at each sales level as shown in the lower part of Figure 12-2, to develop probability distributions for EBIT under Plans A and B. Typical EBIT distributions are shown in the lower section of Figure 12-3. Plan B has a higher expected level of EBIT, but it also entails a much higher probability of large losses. Clearly, Plan B, the one with more fixed costs and a higher degree of operating leverage, is riskier. *In general, holding other things constant, the higher the degree of operating leverage, the greater is the degree of business risk as measured by variability of EBIT.*

To what extent can firms control their operating leverage? To a large extent, operating leverage is determined by technology. Electric utilities, telephone companies, airlines, steel mills, and chemical companies simply *must* have heavy investments in fixed assets; this results in high fixed costs and operating leverage. Grocery stores, on the other hand, generally have significantly lower fixed costs, and hence lower operating leverage. Still, all firms have some control over their operating leverage. For example, an electric utility can expand its generating capacity by building either a nuclear reactor or a coal-fired plant. The nuclear generator would require a larger investment, and hence higher fixed costs,

---

[5]This definition of *breakeven* does not include fixed financial costs. If there are fixed financial costs, the firm will suffer an accounting loss at the breakeven point. Thus, Equation 12-1 defines the *operating* breakeven level of sales. If F represents total fixed costs, including both operating and financial costs, then Equation 12-1 would define the total cost breakeven level.

Figure 12-3
Analysis of Business Risk

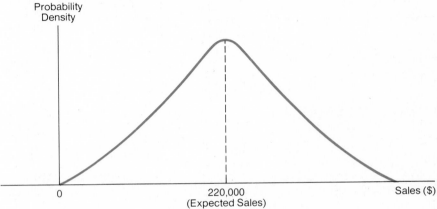

a. Sales Probability Distribution

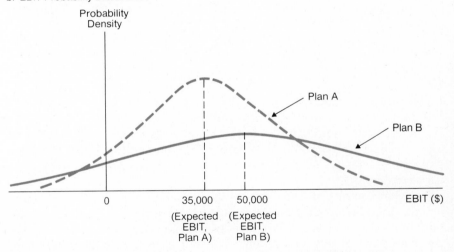

b. EBIT Probability Distribution

Note: We are using continuous distributions to approximate the discrete distributions contained in Figure 12-2.

but its variable operating costs would be relatively low. The coal plant, on the other hand, would require a smaller investment and would have lower fixed costs, but the variable costs (for coal) would be high. Thus, by its capital budgeting decisions, a utility (or any other company) can influence its operating leverage, and hence its basic business risk.

The concept of operating leverage was, in fact, originally developed for use in making capital budgeting decisions. Mutually exclusive projects which involve alternative methods for producing a given product often have different degrees of operating leverage, and hence different breakeven points and different degrees of risk. Porter Electronics (and many other companies) regularly undertakes a type of breakeven analysis (the sensitivity analysis discussed in Chapter 10) as a part of its regular capital budgeting process. Still, once a corporation's operating leverage has been established, the degree of this leverage influences its capital structure decisions. This point is covered next.

Financial leverage refers to the use of fixed charge securities—debt and preferred stock—and *financial risk* is the additional risk placed on the common stockholders as a result of financial leverage. In this section, we show how financial leverage affects a firm's return on equity and the riskiness of this return. Subsequently, we examine the effects of financial leverage on both earnings per share and the price of the firm's stock.

Financial Risk

Conceptually, the firm has a certain amount of risk inherent in its operations—this is its business risk, which is defined as the uncertainty inherent in projections of future EBIT. If a firm uses debt and preferred stock (financial leverage), this concentrates its business risk on the common stockholders. To illustrate, suppose 10 people decide to form a corporation to manufacture steel roof trusses. There is a certain amount of business risk in the operation. If the firm is capitalized only with common equity, and if each person buys 10 percent of the stock, then the investors all share the business risk equally. However, suppose the firm is capitalized with 50 percent debt and 50 percent equity, with 5 of the investors putting up their capital as debt and the other 5 putting up their money as equity. In this case, the investors who put up the equity will have to bear essentially all of the business risk, so the common stock will be twice as risky as it would have been had the firm been financed only with equity. Thus, the use of debt concentrates the firm's business risk on its stockholders.[6]

---

[6]Two additional points should be made about business risk. First, we learned in Chapter 6 that *beta*, or *market*, *risk* is the risk that is relevant to most stockholders. Therefore, a firm can be risky in a *business risk* sense (that is, there can be great uncertainty about its future EBIT), but if its returns are not perfectly correlated with those of other firms, then the stock may still be regarded as being not very risky by diversified investors. In other words, a part of any firm's business risk is company-specific, or diversifiable, risk. Since company-specific risk can be eliminated by diversification, an investor who holds a stock in isolation must bear his or her share of the entire business risk of the firm. By definition, however, well-diversified stockholders render "irrelevant" the company-specific portion of the firm's business risk. Still, the high correlation among the returns on different firms permits us to state as a generality that most increases in business risk result in higher market, or beta, risk, so an increase in business risk will have an adverse effect even on well-diversified investors.

Second, even though debt has a prior claim on the firm's assets and income, under extremely bad business conditions, debtholders can still suffer losses. Therefore, debtholders cannot be totally protected against business risk.

See Baruch Lev, "On the Association between Operating Leverage and Risk," *Journal of Financial and Quantitative Analysis*, September 1974, 627-642; and William H. Beaver and J. Manegold, "The Association between Market-Determined and Accounting-Determined Measures of Systematic Risk: Some Further Evidence," *Journal of Financial and Quantitative Analysis*, June 1975, 231-284.

To illustrate the concentration of business risk, consider a new firm which expects an EBIT of $4 million, requires assets of $20 million, and has a zero tax rate. To begin the analysis, divide expected EBIT by the dollar amount of assets required to produce the EBIT, obtaining *the expected operating rate of return on assets* (ROA), which in this case is ROA = $4/$20 = 0.20 = 20%.[7] If the company uses no debt, then these conditions would exist:

1. Its assets would be equal to its equity.

2. Its return on equity (ROE) would be equal to its return on assets (ROA).

3. Its equity would be exactly as risky as its assets.

Now suppose the firm decides to change its capital structure by issuing $10 million of debt which carries a 15 percent interest rate and substituting these funds for $10 million of equity. Its expected return on equity (which would now be only $10 million) would rise from 20 to 25 percent:

Expected EBIT (unchanged)	$4,000,000
Interest (15% on $10 million of debt)	1,500,000
Income available to common (zero taxes)	$2,500,000
Expected ROE	$2,500,000/$10,000,000 = 25%.

Thus, the use of debt would "leverage" expected ROE up to 25 percent from 20 percent.

However, financial leverage also increases risk to the equity investors. For example, suppose EBIT actually turned out to be $2 million rather than the expected $4 million, so ROA turned out to be 10 percent rather than 20 percent. If the firm uses no debt, then ROE would decline from 20 to 10 percent. However, with debt financing, ROE would fall from 25 to only 5 percent:

	ROA = 10%	
	Zero Debt	$10 Million of Debt
Actual EBIT	$2,000,000	$2,000,000
Interest (15%)	0	1,500,000
Income available to common (zero taxes)	$2,000,000	$ 500,000

Actual ROE:

$2,000,000/$20,000,000 = 10% vs. 20% expected

$500,000/$10,000,000 =   5% vs. 25% expected

---

[7]Here we are defining ROA as EBIT/total assets, which is often called *basic earning power*. An alternate definition of ROA is net income/total assets. Keep in mind that the ROA ratio, and many others, have more than one commonly used definition.

A more complete analysis of the effects of leverage on this firm's ROE is illustrated in Figure 12-4. The two lines in the top graph show the level of ROE that would exist at different levels of ROA under the two different capital structures. The lines were plotted from data developed as described above, and they show that the greater the use of financial leverage, the more sensitive ROE is to changes in the return on assets.[8]

The lower panel of Figure 12-4 shows the effects of leverage on the firm's ROE probability distribution. With zero debt, the company would have an expected ROE of 20 percent, the same as its expected ROA, and a relatively tight distribution. With $10 million of debt, the expected ROE would be 25 percent, but the ROE distribution would be much flatter, indicating a larger standard deviation of returns (σ_{ROE}) and a more risky situation for the equity investors.

Our conclusions from this analysis may be stated as follows:

1. The use of debt generally increases the expected ROE; this situation occurs whenever the expected return on assets exceeds the cost of debt.

2. σ_{ROA} is a measure of business risk, while σ_{ROE} is a measure of the risk borne by stockholders. $\sigma_{ROE} = \sigma_{ROA}$ if the firm does not use any financial leverage, but if the firm does use debt, then $\sigma_{ROE} > \sigma_{ROA}$, indicating that business risk is being concentrated on the stockholders.

3. The difference between σ_{ROA}, the risk that stockholders would bear if no financial leverage were used, and σ_{ROE}, the risk stockholders actually face, is a measure of the risk-increasing effects of financial leverage:[9]

$$\text{Risk from financial leverage} = \sigma_{ROE} - \sigma_{ROA}.$$

[8]If still more debt—say $15 million—were used, the ROE line would be even steeper, while if $5 million of debt were used, the new line would be between the two lines now shown in Figure 12-4. The lines would all intersect at the point where ROE = ROA = 15%, showing that if ROA = k_d, then leverage has no effect on ROE. Note also that the vertical axis intercept shows the fixed interest cost that must be borne by the stockholders; that is, at the intercept, the ROA is zero, but interest must be paid, and this interest must come out of the stockholders' share of the business, and hence it produces an accounting loss and a 15 percent negative return to stockholders. The stockholders' loss would be greater or smaller if the firm uses a greater or lesser amount of debt. For example, if the firm uses only $5 million of debt, then the stockholders would have a 7.5 percent negative return if ROA were zero.

Note also that we have assumed away taxes. If taxes were introduced, the effect would be to lower the ROE. For example, if the tax rate were 50 percent, then the ROE for any ROA would be half the level currently shown in Figure 12-4, and the ROE lines in the top panel of the figure would shift downward so that the lines intersected at ROA = 15%, ROE = 7.5%.

[9]Of course, σ_{ROE} is the total risk which stockholders must bear, and a portion of this risk can be eliminated through diversification. However, as was noted earlier, firms' beta coefficients are highly correlated with their σ_{ROE} values, so any action such as increasing financial leverage which raises σ_{ROE} will also raise beta. This point will be discussed in detail later in this chapter.

Figure 12-4
Effects of Financial Leverage on ROE

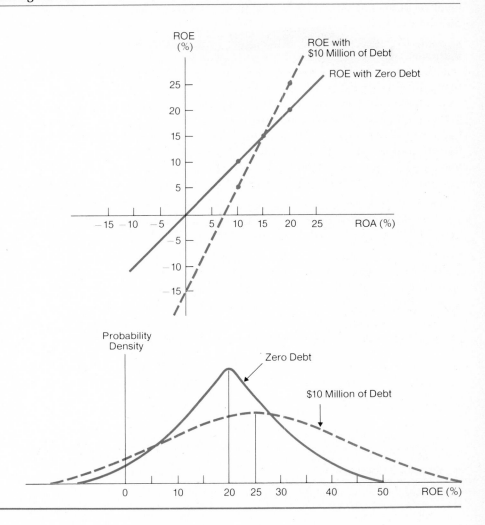

Determining the Optimal Capital Structure

In Chapter 11, we saw that capital structure theory leads to the conclusion that each firm has an optimal capital structure, one which maximizes its value and minimizes its weighted average cost of capital. Financial leverage raises both risk and expected returns. Therefore, when management chooses a capital structure, it must seek to strike that balance between risk and return which maximizes the price of the firm's stock.

In this section, we illustrate how capital structure decisions are made in practice. As we shall see, the process involves a considerable degree of managerial judgment. Many factors, some quantitative and some qualitative, influence the capital structure decision.

Forman Software Systems (FSS) was founded in 1978 to produce a new type of internal memory control system used in personal computers. The basic program was invented and patented by Charles Forman, FSS's founder. Forman also owns a majority of the stock, although a significant portion is held by institutional investors. The company has no debt. FSS's key financial data are shown in Table 12-1. Assets are carried at a book value of $1 million; hence, the common equity also has a balance sheet value of $1 million. However, these balance sheet figures are not very meaningful because (1) the asset figures do not include any value for patents and (2) the fixed assets were purchased several years ago at lower than today's prices.

Charles Forman will retire shortly, and he is planning to sell a major part of his interest in the company to the public, using the proceeds of

Forman Software Systems

Table 12-1
Data on Forman Software Systems

Balance Sheet as of December 31, 1984

Current assets	$ 500,000	Debt	$	0
Net fixed assets	500,000	Common equity		
		(1.0 million shares outstanding)		1,000,000
Total assets	$1,000,000	Total claims		$ 1,000,000

Income Statement for 1984

Sales		$20,000,000
Fixed operating costs	$ 4,000,000	
Variable operating costs	12,000,000	16,000,000
Earnings before interest and taxes (EBIT)		$ 4,000,000
Interest		0
Taxable income		$ 4,000,000
Taxes (40%)		1,600,000
Net income		$ 2,400,000

Other Data

1. Earnings per share = EPS = $2,400,000/1,000,000 shares = $2.40.
2. Dividends per share = DPS = $2,400,000/1,000,000 shares = $2.40. Thus, the company has a 100 percent payout ratio.
3. Book value per share = $1,000,000/1,000,000 shares = $1.
4. Market price per share = P_0 = $20. Thus, the stock sells at 20 times its book value.
5. Price/earnings ratio = P/E = $20/2.40 = 8.33 times.
6. Dividend yield = DPS/P_0 = $2.40/$20 = 12%.

the sale to diversify his personal portfolio. As a part of the planning process, the question of capital structure has arisen. Should the firm continue its policy of using no debt, or should it recapitalize? And if it does decide to substitute debt for equity, how far should it go? As in all such decisions, the correct answer is that *it should choose that capital structure which maximizes the value of the company*. If the company's total market value is maximized, so will be the price of its stock, and its cost of capital will simultaneously be minimized.

To simplify the analysis, we assume that the long-run demand for FSS's products is not expected to grow; hence, its EBIT is expected to continue at $4 million. (However, future sales may turn out to be different from the expected level, so EBIT may actually differ from $4 million.) Also, since the company has no need for new capital, all of its income will be paid out as dividends, and its earnings and dividends are not expected to grow.

Now assume that FSS's financial manager consults with investment bankers and learns that debt can be sold, but the more debt used, the riskier the debt and the higher the interest rate, k_d. Also, the company learns that the more debt it uses, the greater the riskiness of its stock, and hence the higher its required rate of return on equity, k_s. Estimates of k_d, beta, and k_s at different debt levels are given in Figure 12-5, along with a graph of the relationship between k_s and debt.

Given the data in Table 12-1 and Figure 12-5, we can determine FSS's total market value, V, at different capital structures and then use this information to establish its stock price. These equations, which were developed in Chapter 11, are used in the analysis:

$$V = D + S. \tag{12-2}$$

$$S = \frac{\text{Net income after taxes}}{k_s} = \frac{(\text{EBIT} - k_d D)(1 - T)}{k_s}. \tag{12-3}$$

$$P_0 = \frac{\text{DPS}}{k_s} = \frac{\text{EPS}}{k_s}. \tag{12-4}$$

$$k_a = (D/V)(k_d)(1 - T) + (S/V)(k_s). \tag{12-5}$$

Note that we assume that FSS is a zero-growth firm. It pays out all earnings as dividends, thus $g = 0$ and DPS = EPS. We first substitute values for k_d, D, and k_s into Equation 12-3 to obtain values for S, the market value of common equity, at each level of debt, D, then sum S and D to find the total value of the firm. Table 12-2 and Figure 12-6, which plots selected data from the table, were developed by this process. The values shown in Columns 1, 2, and 3 of the table were taken from Figure 12-5, while those in Column 4 were obtained by solving Equation 12-3 at different debt levels. The values for the firm given in Column 5 were obtained by summing Columns 1 and 4: D + S = V.

To see how the stock prices shown in Column 6 were developed, visualize this series of events:

Figure 12-5
FSS's Cost of Debt, Cost of Equity, and Beta

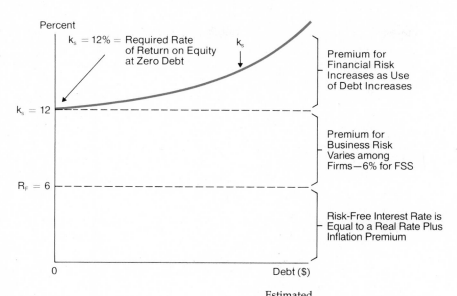

Amount Borrowed[a] (1)	Interest Rate on All Debt, k_d (2)	Estimated Beta Coefficient of Stock, b (3)	Required Rate of Return on Stock, k_a[b] (4)
$ 0	—	1.50	12.0%
2,000,000	8.0%	1.55	12.2
4,000,000	8.3	1.65	12.6
6,000,000	9.0	1.80	13.2
8,000,000	10.0	2.00	14.0
10,000,000	12.0	2.30	15.2
12,000,000	15.0	2.70	16.8
14,000,000	18.0	3.25	19.0

[a]FSS is unable to borrow more than $14 million because of limitations on interest coverage in its corporate charter.

[b]We assume that $R_F = 6\%$ and $k_M = 10\%$. Therefore, at zero debt, $k_s = 6\% + 1.5(10\% - 6\%) = 12\%$. Other values of k_s are calculated similarly.

1. Initially, FSS has no debt. The firm's value is $20 million, or $20 for each of its 1 million shares. (See the top line of Table 12-2.)

2. Management announces a decision to change the capital structure; legally, the firm *must* make an explicit announcement or run the risk of having stockholders sue the directors.

3. The values shown in Columns 1 through 5 of Table 12-2 are estimated as described above. The major institutional investors, and the large bro-

Table 12-2
FSS's Value and Cost of Capital
at Different Debt Levels

Value of Debt, D (in Millions) (1)	k_d (2)	k_s (3)	Value of Stock, S (in Millions) (4)	Value of Firm, V (in Millions) (1) + (4) = (5)	Stock Price, P_0 (6)	D/V (7)	k_a (8)
$ 0.0	—	12.0%	$20.000	$20.000	$20.00	0.0%	12.0%
2.0	8.0%	12.2	18.885	20.885	20.89	9.6	11.5
4.0	8.3	12.6	17.467	21.467	21.47	18.6	11.2
6.0	9.0	13.2	15.727	21.727	21.73 (Max.)	27.6	11.0 (Min.)
8.0	10.0	14.0	13.714	21.714	21.71	36.8	11.1
10.0	12.0	15.2	11.053	21.053	21.05	47.5	11.4
12.0	15.0	16.8	7.857	19.857	19.86	60.4	12.1
14.0	18.0	19.0	3.160	17.160	17.16	81.6	12.3

Notes:

a. Values shown in Columns 1 through 3 were taken from Figure 12-5.

b. Values for S in Column 4 were found by use of Equation 12-3:

$$S = \frac{\text{Net income}}{k_s} = \frac{(EBIT - k_dD)(1 - T)}{k_s}.$$

For example, at D = $0,

$$S = \frac{(\$4.0 - 0)(0.6)}{0.12} = \frac{\$2.4}{0.12} = \$20.0 \text{ million},$$

while at D = $6.0,

$$S = \frac{[\$4.0 - 0.09(\$6.0)](0.6)}{0.132} = \frac{\$2.076}{0.132} = \$15.727 \text{ million}.$$

c. Values for V in Column 5 were obtained as the sum of D + S. For example, at D = $6.0, V = $6.0 + $15.727 = $21.727 million.

d. The stock prices shown in Column 6 are equal to the value of the firm as shown in Column 5 divided by the original number of shares outstanding, which in this case is 1 million. The logic behind this statement is explained in the text.

e. Column 7 is found by dividing Column 1 by Column 5. For example, at D = $6, D/V = $6/$21.727 = 27.6%.

f. Column 8 is found by use of Equation 12-5. For example, at the optimal capital structure,

$$k_a = (D/V)(k_d)(1 - T) + (S/V)(k_s)$$

$$= (0.276)(9\%)(0.6) + (0.724)(13.2\%) = 11.0\%.$$

kerage companies which advise individual investors, have analysts just as capable of making these estimates as the firm's management. These analysts would start making their own estimates as soon as FSS announced the planned change in leverage, and they would presumably reach the same conclusions as the FSS analysts.

4. FSS's stockholders initially own the entire company. (There are not yet any bondholders.) They see, or are told by their advisor-analysts, that very shortly the value of the enterprise will rise from $20 million to some higher amount, presumably the maximum attainable, or $21,727,000. Thus, they anticipate that the value of the firm will increase by $1,727,000.

Figure 12-6
Relationship between FSS's Capital Structure,
Cost of Capital, and Stock Price

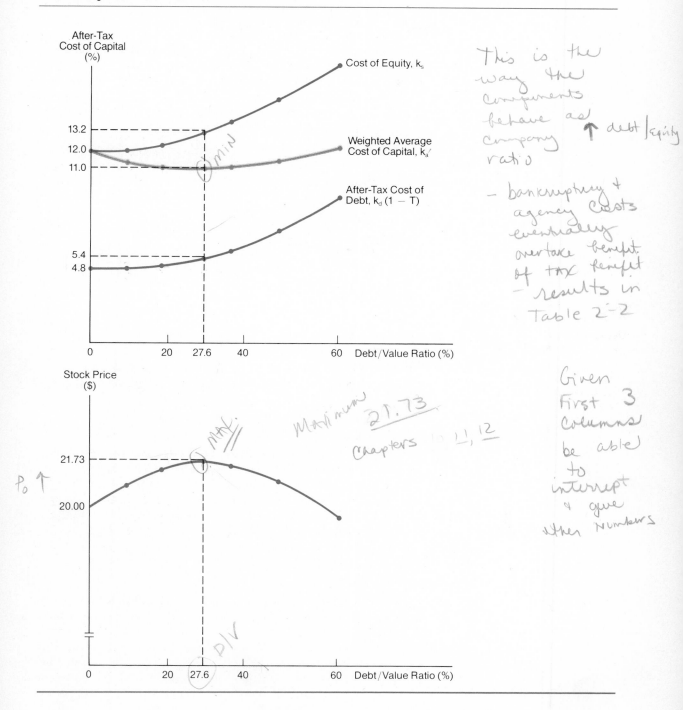

(Handwritten margin notes:)

This is the way the components behave as ↑ debt/equity ratio

– bankruptcy + agency costs eventually overtake benefit of tax benefit.
– results in Table 2-2

Maximum 21.73
chapters 11, 21, 12

P_0 ↑

Given first 3 columns be able to interpret & give other numbers

5. This additional $1,727,000 will accrue to the firm's current stockholders. Since there are 1 million shares of stock, each share will rise in value by $1.73, or from $20 to $21.73.

6. This price increase will occur *before* the transaction is completed. Suppose, for example, that the stock price remained at $20 after the announcement of the recapitalization plan. Shrewd investors would immediately recognize that the stock's price will soon go up to $21.73, and they would place orders to buy at any price below $21.73. This buying pressure would quickly run the price up to $21.73, at which point it would remain constant. Thus, $21.73 is the *equilibrium stock price* for FSS once the announcement has been made to recapitalize.

7. The firm sells $6 million of bonds at an interest rate of 9 percent. This money is used to buy stock at the market price, which is now $21.73, so 276,116 shares are repurchased:

$$\text{Shares repurchased} = \frac{\$6,000,000}{\$21.73} = 276,116.$$

8. The value of the stock after the 276,116 shares have been repurchased is $15,727,000, as shown in Column 4 of Table 12-2. There are $1,000,000 - 276,116 = 723,884$ shares still outstanding, so the value per share of the remaining stock is

$$\text{Value per share} = \frac{\$15,727,000}{723,884} = \$21.73.$$

This confirms our earlier calculation of the equilibrium stock price.

 9. The same process was used to find stock prices at other capital structures; these prices are given in Column 6 of Table 12-2 and plotted in the lower graph of Figure 12-6. *Since the maximum price occurs when FSS uses $6 million of debt, its optimal capital structure calls for $6 million of debt.*

10. In this example, we assume that EBIT would decline from $4 million to $3.52 million if the firm's debt rose to $14 million. The reason for the decline is that, at this level of debt, managers and employees would be worried about the firm's failing and about losing their jobs; suppliers would not sell to the firm on favorable credit terms; orders would be lost because of customers' fears that the company might go bankrupt and thus be unable to deliver; and so on. EBIT is independent of financial leverage at "reasonable" debt levels, but at an extreme degree of leverage, EBIT is adversely affected.

11. Quite obviously, the situation in the real world is much more complex, and less exact, than this example suggests. Most important, different investors will have different estimates for EBIT and k_s, and hence will form different expectations about the equilibrium stock price. This means that the firm might have to pay more than $21.73 to repurchase the 276,116 shares, or perhaps that the shares could be bought at a lower price. These changes would cause the optimal amount of debt to be somewhat higher or lower than $6 million. Still, $6 million represents our best estimate as to the optimal debt level; hence, it is the level we should use as our target capital structure.

12. The average cost of capital for the various levels of debt is shown in Column 8 of Table 12-2. It can be seen that the minimum cost of capital (11.0%) corresponds to the level of debt at which the value of the firm and its stock price are maximized, $6.0 million.

The stock price and cost of capital relationships developed in Table 12-2 are graphed in Figure 12-6. Here we see that FSS's stock price is maximized, and its weighted average cost of capital is minimized, at the same D/V ratio, 27.6 percent.

In the preceding section, we examined the effects of debt on stock prices when FSS went from zero debt to some positive level of debt. Now we will examine the general effects of a change from one debt level to some other level, using this equation:

Extensions of the Example

$$P = \frac{\text{Ending value of firm} - \text{Beginning amount of debt}}{\text{Beginning number of shares}}. \qquad \textbf{(12-6)}$$

Note that the beginning amount of debt could be zero, so Equation 12-6 is general in the sense that it could apply to any analysis, zero initial debt or not. In this section, we examine three different cases.

Example 1. Suppose we wish to determine what would happen to FSS's stock price if it went from zero debt to $4 million of debt. This requires us to find V and P with $4 million of debt:

$$V = D + S = D + \frac{(\text{EBIT} - k_d D)(1 - T)}{k_s}$$

$$= \$4,000,000 + \frac{(\$4,000,000 - \$332,000)(0.6)}{0.126}$$

$$= \$4,000,000 + \$17,466,667 = \$21,466,667.$$

$$P = \frac{\text{Ending value} - \text{Beginning debt}}{\text{Beginning shares}}$$

$$= \frac{\$21,466,667 - \$0}{1,000,000}$$

$$= \$21.47, \text{ versus } \$20 \text{ with zero debt.}$$

As explained above, this stock price would exist *as soon as investors learned of the recapitalization plans, before the plans were actually carried out.* Stockholders would recognize that the company will have a value of

$21,466,667 very shortly, and this value will belong entirely to them because presently there is no debt outstanding. Note also that management must inform all stockholders of the planned recapitalization. If you were a stockholder, you would certainly not be willing to sell your stock back to the company at $20 per share, only to see the stock price then rise to $21.47. You and the other stockholders would insist on receiving as much if you sold your stock back to the company as you would end up with if you chose not to sell it.[10]

Once the plan had been carried out, the shares outstanding would decline from 1,000,000 to 813,694:

$$\text{New shares} = \text{Old shares} - \text{Shares repurchased}$$
$$n_1 = n_0 - \text{Shares repurchased}$$
$$= n_0 - \frac{\text{Incremental debt}}{\text{Price per share}}$$
$$= \$1,000,000 - \frac{\$4,000,000}{\$21.47}$$
$$= 1,000,000 - 186,306$$
$$= 813,694 \text{ shares after repurchase.}$$

Check on stock price:

$$P = \frac{\text{New value of equity}}{\text{New shares outstanding}} = \frac{S_1}{n_1} = \frac{\$17,466,667}{813,694} = \$21.47.$$

Had we made similar calculations, but used $6 million of debt, the resulting stock price would have been $21.73 as shown in Table 12-2.

Example 2. Now assume that we are analyzing another company, called Firm Z, which has exactly the same characteristics as FSS with $4 million of 8.3 percent debt. What would happen to Firm Z's stock price if it increased its leverage from $4 million to $6 million of debt? Assume that its old debt must be retired if new debt is issued, so the entire $6 million of debt will have a cost of 9 percent (from Figure 12-5). Firm Z has these initial values:

---

[10]Indeed, if you and other stockholders were silly enough to sell at $20 per share, then the $4 million of debt could be used to buy and retire even more shares, so the remaining shares would be worth even more than $21.47. In fact, the stock would, under these conditions, be worth $21.83:

$$P = \frac{\$17,466,667}{1,000,000 - (\$4,000,000/\$20)} = \$21.83.$$

Of course, you might be afraid that the recapitalization plan would fall through, so you might be willing to sell out for slightly less than $21.47, say for $21, figuring that $21 in the hand is better than $21.47 in the bush.

$$\text{Initial debt value} = D_0 = \$4,000,000.$$
$$\text{Initial stock value} = S_0 = \$17,466,667.$$
$$\text{Initial total value} = V_0 = \$21,466,667.$$
$$\text{Initial price} = P_0 = \$21.47.$$
$$\text{Initial shares} = n_0 = 813,694.$$

The new equilibrium value will be

$$V_1 = D_1 + S_1$$
$$= \$6,000,000 + \frac{(\$4,000,000 - \$540,000)(0.6)}{0.132}$$
$$= \$6,000,000 + \$15,727,272 = \$21,727,272,$$

and the new equilibrium price will be

$$P_1 = \frac{V_1 - D_0}{n_0} = \frac{\$21,727,272 - \$4,000,000}{813,694}$$
$$= \frac{\$17,727,272}{813,694} = \$21.79.$$

Thus, Firm Z could increase the value of its stock from \$21.47 to \$21.79 by increasing its leverage from \$4 million to \$6 million.[11] Here, the stockholders' aggregate gain is ($21.79 - \$21.47)813,694 = \$260,382.

Example 3. Now assume that Firm Z plans to increase its leverage from \$4 million to \$6 million, but that the old debt need not be retired. Here, the \$4 million in old debt would remain in force with a coupon rate of 8.3 percent. As before, assume that the new debt issue of \$2 million would have a cost of 9 percent. Assuming the same initial values as in Example 2, the new equilibrium values are calculated as follows:

1. $$S_1 = \frac{\left[\text{EBIT} - \left(\begin{matrix}\text{Cost of}\\\text{old debt}\end{matrix}\right)\left(\begin{matrix}\text{Old}\\\text{debt}\end{matrix}\right) - \left(\begin{matrix}\text{Cost of}\\\text{new debt}\end{matrix}\right)\left(\begin{matrix}\text{New}\\\text{debt}\end{matrix}\right)\right](1 - T)}{k_s}$$

$$= \frac{[\$4,000,000 - (0.083)(\$4,000,000) - (0.09)(\$2,000,000)](0.6)}{0.132}$$

$$= \frac{(\$3,488,000)(0.6)}{0.132} = \$15,854,545.$$

---

[11]Notice the slight difference in equilibrium stock prices at \$6 million of debt for FSS and Firm Z: \$21.73 versus \$21.79. This difference demonstrates two points: (1) If FSS could move to its optimal capital structure in stages, it could repurchase shares at a lower average price than the equilibrium price of \$21.73, and (2) if it could buy back shares at a lower price, its final price would be higher because more shares could be repurchased for a given expenditure (debt raised), and hence fewer shares would be outstanding in the end.

2. The old debt has a book value of $4,000,000. However, because more debt is to be issued, the risk of the old debt will rise and consequently its market value will fall to $3,688,889:

$$D_0' = \frac{0.083(\$4,000,000)}{0.09} = \$3,688,889.$$

3. The loss suffered by the old bondholders is $311,111:

$$D_0 - D_0' = \$4,000,000 - \$3,688,889 = \$311,111.$$

4. The new value of the firm will be

$$\begin{aligned} V_1 = D_1 + S_1 &= D_0' + \text{New debt} + S_1 \\ &= \$3,688,889 + \$2,000,000 + \$15,854,545 \\ &= \$21,543,434. \end{aligned}$$

5. The new equilibrium stock price will be

$$P_1 = \frac{\$21,543,434 - \$3,688,889}{813,694} = \$21.943.$$

6. The stockholders will have an aggregate gain calculated as follows:

$$\begin{aligned} \text{Stockholders' gain} &= (P_1 - P_0)n_0 \\ &= (\$21.943 - \$21.467)(813,694) \\ &= \$387,318. \end{aligned}$$

7. Of the stockholders' $387,318 gain, $311,111 will have "come out of the hides of the old bondholders," while $76,207 will have come as a "true gain from leverage" as a result of tax savings net of bankruptcy costs:

$$\begin{aligned} \text{True gain from leverage} &= V_1 - V_0 \\ &= \$21,543,434 - \$21,466,667 \\ &= \$76,767. \end{aligned}$$

(There are rounding errors in these calculations.)

Thus, Firm Z could increase the value of its stock from $21.47 to $21.94 by increasing its leverage from $4 million to $6 million if it did not have to refund its initial lower-cost debt. Of course, this gain to stockholders would come partly at the expense of the old bondholders. The addition of $2 million of new debt would increase the riskiness of all the firm's securities. The stockholders would be compensated, as would the new bondholders, but the old bondholders would still be receiving coupon payments of only 8.3 percent, even though the new debt increased the riskiness of Firm Z's bonds to the point where $k_d = 9\%$.[12] Therefore, the value of the old debt would fall, and there would be a transfer of wealth from the old bondholders to Firm Z's stockholders. Because of the possibility of such events, bond indentures limit the amount of debt a firm can issue; this point is discussed in Chapter 15.

The Effect of Financial Leverage on EPS

Although management's primary focus should be on stock prices, it is difficult to specify exactly the relationships between the amount of debt used and k_d, k_s, and consequently P_0. Therefore, the analysis in the preceding section must in practice be regarded with a degree of skepticism—it is useful to show what is going on, but it should be supplemented by other types of analyses. An alternative approach focuses on the effect of capital structure changes on earnings per share, which can be measured with somewhat more accuracy. Table 12-3 shows how FSS's expected EPS varies with changes in financial leverage. The top third of the table gives operating income data. It begins with a probability distribution of sales and then shows EBIT at sales of $10 million, $20 million, and $30 million. Notice that here *EBIT is assumed not to depend on financial leverage.*[13]

The middle third of Table 12-3 shows the situation if FSS continues to use no debt. Net income after taxes is divided by the 1 million shares outstanding to calculate EPS. If sales were as low as $10 million, EPS would be zero, but EPS would rise to $4.80 at sales of $30 million.

The EPS at each sales level is next multiplied by the probability of that sales level to obtain the expected EPS, which is $2.40 if FSS uses no debt.[14] We also calculate the standard deviation and the coefficient of variation of EPS to get an idea of the firm's risk at a zero debt ratio: σ_{EPS} = $1.52, and CV_{EPS} = 0.63.

The lower third of the table shows the financial results that would occur if the company decided to use $10 million of debt. The interest

---

[12]The $2 million of additional debt might actually have a cost somewhat below 9 percent. This is because retention of the old debt at 8.3 percent would result in a lower total interest payment at the new debt level than if the entire $6 million of debt had cost 9 percent. Given equal business risk, the lower interest payments would lower the probability of bankruptcy, and thus lower the riskiness of the new debt. Additionally, lower bankruptcy risk would mean that equity holders might have a required return somewhat less than the 13.2 percent indicated in Table 12-2. However, these gains come at the expense of the existing bondholders. The addition of new debt makes the old debt more risky, yet the old debtholders will not be compensated for the additional risk. Our analysis does not include these effects; they would, of course, be extremely hard to measure with any degree of confidence.

[13]As we discussed earlier, capital structure does affect EBIT at very high debt levels. We assume that FSS's EBIT would fall from $4 million to $3.52 million if the level of debt rose to $14 million. However, in Table 12-3, the debt is limited to $10 million, so this "excessive leverage effect on EBIT" does not show up.

[14]Expected EPS = 0.2($0.0) + 0.6($2.40) + 0.2($4.80) = $2.40.

Table 12-3
FSS's EPS at Different Amounts of Debt
(Millions of Dollars Except per Share Figures)

Operating Income (EBIT)			
Probability of indicated sales	0.2	0.6	0.2
Sales	$10.00	$20.00	$30.00
Fixed costs	4.00	4.00	4.00
Variable costs (60% of sales)	6.00	12.00	18.00
Total costs (except interest)	$10.00	$16.00	$22.00
Earnings before interest and taxes (EBIT)	$ 0.00	$ 4.00	$ 8.00
Zero Debt			
Less interest	$ 0.00	$ 0.00	$ 0.00
Earnings before taxes	0.00	4.00	8.00
Less taxes (40%)	0.00	1.60	3.20
Net income after taxes	$ 0.00	$ 2.40	$ 4.80
Earnings per share on 1 million shares (EPS)	$ 0.00	$ 2.40	$ 4.80
Expected EPS		$ 2.40	
Standard deviation of EPS[a]		$ 1.52	
Coefficient of variation of EPS[a]		0.63	
$10 Million of Debt			
Less interest (0.12 x $10,000,000)	$ 1.20	$ 1.20	$ 1.20
Earnings before taxes	(1.20)	2.80	6.80
Less taxes (40%)[b]	(0.48)	1.12	2.72
Net income after taxes	($ 0.72)	$ 1.68	$ 4.08
Earnings per share on 524,940 shares (EPS)[c]	($ 1.37)	$ 3.20	$7.77
Expected EPS		$ 3.20	
Standard deviation of EPS[a]		$ 2.90	
Coefficient of variation of EPS[a]		0.91	

[a]Procedures for calculating the standard deviation and the coefficient of variation were discussed in Chapter 6.

[b]Assume tax credit on losses. If credits were not available, expected EPS would be lower, and risk higher, at high debt levels.

[c]Shares outstanding is determined as follows:

$$\text{Shares} = \text{Original shares} - \frac{\text{Debt}}{\text{Stock price}} = 1,000,000 - \frac{\text{Debt}}{\text{Stock price}},$$

where the stock price is taken from Table 12-2, Column 6. With $10 million of debt, P = $21.05. After the recapitalization, 524,940 shares will remain outstanding:

$$\text{Shares} = 1,000,000 - \frac{\$10,000,000}{\$21.05} = 524,940.$$

EPS figures can also be calculated using this formula:

$$\text{EPS} = \frac{(\text{EBIT} - k_d D)(1 - T)}{\text{Original shares} - \text{Debt/Price}}.$$

For example, at D = $10 million,

$$\text{EPS} = \frac{[\$4,000,000 - (0.12)(10,000,000)](0.6)}{1,000,000 - \$10,000,000/\$21.05} = \frac{\$1,680,000}{524,940} = \$3.20.$$

rate on the debt, 12 percent, is taken from Figure 12-5. With $10 million of 12 percent debt outstanding, the company's interest expense in Table 12-3 is $1.2 million per year. This is a fixed cost, and it is deducted from EBIT as calculated in the top section. Next, taxes are taken out, and we work on down to the EPS figures that would result at each sales level. With $10 million of debt, EPS would be −$1.37 if sales were as low as $10 million; it would rise to $3.20 if sales were $20 million; and it would soar to $7.77 if sales were as high as $30 million.

The EPS distributions under the two financial structures are graphed in Figure 12-7, where we use continuous distributions to approximate the discrete distributions contained in Table 12-3. Although expected EPS is much higher if the firm uses financial leverage, the graph makes it clear that the risk of low or even negative EPS is also higher if debt is used.

These relationships among expected EPS, risk, and financial leverage are extended in Figure 12-8. Here we see that expected EPS rises for a while as the use of debt increases—interest charges rise, but a smaller number of shares outstanding as debt is substituted for equity still causes EPS to increase. However, EPS peaks when $12 million of debt is used. Beyond this amount, interest rates rise rapidly, and EBIT begins to fall, so EPS is depressed in spite of the falling number of shares outstanding. Risk, as measured by the coefficient of variation of EPS, rises continuously, and at an increasing rate, as debt is substituted for equity.

Figure 12-7
Probability Distribution of EPS for FSS with
Different Amounts of Financial Leverage

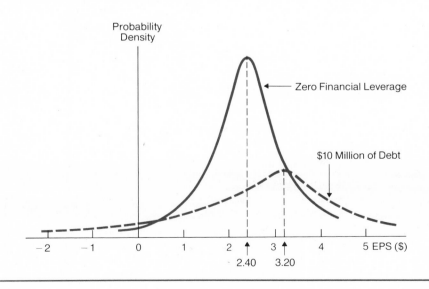

Figure 12-8
Relationship between FSS's Expected EPS,
Risk, and Financial Leverage

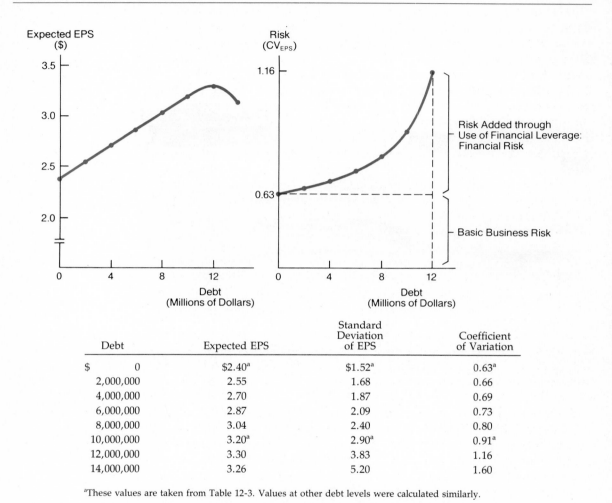

Debt	Expected EPS	Standard Deviation of EPS	Coefficient of Variation
$ 0	$2.40[a]	$1.52[a]	0.63[a]
2,000,000	2.55	1.68	0.66
4,000,000	2.70	1.87	0.69
6,000,000	2.87	2.09	0.73
8,000,000	3.04	2.40	0.80
10,000,000	3.20[a]	2.90[a]	0.91[a]
12,000,000	3.30	3.83	1.16
14,000,000	3.26	5.20	1.60

[a]These values are taken from Table 12-3. Values at other debt levels were calculated similarly.

Figure 12-8 shows clearly that using leverage involves a risk/return trade-off—higher leverage increases expected earnings per share (at least for a while), but using more leverage also increases the firm's risk. It is this increasing risk that causes k_s and k_d to increase in Figure 12-6 at higher amounts of financial leverage.

Using the example of FSS, we have seen how financial leverage affects both stock prices and EPS. In each case, we saw that the variables of interest (stock price and EPS) first rise with leverage, then hit a peak, and finally decline. Does the same amount of debt maximize both price and EPS? The answer is *no*. As we can see in Figure 12-9, FSS's stock price is maximized with $6 million of debt, while expected EPS is maximized by using $12 million of debt. *Since management is primarily interested in maximizing the value of the stock, the optimal capital structure calls for the use of $6 million of debt.*

Why does the expected stock price first rise as the firm begins to use financial leverage, then hit a peak, and finally decline when leverage becomes excessive? This pattern occurs primarily because of *corporate income taxes* and *bankruptcy-related costs*. Interest on debt is tax deductible: The more debt a firm has, the greater is the proportion of its operating income that flows through to investors, and hence the higher the value of the firm. On the other hand, the larger the debt, the greater is the risk of bankruptcy. At very high levels of debt, the odds are high that bankruptcy will occur, and if this happens, lawyers may end up with most of the firm's assets.

Raising New Capital

Thus far in the analysis, we have held constant the firm's assets and simply varied the way those assets are financed. If FSS decided to raise new capital and to expand, how much of that capital should be raised as debt, and how much as equity? The answer is that new capital should be raised in accordance with the value-maximizing D/V ratio. Thus, if FSS, with an optimal D/V ratio of 27.6 percent, needed to raise $100 of new funds, it should issue $27.6 of new debt and raise $72.4 of equity either by retaining earnings or selling new stock. Any other financing mix would fail to maximize the firm's value.

Would the existence of old debt on the balance sheet affect capital structure decisions? The answer is, "Definitely." If the firm had issued a lot of bonds when interest rates were at a peak, then its embedded interest charges would be high, and its ability to use new debt would be constrained. Conversely, if it had a lot of low interest rate debt on the books, then its coverages (discussed in the next section) would look good, and it could safely use more new debt than if its existing debt carried high coupon rates.

Problems with Capital Structure Analysis

Although the examples presented above were reasonably realistic, they were obviously simplified to facilitate the discussion, and we cannot overemphasize the difficulty of the problems which occur when one attempts to find an optimal capital structure in practice. First, the capitalization rates (k_d and especially k_s) are very difficult to estimate. The cost of debt at different debt levels can generally be estimated with a reason-

Figure 12-9
Relationship between FSS's Expected EPS
and Stock Price

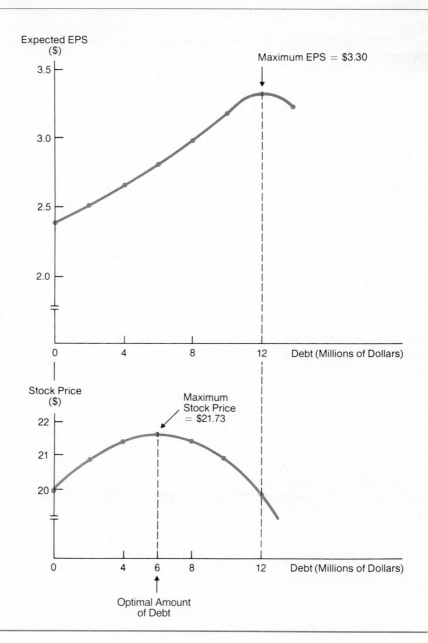

able degree of confidence, but cost of equity estimates must be viewed as very rough approximations.[15]

Second, the mathematics of the valuation process make the outcomes very sensitive to the input estimates. Thus, fairly small errors in the estimates of k_d, k_s, and EBIT can lead to large errors in estimated EPS and stock price.

Third, our formal analysis was restricted to the case of a no-growth firm. Models have been developed for the growth case, but they are quite complex. In view of the input requirements for even the simple no-growth model, and the still greater requirements for the growth model, it is unrealistic to think that a precise optimal capital structure can really be identified.

Finally, many firms are not publicly owned, which obviously makes it difficult to obtain values for k_s and stock prices. If a privately held firm's owners plan never to go public, then potential market value data are really irrelevant. However, an analysis based on market values for a privately owned firm is very useful if the owner is interested in knowing how the firm's market value would be affected by leverage should the decision be made to go public.

Since we cannot determine precisely the optimal capital structure, managers must apply judgment along with quantitative analysis. The judgmental analysis involves several different factors, and in one situation a particular factor might have great importance, while the same factor might be relatively unimportant in another situation. This section discusses some of the more important judgmental issues that should be taken into account.

Other Considerations in the Capital Structure Decision

Managers of large firms, especially those providing vital services such as electricity or telephones, have a responsibility to provide *continuous* service, so they must refrain from using leverage to the point where the firm's long-run viability is endangered. Long-run viability may conflict

Long-Run Viability

---

[15]The statistical relationship between k_s and financial leverage has been studied extensively by use of both cross-sectional and time series data. In the cross-sectional studies, a sample of firms is analyzed, with multiple regression techniques used in an attempt to "hold constant" all factors other than financial leverage that might influence k_s. The general conclusion of the cross-sectional studies is that k_s rises as leverage increases, but statistical problems preclude us from specifying the functional relationship with much confidence.

In the time series studies, a single firm's k_s is analyzed over time in an attempt to see how its k_s value changes in response to changes in its debt ratio, or, perhaps, how k_s changes in relation to changes in the economy. Here again, "other things" do not remain constant, so it is impossible to specify exactly how k_s is affected by financial leverage.

with short-run stock price maximization and cost of capital minimization.[16]

Managerial
Conservatism

Well-diversified investors have eliminated most, if not all, of the diversifiable risk from their portfolios. Also, investors can tolerate some chance of bankruptcy because the bankruptcy losses of one stock could be offset by random gains from other stocks in their portfolio. However, managers generally view potential bankruptcy with more concern—they are not well diversified, and their careers, thus the present value of their expected earnings, can be seriously affected by bankruptcy. Thus, it is not difficult to imagine that managers might be more "conservative" in their use of leverage than the average stockholder; hence, managers may set a somewhat lower target capital structure than the one which maximizes the expected stock price. The managers of a publicly owned firm would never admit this, for unless they owned voting control, they would quickly be removed from office. However, in view of the uncertainties about what constitutes the value-maximizing structure, management could always say that the target capital structure employed is, in its judgment, the value-maximizing structure, and it would be difficult to prove otherwise.[17]

Lender and Rating
Agency Attitudes

Regardless of managers' own analyses of the proper leverage factors for their firms, there is no question but that lenders' and rating agencies' attitudes are frequently important determinants of financial structures. In the majority of cases, the corporation discusses its financial structure with lenders and rating agencies, and gives much weight to their advice. Also, if a particular firm's management is so confident of the future that it seeks to use leverage beyond the norms for its industry, lenders may be unwilling to accept such debt increases, or may do so only at a high price.

---

[16]Recognizing this fact, most public service commissions require utilities to obtain their approval before issuing long-term securities, and Congress has empowered the SEC to supervise the capital structures of public utility holding companies. However, in addition to concern over the firms' safety, which suggests low debt ratios, both managers and regulators recognize a need to keep all costs as low as possible, including the cost of capital. Since a firm's capital structure affects its cost of capital, regulatory commissions and utility managers try to select capital structures that minimize the cost of capital, subject to the constraint that the firm's ability to finance needed construction projects is not endangered.

[17]It is, of course, possible for a particular manager to be less conservative than his or her firm's average stockholder. However, this condition is less likely to occur than is excessive managerial conservatism, which is just another manifestation of the agency problem. If excessive conservatism exists, then managers, as agents of the stockholders, are not acting in the best interests of their principals.

EBIT
Interest

One of the primary measures of bankruptcy risk used by lenders and rating agencies are *coverage ratios*. Accordingly, managements give considerable weight to such ratios as the *times-interest-earned (TIE) ratio*, which is defined as EBIT divided by total interest charges. The lower this ratio, the higher is the probability that a firm will default on its debt, and thus the greater the chance that it will be forced to incur some or all of the previously discussed "bankruptcy costs."

Table 12-4 shows how FSS's expected TIE ratio declines as the use of debt increases. When only $2 million of debt is used, the expected TIE is a high 25 times, but the interest coverage ratio declines rapidly as debt rises. Note, however, that these coverages are expected values—the actual TIE will be higher if sales exceed the expected $20 million level, but lower if sales fall below $20 million.

The variability of the TIE ratios is highlighted in Figure 12-10, which shows the probability distributions of the ratios at $8 million and $12 million of debt. The expected TIE is much higher if only $8 million of debt is used. Even more important, with less debt there is a much lower probability of a TIE of less than 1.0, the level at which the firm is not earning enough to meet its required interest payment and thus becomes seriously exposed to the threat of bankruptcy.

Another ratio that is often used by lenders and rating agencies is the *fixed charge coverage (FCC) ratio*. This is a more precise measure than the TIE ratio because it recognizes that there are fixed charges other than interest payments which could force a company into bankruptcy. The FCC ratio is defined as follows:

$$FCC = \frac{EBIT + \text{Lease payments}}{Interest + \left(\begin{matrix}\text{Lease}\\\text{payments}\end{matrix}\right) + \left(\frac{\text{Sinking fund payments}}{1 - T}\right)}.$$

Table 12-4
Expected Times-Interest-Earned Ratio at Different Amounts of Debt

Amounts of Debt ($ in Millions)	Expected TIE[a]
$ 0	Undefined
2	25.0
4	12.1
6	7.4
8	5.0
10	3.3
12	2.2

[a]TIE = EBIT/Interest. Example: TIE = $4,000,000/$1,200,000 = 3.3 at $10 million of debt. Data are from Table 12-1 and Figure 12-5.

Figure 12-10
Probability Distributions of Times-Interest-Earned Ratio
for FSS with Different Capital Structures

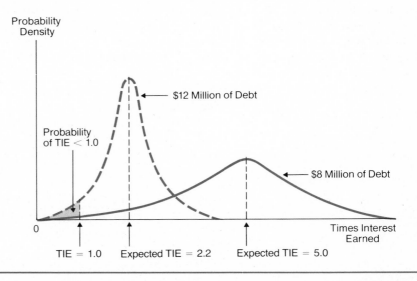

Note that this definition "grosses up" the sinking fund payments in recognition of the fact that these payments must be made with after-tax dollars (net income) because sinking fund payments are not tax deductible.

If FSS had $1 million of lease payments and $1 million of sinking fund payments, its FCC ratio at a debt level of $10 million would be:

$$FCC = \frac{\$4,000,000 + \$1,000,000}{\$1,200,000 + \$1,000,000 + \dfrac{\$1,000,000}{0.6}}$$

$$= \frac{\$5,000,000}{\$3,866,667} = 1.3.$$

Thus, the coverage of total fixed charges is considerably less than the 3.3 times-interest-earned coverage at the $10 million debt level.

Business Risk

We have seen that a firm's investment risk is a function of both business risk and financial risk. If management decides that investment risk should not exceed certain limits, then the company can take on more financial risk if it lowers its business risk, and vice versa. Accordingly, factors such as sales stability and operating leverage, which influence business risk, also indirectly influence firms' optimal capital structures.

Conditions in the stock and bond markets undergo both long-run and *Market Conditions*
short-run changes which can have an important bearing on a firm's optimal capital structure. For example, during the credit crunch in the winter of 1981, there was simply no market at any "reasonable" interest rate
for new long-term bonds rated below A. Low-rated companies that
needed capital were forced to go to the stock market or to the short-term
debt market. At other times, when stock prices are very low, companies
may refrain from selling new stock, choosing instead to let their debt
ratios increase until the stock market improves.

Experienced financial managers always seek to maintain a certain *Financial*
amount of *financial flexibility*, meaning the ability to select the type and *Flexibility*
amount of capital the firm chooses to use at a particular time rather than
to have these choices dictated by the investment bankers or, worse yet,
to be unable to raise capital at all. For example, suppose Firm Y had just
successfully completed an R&D program, and its internal projections
showed much higher earnings in the immediate future. However, the
new earnings are not yet anticipated by investors, and hence are not
reflected in the price of its stock. Firm Y would not want to issue stock—
it would prefer to finance with debt until the higher earnings material-
ized and were reflected in the stock price, at which time it could sell an
issue of common stock, retire the debt, and return to its target capital
structure. Similarly, if the financial manager felt that interest rates were
temporarily low, but likely to rise fairly soon, he or she might want to
issue long-term bonds and thus "lock in" the favorable rates for many
years. To maintain financial flexibility, firms generally tend to use less
debt, and hence to present a stronger financial picture, than they otherwise would. This is not suboptimal from a long-run standpoint, although it might appear so if viewed strictly on a short-run basis.[18]

The effect that its choice of securities has on a management's control *Control*
position may influence its capital structure decision. If a firm's management just barely has voting control (just over 50 percent of the stock),
but it is not in a position to buy any more stock, debt may be the choice
for new financings. On the other hand, a management group that is not
concerned about voting control may decide to use equity rather than
debt if the firm's financial situation is so weak that the use of debt might
subject the company to serious risk of default. If the firm gets into serious difficulties, the creditors (through covenants in the debt agreements)
will assume control and perhaps force a management change. This has

---

[18]In recent years, academicians have begun to develop a formal model, called the *asymmet-
ric information model*, which attempts to relate corporate capital structures to differences in
the information about the firm's investment opportunities between managers and stockholders.

happened to Chrysler, International Harvester, Braniff, Continental Illinois Bank, and a number of other companies in recent years. However, if too little debt is used, management runs the risk of a takeover, where some other company or management group tries to persuade stockholders to turn over control to the new group, which may plan to boost earnings and stock prices by using financial leverage. This happened to Lenox, the china company, in 1983. In general, control considerations do not necessarily suggest the use of debt or of equity, but if management is at all insecure, the effects of capital structure on control will certainly be taken into account.

Additional Considerations

In addition to those factors already listed, the following considerations are relevant to the capital structure decision:

1. Asset structure. Firms whose assets are suitable as security for loans tend to use debt rather heavily. Thus, real estate companies tend to be highly leveraged, while companies involved in technological research employ relatively little debt.

2. Growth rate. Other things the same, faster growing firms must rely more heavily on external capital—slow growth can be financed with retained earnings, but rapid growth generally requires the use of external funds. Further, the flotation costs involved in selling common stock exceed those incurred when selling debt. Thus, rapidly growing firms tend to use somewhat more debt than do slower-growth companies.

3. Profitability. One often observes that firms with very high rates of return on investment use relatively little debt. Although there is no theoretical justification for this fact, the practical reason seems to be that very profitable firms such as IBM, 3M, and Kodak simply do not need to do much debt financing—their high rates of return enable them to do most of their financing with retained earnings.

4. Taxes. Interest is a deductible expense, while dividends are not deductible; hence, the higher a firm's corporate tax rate, the greater the advantage of using corporate debt.

Variations in Capital Structures among Firms

As might be expected, wide variations in the use of financial leverage occur both among industries and among the individual firms in each industry. Table 12-5 illustrates differences for selected industries; the ranks are in descending order of equity ratios as shown in Column 5.[19]

The drug and electronics companies do not use much debt; these companies have generally been quite profitable, and hence able to fi-

---

[19]Information on capital structures and financial strength is available from a multitude of sources. We used the *Compustat* data tapes to develop Table 12-5, but other published sources include *The Value Line Investment Survey, Robert Morris Associates Annual Studies,* and *Dun & Bradstreet Key Business Ratios.*

Table 12-5
Capital Structure Percentages, 1982:
Selected Industries Ranked by Common Equity Ratios

Industry	Short-Term Debt (1)	Long-Term Debt (2)	Total Debt (3)	Preferred Stock (4)	Common Equity (5)	Fixed Charge Coverage Ratio (6)
Drugs	9.6%	13.4%	23.0%	0.2%	76.8%	9.7×
Electrical/electronics	8.2	15.7	23.9	1.4	74.7	5.9
Automotive	11.5	25.7	37.2	2.2	60.6	1.2
Nonfood retailing	10.2	34.2	44.4	0.6	55.0	2.7
Steel	4.6	44.4	49.0	2.6	48.4	Negative
Utilities (electric, gas, and telephone)	3.6	45.1	48.7	6.8	44.5	2.4
Composite (average of all industries, not just those listed above)	6.3	32.4	38.7	2.8	58.5	3.2

Note: These ratios are based on accounting (or book) values. Stated on a market value basis, the results would be somewhat different. Most important, the equity percentage would rise because most stocks sell at prices that are much higher than their book values. If inflation reignites to the same rate as in the 1970s, one could expect to find (1) book value equity ratios declining, but (2) market value ratios remaining reasonably constant.

Source: *Compustat* Data Tapes.

nance through retained earnings, and the uncertainties inherent in industries that are oriented toward research and subject to huge product liability suits render the heavy use of leverage unwise. Retailers, steel, and utility companies, on the other hand, use debt relatively heavily, but for different reasons. Retailers use short-term debt to finance inventories and long-term debt secured by mortgages on their stores. The steel companies have been losing money in recent years, and these losses have reduced their equity positions and also made it difficult for them to sell new common stock. Therefore, the steel companies have been forced to borrow (at very high interest rates) to modernize their plants, and the result is a high debt ratio and negative coverages. The utilities have traditionally used large amounts of debt—their fixed assets make good security for mortgage bonds, and their relatively stable sales and profits enable them to carry more debt than would be true for firms in less-stable industries.

Particular attention should be given to the fixed charge coverage ratios. These ratios are a function of (1) financial leverage and (2) profitability. Generally, the least-levered industries, such as the drug companies, have the highest fixed charge coverage ratios. Also, industries such as the auto industry with profit problems in 1982 had low, or, in the case of the steel industry, negative, fixed charge coverage ratios.

Wide variations in capital structures among firms within given industries also exist. For example, Table 12-5 shows that the average common equity ratio for the drug industry in 1982 was 76.8 percent. However, Upjohn's equity ratio was only 63.1 percent, while Lilly's was over 90 percent. Thus, factors unique to individual firms still play an important role in setting target capital structures.

Book Weights versus Market Weights, Revisited

In Chapter 7, we calculated the weighted average cost of capital with market value rather than book value weights. Further, in all of our discussions of capital structure we have continued to focus on market values, and not book value. However, survey data indicate that financial managers are primarily concerned with book value structures. Thus, there seems to be a conflict between academic theory and business practice. Here are some thoughts on this issue:

1. If stocks and bonds do not sell at exactly book value—and they almost never do—then it is impossible for a growing firm to maintain both a constant book value and a constant market value capital structure over time. One or the other could be maintained, but not both. To illustrate, assume that a company has $50 million of book value debt plus $50 million of book equity, for a total book value of $100 million, but its stock sells at twice book. Here is the situation, with dollars in millions:

	Book Value		Market Value	
Debt	$ 50	50%	$ 50	33%
Equity	50	50	100	67
Total	$100	100%	$150	100%

Now suppose the company needs to raise an additional $50 million. If it sells $25 million of debt and $25 of common stock, it will add these amounts to its balance sheet, so its book value capital structure will remain constant, but its market value capital structure will change. If it raises $16.7 million as debt and $33.3 million as equity, its market value capital structure will remain constant, but its book value structure will change. Thus, it can maintain either its book or its market capital structure, but not both.

2. Book values, as reported on balance sheets, reflect the historical cost of assets. At times, historical costs have little to do with assets' current earning power, with the actual value of these assets, and with their ability to produce cash flows which can be used to service debt. Market values would, almost always, better reflect earning power, cash generation, and debt service ability.

3. As we have discussed throughout this chapter and the last one, the point of capital structure analysis is to find that capital structure which maximizes the firm's market value, and hence its stock price. This optimal capital structure can only be determined by an analysis of market values.

4. Now suppose a firm found its optimal market value structure, but then financed so as to maintain a constant book value structure. This would lead to a departure from value maximization. Therefore, if a firm is growing, it must finance so as to hold constant its market value structure. That will, as we have seen, normally lead to a change in the book value structure.

5. Since the firm should, to keep its value at a maximum, finance so as to hold its market value structure constant, the weighted average cost of capital, k_a, must be found using market value weights.

6. Business executives prefer stability and predictability to volatility and uncertainty. Book values are far more predictable than market values. Further, a financial manager can set a target book value capital structure and then attain it, right on the money. It would be virtually impossible to maintain a market value target structure because of bond and stock price volatility. This is probably why executives generally talk about book value structures rather than more logical market value structures.

7. For purposes of developing the weighted average cost of capital, we recommend the use of market value weights. However, if a company does focus on a book value capital structure, and does seek to maintain that structure, then it will finance in accordance with book value weights, and in this case its weighted average cost of capital should be based on book weights.

8. Some executives have argued against the use of market value weights on the grounds that as stock prices change, so would capital structure weights, with the result being a volatile cost of capital. This argument is incorrect. The cost of capital should be based on *target* weights, and not the actual capital structure, and there is no reason to think that a target market value structure would be any less stable than a target book value structure. In fact, as we discuss below, target market value weights are probably more stable than target book weights.

9. Now consider a fairly typical situation. Firm X currently has a 50/50 debt/equity ratio at book, and a 33/67 ratio at market. It targets on the book value ratio. Several years go by. Inflation occurs, so new assets cost more. Output prices are based on marginal costs, which have risen because of inflation. With the new, higher prices, the rate of return on old assets increases, as does the value of the old assets, and the firm's stock price rises. Book values per share are fairly constant, so the increasing stock price leads to an increase in the market/book ratio. Debt values, on the other hand, remain close to book. Rising stock prices vis-à-vis stable bond prices cause the debt/equity ratio at market to increase from the 33/67 level, even if the firm finances in a 50/50 ratio.

10. Note also that, under our scenario, the rising ROE will lead to improved coverages which, together with everyone's knowledge that the firm's book asset values are understated, will encourage the increased use of debt, that is, an increase in the debt ratio measured at book.

11. The situation described above has been occurring in the United States in recent years. ROEs have moved up sharply (from about 13 percent in the early 1970s to well over 15 percent in the 1980s). Debt/equity ratios at book have gone up from about 33/67 to close to 50/50, while debt/equity ratios at market for most companies have remained fairly constant. Thus, it appears that companies have actually been raising new capital more nearly in proportion to their market value than to their book value capital structures, in spite of the fact that executives say they target on book value ratios.

What can we conclude from all this? We are absolutely convinced that the procedures we recommend are correct—namely, firms should focus on market value capital structures and base their cost of capital on market value weights. Because market values do change, it would be impossible to keep the capital structure on target at all times, but this fact in no way detracts from the validity of market value targets.

Summary

In this chapter, we examined the way in which firms should set their target capital structures. We begin by defining (1) *business risk*, which is the riskiness of the firm if it uses no debt, and (2) *financial risk*, which is the additional risk placed on the common stockholders by the use of debt financing. Business risk and financial risk can be viewed from either a total risk or market risk standpoint.

We next examined the effects of financial leverage on stock prices, earnings per share, and the cost of capital. The analysis suggests that some *optimal capital structure* exists for each firm, which simultaneously maximizes the firm's total market value and stock price while minimizing its average cost of capital. However, although it is theoretically possible to determine the optimal capital structure, as a practical matter, we cannot estimate this structure with precision. Accordingly, financial executives generally treat the optimal capital structure as a range—for example, 40 to 50 percent debt—rather than as a precise point, such as 45 percent debt. Also, we saw that financial executives analyze the effects of different capital structures on expected earnings per share and interest coverage ratios, and they also tend to analyze such factors as business risk, asset structure, effects on control, and so on. Finally, the optimal capital structure should be thought of in market value rather than book value terms, even though managers often seem to pay more attention to book than to market values. In the final analysis, the final target capital structure is more judgmentally than rigorously determined.

Questions

12-1   Define each of the following terms:
     a. Capital structure; optimal capital structure; target capital structure
     b. Business risk; financial risk
     c. Operating leverage; financial leverage
     d. Breakeven point

e. Tax shelter; tax shelter benefit; bankruptcy costs
f. Book weights; market value weights

12-2 What term refers to the uncertainty inherent in projections of future operating income?

12-3 Firms with relatively high nonfinancial fixed costs are said to have a high degree of what?

12-4 "One type of leverage affects both EBIT and EPS. The other type affects only EPS." Explain what the statement means.

12-5 What is the relationship between market, or beta, risk and leverage?

12-6 Why is the following statement true? "Other things being the same, firms with relatively stable sales are able to carry relatively high debt ratios."

12-7 Why do public utility companies usually have capital structures different from those of retail firms?

12-8 Some economists believe that swings in business cycles will not be as wide in the future as they have been in the past. Assuming that they are correct, what effect might this added stability have on the types of financing used by firms in the United States? Would your answer be true for all firms?

12-9 Why is EBIT generally considered to be independent of financial leverage? Why might EBIT actually be influenced by financial leverage at high debt levels?

12-10 If a firm with no debt could buy back and retire its stock at the initial price, would its final stock price be higher than that resulting from the procedure outlined in the chapter? Would it be fair for a firm to buy back its stock without telling stockholders that stock was being repurchased?

12-11 How might increasingly volatile inflation rates, interest rates, and bond prices affect the optimal capital structure for corporations?

12-12 If a firm went from zero debt to successively higher levels of debt, why would you expect its stock price to first rise, then hit a peak, and then begin to decline?

12-13 Why is the debt level that maximizes a firm's expected EPS generally higher than the debt level that maximizes its stock price?

Self-Test Problems

ST-1 Boston Scientific, Inc., produces satellite earth stations which sell for $100,000 each. Boston's fixed costs, F, are $2 million; 50 earth stations are produced and sold each year; profits total $500,000; and Boston's assets (all equity financed) are $5 million. Boston estimates that it can change its production process, adding $4 million to investment and $500,000 to fixed operating costs. This change will (1) reduce variable costs per unit by $10,000 and (2) increase output by 20 units, but (3) the sales price on all units will have to be lowered to $95,000 to permit sales of the additional output. Boston has tax loss carry-forwards that cause its tax rate to be zero, and its cost of capital is 15 percent. Boston uses no debt.

a. Should Boston make the change?

b. Would Boston's operating leverage increase or decrease if it made the change? What about its breakeven point?

c. Would the new situation expose Boston to more or less business risk than the old one?

ST-2 Suppose, some years later, Boston Scientific found itself in this situation: (1) EBIT = $4 million; (2) tax rate, T = 35%; (3) value of debt, D = $2 million; (4) k_d = 10%; (5) k_s = 15%; and (6) shares of stock outstanding, n = 600,000. Boston's market is stable, and it expects no growth, so all earnings are paid out as dividends. The debt consists of perpetual bonds.

a. What is the total market value of Boston's stock, S, its price per share, P_0, and the firm's total market value, V?

b. What is Boston's weighted average cost of capital, k_a?

c. Boston can increase its debt by $8 million, to a total of $10 million, using the new debt to buy back and retire some of its shares. Its interest rate on all debt will be 12 percent (it will have to call and refund the old debt), and its cost of equity will rise from 15 to 17 percent. EBIT will remain constant. Should Boston change its capital structure?

d. If Boston did not have to refund the $2 million of old debt, how would this have affected things? Assume the new and the old debt are equally risky, with k_d = 12%, but the coupon rate on the old debt is 10 percent.

e. What is Boston's TIE ratio under the original conditions and under the conditions in Part c?

Problems   12-1 Here are the estimated EPS distributions for Firms A, B, and C:

	Probability				
	0.1	0.2	0.4	0.2	0.1
Firm A: EPS_A	($1.00)	$1.20	$3.40	$5.60	$7.80
Firm B: EPS_B	($0.80)	$1.00	$2.80	$4.60	$6.40
Firm C: EPS_C	($1.60)	$0.90	$3.40	$5.90	$8.40

a. Calculate the expected value and standard deviation for firm C's EPS. You may assume that EPS_A = $3.40, σ_A = $2.41, EPS_B = $2.80, and σ_B = $1.97.

b. Discuss the relative riskiness of the three firms' earnings.

12-2 Krebs, Inc., has no debt outstanding, and its financial position is given by the following data:

Assets (book = market):	$3,000,000
EBIT:	$500,000
Cost of equity, k_s:	10%
Stock price, P_0:	$15
Shares outstanding, n:	200,000
Tax rate, T:	40%

The firm is considering selling bonds and simultaneously repurchasing some of its stock. If it uses $900,000 of debt, its cost of equity, k_s, will increase to 11 percent to reflect the increased risk. Bonds can be sold at a cost, k_d, of 7 percent.

a. What effect would this use of leverage have on the value of the firm?

b. What would be the price of Krebs' stock?

c. What would happen to the firm's earnings per share after the recapitalization? (Assume all earnings are paid out as dividends.)

12-3 The following data reflect the current financial condition of Micanopy Corporation:

Value of debt (book = market):	$ 1,000,000
Market value of equity:	$ 5,257,143
Sales, last 12 months:	$12,000,000
Variable operating costs (50% of sales):	$ 6,000,000
Fixed operating costs:	$ 5,000,000
Tax rate, T:	40%

At the current level of debt, the cost of debt, k_d, is 8 percent and the cost of equity, k_s, is 10.5 percent. Management questions whether or not the capital structure is optimal, so the financial vice-president has been asked to consider the possibility of issuing an additional $1 million of debt and using the proceeds to repurchase stock. It is estimated that if this were done, the interest rate on the new debt would be 9 percent and k_s would rise to 11.5 percent. The old 8 percent debt is senior to the new debt, and it would remain outstanding and continue to yield 8 percent and to have a market value of $1 million.

a. Should Micanopy increase its debt to $2 million?

b. If the firm decided to increase its level of debt to $3 million, its cost of the additional $2 million of debt would be 12 percent, and k_s would rise to 15 percent. The original 8 percent debt would again remain outstanding, and its market value would remain at $1 million. What level of debt should the firm choose: $1 million, $2 million, or $3 million?

c. The market price of Micanopy Corporation's stock was originally $20 per share. Calculate the new equilibrium stock prices at debt levels of $2 million and $3 million.

d. Calculate the firm's earnings per share if it uses debt of $1 million, $2 million, and $3 million. Assume that the firm pays out all of its earnings as dividends. If you find that EPS increases with more debt, does this mean that the firm should choose to increase its debt to $3 million, or possibly higher?

e. What would happen to the value of the old bonds if Micanopy used more leverage and the old bonds were not senior to the new bonds?

12-4 Milton Coal, Inc., has a total market value of $100 million, consisting of 1 million shares selling for $50 per share and $50 million of 10 percent perpetual bonds now selling at par. The company's EBIT is $15 million, and its tax rate is 30 percent. Milton Coal can change its capital structure by either increasing its debt to $70 million or decreasing it to $30 million. If it decides to *increase* its leverage, it must call its old bonds and issue new ones with a 12 percent coupon. If it decides to *decrease* its leverage, it will call in its old bonds and replace them with new 8 percent coupon bonds. The company will sell or repurchase stock at the new equilibrium price to complete the capital structure change.

Milton Coal pays out all earnings as dividends; hence, its stock is a zero growth stock. If it increases leverage, k_s will rise to 16 percent. If it decreases leverage, k_s will be 13 percent.

a. What is the cost of equity to Milton Coal at present?
b. Should Milton Coal change its capital structure? Explain, and show your work.
c. Suppose the tax rate were changed to 60 percent. This would lower after-tax income and also cause a decline in the price of the stock and the value of the equity, other things held constant. Calculate the new stock price (at $50 million of debt).
d. Continue the scenario of Part c, but now re-examine the question of the optimal amount of debt. Does the tax rate change affect your decision about the optimal use of financial leverage?
e. How would your analysis of the capital structure change be modified if Milton Coal's presently outstanding debt could not be called, and did not have to be replaced, that is, if the $50 million of 10 percent debt continued even if the company issued new 12 percent bonds?

Solutions to Self-Test Problems

ST-1 a. 1. Determine the variable cost per unit at present, V:

$$\text{Profit} = PQ - VQ - F$$
$$\$500,000 = (\$100,000)(50) - V(50) - \$2,000,000$$
$$50V = \$2,500,000$$
$$V = \$50,000.$$

2. Determine the new profit level if the change is made:

$$\begin{aligned}\text{New profit} &= P_2Q_2 - V_2Q_2 - F_2 \\ &= \$95,000(70) - (\$50,000 - \$10,000)(70) - \$2,500,000 \\ &= \$1,350,000.\end{aligned}$$

3. Determine the incremental profit:

$$\text{Incremental profit} = \$1,350,000 - \$500,000 = \$850,000.$$

4. Estimate the approximate rate of return on the new investment:

$$\text{Return} = \frac{\Delta \text{Profit}}{\Delta \text{Investment}} = \frac{\$850,000}{\$4,000,000} = 21.25\%.$$

Since the return exceeds the 15 percent cost of capital, this analysis suggests that Boston should go ahead with the change.

b. If we measure operating leverage by the ratio of fixed costs to total costs (fixed costs plus total variable costs) at the expected output, then the change would increase operating leverage:

Old: $\dfrac{F}{F + VQ} = \dfrac{\$2,000,000}{\$2,000,000 + \$2,500,000} = 44.44\%.$

New: $\quad = \dfrac{\$2,500,000}{\$2,500,000 + \$2,800,000} = 47.17\%.$

The change would also increase the breakeven point:

Breakeven, old: PQ $= F + VQ$

$$Q_{BE} = \frac{F}{P - V} = \frac{\$2,000,000}{\$100,000 - \$50,000} = 40 \text{ units.}$$

Breakeven, new: $Q_{BE} = \dfrac{\$2,500,000}{\$95,000 - \$40,000} = 45.45 \text{ units.}$

If you have read Appendix 12A, you may try to measure the degree of operating leverage (DOL) in the following way:

$$DOL = \frac{Q(P - V)}{Q(P - V) - F} = \frac{50(\$50,000)}{50(\$50,000) - \$2,000,000} = 5.0.$$

The new DOL, at the expected sales level of 70, would be calculated as

$$DOL = \frac{70(\$95,000 - \$40,000)}{70(\$55,000) - \$2,500,000} = 2.85.$$

The problem here is that we have changed both output and sales price, so the DOLs are not comparable as shown in Appendix 12A.

c. It is impossible to state unequivocally whether the new situation would have more or less business risk than the old one. We would need information on both the sales probability distribution and the uncertainty about variable input costs in order to make this determination. However, since a higher breakeven point, other things held constant, is more risky, the change in breakeven points—and also the higher percentage of fixed cost—suggests that the new situation is more risky.

ST-2 a.
$$S = \frac{(EBIT - k_d D)(1 - T)}{k_s}$$

$$= \frac{[\$4,000,000 - 0.10(\$2,000,000)](0.65)}{0.15} = \$16,466,667.$$

$P_0 = S/n = \dfrac{\$16,466,667}{600,000} = \$27.44.$

$V = D + S = \$2,000,000 + \$16,466,667 = \$18,466,667.$

b. $k_a = (D/V)(k_d)(1 - T) + (S/V)(k_s)$

$$= \left(\frac{\$2,000,000}{\$18,466,667}\right)(10\%)(0.65) + \left(\frac{\$16,466,667}{\$18,466,667}\right)(15\%)$$

$$= 14.08\%.$$

c. Under the new capital structure,

$$S = \frac{[\$4,000,000 - 0.12(\$10,000,000)](0.65)}{0.17} = \$10,705,882.$$

$$V = \$10,000,000 + \$10,705,882 = \$20,705,882.$$

The new value of the firm will thus be \$20,705,882. This value belongs to the *present* stockholders and bondholders, so we may calculate the new equilibrium price of the stock, P_1:

$$P_1 = \frac{V_1 - D_0}{n_0} = \frac{\$20,705,882 - \$2,000,000}{600,000} = \$31.1765.$$

Check: Shares repurchased $= \dfrac{\text{New debt}}{P_1} = \dfrac{\$8,000,000}{\$31.1765} = 256,604.$

$$P_1 = \frac{S_1}{n_1} = \frac{\$10,705,882}{600,000 - 256,604} = \$31.1765.$$

$$k_a = \left(\frac{\$10,000,000}{\$20,705,882}\right)(12\%)(0.65) + \left(\frac{\$10,705,882}{\$20,705,882}\right)(17\%) = 12.56\%.$$

Thus, the proposed capital structure change would increase the value of the firm and the price of the stock (from \$27.44 to \$31.18), and lower the cost of capital. Therefore, Boston should increase its use of financial leverage. Of course, it is possible that some amount of debt other then \$10 million would result in an even higher value, but we do not have enough information to make this determination.

d. Offhand, we would expect the value of the equity and the price of the stock to rise. We would also expect the value of the old debt to decline. Here is the situation:

$$S = \frac{(\text{EBIT} - I_{Old} - I_{New})(1 - T)}{k_s}$$

$$= \frac{[\$4,000,000 - 0.10(\$2,000,000) - 0.12(\$8,000,000)](0.65)}{0.17}$$

$$= \$10,858,824.$$

Value of debt $=$ Old debt $+$ New debt
$$= \$200,000/0.12 + \$8,000,000 = \$9,666,667.$$

$$V = D + S$$
$$= \$9,666,667 + \$10,858,824$$
$$= \$20,525,491.$$

$$P_1 = \frac{\text{New total value} - \text{New value of old debt}}{\text{Old shares outstanding}}$$

$$= \frac{\$20,525,491 - (\$200,000/0.12)}{600,000} = \$31.43.$$

In this case, the old stockholders gain from the use of increased leverage, and they also extract a further gain from the old bondholders. This illustrates why bond indentures place restrictions on the sale of future debt issues.

e.
$$\text{TIE} = \frac{\text{EBIT}}{\text{I}}.$$

$$\text{Original TIE} = \frac{\$4,000,000}{\$200,000} = 20 \text{ times.}$$

$$\text{New TIE} = \frac{\$4,000,000}{\$1,200,000} = 3.33 \text{ times.}$$

Selected Additional References and Cases

Chapter 11 provided references on the theory of capital structure; those provided here are oriented more toward applications than theory.

Donaldson's work on the setting of debt targets is old but still relevant:

Donaldson, Gordon, "New Framework for Corporate Debt Capacity," *Harvard Business Review*, March-April 1962, 117-131.

————, "Strategy for Financial Emergencies," *Harvard Business Review*, November-December 1969, 67-79.

Definitive references on the empirical relationships between capital structure and (1) the cost of debt, (2) the cost of equity, (3) earnings, and (4) the price of a firm's stock are virtually nonexistent— statistical problems make the precise estimation of these relationships extraordinarily difficult, if not impossible. Probably the best way to get a feel for the issues involved is to obtain a set of the cost of capital testimonies filed in a major utility rate case. Such testimony is available from state public utility commissions, the Federal Communications Commission, the Federal Energy Regulatory Commission, and utility companies themselves. For an academic discussion of the issues, see

Caks, John, "Corporate Debt Decisions: A New Analytical Framework," *Journal of Finance*, December 1978, 1297-1315.

Gordon, Myron J., *The Cost of Capital to a Public Utility*, Division of Research, Graduate School of Business Administration, Michigan State University, East Lansing, Michigan, 1974.

Hamada, Robert S., "The Effect of the Firm's Capital Structure on the Systematic Risk of Common Stocks," *Journal of Finance*, May 1972, 435-452.

Masulis, Ronald W., "The Impact of Capital Structure Change on Firm Value: Some Estimates," *Journal of Finance*, March 1983, 107-126.

Shalit, Sol S., "On the Mathematics of Financial Leverage," *Financial Management*, Spring 1975, 57-66.

Shiller, Robert J., and Franco Modigliani, "Coupon and Tax Effects on New and Seasoned Bond Yields and the Measurement of the Cost of Debt Capital," *Journal of Financial Economics*, September 1979, 297-318.

To learn more about the link between market risk and the degrees of operating and financial leverage, see

Gahlon, James M., and James A. Gentry, "On the Relationship between Systematic Risk and the Degrees of Operating and Financial Leverage," *Financial Management*, Summer 1982, 15-23.

See the following two articles for additional insights into the relationship between industry characteristics and financial leverage:

Bowen, Robert M., Lane A. Daley, and Charles C. Huber, Jr., "Evidence on the Existence and Determinants of Inter-Industry Differences in Leverage," *Financial Management*, Winter 1982, 10-20.

Scott, David F., Jr., and John D. Martin, "Industry Influence on Financial Structure," *Financial Management*, Spring 1975, 67-73.

The following Brigham-Crum cases contain many of the concepts we present in Chapters 11 and 12:

Case 28, "Medical Innovations Corporation," which shows the effect of leverage on EPS and stock price.

Case 29, "Page Solarlite, Inc.," which concentrates on the effect of financial leverage on firm value and the weighted average cost of capital.

Case 30, "American Telephone and Electronics," which consists of two parts that illustrate how operating and financial leverage interact to affect firm value.

The following Harrington case is pertinent:

"Marriott Corporation," which illustrates several ways to measure debt capacity to determine optimal capital structure.

Degrees of Operating, Financial, and Total Leverage

In Chapter 12, we discussed the concepts of operating and financial leverage. In this appendix, we discuss some specific ways to measure them. To illustrate these measures, we will refer to the two operating plans described in Figure 12-2 in Chapter 12.

The effects of a change in sales on operating profits is influenced by operating leverage, and the precise relationship is measured by the *degree of operating leverage (DOL)*, defined as the percentage change in net operating income associated with a given percentage change in sales volume:

Degree of Operating Leverage

$$
\begin{aligned}
\text{DOL} &= \frac{\%\Delta\text{EBIT}}{\%\Delta Q} = \frac{\dfrac{\Delta\text{EBIT}}{\text{EBIT}}}{\dfrac{\Delta Q}{Q}} \\[2em]
&= \frac{\dfrac{\Delta(PQ - VQ - F)}{PQ - VQ - F}}{\dfrac{\Delta Q}{Q}} \\[2em]
&= \frac{\dfrac{\Delta Q(P - V) - \Delta F}{Q(P - V) - F}}{\dfrac{\Delta Q}{Q}} \\[2em]
&= \frac{Q(P - V)}{Q(P - V) - F}.
\end{aligned}
\tag{12A-1}
$$

Note that $\Delta F = 0$.

In deriving the degree of operating leverage, we assume that P, F, and V are constant, that is, they do not change with changes in output. However, the calculated degree of operating leverage itself is not constant—it changes   529 as Q changes. Thus, the DOL must be measured at a particular projected sales volume, and it would be different for a different projected sales volume. For example, the DOL for Plan A at a planned sales volume of 80,000 units is 2.0:

$$\text{DOL}_A = \frac{80{,}000(\$2.00 - \$1.50)}{80{,}000(\$2.00 - \$1.50) - \$20{,}000} = \frac{\$40{,}000}{\$20{,}000} = 2.0.$$

Thus, an X percent increase in sales will produce a 2X percent increase in EBIT. Note, however, if we target on sales of 100,000 units, DOL_A is 1.67, so here an X percent increase in sales above target would result in only a 1.67X increase in EBIT. Note also that at sales volumes close to the break-even point, DOL is close to infinity, and at the breakeven point, 40,000 units, DOL_A is undefined:

$$\text{DOL}_A = \frac{40{,}000(\$2.00 - \$1.50)}{40{,}000(\$2.00 - \$1.50) - \$20{,}000} = \frac{\$20{,}000}{0} = \text{Undefined.}$$

For Plan B at 80,000 unit sales, we would find $\text{DOL}_B = 4.0$. This verifies the fact that Plan B has much more operating leverage than Plan A; hence, its operating profits are more sensitive to changes in sales.

Degree of Financial Leverage

The *degree of financial leverage (DFL)* is defined as the percentage change in earnings available to common stockholders that is associated with a given percentage change in earnings before interest and taxes (EBIT):

$$\text{DFL} = \frac{\%\Delta \text{ Net income}}{\%\Delta \text{ EBIT}}. \qquad \text{(12A-2)}$$

In other words, DFL shows the sensitivity of net income to changes in EBIT.

Equation 12A-2 can be reduced to the following simplified expression, which is useful in calculating DFL:[1]

$$\text{DFL} = \frac{\text{EBIT}}{\text{EBIT} - I} = \frac{Q(P - V) - F}{Q(P - V) - F - I}. \qquad \text{(12A-2a)}$$

To illustrate, we earlier discussed a firm with an EBIT of $4 million and $10 million of debt at a coupon rate of 15 percent. Using Equation 12A-2a, we find the firm's degree of financial leverage to be 1.6:

---

[1]Equation 12A-2a is developed as follows:

1. Net income available to common stockholders is

$$\text{NI} = (\text{EBIT} - I)(1 - T),$$

where NI is net income, I is the fixed interest payment, and other terms are as defined earlier.

2.
$$\text{DFL} = \frac{\%\Delta \text{NI}}{\%\Delta \text{EBIT}} = \frac{\dfrac{\Delta \text{NI}}{\text{NI}}}{\dfrac{\Delta \text{EBIT}}{\text{EBIT}}} = \frac{\dfrac{(\Delta \text{EBIT} - \Delta I)(1 - T)}{(\text{EBIT} - I)(1 - T)}}{\dfrac{\Delta \text{EBIT}}{\text{EBIT}}}.$$

$$DFL = \frac{\$4 \text{ million}}{\$4 \text{ million} - \$1.5 \text{ million}} = \frac{\$4 \text{ million}}{\$2.5 \text{ million}} = 1.6.$$

Therefore, a 50 percent increase in EBIT would result in a $50\%(1.6) = 80\%$ increase in net income. Had the firm used no debt, its DFL would have been 1.0, so any given percentage change in EBIT would be translated directly into an equal percentage change in net income.

Degree of Total Leverage

We have seen that operating leverage causes a change in sales volume to have a magnified effect on EBIT. Further, if financial leverage is superimposed on operating leverage, changes in EBIT will have a magnified effect on both net income available to common stockholders and earnings per share. Therefore, if a firm uses a considerable amount of both operating leverage and financial leverage, even small changes in the level of sales will produce wide fluctuations in net income and EPS.

Equation 12A-1 for the degree of operating leverage can be combined with Equation 12A-2a for financial leverage to show the *degree of total leverage (DTL)*, or the total leveraging effect of a given change in sales on net income:[2]

$$DTL = \frac{Q(P - V)}{Q(P - V) - F - I} = (DOL)(DFL). \qquad \textbf{(12A-3)}$$

---

3. Recognize that interest payments are fixed, so $\Delta I = 0$. Also, the $(1 - T)$ terms cancel, so

$$DFL = \frac{\dfrac{\Delta EBIT}{EBIT - I}}{\dfrac{\Delta EBIT}{EBIT}} = \frac{EBIT}{EBIT - I}. \qquad \textbf{(12A-2a)}$$

4. Equation 12A-2a would have to be modified if preferred stock were outstanding.

5. We could have defined DFL in terms of earnings per share (EPS) rather than in terms of total income to common. Back in Step 1, and thereafter, we would simply divide through by n, the number of shares of stock outstanding. The solution would have again led to Equation 12A-2a. Therefore, Equation 12A-2a shows how changes in EBIT affect EPS as well as total income available to common stockholders.

[2]Equation 12A-3 is developed as follows:

1. The degree of total leverage (DTL) is defined as the degree of operating leverage times the degree of financial leverage, or Equation 12A-1 times Equation 12A-2a:

$$
\begin{aligned}
DTL &= \left(\frac{Q(P - V)}{Q(P - V) - F}\right)\left(\frac{Q(P - V) - F}{Q(P - V) - F - I}\right) \\
&= \frac{Q(P - V)}{Q(P - V) - F - I}.
\end{aligned}
\qquad \textbf{(12A-3)}
$$

2. Recognizing that sales, $S = QP$ and that total variable costs, $VC = QV$, we can also write Equation 12A-3 as follows:

$$DTL = \frac{S - VC}{S - VC - F - I}. \qquad \textbf{(12A-3a)}$$

To illustrate the degree of total leverage, assume that Firm X has the following operating and financial data:

Expected sales quantity:	2,000,000 units.
Sales price:	$7 per unit.
Variable operating costs:	$3 per unit.
Fixed operating costs:	$4 million.
Interest:	$1.5 million.

Using these data, we find that:

$$DOL = \frac{2,000,000(\$7 - \$3)}{2,000,000(\$7 - \$3) - \$4,000,000} = 2.0.$$

$$DFL = \frac{2,000,000(\$7 - \$3) - \$4,000,000}{2,000,000(\$7 - \$3) - \$4,000,000 - \$1,500,000} = 1.6.$$

$$DTL = \frac{2,000,000(\$7 - \$3)}{2,000,000(\$7 - \$3) - \$4,000,000 - \$1,500,000} = 3.2.$$

Note that we could also determine DTL as follows:

$$DTL = (DOL)(DFL) = (2.0)(1.6) = 3.2.$$

The degree of total leverage concept is useful because it enables us (1) to specify the approximate effect of a change in sales volume on earnings available to common stock, and (2) to show the interrelationship between operating and financial leverage. These concepts can be used to show the owner or manager of a business, for example, that a decision to automate and to finance the new equipment with bonds would result in a situation wherein a 10 percent decline in sales would produce a 50 percent decline in earnings, whereas a different operating and financial leverage package would be such that a 10 percent sales decline would cause earnings to decline by only 20 percent. Having the alternatives stated in this manner gives the decision maker a better idea of the ramifications of the alternative actions.

Problems

12A-1   a.   Refer back to Figure 12-2. Calculate the degrees of operating leverage for Plans A and B at sales of $120,000 and $160,000. At sales of $80,000, DOL_A = undefined and DOL_B = −2.0, while at sales of $240,000, DOL_A = 1.50 and DOL_B = 2.0.

     b.   Is it true that the DOL is approximately equal to infinity just above the breakeven point, implying that a very small increase in sales will produce a huge percentage increase in EBIT, but that DOL declines when calculated at higher levels of sales?

     c.   Is it true for all sales levels where DOL > 0 for both plans that $DOL_B < DOL_A$? Explain.

     d.   Assume that Plans A and B can be financed in either of the following ways: (1) no debt or (2) $90,000 of debt at 10 percent. Calculate the DFL for Plan A at sales of $120,000 and $160,000. The DFLs for Plan B at these sales levels, with debt, equal 0 and 1.82, respectively.

e. Calculate the degree of total leverage (DTL) under Plan A with debt at sales of $120,000 and $160,000. The DTLs under Plan B at these sales levels are -6.67 and 7.27, respectively.

f. Several of the degree of leverage figures were negative; for example, DTL_B at $S = \$120,000$ in Part e was -6.67. Does a negative degree of leverage imply that an increase in sales will *lower* profits?

12A-2 Varifixed Corporation will begin operations next year, producing a single product to be priced at $8 per unit. Varifixed has a choice of two methods of production: Method A, with variable costs of $3 per unit and $400,000 of fixed costs, and Method B, with variable costs of $5 per unit and fixed costs of $200,000. In anticipation of beginning operations, the firm has acquired $1 million in assets, of which $300,000 is financed by debt. The current cost of debt, k_d, to Varifixed is 10 percent. Analysis of the two production methods requires the following calculations: (1) unit contribution margins under each method, (2) breakeven points for each method, and (3) the level of sales in units at which the firm should be indifferent between the two methods with respect to expected earnings.

The sales forecast for the coming year is 150,000 units. Under which method would profits be most adversely affected if sales did not reach expected levels? Given the present debt of the firm, which method would produce the greatest percentage increase in earnings per share for a given increase in EBIT? What is the maximum debt ratio under Method A which would produce the same degree of total leverage as for Method B? If the management of the firm is risk averse, which method of production will most likely be selected? (Hint: Let $DTL_A = DTL_B$ and then solve for I.)

12B Business and Financial Risk Premiums

Our discussion of business and financial risk in Chapter 12 focused on total risk. We used σ_{ROA} as the measure of business risk and σ_{ROE} as the measure of the total risk borne by the stockholders. Thus, in the total risk sense, $\sigma_{ROE} - \sigma_{ROA}$ is the measure of financial risk. In this appendix, we shift our focus from total risk to *market*, or *systematic*, *risk*.

In a very important article, Robert Hamada combined the CAPM with the MM after-tax model, obtaining this expression:[1]

$$
\begin{aligned}
k_{sL} &= \frac{\text{Risk-free}}{\text{rate}} + \frac{\text{Business risk}}{\text{premium}} + \frac{\text{Financial risk}}{\text{premium}} \\
&= R_F + b_U(k_M - R_F) + b_U(k_M - R_F)(1 - T)(D/S). \quad \textbf{(12B-1)}
\end{aligned}
$$

Equation 12B-1 expresses the relationship between the cost of equity to a levered firm, the beta of an unlevered firm with equivalent business risk, and financial leverage. In effect, Equation 12B-1 partitions the required rate of return into three components: R_F, the risk-free rate, which compensates shareholders for the time value of money; a premium for business risk reflected by the term $b_U(k_M - R_F)$; and a premium for financial risk reflected by the third term, $b_U(k_M - R_F)(1 - T)(D/S)$. If a firm has no financial leverage ($D = 0$), then the financial risk premium term is zero, and equity investors are compensated only for the firm's business risk.

As we saw in Chapter 11, the MM model does not hold exactly, and we also know that the CAPM may not fully describe investor behavior. Therefore, Equation 12B-1 must be regarded as a rough approximation. Nevertheless, the Hamada equation can provide the financial manager with useful insights. As an illustration, assume that an unlevered firm with $b_U = 1.5$ and \$100,000 of equity ($S = \$100,000$) is considering replacing \$20,000 of equity with debt. If $R_F = 10\%$, $k_M = 15\%$, and $T = 46\%$, then the firm's current unleveraged required rate of return on equity is 17.5 percent:

---

[1]Hamada, Robert S., "Portfolio Analysis, Market Equilibrium and Corporation Finance," *Journal of Finance*, March 1969, 13-31.

$$k_{sU} = 10\% + 1.5(15\% - 10\%)$$
$$= 10\% + 7.5\% = 17.5\%.$$

This shows that the business risk premium is 7.5 percent. Now, if the firm were to add $20,000 of debt to its capital structure, and assuming that the remaining equity had a market value of $80,000, its new k_s, using the Hamada equation, would rise to 18.5 percent:

$$k_{sL} = 10\% + 1.5(15\% - 10\%) + 1.5(15\% - 10\%)(1 - 0.46)(\$20,000/\$80,000)$$
$$= 10\% + 7.5\% + 1.0\% = 18.5\%.$$

We see that adding $20,000 of debt to the capital structure results in a financial risk premium of 1.0 percent, which is added to the business risk premium of 7.5 percent.

Equation 12B-1 can also be used to develop the relationship between levered and unlevered betas which we presented in Chapter 10. We know that under the CAPM, the SML can be used to determine the required rate of return on equity:

$$\text{SML: } k_{sL} = R_F + b_L(k_M - R_F).$$

Now, by equating the SML with Equation 12B-1, the Hamada equation, we obtain:

$$R_F + b_L(k_M - R_F) = R_F + b_U(k_M - R_F) + b_U(k_M - R_F)(1 - T)(D/S)$$
$$b_L(k_M - R_F) = b_U(k_M - R_F) + b_U(k_M - R_F)(1 - T)(D/S)$$
$$b_L = b_U + b_U(1 - T)(D/S), \tag{12B-2}$$

or

$$b_L = b_U[1 + (1 - T)(D/S)]. \tag{12B-2a}$$

Thus, under the MM assumptions, the beta of a levered firm is equal to the beta the firm would have if it used zero debt, adjusted upward by a factor which depends on the amount of financial leverage and the corporate tax rate. We see that the firm's relevant (or market) risk, measured by b_L, depends on both the firm's business risk and its financial risk. The relevant portion of business risk is measured by b_U, while the relevant portion of financial risk is measured by $b_U(1 - T)(D/S)$.

These relationships can be used to help estimate the company's cost of capital, as we discussed in Chapter 6. Also, as we saw in Chapter 10, and we shall see in the discussion of merger analysis in Chapter 24, they can be used to help establish the cost of capital for a division. In all instances, we would obtain betas for publicly traded firms, then "leverage up or down" these betas to make them consistent with our firm's capital structure. The result would be an estimate of our firm's (or division's) beta, given its business risk as measured by betas of other firms in the same industry and its financial risk as measured by its own capital structure.

Dividend Policy

13

Several years ago, Jim Taggart, financial vice-president for Tampa Electric Company (TECO), and George Schreiber, vice-president of Kidder Peabody & Company, a major investment banking house, met with a group of students at the University of Florida to discuss corporate dividend policy. Taggart led off the discussion. He presented information on TECO's forecasted capital requirements, its cost of money from various sources, the earnings and dividend growth rates that TECO could achieve if it plowed back a higher percentage of its earnings, and the tax advantages that would accrue to stockholders from receiving returns as capital gains rather than as dividends. His conclusion, which the students seemed to second, was that a low-dividend, high-plowback policy was best for TECO's stockholders.

Schreiber then took the floor. He explained that he and the Kidder Peabody sales representatives were in constant contact with investors, and that in their judgment, the higher the payout, the higher the price of a given utility's stock. He went on to say that Kidder Peabody's surveys showed that most utility stocks were owned by investors in low tax brackets (for example, retirees and tax-exempt pension plans), so dividends were just as good as capital gains. Further, he pointed out that utility stockholders often live on their dividend income, and that it was much more convenient to cash a dividend check to obtain cash income than to sell some stock (and incur brokerage costs). Finally, he gave an example of a "typical" investor with $10,000. The person could (1) buy bonds and get an income of $1,500 per year, (2) purchase a low-dividend utility stock and get $900 cash plus perhaps eventually some capital gains, or (3) choose a high-dividend stock and get $1,300 cash plus smaller expected capital gains. Schreiber's strong opinion was that utility investors give little weight to growth, so his conclusion was that the higher the dividend, the more people will pay for a given stock.

After listening to both presentations, the students were thoroughly confused. First, the utility executive had convinced them that maximizing stock prices called for holding down dividend payout ratios. Then the investment banker made a convincing argument for higher payout ratios. The professor was uncharacteristically quiet. After reading Chapter 13, see if you can decide who was right.

Dividend policy involves the decision to pay out earnings versus retaining them for reinvestment in the firm. Our basic constant growth stock price model, $P_0 = D_1/(k_s - g)$, shows that a policy of paying out more cash dividends will raise D_1, which will tend to increase the price of the stock. However, if cash dividends are raised and consequently less money is available for reinvestment, the expected growth rate will be lowered, which in turn will depress the price of the stock. Thus, dividend policy has two opposing effects, and *an optimal dividend policy strikes exactly the balance that investors in the aggregate want between current dividends and future growth and thereby maximizes the price of the firm's stock.*

A firm that pays out some of its earnings as dividends is limiting its retained earnings, and hence the asset expansion it can finance with relatively cheap internal equity. Further expansion is possible, of course, but it will have to be supported by the sale of more expensive new common stock. Thus, for any given rate of asset expansion, decisions on dividend policy also imply decisions on new stock sales, if the optimal capital structure is to be maintained.

In this chapter, we examine factors which affect the optimal dividend policy for the firm. Also, because dividend policy and stock repurchases are so closely connected, we take up stock repurchases as an alternative to dividends in Appendix 13A.

Dividend Policy Theories

A number of factors influence dividend policy, including the differential tax rates on dividends and capital gains, the investment opportunities available to the firm, alternative sources of capital, and stockholders' preferences for current versus future income. Our major goal in this chapter is to show how these and other factors interact to determine a firm's optimal dividend policy. We begin by examining three theories of dividend policy: (1) the dividend irrelevance theory, (2) the "bird-in-the-hand" theory, and (3) the tax differential theory.

Dividend Irrelevance

It has been asserted that dividend policy has no effect on either the price of a firm's stock or its cost of capital, that is, dividend policy is *irrelevant*. The principal proponents of this view are Merton Miller and Franco Modigliani (MM).[1] MM argue that the value of the firm is determined by its basic earnings power and its risk class. Thus, the value of the firm depends on asset investment policy only, and not on how the firm's earnings are split between dividends and retained earnings.

MM prove their proposition theoretically, but only under these assumptions: (1) there are no personal or corporate income taxes, (2) there are no stock flotation or transaction costs, (3) financial leverage has only a very limited effect, if any, on the cost of capital, (4) dividend policy has no effect on the firm's cost of equity, and (5) a firm's capital investment policy is independent of its dividend policy. To show how MM proved dividend irrelevance under these assumptions, we shall use the following terms:

P_0 = stock price at $t = 0$.

P_1 = stock price at $t = 1$.

D_1 = dividend per share paid at $t = 1$.

n = number of shares outstanding at $t = 0$.

m = number of new shares issued at $t = 1$.

I = total new investment during Period 1.

X = net income during Period 1.

k_s = cost of retained earnings = cost of new equity (assumed to be constant).

Now, looking only at a one-period dividend decision, the price of the stock at the beginning of the period, P_0, is equal to the present value of the dividend paid at the end of the period, D_1, plus the present value of the stock price at the end of the period, P_1:

$$P_0 = \frac{D_1 + P_1}{(1 + k_s)}. \tag{13-1}$$

We can obtain the firm's total market value by multiplying both sides of the equation by n, the shares outstanding at $t = 0$:

$$nP_0 = \frac{nD_1 + nP_1}{(1 + k_s)}. \tag{13-2}$$

Now assume that m additional shares will be sold on $t = 1$ at a price P_1, bringing in mP_1 of dollars at $t = 1$. The m shares of new stock will not receive the D_1 dividend. We can add a $+mP_1$ and a $-mP_1$ to the

---

[1]See Merton H. Miller and Franco Modigliani, "Dividend Policy, Growth, and the Valuation of Shares," *Journal of Business*, October 1961, 411-433.

numerator of Equation 13-2 without changing its value, and then re-arrange terms, to produce Equation 13-2a:

$$nP_0 = \frac{nD_1 + nP_1 + mP_1 - mP_1}{(1 + k_s)}$$
$$= \frac{nD_1 + (n + m)P_1 - mP_1}{(1 + k_s)}. \qquad \text{(13-2a)}$$

Equation 13-2a shows that the value of the firm at $t = 0$ is equal to the present value of the dividends plus the total stock value at $t = 1$, minus the value at $t = 1$ that will belong to the new stockholders.

If we assume that no debt is used, the sources and uses of funds at $t = 1$ are as follows:

$$\text{Sources of funds} = \text{Uses of funds}$$
$$mP_1 + X = I + nD_1. \qquad \text{(13-3)}$$

Thus, the sources of funds are the money raised by selling stock and net income, X, for the period, while the uses of these funds are new investment, I, and the dividends paid to the original shareholders.

Rearranging Equation 13-3, we obtain this expression:

$$mP_1 = I + nD_1 - X. \qquad \text{(13-3a)}$$

Now, we substitute Equation 13-3a into Equation 13-2a to produce Equation 13-4,

$$nP_0 = \frac{nD_1 + (n + m)P_1 - (I + nD_1 - X)}{(1 + k_s)}$$
$$= \frac{(n + m)P_1 - I + X}{(1 + k_s)}, \qquad \text{(13-4)}$$

which is MM's basic expression for the current ($t = 0$) value of the firm. Notice that the firm's value, nP_0, does not depend directly on the next period's dividend, for there is no D_1 term in Equation 13-4. Thus, under the MM assumptions, its stock price is not affected by the firm's dividend decision—any gain in the current stock price which results from an increase in dividends is exactly offset by a decrease in the current price due to the decline in the stock's end-of-period value. Therefore, shareholders can receive their cash flows from the firm either as dividends or as capital gains (end-of-period price), and under the MM assumptions, the shareholder should be indifferent to the two alternatives.

MM extend their model to a multi-period setting by looking at subsequent dividend decisions. The results remain the same—under the MM assumptions, dividends are irrelevant. However, the MM assumptions are very strong, and as we shall see, they do not hold precisely. Firms and investors do pay income taxes; firms do incur flotation costs; investors do incur transactions costs; and both taxes and transactions costs may cause k_s to be affected by dividend policy. Thus, the MM conclusions on dividend irrelevancy may not be valid under real-world conditions.

The most critical assumption of MM's dividend irrelevance theory is that dividend policy does not affect investors' required rate of return on equity, k_s. The question of whether or not dividend policy affects the cost of equity has been hotly debated in academic circles. Myron Gordon and John Lintner, on the one hand, argue that k_s increases as the dividend payout is reduced because investors are more sure of receiving dividend payments than income from the capital gains which should result from retained earnings.[2] They say, in effect, that investors value a dollar of expected dividends more highly than a dollar of expected capital gains because the dividend yield component, D_1/P_0, is less risky than the g component in the total expected return equation, $\hat{k}_s = D_1/P_0 + g$.

On the other hand, MM argue that k_s is independent of dividend policy, which implies, if we ignore tax effects, that investors are indifferent between D_1/P_0 and g, and hence between dividends and capital gains. MM call the Gordon-Lintner argument "the bird-in-the-hand fallacy" because, in MM's view, many, if not most, investors are going to reinvest their dividends in the same or similar firms anyway, and, in any event, the riskiness of the firm's cash flows to investors in the long run is determined only by the riskiness of its asset cash flows, and not by its dividend payout policy.

Figure 13-1 presents two graphs which highlight the MM versus Gordon-Lintner arguments. The left panel shows the Miller-Modigliani position. Here the company has $\hat{k}_s = D_1/P_0 + g = R_F + RP = k_s = a$ constant 13.3% for any dividend policy. Thus, the equilibrium total return, k_s, is assumed to be a constant whether it comes entirely as a dividend yield, entirely as expected capital gains, or as a combination of the two.

The right panel adds the Gordon-Lintner view. They argue that a possible capital gain in the bush is riskier than a dividend in the hand, so investors require a larger total return, k_s, if that return has a larger capital gains yield component, g, than dividend yield, D_1/P_0. In other words, Gordon-Lintner argue that _more than 1 percent_ of additional g is required to offset a 1 percent reduction of dividend yield.

"Bird-in-the-Hand" Theory

dividend yield less risky than capital gains yield

Investors want ↑ k_s — on capital gains

[2]See Myron J. Gordon, "Optimal Investment and Financing Policy," *Journal of Finance*, May 1963, 264-272; and John Lintner, "Dividends, Earnings, Leverage, Stock Prices, and the Supply of Capital to Corporations," *Review of Economics and Statistics*, August 1962, 243-269.

Figure 13-1
The Miller-Modigliani and Gordon-Lintner Dividend Hypotheses

a. Dividends Are Irrelevant (MM)

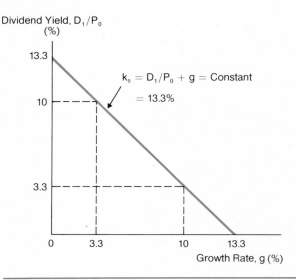

b. Dividends Are Relevant: Investors Like Dividends (GL)

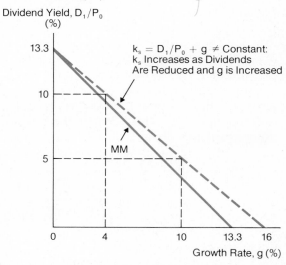

Tax Differential Theory

In Appendix 5A, we discussed the effects of personal taxes on stock and bond valuation. We pointed out that in the United States, only 40 percent of long-term capital gains are taxed, and that this proportion is taxed at the ordinary rate. Thus, an investor in the 48 percent marginal tax bracket would pay 48 percent in taxes on his or her dividend income, but only $(0.4)(0.48) = 19.2\%$ on long-term capital gains.

Suppose our investor is considering the purchase of Stock G, a stock with a high constant growth rate which has an expected total before-tax return of 15 percent, consisting of a 5 percent expected dividend yield and a 10 percent expected capital gains yield, or one-third dividend yield and two-thirds capital gains yield. The after-tax expected return to the investor on Stock G is:

$$\hat{k}_{AT(G)} = (1 - 0.48)(5\%) + (1 - 0.192)(10\%)$$
$$= 2.6\% + 8.1\% = 10.7\%.$$

Now suppose the investor is offered the chance to buy Stock Y, a "yield stock" which is in the same risk class as Stock G, but Y's expected return consists of two-thirds dividend yield and only one-third capital gains yield.

What before-tax return is required to provide the investor with the same after-tax expected return on Y as that offered on G, or 10.7%? If we let X be the total before-tax return for Stock Y, then X must equal 17.4 percent:

$$\hat{k}_{AT(Y)} = 10.7\% = (1 - 0.48)(0.667X) + (1 - 0.192)(0.333X)$$
$$10.7\% = 0.347X + 0.269X = 0.616X$$
$$X = 17.4\%.$$

Thus, the investor would need a 17.4 percent pre-tax return on the high-dividend payout stock if he or she is to receive the same after-tax return as that provided by the 15.0 percent low-dividend, high growth stock. This 17.4 percent pre-tax return consists of a 0.667(17.4%) = 11.6% dividend yield and a 0.333(17.4%) = 5.8% capital gains yield. It follows, therefore, that because of differential personal tax rates on dividends and capital gains, investors should require higher rates of return on high dividend yield stocks than they do on low dividend yield stocks, other things held constant.

Wells Fargo Bank has developed, and trademarked, a model for determining required rates of return which includes dividend yield as well as market risk. This model, called the *Security Market Plane (SMP)*, is based on the premise that an investor's required rate of return depends not only on market risk, but also on stocks' dividend yields. The greater the market risk, the greater is the required return, as in the pure CAPM, but under SMP, in addition, the greater the dividend yield, the greater the required return.

Figure 13-2 shows the SMP as it was estimated in February 1984. The expected (and required) return is shown on the shaded plane, and it increases (1) with dividend yield for any given risk as measured by beta and (2) with beta for any given dividend yield. At the time, $R_F = 10.2$ percent, $k_M = \hat{k}_M = 15\%$, and $RP_M = 15\% - 10.2\% = 4.8\%$. An average stock had $b = 1.0$ and a dividend yield of 4 percent. The upper corner of the shaded plane shows that under this theory, a very high beta, high-yield stock would have a required return of $k_s = 20\%$—this stock would be quite risky, and its returns would be taxed at a relatively high rate.

We are not, at this point, prepared to say which, if any, of these three theories is correct. Before such a conclusion, we must examine the empirical evidence.

In the preceding section, we presented the following three dividend theories:

Tests of Dividend Theories

1. MM argue that dividend policy is irrelevant; that is, dividend policy does not affect a firm's value or its cost of capital. Thus, according to MM, there is no optimal dividend policy—one dividend policy is as good as any other.

Figure 13-2
Security Market Plane

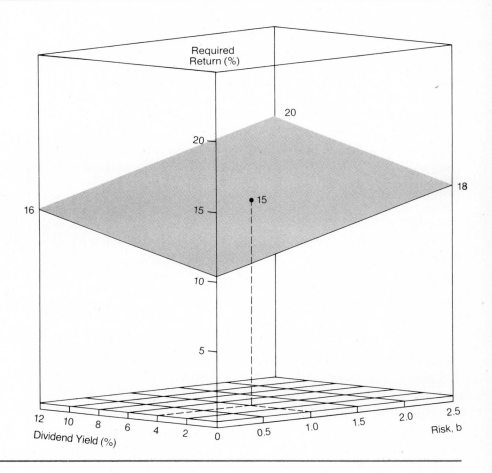

2. Gordon and Lintner disagree with MM, arguing that dividends are less risky than capital gains, so a firm should set a high dividend payout ratio and offer a high dividend yield to minimize its cost of capital. MM call this the "bird-in-the-hand fallacy."

3. The third position is the reverse of the Gordon-Lintner position; namely, that since dividends are taxed at higher rates than capital gains, investors require higher rates of return on high dividend yield stocks. Thus, according to this theory, to minimize its cost of capital and to thereby maximize its value, a firm should establish a low dividend payout ratio. This position is represented by the Security Market Plane (SMP) model.

These three theories offer contradictory advice to corporate managers. Which theory should we believe? The only way to decide, logically, is to examine the empirical tests which have been conducted and then to attempt to choose among the three theories.

Actually, many empirical tests have been used in attempts to determine the true relationship between dividend yield and required return. We will restrict our discussion, however, to only two types of tests. First, academic researchers have attempted to test the alternative theories along the lines set forth in Figure 13-1.[3] In theory, one could take a sample of companies which have different dividend policies, and hence different dividend yield and growth rate components, and plot them on graphs such as those shown in Figure 13-1. If the points all fell on the line in the left graph, so that the slope of the resulting regression line was approximately -1.0, this would support the MM irrelevance hypothesis. If the points all plotted on the dashed line in the right graph, so that the slope was less negative (less steep) than -1.0 (say -0.8), this would support the Gordon-Lintner hypothesis. If the slope were more negative (steeper) than -1.0 (say -1.2), this would support the Wells Fargo position.

In fact, when such tests have been conducted with reasonably good data, the slope of the regression line is found to be about -1.0. This seems to refute both Gordon-Lintner and Wells Fargo, and to support MM, but statistical problems prevent us from saying that this *proves* that MM are right and that dividend policy does not affect k_s. The two statistical problems are these: (1) For a valid statistical test, things other than dividend policy must be held constant, that is, the sample companies must differ only in their dividend policies, and (2) we must be able to measure with a high degree of accuracy the expected growth rates for the sample firms. Neither of these two conditions actually holds. We cannot find a set of publicly owned firms that differ only in their dividend policies, nor can we get precise estimates of investors' expected growth rates. Therefore, we cannot determine with much precision what effect, if any, dividend policy has on the cost of equity. Therefore, this particular type of test does not appear to be capable of solving the dividend policy dilemma.

Academic researchers have also studied the dividend yield effect from a CAPM perspective. These studies hypothesize that required returns are a function of both market risk, as measured by beta, and dividend yield. If so, then a stock's required return could be expressed as follows:

$$k_i = R_F + b_i(k_M - R_F) + \lambda_i(D_i - D_M). \qquad (13\text{-}5)$$

---

[3]The earliest such test was Eugene F. Brigham and Myron J. Gordon, "Leverage, Dividend Policy, and the Cost of Capital," *Journal of Finance*, March 1968, 85-104. In work done in conjunction with writing this chapter, we reexamined the issue and reached the conclusions reported herein.

Here, D_i is the dividend yield of Stock i, D_M is the dividend yield of an average stock, and λ_i is the dividend impact coefficient. Researchers have tested Equation 13-5 by regressing historic values of R_F, k_M, D_i, and D_M against historic values of k_i. If the coefficient of λ_i turns out to be zero, dividend yield would not appear to affect required returns. If λ_i were positive, then investors would appear to require a higher return on stocks with high dividend yields, and vice versa if λ_i were negative.

The results of this line of research have been mixed. Litzenberger and Ramaswamy showed, using NYSE data from 1936 through 1977, that stocks with high dividend yields did have greater total yields than did stocks with low dividend yields, after adjusting for market risk.[4] Their study indicates that investors' required rates of return increased about 0.24 percentage points for every percentage point increase in dividend yield. However, other studies have reached contradictory conclusions, namely, that the λ_i term is zero and consequently that dividend yield has no effect on required returns.[5] The major problem with all of these studies is that they used historic earned rates of return as proxies for required returns, and with such a poor proxy, the tests are almost bound to have mixed results. Thus, these CAPM-based empirical tests, like the pure DCF-based tests, have not led to definitive conclusions as to which dividend theory is most correct. Unfortunately, the issue is still unresolved.

Other Dividend Policy Issues

Before we discuss dividend policy in practice, we need to examine two other theoretical issues that could affect our views toward the three theories presented earlier. These issues are (1) the *information content*, or *signaling*, *hypothesis* and (2) the *clientele effect*.

Information Content, or Signaling, Hypothesis

The MM dividend irrelevancy theory implicitly assumes that all investors have identical opinions about the distributions of the expected future dividend stream. In reality, however, investors have conflicting opinions on both the level of future dividend payments and the degree of uncertainty inherent in those payments.

It has been observed that an increase in the dividend (for example, the annual dividend per share is raised from $2 to $2.50) is often accompanied by an increase in the price of the stock, while a dividend cut

---

[4]See Robert H. Litzenberger and Krishna Ramaswamy, "The Effect of Personal Taxes and Dividends on Capital Asset Prices," *Journal of Financial Economics*, June 1979, 163-196. This paper is reported to have been influential in the development of the Wells Fargo (SMP) model.

[5]For example, see Fischer Black and Myron Scholes, "The Effects of Dividend Yield and Dividend Policy on Common Stock Prices and Returns," *Journal of Financial Economics*, May 1974, 1-22.

generally leads to a stock price decline. This suggests to some that investors, in the aggregate, prefer dividends to capital gains. However, MM argue differently. They note the well-established fact that corporations are always reluctant to cut dividends, and hence do not raise dividends unless they anticipate higher, or at least stable, earnings in the future. Thus, MM argue that a dividend increase is a "signal" to investors that the firm's management forecasts good future earnings.[6] Conversely, a dividend reduction signals that management is forecasting poor earnings in the future. Thus, MM claim that investor reactions to changes in dividend policy do not necessarily show that investors prefer dividends to retained earnings. Rather, the fact that price changes follow dividend actions simply indicates to MM that there is an important *information,* or *signaling, content* in dividend announcements.

Like most other aspects of dividend policy, empirical studies on this topic have been inconclusive. Although there clearly is some information content in dividend announcements, it is not necessarily the complete explanation for the stock price changes that follow increases or decreases in dividends, especially if these increases or decreases include a change in the percentage payout ratio as well as a change in the dollars of dividends paid.

Clientele Effect

MM also suggest that a *clientele effect* might exist; that is, each firm sets a particular dividend payout policy, and then tends to attract a "clientele" consisting of those investors who like its particular dividend policy. For example, some stockholders, such as university endowment funds and retired individuals, prefer current income; they would want the firm to pay out a higher percentage of its earnings. Other stockholders have no need for current investment income; they would simply reinvest any dividends received, after first paying income taxes on the dividend income.

If the firm retains and reinvests income, rather than paying dividends, those stockholders who need current income would be disadvantaged. They would presumably receive capital gains, but they would be forced to go to the trouble and expense of selling off some of their shares to obtain cash. Also, some institutional investors (or trustees for individuals) are precluded from selling stock and then "spending capital." The

---

[6]Stephen Ross has suggested that managers can use capital structure as well as dividends to give signals concerning firms' future prospects. For example, a firm with good earnings prospects could carry more debt than a similar firm with poor earnings prospects. This theory, called "incentive-signaling," rests on the premise that signals based on cash-based variables (either debt interest or dividends) cannot be mimicked by unsuccessful firms because unsuccessful firms do not have the future cash-generating power to maintain the announced interest or dividend payment. Thus, investors are more likely to believe a glowing verbal report when it is accompanied by a dividend increase or a debt-financed expansion program. See Stephen A. Ross, "The Determination of Financial Structure: The Incentive-Signalling Approach," *The Bell Journal of Economics,* Spring 1977, 23-40.

other group, the stockholders who are saving rather than spending dividends, would have to pay taxes and then go to the trouble and expense of reinvesting their dividends. Thus, investors who desire current investment income should own shares in high dividend yield firms, while investors with no need for current investment income should own shares in low dividend yield firms.

To the extent that stockholders can shift their investments among firms, a firm can set the specific policy that seems appropriate to its management, and then have stockholders who do not like this policy sell to other investors who do. However, switching may be inefficient because of (1) brokerage costs, (2) the likelihood that selling stockholders will have to pay capital gains taxes, and (3) a possible shortage of investors, in the aggregate, who like the firm's newly stated dividend policy. Thus, management might be reluctant to change its dividend policy, because such changes might cause current shareholders to sell their stock, forcing the stock price down. Such a price decline might be temporary or it might be permanent—if few investors were attracted to the new dividend policy, that is, if an insufficiently large new clientele develops, then the stock price would remain depressed. Of course, it is possible that the new policy would attract an even larger clientele than the firm had previously, and if so, the stock price would rise.

Evidence from several studies suggests that there is, in fact, a clientele effect.[7] However, MM and others argue that one clientele is as good as another; if so, the existence of a clientele effect does not imply that one dividend policy is better than any other dividend policy. However, MM offer no proof that the aggregate makeup of investors permits firms to disregard clientele effects. Thus this issue, like most others in the dividend arena, is still up in the air.

Dividend Policy in Practice

In the preceding sections, we noted that there are three conflicting theories as to what dividend policy firms *should* follow. We also noted that empirical tests do not answer the question of which theory is correct. In this section, we present four alternative dividend payment policies that firms actually *do* follow. As a part of this discussion, we discuss a multitude of factors which are not generally discussed by the theorists but which do influence dividend policy in practice.

Residual Dividend Policy

In practice, dividend policy is influenced by both investment opportunities and the availability of funds to finance these opportunities. This fact has led to the development of a *residual dividend payment policy*,

---

[7]For example, see R. Richardson Pettit, "Taxes, Transactions Costs and the Clientele Effect of Dividends," *The Journal of Financial Economics*, December 1977, 419-436.

which states that a firm should follow these four steps when deciding its payout ratio: (1) Determine the optimal capital budget; (2) determine the amount of equity needed to finance that budget; (3) use retained earnings to supply this equity to the extent possible; and (4) pay dividends only if more earnings are available than are needed to support the optimal capital budget. The word *residual* implies "left over," and the residual policy implies that dividends should only be paid out of "leftover" earnings.

The basis of the residual policy is the belief that *most investors prefer to have the firm retain and reinvest earnings rather than pay them out in dividends if the rate of return the firm can earn on reinvested earnings exceeds the rate of return investors could themselves obtain on other investments of comparable risk.* If the corporation can reinvest retained earnings at a 14 percent rate of return, while the best rate stockholders can obtain if the earnings were passed on in the form of dividends is 12 percent, then stockholders would prefer to have the firm retain the profits.

To continue, we saw in Chapter 7 that the cost of retained earnings is an *opportunity cost* which reflects rates of return available to equity investors. If a firm's stockholders could buy other stocks of equal risk and obtain a 12 percent dividend-plus-capital-gains yield, then 12 percent is the firm's cost of retained earnings. The cost of new outside equity raised by selling common stock is higher than 12 percent because of the costs of floating the issue.

Also, most firms have a target capital structure that calls for at least some debt, so new financing is done partly with debt and partly with equity. As long as the firm finances with the optimal mix, using the proper amounts of debt and equity, and provided it uses only internally generated equity (retained earnings), its marginal cost of each new dollar of capital will be minimized. Internally generated equity is available for financing a certain amount of new investment, but beyond that amount, the firm must turn to more expensive new common stock. At the point where new stock must be sold, the cost of equity, and consequently the marginal cost of capital, rises.

These concepts, which were developed in Chapters 7 and 10, are illustrated in Figure 13-3 with data from the Texas and Western Transit Company. T&W has a marginal cost of capital of 10 percent as long as retained earnings are available, but its MCC begins to rise at the point where new stock must be sold. T&W has $60 million of net income and a 40 percent optimal debt ratio. Provided it does not pay cash dividends, T&W can make net investments (investments in addition to asset replacements financed from depreciation) of $100 million, consisting of $60 million from retained earnings plus $40 million of new debt supported by the retained earnings, at a 10 percent marginal cost of capital. Therefore, its MCC is constant at 10 percent up to $100 million of capital. Beyond $100 million, the marginal cost of capital rises as the firm begins to use more expensive new common stock.

Figure 13-3
T&W Transit Company:
Marginal Cost of Capital

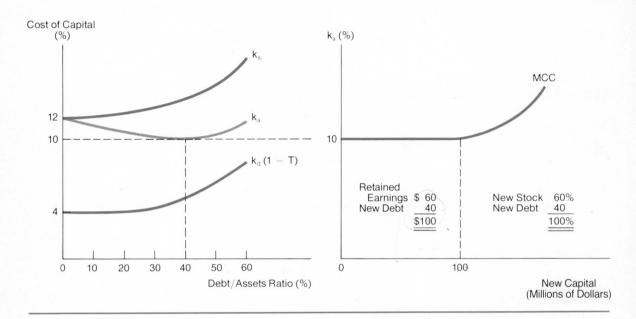

Of course, if T&W does not retain all of its earnings, its MCC will begin to rise before $100 million. For example, if T&W retained only $30 million, then its MCC would begin to rise at $30 million retained earnings + $20 million debt = $50 million.

Now suppose T&W's director of capital budgeting constructs several investment opportunity schedules and plots them on a graph. The investment opportunity schedules for three different years—a good year (IOS_G), a normal year (IOS_N), and a bad year (IOS_B)—are shown in Figure 13-4. T&W can invest the most money, and at the highest rates of return, when the investment opportunities are given as IOS_G.

In Figure 13-5, we combine these investment opportunity schedules with the cost of capital schedule. The point where the relevant IOS curve cuts the MCC curve defines the proper level of new investment. When investment opportunities are relatively bad (IOS_B), the optimal level of investment is $40 million; when opportunities are normal (IOS_N), $70 million should be invested; and when opportunities are relatively good (IOS_G), T&W should make new investments in the amount of $150 million.

Consider the situation where IOS_G is the appropriate schedule. The company should raise and invest $150 million. T&W has $60 million in

Figure 13-4
T&W Transit Company:
Investment Opportunity (or IRR) Schedules

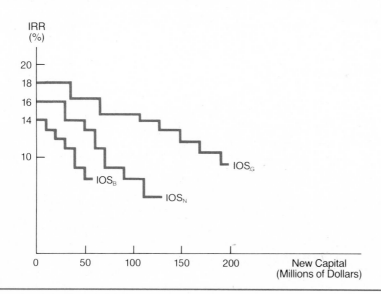

earnings and a 40 percent target debt ratio. Thus, it can finance $100 million, consisting of $60 million of retained earnings plus $40 million of new debt, at an average cost of 10 percent if it retains all of its earnings. The remaining $50 million will include external equity and thus have a higher cost. If T&W pays out part of the earnings in dividends, it will have to begin to use more costly new common stock earlier than need be, so its MCC curve will rise earlier than it otherwise would. *This suggests that under the conditions of IOS$_G$, T&W should retain all of its earnings. According to the residual policy, T&W's payout ratio should be zero if IOS$_G$ applies.*

Under the conditions of IOS$_N$, however, T&W should invest only $70 million. How should this investment be financed? First, notice that if T&W retains all of its earnings, $60 million, it will need to sell only $10 million of new debt. However, if T&W retains $60 million and sells only $10 million of new debt, it will move away from its target capital structure. To stay on target, T&W must finance 60 percent of the required $70 million by equity—retained earnings—and 40 percent by debt; this means T&W must retain $42 million and sell $28 million of new debt. Since T&W retains only $42 million of its $60 million total earnings, it must distribute the residual, $18 million, to its stockholders. Thus, its optimal payout ratio is $18/$60 = 30%.

Figure 13-5
T&W Transit Company:
Interrelation among Cost of Capital,
Investment Opportunities, and New Investment

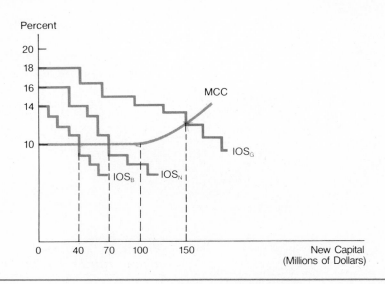

Under the conditions of IOS_B, T&W should invest only $40 million. Because it has $60 million in earnings, it could finance the entire $40 million out of retained earnings and still have $20 million available for dividends. Should this be done? Under our assumptions, this would not be a good decision, because T&W would move away from its optimal capital structure. To stay at the 40 percent target debt/assets ratio, T&W must retain $24 million of earnings and sell $16 million of debt. When the $24 million of retained earnings is subtracted from the $60 million total earnings, T&W is left with a residual of $36 million, the amount that should be paid out in dividends. Thus, the payout ratio, as prescribed by the residual policy, is 60 percent.

If either the IOS schedule or the earnings level varies from year to year, strict adherence to the residual dividend policy would result in dividend variability—one year the firm might declare zero dividends, when investment opportunities are good, while the next year, the same firm, with poor investment opportunities facing it, might declare a large dividend. Similarly, fluctuating earnings would lead to variable dividends even if investment opportunities were stable over time. Thus, a residual dividend policy could be optimal only if investors do not object to fluctuating dividends; if they do object, then k_s will be higher for a firm that follows the residual theory in a strict sense than for an otherwise similar firm which attempts to stabilize its dividends over time.

In the past, many firms set a specific annual dollar dividend per share and then maintained it, increasing the annual dividend only if it seemed clear that future earnings would be sufficient to allow the new dividend to be maintained. A corollary of that policy was this rule: *Try to avoid ever having to reduce the annual dividend.*

More recently, inflation has tended to push up earnings, so most firms that would otherwise have followed the stable dividend payment policy have switched over to what is called the "stable growth rate" policy. Here the firm sets a target growth rate for dividends, say 6 percent per year, and strives to increase dividends by this amount each year. Obviously, earnings must be growing at a reasonably steady rate for this to be feasible.

Both a stable payment policy and a stable growth rate policy are illustrated in Figure 13-6, using data for the Morris Equipment Company over a 35-year period. Initially, earnings were $2 a share and dividends were $1 a share, so the payout ratio was 50 percent. During most of the 1950s, earnings fluctuated, but no clear trend was evident, so the dividend was kept at the $1 level. However, by the early 1960s, earnings

Constant or Steadily Increasing Dividends

Stable growth rate

Figure 13-6
Morris Equipment Company:
Dividends and Earnings over Time

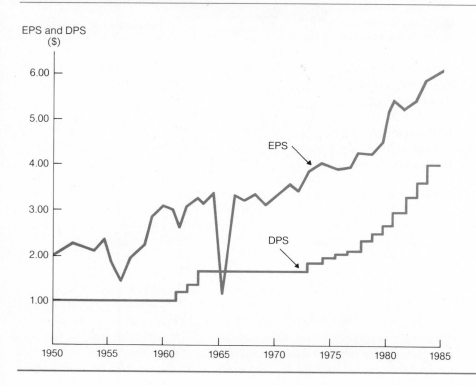

had increased above earlier levels, causing the payout ratio to drop below 50 percent. Further, management believed the new earnings would be sustained, so the company raised the dividend in three steps to $1.50 to reestablish the 50 percent payout. During 1964 and 1965, a strike caused earnings to fall below the regular dividend. Expecting the earnings decline to be temporary, management maintained the $1.50 dividend. Earnings fluctuated on a fairly high plateau from 1966 through 1973, during which time dividends remained constant.

Due in large part to inflation, earnings grew rather steadily during the 1970s and early 1980s, and investors came to expect most successful companies to increase dividends at a rate which, they hoped, would offset inflation. Therefore, after 1973 management adopted the policy of increasing the dividend annually.

There are several logical reasons for following a stable, predictable dividend policy. First, given the existence of the information content idea, a fluctuating payment policy might lead to greater uncertainty, a higher k_s, and a lower stock price than would exist under a stable policy. Second, stockholders who use dividends for current consumption want to be able to count on receiving dividends on a regular basis, so irregular dividends might lower demand for the stock and cause its price to decline. Third, even though the optimal dividend as prescribed by the residual policy might vary somewhat from year to year, actions such as delaying some investment projects, departing from the target capital structure during a particular year, or even selling common stock might all be preferable to cutting the dividend or reducing its growth rate. Finally, setting a steady dividend growth rate will confirm investors' estimates of the g-factor, reduce risk perceptions, and thus enhance the price of the stock.

Constant Payout Ratio

A very few firms follow a policy of paying out a constant percentage of earnings. Earnings will surely fluctuate, so following this policy necessarily means that the dollar amount of dividends will fluctuate. For reasons discussed in the preceding section, this policy is not likely to maximize a firm's stock price. However, before its bankruptcy, Penn Central Railroad did follow the policy of paying out one-half its earnings: "A dollar for the stockholders and a dollar for the company," as one director put it. Logic like this could drive any company to bankruptcy!

Low Regular Dividend plus Extras

A policy of paying a low regular dividend plus a year-end extra in good years is a compromise between the previous two policies. It gives the firm flexibility, yet investors can count on receiving at least a minimum dividend. Therefore, if a firm's earnings and cash flows are quite volatile, this policy may well be its best choice. The directors can set a relatively low regular dividend—low enough so that it can be maintained even in low-profit years or in years when a considerable amount of retained earnings is needed—and then supplement it with an extra dividend in years when excess funds are available. General Motors, whose earnings fluctuate widely from year to year, has long followed the practice of supplementing its regular dividend with an extra dividend paid at the end of the year, when its profits and investment requirements are known.

Dividends are normally paid quarterly. For example, Consolidated Edison paid dividends of $1.88, $0.47 each quarter, during 1983. In common financial language, we say that Con Ed's *regular quarterly dividend* is $0.47, or that its *regular annual dividend* is $1.88. The actual payment procedure is as follows:

Payment Procedures

1. Declaration date. The directors meet, say on November 15, and declare the regular dividend. On this date, the directors issue a statement similar to the following: "On November 15, 1984, the directors of the XYZ Company met and declared the regular quarterly dividend of 50 cents per share, plus an extra dividend of 25 cents per share, payable to holders of record on December 15, payment to be made on January 2, 1985."

2. Holder-of-record date. At the close of business on the *holder-of-record date*, December 15, the company closes its stock transfer books and makes up a list of the shareholders as of that date. If XYZ Company is notified of the sale and transfer of some stock before 5 P.M. on December 15, the new owner receives the dividend. However, if notification is received on or after December 16, the previous owner of the stock gets the dividend check.

3. Ex-dividend date. Suppose Jean Buyer buys 100 shares of stock from John Seller on December 13. Will the company be notified of the transfer in time to list Buyer as the new owner and thus pay the dividend to her? To avoid conflict, the brokerage industry has set up a convention of declaring that the right to the dividend remains with the stock until four business days prior to the holder-of-record date; on the fourth day before the record date, the right to the dividend no longer goes with the shares. The date when the right to the dividend leaves the stock is called the *ex-dividend date*. In this case, the ex-dividend date is four days prior to December 15, or December 11:

	December 10
Ex-dividend date:	December 11
	December 12
	December 13
	December 14
Holder-of-record date:	December 15

Therefore, if Buyer is to receive the dividend, she must buy the stock by December 10. If she buys it on December 11 or later, Seller will receive the dividend.

The XYZ dividend, regular plus extra, amounts to $0.75, so the ex-dividend date is important. Barring fluctuations in the stock market, we would normally expect the price of a stock to drop by approximately the amount of the dividend on the ex-dividend date. Thus, if XYZ closed at $30¾ on December 10, it would probably open at about $30 on December 11.[8]

4. Payment date. The company actually mails the checks to the holders of record on January 2, the payment date.

Dividend Reinvestment Plans

During the 1970s, most of the larger companies instituted *dividend reinvestment plans (DRPs)*, whereby stockholders can automatically reinvest dividends received in the stock of the paying corporation.[9] *There are two types of DRPs: (1) plans which involve only "old" stock that is already outstanding, and (2) plans which involve newly issued stock.* In either case, the stockholder must pay income taxes on the amount of the dividends, even though stock rather than cash is received.

Under the "old stock" type of plan, the stockholder elects either to continue receiving dividend checks or to have the company use the dividends to buy more stock in the corporation. If the stockholder elects reinvestment, a bank, acting as trustee, takes the total funds available for reinvestment (less a fee), purchases the corporation's stock on the open market, and allocates the shares purchased to the participating

---

[8]Tax effects cause the price decline, on average, to be less than the full amount of the dividend. Suppose you were an investor in the 50 percent tax bracket. If you bought XYZ's stock on December 10, you would receive the dividend, but almost immediately pay half of it out in taxes. Thus, you would want to wait until December 11 to buy the stock if you thought you could get it for $0.75 per share less. Your reaction, and that of others, would influence stock prices around dividend payment dates. Here is what would happen:

1. Other things held constant, a stock's price should rise during the quarter, with the daily price increase (for XYZ) equal to $0.75/90 = $0.0083. Therefore, if it started at $30 just after its last ex-dividend date, it would rise to $30.75 on December 10.

2. In the absence of taxes, the stock's price would fall to $30 on December 11, then start up as the next dividend accrual period began. Thus, over time, if everything else were held constant, the stock's price would follow a saw-tooth pattern.

3. Because of taxes, the stock's price will not rise by the full amount of the dividend, or fall by the full dividend amount when it goes ex dividend.

4. The amount of the rise and subsequent fall depends on the average investor's marginal tax rate, and the differential between taxes on dividends and capital gains.

See Edwin J. Elton and Martin J. Gruber, "Marginal Stockholder Tax Rates and the Clientele Effect," *Review of Economics and Statistics*, February 1970, 68-74, for an interesting discussion of all this.

[9]See Richard H. Pettway and R. Phil Malone, "Automatic Dividend Reinvestment Plans," *Financial Management*, Winter 1973, 11-18, for an excellent discussion of the topic.

stockholders' accounts on a *pro rata* basis. The transactions costs of buy-ing shares (brokerage costs) are low because of volume purchases, so these plans benefit small stockholders who do not need cash dividends for current consumption.

The "new stock" type of DRP provides for dividends to be invested in newly issued stock; hence, these plans raise new capital for the firm. AT&T, Florida Power & Light, Union Carbide, and many other compa-nies have had such plans in effect in recent years, using them to raise substantial amounts of new equity capital. No fees are charged to stock-holders, and many companies offer stock at a discount of 5 percent be-low the actual market price. The companies absorb these costs as a trade-off against flotation costs that would be incurred on stock sold through investment bankers rather than through the dividend reinvest-ment plans. Discussions with corporate treasurers suggest that many other companies are seriously considering establishing or switching to new-stock DRPs.[10]

Summary of Factors that Influence Dividend Policy

In earlier sections, we described the major theories dealing with the ef-fects of dividend policy on the value of a firm and discussed four alter-native payment policies. Firms choose a particular policy based on man-agements' beliefs concerning the dividend theories, plus a host of other factors. All of the factors which are taken into account may be grouped into four broad categories: (1) constraints on dividend payments, (2) in-vestment opportunities, (3) availability and cost of alternative sources of capital, and (4) effects of dividend policy on k_s. Each of these categories has several subparts. They are all discussed in the following paragraphs.

Constraints

1. Bond indentures. Debt contracts generally restrict dividend payments to earnings generated after the loan was granted. Also, debt contracts often stipulate that no dividends can be paid unless the current ratio,

---

[10]One interesting aspect of DRPs is that they are forcing corporations to reexamine their basic dividend policies. A high participation rate in a DRP suggests that stockholders might be better off if the firm simply reduced cash dividends, as this would save stock-holders some personal income taxes. Quite a few firms are surveying their stockholders to learn more about their preferences and to find out how they would react to a change in dividend policy. A more rational approach to basic dividend policy decisions may emerge from this research.

Also, it should be noted that the Economic Recovery Tax Act of 1981 permitted investors to exempt from taxable income in 1982 to 1985 up to $750 of dividends ($1,500 on joint returns) paid by public utilities and reinvested in new-stock DRPs. The purpose of this provision was to help the utilities obtain investment capital.

Finally, companies use or stop using new stock DRPs depending on their need for eq-uity capital. Thus, Union Carbide recently stopped offering a new-stock DRP with a 5 percent discount because its need for equity capital declined.

the times-interest-earned ratio, and other safety ratios exceed stated minimums.

2. Impairment of capital rule. Dividend payments cannot exceed the balance sheet item retained earnings. This legal restriction, known as the *impairment of capital rule,* is designed to protect creditors. (*Liquidating dividends* can be paid out of capital, but they must be indicated as such and must not reduce capital below limits stated in the debt contracts.)

3. Availability of cash. Cash dividends can only be paid with cash. Thus, a shortage of cash in the bank can restrict dividend payments. However, unused borrowing capacity can offset this factor.

4. Penalty tax on improperly accumulated earnings. To prevent wealthy individuals from using corporations to avoid personal taxes, the Tax Code provides for a special surtax on improperly accumulated income. Thus, if the IRS can demonstrate that the dividend payout ratio is being deliberately held down to help stockholders avoid personal taxes, the firm is subject to heavy penalties. To date, this factor has been applied only to privately owned firms.

Investment Opportunities

1. Location of the IOS schedule. If the relevant IOS schedule in Figure 13-5 is far to the right, this will tend to produce a low payout ratio, and conversely if the IOS is far to the left. Also, the steeper the slope of the IOS, the more costly is a failure to use the payout prescribed by the residual theory.

2. Possibility of accelerating or delaying projects. The ability to accelerate or postpone projects will permit more flexibility in a firm's dividend policy.

Alternative Sources of Capital

1. Cost of selling new stock. If a firm needs to finance a given level of investment, it can obtain equity by retaining earnings or by selling new common stock. If flotation costs are high, k_e will be well above k_s, making it much better to finance through retention than through sale of new common stock. On the other hand, if these costs are low, dividend policy will be less important. Flotation costs differ among firms. For example, they are generally higher for small firms. Hence, the importance of these costs, and consequently the degree of flexibility in setting a dividend policy, varies among firms.

2. Ability to substitute debt for equity. A firm can finance a given level of investment with either debt or equity. As we have seen, if stock flotation costs are low, a more flexible dividend policy may be followed, because equity can be raised by retaining earnings or by selling new stock. A similar situation holds for debt policy. If the firm is willing to adjust its debt ratio, it can maintain a constant dollar dividend by using a variable debt ratio. The shape of the average cost of capital curve (left panel in Figure 13-3) determines the practical extent to which the debt ratio can be varied. If the average cost of capital curve is relatively flat over a wide range, then dividend policy is less critical than it would be if the curve had a distinct minimum.

3. Control. If management is concerned about maintaining control, it may be reluctant to sell new stock, and hence may retain more earnings than it otherwise would. This factor is especially important for small, closely held firms.

The effects of dividend policy on k_s may be considered in terms of these four factors: (1) differential tax rates, (2) stockholders' desire for current versus future income, (3) perceived riskiness of dividends versus capital gains, and (4) the information content of dividends (signaling). Since we discussed each of these factors in detail earlier, we need only note here that the importance of each factor in terms of its effect on k_s varies from firm to firm, depending on the makeup of its stockholders. Management certainly ought to take its own stockholders into account when it sets its dividend policy.

Effects of Dividend Policy on k_s

It should be apparent from our discussion thus far in the chapter that dividend policy decisions are truly exercises in informed judgment, not decisions which can be quantified precisely. However, to make rational dividend decisions, financial managers need to take account of all the points we have raised in the preceding sections.

Stock dividends and stock splits are related to the firm's cash dividend policy. The rationale for stock dividends and splits can best be explained through an example; we will use the Porter Electronics Company, a $700 million electronic components manufacturer, to illustrate. Since its inception, Porter's markets have been expanding, and as the company continued to grow and to retain earnings, its book value per share also grew. More important, its earnings per share and market price per share also rose. The company began its life with only a few thousand shares outstanding. After some years of growth, each share had a very high EPS and DPS. When a "normal" P/E ratio was applied to the stock, the derived market price was so high that few people could afford to buy a "round lot" of 100 shares. This limited demand for the stock, thus keeping the total market value of the firm below what it would be if more shares, at lower prices, were outstanding. To correct this situation, Porter "split its stock" as described below.

Stock Dividends and Stock Splits

Although there is little empirical evidence to support the contention, there is nevertheless a widespread belief in financial circles that an *optimal price range* exists for stocks. "Optimal" means that if the price is in

Stock Splits

this range, the price/earnings ratio, and hence the value of the firm, will be maximized. Many observers, including Porter's management, believe that the best range for most stocks is from $20 to $80 per share. Accordingly, if the price of Porter's stock rose to $80, management would probably declare a two-for-one stock split, thus doubling the number of shares outstanding, halving the earnings and dividends per share, and thereby lowering the price of the stock. Each stockholder would have more shares, but each share would be worth less. If the post-split price were $40, Porter's stockholders would be exactly as well off as they were before the split. If the price of the stock were to stabilize above $40, stockholders would be better off. Stock splits can be of any size. For example, the stock could be split two-for-one, three-for-one, 1.5-for-one, or in any other way.[11]

| Stock Dividends | *Stock dividends* are similar to stock splits in that they divide the pie into smaller slices without affecting the fundamental position of the current stockholders. On a 5 percent stock dividend, the holder of 100 shares would receive an additional 5 shares (without cost); on a 20 percent stock dividend, the same holder would receive 20 new shares; and so on. Again, the total number of shares is increased, so earnings, dividends, and price per share all decline. |

If a firm wants to reduce the price of its stock, should a stock split or a stock dividend be used? Stock splits are generally used after a sharp price run-up, when a large price reduction is sought. Stock dividends are frequently used on a regular annual basis to keep the stock price more or less constrained. For example, if a firm's earnings and dividends are growing at about 10 percent per year, the price would tend to go up at about that same rate, and it would soon be outside the desired trading range. A 10 percent annual stock dividend would maintain the stock price within the optimal trading range.

| Balance Sheet Effects | Although the economic effects of stock splits and dividends are virtually identical, accountants treat them somewhat differently. On a two-for-one split, the shares outstanding are doubled, and the stock's par value is halved. This treatment is shown in the middle section of Table 13-1 for Porter Electronics, using a pro forma 1986 balance sheet. |

---

[11]*Reverse splits*, which reduce the shares outstanding, can even be used; for example, a company whose stock sells for $5 might employ a one-for-five reverse split, exchanging one new share for five old shares and raising the value of the shares to about $25, which is within the "acceptable" range. LTV Corporation did this after several years of losses drove its stock price down below the "optimal" range.

Table 13-1
Porter Electronics Company:
Stockholders' Equity Accounts, Pro Forma 12/31/86

Before a Stock Split or a Stock Dividend

Common stock (6 million shares authorized, 5 million outstanding, $1 par)	$ 5,000,000
Additional paid-in capital	10,000,000
Retained earnings	155,000,000
Total common stockholders' equity	$170,000,000

After a Two-for-One Stock Split

Common stock (12 million shares authorized, 10 million shares outstanding, $0.50 par)	$ 5,000,000
Additional paid-in capital	10,000,000
Retained earnings	155,000,000
Total common stockholders' equity	$170,000,000

After a 20 Percent Stock Dividend

Common stock (6 million shares authorized, 6 million outstanding, $1 par)[a]	$ 6,000,000
Additional paid-in capital[b]	89,000,000
Retained earnings[b]	75,000,000
Total common stockholders' equity	$170,000,000

[a]Shares outstanding are increased by 20 percent, from 5 million to 6 million.

[b]A transfer equal to the market value of the new shares is made from the retained earnings account to the additional paid-in capital and common stock accounts:

$$\text{Transfer} = (5 \text{ million shares})(0.2)(\$80) = \$80 \text{ million.}$$

Of this $80 million, ($1 par)(1,000,000 shares) = $1 million goes to common stock and $79 million to paid-in capital.

With a stock dividend, the par value is not reduced, but an accounting entry is made transferring capital from the retained earnings account to the common stock and paid-in capital accounts. The transfer from retained earnings is calculated as follows:

$$\begin{pmatrix} \text{Dollars} \\ \text{transferred from} \\ \text{retained earnings} \end{pmatrix} = \begin{pmatrix} \text{Number} \\ \text{of shares} \\ \text{outstanding} \end{pmatrix} \begin{pmatrix} \text{Percentage} \\ \text{of the} \\ \text{stock dividend} \end{pmatrix} \begin{pmatrix} \text{Market} \\ \text{price of} \\ \text{the stock} \end{pmatrix}.$$

For example, if Porter Electronics, with 5 million shares outstanding, selling at $80 each, declared a 20 percent stock dividend, the transfer would be

$$\text{Dollars transferred} = (5 \text{ million})(0.2)(\$80) = \$80,000,000.$$

As shown in the bottom section of Table 13-1, of this $80 million transfer, $1 million is recorded in the common stock account and $79 million in the additional paid-in capital account. The retained earnings account is reduced to $75 million.[12]

Price Effects

Several empirical studies have examined the effects of stock splits and stock dividends on stock prices.[13] The findings of the Barker study are presented in Table 13-2. When stock dividends were associated with a cash dividend increase, the value of the company's stock six months after the ex dividend date had risen by 8 percent. On the other hand, when stock dividends were not accompanied by cash dividend increases, stock values fell by 12 percent, which approximated the percentage of the average stock dividend.

These data seem to suggest that stock dividends are seen for what they are—simply additional pieces of paper—and that they do not represent true income. When stock dividends are accompanied by higher earnings and cash dividends, investors bid up the value of the stock. However, when stock dividends are not accompanied by increases in earnings and cash dividends, the dilution of earnings and dividends per share causes the price of the stock to drop by about the same percentage as the stock dividend. The fundamental determinants of price are the underlying earnings and cash dividends per share.

Table 13-2
Price Effects of Stock Dividends

| | Price at Selected Dates (in Percentages) | | |
	Six Months before Ex-Dividend Date	At Ex-Dividend Date	Six Months after Ex-Dividend Date
Cash dividend increase after stock dividend	100	109	108
No cash dividend increase after stock dividend	100	99	88

---

[12]Note that Porter could not pay a stock dividend that exceeded 38.75 percent; a stock dividend of that percentage would exhaust the retained earnings. Thus, a firm's ability to declare stock dividends is constrained by the amount of its retained earnings. Of course, if Porter had wanted to pay a 50 percent stock dividend, it could just switch to a 1.5-for-1 stock split and accomplish the same thing.

[13]See C. A. Barker, "Evaluation of Stock Dividends," *Harvard Business Review*, July-August 1958, 99-114. Barker's study has been replicated several times in recent years, and his results are still valid—they have withstood the test of time. Another excellent study, using an entirely different methodology yet reaching similar conclusions, is that of Eugene F. Fama, Lawrence Fisher, Michael C. Jensen, and Richard Roll, "The Adjustment of Stock Prices to New Information," *International Economic Review*, February 1969, 1-21.

As we have seen, many factors interact to determine a firm's optimal dividend policy. Moreover, since the interactions are too complex to permit the development of a rigorous model for use as a guide to dividend policy, firms are forced to consider their dividend policies in a relatively subjective manner. Some illustrations of how dividend policies are actually set are given below.

Erie analyzed its situation in terms of the residual theory as shown in Figure 13-5. The residual theory suggested a dividend of $1.80 per share during 1985, or a 30 percent payout ratio. Erie's stock is widely held, and a number of tax-exempt institutions are important stockholders. A questionnaire to its stockholders revealed no strong preferences for dividends versus capital gains. Erie's long-range planning group projected a cost of capital and a set of investment opportunities during the next 3 to 5 years that are similar to those estimated for this year.

Based on this information, Erie's treasurer recommended to the board of directors that it establish a dividend of $1.80 for 1985, payable 45 cents quarterly. The 1984 dividend was $1.70, so the $1.80 represents an increase of about 6 percent. The treasurer also reported to the board that, in the event of an unforeseen earnings downturn, the company could obtain additional debt to meet its capital expenditure requirements. The board accepted the treasurer's recommendation, and in December of 1984 it declared a quarterly dividend of 45 cents per share, payable January 15, 1985. The board also announced its intention of maintaining this dividend for all of 1985.

Watkins Electronics has a residual theory position that resembles IOS_G in Figure 13-5. This suggests that no dividend be paid. Watkins has, in fact, paid no dividend since its inception in 1975, even though it has been continuously profitable and its earnings have recently been growing at a 25 percent rate. Informal conversations with the firm's major stockholders, all of whom are in high tax brackets, suggest that they neither expect nor want dividends—they would prefer to have the firm retain earnings, generate a higher earnings growth rate, and provide capital gains which are taxed at relatively low rates. The stock now sells for $106 per share. Watkins' treasurer recommended a three-for-one split, no cash dividend, and a future policy of declaring an annual stock dividend geared to earnings for the year. The board of directors concurred.

Southwest Electric has an acute need for new equity capital. The company has a major expansion program under way and absolutely must come up with the money to meet construction payments. The debt ratio

Establishing a Dividend Policy: Some Illustrations

Erie Steel Company

Watkins Electronics

Southwest Electric Company

is high, and if the times-interest-earned ratio falls any lower, then (1) the company's bonds will be downgraded, and (2) it will be barred by bond indenture provisions from further debt issues. These facts suggest a cut in dividends from the $2.50 per share paid last year. However, the treasurer knows that many of the stockholders rely on dividends for current living expenses, so if dividends are cut, these stockholders may be forced to sell, thus driving down the price of the stock. This would be especially bad in view of the treasurer's forecast that there will be a need to sell new common stock during the coming year. (New outside equity would be needed even if the company totally eliminated the dividend.) The treasurer is aware that many other utilities face a similar problem. Some have cut their dividends, and their stock prices invariably have fallen by amounts ranging from 30 to 70 percent.

Southwest's earnings were forecasted to increase from $3.33 to $3.60. The treasurer recommended that the dividend be raised from $2.50 to $2.70, with the dividend increase being announced a few weeks before the company floated a new stock issue. The hope was that this action would cause the price of the stock to increase, after which the company could sell a new issue of common stock at a better price.

North American Oil (NAO)

NAO's 1984 dividend was $2.45 per share, up from $2.30 in 1983. Both dividend figures represented about 50 percent of earnings, and this payout was consistent with a residual theory analysis. The company's growth rate in EPS and DPS had been in the 5 to 10 percent range during the previous few years, and management was projecting a continuation of this trend. The financial vice president foresaw a cash flow problem in 1985—earnings were projected to increase in line with the historical average, but an especially large number of good investment opportunities (along with some unprofitable, but required, pollution control expenditures) were expected. A preliminary analysis using the residual theory suggested that the dividend in 1985 should be cut back sharply, if not eliminated.

The financial vice president quickly rejected this cutback, recommending instead a 6 percent *increase* in the dividend, to $2.60. He noted that the company could easily borrow funds during the coming year to meet its capital requirements. The debt ratio would rise somewhat above the target, but the firm's average cost of capital curve was relatively flat, and cash flows from the 1985 investments should permit a reduction in the debt ratio over the next few years. The vice president felt that it was more important to maintain the steady growth in dividends than to adhere strictly to the target debt ratio.

Dividend policy involves the decision to pay out earnings or to retain them for reinvestment in the firm. Any change in dividend policy has both favorable and unfavorable effects on the price of the firm's stock. Higher dividends mean higher cash flows to investors, which is good, but lower future growth, which is bad. The optimal dividend policy balances these opposing forces and maximizes the price of the stock.

We first identified three dividend theories: (1) *dividend irrelevance*, (2) *"bird-in-the-hand,"* and (3) *tax differential*. Then we described a number of factors that bear on dividend policy, including the following: *legal constraints* such as bond indenture provisions, the firm's *investment opportunities*, the *availability and cost of funds from other sources* (new stock and debt), *tax rates*, *stockholders' desire for current income*, and the *information effect* of dividend changes. Because of the large number of factors that bear on dividend policy, and also because the relative importance of these factors changes over time and across companies, it is impossible to develop a precise, generalized model for use in establishing dividend policy.

The *residual dividend policy* is used by most firms to set a target payout, but then firms tend to use one of three payment policies: (1) *a stable or continuously increasing dollar dividend per share*; (2) *a low regular dividend plus extras* that depend on annual earnings; or (3) *a constant payout ratio*, which will cause the dollar dividend to fluctuate. Most firms follow the first policy, a few use the second, and almost none uses the third. Also, we noted that many firms today are using *dividend reinvestment plans (DRPs)* to help stockholders reinvest dividends at minimal brokerage costs. In Appendix 13A, we also show that some firms use stock repurchase plans in lieu of more cash dividends.

Stock splits and *stock dividends* were also discussed. Our conclusion was that these actions may be beneficial if the firm's stock price is quite high, but otherwise they have little effect on the value of the firm.

Summary

Questions

13-1 Define each of the following terms:
  a. Optimal dividend policy
  b. Dividend irrelevance theory
  c. "Bird-in-the-hand" theory
  d. Tax differential theory
  e. Residual dividend policy
  f. Constraints on dividend policy
  g. Clientele effect
  h. Information content of dividends
  i. Extra dividend
  j. Ex-dividend date
  k. Dividend reinvestment plans (each of two types)
  l. Stock split; stock dividend

13-2 As an investor, would you rather invest in a firm that has a policy of maintaining (a) a constant payout ratio, (b) a constant dollar dividend per share, (c) a target dividend growth rate, or (d) a constant regular quarterly dividend plus a year-end extra when earnings are sufficiently high or corporate investment needs are sufficiently low? Explain your answer, stating how these policies would affect your k_s.

13-3 How would each of the following changes probably affect aggregate (that is, the average for all corporations) payout ratios? Explain your answers.
   a. An increase in the personal income tax rate.
   b. A liberalization in depreciation for federal income tax purposes, that is, faster tax writeoffs.
   c. A rise in interest rates.
   d. An increase in corporate profits.
   e. A decline in investment opportunities.

13-4 Discuss the pros and cons of having the directors formally announce what a firm's dividend policy will be in the future.

13-5 Most firms would like to have their stock selling at a high P/E ratio and also have an extensive public ownership (many different shareholders). Explain how stock dividends or stock splits may help achieve these goals.

13-6 What is the difference between a stock dividend and a stock split? As a stockholder, would you prefer to see your company declare a 100 percent stock dividend or a two-for-one split? Assume that either action is feasible.

13-7 "The cost of retained earnings is less than the cost of new outside equity capital. Consequently, it is totally irrational for a firm to sell a new issue of stock and to pay dividends during the same year." Discuss this statement.

13-8 Would it ever be rational for a firm to borrow money in order to pay dividends? Explain.

13-9 Union representatives have presented arguments similar to the following: "Corporations such as General Foods retain about one-half their profits for financing needs. If they financed by selling stock instead of by retaining earnings, they could cut prices substantially and still earn enough to pay the same dividend to their shareholders. Therefore, their profits are too high." Evaluate this statement.

13-10 "Executive salaries have been shown to be more closely correlated to the size of the firm than to its profitability. If a firm's board of directors is controlled by management instead of by outside directors, this might result in the firm's retaining more earnings than can be justified from the stockholders' point of view." Discuss the statement, being sure (a) to use Figure 13-5 in your answer and (b) to explain the implied relationship between dividend policy and stock prices.

Problems

13-1 Modigliani and Miller (MM), on the one hand, and Gordon and Lintner (GL), on the other, have expressed strong views regarding the effect of dividend policy on a firm's cost of capital and value.
   a. In essence, what are the MM and the GL views regarding the effect of dividend policy on cost of capital and value? Illustrate your answer with a graph.
   b. How does the SMP model differ from the views of MM and GL?
   c. According to the text, which position (MM, GL, or SMP) has received statistical confirmation from empirical tests?

d. How could MM use the *information content,* or *signaling, hypothesis*
to counter their opponents' arguments? If you were debating MM,
how would you counter them?

e. How could MM use the *clientele effect* concept to counter their opponents' arguments? If you were debating MM, how would you
counter them?

13-2 One position expressed in the literature is that firms set their dividends as a residual, after using income to support new investment.

a. Explain what a residual dividend policy implies, illustrating your
answer with a graph showing how different conditions could lead
to different dividend payout ratios.

b. Could the residual dividend policy be consistent with (1) a constant
growth rate policy, (2) a constant payout policy, and/or (3) a low-
regular-plus-extras policy? Explain.

c. Think back to Chapters 11 and 12, where we considered the relationship between capital structure and the cost of capital. If the k_a
versus debt ratio plot were shaped like a sharp V, would this have
a different implication for the importance of setting dividends according to the residual policy than if the plot were shaped like a
shallow bowl (or a U)?

d. Companies A and B both have IOS schedules which intersect their
MCC schedules at a point which, under the residual policy, calls
for a 20 percent payout. In both cases, a 20 percent payout would
require a cut in the annual dividend from $2 to $1. One company
cut its dividend, while the other did not. One company had a relatively steep IOS curve, while the other had a relatively flat IOS.
Explain which company probably had the steep, and which the flat,
IOS.

13-3 More NYSE companies had stock dividends and stock splits during the
first 9 months of 1983 than during the whole 12 months of the previous record year, 1971. What was there about 1983 that made stock
splits and dividends so popular? Explain the rationale that a financial
vice president might give his or her board of directors to support a
stock split/dividend recommendation.

13-4 Cartwright Corporation declares a 4 percent stock dividend and a cash
dividend of $0.40 per share. The cash dividend is paid on old shares
plus new shares received from the stock dividend. Construct a pro
forma balance sheet showing the effect of these actions; use one new
balance sheet that incorporates both actions. The stock was selling for
$25 per share, and a condensed version of the Cartwright Corpora-
tion's balance sheet as of December 31, 1984, before the dividends,
follows (millions of dollars):

Cash	$ 50	Debt	$1,000
Other assets	1,950	Common stock (60 million shares authorized, 50 million shares outstanding, $1 par)	50
		Paid-in capital	200
		Retained earnings	750
Total assets	$2,000	Total claims	$2,000

13-5 Tampa Tobacco Company has for many years enjoyed a moderate but stable growth in sales and earnings. However, cigarette consumption and, consequently, Tampa's sales have been falling off recently, partly because of a national awareness of the dangers of smoking to health. Anticipating further declines in tobacco sales for the future, Tampa's management hopes eventually to move almost entirely out of the tobacco business and, instead, to develop a new, diversified product line in growth-oriented industries.

Tampa Tobacco has been especially interested in the prospects for pollution-control devices—its research department has already done much work on the problems of filtering smoke. Right now, the company estimates that an investment of $24 million is necessary to purchase new facilities and begin operations on these products, but the investment could return about 18 percent within a short time. Other investment opportunities total $9.6 million and are expected to return about 12 percent.

The company has been paying a $2.40 dividend on its 6 million shares outstanding. The announced dividend policy has been to maintain a stable dollar dividend, raising it only when it appears that earnings have reached a new, permanently higher level. The directors might, however, change this policy if reasons for doing so are compelling. Total earnings for the year are $22.8 million, the common stock is currently selling for $45, and the firm's current leverage ratio (debt/assets ratio) is 45 percent. Current costs of various forms of financing are listed below:

New bonds, $k_d = 7\%$.

New common stock sold at $45 will yield the firm $41.

Required rate of return on retained earnings, k_s, = 9%.

Tax rate = 50%.

a. Calculate the marginal cost of capital above and below the point of exhaustion of retained earnings for Tampa Tobacco, both with and without the dividend.
b. How large should Tampa's capital budget be for the year?
c. What is an appropriate dividend policy for Tampa Tobacco? How should the capital budget be financed?
d. How might risk factors influence Tampa's cost of capital, capital structure, and dividend policy?
e. What assumptions, if any, do your answers to the above make about investors' preference for dividends versus capital gains, that is, investors' preferences regarding the D_1/P_0 and g components of k_s?

Selected Additional References and Cases

Dividend policy has been studied extensively by academicians. The first major academic work, and still a classic that we recommend highly, is Lintner's analysis of how corporations actually set their dividend payment policies:

Lintner, John, "Distribution of Incomes of Corporations among Dividends, Retained Earnings, and Taxes," *American Economic Review*, May 1956, 97-113.

The effects of dividend policy on stock prices and capital costs have been examined by many researchers. The classic theoretical argument that dividend policy is important, and that stockholders like dividends, was set forth by Gordon, while Miller and Modigliani (MM) developed the notion that dividend policy is not important. Many researchers have extended both Gordon's and MM's theoretical arguments, and have attempted to test the effects of dividend policy in a variety of ways. Although statistical problems have precluded definitive conclusions, the following articles, among others, have helped to clarify the issues:

Brennan, Michael, "Taxes, Market Valuation, and Corporate Financial Policy," *National Tax Journal*, Spring 1975, 417-427.

Hayes, Linda S., "Fresh Evidence That Dividends Don't Matter," *Fortune*, May 4, 1981, 351-354.

Lewellen, Wilbur G., Kenneth L. Stanley, Ronald C. Lease, and Gary G. Schlarbaum, "Some Direct Evidence on the Dividend Clientele Phenomenon," *Journal of Finance*, December 1978, 1385-1399.

Mukherjee, Tarun J., and Larry M. Austin, "An Empirical Investigation of Small Bank Stock Valuation and Dividend Policy," *Financial Management*, Spring 1980, 27-31.

On stock dividends and stock splits, see

Baker, W. Kent, and Patricia L. Gallagher, "Management's View of Stock Splits," *Financial Management*, Summer 1980, 73-77.

Copeland, Thomas E., "Liquidity Changes Following Stock Splits," *Journal of Finance*, March 1979, 115-141.

On repurchases, see

Finnerty, Joseph E., "Corporate Stock Issue and Repurchase," *Financial Management*, Autumn 1975, 62-71.

Stewart, Samuel S., Jr., "Should a Corporation Repurchase Its Own Stock?" *Journal of Finance*, June 1976, 911-921.

Woolridge, J. Randall, and Donald R. Chambers, "Reverse Splits and Shareholder Wealth," *Financial Management*, Autumn 1983, 5-15.

The following cases from the Brigham-Crum casebook focus on the issues contained in this chapter:

Case 34, "Bellweather Oil Company," which emphasizes the effect of dividend policy on stock price.

Case 35, "Genetic Industries, Inc.," which deals with virtually all aspects of dividend policy.

The following Harrington case is also appropriate for this chapter:

"New Hampshire Savings Bank Corporation," which illustrates the traditional arguments set forth as the board of directors attempt to establish the company's dividend policy.

13A   Stock Repurchases

As an alternative to paying cash dividends, a firm may distribute income to stockholders by *repurchasing its own stock*. Stock that has been repurchased by a firm is called *treasury stock*. If some of the outstanding stock is repurchased, fewer shares will remain outstanding. Assuming the repurchase does not adversely affect the firm's earnings, the earnings per share on the remaining shares will increase, resulting in a higher market price per share. Capital gains, then, will have been substituted for dividends. In this appendix, we discuss stock repurchases in more detail.

The Effects of Stock Repurchases

Many companies have been repurchasing their stock in recent years. Until recently, most repurchases amounted to a few million dollars; but in 1984, Standard Oil of Indiana announced plans for the largest repurchase on record, up to 30 million of its shares at a price of about $60 per share, or about $1.8 billion in total. Almost simultaneously, Teledyne announced plans to buy back another 8.7 million of its shares at a price of $200 per share, for a total of $1.7 billion. Other large repurchases have been made by Texaco, IBM, and Consolidated Edison.

The effects of a repurchase can be illustrated with data on American Development Corporation (ADC). The company earned $4.4 million in 1984, and 50 percent of this amount, or $2.2 million, had been allocated for distribution to common shareholders. There were 1.1 million shares outstanding, and the market price was $20 a share. ADC felt that it could use the $2.2 million to repurchase 100,000 of its shares through a tender offer for $22 a share or could pay a cash dividend of $2 a share.[1]

---

[1]Stock repurchases are commonly made in three ways. First, a publicly owned firm can simply buy its own stock through a broker on the open market. Second, it can issue a *tender* under which it permits stockholders to send in (that is, "tender") their shares to the firm in exchange for a specified price per share. When tender offers are made, the firm generally indicates that it will buy up a specified number of shares within a particular time period (usually about two weeks); if more shares are tendered than the company wishes to purchase, then purchases are made on a *pro rata* basis. Finally, the firm can purchase a block of shares from one large holder on a negotiated basis. If a negotiated purchase is

The effect of the repurchase on the EPS and market price per share of the remaining stock can be determined in the following way:

1. Current EPS $= \dfrac{\text{Total earnings}}{\text{Number of shares}} = \dfrac{\$4.4 \text{ million}}{1.1 \text{ million}} = \$4$ per share.

2. P/E ratio $= \dfrac{\$20}{\$4} = 5\times$.

3. $\begin{array}{l}\text{EPS after repurchase} \\ \text{of 100,000 shares}\end{array} = \dfrac{\$4.4 \text{ million}}{1 \text{ million}} = \$4.40$ per share.

4. $\begin{array}{l}\text{Expected market price} \\ \text{after repurchase}\end{array} = (\text{P/E})(\text{EPS}) = (5)(\$4.40) = \$22$ per share.

It should be noticed from this example that investors would receive benefits of $2 per share in any case, either in the form of a $2 cash dividend or a $2 increase in the stock price. This result occurs because we assumed that (1) shares could be repurchased at exactly $22 a share and (2) the P/E ratio would remain constant. If shares could be bought for less than $22, the operation would be even better for *remaining* stockholders, but the reverse would hold if ADC paid more than $22 a share. Furthermore, the P/E ratio might change as a result of the repurchase operation, rising if investors viewed it favorably, and falling if they viewed it unfavorably. Some factors that might affect P/E ratios are considered next.

From the stockholder's viewpoint, advantages of repurchases are as follows:

Advantages of Repurchases from the Stockholder's Viewpoint

1. Profits earned on repurchases are typically taxed at the capital gains rate, whereas a dividend distribution is taxed at the stockholder's marginal tax rate. This is significant. For example, it has been estimated that, on average, individual stockholders pay a tax of about 45 percent on marginal income. Since the capital gains tax rate is generally only 40 percent of the ordinary tax rate, the typical shareholder clearly benefits, other things the same, if the distribution is in the form of a stock repurchase rather than a dividend. Teledyne, a $3 billion conglomerate, earns about $400 million per year, yet it has not paid a cash dividend in 20 years, and it is not expected to pay any dividends in the foreseeable future. Profits are, however, used to repurchase stock and thus stimulate growth. Teledyne's stock rose from $4 in 1975 to $250 in 1984, so the company is clearly doing something right!

2. The stockholder has a choice—to sell or not to sell. On the other hand, one must accept a dividend payment and pay the tax. Thus, Teledyne stock-

employed, care must be taken to insure that this one stockholder does not receive preferential treatment not available to other stockholders, or that if preference is given, that this preference is justified by "sound business reasons." At this time (Summer 1984), Texaco's management is being sued by stockholders who are unhappy over the company's repurchase of about $600 million of stock from the Bass Brothers interests at a substantial premium over the market price. The suit charges that management was afraid the Bass Brothers would attempt a takeover, and the buyback got the Basses off management's back. Such payments have been dubbed "greenmail."

holders who want cash can sell some of their shares, and those who do not need cash can simply retain their stock. From a tax standpoint, both types of stockholders come out ahead.

3. A qualitative advantage advanced by market practitioners is that repurchase can often remove a large block of stock which is overhanging the market and keeping the price per share down.

Advantages of Repurchases from Management's Viewpoint

From management's viewpoint, here are the major advantages of repurchases:

1. As noted in Chapter 13, dividends are "sticky" in the short run because managements are reluctant to raise dividends if the new dividend cannot be maintained in the future—managements dislike cutting cash dividends. Hence, if the excess cash flow is thought to be only *temporary*, management may prefer to make the distribution in the form of a share repurchase rather than to declare a cash dividend they believe cannot be maintained.

2. Repurchased stock can be used for acquisitions or released when stock options are exercised, when convertibles are converted, or when warrants are exercised. Discussions with financial managers indicate that they often like to use repurchased stock rather than newly issued stock for these purposes so as to avoid dilution of per share earnings.

3. If directors have large holdings themselves, they may have especially strong preferences for repurchases rather than dividend payments because of the tax factor.

4. Repurchases can be used to effect large-scale changes in capital structures. For example, at one time, American Standard (a major plumbing supply company) had virtually no long-term debt outstanding. The company decided that its optimal capital structure called for the use of considerably more debt, but even if it had financed only with debt, it would have taken years to get the debt ratio up to the newly defined optimal level. What should the company do? It decided to sell long-term debt and to use the proceeds to repurchase its common stock, thus producing an instantaneous change in its capital structure.

5. Treasury stock can be resold in the open market if the firm needs additional funds.[2]

Disadvantages of Repurchases from the Stockholder's Viewpoint

From the stockholder's viewpoint, disadvantages of repurchases include the following:

1. Stockholders may not be indifferent between the choice of dividends and capital gains, and the price of the stock might benefit more from cash dividends than from repurchases. Cash dividends are generally thought to be

---

[2]Another interesting use of stock repurchases was St. Joe Minerals' strategy of repurchasing its own stock to thwart an attempted takeover. Seagram Company was attempting to acquire a controlling interest in St. Joe through a tender offer of $45 a share. St. Joe's management countered with a tender offer of its own for 7 million shares at $60 per share, to be financed by the sale of several divisions plus borrowings.

relatively dependable, but repurchases are not. Further, if a firm announces a regular, dependable repurchase program, the improper accumulation tax would probably become more of a threat. Although Teledyne has apparently had no problems in this regard, Teledyne's repurchases are somewhat irregular, which may make a difference.

2. The *selling* stockholders may not be fully aware of all the implications of a repurchase, or they may not have all pertinent information about the corporation's present and future activities. Therefore, firms generally announce a repurchase program before embarking on it to avoid potential stockholder suits.

3. The corporation may pay too high a price for the repurchased stock, to the disadvantage of remaining stockholders. If the shares are inactively traded, and if the firm seeks to acquire a relatively large amount of its own stock, the price may be bid above a maintainable price and then fall after the firm ceases its repurchase operations.

From management's viewpoint, disadvantages of repurchases are as follows:

1. Some people have argued that firms which repurchase substantial amounts of stock often have poorer growth rates and fewer good investment opportunities than firms which do not engage in repurchases. Thus, to some extent, announcing a repurchase program is like announcing that management cannot locate good investment projects. One could argue that instituting a repurchase program should be regarded in the same manner as announcing a higher dividend payout; however, if it is true that repurchases are regarded as indicating especially unfavorable growth opportunities, then they could have an adverse impact on the firm's image, and therefore on the price of its stock. There is, in our view, little empirical support for this position.

2. Repurchases might involve some risk from a legal standpoint. If the Internal Revenue Service could establish that the repurchases were primarily for the avoidance of taxes on dividends, then penalties could be imposed on the firm under the improper accumulation of earnings provision of the Tax Code. Such actions have been brought against privately held companies, but we know of no case involving a publicly owned firm, even though some firms have retired over one-half of their outstanding stock.

3. The SEC could raise questions if it appears that the firm may be manipulating the price of its shares. This factor, in particular, keeps firms from doing much repurchasing if they plan offerings of other types of securities in the near future, or if they contemplate merger negotiations where their stock would be exchanged for that of the acquired company.

Disadvantages of Repurchases from Management's Viewpoint

When all the pros and cons on stock repurchases are totaled, where do we stand? Our conclusions may be summarized as follows:

1. Repurchases on a regular, systematic, dependable basis may not be feasible because of uncertainties about the tax treatment of such a program and

Conclusions on Stock Repurchases

uncertainties about such things as the market price of the shares, how many shares would be tendered, and so forth.

2. However, repurchases do offer investors some significant tax advantages over dividends, so this procedure should be given careful consideration on the basis of the firm's unique situation.

3. Repurchases can be especially valuable to a firm that wants to make a significant shift in its capital structure within a short period.

On balance, companies probably ought to be doing more repurchasing than they are, and distributing less cash as dividends. Increases in the size and frequency of repurchases in recent years suggests that companies are increasingly sharing this conclusion.

Types of
Long-Term Capital

Common Stock and the Investment Banking Process

14

In the early 1980s, after several years of strong growth, Apple Computer, Inc., had some excellent investment opportunities, but it lacked the capital necessary to take advantage of them. It could have borrowed the funds, but a debt ratio constraint limited the company's use of debt without additional equity. To take advantage of its growth opportunities, the company needed to sell about $90 million of stock.

At the time, Apple's stock was not publicly traded—the 50 million shares outstanding were all owned by its founders and several venture capital firms. Since the stock was not traded, it had no established price. This presented a problem. To raise the $90 million, Apple would have to create and then sell new shares. It could create 1 million shares and try to sell them for $90 each, 10 million shares for $9 each, 90 million shares for $1 each, or any other combination that would produce $90 million. If it sold a few shares at a high price, the current owners would benefit, since they would end up owning a higher percentage of the company. On the other hand, potential buyers would want to obtain shares at a lower price, so if the offering price were set too high, the issue would fail and Apple would not raise the $90 million. However, if the offering price were set too low, then the original owners would be giving away a larger share of the company than was necessary.

To help resolve the price question, and also to help market the stock, Apple brought in a group of investment bankers, including Morgan Stanley & Company. Based on a careful analysis of Apple's sales, earnings, and assets, as well as of how investors were valuing similarly situated but publicly traded firms at the time, Morgan concluded that Apple should sell 4.4 million shares at a price of $22, for a total of $96.8 million. Morgan Stanley and the other investment bankers were paid about $6 million for their services, and Apple netted just over $90 million.

Immediately after the sale, the stock moved up from the $22 offering price to the $28 to $29 range. The new stockholders were happy—they had made a quick gain of about 30 percent. The old stockholders were also happy, because (1) the public sale indicated a minimum value of 50,000,000($28) = $1.4 billion for their stock, and (2) with a market price established, the old stockholders' liquidity was greatly enhanced. Finally, the investment bankers were happy—they not only had made $6 million, but also had satisfied their clients on both sides of the deal, which meant more business in the future.

Stock offerings do not always work out so well. For example, shortly after the Apple issue, Abt Computer Graphics, a Boston company, tried to sell an issue at $14 per share to raise $5 million. The issue failed to sell, so the company cut the price to $7. That did not work either, and Abt was forced to withdraw the offering entirely and to

Success or failure in the equity market is a function of many things. Obviously, the fundamental position of the company is critical, but two similar firms can have very different experiences, depending on the timing of their issues, how the securities are packaged, and the sales approach taken by the investment bankers. These topics are discussed in this chapter.

In Part III, we examined the analysis firms employ when making decisions regarding the investment in long-term (or fixed) assets, while in Part IV we discussed capital structure and dividend decisions. Any decision to acquire new assets necessitates the raising of new capital, and, generally, long-term assets are financed with long-term capital. In this chapter, we consider in some detail decisions regarding common stock financings. As a part of this analysis, we also examine in detail the procedures used by firms to raise new long-term capital, or the investment banking process.

Balance Sheet Accounts and Definitions

Legal and accounting terminology is vital to both investors and financial managers if they are to avoid misinterpretations and possibly costly mistakes, so we begin our analysis of common stock with a discussion of accounting and legal issues. Consider first Table 14-1, which shows the common stockholders' equity section of Southern Metals Company's balance sheet. Southern's owners, its stockholders, have authorized management to issue a total of 60 million shares, and management has, thus far, actually issued (or sold) 50 million shares. Each share has a *par*

Table 14-1
Southern Metals Company:
Stockholders' Equity Accounts
as of December 31, 1984

Common stock (60 million shares authorized, 50 million shares outstanding, $1 par)	$ 50,000,000
Additional paid-in capital	100,000,000
Retained earnings	750,000,000
Total common stockholders' equity (or common net worth)	$900,000,000

$$\text{Book value per share} = \frac{\text{Total common stockholders' equity}}{\text{Shares outstanding}}$$

$$= \frac{\$900,000,000}{50,000,000} = \$18.$$

value of $1; this is the minimum amount for which new shares can be issued.[1]

Southern Metals is an old company, established in 1873. Its initial equity capital consisted of 5,000 shares sold at the $1 par value, so on its first balance sheet the total stockholders' equity was $5,000. The initial paid-in capital and retained earnings accounts showed zero balances. Over the years, Southern retained earnings, and the firm issued new stock to raise capital from time to time. During 1984, Southern earned $120 million, paid $100 million in dividends, and retained $20 million. The $20 million was added to the $730 million accumulated retained earnings shown on the year-end 1983 balance sheet to produce the $750 million retained earnings at year-end 1984. Thus, since its inception in 1873, Southern has retained, or plowed back, a total of $750 million. This is money that belongs to the stockholders and that they could have received in the form of dividends. Instead, the stockholders chose to let management reinvest the $750 million in the business.

Now consider the $100 million additional paid-in capital. This account shows the difference between the stock's par value and what new stock-

---

[1] A stock's par value is an arbitrary value that indicates the minimum amount of money stockholders have put up, or must put up in the event of bankruptcy. Actually, the firm could legally sell new shares at below par, but any purchaser would be liable for the difference between the issue price and the par value in the event the company went bankrupt. Thus, if Southern sold an investor 10,000 shares at $0.40 per share, for $4,000, the investor would have to put up an additional $6,000 if the company should later go bankrupt. This contingent liability effectively precludes the sale of new common stock at prices below par.

Also, we should point out that firms are not required to establish a par value for their stock. Thus, Southern could have elected to use "no par" stock, in which case the common stock and additional paid-in capital accounts could have been consolidated under one account called *common stock*, which would show a balance of $150 million.

holders paid when they bought newly issued shares. As has been noted, Southern was formed in 1873 with 5,000 shares issued at the $1 par value; thus, the first balance sheet showed a zero balance for additional paid-in capital. By 1888, the company had demonstrated its profitability and was earning $0.50 per share. Further, it had built up the retained earnings account to a total of $10,000, so the total stockholders' equity was $5,000 of par value plus $10,000 of retained earnings = $15,000, and the book value per share was $15,000/5,000 shares = $3. Southern had also borrowed heavily, and, in spite of its retained earnings, the company's debt ratio had built up to an unacceptable level, precluding further use of debt without an infusion of equity.

The company had profitable investment opportunities, so, to take advantage of them, it decided to issue another 2,000 shares of stock. The market price at the time was $4 per share, which was eight times the $0.40 earnings per share (the price/earnings ratio was $8 \times$). This $4 market value per share was well in excess of the $1 par value, and also higher than the $3 book value per share, demonstrating that par value, book value, and market value are not necessarily equal. Had the company lost money since its inception, it would have had negative retained earnings, the book value would have been below par, and the market price might well have been below book. After the 2,000 new shares had been sold to investors back in 1888, at a price of $4 per share, which was the market price then, Southern Metals' partial balance sheet changed as shown in Table 14-2. Each share brought in $4, of which $1 represented the par value and $3 represented the excess of the sale price

Table 14-2
Effects of Stock Sale on
Southern Metals' Equity Accounts

	Before Sale of Stock
Common stock (5,000 shares outstanding, $1 par)	$ 5,000
Additional paid-in capital	0
Retained earnings	10,000
Total stockholders' equity	$15,000
Book value per share = $15,000/5,000 =	$3.00

	After Sale of Stock
Common stock (7,000 shares outstanding, $1 par)	$ 7,000
Additional paid-in capital ($4 − $1) × 2,000 shares	6,000
Retained earnings	10,000
Total stockholders' equity	$23,000
Book value per share = $23,000/7,000 =	$3.29

above par. Since 2,000 shares were involved, a total of $2,000 was added to common stock, while $6,000 was entered in additional paid-in capital. Notice also that book value per share rose from $3 to $3.29; whenever stock is sold at a price above book, the book value increases, and conversely if stock is sold below book.[2]

Similar transactions have taken place down through the years to produce the current situation, as shown on Southern's latest balance sheet in Table 14-1.[3]

Legal Rights and Privileges of Common Stockholders

The common stockholders are the owners of a corporation, and as such they have certain rights and privileges. The most important of these rights are discussed in this section.

Control of the Firm

The stockholders have the right to elect the firm's directors, who in turn select the officers who manage the business. In a small firm, the major stockholder typically assumes the positions of president and chairman of the board of directors. In a large, publicly owned firm, the managers typically have some stock, but their personal holdings are insufficient to exercise voting control. Thus, the management of a publicly owned firm can be removed by the stockholders if the stockholder group decides the management is not effective.

Various state and federal laws stipulate how stockholder control is to be exercised. First, corporations must hold an election of directors periodically, usually once a year, with the vote taken at the annual meeting. Frequently, one-third of the directors are elected each year for a 3-year term. Each share of stock has one vote; thus, the owner of 1,000 shares has 1,000 votes. Stockholders can appear at the annual meeting and vote in person, or they can transfer their right to vote to a second party by means of an instrument known as a *proxy*. Management always solicits stockholders' proxies and usually gets them. However, if earnings are

---

[2]The effects on book value are not important for industrial firms, but they are *very* important for utility companies, whose allowable earnings per share are, in effect, determined by regulators as a percentage of book value. Thus, if a utility's stock is selling below book, and the company sells stock to raise new equity, this dilutes the book value per share of its existing stockholders and drives down their allowable earnings per share, which in turn drives down the market price. Most U.S. electric utilities' stocks were sold below book value during the late 1970s and early 1980s. They needed to raise large amounts of capital, including equity, since they had to keep their capital structures in balance. This meant selling stock at prices below book, which tended to depress the market value of the stock still further.

[3]Stock dividends, stock splits, and stock repurchases (the reverse of stock issues) also affect the capital accounts. These were discussed in Chapter 13 and Appendix 13A.

poor and stockholders are dissatisfied, an outside group may solicit the proxies in an effort to overthrow management and take over control of the business. This is known as a *proxy fight*.

The question of control has become a central issue in finance in recent years. The frequency of proxy fights has increased, as have attempts by one corporation to take over another by purchasing a majority of the outstanding stock. This latter action, which is called a *takeover*, is discussed in detail in Chapter 24. Some well-known examples of recent takeover battles include Du Pont's acquisition of Conoco, and Chevron's acquisition of Gulf Oil. Managers who do not have majority control (over 50 percent) of their firms' stocks are very much concerned about takeovers, and many of them are attempting to get stockholder approval for changes in their corporate charters that would make takeovers more difficult. For example, a number of companies tried in 1984 to get their stockholders to agree (1) to elect only one-third of the directors each year (rather than to elect all directors each year) and (2) to require 75 percent of the stockholders (rather than 50 percent) to approve a merger. Managements seeking such changes generally cite as the reason the fear that the firm will be picked up at a bargain price, but some stockholders wonder whether concern about their jobs might not be an even more important consideration.

The Preemptive Right

Common stockholders often have the right, called the *preemptive right*, to purchase any additional shares sold by the firm. In some states, the preemptive right is automatically included in every corporate charter; in others, it is necessary to specifically insert the preemptive right into the charter.

The purpose of the preemptive right is twofold. First, it protects the power of control of present stockholders. If it were not for this safeguard, the management of a corporation under criticism from stockholders could prevent stockholders from removing it from office by issuing a large number of additional shares and purchasing these shares itself. Management would thereby secure control of the corporation to frustrate the will of the current stockholders.

The second, and by far the more important, protection that the preemptive right affords stockholders regards dilution of value. For example, assume that 1,000 shares of common stock, each with a price $100, are outstanding, making the total market value of the firm $100,000. An additional 1,000 shares are sold at $50 a share, or for $50,000, thus raising the total market value of the firm to $150,000. When the total market value is divided by the new total shares outstanding, a value of $75 a share is obtained. Thus, selling common stock at below market value would dilute the price of the stock and would transfer wealth from the present stockholders to those who purchase the new shares. The preemptive right prevents such occurrences. Procedures for issuing stock to existing shareholders, called a *rights offering*, are discussed in Appendix 14A.

Types of Common Stock

Although most firms have only one type of common stock, in some instances special classifications of stock are created to meet the special needs of the company. Generally, when different types of stock are used, one type is designated *Class A*, the second *Class B*, and so on. Small, new companies seeking to obtain funds from outside sources frequently use different types of common stock. For example, stock designated Class A may be sold to the public, pay a dividend, and have full voting rights. The stock designated Class B, however, may be retained by the organizers of the company, and the legal terms may state that dividends will not be paid on it until the company has established its earning power by building up retained earnings to a designated level. By the use of classified stock, the public can take a position in a conservatively financed growth company without sacrificing income. In situations such as this, the Class B stock is often called *founders' shares* and given *sole* voting rights for a number of years. This permits the organizers to maintain complete control of the operations in the crucial early stages of the firm's development. At the same time, other investors are protected against excessive withdrawals of funds by the original owners.

Note that "Class A," "Class B," and so on have no standard meanings. Most firms have no classified shares. Of the firms that do use classified shares, one may designate its Class B shares as founders' shares and its Class A shares as those sold to the public. Another firm can reverse these designations. Still other firms could use the A and B designations for entirely different purposes.

The Market for Common Stock

Some companies are so small that their common stock is not actively traded—it is owned by only a few people, usually the companies' managers. Such companies are said to be *privately owned*, or *closely held*, and their stock is said to be *closely held stock*. On the other hand, the stocks of most larger companies are owned by a fairly large number of investors, most of whom are not active in management. Such companies are said to be *publicly owned*, and their stock is said to be *publicly held stock*.

As we saw in Chapter 3, the stocks of smaller publicly owned firms are not listed on an exchange; they trade in the *over-the-counter (OTC)* market, and the companies and their stocks are said to be *unlisted*. However, larger publicly owned companies generally apply for listing on an exchange, and these companies and their stocks are said to be *listed*. As a general rule, companies are first listed on a regional exchange such as the Pacific Coast or Midwest, then move up to the American (AMEX), and finally, if they grow large enough, to the "Big Board," the New York Stock Exchange (NYSE). Thousands of stocks are traded in the OTC market, but in terms of market value of both outstanding shares and daily transactions, the NYSE dominates with about 60 percent of the business.

Institutional investors such as pension trusts, insurance companies, and mutual funds own about 35 percent of all common stocks. However, the institutions buy and sell relatively actively, so they account for about 75 percent of all transactions. Thus, the institutions have a heavy influence on the price of individual stocks—in a real sense, institutional investors determine the prices of individual stocks, and hence set the tone of the market.

Types of Stock Market Transactions

We can classify stock market transactions into three distinct categories:

1. Trading in the outstanding shares of established, publicly owned companies: the secondary market. Southern Metals Company has 50 million shares of stock outstanding. If the owner of 100 shares sells his or her stock, the trade is said to have occurred in the *secondary market*. Thus, the market for outstanding shares, or *used shares*, is defined as the secondary market. The company receives no new money when sales occur in the secondary market.

2. Additional shares sold by established, publicly owned companies: the primary market. If Southern Metals decides to sell an additional 1 million shares to raise new equity capital, this transaction is said to occur in the *primary market*.[4]

3. New public offerings by privately held firms: the primary market. In 1975 the Coors Brewing Company, which was owned by the Coors family at the time, decided to sell some stock to raise capital needed for a major expansion program.[5] This type of transaction is defined as *going public*—whenever stock in a closely held corporation is offered to the public for the first time, the company is said to be going public. The market for stock that has recently gone public is often called the *new issue market*.

Firms can go public without raising any additional capital. For example, in its early days, the Ford Motor Company was owned exclusively by

---

[4]Recall that Southern has 60 million shares authorized but only 50 million outstanding. Thus, the company has 10 million authorized but unissued shares. If it had no authorized but unissued shares, management could increase the authorized shares by obtaining stockholders' approval, which would generally be granted without any arguments.

[5]The stock Coors offered to the public was designated Class B, and it was nonvoting. The Coors family retained the founders' shares, called Class A stock, which carried full voting privileges. The company was large enough to obtain a NYSE listing, but this exchange has a requirement that listed common stock must have full voting rights, and this requirement precluded Coors from obtaining a NYSE listing.

the Ford family. When Henry Ford died, he left a substantial part of his stock to the Ford Foundation. When the Foundation later sold some of this stock to the general public, the Ford Motor Company went public, even though the company raised no capital in the transaction.

As noted in Chapter 2, most businesses begin life as proprietorships or partnerships, and then, as the more successful ones grow, they find it desirable at some point to convert into corporations. Initially, these new corporations' stocks are generally owned by the firms' officers, key employees, and/or a very few investors who are not actively involved in management. However, if growth continues, the company may decide at some point to go public. The advantages and disadvantages weighed in making this decision are discussed next.

The Decision to Go Public

1. **Permits diversification.** As a company grows and becomes more valuable, its founders often have most of their wealth tied up in the company. By selling some of their stock in a public offering, they can diversify their holdings, thereby reducing somewhat the riskiness of their personal portfolios.

Advantages of Going Public

2. **Increases liquidity.** The stock of a closely held firm is very illiquid. No ready market exists for it. If one of the holders wants to sell some shares to raise cash, it is hard to find potential buyers, and even if a buyer is located, there is no established price at which to complete the transaction. These problems do not exist with publicly owned firms.

3. **Makes it easier to raise new corporate cash.** If a privately held company wants to raise cash by a sale of new stock, it must either go to its existing owners, who may not have any money or may not want to put any more eggs in this particular basket, or shop around for wealthy investors who may want to make an investment in the company. However, it is usually difficult to get outsiders to put money into a closely held company, because if the outsiders do not have voting control (over 50 percent) of the stock, then the inside stockholders/managers can run roughshod over them. The insiders can pay or not pay dividends, pay themselves exorbitant salaries, have private deals with the company, and so on. For example, the president might buy a warehouse and lease it to the company, or get the use of a Rolls Royce and all-the-frills travel to conventions. The insiders can even keep the outsiders from knowing the company's actual earnings, or its real worth. There are not many positions more vulnerable than that of an outside stockholder in a closely held company, and for this reason it is hard for closely held companies to raise new equity capital. Going public, which brings with it disclosure and regulation by the Securities and Exchange Commission (SEC), greatly reduces these problems and thus makes people more willing to invest in the company.

4. Establishes a value for the firm. For a number of reasons, it is often useful to establish a firm's value in the marketplace. For one thing, when the owner of a privately owned business dies, state and federal inheritance tax appraisers must set a value on the company for estate tax purposes. Often, these appraisers set too high a value, which creates all sorts of problems. However, a company that is publicly owned has its value established, with little room for argument. Similarly, if a company wants to give incentive stock options to key employees, it is useful to know the exact value of these options. Also, employees much prefer to own stock, or options on stock, that is publicly traded, because public trading increases liquidity.

Disadvantages of
Going Public

1. Cost of reporting. A publicly owned company must file quarterly and annual reports with the SEC and/or with various state officials. These reports can be costly, especially for very small firms.

2. Disclosure. Management may not like the idea of reporting operating data, because such data will then be available to competitors. Similarly, the owners of the company may not want people to know their net worth. Since publicly owned companies must disclose the number of shares owned by officers, directors, and major stockholders, it is easy enough for anyone to multiply shares held by price per share to estimate the net worth of insiders.

3. Self-dealings. The owners/managers of closely held companies have many opportunities for various types of questionable but legal self-dealings, including the payment of high salaries, nepotism, personal transactions with the business (such as a leasing arrangement), and not-truly-necessary fringe benefits. Such self-dealing is much harder to arrange if a company is publicly owned—it must be disclosed, and the managers are also subject to stockholder suits.

4. Inactive market/low price. If the firm is very small, and if its shares are not traded with much frequency, its stock will not really be liquid, and the market price may not be representative of the stock's true value. Security analysts and stockbrokers simply will not follow the stock, because there just will not be enough trading activity to generate enough sales commissions to cover the analysts'/brokers' costs of following the stock.

5. Control. Because of the dramatic increase in tender offers and proxy fights in the 1980s, the managers of publicly owned firms who do not have at least 50 percent of the stock must be concerned about maintaining control. Further, there is pressure on such managers to produce annual earnings gains, even when it might be in the shareholders' best long-term interests to adopt a strategy that would penalize short-run earnings but benefit earnings in future years. These factors have led a number of public companies to "go private" in "leveraged buyout" deals where the managers borrow the money to buy out the nonmanagement stockholders.

It should be obvious from this discussion that there are no hard-and-fast rules regarding whether or when a company should go public. This is an individual decision that should be made on the basis of the company's and its stockholders' own unique circumstances.

Conclusions on Going Public

If a company does decide to go public, either by the sale of newly issued stock to raise new capital for the corporation or by the sale of stock by the current owners, one key issue is setting the price at which shares will be offered to the public. The company and its current owners want to set the price as high as possible—the higher the offering price, the smaller the fraction of the company the current owners will have to give up to obtain any specified amount of money. On the other hand, potential buyers will want the price set as low as possible. We will return to the establishment of the offering price later in the chapter, after we have described some other aspects of common stock financing.

The decision to go public is a truly significant milestone in a company's life—it marks a major transition in the relationship between the firm and its owners. The decision to list, on the other hand, is not a major event. The company will have to file a few new reports with an exchange; it will have to abide by the rules of the exchange; stockholders will generally purchase or sell shares through a stockbroker who acts as an *agent* rather than as a *dealer*; and the stock's price will be quoted in the newspaper under a stock exchange rather than in the over-the-counter section. These are not very significant differences.

The Decision to List the Stock

In order to have its stock listed, a company must apply to an exchange, pay a relatively small fee, and meet the exchange's minimum requirements. These requirements relate to the size of the company's net income, as well as to the number of shares outstanding and in the hands of outsiders (as opposed to the number held by insiders who generally do not trade their stock very actively). Also, the company must agree to disclose certain information to the exchange; this information is designed to help the exchange track trading patterns and thus to try to be sure that no one is attempting to manipulate the price of the stock.[6] The size qualifications increase as one moves from the regional exchanges to the AMEX and on to the NYSE.

---

[6]It is illegal for anyone to attempt to manipulate the price of a stock. Prior to the creation of the SEC in the 1930s, syndicates would buy and sell stock back and forth at rigged prices for the purpose of deceiving the public into thinking that a particular stock was worth more or less than its true value. The exchanges, with the encouragement and support of the SEC, utilize sophisticated computer programs to help spot any irregularities that suggest manipulation, and they require disclosures to help identify manipulators. This same system helps to identify illegal insider trading, as discussed in the next section.

Assuming a company qualifies, many people believe that listing is beneficial both to it and to its stockholders. Listed companies receive a certain amount of free advertising and publicity, and their status as a listed company enhances their prestige and reputation. This may have a beneficial effect on the sales of the products of the firm, and it probably is advantageous in terms of lowering the required rate of return on the common stock. Investors respond favorably to increased information, increased liquidity, and confidence that the quoted price is not being manipulated. By providing investors with these benefits in the form of listing their companies' stock, financial managers may lower their firms' costs of capital and increase the value of their stocks.

Regulation of Securities Markets

Sales of new securities, and also operations in the secondary markets, are regulated by the Securities and Exchange Commission (SEC) and, to a lesser extent, by each of the 50 states:

1. Elements in the regulation of new issues by the SEC.

a. The SEC has jurisdiction over all interstate offerings to the public in amounts of $1.5 million or more.

b. Securities must be registered at least 20 days before they are publicly offered. The *registration statement* provides financial, legal, and technical information about the company. A *prospectus* summarizes this information for use in selling the securities. SEC lawyers and accountants analyze both the registration statement and the prospectus, and if the information is inadequate or misleading, the SEC will delay or stop the public offering.

c. After the registration has become effective, the securities may be offered, but any sales solicitation must be accompanied by the prospectus. Preliminary, or "red herring," prospectuses may be distributed to potential buyers during the waiting period, but no sales may be finalized during this period. The "red herring" prospectus contains all the key information that will appear in the final prospectus except the price.

d. If the registration statement or prospectus contains misrepresentations or omissions of material facts, any purchaser who suffers a loss may sue for damages. Severe penalties may be imposed on the issuer or its officers, directors, accountants, engineers, appraisers, underwriters, and all others who participated in the preparation of the registration statement.

2. Elements in the regulation of outstanding securities.

a. The SEC regulates all national securities exchanges. Companies whose securities are listed on an exchange must file annual reports similar to the registration statement with both the SEC and the stock exchange.

b. The SEC has control over corporate *insiders*. Officers, directors, and major stockholders of a corporation must file monthly reports of changes in their holdings of the stock of the corporation. Any short-term profits from such transactions are payable to the corporation.

c. The SEC has the power to prohibit manipulation by such devices as pools (aggregations of funds used to affect prices artificially) or wash sales (sales between members of the same group to record artificial transaction prices).

d. The SEC has control over the form of the proxy and the way the company uses it to solicit votes.

e. Control over the flow of credit into security transactions is exercised by the Board of Governors of the Federal Reserve System. The Fed exercises this control through *margin requirements*, which stipulate the maximum percentage of the purchase price of a security that can be borrowed. If a great deal of margin borrowing has been going on, then a decline in stock prices can result in inadequate coverages; this forces the stockbrokers to issue *margin calls*, which in turn require investors either to put up more money or to have their margined stock sold to pay off their loans. Such forced sales further depress the stock market and can set off a downward spiral. To prevent this, the Fed controls the volume of margin borrowing.

3. **State regulations.**

a. States have some control over the issuance of new securities within their boundaries. This control is usually exercised by a "corporation commissioner" or similar official.

b. State laws relating to security sales are called "blue sky laws" because they were put into effect to keep unscrupulous promoters from selling securities that offered the blue sky but actually had little or no asset backing.

4. **Self-regulation.** The security industry itself realizes the importance of stable markets, sound brokerage firms, and the absence of stock manipulation. Therefore, the various exchanges work closely with the SEC to police transactions on the exchanges and to maintain the integrity and credibility of the system. Similarly, the National Association of Securities Dealers (NASD) cooperates with the SEC to police trading in the OTC market. These industry groups also cooperate with regulatory authorities to set net worth and other standards for securities firms, to develop insurance programs to protect the customers of brokerage houses, and the like.

In general, government regulation of securities trading is designed to insure that investors receive information that is as accurate as possible, that no one artificially manipulates the market price of a given stock, and that corporate insiders do not take advantage of their position to profit in their companies' stocks at the expense of other stockholders. Neither the SEC nor the state regulators can prevent investors from making foolish decisions or from having "bad luck," but they can and do help investors obtain the best data possible for making sound investment decisions.

The Investment Banking Process

The role of investment bankers was discussed in general terms in Chapter 3. There we saw (1) that the major investment banking houses are often divisions of large financial service corporations engaged in a wide range of activities and (2) that the investment banking houses not only help firms issue new securities in the primary markets but also operate as brokers in the secondary markets. Thus, American Express is a major financial services corporation, and it owns a large brokerage house and a large investment banking house. Similarly, Merrill Lynch has a brokerage department which operates thousands of offices and an investment banking department which helps companies issue securities. Of course, Merrill Lynch's and American Express' brokers sell securities issued through their investment banking departments. In this section, we describe in some detail how securities are issued and what the role of investment bankers is in this process.

Stage I Decisions

The firm itself makes some initial, preliminary decisions on its own, including these:

1. **Dollars to be raised.** How much new capital is needed?

2. **Type of securities used.** Should stock or bonds, or a combination, be used? Further, if stock is to be issued, should it be via a rights offering or by a direct sale to the general public? (See Chapter 15 for a discussion of the many different types of bonds.)

3. **Competitive bid versus a negotiated deal.** Should the company simply offer a block of its securities for sale to the highest bidder, or should it sit down with an investment banker and negotiate a deal? These two procedures are called *competitive bids* versus *negotiated deals*. Only the 100 or so largest firms on the NYSE, whose issues would be very lucrative for the investment bankers, typically use the competitive bid process—the investment banks have to do a large amount of work in order to bid on an issue, and the costs are generally too high to make it worthwhile unless the banker is sure of getting the deal. Therefore, most offerings of stock or bonds are on a negotiated basis.

4. **Selection of an investment banker.** Assuming the issue is to be negotiated, the firm must select an investment banker. This can be an important decision for a firm that is going public; older firms that have "been to market" before will have already established a relationship with

---

Table 14-3
Ten Largest Investment Bankers

---

1. Salomon Brothers
2. Merrill Lynch Capital Markets
3. Goldman Sachs
4. First Boston
5. Morgan Stanley
6. Drexel Burnham Lambert
7. Lehman Brothers Kuhn Loeb
8. Kidder Peabody
9. Blyth Eastman Paine Webber
10. E. F. Hutton

Notes:
a. Rankings are based on the dollar volume of domestic underwritings in 1983.
b. Shearson/American Express acquired Lehman Brothers Kuhn Loeb in May 1984.
Source: *The Wall Street Journal*, January 6, 1984.

---

an investment banker, although it is easy enough to change bankers if the firm is dissatisfied. Different investment banking houses are better suited for different companies. The older, larger "establishment houses" like Morgan Stanley deal mainly with companies like AT&T, IBM, and Exxon. Other bankers handle more speculative issues. There are some houses that specialize in new issues, and others that are not well suited to handle new issues because their brokerage clients are relatively conservative. (The investment banking firms sell the issues largely to their own regular investment customers, so the nature of these customers has a major effect on the ability of the house to do a good job for a corporate security issuer.) Table 14-3 lists in rank order the ten largest investment bankers for 1983.

Stage II Decisions

Stage II decisions, which are made jointly by the firm and its selected investment banker, include the following:

1. Reevaluating the initial decisions. The firm and its banker will reevaluate the initial decisions regarding the size and the type of securities to use. For example, the firm may have initially decided to raise $50 million by selling common stock, but the investment banker may convince management that it would be better off, in view of current market conditions, to limit the stock issue to $25 million and to raise the other $25 million as debt.

2. Best efforts or underwritten issues. The firm and its investment banker must decide whether the banker will work on a *best efforts* basis or will *underwrite* the issue. In a best efforts sale, the banker does not guarantee that the securities will be sold or that the company will get the cash it needs. On an underwritten issue, the company does get a guarantee. Therefore, the banker bears significant risks in underwritten offerings. For example, when IBM sold $1 billion of bonds in 1979, interest rates rose sharply, and bond prices fell, after the deal had been set but before the investment bankers could sell the bonds to ultimate purchasers. The bankers lost somewhere between $10 million and $20 million. Had the offering been on a best efforts basis, IBM would have been the loser.

3. Banker's compensation; other expenses. The investment banker's compensation must be negotiated. Also, the firm must estimate the other expenses it will incur in connection with the issue—lawyers' fees, accountants' costs, printing and engraving, and so on. Usually, the banker will buy the issue from the company at a discount below the price at which the securities are to be offered to the public, with this "spread" being set to cover the bankers' costs and to provide a profit.

Table 14-4 gives an indication of the flotation costs associated with public issues of bonds, preferred stock, and common stock. As the table shows, costs as a percentage of the proceeds are higher for stocks than for bonds, and costs are higher for small than for large issues. The relationship between size of issue and flotation costs is due primarily to the existence of fixed costs—certain costs must be incurred regardless of

Table 14-4
Costs of Flotation for Underwritten,
Nonrights Offerings
(Expressed as a Percentage of Gross Proceeds)

Size of Issue (Millions of Dollars)	Bonds			Preferred Stock			Common Stock		
	Underwriting Commission	Other Expenses	Total Costs	Underwriting Commission	Other Expenses	Total Costs	Underwriting Commission	Other Expenses	Total Costs
Under 1.0	10.0%	4.0%	14.0%	—	—	—	13.0%	9.0%	22.0%
1.0 − 1.9	8.0	3.0	11.0	—	—	—	11.0	5.9	16.9
2.0 − 4.9	4.0	2.2	6.2	—	—	—	8.6	3.8	12.4
5.0 − 9.9	2.4	0.8	3.2	1.9%	0.7%	2.6%	6.3	1.9	8.1
10.0 − 19.9	1.2	0.7	1.9	1.4	0.4	1.8	5.1	0.9	6.0
20.0 − 49.9	1.0	0.4	1.4	1.4	0.3	1.7	4.1	0.5	4.6
50.0 and over	0.9	0.2	1.1	1.4	0.2	1.6	3.3	0.2	3.5

Notes:
a. Small issues of preferred are rare, so no data on issues below $5 million are given.
b. Flotation costs tend to rise somewhat when interest rates are cyclically high, indicating that money is in relatively tight supply, and hence investment bankers will have a relatively hard time placing issues with permanent investors. Thus, the figures shown above represent averages, as flotation costs actually vary somewhat over time.

Sources: Securities and Exchange Commission, *Cost of Flotation of Registered Equity Issues* (Washington, D. C.: U.S. Government Printing Office, December 1974); Pettway, Richard H., "A Note on the Flotation Costs of New Equity Capital Issues of Electric Companies," *Public Utilities Fortnightly*, March 18, 1982; and informal surveys of common stock, preferred stock, and bond issues conducted by the authors.

the size of the issue, so the percentage of flotation costs is quite high for small issues.

Also, it should be noted that when relatively small companies go public to raise new capital, the investment bankers frequently take part of their compensation in the form of options to buy stock in the firm. For example, when DEW Technologies, Inc., went public with a $10 million issue in 1984 by selling 1 million shares at a price of $10, its investment bankers not only (1) bought the stock from the company at a price of $9.75, so the direct underwriting fee was only $1,000,000(\$10.00 - \$9.75)$ = $250,000, or 2.5 percent, but (2) also received a 5-year option to buy 200,000 shares at a price of $10. If the stock should go up to $15, which the bankers expected it to do, then the investment banking firm would make a $1 million profit, which would in effect be an additional underwriting fee.

4. Setting the offering price. If the company is already publicly owned, the offering price will be based on the existing market price of the stock or the yield on the bonds. For common stock, the most typical arrangement calls for the investment banker to buy the securities at a prescribed number of points below the closing price on the last day of registration. Suppose that in October 1984, the stock of Southern Metals Company had a current price of $28.50 and that it had traded between $25 and $30 a share during the previous 3 months. Suppose further that Southern and its underwriter agreed that the investment banker would buy 10 million new shares at $1 below the closing price on the last day of registration. If the stock closed at $26 on the day the SEC released the issue, Southern would receive $25 a share. Typically, such agreements have an escape clause that provides for the contract to be voided if the price of the securities ends below some predetermined figure. In the illustrative case, this "upset" price might be set at $25 a share. Thus, if the closing price of the shares on the last day of registration had been $24.50, Southern would have had the option of withdrawing from the agreement.

The investment banker will have an easier job if the issue is priced relatively low, but the issuer of the securities naturally wants as high a price as possible. Some conflict of interest on price therefore arises between the investment banker and the issuer. If the issuer is financially sophisticated and makes comparisons with similar security issues, the investment banker will be forced to price close to the market.

The offering price may have to be set at a price below the preoffering market price. Consider Figure 14-1, in which D_0 is the estimated market demand curve for Southern Metals stock and S_0 is the number of shares outstanding. Initially, there are 50 million shares outstanding, and the equilibrium price of the stock is $28.50. As we saw in Chapter 5, the equilibrium price of a constant-growth stock is found in accordance with the following equation:

Figure 14-1
Estimated Demand Curve for Southern Metals Company's Common Stock

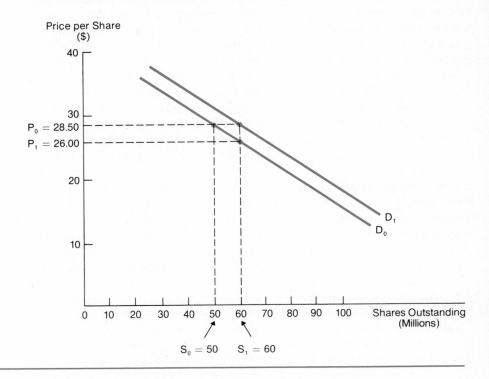

$$P_0 = \hat{P}_0 = \frac{D_1}{k_s - g} = \frac{\$2.00}{0.12 - 0.05} = \$28.57 \approx \$28.50.$$

The values shown for D_1, k_s, and g are the *estimates of the marginal stockholder*. Some stockholders doubtlessly regard Southern as being less risky than others, and hence assign it a lower value for k_s. Similarly, some stockholders will estimate the company's growth rate higher than others, and so use g > 5 percent when calculating the stock's intrinsic value. Thus, there are some investors who think Southern's stock is worth more than $28.50, and others who think it is worth less, but the marginal investor thinks the stock is worth $28.50. Accordingly, this is its current price.

If Southern is to sell another 10 million shares of stock, it will have to either attract some investors who are apparently not willing to own the stock at the $28.50 price or else induce present stockholders to buy additional shares. There are two ways this can be accomplished: (1) by reducing the price of the stock or (2) by "promoting" or "advertising" the company and thus shifting the demand curve to the right.[7] If the demand curve does not shift at all, we see from Figure 14-1 that the only way the 10 million additional shares could be sold would be by setting the offering price at $26 per share. However, if the investment bankers can promote the stock sufficiently to shift the demand curve out to D_1, then the offering price can be set equal to the current market price, $28.50.[8]

The extent to which the demand curve can be shifted depends primarily on two factors: (1) what investors think the company can do with the money brought in by the stock sale, and (2) how effectively the brokers promote the issue. If investors can be convinced that the new money will be invested in highly profitable projects that will substantially raise earnings and the earnings growth rate, then the shift will occur, and the stock price may even go above $28.50. Even if investors do not radically change their expectations about the company's fundamental factors, the fact that thousands of stockbrokers telephone their clients with suggestions that they consider purchasing Southern's stock may shift the demand curve. The extent to which this promotion campaign is successful in shifting the demand curve depends, of course, upon the effectiveness of the investment banking firm. Therefore, Southern's financial manager's perceptions about the effectiveness of different investment bankers will be an important factor in the choice of an underwriter.

One final point is that *if pressure from the new shares drives down the price of the stock, all shares outstanding, and not just the new shares, will be affected*. Thus, if Southern's stock should fall from $28.50 to $26 as a result of the financing, and if the price should remain at this new level, then the company would incur a loss of $2.50 on each of the 50 million shares previously outstanding, or a total market value loss of $125 million. In a very real sense, this loss would be a *flotation cost*, since it would be a cost associated with the new issue. However, most observers feel that even though pressure may drive stock prices down immediately after a

---

[7]It should be noted that investors can buy newly issued stock without paying normal brokerage commissions, and brokers are careful to point this out to potential purchasers. Thus, if an investor were to buy Southern's stock at $28.50 in the regular market, the commission would be about 1 percent, or 28 cents per share. If the stock were purchased in an underwriting, this commission would be avoided.

It should also be noted that many academicians argue that the demand curve for a firm's stock is either horizontal or has only a slight downward slope. Most corporate treasurers, on the other hand, feel that there is a decided downward slope to the curve, especially if the sale occurs at a time when the stock is "out of favor" with the investing public. Recent empirical studies suggest that the demand curve, at least for utility stocks, does have a slight downward slope. See the Bowyer and Yawitz article listed in the references at the end of this chapter.

[8]The supply curve is a vertical line, first at 50 million shares and then, after the new issue, at 60 million.

new issue is announced, demand curves do shift over time, so Southern Metals would not be likely to suffer a permanent loss anywhere close to $125 million on an issue such as this one.

If the company is "going public," there will be no established price, so the bankers will have to estimate the *equilibrium price* at which the stock will sell after issue. Problem 14-1 at the end of this chapter illustrates in some detail the process involved. Note that if the offering price is set below the true equilibrium price, the stock will rise sharply after issue, and the company and its original stockholders will have given away too much stock to raise the required capital. If the offering price is set above the true equilibrium price, either the issue will fail or, if the bankers succeed in selling the stock to their investment clients, these clients will be unhappy when the stock subsequently falls to its equilibrium level. Therefore, it is important that the equilibrium price be closely approximated, but it is hard to estimate this price.

Selling Procedures   Once the company and its investment bankers have decided how much money to raise, the type of securities to issue, and the basis for pricing the issue, they will prepare and file an SEC registration statement and a prospectus as described earlier in the chapter. It generally takes about 20 days for the issue to be approved by the SEC. The final price of the stock (or the interest rate on a bond issue) is set at the close of business the day the issue clears the SEC, and the securities are offered to the public the following day.

Investors are required to pay for the stock within 10 days, and the investment bankers must pay the issuing firm within four days of the time the offering officially begins. Typically, the bankers sell the stock within a day or two after the offering begins, but on occasion, the bankers miscalculate, set the offering price too high, and are unable to move the issue. At still other times, the market declines during the offering period, forcing the bankers to reduce the price of the stock or bonds. In either instance, on an underwritten offering the firm receives the price that was agreed upon, and the bankers must absorb any losses that may be incurred.

Because they are exposed to large potential losses, investment bankers typically do not handle the purchase and distribution of issues single-handedly unless the issue is a very small one. If the sum of money involved is large and the risk of price fluctuations is substantial, investment bankers form *underwriting syndicates* in an effort to minimize the amount of risk each one carries. The banking house which sets up the deal is called the *lead*, or *managing, underwriter*.

In addition to the underwriting syndicate, on larger offerings still more investment bankers are included in a *selling group*, which handles the distribution of securities to individual investors. The selling group includes all members of the underwriting syndicate plus additional dealers who take relatively small participations, or shares of the total issue, from the members of the underwriting syndicate. Thus, the underwriters act as *wholesalers*, while members of the selling group act as *retailers*. The number of houses in a selling group depends partly upon the size of the issue; for example, the one for Communications Satellite Corporation (Comsat) consisted of 385 members.

The selling procedures described above, including the 20-day minimum waiting period between registration with the SEC and sale of the issue, apply to most security sales. However, it should be noted that large, well-known public companies which issue securities frequently may file a *master registration statement* with the SEC and then update it with a *short-form statement* just prior to each individual offering. This procedure is known as *shelf registration* because, in effect, the company puts its new securities "on the shelf" and then sells them to investors when it feels the market is "right."

Shelf Registrations

In the case of a large, established firm such as Southern Metals, the investment banking firm's job is finished after it has disposed of the stock and turned the net proceeds over to the issuing firm. However, in the case of a company going public for the first time, the investment banker is under an obligation to maintain a market in the shares after the issue has been completed. Such stocks are typically traded in the over-the-counter market, and the lead underwriter generally agrees to "make a market" in the stock so as to keep it reasonably liquid. The company wants a good market to exist for its stock, as do the stockholders. Therefore, if the banking house wants to do business with the company in the future, keep its own brokerage customers happy, and have future referral business, it will hold an inventory and help to maintain an active secondary market in the stock.

Maintenance of the Secondary Market

This chapter has focused on these items: (1) the balance sheet treatment of common stock; (2) the legal rights of individual stockholders, especially their control of the firm; (3) the types of common stock that are in use (for example, founders' shares); (4) the market for common stocks; (5) the steps that a firm must go through when issuing new shares; (6) the government's regulation of security markets; (7) the decisions related to a company's going public; and (8) the decisions related to having a company's stock listed on an exchange. The chapter is more descriptive than analytical, but a knowledge of the issues discussed here is essential to an understanding of finance.

Summary

Questions

14-1 Define each of the following terms:
   a. Net worth; common equity; paid-in capital
   b. Book value per share
   c. Proxy; proxy fight
   d. Preemptive right
   e. Class A and Class B stock; founders' stock
   f. Closely held corporations versus publicly held corporations
   g. Secondary market; primary market
   h. Going public; new issue market
   i. Organized exchanges; over-the-counter (OTC) market
   j. Listed stock
   k. Flotation costs; offering price; spread
   l. Market pressure; shift in the stock demand curve
   m. SEC; registration; shelf registration; blue sky law
   n. Underwritten versus best efforts issue
   o. Lead underwriter; selling group
   p. Prospectus; "red herring"
   q. National Association of Securities Dealers (NASD)

14-2 Examine Table 14-1. Suppose Southern sold 2 million shares, with the company netting $25 per share. Construct a pro forma statement of the equity accounts to reflect this sale.

14-3 Is it true that the "flatter," or more nearly horizontal, the demand curve for a particular firm's stock, the more important the role of investment bankers is when the company sells a new issue of stock.

14-4 Company A has assets of $20 million, net income after taxes of $1 million, manufactures widgets, and is publicly owned. Company B is identical to A in every respect except that B's stock is all owned by its founder. If each firm sells stock to the public to raise $5 million of new money for corporate purposes, which would probably have the higher flotation cost? Why?

14-5 The SEC attempts to protect investors who are purchasing newly issued securities by making sure that the information put out by a company and its investment bankers is correct and is not misleading. However, the SEC *does not* provide any information about the real value of the securities; hence, an investor might pay too much for some new stock and consequently lose heavily. Do you think the SEC should, as a part of every new stock or bond offering, render an opinion to investors on the proper value of the securities being offered? Explain.

Problems

14-1 The Callaway Company is a small jewelry manufacturer. The company has been successful and has grown. Now Callaway is planning to sell an issue of common stock to the public for the first time, and it faces the problem of setting an appropriate price on its common stock. The company and its investment bankers feel that the proper procedure is to select firms similar to it with publicly traded common stock and to make relevant comparisons.

Several jewelry manufacturers are reasonably similar to Callaway with respect to product mix, size, asset composition, and debt/equity proportions. Of these companies, Sonnet and Mailers are most similar. Data are given below. When analyzing these data, assume that 1979 and 1984 were reasonably "normal" years for all three companies; that is, these years were neither especially good nor especially bad in terms of sales, earnings, and dividends. At the time of the analysis, R_F was 10 percent and k_M was 15 percent. Sonnet is listed on the American Exchange and Mailers on the NYSE, while Callaway will be traded in the OTC market.

	Sonnet	Mailers	Callaway (Totals)
Earnings per share			
1984	$ 4.50	$ 7.50	$1,200,000
1979	3.00	5.50	816,000
Price per share			
1984	$36.00	$65.00	—
Dividends per share			
1984	$ 2.25	$ 3.75	$ 600,000
1979	1.50	2.75	420,000
Book value per share, 1984	$30.00	$55.00	$9,000,000
Market/book ratio, 1984	120%	118%	—
Total assets, 1984	$28 million	$ 82 million	$20 million
Total debt, 1984	$12 million	$ 30 million	$11 million
Sales, 1984	$41 million	$140 million	$37 million

a. Assume that Callaway has 100 shares of stock outstanding. Use this information to calculate earnings per share (EPS), dividends per share (DPS), and book value per share for Callaway.

b. Based on your answer to Part a, do you think Callaway's stock would sell at a price in the same "ballpark" as that of Sonnet and Mailer, that is, sell in the range of $25 to $100 per share?

c. Assuming that Callaway's management can split the stock so that the 100 shares could be changed to 1,000 shares, 100,000 shares, or any other number, would such an action make sense in this case? Why?

d. Now assume that Callaway did split its stock and has 400,000 shares. Calculate new values for EPS, DPS, and book value per share.

e. What can you say about the relative growth rates of the three companies?

f. What can you say about their dividend payout policies?

g. Return on equity (ROE) can be measured as EPS/book value per share, or as total earnings/total equity. Calculate ROEs for the three companies.

h. Calculate debt/total assets ratios for the three companies.

i.   Calculate P/E ratios for Sonnet and Mailers. Are these P/Es consistent with the growth and ROE data? If not, what other factors would explain the relative P/E ratios?

j.   Now determine a range of values for Callaway's stock price, with 400,000 shares outstanding, by applying Sonnet and Mailers' P/E ratios, price/dividends ratios, and price/book value ratios to your data for Callaway. For example, one possible price for Callaway's stock is (P/E Sonnet)(EPS Callaway) = (8)($3) = $24 per share. Similar calculations would produce a range of prices based on both Sonnet and Mailers data.

k.   Using the equation $k = D_1/P_0 + g$, find approximate k values for Sonnet and Mailers. Then use these values in the constant growth stock price model to find a price for Callaway's stock.

l.   At what price do you think Callaway's shares should be offered to the public? You will want to find the *equilibrium price*, that is, a price that will be low enough to induce investors to buy the stock, but not so low that it will rise sharply immediately after it is issued. Think about relative growth rates, ROEs, dividend yields, and total returns ($k = D/P + g$). Also, as you think about the appropriate price, be aware of the fact that when Howard Hughes let the Hughes Tool Company go public several years ago, different investment bankers proposed prices that ranged from $20 to $30 dollars per share. Hughes naturally accepted the $30 price, and the stock jumped to $40 almost immediately. Nobody's perfect!

m. Would your recommended price be different if the offering were by the Callaway family, selling some of their 400,000 shares, or if it were new stock authorized by the company? For example, another 100,000 shares could be authorized, which when issued would bring the outstanding shares up to 500,000, with 400,000 shares owned by the Callaways and 100,000 shares held by the public. If the Callaways sell their own shares, they receive the proceeds as their own personal funds. If the company sells newly issued shares, the company receives the funds and presumably uses the money to expand the business.

n.   If the price you selected above were actually established as the price at which the stock would be offered to the public, approximately how much money, in total, would Callaway actually receive?

Selected Additional References and Cases

For a wealth of facts and figures on a major segment of the stock market, see

New York Stock Exchange, *Fact Book* (New York, published annually).

For both a description of the stock market and some further facts and figures, see

Frances, Jack C., *Investments: Analysis and Management* (New York: McGraw-Hill, 1980).

Radcliffe, Robert C., *Investment Concepts, Analysis, and Strategy* (Glenview, Ill.: Scott, Foresman, 1982).

Reilly, Frank K., *Investment Analysis: Portfolio Management* (Hinsdale, Ill.: Dryden, 1985).

Sharpe, William F., *Investments* (Englewood Cliffs, N.J.: Prentice-Hall, 1981).

For a discussion of the current state of investment banking and trends in the industry, see

Hayes, S. L., "The Transformation of Investment Banking," *Harvard Business Review*, January-February 1979, 153-170.

Other good references on specific aspects of equity financing include the following:

Block, Stanley, and Marjorie Stanley, "The Financial Characteristics and Price Movement Patterns of Companies Approaching the Unseasoned Securities Market in the Late 1970s," *Financial Management*, Winter 1980, 30-36.

Bowyer, John W., and Jess B. Yawitz, "The Effect of New Equity Issues on Utility Stock Prices," *Public Utilities Fortnightly*, May 22, 1980, 25-28.

Fabozzi, Frank J., "Does Listing on the AMEX Increase the Value of Equity?" *Financial Management*, Spring 1981, 43-50.

Hansen, Robert S., and John M. Pinkerton, "Direct Equity Financing: A Resolution to a Paradox," *Journal of Finance*, June 1982, 651-665.

Logue, Dennis E., and Robert A. Jarrow, "Negotiation versus Competitive Bidding in the Sale of Securities by Public Utilities," *Financial Management*, Autumn 1978, 31-39.

The Harrington casebook contains the following applicable case:

"Hop-in Food Stores, Inc.," which focuses on a firm's decision to go public.

14A   The Use of Rights in Financing

If the preemptive right is contained in a particular firm's charter, it must offer any new common stock to existing stockholders. If the charter does not prescribe a preemptive right, the firm has a choice of making the sale to its existing stockholders or to the public at large. If the sale is to the existing stockholders, the stock flotation is called a *rights offering*. Each stockholder is issued an option to buy a certain number of new shares, and the terms of the option are listed on a certificate called a *right*. The advantages and disadvantages of rights offerings are described in this appendix.

Several issues confront the financial manager who is setting the terms of a rights offering. The various considerations can be made clear by the use of illustrative data on the Southeast Company, whose partial balance sheet and income statement are given in Table 14A-1.

Table 14A-1
Southeast Company:
Financial Statements before Rights Offering

Partial Balance Sheet

		Total debt	$ 40,000,000
		Common stock	10,000,000
		Retained earnings	50,000,000
Total assets	$100,000,000	Total claims	$100,000,000

Partial Income Statement

Earnings before interest and taxes	$20,000,000
Interest on debt	4,000,000
Income before taxes	16,000,000
Taxes (50% assumed)	8,000,000
Net income	$ 8,000,000
Earnings per share (1,000,000 shares)	$8
Market price of stock (price/earnings ratio of 12.5)	$100

Southeast earns $8 million after taxes and has 1 million shares outstanding, so earnings per share are $8. The stock sells at 12.5 times earnings, or for $100 a share. The company plans to raise $10 million of new equity funds through a rights offering, and it decides to sell the new stock to shareholders for $80 a share. The questions facing the financial manager are these:

1. How many rights will be required to purchase a share of the newly issued stock?

2. What is the value of each right?

3. What effect will the rights offering have on the price of the existing stock?

We will now analyze each of these questions.

Southeast plans to raise $10 million in new equity funds and to sell the new stock at a *subscription price* of $80 a share. Dividing the total funds to be raised by the subscription price gives the number of shares to be issued:

Number of Rights Needed to Purchase a New Share

$$\text{Number of new shares} = \frac{\text{Funds to be raised}}{\text{Subscription price}} = \frac{\$10,000,000}{\$80}$$
$$= 125,000 \text{ shares.}$$

The next step is to divide the number of previously outstanding shares by the number of new shares to get the number of rights required to subscribe to one share of the new stock. Note that stockholders always get one right for each share of stock they own, so

$$\text{Number of rights needed to} \atop \text{buy a share of stock} = \frac{\text{Old shares}}{\text{New shares}} = \frac{1,000,000}{125,000}$$
$$= 8 \text{ rights.}$$

Therefore, a stockholder will have to surrender 8 rights plus $80 to receive one of the newly issued shares. Had the subscription price been set at $95 a share, 9.5 rights would have been required to subscribe to each new share; at $10 a share, only one right would have been needed to buy a new share.

It is clearly worth something to be able to buy for less than $100 a share of stock selling for $100. The right provides this privilege, so the right must have a value. To see how the theoretical value of a right is established, we continue with the example of the Southeast Company, assuming that it will raise $10 million by selling 125,000 new shares at $80 a share.

Value of a Right

First, notice that the total *market value* of the old stock was $100 million: $100 a share times 1 million shares. (The book value is irrelevant.) When the firm sells the new stock, it brings in an additional $10 million. As a first approximation, we assume that the total market value of the common stock increases by exactly this $10 million to $110 million. Actually, the market value of all the common stock will go up by more than $10 million if investors think the company will be able to invest these funds at a return substantially in excess of the cost of equity capital, but it will go up by less than $10 million if investors are doubtful of the company's ability to put the new funds to work profitably in the near future.

Under the assumption that market value exactly reflects the new funds brought in, the total market value of the common stock after the new issue will be $110 million. Dividing this new value by the new total number of shares outstanding, 1.125 million, we obtain a new market value of $97.78 a share:

$$\text{New market value} = \frac{\$100,000,000 + \$10,000,000}{1,000,000 + 125,000} = \$97.78.$$

Since the rights give the stockholders the privilege of buying for only $80 a share that will end up being worth $97.78, thus saving $17.78, is $17.78 the value of each right? The answer is *no*, because 8 rights are required to buy one new share. We must divide $17.78 by 8 to get the value of each right. In the example, each right is worth $2.22.

Ex Rights

The Southeast Company's rights have a very definite value, which accrues to the holders of the common stock. What will be the price of the stock if it is traded during the offering period? This depends on who will receive the rights, the old owners or the new. The standard procedure calls for the company to set a *holder-of-record date*, and then for the stock to go *ex rights* four trading days prior to the holder-of-record date. If the stock is sold prior to the ex-rights date, it is sold *rights on*; that is, the new owner will receive the rights. The exact time at which the stock goes ex rights is at the close of business (say 5 P.M.) on the fifth trading day before the holder-of-record date, so the ex-rights date is the fourth day before the record date. The following tabulation indicates what is involved:

	Date	Stock Price
Rights on:	Nov. 9	$100.00
	Nov. 10	100.00
Ex-rights date:	Nov. 11	97.78
	Nov. 12	97.78
	Nov. 13	97.78
	Nov. 14	97.78
Holder-of-record date:	Nov. 15	97.78

On October 24, Southeast Company announced the terms of the new financing, stating that rights would be mailed out on December 1 to stockholders of record as of the close of business on November 15. Anyone who buys the old stock on or before November 10 will receive the rights; anyone who buys the stock on or after November 11 will *not* receive the rights. Thus, November 11 is the *ex-rights date*; before November 11, the stock sells *rights on*. In the case of Southeast Company, the *rights-on price* is $100, while the *ex-rights price* is $97.78.

To simplify the procedures described above, equations have been developed to determine the value of a right.

Formula Value of a Right

Rights On. While the stock is still selling rights on, the value at which the rights will sell when they are issued can be found by use of the following formula:

$$\frac{\text{Value of}}{\text{one right}} = \frac{\text{Market value of stock, rights on} - \text{Subscription price}}{\text{Number of rights required to purchase one share} + 1}$$

$$R = \frac{M_o - S}{N + 1}. \qquad\qquad \textbf{(14A-1)}$$

Here

R = value of one right.

M_o = rights-on price of the stock.

S = subscription price.

N = number of rights required to purchase a new share of stock.

Substituting the appropriate values for the Southeast Company, we obtain

$$R = \frac{\$100 - \$80}{8 + 1} = \frac{\$20}{9} = \$2.22.$$

This agrees with the value of the rights we found by the long procedure.

Ex Rights. Suppose you are a stockholder in the Southeast Company. When you return to the United States from a trip to Europe, you read about the rights offering in the newspaper. The stock is now selling ex rights for $97.78 a share. How can you calculate the theoretical value of a right? Simply by using the following formula, which follows the logic described in preceding sections:[1]

---

[1] We developed Equation 14A-2 directly from the verbal explanation given in the section, "Value of a Right." Equation 14A-1 can then be derived from Equation 14A-2 as follows:

1. Note that

$$M_e = M_o - R. \qquad\qquad \textbf{(14A-3)}$$

2. Substitute 14A-3 into Equation 14A-2, obtaining

$$R = \frac{M_o - R - S}{N}. \qquad\qquad \textbf{(14A-4)}$$

3. Simplify Equation 14A-4 as follows, ending with Equation 14A-1:

$$R = \frac{M_o - S}{N} - \frac{R}{N}$$

$$R + \frac{R}{N} = \frac{M_o - S}{N}$$

$$R\left(\frac{N + 1}{N}\right) = \frac{M_o - S}{N}$$

$$R = \left(\frac{M_o - S}{N}\right)\left(\frac{N}{N + 1}\right)$$

$$R = \frac{M_o - S}{N + 1}. \qquad\qquad \textbf{(14A-1)}$$

This completes the derivation.

$$\frac{\text{Value of}}{\text{one right}} = \frac{\text{Market value of stock, ex rights} - \text{Subscription price}}{\text{Number of rights required to purchase one share}}.$$

$$R = \frac{M_e - S}{N} = \frac{\$97.78 - \$80}{8} = \frac{\$17.78}{8} = \$2.22. \qquad \text{(14A-2)}$$

Here M_e is the ex-rights price of the stock.

Effects on Position of Stockholders

Stockholders have the choice of exercising their rights or selling them. Those who have sufficient funds and want to buy more shares of the company's stock will exercise their rights. Others can sell theirs. In either case, provided the formula value of the right holds true, the stockholder will neither benefit nor lose by the rights offering. This statement can be illustrated by examining the position of a stockholder in the Southeast Company.

Assume the stockholder had 8 shares of stock before the rights offering. Each share had a market value of $100 a share, so the stockholder had a total market value of $800 in the company's stock. If the rights were exercised, one additional share could be purchased for $80, and the investor would own 9 shares of the company's stock, which would have a value of $97.78 a share after the rights offering. The value of the stock would be 9($97.78) = $880, exactly what is invested in it.

Alternatively, if the 8 rights were sold at their value of $2.22 a right, the investor would receive $17.78, ending up with the original 8 shares of stock plus $17.78 in cash. The original 8 shares of stock would have a market price of $97.78 a share. This new $782.24 market value of the stock, plus the $17.78 in cash, is the same as the original $800 market value of the stock except for a rounding error. From a purely mechanical or arithmetical standpoint, the stockholders neither benefit nor lose from the sale of additional shares of stock through rights. Of course, if they forget either to exercise or to sell the rights, or if the brokerage costs of selling their rights are excessive, then stockholders can suffer losses. However, as a rule the issuing firm will make special efforts to minimize brokerage costs and to allow enough time for stockholders to take some action.

Notice that, after a rights offering, the price of the company's stock will be lower than it was prior to the offering. Stockholders have not suffered a loss, however, because they receive the value of the rights. Thus, the stock price decline is similar in nature to a *stock split*, a process we described in some detail in Chapter 13. The larger the underpricing in the rights offering, the greater is the stock split effect—that is, the lower the final stock price. Thus, if a company wants to lower the price of its stock by a substantial amount, it will set the subscription price well below the current market price. If it does not want to lower the price very much, it will set the subscription price just enough below the current price to ensure that the market price will remain above the subscription price during the offering period and thus cause the new shares to be purchased and the new funds to come into the corporation.

Problems

14A-1 The common stock of Irving Development Company is selling for $55 in the market. The stockholders are offered one new share at a subscription price of $25 for every 5 shares held. What is the value of each right?

14A-2 American Appliance Company's common stock is priced at $72 a
   share in the market. Notice is given that stockholders may purchase
   one new share at a price of $40 for every 7 shares held. You hold 120
   shares at the time of notice.
   a. At approximately what price will each right sell in the market?
   b. Why will this be the approximate price?
   c. What effect will the issuance of rights have on the original market
      price? Why?

14A-3 Jane Thompson has 300 shares of Piper Industries. The market price
   per share is $75. The company now offers stockholders one new
   share to be purchased at $60 for every 4 shares held.
   a. Determine the value of each right.
   b. Assume that Jane (1) uses 80 rights and sells the other 220, or (2)
      sells 300 rights at the market price you have calculated. Prepare a
      statement showing the changes in her position in each case.

Long-Term Debt and Preferred Stock Financing

15

On any given day, corporations go to the market for vast amounts of new debt capital, and they use many types and forms of securities. For example, in a recent *Wall Street Journal* it was announced that Houston Lighting and Power had just sold $125 million of 13⅛ percent, 10-year, first mortgage bonds; that a Carolina Power & Light subsidiary was raising $60 million in Europe on 7-year notes guaranteed by the parent company; that Leaseway Transportation Corporation was raising $75 million, using collateral trust notes secured by railroad rolling stock; that Moran Energy of Houston had obtained a $75 million revolving line of credit from a group of banks, with interest to vary over time and to be set at a rate based on the lower of the First National Bank of Houston's prime rate or the London Inter-Bank Offered Rate (LIBOR); that Occidental Petroleum was selling $100 million of long-term debt and using the money to reduce its short-term debt; that Southwestern Bell was selling 40-year, Aaa debenture bonds at a rate of 14⅛ percent; and that Bell Canada was issuing 11,250,000 shares of voting preferred stock which would pay a 13.5 percent dividend and which would be convertible, for 10 years, into common stock on a one-for-one basis. Another story in the same issue of the *Journal* reported that the bond rating of Fedders Corporation, an air conditioning manufacturer, was being lowered, with the result that the company would have to pay more for debt in the future.

Why are there so many different types of debt, with so many different maturities, ratings, and so on? Is it less expensive to raise debt capital by selling 40-year bonds or 7-year notes? What are the pros and cons of making bonds or preferred stocks convertible into common, of paying a fixed rate of interest versus letting the rate on a bond float up and down as rates in the economy fluctuate? How can a company keep its bond rating up, or get it back up if it is lowered? These are some of the issues discussed in this chapter.

Different groups of investors favor different types of securities, and their tastes change over time. Thus, astute financial managers offer a variety of securities, and they "package" their new security offerings at each point in time so as to attract the greatest possible number of potential investors, thereby holding their costs of capital to a minimum.

Long-Term Debt

Long-term debt is often called *funded debt*. When a firm is said to be planning to "fund" its floating debt, it is planning to replace short-term debt with securities of longer maturity. Funding does not imply placing money with a trustee or other repository; it is simply part of the jargon of finance and means "replacing short-term debt with permanent capital." Tampa Electric Company provides a good example of funding. This company has a continuous construction program. Typically, it uses short-term debt initially to finance construction expenditures. However, once short-term debt has built up to about $100 million, the company sells a stock or bond issue, uses the proceeds to pay off its bank loans, and starts the cycle again. There is a fixed cost involved in selling stocks or bonds which makes it prohibitively expensive to issue small amounts of these securities. Therefore, the process used by Tampa Electric and other companies is very logical.

Traditional Debt Instruments

There are many types of long-term debt instruments: term loans, bonds, secured and unsecured notes, marketable and nonmarketable paper, and so on. In this section, we discuss briefly the traditional long-term debt instruments. Then, in the next section, we discuss some important recent innovations in long-term debt financing.

Term Loans

A *term loan* is a contract under which a borrower agrees to make a series of interest and principal payments, on specific dates, to a lender.[1] Term loans are usually negotiated directly between the borrowing firm and a financial institution—generally a bank, an insurance company, or a pension fund. Although the maturities of term loans vary from 2 to 30 years, most are for periods in the 3-year to 15-year range.

Term loans have three major advantages over public offerings—*speed, flexibility,* and *low issuance costs.* Also, because they are negotiated di-

---

[1]Most term loans are *amortized*, which means paid off in equal installments over the life of the loan. See Chapter 4 for a review of amortization. Also, if the interest and maturity payments required under a term loan agreement are not met on schedule, the borrowing firm is said to have *defaulted*, and it can then be forced into bankruptcy. See Chapter 25 for a discussion of bankruptcy.

rectly between the lender and the borrower, formal documentation is minimized. The key provisions of the loan can be worked out much more quickly, and with more flexibility, than can those for a public issue, and it is not necessary for a term loan to go through the Securities and Exchange Commission registration process. A further advantage of term loans over publicly held debt has to do with future flexibility: If a bond issue is held by many different bondholders, it is virtually impossible to obtain permission to alter the terms of the agreement, even though new economic conditions may make such changes desirable. With a term loan, the borrower generally can negotiate with the lender to work out modifications in the contract.

The interest rate on a term loan can be either fixed for the life of the loan or variable. If it is fixed, the rate used will be close to the rate on bonds of equivalent maturity for companies of comparable risk. If the rate is variable, it is usually set at a certain number of percentage points over the prime rate, the commercial paper rate, the T-bill rate, or the London Inter-Bank Offered Rate (LIBOR). Thus, when the index rate goes up or down, so does the rate on the outstanding balance of the term loan. In 1984, about 50 percent of the dollar amount of term loans made by banks had floating rates, up from virtually zero in 1970. Banks "buy" most of the funds they themselves lend to corporations by selling certificates of deposit, and if the CD rate rises along with other market rates, banks need to raise the rate they earn in order to meet their own interest costs. With the increased volatility of interest rates in recent years, lenders have become increasingly reluctant to make long-term, fixed rate loans.

Bonds

A *bond* is a long-term contract under which a borrower agrees to make payments of interest and principal, on specific dates, to the holder of the bond. While bonds have traditionally been issued with maturities of between 20 and 30 years, in the 1980s shorter maturities, such as 7 to 10 years, have been used to an increasing extent. Although bonds are similar to term loans, a bond issue is generally advertised, offered to the public, and actually sold to many different investors. Indeed, thousands of individual and institutional investors may purchase bonds when a firm sells a bond issue, while there is generally only one lender in the case of a term loan.[2] With bonds, the interest rate is generally fixed, although in recent years there has been a sharp increase in the use of various types of floating rate bonds. There are a number of different types of bonds, the more important of which are discussed next.

---

[2]However, for very large term loans, 20 or more financial institutions may form a syndicate to grant the credit. Also, it should be noted that a bond issue can be sold to one lender (or to just a few); in this case, the issue is said to be "privately placed." Companies that place bonds privately do so for the same reasons that they use term loans—speed, flexibility, and low issuance costs.

Mortgage Bonds. Under a *mortgage bond*, the corporation pledges certain assets as security for the bond. To illustrate, suppose $10 million is required to purchase land and to build a plant. Bonds in the amount of $4 million, secured by a mortgage on the property, are issued. If the company defaults on the bonds, the bondholders could foreclose on the plant and sell it to satisfy their claims.

If our illustrative company chose to, it could issue *second mortgage bonds* secured by the same $10 million plant. In the event of liquidation, the holders of these second mortgage bonds would have a claim against the property only after the first mortgage bondholders had been paid off in full. Thus, second mortgages are sometimes called *junior mortgages* because they are junior in priority to claims of *senior mortgages*, or *first mortgage bonds*.

The first mortgage indentures of most major corporations were written 20, 30, 40, or more years ago.[3] These indentures are generally "open ended," meaning that new bonds may be issued from time to time under the existing indenture. However, the amount of new bonds that can be issued is virtually always limited to a specified percentage of the firm's total "bondable property," which generally includes all plant and equipment. For example, Savannah Electric Company can issue first mortgage bonds in total up to 60 percent of its fixed assets. If fixed assets totaled $1 billion, and if the company had $500 million of first mortgage bonds outstanding, then it could, by the property test, issue another $100 million of bonds (60% of $1 billion = $600 million).

In recent years, Savannah Electric has at times been unable to issue any new first mortgage bonds because of another indenture provision: Its times-interest-earned (TIE) ratio was below 2.5, the minimum coverage that it must maintain in order to sell new bonds. Thus, Savannah Electric passed the property test but failed the coverage test; hence, it could not issue first mortgage bonds, and it had to finance with junior securities. Since first mortgage bonds carry lower rates of interest than junior long-term debt, this restriction was a costly one.

Savannah Electric's neighbor, Georgia Power Company, has more flexibility under its indenture; its interest coverage requirement is only 2.0. In hearings before the Georgia Public Service Commission, it was suggested that Savannah Electric should change its indenture coverage to 2.0 so that it could issue more first mortgage bonds. However, this was simply not possible—the holders of the outstanding bonds would have to approve the change, and it is inconceivable that they would vote for a change that would seriously weaken their position.

Debentures. A *debenture* is an unsecured bond, and as such it provides no lien against specific property as security for the obligation. Debenture

---

[3]Bond indentures, which are the actual debt contracts, will be discussed in detail later in this chapter.

holders are, therefore, general creditors whose claims are protected by property not otherwise pledged. In practice, the use of debentures depends on the nature of the firm's assets and its general credit strength. If its credit position is exceptionally strong, the firm can issue debentures—it simply does not need specific security. IBM has used debentures; IBM is such a strong corporation that it does not have to put up property as security for its debt issues. Debentures are also issued by companies in industries where it would not be practical to provide security through a mortgage on fixed assets. Examples of such industries are the large mail-order houses and commercial banks, which characteristically hold most of their assets in the form of inventory or loans, neither of which is satisfactory security for a mortgage bond.

Subordinated Debentures. The term *subordinate* means "below," or "inferior." Thus, in the event of bankruptcy *subordinated debt* has claims on assets only after senior debt has been paid off. Debentures may be subordinated either to designated notes payable—usually bank loans—or to all other debt. In the event of liquidation or reorganization, holders of subordinated debentures cannot be paid until senior debt, as named in the debentures' indenture, has been paid. Precisely how subordination works, and how it strengthens the position of senior debtholders, is shown in Chapter 25.

Other Types of Bonds. Several other types of bonds are used sufficiently often to warrant mention. First, *convertible bonds* are securities that are convertible into shares of common stock, at a fixed price, at the option of the bondholder. Basically, convertibles provide their holders with a chance for capital gains in exchange for a lower coupon rate, while the issuing firm gets the advantage of the low coupon rate. Bonds issued with *warrants* are similar to convertibles. Warrants are options which permit the holder to buy stock for a stated price. Therefore, if the price of the stock rises, the holder of the warrant will earn a capital gain. Bonds that are issued with warrants, like convertibles, carry lower coupon rates than straight bonds. Warrants and convertibles are discussed in detail in Chapter 16.

Income bonds pay interest only when the interest is earned. Thus, these securities cannot bankrupt a company, but from an investor's standpoint, they are riskier than "regular" bonds. Another type of bond that has been discussed in the United States, but not yet used here to any extent, is the *indexed,* or *purchasing power, bond*, which is popular in Brazil, Israel, and a few other countries long plagued by inflation. The interest rate paid on these bonds is based on an inflation index such as the consumer price index; interest paid rises when the inflation rate rises, thus protecting the bondholders against inflation. Mexico has used bonds whose interest rate is pegged to the price of oil to finance the development of its huge petroleum reserves; since oil prices and inflation are correlated, these bonds also protect investors against inflation.

Two other types of bonds that are being used increasingly are *development bonds* and *pollution control bonds*. State and local governments may set up *industrial development agencies* and *pollution control agencies*. These agencies are allowed, under certain circumstances, to sell *tax-exempt bonds*, making the proceeds available to corporations for specific uses deemed (by Congress) to be in the public interest. Thus, a Florida industrial development agency might sell bonds to provide funds for a paper company to build a plant in the Florida Panhandle, where unemployment is high. Similarly, a Pittsburgh pollution control agency might sell bonds to provide U.S. Steel with funds to be used to purchase pollution control equipment. In both cases, the income from the bonds would be tax exempt to the holders; hence, the bonds would sell at relatively low interest rates. Note, however, that these bonds are guaranteed by the corporation that will use the funds, not by a governmental unit.

Recent Innovations

The early 1980s produced several innovations in long-term debt financing. We will discuss four in this section. The first three—zero coupons, floating rates, and bonds redeemable at par—are a result of the extreme volatility in interest rates which characterized the period. The fourth, project financing, permits a firm to tie a debt issue to a specific asset.

Zero (or Very Low) Coupon Bonds

Zero (or very low) coupon bonds are offered at a substantial discount below their par values; hence, they are also called "original issue discount bonds." This type of bond was first used in a major way in 1981, and in recent years IBM, Alcoa, J. C. Penney, ITT, Cities Service, GMAC, Martin-Marietta, and many other companies used them to raise billions of dollars. However, changes in tax laws and the *de facto* creation of zero coupon Treasury bonds has greatly reduced, at least temporarily, the demand for corporate zero coupon bonds issued in the United States. We include a discussion of these securities both to illustrate financial analytical techniques and also to demonstrate how quickly financial markets react to innovation.

To understand what they are, consider Penney's $200 million par value issue of bonds which have no coupons and which pay no annual interest. These zero coupon bonds were sold in 1981 and mature after 8 years, in 1989, at which time holders will be paid $1,000. The bonds were sold at a discount of 66.753 percent below par, or for $332.47 per $1,000 bond. The semiannual compound interest rate which causes $332.47 to grow to $1,000 over 8 years is 7.125 percent, or a nominal annual return of 14.25 percent. (Since most bonds pay interest semiannually, and since people normally compare the yield on zero coupon bonds with yields on "regular" bonds, it is important to calculate the zero's yield on a semiannual basis.) Penney received $66,494,000 less underwriting expenses for the issue, but it will have to pay back $200 million in 1989.

The advantages to Penney include the following: (1) No cash outlays are required for either interest or principal until the bond matures; (2) these bonds have a relatively low yield to maturity (Penney would have had to pay approximately 15 percent versus the actual 14.25 percent had it issued regular coupon bonds at par); and (3) Penney receives an annual tax deduction equal to the yearly amortization of the discount ($667.53/8 = $83.44 per bond), which means that the bonds provide a positive cash flow in the form of tax savings over their life. There are also two disadvantages to Penney: (1) The bond is, in effect, simply not callable since it would have to be called at its $1,000 par value, so Penney cannot refund it if interest rates should fall; and (2) Penney will have a very large nondeductible cash outlay coming up in 1989.

There are two principal advantages to investors in zero coupon bonds: (1) They have no danger whatever of a call, and (2) they are guaranteed a "true" yield (14.25 percent in the Penney case) irrespective of what happens to interest rates—the holders of Penney's bonds do not have to worry about having to reinvest coupons received at low rates if interest rates should fall, which would result in a "true" yield to maturity of less than 14.25 percent. This second feature is extremely important to pension funds, life insurance companies, and other institutions which make actuarial contracts based on assumed reinvestment rates. For such investors, the risk of declining interest rates, and hence an inability to reinvest cash inflows at the assumed rate, is greater than the risk of an increase in rates and the accompanying fall in bond values.

To illustrate, suppose an insurance company or pension plan signed a contract to pay $100,000 in 8 years in exchange for a lump sum premium of $35,056 today. The premium was based on the assumption that the company could invest the $35,056 at a return of 14 percent. If the $35,056 were invested in regular coupon bonds paying a 14 percent coupon rate, then the accumulated value 8 years hence would be equal to the required $100,000 only if all coupon payments could be invested at 14 percent over the next 8 years. If interest rates were to fall, then the accumulated amount would fall short of the required $100,000. Note, however, that if the $35,056 were invested in a zero coupon bond with a 14 percent yield, the insurance company would end up with the required $100,000 irrespective of what happened to interest rates in the future. Thus, the insurance company or pension fund would have been "immunized" against a decline in interest rates.

One might think that there would be a tax advantage to the purchaser of a zero coupon bond in that income would come in the form of capital gains rather than interest income, but this is not true in the United States. The IRS has ruled that the amortization of original-issue discounts must be treated as ordinary income. Further, all zero coupon bonds must be registered, and the issuing corporation must send both the registered owner and the IRS a Form 1099 each year indicating the amount of the amortized discount. However, according to the investment bankers who have handled the underwritings, this is not a material issue, because these bonds have been sold exclusively to tax-exempt organizations, principally pension funds.[4] Yet, since pension funds are by far the largest purchasers of corporate bonds, the potential market for zero coupon bonds is by no means small.

To analyze a zero coupon bond and to compare it with a coupon bond, a corporate treasurer (or pension fund administrator) must employ the valuation models developed in Chapter 5. For simplicity, we will do the analysis on an annual basis. Consider again Penney's bonds. Penney will receive $332.47 per bond at t = 0. Also, Penney will have a tax deduction each year equal to the $83.44 amortization of the discount. This deduction will save taxes each year in the amount of T(Deduction) = 0.46($83.44) = $38.38 per bond. Penney will have to make a payment of $1,000 at t = 8. Thus, the after-tax cash flow time line is as follows:

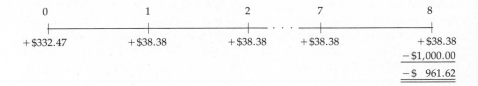

The discount rate which solves this equation is Penney's after-tax cost of debt capital from the zero coupon bond, k_d:

$$\frac{\$332.47}{(1 + k_d)^0} + \frac{\$38.38}{(1 + k_d)^1} + \cdots + \frac{\$38.38}{(1 + k_d)^7} - \frac{\$961.62}{(1 + k_d)^8} = 0.$$

The solution value for k_d is 7.6 percent; this is Penney's after-tax cost of zero coupon debt.

If Penney had sold an annual payment coupon bond, it would have had to pay about 15 percent. Its after-tax interest payments would have been (Coupon)(1 − T) = ($150)(0.54) = $81, and its after-tax cost of debt would have been k_d = 8.1 percent:

$$\frac{\$1,000}{(1 + k_d)^0} - \frac{\$81}{(1 + k_d)^1} - \cdots - \frac{\$81}{(1 + k_d)^7} - \frac{\$1,081}{(1 + k_d)^8} = 0.$$

[4]This statement refers to sales within the United States. There was also a strong market for zero coupon bonds issued by U.S. companies in Europe and the Far East, especially in Japan, where the appreciation of the bonds was treated as capital gains income rather than as interest income. Japan subsequently modified its tax laws to treat the amortization as interest.

Thus, on an after-tax basis, the zero coupon bond has a lower cost to Penney than would a regular coupon bond, 7.6 percent for the zero versus 8.1 percent for the coupon bond.[5] For a purchaser, of course, the reverse is true. A tax-exempt bond buyer would receive the yield to maturity, which is 14.25 percent for the zero coupon bond and 15.0 percent for the coupon bond. Purchasers apparently believed that call protection plus interest rate immunization were worth the 0.75 percentage point cost.

Two events brought about the downfall of domestic corporate zero coupon bonds. First, in 1983 the tax laws were changed so that issuing firms could no longer amortize the discount by the straight-line method. Instead, the discount had to be amortized by an annuity method, which meant that the tax savings in the early years were greatly reduced, while the tax savings in later years were increased. This change increased the after-tax cost of a zero coupon bond to the point where it exactly equaled the after-tax cost of a regular coupon bond with the same before-tax yield.

Second, at about the same time, several brokerage houses introduced a new security based on separating, or "stripping," the interest coupons from the principal amount of a Treasury bond. For example, Merrill Lynch introduced the concept with its Treasury Investment Growth Receipts (TIGRs, or "tigers"). To back its first TIGRs, Merrill Lynch bought $500 million face value of 30-year Treasury bonds, which it placed in trust. Then, Merrill Lynch literally stripped off the coupons that mature each six months over the next 30 years, and used the $2 \times 30 = 60$ sets of coupons to back a series of TIGRs that mature at six-month intervals as the coupon payments on the Treasury bonds come due. The investor receives nothing until the maturity date he or she selects, be it six months or 30 years away. Sold at a discount, the TIGR is redeemed at face value at maturity—the more distant the maturity, the deeper the discount. Thus, with the introduction of TIGRs, insurance companies and pension funds were offered a default-free substitute for corporate zero coupon bonds, and thus far the substitute has proved more acceptable than the original product.

---

[5]Here we have treated the bonds on an annual interest rather than a semiannual interest basis. The same relative situation would hold on a semiannual basis. Also, note that even if Penney could have sold a regular coupon bond at the same yield to maturity as the zero coupon bond, 14.25 percent, there still would have been an after-tax cost advantage to the zero coupon bond. The after-tax cost of a 14.25 percent regular coupon bond would have been 7.7 percent:

$$\frac{\$1,000}{(1 + k_d)^0} - \frac{\$76.95}{(1 + k_d)^1} - \cdot \cdot \cdot - \frac{\$1,076.95}{(1 + k_d)^8} = 0.$$

This compares with 7.6 percent for the zero coupon bond. The difference arises because the zero coupon bond gets its interest tax shelter in advance of the cash outlay for interest, while for a regular bond, the tax deduction and cash payment occur simultaneously.

Floating Rate Debt   In the late 1970s and early 1980s, inflation pushed interest rates up to unprecedented levels. These rising interest rates caused sharp declines in the prices of long-term bonds. Even supposedly "risk-free" U.S. Treasury bonds lost fully half their value, and a similar situation occurred with corporate bonds, mortgages, and other fixed rate, long-term securities. The lenders who held the fixed rate debt were of course hurt very badly. Bankruptcies (or forced mergers to avoid bankruptcy) were commonplace in the banking and especially in the savings and loan industries. Pension fund asset values declined, requiring corporations to increase contributions to their plans, which in turn hurt profits. Insurance company reserves plummeted, causing those companies severe problems, including the bankruptcy of Baldwin-United, a $9 billion diversified insurance firm.

Consequently, lenders became extremely reluctant to lend money at fixed rates on a long-term basis, and they would do so only at high rates. There is normally a *maturity risk premium* embodied in long-term interest rates—this is a risk premium designed to offset the risk of declining bond prices if interest rates rise. Prior to the 1970s, this maturity risk premium is estimated to have been about 1 percentage point, meaning that, under "normal" conditions, a firm might expect to pay about 1 percentage point more to borrow on a long-term basis than on a short-term basis. However, in the late 1970s and early 1980s, the maturity risk premium is estimated to have jumped to about 3 percentage points. This made long-term debt very expensive relative to short-term debt.

Lenders were able and willing to lend on a short-term basis, but corporations were rightly reluctant to borrow short-term to finance long-term assets—such action is, as we shall see in Chapter 18, extremely dangerous. Therefore, we had a situation where lenders did not want to lend on a long-term basis, but corporations had a need for long-term money. The problem was solved by the introduction of *long-term, floating-rate debt*. A typical floating rate issue works like this. The coupon rate is set for, say, the initial six-month period, after which it is adjusted every six months based on some market rate. For example, Gulf Oil sold a floating rate bond that was pegged at 35 basis points above the rate on 30-year Treasury bonds. Other issues were tied to short-term rates. Many additional provisions have been included in floating rate issues; for example, some are convertible to fixed rate debt, while others have a stated minimum coupon rate, and also a cap on how high the rate can go.

Floating rate debt is advantageous to lenders because the interest rate moves up if market rates rise, and this (1) causes the market value of the debt to be stabilized and (2) provides the lender with more income to meet its own obligations (for example, a bank which owns floating rate bonds can use the interest it earns to pay interest on its own deposits). Moreover, floating rate debt is advantageous to corporations because, with this security, they can obtain debt with a long maturity without committing the firm to pay a historically high rate of interest for the entire term of the loan. Of course, if interest rates increase after a floating rate note has been signed, then the borrower would have been better off issuing conventional, fixed rate debt.[6]

Bonds that are *redeemable at par* at the holder's option also protect the holder against a rise in interest rates. If rates rise, fixed rate debt prices decline. However, if the holders have the option of turning their bonds in and having them redeemed at par, they are protected against rising rates. Examples of such debt include Transamerica's $50 million issue of 25-year, 8½ percent bonds. The bonds are not callable by the company, but holders can turn them in for redemption at par 5 years after the date of issue. If interest rates have risen, holders will turn in the bonds and reinvest the proceeds at a higher rate. This feature enabled Transamerica to sell the bonds with an 8½ percent coupon at a time when similar bonds had yields of 9 percent.

Bonds that Are Redeemable at Par

In recent years, many large, individual capital investments have been financed by what is called *project financing*. Project financings have been used to finance energy explorations, oil tankers, refineries, and utility power plants. The firm or firms that will operate the project are called *sponsors*, and the sponsors put up the required equity capital. The remainder of the financing for the project is furnished by lenders or lessors.[7] Most often, a separate legal entity is formed to operate the project. The single most distinguishing feature of project financing is that normally the project's creditors do not have full recourse against the sponsors. In other words, the lenders and lessors must be paid with the cash flows that the project generates, plus the sponsors' equity in the project, for the creditors have no claims against the sponsors' other assets or cash flows. Often the sponsors will write "comfort" letters, giving general assurance that they will strive diligently to make the project successful, but these letters represent only a moral commitment, for they are not legally binding. In this type of project financing, the lenders and

Project Financing

---

[6]For a general discussion of floating rate debt, see Kenneth R. Marks and Warren A. Law, "Hedging against Inflation with Floating-Rate Notes," *Harvard Business Review*, March-April 1980, 106-112.

[7]A *lessor* is an individual or firm that leases, or "rents," buildings and equipment to another firm while retaining ownership of the property. Leasing, and the role of the lessor, is discussed in Chapter 17.

lessors must base their participation on the inherent merits of the project and the equity cushion provided by the sponsors.[8]

Project financing is generally characterized by large size and a high degree of complexity. Moreover, since project financing is tied to a specific project, it can be tailored to meet the specific needs of both the creditors and the sponsors.[9]

Specific Debt Contract Features

A firm's managers are most concerned about (1) the effective cost of debt, and (2) any provisions which might restrict the firm's future alternatives. In this section, we discuss features which could affect either the cost of the firm's debt or its future flexibility.

Bond Indentures

An *indenture* is a legal document that spells out the rights of both the bondholders and the issuing corporation, and a *trustee* is an official (usually of a bank) who represents the bondholders and makes sure that the terms of the indenture are carried out. The indenture may be several hundred pages in length, and it will include *restrictive covenants* that cover such points as the conditions under which the issuer can pay off the bonds prior to maturity, the level at which the issuer's times-interest-earned ratio must be maintained if the company is to sell additional bonds, and restrictions against the payment of dividends unless earnings meet certain specifications. Overall, these covenants relate to the agency problem discussed earlier, and they are designed to insure, insofar as possible, that the firm does nothing to cause the quality of its bonds to deteriorate after they are issued.

The trustee is responsible for making sure the covenants are not violated and for taking appropriate action if a violation occurs. What constitutes "appropriate action" varies with the circumstances. It might be that to insist on immediate compliance would result in bankruptcy and possibly large losses on the bonds. In such a case, the trustee

---

[8]In another type of project financing, each sponsor guarantees its share of the project's debt obligations. Here the creditors would also consider the credit worthiness of the sponsors in addition to the project's own prospects. It should be noted that project financing with multiple sponsors in the utility industry has led to problems when one or more of the sponsors has gotten into financial trouble. In 1984, Long Island Lighting, one of the sponsors in the Nine Mile Point nuclear project, was unable to meet its commitments to the project, and Public Service of New Hampshire similarly defaulted on its payments to the Seabrook nuclear project. These defaults created problems for other participants, and utility executives have stated that these defaults will make other companies reluctant to enter into joint projects in the future.

[9]A number of utility companies whose earnings were too low to satisfy the indenture coverages of their bond indentures have used project financings.

might decide that the bondholders would be better served by giving the company a chance to work out its problems rather than force it into bankruptcy.

The Securities and Exchange Commission (1) approves indentures and (2) makes sure that all indenture provisions are met before allowing a company to sell new securities to the public. Also, it should be noted that the indentures of most larger corporations were actually written back in the 1930s or 1940s, and that many issues of new bonds, all covered by the same indenture, have been sold down through the years. The interest rates on the bonds, and perhaps also the maturities, will change from issue to issue, but bondholders' protection as spelled out in the indenture will be the same for all bonds of a given type.[10]

Call Provisions

A *call provision* gives the issuing corporation the right to call the bond for redemption. If it is used, the call provision generally states that the company must pay an amount greater than the par value for the bond. The additional sum required, defined as the *call premium*, is typically set equal to one year's interest if the bond is called during the first year, with the premium declining at a constant rate of I/n each year thereafter, where I = annual interest and n = original maturity in years. For example, the call premium on a $1,000 par value, 20-year, 8 percent bond would generally be $80 if it were called during the first year, $76 during the second year (calculated by reducing the $80, or 8 percent, premium by one-twentieth), and so on.

The call privilege is valuable to the firm but potentially detrimental to the investor, especially if the bond is issued in a period when interest rates are cyclically high. Accordingly, the interest rate on a new issue of callable bonds will exceed that on a new issue of noncallable bonds. For example, on February 1, 1984, Great Falls Timber Company sold a bond issue yielding 13.375 percent. These bonds were callable immediately. On the same day, Midwest Milling Company sold an issue of similar risk and maturity yielding 13.00 percent. Midwest's bonds were noncallable for 10 years. (This is known as a *deferred call*.) Investors were apparently willing to accept a 0.375 percent lower interest rate on Midwest's bonds for the assurance that the relatively high (by historic standards) rate of interest would be earned for at least 10 years. Great Falls, on the other hand, had to incur a 0.375 percent higher annual interest rate to obtain the option of calling the bonds in the event of a subsequent decline in interest rates. We discuss the analysis for determining when to call an issue in Appendix 15A.

---

[10]A firm will have different indentures for each of the major types of bonds it issues, including its first mortgage bonds, its debentures, and so on. Even though the same indenture is used for all bonds in a class, SEC approval of a new issue can still be a lengthy process.

Sinking Funds

A *sinking fund* is a provision that facilitates the orderly retirement of a bond issue (or, in some cases, an issue of preferred stock). Typically, the sinking fund provision requires the firm to retire a portion of the bond issue each year. On rare occasions, the firm may be required to deposit money with a trustee, who invests the funds and then uses the accumulated sum to retire the bonds when they mature. Sometimes the stipulated sinking fund payment is tied to sales or earnings of the current year, but usually it is a mandatory fixed amount. If it is mandatory, a failure to meet the sinking fund requirement causes the bond issue to be thrown into default, which may force the company into bankruptcy. Obviously, then, a sinking fund can constitute a dangerous cash drain on the firm.

In most cases, the firm is given the right to handle the sinking fund in either of two ways:

1. It may call in for redemption (at par value) a certain percentage of the bonds each year—for example, it might be able to call 2 percent of the total original amount of the issue at a price of $1,000 per bond. The bonds are numbered serially, and the ones called for redemption are determined by a lottery.

2. It may buy the required amount of bonds on the open market.

The firm will choose the least costly method. Therefore, if interest rates have risen, causing bond prices to fall, the company will elect to use the option of buying bonds in the open market at a discount. Otherwise, it will call them. Note that a call for sinking fund purposes is quite different from a refunding call as discussed above. A sinking fund call requires no call premium; however, only a small percentage of the issue is callable in any one year.

Although the sinking fund is designed to protect the bondholders by assuring that the issue is retired in an orderly fashion, it must be recognized that the sinking fund will at times work to the detriment of bondholders. If, for example, the bond carries a 15 percent interest rate, and if yields on similar bonds have fallen to 10 percent, then the bond will sell above par. A sinking fund call at par would thus greatly disadvantage those bondholders whose bonds were called. On balance, however, securities that provide for a sinking fund and continuing redemption are regarded as being safer than bonds without sinking funds, so sinking fund bonds generally have a lower cost of capital to the firm.

Bond Ratings

Since the early 1900s, bonds have been assigned quality ratings that reflect their probability of going into default. The two major rating agencies are Moody's Investors Service (Moody's) and Standard & Poor's

Table 15-1
Comparison of Bond Ratings

	High Quality		Investment Grade	Substandard		Speculative
Moody's	Aaa	Aa	A Baa	Ba	B	Caa to C
S&P	AAA	AA	A BBB	BB	B	CCC to D

Note: Both Moody's and S&P use "modifiers" for bonds rated below triple A. S&P uses a plus and minus system; thus, A+ designates the strongest A rated bonds and A- the weakest. Moody's uses a 1, 2, or 3 designation, with 1 denoting the strongest and 3 the weakest; thus, within the double A category, Aa1 is the best, Aa2 is average, and Aa3 is the weakest.

Corporation (S&P). These agencies' rating designations are shown in Table 15-1.[11]

The triple and double A bonds are extremely safe. Single A and triple B bonds are strong enough to be called *investment grade,* and they are the lowest-rated bonds that many banks and other institutional investors are permitted by law to hold. Double B and lower bonds are speculations; they have a significant probability of going into default, and many financial institutions are prohibited from buying them.

Although the rating assignments are judgmental, they are based on both qualitative and quantitative factors, some of which are listed below:

Bond Rating Criteria

1. Debt ratio.

2. Times-interest-earned ratio.

3. Fixed charge coverage ratio.

4. Current ratio, or current assets/current liabilities.

5. Mortgage provisions: Is the bond secured by a mortgage? If it is, and if the property has a high value in relation to the amount of bonded debt, the bond's rating is enhanced.

6. Subordination provisions: Is the bond subordinated to other debt? If so, it will be rated at least one notch below the rating it would have if it were not subordinated. Conversely, a bond with other debt subordinated to it will have a somewhat higher rating.

7. Guarantee provisions: Some bonds are guaranteed by other firms. If a weak company's debt is guaranteed by a strong company (usually the weak company's parent), then the bond will be given the strong company's rating.

---

[11]In the discussion to follow, reference to the S&P code is intended to imply the Moody code as well. Thus, for example, triple B bonds means both BBB and Baa bonds; double B bonds, both BB and Ba bonds; and so on.

8. Sinking fund: Does the bond have a sinking fund to insure systematic repayment? This feature is a plus factor to the rating agencies.

9. Maturity: Other things the same, a bond with a shorter maturity will be judged less risky than a longer-term bond, and this will be reflected in the ratings.

10. Stability: Are the issuer's sales and earnings stable?

11. Regulation: Is the issuer regulated, and could an adverse regulatory climate cause the company's economic position to decline? Regulation is especially important for utilities, railroads, and telephone companies.

12. Antitrust: Are any antitrust actions pending against the firm that could erode its position?

13. Overseas operations: What percentage of the firm's sales, assets, and profits are from overseas operations, and what is the political climate in the host countries?

14. Environmental factors: Is the firm likely to face heavy expenditures for pollution control equipment?

15. Pension liabilities: Does the firm have unfunded pension liabilities that could pose a future problem?

16. Labor unrest: Are there potential labor problems on the horizon that could weaken the firm's position? As this is written, the entire airline industry faces this problem, and it has caused ratings to be lowered.

17. Resource availability: Is the firm likely to face supply shortages that could force it to curtail operations?

18. Accounting policies: If a firm uses relatively conservative accounting policies, then its reported earnings will be of "higher quality" than if it uses less conservative accounting procedures. Thus, conservative accounting policies are a plus factor in bond ratings.

Representatives of the rating agencies have consistently stated that no precise formula is used to set a firm's rating—all the factors listed, plus others, are taken into account, but not in a mathematically precise manner. Statistical studies have borne out this contention. Researchers who have tried to predict bond ratings on the basis of quantitative data have had only limited success, indicating that the agencies do indeed use a good deal of subjective judgment when establishing a firm's rating.[12]

Importance of Bond Ratings

Bond ratings are important both to firms and to investors. First, a bond's rating is an indicator of its default risk; hence, the rating has a direct, measurable influence on the bond's interest rate and the firm's cost of

---

[12]See Robert S. Kaplan and Gabriel Urwitz, "Statistical Methodological Inquiry," *Journal of Business*, April 1979, 231-261; and Ahmed Belkaoui, *Industrial Bonds and the Rating Process* (London: Quorum Books, 1983).

debt capital. Second, most bonds are purchased by institutional investors, and not by individuals, and these institutions are generally restricted to investment-grade securities. Thus, if a firm's bonds fall below BBB, it will have a difficult time trying to sell new bonds, since most of the potential purchasers will not be allowed to buy them.

Ratings also have an effect on the availability of debt capital. If an institutional investor buys BBB bonds, which are subsequently downgraded to BB or lower, then (1) the institution's regulators will reprimand or perhaps impose restrictions on the institution if it continues to hold the bonds, but (2) since many other institutional investors will no longer be able to purchase the bonds, the institution that owns them will probably not be able to sell them except at a sizable loss. Because of this fear of downgrading, many institutions restrict their bond portfolios to at least A, or even AA, bonds. Some even confine purchases to AAA bonds. Thus, the lower a firm's bond rating, the smaller is the group of available purchasers for its new issues.

As a result of their higher risk and more restricted market, lower-grade bonds have much higher required rates of return, k_d, than do high-grade bonds. Figure 15-1 illustrates this point. In each of the years shown on the graph, U.S. Government bonds have had the lowest yields, AAAs have been next, and the BBB bonds have had the highest yields of the three types.

Figure 15-1 also shows that the gaps between yields on the three types of bonds vary over time; in other words, the cost differentials, or risk premiums, fluctuate from year to year. This point is highlighted in Figure 15-2, which gives the yields on the three types of bonds, and the risk premiums for AAA and BBB bonds, in June 1963, in June 1975, in January 1981, and again in February 1982, when interest rates were at an all-time high.[13] Note first that the riskless rate, or vertical axis intercept, rose over 10 percentage points from 1963 to 1982, reflecting the increase in realized and anticipated inflation. Second, the slope of the line also rose, indicating increased investor risk aversion, from 1963 to 1975, but the slope lessened in 1981 and 1982. Thus, the penalty for

---

[13]The term *risk premium* ought to reflect only the difference in expected (and required) returns between two securities that results from differences in their risk. However, the differences between *yields to maturity* on different types of bonds consist of (1) a true risk premium; (2) a liquidity premium, which reflects the fact that U.S. Treasury bonds are more readily marketable than most corporate bonds; (3) a call premium, because most Treasury bonds are not callable, while corporate bonds are; and (4) an expected loss differential, which reflects the probability of loss on the corporate bonds. As an example of the latter point, suppose the yield to maturity on a BBB bond were 10 percent versus 7 percent on government bonds, but there was a 5 percent probability of total default loss on the corporate bond. In this case, the expected return on the BBB bond would be $0.95(10\%) + 0.05(0\%) = 9.5\%$, and the risk premium would be 2.5 percent, and not the full 3.0 percentage point difference in "promised" yields to maturity. Therefore, the risk premiums given in Figure 15-2 overstate somewhat the true (but unmeasurable) risk premiums.

Figure 15-1
Yields on U.S. Government Bonds, AAA Corporates,
and BBB Corporates, 1953-1984

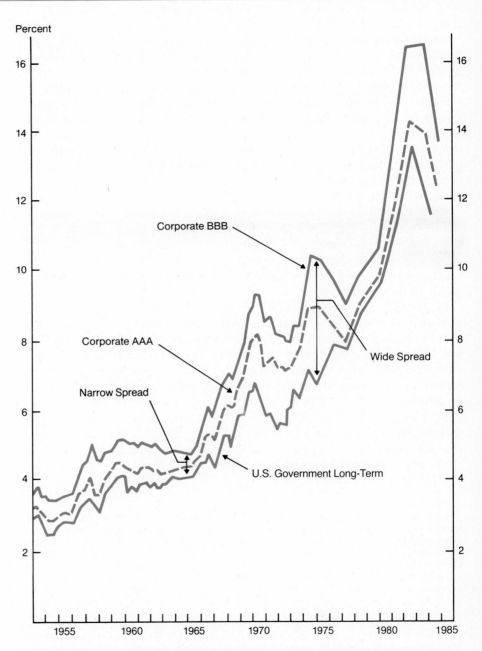

Sources: Federal Reserve Board, *Historical Chart Book,* 1983, and various *Federal Reserve Bulletins.*

**Figure 15-2
Relationship between Bond Ratings
and Bond Yields, 1963, 1975, 1981, and 1982**

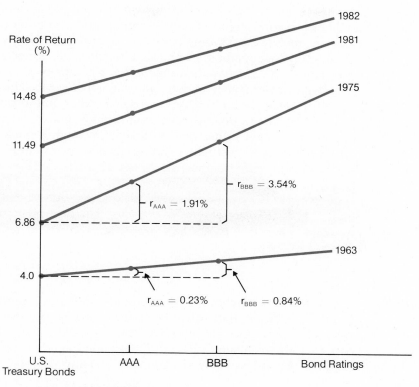

r_{AAA} = risk premium on AAA bonds

r_{BBB} = risk premium on BBB bonds

	Long-Term Government Bonds (Default-Free) (1)	AAA Corporate Bonds (2)	BBB Corporate Bonds (3)	Risk Premiums	
				AAA $(4) = (2) - (1)$	BBB $(5) = (3) - (1)$
June 1963	4.00%	4.23%	4.84%	0.23%	0.84%
June 1975	6.86	8.77	10.40	1.91	3.54
January 1981	11.49	12.83	15.09	1.34	3.60
February 1982	14.48	15.27	17.18	0.79	2.70

Sources: *Federal Reserve Bulletin,* December 1963, December 1975, March 1981, and May 1982.

having a low credit rating varies over time. Occasionally, as in 1963, it is quite small, but at other times, as in 1975, it is quite large.[14]

Changes in Ratings

A change in a firm's bond rating will have a significant effect on its ability to borrow long-term capital, and on the cost of that capital. Rating agencies review outstanding bonds on a periodic basis, occasionally upgrading or downgrading a bond as a result of its issuer's changed circumstances. Also, an announcement that a company plans to sell a new issue will trigger agency reviews and possibly lead to rating changes.[15]

If a firm's situation has deteriorated somewhat, but its bonds have not been reviewed and downgraded, then it may choose to use a term loan or short-term debt rather than to finance through a public bond issue. This will perhaps postpone a rating agency review until the situation has improved. For example, a number of public utilities delayed bond issues in 1981 and 1982, financing with short-term debt until rate increases could be obtained to raise interest coverage ratios to acceptable levels. After rate increases were put into effect and coverages improved, the companies sold bonds and used the proceeds to retire the excess short-term debt.

Preferred Stock Financing

Preferred stock is a hybrid—it is similar to bonds in some respects and to common stock in other ways. Preferred often has a par (or liquidating) value, usually either $25 or $100. The dividend is generally indicated either as a percentage of par, in dollars, or sometimes both ways. For example, Mississippi Power Company recently sold 150,000 shares of

---

[14]The relationship graphed here is akin to the Security Market Line developed in Chapter 6, although bond ratings rather than beta coefficients are used to measure risk. A word about the scaling of the horizontal axis and about the placement of the points is in order. (1) We have shown a linear fit, although there is no theoretical reason to think that yields plotted against bond ratings are necessarily linear. (2) We have shown the interval on the horizontal axis between AAA and BBB to be equal to that between U.S. Government bonds and AAA, but this is an arbitrary scaling. (3) Finally, on an accurate, large-scale graph, it would be clear that the plotted points for the AAA and BBB bonds are not precisely on the straight lines shown in the graph; however, they are sufficiently close to warrant our analysis.

Attempts have been made to calculate beta coefficients for bonds and to plot bonds on the same SML that is used for common stocks. However, these results have not been successful—bonds do not plot on the same linear SML as stocks.

[15]Rating agencies do review ratings without being prompted by the company. However, most reviews associated with new issues are actually requested by the company, not because the company wants a review but because the investment bankers make such a review a condition of their handling the offering. Note also that a company must pay the agency to have its bonds rated. It has been suggested that such payments might lead to a favorable bias in ratings. However, there is no evidence whatever of any bias on the part of the major rating agencies. The value of their service, and hence the agencies' incomes, depends almost entirely on their credibility, so there is every reason to expect the agencies to maintain strict objectivity.

$100 par value preferred stock for a total of $15 million. This preferred had a stated dividend of $12 per share, so the preferred dividend yield was $12/$100 = 0.12, or 12 percent, at the time of issue. The dividend was set when the stock was issued; it will not be changed in the future.[16] Therefore, if the market discount rate for the preferred, k_p, changes from 12 percent after the issue date—as it certainly will—then the market price of the preferred stock will go up or down. For example, if k_p for Mississippi Power's preferred falls to 10 percent, the price of the preferred will rise to $12/0.10 = $120.

If the preferred dividend is not earned, the company does not have to pay it. However, most preferred issues are *cumulative*, meaning that the cumulative total of all unpaid preferred dividends must be paid before dividends can be paid on the common stock. Unpaid preferred dividends are called *arrearages*.[17]

Preferred stock normally have no voting rights, but most preferred issues do stipulate that the preferred stockholders can elect a minority of the directors—say three out of 10—if the preferred dividend is passed (omitted). However, Jersey Central Power & Light, one of the companies that owned a share of the Three Mile Island (TMI) nuclear plant, has preferred stock outstanding which can elect a *majority* of the directors if the preferred dividend is passed for four consecutive quarters. Jersey Central kept paying its preferred dividends even during the dark days following the TMI accident. Had the preferred only been entitled to elect a minority of the directors, the dividend would probably have been passed.

Even though nonpayment of preferred dividends will not bankrupt a company, corporations issue preferred with every intention of paying the dividends. Even if passing the dividend does not give the preferred stockholders control of the company, a failure to pay a preferred dividend precludes payment of common dividends and, in addition, makes it virtually impossible for a firm to raise capital by selling bonds, more preferred, or common stock. However, having preferred stock outstanding does give a firm that experiences temporary problems a chance to overcome its difficulties; had bonds been used instead of preferred stock, the company might have been forced into bankruptcy before it could straighten out its problems. Thus, from the viewpoint of the issuing corporation, preferred stock is less risky than bonds.

Investors, on the other hand, regard preferred stock as being riskier than bonds for two reasons: (1) Preferred stockholders' claims are subordinated to bondholders' in the event of liquidation, and (2) bondhold-

---

[16]Recently, firms have begun to issue preferred stock with floating dividend yields. This type of preferred, which is especially suitable for marketable security holdings by corporations, is discussed in Chapter 20.

[17]Dividends in arrears do not earn interest; thus, arrearages do not increase in a compound interest sense. They only grow from continued nonpayment of the preferred dividend.

ers are more likely to continue receiving income during hard times than are preferred stockholders. Accordingly, investors historically have required a higher rate of return on a given firm's preferred stock than on its bonds. However, the fact that 85 percent of preferred dividends are exempt from the corporate tax has made preferred stock attractive to corporate investors. In recent years, high-grade preferred stock, on average, has sold on a lower yield basis than have high-grade bonds. As an example, in June 1984, Du Pont's preferred stock yielded about 11.0 percent, while its bonds provided a yield of 13.7 percent, or 2.7 percentage points *more* than its preferred. The tax treatment accounted for this differential; the *after-tax yield* to corporate investors was greater on the preferred stock than on the bonds.[18]

About half of all preferred stock issued in recent years has been convertible into common stock. For example, a firm might issue preferred stock which stipulated that one share of preferred could be converted into three shares of common, at the option of the preferred stockholder. Convertibles are discussed at length in the next chapter.

Preferred stock is generally similar to perpetual bonds in that it has no maturity date. However, many preferred shares do have a sinking fund provision; if the sinking fund calls for the retirement of 2 percent of the issue each year, the issue will "mature" in a maximum of 50 years.[19] Also, many preferred issues are callable by the issuing corporation. This feature, if exercised, will also limit the life of the preferred.

Nonconvertible preferred stock is virtually all owned by corporations, which can take advantage of the 85 percent exclusion of dividends to obtain a higher after-tax yield on preferred stock than on bonds. Individuals should not own preferred stocks (except convertible preferreds)—they can get higher yields on safer bonds, so it is simply not logical for them to hold preferreds. The volume of preferred stock financing is geared to the supply of money in the hands of insurance companies and other corporate investors who are looking for tax-favored investments. When the supply of such money is plentiful, the prices of preferred stocks are bid up, their yields fall, and investment bankers suggest to

---

[18]The after-tax yield on a 13.7 percent bond to a corporate investor that is paying a 46 percent marginal tax rate is 13.7%(1 − T) = 13.7%(0.54) = 7.4%. The after-tax yield on an 11 percent preferred stock is 11.0%(1 − Effective T) = 11.0%[1 − (0.15)(0.46)] = 10.2%. Also, note that the 1984 Deficit Reduction Act prohibits firms from issuing debt and then using the proceeds to purchase another firm's preferred or common stock. If debt financing is used for stock purchases, then the 85 percent dividend exclusion is reduced. This provision of the 1984 Act was designed to prevent firms from engaging in "tax arbitrage."

[19]Prior to the late 1970s, virtually all preferred stock was perpetual, and almost no issues had sinking funds. Then, insurance company regulators, worried about the unrealized losses the companies had been incurring on preferred holdings as a result of rising interest rates, put into effect some regulatory changes which essentially mandated that insurance companies buy only preferred issues which contained sinking funds. From that time on, virtually all preferred issues have had sinking funds, and almost no new issues have been perpetuities. This example illustrates how the nature of securities changes due to changes in the economic environment.

companies that they consider issuing preferred stock because (1) it provides financial leverage, yet (2) if earnings fall and the preferred dividend cannot be paid, this will not bankrupt the company.

There are several situations in which firms might retire a bond or preferred stock issue prior to maturity. We discuss three in this section: (1) bond and preferred stock refunding, (2) bond/stock swaps, and (3) defeasance.

Early Retirement of Bonds and Preferred Stock

Suppose a company sells bonds or preferred stock when interest rates are relatively high. Provided the issue is callable, as many are, the company could sell a new issue of low-yielding securities if and when interest rates drop. It could then use the proceeds to retire the high-rate issue and thus reduce its interest or preferred dividend expenses. This is called a *refunding operation*. Refunding operations are discussed in detail in Appendix 15A.

Bond and Preferred Stock Refunding

In the early 1980s, because of the dramatic increase in interest rates, many companies had outstanding low-coupon bonds which were selling at deep discounts. Obviously, it would not pay to refund such bonds in the manner described above, but for some companies, it did make sense to engage in a *bond/stock swap*.[20] Swaps work like this:

Bond/Stock Swaps

1. Duke Power Company arranged for Salomon Brothers, which is a major investment banking company, to buy in the open market about $100 million of Duke's old, low-coupon bonds, which were then selling at about 60 percent of their par value. Thus, Salomon paid about $60 million for $100 million of par value debt.

2. Duke then issued new common stock worth just over $60 million and swapped this new stock with Salomon for the $60 million of bonds. The excess of the stock's value over that of the bonds represented Salomon's fee.

3. Salomon then sold the stock on the open market, closing out its position and netting a profit equal to its fee.

4. Duke canceled the $100 million of debt, and it had issued about $60 million of stock. The difference, $40 million, was reported to stockhold-

---

[20]Of course, the firm could always buy the debt on the open market, using either cash flow from operations or new debt to fund the retirement. However, using high cost new debt to pay off low-rate old debt is not, in general, a sound financial decision. Moreover, using cash flows from operations for open market purchases of bonds would have a tax disadvantage in that the difference between the discounted price paid for the bond and its par value would have to be treated as ordinary income. This would increase the firm's reported net income for the period, and taxes at the marginal rate would have to be paid on the increase, even though the firm would not realize a cash inflow from the transaction.

ers as net income during the year of the swap. However, for tax purposes, the profit was not regarded as income. Had the bonds been purchased by Duke, rather than acquired via a swap, the gain would have been taxable under then existing tax laws.[21]

5. Duke's interest coverages were improved, because it had less debt outstanding. Also, its balance sheet was strengthened, because debt went down by $100 million and equity went up by $100 million ($60 million of common stock plus a $40 million addition to retained earnings).

Defeasance

Sometimes firms want to retire old, low-coupon debt, but they are not able to purchase the quantity desired because the debt is neither callable nor actively traded. For these firms, another alternative exists: *defeasance*. In a defeasance, which means "render null and void," a firm effectively discharges a debt obligation, without actually paying it off prior to maturity, by passing the obligation to a trustee, such as a bank, along with a portfolio of securities, typically Treasury bonds. The trustee uses the income from these securities, and their principal as they mature, to service the old debt during its remaining life and to retire it at maturity. Until recently, only tax-exempt issuers, such as municipalities, found defeasance worthwhile; because municipalities' bonds had much lower coupons than those on Treasury bonds, a state or city government could buy say $50 million of Treasury bonds whose income was sufficient to cover a $75 million obligation. Thus, defeasance—which was also a type of "tax arbitrage" operation for municipalities—looked good.

Defeasance only "works" if treasury securities have yields which exceed those of the corporate bonds that are being "retired." Normally, treasury bonds yield less than corporates. However, the high interest rates of the early 1980s resulted in coupons on new Treasury bonds that were far above the coupons on old corporate debt, so defeasance became feasible for corporations. In the first publicly announced example of a corporate defeasance, Exxon in 1982 handed its trustee, Morgan Guaranty Trust Company, $313 million worth of Treasury and other U.S. Government securities with an overall yield of about 14 percent. The income from these securities was sufficient to pay the interest on 6 Exxon debt issues, whose par value totaled $515 million and whose coupons ranged from 5.8 to 6.7 percent. The excess of interest received over interest paid each year will be added to the pool so that, by the time the last Exxon bond issue matures in 2009, the trustee will have accumulated $515 million, enough to pay off all the principal on the 6 issues.

Exxon was able to remove those 6 issues of debt from its balance sheet for reporting purposes, thus reducing its leverage. In addition, Exxon

---

[21]The Deficit Reduction Act of 1984 now requires corporations to pay taxes on the "profit" from a bond/stock swap. This action will effectively stop such swaps except for ailing firms with effective tax rates near zero.

no longer had to deduct the $31.7 million in interest expense associated with the 6 issues from earnings, since the servicing responsibility had passed to the trustee. Also, because the debt was discharged at less than face value, Exxon posted a gain of about $132 million to reported 1982 after-tax profits. However, for tax purposes, Exxon may continue to deduct the interest expense on the 6 debt issues, and it must pay tax on the income from the government securities.

Why are there so many different types of long-term securities? At least a partial answer to this question may be seen from Figure 15-3, which depicts the now familiar risk/return trade-off function drawn to show the risk and the expected returns for the various securities of the Montpelier Company. First, U.S. Treasury bills, representing the risk-free

Rationale for the Use of Different Types of Securities

Figure 15-3
Montpelier Company: Risk and Expected Returns on Different Classes of Securities

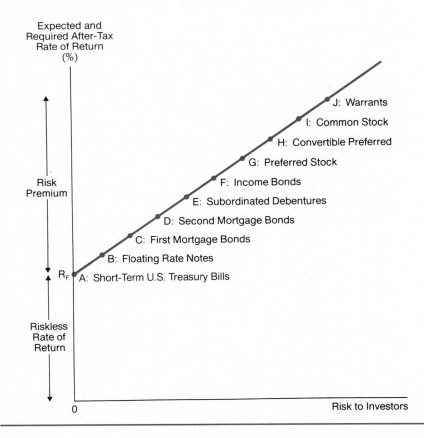

rate, are shown for reference. The lowest risk long-term securities offered by Montpelier are its floating rate notes; these securities are free of interest rate risk, but they are exposed to some risk of default. The first mortgage bonds are somewhat riskier than the notes, and they sell at a somewhat higher required and expected after-tax return. The second mortgage bonds are even riskier, and they have a still higher expected return. Subordinated debentures, income bonds, and preferred stocks are all increasingly risky, and their expected returns increase accordingly. The firm's convertible preferred is riskier than its straight preferred, but less risky than its common stock. Montpelier's warrants, the riskiest security the firm issues, have the highest required return of any of its offerings (warrants and convertibles are discussed in Chapter 16).

Why does Montpelier issue so many different classes of securities? Why not just offer one type of bond plus common stock? The answer lies in the fact that different investors have different risk/return trade-off preferences, so to appeal to the broadest possible market, Montpelier must offer securities that attract as many different types of investors as possible. Also, different securities are especially attractive at different points in time. Used wisely, a policy of selling differentiated securities to take advantage of market conditions can lower a firm's overall cost of capital below what it would be if the firm issued only one class of debt plus common stock.

Factors that Influence Long-Term Financing Decisions

As we show in this section, many factors influence a firm's long-term financing decisions. It is impossible to rank the factors in order of importance, because their relative importance varies (1) among firms at any point in time and (2) for any given firm over time.

Target Capital Structure

One of the most important considerations in any financing decision is how the firm's actual capital structure compares to its target structure. Remember that firms establish an optimal, or target, capital structure and, over time, finance in accordance with this target. Of course, in any one year, few firms finance exactly in accordance with the target capital structure, primarily because of flotation costs: Smaller issues of new securities have proportionally larger flotation costs, so firms tend to use debt one year and stock the next.

For example, assume that Consolidated Tools, Inc., a Cincinnati machine tool manufacturer, anticipates a requirement for $10 million of new external capital in each of the next 2 years. The target capital structure calls for 40 percent debt, so Consolidated, if it were to raise debt each year, would issue $4 million of new bonds each year for 2 years. The flotation costs, based on the data in Table 14-4, would be 6.2 percent of each $4 million issue. To net $4 million, Consolidated would have to sell $4 million/0.938 = $4,264,392 each year, and pay $264,392 in flotation costs on each issue, for a total of $528,784 in flotation costs over the 2 years.

Alternatively, Consolidated could elect to raise the total $8 million of debt in one year. The flotation cost for an $8 million issue would be 3.2 percent, so the firm would float an issue for $8 million/0.968 = $8,264,463 and pay $264,463 in total flotation costs. By issuing debt only once, Consolidated would cut its debt flotation costs almost in half. The same relationship would apply to sales of preferred stock and new common equity issues. Note that making fewer, but larger, security offerings would cause Consolidated's capital structure to fluctuate about its optimal level rather than stay right on target. However, (1) small fluctuations about the optimal capital structure have little effect on a firm's weighted average cost of capital, (2) investors would recognize that this action is prudent, and (3) the firm would save substantial amounts of flotation costs by financing in this manner. So, firms such as Consolidated tend, over the long haul, to finance in accordance with their target capital structures, but flotation costs plus the factors discussed in the following sections do influence the specific financing decisions in any given year.

We should also point out that firms such as Consolidated can, and often do, arrange financings in advance. Thus, if Consolidated concluded that it would need $8 million of debt over a 2-year period, it might arrange with one or more pension funds to borrow $4 million in each of the next 2 years, with the second $4 million being firmly committed by the lenders at the time the first $4 million is borrowed. Such financings can reduce flotation costs because the lenders need make only one detailed credit analysis of Consolidated. Similarly, larger firms can use shelf registrations, which we discussed in Chapter 14, to hold down financing costs even while they sell relatively small blocks of securities. Both commitment financings and shelf registrations make it possible for firms to adhere reasonably closely to their optimal capital structures without incurring unduly high flotation costs.

Maturity Matching

Assume that Consolidated makes the decision to float a single $8 million nonconvertible bond issue, with a sinking fund. It must next choose a maturity for the issue, taking into consideration both the shape of the yield curve and the management's own expectations about future interest rates, as well as the maturity of the assets being financed. To illustrate how asset maturities affect the choice of debt maturities, suppose Consolidated's capital projects over the next 2 years consist primarily of new, automated milling and stamping machinery for its Cincinnati plant. This machinery has an expected economic life of 10 years (even though it falls into the ACRS 5-year class life). Should Consolidated finance the debt portion of this equipment with 5-year, 10-year, 20-year, or 30-year debt, or some other maturity? *The least risky approach to financing is to match the maturities of the liabilities with the maturity of the assets being financed.*

Note that some of the new capital for the machinery will come from common and preferred stock, both of which are generally considered to be perpetual securities with infinite maturities. Of course, preferred stock can have a sinking fund or be redeemable, and common stock can always be repurchased on the open market or by a tender offer, so the effective maturity of preferred and common stock can be reduced significantly.

On the other hand, debt maturities can be specified at the time of issue. If Consolidated financed its capital budgets over the next 2 years with 10-year sinking fund bonds, it would be matching asset and liability maturities. The cash flows resulting from the new machinery could be used to make the interest and sinking fund payments on the issue, so the bonds would be retired as the machinery wore out. If Consolidated had used one-year debt, it would have to pay off this debt with cash flows derived from assets other than the machinery in question. Conversely, if it used 20-year or 30-year debt, it would have to service the debt long after the assets that were purchased with the debt had been scrapped and had ceased providing cash flows. This would worry the lenders.

Of course, the one-year debt could probably be rolled over year after year, out to the 10-year asset maturity. However, if interest rates rise, Consolidated would have to pay a higher rate when it rolled over its debt, or if the company experienced difficulties, it might even be unable to refund the debt at any reasonable rate. On the other hand, if Consolidated financed 10-year assets with 20-year or 30-year bonds, it would still have (1) a liability after the 10-year life of the asset, but (2) it would have generated some excess cash from the assets over their 10-year life. The question then would be: Can we reinvest the accumulated cash flows at a rate which will enable us to pay off the bonds over their remaining 20-year or 30-year life? This strategy clearly imposes uncertainty on the firm, since it cannot know at the time it sells the bonds if profitable capital investment opportunities will be available 10 years later.

For all these reasons, the least risky financing strategy is to match security maturities with asset maturities. In recognition of this fact, firms generally do place great emphasis on maturity matching, and this factor often dominates the debt portion of the financing decision.

Interest Rate Levels

Financial managers also consider interest rate levels, both absolute and relative, when making financing decisions. For example, if long-term interest rates are high by historic standards, many managers will be reluctant to issue long-term debt and thus lock in those costs for long periods. We already know that one solution to this problem is for firms to use a call provision—callability permits refunding of the issue should interest rates drop, but there is a cost, because the firm must pay more for callable debt. Alternatively, the firm may finance with short-term debt whenever long-term rates are historically high and then, assuming interest rates subsequently fall, sell a long-term issue to replace the short-term debt. Of course, this strategy has its risks. If interest rates move even higher, the firm will be forced to renew the debt at higher and higher short-term rates, or to replace the short-term debt with a long-term bond which costs more than it would have when the original decision was made.

One could argue, and many do, that capital markets are efficient. If so—and most evidence supports the efficient markets hypothesis—then it is impossible to predict what future interest rates will be, since these rates will be determined by information which is not now known. Thus, under the efficient markets hypothesis, it would be unproductive for firms to try to "beat the market" by forecasting future capital costs and acting on such forecasts. According to this view, financial managers ought to arrange their capital structures in such a manner that they can ride out almost any economic storm, and this generally calls for (1) using some "reasonable" mix of debt and equity as discussed in Chapter 12, and (2) using debt with maturities which match the maturities of the assets being financed.

Although we personally support the view dictated by the efficient markets hypothesis, there is no question but that many managers disagree. They are influenced by current cost levels, and they act accordingly. One manifestation of this behavior is the heavy use of shelf registrations. In Chapter 14, we noted that the registration of new securities with the Securities and Exchange Commission (SEC) is a costly and lengthy process. To help alleviate the problem, in March 1982, the SEC adopted Rule 415, which permits certain large, well-known corporations to register debt or equity offerings in advance and then sell the securities, in one or more sales, within two years after the filing is completed. Because this allows firms to register an issue and then place it "on the shelf" until conditions are "right" for the sale, Rule 415 registrations have become known as shelf registrations.

By using shelf registrations, issuers are spared the costs of filing several registrations, and they gain flexibility in timing their issues. At the very least, filing a shelf registration saves printing costs and management time, because no preliminary prospectus is required. Critics of shelf registration claim (1) that putting security offerings on the shelf may cause potential investors to be wary about an overhang in the market, thus holding down prices, and (2) that since the SEC approves shelf registrations so speedily, underwriters may not have time to perform their "due diligence" work of gathering information about a company and its offering.[22]

Some firms use shelf registrations because managers believe that financing "windows" exist. Because interest rates have been so volatile in the early 1980s, a company might decide to issue bonds when the rate is 12 percent but then find, 6 weeks later when it has SEC approval to go ahead with the issue, that rates are up to 13 percent. Had it had "bonds on the shelf," it could have gone ahead and sold the issue while the low-cost window was open.

Interest Rate Forecasts

In early September of 1983, the interest rate on AAA corporate bonds was about 12.5 percent, up from 11.5 percent in April. Exxon's investment bankers advised the company to tap the Eurodollar bond market for relatively cheap fixed-rate financing.[23] At the time, Exxon could issue its bonds in London at 0.4 percentage points *below* comparable maturity Treasury bonds. However, one of Exxon's officers was quoted as saying, "I say so what. The absolute level of rates is too high. Our people would rather wait." The managers of Exxon, as well as many other companies, were betting that the next move in interest rates would be down. This belief was also openly expressed by executives of ITT, Ontario Hydro, and RCA, among others.

These attitudes confirm that many firms base their financing decisions on expectations about future interest rates. However, the success of such a strategy requires that interest rate forecasts be right more often than they are wrong, and it is very difficult to find someone with a long-term track record better than 50-50. Turn back to Figure 3-5 and focus on the yield curve for March 1983. That curve shows how much the U.S. government had to pay in 1983 to borrow money for one year, 3 years, 5 years, 10 years, and so on. A business borrower would have had to pay somewhat more, but assume for the moment that we are back in 1983 and the yield curve shown for that year also applies to your company. Now suppose you have decided (1) to build a new plant with a 20-year life which will cost $1 million and (2) to raise the $1 million by selling an issue of debt (or borrowing) rather than by selling stock. If you borrowed in 1983 on a short-term basis, say for one year, your interest cost for that year would be only 9.0 percent, or $90,000, while if you used long-term financing, your cost would be 10.8 percent, or $108,000. Therefore, at first glance, it would seem that you should use short-term debt.

---

[22]Because of these potential problems, shelf registration is restricted to firms with $150 million or more in stock held by outside investors. Thus, large, widely followed companies can use shelf registration, but a lot of companies (29 percent of those listed in the NYSE) are still required to register each individual issue.

[23]A *Eurodollar bond* is a bond sold outside of the United States but denominated in U.S. dollars. See Chapter 26 for a further discussion.

However, this could prove to be a horrible mistake. If you use short-term debt, you will have to renew your loan every year, and the rate charged on each new loan will reflect the then current short-term rate. Interest rates could return to their March 1980 levels, so by 1987, you could be paying 14 percent, or $140,000 per year. These high interest payments would cut into and perhaps eliminate your profits. The reduced profitability could easily increase your firm's risk to the point where your bond rating would be lowered, causing lenders to increase the risk premium built into the interest rate they charge you, which would force you to pay even higher rates. These super high interest rates would further reduce profitability, worrying lenders even more, and making them reluctant even to renew your loan. If the lenders refuse to renew the loan and demand payment, as they have every right to do, you might have trouble raising the cash. If the high interest rates cause a recession, you would certainly find it difficult to convert physical assets to cash without making drastic price cuts, which would mean heavy operating losses or even bankruptcy.

On the other hand, if you used long-term financing in 1983, your interest costs would remain constant at $108,000 per year, and an increase in interest rates would not hurt you. You might even be able to buy up some of your bankrupted competitors at bargain prices—bankruptcies increase dramatically when interest rates rise.

Does all this suggest that firms should always avoid short-term debt? Not necessarily. If you borrowed on a short-term basis for 9 percent in March 1983, and if President Reagan's economic program worked perfectly, then inflation would fall sharply in the next few years, and so would interest rates. In that event, your company would be at a major disadvantage if its debt were locked in at 10.8 percent while its competitors (who used short-term debt in 1983 and thus rode interest rates down in subsequent years) had a borrowing cost of only 5 or 6 percent. On the other hand, President Reagan's economic program may not work, and projected high federal deficits might drive inflation and interest rates up to new record levels. In that case, you would wish you had borrowed long-term in 1983.

Finance would be easy if we could predict future interest rates accurately. Unfortunately, predicting future interest rates with consistent accuracy is somewhere between difficult and impossible—people who make a living selling interest rate forecasts say it is difficult; many others say it is impossible.

Restrictions in Existing Debt Contracts

Earlier we discussed the problems that Savannah Electric has had because they were at times restricted from issuing new first mortgage bonds by their indenture coverage requirements. This is just one example of how indenture covenants can influence a firm's financing decision. Restrictions on the current ratio, on the debt/equity ratio, and so on could also restrict a firm's ability to use different types of financings at a given time.

The Firm's Current and Forecasted Condition

Earlier in the chapter, we discussed bond ratings and the effects of changes in ratings on the cost and availability of capital. If a firm's current financial condition is poor, its managers may be reluctant to issue new debt because (1) a new debt issue would probably trigger a review by the rating agencies, and (2) debt issued when a firm is in poor financial condition would probably cost more and have more severe restrictive covenants than debt issued from strength. Thus, a firm that is in a weakened condition, but which is forecasting a better time in the future, would be inclined to delay permanent financing of any type until things improved. Conversely, a firm that is strong now, but which forecasts a potentially bad time in the period just ahead, would be motivated to finance long term now rather than to wait. Each of these scenarios implies that the capital markets are either inefficient or that investors do not have as much information about the firm's future as does its financial manager. The second situation is undoubtedly true at times, and possibly the first one also in rare cases.

The firm's earnings outlook, and the extent to which forecasted higher earnings per share are reflected in stock prices, also has an effect on the choice of securities. If a successful R&D program has just been concluded, and management forecasts higher earnings than do most investors, then the firm would not want to issue common stock. It would use debt and then, once earnings rise and push up the stock price, sell common to restore the capital structure to its target level.

Amount of Financing Required

Obviously, the amount of financing required will influence the financing decision. This is mainly due to flotation costs. A $1 million debt financing would most likely be done with a term loan or a privately placed bond issue, while a firm seeking $100 million of new debt would most likely use a public offering.

Availability of Collateral

Generally, secured debt will be less costly than unsecured debt. Thus, firms with large amounts of fixed assets which have a ready resale value are likely to use a relatively large amount of debt, especially mortgage bonds. Additionally, each year's financing decision would be influenced by the amount of qualified assets available as security for new bonds.

Using Futures in Corporate Finance

Many of the factors discussed in the previous section imply an ability to forecast future capital market conditions. As we have stated repeatedly, the evidence strongly indicates that managers can forecast their own firms' internal conditions better than outside investors, but that no one can consistently forecast interest rates and the general level of stock prices. If one believes that it is impossible to forecast future capital costs, then his or her major concern should be to minimize the adverse effects of changes in capital costs from today's "spot" costs. This can be done through transactions in the *futures markets*.[24]

Futures Markets and Contracts

Most financial and real asset contracts occur in what is known as the *spot*, or *cash, market*. Here, the asset is delivered immediately (or within a few days). Conversely, *futures*, or *futures contracts*, call for the purchase or sale of a financial or real asset at some future date, but at a price which is fixed today.

In 1984, futures contracts were available on more than 30 physical and financial assets traded on 11 U.S. exchanges, the largest of which are the Chicago Board of Trade (CBT) and the Chicago Mercantile Exchange (CME). Futures contracts are divided into two classes, *commodity futures* and *financial futures*. Commodity futures, which cover various grains and oilseeds, livestock and meats, foods and fibers, metals, and wood, were first traded in the United States in the middle 1800s. Financial futures cover stock market indexes, Treasury bills, Treasury notes and bonds, certificates of deposit, commercial paper, GNMA certificates, and foreign currencies, and they were first traded in the mid-1970s.[25]

To illustrate how futures contracts work, consider the CBT's contract on Treasury bonds. The basic contract is for $100,000 of a hypothetical 8 percent coupon, semiannual-payment Treasury bond with approximately 20 years to first call. On August 9, 1983, futures contracts for March 1984 delivery (7 month futures) of this hypothetical bond sold for $67^{21}/_{36}$ ($675.83 per $1,000 par value bond, or $67,583 for 100 bonds with a par value of $100,000), which translates to a yield to maturity of 12.42 percent. This yield represents investors' beliefs in August 1983 about the interest rate level which will prevail in March 1984.

Now suppose that three months later, on November 9, 1983, interest rates had fallen from the August levels, say to 11 percent, and investors expected this 11 percent rate to persist in the future. Falling interest rates mean rising bond prices, so the March 1984 contract would now be worth about $75,931. Thus, the contract's value would have increased by $75,931 − $67,583 = $8,348.

When futures contracts are purchased, the purchaser does not have to put up the full amount of the purchase price; rather, the purchaser is

---

[24]Our discussion of futures is necessarily limited in scope. For a more detailed description of futures and their use in financial management, see Robert C. Radcliffe, *Investment Concepts, Analysis, and Strategy* (Glenview, Ill.: Scott, Foresman, 1982).

[25]GNMA certificates are issued by the Government National Mortgage Association, known as "Ginnie Mae." GNMA is a wholly owned government agency organized to provide assistance to the housing mortgage market. GNMA certificates are backed by the full faith and credit of the U.S. Government, but have residential mortgages as the underlying asset.

required to post an initial *margin*, which for CBT Treasury bond contracts is $3,000 per $100,000 contract. Thus, if an investor purchased a contract in August, and then sold it in November, he or she would have made a profit of $8,340 on an investment of only $3,000. It is clear, therefore, that futures contracts offer a considerable amount of leverage. Of course, if interest rates had risen, then the value of the contract would have declined, and the investor could easily have lost his or her $3,000.

Futures contracts are rarely delivered, since both buyers and sellers normally close their positions prior to the delivery date. Since they are so similar, it is easy to become confused between futures contracts and options. An *option* is merely the right to conduct a transaction, say the right to buy 100 shares of IBM at $120 per share. The option may or may not be exercised, and the option contract may or may not be sold—it could just expire. On the other hand, a futures contract to buy $100,000 in Treasury bonds requires that the transaction be completed, either by taking delivery, which is rare, or by reversing the trade, which amounts to selling the contract back to the original seller.[26]

Hedging

Futures markets are used for both speculation and hedging. *Speculation* involves anticipating price movements, and taking advantage of the inherent leverage in the contract to enhance expected returns. *Hedging*, on the other hand, is done to protect against unwanted interest rate movements. In a hedge, there is always an underlying transaction which we seek to protect. To illustrate, assume that Porter Electronics plans to issue $10 million in long-term bonds 3 months from now to support a major capital project. The interest rate would be 14 percent if the bonds were issued today, and at that rate, the capital budgeting project has a positive NPV. However, Porter's financial manager fears that interest rates will rise over the next 3 months, and that, when the issue is actually sold, it will have a cost substantially above 14 percent, which would make the project a bad investment. Porter can protect itself against such a rise in rates by hedging in the futures market.

In the example, Porter would be hurt by an increase in interest rates. To hedge against this possibility, Porter would *sell* (or *short*) futures contracts. It would choose a futures contract on the security most similar to the company's underlying security—long-term bonds. In this case, Porter should choose to hedge with Treasury bond futures. Since it has $10 million in underlying securities, Porter would sell $10,000,000/$100,000 = 100 Treasury bond contracts for delivery in 3 months. In doing so, Porter would have to put up margin money as well as pay brokerage

---

[26]The buyers and sellers of futures contracts do not actually trade with one another, even though a contract cannot be bought without a seller, and vice versa. Each trader's contractual obligation is with the futures exchange. This feature helps to guarantee the fiscal integrity of the trade.

commissions. Assuming that each contract has a value of $70,000, the total value of the 100 contracts is $7 million. Now, assume that interest rates rise to 15 percent over the next 3 months. Porter's own 14 percent coupon bonds would bring only $934 per bond, because investors are requiring a 15 percent return. Thus, Porter would lose $66 per bond times 10,000 bonds, or $660,000, because it delayed the financing. However, the increase in interest rates would also bring about a change in the value of Porter's short position in the futures market. Since interest rates have increased, the futures contract value will fall, from $7 million to $6,340,000, or by $660,000, if corporate and Treasury bonds experienced the same relative changes. Porter would then close its position in the futures market by repurchasing for $6,340,000 the contracts which it sold short for $7 million, giving it a profit of $660,000.

Thus, Porter has, if we ignore commissions and the opportunity cost of the margin money, exactly offset the loss on the bond issue. This is known as a perfect hedge. The increase in value of Porter's short position exactly offset its losses due to rising interest rates. In reality, it is difficult to construct perfect hedges, because in most cases, the underlying asset is not identical to the futures asset. Of course, if in our example interest rates had fallen, Porter would have lost on its futures position. However, this loss would have been offset by the fact that Porter could now sell its bonds for more than $1,000.

Similarly, if Porter had been planning an equity offering, and if its stock tended to move fairly closely with one of the stock indexes on which options are written, it could have hedged against falling stock prices by buying a *put* on the index option.[27]

These are two examples of how firms can use the futures and options markets to hedge against changes in interest rates or prices. These markets permit flexibility in the timing of financial policy, because the firm can be protected, at least partially, against changes that occur between the time a decision to acquire assets is made and the financing is completed. The cost of the protection is represented by commissions plus the opportunity cost of the margin money. Whether or not the protection is worth the cost is a matter of judgment, and it depends on management's risk aversion as well as the company's strength and ability to assume the risk of changing money costs. We will discuss the use of the futures market again when we look at inventory management.

Summary

This chapter described the characteristics, advantages, and disadvantages of the major types of long-term debt securities and preferred stocks. The key difference between *bonds* and *term loans* is the fact that term loans are sold

---

[27]A *put* is an option to *sell* at a future time at a specified price, while a *call* is an option to *buy*. Puts and calls are discussed in Chapter 16.

directly by a corporate borrower to between one and 20 lenders, while bonds are generally sold to many public investors through investment bankers. *Preferred stocks* are similar to bonds in that they offer a fixed return. However, preferred stock is less risky than bonds from the corporation's viewpoint because (1) the dividend does not have to be paid if it is not earned, and (2) nonpayment of preferred dividends will not bankrupt the firm. From the investors' standpoint, however, preferred stocks are riskier than bonds, because (1) firms are more likely to omit preferred dividends than to fail to pay interest, and (2) bonds have priority over preferred stock in the event of bankruptcy. Additionally, we discussed three means of retiring securities before they mature: (1) bond and preferred stock *refunding*, (2) *bond/stock swaps*, and (3) *defeasance*. In Appendix 15A, we present a method for evaluating the refunding decision.

It is impossible to state, as a generalization, that debt, preferred stock, or common equity is the "best" method of financing. Each has advantages and disadvantages vis-à-vis the other types of securities, and the relative importance of these advantages/disadvantages varies over time and from company to company. There are many factors that influence a firm's long-term financing decisions. Among the most important are (1) its target capital structure, (2) maturity matching, (3) current interest rate levels, (4) forecasts of future interest rates, (5) restrictive covenants, (6) the firm's current and forecasted condition, (7) the amount of financing, and (8) the availability of collateral.

Finally, we discussed the *futures markets,* and we showed how futures contracts can be used to hedge against changing interest rates and stock prices.

Questions

15-1 Define the following terms:
    a. Bond; preferred stock
    b. Term loan
    c. Mortgage
    d. Debenture
    e. Convertible
    f. Subordinated debenture
    g. Income bond
    h. Development bond
    i. Pollution control bond
    j. Indenture
    k. Restrictive covenant
    l. Call provision
    m. Sinking fund
    n. Amortization schedule
    o. Funded debt
    p. Preferred arrearage
    q. Flotation costs
    r. Floating rate bond
    s. Zero coupon bond
    t. Futures market; hedging

15-2 What effect would each of the following items have on the interest rate a firm must pay on a new issue of long-term debt? Indicate whether each factor will tend to raise, lower, or have an indeterminate effect and then explain *why*.

a. The firm uses bonds rather than a term loan.

b. The firm uses nonsubordinated debentures rather than first mortgage bonds.

c. The firm makes its bonds convertible into common stock.

d. The firm makes its debentures subordinated to its bank debt. What will the effect be
   (1) on the debentures?
   (2) on the bank debt?
   (3) on average total debt?

e. The firm sells income bonds rather than debentures.

f. The firm must raise $100 million, all of which will be used to construct a new plant, and is debating the sale of mortgage bonds or debentures. If it decides to issue $50 million of each type, as opposed to $75 million of mortgage bonds and $25 million of debentures, how will this affect
   (1) the debentures?
   (2) the mortgage bonds?
   (3) the average cost of the $100 million?

g. The firm is planning to raise $25 million of long-term capital. Its outstanding bonds yield 9 percent. If it sells preferred stock, how will this affect the yield on the outstanding debt?

h. The firm puts a call provision on its new issue of bonds.

i. The firm includes a sinking fund on its new issue of bonds.

j. The firm's bonds are downgraded from A to BBB.

15-3 Rank the following securities from lowest (1) to highest (10) in terms of their riskiness for an investor. All securities (except the government bond) are for a given firm. If you think two or more securities are equally risky, so indicate.

a. Income bond   _____

b. Subordinated debentures—noncallable   _____

c. First mortgage bond—no sinking fund   _____

d. Preferred stock   _____

e. Common stock   _____

f. U.S. Treasury bond   _____

g. First mortgage bond—with sinking fund   _____

h. Subordinated debentures-callable   _____

i. Amortized term loan   _____

j. Nonamortized term loan   _____

15-4 A sinking fund can be set up in one of two ways:

1. The corporation makes annual payments to the trustee, who invests the proceeds in securities (frequently government bonds) and uses the accumulated total to retire the bond issue at maturity.

2. The trustee uses the annual payments to retire a portion of the issue each year, either calling a given percentage of the issue by a lottery

and paying a specified price per bond or buying bonds on the open market, whichever is cheaper.

Discuss the advantages and disadvantages of each procedure from the viewpoint of both the firm and the bondholders.

15-5 Draw an SML graph. Put dots on the graph to show (approximately) where you think a particular company's (a) common stock and (b) bonds would lie. Now put on a dot to represent a riskier company's stock.

15-6 Suppose you work for the treasurer of a large, profitable corporation. Your company has some surplus funds to invest. You can buy these securities:
  (1) Aaa-rated Exxon 20-year bonds which sell at par and yield 12 percent.
  (2) Aa-rated Exxon preferred stock which yields 10 percent.
  (3) Ca-rated Eastern Airlines bonds which yield 16 percent.
  (4) C-rated Eastern Airlines preferred stock which yields 17 percent.
  (5) A-rated Alabama Power floating rate preferred stock which currently yields 9 percent.
  (6) Treasury bills which yield 8.5 percent.
  a. Does it appear that these securities are in equilibrium?
  b. If these were your only choices, which would you recommend?

Self-Test Problem   ST-1 The Montreal Development Company has just issued a $100 million, 10-year, 8-percent bond. A sinking fund will retire the issue over its life. Sinking fund payments are of equal amounts and will be made semiannually, and the proceeds will be used to retire bonds as the payments are made. Bonds can be called at par for sinking fund purposes, or the funds paid into the sinking fund can be used to buy bonds in the open market.
  a. How large must each semiannual sinking fund payment be?
  b. What will happen, under the conditions of the problem thus far, to the company's debt service requirements per year for this issue over time?
  c. Now suppose Montreal Development had set its sinking fund so that *equal annual amounts*, payable at the end of each year, were paid into a sinking fund trust held by a bank, with the proceeds being used to buy government bonds that pay 6 percent interest. The payments, plus accumulated interest, must total $100 million at the end of 10 years, and the proceeds will be used to retire the bonds at that time. How large must the annual sinking fund payment now be?
  d. What are the annual cash requirements to cover bond service costs under the trusteeship arrangement? (Note: Interest must be paid on Montreal's outstanding bonds, but not on bonds that have been retired.)
  e. What would have to happen to interest rates to cause the company to buy bonds on the open market rather than call them under the original sinking fund plan?

15-1   Suppose a firm is setting up an amortized term loan. What are the   *Problems*
        annual payments for a $2 million loan under the following terms:
   a. 8 percent, 5 years?
   b. 8 percent, 10 years?
   c. 10 percent, 5 years?
   d. 10 percent, 10 years?

15-2   Set up an amortization schedule for a $1 million, 3-year, 9-percent
        loan.

15-3   In 1936, the Canadian government raised $55 million by issuing per-
        petual bonds at a 3 percent annual rate of interest. Unlike most bonds
        issued today, which have a specific maturity date, these perpetual
        bonds can remain outstanding forever; they are, in fact, perpetuities.

        At the time of issue, the Canadian government stated in the bond
        indenture that cash redemption was *possible* at face value ($100) on or
        after September 1966; in other words, the bonds were callable at par
        after September 1966. Believing that the bonds would in fact be called,
        many investors in the early 1960s purchased these bonds with expec-
        tations of receiving $100 in 1966 for each perpetual they had. In 1963,
        the bonds sold for $55, but a rush of buyers drove the price to just
        below the $100 par value by 1966. Prices fell dramatically, however,
        when the Canadian government announced that these perpetual
        bonds were indeed perpetual and would not be paid off. A new 30-
        year supply of coupons was sent to each bondholder, and the bonds'
        market price declined to $42 in December 1972.

        Because of their severe losses, hundreds of Canadian bondholders
        formed the Perpetual Bond Association to lobby for face value redemp-
        tion of the bonds. Government officials in Ottawa insisted that claims
        for face value payment were nonsense, that the bonds were clearly
        identified as perpetuals, and that they did not mature in 1966 or at any
        other time. One Ottawa official stated, "Our job is to protect the tax-
        payer. Why should we pay $55 million for less than $25 million worth
        of bonds?"
   a. Would it make sense for a business firm to issue bonds such as the
       Canadian bonds described above? Would it matter if the firm was
       a proprietorship or a corporation?
   b. If the U. S. government today offered a 5-year bond, a 50-year
       bond, a "regular" perpetuity, and a Canadian-type perpetuity,
       what do you think the relative order of interest rates would be (that
       is, rank the bonds from the one with the lowest to the one with the
       highest rate of interest)? Explain your answer.
   c. (1) Suppose that because of pressure by the Perpetual Bond Asso-
       ciation, you believe that the Canadian government will redeem this
       particular perpetual bond issue in 5 years. Which course of action
       would be more advantageous to you if you owned the bonds: (a)
       to sell your bonds today at $42 or (b) to wait 5 years and have them
       redeemed? Assume that similar risk bonds earn 8 percent today,
       and that interest rates are expected to remain at this level for the
       next 5 years.
       (2) If you had the opportunity to invest your money in bonds of
       similar risk, at what rate of return would you be indifferent to the

choice of selling your perpetuals today or having them redeemed in 5 years; that is, what is the expected yield-to-maturity on the Canadian bonds?

d. Show, mathematically, the perpetuities' value if they yield 7.15 percent, pay $3 interest annually, and are considered as "regular" perpetuities. Show what would happen to the price of bonds if the going interest rate fell to 2 percent.

e. Are the Canadian bonds more likely to be valued as "regular" perpetuities if the going rate of interest is above or below 3 percent? Why?

f. Do you think the Canadian government would have taken the same action with regard to retiring the bonds if the interest rate had fallen rather than risen after they were issued in 1936?

g. Do you think the Canadian government was "fair" or "unfair" in its actions? Give the pros and cons, and justify your reason for thinking that one outweighs the other.

15-4 Suppose Midland Copper, Inc., needed to raise $500 million, and its investment bankers indicated that 10-year zero coupon bonds could be sold at a YTM of 14 percent while a 15 percent yield would be required on *annual* payment coupon bonds. (Assume that the discount can be amortized by the issuer using the straight-line method.)

a. How many $1,000 par value bonds would Midland have to sell under each plan?

b. What would be the YTM on each type of bond (1) to a holder who is tax exempt and (2) to a taxpayer in the 50 percent bracket?

c. What would be the after-tax cost of each type of bond to Midland?

d. Why would investors be willing to buy the zero coupon bonds?

e. Why might Midland turn down the offer to issue zero coupon bonds?

Solution to Self-Test Problem

ST-1 a. $100,000,000/10 = $10,000,000 per year, or $5 million each 6 months. Since the $5 million will be used to retire bonds immediately, no interest will be earned on it.

b. The debt service requirements will decline. As the amount of bonds outstanding declines, so will the interest requirements (in millions of dollars):

6-Month Period	Sinking Fund Payment	Amount on Which Interest Is Paid	Interest Payment	Total Bond Service
1	$5	$100	$4.0	$9.0
2	5	95	3.8	8.8
3	5	90	3.6	8.6
.	.	.	.	.
.	.	.	.	.
.	.	.	.	.
20	5	5	0.2	5.2

Note that the total servicing requirement for the nth 6-month period $= \$5 + [100 - 5(n - 1)](0.04)$. The company's total cash bond service requirement will be $17.8 million per year for the first year. The requirement will decline by $0.8 million per year for the remaining years, declining to $10.6 million in the tenth year.

c. We have a 10-year, 6-percent annuity whose compound value is $100 million, and we are seeking the annual payment, PMT, in this equation:

$$\$100 \text{ million} = PMT(FVIFA_{6\%,10})$$
$$= PMT(13.1808)$$
$$PMT = \$7,586,793 = \text{Sinking fund payment.}$$

d. Annual debt service costs will be $100,000,000(0.08) + $7,586,793 = $15,586,793.

e. If interest rates rose and the bond prices fell, the company would use open market purchases.

Selected Additional References and Cases

The chapters on fixed-income securities in the investment textbooks listed in the Chapter 14 references provide useful information on bonds and preferred stocks, as well as the markets in which they are traded. In addition, the following articles offer useful insights:

Backer, Morton, and Martin L. Gosman, "The Use of Financial Ratios in Credit Downgrade Decisions," *Financial Management*, Spring 1980, 53-56.

Clark, John J., with Brenton W. Harries, "Some Recent Trends in Municipal and Corporate Securities Markets: An Interview with Brenton W. Harries, President of Standard & Poor's Corporation," *Financial Management*, Spring 1976, 9-17.

Ferri, Michael G., "An Empirical Examination of the Determinants of Bond Yield Spreads," *Financial Management*, Autumn 1978, 40-46.

Kalotay, Andrew J., "Innovations in Corporation Finance: Deep Discount Private Placements," *Financial Management*, Spring 1982, 55-57.

———, "Sinking Funds and the Realized Cost of Debt," *Financial Management*, Spring 1982, 43-54.

Pinches, George E., J. Clay Singleton, and Ali Jahankhani, "Fixed Coverage as a Determinant of Electric Utility Bond Ratings," *Financial Management*, Summer 1978, 45-55.

Smith, Clifford W., and J. B. Warner, "On Financial Contracting: An Analysis of Bond Covenants," *Journal of Financial Economics*, June 1979, 117-161.

Weinsten, Mark I., "The Seasoning Process of New Corporate Bond Issues," *Journal of Finance*, December 1978, 1343-1354.

Zwick, Burton, "Yields on Privately Placed Corporate Bonds," *Journal of Finance*, March 1980, 23-29.

References on bond refunding include the following:

Ang, James S., "The Two Faces of Bond Refunding," *Journal of Finance*, June 1975, 869-874.

———, "The Two Faces of Bond Refunding: Reply," *Journal of Finance*, March 1978, 354-356.

Dyl, Edward A., and Michael D. Joehnk, "Refunding Tax Exempt Bonds," *Financial Management*, Summer 1976, 59-66.

Emery, Douglas R., "Overlapping Interest in Bond Refunding: A Reconsideration," *Financial Management*, Summer 1978, 19-20.

Finnerty, John D., "Evaluating the Economics of Refunding High-Coupon Sinking-Fund Debt," *Financial Management*, Spring 1983, 5-10.

Harris, Robert S., "The Refunding of Discounted Debt: An Adjusted Present Value Analysis," *Financial Management*, Winter 1980, 7-12.

Kalotay, Andrew J., "On the Advanced Refunding of Discounted Debt," *Financial Management*, Summer 1978, 14-18.

————, "On the Structure and Valuation of Debt Refundings," *Financial Management*, Spring 1982, 41-42.

Laber, Gene, "The Effect of Bond Refunding of Discounted Debt," *Financial Management*, June 1979, 795-799.

————, "Implications of Discount Rates and Financing Assumptions for Bond Refunding Decisions," *Financial Management*, Spring 1979, 7-12.

————, "Repurchases of Bonds through Tender Offers: Implications for Shareholder Wealth," *Financial Management*, Summer 1978, 7-13.

Livingston, Miles, "Bond Refunding Reconsidered: Comment," *Journal of Finance*, March 1980, 191-196.

————, "The Effect of Bond Refunding on Shareholder Wealth: Comment," *Journal of Finance*, June 1979, 801-804.

Mayor, Thomas H., and Kenneth G. McCoin, "Bond Refunding: One or Two Faces?" *Journal of Finance*, March 1978, 349-353.

Ofer, Ahron R., and Robert A. Taggart, Jr., "Bond Refunding Reconsidered: Reply," *Journal of Finance*, March 1980, 197-200.

Riener, Kenneth D., "Financial Structure Effects of Bond Refunding," *Financial Management*, Summer 1980, 18-23.

Yawitz, Jess B., and James A. Anderson, "The Effect of Bond Refunding on Shareholder Wealth," *Journal of Finance*, December 1977, 1738-1746.

————, "The Effect of Bond Refunding on Shareholder Wealth: Reply," *Journal of Finance*, June 1979, 805-809.

Zeise, Charles H., and Roger K. Taylor, "Advance Refunding: A Practitioner's Perspective," *Financial Management*, Summer 1977, 73-76.

The following cases focus on the topics covered in this chapter:

Case 17, "Cumberland Gas and Electric," in the Brigham-Crum casebook, which illustrates the bond refunding decision.

The Harrington case, "Exxon Corporation," which describes three early 1980 Exxon debt/equity swaps.

Refunding Operations   15A

Refunding decisions actually involve two separate questions: (1) Is it profitable to call an outstanding issue in the current period and to replace it with a new issue, and (2) even if refunding is currently profitable, would the expected value of the firm be increased even more if the refunding were postponed to a later date? We consider both questions in this appendix.[1]

First, note that the decision to refund a security is analyzed in much the same way as a capital budgeting expenditure. The costs of refunding—the investment outlays—are (1) the call premium paid for the privilege of calling the old issue and (2) the flotation costs incurred in selling the new issue. The annual benefits, in a capital budgeting sense, are the interest payments that are saved each year. For example, if the interest expense on the old issue is $1,000,000 while that on the new issue is $700,000, the $300,000 savings constitutes an annual benefit.

The net present value method is used to analyze the advantages of refunding—discount the future interest savings back to the present, and then compare this discounted value with the cash outlays associated with the refunding. The firm should refund the bond if the present value of savings exceeds the cost, that is, if the NPV of the refunding operation is positive.

In the discounting process, the after-tax cost of the new debt, k_d, should be used as the discount rate. The reason for this is that there is relatively little risk to the savings—cash flows in a refunding are known with relative certainty, which is quite unlike the situation with cash flows in most capital budgeting decisions.

---

[1]During the early 1980s, there was a flurry of work on the pros and cons of refunding bond issues that had fallen to deep discounts as a result of rising interest rates. At such times, the company could go into the market, buy its debt at a low price, and retire it. The difference between the bonds' par value and the price the company paid would be reported as income, and taxes would have to be paid on it. The results of the research on the refunding of discount issues suggest that bonds should not, in general, be refunded after a rise in rates. See Andrew J. Kalotay, "On the Structure and Valuation of Debt Refundings," *Financial Management*, Spring 1982, 41-42; and Robert S. Harris, "The Refunding of Discounted Debt: An Adjusted Present Value Analysis," *Financial Management*, Winter 1980, 7-12.

The easiest way to examine the refunding decision is through an example. Microchip Computer Company has outstanding a $60 million bond issue which has a 15 percent coupon interest rate and 20 years remaining to maturity. This issue, which was sold 5 years ago, had flotation costs of $3 million, which the firm has been amortizing on a straight-line basis over the 25-year original life of the issue. The bond has a call provision which makes it possible for the company to retire the bonds at this time by calling them in at a 10 percent call premium. Investment bankers have assured the company that it could sell an additional $60 million to $70 million worth of new 20-year bonds at an interest rate of 12 percent. To insure that the funds required to pay off the old debt will be available, the new bonds would be sold one month before the old issue is called, so for one month, interest would have to be paid on two issues. Current short-term interest rates are 11 percent. Predictions are that long-term interest rates are unlikely to fall below 12 percent.[2] Flotation costs on a new refunding issue would amount to $2,650,000. Microchip's marginal tax rate is 40 percent. Should the company refund the $60 million of 15 percent bonds?

The following steps outline the decision process; the steps are summarized in worksheet form in Table 15A-1.

Step 1. Determine the investment outlay required to refund the issue.
a. Call premium

$$\text{Before tax: } 0.10(\$60,000,000) = \$6,000,000.$$
$$\text{After tax: } \$6,000,000(1 - T) = \$6,000,000(0.6)$$
$$= \$3,600,000.$$

Although Microchip must expend $6 million on the call premium, this is a deductible expense in the year the call is made. Since the company is in the 40 percent tax bracket, it saves $2.4 million in taxes. Therefore, the after-tax cost of the call is only $3.6 million. This amount is shown on Line 1 of Table 15A-1.

b. Flotation costs on new issue

Flotation costs on the new issue are $2,650,000. For tax purposes, flotation costs must be amortized over the life of the new bond, or 20 years. Therefore, the annual tax deduction is

$$\frac{\$2,650,000}{20} = \$132,500.$$

Since Microchip is in the 40 percent tax bracket, it has a tax savings of $132,500(0.4) = $53,000 a year for 20 years. This is an annuity of $53,000 for 20 years. In a refunding analysis, all cash flows should be discounted at the

---

[2]The firm's management has estimated that interest rates will probably remain at their present level of 12 percent or else rise; there is only a 25 percent probability that they will fall further.

Table 15A-1
Worksheet for the Bond Refunding Decision

	Amount before Tax	Amount after Tax	Time Event Occurs	PV Factor at 7.2%	PV
Cost of Refunding: t = 0					
1. Call premium on old bond	$6,000,000	$3,600,000	0	1.0000	$3,600,000
2. Flotation costs on new issue	2,650,000	2,650,000	0	1.0000	2,650,000
3. Tax savings on new issue flotation cost amortization	(132,500)	(53,000)	1-20	10.4313	(552,859)
4. Immediate tax savings on old flotation cost expense	(2,400,000)	(960,000)	0	1.0000	(960,000)
5. Periodic tax benefits no longer received on old flotation costs	120,000	48,000	1-20	10.4313	500,702
6. Extra interest on old issue	750,000	450,000	0	1.0000	450,000
7. Interest on short-term investment	(550,000)	(330,000)	0	1.0000	(330,000)
8. Total after-tax investment (PV of investment)					$5,357,843
Savings over the Life of the New Issue: t = 1 to 20					
9. Interest on old bond	$9,000,000	$5,400,000			
10. Interest on new bond	(7,200,000)	(4,320,000)			
11. Net savings of interest	$1,800,000	$1,080,000	1-20	10.4313	$11,265,804
Refunding NPV					

12. NPV = PV of interest savings − PV of investment
    = $11,265,804 − $5,357,843
    = $5,907,961.

after-tax cost of new debt, in this case 12%(1 − T) = 12%(0.6) = 7.2%. The present value of the tax savings, discounted at 7.2 percent, is $552,859. Thus, the net after-tax cost of new flotation costs is $2,097,141:

Gross flotation costs on new issue	$2,650,000
PV of associated tax savings	(552,859)
Net after-tax flotation cost on new issue	$2,097,141

The gross costs and tax savings are reflected on Lines 2 and 3 of Table 15A-1.

c. Flotation costs on old issue

The old issue has an unamortized flotation cost of (20/25)($3,000,000) = $2.4 million at this time. If the issue is retired, the unamortized flotation cost may be recognized immediately as an expense, thus creating an after-tax savings of $2,400,000(T) = $960,000. The firm will, however, no longer receive a tax deduction of $120,000 a year for 20 years, or an after-tax benefit of $48,000 a year. The present value of this tax savings, discounted at 7.2 percent, is $500,702. Thus, the net after-tax effect of the old flotation costs is − $459,298:

Tax savings from immediate write-off of old flotation costs	($960,000)
PV of tax savings on old flotation costs had refunding not occurred	500,702
Net after-tax savings on old flotation costs	($459,298)

These figures are reflected on Lines 4 and 5 of the table.

It is important to note that, because of the refunding, the flotation costs provide an immediate tax saving rather than annual savings over the next 20 years. Thus, the $459,298 net savings simply reflects the difference between the present value of benefits received in the future without the refunding versus an immediate benefit if the refunding occurs.

d. Additional interest

One month "extra" interest on the old issue, after taxes, costs $450,000:

$$(\text{Dollar amount})(1/12 \text{ of } 15\%)(1 - T) = \text{Interest cost}$$
$$(\$60,000,000)(0.0125)(0.6) = \$450,000.$$

However, the proceeds from the new issue can be invested in short-term securities for one month. Thus, $60 million invested at a rate of 11 percent will return $330,000 in after-tax interest:

$$(\$60,000,000)(1/12 \text{ of } 11\%)(1 - T) = \text{Interest earned}$$
$$(\$60,000,000)(0.009167)(0.6) = \$330,000.$$

The net after-tax additional interest cost is thus $120,000:

Extra interest paid on old issue	$450,000
Interest earned on short-term securities	(330,000)
Net additional interest	$120,000

These figures are reflected in Lines 6 and 7.

e. Total after-tax investment

The total investment outlay required to refund the bond issue, which will be financed by debt, is thus[3]

---

[3]The investment outlay (in this case, $5,357,843) is usually obtained by increasing the amount of the new bond issue. In the example given, the new issue would be $65,357,843. However, the interest on the additional debt *should not* be deducted at Step 2 because the $5,357,843 itself will be deducted at Step 3. If additional interest on the $5,357,843 were deducted at Step 2, then interest would, in effect, be deducted twice. The situation here is exactly like that in regular capital budgeting decisions. Even though some debt may be used to finance a project, interest on that debt is not subtracted when developing the annual cash flows. Rather, the annual cash flows are *discounted* by the project's cost of capital.

Call premium	$3,600,000
Flotation costs, new, net of tax savings	2,097,141
Flotation costs, old, net savings	(459,298)
Net additional interest	120,000
Total investment	$5,357,843

This total is shown on Line 8 of the table.

Step 2. Calculate the PV of the annual interest savings.

a. Interest on old bond, after tax

The annual after-tax interest on the old issue is $5,400,000:

$$(\$60,000,000)(0.15)(0.6) = \$5,400,000.$$

This is shown on Line 9.

b. Interest on new bond, after tax

The new issue has an annual after-tax cost of $4,320,000:

$$(\$60,000,000)(0.12)(0.6) = \$4,320,000.$$

This is shown on Line 10 as a negative saving.

c. Annual savings

Thus, the annual after-tax savings is $1,080,000:

Interest on old bonds, after tax	$5,400,000
Interest on new bonds, after tax	(4,320,000)
Annual net savings	$1,080,000

This is shown on Line 11.

d. PV of annual savings

The PV of $1,080,000 a year for 20 years is $11,265,804:

$$PV = \$1,080,000(PVIFA_{7.2\%,20})$$
$$= (\$1,080,000)(10.4313) = \$11,265,804.$$

This is also shown on Line 11.

Step 3. Determine the NPV of the refunding.

PV of annual savings	$11,265,804
Net investment	(5,357,843)
NPV from refunding	$ 5,907,961

Since the net present value of the refunding is positive, it would be profitable to refund the old bond issue.

Several other points should be noted. First, since the cash flows are based on differences between contractual obligations, their risk is the same as that of the underlying obligations. Therefore, the present values of the cash flows should be found by discounting at the firm's least risky rate—its after-tax cost of marginal debt. Second, since the refunding operation is advantageous to the firm, it must be disadvantageous to bondholders; they must give up their 15 percent bonds and reinvest in new ones that yield 12 percent. This points out the danger of the call provision to bondholders, and it also explains why bonds without a call provision command higher prices than callable bonds. Third, although it is not emphasized in the example, we assumed that the firm raises the investment required to undertake the refunding operation ($5,357,843 shown on Line 8 of Table 15A-1) as debt. This should be feasible, since the refunding operation will improve the interest coverage ratio even though a larger amount of debt is outstanding.[4] Fourth, we set up our example in such a way that the new issue had the same maturity as the remaining life of the old issue. Often, the old bond has only a relatively short time to maturity (say, 5 to 10 years), while the new bond would have a much longer maturity (say, 25 to 30 years). In this situation, the analysis should only include cash flows up to the maturity of the old issue.[5] Fifth, refunding decisions are well suited for analysis with a computer spreadsheet such as *VisiCalc*, *Lotus 1-2-3*, or *IFPS*. The spreadsheet is easy to set up, and once it is, it is easy to vary the assumptions, especially the assumption about the interest rate on the refunding issue, and see how such changes affect the NPV.

One final point should be addressed: Although our analysis shows that the refunding would increase the value of the firm, would refunding *at this time* truly maximize the firm's expected value? Note that if interest rates continue to fall, then the company might be better off waiting, for this could increase the NPV of the refunding operation even more. The mechanics of calculating the NPV of a refunding are simple, but the decision on *when* to refund is not a simple one at all, because it requires a forecast of future interest rates. Thus, the final decision on refunding now, versus waiting for a possibly more favorable future refunding is a judgmental decision.

---

[4]See Ahron R. Ofer and Robert A. Taggart, Jr., "Bond Refunding: A Clarifying Analysis," *Journal of Finance*, March 1977, 21-30, for a discussion of how the method of financing the refunding affects the analysis. Ofer and Taggart prove that (1) if the refunding investment outlay is to be raised as debt, then the after-tax cost of debt is the proper discount rate, while (2) if these funds are to be raised as common equity, then the before-tax cost of debt is the proper rate. Since a profitable refunding will virtually always raise the firm's debt-carrying capacity (because total interest charges after the refunding will be lower than before the refunding), it is more logical to use debt than either equity or a combination of debt and equity to finance the operation. Therefore, firms generally do use additional debt to finance refunding operations, so we may assume debt financing for the costs of refunding and discount at the after-tax cost of debt.

[5]It should also be noted that, to be exactly precise, the old bond should, in our example, have had a maturity of 20 years plus one month at the time the analysis was undertaken, so that it would have a 20-year remaining maturity when it is actually refunded. This is a detail that should not concern you.

To illustrate the timing decision, assume that Microchip's managers forecast that long-term interest rates have a 50 percent probability of remaining at their present level of 12 percent over the next year. However, there is a 25 percent probability that they could fall to 10 percent, and a 25 percent probability that they could rise to 14 percent. Further, assume that short-term rates are expected to remain one percentage point below long-term rates, and that the call premium would be reduced by one-twentieth if the call were delayed for one year.

The refunding analysis could then be repeated, as above, but assuming it would take place one year from now. Thus, the old bonds would have only 19 years remaining to maturity. We performed the analysis, found the NPVs, discounted them back to the present, and developed the following values:

Probability	Long-Term Interest Rate	NPV from Refunding
25%	10%	$11,783,741
50	12	3,896,583
25	14	(2,441,521)

At first blush, it would seem reasonable to calculate the expected value of the NPV refunding next year based on the above probability distribution and then to compare it with the NPV of refunding now, $5,907,961. However, that would not be correct. If interest rates did rise to 14 percent, Microchip would not refund the issue; therefore, the actual result if rates rise to 14 percent would be zero. The expected NPV today from refunding one year hence is, therefore, $0.25(\$11,783,741) + 0.50(\$3,896,583) + 0.25(\$0) = \$4,894,227$.

The NPV from refunding today is $5,907,961. Clearly, based on the above interest rate forecast, Microchip should refund today. In fact, even if the expected NPV from refunding one year hence had been, say, $6,000,000, Microchip's managers might still have decided to refund today. The $5,907,961 is a certain increase in firm value, while the $6,000,000 is only an expected increase. Microchip's managers should opt to delay refunding only if the expected NPV from later refunding were sufficiently above today's certain NPV to compensate for the risk involved.

The above refunding timing analysis could be easily extended by (1) including possible refunding at more than one future point in time, and (2) specifying future interest rates by a continuous rather than a discrete distribution. However, the essence of the timing decision remains the same.

Problems

15A-1 Systems Analysis Corporation (SAC) is considering whether to refund a $100 million, 15 percent coupon, 20-year original maturity bond issue which was sold 5 years ago. It is amortizing $4 million of flotation costs on the 15 percent bonds over the 20-year life of that issue. SAC's investment bankers have indicated that the company could sell a new $100 million, 15-year issue at an interest rate of 12.5 percent in today's market. SAC's management thinks the chances of an interest rate increase are about equal to the chances of a decrease. Specifically, it estimates a 0.25 probability of rates declining to 10 percent, a 0.5 probability of rates remaining at 12.5 percent, and a 0.25 probability of rates rising to 15 percent.

A call premium of 10 percent would be required to retire the old bonds, and flotation costs on the new issue would amount to $6 million. SAC's marginal tax rate is 40 percent. The new bonds would be issued one month before the old bonds were called, with the proceeds of the new issue being invested in short-term government securities with a 9 percent coupon during the interim period.

a. Calculate the NPV of the bond refunding.

b. What factors would influence SAC's decision to refund now rather than later?

15A-2 Cannon Container Corporation (CCC) is considering whether to refund a $50 million, 14 percent coupon, 30-year bond issue that was sold 5 years ago. It is amortizing $3 million of flotation costs on the 14 percent bonds over the 30-year life of that issue. CCC's investment bankers have indicated that the company could sell a new 25-year issue at an interest rate of 12 percent in today's market.

A call premium of 14 percent would be required to retire the old bonds, and flotation costs on the new issue would amount to $3 million. CCC's marginal tax rate is 50 percent. The new bonds would be issued one month before the old bonds were called, with the proceeds being invested in short-term government securities returning 9 percent annually.

a. Perform a complete bond refunding analysis. What is the bond refunding's NPV?

b. CCC's managers estimate the probability distribution of interest rates one year from now as follows:

Rate	Probability
10%	0.2
12	0.6
13	0.2

Further, assume the following:

(1) Today's bond refunding NPV is $1,000,000.

(2) If interest rates fall to 10 percent next year, the refunding NPV one year from now would be $2,500,000. If interest rates remain at 12 percent, the refunding NPV one year hence would be $833,333. If interest rates rise to 13 percent, the refunding NPV would be negative.

Should Cannon refund the issue this year or wait until next year to make the decision? Why?

Financing the Small Firm

15B

Some firms are small because the nature of their industry dictates that small enterprises are more efficient than large ones, while other firms are small primarily because they are new companies—either new entrants to established industries or new enterprises in developing industries. Regardless of type, small firms' long-term financing decisions are different from those confronting larger businesses because (1) the goals of a small firm are likely to be oriented toward the aspirations of an individual entrepreneur rather than toward investors in general, and (2) the characteristics of the money and capital markets create special problems for small firms. This appendix presents some of the unique aspects of small business financing.

Traditional small firm industries are those where firms, in general, remain small throughout their lives. The industries, or segments of industries, in which traditional small businesses dominate exhibit three common characteristics: (1) a localized market, (2) low capital requirements, and (3) relatively simple technology. The typical traditional small business, even the successful one, cannot look to the general capital markets for funds. If the firm owns any real estate, it may be able to obtain a mortgage from a bank or a savings and loan. Equipment may perhaps be purchased under a term loan, or be leased. After the business has survived for a few years, bank financing may become available on a seasonal basis, but not for permanent growth capital.

Traditional Small Firms

    Traditional small firms cannot sell bonds or stock. Equity must be provided by the owner-manager, while the bulk of the long-term external financing will be provided by banks as term loans.[1]

The second category of small business is the new firm with the potential for substantial growth. Typically, such a firm has developed a new product or an innovative way of providing an old service. The personal computer industry is a good example of the former, while franchised fast food opera-

The Small Firm with Growth Potential

---

[1]The bulk of a traditional small firm's short-term, or working capital, financing will be in trade credit. This form of financing is discussed in Chapter 18.

tions illustrate the latter. In this section, we discuss the financing of potential growth companies as they pass through their life cycle from inception until maturity. First, we describe the life cycle of the firm. Then we discuss the financing sources most used by the small growth company.

Stage 1: Formation. Figure 15B-1 shows the life cycle of a typical firm. In the first stage of its life cycle, the firm is experimenting and working to establish itself.

Stage 2: Rapid Growth. After its inception, a successful firm will enter Stage 2 of its life cycle. Here the firm has achieved initial success, and it is growing rapidly and is reasonably profitable. Cash flows and working capital management have become increasingly important. Also, at this stage the firm will have an extraordinary need for additional outside financing; the need for external funds is a function of the firm's growth rate, so in Stage 2 large amounts of external funds are required. This necessitates good financial planning, for otherwise a shortage of capital may throttle the firm's growth opportunities.

Firms in Stage 2 have an especially difficult time obtaining equity capital because they are not large enough to go public, but they need more than their owners can provide. Typically, they are entering new areas about which little information is available. They may have great potential, but large risks are also involved, and for every glowing success story there are dozens of failures. In addition, even after an innovative growth firm has been established, there are continued pressures because of the financial problems noted above. Also, demonstrated success will stimulate imitators, so growth projections must take into account an influx of new firms and the likelihood of a declining market share and increased competitive pressures. Furthermore, high profits may lead to excessive industry expansion, which will be followed by excess capacity, which in turn will cause problems for every firm in the industry. For all these reasons, the small, rapidly growing firm's existence is precarious, even when the product market opportunities upon which it was conceived are sound.

Figure 15B-1
Hypothetical Life Cycle of a Typical Firm

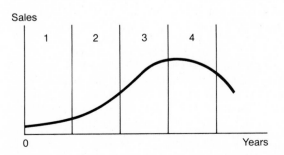

Stage 3: Growth to Maturity. A particularly successful firm may reach Stage 3, where going public becomes feasible. This provides access to the broader money and capital markets, and it represents a true coming-of-age for the small firm. Even at this point, however, the firm must look ahead, analyzing its products and their long-run prospects.

Stage 4: Maturity. Because every product has a life cycle, the firm must be aware that without the continuous development of new products, growth will cease, and eventually the firm will decline. Accordingly, as Stage 4 approaches, the firm must plan for the possibility of share repurchases, mergers, or other long-term strategies. The best time to do this is while the firm still has energy, momentum, and a high price/earnings ratio—in other words, before it leaves Stage 3.

The combination of high risks and great profit potential inherent in Stage 2 firms has led to the development of *venture capital suppliers*—wealthy individuals, partnerships, or corporations whose business is supplying risk capital to small growth companies. When a new business makes an application for financial assistance from a venture capital firm, it receives a rigorous examination. Some development companies use their own staffs for this investigation, while others depend on a board of advisers acting in the capacity of consultants. A high percentage of applications is rejected, but if the application is approved, funds are provided. Venture capital companies generally take an equity position in the firms they finance, but they may also extend debt capital. However, when loans are made, they generally involve convertibles or warrants, or are tied in with the purchase of stock by the investment company.[2]

Venture Capital

Venture capital companies perform a continuing and active role in firms to which they have extended capital. Typically, they do not insist on voting control, but they usually have at least one member on the board of directors of the new enterprise. The matter of control has *not* been one of the crucial considerations in investment companies' decisions to invest—indeed, if the management of a small business is not sufficiently strong to make sound policy decisions, the venture capital firm is not likely to be interested in the first place. The typical investment company does, however, want to maintain continuous contact, to provide management counsel, and to monitor the progress of its investment.

Another distinctive feature of the venture capital firm stems from its ownership by wealthy individuals. (The Rockefellers, for example, are leading venture capitalists.) For tax reasons, such people are interested in receiving their income in the form of capital gains rather than dividend income. They are, furthermore, in a position to take larger risks. Also, special provisions of the tax laws make equity investments in small business (as defined by the Tax Code) especially interesting. First, as noted in Chapter 2, it is pos-

---

[2]Venture capital firms, because of the costs of screening and monitoring, generally do not make investments of less than $500,000. Thus, venture capital financing is not available to the very small firm.

sible to set up a small business as an S corporation, and yet have it taxed as a partnership or a proprietorship, so that operating losses, tax credits, and so on can be passed through to the investor and used to offset ordinary income. Second, while it is generally possible to offset only $2,000 of ordinary income with capital losses, if the losses are on a small business as defined by the Tax Code, up to $50,000 per year of ordinary income may be offset. This provides a powerful inducement for wealthy investors to invest in small businesses.

To illustrate the tax loss advantage, suppose an investor who is in the 60 percent federal-plus-state income tax bracket on ordinary income, and in the 20 percent bracket on long-term capital gains, is considering a $50,000 investment in the stock of a small business. The company is judged to have a 50 percent probability of being worth $110,000 after a year and a 50 percent probability of being worth zero. On a before-tax basis, the expected rate of return on the investment is only 10 percent:

$$\text{Expected before-tax} \atop \text{rate of return} = \frac{0.5(\$110,000) + 0.5(\$0)}{\$50,000} - 1.0 = 0.10 = 10\%.$$

This is not a very good return on an investment that appears to be quite risky. However, consider the after-tax situation:

$$\begin{array}{c}\text{Expected}\\\text{after-tax}\\\text{rate of}\\\text{return}\end{array} = \frac{0.5\left(\begin{array}{c}\text{Invested}\\\text{capital}\end{array} + \begin{array}{c}\text{After-tax}\\\text{gains}\end{array}\right) + 0.5\left(\begin{array}{c}\text{Tax savings}\\\text{from loss}\end{array}\right)}{\text{Invested capital}} - 1.0$$

$$= \frac{0.5[\$50,000 + \$60,000(1.0 - 0.20)] + 0.5[\$50,000(0.60)]}{\$50,000} - 1.0$$

$$= \frac{\$49,000 + \$15,000}{\$50,000} - 1.0 = 0.28 = 28\%.$$

A 28 percent expected after-tax return for a 60 percent bracket investor is not bad at all, especially if the investor takes a position in a number of different small businesses and thus diversifies away much of the risk that exists in each individual investment.

It is possible for corporations as well as individuals to benefit from small business investments. Therefore, in recent years, many large, well-established corporations have invested both money and know-how in small businesses. Corporations with their own venture capital companies include General Electric, Texaco, Citicorp, and Xerox.[3] Other established companies have invested heavily in new businesses in emerging technologies; for ex-

---

[3]More and more bankers are shedding their conservative ways and jumping into the high-risk, high-reward venture capital business. Regulators permit banks to put up to 5 percent of their funds into venture capital subsidiaries. By 1983, about 70 banks had formed such subsidiaries. To illustrate the profit potential, Continental Illinois Corporation's $500,000 investment in Apple Computer 5 years ago is expected to net the bank more than $40 million in profit. As one banker puts it: "One good venture-capital hit brings in more profit than billions of dollars of loans." (Continental appears to have had better skill in picking venture capital investments than in selecting borrowers.)

ample, in recent years Dow, Monsanto, Shell Oil, and Standard Oil of California have been among the many corporate investors in new genetic engineering firms such as Genentech, Cetus, and Genex Corporation. The founders of small, new firms are usually specialists, frequently technical people who need both money and help with administrative services such as accounting, finance, production, and marketing. The small firm's owners contribute entrepreneurship, special talents, a taste for risk taking, and "the willingness to work 18 hours a day for peanuts—or maybe for millions." The major corporations have found that there is a mutual advantage in cooperative ventures with such individuals.

It is clear that small firms face difficulties in obtaining capital, and in recognition of this fact, the federal government established the *Small Business Administration (SBA)*, which operates a number of different programs. One important program is the licensing of *Small Business Investment Companies (SBICs)*.

The Small Business Administration

To assist small companies in overcoming their very real disadvantages in the capital markets, in 1958 Congress passed the Small Business Investment Company Act, which empowered the Small Business Administration to license and regulate SBICs and to provide them with financial assistance. A minimum of $150,000 in private capital is required for the licensing of an SBIC, and this amount can be doubled by selling subordinated debentures to the SBA (at interest rates generally below those prevailing in the market).

In their operations, SBICs have followed two policies similar to those of venture capital companies: (1) Their investments are generally made by the purchase of convertible securities or bonds with warrants, thus giving the SBICs a residual equity position in the companies to which funds are provided; and (2) SBICs emphasize management counsel, for which a fee is charged.

The Small Business Administration also has direct involvement in small business loans through the *Business Loan Program*. Two types of loans are available under this program to small businesses which are unable to obtain funds on reasonable terms from private sources: (1) direct loans and (2) participation loans. In a *direct loan*, the SBA itself makes the loan to a small business borrower. In a *participation loan*, the SBA lends part of the funds, while a bank (or other private lending institution) advances the balance, with the bank's portion guaranteed by the SBA. The maximum amount the SBA may lend to any borrower is $350,000; this maximum applies to either a direct loan or the SBA's portion of a participation loan. Since both SBA loans and guarantees are advantageous to the business recipient, the definition of what constitutes a "small business" is important. The definition varies depending on the industry, but a manufacturing firm is defined as small if it has less than 250 employees (in certain industries, the firm can have up to 1,000 employees and still be classified as small).

In addition to the Business Loan Program, the SBA administers a number of other programs, including the following: (1) Equal Opportunity Loan Program, designed specifically for disadvantaged persons who wish to start or expand an existing business; (2) Development Company Loan Program, which is used to help attract businesses to geographic areas in need of economic stimulation; (3) Displaced Business Loan Program, designed to help small businesses that are forced to relocate because of urban renewal or similar events; (4) Disaster Loan Program, designed to aid both businesses and homeowners who suffer losses as a consequence of some natural disaster; (5) Lease Guarantee Program, designed to help small businesses obtain rental space in the commercial real estate market; (6) Revolving Line-of-Credit Program, designed to aid small building contractors; (7) Surety Bonding Program, designed to aid small business people who must post performance bonds when seeking construction or other contracts; and (8) Minority Enterprise SBIC Program, designed to stimulate SBICs whose clients are minority-owned firms.

Going Public

If Stage 2 growth continues long enough, the firm will experience increasing pressures to add large amounts of equity capital, and its owners may want to establish a market for their own personal stock holdings. At this point, a full assessment of the critical step in a firm's life—that of "going public"—must be made.

Going public leads to four fundamental changes. (1) The firm moves from informal, personal control to a system of formal controls. (2) Information must be reported on a timely basis to the outside investors, even though the founders may continue to have majority control. (3) The firm must have a breadth of management in all areas if it is to operate its expanded business effectively. (4) The publicly owned firm typically draws on a board of directors to help formulate sound plans and policies; the board should include representatives of the public owners and other external interest groups to aid the management group in carrying out its broader responsibilities.

The valuation process is particularly important at the time the firm goes public: At what price will stock be sold to new outside investors? In analyzing the investment value of the small and growing firm, some significant differences in capital costs between large and small firms should be noted:

1. It is especially difficult to obtain reliable estimates of the cost of equity capital for small, privately owned firms.

2. Because of the risks involved, including agency risks for nonmanagement stockholders, the required rate of return tends to be high for small firms. However, portfolio effects from a pooling of risks can reduce this factor somewhat for publicly owned small firms.

3. Tax considerations are generally quite important for privately-owned companies that are large enough to consider going public, since the owner-managers are probably in the top personal tax brackets. This factor can cause the effective after-tax cost of retained earnings to be considerably lower than the after-tax cost of new outside equity.

4. Flotation costs for new security issues, especially new stock issues, are much higher for small than for large firms. This factor, as well as the relatively high after-tax cost of new outside equity noted above in Item 2, causes the marginal cost of capital curve for small firms to rise rapidly once retained earnings have been exhausted.

5. The timing of the decision to go public is very important because the demand for new public offerings tends to change markedly over time. As a

result, a new company with a given set of financial statements and prospects might be worth two or even three times as much in a strong market as in a weak one. For example, Apple Computer went public in December 1980, at a price of $22 per share, which represented a P/E ratio of 92 times. In 1982, when the new issue market was weak, it probably would have commanded a P/E ratio in the 10 to 20 range. Thus, the founders had to give up a far smaller share of the stock to raise new equity capital in 1980 than they would have if the company had gone public two years later.

Of course, the small firm is not always free to choose when it will go public. Small companies often have a slight head start over their larger competitors—as Apple had over IBM—and they must forge ahead rapidly or else watch the market they have developed be picked off by another firm. Clearly, large amounts of capital are needed to keep pace, and the company may not have the luxury of waiting for a strong market before going public.

Note also that equity infusions also make it easier and less expensive to raise debt capital. During periods of tight money and high interest rates, financial institutions, especially commercial banks, find that the quantity of funds demanded exceeds the supply available at "reasonable" rates. One important method used to ration credit is to raise credit standards. At such times, both a stronger balance sheet and a longer and more stable profitability record are required in order to qualify for bank credit. Since financial ratios for small and growing firms tend to be less strong, such firms bear the brunt of credit rationing. Obviously, the small firm that goes public and raises equity capital before a money squeeze occurs is in a better position to ride out a tight money period. This firm has already raised some of its needed capital, and its equity cushion enables it to present a stronger picture to the banks, thus helping it to obtain additional capital in the form of debt.

Options, Warrants, and Convertibles

16

In August 1981, the bond market was in shambles. Interest rates were near all-time highs, and even AAA-rated corporations could only issue fixed rate long-term debt by offering yields close to 18 percent. Yet, MCI Communications Corporation, the biggest and fastest growing of the new competitors in long-distance telephone service, sold a B-rated $100 million issue of 20-year debentures which carried a low 10.25 percent coupon. The issue sold out in an hour, and, within a month, each bond was selling at a premium of $70 over its $1,000 par value. How was MCI able to sell this low-coupon issue so easily? The key was that the issue was convertible—bondholders could swap their bonds for 40 shares of stock. If the price of the stock rose over the next 20 years, the value of the convertible bond would also rise. Thus, the purchaser of an MCI convertible bond was buying (1) a fixed income security with a yield of 10¼ percent plus (2) a chance for capital gains if MCI's stock price rose.

Convertibles, and also warrants, are a specialized type of option used in corporate financing. MCI's convertibles appealed to investors because they yielded steady income and also offered the expectation of capital gains, and the bonds were attractive to the company because they saved it interest expense and also offered the possibility of replacing debt with equity in the future. Of course, there are also disadvantages to both MCI and the buyers of the convertibles. In this chapter, we discuss when companies such as MCI should use convertibles or bonds-with-warrants, how the terms should be set on such securities, and their pros and cons from the standpoint of an investor.

When we discussed long-term financing in Chapters 14 and 15, we concentrated on common stock, preferred stock, and various types of debt. In this chapter, we see how the use of warrants and convertibles can make a company's securities attractive to an even broader range of investors, thereby increasing the potential supply of capital and decreasing its cost. Reducing the cost of capital will, of course, help to maximize the value of the firm's stock. Warrants and convertibles are rapidly gaining popularity, so a knowledge of these instruments is especially important today. As we shall see, both warrants and convertibles are types of option securities, and options themselves represent an important part of today's financial scene. Therefore, we begin the chapter by discussing the rapidly growing option markets, option pricing theory, and the contribution of option pricing theory to corporate finance theory.

Options

An *option* is a contract which gives its holder the right to buy (or sell) an asset at some predetermined price within a specified period of time. "Pure options" are instruments that (1) are created by outsiders (generally investment banking firms) rather than the firm, (2) are bought and sold primarily by investors (or speculators), and (3) are of greater importance to investors than to financial managers. However, financial managers should understand option theory, because such an understanding will help them structure warrant and convertible financings. Additionally, option theory provides some useful insights into many other facets of corporate finance.

Option Types and Markets

There are many types of options and option markets.[1] To illustrate how options work, suppose you owned 100 shares of IBM stock, which, on August 31, 1983, sold for $119.25 per share. You could give (or sell) to someone else the right to buy the 100 shares at any time during the next 5 months at a price of, say, $120 per share. The $120 is called the *striking,* or *exercise, price.* Such options exist, and they are traded on a number of stock exchanges, with the Chicago Board Options Exchange (CBOE) being the oldest and the largest. This type of option is defined as a *call option*, as the purchaser has a "call" on 100 shares of stock, and the seller of the call option is defined as the *writer.* An investor who "writes" a call option against stock held in his or her portfolio is said to be selling *covered options.* Options sold without the stock to back them up are called *naked options.* When the exercise price of an option exceeds the current stock price, the option is called an *out-of-the-money option.* However, when the exercise price is less than the current price of the underlying stock, the option is an *in-the-money option.*

You can also buy an option which gives you the right to *sell* a stock at a specified price at some time in the future—this is called a *put option.*

---

[1]For an in-depth treatment of options, see Robert C. Radcliffe, *Investment Concepts, Analysis, and Strategy* (Glenview, Ill.: Scott, Foresman, 1982).

For example, suppose you think that IBM's stock price is going to decline from its current level of $119.25 sometime during the next 5
months. For $612.50 you could buy a 5-month put option giving you the
right to sell 100 shares (which you would not necessarily own) at a price
of $120 per share ($120 is the striking price). If you bought a 100-share
contract for $612.50 and IBM's stock price actually fell to $100, you
would make ($120 − $100)(100) = $2,000, less the $612.50 you paid for
the put option, for a net profit (before taxes and commissions) of
$1,387.50.

Table 16-1 contains an extract from the September 1, 1983, *Wall Street
Journal* Listed Option Quotations Table. This extract, which focuses on
IBM and Monsanto options, reflects trading which occurred on the previous day. On August 31, 1983, IBM's January (5-month), $120 options
sold on the CBOE for $9.00. Thus, for ($9.00)(100) = $900 you could buy
an option that would give you the right to purchase 100 shares of IBM
at a price of $120 per share at any time during the next 5 months.[2] If the
stock price stayed below $120 during that period, you would lose your
$900, but if it rose to $150, then your $900 investment would have grown
to ($150 − $120)(100) = $3,000. That translates into a very healthy rate
of return. Incidentally, if the stock price did go up, you would probably
not actually exercise your option and buy the stock—you would sell the
option, which would then have a price of at least $30 versus the $9 you
paid, to another option buyer.

Options trading is one of the "hottest" financial activities in the
United States today. The leverage involved makes it possible for specu-

Table 16-1
August 31, 1983, Listed Option Quotations (CBOE)

NYSE Close	Strike Price	Calls—Last Quote			Puts—Last Quote		
		October	January	April	October	January	April
IBM							
119¼	$100	20⅝	23	s	¼	⅝	s
119¼	110	11¾	14⅞	17⅞	13⁄16	2½	4¼
119¼	120	4¾	9	11⅞	4⅛	6⅛	7⅜
119¼	130	1⁷⁄₁₆	4¾	7¾	11	12¼	12⅞
Monsanto							
111¾	$110	6¼	9½	r	3¼	5½	r

Note: s means no option offered; r means not traded on August 31.

---

[2]Actually, the *exercise date*, which is the last date that the option can be exercised, is the
third Friday of the exercise month. Thus, the January options have a term somewhat less
than five months. Also, note that option contracts are generally written in 100-share multiples.

lators with just a few dollars to make a fortune almost overnight. Also, investors with sizable portfolios can sell options against their stocks and earn the value of the option (less brokerage commissions), even if the stock's price remains constant. Still, perhaps those who have profited most from the development of options trading are security brokers, who earn commission income on such trades.

The corporations such as IBM and Monsanto on whose stocks options are written have nothing to do with the options market. The corporations do not raise money in the options market, nor do they have any direct transactions in it, and option holders do not vote for corporate directors (unless they exercise their options to purchase the stock, which few actually do). There have been studies by the SEC and others as to whether options trading stabilizes or destabilizes the stock market, and whether this activity helps or hinders corporations seeking to raise new capital. The studies have not been conclusive, but options trading does seem to be here to stay, and many regard it as the most exciting game in town.

Call Option Valuation

An analysis of Table 16-1 provides some insights into call option valuation. First, we see that there are at least three factors which affect a call option's value: (1) The higher the stock's market price, the higher will be the call option price. Thus, Monsanto's $110 October call option sells for $6.25, while IBM's $110 October option sells for $11.75 because IBM's current stock price is $119.25 versus $111.75 for Monsanto. (2) The higher the striking price, the lower will be the call option price. Thus, all of IBM's call options, regardless of exercise month, decline as the striking price increases. (3) The longer the option period, the higher will be the option price, because with more time before expiration, there is a greater chance that the stock price will climb substantially above the exercise price. Thus, for all striking prices, option prices increase from an October expiration date to a later date.

Formula Value versus Option Price

How is the actual price of an option determined in the market? We shall, shortly, present a widely used model (the Black-Scholes model) for pricing options, but first it is useful to establish some basic concepts. To begin, we define an option's *formula value* as follows:

$$\text{Formula value} = \frac{\text{Current price}}{\text{of the stock}} - \text{Striking price}.$$

For example, if a stock sells for $50, and its options have a striking price of $20, then the formula value of the option is $30. The formula value can be thought of as the value of the option on its expiration date.

Now consider Figure 16-1, which presents some data on Space Technology, Incorporated (STI), a company which recently went public and

Figure 16-1
Space Technology, Inc.: Option Price and Formula Value

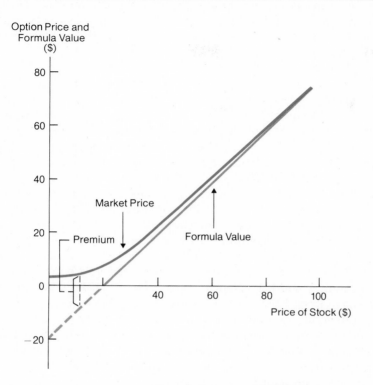

Price of Stock (1)	Striking Price (2)	Formula Value of Option (1) − (2) = (3)	Market Price of Option (4)	Premium (4) − (3) = (5)
$12.00	$20.00	−$ 8.00	$ 5.00	$13.00
20.00	20.00	0.00	9.00	9.00
21.00	20.00	1.00	9.75	8.75
22.00	20.00	2.00	10.50	8.50
35.00	20.00	15.00	21.00	6.00
42.00	20.00	22.00	26.00	4.00
50.00	20.00	30.00	32.00	2.00
73.00	20.00	53.00	54.00	1.00
98.00	20.00	78.00	78.50	0.50

whose stock has fluctuated widely during its short history. The third
column in the lower section shows the formula values for STI's options
when the stock was selling at different prices; the fourth column gives
the actual market prices; and the fifth column shows the premium of
the actual option price over its formula value. At any stock price below
$20, the formula value is negative; beyond $20, each $1 increase in the

price of the stock brings with it a $1 increase in the option's formula value. Note, however, that the actual market price of the option lies above the formula value at each price of the common stock, but the premium declines as the price of the common stock increases. For example, when the common stock sold for $20 and the option had a zero formula value, its actual price, and the premium, was $9. Then, as the price of the stock rose, the *formula value* matched the increase dollar for dollar, but the *market price* of the option climbed less rapidly, and the premium declined. The premium was $9 when the stock sold for $20 a share, but it declined to $1 by the time the stock price had risen to $73 a share. Beyond this point the premium virtually disappeared.

Why does this pattern exist? Why should the option ever sell for more than its formula value, and why does the premium decline as the price of the stock increases? The answer lies in the speculative appeal of options—they enable an individual to gain a high degree of personal leverage when buying securities. To illustrate, suppose STI's options sold for exactly their formula value. Now suppose you were thinking of investing in the company's common stock at a time when it is selling for $21 a share. If you bought a share and the price rose to $42, you would have made a 100 percent capital gain. However, had you bought the option at its formula value ($1 when the stock sells for $21), your capital gain would have been $21 on a $1 investment or 2,000 percent! At the same time, your total loss potential with the option would be only $1, while the potential loss from the purchase of the stock would be $21. The huge capital gains potential, combined with the loss limitation, is clearly worth something—the exact amount it is worth to investors is the amount of the premium.

But why does the premium decline as the price of the stock rises? Part of the answer is that both the leverage effect and the loss protection feature decline at high stock prices. For example, if you were thinking of buying the stock when its price was $73 a share, the formula value of the option would be $53. If the stock price doubled to $146, the formula value of STI's option would go from $53 to $126. The percentage capital gain on the stock would still be 100 percent, but the percentage gain on the warrant would now be only 138 percent versus 2,000 percent in the earlier case. Notice also that the potential loss on the option is much greater when the option is selling at high prices. These two factors, the declining leverage impact and the increasing danger of losses, help explain why the premium diminishes as the price of the common stock rises.

In addition to the stock price and the exercise price, the value of an option depends on three other factors: (1) the option's time to maturity, (2) the variability of the stock price, and (3) the risk-free rate. We will explain precisely how these factors affect option prices in the next section, but for now, note these points:

1. The longer an option has to run, the greater is its value and the larger is its premium. If an option expires at 4 P.M. today, there is not much chance that the stock price will go way up, so the option must sell at close to its formula value, and its premium must be small. On the other hand, if it has a year to go, the stock price could rise sharply, pulling the option's value up with it.

2. An option on an extremely volatile stock will be worth more than one on a very stable stock. If the stock price rarely moves, then there is a small chance of a large gain. However, if the stock price is highly volatile, the option could become very valuable. At the same time, losses on options are limited, so large declines in a stock's price do not have a corresponding bad effect on option holders. Therefore, the more volatile a stock, the higher is the value of its options.

3. Because of points (1) and (2), in a graph such as Figure 16-1, if everything else were constant, then the longer an option's life, the higher its market price line would be above the formula value line. Similarly, the more volatile the price of the underlying stock, the higher is the market price line.

The risk-free rate affects option prices in a complicated way, as we shall see in the next section.

The Option Pricing Model (OPM)

The *Black-Scholes Option Pricing Model (OPM)* was developed in 1973, just as the rapid growth in options trading began.[3] This model, which has actually been programmed into the permanent memory of some handheld calculators, is widely used by option traders. Our interest, however, lies in the insights that option theory provides in valuing all securities subject to contingent claims, including warrants, convertibles, and even the equity of a levered firm.

In deriving their option pricing model, which values call options, Black and Scholes make the following assumptions:

1. The stock underlying the call option provides no dividends or other distributions during the life of the option.

2. There are no transactions costs in buying or selling either the stock or the option.

3. The short-term, risk-free interest rate is a known constant during the life of the option.

4. Any purchaser of a security may borrow any fraction of the purchase price at the short-term, risk-free interest rate.

---

[3]See Fischer Black and Myron Scholes, ''The Pricing of Options and Corporate Liabilities,'' *Journal of Political Economy*, May/June 1973, 637-659.

5. *Short selling* is permitted without penalty, and the short seller will receive immediately the full cash proceeds of today's price for a security sold short.[4]

6. The call option can only be exercised at maturity.

7. Trading in all securities takes place in continuous time, and the stock price follows a *random walk* in continuous time.[5]

The assumption that the option can only be exercised at maturity is characteristic of a *European* option. *American* options can be exercised at any time up to and including the maturity date. However, it has been shown that for nondividend paying stocks, the market price of an American call option is always greater than the value it would have if it were exercised immediately.[6] Hence, a rational investor would not exercise an American call option on a nondividend paying stock before maturity—the investor would sell the option on the open market. Therefore, the value of an American call option is the same as that of a European option.

The derivation of the Black-Scholes Option Pricing Model rests on the concept of the *riskless hedge*. By buying shares of a stock and simultaneously selling options on this stock, an investor can create a risk-free investment position—gains on the stock would exactly offset losses on the option, and vice versa. This riskless hedged position must earn a rate of return equal to the risk-free rate; otherwise, an arbitrage opportunity would exist, and people trying to take advantage of this opportunity would drive the price of the option to the equilibrium level specified by the Black-Scholes model.

The Black-Scholes model consists of the following three equations:

$$V = P[N(d_1)] - Xe^{-R_F t}[N(d_2)]. \tag{16-1}$$

$$d_1 = \frac{\ln(P/X) + [R_F + (\sigma^2/2)]t}{\sigma\sqrt{t}}. \tag{16-2}$$

$$d_2 = d_1 - \sigma\sqrt{t}. \tag{16-3}$$

---

[4]Suppose an investor (or speculator) does not now own any IBM stock. If the investor anticipates a rise in the stock price and consequently buys IBM stock, he or she is said to have *gone long* in IBM. On the other hand, if the investor thinks IBM's stock price is likely to fall, he or she could *go short*, or *sell IBM short*. Since the short seller had no IBM stock, he or she would have to borrow the shares sold short from a broker. If the stock price falls, the short seller could, later on, buy the shares on the open market and return them to the broker. The short seller's profit, before commissions and taxes, would be the difference in the price received from the short sale and the price paid later to purchase the replacement stock.

[5]See Appendix 4A for a review of continuous compounding and discounting.

[6]See Robert C. Merton, "The Theory of Rational Option Pricing," *Bell Journal of Economics and Management Science*, Spring 1973, 141-183.

Here

$\quad$ V = current value of a call option with time t until maturity.

$\quad$ P = current price of the underlying stock.

$N(d_i)$ = probability that a deviation less than d_i will occur in a standard normal distribution. Thus, $N(d_1)$ and $N(d_2)$ represent areas under a standard normal distribution function.

$\quad$ X = exercise, or striking, price of the option.

$\quad$ e = exponential function = 2.7183. . . .

$\quad R_F$ = risk-free interest rate.

$\quad$ t = time until the option expires (the option period).

$\ln(P/X)$ = natural logarithm of P/X.

$\quad \sigma^2$ = variance of the instantaneous rate of return on the stock.

Note that the value of the option is a function of the variables that we discussed earlier: (1) P, the stock's price, (2) t, the option's time to maturity, (3) X, the striking price, (4) σ^2, the price variance of the underlying stock, and (5) R_F, the risk-free rate. We do not derive the Black-Scholes model—the derivation involves some extremely complicated mathematical statistics that go far beyond the scope of this text. However, it is not difficult to use the model, and under the assumptions set forth above, any option price different from the one found by Equation 16-1 would provide the opportunity for arbitrage profits, which would, in turn, force the option price back to the value indicated by the model. As we noted earlier, the Black-Scholes model is widely used by traders, so actual option prices do conform reasonably well to values derived from the model.

It is hard to provide an intuitive explanation of the model. Under certain conditions, the first term of Equation 16-1, $P[N(d_1)]$, can be thought of as the discounted expected value of the terminal stock price, given that the terminal stock price exceeds the exercise price, times the probability that the terminal stock price will be greater than the exercise price, while the second term, $Xe^{-R_Ft}[N(d_2)]$, can be viewed as the discounted exercise price times the probability that the terminal stock price will be greater than the exercise price. However, rather than try to figure out exactly what the equations mean, it is more productive to work out some values and see just how changes in the inputs change the value of the option.

OPM Illustration

The current stock price, P, the exercise price, X, and the time to maturity, t, of the option can be obtained from a current newspaper such as *The Wall Street Journal*. The risk-free rate, R_F, used in the OPM is the

Treasury bill rate with the same maturity date as the option. The stock price variance, σ^2, can be estimated by calculating the variance of the percentage change in daily stock prices for the past year, that is, the variance of $(P_t - P_{t-1})/P_t$ on a daily basis.

Assume that the following information has been obtained:

$P = \$20$.

$X = \$20$.

$t = 3$ months or 0.25 years.

$R_F = 12\% = 0.12$.

$\sigma^2 = 0.16$.

(Note: The average daily price change over the last year was 1.43%; σ was 0.40%, so on about two-thirds of the days, the stock price change was $1.43\% \pm 0.40\%$; and σ^2 was 0.16.) Given this information, we can now proceed to use the OPM by solving Equations 16-1 through 16-3. Since d_1 and d_2 are required inputs for Equation 16-1, we solve Equations 16-2 and 16-3 first:

$$d_1 = \frac{\ln(\$20/\$20) + [0.12 + (0.16/2)](0.25)}{(0.40)(0.50)}$$

$$= \frac{0 + 0.05}{0.20} = 0.25.$$

$$d_2 = d_1 - 0.20 = 0.05.$$

Now we solve Equation 16-1:

$$V = \$20[N(d_1)] - \$20e^{-(0.12)(0.25)}[N(d_2)]$$

$$= \$20[N(0.25)] - \$20(0.9704)[N(0.05)]$$

$$= \$20(0.5987) - \$19.41(0.5199)$$

$$= \$11.97 - \$10.09 = \$1.88.$$

Note that $N(0.25)$ and $N(0.05)$ represent areas under a standard normal distribution function. From Table A-5 in Appendix A at the end of the book, we see that the value $d_1 = 0.25$ implies a probability of $0.0987 + 0.5000 = 0.5987$, so $N(d_1) = 0.5987$. Similarly, $N(d_2) = 0.5199$. Thus, the value of the option, under the assumed conditions, is $1.88. If the actual option price is materially different from this value, then an arbitrageur could simultaneously buy or sell options and the underlying stock and earn a riskless profit. This arbitrage opportunity would, in turn, drive the price of the option back to $1.88. Thus, you would be unwilling to pay much more than $1.88 for the option, and you could not buy it for much less.

To see how each of the five OPM factors affects the value of the option, V, consider Table 16-2. Here the top row shows the base case input

Table 16-2
Effects of OPM Factors on the Value of a Call Option

Case	P	X	t	R_F	σ^2	V
Base case	$20	$20	0.25 years	12%	0.16	$1.88
Increase P by $5	25	20	0.25	12	0.16	5.81
Increase X by $5	20	25	0.25	12	0.16	0.39
Increase t to 6 months	20	20	0.50	12	0.16	2.81
Increase R_F to 16%	20	20	0.25	16	0.16	1.99
Increase σ^2 to 0.25	20	20	0.25	12	0.25	2.27

values and the resulting option value, V = $1.88. The base case input values are those we just used to illustrate the OPM. In each of the subsequent rows, one factor is increased, while the values of the other four are held constant at their base case levels. The value of the call option is given in the last column. Now we examine the effects of changes in each factor.

1. Current stock price. As the current stock price, P, increases from $20 to $25, the option value increases from $1.88 to $5.81. Thus, the value of the call increases as the stock price increases, but not by as much as the stock price increased ($3.93 versus $5.00). Note, though, that the percentage increase in the option value ($5.81 − $1.88)/$1.88 = 209% far exceeds the percentage increase in the stock price ($25 − $20)/$20 = 25%.

2. Exercise price. As the exercise price, X, increases from $20 to $25, the value of the option declines. Again, though, the option value does not decrease in absolute amount by as much as the exercise price increases, but the percentage change in the option value, ($0.39 − $1.88)/$1.88 = −79%, exceeds the percentage change in the exercise price, ($25 − $20)/$20 = 25%.

3. Time to maturity. As time to maturity increases from t = 3 months (or 0.25 years) to t = 6 months (or 0.50 years), the value of the option increases from $1.88 to $2.81. This result should not be surprising. The value of the option depends on an increase in the price of the underlying stock. Obviously, the longer the option runs, the higher the stock price may go. Thus, other things held constant, a six-month option is worth more than a three-month option.

4. Risk-free rate. The next factor is the risk-free rate, R_F. As the risk-free rate increases from 12 to 16 percent, the call option value increases slightly, from $1.88 to $1.99. Equations 16-1, 16-2, and 16-3 suggest that the principal effect of an increase in R_F is the reduction of the present value of the exercise price of the option, Xe^{-R_Ft}, and hence an increase in the current value of the call option.[7] The risk-free rate also plays a role in determining the values of the normal distribution functions $N(d_1)$ and $N(d_2)$, but this effect is of secondary importance. Indeed, option prices in general are not very sensitive to interest rate changes, at least not to changes within the ranges normally encountered.

5. Variance. As the variance increases from the base case level of 0.16 to 0.25, the value of the call option increases from $1.88 to $2.27. That is, if all other factors are held constant, the riskier the underlying security, the more valuable will be the call option. This result is logical. First, if you bought an option to buy a stock that sells at its exercise price with $\sigma^2 = 0$, then there would be a zero probability of the stock going up, and hence a zero probability of making any money on the option. On the other hand, if you bought an option on a high-variance stock, there would be a fairly high probability of the stock price going way up, and hence of making a high profit on the option. Of course, the price of a high-variance stock could go way down, but as an option holder, your losses would be limited to the price paid to buy the option. All of this makes the options of risky stocks more valuable than those of safer, low-variance stocks. (An increase in the price of the stock helps options holders more than a decrease hurts them; thus, the greater the variance, the greater is the value of the option.)

Implications for Corporate Financial Policy

The equity of a levered firm can be thought of as a call option. When a firm issues debt, this is in a sense equivalent to the shareholders selling the assets of the firm to the debtholders, who pay for the assets with cash plus an implied call option with a striking price equal to the principal value plus interest on the debt. If the company is successful, the stockholders will "buy it back" by exercising their call and paying the principal and interest on the debt. Otherwise, they will default on the loan, which means not exercising their call and giving the company to the creditors.

As an illustration, suppose that the One-Shot Corporation is just being formed to make a one-year investment in producing and marketing presidential campaign buttons. The firm requires an investment of $10,000, of which $7,500 will be obtained by selling debt with a 10 percent interest rate, and the other $2,500 will be raised by selling common stock. All cash distributions to debtholders and stockholders are to be made at the end of one year. After this year is up, the value of the firm

---

[7]At this point, you may be wondering why the first term in Equation 13-1, $P[N(d_1)]$, is not discounted. In fact, it has been, because the current stock price, P, already represents the present value of the expected end-of-option-period stock price, so it is a discounted value, and the discount rate used in the maket to determine today's stock price includes the risk-free rate. Thus, Equation 16-1 can be thought of as the present value of the end-of-option-period spread between the stock price and the exercise price, adjusted for the probability that the stock price will be higher than the striking price.

will depend primarily on which candidates make it through the primary elections, plus perhaps some value in the collector's market. The probability distribution of the firm's value is given below:

Probability	Value
0.7	$20,000
0.2	5,000
0.1	0

Thus, the expected value of the firm is 0.1($0) + 0.2($5,000) + 0.7($20,000) = $15,000. The expected value, if it were realized, would provide the shareholders with $6,750 before taxes on their $2,500 investment:

Expected value		$15,000
Less:		
Debt principal	$7,500	
Debt interest	750	8,250
		$ 6,750

However, the expected value is not achievable: The value of the firm will be $0 or $5,000 or $20,000. If the value is either $0 or $5,000, the shareholders will not exercise their call option, that is, they will default. The debtholders would then be entitled to the value of the firm, and the equity holders would receive nothing. However, if the firm's value turns out to be $20,000, the shareholders will exercise the call option by paying off the $8,250 principal and interest, and then pocket a sizable $11,750 before taxes. Thus, equity ownership can be viewed as a call option. In this illustration, an equity investment of $2,500 (the current price of the call) entitles the shareholders to purchase the assets of the firm for $8,250 (the exercise price). This insight has been applied to many of the traditional issues of corporate finance.[8] We look at two issues below, and we will examine the implications of option analysis for mergers in Chapter 24.

Investment Decisions. Suppose a levered firm has a large portfolio of Treasury bills. Management could sell the bills (which are riskless) and use the proceeds to purchase a risky asset that would increase the firm's earnings variance, yet have no effect on the firm's systematic risk. Since the equity can be viewed as a call option, the increased variance would increase the market value of the equity without increasing its market

---

[8]For example, see Dan Galai and Ronald Masulis, "The Option Pricing Model and the Risk Factor of Stock," *The Journal of Financial Economics*, January/March 1976, 53-82. Galai and Masulis combine the CAPM with the OPM. Thus, the assumptions of both models underlie their analysis.

risk. The risk of bankruptcy would increase, but shareholders would have increased their chances of greater gains while their losses would still be limited to the amount of their investment.

However, any gains to shareholders come at the expense of the debt-holders. To illustrate, suppose the initial value of the firm's assets is \$4 million, and it has \$2 million of face (book) value of 2-year debt outstanding. (Interest, which is payable at maturity, is included in the face value of the debt, so the debt is a discount issue.) Further, assume that the variance, σ^2, of the rate of return on the firm's assets is 0.01, and that the risk-free rate is 10 percent. If we view the stock as a call option on the firm's assets, then we would have:

V = current call option value, or current market value of the equity.

P = current value of the firm, or \$4 million.

X = striking price, or face value of the \$2 million of debt.

Then, using Equations 16-1 through 16-3, the market value of the firm's equity is found to be \$2,362,538:

$$d_1 = \frac{\ln(\$4{,}000{,}000/\$2{,}000{,}000) + [0.10 + (0.01/2)](2)}{0.10\sqrt{2}}$$

$$= \frac{\ln 2 + 0.2100}{0.1414} = 6.3872.$$

$$N(d_1) = 1.0$$

$$d_2 = d_1 - \sigma\sqrt{t} = 6.3872 - 0.1414 = 6.2458.$$

$$N(d_2) = 1.0.$$

$$V = \$4{,}000{,}000[N(d_1)] - \$2{,}000{,}000e^{-(0.10)(2)}[N(d_2)]$$

$$= \$4{,}000{,}000(1) - \$1{,}637{,}462(1) = \$2{,}362{,}538.$$

Given that the total value of the firm is \$4,000,000, and that the market value of the equity using the OPM is \$2,362,538, then the implied market value (or present value) of the \$2,000,000 face value of debt must be \$1,637,462.

Now suppose the firm uses some of its liquid assets to buy risky assets, increasing the variance of the firm's rate of return from 0.01 to 0.10. Thus, under the new situation, $\sigma^2 = 0.10$, and $\sigma = 0.3162$. Now we can recalculate the equity and debt values, assuming that the total value of the firm remains unchanged at \$4 million:

$$d_1 = \frac{\ln 2 + [0.10 + (0.02/2)](2)}{0.3162\sqrt{2}}$$

$$= \frac{0.6931 + 0.2200}{0.4472} = 2.0418.$$

$$N(d_1) = 0.9794.$$
$$d_2 = 2.0418 - 0.4472 = 1.5946.$$
$$N(d_2) = 0.9446.$$
$$V = \$4,000,000(0.9794) - \$1,637,462(0.9446)$$
$$= \$2,370,813.$$

The implied market value of the debt is now $\$4,000,000 - \$2,370,813 = \$1,629,187$. Thus, under the assumptions of the OPM and CAPM (both of which must be invoked), and assuming a constant firm value, the equity holders have gained $\$2,370,813 - \$2,362,538 = \$9,275$ at the expense of the debtholders. This illustration highlights the importance of restrictive covenants which debtholders can use to protect themselves against possible shareholder actions which would reduce the value of debt.

Capital Structure Decisions. Suppose a firm plans to double its outstanding debt, with the proceeds from the new debt being used to repurchase stock, so the assets of the firm would be unchanged. Increasing leverage would increase the variance of the firm's net income, and thus the variance of its equity value. This would, other things held constant, increase the value of the equity, because equity holders have a call option on the firm's value. The numerical analysis would be similar to that presented in the previous example. Clearly, the additional debt would put current debtholders in a riskier position, with no additional compensation. Consequently, the value of their debt would fall, and this decrease in value would be equal to the shareholders' gain.

Summary on Option Theory

Options are important in the investments area, so students of finance need to have a knowledge of how they are used and priced in the market. The role of option theory in financial management is less clear. As we have seen, it is possible to use option theory to gain insights into the effects of leverage and asset investments on the value of the firm's debt and equity. However, these insights are really rather obvious, and one can see the general effects of leverage and asset risk changes more easily just by thinking about them than by working through the OPM. However, it may be that the OPM approach can in the future lead to a more precise quantification of certain effects, which would be useful in structuring contracts and in other types of financial policy decisions. Those who advocate the use of the OPM in corporate finance would take that position. Others would argue that these applications may be all right in theory, but that they will never work in practice because, to obtain precise results, the model requires (1) all the assumptions of both the Black-Scholes OPM and the CAPM, plus (2) an estimate of the expected future returns on the firm's assets as seen by an average investor, and this combined set of assumptions and data requirements is just too restrictive for use in any practical application.

We are not ready to make a judgment on all this. We have seen some interesting practical attempts to apply the OPM to corporate finance, but it is not at all clear how things will work out.[9] In any event, students of finance do need to be aware of what is happening in the field; hence, they do need to be aware of developments in the options area.

Warrants

A warrant is an option issued by a company which gives the warrant's owner the right to buy a stated number of shares of the company's stock at a specified price. Generally, warrants are distributed with debt, and they are used to induce investors to buy a firm's long-term debt at a lower interest rate than would otherwise be required. For example, when Pan Pacific Airlines (PPA) wanted to sell $50 million of 20-year bonds in 1983, the company's investment bankers informed the financial vice president that the bonds would be difficult to sell, and that an interest rate of 14 percent would be required. However, as an alternative, the bankers suggested that investors might be willing to buy the bonds with a coupon rate as low as 10⅜ percent if the company would offer 30 warrants with each $1,000 bond, each warrant entitling the holder to buy one share of common stock at a price of $22 per share. The stock was selling for $20 per share at the time. The warrants would expire in 1993 if they had not been exercised previously.

Why would investors be willing to buy Pan Pacific's bonds at a yield of only 10⅜ percent in a 14 percent market just because warrants were also offered as part of the package? The warrants, since they are just long-term options, have value as discussed in the previous section, and this value offsets the low interest rate on the bonds and makes the entire package of below-market-yield bonds plus warrants attractive to investors.

---

[9]The OPM was used in an analysis of the cost of capital to the Alaska Pipeline. The pipeline is owned by a company, which in turn is owned by a group of oil companies. The pipeline is regulated, and as such, it is entitled to a fair rate of return on invested capital. However, its equity capital is not traded (since it is owned by the parent oil companies), and its debt, while it is publicly traded, is guaranteed by the parent companies, so the pipeline's debt cost cannot be used as a basis for estimating its cost of equity. Thus, conventional methods were unsuited for estimating the pipeline's cost of capital, and hence the fair rate of return that should be built into the prices charged for delivering North Slope oil to Valdez, Alaska. However, option pricing concepts were used to determine what the pipeline's cost of debt would have been without the parent companies' guarantees, and hence the cost of equity and the weighted average cost of capital. This application had not, at this writing, been accepted by the pipeline's regulators, but it does illustrate how financial theories may be applied in practice.

The PPA bonds, if they had been issued as straight debt, would have carried a 14 percent interest rate. However, with warrants attached, the bonds were sold to yield 10⅜ percent. Someone buying the bonds at their $1,000 initial offering price would thus be receiving a package consisting of a 10⅜ percent, 20-year bond plus 30 warrants. Since the going interest rate on bonds as risky as those of PPA was 14 percent, we can find the straight-debt value of the bonds, assuming an annual coupon, as follows:

Initial Market Price of Bond with Warrants

$$\text{Value} = \sum_{t=1}^{20} \frac{\$103.75}{(1.14)^t} + \frac{\$1,000}{(1.14)^{20}}$$
$$= \$687.15 + \$72.80 = \$759.95 \approx \$760.$$

Thus, a person buying the bonds in the initial underwriting would pay $1,000 and receive in exchange a straight bond worth about $760 plus warrants presumably worth about $1,000 − $760 = $240:

$$\begin{array}{ccccc} \text{Price paid for} & = & \text{Straight-debt} & + & \text{Value of} \\ \text{bond with warrants} & & \text{value of bond} & & \text{warrants} \\ \$1,000 & = & \$760 & + & \$240. \end{array}$$

Since investors receive 30 warrants with each bond, each warrant has an implied value of $240/30 = $8.

The key issue in setting the terms of a bond-with-warrants offering is valuing the warrants. The straight-debt value of the bond can be estimated quite accurately. However, it is much more difficult to estimate the value of the warrants. Even the Black-Scholes OPM provides only a rough estimate, since its parameters are not easily estimated. If, in setting the terms, the warrants are overvalued relative to their true market value, then it will be difficult to sell the issue at its par value. Conversely, if the warrants are undervalued, then investors in the issue will receive a windfall profit since they can sell the warrants in the market for more than they implicitly paid for them. This windfall profit would come out of the pockets of PPA's stockholders.

In the past, warrants have generally been used by small, rapidly growing firms as "sweeteners" when they were selling either debt or preferred stock. Such firms are frequently regarded by investors as being highly risky. Their bonds could be sold only if they were willing to pay extremely high rates of interest and to accept very restrictive indenture provisions. To avoid this, firms such as Pan Pacific often offered warrants along with the bonds. In the 1970s, however, AT&T raised $1.57 billion by selling bonds with warrants. This was the largest financing of

Use of Warrants in Financing

any type ever undertaken by a business firm, and it marked the first use ever of warrants by a large, strong corporation.[10]

Getting warrants along with bonds enables investors to share in the company's growth, if it does in fact grow and prosper; therefore, investors are willing to accept a lower bond interest rate and less restrictive indenture provisions. A bond with warrants has some characteristics of debt and some characteristics of equity. It is a hybrid security that provides the financial manager with an opportunity to expand the firm's mix of securities, appealing to a broader group of investors, and thus possibly lowering the firm's cost of capital.

Virtually all warrants today are *detachable*. Thus, after a bond with attached warrants is sold, the warrants can be detached and traded separately from the bond. Further, when these warrants are exercised, the bond issue (with its low coupon rate) remains outstanding, so the warrants bring in additional funds to the firm while leaving its interest costs relatively low.

The exercise price is generally set at from 10 to 30 percent above the market price of the stock on the date the bond is issued. If the firm does grow and prosper, and if its stock price rises above the exercise price at which shares may be purchased, warrant holders will exercise their warrants and buy stock at the stated price. However, without some incentive, warrants will never be exercised prior to maturity—their value in the market will be greater than their formula, or exercise, value, and hence holders would sell rather than exercise. There are three conditions which would encourage holders to exercise their warrants: (1) Warrant holders will *surely* exercise warrants and buy stock if the warrants are about to expire and the market price of the stock is above the exercise price. (2) Warrant holders will tend to exercise *voluntarily* and buy stock if the company raises the dividend on the common stock by a sufficient amount. No dividend is earned on the warrant, so it provides no current income. However, if the common stock pays a high dividend, it provides an attractive dividend yield. This induces warrant holders to exercise their option to buy the stock. (3) Warrants sometimes have *stepped-up exercise prices*, which prod owners into exercising them. For

---

[10]It is interesting to note that before the AT&T issue, the New York Stock Exchange's stated policy was that warrants could not be listed because they were "speculative" instruments rather than "investment" securities. When AT&T issued warrants, however, the Exchange changed its policy, agreeing to list warrants that met certain requirements. Many other warrants have since been listed.

It is also interesting to note that, prior to the sale, AT&T's analysts, working with Morgan Stanley analysts, estimated the value of the warrants as a part of the underwriting decision. The package was supposed to sell for a total price in the neighborhood of $1,000. The bond value could be determined accurately, so the trick was to estimate the equilibrium value of the warrant under different possible exercise prices and years to expiration, and then use that exercise price and life that caused bond value + warrant value ≈ $1,000. Using the option pricing model, the AT&T/Morgan Stanley analysts set terms which caused the warrant to sell on the open market at within $0.35 of the estimated price.

example, the Williamson Scientific Company has warrants outstanding with an exercise price of $25 until December 31, 1986, at which time, the exercise price rises to $30. If the price of the common stock is over $25 just before December 31, 1986, many warrant holders will exercise their options before the stepped-up price takes effect.

Another desirable feature of warrants is that they generally bring in funds only if they are needed. If the company grows, it will probably need new equity capital. At the same time, growth will cause the price of the stock to rise, the warrants to be exercised, and the firm to obtain additional cash. If the company is not successful and cannot profitably employ additional money, the price of its stock will probably not rise sufficiently to induce exercise of the options.

Convertibles

Convertible securities are bonds or preferred stocks that, under specified terms and conditions, can be exchanged for common stock at the option of the holder. Unlike the exercise of warrants, which brings in additional funds to the firm, conversion does not bring in additional capital: Debt (or preferred stock) on the balance sheet is simply replaced by common stock. Of course, this reduction of the debt or preferred stock will make it easier to obtain additional fixed charge capital, but this is a separate action.

Conversion Ratio and Conversion Price

One of the most important provisions of a convertible bond is the *conversion ratio*, R, defined as the number of shares of stock a bondholder receives upon conversion. Related to the conversion ratio is the *conversion price*, P_c, which is the effective price the company receives for the common stock when conversion occurs. The relationship between the conversion ratio and the conversion price is illustrated by the Mountain States Oil (MSO) convertible debentures, issued at their $1,000 par value in 1984. At any time prior to maturity on July 1, 2004, a debenture holder can exchange a bond for 20 shares of common stock; therefore, $R = 20$. The bond has a par value of $1,000, so the holder would be relinquishing this amount upon conversion. Dividing the $1,000 par value by the 20 shares received gives a conversion price of $P_c = \$50$ a share:

$$\text{Conversion price} = P_c = \frac{\text{Par value of bond}}{\text{Shares received}}$$

$$= \frac{\$1,000}{R} = \frac{\$1,000}{20} = \$50.$$

Similarly,

$$R = \frac{\$1,000}{P_c} = \frac{\$1,000}{\$50} = 20 \text{ shares.}$$

Once R is set, the value of P_c is established, and vice versa.

Like a warrant's exercise price, the conversion price is characteristically set at from 10 to 30 percent above the prevailing market price of the common stock at the time the convertible issue is sold. Exactly how the conversion price is established can best be understood after examining some of the reasons firms use convertibles.

Generally, the conversion price and ratio are fixed for the life of the bond, although sometimes a stepped-up conversion price is used. Litton Industries' convertible debentures, for example, were convertible into 12.5 shares until 1972; into 11.76 shares from 1972 until 1982; and into 11.11 shares from 1982 until maturity in 1987. The conversion price thus started at $80, rose to $85, and then went to $90. Litton's convertibles, like most, became callable at the option of the company after a 10-year call-protection period.

Another factor that may cause a change in the conversion price and ratio is a standard feature of almost all convertibles—the clause protecting the convertible against dilution from stock splits, stock dividends, and the sale of common stock at prices below the conversion price. The typical provision states that if common stock is sold at a price below the conversion price, then the conversion price must be lowered (and the conversion ratio raised) to the price at which the new stock was issued. Also, if the stock is split, or if a stock dividend is declared, the conversion price must be lowered by the percentage amount of the stock dividend or split. For example, if MSO were to have a two-for-one stock split, the conversion ratio would automatically be adjusted from 20 to 40 and the conversion price lowered from $50 to $25. If this protection were not contained in the contract, a company could completely thwart conversion by the use of stock splits and stock dividends. Warrants are similarly protected against dilution.

The standard protection against dilution from selling new stock at prices below the conversion price can, however, get a company into trouble. For example, Litton Industries' stock had fallen from about $80 to $62 by 1983. Thus, Litton would have had to give the bondholders a tremendous advantage by lowering the conversion price from $85 to $62 if it had wanted to sell new common stock. Problems such as this must be kept in mind by firms considering the use of convertibles or bonds with warrants.

Convertible Bond Model

Suppose MSO is thinking of issuing 20-year convertible bonds at a price of $1,000 per bond; this $1,000 would also be the bond's par (and maturity) value. The bonds would pay a 10 percent annual coupon interest rate, or $100 per year. Each bond could be converted into 20 shares of stock, so the conversion price would be $1,000/20 = $50. The stock is expected to pay a dividend of $2.80 in the coming year, and it sells at $35 per share; this price is expected to grow at a constant rate of 8 percent per year. Therefore, $k_s = \hat{k}_s = D_1/P_0 + g = \$2.80/\$35 + 8\% = 8\%$ $+ 8\% = 16\%$. If the bonds were not made convertible, they would have a yield of 13 percent, given their riskiness and the yields on other bonds. The convertible bonds would not be callable for 10 years, after which they could be called at a price of \$1,050, with this price declining by \$5 per year thereafter. If, after 10 years, the conversion value exceeds the call price by at least 20 percent, management will probably call the bonds.

Figure 16-2 shows the expectations of both an average investor and the company:[11]

1. The horizontal line at M = \$1,000 represents the par (and maturity) value. Also, \$1,000 is the price at which the bond is initially offered to the public.

Figure 16-2
Model of a Convertible Bond

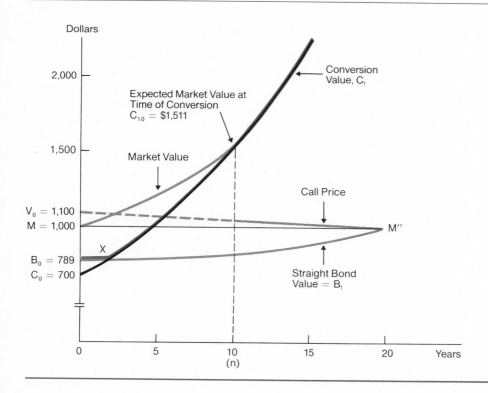

---

[11]For a more complete discussion of how this model can be used to structure the terms of a convertible offering, see Eugene F. Brigham, "An Analysis of Convertible Debentures: Theory and Some Empirical Evidence," *Journal of Finance*, March 1966, 35-54; and M. Wayne Marr and G. Rodney Thompson, "The Pricing of New Convertible Bond Issues," *Financial Management*, Summer 1984, 31-37.

2. The bond is protected against call for 10 years. It is initially callable at a price of $1,050, and the call price declines thereafter by $5 per year. Thus, the call price is represented by the solid section of the line V_0M''.

3. Since the convertible has a 10 percent coupon rate, and since the yield on a nonconvertible bond of similar risk was stated to be 13 percent, the "straight bond" value of the convertible, B_t, must be less than par. At the time of issue, assuming an annual coupon, B_0 is $789:

$$B_0 = \sum_{t=1}^{20} \frac{\$100}{(1.13)^t} + \frac{\$1,000}{(1.13)^{20}} = \$789.$$

Note, however, that the bond's straight debt value must be $1,000 just prior to maturity, so the bond's straight debt value rises over time. B_t follows the line B_0M'' in the graph.

4. The bond's initial *conversion value*, or the value of the stock the investor would receive if the bonds were converted at t = 0, is $700: Conversion value = $P_0(R) = \$35(20 \text{ shares}) = \$700$. Since the stock price is expected to grow at an 8 percent rate, the conversion value of the bond is also expected to rise over time. For example, in Year 5 it should be $P_5(R) = \$35(1.08)^5(20) = \$1,029$. The expected conversion value, over time, is given by the line C_t in Figure 16-2.

5. The actual market price of the bond must always be equal to or greater than the higher of its straight debt value or its conversion value. If the market price were below the straight bond value, those who wanted bonds would recognize the bargain and buy them as bonds. If the market price were below the conversion value, people would buy the bonds, convert them to stock, and sell the stock at a profit. Therefore, the higher of the bond value and conversion value curves in the graph represents a "floor price" for the bond. In Figure 16-2, the floor price is represented by the heavy line B_0XC_t.

6. In fact, the bond's market value will typically exceed its floor value. It will exceed the straight bond value because the option to convert is worth something—a 10 percent bond with conversion possibilities is worth more than a 10 percent bond without this option. The actual price will typically exceed the conversion value because holding the convertible is safer than holding the common stock—the stock can fall to zero, but the convertible bond will not fall below its straight bond value.[12] We cannot say exactly where the market value line will lie, but it will be above the floor set by the straight bond and conversion value lines.

7. At some point, the market value line will hit the conversion value line. This convergence will occur for two reasons. First, the stock should pay higher and higher dividends as the years go by, but the interest

---

[12]Note, though, that the bond value line B_0M'' would fall later on if interest rates rose in the economy, or if the company's credit risk deteriorated and consequently its k_d rose.

payments on the convertible are fixed. For example, MSO's convertibles would pay $100 in interest annually, while the dividends on the 20 shares received upon conversion would initially be 20($2.80) = $56. However, at an 8 percent growth rate, the dividends after 10 years would be up to $120.90, while the interest would still be $100. Thus, at some point, rising dividends could be expected to push against the fixed interest payments, causing investors to convert voluntarily. Second, once the bond becomes callable, its market value cannot get very far above both the conversion value and the call price without exposing investors to the danger of a call. For example, suppose that 10 years after issue (when the bonds were callable), the market value of the MSO bonds was $1,600, the conversion value was $1,500, and the call price was $1,050. If the company called the bonds the day after you bought 10 bonds for $16,000, you would be forced to convert into stock worth only $15,000, so you would suffer a loss of $100 per bond, or $1,000, in one day. Recognizing this danger, you and other investors would simply not pay much of a premium over the higher of the call price or the conversion value. Therefore, in Figure 16-2, we assume that the market value line hits the conversion value line in Year 10, when the bond becomes callable.

8. We can let n represent the year when investors expect conversion to occur, either voluntarily because of rising dividends or because the company calls the convertibles to strengthen its balance sheet by substituting equity for debt. In our example, we assume that $n = 10$, the first call date. Had we assumed a lower initial conversion value, or a lower expected growth rate for the stock, such that C_{10} was less than V_{10}, n would have been greater than 10, the first call date.

9. An investor can find the expected rate of return on the convertible bond, k_c, which is an "internal rate of return," by solving for k_c in the following equation:

$$\begin{array}{l} \text{Price} \\ \text{paid for} \\ \text{bond} \end{array} = \$1,000 = \sum_{t=1}^{n} \frac{\$100}{(1 + k_c)^t} + \frac{\begin{array}{c}\text{Expected market value} \\ \text{at time of conversion}\end{array}}{(1 + k_c)^n}.$$

Since $n = 10$, and the expected market value at Year 10 is $\$35(1.08)^{10}(20) = \$1,511$, we can substitute into this equation and solve for k_c, which turns out to be 12.8 percent:

$$\$1,000 = \sum_{t=1}^{10} \frac{\$100}{(1 + k_c)^t} + \frac{\$1,511}{(1 + k_c)^{10}}.$$

10. The return on a convertible is expected to come partly from interest income and partly from capital gains; in this case, the total return is 12.8 percent, with 10 percent representing interest income and 2.8 percent representing expected capital gains. The interest component is relatively assured, while the capital gains component is more risky. On a new

straight bond, all of the return is in the form of interest. Therefore, a convertible's expected yield is more risky than is that of a straight bond, so k_c should be larger than the cost of straight debt, k_d. Thus, it would seem that the expected rate of return on MSO's convertibles, k_c, should lie between its cost of straight debt, $k_d = 13\%$, and its cost of common stock, $k_s = 16\%$.

Investment bankers use the type of model described here, plus a knowledge of the market, to set the terms on convertibles (conversion ratio and coupon interest rate) so that the security will just "clear the market" at its $1,000 offering price. In this example, the required conditions do not seem to hold—the calculated rate of return on the convertible is only 12.8 percent, which is less, rather than more, than the cost of straight debt. Therefore, it would appear that the terms on the bond must be made more attractive to investors. MSO could increase the coupon interest rate to a level above 10 percent, raise the conversion ratio above 20 (and thereby lower the conversion price from $50 to a level closer to the current $35 market price of the stock), or use a combination of these two such that the expected rate of return on the convertible ends up between 13 and 16 percent.

However, yet another complication should be noted—the differential tax rate on dividends and capital gains. The 13 percent interest on a straight bond would be entirely taxable as interest income, so to an investor in the 50 percent bracket, the after-tax yield on an MSO straight bond would be $0.5(13\%) = 6.5\%$. The after-tax yield on the convertible would be $0.5(10\%) + [1.0 - 0.4(0.5)](2.8\%) = 7.24\%$. So, on an after-tax basis, the convertible could be correctly priced vis-à-vis the firm's other securities.

Use of Convertibles in Financing

Convertibles offer both advantages and disadvantages to issuing corporations.

Advantages of Convertibles. Convertibles have two important advantages from the issuer's standpoint. (1) Convertibles, like bonds with warrants, offer a company the chance to sell debt with lower interest rates and less restrictive covenants in exchange for a chance to share in potential capital gains. (2) Convertibles provide a way to sell common stock at prices higher than those currently prevailing. Many companies actually want to sell common stock, and not debt, but feel that the price of their stock is temporarily depressed. Management may know, for example, that earnings are depressed because of start-up costs associated with a new project, but they expect earnings to rise sharply during the next year or so, pulling the price of the stock up with them. Management thinks that if it sold stock now, it would be giving up more shares than necessary to raise a given amount of money. However, if it set the conversion price 20 to 30 percent above the present market price of the stock, then 20 to 30 percent fewer shares would be given up when the bonds are converted than would be required if stock were sold directly at this time. Notice, however, that management is counting on the stock's price to rise above the conversion price to make the bonds attractive in conversion. If earnings do not rise and pull the stock price up, and hence conversion does not occur, then the company will be saddled with debt in the face of low earnings, which could be disastrous.

How can the company be sure that conversion will occur if the price of the stock rises above the conversion price? Typically, convertibles contain a call provision that enables the issuing firm to force bondholders to convert. Suppose the conversion price is $50, the conversion ratio is 20, the market price of the common stock has risen to $60, and the call price on the convertible bond is $1,050. If the company calls the bond, bondholders can either convert into common stock with a market value of $1,200 or allow the company to redeem the bond for $1,050. Naturally, bondholders prefer $1,200 to $1,050, so conversion occurs. The call provision therefore gives the company a means of forcing conversion, provided the market price of the stock is greater than the conversion price. Note, however, that most convertibles have a fairly long period of call protection—10 years is the general rule. Therefore, if the company wants to be able to force conversion fairly early, then it will have to set a short call protection period. This will, in turn, require that it set a higher coupon rate or a lower conversion price.

Disadvantages of Convertibles. From the standpoint of the issuer, convertibles have three important disadvantages. (1) Although the use of a convertible security does give the issuer the opportunity to sell common stock at a price higher than the price at which it would have to be sold currently, if the common stock greatly increases in price, the issuing firm would probably find that it would have been better off if it had used straight debt in spite of its higher cost and then later sold common stock and refunded the debt. (2) If the company truly wants to raise equity capital, and if the price of the stock does not rise sufficiently after the bond is issued, then the company will be stuck with debt. This debt will, however, have a low interest rate. (3) Convertibles typically have a low coupon interest rate, and the advantage of this low-cost debt will be lost when conversion occurs.

Decisions on Use of Warrants and Convertibles

The Adams Electronics Company (AEC), a high-tech company with assets of $60 million, illustrates a typical case in which convertibles proved useful. AEC's profits had been depressed as a result of its heavy expenditures on research and development for a new microwave filter. This situation held down the growth rate of earnings and dividends, and its price/earnings ratio was only 18 times, as compared with an industry average of 22. At the current $2 earnings per share and P/E of 18, the stock was selling for $36 a share. The Adams family owned 70 percent of the 1.5 million shares outstanding, or 1.05 million shares. It wanted to retain majority control but did not have funds available to buy more stock.

The heavy R&D expenditures had resulted in the development of a new type of filter that management believed would be highly profitable. A total of $25 million was needed to build and equip new production facilities, but profits were not expected to flow into the company for some 18 months after construction on the new plant was started. AEC's debt amounted to $27 million, or 45 percent of assets, well above the 25 percent industry average. Also, its debt indenture provisions restricted the company from selling any additional debt unless the new debt was subordinated to outstanding debt.

Investment bankers informed AEC's financial vice president that subordinated debentures could not be sold at any reasonable interest rate unless they were convertibles or had warrants attached. Convertibles or bonds with warrants could be sold with a 10 percent coupon interest rate, provided the conversion price or warrant option price was set at 15 percent above the current market price of $36, or at $41 per share. Alternatively, the investment bankers were willing to buy convertibles or bonds with warrants at an 11 percent interest rate and a 20 percent conversion premium, or a conversion (or exercise) price of $43.50. Because the company wanted to increase its common equity, any convertibles used would have a relatively short 2-year call protection period, although the warrants would have a 5-year life. If the company wanted to sell common stock directly, it could net $33 per share.

Which of the alternatives should AEC have chosen? First, note that if common stock were used, the company would have to sell 757,576 shares ($25 million divided by $33). Combined with the 450,000 shares already held outside the family, this amounts to approximately 1.2 million shares versus the Adams family holdings of 1.05 million. Thus, the family would lose majority control if common stock were sold.

If the 10 percent convertibles or bonds with warrants were used, and the bonds were converted or the warrants exercised, 609,756 new shares would be added. Combined with the old 450,000, the outside interest would then be 1,059,756, so again the Adams family would lose majority control. However, if the 11 percent convertibles or bonds with warrants were used, then after conversion or exercise, only 574,713 new shares would be created. In this case, the family would have 1,050,000 shares versus 1,024,713 for outsiders; absolute voting control would be maintained.

In addition to assuring control, using the convertibles or warrants would also benefit earnings per share in the long run—the total number of shares would be less because fewer new shares would have to be issued to get the $25 million, so earnings per share would be higher.

Before conversion or exercise, however, the firm would have a considerable amount of debt outstanding. The addition of $25 million would raise the total debt to $52 million against new total assets of $85 million, so the debt ratio would be over 61 percent versus the 25 percent industry average. This could be dangerous: If delays were encountered in bringing the new plant into production, if demand failed to meet expectations, if the company experienced a strike, if the economy went into a recession—if any of these things occurred—the company would be extremely vulnerable because of its high debt ratio.

In the actual case, AEC decided to sell the 11 percent convertible debentures. Two years later, earnings climbed to $3 a share, the P/E ratio to 20, and the price of the stock to $60. The bonds were called, but, of course, conversion occurred. After conversion, debt amounted to approximately $27.5 million against total assets of $87.5 million (some earnings had been retained), so the debt ratio was down to a more reasonable 31 percent.

Convertibles rather than bonds with warrants were chosen for the following reason. The firm had a high debt ratio, and management regarded its near-term prospects as being favorable, so it anticipated a rise in the price of its stock and thus the opportunity to call the bonds and force conversion. The warrants, on the other hand, would have a 5-year life, and even though the price of the firm's stock might rise, the warrants would probably not be exercised until near their expiration date. If, subsequent to the favorable period (during which the convertibles could be called), the firm encountered less favorable developments and the price of its stock fell, the warrants would lose their value and might expire without having been exercised. The heavy debt burden would then not be alleviated. Therefore, the use of convertibles gave the firm greater control over the timing of its future capital structure changes. This factor was of particular importance to AEC because its debt ratio was already high in relation to the risks of its line of business.

If warrants or convertibles are outstanding, a firm could theoretically report earnings per share in one of three ways:

Reporting Earnings when Warrants or Convertibles Are Outstanding

1. *Simple EPS*, where earnings available to common stockholders would be divided by the average number of shares actually outstanding during the period.

2. *Primary EPS*, where earnings available would be divided by the average number of shares that would have been outstanding if warrants and convertibles "likely to be converted in the near future" had actually been exercised or converted. Earnings would be pro formed by "backing out" the interest on the convertibles. Accountants have a formula which basically compares the conversion or exercise price with the actual market

value of the stock to determine the likelihood of conversion when deciding on the need to use this adjustment procedure.

3. *Fully diluted EPS*, which is similar to primary EPS except that *all* warrants and convertibles are assumed to be exercised or converted, regardless of the likelihood of exercise or conversion.

Simple EPS is virtually never reported by firms which have warrants or convertibles likely to be exercised or converted—the SEC requires that primary and fully diluted earnings be shown. For firms with large amounts of option securities outstanding, there can be a substantial difference between the primary and fully diluted EPS figures. The purpose of the provision is, of course, to give investors a more accurate picture of the firm's true profit position.

Summary

Both *warrants* and *convertibles* are forms of options used to finance business firms. The use of such securities is encouraged by an economic environment in which either recessions or booms can occur. The senior position of the fixed charge portion of those securities protects against recessions, while the option feature offers the opportunity for participation in rising stock markets.

Both convertibles and warrants are used as "sweeteners." The option privileges they grant may make it possible for small companies to sell debt or preferred stock that otherwise could not be sold. For large companies, the "sweeteners" result in lower costs of the securities sold.

The conversion of bonds or preferred stock by their holders does not provide additional funds to the company. The exercise of warrants does provide such funds. The conversion of securities results in reduced debt ratios. The exercise of warrants also strengthens the equity position, but it still leaves the debt or preferred stock on the balance sheet. A firm with a high debt ratio should probably choose to use convertibles rather than senior securities that carry warrants. A firm with a moderate or low debt ratio may choose to employ warrants. Note, though, that low interest rate debt remains outstanding when warrants are exercised, but the firm loses the advantage of low-cost debt when convertibles are converted.

In the past, larger and stronger firms tended to favor convertibles over bonds with warrants, so most warrants were issued by smaller, weaker concerns. AT&T's use of warrants in its $1.57 billion financing has caused other large firms to reexamine their positions on warrants, and warrants have come into increasing use since that time.

Partly because of investors' interest in warrants and convertibles, a new market in pure options was developed during the 1970s. Option contracts are created by investors, and not by the firms whose securities are involved in option contracts. The corporations themselves do not raise capital from the sale of these options and, in fact, have no direct involvement with this market. The *Black-Scholes Option Pricing Model (OPM)* can be used to estimate the value of a call option, and it has two major uses for financial managers.

First, the OPM can help when setting the terms on warrant and convertible issues. Second, since the stock of a firm can be viewed as a call option, it provides some insights into such traditional financial management issues as investment decisions and capital structure decisions.

16-1 Define each of the following terms:
    a. Option; call option; put option
    b. Striking price; exercise price; variance
    c. Warrant; detachable warrant
    d. Formula value; exercise value
    e. Stepped-up price
    f. Convertible security
    g. Conversion ratio; conversion price; conversion value
    h. "Sweetener"
    i. Simple EPS; primary EPS; fully diluted EPS

Questions

16-2 Why do options typically sell at prices higher than their formula values?

16-3 What effect does the trend in stock prices (subsequent to issue) have on a firm's ability to raise funds through (a) convertibles and (b) warrants?

16-4 If a firm expects to have additional financial requirements in the future, would you recommend that it use convertibles or bonds with warrants? What factors would influence your decision?

16-5 How does a firm's dividend policy affect each of the following?
    a. The value of its long-term warrants.
    b. The likelihood that its convertible bonds will be converted.
    c. The likelihood that its warrants will be exercised.

16-6 Evaluate the following statement: "Issuing convertible securities represents a means by which a firm can sell common stock at a price above the existing market."

16-7 Why do corporations often sell convertibles on a rights basis?

16-8 Suppose a company simultaneously issues $50 million of convertible bonds with a coupon rate of 10 percent and $50 million of straight bonds with a coupon rate of 14 percent. Both bonds have the same maturity. Does the fact that the convertible issue has the lower coupon rate suggest that it is less risky than the straight bond? Is its cost of capital lower on the convertible than on the straight bond? Explain.

16-1 Savannah Software Corporation (SSC) options are actively traded on one of the regional exchanges. SSC's current stock price is $15, with a 0.16 instantaneous variance of returns. The current 6-month risk-free rate is 12 percent.
    a. What is the value of SSC's 6-month option with an exercise price of $10 according to the Black-Scholes model?
    b. What would be the effect on the option price if SSC redeployed its assets and/or reduced its debt ratio, thereby reducing its variance of returns to 0.09?

Problems

16-2 Weatherford Industries, Inc., has warrants outstanding that permit the holders to purchase one share of stock per warrant at a price of $25.

    a. Calculate the formula value of Weatherford's warrants if the common sells at each of the following prices: (1) $20, (2) $25, (3) $30, and (4) $100. (Use the simple option formula value equation, not the Black-Scholes model.)

    b. At what approximate price do you think the warrants would actually sell under each condition indicated above? What premium is implied in your price? Your answer is a guess, but your prices and premiums should bear reasonable relationships to one another.

    c. How would each of the following factors affect your estimates of the warrants' prices and premiums in Part b?

        (1) The life of the warrant.

        (2) Expected variability in the stock's price.

        (3) The expected growth rate in the stock's EPS.

        (4) The company announces a change in dividend policy: Whereas it formerly paid no dividends, henceforth it will pay out *all* earnings as dividends.

    d. Assume Weatherford's stock now sells for $20 per share. The company wants to sell some 20-year, annual interest, $1,000 par value bonds. Each bond will have attached 50 warrants, each exercisable into one share of stock at an exercise price of $25. Weatherford's straight bonds yield 12 percent. Regardless of your answer to Part b above, assume that the warrants will have a market value of $3 when the stock sells at $20. What coupon interest rate, and dollar coupon, must the company set on the bonds-with-warrants if they are to clear the market?

16-3 The Boca Grande Company was planning to finance an expansion in the summer of 1984. The principal executives of the company were agreed that an industrial company such as theirs should finance growth by means of common stock rather than by debt. However, they felt that the price of the company's common stock did not reflect its true worth, so they decided to sell a convertible security. They considered a convertible debenture but feared the burden of fixed interest charges if the common stock did not rise in price to make conversion attractive. They decided on an issue of convertible preferred stock, which would pay a dividend of $2.10 per share.

    The common stock was selling for $42 a share at the time. Management projected earnings for 1984 at $3 a share and expected a future growth rate of 10 percent a year in 1985 and beyond. It was agreed by the investment bankers and the management that the common stock would sell at 14 times earnings, the current price/earnings ratio.

    a. What conversion price should be set by the issuer? The conversion ratio will be 1.0; that is, each share of convertible preferred can be converted into one share of common. Therefore, the convertible's par value (and also the issue price) will be equal to the conversion price, which in turn will be determined as a percentage over the current market price of the common. Your answer will be a guess but make it a reasonable one.

    b. Should the preferred stock include a call provision? Why?

16-4 In June 1976, U.S. Steel sold $400 million of convertible bonds, the largest issue on record. The bonds had a 25-year maturity and a 5¾ percent coupon rate, and they were sold at their $1,000 par value. The conversion price was set at $62.75 against a current price of $55 per share of common. The bonds were subordinated debentures, and they were given an A rating; straight nonconvertible debentures of the same quality yielded about 8¾ percent at the time.

  a. Calculate the premium on the bonds, that is, the percentage excess of the conversion price over the current stock price.
  b. What is U.S. Steel's annual interest savings on the convertible issue versus a straight debt issue?
  c. Look up U.S. Steel's current stock price in the paper. Based on this price, do you think it likely that the bonds would have been converted? (Calculate the value of the stock one would receive by converting a bond.)
  d. The bonds originally sold for $1,000. If interest rates on A-rated bonds had remained constant at 8¾ percent, what do you think would have happened to the price of the convertible bonds?
  e. Now suppose the price of U.S. Steel's common stock had fallen from $55 on the day the bonds were issued to $20 at present. (At the time this problem was written, that is exactly what had happened.) Suppose also that the rate of interest had fallen from 8¾ to 5¾ percent. (This had not happened when the problem was being written—the interest rate on A-rated bonds was about 11 percent.) Under these conditions, what do you think would have happened to the price of the bonds?
  f. Set up a graphic model to illustrate how investors valued the U.S. Steel convertibles in 1976. How well were these expectations realized?

16-5 The Drake Computer Company has grown rapidly during the past 5 years. Recently, its commercial bank urged the company to consider increasing permanent financing. Its bank loan under a line of credit has risen to $250,000, carrying an 8 percent interest rate. Drake has been 30 to 60 days late in paying trade creditors.

   Discussions with an investment banker have resulted in the decision to raise $500,000 at this time. Investment bankers have assured Drake that the following alternatives are feasible (flotation costs will be ignored):

Alternative 1: Sell common stock at $8.

Alternative 2: Sell convertible bonds at an 8 percent coupon, convertible into 100 shares of common stock for each $1,000 bond (that is, the conversion price is $10 per share).

Alternative 3: Sell debentures at an 8 percent coupon, each $1,000 bond carrying 100 warrants to buy common stock at $10.

Melissa Davis, the president, owns 80 percent of the common stock of Drake and wishes to maintain control of the company. One hundred thousand shares are outstanding. The following are extracts of Drake's latest financial statements:

Balance Sheet

		Current liabilities	$400,000
		Common stock, par $1	100,000
		Retained earnings	50,000
Total assets	$550,000	Total claims	$550,000

Income Statement

Sales	$1,100,000
All costs except interest	990,000
EBIT	$ 110,000
Interest	20,000
EBT	$ 90,000
Taxes at 50%	45,000
Net income	$ 45,000
Shares outstanding	100,000
Earnings per share	$0.45
Price/earnings ratio	19×
Market price of stock	$8.55

a. Show the new balance sheet under each alternative. For Alternatives 2 and 3, show the balance sheet after conversion of the debentures or exercise of the warrants. Assume that one-half of the funds raised will be used to pay off the bank loan and one-half to increase total assets.

b. Show Ms. Davis's control position under each alternative, assuming that she does not purchase additional shares.

c. What is the effect on earnings per share of each alternative, if it is assumed that profits before interest and taxes will be 20 percent of total assets?

d. What will be the debt ratio under each alternative?

e. Which of the three alternatives would you recommend to Davis, and why?

16-6 Disk Drives, Inc. (DDI) needs to raise $25 million to put a new disk drive into production. DDI's straight, nonconvertible debentures currently yield 14 percent. Its stock sells for $30 per share; the last dividend was $2; and the expected growth rate is a constant 9 percent. Investment bankers have tentatively proposed that DDI raise the $25 million by issuing convertible debentures. These convertibles would have a $1,000 par value, carry a coupon rate of 10 percent, have a 20-year maturity, and be convertible into 20 shares of stock. The bonds would be noncallable for 5 years, after which they would be callable at a price of $1,075; this call price would decline by $5 per year in Year 6 and each year thereafter. Management has called convertibles in the past (and presumably it will call them again in the future), once they were eligible for call, when the bonds' conversion value was about 20 percent above the bonds' par value (not their call price).

a. Draw an accurate graph similar to Figure 16-2 representing the expectations set forth above.

b. What is the expected rate of return on the proposed convertible issue?

c. Do you think that these bonds could be successfully offered to the public at par? That is, does $1,000 seem to be an equilibrium price in view of the stated terms? If not, suggest the type of change that would have to be made to cause the bonds to trade at $1,000 in the secondary market, assuming no change in capital market conditions.

d. Suppose the projects outlined above work out on schedule for 2 years, but then DDI begins to experience extremely strong competition from Japanese firms. As a result, DDI's expected growth rate drops from 9 percent to zero. Assume that the dividend at the time of the drop is $2.38. The company's credit strength is not impaired, and its value of k_s is also unchanged. What would happen (1) to stock price and (2) to the convertible bond's price? Be as precise as you can.

The investments texts listed in Chapter 6 provide extended discussions of options, warrants, and convertibles.

The original Black-Scholes article tested the OPM to see how well predicted prices conformed to market values. For additional empirical tests, see

Galai, Dan, "Tests of Market Efficiency of the Chicago Board Options Exchange," *Journal of Business*, April 1977, 167-197.

Gultekin, N. Bulent, Richard J. Rogalski, and Seha M. Tinic, "Option Pricing Model Estimates: Some Empirical Results," *Financial Management*, Spring 1982, 58-69.

MacBeth, James D., and Larry J. Merville, "An Empirical Examination of the Black-Scholes Call Option Pricing Model," *Journal of Finance*, December 1979, 1173-1186.

Quite a bit of work has also been done on warrant pricing. Two of the more prominent articles are

Galai, Dan, and Mier I. Schneller, "The Pricing of Warrants and the Value of the Firm," *Journal of Finance*, December 1978, 1333-1342.

Schwartz, Eduardo S., "The Valuation of Warrants: Implementing a New Approach," *Journal of Financial Economics*, January 1977, 79-93.

For more insights into convertible pricing and use, see

Alexander, Gordon J., and Roger D. Stover, "Pricing in the New Issue Convertible Debt Market," *Financial Management*, Fall 1977, 35-39.

Alexander, Gordon J., Roger D. Stover, and D. B. Kuhnau, "Market Timing Strategies in Convertible Debt Financing," *Journal of Finance*, March 1979, 143-155.

Ingersoll, Jonathan E., "A Contingent Claims Valuation of Convertible Securities," *Journal of Financial Economics*, May 1977, 289-322.

————, "An Examination of Corporate Call Policies on Convertible Securities," *Journal of Finance*, May 1977, 463-478.

The following cases cover issues presented in this chapter:

Case 26, "Kennesaw Edison Power and Light," in the Brigham-Crum casebook, which illustrates convertible bond valuation.

"FLX, Inc.," in the Harrington casebook, which focuses on the retirement of convertible subordinated debentures which are selling below par.

Selected Additional References and Cases

Lease Financing

17

In 1982, U.S. Steel was planning to build a $690 million plant to manufacture seamless pipe. This capital expansion could have been financed conventionally, using both debt and equity. However, the steel industry was in the midst of a severe recession, and U.S. Steel had (1) a depressed stock price, (2) high marginal debt costs, and (3) virtually no retained earnings. Thus, conventional financing would have required U.S. Steel to go to the capital markets at the worst possible time.

Instead, U.S. Steel decided to lease the plant from General Electric Credit Corporation (GECC), one of the largest providers of commercial and industrial financing. GECC lined up 17 banks in six countries to put up most of the required funds, with GECC retaining ownership. U.S. Steel then leased the plant for 10 years, after which it has the option of buying the assets. U.S. Steel's effective financing cost was 40 percent less under leasing than under conventional financing.

The key factor that makes deals such as this possible is the differential value of tax benefits. U.S. Steel, with past losses and a slow recovery in sight, could not immediately use the plant's investment tax credit and depreciation deductions. GECC, on the other hand, consolidates its income with its parent, General Electric, and the tax benefits of the plant could be used immediately to offset General Electric's own current income. In effect, U.S. Steel transferred tax benefits it could not use to General Electric, whose operations were profitable and, hence, to whom tax credits were valuable. General Electric paid U.S. Steel for those tax credits by charging it relatively low lease payments over the 10-year life of the lease.

Firms generally own fixed assets and report them on their balance sheets, but it is the *use* of buildings and equipment that is important, 701 not their ownership per se. One way of obtaining the use of facilities and equipment is to buy them, but an alternative is to lease them. Prior to the 1950s, leasing was generally associated with real estate—land and buildings. Today, however, it is possible to lease virtually any kind of fixed asset, and in 1984 about 20 percent of all new capital equipment acquired by businesses was financed through lease arrangements. It is estimated that $200 billion worth of capital equipment is currently being leased.

Types of Leases

Leasing takes several different forms, the three most important of which are (1) *sale-and-leaseback* arrangements, (2) *operating leases*, and (3) straight *financial*, or *capital*, *leases*.

Sale and Leaseback

Under a *sale-and-leaseback* arrangement, a firm that owns land, buildings, or equipment sells the property to a financial institution and simultaneously executes an agreement to lease the property back for a specified period under specific terms. The financial institution could be an insurance company, a commercial bank, a specialized leasing company, or an individual investor. The sale-and-leaseback plan is an alternative to a mortgage.

Note that the seller, or *lessee*, immediately receives the purchase price put up by the buyer, or *lessor*.[1] At the same time, the seller-lessee retains the use of the property. This parallel to borrowing is carried over to the lease payment schedule. Under a mortgage loan arrangement, the financial institution would normally receive a series of equal payments just sufficient to amortize the loan while providing a specified rate of return to the lender on the outstanding loan balance. Under a sale-and-leaseback arrangement, the lease payments are set up in exactly the same manner—the payments are sufficient to return the full purchase price to the investor, plus a stated return on the lessor's investment.

Operating Leases

Operating leases, sometimes called *service leases*, provide for both *financing* and *maintenance*. IBM is one of the pioneers of the operating lease contract. Computers and office copying machines, together with automobiles and trucks, are the primary types of equipment involved in operating leases. Ordinarily, these leases call for the lessor to maintain and service the leased equipment, and the cost of the maintenance is built into the lease payments.

---

[1]The term *lessee* is pronounced "less-ee," not "lease-ee," and *lessor* is pronounced "less-or."

Another important characteristic of operating leases is the fact that they are frequently *not fully amortized*. In other words, the payments required under the lease contract are not sufficient to recover the full cost of the equipment. However, the lease contract is written for a period considerably less than the expected economic life of the leased equipment, and the lessor expects to recover all costs either in subsequent renewal payments, through leases to other lessees, or by sale of the leased equipment.

A final feature of operating leases is that they frequently contain a *cancellation clause* which gives the lessee the right to cancel the lease and return the equipment before the expiration of the basic lease agreement. This is an important consideration to the lessee, for it means that the equipment can be returned if it is rendered obsolete by technological developments or is no longer needed because of a decline in the lessee's business.

Financial leases, sometimes called *capital leases*, are differentiated from operating leases in that they (1) *do not* provide for maintenance service, (2) *are not* cancelable, and (3) *are* fully amortized (that is, the lessor receives rental payments equal to the full price of the leased equipment plus a return on investment). In a typical arrangement, the firm that will use the equipment (the lessee) selects the specific items it requires, and then it negotiates the price and delivery terms with the manufacturer. The user firm then arranges to have a leasing company (the lessor) buy the equipment from the manufacturer or the distributor. When the equipment is purchased, the user firm simultaneously executes an agreement to lease the equipment from the financial institution. The terms of the lease call for full amortization of the lessor's investment, plus a rate of return on the unamortized balance which is close to the percentage rate the lessee would have paid on a secured term loan. For example, if the lessee would have to pay 10 percent for a term loan, then a rate of about 10 percent would be built into the lease contract. The lessee is generally given an option to renew the lease at a reduced rate on expiration of the basic lease. However, the basic lease usually cannot be canceled unless the lessor is completely paid off. Also, the lessee generally pays the property taxes and insurance on the leased property. Since the lessor receives a return *after*, or *net of*, these payments, this type of lease is often called a "net, net" lease.

Financial leases are almost the same as sale-and-leaseback arrangements, the major difference being that the leased equipment is new and the lessor buys it from a manufacturer or a distributor instead of from the user-lessee. A sale and leaseback may, then, be thought of as a special type of financial lease. Both sale-and-leaseback arrangements and financial leases are analyzed in the same manner.

Financial, or Capital, Leases

Tax Effects

The full amount of the annual lease payment is a deductible expense for income tax purposes *provided the Internal Revenue Service agrees that a particular contract is a genuine lease, and not simply an installment loan called a lease.* This makes it important that a lease contract be written in a form acceptable to the IRS. The IRS considers any agreement to be a sale if (1) the total lease payments are made over a relatively short period and approximate the price of the property, and (2) the lessee may continue to use the property over the remainder of its useful life for relatively nominal renewal payments.

The reason for the IRS's concern about these factors is that without restrictions, a company could set up a "lease" transaction calling for very rapid payments, which would be tax deductions. The effect would be to depreciate the equipment over a much shorter period than its ACRS class life. For example, suppose a firm planned to acquire a $2 million printing press which had a 5-year ACRS class life. The annual depreciation allowances, ignoring the investment tax credit, would be $300,000 in Year 1, $440,000 in Year 2, and $420,000 in each of Years 3-5. If the firm were in the 46 percent tax bracket, the depreciation would provide a tax saving of $138,000 in Year 1, $202,400 in Year 2, and $193,200 in each of Years 3-5, or $920,000 in total. At a 6 percent discount rate, the present value of these tax savings would be $769,941.

Now suppose the firm could acquire the press through a 3-year lease arrangement with a leasing company for payments of $666,666.67 per year with a $1 purchase option. If the $666,666.67 payments were treated as lease payments, they would be fully deductible, and hence would provide a tax saving of 0.46($666,666.67) = $306,666.67 per year for 3 years, with a present value of $819,724 versus a present value of only $769,941 for the depreciation shelters. Thus, the lease payments and the depreciation both provide the same total amount of tax savings (46% of $2 million, or $920,000), but the savings come in faster, and hence have a higher present value, with the 3-year lease. Therefore, if any type of contract could be called a lease and given tax treatment as a lease, then the timing of the tax shelters could be speeded up as compared with ownership depreciation tax shelters. This speedup would benefit the firm, but it would be costly to the government. For this reason, the IRS has established the rules described above for defining a lease for tax purposes.

Even though leasing can be used only within limits to speed up the effective depreciation schedule, there are still times when very substantial tax benefits can be derived from a leasing arrangement. For example, if a firm like U.S. Steel has been experiencing losses and therefore has no tax liabilities, then it cannot immediately use the investment tax credit, and its loss carry-forwards make depreciation shelters not very useful. In this case, a leasing company like General Electric Credit can buy the equipment, receive the tax credit and depreciation shelters, and then share these benefits with the lessee by charging lower lease payments. This point will be discussed in detail later in the chapter, but the point to be made now is that if firms are to obtain tax benefits from leasing, the lease contract must be written in a manner that will qualify it as a true lease under IRS guidelines. If there is any question about the legal status of the contract, the financial manager must be sure to have the firm's lawyers and accountants check the latest IRS regulations.[2]

Lease payments are shown as operating expenses on a firm's income statement, but under certain conditions, neither the leased assets nor the liabilities under the lease contract appear on the firm's balance sheet. For this reason, leasing is often called *off balance sheet* financing. This point is illustrated in Table 17-1 by the balance sheets of two hypothetical firms, P and L. Initially, the balance sheets of both firms are identical, and they both have debt ratios of 50 percent. Next, each firm decides to acquire fixed assets costing $100. Firm P borrows $100 to make the purchase, so both an asset and a liability go on its balance sheet, and its debt ratio is increased to 75 percent. Firm L leases the equipment. The lease may call for fixed charges as high as or even higher than the loan, and the obligations assumed under the lease can be equally or more dangerous from the standpoint of financial analysis, but the firm's debt ratio remains at 50 percent.

To correct this problem, the Financial Accounting Standards Board issued *FASB #13*, which requires that, for an unqualified audit report, firms that enter into financial (or capital) leases must restate their bal-

Financial Statement Effects

Table 17-1
Balance Sheet Effects of Leasing

	Before Asset Increase			After Asset Increase						
	Firms P and L			Firm P, which Borrows and Purchases				Firm L, which Leases		
Current assets	$ 50	Debt	$ 50	Current assets	$ 50	Debt	$150	Current assets	$ 50	Debt	$ 50
Fixed assets	50	Equity	50	Fixed assets	150	Equity	50	Fixed assets	50	Equity	50
Total	$100		$100	Total	$200		$200	Total	$100		$100

[2]Under the Economic Recovery Tax Act of 1981, Congress relaxed the normal IRS rules to permit *safe harbor leases*, which had virtually no IRS restrictions and which were explicitly designed to permit the transfer of the tax benefits under the 1981 Act from low profit companies which could not use them to high profit companies which could. The point of safe harbor leases was to provide incentives for capital investment to companies which had little or no tax liability—companies with a low tax liability could sell the benefit to companies in a high marginal tax bracket. In 1981 and 1982, literally billions of dollars were paid by such profitable firms as IBM and GE for the tax shelters of such unprofitable ones as Ford and Eastern Airlines. However, in 1983, Congress sharply curtailed the use of safe harbor leases.

ance sheets to report the leased asset as a fixed asset and the present value of the future lease payments as a debt. This process is called *capitalizing the lease*, and its net effect is to cause Firms P and L to have similar balance sheets, both of which will, in essence, resemble the one shown for Firm P.[3]

The logic behind FASB #13 is as follows. If a firm signs a lease contract, its obligation to make lease payments is just as binding as if it had signed a loan agreement—the failure to make lease payments can bankrupt a firm just as fast as the failure to make principal and interest payments on a loan. Therefore, for all intents and purposes, a financial lease is identical to a loan.[4] This being the case, if a firm signs a lease agreement, this has the effect of raising its true debt ratio, and its true capital structure is changed. Therefore, if the firm had previously established a target capital structure, and if there is no reason to think that the optimal capital structure has changed, then using lease financing requires additional equity support in exactly the same manner as does debt financing.

If disclosure of the lease in our Table 17-1 example were not made, then Firm L's investors could be deceived into thinking that its financial position is stronger than it really is. Thus, even before FASB #13 was issued in 1976, firms were required to disclose the existence of long-term leases in footnotes to their financial statements. At that time, it was debated as to whether or not investors recognized fully the impact of leases and, in effect, would see that Firms P and L were in essentially the same financial position. Some people argued that leases were not fully recognized, even by sophisticated investors. If this were the case, then leasing could alter the capital structure decision in a really significant manner—a firm could increase its true leverage through a lease arrangement, and this procedure would have a smaller effect on its cost of conventional debt, k_d, and on its cost of equity, k_s, than if it had borrowed directly. These benefits of leasing would accrue to existing investors at the expense of new investors who would, in effect, be deceived by the fact that the firm's balance sheet did not reflect its true liability situation.

---

[3]FASB #13, ''Accounting for Leases,'' November 1976, spells out in detail the conditions under which the lease must be capitalized and the procedures for capitalizing it.

[4]There are, however, certain legal differences between loans and leases. In the event of liquidation in bankruptcy, a lessor is entitled to take possession of the leased asset, and if the value of the asset is less than the required payments under the lease, the lessor can enter a claim (as a general creditor) for one year's lease payments. In a reorganization, the lessor receives the asset plus three years' lease payments if needed to cover the value of the lease. The lender under a secured loan arrangement has a security interest in the asset, meaning that if it is sold, the lender will be given the proceeds, and the full unsatisfied portion of the lender's claim will be treated as a general creditor obligation. (See Chapter 25.) It is not possible to state, as a general rule, whether a supplier of capital is in a stronger position as a secured creditor or as a lessor. Usually, one position is regarded as being about as good as the other at the time the financial arrangements are being made.

The question of whether investors were truly deceived was debated but never resolved. Those who believed strongly in efficient markets thought that investors were not deceived and that footnotes were sufficient, while those who questioned market efficiency thought that leases should be capitalized. FASB #13 represents a compromise between these two positions, though one that is tilted heavily toward those who favor capitalization.

A lease is classified as a capital lease, and hence is capitalized and shown directly on the balance sheet, if one or more of the following conditions exist:

1. Under the terms of the lease, ownership of the property is effectively transferred from the lessor to the lessee.

2. The lessee can purchase the property at less than its true market value when the lease expires.

3. The lease runs for a period equal to or greater than 75 percent of the asset's life. Thus, if an asset has a 10-year life and the lease is written for 8 years, the lease must be capitalized.

4. The present value of the lease payments is equal to or greater than 90 percent of the initial value of the asset, less any tax credit taken by the lessor.[5]

These rules, together with strong footnote disclosure rules for operating leases, are sufficient to insure that no one will be fooled by lease financing; thus, leases will be regarded as debt, and they will have the same effects as debt on k_d and k_s. Therefore, leasing is not likely to permit a firm to use more financial leverage than could be obtained with conventional debt.

Evaluation by the Lessee

Leases are evaluated by both the lessee and the lessor. The lessee must determine whether leasing an asset is less costly than buying the asset, and the lessor must decide what the lease payments must be to produce a target rate of return. This section focuses on the analysis by the lessee.

In the typical case, the events leading to a lease arrangement follow the sequence described below. We should note that a great deal of uncertainty exists regarding the theoretically correct way to evaluate lease versus purchase decisions, and some very complex decision models

---

[5]The discount rate used to calculate the present value of the lease payments must be the lower of (1) the rate used by the lessor to establish the lease payments (this rate is discussed later in the chapter) or (2) the rate of interest which the lessee would have to pay for new debt with a maturity equal to that of the lease.

have been developed to aid in the analysis. However, the simple analysis given here leads to the correct decision in all the cases we have ever encountered.

1. The firm decides to acquire a particular building or piece of equipment; this decision is based on regular capital budgeting procedures. The decision to acquire the machine is not at issue in the typical lease analysis—this decision was made previously as part of the capital budgeting process. In a lease analysis, we are concerned simply with whether to obtain the use of the machine by lease or by purchase. However, if the effective cost of the lease is substantially lower than the cost of debt—and, as explained later in this chapter, this could occur for several reasons, including the situation where the lessor is able to utilize the investment tax credit but the lessee is not—then the cost of capital used in capital budgeting would have to be recalculated, and perhaps projects formerly deemed unacceptable might become acceptable. We discuss a procedure for this reevaluation later in the chapter.

2. Once the firm has decided to acquire the asset, the next question is how to finance its acquisition. Well-run businesses do not have excess cash lying around, so new assets must be financed in some manner.

3. Funds to purchase the asset could be obtained by borrowing, by retaining earnings, or by selling new equity. Alternatively, the asset could be leased. Because of the capitalization/disclosure provision for leases, we assume that a lease would have the same capital structure effect as a loan.

As indicated earlier, a lease is comparable to a loan in the sense that the firm is required to make a specified series of payments and that a failure to meet these payments will result in bankruptcy. Thus, the most appropriate comparison is the cost of lease financing versus the cost of debt financing.[6] The lease versus borrow-and-purchase analysis is illustrated with data on the Porter Electronics Company. The following conditions are assumed:

1. Porter plans to acquire equipment with a cost of $11,111,111, delivered and installed.

2. An investment tax credit of $1,111,111, which is 10 percent, applies. Thus, the net financing required if Porter borrows and buys is $10 million.

---

[6]Note that the analysis should compare the cost of leasing to the cost of debt financing *regardless* of how the asset is actually financed. The asset may be purchased with available cash if not leased, but since leasing is a substitute for debt financing, the appropriate comparison would still be to debt financing.

3. Porter can borrow the required $10 million on a 10 percent loan to be amortized over 5 years. Therefore, the loan will call for payments of $2,637,965.60 per year, calculated as follows:

$$\text{Payment} = \frac{\$10,000,000}{\text{PVIFA}_{(10\%, 5 \text{ years})}} = \frac{\$10,000,000}{3.7908} = \$2,637,965.60.$$

4. The equipment will definitely be used for 5 years, at which time its estimated net salvage value is $715,000. If the operation is profitable, Porter will continue to use the equipment. If not, the equipment will be sold, netting $715,000 after taxes.

5. Porter can lease the equipment for 5 years at a rental charge of $2,791,670 per year, but the lessor will own it upon the expiration of the lease. (The lease payment schedule is established by the potential lessor, as described in the next major section, and Porter can accept it, reject it, or negotiate.) Porter plans to continue to use the equipment after the lease has expired, so a purchase arrangement will have to be negotiated with the lessor. We assume that Porter will have the option to buy the equipment at its estimated net salvage value, $715,000.

6. The lease contract stipulates that the lessor will maintain the equipment. However, if Porter borrows and buys, it will have to bear the cost of maintenance, which will be performed by the equipment manufacturer at a fixed contract rate of $500,000 per year, payable at year-end.

7. The equipment falls in the ACRS 5-year class life, and for this analysis, we assume that Porter's effective tax rate is 40 percent. Also, note that the depreciable basis is the original cost less one-half of the ITC, or $11,111,111 - \$555,556 = \$10,555,555$.

NPV Analysis

Table 17-2 shows the steps involved in an NPV analysis. Columns 2 through 10 are devoted to the costs of borrowing and buying. Within this set, Columns 2 through 5 give the loan amortization schedule; Column 6 shows the maintenance expense; and Column 7 gives depreciation charges. Tax-deductible expenses—interest, maintenance, and depreciation—are summed and shown in Column 8, while Column 9 gives the taxes saved due to these deductions. Column 10 summarizes the preceding columns, giving the annual net cash outflows that Porter will incur if it borrows and buys the equipment.

The lease payments are $2,791,670 per year; this rate, which includes maintenance, was established by the prospective lessor and offered to Porter Electronics. If Porter accepts the lease, the full $2,791,670 will be a deductible expense, so the after-tax cost of the lease is calculated as follows:

Table 17-2
Porter Electronics Company: NPV Analysis
(Thousands of Dollars)

Year (1)	Loan Amortization Schedule				Applicable to Net Cost of Owning					Lease Cost after Tax: (Lease Cost) × (1 − 0.4) (11)	PVIFs for 6% (12)	Comparative Costs	
	Total Payment (2)	Interest (3)	Principal (4)	Remaining Balance (5)	Maintenance Cost (6)	Depreciation (7)	Tax Deductible Expenses: (3)+(6)+(7) (8)	Tax Savings: 0.4 × (8) (9)	Cash Outflow If Owned: (2)+(6)−(9) (10)			PV Cost of Owning: (10)×(12) (13)	PV Cost of Leasing: (11)×(12) (14)
1	$ 2,638	$1,000	$ 1,638	$8,362	$500	$ 1,583	$3,083	$1,233	$1,905	$1,675	0.9434	$1,797	$1,580
2	2,638	836	1,802	6,560	500	2,322	3,658	1,463	1,675	1,675	0.8900	1,491	1,491
3	2,638	656	1,982	4,578	500	2,217	3,373	1,349	1,789	1,675	0.8396	1,502	1,406
4	2,638	458	2,180	2,398	500	2,217	3,175	1,270	1,868	1,675	0.7921	1,480	1,327
5	2,638	240	2,398	0	500	2,217	2,957	1,183	1,955	1,675	0.7473	1,461	1,252
5										715	0.7473		534
	$13,190	$3,190	$10,000			$10,556						$7,731	$7,590

Net advantage to leasing (NAL) = $7,731 − $7,590 = $141

Notes:

a. Two lines are shown for Year 5 in order to account for the net salvage value, $715,000.

b. The net advantage to leasing could be calculated by subtracting Column 11 from Column 10, and then discounting these differences. This procedure is more efficient, and hence preferable in actual practice if hand calculations are used, but the procedure described here is better for explanatory purposes.

c. Leases often involve payments at the *beginning* of the period rather than at the end. Also, a "down payment" may be required under either the lease or the loan. In either event, it would be necessary to set up a "0" year to show payments made at Time 0. Also, if payments were to be made monthly, quarterly, or semiannually, the table would have to show more rows.

d. For a sale-and-leaseback analysis of existing property, the situation often involves such items as capital gains taxes paid when the property is sold, the use of some of the sales proceeds to pay off an existing mortgage, the payment of a finder's fee, and the like. In such cases, one or more "t = 0" rows must be added to the table, and the after-tax consequences of these t = 0 cash flows must be reported, as appropriate, in Column 10 or 11.

e. In practice a lease analysis such as this would probably be done using an electronic spreadsheet such as *Lotus 1-2-3*. Then, rather than use PVIFs, we would insert the function $1/(1.06)^t$ in Column 12.

After-tax cost = Lease payment − Tax savings
             = Lease payment − (Tax rate)(Lease payment)
             = Lease payment(1 − Tax rate)
             = $2,791,670(1 − 0.4)
             = $1,675,002.

This amount is shown in Column 11, Years 1 through 5.

Notice that the last entry in Column 11, $715,000 shown under Year 5, represents the $715,000 expected Year 5 purchase price. We include this amount as a cost of leasing because Porter Electronics will almost certainly want to continue the operation and thus will be forced to purchase the equipment from the lessor. If we had assumed that the operation would not be continued, then no entry would appear in Column 11, but we would then put the $715,000 into Column 10 as an inflow because, if the asset were purchased originally, then it would be sold after 5 years. It would have a minus sign in Column 10 because it would then be an inflow in an outflow column.

The next step is to compare the net cost of owning with the net cost of leasing. However, we must first put the annual cash flows of leasing and borrowing on a common basis. This requires converting them to present values, which brings up the question of the proper rate at which to discount the costs. In Chapter 6, we saw that the riskier the cash flow, the higher will be the discount rate used to find present values. This same principle was observed in our discussion of capital budgeting, and it also applies in lease analysis. Just how risky are the cash flows under consideration here? Most of them are relatively certain, at least when compared with the types of cash flow estimates that were developed in capital budgeting. For example, the loan payment schedule is set by contract, as is the lease payment schedule. The depreciation expenses are also established by law and not subject to change, and the $500,000 annual maintenance cost is fixed by contract as well. The tax savings are somewhat uncertain, but they will be as projected so long as Porter's effective tax rate remains at 40 percent. The residual value is the least certain of the cash flows, but even here, Porter's management is fairly confident that it will want to acquire the property, and that the estimated salvage value distribution is relatively tight.

Since the cash flows under the lease and under the borrow-and-purchase alternatives are both relatively certain, they should be discounted at a relatively low rate. Most analysts recommend that the company's cost of debt be used, and this rate seems reasonable in our example. Further, since all the cash flows are on an after-tax basis, *the after-tax cost of debt, which is 6 percent, should be used*. Accordingly, we multiply the cash outflows in Columns 10 and 11 by the 6 percent PVIFs given in Column 12. The resulting present values are shown in Columns 13 and 14; the sums of these columns are the present values of the costs of owning and leasing. The financing method that produces the smaller present value of costs is the one that should be selected. The example shown in Table 17-2 indicates that leasing has a net advantage over buy-ing: The present value of the costs of leasing is $141,000 less than that of buying. In this instance, it is to Porter Electronics' advantage to lease.[7]

IRR Analysis

Porter's lease versus purchase decision could also be analyzed using an IRR approach. Here we know the after-tax cost of debt, 6 percent, and we now find the *equivalent debt cost* implied in the lease contract. In other words, signing a lease is similar to signing a loan contract, and there is an equivalent loan cost rate embodied in the lease contract. If the equiv-alent after-tax loan rate in the lease is less than the after-tax cost of debt, then there is an advantage to leasing.

Table 17-3 sets forth the cash flows needed to determine the equiva-lent loan cost. Here is an explanation of the table:

1. The net cost to purchase the asset, which is avoided if Porter leases, is shown as a cash inflow at Year 0 (the +$10,000,000 in Column 5). This is equivalent to the amount borrowed in a standard loan analysis.

---

[7]The more complicated methods which exist for analyzing leasing generally focus on the issue of what discount rate should be used to discount the cash flows. Conceptually, we could assign a separate discount rate to each individual cash flow component (the columns in Table 17-2), then find the present values of each of the cash flow components, and finally sum these present values to determine the net advantage or disadvantage of leas-ing. This approach has been taken by Stewart C. Myers, David A. Dill, and Alberto J. Bautista (MDB) in "Valuation of Financial Lease Contracts," *Journal of Finance*, June 1976, 799-819, among others. MDB correctly note that procedures like the one presented in this chapter are valid only if (1) leases and loans are viewed by investors as being equivalent and (2) all cash flows are equally risky, and hence appropriately discounted at the same rate. The first assumption is valid today for virtually all financial leases, and even where it is not, no one knows how to adjust properly for any capital structure effects that leases might have. (MDB, and others, have presented an adjustment formula, but it is based on the assumption that the Modigliani-Miller leverage argument, with no bankruptcy costs, is correct. Since even MM do not regard the pure MM model as being correct, the MDB formula cannot be correct.) Regarding the second assumption, it is generally believed that all of the cash flows in Table 17-2 except the salvage value are of about the same degree of risk, at least to the extent that we are able to evaluate risk. Therefore, the procedures used in Table 17-2 normally meet the MDB assumption; hence, the Table 17-2 analysis is usually correct.

Regarding the application of the discount rate to the salvage value, advocates of multiple discount rates often point out that the salvage value is more uncertain than are the other cash flows and thus recommend discounting it at a higher rate. This would have the effect, in Table 17-2, of lowering the present value of the cost of leasing, thereby making the lease appear even more favorable. However, corporate managers would argue that this conclusion is incorrect. (And we agree; see Chapter 10.) The $715,000 net salvage value is an estimate—it could be higher or lower, and the greater the uncertainty about its actual level, the greater the risk to which Porter's future profits are subject. Thus, if the analysis is to reflect properly the riskiness of the salvage value, one could argue that the greater the variability about the future salvage value, the *lower* is the discount rate that should be used to evaluate it! This problem is confused still further because, in a CAPM sense, all cash flows could be equally risky even though individual items such as the salvage value might have more or less total variability than others.

For all these reasons, most analysts use only one discount rate—the after-tax cost of debt—to evaluate the cash flows in a lease analysis.

Table 17-3
Porter Electronics Company: IRR Analysis
(Thousands of Dollars)

Year (1)	After-Tax Lease Payment (2)	Depreciation Tax Saving (3)	Maintenance Cost after Taxes (4)	Net Cash Flow: Purchase Price or (2) + (3) + (4) (5)
0				$10,000
1	($1,675)	($633)	$300	(2,008)
2	(1,675)	(929)	300	(2,304)
3	(1,675)	(887)	300	(2,262)
4	(1,675)	(887)	300	(2,262)
5	(1,675)	(887)	300	(2,262)
5	(715)			(715)

IRR = 5.5%.

2. Next, we must determine what Porter must give up (or "pay back") if it leases. As we saw in the last section, Porter must make annual lease payments of $2,791,670, which amount to $1,675,002 on an after-tax basis. These amounts are reported in Column 2, Years 1-5.

3. Since Porter plans to continue using the equipment, it will have to buy the asset at the expiration of the lease. This cost is shown at the bottom of Column 2, in Year 5.

4. Note also that if Porter elects to lease, it will have to give up the right to depreciate the asset. The after-tax values of the depreciation tax shelters, which represent an opportunity cost of leasing, are shown in Column 3, Years 1-5.

5. If Porter leases rather than borrows and buys the equipment, it will avoid the maintenance cost of $500 per year, or $300 after taxes. This is shown in Column 4 as a benefit of leasing.

6. Column 5 shows the annual net cash flows. For Years 1-5, Column 5 is the sum of Columns 2-4.

Given the cash flows in Column 5, we can find the IRR for the stream; it is 5.5 percent, and that is the equivalent loan cost implied in the lease contract. If Porter leases, it is using up some of its debt capacity, and the implied cost rate is 5.5 percent. Since this cost rate is less than the 6 percent cost of a straight loan, this IRR lease analysis confirms the NPV analysis; Porter should lease rather than buy the equipment. If the analysis is done correctly, the NPV and IRR approaches will always lead to the same decision. Thus, one method is as good as the other from a decision standpoint. However, the NPV approach is more straightforward, hence most people find it easier to follow and to explain to decision makers. On the other hand, the IRR approach is useful in situations where the financing method might influence the decision to acquire the asset in the first place. This last point is explored in the next section.

Feedback Effect on Capital Budgeting

Up to now, we have assumed that Porter Electronics had already made the decision to acquire the new equipment. Thus, the lease analysis was conducted only to determine whether the equipment should be leased or purchased. But, as we stated earlier, if the cost of leasing is less than the cost of debt, it is possible for projects formerly deemed unacceptable to become acceptable.

To illustrate this point, assume that Porter's target capital structure is 50 percent debt and 50 percent common equity, that Porter's cost of debt, k_d, is 10 percent, and its cost of equity, k_e, is 15 percent. Thus, Porter's weighted average cost of capital is

$$k_a = 0.5(10\%)(0.6) + 0.5(15\%) = 10.5\%.$$

Further, assume that Porter's initial capital budgeting analysis on this equipment, using a 10.5 percent project cost of capital, resulted in an NPV of $-\$50,000$. As we saw in the preceding section, the after-tax cost of leasing for this project is 5.5 percent, compared with Porter's after-tax cost of debt of 6 percent. Thus, this project can be financed at a lower cost than other projects which involve equipment that cannot be leased.

This project would be entirely financed by leasing, but since leasing is a substitute for debt, other projects would have to be financed by a higher percentage of equity if Porter is to maintain its target capital structure. Thus, we must allocate an equity financing component to this project even though it will be entirely lease financed. Its weighted average cost of capital, considering that the equipment can be leased, is 10.26 percent:

$$k_a = 0.5(5.5\%) + 0.5(15\%) = 10.25\%.$$

Porter's capital budgeting director can now recalculate the project's NPV using a cost of capital of 10.25 percent versus the average project cost of capital, ignoring leasing, of 10.5 percent. Assume that the project's NPV is now $+\$100,000$. The availability of lease financing has made the project acceptable, whereas the project would be unacceptable if lease financing were not available.

Evaluation by the Lessor

Thus far, we have considered leasing from the lessee's viewpoint. It is also useful to analyze the transaction as the lessor sees it: Is the lease a good investment for the party who must put up the money? (The lessor will generally be a specialized leasing company, a bank or a bank affiliate, an individual or group of individuals, or a manufacturer such as

IBM that uses leasing as a sales tool.) The potential lessor obviously needs to know the profitability of the lease, and this information is also useful to the prospective lessee: Lease terms on large leases are generally negotiated, so the lessor and the lessee should know one another's position.

The lessor's analysis involves (1) determining the net cash outlay, which is usually the invoice price of the leased equipment less any investment tax credit and/or any lease payments made in advance; (2) determining the periodic cash inflows, which consist of the lease payments minus both income taxes and the lessor's maintenance expense; (3) estimating the after-tax *residual value* of the property when the lease expires; and (4) determining whether the rate of return on the lease exceeds the lessor's opportunity cost of capital or, equivalently, whether the NPV of the lease exceeds zero.

To illustrate the lessor's analysis, we assume the same facts as for the Porter Electronics lease, as well as this situation: (1) The potential lessor is a wealthy individual whose current income is in the form of interest, and whose marginal federal plus state income tax rate, T, is 60 percent. (2) The investor can buy bonds that have a 10 percent yield to maturity, providing an after-tax yield of $(10\%)(1 - T) = (10\%)(0.4) = 4\%$. This is the after-tax return that the investor will obtain if the lease investment is not made. (3) The bonds that the investor would buy are about as risky as the cash flows expected under the lease. (4) The investor will, under the lease, receive the same investment tax credit as did Porter Electronics, and the same depreciation schedule will also be applicable. (5) The net salvage value to the lessor is $715,000.

NPV Analysis

The lease analysis from the investor's standpoint is developed in Table 17-4. Here we see that the lease as an investment has a net present value of $285,000. On a present value basis, the investor who invests in the lease rather than in the 10 percent bonds is better off by this amount, indicating that the investor should be willing to write the lease. Since we saw earlier that the lease is also advantageous to Porter Electronics, the transaction should be completed.[8]

IRR Analysis

IRR analysis for the lessor is less complicated than IRR analysis for the lessee. The lessor must buy the equipment for a net cost of $10 million at t = 0. In return, the lessor receives the net after-tax cash inflows

---

[8]Another point that should be noted here relates to the investment tax credit. Under current IRS regulations, an individual investor may not take the credit if the lease is written for more than one-half the economic life of the equipment. Also, the tax credit can either be taken by the lessor or be passed back to the lessee. These points are ignored in the example.

Table 17-4
Lease Analysis from the Lessor's Viewpoint
(Thousands of Dollars)

Year (1)	Lease Payment (2)	Maintenance Expense (3)	Depreciation (4)	Taxes: [(2) − (3) − (4)]T (5)	Net Cash Flow: (2) − (3) − (5) (6)	PVIFs for 4% (7)	PV of After-Tax Cash Flows (8)
1	$ 2,792	$ 500	$ 1,583	$425	$ 1,867	0.9615	$ 1,795
2	2,792	500	2,322	(18)	2,310	0.9246	2,136
3	2,792	500	2,217	45	2,247	0.8890	1,998
4	2,792	500	2,217	45	2,247	0.8548	1,921
5	2,792	500	2,217	45	2,247	0.8219	1,847
5					715	0.8219	588
	$13,960	$2,500	$10,556	$542	$11,633		$10,285
							10,000[a]

NPV of the lease investment = $ 285

[a]The investment tax credit is deducted from the equipment purchase price to produce the "cost" of $10,000 shown in Column 8.

presented in Column 6 of Table 17-4. The IRR, r, of the lease is that discount rate which equates the sum of the present values of the cash inflows to the net cost of $10 million:

$$\sum_{t=1}^{5} \frac{NCF_t}{(1 + r)^t} = \$10,000,000.$$

The solution value of r = IRR is 4.9 percent. Thus, the lease has an after-tax return to this 60 percent tax rate investor of 4.9 percent, which exceeds the 4 percent after-tax return on 10 percent bonds. So, using either the IRR or the NPV methods, the lease would appear to be a good investment.

Setting the Lease Payment

Just above, we evaluated the lease from the lessor's standpoint when the lease payment had already been specified. As a general rule, in very large leases such as the one between U.S. Steel and GECC, the parties will sit down and work out an agreement as to the size of the lease payment, with this payment being set so as to provide the lessor with some required rate of return. For smaller leases, the lessor does the analysis, again setting terms which provide a target rate of return, and then offers these terms to the potential lessee on a take-it-or-leave-it basis. Competition among leasing companies forces lessors to build market-related returns into their lease payment schedules. To illustrate all this, suppose the potential lessor described above, after examining all alternative investment opportunities, decides that the 4.9 percent return on the Porter Electronics lease is too low, and that the lease should provide an after-tax rate of return of 6 percent. What lease payment schedule should be set?

To answer this question, recognize that Table 17-4 contains the lessor's cash flow analysis. If we let X be the unknown lease payment, then the net after-tax cash flows in Years 1 through 4 are

$$CF(AT)_{1-4} = X - (3) - [X - (3) - (4)]T,$$

where the numbers in parentheses are column numbers. The cash flow in Year 5 is the same value as in Years 1-4, plus the $715,000 residual value. If the lessor requires an after-tax rate of return of 6 percent on the lease investment, then each cash flow, when discounted back to t = 0 at 6 percent, must sum to $10 million. Thus, we can set up the analysis (in thousands of dollars) as:

$$
\begin{aligned}
\$10,000 = {} & \frac{X - \$500 - (X - \$500 - \$1,583)(0.6)}{(1.06)^1} \\
& + \frac{X - \$500 - (X - \$500 - \$2,322)(0.6)}{(1.06)^2} \\
& + \frac{X - \$500 - (X - \$500 - \$2,217)(0.6)}{(1.06)^3} \\
& + \frac{X - \$500 - (X - \$500 - \$2,217)(0.6)}{(1.06)^4} \\
& + \frac{X - \$500 - (X - \$500 - \$2,217)(0.6) + \$715}{(1.06)^5}.
\end{aligned}
$$

This reduces to

$$
\begin{aligned}
\$10,000 = {} & 0.3774X + \$707.3585 + 0.3560X + \$1,061.9438 \\
& + 0.3358X + \$948.9377 + 0.3168X + \$895.2243 \\
& + 0.2989X + \$1,378.8408.
\end{aligned}
$$

Solving further, we get

$$
\begin{aligned}
\$10,000 &= 1.6849X + \$4,992.3051. \\
\$5,007.6949 &= 1.6849X \\
X &= \$2,972.102.
\end{aligned}
$$

Thus, the lessor must set the lease payment at $2,972,102 to obtain an expected after-tax rate of return of 6.0 percent.

Leveraged Lease Analysis

Historically, only two parties have been involved in lease transactions—the lessor, who puts up the money, and the lessee. In recent years, however, a new type of lease, the *leveraged lease*, has come into widespread use. Under a leveraged lease, the lessor arranges to borrow part of the required funds, generally giving the lenders a first mortgage on the plant or equipment being leased. The lessor still receives the full amount of the investment tax credit and the tax shelter associated with accelerated depreciation. However, the lessor now has a riskier position, because the lessor's position is junior to that of the lenders, who have a first mortgage on the plant or equipment.

Such leveraged leases, often with syndicates of wealthy individuals seeking tax shelters acting as owner-lessors, are an important part of the financial scene today. Incidentally, whether or not a lease is leveraged is not important to the lessee; from the lessee's standpoint, the method of analyzing a proposed lease is unaffected by whether or not the lessor borrows part of the required capital.

The example in Table 17-4 is not set up as a leveraged lease. However, it is easy enough to modify the analysis if the lessor borrows all or part of the required $10 million, making the transaction a leveraged lease. First, we would add a set of columns to Table 17-4 to show the loan amortization schedule. The interest component of this schedule would represent another tax deduction, while the loan repayments would constitute additional cash outlays. The "initial cost" would be reduced by the amount of the loan. With these changes made, a new NPV and IRR could be calculated and used to evaluate whether or not the lease represents a good investment.

To illustrate, assume that the lessor can borrow $8 million of the $10 million net purchase price at a rate of 10 percent on an amortized term loan. Table 17-5 contains the lessor's leveraged lease NPV analysis. The present values of the net after-tax cash flows sum to $2,286,000, but the net cost to the lessor is now only $2 million, since $8 million of the total cost was borrowed. Thus, the NPV of the leveraged lease investment is $286,000, which is approximately the same as the $285,000 NPV for the unleveraged lease, but the lessor has only spent $2 million on this lease. Therefore, the lessor could invest in 5 similar leveraged leases for the same $10 million investment required to finance a single unleveraged lease, producing a total added value of $5 \times \$286,000 = \$1,430,000$.

The effects of leverage on the lessor's return is also reflected in the IRR. The IRR is that discount rate which equates the sum of the present values of the Column 10 cash flows to $2 million. Performing the necessary arithmetic, we find the IRR of the leveraged lease to be 8.2 percent, which is substantially higher than the 4.9 percent after-tax return on the unleveraged lease.

Typically, leveraged leases provide the lessor with higher expected rates of return (IRRs) and higher NPVs per dollar of invested capital than unleveraged leases. However, the riskiness of such leases is also higher for the same reason that any leveraged investment is riskier. Since leveraged leases are a relatively new development, no standard methodology has been developed for analyzing them in a risk/return framework. However, sophisticated lessors are now developing simulations similar to those described in Chapter 10. Then, given the apparent riskiness of the lease investment, the lessor can decide whether the returns built into the contract are sufficient to compensate for the risk involved.

Table 17-5
Leveraged Lease Analysis
(Thousands of Dollars)

	Loan Amortization Schedule										
Year (1)	Total Payment (2)	Interest (3)	Amortization Payment (4)	Remaining Balance (5)	Lease Payment (6)	Maintenance Expense (7)	Depreciation (8)	Taxes: [(6)−(3)−(7)−(8)]T (9)	Net Cash Flow: (6)−(2)−(7)−(9) (10)	PVIFs at 4% (11)	PV of After-tax Cash Flows (12)
1	$ 2,110	$ 800	$1,310	$6,690	$ 2,792	$ 500	$ 1,583	$ 55	$ 237	0.9615	$ 228
2	2,110	669	1,441	5,249	2,792	500	2,322	419	601	0.9246	556
3	2,110	525	1,585	3,664	2,792	500	2,217	270	452	0.8890	402
4	2,110	366	1,744	1,920	2,792	500	2,217	175	357	0.8548	305
5	2,110	192	1,918	0	2,792	500	2,217	70	252	0.8219	207
5									715	0.8219	588
	$10,550	$2,552	$7,998		$13,960	$2,500	$10,556	($989)	$2,614		$2,286

Less cost   2,000

NPV of the leveraged lease investment = $ 286

Other Leasing Issues

The basic methods of analysis for both the lessee and the lessor were presented in the previous sections. However, certain other issues warrant additional discussion.

Estimated Residual Value

It is important to note that the lessor owns the property upon the expiration of a lease. The value of the property at that time is called its *residual value*. Superficially, it would appear that if residual values are expected to be large, owning would have an advantage over leasing. However, this apparent advantage of owning is subject to substantial qualification. If expected residual values are large—as they may be under inflation for certain types of equipment and also if real property is involved—competition between leasing companies and other financial sources, as well as competition among leasing companies themselves, will force leasing rates down to the point where potential residual values are fully recognized in the lease contract rates. Thus, the existence of large residual values on equipment is not likely to result in materially lower costs of owning.

Increased Credit Availability

As noted earlier, leasing is sometimes said to have an advantage for firms that are seeking the maximum degree of financial leverage. First, it is sometimes argued that firms can obtain more money for longer terms under a lease arrangement than under a loan secured by a specific piece of equipment. Second, since some leases do not appear on the balance sheet, lease financing has been said to give the firm a stronger appearance in a *superficial* credit analysis and thus to permit the firm to use more leverage than it could use if it did not lease.

There may be some truth to these claims for smaller firms. However, now that large firms are required to capitalize major leases and to report them on their balance sheets, this point is of questionable validity for any firm large enough to have audited financial statements.

Investment Tax Credit and Depreciation

The investment tax credit can be taken only if the firm's profits and taxes exceed prescribed levels. If a firm is unprofitable, or if it is expanding so rapidly and generating such large tax credits that it cannot use all available tax shelters, then it may be worthwhile for it to enter a lease arrangement. Here the lessor (a bank, a leasing company, or a wealthy individual) will take the credit and give the lessee a corresponding reduction in lease charges. Railroads and airlines have been large users of leasing for this reason in recent years, as have industrial companies faced with particular situations. The U.S. Steel lease described at the beginning of the chapter is an example.

Depreciation has the same type of effect as the investment tax credit. A firm that is suffering losses cannot benefit from the tax deductibility of depreciation as much as a lessor who is in a high marginal tax bracket. Tax considerations—the investment tax credit and accelerated depreciation—are without question the dominant motives behind most financial leases that are written today.

Computer Models

Lease analysis, just like capital budgeting analysis, is particularly well suited for computer analysis. Both the lessee and lessor could create computer models for their analyses. Setting the analysis up on a computer is especially useful when negotiations are underway, and when investment banking houses such as Merrill Lynch are working out a leasing deal between a group of investors and a company, the analysis would always be computerized.

Differing Costs of Capital

If the lessor has a substantially lower after-tax cost of capital than the lessee, analyses such as we performed above will generally show that leasing can be made to be advantageous to both parties. Should the cost of capital to these two parties differ? If we ignore tax effects, the answer depends on the risks borne by each lease participant.

There are, essentially, two different risks inherent in a lease agreement. First, there is the risk associated with the asset's depreciation. If the allowed depreciation expense is less than the actual economic loss of value, the owner's return will turn out to be less than was expected. This risk is borne by the lessor under most lease agreements. Second, there is the risk that the asset will not generate the expected net operating cash flows. This risk is generally borne by the lessor if the lease contract is cancelable, but by the lessee if the contract is not cancelable. Of course, the general credit strength of the lessee is a key factor in noncancelable financial leases—lessors are perfectly willing to provide lease financing to a very strong company, such as IBM, for 100 percent of the purchase price of almost any asset. However, a weaker company would only be able to get lease financing on a fraction of the purchase price of most assets. In such cases, the weak lessee would be required to make payments "up front" in the same way a homeowner has to make a down payment when he or she buys a house.

If the leasing market is competitive, then the lease terms as negotiated between lessee and lessor will reflect the proper allocation of risks. Thus, under equilibrium conditions, the cost to the lessee and the return to the lessor will just compensate for the risks borne by each. Theoretically, from a risk-adjusted perspective, a firm in a competitive, efficient market would be indifferent to the choice between leasing and purchase, if tax effects were not considered.[9]

---

[9]For a more extended discussion, see Merton H. Miller and Charles W. Upton, "Leasing, Buying, and the Cost of Capital Services," *Journal of Finance*, June 1976, 761-786.

WACC Effects   A firm that uses significant amounts of lease financing should incorporate this type of financing into its weighted average cost of capital. Carson Foods' average cost of capital was calculated in Chapter 10 to be 12 percent:

$$k_a = w_d(k_d)(1 - T) + w_p k_p + w_s k_s$$
$$= 0.3(10\%)(1 - 0.40) + 0.1(12\%) + 0.6(15\%)$$
$$= 0.3(6\%) + 0.1(12\%) + 0.6(15\%)$$
$$= 12.0\%.$$

However, if Carson decided to use significant amounts of lease financing, with leases representing one-third of the "debt-plus-leases" value, or 10 percent of total funds, then Carson's average cost of capital should be modified to include lease financing effects. For example, if Carson's after-tax cost of leasing were 5 percent, its cost of capital with lease financing included would fall to 11.9 percent:

$$k_a = 0.1(5\%) + 0.2(6\%) + 0.1(12\%) + 0.6(15\%)$$
$$= 11.9\%.$$

Thus, in this example, Carson's average cost of capital would decline when the lower cost of leasing is included.

Note, though, that the effect of leasing on a firm's weighted average cost of capital depends on the situation. If all fixed assets were suitable for leasing, then leasing's effects should be handled as in the Carson Foods example. However, if some assets would be leased but others would not, then it would be more appropriate to calculate different weighted average costs of capital for the different classes of assets as we did earlier in the chapter.

Summary

This chapter discussed the three major types of leases: (1) *operating leases*, (2) *sale-and-leaseback plans*, and (3) *financial leases for new assets*. Operating leases generally provide both for the financing of an asset and for its maintenance, while both sale-and-leaseback plans and regular financial leases usually provide only financing and are alternatives to debt financing.

Financial leases (and sale-and-leaseback plans) are evaluated by a cash flow analysis. We start with the assumption that an asset will be acquired, and that the acquisition will be financed either by debt or by a lease. Next, we develop the annual net cash outflows associated with each financing plan. Then we discount the two sets of outflows at the company's after-tax cost of debt. Finally, we choose the alternative with the lower present value of costs.

Leasing sometimes represents "off balance sheet" financing, which permits a firm to obtain more financial leverage if it leases than if it uses straight debt. This was formerly cited as a major reason for leasing. Today, however, taxes are the primary reason for the growth of financial leasing. Leasing permits the tax shelters (depreciation expenses and the investment tax credit) to be transferred from the user of an asset to the supplier of capital, and if these parties are in different tax brackets, both can benefit from the lease arrangement.

17-1 Define each of the following terms:
   a. Lessee; lessor
   b. Sale and leaseback; operating lease; financial lease; capital lease; leveraged lease
   c. "Off balance sheet" financing
   d. FASB #13
   e. Residual value
   f. Lease analysis
   g. Investment tax credit

17-2 Distinguish between operating leases and financial leases. Would you be more likely to find an operating lease employed for a fleet of trucks or for a manufacturing plant?

17-3 Would you be more likely to find that lessees are in high or low income tax brackets as compared to lessors?

17-4 Commercial banks moved heavily into equipment leasing during the early 1970s, acting as lessors. One major reason for this invasion of the leasing industry was to gain the benefits of accelerated depreciation and the investment tax credit on lease equipment. During this same period, commercial banks were investing heavily in municipal securities, and they were also making loans to real estate investment trusts (REITs). In the mid 1970s, these REITs got into such serious difficulty that many banks suffered large losses on their REIT loans. Explain how its investments in municipal bonds and REITs could reduce a bank's willingness to act as a lessor.

17-5 One alleged advantage of leasing voiced in the past is that it kept liabilities off the balance sheet, thus making it possible for a firm to obtain more leverage than it otherwise could have. This raised the question of whether or not both the lease obligation and the asset involved should be capitalized and shown on the balance sheet. Discuss the pros and cons of capitalizing leases and related assets.

17-6 Suppose there were no IRS restrictions on what constituted a valid lease. Explain, in a manner that a legislator might understand, why some restrictions should be imposed. Illustrate your answer with numbers.

17-7 What are the advantages and disadvantages of leveraged leases from the standpoint of (a) the lessee, (b) the equity investor in the lease, and (c) the supplier of the debt capital?

17-8 Suppose Congress enacted new tax law changes that would (1) permit equipment to be depreciated over a shorter period, (2) lower corporate tax rates, and (3) increase the investment tax credit. Discuss how each of these potential changes would affect the relative volume of leasing versus conventional debt in the U.S. economy.

Self-Test Problem   ST-1 The Olson Company has decided to acquire a new truck. One alternative is to lease the truck on a 4-year contract for a lease payment of $10,000 per year, with payments to be made at the *beginning* of each year. The lease would include maintenance. Alternatively, Olson could purchase the truck outright for $40,000, financing the purchase by a bank loan for the net purchase price and amortizing the loan over a 4-year period at an interest rate of 10 percent per year. Under the borrow-to-purchase arrangement, Olson would have to maintain the truck at a cost of $1,000 per year, payable at year-end. The truck qualifies for a 6 percent investment tax credit; it falls into the ACRS 3-year class; and it has a salvage value of $10,000, which is the expected market value after 4 years, when Olson plans to replace the truck irrespective of whether it leases or buys. Olson has a tax rate of 40 percent.
   a. What is Olson's PV cost of leasing?
   b. What is Olson's PV cost of owning? Should the truck be leased or purchased?
   c. The appropriate discount rate for use in Olson's analysis is the firm's after-tax cost of debt. Why?
   d. The salvage value is the least certain cash flow in the analysis. How might Olson incorporate differential riskiness on this cash flow into the analysis?
   e. Assume that the lessor is in the 50 percent tax bracket. What is the lessor's IRR?

Problems   17-1 Two electronics companies, Minicorp and Microcorp, began operations with identical balance sheets. A year later, both required additional manufacturing capacity at a cost of $50,000. Minicorp obtained a 5-year, $50,000 loan at an 8 percent interest rate from its bank. Microcorp, on the other hand, decided to lease the required $50,000 capacity from Leasecorp for 5 years; an 8 percent return was built into the lease. The balance sheet for each company, before the asset increases, follows:

		Debt	$ 50,000
		Equity	100,000
Total assets	$150,000	Total claims	$150,000

   a. Show the balance sheets for both firms after the asset increase, and calculate each firm's new debt ratio.
   b. Show how Minicorp's balance sheet would look immediately after the financing if it capitalized the lease.
   c. Would the rate of return (1) on assets and (2) on equity be affected by the choice of financing? How?

   17-2 Silverton Mining Company must install $1 million of new machinery in its Colorado mine. It can obtain a bank loan for 100 percent of the required amount, net of ITC. Alternatively, a Denver investment banking firm which represents a group of investors believes that it can arrange for a lease financing plan. *Assume* that these facts apply:
   (1) The equipment falls in the ACRS 3-year class.

(2) An investment tax credit (ITC) of 6 percent is allowed.

(3) Estimated maintenance expenses are $50,000 per year.

(4) Silverton's tax rate is 20 percent.

(5) If the money is borrowed, the bank loan will be at a rate of 14 percent, amortized in 3 equal installments at the end of each year.

(6) The tentative lease terms call for payments of $320,000 per year for 3 years. However, one-half of the payment for the third year must be made in advance.

(7) The potential lessors are in the 70 percent federal, state, and local tax bracket, and if they do not invest in this project, they will invest in taxable bonds that yield 15 percent.

(8) Under the proposed lease terms, the lessee must pay for insurance, property taxes, and maintenance. Thus, the lease is on a net, net, net basis.

(9) Silverton must use the equipment if it is to continue in business, so it will almost certainly want to acquire the property at the end of the lease. If it does, then under the lease terms, it can purchase the machinery at its fair market value at that time. The best estimate of this market value is the $200,000 salvage value, but it could be much higher or lower under certain circumstances.

To assist management in making the proper lease-versus-buy decision, you are asked to answer the following questions:

a. Assuming that the lease can be arranged, should Silverton lease or borrow and buy the equipment? Explain.

b. Does it appear likely that the investment banker will be able to get the investors to agree to accept the terms of the proposed lease? Explain.

c. Consider the $200,000 estimated salvage value. Is it appropriate to discount it at the same rate as the other cash flows? What about the other cash flows; are they all equally risky?

17-3 As part of its overall plant modernization and cost reduction program, Confederate Mills' management has decided to install a new automated weaving loom. In the capital budgeting analysis of this equipment, the IRR of the project was found to be 29 percent versus a project required return of 14 percent.

The loom has an invoice price of $100,000, including delivery and installation charges. The net financing requirement, if Confederate Mills borrows the funds, would be the purchase price less the applicable investment tax credit of 10 percent. The funds needed could be borrowed from the bank on a 4-year amortized loan at a 15 percent interest rate, with payments to be made at the end of each year. The manufacturer will maintain and service the loom, in the event that it is purchased, for a charge of $8,000 per year paid at the end of each year. The loom falls in the ACRS 5-year class, and Confederate's marginal tax rate is 40 percent.

Brooks Automation, Inc., maker of the loom, has offered to lease the loom to Confederate Mills for $27,100 upon delivery and installation, plus 4 additional annual lease payments of $27,100, with these payments to be made at the end of Years 1 to 4. Note that there are 5 lease payments in total. The lease agreement includes maintenance and servicing. Actually, the loom has an expected life of 8 years, at which time its expected salvage value is zero. However, after 4 years, its market value is expected to equal its book value. Confederate Mills plans to build an entire new plant in 4 years, so it has no interest in either leasing or owning the proposed loom for more than 4 years.

a. Should the loom be leased or purchased?

b. Confederate Mills' managers disagree on the proper discount rate to be used in the analysis. Some argue that the proper discount rate is the firm's cost of capital, adjusted for project risk. What effect would a discount rate change have on the lease versus purchase decision?

c. The salvage value is clearly the most uncertain cash flow in the analysis. What effect would a salvage value risk-adjustment have on the analysis? (Assume that the appropriate salvage value discount rate is 18 percent.)

d. The original analysis assumed that Confederate Mills would not need the loom after 4 years. Now assume that the firm will continue to use the loom after the lease expires. Thus, if it leased, Confederate Mills would have to buy the asset after 4 years at the then existing market value, which is assumed to equal the book value. What effect would this requirement have on the basic analysis?

e. Assume that the lessor, Brooks Automation, Inc., has a marginal tax rate of 50 percent. What is the lessor's expected IRR from the lease?

f. Brooks Automation has an existing loan agreement which would permit it to borrow $60,000 against the lease. This loan would be at 10 percent simple interest, with interest only paid at the end of each year and the principal repaid at the end of the fourth year. What effect does leveraging the lease have on the lessor's expected IRR?

g. Assume that the lessor does *not* borrow against the lease, that is, does not use a leveraged lease. What lease payment must Brooks set to have an expected after-tax IRR of 10 percent?

Solution to Self-Test Problem

ST-1 a. Cost of leasing:

Year	After-Tax Lease Payment	PVIF at 6%	Present Value
0	$6,000	1.0000	$6,000
1	6,000	0.9434	5,660
2	6,000	0.8400	5,340
3	6,000	0.8396	5,038
		PV cost of leasing =	$22,038

b. Cost of owning:

Net purchase price = $40,000 − $2,400 ITC = $37,600.
Depreciable basis = $40,000 − 0.5($2,400) = $38,800.

For the cost of owning, we will use an alternate solution technique, which ignores financing effects:

Year (1)	Net Cost (2)	Depreciation (3)	Depreciation Tax Savings: (3)(T) (4)	After-Tax Maintenance Cost (5)	After-Tax Salvage Value (6)	Net Cash Flow: (2) − (4) + (5) − (6) (7)	PVIF at 6% (8)	Present Value (9)
0	$37,600					$37,600	1.0000	$37,600
1		$ 9,700	$3,880	$600		(3,280)	0.9434	(3,094)
2		14,744	5,898	600		(5,298)	0.8900	(4,715)
3		14,356	5,742	600		(5,142)	0.8396	(4,317)
4		0		600	$6,000	(5,400)	0.7921	(4,277)
						PV cost of owning =		$21,197

Since the present value of the cost of owning is less than the present value of the cost of leasing, the truck should be purchased.

c. Use the cost of debt because most cash flows are fixed by contract and consequently are relatively certain; thus, lease cash flows have about the same risk as the firm's debt. Also, leasing is considered as a substitute for debt. Use an after-tax cost rate because the cash flows are stated net of taxes.

d. Olson could increase the discount rate on the salvage value cash flow. Note that since Olson plans to replace the truck after 4 years, the salvage value is treated as an inflow in the cost of owning analysis. This makes it reasonable to raise the discount rate for analysis purposes. However, had Olson planned to continue using the truck, then we would have had to place the estimated salvage value as an additional Year 4 outflow in the leasing section, but without a tax adjustment. Then, higher risk would have been reflected in a *lower* discount rate. This is all very ad hoc, which is why we prefer to use one discount rate throughout the analysis.

e. Lessor's IRR:

Year (1)	Net Cost (2)	After-Tax Lease Payment (3)	After-Tax Maintenance Cost (4)	Depreciation Tax Savings (5)	Net Salvage Value (6)	Net Cash Flow: − (2) + (3) − (4) + (5) + (6) (7)
0	$37,600	$5,000				($32,600)
1		5,000	$500	$4,850		9,350
2		5,000	500	7,372		11,872
3		5,000	500	7,178		11,678
4			500	0	$5,000	4,500

Now the lessor's IRR is the IRR of the Column 7 cash flows, or 6.23 percent.

Selected Additional References and Cases

For a description of lease analysis in practice, as well as a comprehensive bibliography of the leasing literature, see

O'Brien, Thomas J., and Bennie H. Nunnally, Jr., "A 1982 Survey of Corporate Leasing Analysis," *Financial Management*, Summer 1983, 30-36.

Many of the theoretical issues surrounding lease analysis are discussed in the following articles:

Levy, Haim, and Marshall Sarnat, "Leasing, Borrowing, and Financial Risk," *Financial Management*, Winter 1979, 47-54.

Lewellen, Wilbur G., Michael S. Long, and John J. McConnell, "Asset Leasing in Competitive Capital Markets," *Journal of Finance*, June 1976, 787-798.

Miller, Merton H., and Charles W. Upton, "Leasing, Buying, and the Cost of Capital Services," *Journal of Finance*, June 1976, 761-786.

Leveraged lease analysis is discussed in these articles:

Athanasopoulos, Peter J., and Peter W. Bacon, "The Evaluation of Leveraged Leases," *Financial Management*, Spring 1980, 76-80.

Dyl, Edward A., and Stanley A. Martin, Jr., "Setting Terms for Leveraged Leases," *Financial Management*, Winter 1977, 20-27.

Grimlund, Richard A., and Robert Capettini, "A Note on the Evaluation of Leveraged Leases and Other Investments," *Financial Management*, Summer 1982, 68-72.

Perg, Wayne F., "Leveraged Leasing: The Problem of Changing Leverage," *Financial Management*, Autumn 1978, 47-51.

The Option Pricing Model (OPM) has recently been used in lease analysis by

Copeland, Thomas E., and J. Fred Weston, "A Note on the Evaluation of Cancellable Operating Leases," *Financial Management*, Summer 1982, 60-67.

Lee, Wayne J., John D. Martin, and Andrew J. Senchack, "The Case for Using Options to Evaluate Salvage Values in Financial Leases," *Financial Management*, Autumn 1982, 33-41.

The Brigham-Crum casebook contains two cases which deal with lease analysis:

Case 23, "Franklin Foto Finishing," which illustrates the standard lease versus purchase decision.

Case 24, "Pringle, Inc.," which focuses on the analysis of sale and leaseback versus conventional mortgage financing.

Working Capital Management

VI

Working Capital Policy and Short-Term Credit

18

In the late 1970s, Transamerica Corporation, a major financial services company, was financing a significant portion of its total assets with short-term debt. Up until that time, short-term rates had generally been less than long-term rates, and thus Transamerica had reduced its interest expense by following this financing policy. However, in the early 1980s short-term interest rates soared to unprecedented levels, and Transamerica's interest costs rose equally sharply, causing a near-disastrous drop in profits. Transamerica's chairman later described the situation as follows:

> "In the past two years we have reduced our variable-rate (short-term) debt by about $450 million. We aren't going to go through the enormous increase in debt expense again. The company's earnings fell sharply when money rates rose to record levels since we were almost entirely in variable-rate debt. Now, out of total debt of slightly more than $1 billion, about 65 percent is fixed rate and 35 percent variable. We've come a long way, and we'll keep plugging away at it."

Transamerica's earnings and stock price were hurt by the rise in interest rates, but other companies were even less fortunate—they simply could not pay the rising interest charges, and this forced them into bankruptcy.

Working capital policy involves decisions relating to current assets, including decisions about financing them. Since about 40 percent of the typical firm's capital is invested in current assets, working capital policy is vitally important to the firm and its shareholders.

Working Capital Terminology

It is useful to begin our discussion of working capital by introducing some basic definitions and concepts:

1. *Working capital*, sometimes called *gross working capital*, simply refers to current assets.[1]

2. *Net working capital* is defined as current assets minus current liabilities.

3. One key working capital ratio is the *current ratio*, which is computed by dividing current assets by current liabilities. This ratio measures a firm's liquidity, that is, its ability to meet current obligations.

4. The *quick ratio*, or *acid test*, which also measures liquidity, is current assets less inventories, divided by current liabilities. The quick ratio removes inventories from current assets because they are the least liquid of current assets. It is thus an "acid test" of a company's ability to meet its current obligations.

5. *Working capital policy* refers to basic policy decisions regarding (1) target levels for each category of current assets and (2) how current assets will be financed.

6. *Working capital management* involves the administration, within the policy guidelines, of current assets and current liabilities.

Net working capital of Pferree between assets - liabilities.

We must be careful to distinguish between those current liabilities which are specifically used to finance current assets and those current liabilities which (1) simply represent current maturities of long-term debt or (2) represent financing associated with a construction program which will, after the project is completed, be funded with the proceeds of a long-term security issue.

Table 18-1 contains the balance sheet of Drexel Card Company (DCC), a manufacturer of greeting cards. Note that, according to the definitions above, DCC's working capital is $200,000, while its net working capital is $200,000 − $150,000 = $50,000. Also, DCC's current ratio is 1.33, while its quick ratio is 0.67. However, the total current liabilities of $150,000 includes the current portion of long-term debt, which is $40,000. This account is unaffected by changes in working capital policy, since it is a function of the firm's long-term financing decisions. Thus, even though we define the long-term debt coming due in the next accounting period as a current liability, it is not a working capital decision variable. Similarly, if DCC were building a new factory and financing this construction with short-term loans which were to be converted to a mortgage bond when the building was completed, the construction

---

[1]The term *working capital* originated with the old Yankee peddler, who would load up his wagon with goods, and then go off on his route to peddle his wares. The merchandise was defined as his "working capital" because it was what he actually sold, or "turned over," to produce his profits. The wagon and horse were his "fixed assets." He owned the horse and wagon—they were financed by "equity." He borrowed the money to buy the merchandise from a bank—this was a "short-term working capital loan."

Table 18-1
Drexel Card Company: Balance Sheet
as of December 31, 1984
(Thousands of Dollars)

Cash	$ 20	Accounts payable	$ 30[a]
Accounts receivable	80	Accrued wages	15
Inventories	100	Accrued taxes	15
		Notes payable	50
		Current portion of long-term debt	40
Current assets	$200	Current liabilities	$150
Fixed assets	500	Long-term debt	150
		Stockholders equity	400
Total assets	$700	Total claims	$700

[a]DCC takes discounts, so this is "free" trade credit. This point is discussed in detail later in the chapter, but accounts payable are free to a firm which takes discounts, because the firm gets credit and pays no interest on this credit.

---

loans would be segregated out with regard to working capital management.

Table 18-1, presented above, shows the balance sheet of Drexel Card Company (DCC) as of December 31, 1984. The manufacture of greeting cards is a seasonal business. In June of each year, DCC begins producing Christmas cards for sale in the July-November period, and by December 31, it has sold most of its Christmas and New Year cards, so its inventories are relatively low. However, most of its buyers purchase on credit, so the year-end receivables are at a seasonal high. Now look at Table 18-2, which shows DCC's projected balance sheet for June 30, 1985. Here we see that DCC's inventories will be relatively high

The Requirement for External Working Capital Financing

Table 18-2
Drexel Card Company: Projected Balance Sheet
for June 30, 1985
(Thousands of Dollars)

Cash	$ 20	Accounts payable	$ 50
Accounts receivable	20	Accrued wages	10
Inventories	200	Accrued taxes	10
		Notes payable	80[a]
		Current portion of long-term debt	40
Current assets	$240	Current liabilities	$190
Fixed assets	500	Long-term debt	140
		Shareholders equity	410
Total assets	$740	Total claims	$740

($200,000 versus $100,000 the previous December), as will accounts payable ($50,000 versus $30,000), but receivables are projected to be relatively low ($20,000 versus $80,000).

Now consider what happens to DCC's current assets and current liabilities over the period from December 1984 to June 1985. Current assets increase from $200,000 to $240,000, so the firm must finance this $40,000 projected increase—increases on the left side of the balance sheet must be financed by increases on the right-hand side. However, at the same time, the higher volume of purchases and labor expenditures associated with increased production to build inventories will cause payables and accruals to *spontaneously* increase, on net, by $10,000: from $30,000 + $15,000 + $15,000 = $60,000 to $50,000 + $10,000 + $10,000 = $70,000. This leaves a $30,000 projected working capital financing requirement, which we assume will be obtained from the bank as a short-term loan. Therefore, on June 30, 1985, we show notes payable of $80,000, up from $50,000 on December 31, 1984.

These fluctuations for DCC resulted from seasonal factors. Similar fluctuations in working capital requirements, and hence in financing needs, can occur over business cycles—typically, financing needs contract during recessions and expand during booms. In the next two sections, we examine (1) the working capital cash flow cycle and (2) alternative strategies for establishing the level of current assets and the sources of funds to finance these assets.

The Working Capital Cash Flow Cycle

The *working capital cash flow cycle* is an important part of working capital management. This cycle can be described for a typical manufacturing firm as follows: (1) The firm orders and then receives the raw materials which it requires to produce the goods it sells; since firms usually purchase their raw materials on credit, this transaction creates an account payable. (2) Labor is used to convert the raw materials into finished goods; to the extent that wages are not fully paid at the time the work is done, accrued wages build up. (3) The finished goods are sold, usually on credit, which creates receivables; no cash has been received yet. (4) At some point during the cycle, the payables and accruals must be paid; usually, these cash payments must be made before the receivables have been collected, so a net cash drain occurs and must be financed. (5) Finally, the working capital cash flow cycle is completed when the firms' receivables are collected; at this point, the firm is ready to repeat the cycle and/or to pay off the loans that were used to finance the cycle.

Verlyn Richards and Eugene Laughlin developed a useful approach to analyzing the working capital cash cycle.[2] Their approach centers on the

---

[2]See Verlyn D. Richards and Eugene J. Laughlin, "A Cash Conversion Cycle Approach to Liquidity Analysis," *Financial Management*, Spring 1980, 32-38.

conversion of operating events to cash flows, and it is thus called the *cash conversion cycle model*. Here are some terms used in the model:

1. *Inventory conversion period* is the length of time required to convert raw materials into finished goods, and to sell these goods, that is, the length of the production/sales period.

2. *Receivables conversion period* is the length of time required to convert the firm's receivables into cash, that is, the time from a sale to the collection of cash from the sale.

3. *Payables deferral period* is the length of time between the purchase of raw materials and the cash payment for those materials.

4. *Cash conversion cycle* is the length of time between actual cash expenditures on productive resources (raw materials and labor) and actual cash receipts from product sales, that is, the day the receivables are collected.

Now we can use these definitions to analyze the cash conversion cycle. The concept is diagrammed in Figure 18-1. Each component is given a number, and the cash conversion cycle can be expressed by this equation:

$$\underset{(1)}{\begin{array}{c}\text{Inventory}\\\text{conversion}\\\text{period}\end{array}} + \underset{(2)}{\begin{array}{c}\text{Receivables}\\\text{conversion}\\\text{period}\end{array}} - \underset{(3)}{\begin{array}{c}\text{Payables}\\\text{deferral}\\\text{period}\end{array}} = \underset{(4)}{\begin{array}{c}\text{Cash}\\\text{conversion}\\\text{cycle}\end{array}}$$

The firm's goal should be to shorten the cash conversion cycle as much as possible, without hurting operations. This would improve profits, because the longer the cash conversion cycle, the greater the need for external financing, and such financing has a cost to the firm.

The cash conversion cycle can be shortened (1) by reducing the inventory conversion period, (2) by reducing the receivables conversion period, or (3) by lengthening the payables deferral period. To the extent

---

Figure 18-1
The Cash Conversion Cycle

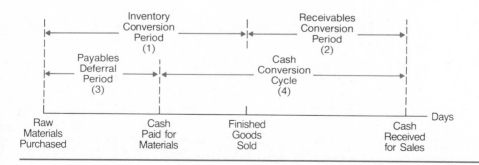

that these actions can be taken *without increasing costs or depressing sales*, they should be done. In fact, as long as the marginal cost increases associated with shortening the cycle are less than the costs of external financing, such costs should be incurred. The cash conversion cycle model is useful in working capital management because it helps managers focus on the determinants of working capital cash flows and various ways to improve them.

Working Capital Investment and Financing Policies

Working capital policy involves two basic questions: (1) What is the appropriate level of current assets, both in total and by specific accounts? (2) How should this level of current assets be financed?

Alternative Current Asset Investment Policies

Figure 18-2 depicts three alternative policies regarding the level of current assets. Essentially, these policies differ in that different amounts of working capital are carried to support a given level of sales. The line with the steepest slope represents a conservative policy. Here, relatively large amounts of cash, marketable securities, and inventories are carried, and sales are stimulated by the use of a credit policy that provides liberal financing to customers and a corresponding high level of receivables. Conversely, with the aggressive policy, the holdings of cash, securities, inventories, and receivables are minimized. The moderate policy is between the two extremes.

Under conditions of certainty—when sales, costs, lead times, payment periods, and so on, are known for sure—all firms would hold the minimum level of current assets. Any larger amounts would increase the need for external funding without a corresponding increase in profits, while any smaller holdings would involve late payments to labor and suppliers, lost sales and production inefficiencies because of inventory shortages, and lost sales due to an overly restrictive credit policy.

However, the picture changes when uncertainty is introduced. Here the firm requires some minimum amount of cash and inventories based on expected payments, expected sales, expected order lead times, and so on, plus additional amounts, or *safety stocks*, which enable it to deal with ex post departures from the expected values. Similarly, accounts receivable are based on credit terms, and the tougher the credit terms, the lower the receivables for any given level of sales. With an aggressive working capital policy, the firm would hold minimal levels of safety stocks for cash and inventories, and it would have a tight credit policy even though this meant running the risk of a decline in sales. Generally, an aggressive policy provides not only the highest expected return on investment, but also the greatest risk, while the converse is true under

Figure 18-2
Alternative Current Asset Investment Policies
(Millions of Dollars)

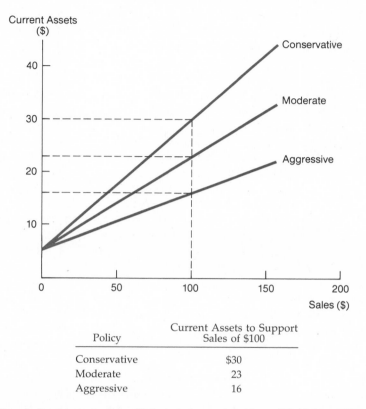

Policy	Current Assets to Support Sales of $100
Conservative	$30
Moderate	23
Aggressive	16

Note: The sales/current assets relationship is shown here as being linear. This is often not the case.

a conservative policy. The moderate policy falls between the two extremes in terms of expected risk and return.

Corporate policy with regard to the level of current assets is never set all by itself—it is always established in conjunction with the firm's working capital financing policy, which we consider next.

Most businesses experience seasonal and/or cyclical fluctuations. For example, construction firms have peaks in the spring and summer, retailers peak around Christmas, and the manufacturers who supply both construction companies and retailers follow similar patterns. Similarly, virtually all businesses must build up working capital when the economy is strong, but they then sell off inventories and have net reductions

Alternative
Financing Policies

of receivables when the economy slacks off. Still, it is apparent that current assets rarely drop to zero, and this realization has led to the development of the idea of *permanent current assets*. These concepts are diagrammed in Figure 18-3. Applying this idea to DCC, Tables 18-1 and 18-2 above suggest that, at this stage in its life, DCC's total assets fluctuate between $700,000 and $740,000. Thus, DCC has $700,000 in permanent assets, composed of $500,000 of fixed assets and $200,000 in permanent current assets, plus *seasonal*, or *temporary*, *current assets* which fluctuate from zero to a maximum of $40,000. The manner in which the permanent and temporary current assets are financed defines the firm's *working capital financing policy*.

Maturity Matching. One policy is to match asset and liability maturities as shown in Panel a of Figure 18-3. This strategy minimizes the risk that the firm will be unable to pay off its maturing obligations. To illustrate, suppose a firm borrows on a 1-year basis and uses the funds obtained to build and equip a plant. Cash flows from the plant (profits plus depreciation) would almost never be sufficient to pay off the loan at the end of only one year, so the loan must be renewed. If for some reason the lender refuses to renew the loan, then the firm has problems. Had the plant been financed with long-term debt, however, the required loan payments would have been better matched with cash flows from profits and depreciation, and the problem of renewal would not have arisen.

At the limit, a firm could attempt to match the maturity structure of its assets and liabilities exactly. Inventory expected to be sold in 30 days could be financed with a 30-day bank loan; a machine expected to last for 5 years could be financed by a 5-year loan; a 20-year building could be financed by a 20-year mortgage bond; and so forth. Actually, of course, uncertainty about the lives of assets prevents this exact maturity matching. For example, a firm may finance inventories with a 30-day loan, expecting to sell the inventories and to use the cash generated to retire the loan. But if sales are slow, the cash will not be forthcoming, and the use of short-term credit may end up causing a problem. Still, if the firm makes an attempt to approximately match asset and liability maturities, we would define this as a moderate working capital financing policy.

Aggressive Approach. Panel b of Figure 18-3 illustrates the situation for an aggressive firm which finances all of its fixed assets with long-term capital but part of its permanent current assets with short-term credit. A look back at Tables 18-1 and 18-2 will show that DCC follows this strategy. Assuming that the $40,000 current portion of long-term debt will be refinanced with new long-term debt, DCC has $500,000 in fixed assets and $590,000 of long-term capital, leaving only $90,000 of long-term capital to finance $200,000 in permanent current assets as shown in Table 18-2. Additionally, DCC has a minimum of $60,000 of "costless" short-term credit consisting of payables and accruals. Thus, DCC uses

Figure 18-3
Alternative Current Asset Financing Policies

a. Moderate Approach (Maturity Matching)

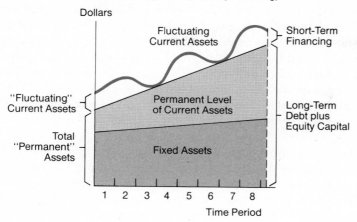

b. Aggressive Approach

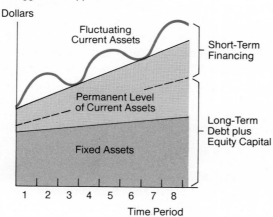

c. Conservative Approach

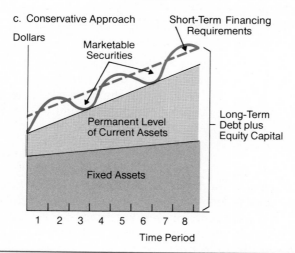

$50,000 of short-term notes payable to help finance its permanent level of current assets.

Returning to Figure 18-3, the dashed line in Panel b could have been drawn *below* the line designating fixed assets, indicating that all of the current assets and part of the fixed assets were financed with short-term credit; this would be a highly aggressive, extremely nonconservative position, and the firm would be very much subject to dangers from rising interest rates as well as to loan renewal problems. However, short-term debt is often cheaper than long-term debt, and some firms are willing to sacrifice safety for the chance of higher profits.

Conservative Approach. As shown in Panel c of Figure 18-3, the dashed line could also be drawn *above* the line designating permanent current assets, indicating that permanent capital is being used to finance all permanent asset requirements and also to meet some or all of the seasonal demands. In the situation depicted in our graph, the firm uses a small amount of short-term credit to meet its peak requirements, but it also meets a part of its seasonal needs by "storing liquidity" in the form of marketable securities during the off-season. The humps above the dashed line represent short-term financing; the troughs below the dashed line represent short-term security holdings. Panel c represents a very safe, conservative working capital financing policy.

Advantages and Disadvantages of Short-Term Credit

The distinction among the three possible financing policies described above was the relative amount of short-term debt financing used under each policy. The aggressive policy called for the greatest amount of short-term debt, while the conservative policy called for the least. Maturity matching fell in between. Although using short-term credit is generally riskier than using long-term credit, short-term credit does have some significant advantages. The pros and cons of financing with short-term credit are considered in this section.

Speed

A short-term loan can be obtained much faster than a long-term loan. Lenders will insist on a more thorough financial examination before granting long-term credit, and the loan agreement will have to be spelled out in considerable detail, because a lot can happen during the life of a 10- to 20-year loan. Therefore, if funds are needed in a hurry, the firm should look to the short-term markets.

Flexibility

If its needs for funds are seasonal or cyclical, a firm may not want to commit itself to long-term debt. In the first place, flotation costs are generally high for long-term debt but trivial for short-term credit. Second, while long-term debt can be repaid early, provided the loan agreement includes a prepayment provision, prepayment penalties can be expensive. Accordingly, if a firm thinks its need for funds will diminish in the near future, it should choose short-term debt for the flexibility it provides. Third, long-term loan agreements always contain provisions, or covenants, which constrain the firm's future actions. Short-term credit agreements are generally much less onerous in this regard.

In Chapter 3, we saw that normally the yield curve is upward sloping, indicating that generally interest rates are lower on short-term than on long-term debt. Thus, under normal conditions, interest expense at the time the funds are obtained will be lower if the firm borrows on a short-term rather than a long-term basis.

Cost of Long-Term versus Short-Term Debt

Even though short-term debt is often less expensive than long-term debt, financing with short-term debt subjects the firm to more risk than does financing with long-term debt. This added risk occurs for two reasons: (1) If a firm borrows on a long-term basis, its interest costs will be relatively stable over time, but if it uses short-term credit, its interest expense will fluctuate widely, at times going quite high. The Transamerica example at the beginning of the chapter illustrated that risk. (2) If a firm borrows heavily on a short-term basis, it may find itself unable to repay this debt, and it may be in such a weak financial position that the lender will not extend the loan; this could force the firm into bankruptcy.[3] Braniff Airlines, which failed during the credit crunch of 1982, is an example.

Risk of Long-Term versus Short-Term Debt

Statements about the flexibility, cost, and riskiness of short-term versus long-term credit depend, to a large extent, on the type of short-term credit that is actually used. To make these distinctions clear, the major types of short-term credit are discussed in the following sections.

Sources of Short-Term Financing

Firms generally pay employees on a weekly, biweekly, or monthly basis, so the balance sheet will typically show some accrued wages. Similarly, the firm's own estimated income taxes, the social security and income

Accruals

---

[3]Some academicians argue that while financial policy as related to working capital affects a firm's *total risk*, it has a much smaller effect on *market*, or *beta, risk*. Hence, they say that from its stockholders' point of view, the riskiness of a firm's working capital policy is not too important. Several comments are appropriate. First, it is difficult to prove this point one way or the other, but most authorities would argue that working capital policy *does* have a significant effect on beta risk. Second, by following a risky working capital policy, a firm can increase greatly the odds of bankruptcy or other types of financial distress, and this can lower its expected future profit stream at the same time that it raises the riskiness of the stream. Thus, working capital policy can have a double-barreled effect on the value of the firm.

taxes withheld from employee payrolls, and the sales taxes collected by the firm are generally paid on a weekly, monthly, or quarterly basis, so the balance sheet will typically show some accrued taxes along with its accrued wages.

Accruals increase automatically as a firm's operations expand. Further, this type of debt is "free" in the sense that no explicit interest is paid on funds raised through accruals. However, a firm cannot ordinarily control its accruals: Payrolls and the timing of wage payments are set by economic forces and industry custom, while tax payment dates are established by law. Thus, firms use all the accruals they can, but they have little control over the levels of these accounts.

Accounts Payable, or Trade Credit

Firms generally make purchases from other firms on credit, recording the debt as an *account payable*. Accounts payable, or *trade credit*, as it is commonly called, is the largest single category of short-term debt, representing about 40 percent of the current liabilities of the average nonfinancial corporation. This percentage is somewhat larger for smaller firms: Because small companies often do not qualify for financing from other sources, they rely especially heavily on trade credit.[4]

Trade credit is a *spontaneous* source of financing in the sense that it arises from ordinary business transactions. For example, suppose a firm makes average purchases of $2,000 a day on terms of net 30, meaning that it must pay for goods 30 days after the invoice date. On average, it will owe 30 times $2,000, or $60,000, to its suppliers. If its sales, and consequently its purchases, were to double, then its accounts payable would also double, to $120,000. Simply by growing, the firm would have spontaneously generated an additional $60,000 of financing. Similarly, if the terms under which it bought were extended from 30 to 40 days, its accounts payable would expand from $60,000 to $80,000. Thus, lengthening the credit period, as well as expanding sales and purchases, generates additional financing.

The Cost of Trade Credit

Firms that sell on credit have a *credit policy* that includes certain *terms of credit*. For example, Porter Electronics Company sells on terms of 2/10, net 30, meaning that a 2 percent discount is given if payment is made within 10 days of the invoice date, with the full invoice amount being due and payable within 30 days if the discount is not taken.

Suppose Pineapple Computers, Inc., (PCI) buys an average of $12 million of electronic components from Porter each year, less a 2 percent

---

[4]In a credit sale, the seller records the transaction as a receivable; the buyer, as a payable. We will examine accounts receivable as an asset investment in Chapter 21. Our focus in this chapter is on accounts payable, a liability item. We might also note that if a firm's accounts payable exceed its receivables, it is said to be *receiving net trade credit*, while if its receivables exceed its payables, it is *extending net trade credit*. Smaller firms frequently receive net credit; larger firms extend it.

discount, for net purchases of $11,760,000/360 = $32,666.67 per day. For simplicity, suppose Porter is PCI's only supplier. If PCI takes the discount, paying at the end of the tenth day, its payables will average (10)($32,666.67) = $326,667; PCI will, on average, be receiving $326,667 of credit from its only supplier, Porter Electronics Company.

Now suppose PCI decides *not* to take the discount; what will happen? First, PCI will begin paying invoices after 30 days, so its accounts payable will increase to (30)($32,666.67) = $980,000.[5] Porter Electronics will now be supplying PCI with an *additional* $653,333 of credit. PCI could use this additional credit to pay off bank loans, to expand inventories, to increase fixed assets, to build up its cash account, or even to increase its own accounts receivable.

PCI's new credit from Porter Electronics has a cost—PCI is foregoing a 2 percent discount on its $12 million of purchases, so its costs will rise by $240,000 per year. Dividing this $240,000 by the additional credit, we find the implicit cost of the added trade credit as follows:

$$\text{Approximate percentage cost} = \frac{\$240,000}{\$653,333} = 36.7\%.$$

Assuming that PCI can borrow from its bank (or from other sources) at an interest rate less than 36.7 percent, it should not expand its payables by foregoing discounts.

The following equation may be used to calculate the approximate percentage cost, on an annual basis, of not taking discounts:

$$\begin{array}{l}\text{Approximate} \\ \text{percentage} \\ \text{cost}\end{array} = \frac{\text{Discount percent}}{100 - \text{Discount percent}} \times \frac{360}{\text{Days credit is} - \text{Discount}} \quad \text{(18-1)}$$
$$\text{outstanding} \quad \text{period}$$

The numerator of the first term, discount percent, is the cost per dollar of credit; while the denominator in this term (100 − Discount percent) represents the funds made available by not taking the discount. The second term shows how many times each year this cost is incurred. To illustrate the equation, the approximate cost of not taking a discount when the terms are 2/10, net 30, is computed as follows:

$$\text{Approximate percentage cost} = \frac{2}{98} \times \frac{360}{20} = 0.0204(18)$$
$$= 0.367 = 36.7\%.$$

In effective annual interest terms, the rate is even higher. In the case of trade discounts, the discount amounts to interest, and with terms of 2/10, net 30, the firm gains use of the funds for 30 − 10 = 20 days, so

---

[5]A question arises here: Should accounts payable reflect gross purchases or purchases net of discounts? Although generally accepted accounting practices permit either treatment on the grounds that the difference is not material, most accountants prefer to record both inventories and payables net of discounts, and then to report the higher payments that result from not taking discounts as an additional expense, called "discounts lost." *Thus, we show accounts payable net of discounts even when the company does not expect to take the discount.*

there are 360/20 = 18 "interest periods" per year. The first term in our equation is (Discount percent)/(100 − Discount percent) = 0.02/0.98 = 0.0204. This "interest rate" is the periodic rate which is "paid" 18 times each year, so the effective annual rate cost of trade credit is

$$\text{Effective rate} = (1.0204)^{18} - 1.0 = 1.438 - 1.0 = 43.8\%.$$

Thus, the 36.7 percent cost calculated by the approximation formula, Equation 18-1, understates the true cost of trade credit.

Notice, however, that the cost of trade credit can be reduced by paying late. Thus, if PCI can get away with paying in 60 days rather than in the specified 30, then the effective credit period becomes 60 − 10 = 50 days, and the approximate cost drops from 36.7 percent to (2/98)(360/50) = 14.7%. The effective annual rate drops from 43.8 to 15.7 percent:

$$\text{Effective rate} = (1.0204)^{7.2} - 1.0 = 1.157 - 1.0 = 15.7\%.$$

In periods of excess capacity, firms may be able to get away with late payments, but they may also suffer a variety of problems associated with "stretching" accounts payable and being branded a "slow payer" account. These problems are discussed later in the chapter.

The cost of additional trade credit that results from not taking discounts can be worked out for other purchase terms. Some illustrative costs are shown below:

Credit Terms	Cost of Additional Credit if Cash Discount Not Taken	
	Approximate Cost	Effective Cost
1/10, net 20	36%	44%
1/10, net 30	18	20
2/10, net 20	73	107
3/15, net 45	37	44

As these figures show, the cost of not taking discounts can be substantial. Incidentally, throughout the chapter, we assume that payments are made either on the *last day* for taking discounts or on the *last day* of the credit period, unless otherwise noted. It would be foolish to pay, say, on the fifth day or on the twentieth day if the credit terms were 2/10, net 30.

Effects of Trade Credit on the Financial Statements

A firm's policy with regard to taking or not taking discounts can have a significant effect on its financial statements. To illustrate, let us assume that PCI is just beginning its operations. On the first day, it makes net purchases of $32,666.67. This amount is recorded on its balance sheet under accounts payable.[6] The second day it buys another $32,666.67.

---

[6]Inventories also increase by $32,666.67, but we are not now concerned with this account.

The first day's purchases are not yet paid for, so at the end of the second day, accounts payable total $65,333.34. Accounts payable increase by another $32,666.67 on the third day, for a total of $98,000, and after 10 days, accounts payable are up to $326,667.

If PCI takes discounts, then on the eleventh day it will have to pay for the $32,666.67 of purchases made on the first day, which will reduce accounts payable. However, it will buy another $32,666.67, which will increase payables. Thus, after the tenth day of operations, PCI's balance sheet will level off, showing a balance of $326,667 in accounts payable, assuming that the company pays on the tenth day in order to take discounts.

Now suppose PCI decides not to take discounts. In this case, on the eleventh day, it will add another $32,666.67 to payables, but it will not pay for the purchases made on the first day. Thus, the balance sheet figure for accounts payable will rise to (11)($32,666.67) = $359,333.37. This buildup will continue through the thirtieth day, at which point payables will total (30)($32,666.67) = $980,000. On the thirty-first day, PCI will buy another $32,667 of goods, which will increase accounts payable, but it will also pay for the purchases made the first day, which will reduce payables. Thus, the balance sheet item accounts payable will stabilize at $980,000 after 30 days, assuming PCI does not take discounts.

Table 18-3, Part I, shows PCI's balance sheet, after it reaches a steady state, under the two trade credit policies. Total assets are unchanged by this policy decision, and we also assume that the accruals and common equity accounts are unchanged. The differences show up in accounts payable and notes payable; when PCI elects to take discounts and thus gives up some of the trade credit it otherwise could have obtained, it will have to raise $653,333 from some other source. It could have sold more common stock, or it could have used long-term bonds, but it chose to use bank credit, which has a 10 percent cost and is reflected in the notes payable account.

Part II of Table 18-3 shows PCI's income statement under the two policies. If the company does not take discounts, then its interest expense is zero, but it will have a $240,000 expense for discounts lost. On the other hand, if it does take discounts, it incurs an interest expense of $65,333, but it avoids the cost of discounts lost. Since discounts lost exceed the interest expense, the take-discounts policy results in the higher net income and, thus, in a higher stock price.

Based on the preceding discussion, trade credit can be divided into two components: (1) *free trade credit*, which involves credit received during the discount period and which for PCI amounts to 10 days' net purchases, or $326,667, and (2) *costly trade credit*, which involves credit in excess of the free credit, and whose cost is an implicit one based on the

Components of Trade Credit: Free versus Costly

Table 18-3
PCI's Financial Statements with
Different Trade Credit Policies

I. Balance Sheets

Do Not Take Discounts; Use Maximum Trade Credit		Take Discounts; Borrow from Bank	
Cash	$ 500,000	Cash	$ 500,000
Receivables	1,000,000	Receivables	1,000,000
Inventories	2,000,000	Inventories	2,000,000
Fixed assets	2,980,000	Fixed assets	2,980,000
	$6,480,000		$6,480,000
Accounts payable	$ 980,000	Accounts payable	$ 326,667
Notes payable	0	Notes payable	653,333
Accruals	500,000	Accruals	500,000
Common equity	5,000,000	Common equity	5,000,000
	$6,480,000		$6,480,000

II. Income Statements

	Do Not Take Discounts	Take Discounts
Sales	$15,000,000	$15,000,000
Less: Purchases	11,760,000	11,760,000
Labor and other costs	2,000,000	2,000,000
Interest	0	65,333
Discounts lost	240,000	0
Net income before tax	1,000,000	1,174,667
Tax (40%)	400,000	469,867
Net income	$ 600,000	$ 704,800

foregone discounts.[7] PCI could obtain $653,333, or 20 days' net purchases, of nonfree trade credit at a cost of approximately 37 percent. *Financial managers should always use the free component, but they should use the costly component only after analyzing the cost of this capital to make sure that it is less than the cost of funds which could be obtained from other sources.* Under the terms of trade found in most industries, the costly component will involve a relatively high percentage cost, so stronger firms will avoid using it.

We noted earlier that firms sometimes can and do deviate from the stated credit terms, thus altering the percentage cost figures cited above. For example, a California manufacturing firm that buys on terms of

---

[7]There is some question as to whether any credit is really "free," because the supplier will have a cost of carrying receivables which must be passed on to the customer in the form of higher prices. Still, where suppliers sell on standard terms such as 2/10, net 30, and where the base price cannot be negotiated downward for early payment, then for all intents and purposes, the 10 days of trade credit is indeed "free."

2/10, net 30, makes a practice of paying in 15 days (rather than 10), but it still takes discounts. Its treasurer simply waits until 15 days after receipt of the goods to pay, and then writes a check for the invoiced amount less the 2 percent discount. The company's suppliers want its business, so they tolerate this practice. Similarly, a Wisconsin firm that also buys on terms of 2/10, net 30, does not take discounts, but it pays in 60 rather than in 30 days, thus "stretching" its trade credit. As we saw earlier, both practices reduce the cost of trade credit. Neither of these firms is "loved" by its suppliers, and neither could continue these practices in times when suppliers were operating at full capacity and had order backlogs, but these practices can and do reduce the costs of trade credit during times when suppliers have excess capacity.

Short-Term Bank Loans

Commercial banks, whose loans generally appear on firms' balance sheets under the notes payable account, are second in importance to trade credit as a source of short-term financing.[8] The banks' influence is actually greater than appears from the dollar amounts they lend, because banks provide *nonspontaneous* funds. As a firm's financing needs increase, it requests its bank to provide the additional funds. If the request is denied, the firm may be forced to abandon attractive growth opportunities.

Bank Loan Features

Some features of bank loans are discussed in the following paragraphs.

Maturity. Although banks do make longer-term loans, *the bulk of their lending is on a short-term basis*—about two-thirds of all bank loans mature in a year or less. Bank loans to businesses are frequently written as 90-day notes, so the loan must be repaid or renewed at the end of 90 days. Of course, if a borrower's financial position has deteriorated, the bank may well refuse to renew the loan. This can mean serious trouble for the borrower.

Promissory Note. When a bank loan is approved, the agreement is executed by signing a *promissory note*. The note specifies (1) the amount borrowed; (2) the percentage interest rate; (3) the repayment schedule, which can involve either a lump sum or a series of installments; (4) any collateral that might have to be put up as security for the loan; and (5) any other terms and conditions to which the bank and the borrower may

---

[8]Although commercial banks remain the primary source of short-term loans, other sources are available. For example, in 1981, General Electric Credit Corporation (GECC) had $2.6 billion in commercial loans outstanding. Firms such as GECC, which were initially established to finance consumers' purchases of GE's durable goods, often find business loans to be more profitable than consumer loans.

have agreed. When the note is signed, the bank credits the borrower's demand deposit with the amount of the loan. On the borrower's balance sheet, both the cash and notes payable accounts increase.

Compensating Balances. Banks typically require that a regular borrower maintain an average demand deposit (checking account) balance equal to at least 10 to 20 percent of the face amount of the loan. This is called a *compensating balance*, and such balances raise the effective interest rate on the loans. For example, if a firm needs $80,000 to pay off outstanding obligations, but if it must maintain a 20 percent compensating balance, then it must borrow $100,000 to obtain a usable $80,000. If the stated interest rate is 8 percent, the effective cost is actually 10 percent: $8,000 interest divided by $80,000 of usable funds equals 10 percent.[9]

Line of Credit. A *line of credit* is a formal or informal understanding between the bank and the borrower indicating the maximum credit the bank will extend to the borrower. For example, on December 31 a bank loan officer may indicate to a financial manager that the bank regards the firm as being "good" for up to $80,000 for the forthcoming year. On January 10 the financial manager signs a promissory note for $15,000 for 90 days; this is called "taking down" $15,000 of the total line of credit. This amount is credited to the firm's checking account at the bank. Before repayment of the $15,000, the firm may borrow additional amounts up to a total outstanding at any one time of $80,000.

Revolving Credit Agreement. A *revolving credit agreement* is a formal line of credit often used by large firms. To illustrate, in 1984 Porter Electronics negotiated a revolving credit agreement for $100 million with a group of banks. The banks were formally committed for 4 years to lend Porter up to $100 million if the funds were needed. Porter, in turn, paid a commitment fee of one-quarter of 1 percent on the unused balance of the commitment to compensate the banks for making the commitment. Thus, if Porter did not take down any of the $100 million commitment during a year, it would still be required to pay a $250,000 fee. If it borrowed $50 million, the unused portion of the line of credit would fall to $50 million, and the fee would fall to $125,000. Of course, interest also had to be paid on the amount of money Porter actually borrowed. As a general rule, the rate of interest on "revolvers" is pegged to the prime rate (see the next section), so the cost of the loan varies over time as interest rates vary. Porter's rate was set at prime plus 0.5 percentage points.

---

[9]Note, however, that the compensating balance may be set as a minimum monthly *average*; if the firm would maintain this average anyway, the compensating balance requirement would not raise the effective interest rate. Also, note that these *loan* compensating balances are added to any compensating balances that the firm's bank may require for *services performed*, such as clearing checks. Service compensating balances are discussed in Chapter 20.

Note that a revolving credit agreement is very similar to a line of credit. However, there is an important distinguishing feature: The bank has a legal obligation to honor a revolving credit agreement, and it receives a commitment fee. Neither the legal obligation nor the fee exists under a less formal line of credit.

As an example of the types of short-term loans made by commercial banks, consider the commercial loans made during the second week of February 1984 as reported in the May 1984 *Federal Reserve Bulletin*. The total amount loaned was approximately $38 billion. The dollar-weighted average maturity was 1.4 months, with fixed rate loans averaging just under one month in maturity and floating rate loans averaging 2.2 months. Of the loans made, 32 percent had a floating rate, and 68 percent had a fixed rate. Also, 64 percent of the loans were made under formal commitment, such as a revolving credit agreement, while only 36 percent were newly arranged credits.

The cost of bank loans varies for different types of borrowers at a given point in time, and for all borrowers over time. Interest rates are higher for riskier borrowers, and rates are also higher on smaller loans because of the fixed costs involved in making and servicing loans. If a firm can qualify as a "prime risk" because of its size and financial strength, it can borrow at the *prime rate*, which has traditionally been the lowest rate banks charge. Rates on other loans tend to be scaled up from the prime rate.[10]

The Cost of Bank Loans

Bank rates vary widely over time depending on economic conditions and Federal Reserve policy. When the economy is weak, then (1) loan demand is usually slack, and (2) the Fed also makes plenty of money available to the system. As a result, rates on all types of loans are relatively low. Conversely, when the economy is booming, loan demand is typically strong and the Fed restricts the money supply; the result is

---

[10]Each bank sets its own prime rate, but, because of competitive forces, most banks' prime rates are identical. Further, most banks follow the rate set by the large New York City banks, and they, in turn, generally follow the rate set by Citibank, New York City's (and the world's) largest. Citibank had a policy of setting the prime rate each week at 1¼ to 1½ percentage points above the average rate on large certificates of deposit (CDs) during the three weeks immediately preceding. CD rates represent the "price" of money in the open market, and they rise and fall with the supply and demand of money, so CD rates are "market-clearing" rates. By tying the prime rate to CD rates, the banking system insured that the prime rate would also be a market-clearing rate.

However, in recent years the prime rate has been held relatively constant even while open market rates have fluctuated sharply. Thus, from January 1983 through April 1984, the prime rate was changed only four times. Also, in recent years many banks have been lending to the very strongest companies at rates below the prime rate. As is noted later in this chapter, larger firms have ready access to the commercial paper market, and if banks want to do a significant volume of business with these larger companies, they must match or at least come close to the commercial paper rate. As competition in financial markets increases, as it has been doing because of the deregulation of banks and other financial institutions, "administered" rates such as the prime rate are giving way to flexible, negotiated rates based on market forces.

high interest rates. As an indication of the kinds of fluctuations that can occur, the prime rate during 1980 rose from 11 percent in August to 21 percent in December. Interest rates on other bank loans also vary, but generally they are kept in phase with the prime rate.

Interest rates on bank loans are calculated in three ways: as *simple interest*, as *discount interest*, and as *add-on interest*. These three methods are explained next.

Regular, or Simple, Interest. Simple interest forms the basis for comparison of all loan rates. In a *simple interest* loan, the borrower receives the face value of the loan and repays the principal and interest at maturity. For example, in a simple interest loan of $10,000 at 12 percent for one year, the borrower receives the $10,000 upon approval of the loan and pays back the $10,000 principal plus $10,000(0.12) = $1,200 in interest at maturity (one year later). The 12 percent is the stated, or nominal, rate. The effective annual rate is also 12 percent:

$$\text{Effective rate}_{\text{Simple}} = \frac{\text{Interest}}{\text{Amount received}} = \frac{\$1,200}{\$10,000} = 12\%.$$

On a simple interest loan of one year or more, the nominal rate equals the effective rate. If the loan had a term of less than one year, say 90 days, then the effective rate would be calculated as follows:

$$\text{Effective rate}_{\text{Simple}} = \left(1 + \frac{k_{\text{Nom}}}{m}\right)^m - 1.0$$
$$= (1 + 0.12/4)^4 - 1.0 = 12.55\%.$$

Here k_{Nom} is the nominal, or stated, rate and m is the number of loan periods per year, or 360/90 = 4. The bank gets the interest sooner than under a 1-year loan, and hence the effective rate is higher.

Discount Interest. In a *discount interest* loan, the bank deducts the interest in advance (*discounts* the loan). Thus, the borrower receives less than the face value of the loan. On a one-year, $10,000 loan with a 12 percent (nominal) rate, discount basis, the interest (discount) is $10,000(0.12) = $1,200, so the borrower obtains the use of only $10,000 − $1,200 = $8,800. The effective rate is 13.64 percent versus 12 percent on a one-year simple interest loan:[11]

---

[11]Note that if the borrowing firm actually requires a loan of $10,000, it must borrow $11,363.64:

$$\text{Face value} = \frac{\text{Funds required}}{1.0 - \text{Nominal rate (fraction)}}$$
$$= \frac{\$10,000}{1.0 - 0.12} = \frac{\$10,000}{0.88} = \$11,363.64.$$

Now, the borrower will receive $11,363.64 − 0.12($11,363.64) = $10,000. Increasing the face value of the loan does not change the effective rate of 13.64 percent on the $10,000 of usable funds.

$$\text{Effective rate}_{\text{Discount}} = \frac{\text{Interest}}{\text{Amount received}}$$

$$= \frac{\text{Interest}}{\text{Face value} - \text{Interest}}$$

$$= \frac{\$1,200}{\$10,000 - \$1,200} = 13.64\%.$$

An alternative procedure for finding the effective annual rate on a discount interest loan is

$$\text{Effective rate}_{\text{Discount}} = \frac{\text{Nominal rate (\%)}}{1.0 - \text{Nominal rate (fraction)}}$$

$$= \frac{12\%}{1.0 - 0.12} = \frac{12\%}{0.88} = 13.64\%$$

If the discount loan is for a period of less than one year, its effective annual rate is found as follows:

$$\text{Effective rate}_{\text{Discount}} = \left(1.0 + \frac{\text{Interest}}{\text{Face value} - \text{Interest}}\right)^m - 1.0.$$

For example, if we borrow \$10,000 face value at a nominal rate of 12 percent, discount interest, for 3 months, then m = 12/3 = 4, and the interest payment is (0.12/4)(\$10,000) = \$300, so

$$\text{Effective rate}_{\text{Discount}} = \left(1.0 + \frac{\$300}{\$10,000 - \$300}\right)^4 - 1.0$$

$$= 0.1296 = 12.96\%.$$

Thus, discount interest imposes less of a penalty on shorter-term than on longer-term loans.

Installment Loans: Add-On Interest. Lenders typically charge *add-on interest* on automobile and other types of small installment loans. The term "add-on" means that the interest is calculated based on the nominal rate and then added to the amount received to obtain the loan's face value. To illustrate, suppose someone borrows \$10,000 on an add-on basis at a nominal rate of 12 percent, with the loan to be repaid in 12 monthly installments. At a 12 percent nominal rate, the borrower pays a total interest charge of \$1,200. Thus, the face amount of the note is \$11,200. However, since the loan is paid off in monthly installments, the borrower has the use of the full \$10,000 for only the first month, and the amount actually advanced by the lender declines until, during the last month, only $\frac{1}{12}$ of the original loan will still be outstanding. Thus, the borrower pays \$1,200 for the use of only about half the loan's face amount, as the average outstanding balance of the loan is only about \$5,000. Therefore, we can approximate the effective rate by

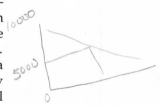

$$\text{Approximate effective rate}_{\text{Add-on}} = \frac{\text{Interest}}{(\text{Amount received})/2}$$

$$= \frac{\$1,200}{\$10,000/2} = 24.0\%.$$

To determine the precise effective rate under add-on, we proceed as follows:

1. The total loan to be repaid is $10,000 of principal, plus $1,200 of interest, or $11,200.

2. The monthly payment is $11,200/12 = $933.33.

3. The bank is, in effect, buying a 12-period annuity of $933.33 for $10,000, so $10,000 is the present value of the annuity. Expressed in equation form,

$$PV = \$10,000 = \sum_{t=1}^{12} \$933.33 \left(\frac{1}{1 + k_d} \right)^t.$$

4. This equation can be solved for k_d, which is the rate per month, using a financial calculator. Here $k_d = 1.788\% = 0.01788$.

5. The precise effective rate is found as follows:[12]

$$
\begin{aligned}
\text{Effective rate}_{\text{Add-on}} &= (1 + k_d)^{12} - 1.0 \\
&= (1.01788)^{12} - 1.0 \\
&= 1.2370 - 1.0 = 23.7\%.
\end{aligned}
$$

Simple Interest with Compensating Balances. Compensating balances tend to raise the effective rate on a loan. To illustrate this, suppose a firm needs $10,000 to pay for some equipment that it recently purchased. A bank offers to lend the company money for one year at a 12 percent simple rate, but the company must maintain a *compensating balance (CB)* equal to 20 percent of the loan amount. If the firm did not take the loan, it would keep no deposits with the bank. What is the effective annual rate on the loan?

First, note that if the firm requires $10,000, it must, assuming it does not have current cash to use as the compensating balance, borrow $12,500:

$$\text{Face value} = \frac{\text{Funds required}}{1.0 - \text{CB (fraction)}} = \frac{\$10,000}{1.0 - 0.20} = \$12,500.$$

The interest paid at the end of the year will be $12,500(0.12) = $1,500,

---

[12]Under the truth-in-lending laws, banks, department stores, and other installment lenders are required to report the *annual percentage rate (APR)* in boldface type on the first page of all installment loan contracts to prevent lenders from calling a loan with an effective rate of 23.7 percent a 12 percent loan. Note, however, that existing laws do not, in all cases, define the effective rate the same way as we do. For example, many institutions would report our example add-on loan as having an APR of 12 × 1.788% = 21.36% versus the 23.7 percent we calculated. Also, note that if an installment loan is paid off ahead of schedule, additional complications arise. For a discussion of this point, see Dick Bonker, "The Rule of 78," *Journal of Finance*, June 1976, 877-888.

but the firm will only get the use of $10,000. Therefore, the effective annual rate is 15 percent:

$$\text{Effective rate}_{\text{Simple/CB}} = \frac{\text{Interest}}{\text{Amount received}}$$

$$= \frac{\$1,500}{\$10,000} = 15\%.$$

An alternative formulation is

$$\text{Effective rate}_{\text{Simple/CB}} = \frac{\text{Nominal rate (\%)}}{1.0 - \text{CB (fraction)}}$$

$$= \frac{12\%}{1.0 - 0.2} = 15\%.$$

Discount Interest with Compensating Balances. The analysis above can be extended to the case where compensating balances are required and the loan is on a discount basis. In this situation, if a firm required $10,000 for one year and a 20 percent compensating balance (CB) is required on a 12 percent discount loan, it must borrow $14,705.88:

$$\text{Face value} = \frac{\text{Funds required}}{1.0 - \text{Nominal rate (fraction)} - \text{CB (fraction)}}$$

$$= \frac{\$10,000}{1.0 - 0.12 - 0.2} = \$10,000/0.68 = \$14,705.88.$$

The firm would record this $14,705.88 as a note payable offset by these asset accounts:

To cash account	$10,000.00
Prepaid interest (12% of $14,705.88)	1,764.71
Compensating balance (20% of $14,705.88)	2,941.18
	$14,705.89

Now the effective annual rate is 17.65 percent:

$$\text{Effective rate}_{\text{Discount/CB}} = \frac{\text{Nominal rate}}{1.0 - \text{Nominal rate (fraction)} - \text{CB (fraction)}}$$

$$= \frac{12\%}{1.0 - 0.12 - 0.2} = 12\%/0.68 = 17.65\%.$$

In our example, compensating balances and discount interest combined to push the effective rate of interest up from 12 to 17.65 percent. Note, however, that in our analysis we assumed that the compensating balance requirements forced the firm to increase its bank deposits. Had the company had transactions balances which could be used to supply all or part of the compensating balances, the effective annual rate would have been less than 17.65 percent. Also, if the firm earns interest on its bank deposits, including the compensating balance, then the effective annual rate would be decreased.

Choosing a Bank

Individuals whose only contact with their bank is through the use of its checking services generally choose a bank for the convenience of its location and the competitive cost of its services. However, a business that borrows from banks must look at other criteria, and a potential borrower seeking banking relations should recognize that important differences exist among banks. Some of these differences are considered below.

Willingness to Assume Risks. Banks have different basic policies toward risk. Some banks are inclined to follow relatively conservative lending practices, while others engage in what are properly termed "creative banking practices." These policies reflect partly the personalities of officers of the bank and partly the characteristics of the bank's deposit liabilities. Thus, a bank with fluctuating deposit liabilities in a static community will tend to be a conservative lender, while a bank whose deposits are growing with little interruption may follow "liberal" credit policies. A large bank with broad diversification over geographic regions or among industries served can obtain the benefit of combining and averaging risks. Thus, marginal credit risks that might be unacceptable to a small bank or to a specialized unit bank can be pooled by a branch banking system to reduce the overall risk of a group of marginal accounts.

Advice and Counsel. Some bank loan officers are active in providing counsel and in stimulating development loans to firms in their early and formative years. Certain banks have specialized departments which make loans to firms expected to grow and thus to become more important customers. The personnel of these departments can provide valuable counseling to customers: The bankers' experience with other firms in growth situations may enable them to spot, and then to warn their customers about, developing problems.

Loyalty to Customers. Banks differ in the extent to which they will support the activities of the borrower in bad times. This characteristic is referred to as the degree of *loyalty* of the bank. Some banks may put great pressure on a business to liquidate its loans when the firm's outlook becomes clouded, whereas others will stand by the firm and work diligently to help it get back on its feet. An especially dramatic illustration of this point was Bank of America's bail-out of Memorex Corporation. The bank could have forced Memorex into bankruptcy, but instead it loaned the company additional capital and helped it survive a bad period. Memorex's stock price subsequently rose on the New York Stock Exchange from $1.50 to $68, so Bank of America's help was indeed substantial.

Specialization. Banks differ greatly in their degrees of loan specialization. Larger banks have separate departments that specialize in different kinds of loans—for example, real estate loans, farm loans, and commercial loans. Within these broad categories, there may be a specialization by line of business, such as steel, machinery, cattle, or textiles. The strengths of banks are also likely to reflect the nature of the business and the economic environment in which they operate. For example, Texas banks have become specialists in lending to oil companies, while many midwestern banks are agricultural specialists. A sound firm can obtain more creative cooperation and more active support by going to the bank that has the greatest experience and familiarity with its particular type of business. The financial manager should therefore choose a bank with care. A bank that is excellent for one firm may be unsatisfactory for another.

Maximum Loan Size. The size of a bank can be an important factor. Since the maximum loan a bank can make to any one customer is limited to 10 percent of the bank's capital accounts (capital stock plus retained earnings), it is generally not appropriate for large firms to develop borrowing relationships with small banks.

Other Services. Banks also provide lockbox systems (see Chapter 20), assist with electronic funds transfers, help firms obtain foreign exchange, and the like, and such services should be taken into account in selecting a bank. Also, if the firm is a small business whose manager owns most of its stock, the bank's willingness and ability to provide trust and estate services should also be considered.

Commercial Paper

Commercial paper is the name given to the unsecured promissory notes of large, strong firms, and it is sold primarily to other business firms, to insurance companies, to pension funds, to money market mutual funds, and to banks. Although the amount of commercial paper outstanding is smaller than bank loans outstanding, this form of financing has grown rapidly in recent years. At the end of February 1984, there was approximately $191 billion of commercial paper outstanding, versus about $421 billion of bank loans to businesses.

Maturity and Cost

Maturities of commercial paper generally vary from two to six months, with an average of about five months.[13] The rates on commercial paper fluctuate with supply and demand conditions—they are determined in the marketplace, varying daily as conditions change. Recently, commer-

---

[13]The maximum maturity without SEC registration is 270 days. Also, commercial paper can only be sold to "sophisticated" investors; otherwise, SEC registration would be required even for maturities of 270 days or less.

cial paper rates have generally ranged from 1¾ to 2½ percentage points below the stated prime rate, and about ¼ of a percentage point above the T-bill rate. For example, in April 1984, the average rate on 3-month commercial paper was 9.92 percent, while the stated prime rate was 12.0 percent and the T-bill rate was 9.64 percent. Also, since compensating balances are not required for commercial paper, the *effective* cost differential is still wider.[14]

Use of Commercial Paper

The use of commercial paper is restricted to a comparatively small number of concerns that are exceptionally good credit risks. Dealers prefer to handle the paper of firms whose net worth is $100 million or more and whose annual borrowing exceeds $10 million. One potential problem with commercial paper is that a debtor who is in temporary financial difficulty may receive little help, because commercial paper dealings are generally less personal than are bank relationships. Thus, banks are generally more able and willing to help a good customer weather a temporary storm than is a commercial paper dealer. On the other hand, using commercial paper permits a corporation to tap a wide range of credit sources, including financial institutions outside its own area and industrial corporations across the country, and this can reduce interest costs.

Secured Short-Term Loans

Thus far, we have not addressed the question of whether or not loans are to be secured. Commercial paper loans are never secured by specific collateral, but all the other types of loans can be if this is deemed necessary or desirable. Given a choice, it is ordinarily better to borrow on an unsecured basis, since the bookkeeping costs of secured loans are often high. However, weak firms may find (1) that they can borrow only if they put up some type of security to protect the lender, or (2) that by using some security they can borrow at a much lower rate.

Several different kinds of collateral can be employed, including marketable stocks or bonds, land or buildings, equipment, inventory, and accounts receivable. Marketable securities make excellent collateral, but few firms hold portfolios of stocks and bonds. Similarly, real property (land and buildings) and equipment are good forms of collateral, but they are generally used as security for long-term loans rather than for working capital loans. Therefore, most secured short-term business bor-

---

[14]However, this factor is offset to some extent by the fact that firms issuing commercial paper are required by commercial paper dealers to have unused revolving credit agreements to back up their outstanding commercial paper, and fees must be paid on these lines. In other words, to sell $1 million of commercial paper, a firm must have revolving credit available to pay off the paper when it matures, and commitment fees on this unused credit line (about ½ percent) increase the effective cost of the paper.

rowing involves the use of accounts receivable and inventories as collateral.

To understand the use of security, consider the case of an Orlando hardware dealer who wanted to modernize and expand his store. He requested a $200,000 bank loan. After examining his business's financial statements, the bank indicated (1) that it would lend him a maximum of $100,000, and (2) that the interest rate would be 15 percent, discount interest, for an effective rate of 17.6 percent. The owner had a substantial personal portfolio of stocks, so he offered to put up $300,000 of high-quality stocks to support the $200,000 loan. The bank then granted the full $200,000 loan, and at a rate of only 13 percent, simple interest. The store owner might also have used his inventories or receivables as security for the loan, but processing costs would have been high.

In the past, state laws varied greatly with regard to the use of security in financing. Today, however, all states except Louisiana operate under the *Uniform Commercial Code*, which standardizes and simplifies the procedure for establishing loan security. The heart of the Uniform Commercial Code is the *Security Agreement*, a standardized document, or form, on which the specific assets that are pledged are stated. The assets can be items of equipment, accounts receivable, or inventories. Procedures under the Uniform Commercial Code for using accounts receivable and inventories as security for short-term credit are described in the following sections. Secured short-term loans involve quite a bit of paperwork and other administrative costs, which makes them relatively expensive. However, this is often the only type of financing available to weaker firms.

Accounts Receivable Financing

Accounts receivable financing involves either the pledging of receivables or the selling of receivables (factoring). The *pledging of accounts receivable* is characterized by the fact that the lender not only has a claim against the receivables but also has recourse to the borrower: If the person or the firm that bought the goods does not pay, the selling firm must take the loss. Therefore, the risk of default on the accounts receivable pledged remains with the borrower. Also, the buyer of the goods is not ordinarily notified about the pledging of the receivables, and the financial institution that lends on the security of accounts receivable is generally either a commercial bank or one of the large industrial finance companies.

Factoring, or *selling accounts receivable*, involves the purchase of accounts receivable by the lender, generally without recourse to the borrower. Under factoring, the buyer of the goods is typically notified of the transfer and is asked to make payment directly to the financial institution. Since the factoring firm assumes the risk of default on bad accounts, it must make the credit check. Accordingly, factors provide not only money but also a credit department for the borrower. Incidentally, the same financial institutions that make loans against pledged receivables also serve as factors. Thus, depending on the circumstances and the wishes of the borrower, a financial institution will provide either form of receivables financing.

Procedure for Pledging Receivables

The financing of accounts receivable is initiated by a legally binding agreement between the seller of the goods and the financing institution. The agreement sets forth in detail the procedures to be followed and the legal obligations of both parties. Once the working relationship has been established, the seller periodically takes a batch of invoices to the financing institution. The lender reviews the invoices and makes credit appraisals of the buyers. Invoices of companies that do not meet the lender's credit standards are not accepted for pledging.

The financial institution seeks to protect itself at every phase of the operation. First, selection of sound invoices is one way the financing institution safeguards itself. Second, if the buyer of the goods does not pay the invoice, the lender still has recourse against the seller. And third, additional protection is afforded the lender in that the loan will generally be for less than 100 percent of the pledged receivables. For example, the lender may advance the selling firm only 75 percent of the amount of the pledged receivables.

Procedure for Factoring Receivables

The procedure for factoring is somewhat different from that for pledging. Again, an agreement between the seller and the factor specifies legal obligations and procedural arrangements. When the seller receives an order from a buyer, a credit approval slip is written and immediately sent to the factoring company for a credit check. If the factor approves the credit, shipment is made and the invoice is stamped to notify the buyer to make payment directly to the factoring company. If the factor does not approve the sale, the seller generally refuses to fill the order, but if the sale is made anyway, the factor will not buy the account.

The factor normally performs three functions: (1) credit checking, (2) lending, and (3) risk bearing. However, the seller can select various combinations of these functions by changing provisions in the factoring agreement. For example, a small- or medium-sized firm can avoid establishing a credit department. The factor's service might well be less costly than a department that would have excess capacity for the firm's credit volume. At the same time, if the selling firm uses part of the time of a noncredit specialist to perform credit checking, then lack of education, training, and experience could result in excessive losses.

The seller may utilize the factor to perform the credit-checking and risk-taking functions without performing the lending function. The following procedure illustrates the handling of a $10,000 order under this arrangement. The factor checks and approves the invoices. The goods are shipped on terms of net 30. Payment is made to the factor, who remits to the seller. But if the buyer defaults, the $10,000 must still be remitted to the seller. If the $10,000 is never paid, the factor sustains a $10,000 loss. Note, though, that in this situation, the factor does not remit funds to the seller until they are received from the buyer of the goods, or until the credit period has expired. Thus, the factor does not supply any credit.

Now consider the more typical situation in which the factor performs a lending function by making payment in advance of collection. The goods are shipped, and even though payment is not due for 30 days, the factor immediately makes funds available to the seller. Suppose $10,000 worth of goods is shipped. Further, assume that the factoring commission for credit checking and risk bearing is 2.5 percent of the invoice price, or $250, and that the interest expense is computed at a 9 percent annual rate on the invoice balance, or $75.[15] The selling firm's accounting entry is as follows:

Cash	$9,175	
Interest expense	75	
Factoring commission	250	
Reserve due from factor on collection of account	500	
Accounts receivable		$10,000

The $500 due from the factor on collection of account is a reserve established by the factor to cover disputes between sellers and buyers on damaged goods, on goods returned by the buyers to the seller, and on the failure to make an outright sale of goods. The reserve is paid to the selling firm when the factor collects on the account.

Factoring is normally a continuous process instead of the single cycle just described. The firm that sells the goods receives orders; it transmits the purchase orders to the factor for approval; upon approval, the firm ships the goods; the factor advances the money to the seller; the buyers pay the factor when payment is due; and the factor periodically remits any excess in the reserve to the seller of the goods. Once a routine is established, a continuous circular flow of goods and funds takes place between the seller, the buyers of the goods, and the factor. Thus, once the factoring agreement is in force, funds from this source are *spontaneous*.

---

[15]Since the interest is only for one month, we multiply $1/12$ of the stated rate (9 percent) by the $10,000 invoice price:

$$(1/12)(0.09)(\$10,000) = \$75.$$

Note that the effective rate of interest is really above 9 percent, because (1) the term is for less than 1 year and (2) a discounting procedure is used and the borrower does not get the full $10,000. In many instances, however, the factoring contract calls for interest to be computed on the invoice price *less* the factoring commission and the reserve account.

*Cost of
Receivables
Financing*

Both accounts receivable pledging and factoring are convenient and advantageous, but they can be costly. The credit-checking and risk-bearing fee is 1 to 3 percent of the amount of invoices accepted by the factor, and even more if the buyers are poor credit risks. The cost of money is reflected in the interest rate (usually 2 to 3 percentage points over the prime rate) charged on the unpaid balance of the funds advanced by the factor.

*Evaluation of
Receivables
Financing*

It cannot be said categorically that accounts receivable financing is always either a good or a poor method of raising funds for an individual business. Among the advantages is, first, the flexibility of this source of financing: As the firm's sales expand, causing more financing to be needed, a larger volume of invoices, and hence receivables financing, is generated automatically. Second, receivables can be used as security for a loan that a firm might otherwise not be able to obtain. Third, factoring can provide the services of a credit department that might otherwise be available to the firm only under much more expensive conditions.

Accounts receivable financing also has disadvantages. First, when invoices are numerous and relatively small in dollar amount, the administrative costs involved may be excessive. Second, the firm is using a highly liquid asset as security. For a long time, accounts receivable financing was frowned upon by most trade creditors. In fact, such financing was regarded as a confession of a firm's unsound financial position. It is no longer regarded in this light, and many sound firms engage in receivables pledging or factoring. However, the traditional attitude causes some trade creditors to refuse to sell on credit to a firm that is factoring or pledging its receivables, on the grounds that this practice removes one of the most liquid of the firm's assets and, accordingly, weakens the position of other creditors.

*Future Use of
Receivables
Financing*

We might make a prediction at this point: In the future, accounts receivable financing will increase in relative importance. Computer technology is rapidly advancing toward the point where credit records of individuals and firms can be kept on disks and magnetic tapes. Systems have been devised so that a retailer can have a device on hand, which when an individual's magnetic credit card is inserted into a box, the box gives a signal that the credit is "good" and that a bank is willing to "buy" the receivable created as soon as the store completes the sale. The cost of handling invoices will be greatly reduced over present-day costs because the new systems will be so highly automated. This will make it possible to use accounts receivable financing for very small sales, and it will reduce the cost of all receivables financing. The net result will be a marked expansion of accounts receivable financing. In fact, when consumers use credit cards such as MasterCard or Visa, the seller is, in effect, factoring receivables. The seller receives the amount of the purchase, less a percentage fee, the next working day. The buyer receives 30 days (or so) credit, at which time he or she remits payment directly to the credit card company or sponsoring bank.

Inventory Financing

A substantial amount of credit is secured by business inventories. If a firm is a relatively good credit risk, the mere existence of the inventory may be a sufficient basis for receiving an unsecured loan. However, if the firm is a relatively poor risk, the lending institution may insist upon security, which often takes the form of a *blanket lien* against the inventory. Alternatively, *trust receipts* or *field warehouse receipts* can be used to secure the loan. These methods of using inventories as security are discussed in this section.

Blanket Liens

The *inventory blanket lien* gives the lending institution a lien against all the borrower's inventories. However, the borrower is free to sell inventories; thus, the value of the collateral can be reduced below the level that existed when the loan was granted.

Trust Receipts

Because of the inherent weakness of the blanket lien, another procedure for inventory financing has been developed—the *trust receipt*, which is an instrument acknowledging that the goods are held in trust for the lender. When trust receipts are used, the borrowing firm, on receiving funds from the lender, signs and delivers a trust receipt for the goods. The goods can be stored in a public warehouse or held on the premises of the borrower. The trust receipt states that the goods are held in trust for the lender or are segregated on the borrower's premises on behalf of the lender, and that any proceeds from the sale of trust goods must be transmitted to the lender at the end of each day. Automobile dealer financing is one of the best examples of trust receipt financing.

One defect of trust receipt financing is the requirement that a trust receipt must be issued for specific goods. For example, if the security is autos in a dealer's inventory, the trust receipts must indicate the cars by registration number. In order to validate its trust receipts, the lending institution must send someone to the premises of the borrower periodically to see that the auto numbers are correctly listed, because auto dealers who are in financial difficulty have been known to sell cars backing trust receipts and then use the funds obtained for other operations rather than to repay the bank. Problems are compounded if borrowers have geographically diversified operations or if they are separated geographically from the lender. To offset these inconveniences, *warehousing* has come into wide use as a method of securing loans with inventory.

*Warehouse
Receipts*

Like trust receipts, warehouse receipt financing uses inventory as security. A *public warehouse* is an independent third party operation engaged in the business of storing goods. Items which must age, such as tobacco and liquor, are often financed and stored in public warehouses. Sometimes a public warehouse is not practical because of the bulkiness of goods and the expense of transporting them to and from the borrower's premises. In such cases, a *field warehouse* may be established at the place of the borrower. To provide inventory supervision, the lending institution employs a third party in the arrangement, the field warehousing company, which acts as an agent for the lending institution.

Field warehousing can be illustrated by a simple example. Suppose a firm which has iron stacked in an open yard on its premises needs a loan. A field warehouse can be established if a field warehousing concern merely places a temporary fence around the iron, erects a sign stating: "This is a field warehouse supervised and conducted by the Lawrence Field Warehousing Corporation," and assigns an employee to supervise and control the inventory.

The example illustrates the three essential elements for the establishment of a field warehouse: (1) public notification, (2) physical control of the inventory, and (3) supervision of the field warehouse by a custodian of the field warehouse concern. When the field warehousing operation is relatively small, the third condition is sometimes violated by hiring an employee of the borrower to supervise the inventory. This practice is viewed as undesirable by most lenders, because there is no control over the collateral by a person independent of the borrowing firm.[16]

The field warehouse financing operation is best described by an actual case. A California tomato cannery was interested in financing its operations by bank borrowing. The cannery had sufficient funds to finance 15 to 20 percent of its operations during the canning season. These funds were adequate to purchase and process an initial batch of tomatoes. As the cans were put into boxes and rolled into the storerooms, the cannery needed additional funds for both raw materials and labor. Because of the cannery's poor credit rating, the bank decided that a field warehousing operation was necessary to secure its loans.

The field warehouse was established, and the custodian notified the bank of the description, by number, of the boxes of canned tomatoes in storage and under warehouse control. Thereupon, the lending institu-

---

[16]This absence of independent control was the main cause of the breakdown that resulted in the $200 million plus losses connected with loans to the Allied Crude Vegetable Oil Company by Bank of America and other banks. American Express Field Warehousing Company was handling the operation, but it hired men from Allied's own staff as custodians. Their dishonesty was not discovered because of another breakdown—the fact that the American Express touring inspector did not actually take a physical inventory of the warehouses. As a consequence, the swindle was not discovered until losses running into the hundreds of millions of dollars had been suffered. See N. C. Miller, *The Great Salad Oil Swindle* (Baltimore: Penguin Books, 1965, 72-77).

tion established a deposit on which the cannery could draw. From this point on, the bank financed the operations. The cannery needed only enough cash to initiate the cycle. The farmers brought in more tomatoes; the cannery processed them; the cans were boxed; the boxes were put into the field warehouse; field warehouse receipts were drawn up and sent to the bank; the bank established further deposits for the cannery on the basis of the receipts; and the cannery could draw on the deposits to continue the cycle.

Of course, the cannery's ultimate objective was to sell the canned tomatoes. As the cannery received purchase orders, it transmitted them to the bank, and the bank directed the custodian to release the inventories. It was agreed that, as remittances were received by the cannery, they would be turned over to the bank. These remittances paid off the loans made by the bank. Note that a seasonal pattern existed. At the beginning of the tomato harvesting and canning season, the cannery's cash needs and loan requirements began to rise, and they reached a peak just as the canning season ended. It was hoped that well before the new canning season begins, the cannery would have sold a sufficient volume to pay off the loan. If for some reason the cannery had a bad year, the bank might carry the loan over for another year to enable the company to work off its inventory.

Acceptable Products. In addition to canned foods, which account for about 17 percent of all field warehouse loans, many other types of products provide a basis for field warehouse financing. Some of these are miscellaneous groceries, which represent about 13 percent; lumber products, about 10 percent; and coal and coke, about 6 percent. These products are relatively nonperishable and are sold in well-developed, organized markets. Nonperishability protects the lender if it should have to take over the security. For this reason, a bank would not make a field warehousing loan on perishables such as fresh fish. However, frozen fish, which can be stored for a long time, can be field warehoused. An organized market aids the lender in disposing of an inventory that it takes over. Banks are not interested in going into the canning or the fish business, so they want to be able to dispose of the inventory with the minimum expenditure of time and effort.

Cost of Financing. The fixed costs of a field warehousing arrangement are relatively high; such financing is therefore not suitable for a very small firm. If a field warehouse company sets up the field warehouse itself, it will typically set a minimum charge of about $5,000 per year, plus about 1 to 2 percent of the amount of credit extended to the borrower. Furthermore, the financing institution will charge an interest rate of 2 to 3 percentage points over the prime rate. An efficient field warehousing operation requires a minimum inventory of at least $1 million.

Evaluation of Inventory Financing. The use of inventory financing, especially field warehouse financing, as a source of funds for business firms has many advantages. First, the amount of funds available is flexible because the financing is tied to the growth of inventories, which in turn is related directly to financing needs. Second, the field warehousing arrangement increases the acceptability of inventories as loan collateral; some inventories simply would not be accepted by a bank as security without a field warehousing arrangement. Third, the necessity for inventory control, safekeeping, and the use of specialists in warehousing has resulted in improved warehouse practice, which saves handling costs, insurance charges, theft, and so on. The services of the field warehouse companies have often saved money for the firm in spite of the costs of financing that we have discussed. The major disadvantages of a field warehousing operation are the paperwork and physical separation requirements and, for small firms, the fixed cost element.

Summary

This chapter began with a discussion of the *working capital cash flow cycle* and alternative *working capital policies*. Working capital policy involves (1) the level of current assets and (2) the manner in which these assets are financed. We saw that because short-term credit offers advantages of greater flexibility, and sometimes lower cost, most firms use at least some current debt to finance current assets, in spite of the fact that short-term debt increases the firm's risk.

The chapter also examined the four major types of short-term credit available to a firm: (1) *accruals*, (2) *accounts payable (or trade credit)*, (3) *bank loans*, and (4) *commercial paper*. Companies use accruals on a regular basis, but this usage is not subject to discretionary actions. The other three types of credit are controllable, at least within limits.

Accounts payable may be divided into two components, *free trade credit* and *costly trade credit*. The cost of the latter is based on discounts lost, and it can be quite high. The financial manager should use all the free trade credit that is available, but costly trade credit should be used only if other credit is not available on better terms.

Bank loans may be negotiated on an individual basis as the need arises, or they may be obtained on a regular basis under a *line of credit*. One frequently encounters three different kinds of interest charges on bank loans: (1) *simple interest*, (2) *discount interest*, and (3) *add-on interest* for installment loans. Also, banks often require borrowers to maintain *compensating balances*. If the required balance exceeds the balance the firm would otherwise maintain, a compensating balance raises the effective cost of a bank loan.

Commercial paper is an important source of short-term credit, but it is available only to large, financially strong firms. Interest rates on commercial paper are generally below the prime bank rate, and the relative cost of paper is even lower when compensating balances on bank loans are considered. However, commercial paper does have disadvantages—if a firm that depends heavily on commercial paper experiences problems, its source of funds will immediately dry up. Commercial bankers are much more likely to help their customers ride out bad times.

Short-term credit is often *secured* by inventories and accounts receivable, which may be either *pledged* as collateral or *factored* (sold). Inventories can be pledged as collateral under (1) *blanket liens*, (2) *trust receipts*, or (3) *warehouse receipts*.

18-1 Define each of the following terms: *Questions*
    a. Working capital level policies
    b. Permanent current assets versus temporary current assets
    c. "Flexibility" as a reason for using short-term debt
    d. Alternative working capital financing policies
    e. Trade credit; free trade credit; costly trade credit
    f. "Stretching" accounts payable
    g. Promissory note; line of credit; revolving credit agreement
    h. Compensating balance; a compensating balance which *does not* increase the cost of a loan
    i. Prime rate
    j. Simple interest; discount interest; add-on interest; revolving credit interest; APR
    k. Commercial paper; commercial paper rate
    l. Secured loan; trust receipt; field warehouse; pledging; factoring

18-2 "Firms can control their accruals within fairly wide limits; depending on the cost of accruals, financing from this source will be increased or decreased." Discuss.

18-3 Is it true that both trade credit and accruals represent a spontaneous source of capital to finance growth? Explain.

18-4 Is it true that most firms are able to obtain some "free" trade credit, and that additional trade credit is often available, but at a cost? Explain.

18-5 What kinds of firms use commercial paper? Could Mamma and Pappa Gus's Corner Grocery borrow on commercial paper?

18-6 From the standpoint of the borrower, is long-term or short-term credit riskier? Explain. Would it ever make sense to borrow on a short-term basis if short-term rates were above long-term rates?

18-7 If long-term credit exposes a borrower to less risk, why would people or firms borrow on a short-term basis?

18-8 Suppose a firm can borrow at the prime rate or also sell commercial paper.
    a. If the prime rate is 12 percent, what is a reasonable estimate for the cost of commercial paper?
    b. If a substantial cost differential exists, why might a firm such as this one actually borrow some of its funds from both markets?

18-1 Suppose a firm makes purchases of $2.4 million per year under terms   *Problems*
of 2/10, net 30. It takes discounts.
    a. What is the average amount of accounts payable, net of discounts? (Assume the $2.4 million purchases are net of discounts; that is,

gross purchases are $2,448,980, discounts are $48,980, and net purchases are $2.4 million. Also, use 360 days in a year.)

b. Is there a cost of the trade credit it uses?

c. If it did not take discounts, what would its average payables be, and what would be the cost of this nonfree trade credit?

d. What would its cost of not taking discounts be if it "stretched" its payments to 40 days?

18-2 Selfridge Corporation projects an increase in sales from $2 million to $3 million, but the company needs an additional $600,000 of current assets to support this expansion. The money can be obtained from the bank at an interest rate of 14 percent discount interest. Alternatively, Selfridge can finance the expansion by no longer taking discounts, and thus increasing accounts payable. Selfridge purchases under terms of 2/10, net 30, but it can delay payment for an additional 30 days, paying in 60 days, and thus becoming 30 days past due, without a penalty at this time.

a. Based strictly on an interest rate comparison, how should Selfridge finance its expansion?

b. What additional qualitative factors should be considered in reaching a decision?

18-3 The Kriebel Corporation had sales of $1.95 million last year and earned a 4 percent return, after taxes, on sales. Although its terms of purchase are 20 days, its accounts payable represent 60 days' purchases. The president of the company is seeking to increase the company's bank borrowings in order to become current (that is, have 20 days' payables outstanding) in meeting its trade obligations. The company's balance sheet is shown below (thousands of dollars):

Cash	$ 25	Accounts payable	$ 300
Accounts receivable	125	Bank loans	250
Inventory	650	Accruals	125
Current assets	$ 800	Current liabilities	$ 675
Land and buildings	250	Mortgage on real estate	250
Equipment	250	Common stock, par 10¢	125
		Retained earnings	250
Total assets	$1,300	Total claims	$1,300

a. How much bank financing is needed to eliminate past-due accounts payable?

b. Would you as a bank loan officer make the loan? Why?

18-4 C. Charles Smith & Sons sells on terms of 2/10, net 40. Sales last year were $6 million. Half of Smith's customers pay on the tenth day and take discounts. What rate of return is Smith earning on its nondiscount receivables, where this rate of return is defined to be equal to the cost of this trade credit to the nondiscount customers?

18-5 Granulated Grain, Inc., buys on terms of 1/10, net 30, but it has not been taking discounts and has actually been paying in 60 days rather than 30 days. Granulated's balance sheet follows (thousands of dollars):

Cash	$ 50	Accounts payable[a]	$ 500
Accounts receivable	450	Notes payable	50
Inventories	750	Accruals	50
Current assets	$1,250	Current liabilities	$ 600
		Long-term debt	150
Fixed assets	750	Common equity	1,250
Total assets	$2,000	Total claims	$2,000

[a]Stated net of discounts.

Now Granulated's suppliers are threatening to stop shipments unless the company begins making prompt payments (that is, pays in 30 days or less). The firm can borrow on a 1-year note (call this a current liability) from its bank at a rate of 15 percent, discount interest, with a 20 percent compensating balance required. (All of the cash now on hand is needed for transactions; it cannot be used as part of the compensating balance.)

a. Determine what action Granulated should take by calculating (1) the cost of nonfree trade credit, and (2) the cost of the bank loan.

b. Based on your decision on Part a, construct a pro forma balance sheet. (Hint: You will need to include an account entitled "prepaid interest" under current assets.)

18-6 The Funtime Company manufactures plastic toys. It buys raw materials, manufactures the toys in the spring and summer, and ships them to department stores and toy stores by late summer or early fall. Funtime factors its receivables. If it did not, Funtime's October 1984 balance sheet might appear as shown below (thousands of dollars):

Cash	$ 40	Accounts payable	$1,200
Receivables	1,200	Notes payable	800
Inventory	800	Accruals	80
Current assets	$2,040	Current liabilities	$2,080
		Mortgages	200
		Common stock	400
Fixed assets	800	Retained earnings	160
Total assets	$2,840	Total claims	$2,840

Funtime provides advanced dating on its sales; thus, its receivables are not due for payment until January 31, 1985. Also, Funtime would have been overdue on some $800,000 of its accounts payable if the above situation had actually existed.

Funtime has had an agreement with a finance company to factor the receivables for the period October 31 through January 31 of each selling season. The factoring company charges a flat commission of 2 percent, plus 6 percent per year interest on the outstanding balance; it deducts a reserve of 8 percent for returned and damaged materials. Interest and commissions are paid in advance. No interest is charged on the reserved funds or on the commission.

a. Show the balance sheet of Funtime on October 31, 1984, including the purchase of all the receivables by the factoring company and the use of the funds to pay accounts payable.

b. If the $1.2 million is the average level of outstanding receivables, and if they turn over four times a year (hence the commission is paid four times a year), what are the total dollar costs of receivables financing (factoring) and the effective annual interest rate?

Selected Additional References and Cases

The following articles provide more information on overall working capital policy and management:

Lambrix, R. J., and S. S. Singhvi, "Managing the Working Capital Cycle," *Financial Executive*, June 1979, 32-41.

Maier, Steven F., and James H. Vander Weide, "A Practical Approach to Short-Run Financial Planning," *Financial Management*, Winter 1978, 10-16.

Merville, Larry J., and Lee A. Tavis, "Optimal Working Capital Policies: A Chance-Constrained Programming Approach," *Journal of Financial and Quantitative Analysis*, January 1973, 47-60.

Yardini, Edward E., "A Portfolio-Balance Model of Corporate Working Capital," *Journal of Finance*, May 1979, 535-552.

For more on trade credit, see

Brosky, John J., *The Implicit Cost of Trade Credit and Theory of Optimal Terms of Sale*, Credit Research Foundation, New York, 1969.

Schwartz, Robert A., "An Economic Analysis of Trade," *Journal of Financial and Quantitative Analysis*, September 1974, 643-658.

For more on bank lending and commercial credit in general, see

Campbell, Tim S., "A Model of the Market for Lines of Credit," *Journal of Finance*, March 1978, 231-243.

Stone, Bernell K., "Allocating Credit Lines, Planned Borrowing, and Tangible Services over a Company's Banking System," *Financial Management*, Summer 1975, 65-78.

For a discussion of effective yields, see

Glasgo, Philip W., William J. Landes, and A. Frank Thompson, "Bank Discount, Coupon Equivalent, and Compound Yields," *Financial Management*, Autumn 1982, 80-84.

Finnerty, John D., "Bank Discount, Coupon Equivalent, and Compound Yields: Comment," *Financial Management*, Summer 1983, 40-44.

The following case is appropriate for use with this chapter:

Case 8, "Brownsville Crate Company," in the Brigham-Crum casebook, which illustrates how changes in working capital policy affect expected profitability and risk.

Inventory Management

19

In 1982, Huffy Corporation, a major bicycle manufacturer, carried a finished goods inventory sufficient to cover four months of sales during the peak spring period. However, by 1984 Huffy had reduced its investment in inventories dramatically. In fact, a bicycle purchased from a retail store in June had probably not been assembled until late May, and Huffy probably did not receive the parts for the bicycle from its suppliers until April. Like many companies, Huffy is betting that, with the aid of computerized inventory controls and closer coordination with suppliers, it can get bikes to its local retail customers on time without keeping the usual warehouse inventories. Huffy forecasts its peak spring inventory in 1984 at $36 million, just over half the $69 million that was invested in the spring of 1982.

So far, the lean-inventory strategy appears to be working well. Huffy is saving millions of dollars in interest and storage costs by keeping a pared-down inventory, and it apparently is losing few sales. However, if the economy strengthens and bicycle sales surge, Huffy's inventories might not be sufficient to meet demand, causing sales to be lost to its rivals, who are continuing to carry higher inventories. Conversely, if higher interest rates suddenly squelch the economic expansion, or if demand shifts to bicycles of different styles, Huffy can adapt easily, but manufacturers with high inventories will be stuck with high carrying costs and/or obsolete bicycles. This chapter deals with the various types of decisions a firm must make in planning and controlling its inventory investment.

Inventories, which may be classified as (1) *raw materials*, (2) *work-in-process*, and (3) *finished goods*, are an essential part of virtually all business operations. As is the case with accounts receivable, inventory levels depend heavily upon sales. However, whereas receivables build up *after* sales have been made, inventories must be acquired *ahead* of sales. This is a critical difference, and the necessity of forecasting sales before establishing target inventory levels makes inventory management a difficult task. Also, since errors in the establishment of inventory levels can lead either to lost sales and profits or to cash flow and profit problems, inventory management is as important as it is difficult.

Typical Inventory Decisions

Two examples will make clear the types of issues involved in inventory management, and the problems poor inventory control can cause.

Retail Clothing Store

Glamour Galore Boutique must order bathing suits for summer sales in January, and it must take delivery by April to be sure of having enough suits to meet the heavy May-June demand. Bathing suits come in many styles, colors, and sizes. If the buyer stocks incorrectly, either in total or in terms of the style-color-size distribution, then the store will have trouble. It will lose potential sales if it stocks too few suits, and it will be forced to mark them down and take losses if it stocks too many or the wrong types.

The effects of inventory changes on the balance sheet are important. For simplicity, assume that Glamour Galore has a $100 base stock of inventories, financed by common stock. Its initial balance sheet is as follows:

Inventories (base stock)	$100	Common stock	$100
Total assets	$100	Total claims	$100

Now it anticipates a seasonal increase in sales of $300 and takes on additional inventories in that amount, financing them with a bank loan:

Inventories	$400	Notes payable to bank	$300
		Common stock	100
Total assets	$400	Total claims	$400

If everything works out as planned, sales will be made, inventories will be converted to cash, the bank loan can be retired, and the company will have earned a profit. The balance sheet, after a successful season, might look like this:

Cash and marketable securities	$ 50	Notes payable to bank	$ 0
Inventories (base stock)	100	Common stock	100
		Retained earnings	50
Total assets	$150	Total claims	$150

The company is now in a highly liquid position and is ready to begin a new season.

But suppose the season had not gone well. Sales were slow, and as fall approached, the balance sheet looked like this:

Inventories	$300	Notes payable to bank	$200
		Common stock	100
Total assets	$300	Total claims	$300

Now suppose the bank insists on repayment of its loan, and it wants cash, and not bathing suits. But if the bathing suits did not sell well in the summer, how will out-of-style suits sell in the fall? Assume that Glamour Galore is forced to mark the suits down to half their cost in order to sell them to raise cash to repay the bank loan. The result will be as follows:

Cash	$150	Notes payable to bank	$200
		Common stock	100
		Retained earnings	(150)
Total assets	$150	Total claims	$150

At this point, Glamour Galore goes bankrupt. The bank gets the $150 of cash and takes a $50 loss on its loan. The stockholders are wiped out, and the company goes out of business.

Now consider a different type of situation, that of Whirlwind Corporation, a well-established appliance manufacturer, whose inventory position, in millions of dollars, follows:

Appliance Manufacturer

Raw materials	$ 200
Work-in-process	200
Finished goods	600
Total inventories	$1,000

Suppose Whirlwind anticipates that the economy is about to get much stronger and that the demand for appliances is likely to rise sharply. If it is to share in the expected boom, Whirlwind will have to increase production. This means it will have to increase inventories, and, since the inventory increase will precede sales, additional financing will be required. The details are not shown here, but some liability account, perhaps notes payable, would have to be increased in order to support the inventory buildup.

Proper inventory management requires close coordination among the sales, purchasing, production, and finance departments. The sales/marketing department is generally the first to spot changes in demand. These changes must be worked into the company's purchasing and manufacturing schedules, and the financial manager must arrange any financing that will be needed to support the inventory buildup.

Improper coordination among departments, poor sales forecasts, or both can lead to disaster. For example, Varner Corporation, a manufacturer of portable computers, was recently forced into bankruptcy because of a poor system of internal controls. The company set its production schedules for 1984 on the basis of 1983 sales. However, introduction of new, improved computers by competitors caused sales to drop sharply during the first half of 1984. Production schedules were not adjusted downward, so both inventories and bank debt built up. By the time the situation was properly assessed, inventories of now obsolete computers had risen to over $10 million. The situation was like this (in millions of dollars):

Cash		$ 1	Accounts payable	$ 3
Receivables		8	Notes payable to bank	15
Inventories:	Good	6	Total current liabilities	$18
	Bad	10	Long-term debt	10
Total current assets		$25	Common equity	7
Fixed assets		10		
Total assets		$35	Total claims	$35

The bank insisted upon payment of the note. Varner simply could not generate the necessary cash, so it was forced into bankruptcy.

Accounting for Inventory

When finished goods are sold, the firm must assign a cost of goods sold. The cost of goods sold appears on the income statement as an expense for the period, and the balance sheet inventory account is reduced by a like amount. There are four methods of valuing cost of goods sold, and hence valuing remaining inventory: (1) specific identification, (2) first-in, first-out (FIFO), (3) last-in, first-out (LIFO), and (4) weighted average.

Specific Identification

Under *specific identification*, a unique cost is attached to each item in inventory. Then, when an item is sold, the inventory value is reduced by that specific amount. This method is used only when the items are high-cost and move relatively slowly, such as would be the case for an automobile dealership or a jeweler.

First-In, First-Out (FIFO)

In the *FIFO* method, the units that are sold during a given period are assumed to be the first units that were placed in inventory. As a result, cost of goods sold will be based on the cost of the older inventory items, and the remaining inventory value will consist of the newer goods. Note that this is purely an accounting convention—the actual physical units sold could be either the earlier or the later units placed in inventory, or some combination.

LIFO is the opposite of FIFO. The cost of goods sold is based on the last units placed in inventory, while the remaining inventory value consists of the first goods placed in inventory.

Last-In, First-Out (LIFO)

This method involves the computation of the *weighted average* unit cost of goods available for sale from inventory. This average cost is then applied to the goods sold to determine the cost of goods sold. This method results in a cost of goods sold and ending inventory value which falls somewhere between the ones obtained by the FIFO and LIFO methods.

Weighted Average

To illustrate these methods and their effects on a firm's financial statements, assume that Porter Electronics manufactured five identical electronic switching systems during a one-year accounting period. During the period, increased parts prices by Porter's suppliers and increases in the price of platinum (a key component) combined to push up prices sharply, so the actual cost of the units also increased over the period:

Comparison of Inventory Accounting Methods

Unit number:	1	2	3	4	5	Total
Cost:	$10,000	$12,000	$14,000	$16,000	$18,000	$70,000

There were no units on hand at the beginning of the period, and Units 1, 3, and 5 were sold during the year.

If Porter used the specific identification method, the cost of goods sold would be reported as $10,000 + $14,000 + $18,000 = $42,000, while the end-of-period inventory value would be $70,000 − $42,000 = $28,000. If Porter used the FIFO method, its cost of goods sold would be $10,000 + $12,000 + $14,000 = $36,000, and the ending inventory value would be $70,000 − $36,000 = $34,000. If Porter used the LIFO method, its cost of goods sold would be $48,000, and its ending inventory value would be $22,000. Finally, if Porter used the weighted average method of inventory valuation, its average cost per unit sold would be $70,000/5 = $14,000, its cost of goods sold would be 3($14,000) = $42,000, and its ending inventory value would be $70,000 − $42,000 = $28,000. If we assume that Porter's actual sales revenues from the systems totaled $80,000, or an average of $26,667 per unit sold, and that its other costs were minimal, here is a summary of the effects of the four inventory methods:

Method	Sales	Cost of Goods Sold	Profit	Ending Inventory Value
Specific identification	$80,000	$42,000	$38,000	$28,000
FIFO	80,000	36,000	44,000	34,000
LIFO	80,000	48,000	32,000	22,000
Weighted average	80,000	42,000	38,000	28,000

Ignoring taxes, Porter's cash flows are not affected by its choice of inventory accounting methods, yet its balance sheet and reported profits do vary with each method. In an inflationary period, FIFO gives the lowest cost of goods sold, and thus the highest reported net income for the period. FIFO also shows the highest inventory value; thus, it produces the strongest apparent liquidity as measured by net working capital or the current ratio. On the other hand, LIFO produces the highest cost of goods sold, the lowest reported profits, and the weakest apparent liquidity position. However, when taxes are considered, LIFO provides the greatest tax deductibility, and thus results in the lowest tax burden. Consequently, after-tax cash flow is greatest using LIFO.

Of course, these results only apply to periods in which costs are increasing. If costs were constant, all four methods would produce the same cost of goods sold, the same ending inventory, the same taxes, and the same cash flows. However, inflation seems to be a fact of life in most industries, so during the rising cost period of the 1970s, a large number of firms switched to LIFO to take advantage of its greater tax and cash flow benefits.[1]

The ABC Method of Inventory Classification

Inventory management, like all other managerial activities, involves costs. Consequently, management's effort should be focused on those items of inventory that are most critical to the firm. To illustrate, Porter Electronics Corporation carries over 30,000 different items in inventory, ranging from very expensive microchips to two-story switching system frames to sheet metal screws. These items vary widely in price, in reorder delivery time, and in terms of the consequences of running out of stock (a stock-out). To manage such a diverse assortment of materials, Porter employs the ABC method of inventory classification. To begin,

---

[1]Note also that inventory valuation methods have cumulative effects that build up over the years. As an example, Del Monte Corporation used LIFO for many years, so it had certain items which, from an accounting standpoint, had been produced back in the 1920s and were still carried on the balance sheet at production costs of that era. Thus, Del Monte had "1923 catsup" and other items whose value was greatly understated. (Of course, Del Monte had no 1923 catsup in storage; there is no necessary relationship between the dating of the physical and the accounting inventory items.) Then, if Del Monte happened to have a bad year, when profits would otherwise be depressed, it would sell off (for accounting purposes) some of the old, undervalued LIFO inventory. This would boost profits and help to "manage" earnings so as to produce a smooth pattern of growth over time.

each inventory item is assigned an order lead time and a stock-out consequence multiplier as illustrated in Table 19-1. The higher the multiplier value, the more important is control over the item.

Porter also has data on the average annual usage and cost of each inventory item. With these data, plus the Table 19-1 multiplier values, Porter assigns a numerical *management importance value* to each inventory item, using the following formula:

$$\begin{matrix}\text{Management} \\ \text{importance} \\ \text{value}\end{matrix} = \left(\begin{matrix}\text{Average} \\ \text{annual} \\ \text{usage}\end{matrix}\right)\left(\begin{matrix}\text{Cost} \\ \text{per} \\ \text{unit}\end{matrix}\right)\left(\begin{matrix}\text{Lead time} \\ \text{multiplier}\end{matrix} + \begin{matrix}\text{Stock-out} \\ \text{multiplier}\end{matrix}\right).$$

For example, Porter's standard blank 8 × 11 circuit board costs the firm $2 per unit, and Porter uses 500,000 boards a year. The boards require an order lead time of 21 days, and they are in the critical stock-out class. Thus, the management importance value is 32 million:

$$\text{Value} = (500,000)(2)(2 + 30) = 32,000,000.$$

Each inventory item is analyzed similarly, the values for the various items are arrayed from highest to lowest, each item's percentage of the total is calculated, and *cumulative* percentage values are plotted as shown in Figure 19-1. Then, the inventory items are separated into three classes, labeled A, B, and C. Notice that only 10 percent of the inventory items are in the A class, but these items involve 50 percent of the cumulative inventory "value," while the 60 percent of the items in Class C

Table 19-1
Inventory Multiplier Values

Order Lead Time Multipliers

Lead Time Class	Multiplier
0−2 days	0
3−7 days	1
8-30 days	2
1-3 months	4
4-6 months	8
7-9 months	12
10-12 months	16

Stock-Out Consequence Multipliers

Consequence Class	Multiplier
Unimportant	1
Average	15
Critical	30

Figure 19-1
ABC Classification Graph

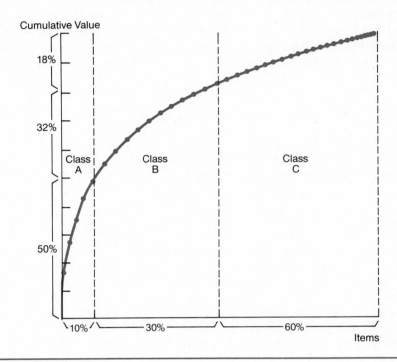

constitute only 18 percent of the total value. By concentrating attention on the items identified as being most critical, Porter better utilizes its managerial resources. The inventory manager reviews the A items' recent usage rates, stock position, and delivery time situation monthly, and adjusts inventory order quantities as necessary. Category B items are reviewed and adjusted less frequently—in Porter's case, every quarter—while C items are only reviewed annually. Thus, the inventory control manager's resources are concentrated where they will do the most good.

Inventory Management

Inventory management focuses on four basic questions. (1) How many units should be ordered (or produced) at a given time? (2) At what point should inventory be ordered (or produced)? (3) What inventory items warrant special attention? (4) Can inventory cost changes be hedged? The remainder of the chapter is devoted to providing answers to these four questions.

The goal of inventory management is to provide the inventories required to sustain operations at the minimum cost. Thus, the first step in inventory management is to identify all the costs involved in purchasing and maintaining inventories in order to minimize them. Table 19-2 gives a listing of the typical costs that are associated with inventories. In the table, we have broken down costs into three categories: those associated with carrying inventories, those associated with ordering and receiving inventories, and those associated with running short of inventory.

Inventory Costs

Although they may well be the most important element, we shall at this point disregard the third category of costs—the costs of running short. These costs are dealt with by adding safety stocks, as we will discuss later. Similarly, we shall discuss quantity discounts in a later section. The costs that remain for consideration at this stage, then, are carrying costs and ordering, shipping, and receiving costs.

Carrying costs generally rise in direct proportion to the average amount of inventory carried. Inventories carried, in turn, depend on the frequency with which orders are placed. To illustrate, if a firm sells S units

Carrying Costs

Table 19-2
Costs Associated with Inventories

	Approximate Annual Percentage Cost
Carrying Costs	
1. Cost of capital tied up	15.0%
2. Storage and handling costs	0.5
3. Insurance	0.5
4. Property taxes	1.0
5. Depreciation and obsolescence	12.0
Total	29.0%
Ordering, Shipping, and Receiving Costs	
1. Cost of placing orders, including production and set-up costs	Varies
2. Shipping and handling costs	2.5%
3. Quantity discounts lost	Varies
Costs of Running Short	
1. Loss of sales	Varies
2. Loss of customer goodwill	Varies
3. Disruption of production schedules	Varies

Note: These costs vary from firm to firm, from item to item, and also over time. The figures shown are U.S. Department of Commerce estimates for an average manufacturing firm. Where costs vary so widely that no meaningful numbers can be assigned, we simply report "Varies."

per year, and places equal sized orders N times per year, then, assuming no safety stocks are carried, the average inventory, A, is:

$$A = \frac{S/N}{2}. \tag{19-1}$$

For example, if a firm sells S = 120,000 units in a year, and orders inventory N = 4 four times a year, then its average inventory will be A = 15,000 units:

$$A = \frac{S/N}{2} = \frac{120,000/4}{2} = \frac{30,000}{2} = 15,000 \text{ units.}$$

Now assume that the firm purchases its inventory at a price P = $2 per unit. The average inventory value is, thus, (P)(A) = ($2)(15,000) = $30,000.

   If the firm has a cost of capital of 10 percent, it incurs $3,000 in capital costs to carry the inventory. Further, assume that each year the firm incurs $2,000 of storage costs (space, utilities, security, taxes, and so forth), $500 of inventory insurance costs, and a cost of $1,000 because of depreciation and obsolescence. The firm's total costs of carrying the $30,000 average inventory is $3,000 + $2,000 + $500 + $1,000 = $6,500. Thus, the percentage cost of carrying the inventory for this firm is $6,500/$30,000 = 0.217 = 21.7%. Defining the percentage cost as C, we can, in general, find the total annual carrying costs, TCC, as the percentage carrying cost, C, times the price per unit, P, times the average number of units, A:

$$TCC = \text{Total carrying costs} = (C)(P)(A). \tag{19-2}$$

In our example,

$$TCC = (0.217)($2)(15,000) \approx $6,500.$$

Ordering Costs   Although carrying costs are entirely variable and rise in direct proportion to the average size of inventories, ordering costs are fixed.[2] For example, the costs of placing and receiving an order—interoffice memos, long-distance telephone calls, setting up a production run, and taking delivery—are essentially fixed costs for each order, so this part of inventory cost is simply the fixed cost of placing and receiving orders

---

[2]For certain purposes, it is useful to add another term to the inventory cost model, *shipping and receiving costs.* This term should be added if there are economies of scale in shipping, such that the cost of shipping a unit is smaller if shipments are larger. However, in most situations, shipping costs are not sensitive to order size, so total shipping costs are simply the shipping cost per unit times the units ordered (and sold) during the year. Under this condition, shipping costs are not influenced by inventory policy, and hence may be disregarded for purposes of determining the optimal inventory level and the optimal order size.

times the number of orders placed. We define the fixed costs associated with ordering inventories as F, and if we place N orders per year, the total annual ordering costs, TOC, are:

$$TOC = (F)(N). \tag{19-3}$$

Here TOC = total ordering costs, F = fixed costs per order, and N = number of orders placed per year.

Equation 19-1 may be rewritten as N = S/2A, and then substituted into Equation 19-3:

$$TOC = \text{Total ordering costs} = F\left(\frac{S}{2A}\right). \tag{19-4}$$

To illustrate the use of Equation 19-4, if F = \$100, S = 120,000 units, and A = 15,000 units, then TOC, the total annual ordering costs, are

$$TOC = \$100\left(\frac{120,000}{30,000}\right) = \$100(4) = \$400.$$

Total Costs

Total carrying costs, TCC, as defined in Equation 19-2, and total ordering costs, TOC, as defined in Equation 19-4, may be combined to find total inventory costs, TIC, as follows:

$$TIC = \text{Total inventory costs} = TCC + TOC$$
$$= (C)(P)(A) + F\left(\frac{S}{2A}\right). \tag{19-5}$$

Recognizing that the average inventory carried is A = Q/2, or one-half the size of each order quantity, Q, Equation 19-5 may be rewritten as follows:

$$TIC = (C)(P)\left(\frac{Q}{2}\right) + \frac{(F)(S)}{Q}. \tag{19-6}$$

We will use this equation in the next section to develop the optimal inventory ordering quantity.

The Optimal Ordering Quantity

Inventories are obviously necessary, but it is equally obvious that a firm will suffer if it has too much or too little inventory. How can we determine the *optimal* inventory level? One approach commonly used is based on the *economic ordering quantity (EOQ)* model as described below.

Derivation of the EOQ Model

Figure 19-2 illustrates the basic premise on which the EOQ model is built, namely, that some costs rise with larger inventories while other costs decline, and there is an optimal order size which minimizes the

Figure 19-2
Determination of the Optimal Order Quantity

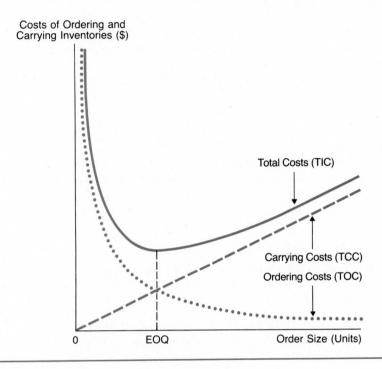

total costs associated with inventories. First, as noted earlier, the average investment in inventories depends on how frequently orders are placed and the size of each order—if we order every day, average inventories will be much smaller than if we order once a year. Further, as Figure 19-2 shows, the firm's carrying costs rise with larger orders: Larger orders mean larger average inventories, so warehousing costs, interest on funds tied up in inventory, insurance, and obsolescence costs will all increase. At the same time, ordering costs decline with larger orders and inventories: The cost of placing orders, costs of supplier production set up, and order handling costs will all decline if we order infrequently and consequently hold larger quantities.

If the carrying and ordering cost curves in Figure 19-2 are added, the sum represents the total cost of ordering and carrying inventories, TIC. The point where the total cost curve is minimized represents the *economic ordering quantity (EOQ)*, and this, in turn, determines the optimal average inventory level.

The EOQ is found by differentiating Equation 19-6 with respect to ordering quantity, Q, and setting the derivative equal to zero:

$$\frac{d(TIC)}{dQ} = \frac{(C)(P)}{2} - \frac{(F)(S)}{Q^2} = 0.$$

Now, solving for Q, we obtain:

$$\frac{(C)(P)}{2} = \frac{(F)(S)}{Q^2}$$

$$Q^2 = \frac{2(F)(S)}{(C)(P)}$$

$$EOQ = \sqrt{\frac{2(F)(S)}{(C)(P)}}. \qquad \textbf{(19-7)}$$

Here

EOQ = economic ordering quantity, or the optimum quantity to be ordered each time an order is placed.

F = fixed costs of placing and receiving an order.

S = annual sales in units.

C = carrying costs expressed as a percentage of inventory value.

P = purchase price the firm must pay per unit of inventory.

Equation 19-7 is the EOQ model.[3] The assumptions of the model, which will be relaxed shortly, include the following: (1) sales can be forecasted perfectly, (2) sales are evenly distributed throughout the year, and (3) orders are received with no delays whatever.

To illustrate the EOQ model, consider the following data, supplied by Cotton Tops, Inc., a distributor of custom designed T-shirts which sells to concessionaires at Daisy World:

*EOQ Model
Illustration*

S = sales = 26,000 shirts per year.

C = percentage carrying cost = 20 percent of inventory value.

P = purchase price per shirt = $6.1538 per shirt. (The sales price is $9, but this is irrelevant for our purposes.)

---

[3]The EOQ model can also be written as

$$EOQ = \sqrt{\frac{2(F)(S)}{C^*}},$$

where C^* is the carrying cost per unit expressed in *dollars*.

F = fixed cost per order = $1,000. The bulk of this cost is the labor cost for setting up the equipment for the production run. The manufacturer bills this cost separately from the $6.1538 cost per shirt.

Substituting these data into Equation 19-7, we obtain an EOQ of 6,500 units:

$$EOQ = \sqrt{\frac{2(F)(S)}{(C)(P)}} = \sqrt{\frac{(2)(\$1,000)(26,000)}{(0.2)(\$6.1538)}}$$
$$= \sqrt{42,250,317} = 6,500 \text{ units.}$$

Notice that average inventory holdings depend directly on the EOQ; this relationship is illustrated graphically in Figure 19-3. Immediately after an order is received, 6,500 shirts are in stock. The usage rate, or sales rate, is 500 shirts per week (26,000/52 weeks), so inventories are drawn down by this amount each week. Thus, the actual number of

Figure 19-3
Inventory Position without Safety Stock

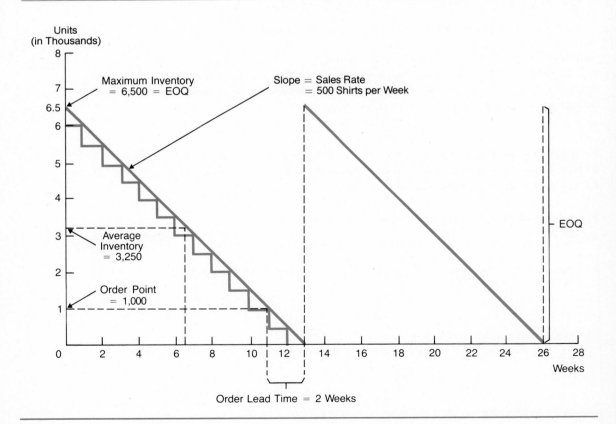

units held in inventory will vary from 6,500 shirts just after an order is received to zero just before a new order arrives. With a 6,500 beginning balance, a zero ending balance, and a uniform sales rate, inventories will average one-half the EOQ, or 3,250 shirts, during the year. At a cost of $6.1538 per shirt, the average investment in inventories will be $(3,250)($6.1538) = $19,999.85 \approx $20,000$. If inventories are financed by bank loans, the loan will vary from a high of $40,000 to a low of $0, but the average amount outstanding over the course of a year will be $20,000.

Notice that the EOQ, and hence average inventory holdings, rises with the square root of sales. Therefore, a given increase in sales will result in a less-than-proportionate increase in inventories, so the inventory/sales ratio will tend to decline as a firm grows. For example, Cotton Tops' EOQ is 6,500 shirts at an annual sales level of 26,000, and the average inventory is 3,250 shirts, or $20,000. However, if sales increase by 100 percent, to 52,000 shirts per year, the EOQ will rise only to 9,192 units, or by 41 percent, and the average inventory will rise by this same percentage. This suggests that there are economies of scale in the holding of inventories.[4]

Setting the Reorder Point

If a two-week lead time is required for production and shipping, what is Cotton Tops' reorder point level? If we use a 52-week year, Cotton Tops sells $26,000/52 = 500$ shirts per week. Thus, if a two-week lag occurs between ordering and receipt, Cotton Tops must place the order when there are $2(500) = 1,000$ shirts on hand. At the end of the two-week production and shipping period, the inventory balance will drop to zero just as the order of new shirts arrives.

Therefore, if Cotton Tops knew for certain that both the sales rate and the order lead time would never vary, it could operate exactly as shown in Figure 19-3. However, sales do change, and production and/or shipping delays are frequently encountered; to guard against these events, the firm will carry additional inventories, or safety stocks, as discussed below.

EOQ Model Extensions

The basic EOQ model was derived under several restrictive assumptions. In this section, we relax some of these assumptions and, in the process, extend the model to make it more useful.

---

[4]Note, however, that these scale economies relate to each particular item, and not to the entire firm. Thus, a large distributor with $500 million of sales might have a higher inventory/sales ratio than a much smaller distributor if the small firm has only a few high-sales-volume items while the large firm distributes a great many low-volume items.

The Concept of
Safety Stocks

The concept of a *safety stock* is illustrated in Figure 19-4. First, note that the slope of the sales line measures the expected rate of sales. The company *expects* sales of 500 shirts per week, but let us assume that the maximum likely sales rate is twice this amount, or 1,000 units each week. Further, assume that Cotton Tops sets the safety stock at 1,000 shirts. Thus, it initially orders 7,500 shirts, the EOQ plus the safety stock. Subsequently, it reorders the EOQ, 6,500 shirts, whenever the inventory level falls to 2,000 shirts, the safety stock of 1,000 shirts plus the 1,000 shirts expected to be used while awaiting delivery of the order. Notice that the company could, over the two-week delivery period, sell 1,000 units a week, or double its normal expected sales. This maximum rate of sales is shown by the steeper dashed line in Figure 19-4. The condition that makes possible this higher maximum sales rate is the safety stock of 1,000 shirts.

The safety stock is also useful to guard against delays in receiving orders. The expected delivery time is two weeks. But, with a 1,000

Figure 19-4
Inventory Position with Safety Stock Included

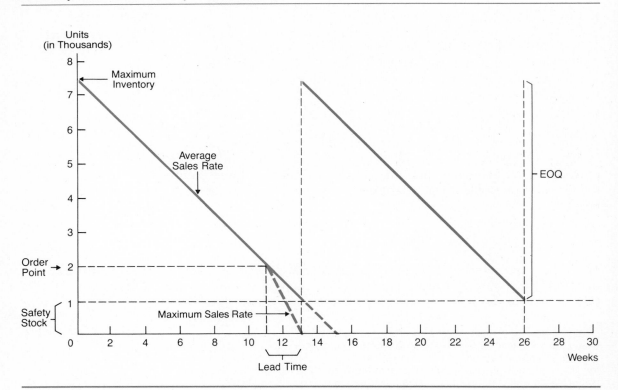

unit safety stock, the company could maintain sales at the expected rate of 500 units per week for an additional two weeks if production or shipping delays held up an order.

However, carrying a safety stock has costs. The average inventory is now EOQ/2 plus safety stock or 6,500/2 + 1,000 = 3,250 + 1,000 = 4,250 shirts, and the average inventory value is now (4,250)($6.1538) = $26,154. This increase in average inventory causes an increase in inventory carrying costs.

The optimum safety stock varies from situation to situation, but, in general, it *increases* with (1) the uncertainty of demand forecasts, (2) the costs (in terms of lost sales and lost goodwill) that result from inventory shortages, and (3) the probability that delays will occur in receiving shipments. The optimum safety stock *decreases* as the cost of carrying this additional inventory increases.

Setting the Safety Stock Level

The critical question with regard to safety stocks is this: How large should the safety stock be? To answer this question, first examine Table 19-3, which contains the probability distribution of Cotton Tops' unit sales for an average 13-week period, the time it takes to sell an order of 6,500 T-shirts. Note that the expected sales over the 13-week inventory cycle is 6,500 units.

Cotton Tops' managers have estimated that the annual carrying cost is 20 percent of inventory value. Since each shirt has an inventory value of $6.1538, the annual carrying cost per unit is 0.20($6.1538) = $1.2308, and the carrying cost for each 13-week inventory period is $1.2308(13/52) = $0.308 per unit. Next, Cotton Tops' managers must estimate the cost of shortages. Assume that when shortages occur, 80 percent of Cotton Tops' buyers are willing to accept back orders, while 20 percent of its potential customers simply do not buy in that 13-week inventory period. Remembering that each shirt sells for $9.00, each one unit shortage produces 0.2($9.00) = $1.80 in expected lost revenues. With this infor-

Table 19-3
Thirteen-Week Sales Probability Distribution

Probability		Unit Sales
0.1		5,500
0.2		6,000
0.4		6,500
0.2		7,000
0.1		7,500
1.0	Expected sales =	6,500

mation, the firm can calculate the costs of different safety stock levels. This is done in Table 19-4.

For each safety stock level listed, we determine the expected cost of a shortage based on the sales probability distribution in Table 19-3. There is an expected shortage cost of $360 if no safety stock is carried; $90 if the safety stock is set at 500 units; and no expected shortage, hence no shortage cost, if a safety stock of 1,000 units is used. The cost of carrying each safety level is merely the cost of carrying a unit of inventory over the 13-week inventory period, $0.308, times the safety stock; for example, the cost of carrying a safety stock of 500 units is $0.308(500) = $154. Finally, we sum the expected shortage cost in Column 6 and the safety stock carrying cost in Column 7 to obtain the total cost figures given in

Table 19-4
Safety Stock Analysis

Safety Stock (1)	Sales (2)	Probability (3)	Shortage[a] (4)	Shortage Cost: $1.80 × (4) = (5)	Product: (3) × (5) = (6)	Safety Stock Carrying Cost: $0.308 × (1) = (7)	Expected Total Cost: (6) + (7) = (8)
0	5,500	0.1	0	$ 0	$ 0		
	6,000	0.2	0	0	0		
	6,500	0.4	0	0	0		
	7,000	0.2	500	900	180		
	7,500	0.1	1,000	1,800	180		
		1.0		Expected shortage cost = $360		$0	$360
500	5,500	0.1	0	$ 0	$ 0		
	6,000	0.2	0	0	0		
	6,500	0.4	0	0	0		
	7,000	0.2	0	0	0		
	7,500	0.1	500	900	90		
		1.0		Expected shortage cost $90		$154	$244
1,000	5,500	0.1	0	$0	$0		
	6,000	0.2	0	0	0		
	6,500	0.4	0	0	0		
	7,000	0.2	0	0	0		
	7,500	0.1	0	0	0		
		1.0		Expected shortage cost $0		$308	$308

[a]Shortage = Actual sales − (6,500 + Safety stock); positive values only.

Column 8. Since the 500-unit safety stock has the lowest expected total cost, Cotton Tops should carry this safety level.[5]

Of course, the resulting optimal safety level is very sensitive to the firm's estimates of the sales probability distribution and shortage costs. Errors here could result in incorrect safety stock levels. Note also that in calculating the $1.80 per unit shortage cost, we implicitly assumed that a lost sale in one period would not result in lost sales in future periods. If shortages cause customer ill will, which in turn leads to permanent sales reductions, the situation is much more serious, stock-out costs are far higher, and the firm should carry a larger safety stock. This is just one example of the many judgments required in inventory management—the mechanics are relatively simple, but the inputs are judgmental and difficult to obtain.

Now suppose the T-shirt manufacturer offered Cotton Tops a *quantity discount* of 2 percent on large orders. If the quantity discount applied to orders of 5,000 or more, then Cotton Tops would continue to place the EOQ order of 6,500 shirts and take the quantity discount. However, if the quantity discount required orders of 10,000 or more, then Cotton Tops' inventory manager would have to compare the savings that would result if its ordering quantity were increased to 10,000 units with the increase in costs caused by the departure from the 6,500 unit EOQ.

Quantity Discounts

First, consider the total costs associated with Cotton Tops' EOQ of 6,500 units. Using Equation 19-6, we find that total inventory costs are $8,000:

$$
\begin{aligned}
\text{TIC} &= \text{TCC} + \text{TOC} \\
&= (C)(P)(Q/2) + F(S/Q) \\
&= (0.20)(\$6.1538)(6,500/2) + \$1,000(26,000/6,500) \\
&= \$4,000 + \$4,000 = \$8,000.
\end{aligned}
$$

Now, what would the total inventory costs be if Cotton Tops ordered 10,000 units instead of 6,500? The answer is $8,631:

$$
\begin{aligned}
\text{TIC} &= (0.20)(\$6.0307)(10,000/2) + \$1,000(26,000/10,000) \\
&= \$6,031 + \$2,600 = \$8,631.
\end{aligned}
$$

Notice that when the discount is taken, the price, P, is reduced by the amount of the discount; the new price per unit would be 0.98($6.1538) = $6.0307. Also note that when the ordering quantity is increased, car-

---

[5]For a more detailed discussion of safety stocks, see Arthur Snyder, "Principles of Inventory Management," *Financial Executive*, April 1964, 13-21. If we also knew the probability distributions of order and lead times, we could determine joint probabilities of stock-outs with various safety stock levels.

rying costs increase because the firm is carrying a larger average inventory, but ordering costs decrease since the number of orders per year decreases. If we were to calculate total inventory costs at an ordering quantity of 5,000, we would find that carrying costs would be less than $4,000 and ordering costs would be more than $4,000, but the total inventory costs would be more than $8,000, since they are at a minimum when 6,500 units are ordered.[6]

Thus, inventory costs would increase by $8,631 − $8,000 = $631 if Cotton Tops were to increase its order size to 10,000 shirts. However, this cost increase must be compared with Cotton Tops' savings if it takes the discount. Taking the discount would save 0.02($6.1538) = $0.1231 per unit. Over the year, Cotton Tops orders 26,000 shirts, so the annual savings is $0.1231(26,000) ≈ $3,200. Thus, the net saving to Cotton Tops, if it were to increase its ordering quantity to 10,000 units and take the discount, is $3,200 in discounts less $631 in increased inventory costs, or $2,569. Obviously, it should order 10,000 units, and thus take the quantity discount.

Inflation

Moderate inflation—say 3 percent per year—can largely be ignored for purposes of inventory management, but at higher rates of inflation, it becomes important to consider this factor. If the rate of inflation in the types of goods the firm stocks tends to be relatively constant, it can be dealt with quite easily—simply deduct the expected annual rate of inflation from the carrying cost percentage, C, in Equation 19-7, and use this modified version of the EOQ model to establish the working stock. The reason for making this deduction is that inflation causes the value of the inventory to rise, thus offsetting somewhat the effects of depreciation and other carrying costs factors. Since C will now be smaller, the calculated EOQ, and hence the average inventory, will increase. However, the higher the rate of inflation, the higher are interest rates, and this factor will cause C to increase, thus lowering the EOQ and average inventories.

On balance, there is no evidence that inflation either raises or lowers the optimal inventories of firms in the aggregate. Inflation should still be explicitly considered, however, for it will raise the individual firm's optimal holdings if the rate of inflation for its own inventories is above average (and is greater than the effects of inflation on interest rates), and vice versa.

---

[6]At an ordering quantity of 5,000 units, total inventory costs are $8,277:

$$\text{TIC} = (0.20)(\$6.1538)(5,000/2) + \$1,000(26,000/5,000)$$
$$= \$3,077 + \$5,200 = \$8,277.$$

For most firms, it is unrealistic to assume that the demand for an inventory item is uniform throughout the year. What happens when there is seasonal demand, as would hold true for an ice cream company? Here the standard EOQ model is obviously not appropriate. However, it does provide a point of departure for setting inventory parameters which are then modified to fit the particular seasonal pattern. The procedure here is to divide the year into seasons in which annualized sales are relatively constant, say the summer, spring and fall, and winter. Then, the EOQ model could be applied separately to each period. During the transition between seasons, inventories would be either run down or built up with a special seasonal order.

Seasonal Demand

Thus far, we have interpreted the EOQ, and the resulting inventory variables, as single point estimates. It has been demonstrated that small deviations from the EOQ do not appreciably affect total inventory costs and, consequently, that the optimal ordering quantity should be viewed more as a range than as a single value.[7]

EOQ Range

To illustrate this point, we can examine the sensitivity of total inventory costs to ordering quantity for Cotton Tops, Inc. Table 19-5 contains the results of our sensitivity analysis. We conclude that the ordering quantity could range from 5,000 to 8,000 units without affecting total inventory costs by more than 3.5 percent. Thus, we see that managers can adjust the ordering quantity within a fairly wide range without fear of significantly increasing inventory costs.

Table 19-5
EOQ Sensitivity Analysis

Ordering Quantity	Percentage Deviation from Optimal	Total Inventory Costs	Percentage Deviation from Optimal
3,000	−54%	$10,513	+31.4%
4,000	−38	8,962	+12.0
5,000	−23	8,277	+3.5
6,000	−8	8,026	+0.3
6,500	0	8,000	0.0
7,000	+8	8,022	+0.2
8,000	+23	8,173	+2.2
9,000	+38	8,427	+5.3
10,000	+54	8,754	+9.4

---

[7]This is somewhat analogous to the optimal capital structure in that small changes in capital structure around the optimum do not have much effect on the firm's weighted average cost of capital. See Snyder, "Principles of Inventory Management."

Inventory Control Systems

The EOQ model, plus safety stocks, helps establish proper inventory levels, but inventory management also involves the *inventory ordering and control system*. One simple control procedure is the *red-line method*—inventory items are stocked in a bin, a red line is drawn around the inside of the bin at the level of the order point, and the inventory clerk places an order when the red line shows. The *two-bin method* has inventory items stocked in two bins. When the working bin is empty, an order is placed and inventory is drawn from the second bin. These procedures work well for parts such as bolts in a manufacturing process, or for many items in retail businesses.

Larger companies employ *computerized inventory control systems*. The computer starts with an inventory count in memory. As withdrawals are made, they are recorded by the computer, and the inventory balance is revised. When the order point is reached, the computer automatically places an order, and when the order is received, the recorded balance is increased. Retail stores have carried this system quite far—each item has a coded tag, and, as an item is checked out, the tag is passed over a reader which adjusts the computer's inventory balance at the same time the price is fed into the cash register tape. When the balance drops to the order point, an order is placed.

A good inventory control system is dynamic, not static. A company such as IBM or General Motors stocks hundreds of thousands of different items. The sales (or use) of these various items can rise or fall quite separately from rising or falling overall corporate sales. As the usage rate for an individual item begins to rise or fall, the inventory manager must adjust its balance to avoid running short or ending up with obsolete items.

Inventory Cost Hedging

In Chapter 15, we introduced the use of financial futures contracts to hedge against changes in interest rate levels. Actually, futures markets were established for many industrial and agricultural commodities long before they began to be used for financial instruments. We can use Porter Electronics, which uses large quantities of copper as well as several precious metals, to illustrate inventory hedging. Suppose that in July 1984, Porter foresaw a need for 100,000 pounds of copper in September 1985 for use in fulfilling a fixed price contract to supply solar power cells to the U.S. Government. Porter's managers are concerned that a strike of the copper mineworkers' union will occur when the union contract expires next spring. A strike would raise the price of copper significantly and possibly turn the expected profit on the solar cell contract into a loss.

Porter could hedge against increasing copper prices in the futures market. The New York Commodity Exchange trades standard copper futures contracts of 25,000 pounds each. Thus, Porter could buy four contracts (go long) for delivery in September 1985. These contracts were trading on July 2, 1984, for about 65 cents per pound. The spot price at that date was about 60 cents per pound. If copper prices do rise appreciably over the next 14 months, the value of Porter's long position in copper futures would increase, thus offsetting some of the price increase in the commodity itself. Of course, if copper prices fall, Porter would lose money on its hedge, but the company would be buying the copper on the spot market at a cheaper price, so it would make a higher profit on its sale of solar cells. Thus, hedging in the futures markets locks in the futures price and removes the inherent price uncertainty of future inventory purchases.

Summary

Inventory management centers around the balancing of a set of costs that increase with larger inventory holdings (storage costs, cost of capital, and physical deterioration) and a set of costs that decline with larger holdings (ordering costs, lost sales, and disruptions of production schedules). Inventory management has been quantified to a greater extent than most aspects of business, with the *EOQ model* being one important part of most inventory systems. This model can be used to determine the optimal order quantity, which, when combined with a specified safety stock, determines the average inventory level. Inventory control systems are used to keep track of actual inventories, and to insure that inventory levels are adjusted to changing sales levels.

Good inventory management will result in a relatively high inventory turnover, low write-offs of obsolete or deteriorated inventories, and few instances of work stoppages or lost sales due to stock-outs. All this, in turn, contributes to a high profit margin, a high rate of return on investment, and a strong stock price.

Questions

19-1   Define each of the following items:
    a. Inventory accounting methods
    b. Specific identification; FIFO; LIFO; weighted average
    c. Carrying costs; ordering costs
    d. EOQ; EOQ model; EOQ range
    e. Reorder point; safety stock
    f. Quantity discount
    g. Inventory control systems
    h. Inventory cost hedging
    i. ABC method; two-bin method

19-2   If a firm calculates its optimal inventory of widgets to be 1,000 units when the general rate of inflation is 2 percent, is it true that the optimal inventory (in units) will almost certainly rise if the general rate of inflation climbs to 10 percent?

19-3   Would each of the following events probably cause average inventories (the sum of the inventories held at the end of each month of the year divided by 12) to rise, fall, or change in an indeterminant manner? Be prepared to explain your answer.

a. Our suppliers switch from delivery by train to air freight.

b. We change from producing to meet seasonal sales to steady year-round production. Sales peak at Christmas.

c. Competition in the markets in which we sell increases.

d. The rate of general inflation increases.

e. Interest rates rise; other things are constant.

Problems

19-1 The following inventory data have been established for the Sealfast Corporation:

(1) Orders must be placed in multiples of 200 units.

(2) Annual sales are 600,000 units.

(3) The purchase price per unit is $6.

(4) Carrying cost is 25 percent of the purchase price of goods.

(5) Cost per order placed is $40.

(6) Desired safety stock is 20,000 units; this amount is on hand initially.

(7) Three days are required for delivery.

a. What is the EOQ?

b. How many orders should Sealfast place each year?

c. At what inventory level should a reorder be made?

d. Calculate the total cost of ordering and carrying the working inventory if the order quantity is (1) 4,000 units, (2) 5,600 units, or (3) 7,000 units. What is the cost of carrying the safety stock?

19-2 Raytech Corporation produces steam turbines used in electric generating plants. Although much of its sales is by special order, the company also maintains a small inventory to meet rush orders for standard units. During 1984, Raytech produced six units for inventory. Raw material prices actually fell during 1984, and concessions by labor resulted in decreased labor costs. The following table contains the cost of each of the six units (in millions of dollars):

Unit Number	Cost
1	$12.4
2	12.0
3	11.6
4	11.2
5	10.8
6	10.6
Total	$68.6

Raytech had zero inventory at the beginning of 1984, and Units 1, 3, and 5 were sold during the year.

a. What would be Raytech's cost of goods sold and ending inventory value for 1984 if the firm used (1) specific identification, (2) FIFO, (3) LIFO, and (4) weighted average accounting methods?

  b. Which method provides the greatest net income? The greatest cash
     flow?
  c. Which method should be used in an inflationary period?
  d. Which method is preferred if costs remain constant throughout the
     year?

19-3 Porter Electronics uses 500,000 standard blank circuit boards a year.
     Each board costs Porter $2.00. The annual percentage cost of carrying
     the circuit board inventory is 20 percent of inventory value. Porter can
     order these boards from either of two competing manufacturers. Man-
     ufacturer A delivers in three days and requires a fixed ordering cost of
     $100 per order. Manufacturer B, which would require a fixed ordering
     cost of $75 per order, takes five days to deliver. To begin the analysis,
     assume that no safety stock is carried.
  a. Calculate Porter's EOQ for blank circuit boards for both suppliers.
  b. How many orders a year must be placed with each supplier (as-
     suming that only one supplier is used)?
  c. What are the reorder point levels for ordering from each supplier?
  d. Considering only inventory costs, should Porter order its blank cir-
     cuit boards from Manufacturer A or Manufacturer B?
  e. Assume that Porter chose Manufacturer B as its circuit board sup-
     plier. Porter has been offered a 1 percent discount if it orders 20,000
     units or more at a time. Should Porter increase the ordering quan-
     tity to 20,000 units and take the discount?
  f. Porter has decided to take the quantity discount, and it now orders
     20,000 boards per order from Manufacturer B. Since Porter uses
     1,389 boards per day, it takes Porter 20,000/1,389 = 14.4 days to
     totally use one order. Porter's usage distribution over the 14.4 day
     inventory period is estimated to be as follows:

Probability	Unit Usage
0.05	15,000
0.20	17,500
0.50	20,000
0.20	22,500
0.05	25,000
1.00	Expected usage = 20,000

     Porter further estimates that a stock-out, if one occurs, would cost
     $2,000 in production stoppage plus $0.10 per unit in special order
     costs. Determine the total costs of holding safety levels of 0; 2,500;
     and 5,000 units. Of these levels, which should Porter hold?

19-4 O'Connell Aircraft has an inventory of over 20,000 items used in the
     maintenance of small aircraft. One item is the basic ⅜" rivet. O'Connell
     orders these rivets every month, so it has a 30-day inventory cycle.
     Each 30 days' expected usage is 10,000 rivets, but usage could be
     greater or less depending on the specific types of aircraft brought in
     for maintenance. The 30-day usage distribution is:

Probability	Unit Usage
0.05	6,000
0.20	7,500
0.50	10,000
0.20	12,500
0.05	14,000
1.00	Expected usage = 10,000

If a shortage occurs, O'Connell faces the following costs:

Lost maintenance time:	$500 per stockout
Special order costs:	$0.05 per unit

O'Connell's management is considering safety stock levels of 0; 2,500; or 4,000 rivets. Each rivet costs $0.50, the inventory carrying cost is estimated to be 10 percent of inventory value, and the carrying cost for each month is $0.50(0.10)(1/12) \approx $0.0042 per unit.

a. What is the expected shortage cost, safety stock carrying cost, and expected total cost if the safety stock is set at zero?

b. What are the total costs (as above) if the safety stock is set at 2,500 rivets?

c. What are the total costs (as above) if the safety stock is set at 4,000 rivets?

d. Which of the three safety stock levels should O'Connell adopt?

19-5 Wellington Dolls, a large manufacturer of toys and dolls, uses large quantities of basic, flesh-colored cloth in its doll production process. Throughout the year, the firm uses 1 million square yards of one particular type of cloth. The fixed costs of placing and receiving an order are $2,500, including a $2,000 set-up charge at the mill.

The annual carrying cost of this inventory item is $0.40 *per unit (square yard)* of inventory, while the cloth costs $2.00 per square yard. Wellington maintains a 10,000 square yard safety stock. The cloth supplier requires a 10-day lead time from order to delivery.

a. What is the EOQ for this inventory item?

b. What is the average inventory dollar value, including safety stock?

c. What is the total cost of ordering and carrying the inventory, including safety stocks? (Assume that the safety stock is on hand at the beginning of the year.)

d. What is Wellington's annual carrying cost expressed as a percentage of inventory value?

e. Using a 360-day year, at what inventory unit level should a reorder be placed? (Again, assume a 10,000 unit on-hand safety stock.)

Selected Additional References and Cases

The following articles provide additional insights into the problems of inventory management:

Bierman, H., Jr., C. P. Bonini, and W. H. Hausman, *Quantitative Analysis for Business Decisions* (Homewood, Ill.: Irwin, 1977).

Brooks, L. D., "Risk-Return Criteria and Optimal Inventory Stocks," *Engineering Economist*, Summer 1980, 275-299.

Magee, John F., "Guides to Inventory Policy, I," *Harvard Business Review*, January-February 1956, 49-60.

———, "Guides to Inventory Policy, II," *Harvard Business Review*, March-April 1956, 103-116.

———, "Guides to Inventory Policy, III," *Harvard Business Review*, May-June 1956, 57-70.

Mehta, Dileep R., *Working Capital Management* (Englewood Cliffs, N.J.: Prentice-Hall, 1974).

Shapiro, A., "Optimal Inventory and Credit Granting Strategies under Inflation and Devaluation," *Journal of Financial and Quantitative Analysis*, January 1973, 37-46.

Smith, Keith V., *Guide to Working Capital Management* (New York: McGraw-Hill, 1979).

The Brigham-Crum casebook has a useful case on inventory management:

Case 7, "Barracuda Marine Corporation," which focuses on the EOQ model and safety stocks.

Cash and Marketable Securities Management

20

Cash is the oil that lubricates the wheels of business. Without adequate oil, machines grind to a halt, and a business with inadequate cash will do likewise. On the other hand, carrying cash is expensive; since it is a nonearning asset, a firm that holds cash beyond its minimum requirements is lowering its potential earnings.

Cash management is developing into a very professional, highly refined activity. The following excerpt from a United California Bank (UCB) advertisement illustrates what is involved:

> Using any lockbox will accelerate cash flow. But a UCB Lock Box System does it with maximum efficiency. One difference is our unique city-wide zip code system for California lockbox customers. It speeds the receipt of your lockbox mail by several hours.
>
> Another difference: We work around the clock, seven days a week. So you can be sure your funds will be deposited, regardless of absenteeism or seasonal work loads.
>
> A third difference: We're the only West Coast bank using helicopters to speed collections of checks, thus reducing float.
>
> Also, using our computerized optimization models, we can determine how many lockboxes you should use, where they should be located, and how much money you'll save with them.
>
> The cost is surprisingly low. Call us, and let us show you how UCB can make your cash work harder.

For some companies, these ideas make good sense. However, firms sometimes go too far with their cash management systems. For example, the general practice in the securities brokerage business (until Merrill Lynch lost a major suit and agreed to stop doing it) was to write checks to customers located east of the Mississippi on a West Coast bank and checks to customers located west of the river on an East Coast bank. This slowed down payment of checks, deprived customers of the use of their money, and gave the brokerage firms the use of millions of dollars of their customers' money for extended periods of time. According to the SEC, this practice, although it increased brokerage firms' profits by millions of dollars each year, was "inconsistent with a broker-dealer's obligation to deal fairly with its customers."

Approximately 1.5 percent of the average industrial firm's assets are held in the form of cash, which is defined as the total of bank demand deposits plus currency. However, sizable holdings of such near-cash short-term marketable securities as U.S. Treasury bills (T-bills) or bank certificates of deposit (CDs) are often reported on corporations' financial statements. Moreover, cash balances vary widely not only among industries but also among the firms within a given industry, depending on the individual firms' specific conditions and on their owners' and managers' aversion to risk. In this chapter, we analyze the factors that determine firms' cash and marketable securities balances. These same factors, incidentally, apply to the cash holdings of individuals and nonprofit organizations, including government agencies.

Cash Management

Cash is often called a "nonearning" asset. It is needed to pay for labor and raw materials, to buy fixed assets, to pay taxes, to service debt, to pay dividends, and so on. However, cash itself (or most commercial checking accounts) earns no interest. Thus, the goal of cash management is to minimize the amount of cash held by the firm without adversely affecting its business activities. We begin our discussion of cash management with the rationale for holding cash.

Rationale for Holding Cash

Firms hold cash for two primary reasons:

1. **Transactions.** Cash balances are necessary to conduct business. Payments must be made in cash, and receipts are deposited in the cash account. Cash balances associated with routine payments and/or collections are known as *transactions balances*.

2. **Compensation to banks for providing loans and services.** Banks make money by lending out funds which have been deposited. Thus, if someone deposits money in a bank, this action helps improve the bank's profit position. Therefore, a bank generally requires firms to leave a certain minimum balance on deposit to help offset the cost of services provided to them. This type of balance, defined as a *compensating balance*, is discussed in detail later in this chapter.

Two other reasons for holding cash have been noted in the finance and economics literature: (1) precaution and (2) speculation. It has been noted that cash inflows and outflows are somewhat unpredictable, with the degree of predictability varying among firms and industries. Therefore, just as firms hold safety stocks of inventories, they also need to hold some cash in reserve for random, unforeseen fluctuations in inflows and outflows; these "safety stocks" are defined as *precautionary balances*. The less predictable the firm's cash flows, the larger are its precautionary balances. However, if the firm has easy access to borrowed funds—that is, if it can borrow on short notice—this borrowing capacity reduces its need to hold cash for precautionary purposes. Also, as we note later in this chapter, firms that would otherwise need large precautionary balances tend to hold highly liquid marketable securities; such holdings accomplish the same purposes as cash balances while providing income in the form of interest.

Some cash balances may be held to enable the firm to take advantage of any bargain purchases that might arise, and also to enable multinational firms to take advantage of exchange rate fluctuations. Such funds are defined as *speculative balances*. However, as with precautionary balances, firms today are more likely to rely on reserve borrowing power and on marketable securities portfolios than on actual cash holdings for speculative purposes.

Although the actual cash account for most firms can be thought of as consisting of transactions balances and compensating balances, we cannot calculate the amount needed for each type, add them together, and produce a total desired cash balance, because the same money often serves both purposes. Firms do, however, consider both factors when establishing their target cash positions.

While there are good reasons for holding *adequate* cash balances, there is a strong reason for not holding *excessive* balances—cash is a nonearning asset, so excessive cash balances simply lower the firm's total asset turnover, thereby reducing both the rate of return on its equity and the value of its stock. Thus, firms are very much interested in establishing procedures for increasing the efficiency of their cash management. If they can make their cash work harder, they can reduce cash balances.

The Cash Flow Cycle

Figure 20-1 shows the cash flow cycle within a firm. Rectangles represent balance sheet accounts—assets and claims against assets—while circles represent actions taken by the firm. Each rectangle may be thought of as a reservoir, with gray rectangles for assets and blue rectangles for claims, and the wavy lines designate the amount in the reservoir (account) on a balance sheet date. Various transactions cause changes in the accounts, just as adding or subtracting water changes the level in a reservoir.

The cash account is the focal point of the graph. Certain events, such as collecting accounts receivable or borrowing money from the bank, will cause the cash account to increase, while the payment of taxes, in-

Figure 20-1
Cash Flows within the Firm

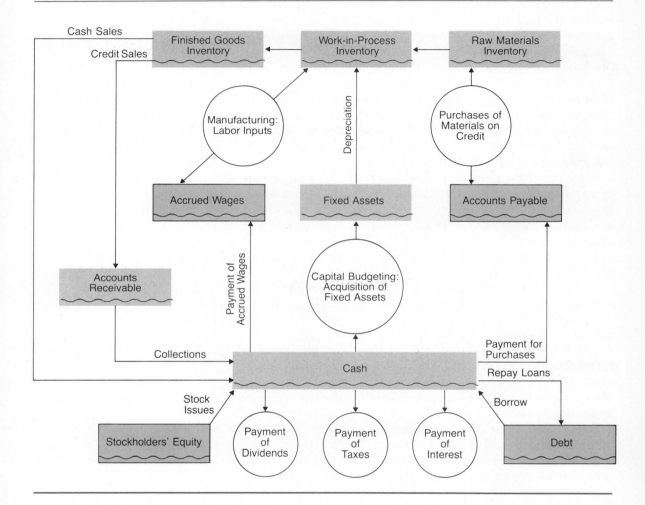

terest, and so on will cause the cash account to decline. Similar comments could be made about all the balance sheet accounts—their balances rise, fall, or remain constant depending on events that occur during the period under study.

Projected sales increases may require the firm to raise cash by borrowing from its bank or selling new stock. For example, if a firm anticipates an increase in sales, it will (1) expend cash to buy or build fixed assets through the capital budgeting process, (2) step up purchases, thereby increasing both raw materials inventories and accounts payable, (3) increase production, which causes an increase in both accrued wages and work-in-process, and (4) eventually build up its finished goods inventory. Some cash will have been expended, and hence removed from the cash account, and the firm will have obligated itself to expend still more cash to pay off its accounts payable and accrued wages within a few weeks. These events will have occurred *before* any new cash has been generated. Even when the expected sales do occur, there will still be a lag in the generation of cash until receivables are collected. For example, if a firm sells on 30-day terms, then about 30 days will lapse after a sale before cash comes in. Depending on how much cash the firm had at the beginning of the buildup, on the length of its cash conversion cycle, and on how long it can delay payment of its own payables and accrued wages, the firm may have to obtain significant amounts of additional cash by issuing stock or bonds, or by borrowing from the bank.

If the firm is profitable, its sales revenues will exceed its costs, and its cash inflows will eventually exceed its cash outlays. However, even a profitable firm can experience a cash shortage if it is growing rapidly. It may have to pay for plant, materials, and labor before cash from the expanded sales starts flowing in. For this reason, rapidly growing firms often require large bank loans or capital from other sources. And like an engine that runs out of oil, a company that runs out of cash will grind to a halt, even if it is otherwise in good shape.

An unprofitable firm, such as International Harvester in recent years, will have larger cash outlays than inflows. Obviously, cash will be drained off, and this, in turn, will typically cause a slowdown in the payment of accrued wages and accounts payable, and it may also lead to heavy borrowings. Thus liabilities—accounts payable, notes payable, and accruals—tend to build up to excessive levels in unprofitable firms. Similarly, an overly ambitious expansion plan will be reflected in an excessive buildup of inventories and fixed assets, while a poor credit/collection policy will produce bad debts and reduced profits that first show up as high accounts receivable. Financial analysts are well aware of these relationships, and they use the analytical techniques discussed in the remainder of this chapter to help discover problems before they become too serious.

The Cash Budget

The firm estimates its needs for cash as a part of its general budgeting, or forecasting, process. First, it forecasts sales and inventory purchases on a monthly basis, along with the times when payments for both fixed assets and inventory purchases must be made. This information is combined with projections about the timing of the collection of accounts receivable, the schedule for payment of taxes, the dates when dividend and interest payments will be made, and so on. All of this information is summarized in the *cash budget*, which shows the firm's projected cash inflows and outflows over some specified period of time. Generally, firms use a monthly cash budget forecasted over the next 6 to 12 months, plus a more detailed daily or weekly cash budget for the coming month. The longer one is used for planning purposes and the shorter one for actual cash control.

Constructing the Cash Budget

As noted above, cash budgets can be constructed on a monthly, a weekly, or even a daily basis. We shall illustrate the process with a monthly cash budget covering the last six months of 1985 for the Drexel Card Company, a leading producer of greeting cards. Drexel's birthday and get-well cards are sold year-round, but the bulk of the company's sales occurs from July through November, with a peak in September, when retailers are stocking up for Christmas. All sales are made on terms that allow a cash discount for payments made within 20 days; if the discount is not taken, the full amount must be paid in 40 days. However, like most other companies, Drexel finds that some of its customers delay payment up to 90 days. Experience shows that on 20 percent of the sales, payment is made during the month in which the sale is made; on 70 percent of the sales, payment is made during the first month after the month of the sale; and on 10 percent of the sales, payment is made during the second month after the month of the sale. Drexel offers a 2 percent discount for payments received within 10 days of sales. Typically, payments received in the month of sale are discount sales.

Rather than produce at a uniform rate throughout the year, Drexel prints cards immediately before they are required for delivery. Paper, ink, and other materials amount to 70 percent of sales and are bought the month before the company expects to sell the finished product. Its own purchase terms permit Drexel to delay payment on its purchases for one month. Accordingly, if July sales are forecast at $10 million, then purchases during June will amount to $7 million, and this amount will actually be paid in July.

Such other cash expenditures as wages and rent are also built into the cash budget, and Drexel must make tax payments of $2 million on September 15 and on December 15, while payment for a new plant must be made in October. Assuming that the company's target cash balance is $2.5 million, and that it has $3 million on July 1, what are Drexel's cash requirements for the period July through December?[1]

The monthly cash requirements are worked out in Table 20-1. The top half of the table provides a worksheet for calculating collections on sales and payments on purchases. The first line in the worksheet gives the sales forecast for the period May through December; May and June sales are necessary to determine collections for July and August. Next, cash collections are given. The first line of this section shows that 20 percent

[1]Setting the target cash balance is an important part of cash management. We will discuss this topic in the next section.

Table 20-1
Drexel Card Company:
Worksheet and Cash Budget
(Thousands of Dollars)

	May	June	July	Aug.	Sept.	Oct.	Nov.	Dec.
Worksheet								
Sales (gross)	$5,000	$5,000	$10,000	$15,000	$20,000	$10,000	$10,000	$5,000
Collections:								
During month of sale (20% less 2% discount)	980	980	1,960	2,940	3,920	1,960	1,960	980
During first month after sale month (70%)		3,500	3,500	7,000	10,500	14,000	7,000	7,000
During second month after sale month (10%)			500	500	1,000	1,500	2,000	1,000
Total collections	$ 980	$4,480	$ 5,960	$10,440	$15,420	$17,460	$10,960	$8,980
Purchases (70% of next month's gross sales)	$3,500	$7,000	$10,500	$14,000	$ 7,000	$ 7,000	$ 3,500	
Payments (one-month lag)		$3,500	$ 7,000	$10,500	$14,000	$ 7,000	$ 7,000	$3,500
Cash Budget								
(1) Collections (from worksheet)			$ 5,960	$10,440	$15,420	$17,460	$10,960	$8,980
(2) Payments:								
(3) Purchases (from worksheet)			$ 7,000	$10,500	$14,000	$ 7,000	$ 7,000	$3,500
(4) Wages and salaries			750	1,000	1,250	750	750	500
(5) Rent			250	250	250	250	250	250
(6) Other expenses			100	150	200	100	100	250
(7) Taxes					2,000			2,000
(8) Payment for plant construction						5,000		
(9) Total payments			$ 8,100	$11,900	$17,700	$13,100	$ 8,100	$6,300
(10) Net cash gain (loss) during month (Line 1 − Line 9)			($ 2,140)	($ 1,460)	($ 2,280)	$ 4,360	$ 2,860	$2,680
(11) Cash at start of month if no borrowing is done (start July with $3,000; calculated thereafter)			3,000	860	(600)	(2,880)	1,480	4,340
(12) Cumulative cash (= cash at start + gains or − losses = Line 10 + Line 11)			$ 860	($ 600)	($ 2,880)	$ 1,480	$ 4,340	$7,020
(13) Deduct: Target cash balance			2,500	2,500	2,500	2,500	2,500	2,500
(14) Total loans outstanding required to maintain $2,500 target cash balance			$ 1,640	$ 3,100	$ 5,380	$ 1,020	—	—
(15) Surplus cash			—	—	—	—	$ 1,840	$4,520

Notes:

a. The amount shown on Line 11 for the first month, the $3,000 balance on July 1, was on hand initially. The values shown for each of the following months on Line 11 represent the cumulative cash as shown on Line 12 for the preceding month; for example, the $860 shown on Line 11 for August is taken from Line 12 in the July column.

b. When the target cash balance of $2,500 (Line 13) is deducted from the cumulative cash balance (Line 12), if a negative figure results, it is shown on Line 14 as a required loan, while if a positive figure results, it is shown on Line 15 as surplus cash.

of the sales during any given month are collected that month. However, customers who pay in the first month typically take the discount; therefore, the actual cash collected in the month of a sale is reduced by 2 percent. The second line shows the collections on the prior month's sales—70 percent of sales in the preceding month. The third line gives collections from sales two months earlier—10 percent of sales in that month. The collections are summed to find the total cash receipts from sales during each month covered by the cash budget.

With the worksheet completed, the cash budget itself can be constructed. Cash from collections is given on Line 1. Next, on Lines 2 through 9, payments during each month are summarized. The difference between cash receipts and cash payments (Line 1 minus Line 9) is the net cash gain or loss during the month; for July there is a net cash loss of $2.140 million. The initial cash on hand at the beginning of the month is added to the net cash gain or loss during the month to obtain the cumulative cash that would be on hand if no financing were done; at the end of July, Drexel would have cumulative cash totaling $860,000 if it did no borrowing.

The target cash balance, $2.5 million, is next subtracted from the cumulative cash to determine the firm's borrowing requirements or surplus cash, whichever the case may be. In July, Drexel expects to have cumulative cash, as shown on Line 12, of $860,000. It has a target cash balance of $2.5 million. Thus, to maintain the target cash balance, it must borrow $1.640 million by the end of July. Assuming that this amount is indeed borrowed, loans outstanding will total $1.640 million at the end of July.

This same procedure is used in the following months. Sales will expand seasonally in August. With the increased sales will come increased payments for purchases, wages, and other items. Receipts from sales will also go up, but the firm will still be left with a $1.460 million net cash outflow during the month. The total financial requirements at the end of August will be $3.100 million, the cumulative cash plus the target cash balance. The $3.100 million is also equal to the $1.640 million needed at the end of July plus the $1.460 million cash deficit for August. Thus, loans outstanding will total $3.100 million at the end of August.

Sales peak in September, and the cash deficit during this month will amount to $2.280 million. The total borrowing requirements through September will increase to $5.380 million. Sales, purchases, and payments for past purchases will fall markedly in October, and collections will be the highest of any month because they reflect the high September sales. As a result, Drexel will enjoy a healthy $4.360 million cash surplus during October. This surplus will be used to pay off borrowings, so loans outstanding will decline by $4.360 million, to $1.020 million.

In November, Drexel will have another cash surplus which will permit it to pay off all of its loans. In fact, the company is expected to have $1.840 million in surplus cash by the month's end, while another cash surplus in December will swell the extra cash to $4.520 million. With such a large amount of unneeded funds, Drexel's treasurer will doubtless want to invest in interest-bearing securities or put the funds to use in some other way.

Before concluding our discussion of the cash budget, we should make six additional points:

1. Our cash budget does not reflect interest on loans or income from the investment of surplus cash. This refinement could be added easily.

2. More important, if cash inflows and outflows are not uniform during the month, we could be seriously understating or overstating our financing requirements. For example, if all payments must be made on the fifth of each month, but collections come in uniformly throughout the month, then we would need to borrow much larger amounts than those shown in Table 20-1. In such a case, we would need to prepare a cash budget centered on the fifth of the month, which would identify the peak borrowing requirements, or, better yet, on a daily basis.

3. Since depreciation is a noncash charge, it does not appear on the cash budget other than through its effect on taxes paid.

4. The cash budget represents a forecast, so all the values in the table are *expected* values. If actual sales, purchases, and so on are different from the forecasted levels, then our forecasted cash deficits and surpluses will also be incorrect. This point is explored further in the next section.

5. Computerized spreadsheet models are particularly well suited for constructing and analyzing the cash budget. Such models are especially useful for analyzing the sensitivity of cash flows to changes in sales levels, collection periods, and the like.

6. Finally, we should note that the target cash balance, set here at $2.5 million, would probably be adjusted over time, rising and falling with seasonal patterns and with long-term changes in the scale of the firm's operations. Factors that influence the target cash balance are discussed in the following sections.

Setting the Target Cash Balance

When we discussed Drexel Card Company's cash budget, we assumed a $2.5 million target cash balance. In this section, we discuss three methods for setting the target cash balance: (1) the Baumol model, (2) the Miller-Orr model, and (3) computer simulation.

The Baumol Model

William Baumol first noted that cash balances are in many respects similar to inventories, and that the EOQ inventory model developed in Chapter 19 can be used to establish the target cash balance.[2] Baumol's

---

[2]See William J. Baumol, "The Transactions Demand for Cash: An Inventory Theoretic Approach," *Quarterly Journal of Economics*, November 1952, 545-556.

model assumes (1) that the firm uses cash at a steady, predictable rate, say $1 million per week, and (2) that the firm's cash inflows from operations also occur at a steady, predictable rate, say $900,000 per week, so (3) its net cash outflows, or net need for cash, also occur at a steady rate, in this case, $100,000 per week.[3] Under these steady-state assumptions, the firm's cash position will resemble the situation shown in Figure 20-2, which is conceptually identical to the inventory position shown in Figure 19-3 in Chapter 19.

If our illustrative firm started at Time 0 with a cash balance of C = $300,000, and its outflows exceeded its inflows by $100,000 per week, then (1) its cash balance would drop to zero at the end of Week 3, and (2) its average cash balance would be C/2 = $300,000/2 = $150,000. At the end of Week 3, the firm would have to replenish its cash balance, either by selling marketable securities, if it has any, or by borrowing.

If C were set at a higher level, say $600,000, then the cash supply would last longer (six weeks), so the firm would have to sell securities (or borrow) less frequently, but its average cash balance would rise from

Figure 20-2
Cash Balances under the Baumol Model's Assumptions

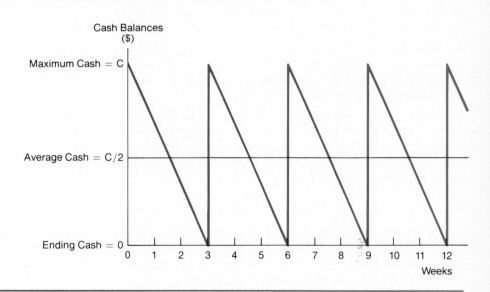

[3]Although our hypothetical firm is experiencing a $100,000 weekly cash shortfall, it is not necessarily headed toward bankruptcy. The firm could, for example, be highly profitable and enjoying high earnings, but be expanding so rapidly that it is subject to chronic cash shortages that must be made up by borrowing or by selling common stock. Similarly, the firm could be in the construction business and therefore receive major cash inflows at wide intervals, but have net cash outflows of $100,000 per week between major inflows.

$150,000 to $300,000. Since a "transactions cost" must be incurred to sell securities (or to borrow), establishing large cash balances will lower the "ordering costs" associated with cash management. On the other hand, cash provides no income, so the larger the average cash balance, the higher the opportunity cost, or the return that could have been earned on securities or other assets held in lieu of cash (or the higher the interest expense on borrowings). The situation is graphed in Figure 20-3, and it is analogous to the one for inventories presented in Figure 19-2. The optimal cash balance is found in the same way as in the EOQ model, but with a different set of variables:

C = amount of cash raised by selling marketable securities or by borrowing. C/2 = average cash balance.

C* = optimal amount of cash to be raised by selling marketable securities or by borrowing. C*/2 = optimal average cash balance.

F = fixed costs of making a securities trade or of borrowing.

Figure 20-3
Determination of the Target Cash Balance

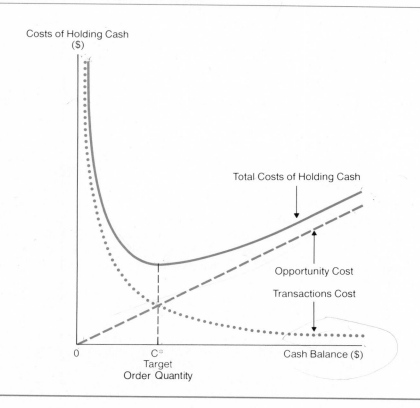

T = total amount of net new cash needed for transactions over the entire period (usually a year, but some other period if cash needs are seasonal).

k = opportunity cost of holding cash (equals the rate of return forgone on marketable securities or the cost of borrowing to hold cash).

The total costs of cash balances consist of a holding, or opportunity, cost plus a transactions cost:[4]

$$\text{Total costs} = \text{Holding cost} + \text{Transactions cost}$$

$$= \frac{C}{2}(k) \quad + \quad \frac{T}{C}(F). \tag{20-1}$$

To minimize total costs, we differentiate Equation 20-1 and set the derivative equal to zero:

$$\frac{d(\text{Total costs})}{dC} = \frac{k}{2} - \frac{(T)(F)}{C^2} = 0. \tag{20-2}$$

Finally, we solve for C^*, the optimal cash transfer:

$$\frac{k}{2} = \frac{(F)(T)}{C^2}$$

$$C^2 = \frac{2(F)(T)}{k}$$

$$C^* = \sqrt{\frac{2(F)(T)}{k}}. \tag{20-3}$$

Equation 20-3 is the Baumol model for determining optimal cash balances. To illustrate its use, suppose F = $150; T = 52 weeks × $100,000 per week = $5,200,000; and k = 15% = 0.15. Then

$$C^* = \sqrt{\frac{2(\$150)(\$5,200,000)}{0.15}} = \$101,980.$$

Therefore, the firm should sell securities in the amount of $101,980 when its cash balance approaches zero, thus building its cash balance back up to $101,980. If we divide T by C^*, we have the number of transactions per year: $5,200,000/$101,980 = 50.99 ≈ 51, or about once a week. The firm's average cash balance would be $101,980/2 = $50,990 ≈ $51,000.

Notice that the target cash balance increases less than proportionately with increases in transactions. For example, if the firm's size and con-

---

[4]Total costs can be expressed on a before-tax basis or on an after-tax basis. Both methods generally lead to the same conclusions regarding target cash balances and comparative costs. Here, for simplicity, we present the model on a before-tax basis.

sequently its net new cash needs doubled, from $5.2 million to $10.4 million per year, average cash balances would increase by only 41 percent, from $51,000 to $72,000. This suggests that there are economies of scale in the holding of cash balances, and this, in turn, gives larger firms an edge over smaller ones.[5]

Of course, just as in the case of inventory holdings, the firm would probably want to hold a "safety stock" of cash designed to reduce the probability of a cash shortage to some specified level. However, if the firm is able to sell securities or to borrow on short notice—and most larger firms can borrow in a matter of a couple of hours simply by making a telephone call—then the safety stock of cash can be quite low.

The Baumol model is obviously simplistic in many respects. Most important, it assumes relatively stable, predictable cash inflows and outflows, and it does not take account of any seasonal or cyclical trends. Other models have been developed to deal with uncertainty in the cash flows and with trends. Two of these models are discussed next.

Merton Miller and Daniel Orr developed a model for setting the target cash balance in which they incorporate uncertainty in the cash inflows and outflows.[6] They assumed that the distribution of daily net cash flows is approximately normal. Each day, the net cash flow could be the expected value or some higher or lower value drawn from a normal distribution. Thus, the daily net cash flow follows a trendless random walk.

The Miller-Orr Model

Figure 20-4 shows how the Miller-Orr model operates over time. The model sets upper and lower control limits, H and L respectively, and a target cash balance, Z. When the cash balance reaches H, such as at Point A, then (H − Z) dollars are transferred from cash to marketable securities, that is, the firm purchases (H − Z) dollars of securities. Similarly, when the cash balance hits L, as at Point B, then (Z − L) dollars are transferred from marketable securities to cash. The lower limit, L, is set by management depending on how much risk of a cash shortfall the firm is willing to accept.

Given L as set by management, the Miller-Orr model determines the cash balance target and the upper limit. We will not show their derivations here, but Miller-Orr found these values for Z and H:

$$Z = \left[\frac{3F\sigma^2}{4k} \right]^{1/3} + L, \qquad \textbf{(20-4)}$$

---

[5]This edge may, of course, be more than offset by other factors—after all, cash management is only one aspect of running a business.

[6]See Merton H. Miller and Daniel Orr, "A Model of the Demand for Money by Firms," *Quarterly Journal of Economics*, August 1966, 413-435.

Figure 20-4
Concept of the Miller-Orr Model

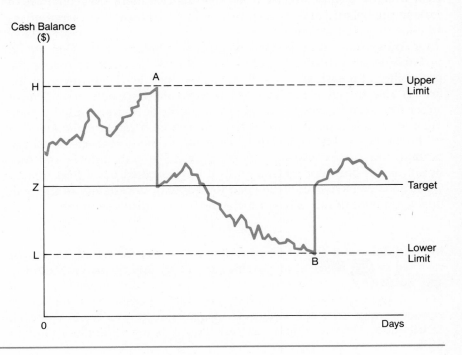

and

$$H = 3\left[\frac{3F\sigma^2}{4k}\right]^{1/3} + L = 3Z - 2L. \qquad \text{(20-5)}$$

Additionally, the average cash balance is

$$\text{Average cash balance} = \frac{4Z - L}{3}. \qquad \text{(20-6)}$$

Here

Z = target cash balance.

H = upper limit.

L = lower limit.

F = fixed transactions cost.

k = opportunity cost on a daily basis.

σ^2 = variance of net daily cash flows.

To illustrate the Miller-Orr model, suppose F = $150, the opportunity cost is 15 percent annually, and the standard deviation (σ) of daily net cash flows is $1,000. The daily opportunity cost and variance of daily net cash flows are, thus,

$$(1 + k)^{360} - 1.0 = 0.15$$
$$(1 + k)^{360} = 1.15$$
$$1 + k = 1.00039$$
$$k = 0.00039,$$

and

$$\sigma^2 = (1,000)^2 = 1,000,000.$$

Further, assume that management sets the lower limit, L, at zero because it can arrange transfers quickly. Substituting these values into Equations 20-4 through 20-6 gives Z = $6,607, H = $19,821, and an average cash balance of $8,809:

$$Z = \left[\frac{3(150)(1,000,000)}{4(0.00039)} \right]^{1/3} + \$0$$
$$= (288,461,500,000)^{1/3} = \$6,607,$$

and

$$H = 3(\$6,607) - 2(\$0) = \$19,821,$$

and

$$\text{Average cash balance} = \frac{4(\$6,607) - \$0}{3} = \$8,809.$$

Several other points should be noted about the Miller-Orr model before we close our discussion:

1. The target cash balance is *not* midway between the upper and lower limits. Therefore, the cash balance will, on average, hit the lower limit more often than the upper limit. Placing the target cash balance midway between the limits would minimize transactions costs, but placing the target cash balance lower than midway decreases opportunity costs. In their derivation of the model, Miller and Orr find, assuming L = $0, that a target of H/3 minimizes total costs.

2. The target cash balance, and consequently the acceptable range, increases with both F and σ^2; a higher F makes it more costly to hit either limit, and a larger σ^2 causes the firm to hit a limit more frequently.

3. The target cash balance decreases with k, because the higher the value of k, the more costly it is to hold cash.

4. The lower limit need not be set at zero. It could be greater than zero because of compensating balance requirements or because of management's desire to maintain a safety stock.

5. The Miller-Orr model has been tested by several firms. It performed as well or better than intuitive cash management. However, it starts to break down when the firm has multiple cash alternatives rather than a single type of marketable security such as T-bills.

6. The Miller-Orr model assumes that the distribution of net cash flows is symmetric about the expected net cash flow. Similar models could be derived with other assumptions concerning the net cash flow distribution. For example, the model could be adjusted for seasonal trends. Here, the distribution of cash flows would not be normal, but would reflect a greater probability of either increasing or decreasing the cash balance, depending on whether the firm was moving into or away from the peak season. The target cash balance in these cases would not be one-third of the way between the lower and upper limits.

Simulation

Monte Carlo simulation can also be used to set the target cash balance.[7] To illustrate this concept, we use the Drexel Card Company cash budget presented earlier in Table 20-1.

Sales and collections are the driving forces in the cash budget. In the Table 20-1 cash budget, we used expected values for sales, and these values were used to derive most of the other cash flow forecasts. Now we repeat the cash budget, but we assume that sales are subject to a probability distribution about the expected value. Specifically, we assume that the distribution of sales for each month is normal, with a coefficient of variation (CV) of 0.10 and a standard deviation which varies with the sales level. In effect, we assume that the relative variability of sales is constant from month to month. Thus in May, when expected sales are $5 million, the standard deviation of sales is $500,000:

$$CV = 0.10 = \frac{\sigma_{Sales}}{\text{Expected sales}} = \frac{\sigma_{Sales}}{\$5,000,000}$$
$$\sigma_{Sales} = 0.10(\$5,000,000) = \$500,000.$$

Similarly, the standard deviation of sales in September is found to be $2 million, and so forth.

Of course, collections are based on actual sales rather than expected sales, so the collections pattern will reflect realized sales. If we assume that the sales realized in any month will not change Drexel's expectations of future sales, then purchases in any month will be based on 70 percent of next month's expected sales, but with upward or downward adjustments to reflect excess inventories on hand due to the current month's sales being less than expected or to inventory shortages that result from above-normal sales. Other payments such as wages, rent,

---

[7]See Eugene M. Lerner, "Simulating a Cash Budget," in *Readings on the Management of Working Capital*, 2nd ed., Keith V. Smith, ed. (St. Paul, Minn.: West Publishing, 1980).

Table 20-2
Simulation of Drexel Card Company's Cash Flows
(Thousands of Dollars)

Month	Point Estimate from Table 20-1[a]	Probability of Monthly Cash Flow Being Greater than				
		90%	70%	50%	30%	10%
July	($2,140)	($2,855)	($2,432)	($2,275)	($2,157)	($1,952)
August	(1,460)	(2,425)	(1,857)	(1,622)	(1,413)	(859)
September	(2,280)	(3,465)	(2,784)	(2,500)	(2,235)	(1,433)
October	4,360	3,786	4,129	4,334	4,712	5,799
November	2,860	2,140	2,553	2,767	2,991	3,478
December	2,680	2,367	2,567	2,684	2,937	3,464

[a]Values taken from Line 10 of Table 20-1. These values should, theoretically, equal the values shown in the 50 percent column. The deviations are caused by randomness in the simulation runs.

and so on are assumed to be fixed for the analysis, although uncertainty could be built into them, too.

Based on these assumptions, we used the *IFPS* modeling system to conduct a Monte Carlo simulation of Drexel's cash budget. The simulation analysis focuses on Line 10 of Table 20-1, the net cash gain (loss) during the month. Table 20-2 summarizes the results and compares the range of likely cash gains or losses with the point estimates taken from Line 10 of Table 20-1.

Now suppose Drexel's managers want to be 90 percent confident that the firm will not run out of cash during July. They would set the beginning of month balance at $2,855,000 (rather than $3,000,000), because there is a 90 percent probability that the cash flow will be no worse than −$2,855,000. Thus, with a beginning cash balance of $2,855,000, there would be only a 10 percent probability that the firm would run out of cash during July. This type of analysis could be extended for the other months and used, in lieu of the fixed $2.5 million, as the target beginning-of-month cash balance.

Note that in our simulation we assumed that sales are independent from month to month. Alternatively, we could have assumed some type of dependence such that a lower-than-expected sales level in July would signal a trend toward lower sales in the following months. This type of dependency would increase the firm's uncertainty with regard to cash flows in any given month and, consequently, increase the required cash balance needed to provide any prescribed level of confidence regarding running out of cash.

Firms' target cash balances are actually set as the larger of (1) their transactions balances plus precautionary (safety stock) balances or (2) their required compensating balances as determined by their agreements with banks. Transactions balances and precautionary balances depend upon the firm's volume of business, the degree of uncertainty inherent in its

Other Factors Influencing the Target Cash Balance

forecasts of cash inflows and outflows, and its ability to borrow on short notice to meet cash shortfalls. Consider again the cash budget shown for Drexel Card Company in Table 20-1. The target cash balance (or desired cash balance) is shown on Line 13 of the table. Other things held constant, the target cash balance would increase if Drexel expanded, while it would decrease if Drexel contracted. Similarly, Drexel could afford to operate with a smaller target balance if it could forecast better and thus be more certain that inflows would come in as scheduled and that no unanticipated outflows such as might result from uninsured fire losses, lawsuits, and the like, would occur.

Statistics are not available on whether transactions balances or compensating balances actually control most firms' target cash balances, but compensating balance requirements do often dominate, especially during periods of high interest rates and tight money.[8]

Increasing the Efficiency of Cash Management

While a carefully prepared cash budget is a necessary starting point, there are other elements in a good cash management program. In this section, we describe some of these other elements.

Cash Flow Synchronization

If you, as an individual, were to receive income on a daily basis instead of once a month, you could operate with a lower average checking account balance. If you could arrange to pay rent, tuition, and other charges on a daily basis, this would further reduce your required average cash balances. If you receive and spend $8,000 in total per year, or about $22 per day, you could operate with an average cash balance of only $11 in a perfectly synchronized world, but you would need an average balance of $4,000 in a one-receipt-a-year world. Exactly the same situation holds for business firms, so by arranging things such that their cash receipts coincide with the timing of their cash outflows, firms can hold their transactions balances to a minimum. Recognizing this point, utility companies, oil companies, and others arrange to bill customers and to pay their own bills on a regular "billing cycle" throughout the

---

[8]This point is underscored by an incident that occurred at a professional finance meeting. A professor presented a scholarly paper that used operations research techniques to determine "optimal cash balances" for a sample of firms. He then reported that actual cash balances of the firms greatly exceeded their "optimal" balances, suggesting inefficiency and the need for more refined techniques. The discussant of the paper made her comments short and sweet. She reported that she had written and asked the sample firms why they had so much cash. They uniformly replied that their cash holdings were set by compensating balance requirements. The model was useful to determine the optimal cash balance in the absence of compensating balance requirements, but it was precisely those requirements that determined actual balances. Since the model did not include compensating balances as a determinant of cash balances, its usefulness was questionable.

month. In our cash budgeting example, if Drexel Card Company could arrange a better synchronization of its cash inflows and outflows, it might be able to reduce somewhat its target cash balance, and therefore its required bank loans.

Float is defined as the difference between the balance shown in a firm's (or an individual's) checkbook and the balance on the bank's books. Suppose a firm writes, on the average, checks in the amount of $5,000 each day, and it takes about six days for these checks to clear and to be deducted from the firm's bank account. Thus, the firm's own checking records show a balance that is $30,000 smaller than the bank's records. If the firm receives checks in the amount of $5,000 daily, but it loses only four days while these checks are being deposited and cleared, its own books will have a balance that is, because of this factor, $20,000 larger than the bank's balance. Thus, the firm's *net float*—the difference between the $30,000 *positive disbursement float* and the $20,000 *negative collection float*—is $10,000.

Using Float

If a firm's own collection and clearing process is more efficient than that of the recipients of its checks—and this is generally true of larger, more efficient firms—then the firm could show a *negative* balance on its own records and a *positive* balance on the books of its bank. Some firms indicate that they *never* have positive book cash balances. One large manufacturer of construction equipment stated that while its account, according to its bank's records, shows an average cash balance of about $20 million, its *book* cash balance is *minus* $20 million; it has $40 million of net float. Obviously, the firm must be able to forecast its positive and negative clearings accurately in order to make such heavy use of float.

Basically, a firm's net float is a function of its ability to speed up the collections on checks received and to slow down the collections on checks written. Efficient firms go to great lengths to speed up the processing of incoming checks, thus putting the funds to work faster, while trying to stretch their own payments out as long as possible.

When a customer writes and mails a check, this *does not* mean that the funds are immediately available to the receiving firm. Most of us have deposited a check in our account and then been told that we cannot write our own checks against this deposit until the check clears. Our bank must (1) make sure that the check we deposited is good and (2) receive funds itself before releasing funds for us to spend.

As shown on the left side of Figure 20-5, quite a bit of time may be required for a firm to process incoming checks and to obtain the use of the money. A check must first be delivered through the mails, and then cleared through the banking system, before the money can be put to use. Checks received from customers in distant cities are especially subject to delays. First, mail delays can obviously cause problems. Second, clearing checks also delays the effective use of funds received. Assume,

Figure 20-5
Diagram of the Check-Clearing Process

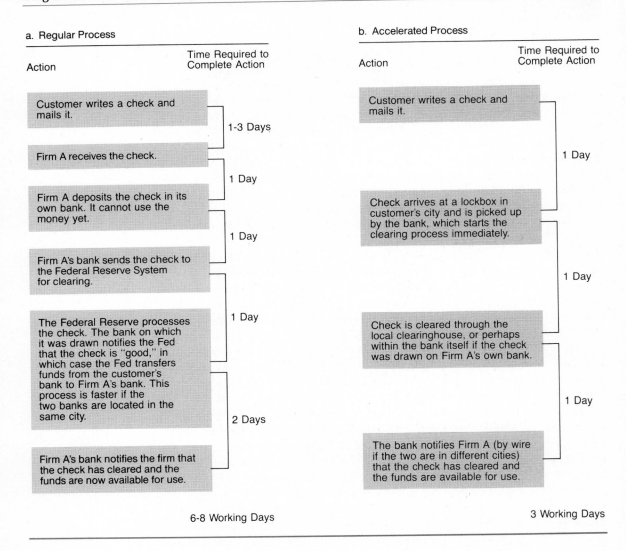

a. Regular Process

Action	Time Required to Complete Action
Customer writes a check and mails it.	1-3 Days
Firm A receives the check.	1 Day
Firm A deposits the check in its own bank. It cannot use the money yet.	1 Day
Firm A's bank sends the check to the Federal Reserve System for clearing.	1 Day
The Federal Reserve processes the check. The bank on which it was drawn notifies the Fed that the check is "good," in which case the Fed transfers funds from the customer's bank to Firm A's bank. This process is faster if the two banks are located in the same city.	2 Days
Firm A's bank notifies the firm that the check has cleared and the funds are now available for use.	

6-8 Working Days

b. Accelerated Process

Action	Time Required to Complete Action
Customer writes a check and mails it.	1 Day
Check arrives at a lockbox in customer's city and is picked up by the bank, which starts the clearing process immediately.	1 Day
Check is cleared through the local clearinghouse, or perhaps within the bank itself if the check was drawn on Firm A's own bank.	1 Day
The bank notifies Firm A (by wire if the two are in different cities) that the check has cleared and the funds are available for use.	

3 Working Days

for example, that we receive a check and deposit it in our bank. Our bank must send the check to the bank on which it was drawn. Only when this latter bank transfers funds to our bank are they available for us to use. Checks are generally cleared through the Federal Reserve System or through a clearinghouse set up by the banks in a particular city. Of course, if the check is deposited in the same bank on which it was drawn, the bank merely transfers funds by bookkeeping entries from one of its depositors to another. The length of time required for other checks to clear is a function of the distance between the payer's and the payee's banks; in the case of private clearinghouses, it can range from one to three days. The maximum time required for checks to clear through the Federal Reserve System is two days.

The right side of Figure 20-5 shows how the process can be speeded up. First, to reduce mail and clearing delays, a *lockbox plan* can be used. Suppose a New York firm makes sales to customers all across the country. It can arrange to have its customers send payments to post office boxes (lockboxes) in their own local areas. A local bank will pick up the checks, have them cleared in the local area, and then transfer the funds by wire to the company's New York bank. In this way, collection time can be reduced by one to five days. Examples of freeing funds in the amount of $5 million or more by this method are not uncommon.

Just as expediting the collection process conserves cash, slowing down disbursements accomplishes the same thing by keeping cash on hand for longer periods. One obviously could simply delay payments, but this involves equally obvious difficulties. Firms have, in the past, devised rather ingenious methods for "legitimately" lengthening the collection period on their own checks, ranging from maintaining deposits in distant banks to using slow, awkward payment procedures. Since such practices are usually recognized for what they are, there are severe limits to their use.

One widely publicized procedure in recent years is the use of drafts. While a check is payable on demand, a draft must be transmitted to the issuer, who approves it and deposits funds to cover it, after which it can be collected. Insurance companies often use drafts. In handling claims, for instance, Aetna can pay a claim by draft on Friday. The recipient deposits the draft at a local bank, which sends it on to Aetna's Hartford bank. It may be Wednesday or Thursday before the draft arrives. The bank then sends it to the company's accounting department, which has until 3 P.M. that day to inspect and approve it. Not until then does Aetna deposit funds in its bank to pay the draft.

In recent years, the Federal Reserve System has speeded up greatly the check clearing process. For example, from 1979 to the first quarter of 1983, the Fed's average daily check float has been reduced from $6.3 billion to $1.8 billion. This effort has reduced, but certainly not removed, the value of such strategies as lockboxes and remote disbursement. However, it has caused changes in existing systems. For example, both Chevron and ITT Corporation recently redeployed their lockbox systems to give greater emphasis to minimizing mail delays and less emphasis to the time lost for checks to clear through the Fed system.[9]

---

[9] The term commonly used for cash control systems that make maximum use of float is *controlled disbursement*. Many banks offer controlled disbursement accounts, wherein the bank informs the corporate customer in the morning how much money is needed, and the firm transfers only the funds necessary to cover the checks clearing that day. At the end of the day, there is a zero cash balance; thus, no funds are left idle.

Cash Management in the Multidivision Firm

The concepts, techniques, and procedures described thus far in the chapter must be extended when applied to large, national firms. Such corporations have plants and sales offices all across the nation (or the world), and they deal with banks in all of their operating territories. These companies must maintain the required compensating balance in each of their banks, and they must be sure that no bank account becomes overdrawn. Cash inflows and outflows are subject to random fluctuations, so in the absence of close control and coordination, there would be a tendency for some accounts to have shortages while excess balances existed in others. Thus, a sound cash management program for such a multibank corporation necessarily includes provisions for keeping strict account of the level of funds in each account and for shifting funds among accounts so as to minimize the total corporate cash balance. Mathematical models and electronic hookups between a central computer and each branch location, often using satellites and roof-top dish antennas, have been developed to help with such situations, but the cash management requirements for a large, multidivision firm can still be substantial.

Cash management in the multidivision firm focuses on the problem of *cash concentration*, which involves the movement of funds between a central cash pool and the various subsidiaries' banks. In general, cash balances are maintained at a minimal level at the division's banks, with all excess funds being wired daily to the central pool for overnight investment. The concentration of excess funds allows the firm to take maximum advantage of economies of scale in cash management and investment.

Bank Relationships

Banks provide a great many services to firms—they clear checks, operate lockbox plans, supply credit information, prepare payroll accounts, operate dividend payment and reinvestment plans, buy or sell foreign currencies, and the like. These services cost the bank money, so the bank must be compensated for rendering them.

Compensating Balances

Banks earn most of their income by lending money at interest, and most of the funds they lend are obtained in the form of deposits. If a firm maintains a deposit account with an average balance of $100,000, and if the bank can lend these funds at a net return of $8,000, then the account is, in a sense, worth $8,000 to the bank. Thus, it is to the bank's advantage to provide services worth up to $8,000 to attract and hold the account.

Banks first determine the costs of the services rendered to their larger customers, and then they estimate the average account balances necessary to provide enough income to compensate for these costs. Firms could make direct payments for these services, but often they find it cheaper to maintain compensating balances in order to avoid paying cash service charges to the bank.[10]

Compensating balances are also required by some banks under loan agreements. During periods when the supply of credit is restricted and interest rates are high, banks frequently insist that borrowers maintain accounts that average a specified percentage of the loan amount as a condition for granting the loan; 15 percent is a typical figure. If the balance is larger than the firm would otherwise maintain, then the effective cost of the loan is increased; the excess balance presumably "compensates" the bank for making a loan at a rate below what it could earn on the funds if they were invested elsewhere.

Compensating balances can be established (1) as an *absolute minimum*, say $100,000, below which the actual balance must never fall, or (2) as a *minimum average* balance, over some period, generally a month. The absolute minimum is a much more restrictive requirement, because the total amount of cash held during the month must be above $100,000 by the amount of the transactions balances. The $100,000 in this case is "dead money" from the firm's standpoint. The minimum average balance, however, could fall to zero one day provided it was $200,000 some other day, with the average working out to $100,000. Thus, the $100,000 in this case is available for transactions.

Statistics on compensating balance requirements are not available, but average balances are typical and absolute minimums rare for business accounts. Discussions with bankers, however, indicate that absolute balance requirements are less rare during times of extremely tight money.

Overdraft Systems

Most countries outside the United States use *overdraft systems*. In such systems, depositors write checks in excess of their actual balances, and the banks automatically extend loans to cover the shortages. The maximum amount of such loans must, of course, be established beforehand. Although statistics are not available on the usage of overdrafts in the United States, a number of firms have worked out informal, and in some cases formal, overdraft arrangements. (Also, both banks and credit card companies regularly establish "cash reserve" systems for individuals.) Thus, the use of overdrafts has been increasing in recent years. If this trend continues, we can anticipate a further reduction of cash balances.

---

[10]Compensating balance arrangements apply to individuals as well as to business firms. Thus, you might get "free" checking services if you maintain a minimum balance of $200, but be charged 10 cents per check if your balance falls below $200 during the month.

Matching the Costs and Benefits of Cash Management

Although a number of procedures may be used to hold down cash balance requirements, implementing these procedures is not a costless operation. How far should a firm go in making its cash operations more efficient? As a general rule, the firm should incur these expenses so long as marginal returns exceed marginal expenses.

For example, suppose that by establishing a lockbox system and increasing the accuracy of cash inflow and outflow forecasts, a firm can reduce its investment in cash by $1 million without increasing the risk of running short of cash. Further, suppose the firm borrows at a cost of 12 percent. The steps taken have released $1 million, which can be used to reduce bank loans and thus save $120,000 per year. If the costs of the procedures necessary to release the $1 million are less than $120,000, the move is a good one; if the costs exceed $120,000, the greater efficiency is not worth the cost. It is clear that larger firms, with larger cash balances, can better afford to hire the personnel necessary to maintain tight control over their cash positions. Cash management is one element of business operations in which economies of scale are present.

Very clearly, the value of careful cash management depends upon the costs of funds invested in cash, which in turn depend upon the current rate of interest. In the 1980s, with interest rates at high levels by historic standards, firms have been devoting a great deal of care to cash management.[11]

Marketable Securities Management

Realistically, cash and marketable securities management cannot be separated—management of one implies management of the other. In the first part of the chapter, we focused on cash management. Now we turn to marketable securities.

Rationale for Holding Marketable Securities

Marketable securities typically provide much lower yields than firms' operating assets; for example, International Business Machines (IBM) recently held a multibillion dollar portfolio of marketable securities that yielded about 9 percent, while its operating assets provided a return of about 18 percent. Why would a company such as IBM have such large holdings of low-yielding assets? There are two basic reasons for these holdings: (1) They serve as a substitute for cash balances, and (2) they are used as a temporary investment. These points are considered below.

Marketable Securities as a Substitute for Cash. Some firms hold portfolios of marketable securities in lieu of larger cash balances, liquidating

---

[11]Banks have also placed considerable emphasis on developing and marketing cash management services. Because of scale economies, banks can generally provide these services to smaller companies at less than the cost of developing in-house cash management systems.

part of the portfolio to increase the cash account when cash outflows exceed inflows. In such situations, the marketable securities could be used as a substitute for transactions balances, for precautionary balances, for speculative balances, or for all three. In most cases, the securities are held primarily for precautionary purposes—most firms prefer to rely on bank credit to make temporary transactions or meet speculative needs, but they may still hold some liquid assets to guard against a possible shortage of bank credit.

During the late 1970s, IBM had approximately $6 billion in marketable securities. This large liquid balance had been built up as a reserve for possible damage payments resulting from pending antitrust suits. When it became clear that IBM would win most of the suits, the liquidity need declined, and the company spent some of the funds on other assets, including repurchases of its own stock. This is a prime example of a firm's building up its precautionary balances to handle possible emergencies.

Marketable Securities Held as a Temporary Investment. Temporary investments in marketable securities generally occur in one of the following three situations:

1. When the firm must finance seasonal or cyclical operations. Firms engaged in seasonal operations frequently have surplus cash flows during one part of the year and deficit cash flows during the other part—Drexel Card Company, described earlier in this chapter, is an example. Such firms may purchase marketable securities during their surplus periods, and then liquidate them when cash deficits occur. Other firms choose to use bank financings to cover shortages.

2. When the firm must meet some known financial requirements. If a major plant construction program is planned for the near future, or if a bond issue is about to mature, a firm may build up its marketable securities portfolio to provide the required funds. Furthermore, marketable securities holdings are frequently large immediately preceding quarterly corporate tax payment dates.

3. When the firm has just sold long-term securities. An expanding firm has to sell long-term securities (stocks or bonds) periodically. The funds from such sales can be invested in marketable securities, which can, in turn, be sold off to provide cash as it is needed to pay for operating assets.

Actually, each of the needs listed above can be met either by taking short-term loans or by holding marketable securities. Consider a firm such as Drexel Card Company, which we discussed earlier, whose sales are growing over time but fluctuate on a seasonal basis. As we saw from Drexel's cash budget (Table 20-1), the firm plans to borrow to meet peak

Marketable Securities Policies

seasonal needs. As an alternative financial policy, Drexel could hold a portfolio of marketable securities, and then liquidate these securities to meet its cash needs.

A firm's marketable securities policy is an integral part of its overall working capital policy. If the firm has a conservative policy as we defined it back in Chapter 18, then its long-term capital will exceed its permanent assets, and marketable securities will be held when inventories and receivables are low. With an aggressive policy, it will never carry any securities, and it will borrow heavily to meet peak needs. With a moderate policy, where maturities are matched, permanent assets will be matched with long-term financing, and most seasonal increases in inventories and receivables will be met by short-term loans, but the firm may also carry marketable securities at certain times.

Figure 20-6 illustrates three possible alternative policies for a firm such as Drexel. Under Plan A, which represents an aggressive financing policy, Drexel would hold no marketable securities, relying completely on bank loans to meet seasonal peaks. Under the conservative Plan B, Drexel would stockpile marketable securities during slack periods, and then sell these securities to raise funds for peak needs. Plan C is a compromise; under this alternative, the company would hold some securities, but not enough to meet all of its peak needs.

There are advantages and disadvantages to each of these strategies. Plan A is clearly the most risky—the firm's current ratio is always lower than under the other plans, indicating that it might encounter difficulties either in borrowing the funds needed or in repaying the loan. On the other hand, Plan A requires no holdings of low-yielding marketable se-

Figure 20-6
Alternative Strategies for Meeting Seasonal Cash Needs

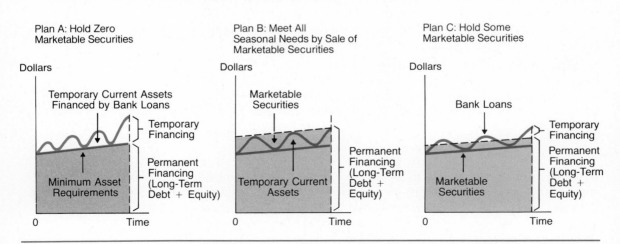

curities, and this will probably lead to a relatively high expected rate of return on both total assets and net worth.

Exactly the same types of choices are involved with regard to meeting such other known financial needs as plant construction, as well as in deciding whether to issue long-term securities before or after the actual need for the funds. Commonwealth Edison, the electric utility serving Chicago, can be used to illustrate the issues involved in timing the sale of long-term securities. Commonwealth has a permanent, ongoing construction program, generating a continuous need for new outside capital. As we saw in Chapters 14 and 15, there are substantial fixed costs involved in stock or bond flotations, so these securities are issued infrequently and in large amounts.

During the 1960s, Commonwealth followed the practice of selling bonds and stock *before* the capital was needed, investing the proceeds in marketable securities, and then liquidating the securities to finance plant construction. Plan A in Figure 20-7 illustrates this procedure. However, during the 1970s and 1980s, Commonwealth encountered financial stress. It was forced to use up its liquid assets and to switch to its present policy of financing plant construction with short-term bank loans, and then selling long-term securities to retire these loans when they

Figure 20-7
Alternative Methods of Financing
a Continuous Construction Program

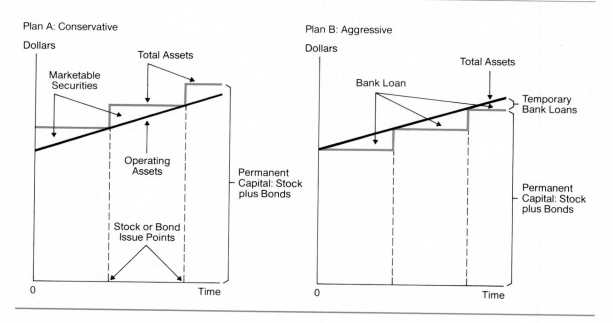

have built up to some target level. This policy is illustrated by Plan B of Figure 20-7.

Plan A is the more conservative, less risky one. First, the company is minimizing its liquidity problems because it has no short-term debt hanging over its head. Second, it is sure of having the funds available to meet construction payments as they come due. On the other hand, firms generally have to pay higher interest rates when they borrow than the return they receive on marketable securities, so following the less risky strategy does have a cost. Again, we are faced with a risk/return trade-off.

It is difficult to "prove" that one strategy is better than another. In principle, the practice of holding marketable securities reduces the expected rate of return, but it also reduces k_s, the required rate of return on the firm's stock. Although we can quantify the costs of following more conservative policies—this cost is the average percentage differential between the return received on marketable securities and the interest rate paid on the long-term debt issued to purchase them—it is almost impossible to quantify the benefits of such a policy in terms of how much it reduces risk and how this risk reduction affects k_s. Accordingly, the basic policies with regard to securities holdings are generally set either on the basis of judgment or, as in the case of Commonwealth Edison, by circumstances beyond the company's control.

Criteria for Selecting Marketable Securities

A wide variety of securities, differing in terms of default risk, interest rate risk, liquidity risk, and expected rate of return, is available to firms that do choose to hold marketable securities. In this section, we first consider the characteristics of different securities, and then we discuss how financial managers select the specific instruments held in their firms' marketable securities portfolios. The same decision criteria are, incidentally, as important for individuals' investment decisions as for firms' decisions.

Default Risk. The risk that an issuer will be unable to make interest payments, or to repay the principal amount on schedule, is known as *default risk*. If the issuer is the U.S. Treasury, default risk is negligible; thus, Treasury securities are regarded as being free of default risk. Corporate securities and bonds issued by state and local governments are subject to some degree of default risk, and they are rated with regard to their chances of going into default.

Interest Rate Risk. Bond prices vary with changes in interest rates. Further, the prices of long-term bonds are much more sensitive to shifts in interest rates than are prices of short-term securities—they have a much greater *interest rate risk*. Therefore, even Treasury securities are not completely free of all risk; as we saw in Chapter 3, U.S. government bonds are subject to risk due to interest rate fluctuations, and they are also subject to loss of purchasing power due to inflation. Thus, if Drexel's treasurer purchased at par $1 million of 25-year U.S. government bonds paying 9 percent interest, and if interest rates rose to 14.5 percent, the market value of the bonds would fall from $1 million to approximately $638,000—a loss of almost 40 percent. (This actually happened from 1980 to 1982.) Had 90-day Treasury bills been held, the capital loss resulting from the change in interest rates would have been negligible.

Purchasing Power Risk. Another type of risk is *purchasing power risk*, or the risk that inflation will reduce the purchasing power of a given sum of money. Purchasing power risk, which is important both to firms and to individual investors during times of inflation, is generally regarded as being lower on assets whose returns can be expected to rise during inflation than on assets whose returns are fixed. Thus, real estate and common stocks are often thought of as being better "hedges against inflation" than are bonds and other long-term fixed income securities.

Liquidity, or Marketability, Risk. An asset that can be sold on short notice for close to its quoted market price is defined as being highly liquid. If Drexel purchased $1 million of infrequently traded bonds of a relatively obscure company such as Gainesville Pork Products, it would probably have to accept a price reduction to sell the bonds on short notice. On the other hand, if Drexel bought $1 million worth of U.S. Treasury bonds, or bonds issued by AT&T, General Motors, or Exxon, it would be able to dispose of them almost instantaneously at close to the quoted market price. These latter bonds are said to have very little *liquidity risk*.

Returns on Securities. As we know from earlier chapters, the higher a security's risk, the higher is the expected and required return on the security. Thus, corporate treasurers, like other investors, must make a trade-off between risk and return when choosing investments for their marketable securities portfolios. Since the liquidity portfolio is generally held for a specific known need, or else for use in emergencies, the firm might be financially embarrassed should the portfolio decline in value. Further, most nonfinancial corporations do not have investment departments specializing in appraising securities and determining the probability of their going into default. Accordingly, the marketable securities portfolio is generally confined to safe, highly liquid, short-term securities issued by either the U.S. government or the very strongest corporations. Given the purpose of the securities portfolio, treasurers are unwilling to sacrifice safety for higher rates of return.

*Types of
Marketable
Securities*

Table 20-3 provides a listing of the major types of securities available for investment, with yields as of June 10, 1977, February 10, 1982, and June 27, 1984. Depending on how long they will be held, the financial manager decides upon a suitable maturity pattern for the firm's holdings. Because the securities' characteristics change with shifts in financial market conditions, it would be misleading to attempt to give detailed descriptions of them here.

It should be noted that larger corporations, with large amounts of surplus cash, tend to make direct purchases of Treasury bills, commercial paper, and CDs, as well as Euromarket securities as described in Chapter 26. Smaller firms, on the other hand, are more likely to use money market mutual funds, because the small firm's volume of investment simply does not warrant its hiring investment specialists to manage the

Table 20-3
Securities Available for Investment of Surplus Cash

Security	Typical Maturity at Time of Issue	Approximate Yields		
		6/10/77	2/10/82	6/27/84
Suitable to Hold as Near-Cash Reserve				
U.S. Treasury bills	91 days to 1 year	4.8%	15.1%	10.5%
Commercial paper	Up to 270 days	5.5	15.3	11.0
Negotiable certificates of deposit (CDs) of U.S. banks	Up to 1 year	6.0	15.5	11.8
Money market mutual funds	Instant liquidity	5.1	14.0	10.4
Floating rate preferred stock mutual funds[a]	Instant liquidity	N.A.	N.A.	12.3
Eurodollar market time deposits	Up to 1 year	6.1	16.2	12.0
Not Suitable to Hold as Near-Cash Reserve				
U.S. Treasury notes	3 to 5 years	6.8	14.8	13.2
U.S. Treasury bonds	Up to 30 years	7.6	14.6	13.6
Corporate bonds (AAA)[b]	Up to 40 years	8.2	16.0	14.6
State and local government bonds (AAA)[b,c]	Up to 30 years	5.7	12.8	10.2
Preferred stocks (AAA)[b,c]	30 years to perpetual	7.5	14.0	10.6
Common stocks of other corporations	Unlimited	Variable	Variable	Variable
Common stock of the firm in question	Unlimited	Variable	Variable	Variable

[a]Floating rate preferred stock is a recent innovation in near-cash securities. It is held by corporations (often through money funds designed for this purpose) because of the 85 percent dividend tax exclusion. First marketed in 1983.

[b]Rates shown for corporate and state/local government bonds and preferred stock are for longer maturities rated AAA. Lower-rated securities have higher yields. The slope of the yield curve determines whether shorter- or longer-term securities of a given rating would have higher yields.

[c]Rates are lower on state/municipal government bonds because the interest they pay is exempt from federal income taxes, and for preferred stocks because 85 percent of the dividends paid on them is exempt from federal taxes for corporate owners, who own most preferred stocks.

portfolio and to make sure that the securities held mature (or can be sold) at the same time cash is required. Such a firm can use a money fund and then literally write a check on the fund to meet cash needs as they arise. Interest rates on money funds are somewhat lower than rates on direct investments of equivalent risk; however, net returns, which have the expenses of managing the portfolio already deducted, are often higher on money funds for smaller companies.

A recent innovation in near-cash securities is floating rate preferred stock. For example, during the three years preceding June 1984, such firms as Chemical Bank, Alabama Power, and Aetna Life and Casualty Company had sold over $7 billion of these new securities. The appeal to corporations, which would otherwise prefer commercial paper and certificates of deposit, is the fact that a corporation can exclude 85 percent of the dividends it receives. This means that preferred stocks provide much higher after-tax returns to corporate owners in high tax brackets than do debt securities. In the past, many firms have resisted purchasing preferred stocks to hold as near-cash reserves because most preferred issues had long (or perpetual) maturities, and hence were subject to a great deal of interest rate risk, even if their default risk was low. However, because the new preferreds have floating rates, their values should remain close to par, which eliminates most interest rate risk.

Banks have been eager issuers of these new preferreds because (1) the banks need to raise nondebt capital, (2) their common stock prices have been low recently, and (3) low profits practically free them from paying taxes for a few years, thus removing a major argument against issuing preferreds—the fact that dividends are not tax deductible to the issuer. At the same time, other corporations have funds to invest and very much like the tax exclusion features of preferred stocks. Because of these supply/demand conditions, some smart money managers set up floating rate preferred stock mutual funds, and then got low tax bracket companies to issue preferreds and high tax bracket companies to buy them. Corporate cash managers of smaller firms can invest their excess cash in these funds, while larger companies can purchase the new preferred shares directly. With the current interest rate structure, the after-tax return on the preferred funds is significantly higher than on money market funds.[12]

---

[12]The Deficit Reduction Act of 1984 contains provisions which reduce the dividend tax advantage previously enjoyed by corporations. Prior to this act, firms could borrow money to buy preferred or common stock, and then deduct their full interest payments while paying reduced taxes on the dividend income, resulting in a perfect arbitrage. For example, if a firm with a 46 percent marginal tax rate borrowed at 12.5 percent and then invested the proceeds in a 9 percent dividend yield preferred stock, its after-tax cost would be $12.5\%(1 - T) = 12.5\%(0.54) = 6.75\%$ while its after-tax return would be $9\%[1 - T(0.15)] = 9\%(1 - 0.069) = 9\%(0.931) = 8.38\%$. Thus, the firm would gain 1.63 percentage points on the transaction after tax. The new law reduces the 85 percent dividend exclusion based on the amount of funds borrowed to buy the stock—the higher the percentage of funds borrowed, the lower the percentage that can be excluded.

Summary

The first topic covered in this chapter was *cash management*. We saw that the key element in any cash management system is the *cash budget*, which is a forecast of cash inflows and outflows during a given planning period. The cash budget shows whether the firm can expect a cash deficit, in which case plans must be made to obtain external capital, or a cash surplus, in which case plans should be made to invest the available funds. The next section of the chapter dealt with the models designed to determine the target cash balance. The Baumol model, based on the standard EOQ inventory model, balances the opportunity cost of holding cash against the transactions costs associated with replenishing the cash account either by selling off marketable securities or by raising cash through the issuance of debt or equity securities. Other models discussed were the Miller-Orr model and simulation. We also discussed ways of speeding up cash flows by the use of *lockboxes*, what *float* is and how it can be used to hold down bank loans, and *compensating balances*.

Our study of marketable securities began with a discussion of why securities are held. Primarily, they are held (1) as a reserve for future contingencies, (2) to meet seasonal needs, with holdings being built up during the slack season and then liquidated when cash requirements are high, (3) to meet known future cash requirements such as construction progress payments or taxes, and (4) immediately after the sale of long-term securities. Given the motives for holding risky securities, treasurers generally do not want to gamble by holding them—safety is the watchword, and rarely will a treasurer sacrifice safety for the higher yields offered on risky securities.

Questions

20-1 Define each of the following terms:
  a. Transactions balance; compensating balance
  b. Cash budget
  c. Target cash balance
  d. Synchronized cash flows
  e. Check clearing
  f. Net float
  g. Overdraft
  h. Lockbox
  i. Marketable securities
  j. Near-cash
  k. Marketable securities versus borrowing strategies
  l. Baumol model
  m. Miller-Orr model

20-2 What are the two principal reasons for holding cash? Can a firm estimate its target cash balance by summing the cash held to satisfy each of the two?

20-3 Explain how each of the following factors would probably affect a firm's target cash balance if all other factors are held constant.
  a. The firm institutes a new billing procedure which better synchronizes its cash inflows and outflows.
  b. The firm develops a new sales forecasting technique which improves its forecasts.

    c. The firm reduces its portfolio of U.S. Treasury bills.

    d. The firm arranges to use an overdraft system for its checking account.

    e. The firm borrows a large amount of money from its bank, and it also begins to write far more checks than it did in the past.

    f. Interest rates on Treasury bills rise from 5 to 10 percent.

20-4 In the cash budget shown in Table 20-1, is the projected maximum funds requirement of $5.38 million in September known with certainty, or should it be regarded as the expected value of a probability distribution? Consider how this peak would probably be affected by each of the following:

    a. A lengthening of the average collection period.

    b. An unanticipated decline in sales that occurred when sales were supposed to peak.

    c. A sharp drop in sales prices required to meet competition.

    d. A sharp increase in interest rates for a firm with a large amount of short-term debt outstanding.

20-5 Would a lockbox plan make more sense for a firm that makes sales all over the United States or for a firm with the same volume of business but concentrated in one city?

20-6 Would a corporate treasurer be more tempted to invest the firm's liquidity portfolio in long-term as opposed to short-term securities when the yield curve was upward sloping or downward sloping?

20-7 What does the term *liquidity* mean? Which would be more important to a firm that held a portfolio of marketable securities as precautionary balances against the possibility of losing a major lawsuit—liquidity or rate of return? Explain.

20-8 Corporate treasurers, when selecting securities for portfolio investments, must make a trade-off between higher risk and higher returns. It is true that most treasurers are willing to assume a fairly high exposure to risk in order to gain higher expected returns?

Problems

20-1 Steve and Susan Ball recently leased space in the Southside Mall and opened a new business, Ball's Coin Shop. Business has been good, but the Balls have frequently run out of cash. This has necessitated late payment on certain orders, and this, in turn, is beginning to cause a problem with suppliers. The Balls plan to borrow money from the bank to have cash ready as needed, but first they need a forecast of just how much they must borrow. Accordingly, they have asked you to prepare a cash budget for the critical period around Christmas, when needs will be especially high.

    Sales are made on a *cash basis only*. The Balls' purchases must be paid for the following month. The Balls pay themselves a salary of $4,800 per month, and the rent is $2,000 per month. In addition, the Balls must make a tax payment of $12,000 in December. The current cash on hand (on December 1) is $400, but the Balls have agreed to maintain an end-of-month bank balance of $6,000—this is their target cash balance. (Disregard till cash, which is insignificant because the Balls keep only a small amount on hand in order to lessen the chances of robbery.)

The estimated sales and purchases for December, January, and February are shown below. Purchases during November amounted to $140,000.

	Sales	Purchases
December	$160,000	$40,000
January	40,000	40,000
February	60,000	40,000

a. Prepare a cash budget for December, January, and February.
b. Now suppose the Balls were to start selling on a credit basis on December 1, giving customers 30 days to pay. All customers accept these terms, and all other facts in the problem are unchanged. What would the company's loan requirements be at the end of December in this case?

20-2 The Torrence Company is planning to request a line of credit from its bank. The following sales forecasts have been made by the firm's marketing department.

May 1984	$ 750,000
June	750,000
July	1,500,000
August	2,250,000
September	3,000,000
October	1,500,000
November	1,500,000
December	375,000
January 1985	750,000

Collection estimates were obtained from the credit and collection department as follows: collected during the month of sale, 5 percent; collected the month following the sale, 80 percent; collected the second month following the sale, 15 percent. Payments for labor and raw materials are typically made during the month following the month in which these costs are incurred. Total labor and raw materials costs are estimated for each month as follows (payments are made the following month):

May 1984	$ 375,000
June	375,000
July	525,000
August	3,675,000
September	1,275,000
October	975,000
November	675,000
December	375,000

General and administrative salaries will amount to approximately $112,000 a month; lease payments under long-term lease contracts will be $37,500 a month; depreciation charges are $150,000 a month; miscellaneous expenses will be $11,500 a month; income tax payments of $262,500 will be due in both September and December; and a progress payment of $750,000 on a new research laboratory must be paid in October. Cash on hand on July 1 will amount to $550,000, and a minimum cash balance of $375,000 should be maintained throughout the cash budget period.

a. Prepare a monthly cash budget for the last six months of 1984.

b. Prepare an estimate of required financing (or excess funds) for each month during the same period, that is, the amount of money that the Torrence Company will need to borrow (or will have available to invest) each month.

c. Suppose receipts from sales come in uniformly during the month—that is, cash payments come in 1/30th each day—but all outflows are paid on the fifth of the month. Would this have an effect on the cash budget, that is, would the cash budget you have prepared be valid under these assumptions? If not, what could be done to make a valid estimation of financing requirements?

d. Torrence produces on a seasonal basis, just ahead of sales. Without making any calculations, discuss how the company's current ratio and debt ratio would vary during the year, assuming all financial requirements are met by short-term bank loans. Could changes in these ratios affect the firm's ability to obtain bank credit?

e. Now suppose a recession occurs, and sales fall below the forecasted, or budgeted, levels. However, the firm continues production according to the indicated plans. Also, because of the recession, customers delay payments, so the lag between sales and collections lengthens. What would all this do to the realized cash surpluses and deficits, and to the external funds requirements?

f. If you prepared the cash budget in Part a correctly, you would show a surplus of $426,000 at the end of July. Suggest some alternative investments for this money. Be sure to consider long-term bonds versus short-term debt instruments, and the appropriateness of investing in common stock.

g. Would your choice of securities in Part f be affected if the cash budget showed continuous cash surpluses versus alternating surpluses and deficits?

20-3 You have just been hired as the cash manager of the Goforth Company. Your first task is to determine the firm's target cash balance. Goforth expects to need $1.5 million of net new cash during the coming year. This requirement occurs at a relatively constant rate over the year. The firm plans to meet this cash requirement by borrowing from Bank A at an annual interest rate of 10 percent. The fixed cost of transferring funds from the bank is $100 per transfer.

a. Assume that the firm will not carry a cash "safety stock." What target cash balance is indicated by the Baumol model? How many cash transfers are expected over the year?

b. Suppose the firm wants to maintain a $5,000 cash "safety stock," which is currently on hand. What would be the new average cash balance?

20-4 The Hardy Hot Tub Company has accumulated $100,000 in excess cash. However, it is expected that the firm will need the entire amount to cover cash outflows anticipated to occur evenly over the coming year. Hardy has the funds invested in commercial paper that pays 10 percent annually. The cost of transferring funds is $50 per transaction.
   a. What is Hardy's target cash balance according to the Baumol model? What is Hardy's total cost of cash balances?
   b. As Hardy's cash manager, you are concerned about whether the Baumol model is on a before-tax or after-tax basis. Hardy's tax rate is 40 percent. What is Hardy's target cash balance and total costs of cash balances on an *after-tax* basis?
   c. Hardy is considering putting its excess cash in a floating rate preferred stock mutual fund. The fund pays 10 percent annually, but only 15 percent of its dividends are taxable. What affect would this decision have on Hardy's target cash balance and cost of cash balances?

20-5 The Karp Corporation has estimated that the standard deviation of its daily net cash flows is $2,500. The firm pays $20 in transaction costs to transfer funds into and out of commercial paper that pays 9.42 percent annual interest. Karp uses the Miller-Orr model to set its target cash balance. Additionally, the firm has decided to maintain a $10,000 minimum cash balance (lower limit).
   a. What is Karp's target cash balance?
   b. What are the upper and lower limits?
   c. What are Karp's decision rules? (That is, when is a transaction called for, and what is the transaction?)
   d. What is Karp's expected average cash balance?

20-6 Piedmont Furniture Company, a prominent manufacturer of early-American style furniture, expects gross sales of $120,000 in January, $140,000 in February, $150,000 in March, $160,000 in April, and $180,000 in May. Piedmont has found, on average, that 50 percent of its customers take the 2 percent discount, and these customers are assumed to pay in the month of sale. Another 25 percent pay the month following the sale, while the remaining 20 percent pay in the second month following the sale. Piedmont's bad debt losses are currently running at 5 percent.

The furniture is produced one month prior to sale. Wages, which are 30 percent of sales, are paid in the month of manufacture. The materials must be purchased two months prior to sale, but Piedmont's terms with its suppliers allow it to pay one month after the materials are purchased. Materials amount to 50 percent of sales.

Piedmont's fixed assets are being depreciated using the appropriate ACRS tables. Depreciation expense is forecast to be $10,000 in March and $9,800 in April. Administrative and selling expenses run $7,000 per month. The plant site is leased, with before-tax lease payments running at $2,000 per month. Piedmont is in the 46 percent tax bracket.

Estimated taxes are paid in the first month of each calendar quarter.

Piedmont's tax liability for the next whole year is estimated at $50,000.

a. Construct Piedmont's cash budget for March and April. What are the net cash flows for March and April?

b. Piedmont's target cash balance is $5,000, which it has on March 1. In order to maintain this balance, Piedmont borrowed $6,400 in January and $3,800 in February against its $50,000 line of credit at the bank. What are Piedmont's cumulative borrowings at the end of April? Is the line of credit sufficient up to this point?

20-7 The Milton Manufacturing Company uses the Miller-Orr model to set its target cash balance. The company's daily net cash flows have a distribution which is approximately normal, with a standard deviation of $500. Excess cash is invested in T-bills which pay 10 percent annually. The cost of converting between T-bills and cash is $100 per transaction. Milton's management is risk averse, so the firm maintains a cash safety stock of $5,000. Milton uses a 360-day year.

a. What is Milton's upper limit, H, lower limit, L, and target cash balance, Z?

b. What are Milton's decision rules; that is, when does it transfer between T-bills and cash, and how much does it transfer?

c. What is Milton's expected average cash balance?

Perhaps the best way to get a good feel for the current state of the art is to look through recent issues of The Journal of Cash Management, *a relatively new publication aimed at professionals in the field.*

Some key references on cash balance models include the following:

Daellenbach, Hans G., "Are Cash Management Optimization Models Worthwhile?" *Journal of Financial and Quantitative Analysis*, September 1974, 607-626.

Miller, Merton H., and Daniel Orr, "The Demand for Money by Firms: Extension of Analytic Results," *Journal of Finance*, December, 1968, 735-759.

Mullins, David Wiley, Jr., and Richard B. Homonoff, "Applications of Inventory Cash Management Models," in *Modern Developments in Financial Management*, S. C. Myers, ed. (New York: Praeger, 1976).

Stone, Bernell K., "The Use of Forecasts for Smoothing in Control-Limit Models for Cash Management," *Financial Management*, Spring 1972, 72-84.

For more information on float management, see

Batlin, C. A., and Susan Hinko, "Lockbox Management and Value Maximization," *Financial Management*, Winter 1981, 39-44.

Gitman, Lawrence J., D. Keith Forrester, and John R. Forrester, Jr., "Maximizing Cash Disbursement Float," *Financial Management*, Summer 1976, 32-41.

Nauss, Robert M., and Robert E. Markland, "Solving Lockbox Location Problems," *Financial Management*, Spring 1979, 21-31.

The following articles provide more information on cash concentration systems:

Stone, Bernell K., and Ned C. Hill, "Cash Transfer Scheduling for Efficient Cash Concentration," *Financial Management*, Autumn 1980, 35-43.

————, "The Design of a Cash Concentration System," *Journal of Financial and Quantitative Analysis*, September 1981, 301-322.

For greater insights into compensating balance requirements, see

Campbell, Tim S., and Leland Brendsel, "The Impact of Compensating Balance Requirements on the Cash Balances of Manufacturing Corporations," *Journal of Finance*, March 1977, 31-40.

Selected Additional References and Cases

Frost, Peter A., "Banking Services, Minimum Cash Balances and the Firm's Demand for Money," *Journal of Finance*, December 1970, 1029-1039.

For more information on marketable securities, see any of the investment textbooks referenced in Chapter 5, or see

Stigum, Marcia, *The Money Market: Myth, Reality, and Practice* (Homewood, Ill.: Dow Jones-Irwin, 1978).

Van Horne, James C., *Financial Market Rates and Flows* (Englewood Cliffs, N. J.: Prentice-Hall, 1984).

The following cases focus on cash management:

Case 5, "Lenox Furniture Company," in the Brigham-Crum casebook, which illustrates the mechanics of the cash budget and the rationale behind its use.

"Austin Limited," in the Harrington casebook, which examines changes in a firm's cash disbursement system.

Receivables Management and Credit Policy

21

All during 1980, security analysts kept expecting Xerox's sales, and consequently its earnings, to plummet. But it didn't happen; earnings rose 10 percent on a 23 percent sales gain. The secret, analysts learned, was that Xerox had begun a policy of lending money to its customers at bargain rates. Profit margins on the added sales more than offset the cost to Xerox of the low-rate loans, boosting the company's net income.

Although Xerox had good success with its liberal credit policy, different companies under other circumstances have increased their profits by reducing or even eliminating credit. In 1982, for example, Atlantic Richfield Company (Arco) sent shock waves through the oil industry by announcing plans to eliminate the use of credit cards at all of its service stations. Its management believed (1) that the recent increases in gasoline prices had made customers very price sensitive; (2) that the combined costs of bad debt losses, processing credit card sales, and having funds tied up in accounts receivable amounted to about 4 cents per gallon; (3) that if it eliminated credit sales and cut gas prices at the pump by 3 cents a gallon, it would lose one out of every three credit card customers, but because of lower prices, gain four new customers for every old one lost; and (4) that consequently it would enjoy a substantial increase in net income. Since then, other firms have adopted similar plans, and it appears that they have generally been successful.

Our goal in this chapter is to examine the factors that must be considered when companies such as Xerox and Arco—or much smaller ones—establish credit policy.

Firms would, in general, rather sell for cash than on credit, but competitive pressures force most firms to offer credit. Thus, goods are shipped, inventories are reduced, and an account receivable is created. Eventually, the customer will pay the account, at which time the firm receives cash and receivables decline. Managing receivables has both direct and indirect costs, but granting credit will enhance sales. The optimal credit policy is the one which maximizes profits over time consistent with the risk assumed.

Receivables Management

Receivables management begins with the decision of whether or not to grant credit. In this section, we discuss the manner in which a firm's receivables build up, and we also present several alternative means of monitoring receivables. Such a system is important, because without it, receivables will build up to excessive levels, cash flows will decline, and bad debts will rise. Corrective action is often needed, and the only way to tell if things are getting out of hand is through a good receivables control system.

The Accumulation of Receivables

The total amount of accounts receivable outstanding at any given time is determined by two factors: (1) the volume of credit sales and (2) the average length of time between sales and collections. For example, suppose someone opens a store on January 1 and, starting the first day, makes sales of $100 each day. Customers are given 10 days in which to pay. At the end of the first day, accounts receivable will be $100; they will rise to $200 by the end of the second day; and by January 10, they will have risen to 10($100) = $1,000. On January 11, another $100 will be added to receivables, but payments for sales made on January 1 will reduce receivables by $100, so total accounts receivable will remain constant at $1,000. In general, once the firm's operations have stabilized, this situation will exist:

$$\text{Accounts receivable} = \text{Credit sales per day} \times \text{Length of collection period}$$
$$= \$100 \times 10 \text{ days} = \$1,000.$$

If either credit sales or the collection period changes, such changes will be reflected in accounts receivable.

Notice that the $1,000 investment in receivables must be financed. To illustrate, suppose that when the store opened on January 1, the owner had put up $100 as common stock and used this money to buy the goods sold the first day. Thus, the initial balance sheet would be as follows:

Inventories	$100	Common equity	$100
Total assets	$100	Total claims	$100

At the end of the day, the balance sheet would look like this:[1]

---

[1] Of course, a profit might have been earned on the sales, but it would, for a retail business, amount to only about 2 percent, or $2. Also, the firm would need other assets such as cash, fixed assets, and a permanent stock of inventory. We abstract from these details here so that we may focus on receivables.

Accounts receivable	$100		
Inventories	0	Common equity	$100
Total assets	$100	Total claims	$100

In order to remain in business, the owner must replenish inventories. To do so requires that $100 of goods be purchased, and this requires $100. Assuming the owner borrows the $100 from the bank, the balance sheet at the start of the second day will be as follows:

Accounts receivable	$100	Notes payable to bank	$100
Inventories	100	Common equity	100
Total assets	$200	Total claims	$200

At the end of the second day, the inventories will have been converted to receivables, and the firm will have to borrow another $100 to restock for the third day.

This process will continue, provided the bank is willing to lend the necessary funds, until the eleventh day, when the balance sheet reads as follows:

Accounts receivable	$1,000	Notes payable to bank	$1,000
Inventories	100	Common equity	100
Total assets	$1,100	Total claims	$1,100

From this point on, $100 of receivables will be collected every day, and these funds can be used to purchase new inventories.

This example should make it clear (1) that accounts receivable depend jointly on the level of credit sales and the collection period, and (2) that any increase in receivables must be financed in some manner. Here we assumed bank financing, but in Chapter 18, we pointed out that there are many alternative ways to finance current assets.

Monitoring the Receivables Position

The optimal credit policy, and hence the optimal level of accounts receivable, depends on the firm's own unique operating conditions. Thus, a firm with excess capacity and low variable production costs should extend credit more liberally and carry a higher level of accounts receivable than a firm operating at full capacity on a slim profit margin. However, even though optimal credit policies vary among firms, or even for a single firm over time, it is still useful to analyze the effectiveness of the firm's credit policy in an overall, aggregate sense. Investors—both stockholders and bank loan officers—should pay close attention to accounts receivable management; otherwise, they could be misled by the current financial statements and later suffer serious losses on their investments.

When a sale is made, the following events occur: (1) Inventories are reduced by the cost of goods sold, (2) accounts receivable are increased by the sales price, and (3) the difference is recorded as a profit. If the sale is for cash, the profit is definitely earned, but if the sale is on credit, the profit is not actually earned unless and until the account is collected. Firms have been known to encourage "sales" to very weak customers in order to inflate reported profits. This could boost the stock price, at least until credit losses begin to lower earnings, at which time, the stock price falls. Analyses along the lines suggested in the following sections would detect any such questionable practice, as well as any unconscious deterioration in the quality of accounts receivable. Such early detection could help both investors and bankers avoid losses.[2]

Average Collection Period. Suppose Super Sets, Inc., a television manufacturer, sells 200,000 television sets a year at $200 each. Further, assume that all sales are on credit with terms of 2/10, net 30. Finally, assume that 70 percent of the customers take discounts and pay on Day 10, while the other 30 percent pay on Day 30.

Super Sets' *average collection period (ACP)* is 16 days:

$$ACP = 0.7(10 \text{ days}) + 0.3(30 \text{ days}) = 16 \text{ days}.$$

The ACP is sometimes called *days sales outstanding (DSO)*.

Super Sets' *average daily sales (ADS)*, assuming a 360-day year, is $111,111.11:

$$ADS = \frac{\text{Annual sales}}{360} = \frac{200,000(\$200)}{360}$$

$$= \frac{\$40,000,000}{360} = \$111,111.11.$$

If the company had made cash as well as credit sales, we would have concentrated on credit sales only, and calculated average daily *credit* sales.

Finally, Super Sets' accounts receivables, assuming a constant, uniform rate of sales all during the year, will at any point in time be $1,777,778:

$$\text{Receivables} = (ADS)(ACP)$$

$$= (\$111,111.11)(16) = \$1,777,778.$$

Thus, the ACP is a measure of the average length of time it takes Super Sets' customers to pay off their credit purchases.[3]

---

[2]Accountants are increasingly interested in these matters. Investors have sued several of the Big Eight accounting firms for substantial damages where (1) profits were overstated and (2) it could be shown that the auditors should have conducted an analysis along the lines described here and then should have reported the results to stockholders on the audited financial statements.

[3]Note that the ACP can be calculated, given a firm's accounts receivable balance and its average daily credit sales, as follows:

$$ACP = \frac{\text{Receivables}}{ADS} = \frac{\$1,777,777}{\$111,111} = 16 \text{ days}.$$

In practice, since the ACP averages the individual collection periods of all the firm's credit customers, and since sales are not generally uniform over time, the ACP provides only limited information. For example, the ACP is often compared with an industry average ACP. If the television manufacturing industry has an average ACP of 25 days versus Super Sets' 16-day ACP, then Super Sets either has a higher percentage of discount customers or else its credit department is exceptionally good at insuring prompt payment.

The ACP can also be compared with the firm's own credit terms. For example, suppose Super Sets' ACP had been running at a level of 35 days versus its 2/10, net 30, credit terms. With a 35-day ACP, some customers would obviously be taking more than 30 days to pay their bills. In fact, if some customers were paying within 10 days to take advantage of the discount, the others would, on average, have to be taking much longer than 35 days. One way to check this possibility is to use an aging schedule as described in the next section.

Aging Schedule. An aging schedule breaks down a firm's receivables by age of account. Super Sets' aging schedule as of December 31, 1984, is shown in Table 21-1. Most of the accounts pay on schedule or after only a slight delay, but a significant number are over one month past due. This might signify potential bad debt problems.

Aging schedules cannot be constructed from the type of summary data that are reported in financial statements; data from a firm's credit department must be used to make the schedule. Although changes in aging schedules over time do provide more information to the firm than does the ACP taken alone, a better way to monitor receivables is the *payments pattern approach*, which we discuss in the next section.

The Payments Pattern Approach. Both the ACP and aging schedules are affected by a firm's pattern of sales. Thus, changes in sales levels, including seasonal or cyclical changes, can change a firm's ACP and aging

---

Table 21-1
Super Sets' Aging Schedule as of December 31, 1984

Age of Account (Days)	Percentage of Total Value of Accounts Receivable
0-10	50%
11-30	22
31-45	13
46-60	4
Over 60	11
	100%

Note: If we knew the day the average customer in each group pays, we could develop a weighted average ACP which would equal the ACP as calculated above. The aging schedule shown here is actually consistent with a 35-day ACP.

schedule even though its customers' payment behavior has not changed. For this reason, a procedure called the *payments pattern approach* has been developed to measure any changes that might be occurring in customers' payment behavior.[4] To illustrate the payments pattern approach, consider the credit sales of Hanover Manufacturing Company (HMC), a small manufacturer of hand tools which commenced operations in January 1984. Table 21-2 contains HMC's credit sales and receivables data for 1984. Column 2 shows that HMC's credit sales are seasonal, with the lowest sales in the fall and winter months and the highest sales during the summer.

Now suppose that HMC's customers have the same payment behavior throughout the year, that is, they take the same length of time to pay.

Table 21-2
Hanover Manufacturing Company:
Receivables Data for 1984
(Thousands of Dollars)

Month (1)	Credit Sales (2)	Receivables (3)	Quarterly ADS[a] (4)	Quarterly ACP[b] (5)	Cumulative ADS (6)	Cumulative ACP (7)
January	$ 60	$ 54				
February	60	90				
March	60	102	$2.00	51 days	$2.00	51 days
April	60	102				
May	90	129				
June	120	174	3.00	58 days	2.50	70 days
July	120	198				
August	90	177				
September	60	132	3.00	44 days	2.67	49 days
October	60	108				
November	60	102				
December	60	102	2.00	51 days	2.50	41 days

[a]ADS = Average daily sales.
[b]ACP = Average collection period.

[4]See Wilbur G. Lewellen and Robert W. Johnson, "A Better Way to Monitor Accounts Receivable," *Harvard Business Review*, May-June 1972, 101-109; and Bernell Stone, "The Payments-Pattern Approach to the Forecasting and Control of Accounts Receivable," *Financial Management*, Autumn 1976, 65-82.

Further, assume that 10 percent of its customers pay in the same month that the sale is made, that 30 percent pay in the first month following the sale, that 40 percent pay in the second month, and that the remaining 20 percent pay in the third month. Based on this payment pattern, Column 3 of Table 21-2 contains HMC's receivables balance at the end of each month. For example, during January, HMC has $60,000 in sales. Ten percent of the customers paid during the month of sale, so the receivables balance at the end of January was $60,000 - 0.1($60,000) = (1.0 - 0.1)($60,000) = $54,000. By the end of February, 10% + 30% = 40% of the customers have paid for January's sales, and 10 percent have paid for February's sales. Thus, the receivables balance at the end of February is (1.0 - 0.4)($60,000) + (1.0 - 0.1)($60,000) = $90,000. By the end of March, 80 percent of January's sales have been paid, 40 percent of February's have been paid, and 10 percent of March's sales have been paid, so the receivables balance is 0.2($60,000) + 0.6($60,000) + 0.9($60,000) = $102,000. And so on.

Columns 4 and 5 give HMC's average daily sales, ADS, and average collection period, ACP, respectively, as these measures would be developed based on the quarterly financial statements. For example, in the April-June quarter, ADS = ($60,000 + $90,000 + $120,000)/90 = $3,000, and ACP = $174,000/$3,000 = 58 days. Columns 6 and 7 list the same measures, but assuming that they are reported on the basis of accumulated sales data. For example, at the end of June, ADS = $450,000/180 = $2,500 and ACP = $174,000/$2,500 = 70 days.

The data in Table 21-2 illustrate two major points. First, the ACP is changing, which suggests that customers are paying faster or slower, even though customer payment patterns are actually not changing at all. Increasing sales causes the calculated ACP to rise, while decreasing sales causes the calculated ACP to fall, even though nothing is changing with regard to when customers pay. This makes it difficult to use the ACP as a monitoring device for a firm whose sales exhibit seasonal or cyclical patterns. Second, since the ACP depends on an averaging procedure, it is difficult to use it for making interfirm comparisons.

Seasonal or cyclical variations also make it difficult to interpret aging schedules. Table 21-3 contains HMC's aging schedules at the end of each quarter of 1984. At the end of June, Table 21-2 showed that HMC's receivables balance is $174,000. Eighty percent of April's $60,000 of sales have been paid, 40 percent of May's $90,000 sales have been paid, and 10 percent of June's $120,000 sales have been paid. Thus, the end-of-June receivables balance consists of 0.2($60,000) = $12,000 of April sales, 0.6($90,000) = $54,000 of May sales, and 0.9($120,000) = $108,000 of June sales. Note again that HMC's customers have not changed their payment patterns. However, rising sales during the second quarter create the impression of faster payments when judged by the percentage aging schedule, and falling sales after July create the opposite appearance. Thus, neither the ACP nor the aging schedule provides the finan-

Table 21-3
Hanover Manufacturing Company:
Aging Schedules for 1984
(Thousands of Dollars)

Age of Accounts (Days)	Value and Percentage of Total Value of Accounts Receivable							
	March 31		June 30		September 30		December 31	
0 – 30	$ 54	53%	$108	62%	$ 54	41%	$ 54	53%
31 – 60	36	35	54	31	54	41	36	35
61 – 90	12	12	12	7	24	18	12	12
	$102	100%	$174	100%	$132	100%	$102	100%

cial manager with an accurate picture of customers' payment patterns in this instance, which is, unfortunately, typical.

With this background, we can now examine another basic tool, the *uncollected balances schedule*. Table 21-4 contains HMC's quarterly uncollected balances schedules. At the end of each quarter, the dollar amount of receivables remaining from each month's sales is divided by that month's sales to obtain the receivables-to-sales ratio. For example, at the end of the first quarter, March, $12,000 of the $60,000 January sales, or 20 percent, are still outstanding; 60 percent of February sales are still out; and 90 percent of March sales are uncollected. Exactly the same situation is revealed at the end of the next three quarters. Thus, Table 21-4 shows HMC's managers that its customers' payment behavior has not changed over the year.

Of course, in the example we assumed a constant payments pattern at the very beginning. In a normal situation, the firm's customers' payments patterns would probably vary over the year. However, this would be detected from the last column of the uncollected balances schedule. For example, say that the May purchasers paid their accounts slower than assumed initially. Then, the second quarter uncollected balances schedule might look like this (in thousands of dollars):

Quarter 2, 1984	Sales	Receivables	Receivables/Sales
April	$ 60	$ 12	20%
May	90	70	78
June	120	108	90
		$190	188%

We see that the receivables-to-sales ratio was higher in May than in February, the corresponding month in the first quarter. This caused the total uncollected balances percentage to rise from 170 to 188 percent, which in turn would alert HMC's managers that customers are paying later than they did earlier in the year.

Table 21-4
Hanover Manufacturing Company:
Quarterly Uncollected Balances Schedules for 1984
(Thousands of Dollars)

	Sales	Receivables	Receivables/Sales
Quarter 1			
January	$ 60	$ 12	20%
February	60	36	60
March	60	54	90
		$102	170%
Quarter 2			
April	$ 60	$ 12	20%
May	90	54	60
June	120	108	90
		$174	170%
Quarter 3			
July	$120	$ 24	20%
August	90	54	60
September	60	54	90
		$132	170%
Quarter 4			
October	$ 60	$ 12	20%
November	60	36	60
December	60	54	90
		$102	170%

The uncollected balances schedule not only permits a firm to monitor its receivables better, but it can also be used to forecast future receivables balances. When the HMC pro forma 1985 quarterly balance sheets are constructed, management can use the receivables-to-sales ratios, coupled with 1985 sales estimates, to project each quarter's receivables balance. For example, with projected sales as given below, and using the same payments pattern as in 1984, HMC could project its end-of-June 1985 receivables balance as follows:

Quarter 2, 1985	Projected Sales	Receivables/Sales	Projected Receivables
April	$ 70,000	20%	$ 14,000
May	100,000	60	60,000
June	140,000	90	126,000
			$200,000

The payment patterns approach permits the separation of seasonal and/or cyclical sales patterns from customers' payment patterns. Thus, it provides financial managers with more information than such summary measures as the average collection period or the aging schedule. Managers can use the payments pattern approach to monitor collection performance as well as to project future receivables requirements.

Use of Computers in Receivables Management

Except possibly in the inventory area, nowhere in the typical firm have computers had more of an impact than in accounts receivable management. A well-run business will use a computer system to record sales, to send out bills, to keep track of when payments are made, to alert the credit manager when an account becomes past due, and to insure that actions are taken to collect past due accounts (for example, to automatically prepare a form letter requesting payment). Additionally, the payment records of each customer can be summarized and used to help establish credit limits for customers and classes of customers, and the data on each account can be aggregated and used for the firm's accounts receivable monitoring system. Finally, historic data can be stored in the firm's data base and used to develop inputs for studies related to credit policy changes.

Technological developments in the computer area are causing fundamental changes in receivables management. Firms that use the new technology in an intelligent manner will be the winners in the new business environment.

Credit Policy

The success or failure of a business depends primarily on the demand for its products—as a rule, the higher its sales, the larger its profits and the healthier the firm. Sales, in turn, depend on a number of factors, some exogenous but others controllable by the firm. The major controllable variables which affect demand are sales prices, product quality, advertising, and *the firm's credit policy*. Credit policy, in turn, consists of these four variables:

1. The *credit period*, which is the length of time buyers have before they must pay for their purchases.

2. The *credit standards*, which refer to the minimum financial strength of acceptable credit customers.

3. The firm's *collection policy*, which is measured by its toughness or laxity in following up on slow-paying accounts.

4. Any *discounts* given for early payment.

The credit manager has the responsibility for administering the firm's credit policy. However, because of the pervasive importance of credit, the credit policy itself is normally established by the executive committee, which usually consists of the president and the vice presidents in charge of finance, marketing, and production.

A firm's regular credit terms, which set the *credit period*, might call for sales on a 2/10, net 30 basis to all "acceptable" customers. Its *credit standards* would be applied to determine which customers qualified for the regular credit terms, and the amount of credit extended. The major factor to consider when setting credit standards and the credit period relates to the likelihood that a given customer will pay slowly or even end up as a bad debt loss. This requires a measurement of credit quality. To begin the discussion, we need to define *credit quality*, and perhaps the best way is in terms of the probability of default. The probability estimate for a given customer is, for the most part, a subjective judgment, but credit evaluation is a well-established practice, and a good credit manager can make reasonably accurate judgments regarding the probability of default by different classes of customers. In this section, we discuss some of the methods used by firms to measure credit quality.

Setting the Credit Period and Standards

One of the traditional methods of measuring credit quality is to investigate the potential buyer with respect to five factors called *the five Cs of credit*:

The Five Cs System

1. *Character* refers to the probability that customers will try to honor their obligations. This factor is of considerable importance, because every credit transaction implies a *promise* to pay. Will debtors make an honest effort to pay their debts, or are they likely to try to get away with something? Experienced credit managers frequently insist that the moral factor is the most important issue in a credit evaluation. Thus, credit reports provide background information on peoples' and firms' past performance. Often, credit analysts will seek this type of information from a firm's bankers, its other suppliers, its customers, and even its competitors. Obviously, "character" is a subjective factor, so good judgment on the part of the analyst is essential.

2. *Capacity* is a subjective judgment regarding customers' *ability* to pay. It is gauged in part by their past records and their business methods, and it may be supplemented by physical observation of customers' plants or stores. Again, credit analysts will obtain information on this factor from a variety of sources.

3. *Capital* is measured by the general financial condition of a firm as indicated by an analysis of its financial statements. Special emphasis is given to risk ratios—the debt/assets ratio, the current ratio, the times-interest-earned ratio, and the fixed charge coverage ratio.

4. *Collateral* is represented by assets that a customer may offer as security to obtain credit.

5. *Conditions* refer to any general economic trends or special developments in certain geographic regions or sectors of the economy that might affect customers' ability to meet their obligations. For example,

suppliers of credit to home builders and building supply companies are very much concerned with local and national housing market trends, for if new homes do not sell, then builders cannot pay off their suppliers, and the suppliers in turn cannot pay off their banks and other creditors.

Information on these five factors is obtained from the firm's previous experience with each customer, supplemented by a well-developed system of external information-gathering groups. More and more firms and industries are setting up computerized data bases for storing and retrieving information on their customers and potential customers.

Of course, once the information on the five Cs is developed, the credit manager must still make a final decision on the potential customer's overall credit quality. This decision is normally judgmental in nature, and credit managers rely on their acquired skills and instincts.

Credit-Scoring Systems

Although most credit decisions are judgmental, many firms are starting to use a sophisticated statistical method called *multiple discriminant analysis (MDA)* to assess credit quality. One advantage of an MDA credit-scoring system is that a customer's credit quality is expressed in a single numerical value, rather than as a judgmental assessment of five separate factors. This is a tremendous advantage for a large firm which must evaluate many customers and which would otherwise have to employ many different credit analysts, who would have a hard time applying equal standards to all credit applicants. Most credit card companies, department stores, oil companies, and the like use credit-scoring systems to determine who gets how much credit, as do the larger building supply chains and manufacturers of electrical products, machinery, and so on.

Multiple discriminant analysis will be discussed in detail in Chapter 25 in connection with bankruptcy prediction. For now, we will briefly describe the concept. Suppose a firm has historical information on 500 of its customers. Of these 500, assume that 400 have always paid on time, but the other 100 either paid late or not at all. Further, the firm has historic data on each business customer's quick ratio, times-interest-earned ratio, debt ratio, years in existence, and so on. Multiple discriminant analysis relates the experienced record (or historic probability) of late payment or nonpayment with various measures of a firm's financial condition, and MDA provides weights for the critical factors.

Then, the values of these factors for a potential customer can be used to develop that firm's credit score. For example, suppose that multiple discriminant analysis indicates that the critical factors affecting prompt payment are the times-interest-earned ratio, quick ratio, and number of years in business. Table 21-5 provides an assumed set of multiple discriminant analysis weights and scoring requirements. Now, suppose that a firm with the following conditions applies for credit:

Table 21-5
Multiple Discriminant Analysis

Weights

Measure	Weight
Times-interest-earned ratio	3.5
Quick ratio	10.0
Years in business	1.3

Scoring Requirements

Credit Score[a]	Credit Quality Class
Less than 40	Poor
40 to 50	Fair
Greater than 50	Good

[a]Score = 3.5(TIE) + 10.0(Quick ratio) + 1.3(Years in business).

$$\text{Times-interest-earned ratio} = 4.2.$$
$$\text{Quick ratio} = 3.1.$$
$$\text{Years in business} = 10.$$

This firm's credit score would be 3.5(4.2) + 10.0(3.1) + 1.3(10) = 58.7. Therefore, it would be considered a good credit risk, and consequently it would be offered favorable credit terms.

Two major sources of external information are available. The first is the work of the *credit associations*, which are local groups that meet frequently and correspond with one another to exchange information on credit customers. These local groups have also banded together to create Credit Interchange, a system developed by the National Association of Credit Management for assembling and distributing information about debtors' past performance. The interchange reports show the paying records of different debtors, the industries from which they are buying, and the geographic areas in which they are making purchases. The second source of external information is the work of the *credit-reporting agencies*, which collect credit information and sell it for a fee. The best known of these agencies are Dun & Bradstreet (D&B) and TRW, Incorporated. D&B, TRW, and other agencies provide factual data that can be used in credit analysis; they also provide ratings similar to those available on corporate bonds.[5]

Sources of Credit Information

---

[5]For additional information, see Christie and Bracuti, *Credit Management*, a publication of the National Association of Credit Management; and also, see Peter Nulty, "An Upstart Takes on Dun & Bradstreet," *Fortune*, April 9, 1979, 98-100.

Managing a credit department requires fast, accurate, up-to-date information, and to help get such information, the National Association of Credit Management (a group with 43,000 member firms) persuaded TRW, Inc., to develop a computer-based telecommunications network for the collection, storage, retrieval, and distribution of credit information. The TRW system is now in existence, and its electronically transmitted credit reports are available within seconds to its thousands of subscribers. Dun & Bradstreet has a similar system plus a service which provides more detailed reports through the U.S. mail.

A typical credit report would include the following pieces of information:

1. A summary balance sheet and income statement.

2. A number of key ratios, with trend information.

3. Information obtained from the firm's suppliers telling whether it has been paying promptly or slowly, and whether it has failed to make payments.

4. A verbal description of the physical condition of the firm's operations.

5. A verbal description of the backgrounds of the firm's owners, including any previous bankruptcies, lawsuits, divorce settlement problems, and the like.

6. A summary rating, ranging from A+ for the best credit risks down to F for those that are most likely to default.

Although a great deal of credit information is available, it must still be processed in a judgmental manner. Computerized information systems can assist in making better credit decisions, but, in the final analysis, most credit decisions are really exercises in informed judgment. Even credit scoring systems require judgment in deciding where to draw the lines, given the set of derived scores.

Management by Exception

Modern credit managers practice *management by exception*. Under such a system, customers are first classified into five or six categories according to degree of risk, after which the credit manager concentrates time and attention on the customers that are most likely to cause problems. For example, the following classes might be established:

Risk Class	Percentage of Uncollectible Credit Sales	Percentage of Customers in This Class
1	0-½%	60%
2	½-2	20
3	2-5	10
4	5-10	5
5	Over 10	5

Firms in Class 1 might be extended credit automatically, and their credit status reviewed only once a year. Those in Class 2 might also receive credit (up to specified limits) automatically, but a ratio analysis of these firms' financial condition would be conducted more frequently (perhaps quarterly), and they would be moved down to Class 3 if their position deteriorated. Specific approvals might be required for credit sales to Classes 3 and 4, while sales to Class 5 might be on a COD (cash on delivery) basis only.

Setting the Collection Policy

Collection policy refers to the procedures the firm follows to collect past-due accounts. For example, a letter may be sent to such accounts when the bill is 10 days past due; a more severe letter, followed by a telephone call, may be used if payment is not received within 30 days; and the account may be turned over to a collection agency after 90 days.

The collection process can be expensive in terms of both out-of-pocket expenditures and lost goodwill, but at least some firmness is needed to prevent an undue lengthening of the collection period and to minimize outright losses. Again, a balance must be struck between the costs and benefits of different collection policies.

Changes in collection policy influence sales, the collection period, the bad debt loss percentage, and the percentage of customers who take discounts. The effects of a change in collection policy, along with changes in the other credit policy variables, will be analyzed later in the chapter.

Cash Discounts

The last element in the credit policy decision, the use of *cash discounts* for early payment, is also analyzed by balancing the costs and benefits of different cash discounts. For example, Stylish Fashions might decide to change its credit terms from "net 30," which means that customers must pay within 30 days, to "2/10, net 30," which means that it will allow a 2 percent discount if payment is received within 10 days, while the full invoice price must otherwise be paid within 30 days. This change should produce two benefits: (1) It should attract new customers who consider discounts to be a type of price reduction, and (2) the discounts should cause a reduction in the average collection period, since some established customers will pay more promptly in order to take advantage of the discount. Offsetting these benefits is the dollar cost of the discounts taken. The optimal discount is established at the point where the marginal costs and benefits are exactly offsetting. The methodology for analyzing changes in the discount is developed later in the chapter.

If sales are seasonal, a firm may use *seasonal dating* on discounts. For example, Slimware, Inc., a swimsuit manufacturer, sells on terms of

2/10, net 30, May 1 dating. This means that the effective invoice date is May 1, even if the sale was made back in January. If the discount is not taken by May 10, the full amount must be paid on May 30. Slimware produces throughout the year, but retail sales of bathing suits are concentrated in the spring and early summer, and by offering seasonal dating, the company induces some customers to stock up early, saving Slimware storage costs and "nailing down sales."

Other Factors Influencing Credit Policy

In addition to the factors discussed above, several other conditions also influence a firm's overall credit policy.

Profit Potential

Thus far, we have emphasized the costs of granting credit. *However, if it is possible to sell on credit and also to assess a carrying charge on the receivables that are outstanding, then credit sales can actually be more profitable than cash sales.* This is especially true for consumer durables (autos, appliances, clothing, and so on), but it is also true for certain types of industrial equipment. Thus, the General Motors Acceptance Corporation (GMAC) unit, which finances automobiles, is highly profitable, as is Sears Roebuck's credit subsidiary.[6] Some encyclopedia companies are even reported to lose money on cash sales but to more than make up these losses from the carrying charges on their credit sales; obviously, such companies would rather sell on credit than for cash!

The carrying charges on outstanding credit are generally about 18 percent on a nominal interest rate basis (1.5 percent per month, so $1.5\% \times 12 = 18\%$); this is equivalent to an effective rate of $(1.015)^{12} - 1.0 = 19.6\%$. Except in the early 1980s, when short-term interest rates rose to unprecedented levels, having receivables outstanding that earn over 18 percent has been highly profitable.

Legal Considerations

It is illegal, under the Robinson-Patman Act, for a firm to charge prices that discriminate among customers unless these differential prices are cost-justified. The same holds true for credit—it is illegal to offer more

---

[6]Companies that do a large volume of sales financing typically set up subsidiary companies called *captive finance companies* to do the actual financing. Thus, General Motors, Chrysler, and Ford all have captive finance companies, as do Sears Roebuck and Montgomery Ward. The reason for this is that consumer finance companies, because their assets are highly liquid, tend to use far more debt, and especially short-term debt, than manufacturers or retailers. Thus, if GM did not use a captive finance company, its balance sheet would show an exceptionally high debt ratio and a very low current ratio. By setting up General Motors Acceptance Corporation (GMAC) as a separate but wholly owned corporation, and then reporting only its equity investment in the subsidiary rather than a fully consolidated balance sheet which included the subsidiary's debt, GM avoids distorting its own balance sheet, presumably helping it to raise capital on more favorable terms.

favorable credit terms to one customer or class of customers than to another, unless the differences are cost-justified.

Most credit is offered on *open account*, which means that the only formal evidence of credit is an invoice which accompanies the shipment and which the buyer signs to indicate that goods have been received. Then, the buyer and the seller each record the purchase on their books of account. Under certain circumstances, the selling firm may require the buyer to sign a *promissory note* evidencing the credit obligation. Promissory notes are useful (1) if the order is very large; (2) if the seller anticipates the possibility of having trouble collecting, because a note is a stronger legal claim than a simple signed invoice; or (3) if the buyer wants a longer-than-usual time in which to pay for the order, because interest charges can be built into a promissory note.

Credit Instruments

Another instrument used in trade credit, especially in international trade, is the *commercial draft*. Here the seller draws up a draft—which is a sort of combination check and a promissory note—calling for the buyer to pay a specific amount to the seller by a specified date. This draft is then sent to the buyer's bank, along with the shipping invoices necessary to take possession of the goods. The bank forwards the draft to the buyer, who signs it and returns it to the bank. The bank then delivers the shipping documents to its customer, who at this point can claim the goods. If the draft is a *sight draft*, then upon delivery of the shipping documents and acceptance of the draft by the buyer, the bank actually withdraws money from the buyer's account and forwards it to the selling firm. If the draft is a *time draft*, payable on a specific future date, then the bank returns it to the selling firm. In this case, the draft is called a *trade acceptance*, and it amounts to a promissory note that the seller can hold for future payment or use as collateral for a loan. The bank, in such a situation, has served as an intermediary, making sure that the buyer does not receive title to the goods until the note (or draft) has been executed for the benefit of the seller.

A seller who lacks confidence in the ability or willingness of the buyer to pay off a time draft may refuse to ship without a guarantee of payment by the buyer's bank. Presumably, the bank knows its customer, and for a fee, the bank will guarantee payment of the draft. In this instance, the draft is called a *banker's acceptance*. Such instruments are widely used, especially in foreign trade. They have a low degree of risk if guaranteed by a strong bank, and there is a ready market for acceptances, making it easy for the seller of the goods to sell the instrument to raise immediate cash. (Banker's acceptances are sold at a discount below face value, and then paid off at face value when they mature, so the discount amounts to interest on the acceptance. The effective interest rate on a strong banker's acceptance is a little above the Treasury bill rate of interest.)

A final type of credit instrument that should be mentioned is the *conditional sales contract*. With a conditional sales contract, the seller retains legal ownership of the goods until the buyer has completed payment. Conditional sales contracts are used primarily for such items as machinery, dental equipment, and the like, which are often paid for on an installment basis over a period of two or three years. The significant advantage of a conditional sales contract is that it is easier for the seller to repossess the equipment in the event of default than it would be if title had passed. This feature makes possible some credit sales that otherwise would not be feasible. Conditional sales contracts generally have a market interest rate built into the payment schedule.

Analyzing Changes in the Credit Policy Variables

If the firm's credit policy is *eased* by such actions as lengthening the credit period, relaxing credit standards, following a less tough collection policy, or offering cash discounts, then sales should increase: *Easing the credit policy stimulates sales*. However, if credit policy is eased and sales do rise, then costs will also rise because more labor, more materials, and so on will be required to produce more goods. Additionally, receivables outstanding will also increase, which will increase carrying costs, and bad debt and/or discount expenses may also rise. Thus, the key question when deciding on a credit policy change is this: Will sales revenues rise more than costs, causing net income to increase, or will the increase in sales revenues be more than offset by higher costs?

Table 21-6 illustrates the general idea behind credit policy analysis. Column 1 shows the projected 1985 income statement under the assumption that the current credit policy is maintained throughout the year. Column 2 shows the expected effects of easing the credit policy—some combination of extending the credit period, offering larger discounts, relaxing credit standards, and relaxing collection efforts. Column 3 shows the projected 1985 income statement incorporating the expected effects of an easing in credit policy. The generally looser policy would be expected to increase sales, but discounts and several other types of costs would rise. The overall, bottom line effect is a $5 million increase in projected profits.

There would, of course, be corresponding changes on the projected balance sheet—the higher sales would necessitate somewhat larger cash balances, inventories, and perhaps (depending on the existence of excess capacity) more fixed assets. Accounts receivable would, of course, also increase. Those increases in assets would have to be financed, so certain liabilities and/or equity would have to be increased.

Whether or not the $5 million expected increase in net income would be deemed sufficient to warrant the credit policy change would require a substantial amount of analysis, and in the end, some judgments. In the first place, there would be some uncertainty, perhaps quite a lot of uncertainty, about the projected $200 million increase in sales. Conceiv-

Table 21-6
Analysis of a Proposed Change in Policy
(Millions of Dollars)

	Projected 1985 Income Statement under Current Credit Policy (1)	Effect of Credit Policy Change (2)	Projected 1985 Income Statement under New Credit Policy (3)
Gross sales	$1,000	+$200	$1,200
Less discounts	10	+20	30
Net sales	$ 990	+$180	$1,170
Production costs, including overhead	700	+120	820
Gross profit before credit costs	$ 290	+$60	$ 350
Credit-related costs:			
Cost of carrying receivables	40	+30	70
Bad debt losses	25	+20	45
Gross profit	$ 225	+$10	$ 235
Taxes	103	+5	108
Net income	$ 122	+$5	$ 127

ably, if the firm's competitors match its changes, sales would not rise at all. Similar uncertainties would be attached to the number of customers who would take discounts, to production costs at higher or lower sales levels, to the costs of carrying additional receivables, and to bad debt losses. Perhaps, in view of all the uncertainties, and also considering the effects on the balance sheet ratios, management would deem the projected $5 million increase in net income insufficient to justify the change.

The preceding paragraphs give an overview of the way changes in credit policy are analyzed. As noted, the most important considerations have to do with changes in sales and in production costs. Specific estimates of these effects are handled by the marketing and production departments, within the framework set forth above. The financial manager has the responsibility for the overall analysis plus the primary responsibility for estimating specific factors—discounts taken, the cost of carrying accounts receivable, and bad debt losses. To evaluate a proposed change in credit policy, one could compare projected income statements, such as Column 1 versus Column 3 in Table 21-6. Alternatively, one could simply analyze Column 2, which shows the incremental effect, or the effect holding other things constant, of the proposed change. Of course, the two approaches are based on exactly the same data, so they must produce identical results. However, it is often preferable to focus on the incremental approach—because firms usually change their credit policies in specific divisions or on specific products, and not across the board, an analysis of complete income statements could be swamped by other factors.

Incremental Analysis

In an incremental analysis, we attempt to determine the increase or decrease in both sales and costs associated with a given easing or tightening of credit policy.[7] The difference between incremental sales and incremental costs is defined as *incremental profit*. If the expected incremental profit is positive, then the proposed credit policy change should be considered.

The Basic Equations

To insure that all relevant factors are considered, it is useful to set up some equations to analyze changes in credit policy. We begin by defining these terms and symbols:

S_0 = current gross sales.

S_N = new gross sales level, after the change in credit policy. Note that this level can be greater or less than the current sales level.

$S_N - S_0$ = incremental, or change in, gross sales.

V = variable costs as a percentage of gross sales. V includes production costs, inventory carrying costs, the cost of administering the credit department, and all other variable costs except bad debt losses, financing costs associated with carrying the investment in receivables, and costs of giving discounts.

$1 - V$ = contribution margin, or the percentage of each gross sales dollar that goes toward covering overhead and increasing profits. The contribution margin is sometimes called the gross profit margin.

k = cost of financing the investment in receivables.

ACP_0 = average collection period prior to the change in credit policy.

ACP_N = new average collection period after the credit policy change.

B_0 = average bad debt loss at the current sales level as a percentage of current gross sales.

B_N = average bad debt loss at the new sales level as a percentage of new gross sales.

P_0 = percentage of total customers who take discounts under the current credit policy.

D_0 = discount percentage at the present time.

P_N = percentage of total customers who will take discounts under the new credit policy.

D_N = discount percentage under the new credit policy.

---

[7]This section is relatively technical. It can be omitted without loss of continuity if time pressures do not permit coverage.

With these definitions in mind, we can calculate values for the incremental change in the level of the firm's investment in receivables, ΔI, and the incremental change in pre-tax profits, ΔP. The formula for calculating ΔI differs depending on whether the change in credit policy results in an increase or decrease in sales. Here we simply present the equations; we discuss and explain them shortly, through use of examples, once all the equations have been set forth.

If the change is expected to *increase* sales—either additional sales to old customers or sales to newly attracted customers, or both—then we have this situation:

Formula for ΔI if sales increase:

$$\Delta I = \begin{bmatrix} \text{Increased investment in} \\ \text{receivables associated with} \\ \text{original sales} \end{bmatrix} + \begin{bmatrix} \text{Increased investment in} \\ \text{receivables associated} \\ \text{with incremental sales} \end{bmatrix}$$

$$= \begin{bmatrix} \text{Change in} \\ \text{collection period} \end{bmatrix} \begin{bmatrix} \text{Old sales} \\ \text{per day} \end{bmatrix} + V \begin{bmatrix} (\text{ACP}_N) \begin{pmatrix} \text{Incremental} \\ \text{sales per day} \end{pmatrix} \end{bmatrix}$$

$$= [(\text{ACP}_N - \text{ACP}_0)(S_0/360)] + V[(\text{ACP}_N)(S_N - S_0)/360]. \qquad \text{(21-1)}$$

However, if the change in credit policy is expected to *decrease* sales, then the change in the level of investment in receivables is calculated as follows:

Formula for ΔI if sales decrease:

$$\Delta I = \begin{bmatrix} \text{Decreased investment in} \\ \text{receivables associated with} \\ \text{remaining original customers} \end{bmatrix} + \begin{bmatrix} \text{Decreased investment in} \\ \text{receivables associated with} \\ \text{customers who left} \end{bmatrix}$$

$$= \begin{bmatrix} \text{Change in} \\ \text{collection} \\ \text{period} \end{bmatrix} \begin{bmatrix} \text{Remaining} \\ \text{sales} \\ \text{per day} \end{bmatrix} + V \begin{bmatrix} (\text{ACP}_0) \begin{pmatrix} \text{Incremental} \\ \text{sales} \\ \text{per day} \end{pmatrix} \end{bmatrix}$$

$$= [(\text{ACP}_N - \text{ACP}_0)(S_N/360)] + V[(\text{ACP}_0)(S_N - S_0)/360]. \qquad \text{(21-2)}$$

With the change in receivables investment calculated, we can now analyze the pre-tax profitability of the proposed change:

Formula for ΔP:

$$\Delta P = \begin{bmatrix} \text{Change in} \\ \text{gross} \\ \text{profit} \end{bmatrix} - \begin{bmatrix} \text{Change in} \\ \text{cost of} \\ \text{carrying} \\ \text{receivables} \end{bmatrix} - \begin{bmatrix} \text{Change in} \\ \text{bad debt} \\ \text{losses} \end{bmatrix} - \begin{bmatrix} \text{Change in} \\ \text{cost of} \\ \text{discounts} \end{bmatrix}$$

$$= (S_N - S_0)(1 - V) - k(\Delta I) - (B_N S_N - B_0 S_0) - (D_N S_N P_N - D_0 S_0 P_0). \qquad \text{(21-3)}$$

Thus, changes in credit policy are analyzed by using either Equation 21-1 or 21-2, depending on whether the proposed change is expected to increase or decrease sales, and Equation 21-3. The rationale behind these equations will become clear as we work through several illustrations. Note that all the terms in Equation 21-3 need not be used in a particular analysis. For example, a change in credit policy might not affect discount sales or bad debt losses, in which case the last two terms of Equation 21-3 would both be zero. Note also that the form of the equations is a function of the way in which the variables are first defined.[8]

Changing the Credit Period

In this section, we examine the effects of changing the credit period, while in the following sections, we consider changes in credit standards, collection policy, and cash discounts. Throughout, we illustrate the situation with data on Stylish Fashions, Inc.

Lengthening the Credit Period. Stylish Fashions currently sells on a cash-only basis. Since it extends no credit, the company has no funds tied up in receivables, has no bad debt losses, and has no credit expenses of any kind. On the other hand, its sales volume is lower than it would be if credit terms were offered. Stylish is now considering offering credit on 30-day terms. Current sales are $100,000 per year, variable costs are 60 percent of sales, excessive production capacity exists (so no new fixed costs will be incurred as a result of expanded sales), and the cost of capital invested in receivables is 10 percent. Stylish estimates that sales would increase to $150,000 per year if credit were extended, and that bad debt losses would be 2 percent of total sales. Thus,

$S_0 = \$100,000.$

$S_N = \$150,000.$

$V = 60\% = 0.6.$

$1 - V = 1 - 0.6 = 0.4.$

$k = 10\% = 0.10.$

$ACP_0 = 0$ days.

$ACP_N = 30$ days. Here we assume that all customers pay on time, so ACP = specified credit period. Generally, some customers pay late, so in most cases ACP is greater than the specified credit period.

---

[8]For example, P_0 and P_N are defined as the percentage of *total* customers who take discounts. If P_0 and P_N were defined as the percentage of *paying* customers (as opposed to bad debts) who take discounts, then Equation 21-3 would become

$$\Delta P = (S_N - S_0)(1 - V) - k(\Delta I) - (B_N S_N - B_0 S_0) - [D_N S_N P_N(1 - B_N) - D_0 S_0 P_0(1 - B_0)].$$

Similarly, changing the definitions of B_0 and B_N would affect the third term of Equation 21-3, as we discuss later.

$B_0 = 0\% = 0.00$. There are currently no bad debt losses.

$B_N = 2\% = 0.02$. These losses apply to the $150,000 of sales.

$D_0 = D_N = 0\%$. No discounts are given under either the current or the proposed credit policies.

Since sales are expected to increase, Equation 21-1 is used to determine the change in the investment in receivables:

$$\Delta I = [(ACP_N - ACP_0)(S_0/360)] + V[(ACP_N)(S_N - S_0)/360]$$
$$= [(30 - 0)(\$100,000/360)] + 0.6[30(\$150,000 - \$100,000)/360]$$
$$= \$8,333 + \$2,500 = \$10,833.$$

Note that the increased investment in accounts receivable associated with *old sales* is based on the full amount of the receivables, whereas the investment associated with *new sales* consists of new receivables multiplied by V, the variable cost percentage. This difference reflects the facts (1) that the firm only invests its variable cost in *new* receivables, but (2) that it would have collected the *full sales price* on the old receivables earlier had it not made the credit policy change. There is an *opportunity cost* associated with the $8,333 additional investment in receivables from old sales and a *direct financing cost* associated with the $2,500 investment in receivables from new sales.

Looking at this another way, *incremental* sales will generate an actual increase in receivables of $(ACP_N)(S_N - S_0)/360 = 30(\$50,000/360) = \$4,167$. However, the only part of that increase which has to be financed (by bank borrowing or from other sources) and reported as a liability on the right side of the balance sheet is the cash outflow generated by the incremental sales, that is, the variable costs, $V(\$4,167) = 0.6(\$4,167) = \$2,500$. The remainder of the receivables increase, $1,667 of accrued before-tax profit, is reflected on the balance sheet not as some type of credit used to finance receivables, but as an increase in retained earnings generated by the sales. On the other hand, the old receivables level was zero, meaning that the original sales produced cash of $100,000/360 = $278 per day, which was immediately available for investing in assets or for reducing capital from other sources. The change in credit policy will cause a delay in the receipt of these funds, and hence will require the firm (1) to borrow to cover the variable costs of the sales and (2) to forego a return on the retained earnings portion, which would have been available immediately had the credit policy change not been made.

Given ΔI, we now determine the incremental profit, ΔP, associated with the proposed credit period change, using Equation 21-3:

$$\Delta P = (S_N - S_0)(1 - V) - k(\Delta I) - (B_N S_N - B_0 S_0) - (D_N S_N P_N - D_0 S_0 P_0)$$
$$= (\$50,000)(0.4) - 0.10(\$10,833) - [0.02(\$150,000) - 0.00(\$100,000)] - \$0$$
$$= \$20,000 - \$1,083 - \$3,000 = \$15,917.$$

Since pre-tax profits are expected to increase by $15,917, the credit policy change appears to be desirable.

Two simplifying assumptions which were made in our analysis should be noted: We assumed (1) that all customers paid on time (ACP = credit period), and (2) that there were no current bad debt losses. The assumption of prompt payment can be relaxed quite easily—we can simply use the actual average collection period (say 40 days), rather than the 30-day credit period, to calculate the investment in receivables, and then use this new (and higher) value of ΔI in Equation 21-3 to calculate ΔP. Thus, if ACP_N = 40 days, then the increased investment in receivables is

$$\Delta I = [(40 - 0)(\$100,000/360)] + 0.6[40(\$50,000/360)]$$
$$= \$11,111 + \$3,333 = \$14,444,$$

and the change in pre-tax profits is

$$\Delta P = \$50,000(0.4) - 0.10(\$14,444) - 0.02(\$150,000)$$
$$= \$20,000 - \$1,444 - \$3,000 = \$15,556.$$

The longer collection period causes incremental profits to fall slightly, but they are still positive, so the credit policy should probably still be relaxed.

If the company had been selling on credit initially and therefore incurring some bad debt losses, then we would have had to include this information in Equation 21-3. In our example, B_0S_0 was equal to zero because Stylish Fashions did not previously sell on credit; therefore, the change in bad debt losses was equal to B_NS_N.

Notice that B_N is defined as the average credit loss percentage on total sales, and not just on incremental sales. Bad debts might be higher for new customers attracted by the credit terms than for old customers who take advantage of them, but B_N is an average of these two groups. Note, though, that if one wanted to keep the two groups separate, it would be easy enough to define B_N as the bad debt percentage of the incremental sales only.

Other factors could be introduced into the analysis. For example, the company could consider a further easing of credit by extending the credit period to 60 days, or it could weigh the effects of a sales expansion so great that fixed assets, and hence additional fixed costs, had to be added. Adding such factors complicates the analysis, but the basic principles are the same—just keep in mind that we are seeking to determine the *incremental sales revenues*, the *incremental costs*, and consequently the *incremental before-tax profit* associated with a given change in credit policy.

Shortening the Credit Period. Suppose that one year after Stylish Fashions began offering 30-day credit terms, management decides to consider the possibility of shortening the credit period from 30 to 20 days. It is expected that sales would decline by $20,000 per year from the current level, $150,000, so S_N = $130,000. It was also believed that the bad debt percentage on these lost sales would be 2 percent, the same as on other sales, and that all other values are as given in the last section.

We first calculate the incremental investment in receivables. Since the change in credit policy is expected to decrease sales, Equation 21-2 is used:

$$\Delta I = [(ACP_N - ACP_0)(S_N/360)] + V[(ACP_0)(S_N - S_0)/360]$$
$$= [(20 - 30)(\$130,000/360)] + 0.6[30(\$130,000 - \$150,000)/360)]$$
$$= (-10)(\$361.11) + 0.6[(30)(-\$55.56)]$$
$$= -\$3,611 - \$1,000 = -\$4,611.$$

With a shorter credit period there is a shorter collection period, so sales are collected sooner; there is also a smaller volume of business, and hence a smaller investment in receivables. The first term captures the speedup in collections, while the second reflects the reduced sales, and hence the lower receivables investment (at variable cost). Notice that V is included in the second term but not in the first one. This treatment can be confusing, so it bears elaboration. V is included in the second term because, by shortening the credit period, Stylish Fashions will drive off some customers and lose sales of $20,000 per year, or $55.56 per day. However, the firm's investment in these sales will only be 60 percent of the average receivables outstanding, or 0.6(30)($55.56) = $1,000, while 0.4(30)($55.56) = $667 is lost pre-tax profit. However, the situation is different for the remaining customers. They would have paid their full purchase price—variable cost plus profit—after 30 days. Now, however, they will pay this amount 10 days sooner, so these funds will be available to meet operating costs or for investment. Thus, the first term should not be reduced by the variable cost factor. Therefore, in total, reducing the credit period would result in a $4,611 reduction in the investment in receivables, consisting of a $3,611 decline in receivables associated with continuing customers and a further $1,000 decline in investment as a result of the reduced sales volume.

With the change in investment calculated, we can now analyze the profitability of the proposed change using Equation 21-3:

$$\Delta P = (S_N - S_0)(1 - V) - k(\Delta I) - (B_N S_N - B_0 S_0) - (D_N S_N P_N - D_0 S_0 P_0)$$
$$= (\$130,000 - \$150,000)(0.4) - 0.10(-\$4,611) - [(0.02)(\$130,000)$$
$$- (0.02)(\$150,000)] - \$0$$
$$= -\$8,000 + \$461 + \$400 = -\$7,139.$$

Since the expected incremental pre-tax profits are negative, the firm should not reduce its credit period from 30 to 20 days.

Changing the Discount Policy

To illustrate how a change in cash discount policy is analyzed, suppose Stylish is considering offering a 2 percent discount for payments made within 10 days, which represents a change in credit terms from its present terms of net 30 to terms of 2/10, net 30. The following conditions currently exist or are expected to occur if the change is made:

S_0 = current gross sales = $150,000.

S_N = new gross sales level if a discount is offered = $160,000.

D_0 = original discount percentage = 0%.

D_N = new discount percentage = 2%.

ACP_0 = old average collection period = 30 days.

ACP_N = new average collection period = 20 days. The new ACP is based on the assumption that 49 percent of the customers will take discounts and pay on the tenth day, another 49 percent will pay on the thirtieth day, and 2 percent will end up as bad debt losses.

P_0 = proportion of total customers who took discounts previously = 0.0.

$B_0 = B_N$ = bad debt losses as a proportion of gross sales = 0.02.

P_N = proportion of total customers who will take discounts under the new policy = 0.49.

V = 60%.

k = 10%.

Since sales are expected to increase, the incremental investment in receivables is found by using Equation 21-1:

$$\Delta I = [(ACP_N - ACP_0)(S_0/360)] + V[(ACP_N)(S_N - S_0)/360]$$
$$= [(20 - 30)(\$150,000/360)] + 0.6[20(\$160,000 - \$150,000)/360]$$
$$= -\$4,167 + \$333 = -\$3,834.$$

Thus, offering discounts will speed up collections and reduce the investment in receivables by $3,834.

The expected change in profits may now be analyzed using Equation 21-3:

$$\Delta P = (S_N - S_0)(1 - V) - k(\Delta I) - (B_N S_N - B_0 S_0) - (D_N S_N P_N - D_0 S_0 P_0)$$
$$= (\$160,000 - \$150,000)(0.4) - (0.1)(-\$3,834)$$
$$- [0.02(\$160,000) - 0.02(\$150,000)]$$
$$- [(0.02)(\$160,000)(0.49) - (0.00)(\$150,000)(0.0)]$$
$$= \$4,000 + \$383 - \$200 - \$1,568 = \$2,615.$$

Since expected incremental pre-tax profits are positive, Stylish should begin to offer discounts.

In the preceding sections, we examined the effects of changes in the credit and discount periods. Changes in other credit policy variables may be analyzed similarly. In general, we follow these steps:

Changes in Other Credit Policy Variables

Step 1. Estimate the effect of the policy change on sales, on ACP, on bad debt losses, and so on.

Step 2. Determine the change in the firm's investment in receivables. If the change will increase sales, then use Equation 21-1 to calculate ΔI. Conversely, if the change will decrease sales, then use Equation 21-2.

Step 3. Use Equation 21-3, or one of its variations, to calculate the effect of the change on pre-tax profits. If profits are expected to increase, the policy change should be made, unless it is judged to increase the firm's risk by a disproportionate amount.

The preceding discussion has considered the effects of changes in credit policy one variable at a time. The firm could, of course, change several or even all policy variables simultaneously. An almost endless variety of equations could be developed, depending on which policy variables are manipulated and on the assumed effects on sales, discounts taken, the collection period, bad debt losses, the existence of excess capacity, changes in credit department costs, changes in the variable cost percentage, and so on. The analysis would get "messy," and the incremental profit equation would be complex, but the principles we have developed could be used to handle any type of policy change.

Simultaneous Changes in Policy Variables

The investment in receivables is dependent on the firm's *credit policy*, and the four credit policy variables are these: (1) the *credit standards*, or the financial strength that customers must exhibit in order to be granted credit; (2) the *credit period*, or length of time for which credit is extended; (3) *cash discounts*, which are designed to encourage rapid payment; and (4) *collection policy*, which helps determine how long accounts remain outstanding. Credit policy has an important impact on the volume of sales, and the optimal credit policy involves a trade-off between the costs inherent in various credit policies and the profits generated by higher sales. From a practical standpoint, it is impossible to determine the optimal credit policy in a mathematical sense—good credit management involves a blending of quantitative analysis and business judgment.

Summary

Monitoring receivables is a very important part of credit management. Firms often use the *average collection period* and *aging schedules* to monitor collections, but these summary measures do not provide a clear picture of changes in payment behavior. A better method of receivables monitoring is the *payments pattern approach*.

Questions   21-1 Define each of the following terms:
   a.   Account receivable
   b.   Credit policy variables
   c.   Credit period
   d.   Credit standards
   e.   Collection policy
   f.   Discounts
   g.   Incremental investment
   h.   Incremental profit
   i.   Five Cs of credit
   j.   Receivables management
   k.   Average collection period
   l.   Aging schedule
   m. Payments pattern approach; uncollected balances schedule

21-2 Is it true that when one firm sells to another on credit, the seller records the transaction as an account receivable while the buyer records it as an account payable, and that, disregarding discounts, the receivable typically exceeds the payable by the amount of profit on the sale?

21-3 What are the four elements in a firm's credit policy? To what extent can firms set their own credit policies as opposed to having to accept credit policies as dictated by "the competition"?

21-4 Suppose a firm makes a purchase and receives the shipment on February 1. The terms of trade as stated on the invoice read, "2/10, net 40, May 1 dating." What is the latest date on which payment can be made and the discount still be taken? What is the date on which payment must be made if the discount is not taken?

21-5 a. What is the average collection period for a firm whose sales are $2,880,000 per year and whose accounts receivable are $312,000? (Use 360 days per year.)
      b. Is it true that if this firm sells on terms of 3/10, net 40, its customers probably all pay on time?

21-6 Is it true that if a firm calculates its average collection period, it has no need for an aging schedule?

21-7 Firm A had no credit losses last year, but 1 percent of Firm B's accounts receivable proved to be uncollectible and resulted in losses. Should Firm B fire its credit manager and hire A's?

21-8 Indicate by a +, −, or 0 whether each of the following events would probably cause accounts receivable (A/R), sales, and profits to increase, to decrease, or to be affected in an indeterminant manner:

	A/R	Sales	Profits
a. The firm tightens its credit standards.	____	____	____
b. The terms of trade are changed from 2/10, net 30, to 3/10, net 30.	____	____	____
c. The terms are changed from 2/10, net 30, to 3/10, net 40.	____	____	____

    d. The credit manager gets tough with
       past-due accounts.

ST-1 Fashion Distributors, Inc., currently sells on terms of 1/10, net 30, with *Self-Test Problem*
bad debt losses at 1 percent of gross sales. Of the 99 percent of the
customers which pay, 50 percent take the discount and pay on Day
10; the remaining 50 percent pay on Day 30.

    Fashion's gross sales are currently $2 million per year, with variable
costs amounting to 75 percent of sales. The firm finances its receivables
with a 10 percent line of credit, and there are sufficient fixed assets to
support a doubling in sales.

    Fashion's credit manager has proposed that credit terms be changed
to 2/10, net 40. He estimates that these terms would boost sales to $2.5
million per year. However, bad debt losses would double to 2 percent
of the new sales level. It is expected that 50 percent of the paying
customers will continue to take the discount and pay on Day 10, and
the other 50 percent will pay on Day 40.

    a. What are the old and new average collection periods?
    b. Find ΔI, the incremental change in Fashion's receivables invest-
       ment, and ΔP, the incremental change in pre-tax profits. Should the
       change in credit terms be made?
    c. Assume that Fashion's new credit terms are the existing credit
       terms, that is, Fashion currently gives 2/10, net 40. Analyze the
       change to terms of 1/10, net 30. Assume that all the variables ini-
       tially stated continue to hold. In other words, reverse the analysis
       and see what results you get.
    d. Assume that Fashion's competitors react to the change as originally
       stated in the problem by also granting more liberal credit terms.
       This causes Fashion's sales to remain at the original level of $2 mil-
       lion. Additionally, bad debt losses remain at the original 1 percent.
       What is the effect on Fashion's profits?

21-1 Provencial, Inc., sells on terms of 2/10, net 30. Total sales for the year *Problems*
are $600,000. Forty percent of the customers pay on the tenth day and
take discounts; the other 60 percent pay, on average, 40 days after
their purchases.
    a. What is the average collection period?
    b. What is the average investment in receivables?
    c. What would happen to the average investment in receivables if
       Provencial toughened up on its collection policy, with the result
       that all nondiscount customers paid on the thirtieth day?

21-2 The Rose Company expects to have sales of $20 million this year under
current operating policies. Its variable costs as a proportion of sales is
0.8, and its cost of receivables financing is 8 percent. Currently, Rose's
credit policy is net 25. However, its average collection period is 30
days, indicating that some customers are paying late, and its bad debt
losses are 3 percent of sales.
    Rose's credit manager is considering two alternative credit policies:

Proposal 1. Lengthen the credit period to net 40. If this were done, it is estimated that sales would increase to $20.5 million, that the average collection period would increase to 45 days, and that the bad debt losses on the *incremental sales* would be 5 percent. Existing customer bad debt losses would remain at 3 percent.

Proposal 2. Shorten the credit period to net 20. Under these terms, sales would be expected to decrease to $18 million, the average collection period would drop to 22 days, and bad debt losses would decrease to 1 percent of the new sales level.

a. Evaluate Proposal 1. What is the expected change in investment in receivables and the expected change in before-tax profit?

b. Evaluate Proposal 2. What is the expected change in investment in receivables and the expected change in before-tax profit?

c. Should either proposal be adopted? If so, which one? Why?

21-3 The Melville Company, a small manufacturer of cordless telephones, began operations on January 1, 1984. Its credit sales for the first six months of operations were as follows:

Month	Credit Sales
January	$ 50,000
February	100,000
March	120,000
April	105,000
May	140,000
June	160,000

Throughout this entire period, Melville's credit customers maintained a constant payment pattern: 20 percent paid in the month of sale, 30 percent paid in the month following the sale, and 50 percent paid in the second month following the sale.

a. What was Melville's receivables balance at the end of March and at the end of June?

b. Assume 90 days per calendar quarter. What was the average daily sales (ADS) and average collection period (ACP) for the first quarter and for the second quarter? What was the cumulative ADS and ACP for the first half-year?

c. Construct an aging schedule as of June 30. Use 0-30, 31-60, and 61-90 day account ages.

d. Construct the uncollected balances schedule for the second quarter as of June 30.

21-4 Sophisticated Shirts, Inc., currently sells on terms of 2/10, net 40, with bad debt losses running at 2 percent of gross sales. Of the 98 percent of the customers who pay, 60 percent take the discount and pay on Day 10; the remaining 40 percent pay on Day 40.

The firm's gross sales are currently $1 million per year, with variable costs amounting to 60 percent of sales. The firm finances its receivables with a 10 percent line of credit, and there are sufficient fixed assets to support a doubling in sales.

The firm's credit manager has proposed that credit terms be changed to 2/20, net 60. She estimates that the change would increase sales to $1.1 million. However, bad debt losses on the new sales level would be 3 percent, compared with only 2 percent on the old sales level. It is expected that 75 percent of the paying customers would take the discount under the new terms, paying on Day 20, while the remaining 25 percent would now pay on Day 60.

a. What are the old and new average collection periods?

b. Find ΔI, the incremental change in Sophisticated's investment in receivables.

c. Find ΔP, the incremental change in pre-tax profits. Should the change in credit terms be made?

d. Assume that Sophisticated's competitors immediately react to the change in credit terms by easing their own terms. This causes Sophisticated to gain no new customers; however, of the existing buyers who pay (2 percent continue as bad debt losses), 75 percent now take the discount and pay on Day 20, while 25 percent pay on Day 60. What is the effect on the firm's pre-tax profits?

21-5   This problem extends Problem 21-2 above. Read the basic problem and Proposals 1 and 2, and then analyze Proposals 3, 4, and 5.

Proposal 3. Relax credit standards and sell to less credit-worthy customers. It is estimated that this action would increase sales by $2 million. The *incremental* sales would have a bad debt loss of 6 percent and an average collection period of 40 days. (Note that current customers would continue to have an average collection period of 30 days and bad debt losses of 3 percent.)

Proposal 4. Tighten credit collection policy. The estimated impact of this change is to decrease sales by $1.5 million, decrease the bad debt losses on total sales to 1.5 percent, and decrease the average collection period on total sales to 25 days.

Proposal 5. Offer a 2 percent discount for payment within 10 days, that is, offer terms of 2/10, net 25. It is estimated that 50 percent of the paying customers would take the discount. Further, the new terms would (1) increase sales by $2 million, (2) decrease bad debt losses to 2 percent of total new sales, and (3) decrease the average collection period to 20 days.

Solution to Self-Test Problem

ST-1

a. $ACP_0 = 0.50(10 \text{ days}) + 0.50(30 \text{ days}) = 20 \text{ days}.$

   $ACP_N = 0.50(10 \text{ days}) + 0.50(40 \text{ days}) = 25 \text{ days}.$

b.   For an increase in sales, use

$$\Delta I = [(ACP_N - ACP_0)(S_0/360)] + V[(ACP_N)(S_N - S_0)/360]$$

$$= [(25 - 20)(\$2,000,000/360)] + 0.75[(25)(\$500,000/360)]$$

$$= \$27,778 + \$26,042 = \$53,820.$$

Then, determine the incremental profit, ΔP:

$$\Delta P = (S_N - S_0)(1 - V) - k(\Delta I) - (B_N S_N - B_0 S_0)$$
$$- [D_N S_N P_N(1 - B_N) - D_0 S_0 P_0(1 - B_0)]$$
$$= \$500{,}000(1 - 0.75) - 0.10(\$53{,}820)$$
$$- [(0.02)(\$2{,}500{,}000) - (0.01)(\$2{,}000{,}000)]$$
$$- [(0.02)(\$2{,}500{,}000)(0.50)(1 - 0.02)$$
$$- (0.01)(\$2{,}000{,}000)(0.50)(1 - 0.01)]$$
$$= \$125{,}000 - \$5{,}382 - \$30{,}000 - \$14{,}600 = \$75{,}018.$$

c.   For a decrease in sales, use

$$\Delta I = [(ACP_N - ACP_0)(S_N/360)] + V[(ACP_0)(S_N - S_0)/360]$$
$$= [(20 - 25)(\$2{,}000{,}000/360)] + (0.75)[(25)(-\$500{,}000/360)]$$
$$= -\$27{,}778 - \$26{,}042 = -\$53{,}820.$$

Then, determine the incremental profit, ΔP:

$$\Delta P = (S_N - S_0)(1 - V) - k(\Delta I) - (B_N S_N - B_0 S_0)$$
$$- [D_N S_N P_N(1 - B_N) - D_0 S_0 P_0(1 - B_0)]$$
$$= -\$500{,}000(0.25) - 0.10(-\$53{,}820)$$
$$- [(0.01)(\$2{,}000{,}000) - (0.02)(\$2{,}500{,}000)]$$
$$- [(0.01)(\$2{,}000{,}000)(0.50)(0.99)$$
$$- (0.02)(\$2{,}500{,}000)(0.50)(0.98)]$$
$$= -\$125{,}000 + \$5{,}382 + \$30{,}000 + \$14{,}600 = -\$75{,}018.$$

d.   If there is no change in sales, then either ΔI formula can be used. Say,

$$\Delta I = [(ACP_N - ACP_0)(S_0/360)]$$
$$= [(25 - 20)(\$2{,}000{,}000/360)]$$
$$= \$27{,}778.$$

Then, determine the incremental profit, ΔP:

$$\Delta P = (S_N - S_0)(1 - V) - k(\Delta I) - (B_N S_N - B_0 S_0)$$
$$- [D_N S_N P_N(1 - B_N) - D_0 S_0 P_0(1 - B_0)]$$
$$= \$0(1 - 0.75) - 0.10(\$27{,}778) - \$0$$
$$- [(0.02)(\$2{,}000{,}000)(0.50)(0.99)$$
$$- (0.01)(\$2{,}000{,}000)(0.50)(0.99)]$$
$$= -\$2{,}777.80 - \$9{,}900 = -\$12{,}677.80.$$

Selected Additional References and Cases

Some recent articles which address credit policy and receivables management include the following:

Atkins, Joseph C., and Yong H. Kim, "Comment and Correction: Opportunity Cost in the Evaluation of Investment in Accounts Receivable," *Financial Management*, Winter 1977, 71-74.

Ben-Horim, Moshe, and Haim Levy, "Management of Accounts Receivable under Inflation," *Financial Management*, Spring 1983, 42-48.

Dyl, Edward A., "Another Look at the Evaluation of Interest in Accounts Receivable," *Financial Management*, Winter 1977, 67-70.

Hill, Ned C., and Kenneth D. Riener, "Determining the Cash Discount in the Firm's Credit Policy," *Financial Management*, Spring 1979, 68-73.

Kim, Yong H., and Joseph C. Atkins, "Evaluating Investments in Accounts Receivable: A Wealth Maximizing Framework," *Journal of Finance*, May 1978, 403-412.

Oh, John S., "Opportunity Cost in the Evaluation of Investment in Accounts Receivable," *Financial Manangement*, Summer 1976, 32-36.

Roberts, Gordon S., and Jeremy A. Viscione, "Captive Finance Subsidiaries: The Manager's View," *Financial Management*, Spring 1981, 36-42.

Sachdeva, Kanwal S., and Lawrence J. Gitman, "Accounts Receivable Decisions in a Capital Budgeting Framework," *Financial Management*, Winter 1981, 45-49.

Walia, Tinlochan S., "Explicit and Implicit Cost of Changes in the Level of Accounts Receivable and the Credit Policy Decision of the Firm," *Financial Management*, Winter 1977, 75-78.

Weston, J. Fred, and Pham D. Tuan, "Comment on Analysis of Credit Policy Changes," *Financial Management*, Winter 1980, 59-63.

The following cases focus on the credit policy decision:

"Zukowski Meats, Inc.," in the Harrington casebook, which stresses forecasting the effect of a credit policy change on the working capital accounts.

Case 6, "Kendall Dairies," in the Brigham-Crum casebook, which demonstrates how the various credit policy variables interact to determine (1) the firm's level of accounts receivable and (2) its risk and rate of return.

Financial Analysis and Planning

VII

Financial Statement Analysis

22

A firm's stock price depends to a large extent on the rate of return management is able to generate on the stockholders' equity (ROE). Consequently, management has as a key goal increasing the firm's ROE, and investors are very much interested in past and prospective ROE levels.

Every year, *Fortune*, *Business Week*, and other business magazines publish "report cards" on the larger firms, breaking them down into such groups as industrials (manufacturing firms), retailers, utilities, and banks. A feature of these reports is the level of, and changes in, ROE, along with clues as to why changes occur. Data from representative companies in the grocery, electric power, and manufacturing industries are given below:

	ROE	=	Profit margin	× Turnover ×	Leverage multiplier
	$\left(\dfrac{\text{Net income}}{\text{Common equity}}\right)$	=	$\left(\dfrac{\text{Profits}}{\text{Sales}}\right)$ ×	$\left(\dfrac{\text{Sales}}{\text{Assets}}\right)$ ×	$\left(\dfrac{\text{Assets}}{\text{Equity}}\right)$
Kroger Stores	14.1%		0.92%	9.53×	1.61×
Union Carbide	14.1		6.73	1.13	1.85
Texas Utilities	14.3		15.69	0.41	2.22

The three companies had about the same ROE, but they achieved it in very different ways. Kroger, a leading food chain, made only a small profit per dollar of sales, but on an average, it turned over its assets 9.53 times per year; hence, it made up in volume for the small markup per item sold. Texas Utilities had a high profit per dollar of sales, but its turnover was low because it required a huge investment in assets to generate a dollar of sales revenue. Union Carbide, a typical manufacturing company, lies between the extremes of the utility and the grocery chain. Notice that the three companies all used leverage to boost their ROEs, and this was especially true for the utility.

If a company wants to increase its ROE, it must raise its profit margin on sales, boost its turnover, or increase its leverage. Of course, there are limits to raising these ratios, and hence to the level of ROE, but the better management is, the better the firm's ROE performance will be. In this chapter, we look in more depth at the determinants of ROE, see how managers can analyze operations and improve performance, and discuss how investors can analyze financial statements to anticipate future changes in profitability, and hence in stock prices.

Financial analysis is of interest to corporate managers, security analysts, investors, and lenders, all of whom use it for a variety of purposes. Indeed, the scope of any financial analysis depends on its purpose, which may range from a total analysis of a firm's strengths and weaknesses to a relatively simple analysis of its short-term liquidity. Since the foundation of most types of financial analysis is the firm's financial statements, we focus on statement analysis in this chapter.

Financial Statements and Reports

Of the various reports that corporations issue to their stockholders, the *annual report* is by far the most important. Two types of information are given in this report. First, there is a verbal section which describes the firm's operating results during the past year and discusses new developments that will affect its future operations. Second, the report presents four basic financial statements—the *income statement*, the *balance sheet*, the *statement of retained earnings*, and the *statement of changes in financial position*. Taken together, these statements give an accounting picture of the firm's operations and its financial position. Detailed data are provided for the two most recent years, along with brief historical summaries of key operating statistics for the past 5 or 10 years.[1]

The quantitative and verbal parts of the report are equally important. The financial statements report *what has actually happened* to earnings and dividends over the past few years, while the verbal statements attempt to explain why things turned out the way they did. For example, Texas Instruments' earnings dropped sharply in 1983. Management reported that the drop resulted from losses in the home computer division, but

---

[1]Firms also provide quarterly reports, but these are much less comprehensive than the annual reports. In addition, larger firms file even more detailed statements, giving the particulars of each major division or subsidiary, with the Securities and Exchange Commission (SEC). These reports, called *10-K reports*, are made available to stockholders upon request to a company's secretary. Finally, many larger firms also publish *statistical supplements*, which give financial statement data and key ratios going back about 10 years. Like the 10-K, statistical supplements may be obtained from the corporate secretary.

they then went on to state that the home computer line had been dropped, and that future profits were expected to bounce back. Of course, this return to profitability may not occur, and analysts should compare management's past statements with subsequent results. *In any event, the information contained in the annual report is used by investors and credit analysts to form expectations about future earnings and dividends, and about the riskiness of these expected values.* Therefore, the annual report is obviously of great interest to investors, managers, and analysts alike.

Table 22-1 contains the 1983 and 1984 income statements for Southern Metals Company, a major producer of fabricated aluminum products. Net sales are shown at the top of the statements, after which various costs, including income taxes, are subtracted to obtain the net income available to common stockholders. A report of earnings per share and dividends per share is given at the bottom of the statements. In financial management, earnings per share (EPS) is often called "the bottom line," denoting that of all the items on the income statement, EPS is the most important.[2] Southern earned $2.20 per share in 1984, down from $2.40 in 1983, but it raised the dividend from $1.60 to $1.80.

The Income Statement

EPS— most important

The left-hand side of Southern's balance sheet, which is given in Table 22-2, shows the firm's assets, while the right-hand side of the statement shows claims against these assets. The assets are listed in order of their liquidity, or the length of time it typically takes to convert them to cash. Similarly, the claims are listed in the order in which they must be paid: Accounts payable must generally be paid within 30 days; notes payable are generally due within 90 days; and so on, down to the stockholders' equity accounts, which represent ownership and need never be "paid off."

The Balance Sheet

Some additional points about the balance sheet are worth noting:

1. **Cash versus other assets.** Although the assets are all stated in terms of dollars, only cash represents actual money. Southern can write checks at present for a total of $50 million (versus current liabilities of $300 million due within a year). The noncash assets will presumably be converted to cash eventually, but they do not represent cash-in-hand.

---

[2]Dividends are important too, but the firm's ability to pay dividends is dependent on its earnings. We should also note that the firm's cash flow from operations is equal to net income plus any noncash expenses. In 1984, Southern's cash flow from operations, after preferred stock dividends, was $110 million net income plus $100 million depreciation expense, for a total cash flow of $210 million. Depreciation does not really *provide* funds; it is simply a noncash charge which is added back to net income to obtain an estimate of the cash flow from operations. However, if the firm made no sales, then depreciation would certainly not provide cash flows.

Table 22-1
Southern Metals Company:
Income Statements for the Years Ended December 31
(Millions of Dollars, except for per Share Data)

	1984	1983
Net sales	$3,000	$2,850
Costs and expenses:		
Labor and materials	$2,544	$2,413
Depreciation	100	90
Selling	22	20
General and administrative	40	35
Lease payments	28	28
Total costs	$2,734	$2,586
Net operating income, or earnings before interest and taxes (EBIT)	$ 266	$ 264
Less interest expense:		
Interest on notes payable	$ 8	$ 2
Interest on first mortgage bonds	40	42
Interest on debentures	18	3
Total interest	$ 66	$ 47
Earnings before taxes	$ 200	$ 217
Taxes (at 40%)	80	87
Net income before preferred dividends	$ 120	$ 130
Dividends to preferred stockholders	10	10
Net income available to common stockholders	$ 110	$ 120
Disposition of net income:		
Dividends to common stockholders	$ 90	$ 80
Addition to retained earnings	$ 20	$ 40
Per share of common stock:		
Stock price	$28.50	$29.00
Earnings per share (EPS)[a]	$ 2.20	$ 2.40
Dividends per share (DPS)[a]	$ 1.80	$ 1.60

[a]There are 50 million common shares outstanding; see Table 22-2. Note that according to generally accepted accounting principles, EPS should be based on earnings after preferred dividends, that is, on net income available to common stockholders. Calculations of EPS and DPS for 1984 are as follows:

$$\text{EPS} = \frac{\text{Net income available to common stockholders}}{\text{Shares outstanding}} = \frac{\$110,000,000}{50,000,000} = \$2.20.$$

$$\text{DPS} = \frac{\text{Dividends paid to common stockholders}}{\text{Shares outstanding}} = \frac{\$90,000,000}{50,000,000} = \$1.80.$$

Table 22-2
Southern Metals Company:
December 31 Balance Sheets
(Millions of Dollars)

Assets	1984	1983	Claims on Assets	1984	1983
Cash	$ 50	$ 55	Accounts payable	$ 60	$ 30
Marketable securities	0	25	Notes payable	100	60
Accounts receivable	350	315	Accrued wages	10	10
Inventories	300	215	Accrued taxes	130	120
Total current assets	$ 700	$ 610	Total current liabilities	$ 300	$ 220
Gross plant & equipment	1,800	1,470	First mortgage bonds	500	520
Less depreciation	500	400	Debentures	300	60
Net plant & equipment	$1,300	$1,070	Total long-term debt	$ 800	$ 580
			Stockholders' equity:		
			Preferred stock		
			(1,000,000 shares,		
			$10 participating preferred,		
			$1 par value)	10	10
			Common stock		
			(50,000,000 shares,		
			$1 par value)	50	50
			Additional paid-in capital	90	90
			Retained earnings	750	730
			Total common equity	$ 890	$ 870
			Total stockholders' equity	900	880
Total assets	$2,000	$1,680	Total claims	$2,000	$1,680

Notes:

a. The first mortgage bonds have a sinking fund requirement of $20 million a year.

b. Southern had $28 million in uncapitalized lease payments in both 1983 and 1984; see Table 22-1.

2. Liabilities versus stockholders' equity. The claims against assets are of two types—liabilities, or money the company owes, and the stockholders' ownership position.[3] The equity, or net worth, is a residual; that is, for 1984

$$\text{Assets} \quad - \quad \text{Liabilities} \quad = \text{Stockholders' equity.}$$
$$\$2{,}000{,}000{,}000 - \$1{,}100{,}000{,}000 = \quad \$900{,}000{,}000.$$

Suppose assets decline in value. For example, assume some of the accounts receivable are written off as bad debts. Liabilities remain constant, so the value of the equity declines. Therefore, the risk of asset

---

[3]One could divide liabilities into (1) debts owed to a specific firm or individual and (2) other items such as deferred taxes and reserves. We do not make this distinction, so the terms *debt* and *liabilities* are used synonymously.

value fluctuations is borne entirely by the stockholders, and specifically by the common stockholders. Note, however, that if asset values rise, these benefits accrue exclusively to the common stockholders.

3. Breakdown of the stockholders' equity account. Note that the equity section is divided into four accounts—preferred stock, common stock, paid-in capital, and retained earnings. The retained earnings account is built up over time by the firm's "saving" a part of its earnings rather than paying all earnings out as dividends. The other three accounts arose from the sale of stock by the firm to raise capital. Accountants generally assign a *par value* to common stock—Southern's stock has a par value of $1. Now suppose Southern were to sell 1 million additional shares at a price of $30 per share. The company would raise $30 million, and the cash accounts would go up by this amount. Of the total, $1 million would be added to common stock, and $29 million would be added to paid-in capital. Thus, after the sale, common stock would show $51 million, paid-in capital would show $119 million, and there would be 51 million shares outstanding.

The breakdown of the equity accounts is important for some purposes but not for others. For example, a potential stockholder would want to know if the company had earned the funds in its equity accounts, or if funds had come mainly from selling stock. A potential creditor, on the other hand, would be more interested in the amount of money the owners had put up than in the form in which they put it up. In the remainder of this chapter, we generally aggregate the three common equity accounts and call this sum *common equity*, or *net worth*.

4. The time dimension. The balance sheet may be thought of as a snapshot of the firm's financial position *at a point in time*—for example, on December 31, 1984. The income statement, on the other hand, reports on operations *over a period of time*—for example, during the calendar year 1984.

Statement of Retained Earnings

Changes in the common equity accounts between balance sheet dates are reported in the statement of retained earnings; Southern's statement is shown in Table 22-3. The company earned $120 million during 1984,

Table 22-3
Southern Metals Company:
Statement of Retained Earnings for the Year Ended
December 31, 1984
(Millions of Dollars)

Balance of retained earnings, December 31, 1983	$730
Net income available to common stockholders, 1984	110
Dividends to common stockholders	(90)
Balance of retained earnings, December 31, 1984	$750

paid out $10 million in preferred dividends and $90 million in common dividends, and plowed $20 million back into the business. Thus, the balance sheet item retained earnings increased from $730 million at the end of 1983 to $750 million at the end of 1984.

Note that the balance sheet account retained earnings represents a *claim against assets*, and not assets per se. Further, firms retain earnings primarily to expand the business. This means investing in plant and equipment, inventories, and so on, and *not* in a bank account. *Thus, retained earnings as reported on the balance sheet do not represent cash and are not "available" for the payment of dividends or anything else.*[4]

The statement of changes in financial position is designed to answer three questions: (1) Where did the firm get its funds during the year? (2) What did it do with its available funds? (3) Did operations during the year tend to increase or decrease the firm's liquidity as measured by the change in net working capital?[5]

Statement of Changes in Financial Position

The starting point in preparing a statement of changes in financial position is to determine the change in each balance sheet item, and then to record it as either a source or a use of funds in accordance with the following rules:

Sources: 1. Increases in claims, that is, in a liability or capital account. Borrowing is an example.

2. Decreases in asset accounts. Selling some inventories is an example.

Uses: 1. Decreases in claims against assets. Paying off a loan is an example.

2. Increases in asset accounts. Buying fixed assets is an example.

Thus, sources of funds include bank loans and retained earnings, as well as money generated by selling assets, collecting receivables, and even drawing down the cash account. Uses include acquiring fixed assets, building up inventories, and paying off debts.

Table 22-4 shows the changes in Southern Metals' balance sheet accounts during the calendar year 1984, with each change designated as

---

[4]Recall from your accounting course that the amount recorded in the retained earnings account is not an indication of the amount of cash the firm has. That amount (as of the balance sheet date) is found in the cash account—an asset account. A positive number in the retained earnings account only indicates that, in the past, according to generally accepted accounting principles, the firm has earned an income, and that its dividends have been less than its reported income. Also, recall the difference between accrual and cash accounting. Even though a company reports record earnings and shows an increase in the retained earnings account, it may still be short of cash.

[5]There are several different formats for presenting the statement of changes in financial position. The format we present here focuses on changes in net working capital.

Table 22-4
Southern Metals Company:
Changes in Balance Sheet Accounts during 1984
(Millions of Dollars)

	12/31/84	12/31/83	Change Source	Use
Cash	$ 50	$ 55	$ 5	
Marketable securities	0	25	25	
Accounts receivable	350	315		$ 35
Inventories	300	215		85
Gross plant and equipment	1,800	1,470		330
Accumulated depreciation[a]	500	400	100	
Accounts payable	60	30	30	
Notes payable	100	60	40	
Accrued wages	10	10		
Accrued taxes	130	120	10	
Mortgage bonds	500	520		20
Debentures	300	60	240	
Preferred stock	10	10		
Common stock	50	50		
Paid-in capital	90	90		
Retained earnings	750	730	20	
			$470	$470

[a]Depreciation is a *contra-asset*, and not an asset. Hence, an increase in depreciation is a source of funds.

a source or a use. Sources and uses each total $470 million.[6] Note that Table 22-4 does not contain any summary accounts such as total current assets and net plant and equipment. If we included summary accounts in Table 22-4, and then used these accounts to prepare the statement of changes in financial position, we would be "double counting."

The data contained in Table 22-4 are next used as inputs to the formal statement of changes in financial position, or sources and uses of funds statement. The one contained in Southern Metals' annual report is shown in Table 22-5. Note that every item in the "change" columns of Table 22-4 is carried over to Table 22-5 except retained earnings: The statement of changes in financial position reports net income as a source and dividends as a use, rather than netting these items out and just reporting the increase in retained earnings.

Notice also that the statement provides answers to the three questions asked at the beginning of this section: (1) The top part answers the question regarding Southern's major sources of long-term funds; (2) the mid-

[6]Adjustments must normally be made if fixed assets were sold or retired during the year. Southern had no sales of fixed assets or major retirements during 1984.

Table 22-5
Southern Metals Company:
1984 Statement of Changes in Financial Position
(Millions of Dollars)

Sources of funds	
Net income before preferred and common dividends	$120
Depreciation	100
Total funds from operations	$220
Proceeds from sale of debentures	240
Total sources	$460
Uses of funds	
Repayment of mortgage bonds	$ 20
Increase in gross fixed assets	330
Dividend payments to preferred stockholders	10
Dividend payments to common stockholders	90
Total nonworking capital uses	$450
Increase in net working capital[a]	10
Total uses	$460
Analysis of changes in working capital[a]	
Increase (decrease) in current assets:	
Cash	($ 5)
Marketable securities	(25)
Accounts receivable	35
Inventories	85
Net increase in current assets	$ 90
Increase (decrease) in current liabilities:	
Accounts payable	$ 30
Notes payable	40
Accrued taxes	10
Net increase in current liabilities	$ 80
Increase (decrease) in net working capital	$ 10

[a]If the company increased its net working capital, as Southern did, this is a sign of strength. If net working capital had declined, this would have represented a weakening position. A decrease in net working capital as calculated in the lower section would have been reported in the top section as a source of funds.

dle section answers the question about how Southern used its available funds for nonworking capital purposes; and (3) the lower section, which deals with current assets and liabilities, shows how the company's liquidity position changed during the year. We see that Southern's major sources of funds were net income, depreciation, and the sale of debentures. These funds were used to reduce the mortgage debt, to increase fixed assets, and to pay dividends on common stock. Also, $10 million was used to increase net working capital.

As shown in the bottom section, Southern decreased its cash and marketable securities but increased accounts receivable and inventories, for a net increase in current assets of $90 million. Current liabilities also increased by $80 million, so there was an increase of $10 million in net working capital (current assets minus current liabilities). This increase in net working capital is reported as a use of funds in the middle section.

Southern is a strong, well-managed company, and its sources and uses statement shows nothing unusual or alarming. One does, however, occasionally see situations where huge increases in fixed assets are financed primarily by short-term debt, which must be repaid within a few months if the lender demands repayment. This would show up in the lower third of the table as a decrease in net working capital, and it could indicate a most dangerous situation.

Financial Statement Analysis

Financial statements report both on a firm's position at a point in time and on its operations over some past period. However, their real value lies in the fact that they can be used to help predict the firm's future earnings and dividends, as well as the riskiness of these cash flows. From an investor's standpoint, *predicting the future is what financial statement analysis is all about*. From management's standpoint, *financial statement analysis is useful both as a way to anticipate future conditions and, more important, as a starting point for planning actions that will influence the future course of events*. In the remainder of this chapter, we discuss three procedures used by both investors and managers to analyze and interpret financial statements: (1) ratio analysis, (2) common-size analysis, and (3) the Du Pont system. Additionally, we discuss some of the problems which arise in financial statement analysis. Then, in the following chapter, we show how analysts construct *projected*, or *pro forma*, statements, and use them to gauge the effects of alternative actions on the firm's future riskiness and profitability.

Ratio Analysis

Financial ratios are designed to show relationships among financial statement accounts. Ratios put numbers into perspective. For example, Firm A might have $5,248,760 of debt and annual interest charges of $419,900, while Firm B has debt of $52,647,980 and interest charges of $3,948,600. The true burden of these debts, and the companies' ability to repay them, can be ascertained by comparing each firm's debt to its assets, and its interest charges to the income available for payment of interest. One way of making such comparisons is by *ratio analysis*. We next discuss ratio analysis and illustrate the procedures with data on Southern Metals.

One of the first concerns of most financial analysts is liquidity: Will the firm be able to meet its maturing obligations? A full liquidity analysis requires the use of cash budgets and an analysis of the cash conversion cycle (see Chapter 20); however, by relating the amount of cash and other current assets to the current obligations, ratio analysis provides a quick, easy-to-use measure of liquidity. Two commonly used liquidity ratios are discussed below.

Liquidity Ratios

Current Ratio. The *current ratio* is computed by dividing current assets by current liabilities:

$$\text{Current ratio} = \frac{\text{Current assets}}{\text{Current liabilities}} = \frac{\$700}{\$300} = 2.3 \text{ times.}$$

Current assets normally include cash, marketable securities, accounts receivable, and inventories. Current liabilities consist of accounts payable, short-term notes payable, current maturities of long-term debt, accrued income taxes, and other accrued expenses (principally wages). We illustrate the calculation of the current ratio, and all succeeding ratios, with Southern Metals' 1984 year-end data. (All dollar amounts in this section are in millions.)

If a company is getting into financial difficulty, it begins paying its bills (accounts payable) more slowly, building up bank loans, and so on. If current liabilities are rising faster than current assets, the current ratio will fall, and this could spell trouble. The current ratio provides the best single indicator of the extent to which the claims of short-term creditors are covered by assets that are expected to be converted to cash in a period roughly corresponding to the maturity of the claims. Therefore, it is the most commonly used measure of short-term solvency.

It is virtually impossible to look at a ratio in isolation and determine if it is good, bad, or indifferent. One must compare it with something, generally either with ratios of other firms or with the firm's own ratios in earlier years. However, rather than analyzing each ratio as we discuss its calculation, we shall defer our comparative analyses until a later section.

Quick, or Acid Test, Ratio. The *quick ratio* is calculated by deducting inventories from current assets and dividing the remainder by current liabilities:

$$\frac{\text{Quick, or acid}}{\text{test, ratio}} = \frac{\text{Current assets} - \text{Inventories}}{\text{Current liabilities}} = \frac{\$400}{\$300} = 1.3 \text{ times.}$$

Inventories are typically the least liquid of a firm's current assets, and hence the assets on which losses are most likely to occur in the event of liquidation. Therefore, this measure of the firm's ability to pay off short-term obligations, without relying on the sale of inventories, is important.

Asset Management Ratios

The second group of ratios is designed to measure how effectively the firm is managing its assets. In particular, the asset management ratios answer this question: Does the total amount of each type of asset as reported on the balance sheet seem "reasonable," too high, or too low in view of current and projected operating levels? Companies must borrow or obtain capital from other sources in order to acquire assets. If they have too many assets, then their interest expenses will be too high, and hence their profits too low. On the other hand, if assets are too low, their operations will be inefficient.

Inventory Utilization. The *inventory utilization ratio*, often called the *inventory turnover ratio*, is defined as sales divided by inventories:

$$\text{Inventory utilization, or inventory turnover, ratio} = \frac{\text{Sales}}{\text{Inventory}} = \frac{\$3,000}{\$300} = 10.0 \text{ times.}$$

Two problems arise in calculating and analyzing the inventory utilization ratio. First, sales are stated at market prices, so if inventories are carried at cost, as they generally are, it would be more appropriate to use cost of goods sold in place of sales in the numerator of the formula. Established compilers of financial ratio statistics such as Dun & Bradstreet, however, use the ratio of sales to inventories carried at cost. To develop a figure that can be compared with those developed by Dun & Bradstreet, it is necessary to measure the inventory turnover ratio with sales in the numerator, as we do here.

The second problem lies in the fact that sales occur over the entire year, whereas the inventory figure is for one point in time. This makes it better to use an average inventory. The average inventory could be calculated by adding beginning and ending figures and dividing by 2, but it would be preferable to sum the monthly inventory figures and divide by 12. If it were determined that the firm's business is highly seasonal, or if there has been a strong upward or downward sales trend during the year, it becomes essential to make some such adjustment. To maintain comparability with industry averages, however, we did not use the average inventory figure.

Average Collection Period. The *average collection period (ACP)* represents the average length of time that the firm must wait after making a sale before receiving cash. Used to appraise the accounts receivable, the average collection period is computed by dividing accounts receivable by average daily sales to find the number of days' sales tied up in receivables. The calculations for Southern show an average collection period of 42 days:

$$\text{ACP} = \frac{\text{Average collection period}}{} = \frac{\text{Receivables}}{\text{Average daily sales}} = \frac{\text{Receivables}}{\text{Annual sales}/360}$$

$$= \frac{\$350}{\$3,000/360} = \frac{\$350}{\$8.333} = 42.0 \text{ days.}$$

Because information on credit sales is generally unavailable, total sales must be used. Since all firms do not have the same percentage of credit sales, there is a chance that the average collection period will be somewhat in error. Also, note that for convenience, the financial community generally uses 360 rather than 365 as the number of days in the year for purposes such as these, but some financial compilers do use 365-day years, so the analyst must be careful. Finally, it would be better to use *average* receivables = (beginning + ending)/2 = ($315 + $350)/2 = $332.5 (or else a 12-month average) in the formula. Had this been done, the ACP would have been $332.5/$8.333 = 40.0 days.

As we know from our discussion in Chapter 21, the ACP does have weaknesses from the standpoint of appraising a company's credit management program. Therefore, the problems we discussed in Chapter 21 should be kept in mind with regard to this ratio.

Fixed Assets Utilization. The ratio of sales to net fixed assets, often called the *fixed assets turnover ratio*, measures the utilization of plant and equipment:

$$\text{Fixed assets utilization, or turnover, ratio} = \frac{\text{Sales}}{\text{Net fixed assets}} = \frac{\$3,000}{\$1,300} = 2.3 \text{ times.}$$

A major potential problem exists with the use of this ratio for comparative purposes. Inflation has caused the value of many assets that were purchased in the past to be seriously understated. Therefore, if we were comparing an old firm which acquired many of its fixed assets years ago at low prices with a new company which acquired its fixed assets only recently, the old firm would have the higher turnover. However, this would be more reflective of problems with accounting statements than of inefficiency on the part of the new firm. Inflation's effects are discussed in detail later in the chapter.

Total Assets Utilization. The final asset utilization ratio measures the utilization, or turnover, of all the firm's assets; it is calculated as follows:

$$\text{Total assets utilization, or turnover, ratio} = \frac{\text{Sales}}{\text{Total assets}} = \frac{\$3,000}{\$2,000} = 1.5 \text{ times.}$$

The extent to which a firm uses debt financing, or financial leverage, has three important implications. (1) By raising funds through debt, the owners maintain control of the firm with a limited investment. (2) Creditors look to the equity, or owner-supplied funds, to provide a margin of safety; if the owners have provided only a small proportion of total financing, the risks of the enterprise are borne mainly by the creditors. (3) If the firm earns more on borrowed funds than it pays in interest, then the return on the owners' capital is magnified, or "leveraged."

Debt Management Ratios

Analysts examine the firm's use of debt in two basic ways: (1) They check balance sheet ratios to determine the extent to which borrowed funds have been used to finance the firm, and (2) they review income statement ratios to determine the number of times fixed charges are covered by operating profits. These two types of ratios are complementary, so most analysts examine both types.

Total Debt to Total Assets. The ratio of total debt to total assets, generally called the *debt ratio*, measures the percentage of total funds provided by creditors:

$$\text{Debt ratio} = \frac{\text{Total debt}}{\text{Total assets}} = \frac{\$1,100}{\$2,000} = 55\%.$$

Debt is generally defined to include current liabilities plus all long-term debt. Creditors prefer a low debt ratio, since the lower the ratio, the greater the cushion against creditors' losses in the event of liquidation. The owners, on the other hand, may seek high leverage either to magnify earnings or because selling new stock would mean giving up some degree of control.

The *debt/equity* ratio is also used in financial analysis. The debt to assets (D/A) and debt to equity (D/E) ratios are simply transformations of one another:[7]

$$\text{D/A} = \frac{\text{D/E}}{1 + \text{D/E}}, \text{ and D/E} = \frac{\text{D/A}}{1 - \text{D/A}}.$$

Thus, given one ratio, it is easy to convert to the other. Note that both ratios increase as a firm of a given size (total assets) uses a greater proportion of debt. However, D/A rises linearly and approaches a limit of 100 percent (for any solvent firm), while D/E rises exponentially and approaches infinity.

As we know, for purposes of calculating the average cost of capital, the debt ratio should in theory be based on the market value of the firm's assets, that is, the sum of the market values of its debt and equity. Market values are especially important if the accounting values as shown on the balance sheet are significantly different from the market values, as is true of many technology companies and natural resource firms.

---

[7]The proofs of these two relationships are straightforward:

$$\frac{\text{D}}{\text{A}} = \frac{\text{D}}{\text{E} + \text{D}} = \frac{\text{D/E}}{\text{E/E} + \text{D/E}} = \frac{\text{D/E}}{1 + \text{D/E}},$$

and

$$\frac{\text{D}}{\text{E}} = \frac{\text{D}}{\text{A} - \text{D}} = \frac{\text{D/A}}{\text{A/A} - \text{D/A}} = \frac{\text{D/A}}{1 - \text{D/A}}.$$

Times Interest Earned. The *times-interest-earned (TIE) ratio* is determined by dividing earnings before interest and taxes (EBIT in Table 22-1) by the interest charges:

$$\text{Times-interest-earned (TIE) ratio} = \frac{\text{EBIT}}{\text{Interest charges}} = \frac{\$266}{\$66} = 4.0 \text{ times.}$$

The TIE ratio measures the extent to which earnings can decline before the firm is unable to meet its annual interest costs. Failure to meet this obligation can bring legal action by the creditors, possibly resulting in bankruptcy. Note that the before-tax profit figure is used in the numerator, because interest is paid with pre-tax dollars.

Fixed Charge Coverage Ratio. The *fixed charge coverage ratio* measures the extent to which operating income can decline without endangering a firm's ability to meet its fixed financial charges:

$$\begin{aligned}\text{Fixed charge coverage ratio} &= \frac{\text{EBIT + Lease payments}}{\text{Interest charges} + \text{Lease payments} + \dfrac{\text{Sinking fund payments}}{(1 - T)}} \\[2mm] &= \frac{\$266 + \$28}{\$66 + \$28 + \$20/0.6} = 2.3 \text{ times.}\end{aligned}$$

Whereas interest charges and lease payments are tax deductible, hence are paid with pre-tax dollars, sinking fund payments must be paid with after-tax dollars. Thus, in the equation, sinking fund payments are "grossed up" by dividing by $(1 - T)$, where T is the firm's marginal tax rate, to find the before-tax income required both to pay taxes and to cover the sinking fund payment. The fixed charge coverage ratio recognizes that failure to meet lease payments or sinking fund payments can result in bankruptcy just as surely as failure to meet interest payments.[8]

---

[8]For certain purposes, primarily ascertaining whether or not coverage ratios as specified in bond indentures are met before issuing new bonds, companies are required to use a coverage ratio which is prescribed by the SEC:

$$\text{SEC coverage ratio} = \frac{\text{EBIT} + (1/3)(\text{Lease payments})}{\text{Interest charges} + (1/3)(\text{Lease payments})}.$$

There is no particular reason for using one-third of the lease payments, but the formula is a rule-of-thumb that has been used since the 1930s. Another ratio that is frequently used is the following:

$$\text{Rate of return on investors' capital} = \frac{\text{Interest charges + Net income}}{\text{Long-term debt + Equity}}.$$

This ratio is especially important in the public utility industries, where regulators are concerned about the companies' using their monopoly positions to earn excessive returns on investors' capital. In fact, regulators try to set utility prices (service rates) at levels that will force the return on investors' capital as defined above to equal the company's cost of capital.

Profitability
Ratios

Profitability is the net result of a large number of policies and decisions. The ratios examined thus far provide some useful information about the way the firm is operating, but the profitability ratios show the combined effects of liquidity, asset management, and debt management on operating results.

Profit Margin on Sales. The *profit margin on sales*, computed by dividing net income after taxes by sales, gives the profit per dollar of sales:

$$\text{Profit margin} = \frac{\text{Net income}}{\text{Sales}} = \frac{\$110}{\$3,000} = 3.7\%.$$

Basic Earning Power Ratio. The *basic earning power ratio* is calculated by dividing the earnings before interest and taxes (EBIT) by total assets:

$$\text{Basic earning power ratio} = \frac{\text{EBIT}}{\text{Total assets}} = \frac{\$266}{\$2,000} = 13.3\%.$$

This ratio is useful for comparing firms in different tax situations and with different degrees of financial leverage. Notice, however, that EBIT is earned all during the year, whereas the total assets figure is as of the end of the year. Therefore, it would be conceptually better to calculate the ratio as EBIT/Average assets = EBIT/[(Beginning assets + Ending assets)/2]. We have not made this adjustment because the published ratios used for comparative purposes do not include it. However, when we develop our own comparative industry ratios from basic data, we do make the adjustment. Also, note that the same adjustment would be appropriate for the next two ratios, ROA and ROE.

Return on Total Assets (ROA). The ratio of net income available to common stockholders to total assets measures the *return, after interest and taxes, on total assets*:

$$\begin{array}{c}\text{Return on total assets}\\ \text{(ROA)}\end{array} = \frac{\text{Net income}}{\text{Total assets}} = \frac{\$110}{\$2,000} = 5.5\%.$$

Although this ratio is useful for certain purposes, it is not very useful for making interfirm comparisons because it is sensitive to differences in capital structures. Therefore, for interfirm profitability comparisons, either the basic earning power ratio or the ROE, described below, should generally be used.

Return on Equity (ROE). The ratio of net income to common equity measures the *rate of return on the common stockholders' investment*, *ROE*:

$$\begin{array}{c}\text{Return on}\\ \text{equity (ROE)}\end{array} = \frac{\begin{array}{c}\text{Net income available to}\\ \text{common stockholders}\end{array}}{\text{Common equity}} = \frac{\$110}{\$890} = 12.4\%.$$

Note that equity here really means *common* equity, which was obtained by deducting preferred stock from Southern's total equity as reported on the balance sheet. It would, of course, be possible to calculate a return on common plus preferred equity, and some analytical services do report it, but in our view, the ROE based on common equity only is far more useful.

A final group of ratios relates the firm's stock price to its earnings and book value per share. These ratios give management an indication of what investors think of the company's past performance and future prospects. If the firm's liquidity, asset management, debt management, and profitability ratios are all good, then its market value ratios will be high, and the stock price will probably be as high as can be expected.

Market Value Ratios

Price/Earnings Ratio. The *price/earnings (P/E)* ratio shows how much investors are willing to pay per dollar of reported profits. Southern's stock sells for $28.50, so with an EPS of $2.20, its P/E ratio is 13.0:

$$\text{Price/earnings (P/E) ratio} = \frac{\text{Price per share}}{\text{Earnings per share}} = \frac{\$28.50}{\$2.20} = 13.0 \text{ times.}$$

Other things held constant, companies with better growth prospects have higher P/E ratios. Similarly, the lower a company's risk, the higher is its P/E ratio, other things held constant.[9]

Market/Book Ratio. The ratio of a stock's market price to its book value gives another indication of how investors regard the company. Companies with high rates of return on equity in relation to their cost of equity sell at higher multiples of book value than those with low returns. Southern Metals' book value per share is $17.80:

$$\text{Book value per share} = \frac{\text{Common equity}}{\text{Shares outstanding}} = \frac{\$890}{50} = \$17.80.$$

Dividing the price per share by the book value gives a market/book ratio of 1.6 times:

$$\text{Market/book ratio} = \frac{\text{Price per share}}{\text{Book value per share}} = \frac{\$28.50}{\$17.80} = 1.6 \text{ times.}$$

[9]Since earnings per share are generally somewhat volatile, a high or low "spot" P/E ratio may simply reflect the fact that investors expect a change in earnings, that is, that this year's earnings are different from "normalized" or "trend line" earnings on which market prices are based. Thus, General Motors sold at a P/E of 21 in 1982, when earnings were depressed, but at a P/E of only 3.7 in 1984, when earnings were inflated due to a combination of "catch-up demand," restrictions on Japanese imports, and the effects of labor union give-backs carried over from the 1982 recession. GM's P/E based on "normalized" earnings is about 8.

We should also note that the EPS used to calculate the P/E ratio can be either EPS over the *past* year, as in our example, or the EPS projected for the *next* 12 months. Projected P/Es are often used by security analysts. For our purposes, either definition is all right, so long as we maintain consistency.

Note also that the degree of conservatism used by the company's accountants can affect the market/book ratio: The more conservative the accountants, the higher the market/book ratio will be, other things held constant. The same holds true for the P/E ratio.

Analyzing the Ratios

Financial ratios are analyzed (1) by comparing a firm's ratios with the industry average ratios and (2) by comparing the trends in a firm's ratios over time.[10] Industry comparisons provide an indication of the comparative financial condition of the firm being analyzed, while trend analysis gives clues as to whether the financial condition is improving or deteriorating. We will use both techniques to assess the financial condition of Southern Metals Company.

Table 22-6 summarizes Southern's financial ratios, as well as provides industry average ratios for the aluminum fabricating industry. We use these data to analyze Southern's financial condition in the following sections.

Liquidity. Southern's *current ratio* is slightly below the industry average, but not enough to cause concern. Since current assets are scheduled to be converted to cash in the near future, it is highly probable that they could be liquidated at close to their stated value. With a current ratio of 2.3, Southern could liquidate current assets at only 43 percent of book value and still pay off current creditors in full.[11]

The industry average quick ratio is 1.1, so Southern's 1.3 ratio compares favorably with other firms in the industry. If the accounts receivable could be collected, the company could pay off current liabilities even without selling any inventory. However, it should be noted that the trend is downward for both the current and quick ratios. In summary, Southern's liquidity position is adequate, but it bears watching in the future.

Asset Utilization. Southern's *inventory turnover* of 10.0 times compares favorably with an industry average of 9.3 times. This suggests that the company does not hold excessive stocks of inventory; excess stocks are, of course, unproductive and represent an investment with a low or zero rate of return. This high inventory turnover ratio also reinforces our faith in the current ratio. If the turnover were low—say 3 or 4 times— we might wonder whether the firm was holding damaged or obsolete materials not actually worth their stated value.

Southern's *average collection period* is almost 6 days longer than the industry average, indicating either poor collection procedures or credit

---

[10]These two analytical techniques are often called (1) *cross-sectional analysis* and (2) *time-series analysis*, respectively.

[11]$1/2.3 = 0.43 = 43\%$. Note that $0.43(\$700) \approx \$300$, the amount of current liabilities.

Table 22-6
Southern Metals Company:
Summary of Financial Ratios

Ratio	Formula for Calculation	1983	1984	1984 Industry Average	Comment
Liquidity					
Current	$\dfrac{\text{Current assets}}{\text{Current liabilities}}$	2.8×	2.3×	2.5×	Slightly low; bad trend
Quick, or acid test	$\dfrac{\text{Current assets} - \text{Inventories}}{\text{Current liabilities}}$	1.8×	1.3×	1.1×	Slightly low; bad trend
Asset Management					
Inventory turnover	$\dfrac{\text{Sales}}{\text{Inventory}}$	13.3×	10.0×	9.3×	OK, but bad trend
Average collection period	$\dfrac{\text{Receivables}}{\text{Sales}/360}$	39.8 days	42.0 days	36.2 days	Poor
Fixed assets turnover	$\dfrac{\text{Sales}}{\text{Fixed assets}}$	2.7×	2.3×	3.1×	Poor
Total assets turnover	$\dfrac{\text{Sales}}{\text{Total assets}}$	1.7×	1.5×	1.8×	Poor
Debt Management					
Debt to total assets	$\dfrac{\text{Total debt}}{\text{Total assets}}$	47.6%	55.0%	40.1%	High
Times interest earned (TIE)	$\dfrac{\text{EBIT}}{\text{Interest charges}}$	5.6×	4.0×	6.2×	Low
Fixed charge coverage	$\dfrac{\text{EBIT} + \text{Lease payments}}{\text{Interest charges} + \text{Lease payments} + \dfrac{\text{Sinking fund payments}}{(1-T)}}$	2.7×	2.3×	4.0×	Very low
Profitability					
Profit margin on sales	$\dfrac{\text{Net income}^{a}}{\text{Sales}}$	4.2%	3.7%	5.1%	Low
Basic earning power	$\dfrac{\text{EBIT}}{\text{Total assets}}$	15.7%	13.3%	17.2%	Low
Return on total assets (ROA)	$\dfrac{\text{Net income}^{a}}{\text{Total assets}}$	7.1%	5.5%	9.0%	Very low
Return on equity (ROE)	$\dfrac{\text{Net income available to common stockholders}}{\text{Common equity}}$	13.8%	12.4%	15.0%	Low
Market Value					
Price/earnings (P/E)	$\dfrac{\text{Price per share}}{\text{Earnings per share}}$	12.1×	13.0×	13.5×	Slightly low
Market/book	$\dfrac{\text{Market price per share}}{\text{Book value per share}}$	1.6×	1.7×	1.8×	OK

aNet income after preferred dividends.

terms that are more lenient than the industry in general. Moreover, Southern's credit terms call for payment within 30 days, so the 42-day collection period indicates that customers, on the average, are not paying their bills on time. Also, note that the average collection period has been rising over the past two years. If the credit policy has not been changed, this would be evidence that steps should be taken to expedite the collection of accounts receivable. Recall from Chapter 21, though, that if sales are seasonal or cyclical, the ACP could be misleading, so care must be taken when analyzing this ratio.

Southern's *fixed asset turnover* ratio of 2.3 times compares poorly with the industry average of 3.1 times, indicating that the firm is not using its fixed assets to as high a percentage of capacity as are the other firms in the industry. The financial manager should bear this fact in mind when production people request funds for new capital investments.

Southern's *total asset turnover* ratio is somewhat below the industry average. The company is not generating a sufficient volume of business for the size of its asset investment. Sales should be increased, some assets should be disposed of, or both steps should be taken.

Debt Management. Southern's *debt ratio* is 55.0 percent, meaning that creditors have supplied more than half the firm's total financing. Since the average debt ratio for this industry—and for manufacturing generally—is about 40 percent, Southern would find it difficult to borrow additional funds at a reasonable cost without first raising more equity capital. Creditors would be reluctant to lend the firm more money, and management would probably be subjecting the firm to the risk of bankruptcy if it sought to increase the debt ratio still more by borrowing.

Southern's *interest coverage (TIE)* is 4.0 times. Since the industry average is 6.2 times, the company is covering its interest charges by a relatively low margin of safety and deserves a poor rating. Additionally, Southern's *fixed charge coverage* ratio is even further below the industry average (on a proportional basis). These ratios reinforce our conclusion, based on the debt ratio, that the company might face some difficulties if it attempts to borrow additional funds, and a small decrease in earnings would place Southern in jeopardy of bankruptcy.

Profitability. Southern's *profit margin* is somewhat below the industry average of 5.1 percent, indicating that its sales prices are relatively low, that its costs are relatively high, or both. Additionally, Southern's *basic earning power* ratio is well below the industry average. Thus, because of its low turnover ratios and its low profit margin on sales, Southern is not getting as much operating income out of its assets as is the average metals company.

Southern's 5.0 percent *return on total assets* is well below the 9.0 percent average for the industry. This low rate results in part from Southern's low basic earning power and in part from its above average use of debt, causing its interest payments to be high and its profits to be correspondingly low. Southern's 12.4 percent *return on equity* is below the 15 percent industry average, but not as far below as the return on total assets. This results from Southern's greater use of debt, a point analyzed in detail later in the chapter.

Southern's *P/E ratio* is slightly below the average of other large aluminum fabricators, suggesting that the company is regarded as being somewhat riskier than most, as having poorer growth prospects, or both. Investors are also willing to pay slightly less for Southern's book value than for that of an average metals company.

In a common size analysis, all income statement items are divided by sales, and all balance sheet items are divided by total assets. Thus, a *common size income statement* shows each item as a percentage of sales, and a *common size balance sheet* shows each item as a percentage of total assets. The significant advantage of common size statements is that they facilitate comparisons of balance sheets and income statements over time and across companies.

Table 22-7 contains common size income statements for Southern Metals Company, along with the composite statement for the industry. Southern's labor and materials costs are somewhat above average, as is

Common Size Analysis

Table 22-7
Southern Metals Company:
Common Size Income Statements

	1983	1984	1984 Industry Average
Net sales	100%	100%	100%
Costs and expenses:			
Labor and materials	85%	85%	83%
Depreciation	3	3	2
Selling	1	1	2
General and administrative	1	1	1
Lease payments	1	1	1
Total costs	91%	91%	89%
Earnings before interest and taxes	9%	9%	11%
Interest expense:			
Interest on notes payable	0%	0%	0%
Interest on first mortgage bonds	1	1	1
Interest on debentures	0	1	0
Total interest	1%	2%	1%
Earnings before taxes	8%	7%	10%
Taxes	3	3	5
Net income	5%	4%	5%

its depreciation. However, Southern's selling expenses are lower than average, which could be one reason why Southern is not generating sales commensurate with its asset base, and hence has low asset turnover ratios. Southern's interest expenses are also relatively high, but its taxes are relatively low because of its low EBIT. The net effect of all these forces is a relatively low profit margin.

Table 22-8 contains Southern's common size balance sheets, along with the industry average. Here, the three striking differences are that (1) Southern's receivables are significantly higher than the industry average, (2) its inventories are significantly lower, and (3) Southern uses much more long-term debt than the industry average.

The conclusions reached in a common size analysis generally parallel those derived from ratio analysis. However, occasionally a serious deficiency is highlighted only by one of the two analytical techniques. Thus,

Table 22-8
Southern Metals Company:
Common Size Balance Sheets

	1983	1984	1984 Industry Average
Assets			
Cash	3%	2%	2%
Marketable securities	1	0	1
Accounts receivable	19	18	13
Inventories	13	15	20
Total current assets	36%	35%	36%
Gross plant and equipment	88	90	85
Less: Depreciation	24	25	21
Net plant and equipment	64%	65%	64%
Total assets	100%	100%	100%
Claims on Assets			
Accounts payable	2%	3%	4%
Notes payable	4	5	3
Accrued wages	1	0	0
Accrued taxes	7	6	7
Total current liabilities	13%	14%	14%
First mortgage bonds	31	25	17
Debentures	4	15	9
Total long-term debt	35%	40%	26%
Preferred equity	1	1	0
Common equity	52	45	60
Total equity	52%	46%	60%
Total claims	100%	100%	100%

a thorough financial statement analysis will include both ratio and common size analyses, as well as a Du Pont analysis, our next topic.

Du Pont Analysis

Figure 22-1, which is called a *modified Du Pont chart* because that company's managers developed the general approach, shows the relationships between debt, asset turnover, and the profit margin. The left-hand side of the chart develops the *profit margin on sales*. The various expense items are listed, and then summed to obtain Southern's total costs. Subtracting costs from sales yields the company's net income, which when divided by sales indicates that 3.7 percent of each sales dollar is left over for stockholders.

The right-hand side of the chart lists the various categories of assets, which are summed, and then sales are divided by the sum to find the

**Figure 22-1
Southern Metals Company:
Modified Du Pont Chart (Millions of Dollars)**

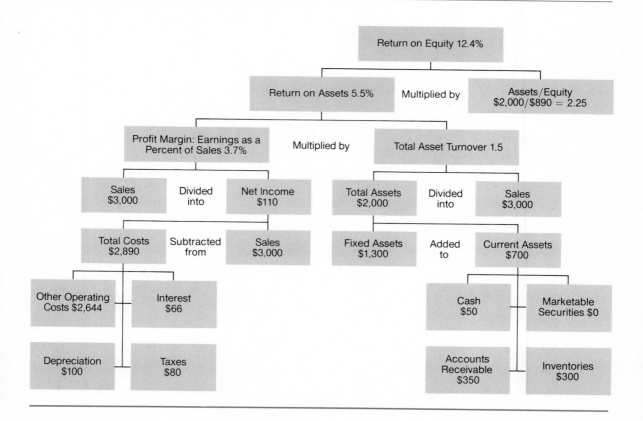

number of times Southern "turns its assets over" each year. Southern's total asset turnover ratio is 1.5 times.

The profit margin times the total asset turnover ratio is defined as the *Du Pont equation*, which gives the rate of return on total assets (ROA):

$$\begin{array}{l} \text{Rate of}\\ \text{return on}\\ \text{total assets} \end{array} = (\text{Profit margin})(\text{Total asset turnover})$$

$$\text{ROA} = \left(\frac{\text{Net income}}{\text{Sales}}\right)\left(\frac{\text{Sales}}{\text{Total assets}}\right) \tag{22-1}$$

$$= (3.7\%)(1.5) = 5.5\%.$$

Southern made 3.7 percent, or 3.7 cents, on each dollar of sales, and assets were "turned over" 1.5 times during the year, so Southern earned a return of 5.5 percent on its assets.

If Southern used only equity, the 5.5 percent rate of return on assets would equal the rate of return on equity. However, 55 percent of the firm's capital was supplied by creditors and preferred stockholders. Since the 5.5 percent return on total assets all goes to common stockholders, who put up only 45 percent of the capital, the return on equity is higher than 5.5 percent. Specifically, the rate of return on assets (ROA) must be multiplied by the *equity multiplier*, which is the ratio of total assets to common equity, to obtain the rate of return on equity (ROE):

$$\text{ROE} = (\text{ROA})(\text{Equity multiplier})$$

$$= \left(\frac{\text{Net income}}{\text{Total assets}}\right)\left(\frac{\text{Total assets}}{\text{Common equity}}\right) \tag{22-2}$$

$$= (5.5\%)(\$2,000/\$890)$$

$$= (5.5\%)(2.25) = 12.4\%.$$

We can combine Equations 22-1 and 22-2 to form the *extended Du Pont equation*:

$$\text{ROE} = \left(\begin{array}{c}\text{Profit}\\\text{margin}\end{array}\right)\left(\begin{array}{c}\text{Total asset}\\\text{turnover}\end{array}\right)\left(\begin{array}{c}\text{Equity}\\\text{multiplier}\end{array}\right)$$

$$= \left(\frac{\text{Net income}}{\text{Sales}}\right)\left(\frac{\text{Sales}}{\text{Total assets}}\right)\left(\frac{\text{Total assets}}{\text{Common equity}}\right) \tag{22-3}$$

$$= \frac{\text{Net income}}{\text{Common equity}}.$$

For Southern Metals, we thus have

$$\text{ROE} = (3.7\%)(1.5)(2.25) = 12.4\%.$$

This 12.4 percent return on equity could, of course, be calculated directly: Net income/Common equity = \$110/\$890 = 12.4%. However, the extended Du Pont equation shows how profit margin, turnover, and leverage interact to determine the return on equity.[12]

Management can use the Du Pont system to analyze ways of improving the firm's performance. On the left, or "profit margin," side of the chart, marketing people can study the effects of raising sales prices (or lowering them to increase volume), of moving into new products or markets with higher margins, and so on. Cost accountants can study the expense items and, working with engineers, purchasing agents, and other operating personnel, seek ways to hold down costs. On the "turnover" side, financial analysts, working with both production and marketing people, can investigate ways of reducing investments in various types of assets. At the same time, the treasurer can analyze the effects of alternative financing strategies, seeking to hold down interest expenses and the risks of debt while still using debt to increase the rate of return on equity.

Equation 22-3 provides an excellent "first look" comparison between a firm's performances as measured by ROE and the performance of an average firm in the industry:

$$\text{Southern Metals: ROE} = (3.7\%)(1.5)(2.25) = 12.4\%.$$
$$\text{Aluminum industry: ROE} = (5.1\%)(1.8)(1.67) = 15.3\%.$$

In comparing Southern with its industry, we find (1) that the average firm in the industry has a higher profit margin, and thus better control over expenses; (2) that the average firm has a higher total asset utilization, and thus is using its assets more productively; and (3) that Southern has offset some of these advantages with its higher financial leverage, although this increased use of leverage increases Southern's risk.

Divisional Analysis

Thus far we have discussed ratio analysis, and financial analysis generally, on a total corporation basis. Total corporation analysis is done and it is quite useful for security analysts and lending officers, but financial managers utilize the procedures described in this chapter primarily on a divisional basis. Most U.S. businesses have a large number of *profit centers*; indeed, the 1,000 largest U.S. companies, which produce over half the private sector's goods and services, each has an average of 25 profit centers. Each profit center has its own investment base and each is expected to contribute to the corporation's total profitability. Each profit center's management utilizes the Du Pont system to monitor its per-

---

[12]Note that in our Du Pont analysis, we have treated preferred stock as debt. Thus, the relevant net income is that available to common stockholders, and the relevant equity multiplier is Total assets/Common equity. The resulting ROE is, therefore, a measure of return to common stockholders. This treatment is consistent with the facts (1) that the common stockholders have voting control of the firm and (2) that preferred stock, with its fixed dividend payments, is really closer to debt financing than to common stock for analytical purposes.

formance, and these data are transmitted (electronically) to corporate headquarters, where financial analysts keep tabs on the various divisions. If the divisions all perform well, then the corporation's ROE and market value ratios will also look good.

Top management continuously monitors summary reports on each division, and uses this information to take corrective actions when necessary. Such a *financial control system,* used with good judgment, is absolutely essential for the proper management of any corporation with sales over a few million dollars. Almost without exception, companies like Du Pont, IBM, GM, and GE, which have had excellent performance over a long period, have in place, and utilize constantly, a good system of financial controls. Conversely, when larger companies get into trouble, their difficulties can usually be traced either to a breakdown in their control system or a failure to heed the signals the system was giving.[13]

Sources of Industry Data

The preceding analysis pointed out the need to compare a company's ratios and common size statements with those of other firms in its industry. In this section, we describe some of the sources of industry data.

External Sources

One useful set of comparative data is compiled by Dun & Bradstreet, Inc. D&B provides 14 ratios for a large number of industries. Useful ratios can also be found in the *Annual Statement Studies* published by Robert Morris Associates, the national association of bank loan officers. The Federal Trade Commission's *Quarterly Financial Report,* which is found in most libraries, gives a set of ratios for manufacturing firms by industry group and size of firm. Trade associations and individual firms' credit departments also compile industry average financial ratios. Finally, financial statements for thousands of corporations are available on magnetic tapes, and since most of the larger brokerage houses, banks, and other financial institutions have access to these data, security

---

[13]An extended discussion of financial controls would go beyond the scope of this book, but we should point out a few problems with such systems: (1) Different divisions will have assets of different ages. This will affect depreciation, hence profits, and also the investment base, hence ROA and ROE. (2) Frequently, one division sells to another and the transfer price used in such intercorporate sales will have a major effect on the divisions' relative profitability. (3) The allocation of corporate overheads will affect relative profitability. (4) Certain types of investments may have no payoff for a number of years, and if divisional managers are rewarded only on the basis of short-term results, this may bias decisions against long-run projects. (5) Certain divisions have more debt capacity than others, yet borrowing is generally done at the corporate level; this must be taken into account. These are just a few of the problems that arise when one attempts to utilize a system of divisional financial controls. Some top managers, when faced with these problems, have just given up and let their division managers operate autonomously. This is a sure path to corporate destruction. Well-run corporations recognize and deal with the problems.

analysts can and do generate comparative ratios tailored to their own individual needs.

Each of the listed organizations uses a somewhat different set of ratios, designed for its own purposes. For example, D&B deals mainly with small firms, many of which are proprietorships, and it is concerned largely with the creditors' viewpoint. Accordingly, D&B's ratios emphasize current assets and liabilities, and it is completely unconcerned with market value ratios. Therefore, when you select a comparative data source, be sure that your emphasis is similar to that of the organization whose data you use, or else recognize the limitations of its ratios for your purposes. Additionally, there are often minor definitional differences in the ratios presented by different sources. Before using any source, be sure to verify the exact definitions of the ratios used.

Internal Sources

Larger firms will generally create their own comparative data using a data base on magnetic tape supplied by a financial services firm. For example, Standard and Poor's Compustat Services, Inc., markets a number of tape libraries of financial, statistical, and market information covering several thousand industrial and nonindustrial companies.

To illustrate, the *Compustat* primary industry file consists of data on approximately 900 companies. For most companies, annual data are available for the past 20 years, and quarterly data for the latest 20 quarters. The data are in the form of annual report statements, and the tapes are updated on a weekly basis to pick up new data as companies report them. Firms which subscribe to the *Compustat* service can use this data base to create their own industry averages, common size statements, and so on. Thus, users can tailor the data to meet their own unique requirements. Additionally, because of the weekly updates, the data are very current.

Problems in Financial Statement Analysis

Financial statement analysis can provide a considerable amount of information concerning a company's operations and financial condition. However, financial statement analysis does have some inherent limitations which necessitate care and judgment in its use. We discuss some of these limitations and problems in this section.

Development of Comparative Data

Many large firms operate a number of different divisions in quite different industries; in such cases, it is difficult to develop a meaningful set of industry averages for comparative purposes. This tends to make financial statement analysis more useful for small firms than for large ones. Additionally, most firms want to be better than average (although half will be above and half below the median), so merely attaining average performance is not necessarily good. As a target for high-level performance, it is preferable to look at the industry leaders' ratios.

Compilers of ratios such as D&B and Robert Morris Associates generally report industry ratios in quartiles; for example, they might report that 25 percent of the firms in the aluminum industry have a current ratio above 6.2, that the median is 4.8, and that 25 percent are below 2.1. Thus, the analyst can obtain some idea of the distribution of ratios within an industry, and make better judgments about the performance of the top firms in the industry as measured by that particular ratio.

Distortion of
Comparative Data

Inflation has badly distorted firms' balance sheets. Further, since inflation affects both depreciation charges and inventory costs, profits are also affected. Thus, a financial statement analysis for one firm over time, or a comparative analysis of firms of different ages, must be interpreted with caution and judgment. Inflation's effects are discussed in detail in a later section.

Seasonal factors can also distort ratio analysis. For example, the inventory turnover ratio for a food processor will be radically different if the balance sheet figure used for inventory is the one just before versus just after the close of the canning season. Receivables, and also current liabilities, are often affected similarly. These problems can be minimized by using average figures.

Interpretation
of Results

It is difficult to generalize about whether a particular ratio is "good" or "bad." For example, a high quick ratio may show a strong liquidity position, which is good, or excessive cash, which is bad because cash is a nonearning asset. Similarly, a high asset turnover ratio may denote either a firm that uses its assets efficiently or one that is undercapitalized and simply cannot afford to buy enough assets. Also, firms often have some ratios which look "good" and others which look "bad," making it difficult to tell whether the firm is, on balance, in a strong or a weak position. We discuss, in Chapter 25, a procedure based on multiple discriminant analysis which can be used to assign weights to different ratios for predicting bankruptcy. However, in general, a ratio analysis must be used as an input to judgmental decisions.

Differences in
Accounting
Treatment

Different accounting practices can distort ratio comparisons. For example, consider the effect of different inventory valuation methods. In Chapter 19, we discussed four inventory valuation methods: (1) specific identification, (2) first-in, first-out (FIFO), (3) last-in, first-out (LIFO), and (4) weighted average. Here we will focus on the effects of using FIFO versus LIFO.

During inflationary periods, LIFO produces a higher cost of goods sold and a lower end-of-period inventory valuation. Table 22-9 contains the simplified financial statements for two firms: Firm L, which uses

Table 22-9
LIFO versus FIFO Financial Statements

| | Both Firms at Beginning of Year | End of Year | |
		Firm L	Firm F
Balance Sheet			
Assets:			
Cash	$ 10	$ 60	$ 35
Inventories	50[a]	50[d]	100[d]
Net plant	100	100	100
Total assets	$160	$210	$235
Claims on assets:			
Current liabilities	10	10	10
Long-term debt	50	50	50
Common equity	100	150	175
Total claims	$160	$210	$235
Income Statement			
Revenues[b]		$300	$300
Cost of goods sold[c]		150	100
Gross profit		150	200
Other expenses		50	50
Earnings before tax		100	150
Tax (0.50)		50	75
Net income		$ 50	$ 75

[a]Beginning inventory for both firms is 200 units, valued at $0.25 per unit for a total of $50. Each firm adds to its inventory by purchasing 300 units at $0.50 each, or a total of $150.

[b]Each firm sells 300 units at a price of $1.00 per unit to produce sales revenues of $300.

[c]Cost of goods sold = (Units sold)(Appropriate purchase price)

$$L = 300(\$0.50) = \$150.$$
$$F = 200(\$0.25) + 100(\$0.50) = \$100.$$

[d]Ending inventory = Beginning inventory + Purchases − Cost of goods sold

$$L = \$50 + \$150 - \$150 = \$50.$$
$$F = \$50 + \$150 - \$100 = \$100.$$

LIFO inventory accounting, and Firm F, which uses FIFO accounting. The footnotes to Table 22-9 explain how the costs of goods sold and ending inventories were calculated. We assume that neither firm pays any dividends, and that cash flows not needed for taxes or inventory maintenance go into the cash account.

Here is what a Du Pont analysis would indicate about the two firms:

	Profit Margin		Total Asset Turnover		Equity Multiplier		ROE
Firm L:	16.7%	×	1.4	×	1.4	=	33.3%
Firm F:	25.0%	×	1.3	×	1.3	=	42.8%

An analyst would be tempted to conclude that the firms are reasonably similar in asset and debt utilization, but that Firm F has better expense control and is, therefore, more profitable. But that would be misleading. The firms are identical from an operating standpoint. However, Firm L, the one which looks worse on a superficial analysis, is actually in the best shape because it paid $25 less in taxes. Thus, Firm L is the stronger and more profitable of the two in a cash flow sense, yet this fact is disguised by the difference in inventory accounting methods.

Other accounting practices can also create distortions. For example, if one firm uses short-term, noncapitalized leases to obtain a substantial amount of its productive equipment, then its reported assets may be low relative to its sales. At the same time, if the lease liability is not shown as a debt, then leasing may artificially improve the debt and turnover ratios.

Window Dressing

Firms sometimes employ "window dressing" techniques to make their financial statements look better to analysts. To illustrate, a Chicago builder borrowed on a two-year basis on December 29, 1984, held the proceeds of the loan as cash for a few days, and then paid off the loan ahead of time on January 4, 1985. This improved his current and quick ratios, and made his year-end 1984 balance sheet look good. However, the improvement was strictly temporary; a week later, the balance sheet was back at the old level.

Financial statement analysis is useful, but analysts should be aware of window dressing and accounting problems and make adjustments as necessary. Financial statement analysis conducted in a mechanical, unthinking manner is dangerous; however, used intelligently and with good judgment, it can provide useful insights into a firm's operations.

Inflation Effects

Double-digit inflation has drawn increased attention to the need to assess both the impact of inflation on business and the success of management in coping with it.[14] Numerous reporting methods have been proposed to provide such an assessment, but no consensus has been reached either on the preferability of any one method or on the practical usefulness of the resulting data. Nevertheless, in September 1979, the Financial Accounting Standards Board (FASB) issued Statement of Financial Accounting Standards #33, which requires businesses to disclose supplementary data to reflect the effects of general inflation.

---

[14]This section draws heavily on the description of inflation accounting on pages 44-47 of AT&T's 1982 Annual Report. See Financial Accounting Standards Board Statement #33, "Financial Reporting and Changing Prices," September 1979, for a discussion of the effects of inflation on financial statements, and for what the accounting profession is trying to do to provide better and more useful balance sheets and income statements.

Traditionally, financial statements have been prepared on the basis of historical costs, that is, the actual number of dollars exchanged at the time each transaction takes place. However, it must be recognized that general inflation has caused the purchasing power of dollars to change, resulting in the presentation of financial statement elements in dollars of varying purchasing power. To illustrate, a $100,000 expenditure on industrial land in 1983 would, in general, purchase far less acreage than a $100,000 expenditure in 1943, so adding 1983 dollars and 1943 dollars is much like adding apples and oranges. Nevertheless, this is done when the typical balance sheet is constructed. To help eliminate this disparity, the assets acquired in different years may be restated in *constant dollars*, each of which has equal purchasing power.

Financial Statement Effects

To reflect the effects of inflation, and thus to express operating results in dollars of comparable purchasing power, FASB #33 requires a company to show what the FASB characterizes as "income from continuing operations" calculated as if all depreciable assets had been purchased with current-year dollars, and consequently depreciation was based on higher-valued assets. Such an adjustment comes closer to showing what profits might be in the long run, when the old, under-valued assets have been replaced with new, inflated-value assets, and depreciation is correspondingly higher. Table 22-10 contains the adjusted amounts as reported by AT&T in its 1982 Annual Report.[15]

It is clear from the data in Table 22-10 that AT&T's reported income would have been much lower had depreciation been based on inflated assets rather than on the historical costs of depreciable assets, with other things held constant. However, it seems most unrealistic to report higher depreciation without recognizing that, if this higher depreciation were used in the basic income determination, then AT&T's regulators would have permitted it to charge higher rates. With higher rates, AT&T would have had higher revenues, and net income would have moved back toward, if not all the way up to, the level reported in Column 1 of Table 22-10. Further, if its revenues had not gone up, then its taxes would have fallen and that would have boosted after-tax income. Clearly, the inflation adjustment in Table 22-10 has problems.

FASB #33 also requires firms to present a supplementary five-year comparison of selected financial data in current dollars. This type of comparison is shown in Table 22-11, where selected financial data are given for AT&T for the years 1978 through 1982. Operating revenues, cash dividends per common share, and the price per share of common stock have been restated in constant 1982 dollars. The effect of these calculations is to increase the number of dollars shown for each year as compared to the actual number of dollars received or spent.

---

[15]In addition to reporting the effects of general inflation, certain companies are also required to report specific cost changes in their particular industries. This adjustment is not addressed here.

Table 22-10
AT&T: Financial Data Adjusted for Inflation,
December 31, 1982
(Millions of Dollars, except for per Share Amounts)

	As Reported in the Basic Financial Statements (Historical Cost) (1)	Adjusted for General Inflation (Constant Dollars) (2)
Operating revenues	$65,093	$65,093
Expenses:		
Depreciation	8,734	15,676
Other operating expenses	36,291	36,291
Operating federal income taxes	4,411	4,411
Other operating taxes	5,398	5,398
Other income	(664)	(664)
Interest expenses	3,930	3,930
Total expenses	58,100	65,042
Net income from continuing operations	$ 6,993	$ 51
Income per common share (after preferred dividends)	$8.06	($0.11)

Table 22-11
AT&T: Supplementary Five-Year Comparison
of Selected Financial Data Adjusted for the Effects of
Changing Prices (Millions of Dollars, except for per
Share Amounts)

	1982	1981	1980	1979	1978
Sales revenues:					
As reported	$65,093	$59,229	$51,755	$46,183	$41,744
In 1982 dollars	65,093	61,647	59,361	60,405	60,700
Cash dividends declared per common share:					
At historical cost	$5.40	$5.40	$5.00	$5.00	$4.60
In 1982 dollars	5.40	5.73	5.86	6.65	6.81
Market price per common share at year end:					
At historical cost	$59.38	$58.75	$47.88	$52.13	$60.50
In 1982 dollars	58.43	60.36	53.58	65.31	86.27
Consumer Price Index	289.2	272.4	246.5	217.4	195.4

The data in Table 22-11 make it clear that much of AT&T's sales growth was caused by rising prices, and not by increases in unit sales. Also, it is clear that AT&T's stockholders have fared worse, considering inflation, than the raw data indicate. Using the raw data, it looks as if dividends have grown from $4.60 to $5.40, or by 4 percent per year.

However, the real value of the dividends received has actually decreased by 6 percent per year. Further, the historical stock price data suggest that the value of AT&T's stock has been reasonably stable, but the inflation-adjusted data reveal that the real value of a share of AT&T stock has declined from $86.27 to $58.43, or by 32 percent.

Ratio Analysis Effects

If a ratio analysis is based on "regular" financial statements, unadjusted for inflation, then distortions can creep in. Obviously, there will be a tendency for the value of the fixed assets to be understated, and inventories will also be understated if the firm uses last-in, first-out (LIFO) accounting. At the same time, increasing rates of inflation will cause increases in interest rates, which in turn will cause the value of the outstanding long-term debt to decline. Further, profits will vary from year to year as the inflation rate changes, and these variations will be especially severe if inventory is charged to cost of goods sold on the first-in, first-out (FIFO) basis.

These factors tend to make ratio comparisons over time for a given company, and across companies at a point in time, less reliable than would be the case in the absence of inflation. This is especially true if a company changes its accounting procedures (say, from straight-line to accelerated depreciation, or from FIFO to LIFO), or if various companies in a given industry use different accounting methods. Analysts can attempt to restate financial statements to put everything on a common basis, but at best, this can only reduce the problem, but not eliminate it. With the present state of the art, financial analysts cannot do much more than base their financial statement analysis of a firm on the existing accounting data. However, they ought to recognize that there are weaknesses in this approach, and to apply judgment in interpreting the data.

Summary

The primary purposes of this chapter were (1) to describe the basic financial statements and (2) to discuss techniques used by investors and managers to analyze these statements. Four basic statements were covered: the *income statement*, the *balance sheet*, the *statement of retained earnings*, and the *statement of changes in financial position*.

Financial analysis is designed to determine the relative strengths and weaknesses of a company—whether the firm is financially sound and profitable relative to other firms in its industry, and whether its position is improving or deteriorating over time. Investors need such information in order to estimate both future profits of the firm and the riskiness inherent in those profits. Managers need to be aware of their firms' financial positions in order to detect and strengthen weaknesses, and capitalize on strengths, in a continuous quest for improvement.

Our study of financial analysis concentrated on a set of ratios designed to highlight the key aspects of a firm's operations. These ratios were broken down into five categories: (1) *liquidity ratios*, (2) *asset management ratios*, (3) *debt management ratios*, (4) *profitability ratios*, and (5) *market value ratios*. The ratios for a given firm are calculated, and then compared with those of other firms in the same industry to judge the relative strength of the firm in question. Trends in the ratios are also analyzed. Another comparative technique is *common size analysis*. Here financial statements are expressed as percentages and a comparative analysis is performed. Additionally, *Du Pont analysis* is especially suited for a preliminary view of how a company compares with the average firm in the industry in the areas of expense control, total asset utilization, and debt utilization.

In closing, we discussed some of the problems encountered in financial statement analysis. Financial statement analysis has limitations, but, used with care and judgment, it can be most helpful.

Questions

22-1 Define each of the following terms:
  a. Balance sheet; income statement
  b. Stockholders' equity; paid-in capital; retained earnings
  c. Source of funds; use of funds
  d. Statement of changes in financial position
  e. Liquidity ratio; current ratio; quick ratio
  f. Asset management ratio; turnover; inventory turnover; fixed assets turnover; total assets turnover
  g. Average collection period (ACP)
  h. Profitability ratio; profit margin; basic earning power; return on assets (ROA); return on equity (ROE)
  i. Market value ratio; price/earnings (P/E) ratio; market/book ratio
  j. Trend analysis; comparative analysis
  k. Common size analysis
  l. Du Pont system; Du Pont equation modified to show effects of debt financing
  m. "Window dressing"
  n. Inflation effects

22-2 What four statements are contained in most annual reports?

22-3 Is it true that if a "typical" firm reports $20 million of retained earnings on its balance sheet, that firm's directors could declare a $20 million cash dividend without any qualms whatsoever?

22-4 How does inflation distort ratio analysis comparisons, both for one company over time (trend analysis) and when different companies are compared? Are only balance sheet items, or both balance sheet and income statement items, affected?

22-5 If a firm's ROE is low, and management wants to improve it, explain how using more debt might provide a solution.

22-6 Suppose a firm used debt to leverage up its ROE, and in the process its EPS was also boosted. Would this necessarily lead to an increase in the price of the firm's stock?

22-7 How might (a) seasonal factors and (b) different growth rates over time or across companies distort a comparative ratio analysis? Give some examples. How might these problems be alleviated?

22-8 Indicate the effects of the transactions listed below on each of the following: total current assets, net working capital, current ratio, and net income. Use + to indicate an increase, − to indicate a decrease, and 0 to indicate no effect or an indeterminate effect. Be prepared to state any necessary assumptions, and assume an initial current ratio of more than 1.0. Note: A good accounting background is necessary to answer some of these questions; if your background is not strong, just answer the questions you can handle.

	Total Current Assets	Net Working Capital	Current Ratio	Net Income
a. Cash is acquired through issuance of additional common stock.				
b. Merchandise is sold for cash.				
c. Federal income tax due for the previous year is paid.				
d. A fixed asset is sold for less than book value.				
e. A fixed asset is sold for more than book value.				
f. Merchandise is sold on credit.				
g. Payment is made to trade creditors for previous purchases.				
h. A cash dividend is declared and paid.				
i. Cash is obtained through short-term bank loans.				
j. Short-term notes receivable are sold at a discount.				
k. Marketable securities are sold below cost.				
l. Advances are made to employees.				
m. Current operating expenses are paid.				
n. Short-term promissory notes are issued to trade creditors for past due accounts receivable.				
o. Ten-year notes are issued to pay off accounts payable.				
p. A fully depreciated asset is retired.				
q. Accounts receivable are collected.				
r. Equipment is purchased with short-term notes.				
s. Merchandise is purchased on credit.				
t. The estimated taxes payable are increased.				

ST-1 The following data apply to Cadwalader & Company (in millions of dollars): *Self-Test Problem*

Cash and marketable securities	$100.00
Fixed assets	$283.50
Sales	$1,000.00
Net income	$50.00
Quick ratio	2.0×
Current ratio	3.0×
ACP	40 days
ROE	12%

Cadwalader has no preferred stock—only common equity, current liabilities, and long-term debt.

a. Find Cadwalader's (1) accounts receivable (A/R), (2) current liabilities, (3) current assets, (4) total assets, (5) ROA, (6) common equity, and (7) long-term debt.

b. In Part a, you should have found Cadwalader's accounts receivable (A/R) = $111.1 million. If Cadwalader could reduce its ACP from 40 days to 30 days while holding other things constant, how much cash would it generate? If this cash were used to buy back common stock (at book value), and thus to reduce the amount of common equity, how would this affect (1) the ROE, (2) the ROA, and (3) the total debt/total assets ratio?

Problems

22-1 Data for the Mainframe Company, and its industry averages, are given below.

a. Calculate the indicated ratios for Mainframe.

b. Construct the extended Du Pont equation for both Mainframe and the industry.

c. Outline Mainframe's strengths and weaknesses as revealed by your analysis.

d. Suppose Mainframe had doubled its sales and also its inventories, accounts receivable, and common equity during 1984. How would that information affect the validity of your ratio analysis?

Balance Sheet as of December 31, 1984

Cash	$ 220,000	Accounts payable	$ 165,000
Receivables	275,000	Notes payable	220,000
Inventory	825,000	Other current liabilities	110,000
Total current assets	$1,320,000	Total current liabilities	$495,000
Net fixed assets	605,000	Long-term debt	220,000
		Common equity	1,210,000
Total assets	$1,925,000	Total claims	$1,925,000

Income Statement for the Year Ended 1984

Sales		$2,750,000
Cost of goods sold:		
Materials	$1,045,000	
Labor	660,000	
Heat, light, and power	99,000	
Indirect labor	165,000	
Depreciation	60,500	2,029,500
Gross profit		$ 720,500
Selling expenses		275,000
General and administrative expenses		316,800

Earnings before interest and taxes	$ 128,700
Less interest expense	13,200
Net profit before taxes	$ 115,500
Less federal income taxes (50%)	57,750
Net income	$ 57,750

Industry Average Ratios

	Ratios	
Ratio	Mainframe	Industry Average
Current assets/current liabilities	_____	2.4×
Average collection period	_____	43 days
Sales/inventories	_____	9.8×
Sales/total assets	_____	2×
Net income/sales	_____	3.3%
Net income/total assets	_____	6.6%
Net income/net worth	_____	18.1%
Total debt/total assets	_____	63.5%

[handwritten annotations: "– Inventories are high – low" next to Current assets/Average collection period; "} Profitability too low   assets which are not contributing to profitability" next to Net income rows]

22-2   The Blacksburg Furniture Company, a manufacturer and wholesaler of high-quality home furnishings, has been experiencing low profitability in recent years. As a result, the board of directors has replaced the president of the firm with a new president, John Stockwell, who asks you to make an analysis of the firm's financial position using the Du Pont system. The most recent industry average ratios, and Blacksburg's financial statements, are reproduced below (in millions of dollars).

Industry Average Ratios

Current ratio	2×	Sales/fixed assets	6×
Debt/total assets	30%	Sales/total assets	3×
Times interest earned	7×	Net profit on sales	3%
Sales/inventory	10×	Return on total assets	9%
Average collection period	24 days	Return on common equity	12.8%

Balance Sheet as of December 31, 1984

Cash	$ 30	Accounts payable	$ 30
Marketable securities	22	Notes payable	30
Net receivables	44	Other current liabilities	14
Inventories	106	Total current liabilities	$ 74
Total current assets	$202	Long-term debt	16
		Total liabilities	$ 90
Gross fixed assets	150		
Less depreciation	52	Common stock	76
Net fixed assets	$ 98	Retained earnings	134
		Total stockholder equity	$210
Total assets	$300	Total claims	$300

Income Statement for the Year Ended 1984

Net sales	$530
Cost of goods sold	440
Gross profit	$ 90
Operating expenses	49
Depreciation expense	8
Interest expense	3
Total expense	$ 60
Net income before tax	$ 30
Taxes (50%)	15
Net income	$ 15

a. Calculate those ratios which you feel would be useful in this analysis.
b. Do the balance sheet accounts or the income statement figures seem to be primarily responsible for the low profits?
c. Which specific accounts seem to be most out of line in relation to other firms in the industry?
d. If Blacksburg had a pronounced seasonal sales pattern, or if it grew rapidly during the year, how might this affect the validity of your ratio analysis? How might you correct for such potential problems?

22-3 The consolidated balance sheets for the Alabama-Atlantic Lumber Company at the beginning and end of 1984 follow (in millions of dollars). The company bought $75 million worth of fixed assets. The charge for depreciation in 1984 was $15 million. Earnings after taxes were $38 million, and the company paid out $10 million in dividends.
a. Fill in the amount of source or use in the appropriate column.

	Jan. 1	Dec. 31	Change Source	Use
Cash	$ 15	$ 7		
Marketable securities	11	0		
Net receivables	22	30		
Inventories	53	75		
Total current assets	$101	$112		
Gross fixed assets	75	150		
Less depreciation	26	41		
Net fixed assets	$ 49	$109		
Total assets	$150	$221		
Accounts payable	$ 15	$ 18		
Notes payable	15	3		
Other current liabilities	7	15		
Long-term debt	8	26		
Common stock	38	64		
Retained earnings	67	95		
Total claims	$150	$221		

b. Prepare a statement of changes in financial position.

c. Briefly summarize your findings.

22-4 The Ameritronic Corporation's balance sheets for 1984 and 1983 are as follows (in millions of dollars):

	1984	1983
Assets		
Cash	$ 21	$ 45
Marketable securities	0	33
Receivables	90	66
Inventories	225	159
Total current assets	$336	$303
Gross fixed assets	450	225
Less accumulated depreciation	123	78
Net fixed assets	$327	$147
Total assets	$663	$450
Claims on Assets		
Accounts payable	$ 54	$ 45
Notes payable	9	45
Accruals	45	21
Total current liabilities	$108	$111
Long-term debt	78	24
Common stock	192	114
Retained earnings	285	201
Total long-term capital	$555	$339
Total claims	$663	$450

Additionally, Ameritronic's 1984 income statement is as follows (in millions of dollars):

Sales	$1,365
Cost of goods sold	888
General expenses	282
EBIT	$ 195
Interest	10
EBT	$ 185
Taxes (46%)	85
Net income	$ 100

a. What was Ameritronic's dividend payout ratio in 1984?

b. The following extended Du Pont equation is the industry average for 1984:

$$\frac{\text{Profit}}{\text{margin}} \times \frac{\text{Asset}}{\text{turnover}} \times \frac{\text{Equity}}{\text{multiplier}} = \text{ROE}$$

$$6.52\% \times 1.82 \times 1.77 = 21.00\%.$$

Construct Ameritronic's 1984 extended Du Pont equation. What does the Du Pont analysis indicate about Ameritronics' expense control, asset utilization, and debt utilization? What is the industry's assets to debt (A/D) ratio?

c. Construct Ameritronic's 1984 statement of changes in financial position.

Solution to Self-Test Problem

ST-1

a.

(1)

$$ACP = \frac{\text{Accounts receivable}}{\text{Sales}/360}$$

$$40 = \frac{A/R}{\$1,000/360}$$

$$A/R = \$111.1$$

(2)

$$\text{Quick ratio} = \frac{\text{Current assets} - \text{Inventories}}{\text{Current liabilities}} = 2.0$$

$$\frac{\text{Cash and marketable securities} + A/R}{\text{Current liabilities}} = 2.0$$

$$2 = \frac{\$100 + \$111.1}{\text{Current liabilities}}$$

Current liabilities = ($100 + $111.1)/2 = $105.5 million.

(3)

$$\text{Current ratio} = \frac{\text{Current assets}}{\text{Current liabilities}} = 3.0$$

$$\frac{\text{Current assets}}{\$105.5} = 3.0$$

Current assets = 3.0($105.5) = $316.50 million.

(4)

Total assets = Current assets + Fixed assets
= $316.5 + $283.5 = $600 million.

(5)

ROA = Profit margin × Total asset turnover

$$= \frac{\text{Net income}}{\text{Sales}} \times \frac{\text{Sales}}{\text{Total assets}}$$

$$= \frac{\$50}{\$1,000} \times \frac{\$1,000}{\$600}$$

= 0.05 × 1.667 = 0.833 = 8.33%.

(6)

$$\text{ROE} = \text{ROA} \times \frac{\text{Assets}}{\text{Equity}}$$

$$12.0\% = 8.33\% \times \frac{\$600}{\text{Equity}}.$$

$$\text{Equity} = \frac{(8.33\%)(\$600)}{12.0\%} = \$416.50 \text{ million.}$$

Note: We could have found equity as follows:

$$\text{ROE} = \frac{\text{Net income}}{\text{Equity}}$$

$$0.12 = \frac{\$50}{\text{Equity}}$$

$$\text{Equity} = \$50/0.12$$

$$= \$416.67 \text{ million (rounding error difference)}.$$

(7)   Total assets = Total claims = $600

Current liabilities + Long-term debt + Equity = $600

$105.5 + Long-term debt + $416.5 = $600

Long-term debt = $600 − $105.5 − $416.5 = $78 million.

b.   Cadwalader's average sales per day were $1,000/360 = $2.777777 million. Its ACP was 40, so A/R = 40($2,777,777) = $111,111,111. Its new ACP of 30 would cause A/R = 30($2,777,777) = $833,333,333. The reduction in receivables would be $111,111,111 − $83,333,333 = $27,777,777, which would equal the amount of new cash generated.

(1)   New equity = Old equity − Stock bought back

$$= \$416,500,000 - \$27,777,777$$

$$= \$388,722,223.$$

Thus,

$$\text{New ROE} = \frac{\text{Net income}}{\text{New equity}}$$

$$= \frac{\$50,000,000}{\$388,722,223}$$

$$= 12.86\% \text{ (versus old ROE of 12.0\%)}.$$

(2)

$$\text{New ROA} = \frac{\text{Net income}}{\text{Total assets} - \text{Reduction in A/R}}$$

$$= \frac{\$50,000,000}{\$600,000,000 - \$27,777,777}$$

$$= 8.74\% \text{ (versus old ROA of 8.33\%)}.$$

(3) The old debt is the same as the new debt:

$$\text{Debt} = \text{Total claims} - \text{Equity}$$

$$= \$600 - \$416.5 = \$183.5 \text{ million}$$

Old total assets = $600 million

New total assets = Old total assets − Reduction in A/R

$$= \$600 - \$27.78$$

$$= \$572.22 \text{ million}.$$

Therefore,

$$\frac{\text{Debt}}{\text{Old total assets}} = \frac{\$183.5}{\$600} = 30.6\%,$$

while

$$\frac{\text{Debt}}{\text{New total assets}} = \frac{\$183.5}{\$572.22} = 32.1\%.$$

Selected Additional References and Cases

The effects of alternative accounting policies on both financial statements and ratios based on these statements are discussed in the investment textbooks referenced in Chapter 5, and also in the many excellent texts on financial accounting. For example, see

Kieso, Donald E., and Jeremy J. Weygandt, *Intermediate Accounting* (New York: Wiley, 1980).

Smith, Jay M., and Fred K. Skousen, *Intermediate Accounting* (Cincinnati: Southwestern, 1981).

For further information on the relative usefulness of various financial ratios, see

Chen, Kung H., and Thomas A. Shimerda, "An Empirical Analysis of Useful Financial Ratios," *Financial Management*, Spring 1981, 51-60.

Considerable work has been done to establish the relationship between bond ratings and financial ratios. For one example, see

Belkaoui, Ahmed, *Industrial Bonds and the Rating Process* (London: Quorum Books, 1983).

For sources of ratios and common size statements, see the following:

Dun & Bradstreet, *Key Business Ratios* (New York: Updated annually).

Financial Research Associates, *Financial Studies of the Small Business* (Arlington, Va.: Updated annually).

Robert Morris Associates, *Annual Statement Studies* (Philadelphia: Updated annually).

Troy, Leo, *Almanac of Business and Industrial Financial Ratios* (Englewood Cliffs, N. J.: Prentice-Hall, Updated annually).

Additionally, there has been considerable research on the relationship between financial ratios and potential bankruptcy; see the Chapter 25 references.

The following case focuses on ratio analysis:

Case 1, "Forest Resources Corporation," in the Brigham-Crum casebook, which illustrates the use of ratio analysis in the evaluation of a firm's existing and potential financial positions.

Financial Planning and Control

23

"We are navigating through icebergs, and any one of them could tear the bottom out of the boat." That's how Chairman Charles Black described the situation at AM International, an office equipment manufacturer with sales of close to $1 billion. AM's problems had begun a few years earlier, when Roy Ash, one of the founders of Litton Industries, took control of the company. Ash decided to change AM from a producer/distributor of relatively staid duplicating equipment into a major provider of "the technologically advanced office of the future." With this decision made, he began pumping the company's cash into R&D on new products, and into facilities for manufacturing these products.

Ash subsequently lost his job because of two strategic errors which combined to cause the company to lose $245 million, or 80 percent of its beginning-of-year common equity, in a single year. First, Ash underestimated how long it would take to bring the new products on line so that they could begin producing positive cash flows, and, second, he overestimated AM's ability to finance the company's extremely rapid projected growth rate. Ash and his management team failed to recognize fully that to get additional sales in the future, the firm must spend money on R&D, plant and equipment, and inventories well in advance of the new sales, and that if the firm runs out of money before it completes the R&D, gets the plant and equipment in place, and builds up the inventories, then the whole plan will collapse. A study of Chapter 23 might have helped Ash avoid the problems he and AM International got into.

In the last chapter, we saw how to analyze a set of financial statements in order to identify a firm's strengths and weaknesses. Now we go on to consider actions a firm can take to exploit its strengths and to overcome its weaknesses. As we shall see, managers are vitally concerned with projected, or pro forma, financial statements, and with the effect of alternative policies on these statements. A good analysis of the effects of alternative actions is indeed the key ingredient of financial planning. However, a good financial plan cannot, by itself, insure that the firm's goals will be met; it must be backed up by a financial control system for monitoring the situation both to insure that the plan is carried out properly and to permit rapid adjustments to the basic plan if economic and operating conditions change from projected levels. In this chapter, we examine the financial planning and control processes.

Strategic Plans

Financial planning must occur within the framework of the firm's strategic and operating plans. Thus, we begin our discussion with an overview of the strategic planning process.[1]

Corporate Purpose

The long-run strategic plan should begin with a statement of the *corporate purpose*, which defines the overall mission of the firm. The purpose can be defined either specifically or in general terms. For example, one firm might state that its corporate purpose is "to increase the intrinsic value of our common stock." Another might say that its purpose is "to maximize the growth rate in earnings and dividends per share while avoiding excessive risk." Yet another might state that its principal goal is "to provide our customers with state-of-the-art computing systems at the lowest attainable cost, which in our opinion will also maximize benefits to our employees and stockholders."

There should be no conflict between sound operations and stockholders' benefits, but occasionally there is. For example, Varian Associates, Inc., a NYSE company with 1984 sales of about $920 million, was for years regarded as one of the most technologically advanced companies in the electronics devices and semiconductor fields. However, Varian's management was reputed to be more concerned with developing new technology than with marketing it, and the stock price was lower in 1979 than it had been 10 years earlier. Some of the larger stockholders were intensely unhappy with the state of affairs, and management was faced with the threat of a proxy fight or forced merger. At that point, management announced a conscious change in policy and stated that it would, in the future, emphasize both technological excellence *and* profitability, rather than focus primarily on technology. Earnings improved dramatically, and the stock price rose from a low of $6.75 in 1979 to over $60 in 1983.

---

[1]One can take many approaches to corporate planning. For more insights into the corporate planning process, see Benton E. Gup, *Guide to Strategic Planning* (New York: McGraw-Hill, 1980).

The Varian example illustrates both the importance of the corporate purpose as viewed by management and also the discipline of the market. Well-run companies need to define an area and then develop competence with regard to meeting the needs of their customers, but they will be forced by the market to translate that competence into earnings.

The *corporate scope* defines a firm's lines of business and geographic area of operations. Again, the corporate scope can be spelled out in great detail or put merely in general terms. Here is Western Electronics' statement of corporate scope:

Corporate Scope

> Our current operations are concentrated in the manufacture and sales of electronic components. We expect to continue this emphasis, primarily because the electronics industry offers above-average growth opportunities.
>
> The company is not confined to any geographical area of operations, but, for now, international expansion is not envisioned. However, domestic expansion will continue until the firm fully realizes its marketing potential.
>
> In order to accomplish our corporate purpose, it may be necessary or desirable to provide products which supplement, complement, or enhance our principal lines of business. Any such activities will be consistent with our responsibilities to our investors, customers, employees, suppliers, and the public in general.

The corporate purpose and scope outline the general philosophy and approach of the business, but they do not provide managers with operational objectives. The *corporate objectives* set forth specific goals that management strives to attain. Corporate objectives can be quantitative, such as specifying a target market share, target ROE, or earnings per share growth rate, or they can be qualitative, such as "keeping the firm's research and development efforts at the cutting edge of the industry." Corporate goals are not static—they should be changed when required by changing conditions. They should also be challenging, yet realistically attainable, and it is appropriate that management compensation be based on the extent to which objectives are met.

Corporate Objectives

Once a firm has defined its purpose, scope, and objectives, it should develop a strategy designed to help it achieve its stated objectives. *Corporate strategies* are broad approaches rather than detailed plans. For example, one airline may have a strategy of offering "no frills" service between a limited number of cities, while another may plan to offer "staterooms in the sky." Strategies must be attainable and compatible with the firm's purpose, scope, and objectives.

Corporate Strategies

Perhaps the most interesting and important set of strategies that has been developed in recent years is that of AT&T and the Bell operating companies in the wake of the breakup of AT&T. The seven regional telephone holding companies which emerged from the breakup will all provide basic local telephone service, but beyond that, they appear at this writing to be developing different strategies which will take them in different directions. Some plan to sell a broad array of telecommunications equipment, while others will have more limited offerings. Some hope to get into the long distance business, even in the territories of their sister companies and in competition with their erstwhile parent, AT&T, while others will avoid long distance markets, or at least not emphasize them.

The surviving AT&T faces perhaps even greater challenges in setting its corporate strategy. On the one hand, it faces increasing competition in its two major markets, long distance transmission and telephone equipment manufacturing. Currently, it has most of the industry's capacity in these areas, so to some extent, it can price high and enjoy high short-run profits, but at the expense of a rapid erosion of its share of the business. Alternatively, it can price low, maintain a greater market share, but not maximize short-run (and perhaps also long-run) profits. Also, AT&T must decide whether to stick to its knitting in telecommunications, or to jump with both feet into the computer business, which would mean direct competition with IBM, a decision that is not to be taken lightly. IBM, meanwhile, has invested heavily in the telecommunications business (both manufacturing and satellite transmissions), so AT&T will probably face competition from IBM regardless what it does.

The AT&T/Bell companies' strategic decisions are more dramatic than most, but they do illustrate the kinds of issues that arise when companies develop their strategic plans.

Operating Plans

Operating plans can be developed for any time horizon, but most companies use a five-year horizon, and thus the name *five-year plan* has become common. In a five-year plan, the plans are most detailed for the first year, with each succeeding year's plan becoming less specific. The operating plan is intended to provide detailed implementation guidance, based on the corporate strategy, in order to meet the corporate objectives. The five-year plan explains in considerable detail who is responsible for what particular function, and when specific tasks are to be accomplished.

Table 23-1 contains the annual planning schedule for Telecomp Corporation, a leading manufacturer of computer and telecommunications equipment. This schedule illustrates the fact that for larger companies, the planning process is essentially continuous. Next, Table 23-2 outlines the key elements of Telecomp's five-year plan. A full outline would require several pages, but Table 23-2 does at least provide insights into the format and content of a five-year plan. It should be noted that Te-

Table 23-1
Telecomp Corporation:
Annual Planning Schedule

Months	Action
April-May	Planning department analyzes environmental and industry factors. Marketing department prepares sales forecast.
June-July	Engineering department prepares cost estimates for new manufacturing facilities and plant modernization programs.
August-September	Financial analysts evaluate proposed capital expenditures, divisional operating plans, and proposed sources and uses of funds.
October-November	Five-year plan is finalized by planning department, reviewed by divisional officers, and put into "semi-final" form.
December	Five-year plan is approved by the executive committee and submitted to the board of directors for final approval.

Table 23-2
Telecomp Corporation:
Five-Year Operating Plan Outline

A. Corporate mission
B. Corporate scope
C. Corporate objectives
D. Projected business environment
E. Corporate strategies
F. Summary of projected business results
G. Product line plans and policies
  1. Marketing
  2. Manufacturing
  3. Finance
    a. Working capital
      (1) Overall working capital policy
      (2) Cash and marketable securities management
      (3) Inventory management
      (4) Credit policy and receivables management
    b. Dividend policy
    c. Financial forecast
      (1) Capital budget
      (2) Cash budget
      (3) Pro forma financial statements
      (4) External financing requirements
      (5) Financial condition analysis
    d. Accounting plan
    e. Control plan
  4. Administrative and personnel
  5. Research and development
  6. New products
H. Consolidated corporate plan

lecomp, like other large, multidivisional companies, breaks down its operating plan by divisions. Thus, each division has its own goals, mission, and plan for meeting its objectives, and these plans are then consolidated to form the corporate plan.

The Financial Plan

Financial planning is a key part of the overall planning process, both because the availability and cost of funds set limits on a firm's business activities and also because the financial plan provides a framework for determining the probable effects of alternative courses of action. Financial planning can be broken down into five steps:

1. Set up a system of projected financial statements which can be used to analyze the effects of the operating plan on projected profits and other financial condition indicators. This system can also be used to monitor operations after the plan has been finalized and put into effect. Rapid awareness of deviations from plans is essential to a good control system, which in turn is essential to corporate success in a changing world.

2. Determine the specific financial requirements to support the company's five-year plan. This includes funds for capital expenditures as well as for inventory and receivables buildups, for R&D programs, and for major advertising campaigns.

3. Forecast the financing sources to be used over the next five years. This involves estimating the funds to be generated internally as well as those required from external sources. Any constraints on operating plans imposed by financial limitations—for example, debt/assets ratio or current ratio restrictions which would limit the use of total and/or short-term debt—should be incorporated into the plan.

4. Establish and maintain a system of controls governing the allocation and use of funds within the firm. Essentially, this involves the effort to insure that the basic plan is carried out properly.

5. Develop procedures for adjusting the basic plan if conditions deviate from the forecasted conditions upon which the plan was based. For example, if the economy turns out to be stronger than was forecasted when the basic plan was drawn up, then these new conditions must be recognized and incorporated into production schedules, marketing quotas, and the like as rapidly as possible. Thus, Step 5 is really a "feedback loop" which triggers modifications to the plan.

The principal components of the financial plan are (1) the sales forecast, (2) the capital budget, (3) the cash budget, (4) the pro forma financial statements, (5) the external financing plan, and (6) the financial condition analysis. We have discussed the capital budget, the cash budget, and financial statement analysis in detail. In the remainder of this chapter, we focus on constructing pro forma financial statements and using them in financial planning.

Pro Forma Financial Statements

Pro forma, or projected, financial statements are constructed by financial managers and used (1) to evaluate the expected future financial condition of the firm, (2) to project financing requirements, (3) to determine how alternative courses of action are likely to affect both the firm's financial condition and its financial requirements, and (4) to provide a standard against which to evaluate actual results.

Sales Forecasts

The first, and perhaps the most critical, step in constructing a set of pro forma financial statements is the sales forecast. Actually, this is part of the firm's marketing plan, but it is of such pervasive importance that we need to discuss it here. The sales forecast generally starts with a review of sales over the past 5 to 10 years, expressed in a graph such as Figure 23-1. The first part of the graph shows actual sales for Telecomp Cor-

Figure 23-1
Telecomp Corporation: 1985 Sales Projection

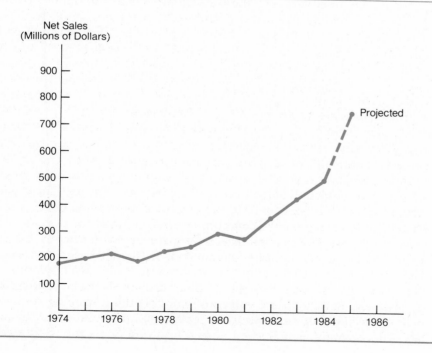

poration from 1974 through 1984. During this 10-year period, sales grew from $175 million to $500 million, or at a compound annual growth rate of 11.1 percent. However, the growth rate has accelerated sharply in recent years, primarily as a result of regulatory changes in the telecommunications market which forced the major national telephone companies to start buying from companies such as Telecomp when they had products that were competitive with the telephone companies' own captive manufacturing companies. Also, Telecomp's R&D program had been especially successful, so when the telecommunications market broke open, Telecomp was ready.

Based on the recent trend in sales, on new product introductions, and on a forecast by Telecomp's economics staff that the national economy will be strong during the coming year, Telecomp's planning group projects a 50 percent growth rate during 1985, to a sales level of $750 million.

Of course, a great deal of work lies behind all good sales forecasts. Companies must project the state of the national economy, economic conditions within their own geographic areas, and conditions in the product markets they serve. Further, they must consider their own pricing strategies, credit policies, advertising programs, capacity limitations, and the like. They must also consider the strategies and policies of their competitors—the introduction of new products by IBM, AT&T, or the Japanese, and also more aggressive pricing by these and other companies, could seriously affect Telecomp's 1985 sales forecast.

If the sales forecast is off, the consequences could be serious. If the market expanded *more* than Telecomp expected and geared up for, then it would not be able to meet its customers' needs. Orders would back up, delivery times would lengthen, repair and installations would be harder to schedule, and customer unhappiness would increase. Customers would end up going elsewhere, Telecomp would lose market share, and it would have missed a major opportunity. On the other hand, if its projections are overly optimistic, Telecomp would end up with too much plant, equipment, and inventories, resulting in unneeded capital costs, low turnover ratios, high costs for depreciation and storage, and, possibly, write-offs of obsolete inventory and equipment. All of this would result in a low rate of return on equity, which in turn would depress the company's stock price. If Telecomp had financed the expansion with debt, its problems would, of course, be compounded. Thus, an accurate sales forecast is critical to the well-being of the firm.

Note that the $750 million sales forecast for 1985 is actually the expected value of a probability distribution of possible levels of sales. Thus, we are interested not only in the expected sales level, but also in the distribution about the expected value. If the probability distribution is relatively tight, then the company will have more confidence in its sales projection. In that event, its operating plans can be relatively firm—for example, it can afford to sign firm purchase contracts for materials on a long-term basis, to make long-run commitments during labor negotiations, and so on. On the other hand, if the sales projections are "iffy," then the company will want to build flexibility into its operating plans, to monitor sales trends very closely, and to cut back production immediately if demand falls below the forecasted level.

Percentage of Sales Forecasting

Several methods are used to forecast financial statements, and in this chapter, we present five of them: (1) percentage of sales, (2) linear regression, (3) curvilinear regression, (4) multiple regression, and (5) specific item forecasting. We begin with the *percentage of sales* method, a simple but often practical procedure for forecasting financial statement variables. The procedure is based on two assumptions: (1) that all variables are tied directly to sales, and (2) that the current levels of most balance sheet items are optimal for the current sales level. We illustrate the process with Telecomp Corporation, whose 1984 financial statements are given in Table 23-3. Telecomp was required to operate its fixed assets at full capacity to support the $500 million in sales in 1984; it had no excess stocks of inventories; and its cash balances were in line with sales of $500 million. Its 1984 profit margin was 4 percent, and it distributed 40 percent of its net income to stockholders as dividends. If Telecomp's sales increase to $750 million in 1985, what will its pro forma 1985 income statement, balance sheet, and statement of changes in financial position look like, and how much external financing will the company require during 1985?

The first step in the percentage of sales forecast is to isolate those income statement and balance sheet items that vary directly with sales. On the income statement, increased sales are expected to bring direct increases in all of the variables except interest expense. That is, cost of goods sold and selling and administrative expenses are assumed to be tied directly to sales, but interest expense is a function of financing decisions. Further, Telecomp's federal, state, and local taxes are expected to continue to amount to 50 percent of pre-tax income.

Turning to the balance sheet, since Telecomp was operating at full capacity, fixed assets as well as current assets must increase if sales are to rise. Thus, each asset item must increase if the higher level of sales is to be attained. More cash will be needed for transactions, receivables will be higher, additional inventory must be stocked, and new plant must be added.[2]

If Telecomp's assets are to increase, its liabilities and/or net worth must likewise rise—the balance sheet must balance, and increases in

---

[2]Some assets, such as marketable securities, are not tied directly to operations, and hence do not vary directly with sales. In fact, marketable securities, if they had been held, could be run down to zero, thus reducing the external funding requirement.

Table 23-3
Telecomp Corporation: Financial Statements
(Millions of Dollars)

	For the Year Ended December 31, 1984
Income Statement	
Net sales	$500
Cost of goods sold	400
Selling and administrative expenses	52
Earnings before interest and taxes	$ 48
Interest expense	8
Earnings before taxes	$ 40
Taxes (50%)	20
Net income	$ 20
Dividends (payout: 40%)	$ 8
Addition to retained earnings	$ 12

	As of December 31, 1984
Balance Sheet	
Cash	$ 10
Receivables	85
Inventories	100
Total current assets	$195
Net fixed assets	150
Total assets	$345
Accounts payable	$ 40
Notes payable (8%)	10
Accrued wages and taxes	25
Total current liabilities	$ 75
Mortgage bonds (10%)	72
Common stock	150
Retained earnings	48
Total claims	$345

assets must be financed in some manner. Accounts payable and accruals will rise *spontaneously* with sales: As sales increase, so will purchases, and larger purchases will result in higher levels of accounts payable. Thus, if sales double, accounts payable will also double. Similarly, a higher level of operations will require more labor, so accrued wages will increase, and, assuming profit margins are maintained, an increase in profits will pull up accrued taxes. Retained earnings should also increase, but not in direct proportion to the increase in sales. Neither notes payable, nor mortgage bonds, nor common stock will rise spontaneously with sales—higher sales do not *automatically* trigger increases in these items.

We can construct pro forma financial statements for December 31, 1985, proceeding as outlined in the following paragraphs.

Step 1. In Table 23-4, Column 1, we express those income statement and balance sheet items that vary directly with sales as a percentage of 1984 sales. An item such as notes payable that does not vary directly with sales is designated n.a., or "not applicable."

Step 2. Next, we multiply these percentages (their fractions, really) by the $750 million projected 1985 sales to obtain the projected 1985 amounts. These are shown in Column 2 of the table.

Step 3. We simply insert figures for interest expense, dividends, notes payable, mortgage bonds, and common stock from 1984. At least one of these accounts will have to be changed later in the analysis.

Step 4. We next add the addition to retained earnings estimated for 1985 to the figure shown on the December 31, 1984, balance sheet to obtain the December 31, 1985, projected retained earnings. Telecomp, ignoring any additional interest expense, would have a net income of $32 million in 1985. If the firm does not increase its dividend in 1985, the total dividend payment would be $8 million, leaving $32 million − $8 million = $24 million of new retained earnings.[3] Thus, the 1985 balance sheet account retained earnings would be $48 million + $24 million = $72 million.

Step 5. Next, we sum the balance sheet asset accounts, obtaining a projected total assets figure of $518 million, and we also sum the projected liabilities and net worth items to obtain $402 million, the estimated available funds. Since claims must total $518 million, but only $402 million is projected, we have a shortfall of $116 million, which will presumably be raised by bank borrowing and/or by selling securities. For simplicity, we disregard depreciation by assuming that cash flows generated by depreciation are used to replace worn-out fixed assets.

---

[3]Normally, companies attempt to "grow" their dividends at a relatively stable rate, and they also have a long-run target payout ratio in mind which is reasonably consistent with the targeted growth rate. However, dividend policy is invariably reviewed as a part of the financial planning process. In its planning, Telecomp begins by holding constant the dollar dividend per share at the earlier year level, but it modifies this figure at a later stage in the process.

Table 23-4
Telecomp Corporation: Pro Forma Financial Statements
(Millions of Dollars)

	Percent of 1984 Sales (1)	1985 Projections[a] (2)
Income Statement		
Net sales	100.0%	$750
Cost of goods sold	80.0	600
Selling and administrative expenses	10.4	78
Earnings before interest and taxes	9.6%	$ 72
Interest expense	n.a.[b]	8[c]
Earnings before taxes	n.a.	$ 64
Taxes (50%)	n.a.	32
Net income	n.a.	$ 32
Dividends	n.a.	$ 8[c]
Addition to retained earnings	n.a.	$ 24

	Percent of 1984 Sales (1)	1985 Projections[a] (2)
Balance Sheet		
Cash	2.0%	$ 15
Receivables	17.0	128
Inventories	20.0	150
Total current assets	39.0%	$293
Net fixed assets	30.0	225
Total assets	69.0%	$518
Accounts payable	8.0%	$ 60
Notes payable (8%)	n.a.	10[c]
Accrued wages and taxes	5.0	38
Total current liabilities	n.a.	$108
Mortgage bonds (10%)	n.a.	72[c]
Common stock	n.a.	150[c]
Retained earnings	n.a.	72[d]
Total claims	n.a.	$402

External funds needed = Projected total assets − Projected claims
= $518 million − $402 million = $116 million.

[a]1985 projection = Column 1 fraction x $750 projected sales level.

[b]Not applicable (item does not vary spontaneously with sales).

[c]Initially projected at the 1984 level. Later financing decisions might change this level.

[d]1984 retained earnings balance plus projected 1985 addition to retained earnings = $48 million + $24 million = $72 million.

Telecomp could use short-term notes, mortgage bonds, common stock, or a combination of these securities to make up the shortfall. Ordinarily, it would make this choice on the basis of its target capital structure, the relative costs of different types of securities, maturity matching considerations, and so on. However, in Telecomp's case, the company has a contractual agreement with its mortgage bondholders to keep total debt at or below 50 percent of total assets, and also to keep the current ratio at a level of 2.5 or greater. These provisions restrict the financing choices as follows (in millions of dollars):

Financing the External Requirements

1. **Restriction on additional debt**

$$\text{Maximum debt permitted} = (0.5)(\text{Total assets})$$
$$= (0.5)(\$518) = \qquad \$259$$

Subtract debt already projected
for December 31, 1985:

Current liabilities	$108	
Mortgage bonds	72	180
Maximum additional debt		$ 79

2. **Restriction on additional current liabilities to maintain 2.5× current ratio**

$$\frac{\text{Projected current assets}}{\text{Maximum current liabilities}} = 2.5$$

Maximum current liabilities = Projected current assets/2.5	
= $293/2.5 =	$117
Subtract current liabilities already projected	108
Maximum additional current liabilities	$ 9

3. **Common equity requirements**

Total external funds needed	$116
Maximum additional debt permitted	79
Common equity funds required	$ 37

From Table 23-4, we saw that, as a first approximation, Telecomp needs a total of $116 million from external sources. Its existing debt contract limits new debt to $79 million, and of that amount, only $9 million can be short-term debt. Thus, assuming that Telecomp wants to make maximum use of debt financing, it must plan to sell common stock in the amount of $37 million, in addition to its debt financing, to cover its financial requirements.

However, the use of external funds will change the forecasted income statement for 1985 as set forth in Table 23-4. First, the issuance of new debt will increase the firm's 1985 interest expense. Second, the sale of new common stock will increase the total dividend payments, assuming that dividends per share are not reduced. Telecomp is forecasting that new short-term debt will cost 10 percent, and that new long-term debt will cost 12 percent. Additionally, Telecomp has 10 million shares of common stock outstanding, and it currently sells for $30 per share. Thus, Telecomp's shareholders received $8 million/10 million = $0.80 dividends per share in 1984, and management has stated that the dividend is not to be cut.

Now, if Telecomp finances in 1985 as outlined above, and if the external financing occurs on January 1, 1985, then its income statement expenses and dividends would increase by the following amounts:

Additional Interest Requirements

Short-term interest = 0.10($9,000,000)   = $ 900,000
Long-term interest = 0.12($70,000,000)   = 8,400,000
      Total additional interest   = $9,300,000 ≈ $9 million.

Additional Dividend Requirements

New shares = $37,000,000/$30 per share = 1,233,333.
Additional dividends = $0.80(1,233,333) = $986,667 ≈ $1 million.

The projected 1985 income statement and balance sheet, including financing feedback effects, are contained in Table 23-5. We see that Telecomp is still $6 million short in meeting its financing requirements, because interest and dividends associated with external financing reduced the addition to retained earnings from $24 million, before feedback effects were considered, to $18 million. Telecomp's managers could repeat the above process with an additional $6 million of external financing. In this case, the additional $6 million would have to be raised as equity, because Telecomp has already issued debt up to its limit. The addition to retained earnings would be further reduced by additional dividend requirements, but the balance sheet would be closer to being in balance. Successive iterations would continue to reduce the discrepancy. If the budget process is computerized, as would be true for most firms, an exact solution can be reached very rapidly. Otherwise, firms will go through two or three iterations and then stop. At this point, the projected statements will generally be very close to being in balance, and they will certainly be close enough for practical purposes, given the uncertainty inherent in the projections themselves.

For Telecomp, the additional $6 million of new equity will have a minimal feedback effect. Thus, we could use Table 23-5, with $193 million in common stock, as the projected 1985 income statement and balance sheet. These statements can then be used (1) to create the pro forma statement of changes in financial condition and (2) to check Telecomp's critical financial ratios. This is done in Table 23-6.

Table 23-5
Telecomp Corporation: Pro Forma Financial Statements
Including Feedback Effect
(Millions of Dollars)

Income Statement	1985 Projection
Net sales	$750
Cost of goods sold	600
Selling and administrative expense	78
Earnings before interest and taxes	$ 72
Interest expense	17[a]
Earnings before taxes	$ 55
Taxes (50%)	28
Net income	$ 27
Dividends	9[b]
Addition to retained earnings	$ 18

Balance Sheet	1985 Projection
Cash	$ 15
Receivables	128
Inventories	150
Total current assets	$293
Net fixed assets	225
Total assets	$518
Accounts payable	$ 60
Notes payable (8% and 10%)	19[c]
Accrued wages and taxes	38
Total current liabilities	$117
Mortgage bonds (10% and 12%)	142[d]
Common stock	187[e]
Retained earnings	66[f]
Total claims	$512

External financing requirements = $518 million − $512 million = $6 million.

[a]$8 million from 1984 plus $9 million from new debt financing.

[b]$8 million on old shares plus $1 million on new shares.

[c]$10 million of old notes payable plus $9 million of new short-term debt.

[d]$72 million of old mortgage bonds plus $70 million of new bonds.

[e]$150 of old common stock plus a new issue of $37 million.

[f]1984 retained earnings balance plus projected 1985 additions = $48 million + $18 million = $66 million.

Table 23-6
Telecomp Corporation: Pro Forma Statement
of Changes in Financial Position
for the Year Ending December 31, 1985
(Millions of Dollars)

Projected Sources of Funds

Funds from operations: net income[a]	$ 27
Proceeds from sale of bonds	70
Proceeds from sale of common stock	43
Total sources	$140

Projected Uses of Funds

Dividend payments	$ 9
Increase in net fixed assets	75
Increase in net working capital	56
Total uses	$140

Analysis of Changes in Working Capital

Increase (decrease) in current assets:	
Cash	$ 5
Accounts receivable	43
Inventories	50
Net increase (decrease) in current assets	$ 98
Increase (decrease) in current liabilities:	
Accounts payable	$ 20
Notes payable	9
Accruals	13
Net increase (decrease) in current liabilities	$ 42
Increase (decrease) in net working capital	$ 56

Key Ratios Projected for December 31, 1985

1. Current ratio	2.5 times
2. Total debt/total assets	50%
3. Rate of return on equity	10.4%

(Other ratios could also be calculated and analyzed, and a Du Pont chart could be developed.)

[a]Normally "Funds from operations" would include depreciation. Here, we have assumed that depreciation is reinvested in fixed assets; that is, depreciation is netted out against fixed asset additions.

Factors Influencing External Financing Requirements

The five factors which have the greatest influence on a firm's external funding requirements are (1) its projected sales growth, (2) its initial fixed asset utilization, (3) its capital intensity, (4) its profit margin, and (5) its dividend policy. We discuss each of these factors in this section.

The faster Telecomp's sales grow, the greater is its need for external financing. At very low growth rates, Telecomp needs no external financing; all required funds can be obtained by spontaneous increases in current liability accounts plus retained earnings. However, if the company's projected sales growth rate increases beyond a certain level, then it must seek outside financing, and the faster the projected growth rate, the greater the need for outside capital. The reasoning here is as follows: *Sales Growth*

1. Increases in sales normally require increases in assets. If sales were not projected to grow, no new assets would be needed. The projected asset increases require financing of some type.

2. Some of the financing needed to support asset increases comes from spontaneously generated liabilities. Also, assuming a positive profit margin and a payout ratio of less than 100 percent, the firm will generate some retained earnings.

3. If the sales growth rate is low enough, spontaneously generated funds plus retained earnings will be sufficient to support the asset growth. However, if the sales growth rate exceeds a certain level, then external funds will be needed. If management foresees difficulties in raising this capital—perhaps because the current owners do not want to sell additional stock—then they may need to reconsider the feasibility of expansion plans.

In determining Telecomp's external financing requirements for 1985, we assumed that its fixed assets were being fully utilized.[4] Thus, any material increase in sales would require an increase in fixed assets. What would be the effect if Telecomp had been operating its fixed assets at only 70 percent of capacity? Under this condition, fixed assets would not have had to increase until sales have reached that level at which fixed assets were being fully utilized, defined as *capacity sales*. Since *Output/Capacity Relationship*

$$\text{Utilization rate} = \frac{\text{Current sales}}{\text{Capacity sales}},$$

we see that

$$\text{Capacity sales} = \frac{\text{Current sales}}{\text{Utilization rate}}.$$

If Telecomp were operating in 1984 at 70 percent of capacity, then its capacity sales would be $714 million:

$$\text{Capacity sales} = \frac{\$500 \text{ million}}{0.70} = \$714 \text{ million}.$$

---

[4]We also assumed that depreciation-generated funds were being used to replace worn-out assets, and that no excess stocks of current assets existed.

Thus, Telecomp could increase sales to $714 million with no increase in fixed assets, and to reach its projected sales of $750 million in 1985, it would require only enough new fixed assets to support the sales increase from $714 million to $750 million, or $36 million of new sales.

Operating at less than full capacity can be incorporated into the pro forma balance sheet as follows:

1. Calculate a new target fixed assets percentage of sales based on capacity sales rather than on current sales. If Telecomp were operating at 70 percent of capacity in 1984, then its target fixed assets percentage of sales would be $150/$714 = 0.21, rather than the $150/$500 = 0.30 that we calculated earlier and used in Table 23-4 to determine the 1985 fixed assets requirement.

2. Use the new percentage of sales to forecast the 1985 level of fixed assets. For Telecomp, the 1985 level would be 0.21($750) = $158 million, rather than the $225 million originally projected. Thus, operating at only 70 percent of capacity in 1984 reduces the 1985 projected net fixed assets account by $225 million − $158 million = $67 million. This decrease in projected assets, in turn, reduces external funding requirements by a like amount. Obviously, operating at less than full capacity has a significant impact on the need for external funds.

Capital Intensity

The amount of assets required per dollar of sales is often called the *capital intensity ratio*. Notice that the capital intensity ratio is the reciprocal of the total asset turnover ratio. This factor has a major effect on capital requirements per unit of sales growth. If the capital intensity ratio is low, then sales can grow rapidly without much outside capital. However, if the firm is capital intensive, then even a small growth in output will require a great deal of outside capital.

Profit Margin

The profit margin is also an important determinant of external funds requirements—the higher the profit margin, the lower the external financing requirement, other things held constant. Telecomp's profit margin in 1984 was 4 percent. Now suppose its profit margin increased to 10 percent through higher sales prices and better expense control. This would increase net income, and hence retained earnings (assuming a constant payout), which in turn would decrease the requirement for external funds.

Because of the relationship between profit margin and external capital requirements, some very rapidly growing firms do not need much external capital. For example, for many years Xerox grew rapidly with very little borrowing or stock sales. However, as the company lost patent protection, and as competition intensified in the copier industry, Xerox's profit margin declined, its needs for external capital rose, and it began to borrow from banks and other sources. IBM and a number of other companies have had similar experiences.

Dividend policy also affects external capital requirements, so if Telecomp foresees difficulties in raising capital, it might want to consider a reduction in its dividend payout ratio. However, before making this decision, management should consider the effects of changes in dividends on stock prices.[5]

Dividend Policy

Problems with the Percentage of Sales Approach

To this point, we have generally assumed that the financial statement ratios are expected to remain constant over time. For the ratios to remain constant, each item must increase at the same rate as sales. In graph form, this assumption suggests the existence of the type of relationship indicated in Panel a of Figure 23-2, where we graph inventory versus sales. Here the plotted relationship is linear and passes through the origin. Thus, if the company grows and sales expand from $200 million to $400 million, inventories will increase proportionately, from $100 million to $200 million.

The assumption of constant ratios is appropriate at times, but there are times when it is incorrect. Three such conditions are described in the following sections.

There are economies of scale in the use of many kinds of assets, and where they occur, the ratios are likely to change over time as the size of the firm increases. Often, for example, firms need to maintain base stocks of different inventory items, even if sales levels are quite low. Then, as sales expand, inventories tend to grow less rapidly than sales, so the ratio of inventory to sales declines. This situation is depicted in Panel b of Figure 23-2. Here we see that the inventory/sales ratio is 1.5, or 150 percent, when sales are $200 million, but the ratio declines to 1.0 when sales climb to $400 million.

Economies of Scale

Panel b still shows a linear relationship between inventories and sales, but even this is not necessarily the case. Indeed, as we saw in Chapter 19, if a firm employs the EOQ model to establish inventory levels, then inventory will rise with the square root of sales. This means that the graph in Panel b would tend to be a curved line whose slope decreases at higher sales levels.

---

[5]Dividend policy was discussed in detail in Chapter 13. Note that if management believes that dividends are irrelevant, Telecomp could adopt a residual dividend policy and use retained earnings to the maximum extent to meet equity financing requirements. However, if dividend irrelevance is not considered valid, then changes in dividend policy would be assumed to affect stock prices, and the trade-off between retained earnings financing and new stock financing would become more complex.

Figure 23-2
Three Possible Ratio Relationships
(Millions of Dollars)

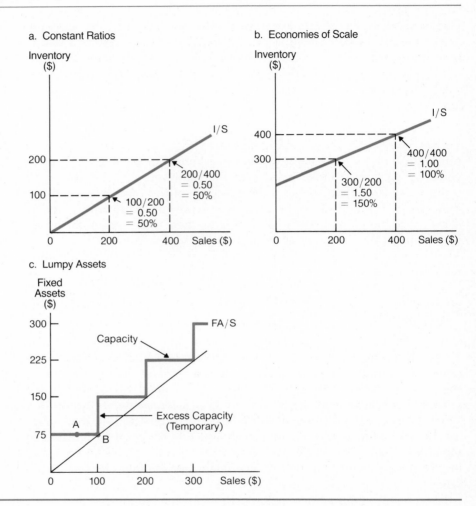

a. Constant Ratios

Inventory
($)

200/400
= 0.50
= 50%

100/200
= 0.50
= 50%

b. Economies of Scale

Inventory
($)

400/400
= 1.00
= 100%

300/200
= 1.50
= 150%

c. Lumpy Assets

Fixed
Assets
($)

Capacity

Excess Capacity
(Temporary)

"Lumpy" Assets   In many industries, technological considerations dictate that if a firm is to be competitive, it must add fixed assets in large, discrete units. For example, in the paper industry, there are strong economies of scale in basic paper mill equipment, so when paper companies expand capacity, they must do so in large increments. This type of situation is depicted in Panel c of Figure 23-2. Here we assume that the minimum-sized feasible plant has a cost of $75 million, and that such a plant can produce enough output to attain a sales level of $100 million per year. If the firm is to be competitive, it simply must have at least $75 million of fixed assets.

This situation has a major effect on the fixed assets/sales (FA/S) ratio at different sales levels, and consequently on financial requirements. At Point A in Panel c, which represents a sales level of $50 million, the fixed assets are $75 million, so the ratio FA/S = $75/$50 = 1.5. However, sales can expand by $50 million, out to $100 million, with no required increase in fixed assets. At that point, represented by Point B, the ratio FA/S = $75/$100 = 0.75. From capacity operations, even a small increase in sales would require the firm to double its plant capacity, so a small projected sales increase would bring with it very large financial requirements.[6]

Panels a, b, and c of Figure 23-2 all focus on target, or projected, relationships between sales and assets. Actual sales, however, are often different from projected sales, and the actual asset/sales ratio for a given period may thus be quite different from the planned ratio. To illustrate, the firm depicted in Panel b might, when its sales are at $200 million and its inventories at $300 million, predict a sales expansion to $400 million and then increase its inventories to $400 million in anticipation of the sales expansion. But suppose an unforeseen economic downturn holds sales to only $300 million. In this case, actual inventories would be $400 million versus only about $350 million needed to support sales of $300 million. In this situation, if the firm were forecasting its financial requirements, it should recognize that sales can be expanded by $100 million with no increase in inventories, but that any sales expansion beyond $100 million would require additional financing to build inventories.

If any of the ratios are subject to any of the conditions noted above, the simple percentage of sales method of forecasting financial requirements should not be used. Rather, other techniques must be used to forecast financial statement item levels and the resulting external financing requirements. Some of these methods are discussed in the following sections.

Cyclical Changes

---

[6]Several other points should be noted about Panel c of Figure 23-2. First, if the firm is operating at a sales level of $100 million or less, then any expansion that calls for a sales increase above $100 million will require a *doubling* of the firm's fixed assets. Much smaller percentage increases would be involved if the firm is large enough to be operating a number of plants. Second, firms generally go to multiple shifts and take other actions to minimize the need for new fixed asset capacity as they approach Point B. However, these efforts can go only so far, and eventually a fixed asset expansion is required. Third, firms often make arrangements to purchase excess capacity output from other firms in their industry, or to sell excess capacity to other firms. For example, consider the situation in the electric utility industry. It is very much like that depicted in Panel c. Electric companies often arrange to buy excess capacity from other companies in order to avoid building a new plant that will be underutilized. At other times, they sell excess power from a newly completed plant for a number of years, until their own customer demand catches up with their output capacity.

Simple Linear Regression

If we assume that the relationship between a variable and sales is linear, then we can use simple linear regression techniques to estimate the asset requirements for any given sales increase. For example, Telecomp's sales, receivables, inventories, and net fixed asset levels over the last 11 years are contained in Table 23-7. These values are then plotted in Figure 23-3 as scatter diagrams of receivables, inventories, and net fixed assets versus sales. Estimated regression equations as found with a hand calculator are also shown in Figure 23-3. For example, the estimated relationship between inventories and sales (in millions of dollars) is

$$\text{Inventories} = \$20 + 0.16 \, (\text{Sales}).$$

The plotted points are quite close to the regression line. In fact, the correlation coefficient between inventories and sales is 0.98, indicating that there is a very strong linear relationship between these two variables. Why might this be the case for Telecomp? According to the EOQ model, inventories should increase with the square root of sales, which would cause the scatter diagram to be nonlinear—the true regression line would rise at a decreasing rate. However, Telecomp has greatly expanded its product line over the last decade, and the base stocks associated with new products could cause inventories to rise proportionately more than sales. These two influences—economies of scale in existing products and base stocks for new products—appear to be offsetting, resulting in a linear relationship between inventories and sales.

Forecasting by Linear Regression

We can use the estimated relationship between inventories and sales to forecast 1985 inventory levels. Since 1985 sales are projected at $750 million, 1985 inventories should be $140 million:

$$\text{Inventories} = \$20 + 0.16(\$750) = \$140 \text{ million.}$$

Table 23-7
Telecomp Corporation:
Selected Financial Statement Levels
(Millions of Dollars)

Year	Sales	Accounts Receivable	Inventories	Net Fixed Assets
1974	$175	$33	$ 44	$ 78
1975	200	38	48	83
1976	215	44	53	86
1977	185	35	57	79
1978	235	43	60	91
1979	265	45	66	98
1980	300	52	73	106
1981	280	47	70	101
1982	350	61	78	118
1983	420	71	90	135
1984	500	85	100	150

Figure 23-3
Telecomp Corporation: Linear Regression Models
(Millions of Dollars)

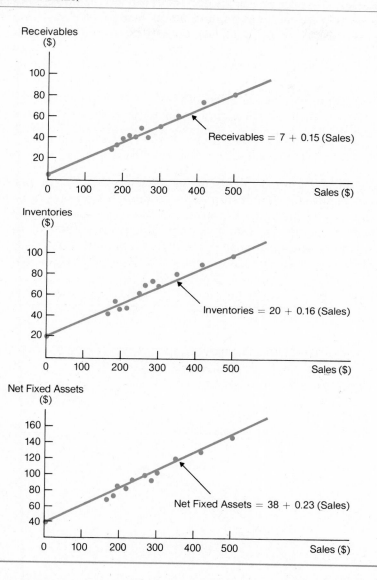

This is $10 million less than our earlier forecast based on the percentage of sales method. The difference occurs because the percentage of sales method assumes that the ratio of inventories to sales remains constant, but it actually declines because the regression line in Figure 23-3 does not pass through the origin.

We have illustrated the use of the regression method for forecasting just one account—inventories. However, we also estimated the relationships between both receivables and net fixed assets versus sales, and we will use these relationships later in the chapter, where we develop a computerized forecasting model for Telecomp. We could actually use the same process for all appropriate financial statement items, but first, in the next section, we discuss several other forecasting techniques.

Other Forecasting Methods

In this section, we discuss three additional forecasting methods that are commonly used in practice: curvilinear regression, multiple regression, and specific item forecasting using such procedures as the EOQ model.

Simple Curvilinear Regression

Simple linear regression as discussed above is based on the assumption that a straight-line relationship exists. Although linear relationships between financial statement variables and sales do exist frequently, this is not a universal rule. For example, if the EOQ relationship had dominated the inventory-sales relationship, the plot of inventory versus sales would have been a concave curve such as the one depicted in Figure 23-4. Here,

Figure 23-4
Simple Curvilinear Regression
(Millions of Dollars)

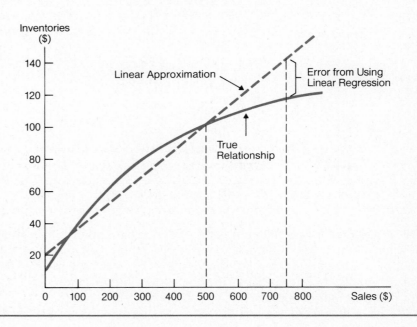

the true relationship between inventories and sales is shown by the curved solid line, and not by the dashed line linear approximation. If we forecast 1985 inventories based on the linear relationship, but the true relationship were actually curvilinear, we would forecast too high an inventory level.

Firms have in their data bases historical data on their own company by divisions, product lines, and individual products. They also have or can easily obtain certain types of data for other firms in their industry. These data can be analyzed using computer programs based on advanced statistical techniques which can be utilized (1) to help determine whether a relationship is curvilinear or linear and (2) to estimate the curvilinear relationship. Once the best-fit relationship has been estimated, it can be used to project future levels of items such as inventories, given a specific sales forecast.

Multiple Regression

If the relationship between a variable such as inventories and sales appears to be either linear or curvilinear, but the individual points are widely scattered about the regression line, and hence the correlation coefficient is low, then there is a good chance that other factors, in addition to sales, affect the level of that variable. For example, inventory levels might be a function of both sales level and number of different products sold. In this case, we would obtain the best forecast for inventory level by using multiple regression techniques, where inventories would be regressed against both sales and the number of products sold. Then, the projected inventories would be based on forecasts of number of products in addition to total sales. Most computer installations now have complete regression software packages, making it easy to apply multiple and curvilinear regression techniques. We anticipate that even personal computers will be able to handle these techniques within a year or two.

Specific Item Forecasting

A final approach to financial forecasting is to develop a specific model for each variable. For example, inventories could be forecasted using the EOQ model; target cash balances could be forecasted using the Baumol model; receivables could be forecasted using the payments pattern model; and fixed assets could be forecasted on the basis of the firm's capital budget and depreciation schedule. Of course, projected sales demand is still the driving force behind each of these specific forecasts, but each item could be analyzed by its own unique forecasting method. Similarly, on the income statement side, a firm could forecast its cost of goods sold by conducting an engineering/production analysis of each major product. Specific item analysis is likely to provide the most accurate forecasts, but it is also the most expensive and time consuming forecasting method.

Comparison of Forecasting Methods

The percentage of sales method assumes that different financial statement items vary directly with sales. It is the easiest and least expensive method, but often its forecasts are of questionable accuracy. Simple linear regression differs from the percentage of sales method in that linear regression does not assume constant ratios. This technique can improve on the forecasts for many financial statement items. Curvilinear and multiple regression techniques can provide still better forecasts when relationships (1) are not linear or (2) depend on other variables in addition to sales. Finally, specific item forecasting that utilizes various decision models can be used.

As we move down the list of forecasting methods, accuracy increases, but so do costs. The need to employ more complicated, and more costly, methods varies from situation to situation. As in all applications, the costs of using more refined techniques must be balanced against the benefits of increased accuracy.

Computerized Financial Planning Models

Although the types of financial forecasting described in this chapter can be done with a hand calculator, most well-managed firms with sales greater than a few million dollars employ some type of computerized financial planning model. Such models can be programmed to show the effects of different sales levels, different relationships between sales and operating assets, and even different assumptions about sales prices and input costs (labor, materials, and so forth). Plans are then made regarding how projected financial requirements are to be met—through short-term bank loans, by selling long-term bonds, or by selling new common or preferred stock. Pro forma balance sheets and income statements are generated under the different financing plans, and earnings per share are projected, along with such risk and profitability measures as the current ratio, the debt/assets ratio, the times-interest-earned ratio, return on assets, and return on equity.

Depending on how these projections look, management may modify the initial plan. For example, the firm may conclude that its projected growth rate must be cut because external capital requirements exceed the firm's ability to raise money. Or, management may decide to reduce dividends and thus generate more funds internally. Alternatively, the company may investigate production processes that require fewer fixed assets, or consider the possibility of buying rather than manufacturing certain components, thus eliminating some raw materials and work-in-process inventories, as well as certain manufacturing facilities.

To illustrate how computerized forecasting models work, we have constructed a financial statement generation model for Telecomp Corporation using *IFPS*.[7] In the model, we defined the key variables' relationship with sales as shown in Table 23-8; these relationships were developed through a linear regression analysis. Further, we assumed (1) that sales will grow at an annual rate of 50 percent in both 1985 and 1986, at a 25 percent rate in 1987, and at a 15 percent rate in 1988 and 1989; (2) that dividends will be increased by 10 percent per year over the next five years; (3) that the stock price will grow at an annual rate of 20 percent during the next five years; (4) that the state-plus-federal income tax rate will be 50 percent for the next five years; (5) that 4 percent of any external financing needs will be met with short-term notes, 26 percent of requirements will be met with bonds, and 70 percent with equity; (6) that all new financing will occur on January 1 of the year in which it is needed; (7) that new short-term debt will cost 10 percent and new long-term debt will cost 12 percent; and (8) that flotation costs are insignificant and thus can be ignored.

The *IFPS* model automatically performs the financing feedback iterations and prints the final results. In Table 23-9, we show the set of pro forma income statements and balance sheets, along with projected EPS and some selected financial ratios. Of course, we could have also produced a statement of changes in financial position as well as a full set of financial ratios. We see that, under the above assumptions, Telecomp's financial condition will improve continually over the next five years. However, to support the growth in sales, Telecomp must raise a total of over $256 million through external funding.

*The Basic
Forecasting Model*

Table 23-8
**Variable to Sales Relationships
(Millions of Dollars)**

Variable	Relationship to Sales
Cost of goods sold	0.80 (Sales)
Administrative and selling expenses	$27 + 0.05 (Sales)
Cash	0.02 (Sales)
Receivables	$7 + 0.15 (Sales)
Inventories	$20 + 0.16 (Sales)
Net fixed assets	$38 + 0.23 (Sales)
Accounts payable	0.08 (Sales)
Accrued wages and taxes	0.05 (Sales)

---

[7] Appendix 10E for Chapter 10 in the *Instructor's Manual* discusses the *Interactive Financial Planning System (IFPS)*. We also set up the Telecomp forecast on an electronic spreadsheet (*VisiCalc*). That simplified the work greatly vis-à-vis generating the statements by hand, but spreadsheets are unable to automatically iterate and zero in on the set of values for all variables which balances the accounts. *IFPS* has a procedure for solving a set of simultaneous equations which brings about this balance almost instantaneously.

Table 23-9
Telecomp Corporation: Base Case
Pro Forma Financial Statements
(Millions of Dollars, except for per Share Amounts)

	1984	1985	1986	1987	1988	1989
Stock price	$ 30.00	$ 36.00	$ 43.20	$ 51.84	$ 62.21	$ 74.65
DPS	$ 0.80	$ 0.88	$ 0.97	$ 1.07	$ 1.17	$ 1.29
Growth rate	n.a.	50%	50%	25%	15%	15%
Income Statements						
Net sales	$500.00	$750.00	$1,125.00	$1,406.00	$1,616.00	$1,860.00
Cost of goods sold	400.00	600.00	900.00	1,125.00	1,294.00	1,488.00
Operating expenses	52.00	64.50	83.25	97.31	107.90	120.00
EBIT	$ 48.00	$ 85.50	$ 141.50	$ 183.90	$ 215.60	$ 252.00
Interest expense	8.00	10.83	14.72	16.56	16.84	17.02
EBT	$ 40.00	$ 74.67	$ 127.00	$ 167.40	$ 198.70	$ 234.90
Taxes	20.00	37.34	63.51	83.69	99.37	117.50
Net income	$ 20.00	$ 37.34	$ 63.51	$ 83.69	$ 99.37	$ 117.50
Dividends	$ 8.00	$ 10.17	$ 12.93	$ 14.97	$ 16.57	$ 18.29
Addition to retained earnings	$ 12.00	$ 27.16	$ 50.59	$ 68.72	$ 82.80	$ 99.18
EPS	$ 2.00	$ 3.23	$ 4.76	$ 5.95	$ 7.02	$ 8.27
Balance Sheets						
Assets						
Cash	$ 10.00	$ 15.00	$ 22.50	$ 28.13	$ 32.34	$ 37.20
Receivables	82.00	119.50	175.80	217.90	249.60	286.00
Inventories	100.00	140.00	200.00	245.00	278.80	317.60
Total current assets	$192.00	$274.50	$ 398.30	$ 491.10	$ 560.70	$ 640.70
Net fixed assets	153.00	210.50	396.80	361.40	410.00	465.70
Total assets	$345.00	$485.00	$ 695.00	$ 852.50	$ 970.60	$1,106.00
Liabilities						
Accounts payable	$ 40.00	60.00	90.00	112.50	129.40	148.80
Notes payable	10.00	13.21	17.64	19.73	20.05	20.25
Accrued wages and taxes	25.00	37.50	56.25	70.31	80.86	92.99
Total current liabilities	$ 75.00	$110.70	$ 163.90	$ 202.50	$ 230.30	$ 262.00
Bonds	72.00	92.89	121.70	125.20	137.30	138.60
Common stock	150.00	206.20	283.70	320.30	325.80	329.40
Retained earnings	48.00	75.16	125.70	194.50	277.30	376.40
Total claims	$345.00	$485.00	$ 695.00	$ 852.50	$ 970.60	$1,106.00

Table 23-9 *(continued)*

	1984	1985	1986	1987	1988	1989
Funding Requirements						
External funding	n.a.	$80.34	$110.70	$52.22	$7.91	$5.13
Surplus cash	n.a.	$ 0	$ 0	$ 0	$ 0	$ 0
New notes payable	n.a.	$ 3.21	$ 4.43	$ 2.09	$0.35	$0.21
New bonds	n.a.	$20.89	$ 28.77	$13.58	$2.06	$1.33
New stock	n.a.	$56.24	$ 77.47	$36.55	$5.54	$3.59
New shares sold	n.a.	1.56	1.79	0.71	0.09	0.05
Total shares outstanding	10.00	11.56	13.36	14.06	14.15	14.20
Financial Ratios						
Current ratio	2.56×	2.48×	2.43×	2.43×	2.44×	2.45×
Total asset turnover	1.45×	1.55×	1.62×	1.65×	1.67×	1.68×
Debt ratio	43%	42%	41%	40%	38%	36%
TIE	6.00×	7.90×	9.63×	11.11×	12.80×	14.80×
ROA	6%	8%	9%	10%	10%	11%
ROE	13%	18%	22%	26%	31%	36%

The forecasted situation could look good or bad. In this case, it looks almost too good. The dramatic stock price increase, the high earnings per share growth rate, and especially the extremely high ROE would probably attract new entry into Telecomp's markets. This new competition could drive down prices, profit margins, EPSs, and ROEs. Thus, Telecomp might want to reexamine its basic assumptions and rerun the model using more conservative forecasts.

Changing Assumptions and Policies

The most important benefit of a financial statement generator is that it permits financial managers to see the effects of changing both basic assumptions and specific financial policies. For example, what would Telecomp's financial condition be if competition lowered its growth rate over the next five years to only 30 percent for 1985 and 1986, to 20 percent for 1987, and to 10 percent for 1988 and 1989? Table 23-10 contains the *IFPS*-generated pro forma financial statements based on these lower sales growth estimates. All other assumptions and financial policies remain as defined by the base case. Here we see that Telecomp's general financial condition and profitability still improve over the next five years, but not as dramatically as in the base case. However, external funding requirements are significantly reduced, totaling less than $103

Table 23-10
Telecomp Corporation: Low-Growth Case
Pro Forma Financial Statements
(Millions of Dollars, except for per Share Amounts)

	1984	1985	1986	1987	1988	1989
Stock price	$ 30.00	$ 36.00	$ 43.20	$ 51.84	$ 62.21	$ 74.65
DPS	$ 0.80	$ 0.88	$ 0.97	$ 1.07	$ 1.17	$ 1.29
Growth rate	n.a.	30%	30%	20%	10%	10%
Income Statements						
Net sales	$500.00	$650.00	$845.00	$1,014.00	$1,115.00	$1,227.00
Cost of goods sold	400.00	520.00	676.00	811.20	892.30	981.60
Operating expenses	52.00	59.50	69.25	77.70	82.77	88.35
EBIT	$ 48.00	$ 70.50	$ 99.75	$ 125.10	$ 140.30	$ 157.00
Interest expense	8.00	9.53	11.33	12.35	12.35	12.35
EBT	$ 40.00	$ 60.97	$ 88.42	$ 112.70	$ 128.00	$ 144.70
Taxes	20.00	30.48	44.21	56.37	63.98	72.34
Net income	$ 20.00	$ 30.48	$ 44.21	$ 56.37	$ 63.98	$ 72.34
Dividends	$ 8.00	$ 9.55	$ 11.30	$ 12.85	$ 14.13	$ 15.55
Addition to retained earnings	$ 12.00	$ 20.94	$ 32.91	$ 43.53	$ 49.85	$ 56.80
EPS	$ 2.00	$ 2.81	$ 3.79	$ 5.67	$ 5.30	$ 6.00
Balance Sheets						
Assets						
Cash	$ 10.00	$ 13.00	$ 16.90	$ 20.28	$ 28.50	$ 39.70
Receivables	82.00	104.50	133.80	159.10	174.30	191.00
Inventories	100.00	124.00	155.20	182.20	198.50	216.30
Total current assets	$192.00	$241.50	$305.90	$ 361.60	$ 401.30	$ 447.00
Net fixed assets	153.00	187.50	232.40	271.20	294.50	320.20
Total assets	$345.00	$429.00	$538.20	$ 632.80	$ 695.90	$ 767.20
Liabilities						
Accounts payable	$ 40.00	$ 52.00	$ 67.60	$ 81.12	$ 89.23	$ 98.16
Notes payable	10.00	11.74	13.78	14.95	14.95	14.95
Accrued wages and taxes	25.00	32.50	42.25	50.70	55.77	61.35
Total current liabilities	$ 75.00	$ 96.24	$123.60	$ 146.80	$ 159.90	$ 174.40
Bonds	72.00	83.33	96.57	104.10	104.10	104.10
Common stock	150.00	180.50	216.10	236.60	236.60	236.60
Retained earnings	48.00	68.94	101.90	145.40	195.20	252.00
Total claims	$345.00	$429.00	$538.20	$ 632.80	$ 695.90	$ 767.20

Table 23-10 (continued)

	1984	1985	1986	1987	1988	1989
Funding Requirements						
External funding	n.a.	$43.56	$50.94	$29.14	($6.24)	($15.08)
Surplus cash	n.a.	$ 0	$ 0	$ 0	$6.24	$15.08
New notes payable	n.a.	$ 1.74	$ 2.04	$ 1.17	$ 0	$ 0
New bonds	n.a.	$11.33	$13.24	$ 7.58	$ 0	$ 0
New stock	n.a.	$30.49	$35.66	$20.40	$ 0	$ 0
New shares sold	n.a.	0.85	0.83	0.39	0	0
Total shares outstanding	10.00	10.85	11.67	12.07	12.07	12.07
Financial Ratios						
Current ratio	2.56×	2.51×	2.47×	2.46×	2.51×	2.56×
Total asset turnover	1.45×	1.52×	1.57×	1.60×	1.60×	1.60×
Debt ratio	43%	42%	41%	40%	38%	36%
TIE	6.00×	7.40×	8.81×	10.13×	11.36×	12.71×
ROA	6%	7%	8%	9%	9%	9%
ROE	13%	17%	21%	24%	27%	31%

million over the five years. Additionally, we see that a cash surplus is generated in 1988 and 1989.[8]

The pro forma financial statements could be rerun over and over, each time changing one or more assumptions concerning sales growth rates, cost relationships, future interest rates, and so on. We could also rerun the model with changes in financial policies, such as increasing or decreasing the dividend growth rate, changing the external financing mix, and so on. Thus, the results of differing assumptions and financial policies could be compared. It is important, however, to note (1) that the financial manager still has to interpret the results of alternative financial policies and (2) that the analysis could encompass virtually hundreds of combinations of assumptions and policies, and thus we could generate hundreds of different sets of pro forma financial statements.

One way to reduce the number of different possible scenarios is to perform a sensitivity analysis on the assumptions—those assumptions that have little effect on the key financial condition and profitability ratios need not be changed from their base case levels. Another approach to reducing the number of scenarios is to perform a Monte Carlo simulation analysis. For example, instead of specifying sales growth, the cost of goods sold, and so on at discrete levels, probability distributions

---

[8]We could have extended the model by placing the cash surplus into interest-earning marketable securities, or by using the surplus to retire debt or repurchase stock.

could be specified. Then, the key results would be presented as distributions rather than as point estimates.[9]

Optimization Models

The *IFPS* model described in the previous section projects the financial consequences of alternative policies under particular assumptions. The results could then be used by management to choose among alternative policies. The model itself is not a decision model—it cannot analyze potential policies and choose the best one.

Considerable effort has been expended by financial researchers to develop integrated financial planning models (1) that incorporate all the major financial planning decisions into a single model, (2) that are based on finance theory rather than on accounting rules, and (3) that identify the optimal policies to be followed. However, this type of model is extremely complex, and, although some progress is being made, financial optimization models are not being used by firms to any significant extent.

One example of an optimization model is *LONGER*, a linear programming financial planning model developed by Stewart Myers and Gerald Pogue.[10] *LONGER* had as its objective function the maximization of shareholder wealth as measured by the market value of net worth. The firm's value was based on the Modigliani and Miller (MM) after-tax model.[11] To use *LONGER*, a firm's managers must have already evaluated potential capital projects over a particular planning horizon. The present values, assuming all-equity financing, of these projects were used as exogenous inputs in the *LONGER* model. The model user also had to specify dividend, new equity, debt, liquidity, and investment project (mutual exclusion) constraints. The model then determined the optimal set of investment projects and financing decisions over the planning horizon. By optimal, we mean that set of decisions which maximizes shareholder wealth.

Although *LONGER* represented a promising first step toward optimization financial planning models, considerable refinement would still be required to make such models truly operational. Execucom Corporation, the developer of *IFPS*, is now marketing a commercial optimization package based on linear programming techniques. The system is prom-

---

[9]This is a good time to mention the basic axiom of computer modeling: GIGO, which means "garbage in, garbage out." Stated another way, the output of a financial model is no better than the assumptions and other inputs used to construct it. So, when you build models, proceed with caution. Note, though, that one advantage of computer modeling is that it does bring the key assumptions out into the open, where their realism can be examined. Critics of models often attack the models' assumptions, but they forget that in their own forecasts, they simply assume the answer.

[10]See Stewart C. Myers and Gerald A. Pogue, "A Programming Approach to Corporate Financial Management," *Journal of Finance*, May 1974, 579-599.

[11]See Chapter 11 for a discussion of the MM model.

ising, but it is our understanding that *IFPS:Optimal* is currently being used only for suboptimization problems such as cash management or production scheduling, and not for full scale financial modeling.

Financial forecasting and planning is vital to successful operations, but planning is for nought unless the firm has a control system (1) that insures implementation of the planned policies and (2) that provides an information feedback loop which permits rapid adjustments if market conditions change. In a financial control system, the key question is not "How did the firm do in 1985 as compared with 1984?" Rather, it is "How is the firm doing in 1985 as compared with our forecasts, and if actual results differ from the budget, what can we do to get back on track?"

Financial Controls

The basic tools of financial control are budgets and pro forma financial statements. These statements set forth expected performance, and, thus, they express management's targets. These targets are then compared with actual corporate performance—on a daily, weekly, or monthly basis—to determine the variance, which is defined here as the difference between the actual value and the target value. Thus, the control system identifies those areas where performance is not meeting target levels. If a division's actuals are better than its targets, this could signify that the manager should be given a raise, or perhaps that the targets were simply set too low and thus should be raised in the future. Conversely, failure to meet the financial targets could mean that market conditions are changing, that some managers are not performing up to par, or that the targets were set initially at unrealistic, unattainable levels. In any event, some action should be taken, and perhaps quickly, if the situation is deteriorating rapidly. By focusing on variances, managers can "manage by exception," concentrating on those variables that are most in need of improvement and leaving alone those operations that are running smoothly.[12]

This chapter has focused on the financial planning and control process. Financial planning must be performed within the overall context of the firm's *strategic* and *operating* plans. The heart of financial planning is the construction of *pro forma financial statements*, and the accuracy of these statements

Summary

---

[12]Of course, entire textbooks have been written on financial controls, and much of the subject of financial control overlaps with managerial, or cost, accounting. Here, we want only to emphasize that financial controls are as critical to financial performance as are financial planning and forecasting. We must also add that financial control systems are not costless. Thus, the control system must balance its costs against the savings it is intended to produce.

rests on the estimates of the relationships between the financial statement variables and sales. There are five basic methods for estimating these relationships: (1) *percentage of sales*, (2) *linear regression*, (3) *curvilinear regression*, (4) *multiple regression*, and (5) *specific item forecasting*.

Pro forma financial statements help financial managers (1) to evaluate the expected future financial health of the firm, (2) to determine financing requirements, and (3) to determine how alternative financial policies affect financial condition and financing requirements. Because of *financing feedback effects*, the construction of pro forma financial statements is best done by computer programs such as *IFPS*.

Financial planning is of little value if the firm does not have a control system to monitor the plan's implementation and to provide information needed to develop future financial plans. However, financial planning and control is a costly process, in terms of both human and financial resources. Thus, in designing the planning and control process, one must balance the costs against the benefits to be gained.

Questions

23-1 Define each of the following terms:
  a. Corporate purpose; corporate objective; corporate strategy
  b. Operating plan; financial plan; pro forma
  c. Sales forecast; percentage of sales method
  d. Excess capacity
  e. Spontaneously generated funds
  f. Capital intensity; "lumpy" assets
  g. Simple linear regression; simple curvilinear regression; multiple regression; specific item forecasting
  h. Financing feedback effects

23-2 Certain liability and net worth items generally increase spontaneously with increases in sales. Which of the following items typically increase spontaneously?
  a. Accounts payable
  b. Notes payable to banks
  c. Accrued wages
  d. Accrued taxes
  e. Mortgage bonds
  f. Common stock
  g. Retained earnings
  h. Marketable securities

23-3 Assume that an average firm in the office supply business has a 6-percent after-tax profit margin, a 40-percent debt/assets ratio, a total asset turnover of 2 times, and a dividend payout ratio of 40 percent. Is it true that if such a firm is to have *any* sales growth (g > 0), it will be forced to sell either bonds or common stock (that is, it will need some nonspontaneous external capital, and this will be true even if g is very small)?

23-4 Is it true that computerized corporate planning models were a fad during the 1970s, but, because of a need for flexibility in corporate planning, they have been dropped by most firms?

23-5 Suppose a firm makes the following policy changes. If the change means that external, nonspontaneous financial requirements for any rate of growth will increase, indicate this by a $+$; indicate decreases by a $-$; and indicate indeterminant and/or no effect by a 0. Think in terms of the immediate, short-run effect on funds requirements.

a. The dividend payout ratio is increased. _____

b. The firm contracts to buy rather than make certain components used in its products. _____

c. The firm decides to pay all suppliers on delivery, rather than after a 30-day delay, in order to take advantage of discounts for rapid payment. _____

d. The firm begins to sell on credit; previously, all sales had been on a cash basis. _____

e. The firm's profit margin is eroded by increased competition; sales are steady. _____

f. Advertising expenditures are stepped up. _____

g. A decision is made to substitute long-term mortgage bonds for short-term bank loans. _____

h. The firm begins to pay employees on a weekly basis; previously, it paid them at the end each month. _____

Problems

23-1 A group of investors is planning to set up a new company to manufacture and distribute a novel type of running shoe. To help plan the new operation's financial requirements, you have been asked to construct a pro forma balance sheet for December 31, 1985, the end of the first year of operations. Sales for 1985 are projected at $20 million, and the following are industry average ratios for athletic shoe companies:

Sales to common equity	$5\times$
Current debt to equity	50%
Total debt to equity	80%
Current ratio	$2.2\times$
Net sales to inventory	$9\times$
Accounts receivable to sales	10%
Fixed assets to equity	70%
Profit margin	3%
Dividend payout ratio	30%

a. Complete the pro forma balance sheet below, assuming that 1985 sales are $20 million and that the firm maintains industry average ratios.

Cash	$	Current debt	$	
Accounts receivable		Long-term debt		
Inventories		Total debt	_____	
Total current assets	_____	Equity		
Fixed assets	_____			
Total assets	$_____	Total claims	$_____	

b. If our group supplies all of the new firm's equity, how much capital will we be required to put up during 1985?

23-2 Tom River Textile's 1984 sales were $72 million. The percentage of sales of each balance sheet item except notes payable, mortgage bonds, and common stock is given below:

Cash	4%
Receivables	25
Inventories	30
Net fixed assets	50
Accounts payable	15
Accruals	5
Profit margin	5

The dividend payout ratio is 60 percent; the December 31, 1983, balance sheet account for retained earnings was $41.80 million; and both common stock and mortgage bonds are constant and equal to the amounts shown on the following balance sheet.

a. Complete the balance sheet below as of December 31, 1984:

Cash	$	Accounts payable	$
Receivables		Notes payable	6,840
Inventories	_____	Accruals	_____
Total current assets		Total current liabilities	
Net fixed assets		Mortgage bonds	10,000
		Common stock	4,000
		Retained earnings	_____
	_____		
Total assets	$_____	Total claims	$_____

b. Assume that the company was operating at full capacity in 1984 with regard to all items *except* fixed assets. If the fixed assets had been used to full capacity, the fixed assets/sales ratio would have been 40 percent in 1984. By what percentage could 1985 sales increase over 1984 sales without the need for an increase in fixed assets?

c. Now suppose that 1985 sales increase by 20 percent over 1984 sales. How much additional external capital will be required? Assume that Tom River Textile cannot sell any fixed assets and that any required financing is borrowed as notes payable.

d. Suppose that the industry percentage of sales averages for receivables and inventories are 20 and 25 percent, respectively, and that Tom River Textile matches these figures in 1985 and then uses the funds released to reduce equity. (It could pay a special dividend out of retained earnings.) What would this do to the rate of return on year-end 1985 equity?

23-3 The 1984 income statement and balance sheet for Dana Industries is presented below (in thousands of dollars):

Income Statement

Net sales	$10,000
Cost of goods sold	6,500
Gross profit	$ 3,500
Administrative expenses	1,000
Miscellaneous expenses	500
EBIT	$ 2,000
Interest expense	200
EBT	$ 1,800
Taxes (48%)	864
Net income	$ 936
Dividends	$ 468
Addition to retained earnings	$ 468

Balance Sheet

Cash	$ 50
Accounts receivable	423
Inventory	513
Total current assets	$ 986
Net plant	4,014
Total assets	$ 5,000
Accounts payable	$ 250
Notes payable	200
Accruals	50
Total current liabilities	$ 500
Long-term debt	1,500
Common stock	1,500
Retained earnings	1,500
Total claims	$ 5,000

As the financial manager, you want to construct a pro forma income statement, balance sheet, and statement of changes in financial position for 1985. As a first step, you develop the following relationships between the financial statement variables and sales (in thousands of dollars):

Variable	Relationship to Sales
Cost of goods sold	0.65(Sales)
Administrative expenses	$500 + 0.05(Sales)
Miscellaneous expenses	0.05(Sales)
Cash	0.005(Sales)
Accounts receivable	0.0423(Sales)
Inventory	$200 + 0.03(Sales)
Net plant	0.40(Sales)
Accounts payable	0.025(Sales)
Accruals	0.005(Sales)

Taxes are expected to continue at 48 percent; sales in 1985 are forecast to increase by 30 percent over 1984; and fixed assets were fully utilized in 1984. Any external funding required for 1985 will be financed in the proportion of 4 percent notes payable, 36 percent long-term debt, and 60 percent new equity. Dana's stock currently sells for $25 per share, and there are 1 million shares outstanding. Thus, the 1984 DPS was $468,000/1,000,000 = $0.468. However, Dana wants to increase the dividend in 1985 to $0.50 per share. New short-term debt is expected to cost 12 percent, while new long-term debt will cost 14 percent.

a. Construct the initial 1985 pro forma income statement and balance sheet. What is the external funding requirement? How will it be met? (For now, ignore financing feedback effects.)

b. Recast the 1985 pro forma income statement and balance sheet considering financing feedback effects. How much of an external financing shortfall still exists?

c. Perform one more iteration on the pro forma income statement and balance sheet. Construct the pro forma 1985 statement of changes in financial position. (You should still have a shortfall of $1,000 after the second iteration. Use $1,000 worth of new equity to balance the balance sheet.)

d. Dana's current bond indenture limits the firm to a minimum current ratio of 1.5, a maximum debt ratio of 35 percent, and a minimum times-interest-earned ratio of 8.0. Are any of these restrictions violated in the pro forma statements? If so, how must the financing program be modified to meet these restrictions?

e. What would be the effect on external financing requirements if the firm had been operating at only 80 percent of capacity in 1984? (Note that the net plant is forecast using the percentage of sales technique.)

23-4 The 1984 income statement and balance sheet for Commonwealth Pulp and Paper are shown below (in thousands of dollars):

Income Statement

Sales	$500
Operating expenses	320
General expenses	80
EBIT	$100
Interest expense	20
EBT	$ 80
Taxes (50%)	40
Net income	$ 40

Balance Sheet

Cash	$ 30	Accounts payable	$ 40
Receivables	50	Accruals	20
Inventories	420	Notes payable	20
Net fixed assets	500	Long-term debt	180
		Common stock	200
		Retained earnings	540
Total assets	$1,000	Total claims	$1,000

The firm has 40,000 shares outstanding, and next year's dividend is forecast at $0.55 per share. Commonwealth has fixed assets sufficient to support a sales level of $750,000. Next year's sales are forecast to be $700,000. The stock is currently selling at $2.86 per share, and the stock price is expected to be flat over the next year. Any external financing needs would be met with a mix of 60 percent long-term debt, at an estimated cost of 12.82 percent and 40 percent common equity. No new short-term debt would be used, but the old short-term debt would be rolled over at the current rate.

The relationships between certain financial statement variables and sales are given below (thousands of dollars):

Variable	Relationship to Sales
General expenses	$ 30 + 0.10(Sales)
Inventories	$200 + 0.44(Sales)

All other variables are forecast using the percentage of sales method. The 1984 levels of these variables are appropriate for a sales level of $500,000.

a. Construct the initial 1985 pro forma income statement and balance sheet, excluding financial feedback effects. What amount of external financing is required? How will it be obtained?

b. Construct the first iteration pro forma income statement and balance sheet, that is, the statements which include financing feedback effects. What is the additional interest expense resulting from external financing? What is the additional dividend payment? How much external financing is still required after this iteration?

The heart of successful financial planning is the sales forecast. On this key subject, see

Pan, Judy, Donald R. Nichols, and O. Maurice Joy, "Sales Forecasting Practices of Large U.S. Industrial Firms," *Financial Management*, Fall 1977, 72-77.

Pappas, James L., Eugene F. Brigham, and Mark Hirschey, *Managerial Economics* (Hinsdale, Ill.: Dryden, 1983).

Computer modeling is becoming increasingly important. For general references, see

Carleton, Willard T., Charles L. Dick, Jr., and David H. Downes, "Financial Policy Models: Theory and Practice," *Journal of Financial and Quantitative Analysis*, December 1973, 691-709.

Francis, Jack Clark, and Dexter R. Rowell, "A Simultaneous Equation Model of the Firm for Financial Analysis and Planning," *Financial Management*, Spring 1978, 29-44.

Grinyer, P. H., and J. Wooller, *Corporate Models Today—A New Tool for Financial Management* (London: Institute of Chartered Accountants, 1978).

Pappas, James L., and George P. Huber, "Probabilistic Short-Term Financial Planning," *Financial Management*, Autumn 1973, 36-44.

Traenkle, J. W., E. B. Cox, and J. A. Bullard, *The Use of Financial Models in Business* (New York: Financial Executives' Research Foundation, 1975).

The Brigham-Crum casebook contains the following applicable cases:

Case 3, "Structural Analytics Corporation," which focuses on the importance and mechanics of financial planning.

Case 4, "Sharman Industries, Inc.," which illustrates some of the basic problems involved in maintaining financial control.

The following classic case is available from Harvard Business School (HBS) Case Services:

"The O. M. Scott & Sons Company," which illustrates financial forecasting and analysis as well as working capital management.

*Selected
Additional
References and
Cases*

Special Topics in Financial Management

VIII

Mergers, Divestitures, and Holding Companies

24

In early 1984, the Federal Trade Commission granted approval for the Chevron Corporation to buy Gulf Oil for a record $13.3 billion. Chevron offered $80 per share for Gulf, which had been selling for $42 shortly before the tender offer was announced. Chevron's primary motive for the offer was Gulf's 800 million barrels of domestic oil reserves. Chevron has been significantly affected by the wide swings in crude oil prices. Earnings hit $2.4 billion in 1980, and then fell to $1.6 billion in 1983. Chevron is heavily dependent on heavy, harder-to-refine California crude oil, and the merger will provide a supply of light, cheaper-to-refine reserves.

But the price was high. Chevron arranged a $14 billion line of credit, and it will end up borrowing an estimated $11 billion to $12 billion to finance the purchase. This caused Moody's Investors Service to downgrade certain Chevron and Gulf debt issues. However, the new ratings are still AA, and Moody's indicated that the downgrading was not more severe because Chevron plans to reduce debt through the sale of about $1 billion worth of Gulf's assets.

Who are the winners in this biggest-of-all merger? The Gulf shareholders who saw their stock almost double in price in six months are certainly winners. However, perhaps the clearest winners are the investment bankers who helped orchestrate the deal. Salomon Brothers and Merrill Lynch will split a $46.5 million fee for advising Gulf, and Morgan Stanley will get $16.5 million for helping Chevron fashion its bid. But are there no losers? Right now it's hard to say. If Gulf's assets were truly undervalued at $42 per share, or if Chevron is able to assimilate and use these assets significantly more efficiently than Gulf did, then the Chevron shareholders will also benefit from the merger. Only time will tell.

Most corporate growth occurs through *internal expansion*, which takes place when the firm's existing divisions grow through normal capital budgeting activities. However, the most dramatic examples of growth, and often the largest increases in firms' stock prices, are the result of mergers, one subject of this chapter.[1] On the other hand, the conditions of corporate life do change over time, and, as a result, firms occasionally find it desirable to *divest,* or sell off, major divisions to other firms which can better utilize the divested assets. This topic is also discussed in the chapter. Finally, we discuss the *holding company* form of organization, wherein one corporation owns the stock of one or more other companies.

Rationale for Mergers

Many reasons have been proposed by both financial managers and theorists to account for the high level of merger activity in the United States. In this section, we present some of the motives behind corporate mergers.

Synergy

The primary motivation for most mergers is to increase the value of the combined enterprise. If Companies A and B merge to form Company C, and if C's value exceeds that of A and B taken separately, then *synergy* is said to exist. Such a merger should be beneficial to both A's and B's stockholders.[2] Synergistic effects can arise from four sources: (1) *operating economies*, which result from economies of scale in management, production, or distribution; (2) *financial economies*, including a higher price/earnings ratio, a lower cost of debt, and/or a greater debt capacity; (3) *differential efficiency*, which implies that the management of one firm is inefficient, and that its managerial effectiveness can be improved by merger; and (4) *increased market power* due to reduced competition. Operating and financial economies are socially desirable, as are mergers which increase managerial efficiency, but mergers that reduce competition are both undesirable and illegal.[3]

---

[1]As we use the term, *merger* means any combination that forms one economic unit from two or more previous ones. For legal purposes, there are distinctions among the various ways these combinations can occur, but our emphasis is on the fundamental business and financial aspects of mergers.

[2]If synergy exists, then the whole is greater than the sum of the parts. Synergy is also called the "2 plus 2 equals 5 effect." The distribution of the synergistic gain between A's and B's stockholders is determined by negotiation. This point is discussed later in the chapter.

[3]In the 1880s and 1890s, many mergers occurred in the United States, and some of them were rather obviously directed toward gaining market power rather than increasing operating efficiency. As a result, Congress passed a series of acts designed to insure that mergers are not used as a method of reducing competition. The principal acts include the Sherman Act (1890), the Clayton Act (1914), and the Celler Act (1950). These acts make it illegal for firms to combine in any manner if the combination tends to lessen competition. The acts are administered by the antitrust division of the Justice Department and by the Federal Trade Commission.

Tax considerations have stimulated a number of mergers. For example, a firm which is highly profitable and in the highest corporate tax bracket could acquire a firm with large accumulated tax losses. These losses could then be turned into immediate tax savings rather than waiting to carry forward the losses.[4] Also, mergers can provide an outlet for excess cash. If a firm has a shortage of internal investment opportunities compared to its cash flow, it could (1) pay an extra dividend, (2) invest in marketable securities, (3) repurchase its own stock, or (4) purchase another firm. If the firm pays an extra dividend, the stockholders would have to pay ordinary taxes on the distribution. Marketable securities often provide a good temporary parking place for money, but generally the rate of return on such securities is less than that required by stockholders. Stock repurchase would result in a capital gain for the remaining stockholders, but (1) a repurchase might push up the firm's stock price to a level which is temporarily above the equilibrium price, so the company will have paid too much for the repurchased shares, which will be disadvantageous to remaining stockholders, and (2) a repurchase designed solely to avoid dividend payment might be challenged by the IRS. However, using surplus cash to acquire another firm has no immediate tax consequences to the acquiring firm or its stockholders, and this fact has motivated a number of mergers.

*Tax
Considerations*

Sometimes a firm will be touted as a possible acquisition candidate because the cost of replacing its assets is considerably higher than its market value. For example, in the 1980s oil companies could acquire reserves cheaper by buying out other oil companies than by exploratory drilling. Thus, in 1984 Chevron Corporation acquired Gulf Oil in order to augment its reserves. Similarly, steel companies have stated that it is "cheaper" to buy an existing steel company than to construct a new mill, and in 1984, LTV (the fourth largest steel company) acquired Republic Steel (the sixth largest) for $700 million in a merger that created the second largest firm in the industry.

*Purchase of Assets
below Their
Replacement Cost*

At the time the LTV-Republic merger was announced, Republic was selling for less than one-third of its book value. Even though LTV bought Republic's capacity at a lower cost than would have been required to build new plants, the logic of the purchase may be weak unless LTV can do something with Republic Steel's assets beyond what was previously being done. That is, the market value of any firm should be based on the earnings power, or the economic value, of its assets. If the firm is fairly valued (markets are efficient), then the market value must reflect the economic value of the assets. The real question, then, is this: Can LTV operate the merged company more efficiently than the

---

[4]Mergers undertaken only to use accumulated tax losses would probably be challenged by the IRS. However, because many factors are present in any given merger, it is hard to prove that a merger was motivated only, or even primarily, by tax considerations.

two companies had been operating before the merger? LTV argues that sufficient economies of scale exist to make the merger synergistic. The least efficient plants of both companies will be closed; plants that make similar products (say sheet steel for autos, or oil drilling pipe) will be consolidated; and distribution systems will be integrated. If these moves do result in sizable cost savings, then the merger will be successful. Otherwise, the fact that LTV could buy Republic's assets at below their replacement value will be immaterial, and the consolidated company will have trouble.

Diversification

Often, managers claim that diversification is a reason for mergers. The contention is that diversification helps to stabilize the firm's earnings stream and thus benefits its owners. Certainly, stabilization of earnings is beneficial to employees, suppliers, and customers, but what is the value of firm diversification to the stockholders and to the debtholders? If a stockholder is worried about the variability of a firm's earnings, he or she could probably diversify more easily than could the firm. Why should Firms A and B merge to stabilize earnings when a stockholder in Firm A could sell half of his or her stock in A and use the proceeds to purchase stock in Firm B? Stockholders can generally create diversification more easily than can the firm.

Of course, if you were the owner-manager of a closely held firm, it might be well nigh impossible for you to sell part of your stock to diversify, because this would dilute your ownership and also generate a large capital gains tax liability. In this case, a diversification merger might well be the best way to effect personal diversification.

We can use option pricing theory to gain some insights into how stockholders and debtholders are affected by mergers. In Chapter 16, we discussed the Galai and Masulis application of option pricing theory to corporate decisions.[5] If we view stock ownership as a call option, then the value of the stock is increased by an increase in earnings variability, but lowered by a decrease in variability. Assume that two firms have the same variability of earnings. If these two firms merge, and their earnings are not perfectly positively correlated, then the earnings of the combined firm will have less variability than the pre-merger earnings. This decrease in earnings variability would, according to option theory, lower the value of the combined firm's equity. Conversely, the value of the debt would increase, because the probability of default would lessen. According to Galai and Masulis, using mergers for diversification results in a transfer of wealth from stockholders to debtholders, leaving the

---

[5]See Dan Galai and Ronald W. Masulis, "The Option Pricing Model and the Risk Factor of Stock," *Journal of Financial Economics*, January/March 1976, 53-82.

total value of the combined firm at the sum of the pre-merger values, assuming no synergistic effects.

However, it is possible for the stockholders to avoid these theoretical losses by financing the merger with debt, or to recoup them by issuing additional debt based on the increased debt capacity of the combined firm, and then using the proceeds to repurchase equity. Also, note that the Galai-Masulis results depend on the CAPM conclusion that only systematic risk is relevant to stockholders, and that corporate stability has no beneficial effects on operating income. To the extent that these assumptions are not correct, then corporate diversification could benefit stockholders even in the absence of synergy.

Types of Mergers

Economists classify mergers into four groups: (1) horizontal, (2) vertical, (3) congeneric, and (4) conglomerate. A *horizontal merger* occurs when, for example, one widget manufacturer acquires another, or one retail food chain merges with a second; that is, when one firm combines with another in its same line of business. An example of a *vertical merger* is a steel producer's acquisition of one of its own suppliers, such as an iron or coal mining firm (an "upstream merger"), or an oil producer's acquisition of a company which uses its products, such as a petrochemical company (a "downstream merger"). *Congeneric* means "allied in nature or action"; hence, a *congeneric merger* involves related enterprises, but not producers of the same product (horizontal) or firms in a producer-supplier relationship (vertical). Examples of congeneric mergers would be American Express's 1981 takeover of Shearson Hammill, or Prudential's acquisition of Bache & Company. A *conglomerate merger* occurs when unrelated enterprises combine; Mobil Oil's acquisition of Montgomery Ward illustrates a conglomerate merger.

Operating economies (and also anticompetitive effects) are at least partially dependent on the type of merger involved. Vertical and horizontal mergers generally provide the greatest operating benefits, but they are also the ones most likely to be attacked by the U.S. Department of Justice. In any event, it is useful to think of these economic classifications when analyzing the feasibility of a prospective merger.

Level of Merger Activity

There have been four major periods of merger activity in the United States. The first was in the late 1800s, when consolidations occurred in oil, steel, tobacco, and other basic industries. The second was in the 1920s, when the stock market boom helped financial promoters consolidate firms in a number of industries, including utilities and communication companies. The third was in the 1960s, when conglomerate mergers were the rage. And the fourth began in the early 1980s and is still going on.

The "merger mania" of the 1980s has been sparked by four factors: (1) the relatively depressed condition of the stock market (for example, the Dow Jones Industrial Index in early 1982 was below its 1968 level); (2) the unprecedented level of inflation that existed during the 1970s and early 1980s; (3) the Reagan administration's stated view that "bigness is not necessarily badness" and its generally more tolerant attitude toward mergers; and (4) the general belief among the major natural resource companies that it is cheaper to "buy reserves on Wall Street" through mergers than to explore and find them in the field. Financial historians have not yet compiled the statistics and done the analysis necessary to compare the 1980s merger wave with the earlier ones, but it is virtually certain that the 1980s wave will rank among the largest. As illustrated in Table 24-1, the top five mergers of all time in terms of dollar value have occurred in the 1980s.

Brief descriptions of some different types of recent mergers will help explain how the deals are worked out:

1. Getty Oil, the fourteenth largest U.S. oil company, was acquired by Texaco, the fourth largest, in February 1984 at a cost of $10.1 billion. Prior to the merger activity, Getty's shares were selling at around $65, and the descendants of J. Paul Getty, the founder, were complaining of inefficient management. Then the controlling trustees of the Sarah C. Getty Trust, together with Pennzoil Company, announced plans to take the firm private through an offering to buy the shares which they did not already control at a price of $112.50 per share. Texaco then jumped in with an offer of $125 per share.

The merger doubled Texaco's domestic oil and gas reserves, and with Getty's retail outlets, gave Texaco a larger share of the gasoline market.

Table 24-1
The Five Biggest Mergers
(Billions of Dollars)

Companies	Year	Value	Percent of Book Value	Type of Transaction
Chevron-Gulf	1984	$13.3	136%	Acquisition for cash
Texaco-Getty	1984	10.1	191	Acquisition for cash and notes
Du Pont-Conoco	1981	7.2	156	Acquisition for cash and common stock
U.S. Steel-Marathon	1982	6.0	289	Acquisition for cash and notes
ELF Aquitaine-Texas Gulf	1981	4.3	212	Acquisition for cash

Some analysts claim that Texaco, with its sprawling network of refineries and rapidly dwindling reserves, made the correct decision by acquiring Getty, with its large reserves and minimal refining operations. Other analysts contend that Texaco paid too much for Getty. Whether Texaco will get its money's worth remains to be seen. For Texaco, acquiring Getty's reserves may be cheaper than finding new oil, but the value of these reserves depends on the price of oil, which in 1984 fell by more than 15 percent.

A side issue which arose at the end of the merger concerned the Bass Brothers of Texas, an immensely wealthy family which had acquired over $1 billion of Texaco stock during all the action. Texaco's management was afraid the Basses planned to try to take over Texaco, so they bought out the Bass interests at a premium of about 20 percent over the market value. Some of Texaco's stockholders argued that the payment amounted to "greenmail" and that it was made with stockholders' money just to insure that Texaco's managers could keep their jobs. This situation, along with several others that were similar, has led to the introduction of bills in Congress to limit the actions that a management group can take in its efforts to avoid being taken over.

2. Conoco, which had book value assets of $11 billion and which was, based on sales, the fourteenth largest company in the United States, was recently the target of Mobil (the second largest company in the United States), Du Pont (the fifteenth largest company in the United States), and Seagram (a large Canadian company). This 1981 merger alone almost surpassed in dollar amount the previous record of all mergers in a single year (book value assets of $12 billion in 1968). Conoco's stock sold for about $50 just before the bidding for it started; the bid price got up to over $100 per share. Conoco's oil and coal reserves, plus its plant and equipment, were thought to be worth far more than their book, and market, values.

If Mobil had won, it would have been a horizontal merger. If Seagram had won, it would have been a conglomerate merger. Yet Du Pont won, and it was a vertical merger because Du Pont uses petroleum in its production processes. The Justice Department did not indicate that it would fight a merger with Seagram or Du Pont, but it apparently would have fought a merger with Mobil. Thus, although Mobil made the highest bid ($115 per share), Du Pont ended up the winner with a bid of $98; stockholders chose the Du Pont bid over that of Mobil because they were afraid the Mobil merger would be blocked and that Conoco's stock would then fall below the level of the Du Pont bid price.

This was a *hostile merger*—Conoco's management would rather have had the company remain an independent entity. Obviously, though, this was not to be, and Conoco's top managers found themselves working for someone else (or out of a job). This is a good illustration of a point made in Chapter 1, namely, that managers have a very strong motivation to operate in a manner that will maximize the value of their firms' stock. Otherwise, they could find themselves in the same boat as Conoco's managers.

Du Pont shelled out $7.2 billion for Conoco's equity. Most of these funds were borrowed, and the Conoco purchase more than quadrupled Du Pont's $1.6 billion debt, to $7.4 billion. This caused Du Pont to lose its AAA credit status. Du Pont has since sliced its debt by $1.5 billion, and its managers are optimistic about the merger results. However, oil prices have fallen since the acquisition, and the final verdict on the wisdom of this merger, as well as the other mergers discussed in this section, will not be known for years.

3. Marathon Oil, a company only slightly smaller than Conoco, was the object of an attempted acquisition by Mobil after that company lost its bid for Conoco. Marathon's management resisted strongly, and again other bidders entered the picture. In March of 1982, U.S. Steel picked up Marathon for about $6 billion, making this the fourth largest merger of all time. (In this and the Conoco merger, the prices we quote refer to the price paid for the equity of the acquired firms. The acquired firms also had debt, which remained outstanding after the mergers, so the assets involved were larger than the amounts we quote.) The U.S. Steel-Marathon Oil merger will be discussed in more detail later in the chapter.

4. Bendix, after one of the most dramatic merger fights of all time, was acquired in 1982 by Allied Corporation. A four-way takeover battle began when Bendix, directed by William Agee and Mary Cunningham, made an unfriendly takeover offer for Martin Marietta. However, Martin Marietta responded with a "shark eats shark" bid to buy Bendix. Additionally, Martin Marietta enlisted the aid of United Technologies, which also made a separate bid for Bendix. While this three-way struggle was going on, it looked as though Bendix would own 70 percent of Martin Marietta, but Martin Marietta would own over 50 percent of Bendix. Then, who controlled whom would depend on who could vote the other's shares first in the annual election of directors. Naturally, this led to lawsuits regarding the two companies' voting of each other's shares.

This co-ownership situation would probably have meant a stalemate which would drag on in the courts for years, with both companies essentially paralyzed in the meantime. At this point, Allied Corporation entered the fray with a bid for Bendix. The final agreement found Allied acquiring Bendix for over $1.8 billion, and Bendix and Martin Marietta swapping the shares each held of the other on the basis of the shares' market values. This left Allied with 8.8 million shares of Martin Marietta, which it got when it completed the purchase of Bendix. Martin Marietta retained its independence, but at a heavy price: The company had taken on $892 million of new debt to buy its Bendix stock, and then it had to issue $346 million of new stock to the public to buy back Allied's shares. Wall Street analysts predict that it will take Martin Marietta seven years to straighten out its balance sheet.

This monumental struggle between corporate giants has been characterized as more of a battle of personal egos than a battle to increase shareholder wealth. Even so, it demonstrated once more that the threat of a takeover is one of the best incentives to a manager to run his or her firm at its best.

5. Schlitz, once the largest U.S. brewer, had been losing both money and market share. By 1980 it had become only the fourth largest brewer, with a market share of 8.5 percent, and in 1982 it seemed to be on a collision course with bankruptcy. Schlitz's troubles arose from its poor marketing strategy, a problem which it was unable to conquer. G. Heileman, the sixth largest brewer, with a 1980 market share of 7.5 percent, had been better managed, and its sales had been growing rapidly. (Heileman's ROE in 1980 was 27.3 percent; Schlitz's was negative.) Because of its successful marketing programs, Heileman needed more brewing capacity, while because of its poor sales performance, Schlitz had 50 percent excess capacity. In July 1981, Heileman offered to buy Schlitz's common stock for $494 million. If the takeover attempt had been successful, Heileman would have acquired capacity at an effective cost of $19 per barrel versus a construction cost of about $50 per barrel. The merger would also have made Heileman the third largest brewer in the nation. Although the U.S. Department of Justice under the Reagan administration had previously taken the position that "bigness is not necessarily badness," it opposed the merger because in its judgment such a merger would substantially reduce competition in the brewing industry. Therefore, the merger was abandoned. However, Schlitz was still in trouble, and in 1982, Schlitz was acquired by Stroh Brewery (another good marketer) for over $500 million.

6. In the summer of 1984, General Motors announced that it planned to buy Electronic Data Systems (EDS), the world's largest data processing company, for $2.2 billion. GM had excess cash; it wanted to diversify outside the auto industry in order to stabilize earnings; and EDS can help GM set up better internal data management systems. Ross Perot, the founder and a 50 percent owner of EDS, was offered over $1 billion plus a seat on the GM board for his stock, and he will continue to run EDS. GM is reportedly looking at other large acquisition candidates.

As we write this, the merger wave of the 1980s is still alive and well, and no end is in sight.

Procedures for Combining Firms

In the vast majority of merger situations, one firm (generally the larger of the two) simply decides to buy another company, negotiates over the price, and then acquires the target company. Occasionally, the acquired firm will initiate the action, but it is much more common for a firm to seek acquisitions than to seek to be acquired.[6] Following convention, we shall call a company that seeks to acquire another the *acquiring company* and the one which it seeks to acquire the *target company*.

Once an acquiring company has identified a possible target, it must establish a suitable price, or range of prices, that it is willing to pay. With this in mind, the acquiring firm's managers must decide how to approach the target company's managers. If the acquiring firm has reason to believe that the target company's management will approve the merger, then it will simply propose a merger and try to work out some suitable terms. If an agreement can be reached, then the two management groups will issue statements to their stockholders recommending that they approve the merger. Assuming that the stockholders do approve, the acquiring firm will simply buy the target company's shares from its stockholders, paying for them either with its own shares (in which case the target company's stockholders become stockholders of the acquiring company) or with cash.

Under other circumstances, the target company's management may resist the merger. Perhaps it feels that the price offered for the stock is too low, or perhaps the target firm's managers simply want to maintain their jobs. In either case, the target firm's management is said to be *hostile* rather than *friendly*, and the acquiring firm must make a direct appeal to the target firm's stockholders. In hostile mergers, the acquiring company generally makes a *tender offer*, in which it asks the stockholders of the firm it is seeking to control to submit, or "tender," their shares in exchange for a specified price. The price is generally stated as so many dollars per share of the stock to be acquired, although it can be stated in terms of shares of stock in the acquiring firm. The tender offer is a direct appeal to stockholders, so it need not be approved by the management of the target firm. Tender offers are not new, but the frequency of their use has increased greatly in recent years.[7]

U.S. Steel's acquisition of Marathon Oil can be used to illustrate how a tender offer works. In late 1981, Marathon's stock was selling for about $65 per share. Then Mobil announced that it wanted to acquire Marathon, and it offered $85 per share for all shares, provided it received a majority of the shares. This was a typical tender offer. Shortly thereafter, U.S. Steel entered the fight with a stock/bond tender offer. It offered to buy 51 percent of Marathon's 59 million shares, or about 30 million shares, at a price of $125 per share. U.S. Steel stated at the time it made

---

[6]However, if a firm is in financial difficulty, if the managers are elderly and do not feel that suitable replacements are on hand, or if the firm needs the support (often the capital) of a larger company, then it may seek to be acquired. Thus, when Continental Illinois bank was in great trouble in 1984, it lobbied to get the Illinois legislature to pass a law that would make it easier for the bank to be acquired, and management actively sought a strong bank which would take it over.

[7]Tender offers can be friendly, with the target firm's management recommending that stockholders go ahead and tender their stock.

the offer that if it succeeded in purchasing the 30 million shares, it would then merge Marathon into U.S. Steel and pay the holders of the remaining 29 million shares with 12-year notes which had a par value of $100, a 12.5 percent coupon, and a market value of $85 at the time of the offer. If less than 51 percent of the Marathon stock was submitted to U.S. Steel, then it would cancel the offer and return the stock. If more than 51 percent was submitted, U.S. Steel would buy 51 percent, or 30 million shares, on a pro rata basis and return the excess stock for later exchange into bonds when the merger was completed.

Mobil immediately countered U.S. Steel's offer with a new offer of its own, $126 for 51 percent of the stock, plus notes with a value of $90 for the remaining shares. Mobil's new offer was higher than that of U.S. Steel—it worked out to an average price per Marathon share of $0.51(\$126) + 0.49(\$90) = \$108.36$ versus $0.51(\$125) + 0.49(\$85) = \$105.40$ for the U.S. Steel offer.

Even though Mobil's offer was higher, investors were still on the horns of a dilemma. In the first place, it appeared that the Justice Department would not try to block a merger with U.S. Steel, but that the Department would fight a merger with Mobil. If Mobil won the tender fight but the merger was blocked, then Marathon's stock would drop back toward $65, for without competition, U.S. Steel could bid much lower the next time around. Realizing this, some Marathon stockholders leaned toward U.S. Steel. The second horn of the dilemma resulted from the two-tiered nature of the tender offers, which made it very important to tender one's stock to the eventual winner. To illustrate, suppose that Mr. Pig and a group of like-minded investors tendered their stock to Mobil, hoping that the Justice Department would not interfere, while Ms. Prudence and some others tendered to U.S. Steel, and that U.S. Steel ended up with exactly 51 percent of the stock. In this case Ms. Prudence and her friends would receive $125 per Marathon share, while Mr. Pig and his group would get only $85 per share. Of course, if there were more Pigs than Prudences, and the Justice Department did not block the merger, then Mr. Pig would get $126 per share and Ms. Prudence $90.

In the Marathon case, 87 percent of the stockholders tendered to U.S. Steel. Mobil's offer was canceled, and the stock which had been tendered to it was returned to the shareholders. U.S. Steel accepted, on a pro rata basis, $51\%/0.87 = 58.62\%$ of the stock submitted to it; it paid $125 each for these shares; and it returned the remainder of the shares to their owners.

Several months later, in March of 1982, Marathon held a stockholders' meeting to finalize the merger. Since U.S. Steel already owned 51 percent of the stock, and since the holders of most of the rest were already committed to voting for the merger, the transaction was quickly completed. In the end, people who had tendered to U.S. Steel received $0.5862(\$125) + 0.4138(\$85) = \$108.45$ for their shares, while those who tendered to Mobil (or who did not tender to either) received $85 per share.[8]

Mobil's original $85 tender offer for 100 percent of the Marathon stock is the way most tender offers had been made in the past. U.S. Steel's offer for 51 percent of the stock was unusual, and many investment bankers have argued that this type of offer will dominate in the future. However, both the SEC and Congress have voiced opposition to two-tier tender offers on the grounds that professional investors, including *merger arbitrageurs* (traders, often affiliated with investment banking houses, who make a business of speculating in the shares of merger candidates), have a distinct advantage over individual investors. The professionals have more information about how shares are likely to be tendered, and they can wait until the last minute and have shares delivered by courier rather than through the mails. So, companies may be required to use straightforward, one-price tender offers in the future.

Merger Analysis

In theory, merger analysis is quite simple. The acquiring firm simply performs a capital budgeting analysis to determine whether the present value of the expected future income from the merger exceeds the price it must pay for the target company. The target company's stockholders, on the other hand, should accept the proposal if the price offered exceeds the present value of its expected future cash flows, assuming that it continues to operate independently. However, some difficult issues are involved: (1) The acquiring company must estimate the cash flow benefits that will be obtained from the acquisition. (2) The acquiring firm must determine what effect, if any, the merger will have on its required rate of return on equity. (3) The acquiring company will have to decide how to pay for the merger if it is not done on an exchange-of-stock basis. (4) Having estimated the benefits of the merger, the acquiring and target firms' managers and stockholders must bargain over how to share these benefits. The Conoco and Marathon cases illustrate just how complex this analysis can actually be.

Operating Mergers versus Financial Mergers

From the standpoint of financial analysis, there are two basic types of mergers:

1. One is an *operating merger*, in which the operations of two companies are integrated with the expectation of obtaining synergistic effects. The Schlitz-Stroh combination is a good example of an operating merger.

---

[8]Actually, interest rates had risen somewhat by March, causing the value of the notes to decline from $85 to $79 on the day the merger was completed. Also, Marathon was headquartered in Ohio, where by state law dissenting stockholders in a merger may petition in court for an improved settlement based on an independent appraisal of the acquired company's value. A few of the 49 percent stockholders refused to accept the $79 worth of bonds and petitioned for an appraisal. At this time, the case is still under review, but since oil prices have fallen, Marathon's appraised value could easily be less than $79, so the dissenting stockholders have little cause for optimism.

2. The other extreme is a *pure financial* merger, in which the merged companies will not be operated as a single unit and from which no operating economies are expected. The 1982 acquisition of Columbia Pictures by Coca-Cola for $748 million is an example of a pure financial merger.

Of course, mergers may actually combine these two features. Thus, if Mobil had acquired Conoco or Marathon, the merger would have been primarily an operating one. However, with Du Pont and U.S. Steel emerging as the victors, the mergers were partly operating and partly financial.

In a pure financial merger, the postmerger cash flows are simply the sum of the expected cash flows of the two companies if they were to continue to operate independently. However, if the two firms' operations are to be integrated, or if the acquiring firm plans to change the target firm's management and expects to get better results, then accurate projected cash flow statements, which are absolutely essential to sound merger decisions, will be even more difficult to construct.

Estimating Future Operating Income

The basic rationale for any operating merger is synergy. Del Monte Corporation provides a good example of a series of well thought out, favorable operating mergers. Del Monte successfully merged and integrated numerous small canning companies into a very efficient, highly profitable organization. It used standardized production techniques to increase the efficiency of all its plants, a national brand name and national advertising to develop customer loyalty, a consolidated distribution system, and a centralized purchasing office that obtained substantial discounts from volume purchases. Because of these economies, Del Monte became the most efficient and profitable U.S. canning company, and its merger activities helped make possible the size that produced these economies. Consumers also benefited, because Del Monte's efficiency enabled the company to sell high-quality products at relatively low prices.

An example of poor pro forma analysis that resulted in a disastrous merger was the consolidation of the Pennsylvania and New York Central railroads. The premerger analysis was grossly misleading, failing to reveal the fact that certain key elements in the two rail systems were incompatible, and hence could not be meshed together. Rather than gaining synergistic benefits, the combined system actually incurred additional overhead costs that helped lead to its bankruptcy. *Thus, in planning operating mergers, the development of pro forma statements is the single most important aspect of the merger analysis.*[9]

---

[9] It should be noted that firms heavily engaged in mergers have "acquisition departments" whose functions include (1) seeking suitable merger candidates and (2) taking over and integrating acquired firms into the parent corporation. The first step involves the development of both pro forma statements and a plan for making the projections materialize. The second step involves (1) streamlining operations of the acquired firm, if necessary, and (2) instituting a system of controls that will permit the parent to effectively manage the new division and to coordinate its operations with those of other units.

Merger Terms

The terms of a merger include two important elements. (1) Who will control the combined enterprise? (2) How much will the acquiring firm pay for the acquired company? These points are discussed next.

Postmerger Control. The employment/control situation is often of vital interest. First, consider the situation where a small, owner-managed firm sells out to a larger concern. The owner-manager may be anxious to retain a high-status position, and he or she may also have developed a camaraderie with the employees and thus be concerned about keeping operating control of the organization after the merger. Thus, these points are likely to be stressed during the merger negotiations.[10] When a publicly owned firm not controlled by its managers is merged into another company, the acquired firm's management also is worried about its postmerger position. If the acquiring firm agrees to keep the old management, then management may be willing to support the merger and to recommend its acceptance to the stockholders. If the old management is to be removed, then it will probably resist the merger.[11]

The Price Paid. The second key element in a merger is the price to be paid for the target company—the cash or shares of stock to be given in exchange for the firm. The analysis is similar to a regular capital budgeting analysis: The incremental earnings are estimated; a discount rate is applied to find the present value of these earnings; and, if the present value of the future incremental earnings exceeds the price to be paid for the target firm, then the merger is approved. Thus, only if the target firm is worth more to the acquiring firm than its market value as a separate entity will the merger be feasible. Obviously, the acquiring firm tries to buy at as low a price as possible, while the target firm tries to

---

[10]The acquiring firm may also be concerned about this point, especially if the acquired firm's management is quite good. A condition of the merger may be that the management team agrees to stay on for a period, such as five years, after the merger. Also, the price paid may be contingent on the acquired firm's performance subsequent to the merger. For example, when International Holdings acquired Walker Products, the price set was 100,000 shares of International Holdings stock at the time the deal was closed plus an additional 30,000 shares each year for the next three years, provided Walker Products earned at least $500,000 during each of these years. Since Walker's managers owned the stock and would receive the bonus, they had incentive to stay on and to help the firm meet its targets.

If the managers of the target company are highly competent but do not wish to remain on after the merger, the acquiring firm will often build into the merger contract a noncompetitive agreement with the old management. Typically, the acquired firm's principal managers must agree not to affiliate with a new business which is competitive with the business they sold for a period, such as five years. Such agreements are especially important with service-oriented businesses.

[11]Managements of firms that are thought to be attractive merger candidates occasionally arrange "golden parachutes" for themselves. These are extremely lucrative retirement plans which take effect if a merger is consummated. Thus, when Bendix was acquired by Allied, Bill Agee, Bendix's chairman, pulled the ripcord of his golden parachute and walked away with $4 million. Congress is currently considering controls on golden parachutes as a part of its "greenmail" legislative proposals.

sell out at the highest possible price. The final price is determined by negotiations, with the side that negotiates better capturing most of the incremental value. *The larger the synergistic benefits, the more room there is for bargaining and the higher the probability that the merger will actually be consummated.*[12]

To determine the value of the target firm, we need two key items: (1) a set of pro forma financial statements, and (2) a discount rate, or cost of capital, to apply to the projected cash flows.

Valuing the Target Firm

Table 24-2 contains the projected income statements for the Target Corporation, a firm which is being considered for acquisition by Allied Technologies, a large conglomerate. The projected data are postmerger, so all synergistic effects are included. Target currently uses 30 percent debt, but, if acquired, Allied would increase Target's debt ratio to 50 percent. Both Allied and Target have 46 percent marginal tax rates.

The Pro Forma Income Statements

The net cash flows are those flows which are available to Allied's stockholders, and these flows are the basis of the valuation.[13] Of course, the postmerger flows attributable to the target firm are extremely difficult to estimate. In a complete merger valuation, just as in a complete capital budgeting analysis, the component cash flow distributions should be specified, and sensitivity, scenario, and simulation analyses should be conducted. Indeed, in friendly mergers, the acquiring firm will often send a team consisting of literally dozens of accountants, engineers, and so forth, to the target firm's headquarters to go over its books, estimate required maintenance expenditures, set values on assets such as petroleum reserves, and the like.

The bottom line net cash flows shown in Table 24-2 are equity flows, so they should be discounted at the cost of equity rather than at the overall cost of capital. Further, the cost of equity used must reflect the riskiness of the net cash flows in Table 24-2; thus, the appropriate discount rate is Target's cost of equity, and not that of Allied or the consolidated post-

Estimating the Discount Rate

---

[12]It has been estimated that of all merger negotiations seriously begun, only about one-third actually results in merger. Also, note that in contested merger situations the company that offers the most will usually make the acquisition, and the company that will gain the greatest synergistic benefits should bid the most.

[13]We purposely keep the cash flows relatively simple to help focus on the key issues of the valuation process. In an actual merger valuation the cash flows would be much more complex, normally including such items as additional capital furnished by the acquiring firm, tax loss carry-forwards, and tax effects of plant and equipment valuation adjustments.

Table 24-2
Target Corporation: Projected Postmerger Income Statements
(Millions of Dollars)

	1985	1986	1987	1988	1989
Net sales	$105	$126	$151	$174	$191
Cost of goods sold	80	94	111	127	137
Selling/administrative costs	10	12	13	15	16
EBIT	$ 15	$ 20	$ 27	$ 32	$ 38
Interest[a]	3	4	5	6	6
EBT	$ 12	$ 16	$ 22	$ 26	$ 32
Taxes[b]	6	7	10	12	15
Net income	$ 6	$ 9	$ 12	$ 14	$ 17
Retentions for growth[c]	2	2	4	6	8
Cash available to Allied	$ 4	$ 7	$ 8	$ 8	$ 9
Terminal value[d]					121
Net cash flow[e]	$ 4	$ 7	$ 8	$ 8	$130

[a]Interest payment estimates are based on current debt plus additional debt to increase debt ratio to 50 percent, plus additional debt after the merger to finance asset expansion.

[b]Allied will file a consolidated tax return after the merger. Thus, the taxes shown here are the full corporate taxes attributable to Target's operations; there will be no additional taxes on the cash flowing from Target to Allied because a consolidated tax return will be filed.

[c]Some of the net income generated by Target after the merger will be retained to finance asset growth, while some will be transferred to Allied to pay dividends on its stock or for redeployment in the corporation. It is assumed that depreciation-generated funds are used to replace worn-out and obsolete plant and equipment.

[d]Target's earnings are expected to grow at a constant 10 percent after 1989. The value of all post-1989 dividends to Allied, as of December 31, 1989, is estimated by use of the constant growth model to be $121 million: $V_{1989} = \$9(1.10)/(0.1815 - 0.10) = \$121$ million. In the next section, we discuss the estimation of the 18.15 percent cost of equity.

[e]These are the net cash flows which are available to Allied by virtue of the acquisition of Target Company. They may be used for dividend payments to Allied's stockholders or to finance asset expansion in Allied's other divisions.

merger firm. Target's market-determined premerger beta was 1.30. However, this reflects Target's premerger 30 percent debt ratio, while Target's postmerger debt ratio will increase to 50 percent. The Hamada equations, which were developed in Chapter 10, can be used to approximate the effects of the leverage change on beta. First, we obtain the unlevered beta of Target's assets:

$$b_U = \frac{b_L}{1 + (1 - T)(D/E)} = \frac{1.30}{1 + (1 - 0.46)(0.30/0.70)} = \frac{1.30}{1.23} = 1.06.$$

Next, we recalculate Target's beta to reflect the new 50 percent debt ratio:

$$\begin{aligned}
b_L &= b_U [1 + (1 - T)(D/E)] \\
&= 1.06[1 + (1 - 0.46)(0.50/0.50)] \\
&= 1.06(1.54) = 1.63.
\end{aligned}$$

Finally, we use the Security Market Line to determine Target's approximate cost of equity. If the risk-free rate is 10 percent and the market risk premium is 5 percent, then Target's cost of equity, k_s, after the merger with Allied, would be 18.15 percent:[14]

$$k_s = R_F + b(RP_M)$$
$$= 10\% + 1.63(5\%) = 18.15\%.$$

Valuing the Cash Flows

The value of Target to Allied in 1984 is the present value of the cash flows accruing to Allied, discounted at 18.15 percent (in millions of dollars):

$$V_{1984} = \frac{\$4}{(1.1815)^1} + \frac{\$7}{(1.1815)^2} + \frac{\$8}{(1.1815)^3} + \frac{\$8}{(1.1815)^4} + \frac{\$130}{(1.1815)^5} = \$74.$$

Thus, if Allied could acquire Target for $74 million or less, the merger would appear to be acceptable from Allied's standpoint.

The Role of the Investment Banker

The investment banking community is involved with mergers in a number of ways: (1) helping to arrange mergers, (2) aiding target companies resist mergers, and (3) helping to value target companies. These merger-related activities have been quite profitable. For example, the investment bankers who arranged RCA's acquisition of C.I.T. Financial earned fees of $5.8 million. Du Pont's investment banker in the Conoco contest, First Boston, earned fees of over $15 million, while Morgan Stanley, Conoco's investment banker, had an arrangement under which it earned fees of about $15 million regardless of who won. No wonder investment banking houses are able to make top offers to finance graduates!

---

[14]In this example, we used the Capital Asset Pricing Model to estimate Target's cost of equity. This assumes that investors require a premium for market risk only. We could have also conducted a total risk analysis, in which the relevant total risk is the contribution of Target's cash flows to the total risk of the postmerger firm. That is, the postmerger firm's cash flows could be more risky or less risky than the premerger flows, or have the same risk.

In actual merger situations, the companies often hire investment banking firms to help develop valuation estimates. For example, when General Electric acquired Utah International in the late 1970s, the largest merger up to that time, GE hired Morgan Stanley to determine Utah's value. We discussed the valuation process with the Morgan Stanley analyst in charge of the appraisal. Morgan Stanley considered using the CAPM, but chose instead to base the discount rate on DCF methodology. However, other analysts, and the Morgan Stanley people in other situations, have used CAPM analysis as we describe it here. Merger analysis, like the analysis of any other complex issue, requires judgment, and people's judgment differs as to which method is most appropriate for any given situation.

Arranging Mergers

The major investment banking firms have merger and acquisition groups which operate within their corporate finance departments. (Corporate finance departments offer advice, as opposed to underwriting services, to business firms.) Members of these groups strive to identify firms with excess cash that might want to buy other firms, firms that might be willing to be bought, and firms that may for a number of reasons be attractive to others. Also, if a firm, say an oil company, decided to expand into coal mining, then it might enlist the aid of an investment banker to help it locate and then negotiate with a target coal company. Similarly, dissident stockholder groups of firms with poor track records may work with investment bankers to oust management through a merger.

Fighting Off Mergers

Target firms that do not want to be acquired generally enlist the help of an investment banking firm, along with a law firm that specializes in helping to block mergers. Defenses include such tactics as (1) changing the by-laws so that only one-third of the directors are elected each year and/or so that a 75 percent approval versus a simple majority is required to approve a merger, (2) trying to convince the target firm's stockholders that the price being offered is too low, (3) raising antitrust issues in hopes that the Justice Department will intervene, (4) repurchasing stock in the open market in an effort to push the price above that being offered by the potential acquirer, and (5) getting a "white knight" that is more acceptable to the target firm's management to compete with the potential acquirer. More extreme measures are also available. For example, some firms have virtually committed suicide by such tactics as borrowing on terms that require immediate repayment of all loans if the firm is acquired, selling off at bargain prices the assets that made them desirable targets, and granting such lucrative "golden parachutes" to their executives that the cash drain from these payments would render the merger infeasible. These extreme tactics are known as "poison pills," and their use is constrained by directors' awareness that blatant use of them will trigger personal suits by stockholders against directors who vote for them and, perhaps in the near future, by laws that will limit management's use of them.

Establishing a Price

If a friendly merger is being worked out between two firms' managements, it is important to be able to prove that the agreed-upon price is a fair one. Otherwise, the stockholders of either company may sue to block the merger. Therefore, in many larger mergers, each side will engage an investment banking firm to evaluate the target company and to help establish the fair price. For example, General Electric employed Morgan Stanley to determine a fair price for Utah International in their merger, and Royal Dutch used the same organization to help establish the price it paid for Shell Oil in 1984. (Royal Dutch owned 70 percent of Shell Oil's stock, and in 1984 it sought to buy the remaining 30 percent and to then merge Shell into Royal Dutch. With a 70 percent ownership, it could have forced a merger anyway, but the controlling ownership position would insure a stockholder suit charging an unfairly low price. At any rate, Morgan Stanley worked with Royal Dutch to establish an offer price and then to defend this price in the courts.) Even if the merger is not friendly, investment bankers may still be asked to help establish a price. If a surprise tender offer is to be made, the acquiring firm will want to know the lowest price at which it might be able to acquire the stock, while the target firm may seek help in "proving" that the price being offered is too low.[15]

Accounting Treatment for Mergers

Although a detailed discussion of accounting is best left to accounting courses, at least some mention should be made of the alternative ways of accounting for mergers. Mergers are handled in either of two basic ways: (1) as a *pooling of interests* or (2) as a *purchase*. The method used can have a significant effect on postmerger reported profits, and this, in turn, can influence the desirability of the merger.

A pooling of interests is, in theory, a merger among equals, whereas in a purchase one firm simply buys another. (Actually, in a pooling, one firm may be clearly dominant, and both its name and its management may be the survivors.) The specific rules that determine when a merger can be treated as a pooling are also discussed in this section.

Pooling of Interests Accounting

In a pooling of interests, the consolidated balance sheet is constructed by simply adding together the balance sheets of the merged companies. Table 24-3 shows the essential elements of the consolidated balance sheet after Firms A and B have merged under a pooling of interests. This final balance sheet holds regardless of how many shares Firm A (the survivor) gave up to acquire Firm B. (In a pooling, shares, not cash, must be exchanged.)

---

[15]Such investigations must obviously be done in secret, for if someone knew that Company A was thinking of offering, say, $50 per share for Company T, which was currently selling at $35 per share, then huge profits could be made. The biggest scandal to hit Wall Street thus far in the 1980s was the disclosure that a member of Morgan Stanley's merger group was himself buying the stock of target companies which he was analyzing for others. His purchases, of course, raised the prices of the stocks and thus caused his clients to pay more than they would otherwise have had to pay. Incidentally, he went to jail for improper use of inside information.

Table 24-3
Pooling of Interests Accounting

	Firm A	Firm B	Postmerger: Firm A
Current assets	$ 50	$25	$ 75
Fixed assets	50	25	75
Total assets	$100	$50	$150
Debt	$ 40	$20	$ 60
Common equity	60	30	90
Total claims	$100	$50	$150

Purchase Accounting

Under purchase accounting, the acquiring firm is assumed to have "bought" the acquired company in much the same way it would buy any capital asset, paying for it with cash, debt, or stock of the acquiring company. If the price paid is exactly equal to the *net asset value*, which is defined as total assets minus liabilities, then the consolidated balance sheet is identical to that under pooling. Otherwise, there is an important difference. If the price paid exceeds the net asset value, then asset values will be increased to reflect the price actually paid, while if the price paid is less than the net asset value, then assets must be written down when preparing the consolidated balance sheet.

Table 24-4 illustrates purchase accounting, using the same data as for the pooled companies. Note that Firm B's net asset value is $30, which is also its reported common equity value. This $30 book value could be equal to the market value (which is determined by the firm's earning power), but book value could also be more or less than the market value. Three situations are considered in Table 24-4. First, in Column 3 we assume that Firm A gives cash or stock worth $20 for Firm B. Thus, B's assets as reported on its balance sheet were overvalued, and A pays less than B's net asset value. The overvaluation could be in either fixed or current assets; an appraisal would be made, but we assume that it is fixed assets which are overvalued. Accordingly, we reduce B's fixed assets and also its common equity by $10 before constructing the consolidated balance sheet shown in Column 3. Next, in Column 4 we assume that A pays exactly the net asset value for B. In this case, pooling and purchase accounting would produce identical balance sheets.

Finally, in Column 5 we assume that A pays more than the net asset value for B: $50 is paid for $30 of net assets. This excess is assumed to be partly attributed to under-valued assets (land, buildings, machinery, and inventories), so to reflect this undervaluation, current and fixed assets are each increased by $5. In addition, we assume that $10 of the $20 excess of market over book value is due to a superior sales organization, or some other intangible factor, and we post this excess as *goodwill*. B's common equity is increased by $20, the sum of the increases in cur-

Table 24-4
Purchase Accounting

	Firm A (1)	Firm B (2)	Postmerger: Firm A		
			$20 Paid (3)	$30 Paid[a] (4)	$50 Paid (5)
Current assets	$ 50	$25	$ 75	$ 75	$ 80
Fixed assets	50	25	65[b]	75	80
Goodwill[c]	0	0	0	0	10
Total assets	$100	$50	$140	$150	$170
Debt	$ 40	$20	$ 60	$ 60	$ 60
Equity	60	30	80[d]	90	110[e]
Total claims	$100	$50	$140	$150	$170

[a]The price paid is the *net* asset value, that is, total assets minus debt.

[b]Here we assume that Firm B's fixed assets are written down to $15 before constructing the consolidated balance sheet.

[c]"Goodwill" refers to the excess paid for a firm over and above the appraised value of the physical assets purchased. Goodwill represents payment both for intangibles such as patents and for "organization value" that might arise from having an effective sales force.

[d]Firm B's common equity is reduced by $10 prior to consolidation to reflect the fixed asset write-off.

[e]Firm B's equity is increased prior to consolidation to reflect the above-book purchase price.

rent and fixed assets plus goodwill, and this markup is also reflected in A's postmerger equity account.[16]

Income Statement Effects

Significant differences can arise in reported profits under the two accounting methods. If asset values are increased, as they often are under a purchase, this must be reflected in higher depreciation charges (and also in a higher cost of goods sold if inventories are written up). This, in turn, will reduce future reported profits. Also, goodwill represents the excess paid for a firm over its adjusted net asset value. This excess is presumably paid because of the acquired firm's superior earning power, which will probably be eroded over time as patents expire, as new firms enter the industry, and so forth. Thus, the accountants (in Accounting Principles Board Opinion #17) require that goodwill be written off, or "amortized," with the write-off period corresponding to the expected life of the superior earning power but in no case being more than 40 years. Goodwill is certainly not a trivial issue. For example, when Philip Morris, Inc., acquired Seven-Up Corporation for a price of $520 million, approximately $390 million of the purchase price represented goodwill.

[16]This example assumes that additional debt was not issued to help finance the acquisition. If the acquisition were totally debt financed, the postmerger balance sheet would show increases in the debt account rather than increases in the equity account. If it were financed by a mix of debt and equity, both accounts would be changed.

Table 24-5 illustrates the income statement effects of the higher current and fixed assets, and also the write-off of goodwill, under pooling versus purchase. For the purchase, we assume that A purchased B for $50, creating $10 of goodwill and $10 of higher physical asset value. Further, we assume that this $20 will be written off over 10 years.[17] As Column 4 indicates, writing off goodwill and the higher asset values under purchase accounting causes reported profits to be lower than they would be under pooling.

The write-off of goodwill is also reflected in earnings per share. In our hypothetical merger, we assume that nine shares exist in the consolidated firm. (Six of these shares went to A's stockholders, and three to B's.) Under pooling, EPS = $2.00, while under purchase, EPS = $1.83. Further, the greater the amount of goodwill, the larger is the write-off and the more significant is the dilution in reported earnings per share. This fact causes managers to prefer pooling to purchase accounting.

Table 24-5
Income Effects of Pooling versus Purchase Accounting

	Premerger		Postmerger: Firm A	
	Firm A (1)	Firm B (2)	Pooling (3)	Purchase (4)
Sales	$100	$50	$150	$150
Operating costs	72	36	108	$109[a]
Operating income	$ 28	$14	$ 42	$ 41
Interest (10%)	4	2	6	6
Taxable income	$ 24	$12	$ 36	$ 35
Taxes (50%)	12	6	18	17.5
Earnings after tax	$ 12	$ 6	$ 18	$ 17.5
Goodwill write-off	0	0	0	1[b]
Net income	$ 12	$ 6	$ 18	$ 16.5
EPS[c]	$ 2	$ 2	$ 2	$ 1.83

[a]Operating costs are $1 higher than they otherwise would be to reflect the higher reported costs (depreciation and cost of goods sold) caused by the physical asset markup at the time of purchase.

[b]($10 of increased goodwill)/10 years = $1 write-off per year.

[c]Firm A had six shares and Firm B had three shares before the merger. A gives one of its shares for each of B's, so A has nine shares outstanding after the merger.

[17]The write-off of goodwill is not a deduction for income tax purposes, but the other excess write-offs (fixed assets and inventories) are deductible. Also, "negative goodwill" is eliminated at the time of the merger, so negative goodwill, had it existed, could not be used to increase reported profits in later years.

Six conditions must be met before the pooling method may be used:

1. The acquired firm's stockholders must maintain an ownership position in the surviving firm.

2. The basis of accounting for the assets of the acquired entity (LIFO versus FIFO, depreciation methods, and so forth) must remain unchanged.

3. Only independent interests may be combined; each entity must have had autonomy for two years prior to the initiation of the plan to combine, and no more than 10 percent ownership of voting common stock may be held as intercorporate investments.

4. The combination must be effected in a single transaction; contingent payouts are not permitted in poolings, but they may be used in purchases.

5. The acquiring corporation may issue only common stock identical to its outstanding voting common stock in exchange for substantially all the voting common stock of the other company; "substantially" is defined as 90 percent. Therefore, the cash portion of a pooled merger can be no more than 10 percent.

6. The combined entity cannot dispose of a significant portion of the assets of the combined companies for two years after the merger.

If all of these conditions are met, then the combination is, in an accounting sense, a "merger between equals," and a pooling of interests has occurred. In contrast, a purchase generally involves (1) a fundamental change in ownership and management, (2) an appraisal of the acquired firm's physical assets with a restatement of the balance sheet to reflect these values, and (3) the possible creation of goodwill.[18]

A merger is not the only way in which the resources of two firms can be combined. In contrast to mergers, in which all resources are combined under a single management, joint ventures involve the joining together of parts of companies to accomplish specific, limited objectives.[19] Joint ventures are controlled by the combined management of the two (or more) parent companies.

Joint Ventures

---

[18]See Accounting Principles Board Opinions #16 and #17.

[19]Cross-licensing, consortia, joint bidding, and franchising are still other ways for firms to combine resources. For more information on joint ventures, see Sanford V. Berg, Jerome Duncan, and Phillip Friedman, *Joint Venture Strategies and Corporate Innovation* (Cambridge, Mass.: Oelgeschlager, Gunn and Hain, 1982).

In one widely publicized joint venture, General Motors and Toyota, the first and third largest automakers in the world, began production in 1984 of 200,000 cars annually at an idle GM plant in Fremont, California. Toyota contributed an estimated $150 million to the venture, while GM put up $20 million in cash in addition to the California plant. Although both firms appointed an equal number of directors, Toyota got to name the chief executive. GM is reported to have sought the venture in order to gain better insights into how the Japanese can produce higher quality cars at a substantially lower cost than do U.S. automakers, while Toyota wanted to increase its production in the United States because of import quota limitations.

Divestitures

Although corporations do more buying than selling of productive facilities, a good bit of selling does occur. In this section, we briefly discuss the major types of divestitures, and then present some recent examples and rationales for divestitures.

Types of Divestitures

There are four primary types of divestitures: (1) sale of an operating unit to another firm, (2) sale to the managers of the unit being divested, (3) setting up the business to be divested as a separate corporation and then giving (or "spinning off") its stock on a pro rata basis to the divesting firm's stockholders, and (4) outright liquidation of assets.

Sale to another firm generally involves the sale of an entire division or unit, usually for cash but sometimes for stock of the acquiring firm. In a *managerial buyout*, the managers of the division purchase the division themselves, usually for cash plus notes. Then, as owners/managers, they reorganize the division as a closely held firm. Managerial buyouts are often called *leveraged buyouts*, or *LBOs*, because the managers generally put up only a small percentage of the purchase price in personal funds, while borrowing the rest. In a *spin-off*, the firm's existing stockholders are given new stock representing separate ownership rights in the division which was divested. The division establishes its own board of directors and officers, and becomes a separate company. The stockholders end up owning shares of two firms instead of one, but no cash has been transferred. Finally, in a *liquidation*, the assets of a division are sold off piecemeal, rather than as a single entity. To illustrate the different types of divestitures, we present some recent examples in the next section.

Divestiture Illustrations

1. Esmark, Inc., a holding company which primarily owns consumer products companies such as Swift meats and Playtex, has been aggressively selling off nonconsumer-oriented divisions. In 1980, Esmark sold

its petroleum properties for $1.1 billion to Mobil, Petro-Lewis, and Total North American. People thought of Esmark as a meat packing and consumer products company, and its stock price reflected this image rather than that of a company with huge holdings of valuable oil reserves. Thus, according to its managers, Esmark's stock was undervalued, and it was in danger of a Conoco-type takeover bid. Selling the oil properties helped Esmark raise its market value from $19 in 1980 to $45 in 1982. The Esmark divestiture is an example of selling assets to another company.

2. ITT, in a move to streamline and rationalize its holdings, recently divested itself of 27 separate companies, with a value of $1.2 billion. Some of these divisions were suffering losses and were holding down the parent company's earnings, while others simply no longer fitted into ITT's corporate strategy. Also, ITT had a debt ratio that many regarded as excessive, and it used the proceeds from its asset sales to reduce debt.

3. International Paper (IP) recently sold its Canadian subsidiary to Canadian Pacific for $1.1 billion. IP plans to spend $4 billion during the next five years to modernize its facilities, and the sale of the Canadian unit will help finance these expenditures.

4. IU International, a multimillion dollar conglomerate listed on the NYSE, recently spun off or sold three major subsidiaries—Gotaas-Larson, an ocean shipping company involved in petroleum products transportation; Canadian Utilities, an electric utility; and Echo Bay Mining, a gold mining company. The Gotaas-Larson and Echo Bay stock was distributed to IU's own stockholders, while Canadian Utilities was sold for cash, which IU then used to repurchase its own shares. IU also owned (and retained) some major trucking companies (Ryder and PIE), several manufacturing businesses, and some large agribusiness operations. IU's management originally planned to combine highly cyclical businesses such as ocean shipping and gold mining with stable ones such as utilities, thereby gaining overall corporate stability through diversification. The strategy worked reasonably well from an operating standpoint, but it failed in the financial markets. According to its management, IU's very diversity kept it from being assigned to any particular industrial classification, so security analysts tended not to follow the company and therefore did not recommend it to investors. (Analysts tend to concentrate on an industry, and they do not like to recommend, and investors do not like to invest in, a company they do not understand.) As a result, IU had a low P/E ratio and a low market price. After the divestitures, IU's stock price rose from $10 to $25.

5. In late 1981, U.S. Steel sold certain coal operations to Standard Oil of Ohio for $600 million. Sohio wanted the properties to diversify its energy base, and U.S. Steel apparently wanted to start building its "war chest" for the early 1982 Marathon Oil acquisition.

6. Occidental Petroleum (Oxy), facing over $800 million in annual debt service requirements, mostly because of its acquisition of Cities Service, was recently scrambling to sell assets to help reduce the debt burden. At the time, Oxy had already sold Cities Service Gas Company for $530 million; a copper division for $75 million; and all of Cities Service's refining and marketing operations, including a giant refinery in Lake Charles, Louisiana, and over 900 service stations and convenience stores, to the Southland Corporation, operator and franchiser of over 7,000 7-Eleven stores.

7. In 1984, AT&T was broken up to settle a Justice Department antitrust suit against AT&T. For almost 100 years, AT&T had operated as a holding company which owned Western Electric (its manufacturing subsidiary), Bell Labs (its research arm), a huge long distance network system which was operated as a division of the parent company, and 22 Bell operating companies such as Pacific Telephone, New York Telephone, Southern Bell, and Southwestern Bell. Under the settlement, AT&T was reorganized into eight separate companies—a slimmed down AT&T, which kept Western Electric, Bell Labs, and all interstate long distance operations, plus seven new regional telephone holding companies which were created from the 22 old operating telephone companies. The stock of the seven new telephone companies was spun off to AT&T's stockholders. A person who held 10 shares of AT&T stock owned, after the divestiture, 10 shares of the new AT&T plus one share in each of the seven new operating companies. The 17 shares were backed by the same assets that had previously backed 10 shares of AT&T common.

The AT&T divestiture occurred at the insistence of the Justice Department, which wanted to break up the Bell System into a regulated monopoly segment (the telephone companies) and a segment which would be subjected to competition and which would not have a huge captive market. The breakup was designed to strengthen competition in those parts of the telecommunications industry which are not natural monopolies.

8. In late 1982 Woolworth liquidated every one of its 336 Woolco discount stores in the United States. This reduced the company, which had 1981 sales of $7.2 billion, by 30 percent. Woolco had posted operating losses of $19 million in 1981, and losses in the first half of 1982 had climbed to an alarming $21 million. Woolworth's CEO, Edward F. Gibbons, was quoted as saying: "How many losses can you take?" Woolco's demise cost the parent company some $325 million, taken as a one-time, after-tax write-off.

9. In early 1982 RCA sold Gibson Greeting Cards to a group which included Gibson's managers and some financiers for $81 million. The purchasing group put up $1 million in cash and raised the remaining $80 million through bank loans and real estate leasebacks. A year later, in May 1983, Gibson went public, and the 50 percent interest held by

the financiers had a market value of $140 million, which is not a bad return on a $1 million investment. This is one example of a hot new divestiture technique called a *leveraged buyout,* in which managers buy a company by borrowing heavily against its assets.

There are two opposing views expressed on leveraged buyouts. One view is that leveraged buyouts present managers with the opportunity to get an equity stake in the business they run, thus fostering entrepreneurship. The opposing view is that the buyout is a classic insider's technique for snapping up a company at a cut-rate price. There is some truth in each view, and, as a result, the SEC examines such deals closely, as do sophisticated stockholders, and suits can and will be filed to block unfair management buyouts.[20]

10. Continental Illinois, one of the largest U.S. bank holding companies, was struggling to avoid bankruptcy in 1984 as a result of imprudent loans to oil companies and developing nations. Continental sold off profitable divisions, such as its leasing and credit card operations, in an effort to raise the funds it needed to cover its bad loan losses and deposit withdrawals. Thus, Continental's asset sales were part of an effort to stay alive. Ultimately, Continental was bailed out by the Federal Deposit Insurance Corporation and the Federal Reserve, which arranged a $7.5 billion rescue package and which gave a blanket guarantee for Continental's entire $40 billion of liabilities.

The above examples illustrate the varied reasons for divestitures. Sometimes, the market does not appear to properly recognize the value of a firm's assets when they are held as part of a conglomerate; the Esmark oil properties case is an example. Also, if IU International's management is correct, there are cases where a company becomes so complex and so diverse that analysts and investors just do not understand it and consequently ignore it.

Often, a company will need cash either to finance expansion in its primary business lines or to reduce a large debt burden, and divestitures can be used to raise cash, as illustrated by the International Paper and Occidental Petroleum examples. The ITT example illustrates the fact that business is dynamic—conditions change, corporate strategies change in response, and, as a result, firms alter their asset portfolios by both acquisitions and divestitures. Some divestitures, such as Woolworth's liquidation of its Woolco stores, occur to unload losing assets that cannot

---

[20]For example, David Mahoney, chairman of Norton Simon Corporation, a NYSE-listed company which owned Hunt Foods, Avis, and Max Factor, among others, attempted to obtain the company in a leveraged buyout. Wall Street analysts were reported to feel that the $29 per share Mahoney offered was too low, and Norton Simon's market price soon went well above $29. Several companies then began bidding for Norton Simon. In the end, Esmark (discussed above) won with a bid of $35.50 per share, or a total cost of $1 billion. Esmark used some of the money it had raised from the sale of its oil properties to help finance the Norton Simon acquisition.

be divested by another method. The AT&T example illustrates one of the many instances in which a divestiture is the result of an antitrust settlement. Finally, Continental Illinois' sales represent a desperate effort to get the cash needed to stay alive.

Holding Companies

Holding companies date from 1889, when New Jersey became the first state to pass a law permitting corporations to be formed for the sole purpose of owning the stocks of other companies. Many of the advantages and disadvantages of holding companies are identical to those of large-scale operations already discussed in connection with mergers and consolidations. Whether a company is organized on a divisional basis or with the divisions kept as separate companies does not affect the basic reasons for conducting a large-scale, multiproduct, multiplant operation. However, as we show next, the holding company form of large-scale operations has some distinct advantages and disadvantages over those of completely integrated divisionalized operations.

Advantages of Holding Companies

Holding companies have two major advantages: (1) control with fractional ownership and (2) isolation of risks.

1. **Control with fractional ownership.** Through a holding company operation, a firm may buy 5, 10, or 50 percent of the stock of another corporation. Such fractional ownership may be sufficient to give the acquiring company effective working control or substantial influence over the operations of the company in which it has acquired stock ownership. Working control is often considered to entail more than 25 percent of the common stock, but it can be as low as 10 percent if the stock is widely distributed. One financier says that the attitude of management is more important than the number of shares owned: "If they think you can control the company, then you do." In addition, control on a very slim margin can be held through friendship with large stockholders outside the holding company group.

2. **Isolation of risks.** Because the various operating companies in a holding company system are separate legal entities, the obligations of any one unit are separate from those of the other units. Catastrophic losses incurred by one unit of the holding company system are therefore not transmitted as claims on the assets of the other units. However, we should note that while this is a customary generalization, it is not always valid. First, the parent company may feel obligated to make good on the subsidiary's debts, even though it is not legally bound to do so, in order to keep its good name and thus retain customers. Examples of this would include American Express's payment of over $100 million in connection with a swindle that was the responsibility of one of its subsidi-

aries, and United California Bank's coverage of its Swiss affiliate's multimillion dollar fraud loss in the 1970s. Second, a parent company may feel obligated to supply capital to an affiliate in order to protect its initial investment; General Public Utilities' continued support of its subsidiaries' Three Mile Island nuclear plant is an example. And, third, when lending to one of the units of a holding company system, an astute loan officer may require a guarantee by the parent holding company. To some degree, therefore, the assets in the various elements of a holding company are joined. Still, a catastrophic loss, as could occur if a drug company's subsidiary distributed a batch of toxic medicine, can be avoided.

Disadvantages of Holding Companies

Holding companies have two major disadvantages: (1) partial multiple taxation and (2) ease of enforced dissolution.

1. **Partial multiple taxation.** Provided the holding company owns at least 80 percent of a subsidiary's voting stock, the IRS permits the filing of consolidated returns, in which case dividends received by the parent are not taxed. However, if less than 80 percent of the stock is owned, then returns cannot be consolidated and only 85 percent of the dividends received by the holding company may be excluded. With a tax rate of 46 percent, this means that the effective tax rate on intercorporate dividends is 6.9 percent. This partial double taxation somewhat offsets the benefits of holding company control with limited ownership, but whether the penalty of 6.9 percent of dividends received is sufficient to offset other possible advantages is a matter that must be decided in individual situations.

2. **Ease of enforced dissolution.** It is relatively easy for the U.S. Department of Justice to require dissolution by disposal of stock ownership of a holding company operation it finds unacceptable. For instance, in the 1950s Du Pont was required to dispose of its 23 percent stock interest in General Motors Corporation, acquired in the early 1920s. Because there was no fusion between the corporations, there were no difficulties, from an operating standpoint, in requiring the separation of the two companies. However, if complete amalgamation had taken place, it would have been much more difficult to break up the company after so many years, and the likelihood of forced divestiture would have been reduced.

Holding Companies as a Leveraging Device

The holding company vehicle has been used to obtain huge degrees of financial leverage. In the 1920s, several tiers of holding companies were established in the electric utility and other industries. In those days, at the bottom of the pyramid, an operating company might have $100 million of assets, financed by $50 million of debt and $50 million of equity. Then, a first-tier holding company might own the stock of the operating firm as its only asset and be financed with $25 million of debt and $25 million of equity. A second-tier holding company, which owned the stock of the first-tier company, might be financed with $12.5 million of debt and $12.5 million of equity. Such systems were extended to four or more levels, but with only two holding companies, we see that $100 million of operating assets could be controlled at the top by $12.5 million of equity, and that these assets must provide enough cash income to support $87.5 million of debt. *Such a holding company system is highly leveraged, even though the individual components only have 50 percent debt/assets ratios.* Because of this *consolidated leverage,* even a small decline in profits at the operating company level could bring the whole system down like a house of cards.[21]

Cost of Capital Implications

A question arises as to the cost of capital to the subsidiaries of a holding company system. To see the problem, consider Table 24-6, which shows the balance sheets of a pure holding company, H, its two operating subsidiaries, A and B, and the consolidated corporation. H's only asset is the stock of A and B. Each of the operating companies has issued its own debt, and the parent company, H, has also issued debt. All of the operating companies' equity is owned by the parent.

Table 24-6
Holding Company System Balance Sheets

		Operating Company A				Operating Company B	
		Debt	$ 50			Debt	$ 50
		Equity	50			Equity	50
Total assets	$100	Total claims	$100	Total assets	$100	Total claims	$100
		Holding Company H				Consolidated Balance Sheet	
Stock A	$ 50	Debt	$ 50	Operating assets	$200	Operating company debt	$100
Stock B	50	Equity	50			Holding company debt	50
						Holding company equity	50
Total assets	$100	Total claims	$100	Total assets	$200	Total claims	$200

[21]Excessive leverage through holding companies caused problems for the electric utilities during the 1930s. Accordingly, Congress passed the Holding Company Act, which specifically forbids electric utility holding companies from issuing debt for the purpose of buying the stock of operating electric utilities. The same situation does not exist in the telephone industry. Therefore, telephone holding companies can and do sell bonds and use the proceeds to buy stock in operating companies. The purpose is to obtain capital at the lowest overall cost.

Here are some points to note:

1. The holding company's debt interest must be paid out of dividend income paid by the operating companies after they have paid interest on their own debt. Similarly, the operating companies' debt has first claim on the assets in the event of bankruptcy. Therefore, the debt of the operating companies is less risky than that of the holding company. Conceivably, if there were many operating companies, diversification would cause the debt of the holding company to be better regarded than that of the operating companies, but this is unlikely.

2. Equity investors in the market see only the consolidated balance sheet—this is the one in the annual report. Thus, in the illustrative situation, stockholders would think of the debt ratio as being ($100 + $50)/$200 = 75%, and the risk associated with a 75 percent debt ratio would be incorporated into the cost of equity. (Bond investors, on the other hand, would see the balance sheet of the entity whose bonds they bought—A, B, or H, but if H, they would certainly know that operating company debt stood between them and physical assets and operating cash flows.)

3. If the two operating companies had equally risky assets, then the cost of capital for capital budgeting purposes should be based on the marginal cost of capital at the *consolidated* level. For example, if the after-tax debt cost to the operating companies were 5 percent, the cost of debt to the holding company were 6 percent, and the cost of common equity to the holding company were 15 percent, then the cost of capital for capital budgeting at the subsidiary level would be

$$k_a(A\&B) = 0.5(5\%) + 0.25(6\%) + 0.25(15\%) = 7.75\%.$$

Alternatively, one could calculate the cost of capital to the *unconsolidated* holding company and then use that cost as the cost of equity to the operating companies:

$$k_a(H) = 0.5(6\%) + 0.5(15\%) = 10.5\%.$$
$$k_a(A\&B) = 0.5(5\%) + 0.5(10.5\%) = 7.75\%.$$

Either way, we see that the cost of capital to the operating companies is 7.75 percent.

The situation would become much more complicated if the debt ratios of Companies A and B were not identical, if A and B operated in different industries and consequently had different business risks, or if the holding company owned operating assets as well as the stock of A and B. In any of these cases, it becomes difficult to determine the appropriate cost of capital for either the operating companies or for the holding company. We can estimate a cost of equity, and hence an overall cost of capital, at the consolidated level, but it is difficult to "unscramble the egg" to determine the separate units' capital costs. The cost of capital estimating process here is conceptually identical to that described in the capital budgeting chapters for multidivisional firms, and it should be approached in the same way.

Summary

A *merger* involves the consolidation of two or more firms. Mergers can provide economic benefits through economies of scale or through the concentration of assets in the hands of more efficient managers, but they also have the potential for reducing competition, and for this reason, they are carefully regulated by governmental agencies.

In most mergers, one company (the acquiring firm) initiates action to take over another (the target firm). The acquiring company must analyze the situation and determine the value of the target company. Often there will be operating economies, or synergistic benefits, which will raise the earnings of the combined enterprise over the sum of the earnings of the two separate companies. In this circumstance, the merger is potentially beneficial to both sets of stockholders, but the two firms' managers and stockholders must agree on how the net benefits will be shared. This all boils down to how much the acquiring company is willing to pay, either in cash or in shares of its own stock, for the target company.

Although the acquisition of assets through merger is more common, firms do on occasion get rid of assets—this is called a *divestiture*. Sometimes divestitures involve a firm's *selling* one of its division's assets to some other firm. At other times, the divestiture involves setting up a separate corporation and then *spinning off* the stock of the new company to the stockholders of the old company. The reasons for divestitures vary from antitrust to cleaning up a company's image to raising capital needed for strengthening the corporation's core business.

In a merger, one firm disappears. However, an acquiring firm may wish to buy all or a majority of the common stock of another and to run the acquired firm as an operating subsidiary. When this occurs, the acquiring firm is said to be a *holding company*. Holding company operations have both advantages and disadvantages. The major advantage is the fact that control can often be obtained for a smaller cash outlay. The disadvantages include tax penalties and the fact of incomplete ownership.

We go on, in Appendix 24A, to show how mergers can be used to create an illusion of growth when no true growth is present.

Questions

24-1 Define each of the following terms:
   a. Horizontal, vertical, congeneric, and conglomerate mergers
   b. Hostile versus friendly tender offer
   c. Synergy
   d. Operating versus financial merger
   e. Merger analysis; valuation analysis
   f. Pooling of interests; purchase accounting; goodwill
   g. Joint venture
   h. Holding company; operating company; parent company
   i. Divestiture; spin-off; leveraged buyout

24-2 Four economic classifications of mergers are (a) horizontal, (b) vertical, (c) conglomerate, and (d) congeneric. Explain the significance of these terms in merger analysis with regard to (1) the likelihood of governmental intervention and (2) possibilities for operating synergy.

24-3 Firm A wants to acquire Firm B. Firm B's management thinks the merger is a good idea. Might a tender offer be used?

24-4 Distinguish between operating mergers and pure financial mergers.

24-5 In the spring of 1984, Disney Productions' stock was selling for about $50 per share. Then Saul Steinberg, a New York financier, began acquiring it, and after he had 12 percent, he announced a tender offer for another 37 percent of the stock, which would bring his holdings up to 49 percent, at a price of $67.50 per share. Disney's management then announced plans to buy Gibson Greeting Cards and Arvida properties, paying for them with stock, and Disney also lined up bank credit and (according to Steinberg) was prepared to borrow up to $2 billion and use the funds to repurchase shares at a higher price than Steinberg was offering. All of these efforts were designed to keep Steinberg from taking control. In June, Disney's management agreed to pay Steinberg $77.45 per share, which gave him a gain of about $60 million on a two-month investment of about $26.5 million.

When Disney's buyback of Steinberg's shares was announced, the stock price fell almost immediately from $68 to $46. Many Disney stockholders were irate, and they sued to block the buyout. Also, the Disney affair added fuel to a fire in a Congressional committee that was holding hearings on proposed legislation that would (1) prohibit someone from acquiring more than 10 percent of a firm's stock without making a tender offer for all the remaining shares, (2) prohibit "poison pill" tactics such as those Disney's management used to fight off Steinberg, (3) prohibit buybacks such as the deal eventually offered to Steinberg unless there was an approving vote by stockholders, and (4) prohibit (or significantly curtail) the use of "golden parachutes" (the one thing Disney's management did not try).

Set forth the arguments for and against the type of legislation discussed above. What provisions, if any, should be in such legislation?

24-6 Suppose a holding company has subsidiaries which have issued preferred stock and bonds to public investors (all of the subsidiaries' common stock is owned by the holding company). The holding company's major asset is its stock in its subsidiaries, but the parent company does own in its own right certain operating assets. The holding company also issues its own bonds and preferred stock.

Given this information, describe the relative riskiness of investments in the common, preferred, and bonds both of the holding company itself (the parent) and of the operating subsidiaries. Assume that all the operating assets are equally risky.

24-7 Philip Morris, Inc., recently acquired Seven-Up Corporation for $520 million. Seven-Up had a book value of $130 million. Do you think Philip Morris's management would prefer to treat the merger as a pooling or a purchase? Would your reaction be the same if the book value had been $520 million and the price paid $130 million? Explain.

24-8 Two large, publicly owned firms are contemplating a merger. No operating synergy is expected, but returns on the two firms are not perfectly positively correlated, so the standard deviation of earnings would be reduced for the combined corporation. One group of consultants argues that this risk reduction is sufficient grounds for the merger. Another group thinks this type of risk reduction is irrelevant because stockholders could themselves hold the stock of both companies and thus gain the risk reduction benefits without all the hassles and expenses of the merger. Whose position is correct?

Problems

24-1 Macon Mattress Company is being acquired by the Royal Knight Bedding Corporation for $2 million. (In addition to the $2 million paid to Macon's stockholders, Royal will also assume Macon's debt.) No synergistic effects are expected. The two companies' premerger balance sheets and income statements are as follows (in thousands of dollars except EPS):

Balance Sheets

Macon

Current assets	$ 750	Debt	$ 875
Fixed assets	1,125	Common equity	1,000
Total assets	$1,875	Total claims	$1,875

Royal

Current assets	$1,500	Debt	$2,000
Fixed assets	1,625	Common equity	1,125
Total assets	$3,125	Total claims	$3,125

Income Statements

	Macon	Royal
Sales	$ 750	$1,300
Operating costs	488	830
EBIT	$ 262	$ 470
Interest expense	100	200
EBT	$ 162	$ 270
Taxes (50%)	81	135
Net income	$ 81	$ 135
Common shares	60,000	100,000
EPS	$1.35	$ 1.35

a. Construct Royal's postmerger balance sheet assuming that the acquisition is treated as a pooling of interests.
b. Assume that the merger is treated as a purchase rather than a pooling of interests. Now, what would be the postmerger balance sheet? (Assume that any excess paid above net asset value will be recorded as goodwill.)

c. Construct the postmerger income statements for both pooling of interests and purchase, assuming a one-for-one exchange of stock. Goodwill will be written off over 25 years. What would be the post-merger EPS under each accounting method?

d. What are the postmerger cash flows under each accounting method assuming that the postmerger depreciation expense, which is included as an operating cost, is $300,000?

24-2 Giant, Inc., a large conglomerate, is evaluating the possible acquisition of the Home Company, a small aluminum window manufacturer. Giant's analyst projects the following postmerger data for Home (in thousands of dollars):

	1985	1986	1987	1988
Net sales	$200	$230	$250	$270
Cost of goods sold	130	140	145	150
Selling/administrative expense	20	25	30	32
EBIT	$ 50	$ 65	$ 75	$ 88
Interest	10	12	13	14
EBT	$ 40	$ 53	$ 62	$ 74
Taxes	16	21	25	30
Net income	$ 24	$ 32	$ 37	$ 44
Retentions	10	12	12	14
Cash available to Giant	$ 14	$ 20	$ 25	$ 30
Terminal value				450
Net cash flow	$ 14	$ 20	$ 25	$480

The acquisition, if made, would occur on January 1, 1985. All cash flows shown in the income statements are assumed to occur at end-of-year. Home currently has a market value capital structure of 40 percent debt, but Giant would increase the debt to 50 percent if the acquisition were made. Home, if independent, pays taxes at 30 percent, but its income would be taxed at 40 percent if it were consolidated. Home's current market-determined beta is 1.50.

The cash flows shown in the projected income statements include the additional interest payments due to increased leverage and asset expansion, and the full taxes paid by Giant on the Home income stream. Depreciation-generated funds would be used to replace worn-out equipment, so they would not be available to Giant's shareholders. Retentions are to be used, along with new debt, to finance Home's projected asset expansion. Thus, the net cash flows shown are the flows that would accrue to Giant's stockholders. The risk-free rate is 10 percent, and the market risk premium is 6 percent.

a. What is the appropriate discount rate for valuing the acquisition?

b. What is the value of the Home Company to Giant?

24-3 Jensen Electric Corporation is considering a merger with the Shady Lamp Company. Shady is a publicly traded company, and its current beta is 1.40. Shady has barely been profitable, so it has paid only 20 percent in taxes over the last several years. Additionally, Shady uses little debt, having a market value debt ratio of just 25 percent.

If the acquisition is made, Jensen plans to operate Shady as a separate, wholly owned subsidiary. Jensen would pay taxes on a consolidated basis, and thus the federal-plus-state tax rate would increase to 50 percent. Additionally, Jensen would increase the debt capitalization in the Shady subsidiary to a market value of 40 percent of assets. Jensen's acquisition department estimates that Shady, if acquired, would produce the following net cash flows to Jensen's shareholders (in millions of dollars):

Year	Net Cash Flow
1	$1.20
2	1.40
3	1.65
4	1.80
5 and beyond	Constant growth at 5%

These cash flows include all acquisition effects. Jensen's cost of equity is 16 percent, its beta is 1.0, and its cost of debt is 12 percent. The risk-free rate is 10 percent.

a. What discount rate should be used to discount the above cash flows?

b. What is the dollar value of Shady to Jensen?

c. Shady has 1.2 million common shares outstanding. What is the maximum price per share that Jensen should offer for Shady? If the tender offer is accepted at this price, what would happen to Jensen's stock price?

Selected Additional References and Cases

Considerable empirical investigation has been conducted to determine whether stockholders of acquiring or acquired companies benefit most from corporate mergers. One of the classic works in this field is

Mandelker, Gershon, "Risk and Return: The Case of Merging Firms," *Journal of Financial Economics*, December 1974, 303-335,

while one of the most recent works is

Wansley, James W., William R. Lane, and Ho C. Yang, "Abnormal Returns to Acquired Firms by Type of Acquisition and Method of Payment," *Financial Management*, Autumn 1983, 16-22.

For a comprehensive review of the empirical literature on mergers, see

Elgers, Pieter T., and John J. Clark, "Merger Types and Shareholder Returns: Additional Evidence," *Financial Management*, Summer 1980, 66-72.

Mueller, Dennis C., "The Effects of Conglomerate Mergers," *Journal of Banking and Finance*, December 1977, 315-347.

For an interesting test of the existence of synergy in mergers, see

Haugen, Robert A., and Terence C. Langetieg, "An Empirical Test for Synergism in Merger," *Journal of Finance*, September 1975, 1003-1014.

For more insights into the likelihood of acceptance of a cash tender offer, see

Hoffmeister, J. Ronald, and Edward A. Dyl, "Predicting Outcomes of Cash Tender Offers," *Financial Management*, Winter 1981, 50-58.

Some additional works on tender offers include

Dodd, Peter, and Richard Ruback, "Tender Offers and Stockholder Returns," *Journal of Financial Economics*, November 1977, 351-373.

Kummer, Donald R., and J. Ronald Hoffmeister, "Valuation Consequences of Cash Tender Offers," *Journal of Finance,* May 1978, 505-516.

The following article examines the effect of merger accounting on stock price:

Hong, Hai, Gershon Mandelker, and R. S. Kaplan, "Pooling versus Purchase: The Effects of Accounting for Mergers on Stock Prices," *Accounting Review,* January 1978, 31-47.

The following case in the Brigham-Crum casebook illustrates merger analysis:

Case 37, "Armada Corporation," which examines the effects of different types of mergers on EPS, P/E ratios, and stock prices.

The following cases in the Harrington casebook focus on Chapter 24 material:

"Philip Morris," which describes the firm's acquisition goals and its success in the acquisition of Miller Brewing Company.

"Kennecott Copper," which illustrates how management's attempt to maintain its position can conflict with shareholder interests.

"Diamond Shamrock," which illustrates divestiture analysis.

Using Mergers to Create an Illusion of Growth

If a company with a high P/E ratio buys a firm with a lower P/E ratio, then an increase in the acquiring firm's EPS results from the merger. If a firm carries out a series of such mergers, this activity will produce a pattern of rising earnings per share, even though no real growth in operating income exists. This illusion of growth, in turn, can lead to an overvaluation of the firm's stock, and this overvaluation may continue as long as the firm is able to continue to buy low P/E companies.

This point is illustrated by the data in Table 24A-1. In Section 1, Column A, we see that Firm A experienced a 20 percent growth rate in after-tax earnings from 1979 to 1981. However, its growth period is over, and, without mergers, total income would level out at $10 million and EPS at $1. Investors, however, do not know that Firm A's growth is over, so the stock has a P/E of 16 and is priced at $16 per share.

Table 24A-1
Merger Analysis: Growth Illusion

1. Net Income of Firms A, B, C, and D

	A	B	C	D	Consolidated
1979	$ 6,944,444	$5,000,000	$7,500,000	$11,250,000	$30,694,444
1980	8,333,333	5,000,000	7,500,000	11,250,000	32,083,333
1981	10,000,000	5,000,000	7,500,000	11,250,000	33,750,000
1982	10,000,000	5,000,000	7,500,000	11,250,000	33,750,000
1983	10,000,000	5,000,000	7,500,000	11,250,000	33,750,000
1984	10,000,000	5,000,000	7,500,000	11,250,000	33,750,000

2. Assumptions and Basic Premerger Data (1981)

a. P/E ratios: A's P/E = 16; other firms' P/Es = 8.
b. Exchange ratio (ER): Based on market values.
c. Shares of acquired companies: Equal to earnings.
d. Other companies' EPS = $1.
e. Other companies' prices = $8.

Table 24A-1 *(continued)*

3. Earnings per Share and Price Calculations

a. 1982: A merges with B.

$P_A = \$16 = 16(\$1)$

$P_B = \$8 = 8(\$1)$.

$ER = \$8/\$16 = 0.5$ shares of A per share of B.

Additional shares $= 0.5(5$ million$) = 2.5$ million.

New EPS $= (\$10 + \$5)/(10 + 2.5) = \$1.20$.

New price $= \$1.20(16) = \$19.20$.

b. 1983: Merge with C.

$P_A = \$19.20$.

$P_C = \$8$.

$ER = 0.4167$.

Additional shares $= 0.4167(7.5$ million$) = 3.125$ million.

New EPS $= (\$10 + \$5 + \$7.5)/(12.5 + 3.125)$

$\quad\quad = \$22.5/15.625 = \$1.44$.

New price $= \$1.44(16) = \$23.04$.

c. 1984: Merge with D.

$P_A = \$23.04$.

$P_D = \$8$.

$ER = 0.3472$.

Additional shares $= 0.3472(11.25$ million$) = 3.906$ million.

New EPS $= (\$10 + \$5 + \$78.5 + \$11.25)/(15.625 + 3.906)$

$\quad\quad = \$33.75/19.531 = \$1.73$.

New price $= \$1.73(16) = \$27.68$.

4. Calculated Earnings per Share for Firm A

	A	B	C	D	Consolidated
1979	$0.69	$1.00	$1.00	$1.00	$1.57
1980	0.83	1.00	1.00	1.00	1.64
1981	1.00	1.00	1.00	1.00	1.73
1982	$EPS_A = \$1.20$		1.00	1.00	1.73
1983		$EPS_A = \$1.44$		1.00	1.73
1984			$EPS_A = \$1.73$		

5. Annual Growth Rate in EPS

For A: $0.69 to $1.73 for 20 percent.

Annual growth rate in consolidated EPS: $1.57 to $1.73 for 2 percent, all of which occurred in 1979 and 1980, when A's operating income was growing.

In 1982, A merges with B, a no-growth company that earns $1 per share and sells for $8, or 8 times earnings. No synergy is present, and the exchange ratio, which is the number of shares of stock A given for each share of stock B, is based on relative market price, so $ER = \$8/\$16 = 0.5$. Therefore, A gives up 0.5 shares for each of B's 5 million shares, or 2.5 million shares in total. This produces the following 1982 EPS for the now enlarged Firm A:

$$EPS = \frac{A's\ earnings\ +\ B's\ earnings}{A's\ shares\ +\ Shares\ given\ for\ B}$$

$$= \frac{\$10,000,000\ +\ \$5,000,000}{10,000,000\ +\ 2,500,000} = \$1.20.$$

Thus, as shown in Section 3a, A's earnings per share for 1982 increase by 20 percent over 1981 EPS. Without the merger, EPS would have been $1.00, with zero growth.

Because A's 20 percent historic EPS growth rate was maintained, its P/E remains at 16 times. Now, in 1983, A buys C, another no-growth company similar to B except that C is 50 percent larger than B. Working through the arithmetic, we see in Section 3b that because of the merger, A's 1983 EPS rises to $1.44, so the 20 percent growth rate is again maintained. Although there is no real growth in any of the companies—operating earnings are flat—the fact that A started off with a high P/E ratio and then bought a series of low P/E ratio companies has produced growth in its EPS. Note, however, that A must buy increasingly larger firms to maintain this growth.

Now suppose the merger string is broken at some point—for example, the Justice Department blocks a particular merger. (As the mergers get larger, there is increasing danger of Justice Department intervention.) A's EPS growth rate would fall to zero, and analysts would examine the company closely. This would probably cause the P/E ratio to decline, and if the P/E ratio dropped back to 8 times, the assumed norm for a no-growth company, then A could no longer play the merger game to obtain growth in EPS, and A's 1984 stock price would fall from the $27.68 shown in Section 3c to $1.72(8) = $13.84.

Exactly this kind of thing happened during the conglomerate boom of the 1960s, and it has also occurred, though on a smaller scale, in the 1980s. In a very real sense, the growth obtained is illusory—it is not the kind of real growth that can be sustained. Buying stock in a firm that is using mergers to produce growth in EPS is very much like buying a chain letter; it may work out okay, but you had better know what you are doing, and you had better get in and out before the bubble bursts!

Bankruptcy and Reorganization

25

On April 22, 1983, Wilson Foods Corporation, the fifth largest meat packer in the United States, stunned its investors, creditors, and employees by filing for bankruptcy under Chapter 11 of the Bankruptcy Act. The filing was controversial because Wilson had an estimated net worth of about $67 million at the time of filing. Wilson had made $12.9 million on sales of $2.23 billion in fiscal 1982, but it reported a loss of $2.8 million for the first half of fiscal 1983, largely because of its high labor costs.

Wilson had a $60 million credit line with five banks, headed by Continental Illinois; such a credit line is essential in the meat packing business, because livestock must be paid with cash at the time of delivery. However, Wilson's credit line had a restrictive covenant calling for the company to maintain a net worth of at least $67 million. With the prospect of continuing losses, this provision would have been breached in the near future, which could have put the company out of business. Although filing under Chapter 11 violated Wilson's loan agreements, making the entire outstanding loan balance of $27 million due immediately, the bankers agreed not to require immediate repayment in order to give Wilson time to straighten out its affairs.

Wilson then lined up a new $80 million credit line from Citibank, and, with the approval of the bankruptcy court, announced its intention to use this to replace the previous credit line provided by Continental Illinois.

In a reorganization under Chapter 11, existing contracts can be modified, and Wilson used this aspect of the Bankruptcy Act to unilaterally abrogate its union wage agreement. Indeed, critics of the filing claim that Wilson filed for the sole purpose of reducing labor costs. Wilson, which traces its roots back to the mid-1800s, had agreed to wage rates and signed a long-term union contract shortly before a group of new,

---

This chapter was coauthored by Arthur L. Herrmann of the University of Hartford. 995

nonunion, low-cost competitors entered the meat packing business. These new competitors' labor costs were much lower than Wilson's, and Wilson claimed that its labor costs were too high to enable it to be competitive. However, because of severance clauses negotiated into the contract years earlier, Wilson could neither reduce wages nor, as a practical matter, cut its labor force.

Under provisions of Chapter 11, Wilson announced it was terminating its collective bargaining agreement and cutting its wage scale by almost half. The union filed unfair-labor-practice charges, and, in June, struck seven of Wilson's eleven plants. In July, Wilson negotiated a new union contract, providing hourly wages of $8.00, up from the $6.50 level that the company imposed upon filing under Chapter 11, but still well below the $10.69 hourly rate that prevailed prior to the filing. As of this writing, the contract, as well as all provisions of the proposed Chapter 11 reorganization, await approval by the bankruptcy court. Finally, it should be noted that in 1984 Congress passed new legislation which makes actions such as the one Wilson took somewhat more difficult, but still possible.

Thus far, the text has dealt with issues faced by growing, successful enterprises. However, many firms encounter financial difficulties, and some fail. Indeed, the combination of (1) record interest rates and (2) the longest recession since the 1930s led to the greatest number of bankruptcies in history, and the largest ones, during 1982, 1983, and 1984. The financial manager of a failing firm must know how to ward off his or her firm's total collapse and thereby reduce its losses. The ability to hang on during rough times often means the difference between the firm's forced liquidation versus its rehabilitation and eventual success. At the same time, an understanding of business failures, their causes, and their possible remedies is also important to financial managers of successful firms, because they must know their rights when customers or suppliers go bankrupt.

Types of Business Failure

Failure can be defined in several ways, depending on the problems involved or the situation facing the firm.

1. Economic failure. Failure in an economic sense signifies that a firm's revenues do not cover its total costs, including its cost of capital. Businesses that are *economic failures* can continue operating as long as their owners are willing to accept lower rates of return. Eventually, though, as assets are worn out and not replaced, such firms either close down or else contract to the point where the smaller level of output provides a "normal" return.

2. Business failure. The term *business failure* is used by Dun & Bradstreet, which is the major compiler of failure statistics, to include any business that has terminated with a resultant loss to creditors.[1]

3. Technical insolvency. A firm is considered *technically insolvent* if it cannot meet its current obligations as they fall due. Technical insolvency denotes a lack of liquidity and may be only temporary, that is, given time, a firm that is technically insolvent may be able to raise cash, pay off its obligations, and survive.

4. Insolvency in bankruptcy. A firm is *insolvent in bankruptcy* when its total liabilities exceed the true valuation of its assets. This is a more serious condition than technical insolvency, and it often leads to liquidation of the business.

5. Legal bankruptcy. Although many people use the term *bankrupt* to refer to any firm that has "failed," a firm is not *legally bankrupt* unless (1) it has failed according to criteria established by the Federal Bankruptcy Act and (2) it has been adjudged bankrupt by a federal court. Bankruptcy is a legal procedure for liquidating or reorganizing a business, with the liquidation or reorganization being carried out under special courts of law. Bankruptcy can be either *voluntary,* with the failing firm petitioning the court, or *involuntary,* with the firm's creditors petitioning the court and proving that the debtor is not paying debts as they mature. Formal bankruptcy proceedings are designed to protect both the firm and its creditors. If the problem is technical insolvency, then the firm may use the Bankruptcy Act to gain time to solve its cash flow problems without foreclosure by its creditors. However, if the firm is bankrupt in the sense that liabilities exceed assets, the creditors can use the bankruptcy procedures to insure that the firm's owners do not siphon off assets which should go to creditors.

Causes of Failure

The causes of financial failure are numerous, and they vary from situation to situation. However, it is useful to understand the major underlying causes in order to avoid them if possible, or to correct them in the event a reorganization is necessary.

A recent Dun & Bradstreet compilation assigned percentage values to bankruptcy causes as shown in Table 25-1. Management incompetence includes the failure to anticipate and then to adjust to recessions, high interest rates, or unfavorable industry trends. This is logical, since managements should plan ahead and be prepared for all types of economic conditions. Further, case studies show that financial difficulties are usually the result of a series of errors, misjudgments, and interrelated weak-

---

[1]Dun & Bradstreet, Inc., *The Business Failure Record* (New York, updated annually).

Table 25-1
Causes of Business Failure

Cause of Failure	Percentage of Total
Management incompetence	45.6%
Lack of managerial experience	12.5
Unbalanced experience in finance, sales, production, and so on	19.2
Lack of experience in line of business	11.1
Neglect	0.7
Disaster	0.5
Fraud	0.3
Reason unknown	10.1
	100.0%

Source: Dun & Bradstreet, Inc., *The Business Failure Record* (New York, 1983).

nesses that can be attributed directly or indirectly to management, and signs of potential financial distress are generally evident before the firm actually fails.

Research to isolate and identify the causes of business failure, and thus to predict or prevent it, is extremely important.[2] A number of financial remedies are available to management when it becomes aware of the imminence or occurrence of insolvency. These remedies are described later in this chapter.

The Failure Record

How widespread is business failure in the United States? In Table 25-2, we see that a fairly large number of businesses fail each year, although the failures in any one year are not a large percentage of the total business population. In 1982, for example, there were 25,346 business failures (as defined by Dun & Bradstreet), but this was only 0.89 percent of all business firms. It is interesting to note that while the failure rate per 10,000 businesses fluctuates with the economy, the average liability per failure has tended to increase over time. This is due both to inflation and to an increase in the number of billion dollar bankruptcies in recent years.

While bankruptcy is more frequent among smaller firms, it is clear from Table 25-3 that large firms are not immune. These data actually understate the financial problems among larger firms, because mergers

---

[2]Much of the current academic work in this area is based on writings by Edward I. Altman. For a summary of his work, and that of others, see Edward I. Altman, "Bankruptcy and Reorganization," in *Financial Handbook*, Edward I. Altman, ed. (New York: Wiley, 1981), Chapter 35.

Table 25-2
Historical Failure Rate of U.S. Businesses

Years	Number of Failures	Average Failure Rate per 10,000 Concerns	Average Liability per Failure
1857-1968	11,233[a]	87	$ 28,292
1900-1968	13,659[a]	70	32,889
1946-1968	11,089[a]	42	61,101
1959-1969	13,881[a]	54	84,724
1970	10,748	44	175,638
1971	10,326	42	185,641
1972	9,566	38	209,099
1973	9,345	36	245,972
1974	9,915	38	307,931
1975	11,432	42	383,150
1976	9,628	35	312,762
1977	7,919	28	390,872
1978	6,619	24	401,270
1979	7,564	28	352,639
1980	11,742	42	394,744
1981	16,794	61	414,147
1982	25,346	89	b
1983	31,334	b	b

[a]Average per year.

[b]Data not available.

Sources: Edward I. Altman, *Corporate Bankruptcy in America* (Lexington, Mass.: Heath Lexington, 1972); and Dun & Bradstreet, Inc., *The Business Failure Record* (New York, 1983).

Table 25-3
The Ten Biggest Nonbank Bankruptcies
(Billions of Dollars)

	Liabilities	Date
Penn Central Transportation Company	$3.3	June 1970
Wickes	2.0	April 1982
Itel	1.7	January 1981
Baldwin-United	1.6	September 1983
GHR Energy Corporation	1.2	January 1983
Manville Corporation	1.1	August 1982
Braniff Airlines	1.1	May 1982
Continental Airlines	1.1	September 1983
W. T. Grant Company	1.0	October 1975
Seatrain Lines	0.8	February 1981

Note: Several banks and savings and loan failures would have made the top ten, but when these institutions fail, they are either taken over by the federal deposit insurance authorities or else merged into healthy institutions.

Source: Data supplied by Edward I. Altman.

or governmental intervention are often used as an alternative to outright bankruptcy. The decision to give federal aid to Chrysler is an excellent illustration. Also, in recent years the Federal Home Loan Bank System has arranged the absorption of several very large "problem" savings and loan associations by sound institutions, and the Federal Reserve System has done the same thing for banks. In 1984, the Federal Deposit Insurance Corporation, along with the Fed, supplied the capital needed to keep Continental Illinois Bank alive. Several U.S. government agencies, principally the Defense Department, were able to "bail out" Lockheed when it otherwise would have failed, and the "shotgun marriage" of Douglas Aircraft and McDonnell was designed to prevent Douglas's failure. Merrill Lynch took over Goodbody & Company, which would otherwise have gone bankrupt and would have frozen the accounts of its 225,000 customers while the bankruptcy settlement was worked out. Goodbody's failure would have panicked investors across the country, so New York Stock Exchange member firms put up $30 million as an inducement to get Merrill Lynch to keep Goodbody from folding. Similar instances could be cited in other industries.

Why do government and industry seek to avoid bankruptcy among larger firms? There are many reasons. In the case of the financial institutions, the main one is to prevent an erosion of confidence and a consequent run on the banks. With Lockheed and Douglas, the Defense Department wanted not only to maintain viable suppliers but also to avoid disrupting local communities. With Chrysler, the government wanted to preserve both jobs and a competitor in the U.S. auto industry. Even when "the public interest" is not at stake, the fact that bankruptcy is a very expensive process gives private industry strong incentives to avoid out-and-out bankruptcy. The costs and complexities of bankruptcy are discussed in subsequent sections of this chapter, but first some less formal and less expensive remedies and legal actions are examined.

Settlements Short of Formal Bankruptcy

In the case of a fundamentally sound company whose financial difficulties appear to be temporary, the creditors generally prefer to work directly with the company, helping it to recover and reestablish itself on a sound financial basis. Such voluntary plans usually require some type of *restructuring* of the firm's debt, involving either *extension*, which postpones the date of required payment of past-due obligations, or *composition*, by which the creditors voluntarily reduce their claims on the debtor. Both procedures are designed to keep the debtor in business and to avoid the court costs associated with formal bankruptcy. Although creditors do not obtain immediate payment and may even have to accept less than is owed them, they often recover more money, and sooner, than if formal bankruptcy is filed. Also, chances are good that a customer will be preserved.

The debt restructuring begins with a meeting between the failing firm's managers and creditors. The creditors appoint a committee consisting of four or five of the largest creditors, plus one or two of the smaller ones. This meeting is typically arranged and conducted by an *adjustment bureau* associated with and run by the local credit managers' association.[3] Once the decision has been reached that the problems can be worked out, the bureau assigns investigators to make an exhaustive report. Then the bureau and the creditors' committee use the facts of the report to formulate a plan for adjustment of claims. Another meeting between the debtor and the creditors is then held in an attempt to work out an extension, a composition, or a combination of the two. Several meetings may be required to reach final agreements.

At least three conditions are usually necessary to make an informal debt restructuring feasible: (1) The debtor must be a good moral risk, (2) the debtor must show an ability to make a recovery, and (3) general business conditions must be favorable to recovery.

Creditors prefer *extension* because it provides for payment in full. The debtor buys current purchases on a cash basis and pays off the past balance over an extended time. In some cases, creditors may agree not only to extend the time of payment but also to subordinate existing claims to vendors who are willing to extend new credit during the extension period. Similarly, creditors may agree to accept a lower interest rate on loans during the extension. Because of the sacrifices involved, the creditors must have faith that the debtor firm will be able to solve its problems.

In a *composition*, a reduced cash settlement is made. Creditors receive in cash from the debtor a uniform percentage of the amounts owed them. The cash received, which may be as low as 10 cents on the dollar, is taken as full settlement of the debt. Bargaining will take place between the debtor and the creditors over the savings that result from avoiding costs associated with legal bankruptcy: administrative costs, legal fees, investigative costs, and so on. In addition to escaping such costs, the debtor gains in that the stigma of bankruptcy may be avoided; as a result, the debtor may be induced to part with most of the savings that result from avoiding a formal bankruptcy.

Often the bargaining process will result in a restructuring which involves both an extension and a composition. For example, the settlement may provide for a cash payment of 25 percent of the debt immediately, plus six future installments of 10 percent each, for a total payment of 85 percent. Installment payments are usually evidenced by

---

[3]There is a nationwide group called the National Association of Credit Management, which consists of bankers and industrial companies' credit managers. This group sponsors research on credit policy and problems, conducts seminars on credit management, and operates local chapters in cities throughout the nation. These local chapters frequently operate adjustment bureaus.

notes, and creditors will also seek protective controls over the firm's operations.

Voluntary settlements are not only informal and simple, but they are also relatively inexpensive because legal and administrative expenses are held to a minimum. Thus, voluntary procedures often result in the largest return to creditors. In addition, the almost-bankrupt business may be saved to continue as a future customer. One possible disadvantage of voluntary extensions/compositions is that the debtor is left to manage the business. This situation may result in an erosion of assets, but there are numerous controls available to protect the creditors. It should also be noted that small creditors may play a nuisance role by insisting on payment in full. As a consequence, settlements typically provide for payment in full for claims under $500 or $1,000. If a composition is involved and all claims under $500 are paid, all creditors will receive a base of $500 plus the agreed-upon percentage for the balance of their claims.

We should point out that informal voluntary settlements are not reserved for small firms. International Harvester, which we will discuss later in the chapter, avoided formal bankruptcy proceedings by getting its creditors to agree to restructure some $3.5 billion of debt. Likewise, Chrysler's creditors accepted both an extension and a composition to help it through its bad years.

Federal Bankruptcy Laws

Bankruptcy actually begins when a debtor is unable to meet scheduled payments to creditors, or when the firm's cash flow projections indicate that it will soon be unable to do so. As the bankruptcy proceedings go forward, these central issues arise:

1. Is the firm's inability to meet scheduled debt payments a temporary cash flow problem (technical insolvency), or is it a permanent problem caused by asset values having fallen below debt obligations (insolvency in bankruptcy)?

2. If the problem is a temporary one, then an extension which gives the firm time to recover and to satisfy everyone will be worked out. However, if basic long-run asset values have truly declined, then economic losses have occurred. In this event, who should bear the losses? Two theories exist: (1) the *absolute priority doctrine*, which states that claims must be paid in strict accordance with the priority of each claim, regardless of the consequence to other claimants, and (2) the *relative priority doctrine*, which is more flexible and which gives a more balanced consideration to all claimants. These doctrines will be discussed later in the chapter.

3. Is the company "worth more dead than alive," that is, would the business be more valuable if it were maintained and continued in oper-

ation or if it were liquidated and sold off in pieces? Under the absolute priority doctrine, liquidations are more likely because this generally permits senior creditors to be paid off sooner, but often at the expense of junior creditors and stockholders. Under the relative priority doctrine, senior creditors are more likely to be required to wait for payment in order to increase the chances of providing some returns to junior creditors and stockholders.

4. Who should control the firm while it is being liquidated or rehabilitated? Should the existing management be left in control, or should a *trustee* be placed in charge of operations?

These are the primary issues that are addressed in the federal bankruptcy statutes.

Our bankruptcy laws were first enacted in 1898. They were modified substantially in 1938, then they were changed substantially again in 1978, and some fine-tuning was done in 1984. The 1978 act was a major revision designed to streamline and expedite proceedings. During the 1970s, as bankruptcies became larger and more complex, it was simply taking too long to conclude bankruptcy proceedings, so Congress changed the law to speed things up. Also, the 1978 act represented a shift from the absolute priority doctrine toward the relative priority doctrine. (These doctrines should be thought of as a continuum, and not as absolute points. The 1978 law represented a movement along the continuum, and not a jump from one polar position to the other.)

The 1938 act consisted of 15 chapters designated with Roman numerals. The 1978 act eliminated all even-numbered chapters and now consists of eight odd-numbered chapters, designated by Arabic numbers. Chapters 1, 3, and 5 of the 1978 act contain general provisions applicable to the other chapters. Chapter 7 details the procedures to be followed when liquidating a firm; generally, Chapter 7 is not used unless it has been determined that reorganization under Chapter 11 is not feasible. Chapter 9 deals with financially distressed municipalities; Chapter 11 is the business reorganization chapter; Chapter 13 covers the adjustment of debts for "individuals with regular income"; and Chapter 15 sets up a system of trustees who help administer proceedings under the new act.

Prior to passage of the 1978 act, reorganizations in bankruptcy were of two types: either (1) Chapter XI proceedings, which were voluntary reorganizations originated by the existing management, or (2) Chapter X proceedings, which were involuntary, originated by creditors, and called for a court-appointed trustee to restructure completely the finances of the firm or else to liquidate it. Long, drawn-out court fights occurred over whether the proceedings should be conducted under Chapter X or Chapter XI.

The 1978 act combined the old Chapters X and XI into a single procedure (the new Chapter 11), which is more flexible and which provides more scope for informal negotiations between a company and its creditors and stockholders. Under the new act, a case is opened by the filing of a petition with a federal district bankruptcy court. The petition may be either voluntary or involuntary; that is, it may be filed either by the firm's management or by its creditors. A committee of unsecured creditors is then appointed by the court to negotiate with management for a reorganization, which may include the restructuring of debt and other claims against the firm. A trustee may be appointed by the court if it is in the best interests of the creditors and stockholders; otherwise, the existing management will retain control. Under the new Chapter 11, if no fair and feasible reorganization can be worked out, the firm will be liquidated under the procedures spelled out in Chapter 7.

Financial Decisions in Bankruptcy

When a business becomes insolvent, a decision must be made whether to dissolve the firm through *liquidation* or to keep it alive through *reorganization.* Fundamentally, this decision depends on a determination of the value of the firm if it is rehabilitated versus the value of its assets if they are sold off individually. The procedure that promises higher returns to the creditors and owners will be adopted. Often, the greater indicated value of the firm in reorganization as compared with its value in liquidation is used to force a compromise agreement among the claimants in a reorganization, even when each group feels that its relative position has not been treated fairly in the reorganization plan. The courts, and possibly the SEC, are called upon to determine the *fairness* and the *feasibility* of proposed plans of reorganization.[4]

Standard of Fairness

The basic doctrine of *fairness* states that claims must be recognized in the order of their legal and contractual priority. Carrying out this concept of fairness in a reorganization involves the following steps:

1. Future sales must be estimated.

2. Operating conditions must be analyzed so that the future earnings and cash flows can be predicted.

3. A capitalization rate to be applied to these future cash flows must be determined.

4. This capitalization rate must then be applied to the estimated cash flows to obtain an indicated value for the company.

5. Provision for distributions to the claimants must then be made.

---

[4]Reorganization plans must be submitted to the SEC if (1) the securities of the debtor are publicly held and (2) total indebtedness exceeds $3 million. However, the SEC recently announced that it would only become involved in bankruptcy cases which are either precedent setting or which involve issues of national interest.

The meaning and content of these procedures may best be shown by the use of an example of a reorganization involving the Columbia Chemical Corporation.[5] Table 25-4 gives Columbia's balance sheet as of March 31, 1983. The company had been suffering losses running to $2.5 million a year, and, as will be made clear in the following discussion, the asset values in the March 31, 1983, balance sheet are overstated. Since the firm was insolvent, it filed a petition with a federal court for reorganization under Chapter 11. The court, in accordance with the law, appointed a disinterested trustee. On June 13, 1983, the trustee filed a plan of reorganization with the court; the plan was subsequently reviewed by the SEC.

The trustee found that the company could not be internally reorganized, and he concluded that the only feasible program would be to combine Columbia with a larger, integrated chemical company. Accordingly, the trustee solicited the interest of a number of chemical companies. Late in July 1983, International Chemical Company showed an interest in Columbia. On August 3, 1983, International made a formal proposal to take over Columbia's $6 million of 7½ percent first-mortgage bonds, to pay the $250,000 in taxes owed by Columbia, and to pay

Table 25-4
Columbia Chemical Corporation:
Balance Sheet as of March 31, 1983
(Millions of Dollars)

Assets	
Current assets	$ 3.50
Net property	12.50
Miscellaneous	0.70
Total assets	$16.70
Liabilities and Capital	
Accounts payable	$ 1.00
Accrued taxes	0.25
Notes payable	0.25
Other current liabilities	1.75
7½% first-mortgage bonds, due 1995	6.00
9% subordinated debentures, due 1990[a]	7.00
Common stock ($1 par)	1.00
Paid-in capital	3.45
Retained earnings	(4.00)
Total claims	$16.70

[a]The debentures are subordinated to the notes payable.

[5]This example is based on an actual reorganization, although the company name has been changed and the numbers have been changed slightly to simplify the analysis.

40,000 shares of International common stock to the company. Since the International stock had a market price of $75 a share, the value of the stock was $3 million. Thus, International was offering $3 million of stock plus the takeover of $6 million of loans and $250,000 of taxes—a total of $9.25 million for assets that had a book value of $16.7 million.

Trustee's Plan. The trustee's plan, based on 40,000 shares at $75 equaling $3 million, is shown in Table 25-5. As in all Chapter 11 plans, the secured creditors' claims are paid in full (in this case, the mortgage bonds are taken over by International Chemical). However, the total remaining claims of the unsecured creditors equal $10 million against only $3 million of available funds. Thus, each claimant would be entitled to receive 30 percent before the adjustment for subordination. Before this adjustment, holders of notes payable would receive 30 percent of their $250,000 claim, or $75,000. However, the debentures are subordinated to the notes payable, so an additional $175,000 must be allocated to notes payable from the subordinated debentures. In Column 5, the dollar claims of each class of debt are restated in terms of the number of shares of International Chemical common stock received by each class of unsecured creditors. Finally, Column 6 shows the percentage of the original claim each group received. Of course, both the taxes and the secured creditors were paid off in full, while the stockholders received nothing.

SEC Evaluation. The Securities and Exchange Commission evaluated the proposal from the standpoint of fairness. The SEC began by esti-

---

Table 25-5
Columbia Chemical Corporation: Trustee's Plan

1. Senior claims:

Taxes	$250,000	Paid off by International
Mortgage bonds	$6,000,000	Assumed by International

2. Trustee's plan for the remaining $10 million of liabilities, based on 40,000 shares at $75 worth a total of $3 million, or 30 percent of remaining liabilities:

Remaining Claims (1)	Original Amount (2)	30% × Amount of Claim (3)	Claim after Subordination (4)	Number of Shares of Common Stock (5)	Percentage of Original Claim Actually Received (6)
Notes payable	$ 250,000	$ 75,000	$ 250,000	3,333	100%
General unsecured creditors	2,750,000	825,000	825,000	11,000	30
Subordinated debentures	7,000,000	2,100,000	1,925,000[a]	25,667	28
	$10,000,000	$3,000,000	$3,000,000	40,000	30%

[a]Because the debentures are subordinated to the notes payable, $250,000 − $75,000 = $175,000 must be allocated from the debentures to the notes payable.

mating the value of Columbia Chemical. This evaluation is presented in Table 25-6. After a survey and discussion with various experts, it arrived at estimated sales of $25 million a year. It further estimated that the profit margin on sales would equal 6 percent, thus giving indicated future earnings of $1.5 million a year.

The SEC analyzed price/earnings ratios for comparable chemical companies and arrived at eight times future earnings for a capitalization factor. Multiplying 8 by $1.5 million gave an indicated total value of the company of $12 million. Since the mortgage bonds assumed and taxes paid by International Chemical totaled $6,250,000, a net value of $5,750,000 was left for the other claims. This value is almost double that of the 40,000 shares of International Chemical stock offered for the remainder of the company. Because the SEC thought that the value of these claims was $5.75 million, almost twice the $3 million offered, it concluded that the trustee's plan for reorganization did not meet the test of fairness. Note that under both the trustee's plan and the SEC evaluation, the holders of common stock were to receive nothing, which is one of the risks of ownership, while the holders of the first-mortgage bonds were to be paid in full.

International Chemical was told of the SEC's conclusions and was asked to increase the number of shares it offered. International refused, and no other company offered to acquire Columbia. Because no better alternative offer could be obtained, and the only alternative to the trustee's plan was liquidation (with an even lower realized value), International Chemical's proposal was accepted despite the SEC's disagreement with the valuation.

Table 25-6
Columbia Chemical Corporation: SEC Evaluation

Estimated annual sales				$25,000,000
Earnings at 6% of sales				1,500,000
Value with P/E ratio of 8 times earnings				12,000,000
Mortgage bonds assumed and taxes paid by International				6,250,000
Net value				$ 5,750,000

Remaining Claims	Amount	0.575 × Amount of Claim[a]	Claim after Subordination	Percentage of Original Claim
Notes payable	$ 250,000	$ 143,750	$ 250,000	100.0%
General unsecured creditors	2,750,000	1,581,250	1,581,250	57.5
Subordinated debentures (subordinated to notes payable)	7,000,000	4,025,000	3,918,750	56.0
Total	$10,000,000	$5,750,000	$5,750,000	57.5

[a]$5,750,000/$10,000,000 = 0.575.

Standard of Feasibility

The primary test of feasibility in a reorganization is whether the fixed charges after reorganization will be adequately covered by earnings. Adequate coverage generally requires an improvement in earnings, a reduction of fixed charges, or both. Among the actions that must generally be taken are the following:

1. Debt maturities are usually lengthened, and some debt is usually converted into equity.

2. When the quality of management has been substandard, a new team must be given control of the company.

3. If inventories have become obsolete or depleted, they must be replaced.

4. Sometimes the plant and equipment must be modernized before the firm can operate and compete successfully on a cost basis.

5. Reorganization may also require an improvement in production, marketing, advertising, and other functions.

6. It is sometimes necessary to develop new products or markets to enable the firm to move from areas where economic trends are poor into areas with more potential for growth or at least stability.

To illustrate how the feasibility tests are applied, let us refer again to the Columbia Chemical Corporation example. The SEC observed that in the reorganization International Chemical Company would take over the properties of the Columbia Chemical Corporation. The SEC judged that the direction and aid of International Chemical would remedy the production deficiencies that had troubled Columbia. Whereas the debt/assets ratio of Columbia Chemical had become unbalanced, International Chemical went into the purchase with only a moderate amount of debt. After consolidation, International Chemical would still have a relatively low 27 percent debt ratio.

International Chemical's net income before interest and taxes had been running at a level of approximately $15 million. The interest on its long-term debt after the merger would be $1.5 million and, taking short-term borrowings into account, would total a maximum of $2 million a year. The $15 million earnings before interest and taxes would therefore provide a 7.5 times coverage of interest charges, exceeding the norm of 5 times for the industry.

Notice that the question of feasibility would have been irrelevant (from the standpoint of the SEC) had International Chemical offered $3 million in cash rather than in stock, and had it offered to pay off the bonds rather than take them over. It is the SEC's function to protect the interests of Columbia Chemical's creditors. Since the creditors are being forced to take common stock or bonds guaranteed by another firm, the SEC felt the need to look into the feasibility of the transaction. If International Chemical had made a cash offer, however, the feasibility of its own operation after the transaction was completed would have been none of the SEC's concern.

If a company is too far gone to be reorganized, then it must be liquidated. Liquidation can occur in two ways: (1) through an *assignment*,
which is an informal liquidation procedure that does not go through the
courts, or (2) through a *formal bankruptcy* carried out under the jurisdiction of a federal district bankruptcy court. Liquidation should occur
when the business is worth more dead than alive, or when the possibility of restoring the firm to financial health is so remote that the creditors
run a high risk of loss if operations are continued.

*Liquidation
Procedures*

Assignment is an informal procedure for liquidating debts, and it usually yields creditors a larger amount than they would receive in a formal
Chapter 7 liquidation. However, assignments are feasible only if the firm
is small, and its affairs are not too complex. An assignment calls for title
to the debtor's assets to be transferred to a third person, known as an
assignee or *trustee*. The assignee is instructed to liquidate the assets
through a private sale or a public auction, and then to distribute the
proceeds among the creditors on a pro rata basis. The assignment does
not automatically discharge the debtor's obligations. However, the
debtor may have the assignee write on the check to each creditor the
requisite legal language to make endorsement of the check acknowledg-
ment of full settlement of the claim.

Assignment

Assignment has some advantages over Chapter 7 liquidation, which
involves more time, legal formality, and expense. The assignee has more
flexibility in disposing of property than does a bankruptcy trustee. Action can be taken sooner, before the inventory becomes obsolete or the
machinery rusts, and, since the assignee is often familiar with the chan-
nels of trade in the debtor's business, better results may be achieved.
However, an assignment does not automatically result in a full and legal
discharge of all the debtor's liabilities, nor does it protect the creditors
against fraud. Both of these problems can be overcome by formal liquidation in bankruptcy, which is discussed next.

Chapter 7 of the Federal Bankruptcy Reform Act accomplishes three important tasks during a liquidation: (1) It provides safeguards against
fraud by the debtor; (2) it provides for an equitable distribution of the
debtor's assets among the creditors; and (3) it allows insolvent debtors
to discharge all their obligations and to start new businesses unham-
pered by a burden of prior debt. However, formal liquidation is time-
consuming, it can be costly, and it results in the extinction of the
business.

*Liquidation in
Bankruptcy*

The distribution of assets in a liquidation under Chapter 7 of the
Bankruptcy Act is governed by the following priority of claims:

1. *Secured creditors, who are entitled to the proceeds of the sale of specific
property pledged for a lien or a mortgage.* If the proceeds from the sale of

property do not fully satisfy the secured creditors' claims, the remaining balance is treated as a general creditor claim. See Item 9 below.[6]

2. *Trustee's costs to administer and operate the bankrupt firm.*

3. *Expenses incurred after an involuntary case has begun but before a trustee is appointed.*

4. *Wages due workers if earned within three months prior to the filing of the petition in bankruptcy.* The amount of wages is limited to $2,000 per person.

5. *Claims for unpaid contributions to employee benefit plans that were to be paid within six months prior to filing.* These claims, plus wages in Item 4, are not to exceed the $2,000 per wage-earner limit.

6. *Unsecured claims for customer deposits, not to exceed a maximum of $900 per individual.*

7. *Taxes due to federal, state, county, and any other government agency.*

8. *Unfunded pension plan liabilities.* Unfunded pension plan liabilities have a claim above that of the general creditors for an amount up to 30 percent of the common and preferred equity, and any remaining unfunded pension claims rank with the general creditors.[7]

9. *General, or unsecured, creditors.* Trade credit, unsecured loans, the unsatisfied portion of secured loans, and debenture bonds are classified as *general creditors.* Holders of subordinated debt also fall into this cate-

---

[6]When a firm or individual who goes bankrupt has a bank loan, the bank will attach any deposit balances. The loan agreement may stipulate that the bank has a first-priority claim on any deposits. If so, the deposits are used to offset all or part of the bank loan; this is called, in legal terms, "the right of offset." In this case, the bank will not have to share the deposits with other creditors. Loan contracts often designate compensating balances as security against a loan. Even if the bank has no explicit claim against deposits, the bank will attach the deposits and hold them for the general body of creditors, including the bank itself. Without an explicit statement in the loan agreement, the bank does not receive preferential treatment with regard to attached deposits.

[7]Pension plan liabilities have a significant bearing on bankruptcy settlements. As we discuss in Chapter 27, pension plans are of two types, *funded* and *unfunded*. Under a funded plan, the firm makes cash payments to an insurance company or to a trustee (generally a bank), which then uses these funds (and interest earned on them) to pay retirees' pensions. Under an unfunded plan, the firm is obligated to make payments to retirees, but it does not provide cash in advance. Many plans are actually partially funded—some money has been paid in advance, but not enough to provide full pension benefits to all employees.

If a firm goes bankrupt, the funded part of the pension plan remains intact and is available for retirees. Prior to 1974, employees had no explicit claims for unfunded pension liabilities, but under the Employees' Retirement Income Security Act of 1974 (ERISA), an amount up to 30 percent of the equity (common and preferred) is earmarked for employees' pension plans and has a priority over the general creditors, with any remaining pension claims having equal status to that of the general creditors. This means, in effect, that the funded portion of a bankrupt firm's pension plan is completely secured, but that the unfunded portion ranks somewhat above the general creditors. Pension funds are discussed in more detail in Chapter 27, but quite obviously, unfunded pension fund liabilities should be of great concern to a firm's unsecured creditors.

gory, but they must turn over required amounts to the holders of senior debt.

10. *Preferred stockholders, who can receive an amount up to the par value of the issue.*

11. *Common stockholders, who receive any remaining funds.*[8]

To illustrate how this priority system works, consider the balance sheet of Whitman, Inc., shown in Table 25-7. Assets total $90 million. The claims are indicated on the right-hand side of the balance sheet. Note that the debentures are subordinated to the notes payable to banks. Whitman has filed for bankruptcy under Chapter 11, and since no fair and feasible reorganization could be arranged, the trustee is liquidating the firm under Chapter 7.

The assets as reported in the balance sheet in Table 25-7 are greatly overstated; they are, in fact, worth less than half of the $90 million at which they are carried. The following amounts are realized on liquidation:

From sale of current assets	$28,000,000
From sale of fixed assets	5,000,000
Total receipts	$33,000,000

Table 25-7
Whitman, Inc.: Balance Sheet at Liquidation
(Thousands of Dollars)

Current assets	$80,000	Accounts payable	$20,000
Net fixed assets	10,000	Notes payable (due bank)	10,000
		Accrued wages, 1,400 at $500	700
		U.S. taxes	1,000
		State and local taxes	300
		Current liabilities	$32,000
		First mortgage	$ 6,000
		Second mortgage	1,000
		Subordinated debentures[a]	8,000
		Total long-term debt	$15,000
		Preferred stock	$ 2,000
		Common stock	26,000
		Paid-in capital	4,000
		Retained earnings	11,000
		Total equity	$43,000
Total assets	$90,000	Total claims	$90,000

[a]Subordinated to $10 million notes payable to the bank.

[8]Note that if different classes of common stock have been issued, differential priorities may exist in stockholder claims.

The order of priority of the claims is shown in Table 25-8. The first mortgage holders receive the $5 million in net proceeds from the sale of fixed property, leaving $28 million available to the remaining creditors, including a $1 million unsatisfied claim of the first mortgage holders. Next come the fees and expenses of administration, which are typically about 20 percent of gross proceeds; in this example, they are assumed to be $6 million. Next in priority are wages due workers, which total $700,000, and taxes due, which amount to $1.3 million. Thus far, the total of claims paid from the $33 million is $13 million, leaving $20 million for the general creditors. In this example, we assume that there are no claims for unpaid benefit plans or unfunded pension liabilities.

Table 25-8
Whitman, Inc.: Order of Priority of Claims

Distribution of Proceeds on Liquidation

1. Proceeds of sale of assets	$33,000,000
2. First mortgage, paid from sale of fixed assets	5,000,000
3. Fees and expenses of administration of bankruptcy	6,000,000
4. Wages due workers earned three months prior to filing of bankruptcy petition	700,000
5. Taxes	1,300,000
6. Available to general creditors	$20,000,000

Distribution to General Creditors

Claims of General Creditors	Claim (1)	Application of 50 Percent (2)	After Subordination Adjustment (3)	Percentage of Original Claims Received (4)
Unsatisfied portion of first mortgage	$ 1,000,000	$ 500,000	$ 500,000	92%
Unsatisfied portion of second mortgage	1,000,000	500,000	500,000	50
Notes payable	10,000,000	5,000,000	9,000,000	90
Accounts payable	20,000,000	10,000,000	10,000,000	50
Subordinated debentures	8,000,000	4,000,000	0	0
	$40,000,000	$20,000,000	$20,000,000	

Notes:

a. Column 1 is the claim of each class of general creditor. Total claims equal $40 million.

b. From Line 6 in the upper section of the table, we see that $20 million is available. This sum, divided by the $40 million of claims, indicates that general creditors will initially receive 50 percent of their claims. This is shown in Column 2.

c. The debentures are subordinated to the notes payable, so $4 million is reallocated from debentures to notes payable in Column 3.

d. Column 4 shows the results of dividing the amount in Column 3 by the original claim amount given in Column 1, except for the first mortgage, where the $5 million received from the sale of fixed assets is included.

The claims of the general creditors total $40 million. Since $20 million is available, claimants would initially be allocated 50 percent of their claims, as shown in Column 2, before the subordination adjustment. This adjustment requires that the subordinated debentures turn over to the notes payable all amounts received until the notes are satisfied. In this situation, the claim of the notes payable is $10 million, but only $5 million is available; the deficiency is therefore $5 million. After transfer of $4 million from the subordinated debentures, there remains a deficiency of $1 million on the notes; this amount will remain unsatisfied.

Note that 90 percent of the bank claim is satisfied, whereas a maximum of 50 percent of other unsecured claims will be satisfied. These figures illustrate the usefulness of the subordination provision to the security to which the subordination is made. Since no other funds remain, the claims of the holders of preferred and common stocks are completely wiped out.

Studies of the proceeds in bankruptcy liquidations reveal that unsecured creditors receive, on the average, about 15 cents on the dollar, while common stockholders generally receive nothing.

Recent Business Failures

This section sketches two of the more prominent recent business failures.

Continental Airlines

On September 24, 1983, Continental Airlines filed for protection from its creditors under Chapter 11. The reorganization plan included a restructuring of the company's $650 million in long-term debt and capital leases, including swapping some debt for stock with warrants attached.

Continental's problems began in 1978, when Congress deregulated the airlines. Under regulation, airlines were granted monopolies over specific routes, and they were allowed to charge prices which covered costs plus a return on invested capital. Thus, the airlines worked on a "cost-plus" basis, with little incentive to hold down costs. As a result, some pilots were paid $100,000 or more per year for what most of us would regard as extremely short work hours, and other wage rates were similarly high. With deregulation, new airlines, such as People Express, sprung up, hiring qualified pilots who would work longer hours than union pilots for $25,000 to $35,000 per year. These new, low-cost airlines sliced fares, yet were still profitable. When established, unionized carriers such as Continental tried to match them to maintain market share, the older carriers ran up huge losses. (Fixed costs are high in airline operations, so Continental had no choice but to cut fares.) A reorganization under Chapter 11, and an abrogation of its union contract, was Continental's answer to the problem.

Critics claimed that the Chapter 11 filing was merely a vehicle to re-distribute income from the labor force to the stockholders, and that the solvency of the company was never in question. However, Continental noted that the Bankruptcy Act does not require insolvency as a condition for filing under Chapter 11—only projections which demonstrate that if a company does not make radical changes, it will soon become insolvent. The 1984 modification to the act would have required Continental to prove that it was becoming insolvent before it abrogated its contract, rather than abrogate the contract and then justify it in the courts.

Reactions to Continental's actions were predictable. One executive of a competitive airline said, "I've got to give Continental credit. They were going right down the tubes, so they took action before they got there. They saw Braniff fold, and they decided to do something while they still had time." Conversely, one union official said, "They're using the pretext of bankruptcy to try to bust the unions." The unions lobbied very hard, and they did get Congress to amend the law as indicated above.

International Harvester

International Harvester is a huge company whose annual sales were $8.3 billion in 1979, when its earnings per share were over $12 and its stock sold for $45 per share. But then a series of disasters struck. Harvester hired a new chief executive, Archie McCardle, who had been president of Xerox, and McCardle decided to take a strike rather than agree to a large wage increase. The shutdown was longer than McCardle anticipated, costing Harvester millions in lost sales and profits. About the time the company started up again, the 1981-1983 recession struck, and since Harvester is a capital goods supplier, its sales and profits were hit especially hard. Finally, Harvester had entered this period with a high debt ratio, and it was forced to borrow even more, and at very high interest rates, to cover its operating losses.

Harvester's total liabilities in 1982 were about $3.5 billion, and it was unable to meet its required interest and principal payments, and to keep current on its accounts payable. The stock price plunged from a 1979 high of $45.50 to a 1982 low of $2.75. The company's common equity was a *negative* $800 million at year-end 1982, and it was forecasted to lose another $500 million in 1983. Clearly, bankruptcy was imminent, and if it had gone under, Harvester would have topped our Table 25-3 list of the largest U.S. bankruptcies.

But Harvester avoided formal bankruptcy proceedings. Its 200-odd major creditors concluded, in October 1983, that the company would be better off alive than dead, and that they would recover more of their money by letting Harvester continue in business. Therefore, the creditors agreed to restructure $3.5 billion of debt. Some $500 million of debt was exchanged for convertible preferred stock, and other relatively short-term debt was converted to longer-term notes with warrants to buy common stock. The plan was conditional upon the company selling $100 million of new common stock.

We can use Harvester's experience to make several points:

1. Companies are often worth more alive than dead, and when they are viable, creditors will strive to keep them operating.

2. Some debt generally has to be exchanged for equity to reduce fixed charges, and the maturity of the remaining debt often has to be lengthened.

3. The common stockholders often have to put up more capital ($100 million in this case) in order to retain their position in the business.

4. The creditors often receive a substantial equity position in exchange for their sacrifices. In Harvester's case, the creditors will own almost 80 percent of the stock if the company survives, the new convertibles are converted, and the warrants are exercised.

As we have seen, bankruptcy, or even the possibility of bankruptcy, can cause significant trauma for a firm's managers, investors, suppliers, customers, and community. Thus, it would be beneficial to be able to predict the possibility of bankruptcy so that steps could be taken to avoid it, or, if that is impossible, to at least reduce its impact. The most successful approach to bankruptcy prediction is *Multiple Discriminant Analysis (MDA)*, a statistical technique similar to regression analysis.[9] MDA can be used to classify companies into two groups, those with a high probability of going bankrupt and those with a low probability of failure. This classification is made on the basis of each company's characteristics as measured by its financial ratios.

Using Multiple Discriminant Analysis to Predict Bankruptcy

Common sense tells us that the probability of bankruptcy is, other things held constant, higher for a firm with a low current ratio than a high one. Similarly, the probability of bankruptcy is higher the higher the debt/assets ratio, the lower the rate of return on assets, the lower the times-interest-earned ratio, and so on. Figure 25-1 shows the general nature of the relationship between bankruptcy and a few illustrative ratios.

There are two difficulties with the type of analysis shown in Figure 25-1: (1) It is difficult to measure the probability of bankruptcy, as firms

Relationship between Ratios and Bankruptcy Probability

---

[9]This section is based largely on the work of Edward I. Altman, especially these two papers: (1) "Financial Ratios, Discriminant Analysis, and the Prediction of Corporate Bankruptcy," *Journal of Finance*, September 1968, 589-609; and (2) with Robert G. Haldeman and P. Narayanan, "Zeta Analysis: A New Model to Identify Bankruptcy Risk of Corporations," *Journal of Banking and Finance*, June 1977, 29-54.

Figure 25-1
General Relationship between Selected Financial
Ratios and the Probability of Bankruptcy

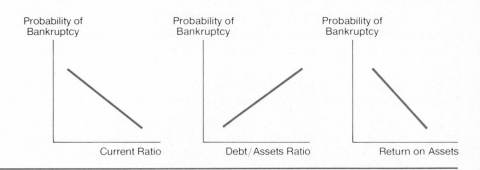

either go bankrupt or remain solvent, and (2) some type of index which blends together the effects of the current ratio, the debt ratio, the rate of return on assets, and all the other factors that affect the likelihood of bankruptcy is needed. Multiple discriminant analysis is designed to solve both of these problems.[10]

Multiple Discriminant Analysis

Suppose a bank loan officer wants to segregate corporate loan applicants into those likely to default or not default. Assume that data for some past period are available on a group of firms which includes both companies that went bankrupt and companies which were successful. For simplicity, we assume that only the current ratio and the debt/assets ratio are analyzed. These ratios for our sample of firms are given in Columns 2 and 3 of Table 25-9.

The data given in Table 25-9 are plotted in Figure 25-2. The X's represent firms that went bankrupt, while the dots represent firms that remained solvent. For example, Point A in the upper left section is the point for Firm 2, which had a current ratio of 3.0, a debt ratio of 20 percent, and the dot indicates that the firm did not go bankrupt. Point B, in the lower right section, represents Firm 19, which had a current ratio of 1.0, a debt ratio of 60 percent, and the X indicates that it did go bankrupt.

---

[10]In general, MDA can use any quantifiable factor to help classify populations. For example, to analyze a business firm, we use financial ratios as the bankruptcy determinants, while in the area of consumer credit, loan applicants may be classified into those likely to default and those not likely to default on the basis of such variables as years employed, annual income, whether the applicant has a telephone, and so on. This is called "credit scoring," and banks, small loan companies, credit card companies, and retailers use MDA extensively for this purpose. See Chapter 21 for a discussion.

Table 25-9
Data on Bankrupt and Solvent Firms

Firm Number (1)	Current Ratio (2)	Debt/Assets Ratio (3)	Did Firm Go Bankrupt? (4)	Z Score (5)	Probability of Bankruptcy (6)
1	3.6	60%	No	−0.780	17.2%
2	3.0	20	No	−2.451	0.8
3	3.0	60	No	−0.135	42.0
4	3.0	76	Yes	0.791	81.2
5	2.8	44	No	−0.847	15.5
6	2.6	56	Yes	0.062	51.5
7	2.6	68	Yes	0.757	80.2
8	2.4	40	Yes[a]	−0.649	21.1
9	2.4	60	No[a]	0.509	71.5
10	2.2	28	No	−1.129	9.6
11	2.0	40	No	−0.220	38.1
12	2.0	48	No[a]	0.244	60.1
13	1.8	60	Yes	1.153	89.7
14	1.6	20	No	−0.948	13.1
15	1.6	44	Yes	0.441	68.8
16	1.2	44	Yes	0.871	83.5
17	1.0	24	No	−0.072	45.0
18	1.0	32	Yes	0.391	66.7
19	1.0	60	Yes	2.012	97.9

[a]Denotes a misclassification. Firm 8 had Z = −0.649, so MDA predicted no bankruptcy, but it did go bankrupt. Similarly, MDA predicted bankruptcy for Firms 9 and 12, but they did not go bankrupt. The following tabulation shows bankruptcy and solvency predictions and actual results:

	Z Positive: MDA Predicts Bankruptcy	Z Negative: MDA Predicts Solvency
Went bankrupt	8	1
Remained solvent	2	8

The model did not perform perfectly, as two predicted bankruptcies remained solvent, while one firm that was expected to remain solvent went bankrupt. Thus, the model misclassified 3 out of 19 firms, or 16 percent of the sample. Its success rate was 84 percent.

The objective of discriminant analysis is to construct a boundary line through the graph such that, if the firm is to the left of the line, it is not likely to become insolvent, while it is likely to go bankrupt if it falls to the right. This boundary line is called the *discriminant function*, and in our example it takes this form:

$$Z = a + b_1(\text{Current ratio}) + b_2(\text{Debt ratio}).$$

Here Z is called the "Z score," a is a constant term, and b_1 and b_2 indicate the effect of the current ratio and the debt ratio on the probability of a firm's going bankrupt.

Figure 25-2
Discriminant Boundary between Bankrupt and
Solvent Firms Based on Current and Debt Ratios

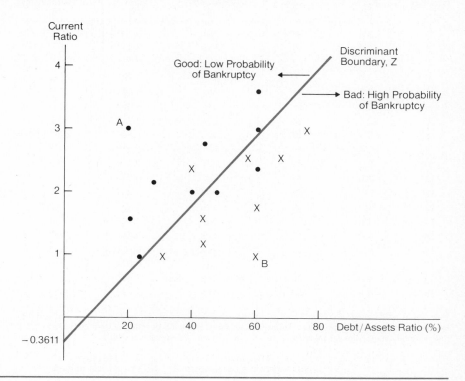

Although a full discussion of discriminant analysis would go well beyond the scope of this book, some useful insights may be gained by observing these points:

1. The discriminant function is fitted (that is, the values of a, b_1, and b_2 are obtained) using historical data for a sample of firms that either went bankrupt or did not during some past period. Table 25-9 gave the data for our illustrative sample. When the data were fed into a "canned" discriminant analysis program (the computing centers of most universities and large corporations have such programs), the following discriminant function was obtained:

$$Z = -0.3877 - 1.0736(\text{Current ratio}) + 0.0579(\text{Debt ratio}).$$

2. This equation was plotted on Figure 25-2 as the locus of points for which $Z = 0$. All combinations of current ratios and debt ratios shown on the line result in Z = 0.[11] Companies that lie to the left of the line are not likely to go bankrupt, while those to the right are likely to fail. It may be seen from the graph that one X, indicating a failing company, lies to the left of the line, while two dots, indicating nonbankrupt companies, lie to the right of the line. Thus, the discriminant analysis failed to classify properly three companies.

3. If we have determined the parameters of the discriminant function, then we can calculate the Z score for other companies, say loan applicants at a bank. The Z scores for our hypothetical companies, given in Column 5 of Table 25-9, may be interpreted as follows:

Z = 0: 50-50 probability of future bankruptcy (say within two years). The company lies on the boundary line.

Z < 0: If Z is negative, there is less than a 50 percent probability of bankruptcy. The smaller (more negative) the Z score, the lower is the probability of bankruptcy. The computer output from MDA programs gives this probability. It is shown in Column 6 of Table 25-9.

Z > 0: If Z is positive, the probability of bankruptcy is greater than 50 percent. The larger Z is, the greater the probability of bankruptcy.

4. The mean Z score of our companies that did not go bankrupt is −0.583, while that for the bankrupt firms is +0.648. These means, along with approximations of the Z score probability distributions of the two groups, are shown in Figure 25-3. We may interpret this graph as indicating that if Z is less than about −0.3, there is a very small probability that the firm will go bankrupt, while if Z is greater than +0.3, there is only a small probability that it will remain solvent. If Z is in the range ±0.3, called the *zone of ignorance*, we are uncertain about how the firm should be classified.

5. The signs of the coefficients of the discriminant function are logical. Since its coefficient is negative, the larger the current ratio, the lower is a company's Z score, and the lower the Z score, the smaller is the probability of failure. Similarly, high debt ratios produce high Z scores, and this is directly translated into a higher probability of bankruptcy.

---

[11]To plot the boundary line, let D/A = 0% and 80%, and then find the current ratio that forces Z = 0. For example, at D/A = 0,

$$Z = -0.3877 - 1.0736(\text{Current ratio}) + 0.0579(0) = 0$$
$$0.3877 = -1.0736(\text{Current ratio})$$
$$\text{Current ratio} = 0.3877/(-1.0736) = -0.3611.$$

Thus, −0.3611 is the vertical axis intercept. Similarly, the current ratio at D/A = 80% is found to be 3.9533. Plotting these two points on Figure 25-2, and then connecting them, provides the discriminant boundary line. It is the line that best partitions the companies into bankrupt and nonbankrupt. It should be noted that nonlinear discriminant functions may also be used.

Figure 25-3
Probability Distributions of Z Scores

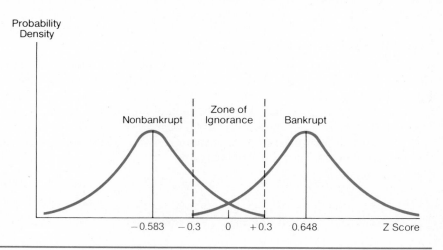

6. Our illustrative discriminant function has only two variables, but other characteristics could be introduced. For example, we could add such variables as the rate of return on assets, the times-interest-earned ratio, the average collection period, the quick ratio, and so forth.[12] Had the rate of return on assets been introduced, it might have turned out that Firm 8 (which failed) had a low ROA, while firm 9 (which did not fail) had a high ROA. A new discriminant function would be calculated:

$$Z = a + b_1(\text{Current ratio}) + b_2(\text{D/A}) + b_3(\text{ROA}).$$

Firm 8 might now have a positive Z, while Firm 9's Z might become negative. Thus, it is quite possible that by adding more characteristics we could improve the accuracy of our bankruptcy forecasts. In terms of Figure 25-3, this would spread the probability distributions apart and narrow the zone of ignorance.

Altman's Model

In a classic paper, Edward Altman applied MDA to a sample of corporations and developed a discriminant function that has seen wide use in actual practice. Altman's function was fitted as follows:

$$Z = 0.012X_1 + 0.014X_2 + 0.033X_3 + 0.006X_4 + 0.999X_5.$$

---

[12]With more than two variables, it is difficult to graph the function, but this presents no problem in actual usage because graphs are only used to explain MDA.

Here

X_1 = net working capital/total assets.

X_2 = retained earnings (balance sheet figure)/total assets.

X_3 = EBIT/total assets.

X_4 = market value of common and preferred stock/book value of debt.[13]

X_5 = sales/total assets.

The first four variables are expressed as percentages rather than as decimals. Also, Altman's 50-50 point was 2.675, and not 0.0 as in our hypothetical example; his zone of ignorance was from Z = 1.81 to Z = 2.99; and the *larger* the Z score, the less the probability of bankruptcy.[14]

Altman's function can be used to calculate a Z score for Southern Metals Company based on the data in Chapter 22. (See Tables 22-1 and 22-2.) This calculation, ignoring preferred stock, is shown below for 1984:

$$
\begin{aligned}
X_1 &= 400/2{,}000 = 20.0\% & \times\ 0.012 &= 0.240 \\
X_2 &= 750/2{,}000 = 37.5\% & \times\ 0.014 &= 0.525 \\
X_3 &= 266/2{,}000 = 13.3\% & \times\ 0.033 &= 0.439 \\
X_4 &= (50)(28.50)/(300 + 800) = 129.5\% & \times\ 0.006 &= 0.777 \\
X_5 &= 3{,}000/2{,}000 = 1.5 & \times\ 0.999 &= \underline{1.499} \\
& & Z &= \underline{\underline{3.480}}
\end{aligned}
$$

Since Southern's Z score of 3.480 is well above the 2.99 upper limit of Altman's zone of ignorance, the data indicate that there is virtually no chance that Southern will go bankrupt within the next two years. (Altman's model predicts bankruptcy reasonably well for about two years into the future.)

Altman and his colleagues' later work updated and improved his original study. In their more recent work, they explicitly considered such factors as capitalized lease obligations, and they used a larger sample with more current financial data. In addition, they applied smoothing techniques to level out random fluctuations in the data. The new model was able to predict bankruptcy with a high degree of accuracy for two years into the future, and with a slightly lower but still reasonable degree of accuracy (70 percent) for about five years.

MDA has been used with success to quantify ratio analysis, by credit analysts to establish default probabilities for both consumer and corpo-

---

[13][(Shares of common outstanding)(Price per share) + (Shares of preferred)(Price per share of preferred)]/Balance sheet value of total debt.

[14]These differences reflect the software package used to generate the discriminant function. Altman's program operated from a base of 2.675 rather than 0.0, and his program simply reversed the sign of Z from ours.

rate loan applicants, and by portfolio managers considering both stock and bond investments. It can also be used to evaluate a set of pro forma ratios as developed in Chapter 23, or to gain insights into the feasibility of a reorganization plan filed under the Bankruptcy Act. The technique is described in detail in many statistics texts, while articles cited at the end of the chapter discuss financial applications of the model. The interested reader is urged to study this literature, for MDA does have many potentially valuable applications in finance.

Summary

The major cause of business failure is incompetent management. Bad managers should, of course, be removed as promptly as possible, but if failure has occurred, a number of remedies are open to the interested parties.

The first question to be answered is whether the firm is better off "dead or alive"; that is, whether it should be liquidated and sold off piecemeal or be rehabilitated. If the company is basically sound, the debtor and the creditors may work out a voluntary plan for its recovery. Legal procedures are always costly, especially in the case of a business failure. Therefore, if it is at all possible, both the debtor and the creditors are better off if matters can be handled on an informal basis rather than through the courts. The informal procedures used in rehabilitation are (1) *extension*, which postpones the date of settlement, and (2) *composition*, which reduces the amount owed.

If voluntary settlement is not possible, the matter is thrown into the bankruptcy courts. If the court decides on *reorganization* rather than *liquidation*, it will appoint a trustee (1) to control the firm going through reorganization and (2) to prepare a formal plan for reorganization. The plan, which for large, publicly held firms may have to be reviewed by the SEC, must meet the standards of *fairness* to all parties and *feasibility* in the sense that the reorganized enterprise will stand a good chance of surviving instead of being thrown back into the bankruptcy courts.

The application of the standards of fairness and feasibility developed in this chapter can help determine the probable success of a particular plan for reorganization. The concept of fairness involves the estimation of sales and earnings and the application of a capitalization rate to earnings to determine the appropriate distribution to each claimant. The feasibility test examines the ability of the new enterprise to carry the fixed charges resulting from the reorganization plan. The quality of management and the company's assets must be assured. Production and marketing may also require improvement.

If liquidation is regarded as the only solution to the debtor's insolvency, the creditors should adopt procedures that will net them the largest recovery. *Assignment* of the debtor's property is the cheaper and the faster procedure. Furthermore, there is more flexibility in disposing of the debtor's property and thus providing larger returns. *Bankruptcy* provides formal procedures for liquidation to safeguard the debtor's property from fraud and to insure equitable distribution to the creditors. Nonetheless, it is a long and cumbersome process, and unless the trustee is closely supervised by the creditors, the debtor's property may be poorly managed during bankruptcy proceedings. The debtor does, however, obtain a full legal release from liability.

Finally, we discussed the use of *Multiple Discriminant Analysis (MDA)* to predict bankruptcy. MDA takes a set of variables such as the current ratio, debt ratio, and return on assets, and then uses them to establish a probability for failure. MDA can be used to evaluate existing firms or to judge the feasibility of a plan for reorganization.

Questions

25-1 Define each of the following terms:
  a. Failure; insolvency; legal bankruptcy
  b. Informal restructuring; reorganization in bankruptcy
  c. Assignment; liquidation in bankruptcy
  d. Fairness; feasibility
  e. Absolute priority doctrine; relative priority doctrine
  f. Bankruptcy Reform Act of 1978; Chapter 11; Chapter 7
  g. Priority of claims in liquidation
  h. Multiple discriminant analysis; Z score

25-2 "A certain number of business failures is a healthy sign. If there are no failures, this is an indication (a) that entrepreneurs are overly cautious, and hence not as inventive and as willing to take risks as a healthy, growing economy requires; (b) that competition is not functioning to weed out inefficient producers; or (c) that both situations exist." Discuss this statement.

25-3 How could financial analysis be used to forecast the probability of a given firm's failure? Assuming that such analysis is properly applied, could it always predict failure?

25-4 Why do creditors usually accept a plan for financial rehabilitation rather than demand liquidation of the business?

25-5 Would it be possible to form a profitable company by merging two companies, both of which are business failures? Explain.

25-6 Would it be a sound rule to liquidate whenever the liquidation value is above the value of the corporation as a going concern? Discuss.

25-7 Why do liquidations usually result in losses for the creditors or the owners, or both? Would partial liquidation or liquidation over a period limit their losses? Explain.

25-8 Are liquidations likely to be more common for public utility, railroad, or industrial corporations? Why?

Problems

25-1 The Trifts Publishing Company's 1984 balance sheet and income statement are shown on page 1024 (in millions of dollars). Trifts and its creditors have agreed upon a voluntary reorganization plan. In this plan, each share of the $6 preferred will be exchanged for one share of $2.40 preferred with a par value of $37.50 plus one 8 percent subordinated income debenture with a par value of $75. The $10.50 preferred issue will be retired with cash.

Balance Sheet

Current assets	$168		Current liabilities	$ 42
Net fixed assets	153		Advance payments	78
Goodwill	15		Reserves	6
			$6 preferred stock, $112.50 par value (1,200,000 shares)	135
			$10.50 preferred stock, no par, callable at $150 (60,000 shares)	9
			Common stock, $1.50 par value (6,000,000 shares)	9
			Retained earnings	57
Total assets	$336		Total claims	$336

Income Statement

Net sales	$540.0
Operating expense	516.0
Net operating income	$ 24.0
Other income	3.0
EBT	$ 27.0
Taxes (50%)	13.5
Net income	$ 13.5
Dividends on $6 preferred	7.2
Dividends on $10.50 preferred	0.6
Income available to common stockholders	$ 5.7

a. Construct the pro forma balance sheet assuming that reorganization takes place. Show the new preferred at its par value.

b. Construct the pro forma income statement. How much does the proposed recapitalization increase income available to common shareholders?

c. *Required earnings* is defined as the amount that is just enough to meet fixed charges (debenture interest and/or preferred dividends). What are the required pre-tax earnings before and after the recapitalization?

d. How is the debt ratio affected by the recapitalization? If you were a holder of Trifts' common stock, would you vote in favor of the recapitalization?

25-2 At the time it defaulted on its interest payments and filed for bankruptcy, the Martin Mining Company had the following balance sheet (in thousands of dollars). The court, after trying unsuccessfully to reorganize the firm, decided that the only recourse was liquidation under Chapter 7. Sale of the fixed assets, which were pledged as collateral to the mortgage bondholders, brought in $400,000, while the current assets were sold for another $200,000. Thus, the total proceeds from the liquidation sale were $600,000. Trustee's costs amounted to $50,000; no single worker was due more than $2,000 in wages; and there were no unfunded pension plan liabilities.

Current assets	$ 400	Accounts payable	$ 50
Net fixed assets	600	Accrued taxes	40
		Accrued wages	30
		Notes payable	180
		Total current liabilities	$ 300
		First mortgage bonds[a]	300
		Second mortgage bonds[a]	200
		Debentures	200
		Subordinated debentures[b]	100
		Common stock	50
		Retained earnings	(150)
Total assets	$1,000	Total claims	$1,000

[a]All fixed assets are pledged as collateral to the mortgage bonds.
[b]Subordinated to notes payable only.

a. How much will Martin's shareholders receive from the liquidation?
b. How much will the mortgage bondholders receive?
c. Who are the other priority claimants in addition to the mortgage bondholders? How much will they receive from the liquidation?
d. Who are the remaining general creditors? How much will each receive from the distribution before subordination adjustment? What is the effect of adjusting for subordination?

25-3 The balance sheet of the Martin Mining Company at the time it filed for bankruptcy is given in Problem 25-2. Martin's EBIT was $80,000 based on sales of $1,200,000, and its common stock market value was $200,000. Use the Altman multiple discriminant bankruptcy prediction model in answering the following questions.
a. What does the Altman model predict about the bankruptcy potential of Martin Mining?
b. Is the Altman model more sensitive to some variables than to others?

25-4 The following balance sheet represents Crown Electronics Corporation's position at the time it filed for bankruptcy (in thousands of dollars):

Cash	$ 10	Accounts payable	$ 1,600
Receivables	100	Notes payable	500
Inventories	890	Wages payable	150
		Taxes payable	50
Total current assets	$ 1,000	Total current liabilities	$ 2,300
Net plant	4,000	Mortgage bonds	2,000
Net equipment	5,000	Subordinated debentures	2,500
		Preferred stock	1,500
		Common stock	1,700
Total assets	$10,000	Total claims	$10,000

The mortgage bonds are secured by the plant, but not by the equipment. The subordinated debentures are subordinated to notes payable. The firm was unable to reorganize under Chapter 11; therefore, it was liquidated under Chapter 7. The trustee, whose legal and administrative fees amounted to $200,000, sold off the assets and received the following proceeds (in thousands of dollars):

Asset	Proceeds
Plant	$1,600
Equipment	1,300
Receivables	50
Inventories	240
Total	$3,190

In addition, the firm had $10,000 in cash available for distribution. No single wage earner had over $2,000 in claims, and there were no unfunded pension plan liabilities.

a. What is the total amount available for distribution to all claimants? What is the total of creditor and trustee claims? Will the preferred and common stockholders receive any distributions?

b. Determine the dollar distribution to each creditor and to the trustee. What percentage of each claim is satisfied?

Selected Additional References and Cases

For a better understanding of multiple discriminant analysis and its use to predict corporate bankruptcy, see

Collins, Robert A., "An Empirical Comparison of Bankruptcy Prediction Models," *Financial Management,* Summer 1980, 52-57.

Eisenbeis, Robert A., "Pitfalls in the Application of Discriminant Analysis in Business Finance and Economics," *Journal of Finance,* June 1977, 875-900.

Joy, O. Maurice, and John O. Tollefson, "On the Financial Application of Discriminant Analysis," *Journal of Financial and Quantitative Analysis,* December 1975, 723-739.

The following articles provide insights into various aspects of bankruptcy:

Altman, Edward I., "A Further Empirical Investigation of the Bankruptcy Cost Question," *Journal of Finance,* September 1984, 1067-1089.

Dun & Bradstreet, Inc., *The Business Failure Record* (New York: updated annually).

Harris, Richard, "The Consequences of Costly Default," *Economic Inquiry,* October 1978, 477-496.

Miller, Danny, "Common Syndromes of Business Failure," *Business Horizons,* December 1977, 43-53.

Warner, Jerold B., "Bankruptcy Costs: Some Evidence," *Journal of Finance,* May 1977, 337-347.

The following bankruptcy case can be found in the Brigham-Crum casebook:

Case 38, "Miller Hardware and Supply," which examines both liquidation and refinancing alternatives for a firm facing financial failure.

Multinational Finance

26

In 1983, roughly 25 percent of the assets of U.S.-based manufacturing corporations were located outside the United States, and even more than 25 percent of the total income of these companies was generated by overseas operations. Moreover, the rate of growth of international investment now exceeds the growth rate of aggregate U.S. domestic investment. This rapid expansion of direct foreign investment by U.S. companies has been caused in large part by the generally higher rates of return available on foreign investments, especially in developing nations, as compared with equivalent-risk domestic projects. Thus, it is not surprising that General Electric has television assembly plants in Mexico, South Korea, and Singapore; that IBM has computer hardware manufacturing and servicing subsidiaries in many parts of Europe and the Far East; that Caterpillar produces tractors and farm equipment in the Middle East, Europe, the Far East, and Africa; and so on.

The past decade has also seen an increasing amount of direct investment in the United States by foreign corporations. This "reverse" investment, which is of growing concern to U.S. government officials, has been expanding at a far higher rate in the past few years than has U.S. investment abroad. By the end of 1982, the level of foreign investment in the United States was about 46 percent of U.S. international investment, and it was concentrated in manufacturing operations, trading companies, and the petroleum industry. The fastest growth has been by Japanese firms in the manufacturing and trade sectors.

These trends are significant because of their implications for eroding the traditional doctrine of independence and self-reliance that has always been a hallmark of U.S. policy. Just as American corporations with extensive overseas operations are said to use their enormous economic power to exert substantial economic and political influence over

---

This chapter was coauthored by Roy L. Crum of the University of Florida.

host governments in many parts of the world, it is feared that foreign corporations will gain similar sway over U.S. policy. Taken together, these developments suggest an increasing degree of mutual influence and interdependence among business enterprises and nations from which even the United States is not immune.

We should state at the outset that international finance is, in a sense, like taxes—it is too important for you to know nothing about, but too complicated for us to cover adequately in one chapter. However, even a quick reading of the chapter will give you a good idea of what is involved in the financial management of a multinational firm, get you ready to talk with people actually involved in multinational operations, and, better yet, prepare you to take a course in international business.

The Multinational Corporation

The term *multinational corporation* is used to describe a firm that operates in two or more nations. However, such a simple characterization obscures some essential attributes of the modern corporation with operations spanning many countries. In the period since World War II, a new and fundamentally different format for international commercial activity has emerged, and it has altered the world's economic infrastructure and led to increased economic and political interdependence. The distinguishing characteristic between the new form of commercial transactions and earlier activities is that, rather than merely buying resources from foreign concerns, firms now make direct investment in operations, and single worldwide entities control all phases of the production process—from extraction of raw materials, through the manufacturing process, to distribution to consumers throughout the world. Today, multinational corporate networks control a large, and increasing, share of the world's technological, marketing, and productive capabilities.

For the most part, these supranational corporations are relatively unconstrained in how the resources—and the profits they generate—are allocated among the various host nations. Thus, goods and services can often be moved among the different elements of the corporate system at "prices" that do not reflect arm's length transactions or market values. Rather, transfer prices can be set to enable the organization to locate production and marketing where these activities can be done most efficiently while simultaneously shifting taxable income so it is recognized in countries that have low tax rates. This maneuvering can break the link between the country in which the economic value is created and the country in which it is recognized. Not surprisingly, such activities lead to frictions between multinational corporations and nations, and among nations in their quest for a larger share of the benefits of international commerce. Perhaps the most serious challenge to multinational corporations today comes from developing (formerly called "underdeveloped") countries which charge that the fair value of their national resources has been—and continues to be—siphoned off and transferred to the owners of the firms, who are located in the developed world, particularly the United States and Europe.

In theory, the models and analytical procedures developed in Chapters 1 through 25 for traditional financial management remain valid even when the operating environment is expanded to include operations in more than a single country. However, problems uniquely associated with multinational operations increase the complexity of the management task and often lead to situations in which it is necessary to alter the way alternative courses of action are evaluated and compared. The complexity arises because it becomes necessary to consider explicitly, as an integral part of the analyses, various issues that are unimportant—or even nonexistent—in traditional financial decision making. The five major factors that distinguish financial management theory and practice between firms operating entirely in a single country from those having operations that span several countries are listed below:

Multinational versus Traditional Financial Management

1. Cash flows in various parts of the corporate system may be denominated in different currencies. Hence, exchange rates and the impact of changing currency values must be included in financial analyses.

2. Each country in which the firm operates has its own unique political and economic institutions. Institutional differences among countries can cause significant problems when the corporation tries to coordinate and control the worldwide operations of its subsidiaries. For instance, differences in tax laws among countries can cause a given economic transaction to have strikingly dissimilar after-tax consequences depending on where it occurred. Similarly, differences in legal systems of host nations, such as the Common Law of Great Britain versus the French Civil Law, complicate matters ranging from the simple recording of a business transaction to the role played by the judiciary in resolving conflicts. Such differences can restrict the flexibility of multinational corporations to deploy resources as they wish, or even preclude certain practices in one part of the company that are required in another part. These differences also make it difficult for executives trained under one system to function or control operations effectively in another.

3. Even within geographic regions that have long been considered relatively homogeneous, different countries have their own unique cultural heritages which shape their values and define the role of business in the society. Multinational corporations find that such matters as the appropriate goals of the firm and attitudes toward risk-taking can vary dramatically from one country to the next. For instance, capital structure norms, and even the concept of equity capital, are perceived differently in Japan and in the United States.[1]

4. Most traditional models in finance assume the existence of a competitive marketplace, in which the terms of competition are determined through the actions of participants. The government, through its power to establish broad ground rules, is only slightly involved in this process. Thus, the market provides both the primary barometer of success and the indicator of actions that need to be taken to remain competitive. This view of the process is reasonably correct for the United States and several other major Western industrialized nations, but it does not accurately describe the situation in most countries of the world. In many countries, the terms of competition, actions that must be taken or avoided, and the terms of trade on various transactions are largely defined not in the marketplace, but by direct negotiation between the host government and the multinational corporation. This is essentially a political process and must be treated as such. Thus, traditional financial models have to be recast to include this and other noneconomic facets of the decision.

5. The distinguishing characteristic of a nation state that differentiates it from a multinational corporation is that the nation state exercises sovereignty over people and property in its territory. Hence, a nation state is free to place constraints on corporate resource transfers and even to expropriate without compensation the assets of the firm. This political risk tends to be largely a given risk rather than a risk which can be changed by negotiation. It varies from country to country, and it must be addressed explicitly in financial analyses.

These five major differences complicate the financial management process, and they clearly increase the business risk of the firms involved. However, the higher profitability that we mentioned earlier often makes it well worthwhile for firms to accept these risks, and to learn how to minimize or at least live with them. The necessary adjustments are discussed in the remainder of this chapter.

Exchange Rates and the International Monetary System

In this section, we examine currency exchange rates, show how to convert among rates expressed in different currencies, and then discuss the world monetary system and its impact on exchange rates.

---

[1]In Japan, it is not unusual for a firm to have a debt ratio of 90 to 95 percent, with most of these funds being supplied by large banks. Thus, banks have an influence over corporate affairs well beyond that of a typical creditor in the United States. Additionally, banks in Japan can hold both debt and equity positions in a firm, whereas U.S. banks are precluded from owning stocks in nonfinancial corporations.

An *exchange rate* designates the number of units of a given currency that can be purchased for one unit of another currency. Hence, it is the price of one currency stated in terms of another. Exchange rates for the leading trading partners of the United States appear each day in *The Wall Street Journal;* selected rates on September 23, 1983, are given in Table 26-1. The value shown in Column 1 of Table 26-1 gives the number of U.S. dollars required to purchase one unit of foreign currency. From the perspective of the United States, exchange rates stated in this manner are called *direct quotations.* Thus, the direct U.S. dollar quotation for the Swiss franc is $0.4655, as one Swiss franc can be bought for $0.4655. The exchange rate given in Column 2 is the number of units of foreign currency that can be purchased for one U.S. dollar; this is an *indirect quotation* to a person living in the United States. The indirect quotation for the Swiss franc is SF2.1480. Note that SF2.1480/$1 is the direct quotation from the perspective of a person residing in Zurich. Normal practice in the United States is to use indirect quotations (Column 2) for all currencies other than British pounds, for which direct quotations are given.

Exchange Rates

Table 26-1
Selected Exchange Rates, September 23, 1983

	U.S. Dollars Required to Buy One Unit of Foreign Currency (1)	Number of Units of Foreign Currency per U.S. Dollar[a] (2)
Austria (schilling)	0.0535	18.67
Britain (pound)	1.5030	0.6653
Canada (dollar)	0.8118	1.2318
Denmark (krone)	0.1047	9.5500
France (franc)	0.1245	8.0325
Greece (drachma)	0.01077	92.80
Hong Kong (dollar)	0.1156	8.6500
India (rupee)	0.0981	10.19
Italy (lira)	0.000623	1603.50
Japan (yen)	0.00417	239.75
Netherlands (guilder)	0.33715	2.9660
Norway (krone)	0.13527	7.3925
Saudi Arabia (riyal)	0.28735	3.48
South Africa (rand)	0.9040	1.1062
Spain (peseta)	0.00657	152.00
Sweden (krona)	0.12755	7.8400
Switzerland (franc)	0.4655	2.1480
Taiwan (dollar)	0.0249	40.15
Venezuela (bolivar)	0.07519	13.30
West Germany (mark)	0.3767	2.6540

[a]Column 2 = 1.0/Column 1.

Source: *The Wall Street Journal,* September 26, 1983.

Thus, we speak of the pound as "selling at $1.50" but of the mark as "being at 2.65."

It is a universal convention on the world's foreign currency exchanges to state all exchange rates except British pounds on a "dollar basis"—the foreign currency price of one U.S. dollar. This conforms to the practice of using direct quotes everywhere except in the United States (and Great Britain), but it goes one step further. In all currency trading centers, whether New York or London or Tokyo or anywhere else, the exchange rate for the Swiss franc on September 23, 1983, would be displayed as SF2.1480.[2] This convention eliminates confusion when comparing quotes from one trading center with quotations from another.

Suppose a tourist from the United States flies from New York to London, then to Paris, then on to Munich, and finally back to New York at the end of the holiday. She checks the foreign exchange listing at Kennedy airport and sees $1.5030 for the British pound. To her, this is a direct quotation that tells her how many dollars she must spend to purchase one British pound. When she arrives at London's Heathrow airport, she goes to the bank to check the foreign exchange listing. The rate she observes for U.S. dollars is $1.5030. This is an indirect rate from the perspective of the British but a direct rate from her point of view. Assume that she exchanges her dollars for pounds and enjoys a week's vacation in London.

At the end of the week she travels to Dover to catch the hovercraft to Calais on the coast of France, and realizes that she needs to exchange her British pounds for French francs. However, what she sees on the board are the quotations between pounds and dollars ($1.5030) and between francs and dollars (FF8.0325). The exchange rate between pounds and francs is called a *cross rate*, and it is computed as follows:

$$\frac{1.5030 \text{ dollars}}{\text{per pound}} \times \frac{8.0325 \text{ francs}}{\text{per dollar}} = \frac{12.0728 \text{ francs}}{\text{per pound}}$$

So, for every British pound she has she would receive 12.0728 French francs.[3]

---

[2]Actually, two rates would be given. The first rate is the *bid* rate, or the exchange rate at which the dealer is willing to buy U.S. dollars. This is the rate to use if you have U.S. dollars and wish to exchange them for Swiss francs. The second rate is the *ask*, or *offer*, *rate*, or the exchange rate at which the dealer is willing to sell U.S. dollars. If a tourist is returning to the United States and wants to exchange unspent francs for U.S. dollars, the ask rate is the correct one to use. Convention dictates that the first rate given is always the bid rate. The difference between the bid rate and the offer rate is the *spread*, or dealer's profit, on offsetting transactions. Since the spread tends to be fairly small for most major currencies, only a single rate will be used in the examples we discuss in this chapter.

[3]At the retail level, the larger stores and hotels would most likely display the franc-pound cross rate, so that no computations would actually be required. This would also hold true for other commonly used cross rates, such as the franc-mark and franc-yen rates. Obviously, though, it would be almost impossible to display all possible cross rates, so travelers often use little calculators to calculate cross rates, as well as to convert foreign prices to their domestic currency prices.

When she finishes her touring in France and travels to Germany, she again needs to determine a cross exchange rate, this time between French francs and West German marks. The dollar basis quotes she sees are FF8.0325 and DM2.6540, both indirect quotes to her. To find the cross rate she desires, she need only divide the two dollar-basis rates:

$$\frac{DM2.6540/\$}{FF8.0325/\$} = DM0.3304/FF,$$

or

$$\frac{FF8.0325/\$}{DM2.6540/\$} = FF3.0266/DM.$$

Finally, her vacation ends and she returns to New York. The quotation given for U.S. dollars is DM2.6540, a direct quotation from the perspective of the West Germans but an indirect quotation to her. However, she now holds marks, and not dollars, and wants to know how many U.S. dollars she will receive for her marks. This, of course, is the direct exchange rate from her perspective, and it is simply the reciprocal of the indirect rate:

$$\frac{1}{Indirect\ rate} = Direct\ rate$$

$$\frac{1}{DM2.6540} = \$0.3767/DM.$$

In this example, we have made a very strong assumption: that the exchange rates are constant over time. Actually, exchange rates can vary dramatically even in a relatively short period of time. For instance, the dollar-basis exchange rate for the French franc was FF8.0325 on September 23, 1983, but had risen to FF9.4875 by September 18, 1984. Thus, it took more francs to purchase one U.S. dollar in September 1984 than it had in September 1983, and this strengthening of the dollar (or cheapening of the franc) would be of sufficient magnitude to introduce serious errors in financial decisions if it were not anticipated. To understand what causes exchange rates to change over time, it is necessary to look at those factors which affect currencies and the world monetary system.

Recent History of the World Monetary System

From the end of World War II until August 1971, the world was on a *fixed exchange rate system* administered by the *International Monetary Fund (IMF)*. Under this system, the U.S. dollar was linked to gold ($35 per ounce), and other currencies were then tied to the dollar. Exchange rates between other currencies and the dollar were controlled within narrow limits. For example, in 1964 the British pound was fixed at 2.80 dollars for one pound, and it was allowed to fluctuate within only 1 percent of this rate:

	Value of the Pound (Exchange Rate in Dollars per Pound)
Upper limit $(+1\%)$	2.828
Official rate	2.800
Lower limit (-1%)	2.772

Fluctuations occurred because of changes in the supply of and demand for pounds. The demand for pounds tends to increase whenever Britain's exports exceed its imports—people in other nations must buy more pounds to pay for British goods than they receive in payment for shipments to Britain. This increased demand for pounds, in turn, tends to drive up their price relative to other currencies—for example, more dollars would have to be paid for each pound. Under the fixed exchange rate system, this increase in value was, of course, subject to the 1 percent upper limit.[4]

The demand for different currencies, and hence exchange rate fluctuations, also depends on capital movements. For example, suppose interest rates in Britain were higher than those in the United States. Americans would buy pounds with dollars, and then use those pounds to purchase high-yielding British securities. This action would tend to drive up the price of pounds.[5]

Finally, current rates are affected by international speculators (including the Arab money managers and the Swiss, as well as the treasurers of major U.S. banks) who buy a currency whenever they expect the value of that currency to rise relative to other currencies.

Prior to 1972, the effects of supply/demand fluctuations were kept within the narrow 1 percent limit by regular market intervention by the British government. When the value of the pound was falling, and

---

[4]For example, the dollar value of the pound might move up from $2.800 to $2.828. This increase in the value of the pound would mean that British goods would now be more expensive in export markets. Thus, a box of candy costing one pound in England would rise in price in the United States from $2.80 to $2.828. Conversely, U.S. goods would be cheaper in England: The British could now buy goods worth $2.828 for one pound, whereas before the exchange rate change, one pound would only buy merchandise worth $2.80. These price changes would, of course, tend to *reduce* British exports and to *increase* imports, and this, in turn, would lower the exchange rate because people in other nations would be buying fewer pounds to pay for English goods. However, the 1 percent limit severely constrained the market's ability to reach an equilibrium between trade balances and exchange rates.

[5]Such capital inflows would also tend to drive down British interest rates. If rates were high in the first place because of efforts by the British monetary authorities to curb inflation, then international currency flows would tend to thwart that effort. This is one of the reasons why domestic and international economics are so closely linked.

A good example of the effects of capital flows occurred during 1984. In an effort to control inflation, the Federal Reserve pushed U.S. interest rates up to high levels. This, in turn, caused an outflow of capital from European nations to the United States. The Europeans were suffering from a severe recession and wanted to keep interest rates down, and capital plentiful, in order to stimulate investment, but the U.S. policy combined with the ease of international capital flows made this difficult.

threatening to go below the 1 percent limit, the Bank of England would step in and buy pounds, offering gold or foreign currencies in exchange. These government purchases would hold up the pound rate. Conversely, when the pound rate was rising, the Bank of England would sell pounds. The central banks of other countries operated similarly.

If the Bank of England (or some other central bank) was running short on gold and foreign currencies, and hence becoming unable to hold to the 1 percent limit, then (1) it could borrow from the International Monetary Fund (IMF) or (2) it could, with the approval of the IMF, *devalue* its currency if it experienced persistent difficulty over a long period in preventing its exchange rate from falling below the lower limit. For just these reasons, the British pound was devalued from $2.80 per pound to $2.50 per pound in 1967. This lowered the price of British goods in the United States and elsewhere and raised the prices of foreign goods in Britain, thus stopping the British export deficit which had been putting pressure on the pound in the first place. Conversely, a nation with an export surplus and a strong currency could, under the old system, *revalue* its currency upwards, as West Germany did twice in the 1960s.

Devaluations and revaluations occurred only rarely before 1971. They were usually accompanied by severe international financial repercussions, partly because nations tended to postpone these needed measures until economic pressures had built up to explosive proportions. For this and other reasons, the old international monetary system came to a dramatic close in the early 1970s, when the U.S. dollar, the foundation upon which all other currencies were anchored, was cut loose from gold and, in effect, allowed to "float."

Today's Floating Exchange Rate System

Under a system of *floating exchange rates,* currency prices are allowed to seek their own levels without much governmental intervention. The present world monetary system is known as a *managed floating system:* Major world currency rates move (float) with market forces, unrestricted by any internationally agreed-upon limits. However, the central bank of each country does intervene to some extent in the foreign exchange market, buying and selling its currency to smooth out exchange rate fluctuations. Each central bank also tries to keep its average exchange rate at a level deemed desirable by its government's exchange policy. This is important, because exchange rates have a profound effect on the levels of imports and exports, which in turn influence the level of domestic employment. For example, if a country were having a problem with high unemployment, its central bank might encourage a decline in the value of its currency, causing its goods to be cheaper in world markets and thus stimulating exports, production, and domestic employment. Conversely, the central bank of a country that is in full production and experiencing inflation might try to raise the value of its currency in order to reduce exports and increase imports. However, under the current floating rate system, such intervention can affect the situation only temporarily—market forces will prevail in the long run.

Figure 26-1 shows how German marks, Japanese yen, and British pounds moved in comparison to the dollar from 1960 through 1983. Until 1971, when the fixed rate system was terminated, rates were stable except for an occasional revaluation or devaluation. The pound's fluctuations against the dollar were too small to even show up on the graph prior to 1967, when a devaluation occurred. The mark was revalued upward in 1961 and again in 1969. The yen was stable until 1971, when the dollar was allowed to float.

After 1971, economic forces became the major factor in setting relative currency values, and Figure 26-1 illustrates the volatility that has occurred since 1971. (Note that Figure 26-1 plots *cumulative* changes in relative value.) The pound has drifted down, while the yen has risen against the dollar since 1971. The mark rose sharply against the dollar until 1980, but it has fallen rapidly since then. The root causes of these trends have been (1) the strength of the British, German, and Japanese economies relative to that of the United States and (2) the relative infla-

Figure 26-1
Changes in the Value of Marks, Yen, and Pounds
Relative to the Value of the U.S. Dollar, 1960–1983

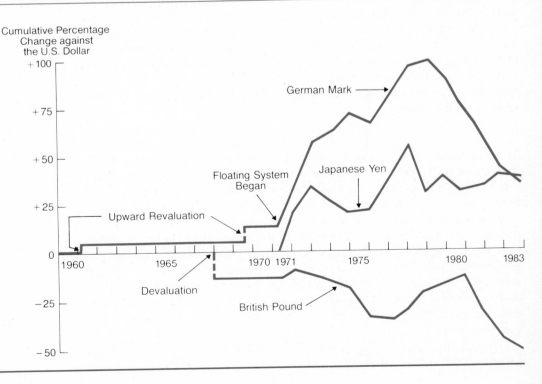

tion rates in the four countries. These points are discussed in detail in a later section.

Volatility of exchange rates under a floating system increases the uncertainty of the cash flows of a multinational corporation. Because its cash flows are generated in many parts of the world, they are denominated in numerous currency units. Therefore, the consolidated value of these streams in terms of a common currency, such as U.S. dollars, depends on both the amount of cash generated by each unit and also on the exchange rates between the respective currencies and dollars. Since these rates change, the dollar-equivalent value of the consolidated cash flow is uncertain, even if the local currency amounts and dates of receipt are known with certainty. This is known as *exchange rate risk*, and it is a major factor that differentiates the multinational corporation from a purely domestic one. However, there are numerous ways for a multinational corporation to manage and limit its exchange rate risk, and several will be discussed in later sections.

Trading in the Foreign Exchange Market

Importers, exporters, and tourists, as well as governments, buy and sell currencies in the foreign exchange market. For example, when a U.S. trader imports automobiles from West Germany, payment will probably be made in German marks. The importer buys marks (through its bank) in the foreign exchange market, much as one buys common stocks on the New York Stock Exchange or pork bellies on the Chicago Mercantile Exchange. However, while the stock and commodity exchanges have organized trading floors, the foreign exchange market consists of a network of brokers and banks based in New York, London, Tokyo, and other financial centers. Most buy and sell orders are conducted by cablegram and telephone.[6]

Spot Rates and Forward Rates

The exchange rates shown in Table 26-1 are known as *spot rates*, which means the rates paid for delivery of the currencies "on the spot" or, really, two days after the day of the trade. For most of the world's major currencies, it is also possible to buy (or sell) currency for delivery at some agreed-upon future date, usually 30, 90, or 180 days from the day the transaction is negotiated. This rate is known as a *forward exchange rate*. For example, if a U.S. firm must make payment to a Swiss firm in 90 days, the U.S. firm's treasurer can buy Swiss francs today for delivery in 90 days, paying the 90-day forward rate. The contract is signed today, and the dollar cost of the Swiss francs is then known with certainty.

---

[6]For a more detailed explanation of exchange rate determination and operations of the foreign exchange market, see Steven Bell and Bryan Kettell, *Foreign Exchange Handbook* (Westport, Conn.: Quorum Books, 1983).

Purchase of a forward contract is one technique for eliminating the volatility of future cash flows caused by fluctuations in exchange rates.

Forward rates for 30-, 90-, and 180-day delivery, along with the spot rates, for October 18, 1983, are given in Table 26-2. If one can obtain *more* of the foreign currency for a dollar in the forward than in the spot market, then the forward currency is less valuable than the current currency, and forward currency is said to be selling at a *discount*. Thus, one dollar could buy 7.8900 French francs in the spot market, but 8.1260 francs in the 180-day forward market, so forward francs sell at a discount vis-à-vis current francs. Conversely, if a dollar will buy *fewer* units of a currency in the forward than in the spot market, then the forward currency is worth more dollars than the current currency, and the forward currency is said to be selling at a premium. Thus, we see in Table 26-2 that the French franc was selling at a discount, but the forward pound, yen, Swiss franc, and mark were all selling at a premium.

Hedging in the Exchange Markets

Individuals and corporations buy or sell forward currencies to protect against future changes in exchange rates. For example, suppose that on October 18, 1983, a U.S. jeweler buys 5,000 watches from a Swiss manufacturer for 1 million Swiss francs. Payment is to be made in Swiss francs in 90 days, so the Swiss firm is extending trade credit for 90 days. The Swiss franc has been strong recently, and the U.S. company is apprehensive that the dollar will weaken because of large trade deficits. If the franc appreciates (dollar depreciates), each dollar will buy fewer francs, so more dollars will be required to buy the 1 million francs, and the profits on the watches could be lost. Still, the U.S. firm does not want to forego the trade credit by paying cash, so it protects itself by

Table 26-2
Selected Spot and Forward Exchange Rates, October 18, 1983
(Number of Units of Foreign Currency per U.S. Dollar)

	Spot Rate	Forward Rates			Premium or Discount
		30 days	90 days	180 days	
Britain (pound)	0.6660	0.6657	0.6652	0.6648	Premium
France (franc)	7.8900	7.9100	7.9850	8.1260	Discount
Japan (yen)	231.95	231.31	231.10	228.15	Premium
Switzerland (franc)	2.0945	2.0833	2.0655	2.0385	Premium
West Germany (mark)	2.5788	2.5695	2.5541	2.5295	Premium

Note: These are representative quotes as provided by a sample of New York banks. Forward rates for other currencies, and for other lengths of time, can be arranged.

Source: *The Wall Street Journal*, October 19, 1983.

purchasing 1 million Swiss francs for delivery in 90 days. The 90-day rate is SF2.0655, so the dollar cost is SF1,000,000/SF2.0655 = $484,144. When payment comes due in 90 days, regardless of the spot rate on that day, the U.S. company will have the needed 1 million Swiss francs at a cost of $484,144. The U.S. firm is said to have *covered* its trade payable by a *forward market hedge*.

If instead of having to pay 1 million Swiss francs, the U.S. company was owed 1 million Swiss francs due in 90 days, the forward exchange market could also be used to protect against exchange rate movements. In this case, the U.S. firm would sell 1 million francs 90 days forward for U.S. dollars. The same forward rate, SF2.0655, applies in this case, so the 1 million francs received from the Swiss customer could be exchanged for $484,144. Again, the U.S. company has used a forward market hedge, this time to cover a receivable.

The forward market gives multinational corporation managers a device for passing exchange rate risk on to professional risk takers, for a price. Forward contracts can be written for any amount, any length of time, and between any two currencies as long as the parties to the contract are in agreement. Some forward contracts are entered into by individuals or firms without going through an intermediary. Usually, though, forward contracts are negotiated between banks and their clients, and are tailored to the specific needs of the clients. For example, Citibank might contract with the watch importer to supply the SF1,000,000 in 90 days for $484,144.

To supplement these specialized instruments, the International Money Market (IMM) was organized in 1972 by the Chicago Mercantile Exchange to trade in foreign currency futures contracts. Conceptually, a negotiated forward contract and an IMM futures contract are virtually identical, the only distinction being in the institutional arrangements. Whereas forward contracts are negotiated, futures contracts are traded on organized exchanges such as the IMM, and like futures for agricultural commodities, futures for foreign currencies involve standardized contracts of a specific type, size, and maturity date. Because an organized market exists for futures contracts, they can be executed much more rapidly than forward contracts can be negotiated. However, the currencies for which future contracts are offered are few, and only a limited number of maturity dates are available.

Futures trading in currencies on the IMM is mainly for hedging or for pure speculation, with only a small percentage of the contracts actually settled by delivery. Firms engaged in international trade can hedge with futures contracts in exactly the same way that firms use futures contracts to hedge against interest rate changes (see Chapter 15). Thus, the watch importer could buy 90-day Swiss franc futures, and the profit or loss on this contract would approximately offset any changes in exchange rates in the spot market. In contrast, in the interbank market for forward contracts, the vast majority are actually settled by delivery of the requisite currency. As futures markets continue to develop and expand to more and more currencies, many firms, particularly smaller ones which do not usually enter into transactions large enough for the interbank forward market, are finding that futures provide a valuable way to hedge their exchange rate risks.

Inflation, Interest Rates, and Exchange Rates

Relative inflation rates, or the rates of inflation in foreign countries as compared to that in the United States, have many implications for multinational financial decisions. Obviously, relative inflation rates will greatly influence production costs at home and those abroad. Equally important, inflation rates have a dominant influence on both relative interest rates and exchange rates. Relative interest rates and exchange rates influence the methods chosen by multinational corporations for financing their foreign investments, and both of these factors also have a major impact on the profitability of foreign investments.

The currencies of countries with inflation rates higher than that of the United States tend to depreciate against the dollar. Some countries where this is the case are France, Italy, Mexico, and all the South American nations. On the other hand, prior to 1981 the currencies of countries such as West Germany, Switzerland, and Japan, which have had less inflation than the United States, have tended to appreciate relative to the dollar. *In fact, a foreign currency will, on average over the long run, depreciate against the dollar at a percentage rate approximately equal to the amount by which that country's inflation rate exceeds our own.*

Relative inflation rates are also reflected in interest rates. The interest rate in any country is largely determined by its inflation rate; this point was made back in Chapter 3. Therefore, countries which are experiencing higher rates of inflation than the U.S. tend to have higher interest rates, while the reverse is true for countries with lower inflation rates.

It might be tempting for the treasurer of a multinational corporation to borrow in countries with the lowest interest rates. However, this is not necessarily the best strategy. For example, suppose interest rates in West Germany were lower than those in the United States because of Germany's lower inflation rate. A U.S. multinational firm could save interest by borrowing in Germany, but the mark could be expected to appreciate in the future, causing annual interest and principal payments on this debt to cost an increasing number of dollars over time. Thus, the lower interest rate could be more than offset by losses from currency appreciation. Similarly, one should not expect multinational corporations to avoid borrowing in a country like Brazil where interest rates are very high, because future depreciation of the Brazilian cruzeiro might make such borrowing relatively inexpensive.

Direct foreign investment by U.S. multinational corporations is one way for Americans to invest in world markets. Another way is for U.S. citizens to purchase stocks, bonds, or various money market instruments issued by foreign corporations and governments. Americans actually do invest substantial amounts in the stocks and bonds of large corporations headquartered in Europe, and to a lesser extent in those operating out of the Far East and South Africa. They also buy securities issued by foreign governments. Such investments in foreign capital markets are known as *portfolio investments* (as distinguished from *direct investments* by U.S. corporations in physical assets).

A *Eurodollar* is a U.S. dollar placed in a time deposit in a bank outside the United States. The bank in which the deposit is made may be a host country institution such as Barclay's Bank in London, the foreign branch of a U.S. bank, or even a foreign branch of a third-country bank. Most Eurodollar deposits are for $500,000 or more, and they have maturities ranging from call money (or overnight funds) up to 5 years. Approximately 85 percent of all Eurodollars are held as call money, or straight withdrawable interest-bearing deposits; the remaining 15 percent take the form of negotiable certificates of deposit (CDs).[7]

The major difference between a dollar-denominated time deposit in Chicago and a Eurodollar deposit in Paris is the geographic location of the deposit. The deposits do not involve different currencies, so exchange rate considerations do not arise. However, Eurodollars are outside the direct control of the U.S. monetary authorities, so such requirements as fractional reserves, interest rate ceilings, and FDIC insurance premiums do not apply. Absence of these costs means that the interest rate paid on Eurodollar deposits tends to be higher than domestic U.S. rates on equivalent instruments.[8] Hence, Eurodollar deposits serve as a

International Money and Capital Markets

Eurocurrency Market

---

[7]It should be noted that today U.S. dollar deposits in any part of the world outside the United States, and not just in Europe, are called Eurodollars. It is also interesting to note that Eurodollars were first created by the Russians in Paris in the late 1940s. The Russians wanted to use dollars to conduct trade with parties who did not want to be paid in Russian currency. At the same time, the Russians did not want to leave dollar balances in U.S. banks for fear that these balances would be taken over and used to pay off defaulted Czarist bonds. Thus, they decided to purchase dollars, leave them on deposit in a Paris bank, and use them to conduct trade. The idea of Eurodollars expanded rapidly thereafter. The dollar was a strong and stable currency, which made it ideal for international trade. Gold had been used earlier to settle international balances, but it is much simpler to make electronic transfers of bank accounts than to ship gold bullion.

[8]Interest rates on Eurodollar deposits (and loans) are tied to a standard rate known by the acronym *LIBOR*, which stands for *London Inter-Bank Offer Rate*. LIBOR is the rate of interest offered on deposits of other large banks by the largest London banks of the highest credit standing. In October 1983, LIBOR rates were approximately ⅝ percentage point above domestic U.S. bank rates on time deposits of the same maturity: 9 percent for 3-month CDs versus 9⅝ percent for LIBOR CDs.

favorite short-term investment for banks, governments, and multinational corporations with temporary excess dollar-denominated liquidity.

Eurobanks lend their Eurodollar deposits to other banks or to nonbank users such as multinational corporations or governments. The loans are for large amounts ($500,000 or more) and are made on an unsecured basis. Since only large organizations of the highest credit standing can qualify for these loans, both processing and overhead costs tend to be relatively low. Hence, Euromarkets are considered to be "wholesale" markets. The Eurodollar market is a prime source for short-term funds for financing the working capital requirements of the multinational giants.

Note also that while the dollar is the leading international currency, and Eurodollars are especially important, German marks, Swiss francs, and so on are also deposited outside their home countries, and these *Eurocurrencies* are handled in exactly the same way as Eurodollars.

Asian Currency Market

While the term *Eurodollar* is almost generic in the sense that it is used to denote dollar deposits in banks throughout the world, and not just in Europe, the highly developed money market dealing in foreign currencies that is located in Singapore has come to be known as the *Asian Currency Market*. The operation of this market is essentially the same as for other Eurocurrency markets, but the Singapore market is in a unique position to serve several very important functions.

First, it bridges the time gap between Eurodollar markets in Europe and the U.S. Pacific Coast, so there is now a market for dollar deposits open 24 hours a day. This availability allows for more effective working capital management by multinational corporations. Second, the Asian Currency Market provides an efficient mechanism by which currencies held by wealthy Asians can be channeled into productive use by capital-starved firms in the region instead of flowing to Europe and the United States. Finally, the Asian Currency Market serves as an intermediary between banks and corporations located in the Far East and the Eurocurrency markets in Europe. This role effectively increases the supply of easily accessible investment capital available to banks and companies operating in the Far East.

International Bond Markets

The Eurocurrency market is essentially a short-term money market—most deposits and loans are for less than one year. However, for corporations, governments, and similar entities that desire to acquire long-term debt capital, several international bond markets have developed. Any bond sold outside the country of the borrower is called an *international bond*, but it is necessary to distinguish further between two types of international bonds that are issued under sharply different institutional arrangements and lead to dissimilar consequences from the perspectives of both borrowers and investors.

Foreign Bonds. Borrowers sometimes raise long-term debt capital in the domestic capital market of a foreign country. For instance, Bell Canada may need U.S. dollars to finance the operations of its subsidiaries located in the United States. If it decides to raise the needed capital in the domestic U.S. bond market, the bond would be underwritten by a syndicate of U.S. investment bankers, would be denominated in U.S. dollars, and would be sold to investors in the United States in accordance with SEC and applicable state regulations. Except for the foreign origin of the borrower—Canada—this bond would be indistinguishable from bonds issued by equivalent U.S. corporations. Since Bell Canada is a foreign corporation, though, this bond would be called a *foreign bond.* Formally, a foreign bond is a bond that is issued by a foreign borrower and underwritten by a syndicate whose members all come from the same country, is denominated in the currency of that same country, and is sold entirely within that country. Foreign bonds sold in the United States are sometimes called "Yankee bonds," while foreign bonds sold in Japan are often referred to as "Samurai bonds."

Eurobonds. The second type of international bond is the *Eurobond,* which is internationally syndicated and has several attributes in common with Eurocurrencies. First, Eurobonds are denominated in a currency other than that of the country in which they are sold. In addition, the institutional arrangements by which they are placed in the market are different from those for most other bond issues. To a corporation issuing a Eurobond, perhaps the most important feature of the process is the far lower level of required disclosure than would usually be found for bonds issued in domestic markets, particularly in the United States. Also, governments tend not to apply such strict regulations to securities denominated in foreign currencies but sold in domestic markets to investors holding foreign currencies as they would for home-currency securities. This often leads to lower total transaction costs for the issue.

Investors also like Eurobonds for several reasons. Generally, they are issued in bearer form so that the name and nationality of the investor is not recorded. Individuals who desire anonymity, whether for privacy reasons or for less worthy motives such as tax avoidance, find Eurobonds to their liking. Similarly, most governments do not withhold tax on interest payments associated with Eurobonds. If the investor requires an effective yield of 10 percent, a Eurobond that is exempt from tax withholding would need a coupon rate of 10 percent. Another bond issue—for instance, a domestic issue subject to a 30 percent withholding tax on interest—would need a coupon rate of roughly 14.3 percent to yield an after-withholding rate of 10 percent. Investors who desire secrecy would not want to file for a refund of the tax, so they would prefer to hold the Eurobond.

Over half of all Eurobonds are denominated in dollars; bonds in German marks and Dutch guilders account for most of the rest. Although centered in Europe, Eurobonds are truly international. Their underwriting syndicates include investment bankers from all parts of the world, and the bonds are sold to investors not only in Europe but also in such faraway places as Bahrain and Singapore. Thus, multinational corporations, together with international financial institutions and national governments, play an important role in mobilizing capital in all parts of the world to finance production and economic growth. For better or for worse, this has resulted in great interdependence among world economies.

International Portfolio Diversification

One reason for investing in foreign securities is to obtain global diversification. To see what is involved, consider Figure 26-2, which shows the Capital Market Line (CML) as we developed it back in Figure 6B-7. The blue shaded area represents the feasible set of portfolios of domestic

Figure 26-2
Portfolio Analysis with Global Diversification

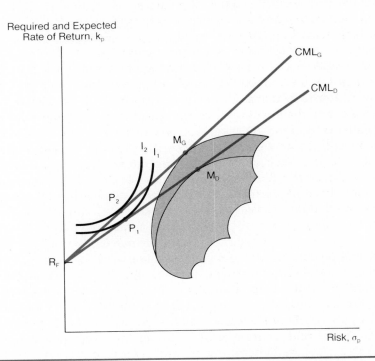

risky assets; the grey shaded area represents the addition to the feasible set when international assets are included; R_F represents the rate of return on domestic riskless assets; M_D is the domestic market portfolio; and M_G is the *global market portfolio*, which contains foreign as well as domestic risky securities. Note that there are no riskless foreign assets—even foreign treasury bills are risky because of exchange risk. Since returns on foreign securities are not perfectly correlated with those on domestic securities, the inclusion of foreign assets in the portfolio shifts the boundary (or feasible) set of portfolios upward and to the left. This has the effect of rotating the CML upward, from CML_D to CML_G. This, in turn, permits an investor to move from portfolio P_1, on indifference curve I_1, to portfolio P_2, on the higher indifference curve I_2. P_2 contains a combination of domestic and foreign stocks, plus riskless domestic government securities, and it is better than P_1 in that it provides a higher expected return for a lower level of risk.

In Chapter 1, we stated that the primary objective of the firm is to maximize shareholder wealth. This remains a valid statement when international activities are added to the firm's operations. However, several new facets are added to the problem, so identifying those actions which will maximize the stock price becomes a more complex task. We have already seen how multinational corporations have access to money and capital markets that are normally closed to purely domestic corporations. These augmented supplies of capital could shift the marginal cost of capital curve of a multinational company down and to the right. Hence, such corporations could have an advantage over domestic firms in that they could be able to invest profitably in projects that domestic companies would have to reject. However, when operating in many different currencies, multinational corporations open themselves to exchange rate risk that could potentially cancel out any increased profit. The hedging techniques described earlier can offset, or at least partially mitigate, exchange rate risk associated with future foreign currency cash flows. Even so, exposure to currency fluctuations is still a far broader problem for multinational companies than one might gather from the previous discussion, and it deserves further exploration.

Financial Management of the Multinational Firm

Because of the high volume of commercial transactions among countries, and the ramifications of these transactions for all sectors of the economy, it is unlikely that any person or firm is immune from the effects of changes in exchange rates. Just after the 1983 devaluation of the Mexican peso, a U.S. tourist who visited Mexico City would have quickly associated the change in currency value with the vastly increased purchasing power of the dollars in her purse. At the same time, though, the home-

Foreign Exchange Exposure

maker who purchased a pineapple at the local supermarket may or may not have been aware that it was grown in Mexico, but she would probably have noticed that its price had fallen recently. While the linkage is not quite as obvious, the same economic event that led to the purchasing bonanza while visiting Mexico City—the devaluation of the peso—caused the dollar price of the pineapple to fall. Domestic companies also experience similar changes in the prices they must pay for goods and services as a result of exchange rate fluctuations.

Even though individuals and domestic companies feel the effects of exchange rate changes, it is the multinational corporations that are most affected by changing exchange rates. The broad term usually used to describe the degree of susceptibility to currency fluctuations is *foreign exchange exposure*. Traditionally, foreign exchange exposure is divided into three types: economic, transaction, and translation.

Economic Exposure. *Economic exposure* refers to the impact of exchange rate fluctuations on cash flows prior to their conversion into domestic currency. For example, a depreciation in the value of the mark against the franc could increase the competitiveness of German products vis-à-vis U.S. products in France, which, in turn, would decrease a U.S. firm's sales in France and cause a reduction in its cash flows prior to the conversion from francs to dollars. Additionally, a series of unexpected changes in exchange rates could alter the perceived *riskiness* of the cash flows. This could happen, for instance, if the currency movement caused the firm to revise its estimate of the economic stability of the country. Also, such fluctuations could lead to fears that the government might be more inclined to institute exchange and/or capital controls, which would impede international transfers.

Almost every decision made by a firm's management, going back to the day it started operations in a foreign country, could have implications for its economic exposure. Hence, the company should plan its reaction to exchange rate changes before it makes its first investment. Further, these plans should be reviewed frequently to ensure their continued appropriateness, and any needed modifications should be made.[9]

Transaction Exposure. A firm which makes an agreement with terms which are (1) fixed at the time of signing, (2) stated in a foreign currency, but (3) will not be consummated or settled until some future date, stands to gain or lose if the exchange rate changes. Such agreements are said to have *transaction exposure*. Our earlier example of the importer of Swiss watches involved this type of exposure. In fact, any uncovered money market or forward exchange contract stated in terms of a foreign

---

[9]An excellent discussion of economic exposure and a procedure for calculating an exposure coefficient for a company can be found in R. C. Hekman, "Foreign Exchange Exposure: Accounting Measures and Economic Reality," *Journal of Cash Management*, February-March 1983, 34-45.

currency leads to transaction exposure. Covering the transaction by contracting to buy at a fixed price the exact amount of the required foreign currency, to be delivered at the time needed to complete the transaction, serves to hedge the exposure. This was the procedure used in the example discussed earlier.

Translation Exposure. Economic exposure and transaction exposure involve real economic gains and losses as exchange rates change. A third exposure concept, *translation exposure,* deals with unrealized accounting gains and losses that are attributable to currency fluctuations. For example, suppose Du Pont had a Canadian mining subsidiary which had assets whose value was $1 million stated in Canadian dollars, and the subsidiary was financed only with equity supplied by Du Pont. Now assume that the Canadian dollar appreciated against the U.S. dollar, doubling from $0.75 U.S. per Canadian dollar to $1.50 U.S. per Canadian dollar. The Du Pont subsidiary's assets, stated in Canadian dollars, would remain unchanged, but since Canadian dollars would now be worth twice as many U.S. dollars, the subsidiary's value in U.S. dollars would now be $2 million, and one could argue that Du Pont gained $1 million as a result of this exchange rate change. (Du Pont would now have to spend $2 million U.S. dollars to acquire the same physical assets, assuming the accounting statements correctly reflect true values.) Conversely, had the Canadian dollar declined, Du Pont would in a sense have suffered a loss. Such gains and losses are defined as *translation gains and losses,* and exposure to them is called *translation exposure.*

Note, though, that if Du Pont had used only Canadian-denominated debt (and zero equity) to finance the subsidiary, a change in the value of the Canadian dollar would have resulted not only in a gain or loss on the assets, but also in an offsetting gain or loss on the liabilities, so the *net gain or loss* would have been zero. For example, if the Canadian dollar had doubled in value, the assets value would have gone up to $2 million, but the $1 million Canadian debt would now have a U.S. value of $2 million, so the net gain would have been zero. Thus, having the subsidiary use debt denominated in the currency of the host country reduces *net translation exposure.* Most companies use some foreign-denominated debt, but far from 100 percent, so they do face some degree of translation exposure. Note also these points: (1) If foreign currencies fluctuate around a stable mean value, then gains in one period will offset losses in another, and over time translation losses will be small, and (2) accounting conventions determine when and how any translation gains or losses are recognized and reported to stockholders. We elaborate on these points in the next section.

Translation exposure derives from financial reporting requirements that mandate the periodic preparation of consolidated financial statements. In a multinational corporation with subsidiary operations in numerous

*Reporting
Requirements*

foreign countries, the job of consolidation is rendered especially difficult by the fact that host nations require the local subsidiaries to keep their financial records in terms of the local currency. Therefore, when a firm prepares consolidated financial statements, it must *translate* the local currency accounts of the subsidiary into the currency used for reporting purposes (usually the currency of the home country). If the exchange rate between these two currencies changes during the accounting period, this can lead to accounting gains or losses. Two issues arise in the accounting area: (1) What is the appropriate rate to use in translating each balance sheet account? (2) How should unrealized accounting gains and losses be handled in the consolidated financial statements?

Translations are done under rules prescribed in Financial Accounting Standards Board (FASB) Statement #52, "Foreign Currency Translation," which was issued in December 1981. The reporting requirements are designed to address objections to earlier rules, which were alleged to have caused substantial distortions of the true economic positions of multinational corporations. Under FASB #52, all assets and liabilities must be translated from the subsidiary's currency into the parent company's currency using the exchange rate that prevailed on the balance sheet date, while revenues and expense items are translated at the average exchange rate for the accounting period. Thus, the accounting principles for foreign currency translation require the *all-current-rate* method.[10]

If changes such as the ones in our Du Pont/Canada example occurred, the gain or loss would *not*, under FASB #52, run through the parent company's income statement. (Before 1982, under FASB #8, these gains and losses would have affected reported income.) Rather, any such gains and losses must be accumulated and reported in a special account within the shareholders' equity section of the balance sheet. Thus, in general, their impact will not be recognized in net income until the underlying investment is sold or otherwise liquidated.

Cash Flow Repatriation

One of the major considerations in choosing the location of corporate subsidiaries around the world is the potential for using local resources for the mutual benefit of the host economy and the multinational corporation. However, before a decision is made to establish a subsidiary in a given location, the firm must consider a number of issues that focus not only on the expected magnitude, timing, and risks of project cash

---

[10]There are two special cases for which this is not true: (1) Where a foreign subsidiary itself works with a currency other than the monetary unit in which the accounting records are kept, and (2) where the subsidiary operates in an economy where the 3-year cumulative inflation rate is 100 percent or more, special translation provisions apply. Under the old FASB #8, some accounts were based on old, historic exchange rates and others on current rates, and these differences lead to large, random translation gains and losses, and hence unstable reported income by the parent company.

flows, but also on the company's flexibility to withdraw its resources and to redeploy them in different locations to take advantage of various opportunities. As we discuss in this section, there are several devices which a multinational corporation can use to shift cash flows among its component parts from a less profitable to a more profitable locale. These same devices can also be useful for minimizing political risk exposure, for preserving value when exchange rates are expected to fall, and for tax planning.

When a corporation makes an investment in a foreign country, resources in the form of an equity investment flow from the parent to the subsidiary. To be a profitable undertaking, future value must flow back to the parent in an amount sufficient to compensate for undertaking the investment. Foreign governments, though, often place restrictions on the flow of capital back to the parent. For example, some governments place a ceiling, usually stated as a percentage of the subsidiary's net worth, on the amount of cash dividends that may be sent back, or *repatriated*, to the parent company. Restrictions may also be placed on the firm's ability to transfer depreciation cash flows back to the parent, or to other countries, until the subsidiary is sold or liquidated, and perhaps not even then. Such restrictions are normally intended to force multinational corporations to reinvest earnings in the host country, although they are also imposed to prevent large currency outflows that might destabilize the exchange rate. Capital that cannot be sent out of the country is said to be *blocked*, and blocked capital is unavailable to the parent to pay cash dividends to its shareholders or for other purposes. There are several means available to reduce the amount of blocked funds, including (1) transfer pricing, (2) royalties, and (3) management fees.

Transfer Pricing. The first device that can be used to repatriate blocked funds is *transfer pricing*, which refers to the prices set by the company on sales between two elements of the corporate system. Assume that the government of the island of Caribia places severe restrictions on the company's ability to repatriate capital and profits back to the parent. The Caribian subsidiary buys most of the subassemblies used in its production process from the parent in the United States, and ships all of its finished products to the parent's marketing subsidiary in Curacao for worldwide distribution. The cost of goods sold for the subassemblies in the United States is $100, and the normal mark-up is 25 percent, but the firm desires to set transfer prices between the United States and Caribia, and between Caribia and Curacao, to minimize the profits realized in Caribia.

Table 26-3 shows an example of this kind of transfer pricing strategy as compared to arm's length transfer prices. By setting the price at $150 instead of $125, an extra profit of $25 is realized in the United States. Also, the cost of goods sold in Caribia is elevated by the same $25. Then,

Table 26-3
Using Transfer Pricing to Circumvent Blocked Funds

	Arm's Length Transfer Prices		Manipulated Transfer Prices	
U.S. cost of goods sold	$100		$100	
U.S. selling price	125		150	
U.S. profit		$ 25		$ 50
Caribian cost from the United States	$125		$150	
Caribian local costs added	50		50	
Caribian cost of goods sold	$175		$200	
Caribian selling price	250		205	
Caribian profit		$ 75		$ 5
Curacao's cost from Caribia	$250		$205	
Curacao's selling price	310		310	
Curacao's profit		$ 60		$105
Total corporate profit		$160		$160

an artificially low transfer price of $205, instead of the arm's length price of $250, is used to reduce Caribian profit to only $5 instead of $75. This low transfer price allows the Curacao marketing subsidiary to earn a profit of $105, a net increase of $45 over the arm's length profit. The world price of $310 at which Curacao sells the goods is determined by free market forces, so it is not subject to arbitrary manipulation. Note that in both cases, the total corporate profit is $160, but *where* the profit is realized was changed via transfer pricing. In essence, $70 of profit has been brought out of Caribia in spite of restrictions on the repatriation of profits from that country.

Transfer pricing manipulation can also be valuable to the firm, even if repatriation of profits is not restricted. If the corporate tax rate in Caribia is higher than in the United States or Curacao, the scheme described in Table 26-3 could be used to shift the profits to lower tax areas. Thus, on an after-tax basis, the company increases its cash flow, and hence its value, by manipulating transfer prices. This is an important aspect of tax planning by the multinational firm.

The Minister of Commerce of Caribia also understands how transfer prices can be manipulated to the benefit of the multinational corporation. The minister's concerns are with the lost tax revenue and the reduction of capital for reinvestment locally caused by the company's actions. To the extent that the minister is able to determine fair arm's length prices for both the subassemblies and the finished goods, the minister will recast Table 26-3 as shown in the left column and base the corporation's taxes on the $75 figure. Also, this amount, less taxes and penalties for trying to circumvent local regulations, will be added to the equity accounts in the balance sheet. Transfer pricing strategies can be used as devices for removing value from a subsidiary in violation of local regulations, so they are watched very carefully by local authorities.

It is much easier to determine fair market prices for some goods than for others. In general, the closer the product is to a standardized commodity, the easier it is to estimate an arm's length price. Specialized intermediate goods involving new technology probably afford the company the greatest opportunity to exercise creativity in setting transfer prices. However, since this device is so well known and so carefully watched, most companies avoid abusing transfer prices, except, perhaps, in special circumstances where political risks are high. Such conditions are less likely to arise when corporate relations with the host government are cordial.

Royalties. *Royalties* are payments made by a subsidiary to another element of the firm for use of patents, processes, or other technical expertise. Host country governments realize that these are legitimate payments for value received, but they do monitor royalty payments carefully to ensure that they are not excessive. Often, the amount of the royalty is set in direct negotiations between the company and the host government. If the host country perceives that, contrary to government policy, the corporation is attempting to use royalties as a conduit for channeling profits out of the country, fines and severe restrictions are likely.

Management Fees. Payments for services rendered, such as the subsidiary's share of centralized management functions, are included in *management fees.* Thus, fees are in a sense similar to royalties, but host government officials, particularly in developing countries, tend to be less willing to approve the payment of management fees. When using this device to remove funds from a subsidiary, the company needs to be particularly careful to justify the charges. Otherwise, the payments may be regarded as disguised dividends and disallowed.

Although the same basic principles of investment analysis apply to both foreign and domestic operations, there are several crucial differences: (1) Cash flow estimation is generally much more complex for overseas investments. (2) Cash flows are not denominated in dollars, so exchange rate risk is now an issue. (3) The possibility of deliberate government acts that truncate or divert cash flows must be considered.

Procedures for Analyzing Foreign Investments[11]

---

[11]This section discusses verbally the process of analyzing a potential foreign investment. Appendix 26A provides an actual illustration, with quantitative data.

The usual form of organization for multinational operations is the establishment of a separate subsidiary in each foreign country in which business activity takes place. If the Dutch subsidiary of a U.S. multinational corporation is evaluating a capital investment, what cash flows are relevant to the decision? Is it the project cash flows accruing to the subsidiary, or is it the incremental cash flow that could be sent back to the U.S. parent? As long as there are no restrictions on the repatriation of dividends and depreciation cash flows, there is no major difference between the two cash flow streams. However, if there are local withholding taxes on dividends, restrictions on return of capital, or other blockages of international cash flows, both the timing and the magnitude of the cash flows back to the parent will be different from the operating cash flows of the project. The parent corporation cannot use cash flows blocked in a foreign country to pay current dividends to its shareholders, nor does it have the flexibility to reinvest them elsewhere in the world, where expected risk-adjusted returns may be higher. Hence, from the perspective of the parent organization, *the relevant cash flows for analysis of an international investment are the financial cash flows that the subsidiary can legally send back to the parent*. Note that the actual cash flows expected to be repatriated to the parent may be less than the cash flows generated by the subsidiary. The company may decide for valid business reasons to retain and reinvest some of the cash flows in the local subsidiary. Thus, the key to assessing the acceptability of the project is how much cash flow is sent back to the parent.

Cash flows that can legally be repatriated to the parent over the life of the project are reduced to their present values by applying an appropriate discount rate. This present value is then compared to the present value of the parent's investment in the project to ascertain the net present value of the project. Cash flows from the parent to the subsidiary, and from the subsidiary back to the parent, are *financial*, and not operating cash flows, so the method of financing the project must be explicitly considered in international capital budgeting. This is a significant conceptual difference from the capital budgeting analysis described in Chapters 8-10, and it leads to a second major difference: If part of the capital used to finance the project is obtained by the subsidiary from local banks or other similar sources, then the loan itself and both principal and interest payments must be reflected in the cash flows used in the analysis.

Exchange rate effects can be included in the project analysis in two different ways: (1) The foreign currency cash flows can be converted into equivalent home currency values by translating them at the expected future exchange rates. However, sensitivity or simulation analyses should be conducted to ascertain the effects of exchange rate variations, and based on this analysis, an *exchange rate premium* should be added to the cost of capital used to discount the cash flows. (2) From earlier sections of this chapter, we know that it is conceptually possible to eliminate exchange rate risk completely by an appropriate hedge. Thus, the second method of incorporating exchange rate risk into the capital budgeting analysis is to fix the home currency value of all future foreign currency cash flows by hedging. The cost of the hedge is then subtracted from the cash flows themselves, so no adjustment is required in the discount rate. Conceptually, this second method for handling exchange rate risk is superior to the first method. However, it is not always possible to hedge cash flows expected in the distant future, and unless the foreign currency is one of the leading western currencies actively traded on the exchange markets, it may not be possible to hedge even short-run cash flows.

The final characteristic of international investment decisions that differentiates them from domestic capital budgeting is the existence of *sovereignty risk*. *Sovereignty* refers to the supreme and independent political authority of a nation state to do as it pleases within its own borders. Since foreign subsidiaries are physically located within the jurisdiction of the host country, they are subject to rules and regulations established by local government authorities, no matter how arbitrary and unfair such requirements may be. Sovereignty risk includes both the possibility of expropriation or nationalization without adequate compensation, and unanticipated restrictions of cash flows to the parent company, such as tighter controls on repatriation of dividends or higher taxes. The risk of expropriation of U.S. assets abroad is small in traditionally friendly and stable countries such as the United Kingdom or Switzerland. However, in Eastern Bloc countries, and in most parts of the developing world of Latin America, Africa, and the Far East, the risk may be substantial. Past expropriations include those of ITT and Anaconda Copper in Chile, Gulf Oil in Bolivia, Occidental Petroleum in Libya, International Petroleum in Peru, and many companies in both Cuba and Iran.

The combined impact of exchange and sovereignty risks, as well as such "regular" risk factors as the stability and predictability of product markets, labor supplies, and government regulations, can be summarized as the *investment climate* of a foreign country. A number of organizations provide, for a fee, advice to multinational companies regarding investment climates. An illustrative list is shown in Table 26-4. The countries are rated in descending order from AAA to B, in much the same way that Moody's rates corporate bonds for risk of default. These ratings, or other procedures as established by an individual multinational corporation, may be used as a basis for estimating the costs of capital for capital budgeting purposes in each country in which the firm operates.

Generally, sovereignty risk premiums are not added to the cost of capital to adjust for sovereignty risk. If corporate management has a serious concern that a given country might expropriate foreign assets, no significant investment will be made. Expropriation is viewed as a catastrophic or ruinous event, and managers have been shown to be

Table 26-4
The Risks of Foreign Investment in Various Countries

Country	Risk Rating	Country	Risk Rating
United States	AAA	Singapore	BBB
West Germany	AAA	Portugal	BBB
Canada	AA	Brazil	BBB
France	AA	Mexico	BBB
Australia	AA	Malaysia	BBB
Sweden	AA	Indonesia	BBB
Netherlands	AA	Philippines	BBB
Japan	AA	Argentina	BB
Saudi Arabia	AA	Chile	BB
Belgium	A	Kenya	BB
Spain	A	Pakistan	BB
Great Britain	A	South Korea	BB
New Zealand	A	Peru	BB
South Africa	A	Thailand	BB
Italy	A	Egypt	BB
		India	B

extraordinarily risk averse in the presence of ruinous loss possibilities. However, as we will discuss later, companies can take steps to reduce the potential loss from expropriation by financing the subsidiary with local sources of capital or by structuring operations so that the subsidiary has value only as a part of the integrated corporate system. Thus, standing alone, the subsidiary would have little or no value. To eliminate substantially or completely economic losses from expropriation, insurance is often obtained from such sources as the Overseas Private Investment Corporation (OPIC). Insurance premiums would then be added to the project cost to cover sovereignty risk. Appendix 26A provides a detailed illustration of multinational capital budgeting.

Sources of Funds for Foreign Investments

Foreign subsidiaries generally obtain a major part of their capital as common equity supplied by their parent companies. Several other sources of funds exist, including (1) sale of common stock to local residents, (2) borrowing from local residents, and (3) borrowing in world financial markets.

Selling common stock to residents of foreign countries has both advantages and disadvantages. For example, it can result in loss of control of the subsidiary if the parent company owns less than 50 percent of the shares. Some countries require majority ownership by local residents, allowing them to have some control over major decisions made by corporations operating within their boundaries and enabling them to retain part of the companies' profits. However, this is not necessarily bad from the point of view of the multinational corporation—local participation may be a desirable feature in countries with less stable governments, since it provides an incentive for the local residents to exert pressure against the threat of expropriation or other interference. Similar protection is obtained by borrowing funds in the subsidiary's country: If the subsidiary is highly leveraged with debt from local sources, expropriation will result in only minimal losses to the parent.

Aside from protecting against expropriation, borrowing locally may be advantageous if local sources of funds offer attractive interest rates. In comparing foreign and domestic interest rates, however, one must be careful to take into account expected future changes in the exchange rate. As was pointed out earlier, a country with interest rates lower than those in the United States also has a currency that is likely to appreciate, causing the number of dollars required to meet interest and principal payments to increase over time and thus to offset the lower foreign interest rate.

The decision to use local or parent country financing necessarily depends in part on projections of future trends in foreign exchange rates. Because such projections are not always accurate, using foreign debt may be riskier than using domestic debt. With the growth of multinational corporations, and the uncertainties of world inflation and floating rates, corporate treasurers are making increasing use of expertise offered by commercial bankers, who make such projections and advise firms on the best way to meet their foreign currency requirements. It should come as no surprise to learn that the international divisions have been among the fastest-growing departments of the larger banks in recent years.

Summary

As the world economy becomes more integrated, the role of *multinational firms* is ever increasing, and new companies are joining the ranks of the multinationals every day. Although the same basic principles of financial management apply to multinational corporations as to domestic ones, the financial manager of a multinational firm faces a much more complex task. The primary problem, from a financial standpoint, is the fact that cash flows must cross national boundaries. These flows may be constrained in various ways, and, equally important, their value in dollars may rise or fall depending on exchange rate fluctuations. Thus, the multinational manager must be constantly aware of the many complex interactions among national economies, and the effects of these interactions on multinational operations.

Efficient markets for foreign currencies and securities tie together the various national money markets, and the *forward* and *spot currency markets* can be used to smooth out the effects of exchange rate fluctuations over time. Because of the central role the U.S. dollar plays in international commerce, large markets have developed for U.S. dollar deposits (*Eurodollars*) and dollar-denominated bonds (*Eurobonds*) in Europe and Asia. These markets have also expanded to include many other currencies held in Euro-form. The *Euromarkets* are popular with multinational corporations and banks, as well as with governments, because they offer safe yet relatively high-return havens for those with an excess of liquid assets, and they offer very competitive rates for those needing working capital loans.

Managers have to cope with many more risks in order to obtain opportunities when operating in the international arena. The ability to redeploy worldwide resources quickly in response to environmental signals gives multinational corporations a distinct advantage over domestic firms. However, there are many complex issues that have to be taken into consideration in order to make good decisions. At times, it is even necessary to modify the theoretical underpinnings of conventional financial models to increase their relevance and their ability to deal with situations that occur in an international environment but are nonexistent in purely domestic finance.

Financial management in a multinational firm is both important and challenging. The risks inherent in international operations are high, but so are the potential rewards. In a world economy that grows more interdependent each year, the multinational manager can look forward to an ever expanding role in the corporate boardroom.

Questions

26-1 Define each of the following terms:
    a. Multinational corporation; parent company; host country
    b. Foreign exchange; exchange rates
    c. Fixed exchange rate system; floating exchange rates; devaluation
    d. Spot rate; forward rate; premium or discount on forward rates
    e. Repatriation of earnings; transfer price
    f. Sovereign risk; exchange risk
    g. FASB #52; translation gain or loss; foreign exchange exposure
    h. Hedging exchange rate exposure
    i. Eurodollar
    j. Foreign bond; Eurobond

26-2 Under the fixed exchange rate system, what was the currency against which all other currency values were defined? How did gold enter the picture?

26-3 Exchange rates fluctuate under both the fixed exchange rate and floating exchange rate systems. What, then, is the difference between the two systems?

26-4 If the French franc depreciates against the U.S. dollar, can a dollar buy more or fewer French francs as a result?

26-5 If the United States imports more goods from abroad than it exports, foreigners will tend to have a surplus of U.S. dollars. What will this do to the value of the dollar with respect to foreign currencies? What is the corresponding effect on Arab investments in the United States?

26-6 Why do U.S. corporations build manufacturing plants abroad when they could build them at home?

26-7 Most firms require higher rates of return of foreign projects then on identical projects located at home. Why?

26-8 What is a Eurodollar? If a French citizen deposits $10,000 in Chase Manhattan Bank in New York, have Eurodollars been created? What if the deposit is made in Barclay's Bank in London? Chase Manhattan's Paris branch?

26-9 Discuss in general terms how, under FASB #52, the financial statements of foreign subsidiaries are consolidated into the statements of their U.S. parent companies. What effect does the method used to translate foreign currencies into U.S. dollars have on the parent's reported net income?

26-1 If British pounds sold for $1.50 per pound, what should dollars sell for in pounds per dollar?   *Problems*

26-2 Suppose one French franc could be purchased in the foreign exchange market for 20 cents today. If the franc appreciated 10 percent tomorrow against the dollar, how many francs would a dollar buy?

26-3 After all foreign and U.S. taxes, a U.S. corporation expects to receive 2 pounds of dividends per share from a British subsidiary this year. The exchange rate at the end of the year is expected to be $1.80 per pound, and the pound is expected to depreciate 5 percent against the dollar each year for an indefinite period. The dividend (in pounds) is expected to grow at 10 percent a year indefinitely. The parent U.S. corporation owns 10 million shares of the subsidiary. What is the present value of its equity ownership in the subsidiary? Assume a cost of equity capital of 12 percent for the subsidiary.

26-4 You are the financial vice president of International Widgets, Inc., headquartered in Miami, Florida. All shareholders of International Widgets live in the United States. Earlier this month, you obtained a loan of 10 million Canadian dollars from a bank in Toronto to finance the construction of a new plant in Montreal. At the time the loan was received, the exchange rate was 78 U.S. cents to the Canadian dollar. By the end of the month, it has unexpectedly dropped to 74 cents. Has your company made a gain or loss as a result, and by how much?

26-5 International Trading Corporation (ITC) has just made a sale worth 400,000 ringos to a Paralivian importer, but payment will not be made for 3 months. To protect against exchange rate fluctuations, ITC will borrow ringos today from a Paralivian bank. The amount borrowed will be such that the repayment 3 months hence will equal 400,000 ringos. The annual interest rate on this loan is 20 percent. ITC will use the borrowed funds to purchase dollars at the current spot rate of 2.0 ringos per dollar, and then invest these dollars in a U.S. bank for 3 months at an annual rate of 10 percent. At the end of 3 months, ITC will use the 400,000 ringos received from the importer to pay off the Paralivian bank loan. ITC's tax rate in each country is 40 percent.
   a. What dollar amount will ITC receive upon liquidating its investment with the U.S. bank?
   b. How much would ITC have in dollars if it merely waited and converted the 400,000 ringos when received 3 months hence if the ex-

change rate remained at 2.0 ringos per dollar? What if the ringo appreciated to 1.8 per dollar, or depreciated to 2.2 per dollar?

c. The borrowing and investing strategy outlined in the problem is equivalent to purchasing insurance to protect against adverse exchange rate fluctuations. What is the cost of this insurance?

d. ITC could also have hedged its position in the futures market. At what forward rate would ITC realize the same ending amount as it did with its capital market strategy?

Selected Additional References and Cases

Useful texts and other books that describe international financial management in some detail include, among others, the following:

Aggarwal, Raj Kumar, *The Management of Foreign Exchange: Optimal Policies of a Multinational Company* (New York: Arno, 1980).

Aliber, Robert C., *Exchange Risk and Corporate International Finance* (New York: Wiley, 1978).

Eiteman, David K., and Arthur I. Stonehill, *Multinational Business Finance* (Reading, Mass.: Addison-Wesley, 1982).

Levi, M., *International Finance: Financial Management and the International Economy* (New York: McGraw-Hill, 1983).

Rodriguez, Rita M., and E. Eugene Carter, *International Financial Management* (Englewood Cliffs, N. J.: Prentice-Hall, 1979).

For more on capital budgeting by multinational firms, see

Oblak, David J., and Roy J. Helm, Jr., "Survey and Analysis of Capital Budgeting Methods Used by Multinationals," *Financial Management*, Winter 1980, 37-41.

Shapiro, Alan C., "Capital Budgeting for the Multinational Corporation," *Financial Management*, Spring 1978, 7-16.

Papers dealing with exchange rate risk include the following:

Calderon-Rossell, Jorge R., "Covering Foreign Exchange Risks of Single Transactions," *Financial Management*, Autumn 1979, 78-85.

Eaker, Mark R., "Covering Foreign Exchange Risks: Comment," *Financial Management*, Winter 1980, 64-65.

Feiger, George, and Bertrand Jacquillat, "Currency Option Bonds, Puts and Calls on Spot Exchange, and the Hedging of Contingent Foreign Earnings," *Journal of Finance*, December 1979, 1129-1139.

Goodman, Stephen H., "Foreign Exchange-Rate Forecasting Techniques: Implications for Business and Policy," *Journal of Finance*, May 1979, 415-427.

Regarding decisions to use financing outside the parent company's home country, see

Eaker, Mark R., "Denomination Decision for Multinational Transactions," *Financial Management*, Autumn 1980, 23-29.

Folks, William R., Jr., and Ramesh Advani, "Raising Funds with Foreign Currency," *Financial Executive*, February 1980, 44-49.

Severn, Alan K., and David R. Meinster, "The Use of Multicurrency Financing by the Financial Manager," *Financial Management*, Winter 1978, 45-53.

Other recent works of interest include these:

Elliott, J. Walter, "The Expected Return on Equity and International Asset Prices," *Journal of Financial and Quantitative Analysis*, December 1978, 987-1002.

Meadows, Edward, "How the Euromarket Fends Off Global Disaster," *Fortune*, September 24, 1979, 122-135.

Shapiro, Alan C., "Financial Structure and Cost of Capital in the Multinational Corporation," *Journal of Financial and Quantitative Analysis*, June 1978, 211-226.

Cases in Managerial Finance (Brigham-Crum) contains two cases which deal with multinational financial decisions:

Case 39, ''Geodyne Exploration,'' which focuses on the overall riskiness of international capital investment.

Case 40, ''Russo Winery, Inc.,'' which illustrates the complexities of international capital budgeting cash flow estimation.

Cases in Financial Decision Making (Harrington) contains the following applicable cases:

''Philip Morris Incorporated: Swiss Franc Financing,'' which focuses on the choice between foreign and U.S. debt financing.

''International Products Corporation,'' which illustrates the complexities of multinational cash flow estimation.

26A An Illustration of Multinational Capital Budgeting

The principles of capital budgeting in a multinational setting can be illustrated with data from International Electronics Corporation (IEC), which is analyzing a proposal to build a plant in Caribia to assemble electronic monitoring and testing equipment for sale worldwide through the company's marketing and distribution facility in Curacao. If the project is accepted, a new subsidiary, IEC Caribia, will be incorporated in Caribia. It will be financed only with common stock, all of which will be owned by the parent firm.

While the corporate income tax in Caribia is a low 20 percent compared with the 50 percent federal-plus-state rate that IEC pays in the United States, the government of Caribia places several restrictions on multinational corporations that will have an impact on the analysis. To preserve investment capital in Caribia, the government prohibits the removal of contributed equity until the investment is sold or otherwise liquidated. Thus, depreciation cash flows may not be repatriated until the end of the project's life. Dividends are not subjected to a withholding tax, but they must come only from net income, and they are restricted to a maximum of 20 percent of the contributed equity in any year. At the end of the project's life, any reinvested earnings can be repatriated to the parent. The investment, to be made in January 1985, consists almost entirely of plant and equipment, and the cost will be $10 million or 50 million Caribian pesos (P50 million). Because of the nature of technological change in the electronics industry, IEC bases its analysis on a time horizon of five years. At the end of the five years (in December 1989), the company estimates that the book value of the facility, 25 million Caribian pesos, is the best estimate of its market value.

The Caribian government recognizes that IEC has developed and patented much of the technology employed in the operations, and is willing to compensate the company for its use. IEC and the Minister of Commerce have reached an agreement that establishes a royalty rate of 10 percent of gross revenues to be paid directly to the parent. Management fees, however, are prohibited by law in Caribia. Table 26A-1 summarizes the projected income statements for the Caribian subsidiary.

The data in Table 26A-1 are straightforward down to "Dividend repatriated." In the 1985 column, we see that net income, 8 million pesos, is less

Table 26A-1
Projected End-of-Year Financial Cash Flows to the U.S. Parent
(Millions of Caribian Pesos)

	1985	1986	1987	1988	1989
Revenues	50.0	55.0	60.0	65.0	70.0
Operating costs	30.0	30.0	35.0	35.0	40.0
Depreciation	5.0	5.0	5.0	5.0	5.0
Royalties (10% of revenue)	5.0	5.5	6.0	6.5	7.0
Income before tax	10.0	14.5	14.0	18.5	18.0
Caribian tax (20%)	2.0	2.9	2.8	3.7	3.6
Net income	8.0	11.6	11.2	14.8	14.4
Dividend repatriated (10.0 maximum)	8.0	10.0	10.0	10.0	10.0
U.S. tax on dividend	3.0	3.75	3.75	3.75	3.75
After-tax dividend	5.0	6.25	6.25	6.25	6.25
Royalty (10% of gross revenues)	5.0	5.50	6.00	6.50	7.00
U.S. tax on royalty (50%)	2.5	2.75	3.00	3.25	3.50
After-tax royalty	2.5	2.75	3.00	3.25	3.50
After-tax cash flow	7.5	9.00	9.25	9.50	9.75

than 20 percent of the 50 million pesos of original equity (0.2 × 50 million = 10 million pesos, which is the maximum dividend in any year), so the entire 8 million pesos can be returned to the parent as a dividend. Dividends in subsequent years are limited to 10 million pesos. IEC reports its world-wide net income to the U.S. Internal Revenue Service, but it receives *tax credits* for taxes paid overseas, including a credit for taxes paid by its subsidiary to the Caribian tax authorities. The amount of the credit depends on the dividend payout ratio of the subsidiary. With a 100 percent payout, the parent would pay the difference between the U.S. tax rate of 50 percent and the Caribian tax rate of 20 percent. For example, in 1985, when the payout was 100 percent, the subsidiary earned 10 million pesos before Caribian tax and paid 2 million in tax (20 percent) to the Caribian government, so an additional 30 percent tax, or 3 million pesos, must be paid to the U.S. government. The total tax paid on the dividend is limited to 5 million pesos, or 50 percent of taxable income; this is the same rate as would be paid if the subsidiary had been located in the United States, in which case, it would have paid a 50 percent tax on 10 million of net income.[1]

In 1986 through 1989, net income exceeds 10 million pesos, the maximum dividend payment allowed under Caribian law, so dividends are set at 10

---

[1] If the foreign tax rate had been higher than the U.S. tax rate, the tax credit would be greater than the taxes owed to the U.S. government on equivalent before-tax earnings by a U.S. firm. This deficit could be used to offset U.S. taxes on income from other foreign subsidiaries in any part of the world. For a more detailed explanation of multinational taxation, see the U.S. Tax Reform Act of 1976, or Price Waterhouse, *U.S. Corporations Doing Business Abroad* (New York, 1976).

million. To see what is involved, consider 1986. Theoretically, the United States could tax the 14.5 million peso pre-tax income, getting 14.5(0.5) = 7.25 million pesos, less a credit of 2.9 pesos, for a net tax bill of 4.35 pesos, but this is not done. Alternatively, the United States could treat as taxable income only the dividends repatriated, which would produce a net tax bill of 10(0.5) − 2.9 = 2.1 million pesos, but this is not done either. Under U.S. law, taxes are collected on the portion of income that is actually repatriated. In the years 1986-1989, we proceed as follows: (1) We "gross up" the dividend payment to determine the before-tax net income which would be required to produce the actual dividend payment. This is equal to the dividend repatriated divided by (1.0 − Caribian tax rate), or 10/0.8 = 12.5 million pesos. Had IEC Caribia had 12.5 million pesos of income, it would have paid 20 percent, or 2.5 million pesos, in taxes and had 10 million left for the dividend which it actually paid. (2) We now multiply this 12.5 million before-tax equivalent amount by the difference between the tax rate in the United States and the Caribian rate, or 30 percent, getting 0.30(12.5) = 3.75 million pesos. This is the additional tax liability in the United States on the income repatriated.[2]

However, 3.75 million pesos is not the total U.S. tax liability. An additional source of taxable income to the parent is the royalties paid by IEC Caribia. Royalties are an operating expense to the subsidiary, so they are not subject to Caribian tax. To the parent, however, they are income, and the royalties are taxed at the full 50 percent tax rate. Total operating cash flow to the U.S. parent, then, is the sum of the after-tax dividend and the after-tax royalty. This is shown in the last line of Table 26A-1.

Since cash flows from depreciation cannot be repatriated until the company is liquidated at the end of 1989, they must be reinvested locally. Assume that there are no other attractive real asset investments available, so the depreciation cash flows will be invested in Caribian government bonds which earn 8 percent annual interest, with interest not subject to tax until it is repatriated. The accumulated and interest-compounded depreciation cash flow at the termination of the project is shown in Table 26A-2 to be 27.166 million pesos after adjusting for Caribian and U.S. taxes.

Operating profits that exceed the dividend repatriation restrictions are also assumed to be invested in 8 percent Caribian government bonds. As shown in Table 26A-3, the U.S. tax adjustment is more complex than it was for the depreciation cash flows because Caribian tax is only due on the interest income, but U.S. tax is due on both interest and "grossed up" operating profits. The total after-tax cash flow from blocked operating profits, approximately 8 million pesos, will be added to the 1989 end-of-project cash flow.

The next steps in the analysis are (1) to convert the annual cash flows as developed in Tables 26A-1, 26A-2, and 26A-3, plus the terminal value (as-

---

[2]Notice that the foreign subsidiary's payout ratio has a major effect on total corporate taxes paid—if no dividends are repatriated, no U.S. taxes are paid. This works as an incentive for multinational corporations to reinvest earnings overseas. It also explains why U.S. oil companies and other multinationals often have very low U.S. taxes in relation to their reported income.

Table 26A-2
Depreciation Cash Flows Repatriated
(Millions of Caribian Pesos)

Year of Depreciation	Amount of Depreciation	Future Value Interest Factor at 8 Percent	Terminal Value in 1989
1985	5.0	1.3605	6.802
1986	5.0	1.2597	6.299
1987	5.0	1.1664	5.832
1988	5.0	1.0800	5.400
1989	5.0	1.0000	5.000
	25.0		
		Total	29.333
		Less depreciation	25.000
		Taxable income	4.333
		Caribian tax (20%)	0.867
		After Caribian tax	28.466
		U.S. tax	1.300
		After U.S. tax	27.166

Table 26A-3
Blocked Operating Profits
(Millions of Caribian Pesos)

Year Earned	Amount of Blocked Profits	Future Value Interest Factor at 8 Percent	Terminal Value in 1989
1985	0.0	1.3605	0.000
1986	1.6	1.2597	2.015
1987	1.2	1.1664	1.399
1988	4.8	1.0800	5.184
1989	4.4	1.0000	4.400
	12.0		
		Total	12.998
		Less investment	12.000
		Taxable income	0.998
		Caribian tax (20%)	0.200
		After Caribian tax	12.798
		U.S. tax[a]	4.799
		After U.S. tax	7.999

[a]Caribian taxes have already been paid on the blocked profits. The pre-tax income that gave rise to the 12.0 of blocked profits was 12.0/0.8 = 15.0. U.S. taxes at a rate of 30 percent must be paid on this income: 15.0(0.3) = 4.50. In addition, a 30 percent U.S. tax must be paid on the 0.998 of interest income: 0.998(0.3) = 0.299. Therefore, the total U.S. taxes payable upon repatriation of the interest-accumulated blocked profits are 4.50 + 0.299 = 4.799 million pesos.

Table 26A-4
Project Cash Flows
(Millions of Dollars)

Year	Cash Flow (Millions of Pesos)				Total Cash Flow (5)	Exchange Rate (6)	Dollar Cash Flow (7)	PVIF at 12% (8)	PV of Cash Flow (9)
	Opera-tions (1)	Depre-ciation (2)	Profits Blocked (3)	Terminal Value (4)					
1985	7.500				7.500	5.00	$1.500	0.8929	$ 1.339
1986	9.000				9.000	5.25	1.714	0.7972	1.366
1987	9.250				9.250	5.51	1.679	0.7118	1.195
1988	9.500				9.500	5.79	1.641	0.6355	1.043
1989	9.750	27.166	7.999	25.000	69.915	6.08	11.499	0.5674	6.525

	$11.468
Less investment of 50 million pesos at 5 pesos/$	10.000
NPV of project	$ 1.468

sumed to be equal to the ending book value), from pesos to dollars, and (2) to find the net present value of the project. We will assume that a 12 percent cost of capital is appropriate for this investment.[3] These steps are shown in Table 26A-4. Column 5 gives the annual cash flows in pesos; the component parts of these cash flows are indicated in the four preceding columns. The estimated exchange rates are shown in Column 6. The current rate, 5 pesos to the dollar, is expected to hold during 1985, but the peso is expected to depreciate thereafter at a rate of 5 percent per year.

Dividing the cash flows in pesos (Column 5) by the exchange rates (Column 6) gives the expected cash flows in dollars (Column 7). The dollar cash flows are converted to a present value basis (Column 9), and the sum of the present values of the annual cash flows is $11.468 million. By subtracting the initial cost of the project, $10 million, from this sum, we obtain the project's NPV, $1,468,000. Since its NPV is positive, the project should be accepted.

Problem

26A-1 The Smith-Capone Corporation of Chicago manufactures typewriters for the world market. In early 1985, the company's board of directors requests the international planning department of the company to evaluate a proposal for setting up a wholly owned subsidiary in Paralivia, a country of 50 million people in South America. The subsidiary will make typewriters for the Paralivian market. Paralivia is a rapidly developing country which has effectively invested its rich oil revenues to support a growing industrial economy. Currently, it im-

---

[3]This hurdle rate is based on the cost of capital employed in the project, adjusted as appropriate for risks associated with the foreign environment and any diversification or other benefits that are applicable.

ports all of its typewriters from abroad, and Smith-Capone is expected to capture a large portion of this market.

Political sentiment in Paralivia regarding foreign investments has been somewhat lukewarm because such investments have overtones of foreign economic control. Not long ago, the government passed a law requiring all foreign investments to pass to local ownership after 6 years or less. Paralivia recently adopted a parliamentary system of government after 20 years of military dictatorship under General Francisco, but the transition of power was peaceful. Gordon Lidder, chairman of the board of Smith-Capone, has expressed concern about the stability of the new government, but "usually reliable" sources indicate that the government has popular support and is unlikely to be toppled for at least 5 to 10 years.

The following financial information on the proposed project is available:

Paralivian currency: Because the inflation rate in Paralivia is about 5 percent higher than that in the United States, the Paralivian ringo is expected to depreciate relative to the dollar by about 5 percent a year. In 1986, when the investment will be made, the exchange rate is expected to be 2 ringos per dollar.

Investment: The estimated investment to be made in 1986 is $60 million in inventory, plant, and equipment. The parent corporation, Smith-Capone, will provide all the capital in the form of equity in the subsidiary. The project will begin to generate earnings in 1987. At the end of 6 years, in 1992, all plant and equipment will be sold to the Paralivian government for 20 million ringos. This amount of money, plus all accumulated cash, will be repatriated as a liquidating dividend.

Repatriation: Only dividends may be repatriated by the subsidiary to the parent company. Cash flows from depreciation may not be repatriated except as part of the liquidating dividend in 1989. However, these cash flows can, in the meantime, be invested in local money market instruments to yield a 15 percent tax-free return.

Taxes: The Paralivian corporate income tax rate is 25 percent. There is also a 10 percent withholding tax on dividends. The U.S. tax rate is 50 percent on the gross earnings of the foreign subsidiary. However, the parent company gets a tax credit for taxes already paid to foreign governments. In the case of the liquidating dividend, the tax treatment is quite different. The Paralivian government will not tax this dividend. Smith-Capone has obtained a ruling from the U.S. Internal Revenue Service that the liquidating dividend will not be taxed by the U.S. government either.

Cost of capital: Based on the sovereign and exchange risk characteristics of Paralivia, Smith-Capone gives Paralivia a BB rating and requires a rate of return of 20 percent on equity.

Projected demand, costs, and exchange rates:

Year	Demand for Typewriters (Thousands)	Price (Ringos)	Unit Variable Operating Cost (Ringos)	Exchange Rate (Ringos per Dollar)
1987	50	1,000	400	2.1
1988	55	1,000	420	2.2
1989	60	1,100	440	2.3
1990	70	1,100	460	2.4
1991	80	1,200	490	2.5
1992	90	1,200	540	2.6

Fixed cost: Depreciation expense is 10 million ringos per year. Consider this to be the only fixed cost of the project.

Use the information above to answer the following questions.

a. Excluding the liquidating dividend, estimate the after-tax dividend received by the parent company each year.

b. Estimate the liquidating dividend, remembering that blocked depreciation flows are reinvested at 15 percent.

c. What is your recommendation for the project? (Consider its NPV, and specify any other relevant considerations.)

Pension Plan Management

27

On March 30, 1984, after 58 years of successful operations, the Wagner Manufacturing Company filed for bankruptcy. Although its sales were down, the company would still be selling enough units, at prices sufficiently above costs, to earn a profit except for one thing—in 1968, management had agreed to an increase in pension benefits that now, 16 years later, were simply beyond the company's means. The financial vice president had protested the 1968 switch from a defined contribution to a defined benefit plan, and he had pointed out, over the intervening years, that each pay increase granted was increasing future pension requirements, but he was never able to quantify and articulate exactly what was going on until it was too late.

Pension plans are, in effect, potential time bombs ticking away deep inside many businesses and governmental units. These problems, where they exist, are generally the result of poor planning based on a lack of knowledge about pension plans and their long-run implications. A careful reading of this chapter will show you how to keep time bombs out of your firm's future, or how to identify and defuse them if one is there now. This chapter is important for managers, investors, and potential retirees alike.

Most companies—and practically all governmental units—have some type of employee pension plan. Typically, the chief financial officer, as administrator of the plan, has three specific responsibilities: (1) deciding on the general nature of the plan, (2) determining the required annual

---

This chapter was coauthored by H. Russell Fogler of the University of Florida.

1067

payments into the plan, and (3) managing the plan's assets. Obviously, the company does not have total control over these decisions—employees, primarily through their unions, have a major say about the plan's structure, and the federal government has a set of rules which must be followed. Still, companies do have a fair amount of latitude regarding the key decisions, and how a plan is set up and administered can materially affect both the firm's performance and its employees' welfare.

Although a few firms have had pension plans for many years, the real start of large-scale plans dates from 1949, when the United Steelworkers negotiated a comprehensive pension plan in their contract with the steel companies. Other companies followed, and the funds grew rapidly thereafter. Under a typical pension plan, the company (or governmental unit) agrees to provide some type of retirement payments for employees. These promised payments constitute a liability, so the employer establishes a pension fund and places money in it each year, with the idea being to have assets sufficient to cover the pension liabilities as they come due. Under current accounting rules, neither the assets nor the liabilities of a pension plan are reflected on a company's balance sheet, although footnotes to the financial statements do generally disclose information on these items.

In 1984, corporate pension plans constituted the largest and the fastest growing major class of investors: These funds had assets of approximately $300 billion; they were growing at a rate of about 15 percent per year; they accounted for approximately one half of all trading in the stock market; and they purchased well over half of all new corporate bonds issued. Pension assets are also large in relation to corporations' assets and equity. Before its 1984 breakup, AT&T had $54 billion in its pension fund versus assets of $150 billion and equity of $80 billion. At the same time, General Motors had over $15 billion in its fund, and GE and IBM each had about $10 billion. For these companies, and most other NYSE firms, pension fund assets were about 30 percent as large as their operating assets. If the pension fund is managed well and has relatively high returns, the firm's contributions—which are a cost and reduce earnings—can be minimized. If the fund does not do well, or if its assets are not sufficient to cover retirement benefits promised to employees, then the firm can be required to step up contributions, which can have a material adverse effect on profits.

It is clear that the management of pension funds is an important job. However, pension fund administration requires specialized technical knowledge, so companies typically hire specialists as consultants to help design, modify, and administer their plans. Still, because the plans are under the general supervision of the financial staff, and because they have such significant implications for the firm as a whole, it is important that students of financial management understand the basics of pension plan management.

Certain terms are used frequently in pension plan management, and it is useful to define them at the outset.

Defined Benefit Plan. Under any pension plan, the employer agrees to give something to the employees when they retire. Under a *defined benefit plan*, the employer agrees to give retirees a specifically defined benefit, such as $500 per month, 80 percent of his or her average salary over the five years preceding retirement, or 2.5 percent of his or her highest annual salary for each year of employment. The payments could be set in final form as of the retirement date, or they could be indexed to increase as the cost of living increases. In any event, under the defined benefit type of plan, the retirement benefits are defined in a specific manner.

Defined Contribution Plan. Rather than specifying exactly how much each retiree will receive, companies can agree to make specific payments into a retirement fund, and then have retirees receive benefits from the plan depending on the investment success of the plan. This is called a *defined contribution plan.* For example, a trucking firm might agree to make payments equal to 15 percent of all union members' wages each year into a pension fund administered by the Teamsters' union, and the fund would then dispense benefits to retirees.

Profit Sharing Plan. A third procedure also calls for the employer to make payments into the retirement fund, but this time with the payments varying with the level of corporate profits; this is a *profit sharing plan.* For example, a computer manufacturer might agree to pay 10 percent of its pre-tax profits into a fund which would then invest the proceeds and pay benefits to employees upon their retirement. Profit sharing plans may be used in conjunction with defined benefit or defined contribution plans. For example, a drug company might have a defined benefit plan which pays employees 1½ percent of their final average salary for each year of employment and, in addition, have a profit sharing plan which calls for putting 5 percent of pre-tax profits into an account for retired employees. Under most profit sharing plans, a separate account is maintained for each employee, and each employee gets a "share" of the contribution each year based upon his or her salary. The employee's account builds up over time just as if he or she were putting money into a mutual fund.

Vesting. If employees have a claim on the assets of a pension fund even if they leave the company prior to retirement, then their pension rights are said to be *vested.* If the employee loses his or her pension rights if he or she leaves the company prior to retirement, the rights are said to be *nonvested.* Most plans today have *deferred vesting,* that is, pension rights are nonvested for the first few years, but become fully vested if the employee remains with the company for a prescribed period, say five years. The costs to the company are clearly lower for plans with nonvested rights, because such plans do not cover employees who leave prior to retirement. Moreover, nonvested plans tend to reduce turnover, which in turn lowers training costs. However, it is much easier to recruit employees if the plan offers some type of vesting.

Portability. Portable means "capable of being carried," and a *portable pension plan* is one that an employee can carry from one employer to another. Portability is extremely important in occupations such as construction, where workers move from one employer to another fairly frequently. However, for a plan to be portable, both the old and the new employer must be part of the same plan—it would simply not be feasible for an IBM employee to leave IBM and go to work for Delta Airlines and take along a share of the IBM plan. (Note, however, that if the employee's rights under the IBM plan were vested, then he or she could receive payments from both Delta's and IBM's plans upon retirement.) Where job changes are frequent—as in trucking, construction, and coal mining—union administered plans are used to make portability possible.

Funding. Under a defined contribution or a profit sharing plan, the company's obligations are satisfied when it makes its required annual contributions to the plan. However, under a defined benefit plan, the company promises to give employees pensions for some unknown number of future years. Pension fund actuaries can determine the present value of the expected future benefits under a defined benefit plan, and this present value constitutes a liability to the plan. Also, the value of the fund's assets can easily be determined. If the present value of expected retirement benefits is equal to assets on hand, then the plan is said to be *fully funded*. If assets exceed the present value of benefits, the plan is *overfunded*, while if the present value of benefits exceeds assets, the plan is *underfunded*, and an *unfunded pension liability* exists.

Funding Ratio. If the fund's assets are divided by its present value of benefits, the result is the *funding ratio;* a ratio less than 1.0 indicates an underfunded plan and a corresponding liability which the company will eventually have to satisfy. When calculating the funding ratio, the assets are reported at market value and the liabilities are either (1) the present value of *all projected* benefits accrued by present workers or (2) the present value of *vested* benefits earned to date. The vested number is obviously smaller, and it represents the actual present value of benefits to workers if the firm went out of business today, or if all workers resigned today.

Actuarial Rate of Return. The discount rate used to determine the present value of future benefits under the plan is called the *actuarial rate of return*. The actuarial rate is also the rate of return at which the fund's assets are assumed to be invested.

ERISA. The *Employee Retirement Income Security Act of 1974 (ERISA)* is the basic federal law governing the administration and structure of corporate pension plans. ERISA requires that companies fully fund their pension plans, although it gives them up to 30 years to correct for underfunding of past service benefits such as would exist if a company agreed in 1984 to double payments to all employees who retire in the future. This "retroactive benefit" would create an immediate and large underfunding problem. The prolonged adjustment period is especially important in such a situation. Relevant provisions of ERISA are discussed throughout the chapter.

PBGC. One section of ERISA created the *Pension Benefit Guarantee Corporation (PBGC)*, which is a government run insurance system set up to ensure that employees of companies which go bankrupt before their plans are fully funded will receive benefits. PBGC serves much the same general purpose as the Federal Deposit Insurance Corporation (FDIC). Companies currently (1984) pay an insurance premium in the form of a "head tax" of $2.60 per employee per year, which goes into a fund which is then used to protect the employees of firms which go bankrupt and leave behind underfunded pension plans.

Contributions to the Plan. Actuaries calculate each year how much a company must pay into a defined benefit pension fund in order to keep it fully funded (or to move it toward full funding). These contributions are a tax-deductible cost, just as are wages. Obviously, if a company agrees to an increase in benefits, this increases its required contribution and consequently lowers its reported profits. Also, if the fund's managers do a good job of investing the fund's assets, and consequently earn a return which is greater than the actuarial rate of return built into the present value of benefits calculation, the required contributions are reduced, and vice versa if the fund's investment performance is poor.

FASB. The Financial Accounting Standards Board (FASB), together with the SEC, establishes the rules under which a firm reports its financial results, including its income and its balance sheet position, to stockholders. The costs for the year, and hence reported profits, are heavily dependent on the required pension fund contribution. Also, any shortfall between the fund's assets and the present value of vested benefits must be disclosed in a footnote to the statements. However, the FASB is currently studying the whole issue of pension fund reporting, and the

Board is expected to issue new guidelines in late 1984 or early 1985. The two major changes that are contemplated are as follows: (1) The present value of benefits which must be reported might be changed (increased) from *vested* to *total*. (2) Pension fund assets might have to be shown directly on the balance sheet as an asset, with the present value of total expected benefits shown as a liability, rather than have those amounts disclosed in a footnote.

Pension Fund Mathematics

It is clear from the preceding definitions that the calculation of the present value of expected future benefits is of primary importance in pension plan operations. These calculations determine both the required contribution to the fund for the year and also the reported unfunded liability or surplus. Thus, it is essential that financial managers understand the basic mathematics which underlies the benefits calculation.[1]

To illustrate the process, let us begin with the following assumptions:

1. A firm has only one employee, age 40, who will retire 25 years from now, at age 65, and die at age 80. There is no uncertainty about these facts.

2. The firm has promised a benefit of $10,000 at the end of each year from retirement until death. For accounting purposes, 1/25th of this $10,000 payment will be vested each year the employee works for the company.

3. No uncertainty exists regarding the contribution stream; that is, the company will definitely make the required payments, in equal annual installments, over the next 25 years to build the fund to the amount needed to make the payments of $10,000 per year during the employee's 15-year retirement life.

4. The pension fund will earn 8 percent on its assets; this rate of return is known with certainty.

The problem is to find (1) the present value of the future benefits and (2) the company's required annual contributions. We find these values as follows:

Step 1. Find the value of a 15-year regular annuity of $10,000 per year:

$$\text{PV of an annuity of \$10,000 per year for 15 years at 8\%} = \$10,000(\text{PVIFA}_{8\%,15}) = \$85,594.79.$$

---

[1] For a detailed treatment of pension fund mathematics, see C. L. Trowbridge and C. E. Farr, *The Theory and Practice of Pension Funding* (Homewood, Ill.: Irwin, 1976).

Step 2. Find the set of equal annual cash contributions required to accumulate $85,594.79 over 25 years:

$$\begin{array}{c}\text{Annual cash contribution} \\ \text{to establish a fund of} \\ \$85,594.79 \text{ over a 25-year} \\ \text{period at 8\%}\end{array} = \frac{\$85,594.79}{\text{FVIFA}_{8\%,25}} = \$1,170.85.$$

Thus, the company must contribute $1,170.85 per year to satisfy its pension requirements; such payments will also enable it to report a fully funded position.

A graphical representation of the contribution and benefit cash flows and fund value is presented in Figure 27-1. The "Value of Fund" line is drawn continuously, although in reality, it would be a step function. Note also that setting up a pension plan for this "middle life" worker involves investing over a 40-year horizon.

Sensitivity to the assumed rate of return can be substantial. If we had assumed a 9 percent return rather than 8 percent, the annual contributions would have dropped from $1,170.85 to $951.67. Thus, annual con-

Figure 27-1
Pension Fund Cash Flows
and Value under Certainty

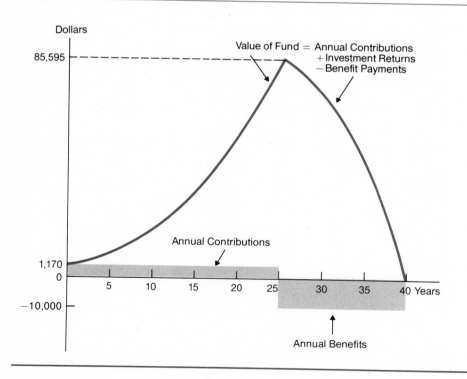

tributions would have fallen by 18.7 percent from only a one percentage point change in the assumed investment rate. Conversely, if we had assumed a 7 percent return, the annual contributions would have increased to $1,842.49, a 57 percent increase.

Types of Pension Fund Plans

By modifying the certainty assumption used to construct Figure 27-1, the three basic types of plans can be illustrated. In Figure 27-2, the left panel shows the funding and value for a defined contribution plan; the middle panel depicts a profit sharing plan; and the right panel represents a defined benefit plan. Each type of plan differs in regard to the certainty of cash contributions, investment earnings, and/or the promised benefit at retirement.

In a *defined contribution plan*, shown in Panel a, the corporation, or *plan sponsor*, contributes a guaranteed amount which will be invested for eventual retirement payments to the beneficiaries of the plan. No guarantee, however, is made about either the rate of return earned on funds or the final payments. Thus, the beneficiaries assume the risk of fluctuations in the rate of return on the invested money, which would result

Figure 27-2
Funding and Value of Different
Types of Pension Plans

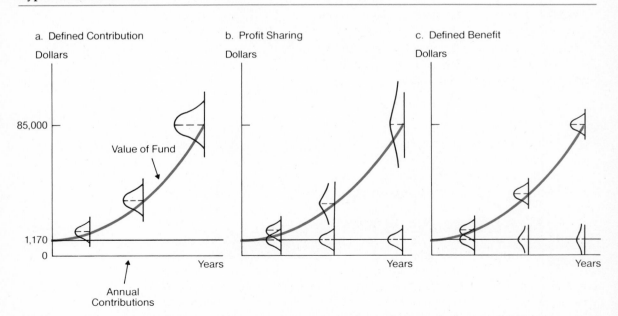

a. Defined Contribution

b. Profit Sharing

c. Defined Benefit

in corresponding uncertainty about their retirement incomes. Thus, uncertainty is shown around the value line, but the contributions line is fixed.

A *profit sharing plan*, shown in Panel b, is similar to a defined contribution plan, except that the sponsor's cash contributions are also uncertain. Because of this uncertainty, the value line has additional dispersion around its forecasts—uncertainty about the value of the fund increases over time because of the cumulative effects of uncertainty about both the size of the annual contribution and the rate of return earned on the fund's assets. The final value of the fund, and hence retirees' incomes, could be quite large or quite small, depending on how well the corporation does and the returns generated on the plan's assets.

Finally, Panel c of Figure 27-2 depicts a *defined benefit plan*, which guarantees to pay a stated amount at retirement. We show a small range around both the value line and the contributions line to reflect possible variations in required contributions and fund assets due to rate of return fluctuations because, under the typical defined benefit plan, the corporate sponsor assumes the risks of unexpected variations in rates of return on investment. Also, the required level of the fund, and the resulting annual contributions, could vary if the defined benefits are based on some average of the final years' salaries, for salaries can grow at a rate different from the assumed level. Thus, the future cash contribution requirements are relatively uncertain, and these contributions cannot be reduced if the corporation's profits fall, as in a profit sharing plan. *Therefore, a defined benefit plan is by far the riskiest from the standpoint of the sponsoring corporation, but the least risky from the standpoint of the employees.* Given this risk, it is reasonable to ask, "Why do most large corporations use defined benefit plans?" Although a simple answer might be "unions," maintaining a loyal and productive work force also plays a part, as does an appreciation of the relative abilities of employers versus employees to assume these risks.

Risks to the Corporation

From the foregoing discussion, we see that risks are inherent in pension fund operations depending on how the plan is structured. Under a defined benefit plan, these risks fall primarily on the corporation (through the uncertainty of its future contributions). If the plan calls for defined contributions, then risks are shared, while under a profit-sharing plan, most risks fall on the beneficiaries (through uncertainty regarding the benefits to be received). Risk to the corporation under a defined benefit plan can be further subdivided into (1) uncertainty about the annual cash contribution, (2) uncertainty about the firm's obligations in the event it goes bankrupt, and (3) a possible penalty on the firm's stock price because of investors' uncertainty about unfunded liabilities and future pension expenses, as we demonstrate in the following sections.

*Annual Cash
Contribution Risk*

The *minimum annual cash contribution* is the sum of (1) the amount needed to fund projected future benefit payments that were accrued (vested) during the current period, (2) the amount (which could be zero) that must be contributed to pay for not having funded all benefits for service that occurred prior to the current period, and (3) an additional amount (which could be zero or negative) required to offset unexpected deviations from the plan's actuarial assumptions, especially deviations in the earned rate of return and in employee turnover and wage rates. This minimum cash contribution can be formalized by the following equation:

$$\text{Minimum cash contribution} = NC + PS + AG,$$

where

NC = normal contribution, which is a figure based on funding the present value of benefits earned for service during the current period, discounted at the actuarial rate. NC can vary considerably depending on the assumptions made about the return on pension plan assets, future employee turnover, and future salary increases.

PS = past service, which is the make-up contribution for unfunded past service. The minimum PS make-up under ERISA is the amount required to amortize the unfunded liability on a straight line basis over 30 years at the plan's actuarial rate. The company can, if it has the cash and chooses to do so, set PS equal to the full unfunded liability and, thus, immediately bring the plan up to full funding. However, for tax purposes, the IRS will allow as a deduction only amounts based on amortization over a 10-year or longer period.

AG = actuarial gains and losses from the assumed actuarial forecast, amortized over 15 years at the plan's assumed rate of interest. These actuarial gains or losses could occur because of deviations in employees' turnover, final salaries, life expectancy, and so on, and also because of deviations between actual and expected investment performance for the fund's assets.

To help explain all this, two concepts should be discussed in detail: (1) *actuarial assumptions* and (2) *funding methods.* In the preceding illustration of pension fund mathematics, we assumed certainty. In actual plans, there are three key types of actuarial assumptions: (1) *decrement assumptions,* which allow the actuary to adjust annually for the probability that any employee will leave the company (that is, terminate employment, become disabled, retire, or die); (2) *future salary assumptions,* which take into account expected future average wage and merit-pay increases, which will, of course, affect the final salary, and hence defined benefit payments based on the final salary; and (3) *discount rate assumptions,* which explicitly forecast the portfolio's expected future rate of return, which is used both to forecast the fund's growth from investment and also to find the present value of future benefit payments.

At the end of each year, deviations between the fund's actual value and the actuarially forecasted required value based on the modified assumptions become part of the "total cumulative actuarial gains and losses." Then the annual required contribution is adjusted by an amount sufficient to amortize this cumulative amount over a 15-year period. For example, suppose a fund was set up on January 1, 1980, and money was deposited based on a set of actuarial assumptions. Then, at the end of the year, the actual actuarial conditions would be examined and compared with the assumed conditions, and the money in the fund would be compared with the money that would be needed for full funding under revised actuarial assumptions. Any difference between the actual and required fund balance would be recorded in an account labeled "cumulative actuarial gains and losses," and the required annual contribution would be increased or decreased by an amount sufficient to amortize this account's balance over a 15-year period. The same thing would be done the next year; the cumulative gains and losses account would be adjusted; and a new 15-year amortization payment for actuarial gains and losses would be determined. To illustrate, suppose the cumulative amount in the actuarial gains and losses account at the end of 1980 was a $15 million shortfall, and the actuarial earnings rate was 8 percent. Under these conditions, in 1981 the minimum value of AG would be $552,443, because this level of AG would eliminate the $15 million deficiency in 15 years. If everything else remained constant, then AG would remain at $552,443 for 15 years. However, in future years new deviations are bound to occur and the cumulative amount of actuarial gains and losses will rise or fall, requiring new calculations and new values for AG. All of this is designed to build the fund up to its required level but, at the same time, to smooth out the annual cash contribution charge and, hence, to smooth out the firm's reported profits and cash flows.

Many *funding methods* can be used to determine the employer's normal contribution (NC) for the year. One commonly used method, called the *unit credit* method, requires current funding for the additional benefit each employee earns during the year, under the assumption that he or she will quit at the end of the year and thus will receive retirement benefits based on present salary levels. For example, if an employee were earning $30,000 and was to get a pension equal to 2 percent of the final salary per year of service, then this employee would earn a retirement benefit of 0.02($30,000) = $600 per year for that year's service. If the employee was 30 years old and was expected to retire in 35 years and then to live for another 15 years, and if the assumed rate of return was 8 percent, then the company would need to have $5,135.69 in the fund 35 years from now, and a payment of $347.35 could be made today to reach that future goal. Note, though, that if the employee receives a raise in the future, his or her retirement income based on this year's work will be greater than $600, and hence the $347.35 payment will not be sufficient to cover the benefits. Thus, the unit credit funding method is not realistic for a great many situations. Note also that younger employees, who could not collect any benefits for many years, would require smaller funding amounts under the unit credit method than would workers nearing retirement, because the funding requirement is the present value of future benefits, which is obviously less for a 30-year-old worker who will not start receiving benefits for 35 years than for a 60-year-old worker who will start drawing the same benefits 5 years hence. Thus, had the worker in our example been 60 rather than 30 years old, his or her pension cost would have been $3,495.26 rather than $507.26.

The unit credit method is actually used primarily for hourly pay workers. Another commonly used method, *entry age normal*, is typically used for salaried (as opposed to hourly) workers, and it projects the worker's salary into the future, factors in the probability the employee will quit before retirement, and then finds the present value of the resulting expected benefits.[2]

A significant change in the benefits offered or in the funding method would lead to a change in required annual contributions, but, in the normal course of events, where salary increases are projected with a reasonable degree of accuracy, most contribution level changes result from fluctuations in the value of the pension fund's assets due to increases or decreases in stock and bond prices. If a decline in market prices causes the value of the fund's assets to fall below the present value of the benefits, then annual contributions will have to be increased, and the company's profits will suffer. Conversely, if good investment experience raises the value of the assets, the required annual contribution will decline, and profits will benefit.

Bankruptcy Liens   Prior to the passage of the Employee Retirement Income Security Act (ERISA) in 1974, employees had no claim against a corporation's assets in the event of bankruptcy. Of course, if a plan were fully funded, bankruptcy would present no problem for employees, but it did work a serious hardship on members of plans that were not fully funded. ERISA had the major effect of elevating the priority of unfunded vested pension liabilities in the event of bankruptcy. Today, in the event of a pen-

---

[2]At first glance, it might appear that the unit credit method would defer a huge liability until workers are near retirement. However, for growing firms that are continually hiring younger workers, the situation might not be bad, since excessive funding for the younger workers may offset the funding shortfall for the older workers. On the other hand, a unit credit plan for a firm with an aging work force in a mature industry subject to increasing automation, and hence declining employment, could indeed result in serious underfunding. Therefore, such a corporation should require its actuaries to project the present plan's contributions for the next 10 or so years, in addition to the standard one-year forecast, and use this information in its internal planning and labor negotiations.

sion plan termination due to bankruptcy, unfunded vested liabilities have an automatic priority lien on a par with federal taxes on up to 30 percent of the stockholders' equity. Thus, the pension fund ranks above the unsecured creditors for up to 30 percent of the equity. Any unsatisfied pension claims rank with the general creditors. The rights of the pension fund are enforced by the Pension Benefit Guarantee Corporation (PBGC), which was created to guarantee beneficiaries of their vested pension benefits.[3] PBGC is funded by an annual "head tax" of $2.60 per beneficiary. However, because of the high level of bankruptcies that occurred in the early 1980s, it is now clear that $2.60 is not sufficient, and drawdowns from PBGC have been exceeding inflows. Thus, higher taxes are likely in the future.[4]

Note also that if one of the subsidiaries of a holding company had been operating at a loss, and consequently had a low net worth, and if the subsidiary also had an unfunded pension liability which was greater than its net worth, then the parent company would probably be better off without the subsidiary than with it. This situation has undoubtedly led some companies to contemplate spinning off or otherwise disposing of some subsidiaries. Such spinoffs would have detrimental effects on the PBGC, which in fact sued International Harvester for having sold its Wisconsin Steel subsidiary three years before the subsidiary went bankrupt and turned its underfunded pension plan over to the PBGC. PBGC claimed that the purpose of the sale was to rid the parent company of the pension liability. Some people suspect that several of the leveraged buyouts of divisions of corporations that have been so prevalent recently may have been motivated in part by the pension situation.

The value of a firm's stock may be affected if investors are confused by an unfunded pension plan shown on its financial statements. Because of the long-term nature of pension liabilities, accounting standards for

Stock Market Effects

---

[3]Actual benefit payments to employees are subject to a maximum limit. Thus, when bankruptcy occurs, highly paid employees would obtain less from the PBGC than they would had the company survived. Note also that if a company has been suffering losses prior to bankruptcy, which is generally the case, its equity will be low, and 30 percent of a low number is lower yet. Nevertheless, PBGC must still make payments as specified to vested pension holders.

[4]The shortfall between PBGC's assets and the present value of its liabilities was over $230 million in 1982, and thus it has asked for an increase in the head tax. Critics argue that the flat tax currently being used is unfair to plans which are fully funded, and that the tax rate ought to penalize unfunded plans. As with any issue in the political arena, there are many contradictory opinions. Experience to date suggests that approximately 97 percent of terminating plans have assets sufficient to cover their current vested benefits. However, bankruptcies by some large companies such as Chrysler or International Harvester, had they occurred, would have increased PBGC's liability by another $1.5 to $2.0 billion and truly bankrupted it. For a theoretical discussion of the insurance features of the PBGC, see William F. Sharpe, "Corporate Pension Funding Policy," *Journal of Financial Economics*, June 1976, 183-193.

reporting income and liabilities are most difficult to devise. Currently, under the Financial Accounting Standard Board's Statement #36, corporations are required to disclose both the present value of vested benefits and the actuarial discount rate used to calculate this value, along with the fund's actual assets. The present value is computed *as of the statement date*, under the assumption that each employee is terminated immediately after the statement date (that is, under an assumption similar to that used in the *unit credit* funding method). The theory is that this treatment will ensure comparability between companies with hourly pay plans versus those with final-salary plans, even though the true liability is almost certainly understated for both groups.[5] The assumed actuarial rate of return for reporting purposes under FASB #36 does not have to be the same as that used for actual funding. For example, Firestone used 15.9 percent to calculate the present value of benefits for disclosure (or reporting) purposes but 9.8 percent for actual funding in 1982; had it used 9.8 percent for both purposes, its reported pension liabilities would have been much higher.

Can investors make sense of such accounting data, especially with each corporation using whatever actuarial rate best suits its purpose and without full consideration of probable future salary increases? To help answer this question, Martin Feldstein and Randall Morck examined the relationship between corporations' market values and their pension fund liabilities.[6] Their procedure was to divide the market value of a corporation's assets, V, by the replacement value of its assets, A, and then to regress this "market value/replacement value" ratio against six variables: EBIT/total assets (EBIT/A), growth of profits over the past decade (GROW), research and development expenditures as a proportion of the firm's assets (RD/A), beta, the market value of the firm's net debt (DEBT), and the unfunded vested pension liability (UVPL); that is,

$$V/A = f(EBIT/A, GROW, RD/A, BETA, DEBT, UVPL).$$

If the sign of UVPL turned out to be negative, this would indicate that investors recognize the existence of the unfunded pension liability and

---

[5]Hourly pay plans are usually negotiated under limited-term union contracts (say 3 years), and this can create problems for corporate planning. While management might actually plan for the next 10 years (and recognize that pension costs will probably rise sharply), the IRS allows contributions to reflect only the current contract. (Under final-salary plans, tax-deductible contributions can be based on projected salary increases over employees' entire working lives.) Thus, for an hourly wage plan, any forecast of inflation in pay and benefits for the period after the contract will not qualify for current tax deductibility. The impact of this situation varies from company to company, depending largely on the age distribution of the company's potential beneficiaries. Because of the lower vested benefits for young hires, the net effect is not too great for many companies, especially those that are growing rapidly, but it does create a problem for mature, slow growing firms, and for those that are increasing the use of automated production equipment, and hence decreasing their labor forces.

[6]See Martin Feldstein and Randall Morck, "Pension Funds and the Value of Equities," *Financial Analysts Journal*, September-October 1983, 29-39.

lower the firm's value accordingly. The sign of the coefficient did turn out to be significantly negative. As with most empirical studies, one can argue about the measurement, the choice of variables, or both, but this and other evidence indicates that investors are well aware of companies' pension situations, and that unfunded pension liabilities do reduce corporate value.

As noted earlier, to increase comparability among different companies' financial statements, and also to increase the relevance of such statements to investors, the FASB has recently distributed a memorandum suggesting that pension liabilities may in the future have to be included directly on the balance sheet. The proposal in this memorandum represents an attempt to remedy some of the weaknesses of FASB #36. For example, the calculated liability under the FASB proposal would reflect a forecast of the future growth rate in salaries for plans that define benefits in terms of final pay. The FASB proposal would also require a change in the actuarial rate used to calculate the present value of benefits whenever market conditions necessitated such a change. Another change contained in the FASB proposal is the creation of a balance sheet account called *measurement valuation allowance (MVA)*. This account is designed to reduce the volatility of reported net income caused by pension fund accounting. Its value would initially be zero, but each year, as the plan's liabilities were changed by either experienced portfolio gains or losses or because of changes in the actuarial rate, the change would be added to the MVA, which would then be amortized at a rate in the 5 to 7 percent range per year, depending on the average remaining service life of employees. Only the amortization charges would be reflected in reported income, so even major changes in asset values would have only a small effect on income during any given year, and positive and negative changes in the MVA from year to year would tend to offset one another and further reduce income volatility.

If the new rule is put into effect, corporations would have to face up to the difficult issue of determining an appropriate actuarial rate each year. Given our lack of success in forecasting inflation and interest rates, this would not be an easy task. Still, the proposed rule might provide a more accurate and comparable set of financial statements than those currently provided under FASB #36.

Risks to Beneficiaries

While the preceding section might suggest that all the risks inherent in defined benefit pension plans are borne by the PBGC or the corporate sponsor and its investors, this is not entirely true. For example, suppose that in 1984 a corporation goes bankrupt and its employees are laid off. It is true that the PBGC will provide the promised retirement payments when the employee actually retires. But suppose the employee is 50 years old now, the benefits are $10,000 per year, and retirement is 15 years away. If the firm is in an industry where employment is contracting, such as steel or auto production, the worker will have a hard time finding a new job offering comparable wages. Moreover, even if the worker could get another job at the same salary and with an equivalent pension plan, his or her benefits will be adversely affected. The benefits under the bankrupt company's plan would be frozen—the past benefits from the now-bankrupt firm would not be increased as a result of pay increases over the worker's remaining employment life, as they probably would have been had the original employer not gone bankrupt. The worker's benefits under his or her new plan, assuming he or she does get a new job, would rise with inflation, but the worker's retirement income will be the sum of payments under the old frozen plan and the new one, and these benefits will almost certainly be lower than they would have been had no bankruptcy occurred. Thus, under bankruptcy, workers still face risks, and a realization of this fact has been a major factor in unions' acceptance of reduced wages and benefits in situations where corporate bankruptcy with corresponding layoffs would otherwise have occurred.

It should also be recognized (1) that prior to the 1930s, most people had to depend on personal savings (and their children) to support them in their old age, (2) that Social Security was put into effect in 1933 to provide a formalized retirement system for workers, (3) that corporate pension plans did not really "take off" until after World War II, and (4) that even today many workers, especially those employed by smaller firms, have no formal retirement plan other than Social Security. Also, when it was passed into law, the Social Security program was supposed to be based on insurance principles in the sense that each person was supposed to pay into the system and then receive benefits which, actuarially, were equivalent to what he or she had paid in. Thus, Social Security was designed to help workers provide for their own future. Today, Social Security has become an income transfer mechanism in the sense that workers with high salaries get less out of the system than they pay in, while low salaried workers get more out than they pay in. In a sense, the Social Security system, including Medicare, is becoming a "safety net" for all older Americans, irrespective of their payments into the system. Even so, few people want to have to live on the income provided by Social Security, so private pension plans are still a vital part of the American economic scene.

Illustration of a Defined Benefit versus a Defined Contribution Plan

Like corporations, some universities (and government organizations) provide their faculty with defined benefit plans, while others use defined contribution plans. The implications of these plans ought to be understood by people working under them and by the agencies responsible for paying the prescribed benefits. While pension plan status would rarely be the primary factor in a job selection decision, it is a factor that ought to be given at least some consideration. Our example does not correspond (to our knowledge) exactly with the plan of any university, but the University of Florida and UCLA do have plans that are similar to our hypothetical University DB (for defined benefit), while the University of Wisconsin and many private colleges have plans similar to our University DC (for defined contribution).

Here are the assumptions used in the illustration:

1. It is now 1985.

2. The employee is 30 years old, earns $30,000 per year, and plans to retire in 35 years, at age 65.

3. Both universities provide for immediate vesting. (This is not always the case.)

4. The rate of inflation is expected to be 6 percent per year. Salaries will also increase at this same rate.

5. Pension fund assets are expected to earn a return of 10 percent.

6. The employee is expected to live for 15 years past retirement at age 65, or to age 80.

This school has a defined benefit plan which offers 2 percent of the average salary over the last year of an employee's employment at the university for each year of service at the university. Thus, if the employee worked for one year and then resigned, we would have the following situation:

University DB: Defined Benefit

1. The annual benefit at age 65 would be 0.02($30,000) = $600.

2. The amount needed to establish an annuity of $600 per year for 15 years (assume payment at the end of each year) would be

$$\text{PV of the annuity} = \$600(\text{PVIFA}_{10\%,15}) = \$4,564.$$

3. The university will have to put up $162 today to provide the required annuity 35 years from now:[7]

$$\text{PV of the PV of the annuity} = \$4,564(\text{PVIF}_{10\%,35}) = \$162.$$

Thus, the cost to the university is $162. (The cost to the university would have been $4,564 had the employee been 64 years old instead of 30; does this help explain why older workers sometimes have a hard time landing jobs?)

4. Given an inflation rate of 6 percent, the real (1985) value of the income for the employee from this pension would be $78 in the first year of retirement:

---

[7]We have assumed that inflation in wages is not built into the funding requirement. If a 6 percent wage inflation were built in, then the cost would rise from $162 to $1,245 (as determined by a simple *Lotus 1-2-3* spreadsheet model).

$$\text{Real income} = \$600(PVIF_{6\%,35}) = \$78.$$

If the person remained at University DB until retirement, and if his or her salary increased with inflation, then the final salary would be $30,000(FVIF6%,35) = $230,583 per year, and his or her retirement income would be 0.02(35)($230,583) = $161,408, which, in 1985 dollars, would be $21,000, or 70 percent of the 1985 employment income.

University DC: Defined Contribution

This school has a defined contribution plan under which an amount equal to 6 percent of each employee's salary is put into a pension fund account. The fund keeps track of the dollar amount of the contribution attributable to each employee, just as if the university had put the money into a bank time deposit for the employee. Here is the situation that would exist if the employee worked for one year and then resigned:

1. The university would contribute 0.06($30,000) = $1,800 to the employee's account in the pension fund. This is the university's cost, and it would be the same irrespective of the professor's age.

2. The fund's assets would earn 10 percent per year, so when the employee retired, the value of his or her share of the fund would be

$$\text{Value in fund} = \$1,800(FVIF_{10\%,35}) = \$50,584.$$

3. At a 10 percent rate of return, this $50,584 would provide an annuity of $6,650 per year for 15 years:

$$\text{Annuity} = \frac{\$50,584}{PVIFA_{10\%,15}} = \frac{\$50,584}{7.6061} = \$6,650.$$

4. The real (1985) retirement income for this person would be

$$\text{Real income} = \$6,650(PVIF_{6\%,35}) = \$865.$$

If the person remained at University DC, his or her retirement fund would accumulate to $1,024,444 over the 35-year employment period (we worked this amount out on a personal computer using *Lotus 1-2-3*). This would provide a retirement income of $134,688, or 58 percent of the $230,583 final salary. The real (1985 dollar) retirement income would be $17,524.

Conclusions

1. A young professor, who has a high probability of moving, would be better off under a defined contribution plan such as the one offered by University DC.

2. A worker who planned to spend his or her entire career at one school would be better off at University DB, with its defined benefit plan.

3. The economic consequences of changing jobs are much worse under the defined benefit plan. Therefore, defined benefit plans contribute to lower employee turnover, other things held constant.

4. It is much more costly to a university (or to a company) to hire older workers if it operates under a defined benefit plan than if it operates under a defined contribution plan. In our example, the current year cost to provide pension benefits to a 30-year-old employee under the defined benefit plan is $162 versus $4,564 for a 64-year-old employee earning the same salary. The average cost per employee to the university would depend on the age distribution of employees. The cost would be $1,800 per employee, irrespective of age, under the defined contribution plan. Thus, defined benefit plans carry with them economic incentive to discriminate against older workers in hiring, while defined contribution plans are neutral in this regard.

5. If one were to vary the assumptions, it would be easy to show that employees are generally exposed to more risks under a defined contribution plan, while employers face more risks under a defined benefit plan. In particular, the pension benefits of the defined contribution plan are highly sensitive to changes in the actuarial rate of return on the pension fund's investments. Likewise, the costs to University DB would vary greatly depending on investment performance, but University DC's costs would not vary with respect to changes in investment performance.

6. We could have changed the facts of the example to deal with an "average man" with a life expectancy of 70.6 years and an "average woman" with a 78.2-year life expectancy. Obviously, an average woman would receive benefits over a longer period and thus would need a larger accumulated sum in the plan upon retirement, and hence would have a higher actuarial annual required cost to the university than an average man under the defined benefit plan. Thus, other things held constant, there is an economic incentive for employers to discriminate against women in their hiring practices if they use defined benefit plans. Defined contribution plans are again neutral in this regard.

Developing a Plan Strategy

The actual choice of a plan type is often dictated by competitive conditions in the labor market. For example, unions generally seek defined benefit plans in order to cushion the beneficiaries from the investment risks that would exist under a defined contribution or a profit sharing plan. Even if the firm has the economic power to resist a defined benefit plan, it may still agree to one on the grounds that such a plan would, for the reasons set forth above, reduce its turnover rate. However, this advantage must be weighed against the fact that the use of a defined contribution plan would relieve the corporation of the risks of both underfunding and accounting interpretations. In practice, defined contribution and/or profit sharing plans are often used by small firms when they first agree to offer corporate retirement plans to their employees, while larger and more stable firms generally have defined benefit plans.

Assuming that a firm has decided on a defined benefit plan, proper strategic planning requires integrating the plan's funding and investment policies into the company's general corporate policies. The *funding strategy* involves two decisions: (1) How fast should any unfunded liability be reduced, and (2) what rate of return should be assumed in the actuarial calculations? The *investment strategy* also involves two decisions: (1) What rate of return should be targeted, given investment risk considerations, and (2) how should a portfolio that minimizes the risk of not achieving that return be structured?

Pension fund managers use models called *asset allocation models* to help them plan funding and investment strategies. These models examine the risk/return relationship of portfolios with various mixes of assets, including stocks, bonds, T-bills, real estate, international assets, and so on. Several conclusions emerge from a study of these models. First, the very nature of pension funds suggests that safety of principal is a paramount consideration, so pension fund managers ought not to "reach" for the highest possible return levels. Second, as we learned from Chapter 6, for a given level of return, the inclusion of more types of assets generally reduces the portfolio's standard deviation, because asset types are not perfectly correlated. And third, choices among the possible portfolios are limited by the introduction of managerial constraints, such as (1) that the portfolio should not drop more than 30 percent if a 1930s-style depression occurs, and (2) that the portfolio should earn at least 10 percent if a 1970s-style inflation occurs.

Another step in funding and investment strategy is to combine the asset allocation model with the pension plan's assumed actuarial rate of return. For example, if the plan's actuaries assume that an 8 percent annual rate of return will be earned, it would be possible to calculate the difference between each possible portfolio's expected results and the actuarial assumption of 8 percent, as well as the probability of being off the 8 percent mark. Such differences can then be translated into increases or decreases in the company's required pension fund contributions, and hence to effects on reported profits.

In addition, pension fund managers must also consider the impact of portfolio selection and actuarial assumptions on required contributions. First, note that the most commonly used measure of pension plan cost is the ratio of pension contributions to payroll. Now suppose salary inflation heats up to 15 percent, and therefore the company's projected benefit payments under a final pay plan are growing at 15 percent per year for active participants. Such a situation might not affect the percentage of pension costs to payroll costs, because payroll costs inflate rapidly during such times. However, if a company has a large number of retirees, relative to actives, and if the payments to retirees are raised at a rate lower than the inflation rate, while the reinvestment rate rises on those assets held for retirees (because inflation pushes up interest rates), then pension costs as a percentage of payroll could even go down. On the other hand, in a 1930s-style depression, a company with a lot of retirees on defined benefits might be in substantial trouble. For example, suppose production cutbacks caused nonvested employees to be laid off, thereby reducing payroll expenses, while the pension fund, which was heavily invested in stocks, declined substantially in price. For such a company, the now-higher pension expenses could become an extremely high percentage of the reduced payroll (and operating income).

These examples illustrate the interdependence among business policies, economic conditions, and pension fund planning. Understanding these relationships under alternative economic scenarios requires that managers have access to actuarial forecasts of plan liabilities under different scenarios. Pension fund consultants can supply these. Such "asset-liability simulators" develop probability distributions for the plan under different portfolio mixes, and they calculate probability distributions for plan contributions over time assuming different investment strategies.[8] These models are helpful, but it is often difficult to develop reasonable assumptions about asset and liability interrelationships under different economic scenarios.

In summary, it is important to understand how a plan's liabilities will change under alternative economic scenarios, and to combine this understanding with projected asset returns under the same scenarios. Application of asset allocation models has resulted in the widespread recognition that portfolios consisting of between 25 to 50 percent bonds, and 50 to 75 percent stocks, provide adequate diversification for safety along with a satisfactory expected return. Additionally, it is now recognized that further benefits can be gained by investing in assets other than stocks and bonds. Indeed, many pension funds now make minimum commitments to several asset categories. A typical minimum commitment might be 25 percent in bills and bonds, 30 percent in domestic stocks, 15 percent in real estate, and 10 percent in international assets, with the remaining 20 percent of the portfolio being available for discretionary investment in whichever category seems best at a particular time.

Pension Fund Investment Tactics

Three characteristics have a major influence on pension funds' investment tactics: (1) the dollar size of a fund's investable assets, (2) the mix of the funds' liabilities between those attributable to active workers and those attributable to retired beneficiaries, and (3) the tax situation facing

---

[8]An excellent description of several such simulation models is found in the May 1982 *Journal of Finance*. Included are articles by Louis Kingsland, Howard E. Winklevoss, and Alice B. Goldstein and Barbara G. Markowitz, plus excellent discussions of these articles by William F. Sharpe and Irwin Tepper.

the corporate sponsor. To show how these characteristics affect funds' investment tactics, we next discuss four topics: (1) performance measurement, (2) equity portfolio risk, (3) bond portfolio risk, and (4) procedures for controlling management fees and transactions costs.

Performance Measurement

Pension fund sponsors need to evaluate the performance of their portfolio managers on a regular basis, and then to use this performance evaluation information as a basis for allocating the fund's assets among portfolio managers. Suppose a fund's common stock portfolio increased in value by 16 percent during a recent year—is this good, bad, or average performance? To answer this question, the portfolio's systematic risk (beta) should be estimated, and then the portfolio's return should be compared to the Security Market Line (SML) as described in Chapter 6. Suppose, for example, that the "market" portfolio, say the S&P 500, returned 15 percent, that 20-year Treasury bonds returned 9 percent, and that our fund's equity portfolio had a beta of 0.9 (that is, it was invested in stocks that had lower systematic risk than the market). An SML analysis would lead to the visual comparison shown in Figure 27-3, which

Figure 27-3
SML Analysis

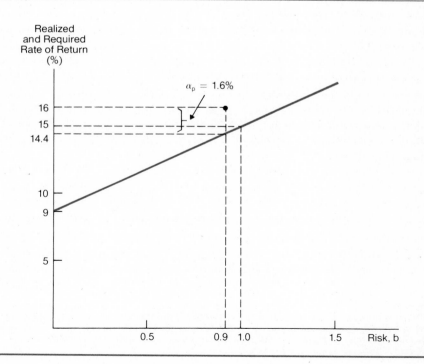

indicates that the portfolio did better than expected—it is said to have an *alpha* (α) of 1.6 percentage points. Alpha measures the vertical distance of a portfolio's return above or below the Security Market Line. Looked at another way, alpha is the portfolio's extra return (positive or negative) after adjustment for the portfolio's beta risk.[9]

To measure portfolio performance over several periods, returns must also be adjusted for cash flow timing. For example, assume that a portfolio consists of $10 million dollars at Year 0, and that the fund manager receives one cash contribution, $1 million at the beginning of Year 2. This situation is set forth below, along with the assumed investment returns on the portfolio during each year:

Year (t)	Portfolio in Return Year t	Cash Flow at Beginning of Year t	Portfolio Value at End of Year t	Portfolio Value at End of Year t, Ignoring Cash Contribution
0	—	—	$10,000,000	$10,000,000
1	−0.10	$ 0	9,000,000	9,000,000
2	+0.25	1,000,000	12,500,000	11,250,000
3	+0.05	0	13,125,000	11,812,500

In our example, the portfolio's value grows from $10 million to $13,125,000—an increase of 31.2 percent over the 3-year period. However, the actual growth without the cash flow would have been 18.1 percent over the 3 years. The 18.1 percent is found by compounding each annual rate of return, $(0.90)(1.25)(1.05) - 1.0 = 0.181 = 18.1\%$, or, equivalently, by using the last column to calculate the total growth in the portfolio.

Now suppose that the last two columns in the table represented the results of two different pension funds which had started with identical portfolios. The manager of the first fund actually received the interim $1 million cash contribution in a year when returns were high, so this manager has an increase in his or her portfolio of 31.2 percent, while the other has achieved a growth of only 18.1 percent. However, the two managers really had identical performance records, because the observed difference was caused entirely by the cash inflow. Therefore, a valid comparison of portfolio managers requires that portfolio returns be adjusted to eliminate cash flow timing effects. The problem appears trivial in our simple example, but when the fund has frequent inflows and

---

[9]The Jensen alpha, so-called because this performance measure was first suggested by Professor Michael Jensen, is very popular because of its ease of calculation. Theoretically, its purpose is to measure the performance of a single portfolio versus the market portfolio, after adjusting for the portfolio's beta. However, this measure is not useful in comparing the performance of two portfolios which include real estate and other assets which do not trade actively on the market. This fact has led to the development of a number of other portfolio performance measures. For a discussion of these measures, see Jack L. Treynor and Fischer Black, "How to Use Security Analysis to Improve Portfolio Selection," *Journal of Business*, January 1973, 66-86.

outflows, on a monthly basis over many years, proper adjustments are quite complex.[10]

The type of performance analysis described above adds substantially to a pension manager's knowledge about his or her equity portfolio's results, but several shortcomings must be recognized. First, alpha analysis relies on the CAPM, which, as we discussed in Chapter 6, is an ex ante equilibrium concept which in theory requires that all earning assets be included in the market portfolio (for example, human capital and residential real estate), so market proxies such as the Standard and Poor's Index result in some degree of measurement error.[11] Second, the statistical significance of alpha is often too low to make strong statements about the portfolio's relative performance. And third, all of our measurements are based on ex post results which contain both expected returns plus unanticipated returns that resulted from unexpected random economic events. Thus, a large positive alpha may indicate good luck rather than good management, and vice versa.

Equity Portfolio Risk

In Chapter 6, we saw that the standard deviation of returns on a portfolio is reduced when assets with less than perfect positive correlation are combined. The same principle applies to combining portfolios under different management. Further, it is common practice to classify portfolio managers by their stated investment objectives. For example, some managers specialize in emerging high-growth firms, others specialize in energy-related companies, and still others invest in well-established, large capitalization firms. One pension fund consulting firm divides all managers into five groups, depending on the types of firms included in their portfolios: Group A: high-quality growth firms; Group B: high-yield, low-price volatility firms; Group C: small, aggressive growth companies; Group D: broadly diversified companies; and Group E: a mix of all types of firms. Since the groups are not perfectly correlated, a pension fund manager could, by diversification among portfolio managers within different groups, control the pension fund's expected risk/return relationship. If a pension fund manager targets on equaling a specific index, such as the S&P 500, then the weights assigned to each group would be chosen to correspond to the weightings of these

---

[10]The adjustment for cash flow timing is called *time weighting*. See Bank Administration Institute, *Measuring the Investment Performance of Pension Funds* (Park Ridge, Ill.: 1968) for more information on time weighting.

[11]Although managerial performance statistics exhibit about 80 to 90 percent correlation regardless of the index used, Richard Roll presents some interesting examples of how easily different rankings can be created. See Richard Roll, "Ambiguity When Performance Is Measured by the Securities Market Line," *Journal of Finance*, September 1978, 1051-1069.

groups in the index. If a pension fund manager wants to try to "beat the market," then he or she should attempt to forecast which groups will perform best, and then "tilt" the allocation to favor those particular groups.

Fund administrators can manage their funds' assets with company employees (in-house management) or with external managers (out-of-house management). Insurance companies and bank trust departments are often used as external managers, but "boutique" managers, who have more flexibility than the major institutions, have had strikingly better performance and are capturing an ever increasing share of the money management market. Regardless of whether a fund is using internal or external managers, if different managers specialize in different types of stocks, then it will be necessary to diversify among managers.

Bond Portfolio Risk

By diversifying broadly to eliminate diversifiable risk, and by selecting stocks with low betas, a firm can reduce the riskiness inherent in its stock portfolio. Several devices are also available to help reduce the riskiness of a pension fund's bond portfolio. First, there is obviously some credit (or default) risk inherent in any bond other than those issued by the U.S. Treasury (foreign government bonds have exchange rate risk to U.S. investors), so some type of credit analysis is obviously required. To a large extent, fund managers generally restrict their bond holdings to selected bond ratings: The most conservative plans hold only Treasury bonds, or perhaps Treasuries plus triple A's, but as the corporate sponsor's tolerance for risk and quest for returns increases, the fund will purchase lower and lower rated bonds.

In addition to default risk, pension plans' bond portfolios are also exposed to *interest rate risk*, but this risk takes a different form than we discussed in Chapter 5. To illustrate this, consider the situation where a firm is obligated to pay a worker a lump sum retirement benefit of $10,000 at the end of 10 years. Assume that the yield curve is horizontal, so the current interest rate on all Treasury securities is 9 percent, and the fund is restricted to Treasury debt. The present value of $10,000 discounted back 10 years at 9 percent is $10,000(0.4224) = $4,224. Therefore, the firm could invest $4,224 in Treasury bonds and expect to be able to meet its obligation 10 years hence.

Suppose, however, that interest rates change from the current 9 percent rate immediately after the firm has funded its pension plan. How would this affect the situation? The answer is, "It all depends." If rates fall, then the value of the bonds in the portfolio will rise, but this benefit will be offset to a greater or lesser degree by a decline in the rate at which the coupon payment of 0.09($4,224) = $380.16 can be reinvested. The reverse would hold if interest rates rise above 9 percent. Here are some examples (for simplicity, we assume annual coupons):

1. *The fund buys $4,224 of 9 percent, 10-year bonds; rates fall to 7 percent immediately after the purchase and remain at that level:*

$$\begin{array}{rl}
\text{Portfolio value at} & = (0.09)(\$4,224)(\text{FVIFA}_{7\%,10}) + \$4,224 \\
\text{the end of 10 years} & \\
& = \$380.16(13.816) + \$4,224 \\
& = \$5,252 + \$4,224 = \$9,476.
\end{array}$$

Therefore, the fund cannot meet its $10,000 obligation, and the corporation must contribute additional funds.

2. *The fund buys $4,224 of 9 percent, 40-year bonds; rates fall to 7 percent immediately after the purchase and remain at that level:*

$$\begin{array}{rl}
\text{Portfolio value at} & = (0.09)(\$4,224)(\text{FVIFA}_{7\%,10}) + \begin{array}{c}\text{Value of 30-year, 9\% bonds} \\ \text{when } k_d = 7\%\end{array} \\
\text{the end of 10 years} & \\
& = \$5,252 + \$5,272 = \$10,524.
\end{array}$$

In this situation, the fund has excess capital and can return money to the sponsor at the end of the 10-year period.

3. *The fund buys $4,224 of 9 percent, 10-year bonds; rates rise to 12 percent immediately after the purchase and remain at that level:*

$$\begin{array}{rl}
\text{Portfolio value at} & = (\$380.16)(\text{FVIFA}_{12\%,10}) + \$4,224 \\
\text{the end of 10 years} & \\
& = \$380.16(17.548) + \$4,224 \\
& = \$6,671 + \$4,224 = \$10,895.
\end{array}$$

This situation also produces a funding surplus.

4. *The fund buys $4,224 of 9 percent, 40-year bonds; rates rise to 12 percent immediately after the purchase and remain at that level:*

$$\begin{array}{rl}
\text{Portfolio value at} & = \$6,771 + \begin{array}{c}\text{Value of 30-year, 9\% bonds} \\ \text{when } k_d = 12\%\end{array} \\
\text{the end of 10 years} & \\
& = \$6,771 + \$3,203 = \$9,974.
\end{array}$$

This time, a shortfall occurs.

Here are some generalizations we can draw from the examples:

1. If interest rates *fall,* and the portfolio is invested in relatively short-term bonds, then the reinvestment rate penalty exceeds the capital gains, so a net shortfall occurs. However, if the portfolio has been invested in relatively long-term bonds, a drop in rates will produce capital gains which can offset the shortfall caused by low reinvestment rates.

2. If interest rates *rise,* and the portfolio is invested in relatively short-term bonds, then gains from high reinvestment rates will more than offset capital losses, and the final portfolio value will exceed the required amount. However, if the portfolio has been invested in long-term bonds, then capital losses will more than offset reinvestment gains, and a net shortfall will result.

If a company has many employees, who planned to retire at varying times in the future, and if benefits are to be paid on an annual (or monthly) basis from retirement to death rather than as lump sums, the complexity of estimating the effects of interest rate changes is obviously expanded. Still, methods have been devised to help deal with interest rate risk in the management of pension funds. Several methods are discussed in the following sections.

Zero Coupon Bonds and Stripped Treasuries. We discussed zero coupon bonds and stripped Treasury bonds in Chapter 15, where we indicated that they were devised for and are primarily held by pension funds. In our example, where the fund manager needs $10,000 in 10 years, the purchase of a 10-year zero coupon corporate bond, or a bond due in 10 years that is backed by coupons stripped from Treasury bonds, would eliminate all risks associated with changes in interest rates. The fund manager would, in our example, simply purchase for $4,224 a zero coupon bond which promised to pay $10,000 in 10 years. Note also that if a fund had many employees who were likely to retire at different future dates and who would take annuities rather than lump sum payments, and if the actuaries could make accurate forecasts of cash requirements for each future date, then the fund manager could simply buy many different zero coupon bonds whose maturities matched the fund's cash flow requirements. Thus, zero coupon bonds and bonds backed by stripped Treasuries can be used to take a lot of the uncertainty out of pension fund management. Of course, there may be a cost to this uncertainty reduction—the expected returns on zeroes and stripped Treasuries are often lower than are returns available on many other types of securities.

Immunization. Bond portfolios can be *immunized* against interest rate risk. The details of immunization are best left to investments courses, but, in brief, the process involves selecting maturities for the bonds in a portfolio such that gains or losses from reinvestment exactly match capital gains or losses. To see what is involved, refer back to the example where the fund bought $4,224 of 9 percent Treasury bonds to meet an obligation due 10 years hence. Where interest rates fell from 9 to 7 percent, we saw that a shortfall occurred if the fund bought 10-year bonds, but a surplus arose if the fund bought 40-year bonds. There is some maturity between 10 and 40 years where a breakeven would have occurred. Similarly, in the example where rates rose, there also exists a breakeven maturity within the range from 10 to 40 years.

In investments terminology, what we are seeking is a bond whose *duration* is 10 years, because that is when the $10,000 benefit is due.[12] It is not too difficult to find a bond with a 10-year duration, purchase it, and thus immunize the fund from changes in interest rates with respect to this one future benefit claim. However, the problem becomes vastly more complex when we bring in multiple beneficiaries with nonlump sum claims. Still, it is possible to view a series of future liabilities as a series of separate, single payments, and for a fund manager to immunize each of them by appropriate bond selection.

Unfortunately, other complications arise. Our simple example looked at a single interest rate change which occurred immediately after funding. In reality, interest rates change every day; this causes a bond's duration to change; and this, in turn, requires that bond portfolios be *rebalanced* periodically to maintain immunization. Still, this can be done, and computer programs are available to assist in the rebalancing pro-

---

[12]A bond's duration can be thought of as the "average date" that a holder will receive cash flows (interest and principal repayment) on the bond. For a zero coupon bond, with only one cash inflow, the duration is the same as the maturity. For coupon bonds, the duration is less than the years to maturity. Duration is calculated by use of this formula:

$$\text{Duration} = \sum_{t=1}^{n} \frac{t(PVCF_t)}{\sum_{t=1}^{n} PVCF_t} = \sum_{t=1}^{n} \frac{t(PVCF_t)}{\text{Value}}.$$

Here n is the bond's years to maturity, t is the year each cash flow occurs, and $PVCF_t$ is the present value of the cash flow at Year t discounted at the current rate of interest. Note that the denominator of the equation is merely the current value of the bond. To illustrate the process, consider a 20-year, 9 percent bond bought at its par value of $4,224. It provides cash flows of $0.09(\$4,224) = \$380.16$ per year for 19 years, and $\$380.16 + \$4,224 = \$4,604.16$ in the twentieth year. For calculating purposes, we use the following format:

t	CF	PVCF (9%)	PVCF/Value = PVCF/$4,224	t(PVCF/Value)
1	$ 380.16	$348.77	0.08257	0.08257
2	380.16	319.97	0.07575	0.15150
.	.	.	.	.
.	.	.	.	.
.	.	.	.	.
19	380.16	73.94	0.01750	0.33258
20	4,604.16	821.52	0.19449	3.88979
			Duration =	9.95011

Since this 20-year bond's duration is close to that of the pension fund's liability, if the fund manager bought it and reinvested the coupons as they came in, the accumulated interest payments, plus the value of the bond after 10 years, would be close to $10,000 irrespective of whether interest rates rose, fell, or remained constant at 9 percent. A bond with a maturity slightly over 20 years would have exactly the 10-year duration needed to exactly immunize the fund from interest rate risk.

cess, but there is yet another critical requirement for immunization to work for the entire pension fund: The future liabilities must be fixed. However, for most pension liabilities, inflation indexing causes future payments to be variable, not fixed. Such indexing is, of course, clearly inherent in plans with liabilities that are defined in terms of future salaries, which includes most plans. One class of pension liabilities, however, is relatively constant—the benefits owed to those employees who are already retired (termed *retired lives*). Because benefits to present retirees are relatively constant, a recent practice has been to set aside a *dedicated asset pool* in an immunized bond portfolio to provide for these liabilities. Such a practice can reduce and stabilize unfunded liabilities, especially if a company has a large portion of retirees in its plan.

Management of Pension Fund Managers

As indicated in the section on equity portfolio risk, large pension funds usually employ more than one investment manager. The use of multiple managers can help a firm achieve better diversification and earn higher returns by utilizing different managers' specialized knowledge of particular segments of the market. In general, the fund's assets are invested on either an *active* or a *passive* basis. Active management selects stocks with the idea of "beating the market," while passive management is based on the idea of achieving average returns while minimizing transactions costs and management fees.

The simplest method of passive management is to utilize an *index fund*, which is a portfolio whose securities are selected and rebalanced periodically to achieve a rate of return that will be nearly the same as that of an index such as the S&P 500. The goal is to minimize transactions costs and management fees while achieving average returns. The hypothesis underlying this approach is market efficiency, for *if the market is efficient, then all costs and fees associated with active management merely reduce the fund's return.* In practice, index funds often concentrate their purchases in a subset of the securities in the broad index. Recall from our discussion of working capital that an increase in "order size" produces a corresponding reduction in transaction costs. This principle also applies in portfolio management, and it leads to "S&P-like portfolios" which actually have fewer stocks than the S&P 500. Selection of securities for the proxy portfolio is usually done by matching the industrial sector percentages of the portfolio to the mix of the target index.[13]

Some fund administrators have employed what is called the *active-passive* concept in an attempt to have the pension fund earn more than an index such as the S&P 500. The fund would be set up as follows.

---

[13]For an excellent discussion of constructing passive portfolios, see Andrew Rudd, "Optimal Selection of Passive Portfolios," *Financial Management,* Spring 1980, 57-66.

First, the plan administrator selects a series of managers with expertise in different segments of the market, and each manager is required to confine his or her purchases to the type of stocks in which the respective managers specialize. Second, each manager is allocated a percentage of the pension fund's equity assets equal to the percentage of the particular group to the index. For example, if a particular manager specializes in energy stocks, and if energy stocks represent 20 percent of the capitalization of the S&P 500 Index, then this manager would be given 20 percent of the pension fund's equity assets to invest. Each manager's allocation would be based on this same principle, and any remaining assets of the fund would be invested on a pro rata basis in those stocks that are not on any manager's list. These residual assets would thus be invested in a passive fund that merely buys and holds the required stocks. Thus, every stock in the index (say the S&P 500) would either be available for purchase by one of the active managers or else held in the passive fund. If the active managers are indeed superior stock-pickers in their specialized areas, then the overall portfolio's excess risk-adjusted return (or "alpha") will be positive.

The effectiveness of the active-passive approach to fund management depends on (1) whether the active managers can produce positive alphas net of fees and transactions costs and (2) the management and transactions costs associated with the passive fund. Thus, the keys to success in using this approach are to select the best active managers and to limit passive funds costs.

"Tapping" Pension Fund Assets

Corporate sponsors administer defined benefit plans which have assets running into the hundreds of billions of dollars. To what extent should a corporation be able to invest its fund's assets to the corporation's own advantage? Or, if the plan is overfunded because, for example, investment results were better than the actuaries had assumed, or for any other reason, should the company be able to take assets out of the plan? (Obviously, we are talking about defined benefit plans only; companies clearly cannot tinker with the assets of a defined contribution or profit sharing plan.) Here are some examples of recent actions which have been called to question:

1. Occidental Petroleum acquired Cities Service in 1982. The combined pension plans had assets of $700 million, but the vested funding requirement was only $300 million. Occidental replaced the two old plans with a new one, and took $400 million out of the fund's assets. Similarly, Celanese Corporation has filed an application to change its $700 million plan and to recoup $300 million from it. Estimates made in 1984 suggest that, in total, corporate pension funds are overfunded by about $100 billion, so there is a lot of scope for actions such as those of Occidental

and Celanese. Incidentally, the old Occidental plan was a defined benefit plan; the new one is a defined contribution plan.[14]

2. Some cash-short companies have been contributing their own stock, bonds, and real property used in their operations, rather than cash, to their funds. This is legal under ERISA provided that a fund has no more than 10 percent of its sponsor's own securities and assets, and provided that the Department of Labor agrees that the transaction is made at a fair price. Thus, Exxon in 1982 contributed a $5.4 million office complex to its plan; Boise Cascade sold timberland worth $16 million to its plan; and U.S. Steel, Alcoa, Armco, Reynolds Meals, and Republic Steel all contributed their own newly issued securities rather than cash.

3. Grumman Corporation, Bendix Corporation, and others have tried to use their pension funds to help thwart hostile takeover attempts, or to help the sponsoring company take over another firm. For example, Grumman's pension fund bought 1.2 million of its shares, paying a 43 percent premium over the pre-bid price, to help fend off a takeover attempt by LTV. The takeover failed, but the fund incurred an immediate $16 million paper loss on these shares. Similarly, Bendix tried (unsuccessfully) to stop its fund's trustee from tendering 4.5 million shares of its stock to Martin Marietta.

These examples raise some interesting issues: Do the excess assets in a defined benefit plan belong to the sponsoring company or to the employees? Legally, they belong to the company, but a number of union leaders have argued that they ought to belong to the workers. Should the PBGC get involved in revisions such as Occidental's? Since Occidental switched from a defined benefit to a defined contribution plan, it left the PBGC's jurisdiction (and also eliminated the $2.60 per employee per year "head tax"), but if it had simply reduced the funding level of a defined benefit plan from overfunded to fully funded, the plan would have been exposed to more risk after assets were removed. Should companies be able to use fund assets to help fight off takeovers? There are no easy answers to these questions. Obviously, actions which would either violate existing laws or jeopardize the safety of the plan should not be permitted, but many actions are not at all clear-cut. Given the importance of pension plans, it is safe to assume that the debate will continue.

---

[14]We should point out that this type of action can be taken only (1) when approved by the plan's beneficiaries and (2) in conjunction with the establishment of a new pension plan. Still, siphoning off pension fund assets when stock prices, and hence the value of stock portfolios, are at or near all-time highs could leave the new fund significantly underfunded should stock prices subsequently fall.

Summary

Because the management of pension fund assets and liabilities has major long-term implications for both corporations and workers, financial managers must plan carefully their strategies for pension fund management. The development of a good strategy requires both a basic knowledge of actuarial concepts and a knowledge of operating and financial characteristics of the firm. Additionally, an investment strategy must be developed based on (1) the portfolio's average volatility and (2) its relationship to both future pension liabilities and corporate profitability under alternative economic scenarios. The development of such strategies is complex, but extremely important to both workers and investors.

Questions

27-1 Define each of the following terms:
   a. Defined benefit plan; defined contribution plan; profit sharing plan
   b. Vesting; portability
   c. Funding; overfunded; underfunded; funding ratio
   d. Actuarial rate of return
   e. ERISA; PBGC
   f. Minimum annual cash contribution
   g. Funding strategy
   h. Investment strategy
   i. Performance measurement; alpha
   j. Interest rate risk; reinvestment rate risk
   k. Duration; immunization
   l. Active management; passive management; index fund
   m. Pension fund "tapping"

27-2 Examine the annual report of any large U.S. corporation. Where are the pension fund data located? What effect would these data have if incorporated into the firm's balance sheet?

27-3 What impact has ERISA had on beneficiary risk? On corporate risk?

27-4 Assume that a firm has a defined benefit plan based on the final year's salary of the worker. Also, assume that once retired, a worker's pension benefits are fixed. What effect will an increase in the inflation rate have on the firm's funding ratio?

27-5 A firm's pension fund assets are currently invested only in domestic stocks and bonds. The outside manager recommends that assets such as precious metals, real estate, and foreign financial assets be added to the fund. What effect would the addition of these assets have on the fund's risk/return trade-off?

27-6 How does the type of pension fund a company uses influence each of the following:
   a. The likelihood of age discrimination in hiring?
   b. The likelihood of sex discrimination in hiring?
   c. Employee training costs?
   d. The likelihood that union leaders will be "flexible" if a company faces a changed economic environment such as have faced the airline, steel, and auto industries in recent years?

27-7 Should employers be required to pay the same "head tax" to PBGC irrespective of the financial condition of the plan?

27-1 The Certainty Company (CC) operates in a world of certainty. It has just hired Mr. Jones, age 20, who will retire at age 65, draw retirement benefits for 15 years, and die at age 80. Mr. Jones's salary is $20,000 per year, but wages are expected to increase at the 5 percent annual rate of inflation. CC has a defined benefit plan in which workers receive 1 percent of the final year's wage for each year employed. The retirement benefit, once started, does not have a cost of living adjustment. CC earns 10 percent annually on its pension fund assets. Assume that pension contribution and benefit cash flows occur at year end.

a. How much will Mr. Jones receive in annual retirement benefits?

b. What is CC's required annual contribution to fully fund Mr. Jones's retirement benefits?

c. Assume now that CC hires Mr. Smith at the same $20,000 salary as Mr. Jones. However, Mr. Smith is 45 years old. Repeat the analysis in Parts a and b above under the same assumptions used for Mr. Jones. What do the results imply about the costs of hiring older versus younger workers?

d. Now assume that CC hires Ms. Brown at the same time that it hires Mr. Smith. Ms. Brown is expected to live to age 90. What is CC's annual pension cost for Ms. Brown? If Mr. Smith and Ms. Brown are doing the same work, are they truly doing it for the same pay? Would it be "reasonable" for CC to lower Ms. Brown's annual retirement benefit to a level that would mean that she received the same present value as Mr. Smith?

27-2 Mobile Metals, Inc., has a small pension fund which is managed by a professional portfolio manager. All of the fund's assets are invested in corporate equities. Last year, the portfolio manager realized a rate of return of 18 percent. The risk-free rate was 10 percent and the market risk premium was 6 percent. The portfolio's beta was 1.2.

a. Compute the portfolio's alpha.

b. What does the portfolio alpha imply about the manager's performance last year? What can Mobile Metal's financial manager conclude about the portfolio's manager's performance next year?

27-3 Slick Industries is planning to operate for 10 more years and then to cease operations. At that time (in 10 years), it expects to have the following pension benefit obligations:

For Years	Annual Total Payments during Each of These Years
11-15	$2,500,000
16-20	2,000,000
21-25	1,500,000
26-30	1,000,000
31-35	500,000

The current value of Slick's pension fund is $6 million. Assume that all cash flows occur at year end.

a. Slick's actuarial rate of return is 10 percent. What is the present value of Slick's pension fund benefits?

   b. Calculate Slick's funding ratio. Is the plan underfunded or over-
      funded?

27-4 Two portfolio managers, A and B, achieved the same realized rates of
   return over the years 1981 through 1984. However, the managers experienced different contribution patterns during that period. The following data summarize their performance:

| Year | Rate of Return during Year | Cash In-Flow from Corporate Sponsor at Beginning of Year | |
		Portfolio A	Portfolio B
1981	10%	$ 1,000,000	$ 5,000,000
1982	−5	5,000,000	1,000,000
1983	30	1,000,000	5,000,000
1984	−10	5,000,000	1,000,000
Total contributions		$12,000,000	$12,000,000

   a. Assume that each portfolio had $10 million in assets as of December
      31, 1980. Find the value of each portfolio at the end of each year.
   b. Consider only end-of-year portfolio values. What was each manag-
      er's total realized return over the four years? What was each man-
      ager's average annual return?
   c. Now consider contribution effects. What were the actual total and
      average annual rates of return?

Selected Additional References

For more information on how pension fund management has been affected by the Employee Retirement Income Security Act of 1974 (ERISA), including the establishment of the Pension Benefit
Guarantee Corporation (PBGC), see

Treynor, Jack L., W. Priest, and Patrick J. Regan, *The Financial Reality of Pension Funding
Under ERISA* (Homewood, Ill.: Dow Jones-Irwin, 1976).

The following articles provide additional insights into the relationship between pension plan funding
and capital costs:

Malley, Susan L., "Unfunded Pension Liabilities and the Cost of Equity Capital," *Financial
Review*, May 1983, 133-145.

Regan, Patrick J., "Pension Fund Perspective: Credit Ratings and Pension Costs," *Financial
Analysts Journal*, September-October 1983, 19-23.

Other pertinent works include

Bodie, Zvi, and J. Shoren, eds., *Financial Aspects of the United States Pension System* (Chicago: University of Chicago Press, 1983).

Black, Fischer, "The Tax Consequences of Long-Run Pension Policy," *Financial Analysts
Journal*, July-August 1980, 25-31.

Munnell, Alicia H., "Guaranteeing Private Pension Benefits: A Potentially Expensive Business," *New England Economic Review*, March-April 1982, 24-47.

Oldfield, G. S., "Financial Aspects of the Private Pension System," *Journal of Money, Credit
and Banking*, February 1977, 48-54.

For an excellent discussion of the relationship between pension funding policy and the firm's overall
financial policy, see

Bodie, Zvi, Jay O. Light, Randall Morck, and Robert A. Taggart, Jr., "Funding and Asset
Allocation in Corporate Pension Plans: An Empirical Investigation," National Bureau of
Economic Research Working Paper #1315.

Mathematical Tables

A

Table A-1
Present Value of $1 Due at the End of n Periods

$$PVIF_{k,n} = \frac{1}{(1 + k)^n}$$

Period	1%	2%	3%	4%	5%	6%	7%	8%	9%	10%
1	.9901	.9804	.9709	.9615	.9524	.9434	.9346	.9259	.9174	.9091
2	.9803	.9612	.9426	.9246	.9070	.8900	.8734	.8573	.8417	.8264
3	.9706	.9423	.9151	.8890	.8638	.8396	.8163	.7938	.7722	.7513
4	.9610	.9238	.8885	.8548	.8227	.7921	.7629	.7350	.7084	.6830
5	.9515	.9057	.8626	.8219	.7835	.7473	.7130	.6806	.6499	.6209
6	.9420	.8880	.8375	.7903	.7462	.7050	.6663	.6302	.5963	.5645
7	.9327	.8706	.8131	.7599	.7107	.6651	.6227	.5835	.5470	.5132
8	.9235	.8535	.7894	.7307	.6768	.6274	.5820	.5403	.5019	.4665
9	.9143	.8368	.7664	.7026	.6446	.5919	.5439	.5002	.4604	.4241
10	.9053	.8203	.7441	.6756	.6139	.5584	.5083	.4632	.4224	.3855
11	.8963	.8043	.7224	.6496	.5847	.5268	.4751	.4289	.3875	.3505
12	.8874	.7885	.7014	.6246	.5568	.4970	.4440	.3971	.3555	.3186
13	.8787	.7730	.6810	.6006	.5303	.4688	.4150	.3677	.3262	.2897
14	.8700	.7579	.6611	.5775	.5051	.4423	.3878	.3405	.2992	.2633
15	.8613	.7430	.6419	.5553	.4810	.4173	.3624	.3152	.2745	.2394
16	.8528	.7284	.6232	.5339	.4581	.3936	.3387	.2919	.2519	.2176
17	.8444	.7142	.6050	.5134	.4363	.3714	.3166	.2703	.2311	.1978
18	.8360	.7002	.5874	.4936	.4155	.3503	.2959	.2502	.2120	.1799
19	.8277	.6864	.5703	.4746	.3957	.3305	.2765	.2317	.1945	.1635
20	.8195	.6730	.5537	.4564	.3769	.3118	.2584	.2145	.1784	.1486
21	.8114	.6598	.5375	.4388	.3589	.2942	.2415	.1987	.1637	.1351
22	.8034	.6468	.5219	.4220	.3418	.2775	.2257	.1839	.1502	.1228
23	.7954	.6342	.5067	.4057	.3256	.2618	.2109	.1703	.1378	.1117
24	.7876	.6217	.4919	.3901	.3101	.2470	.1971	.1577	.1264	.1015
25	.7798	.6095	.4776	.3751	.2953	.2330	.1842	.1460	.1160	.0923
26	.7720	.5976	.4637	.3604	.2812	.2198	.1722	.1352	.1064	.0839
27	.7644	.5859	.4502	.3468	.2678	.2074	.1609	.1252	.0976	.0763
28	.7568	.5744	.4371	.3335	.2551	.1956	.1504	.1159	.0895	.0693
29	.7493	.5631	.4243	.3207	.2429	.1846	.1406	.1073	.0822	.0630
30	.7419	.5521	.4120	.3083	.2314	.1741	.1314	.0994	.0754	.0573
35	.7059	.5000	.3554	.2534	.1813	.1301	.0937	.0676	.0490	.0356
40	.6717	.4529	.3066	.2083	.1420	.0972	.0668	.0460	.0318	.0221
45	.6391	.4102	.2644	.1712	.1113	.0727	.0476	.0313	.0207	.0137
50	.6080	.3715	.2281	.1407	.0872	.0543	.0339	.0213	.0134	.0085
55	.5785	.3365	.1968	.1157	.0683	.0406	.0242	.0145	.0087	.0053

Table A-1
Continued

Period	12%	14%	15%	16%	18%	20%	24%	28%	32%	36%
1	.8929	8772	.8696	.8621	.8475	.8333	.8065	.7813	.7576	.7353
2	.7972	.7695	.7561	.7432	.7182	.6944	.6504	.6104	.5739	.5407
3	.7118	.6750	.6575	.6407	.6086	.5787	.5245	.4768	.4348	.3975
4	.6355	.5921	.5718	.5523	.5158	.4823	.4230	.3725	.3294	.2923
5	.5674	.5194	.4972	.4761	.4371	.4019	.3411	.2910	.2495	.2149
6	.5066	.4556	.4323	.4104	.3704	.3349	.2751	.2274	.1890	.1580
7	.4523	.3996	.3759	.3538	.3139	.2791	.2218	.1776	.1432	.1162
8	.4039	.3506	.3269	.3050	.2660	.2326	.1789	.1388	.1085	.0854
9	.3606	.3075	.2843	.2630	.2255	.1938	.1443	.1084	.0822	.0628
10	.3220	.2697	.2472	.2267	.1911	.1615	.1164	.0847	.0623	.0462
11	.2875	.2366	.2149	.1954	.1619	.1346	.0938	.0662	.0472	.0340
12	.2567	.2076	.1869	.1685	.1372	.1122	.0757	.0517	.0357	.0250
13	.2292	.1821	.1625	.1452	.1163	.0935	.0610	.0404	.0271	.0184
14	.2046	.1597	.1413	.1252	.0985	.0779	.0492	.0316	.0205	.0135
15	.1827	.1401	.1229	.1079	.0835	.0649	.0397	.0247	.0155	.0099
16	.1631	.1229	.1069	.0980	.0708	.0541	.0320	.0193	.0118	.0073
17	.1456	.1078	.0929	.0802	.0600	.0451	.0258	.0150	.0089	.0054
18	.1300	.0946	.0808	.0691	.0508	.0376	.0208	.0118	.0068	.0039
19	.1161	.0829	.0703	.0596	.0431	.0313	.0168	.0092	.0051	.0029
20	.1037	.0728	.0611	.0514	.0365	.0261	.0135	.0072	.0039	.0021
21	.0926	.0638	.0531	.0443	.0309	.0217	.0109	.0056	.0029	.0016
22	.0826	.0560	.0462	.0382	.0262	.0181	.0088	.0044	.0022	.0012
23	.0738	.0491	.0402	.0329	.0222	.0151	.0071	.0034	.0017	.0008
24	.0659	.0431	.0349	.0284	.0188	.0126	.0057	.0027	.0013	.0006
25	.0588	.0378	.0304	.0245	.0160	.0105	.0046	.0021	.0010	.0005
26	.0525	.0331	.0264	.0211	.0135	.0087	.0037	.0016	.0007	.0003
27	.0469	.0291	.0230	.0182	.0115	.0073	.0030	.0013	.0006	.0002
28	.0419	.0255	.0200	.0157	.0097	.0061	.0024	.0010	.0004	.0002
29	.0374	.0224	.0174	.0135	.0082	.0051	.0020	.0008	.0003	.0001
30	.0334	.0196	.0151	.0116	.0070	.0042	.0016	.0006	.0002	.0001
35	.0189	.0102	.0075	.0055	.0030	.0017	.0005	.0002	.0001	*
40	.0107	.0053	.0037	.0026	.0013	.0007	.0002	.0001	*	*
45	.0061	.0027	.0019	.0013	.0006	.0003	.0001	*	*	*
50	.0035	.0014	.0009	.0006	.0003	.0001	*	*	*	*
55	.0020	.0007	.0005	.0003	.0001	*	*	*	*	*

*The factor is zero to four decimal places.

Table A-2
Present Value of an Annuity
of $1 per Period for n Periods

$$PVIFA_{k,n} = \sum_{t=1}^{n} \frac{1}{(1+k)^t} = \frac{1 - \dfrac{1}{(1+k)^n}}{k} = \frac{1}{k} - \frac{1}{k(1+k)^n}$$

Number of Periods	1%	2%	3%	4%	5%	6%	7%	8%	9%
1	0.9901	0.9804	0.9709	0.9615	0.9524	0.9434	0.9346	0.9259	0.9174
2	1.9704	1.9416	1.9135	1.8861	1.8594	1.8334	1.8080	1.7833	1.7591
3	2.9410	2.8839	2.8286	2.7751	2.7232	2.6730	2.6243	2.5771	2.5313
4	3.9020	3.8077	3.7171	3.6299	3.5460	3.4651	3.3872	3.3121	3.2397
5	4.8534	4.7135	4.5797	4.4518	4.3295	4.2124	4.1002	3.9927	3.8897
6	5.7955	5.6014	5.4172	5.2421	5.0757	4.9173	4.7665	4.6229	4.4859
7	6.7282	6.4720	6.2303	6.0021	5.7864	5.5824	5.3893	5.2064	5.0330
8	7.6517	7.3255	7.0197	6.7327	6.4632	6.2098	5.9713	5.7466	5.5348
9	8.5660	8.1622	7.7861	7.4353	7.1078	6.8017	6.5152	6.2469	5.9952
10	9.4713	8.9826	8.5302	8.1109	7.7217	7.3601	7.0236	6.7101	6.4177
11	10.3676	9.7868	9.2526	8.7605	8.3064	7.8869	7.4987	7.1390	6.8052
12	11.2551	10.5753	9.9540	9.3851	8.8633	8.3838	7.9427	7.5361	7.1607
13	12.1337	11.3484	10.6350	9.9856	9.3936	8.8527	8.3577	7.9038	7.4869
14	13.0037	12.1062	11.2961	10.5631	9.8986	9.2950	8.7455	8.2442	7.7862
15	13.8651	12.8493	11.9379	11.1184	10.3797	9.7122	9.1079	8.5595	8.0607
16	14.7179	13.5777	12.5611	11.6523	10.8378	10.1059	9.4466	8.8514	8.3126
17	15.5623	14.2919	13.1661	12.1657	11.2741	10.4773	9.7632	9.1216	8.5436
18	16.3983	14.9920	13.7535	12.6593	11.6896	10.8276	10.0591	9.3719	8.7556
19	17.2260	15.6785	14.3238	13.1339	12.0853	11.1581	10.3356	9.6036	8.9501
20	18.0456	16.3514	14.8775	13.5903	12.4622	11.4699	10.5940	9.8181	9.1285
21	18.8570	17.0112	15.4150	14.0292	12.8212	11.7641	10.8355	10.0168	9.2922
22	19.6604	17.6580	15.9369	14.4511	13.1630	12.0416	11.0612	10.2007	9.4424
23	20.4558	18.2922	16.4436	14.8568	13.4886	12.3034	11.2722	10.3711	9.5802
24	21.2434	18.9139	16.9355	15.2470	13.7986	12.5504	11.4693	10.5288	9.7066
25	22.0232	19.5235	17.4131	15.6221	14.0939	12.7834	11.6536	10.6748	9.8226
26	22.7952	20.1210	17.8768	15.9828	14.3752	13.0032	11.8258	10.8100	9.9290
27	23.5596	20.7069	18.3270	16.3296	14.6430	13.2105	11.9867	10.9352	10.0266
28	24.3164	21.2813	18.7641	16.6631	14.8981	13.4062	12.1371	11.0511	10.1161
29	25.0658	21.8444	19.1885	16.9837	15.1411	13.5907	12.2777	11.1584	10.1983
30	25.8077	22.3965	19.6004	17.2920	15.3725	13.7648	12.4090	11.2578	10.2737
35	29.4086	24.9986	21.4872	18.6646	16.3742	14.4982	12.9477	11.6546	10.5668
40	32.8347	27.3555	23.1148	19.7928	17.1591	15.0463	13.3317	11.9246	10.7574
45	36.0945	29.4902	24.5187	20.7200	17.7741	15.4558	13.6055	12.1084	10.8812
50	39.1961	31.4236	25.7298	21.4822	18.2559	15.7619	13.8007	12.2335	10.9617
55	42.1472	33.1748	26.7744	22.1086	18.6335	15.9905	13.9399	12.3186	11.0140

Table A-2
Continued

Number of Periods	10%	12%	14%	15%	16%	18%	20%	24%	28%	32%
1	0.9091	0.8929	0.8772	0.8696	0.8621	0.8475	0.8333	0.8065	0.7813	0.7576
2	1.7355	1.6901	1.6467	1.6257	1.6052	1.5656	1.5278	1.4568	1.3916	1.3315
3	2.4869	2.4018	2.3216	2.2832	2.2459	2.1743	2.1065	1.9813	1.8684	1.7663
4	3.1699	3.0373	2.9137	2.8550	2.7982	2.6901	2.5887	2.4043	2.2410	2.0957
5	3.7908	3.6048	3.4331	3.3522	3.2743	3.1272	2.9906	2.7454	2.5320	2.3452
6	4.3553	4.1114	3.8887	3.7845	3.6847	3.4976	3.3255	3.0205	2.7594	2.5342
7	4.8684	4.5638	4.2883	4.1604	4.0386	3.8115	3.6046	3.2423	2.9370	2.6775
8	5.3349	4.9676	4.6389	4.4873	4.3436	4.0776	3.8372	3.4212	3.0758	2.7860
9	5.7590	5.3282	4.9464	4.7716	4.6065	4.3030	4.0310	3.5655	3.1842	2.8681
10	6.1446	5.6502	5.2161	5.0188	4.8332	4.4941	4.1925	3.6819	3.2689	2.9304
11	6.4951	5.9377	5.4527	5.2337	5.0286	4.6560	4.3271	3.7757	3.3351	2.9776
12	6.8137	6.1944	5.6603	5.4206	5.1971	4.7932	4.4392	3.8514	3.3868	3.0133
13	7.1034	6.4235	5.8424	5.5831	5.3423	4.9095	4.5327	3.9124	3.4272	3.0404
14	7.3667	6.6282	6.0021	5.7245	5.4675	5.0081	4.6106	3.9616	3.4587	3.0609
15	7.6061	6.8109	6.1422	5.8474	5.5755	5.0916	4.6755	4.0013	3.4834	3.0764
16	7.8237	6.9740	6.2651	5.9542	5.6685	5.1624	4.7296	4.0333	3.5026	3.0882
17	8.0216	7.1196	6.3729	6.0472	5.7487	5.2223	4.7746	4.0591	3.5177	3.0971
18	8.2014	7.2497	6.4674	6.1280	5.8178	5.2732	4.8122	4.0799	3.5294	3.1039
19	8.3649	7.3658	6.5504	6.1982	5.8775	5.3162	4.8435	4.0967	3.5386	3.1090
20	8.5136	7.4694	6.6231	6.2593	5.9288	5.3527	4.8696	4.1103	3.5458	3.1129
21	8.6487	7.5620	6.6870	6.3125	5.9731	5.3837	4.8913	4.1212	3.5514	3.1158
22	8.7715	7.6446	6.7429	6.3587	6.0113	5.4099	4.9094	4.1300	3.5558	3.1180
23	8.8832	7.7184	6.7921	6.3988	6.0442	5.4321	4.9245	4.1371	3.5592	3.1197
24	8.9847	7.7843	6.8351	6.4338	6.0726	5.4509	4.9371	4.1428	3.5619	3.1210
25	9.0770	7.8431	6.8729	6.4641	6.0971	5.4669	4.9476	4.1474	3.5640	3.1220
26	9.1609	7.8957	6.9061	6.4906	6.1182	5.4804	4.9563	4.1511	3.5656	3.1227
27	9.2372	7.9426	6.9352	6.5135	6.1364	5.4919	4.9636	4.1542	3.5669	3.1233
28	9.3066	7.9844	6.9607	6.5335	6.1520	5.5016	4.9697	4.1566	3.5679	3.1237
29	9.3696	8.0218	6.9830	6.5509	6.1656	5.5098	4.9747	4.1585	3.5687	3.1240
30	9.4269	8.0552	7.0027	6.5660	6.1772	5.5168	4.9789	4.1601	3.5693	3.1242
35	9.6442	8.1755	7.0700	6.6166	6.2153	5.5386	4.9915	4.1644	3.5708	3.1248
40	9.7791	8.2438	7.1050	6.6418	6.2335	5.5482	4.9966	4.1659	3.5712	3.1250
45	9.8628	8.2825	7.1232	6.6543	6.2421	5.5523	4.9986	4.1664	3.5714	3.1250
50	9.9148	8.3045	7.1327	6.6605	6.2463	5.5541	4.9995	4.1666	3.5714	3.1250
55	9.9471	8.3170	7.1376	6.6636	6.2482	5.5549	4.9998	4.1666	3.5714	3.1250

Table A-3
Future Value of $1 at the End of n Periods

$$FVIF_{k,n} = (1 + k)^n$$

Period	1%	2%	3%	4%	5%	6%	7%	8%	9%	10%
1	1.0100	1.0200	1.0300	1.0400	1.0500	1.0600	1.0700	1.0800	1.0900	1.1000
2	1.0201	1.0404	1.0609	1.0816	1.1025	1.1236	1.1449	1.1664	1.1881	1.2100
3	1.0303	1.0612	1.0927	1.1249	1.1576	1.1910	1.2250	1.2597	1.2950	1.3310
4	1.0406	1.0824	1.1255	1.1699	1.2155	1.2625	1.3108	1.3605	1.4116	1.4641
5	1.0510	1.1041	1.1593	1.2167	1.2763	1.3382	1.4026	1.4693	1.5386	1.6105
6	1.0615	1.1262	1.1941	1.2653	1.3401	1.4185	1.5007	1.5869	1.6771	1.7716
7	1.0721	1.1487	1.2299	1.3159	1.4071	1.5036	1.6058	1.7138	1.8280	1.9487
8	1.0829	1.1717	1.2668	1.3686	1.4775	1.5938	1.7182	1.8509	1.9926	2.1436
9	1.0937	1.1951	1.3048	1.4233	1.5513	1.6895	1.8385	1.9990	2.1719	2.3579
10	1.1046	1.2190	1.3439	1.4802	1.6289	1.7908	1.9672	2.1589	2.3674	2.5937
11	1.1157	1.2434	1.3842	1.5395	1.7103	1.8983	2.1049	2.3316	2.5804	2.8531
12	1.1268	1.2682	1.4258	1.6010	1.7959	2.0122	2.2522	2.5182	2.8127	3.1384
13	1.1381	1.2936	1.4685	1.6651	1.8856	2.1329	2.4098	2.7196	3.0658	3.4523
14	1.1495	1.3195	1.5126	1.7317	1.9799	2.2609	2.5785	2.9372	3.3417	3.7975
15	1.1610	1.3459	1.5580	1.8009	2.0789	2.3966	2.7590	3.1722	3.6425	4.1772
16	1.1726	1.3728	1.6047	1.8730	2.1829	2.5404	2.9522	3.4259	3.9703	4.5950
17	1.1843	1.4002	1.6528	1.9479	2.2920	2.6928	3.1588	3.7000	4.3276	5.0545
18	1.1961	1.4282	1.7024	2.0258	2.4066	2.8543	3.3799	3.9960	4.7171	5.5599
19	1.2081	1.4568	1.7535	2.1068	2.5270	3.0256	3.6165	4.3157	5.1417	6.1159
20	1.2202	1.4859	1.8061	2.1911	2.6533	3.2071	3.8697	4.6610	5.6044	6.7275
21	1.2324	1.5157	1.8603	2.2788	2.7860	3.3996	4.1406	5.0338	6.1088	7.4002
22	1.2447	1.5460	1.9161	2.3699	2.9253	3.6035	4.4304	5.4365	6.6586	8.1403
23	1.2572	1.5769	1.9736	2.4647	3.0715	3.8197	4.7405	5.8715	7.2579	8.9543
24	1.2697	1.6084	2.0328	2.5633	3.2251	4.0489	5.0724	6.3412	7.9111	9.8497
25	1.2824	1.6406	2.0938	2.6658	3.3864	4.2919	5.4274	6.8485	8.6231	10.835
26	1.2953	1.6734	2.1566	2.7725	3.5557	4.5494	5.8074	7.3964	9.3992	11.918
27	1.3082	1.7069	2.2213	2.8834	3.7335	4.8223	6.2139	7.9881	10.245	13.110
28	1.3213	1.7410	2.2879	2.9987	3.9201	5.1117	6.6488	8.6271	11.167	14.421
29	1.3345	1.7758	2.3566	3.1187	4.1161	5.4184	7.1143	9.3173	12.172	15.863
30	1.3478	1.8114	2.4273	3.2434	4.3219	5.7435	7.6123	10.063	13.268	17.449
40	1.4889	2.2080	3.2620	4.8010	7.0400	10.286	14.974	21.725	31.409	45.259
50	1.6446	2.6916	4.3839	7.1067	11.467	18.420	29.457	46.902	74.358	117.39
60	1.8167	3.2810	5.8916	10.520	18.679	32.988	57.946	101.26	176.03	304.48

Table A-3
Continued

Period	12%	14%	15%	16%	18%	20%	24%	28%	32%	36%
1	1.1200	1.1400	1.1500	1.1600	1.1800	1.2000	1.2400	1.2800	1.3200	1.3600
2	1.2544	1.2996	1.3225	1.3456	1.3924	1.4400	1.5376	1.6384	1.7424	1.8496
3	1.4049	1.4815	1.5209	1.5609	1.6430	1.7280	1.9066	2.0972	2.3000	2.5155
4	1.5735	1.6890	1.7490	1.8106	1.9388	2.0736	2.3642	2.6844	3.0360	3.4210
5	1.7623	1.9254	2.0114	2.1003	2.2878	2.4883	2.9316	3.4360	4.0075	4.6526
6	1.9738	2.1950	2.3131	2.4364	2.6996	2.9860	3.6352	4.3980	5.2899	6.3275
7	2.2107	2.5023	2.6600	2.8262	3.1855	3.5832	4.5077	5.6295	6.9826	8.6054
8	2.4760	2.8526	3.0590	3.2784	3.7589	4.2998	5.5895	7.2058	9.2170	11.703
9	2.7731	3.2519	3.5179	3.8030	4.4355	5.1598	6.9310	9.2234	12.166	15.917
10	3.1058	3.7072	4.0456	4.4114	5.2338	6.1917	8.5944	11.806	16.060	21.647
11	3.4785	4.2262	4.6524	5.1173	6.1759	7.4301	10.657	15.112	21.199	29.439
12	3.8960	4.8179	5.3503	5.9360	7.2876	8.9161	13.215	19.343	27.983	40.037
13	4.3635	5.4924	6.1528	6.8858	8.5994	10.699	16.386	24.759	36.937	54.451
14	4.8871	6.2613	7.0757	7.9875	10.147	12.839	20.319	31.691	48.757	74.053
15	5.4736	7.1379	8.1371	9.2655	11.974	15.407	25.196	40.565	64.359	100.71
16	6.1304	8.1372	9.3576	10.748	14.129	18.488	31.243	51.923	84.954	136.97
17	6.8660	9.2765	10.761	12.468	16.672	22.186	38.741	66.461	112.14	186.28
18	7.6900	10.575	12.375	14.463	19.673	26.623	48.039	85.071	148.02	253.34
19	8.6128	12.056	14.232	16.777	23.214	31.948	59.568	108.89	195.39	344.54
20	9.6463	13.743	16.367	19.461	27.393	38.338	73.864	139.38	257.92	468.57
21	10.804	15.668	18.822	22.574	32.324	46.005	91.592	178.41	340.45	637.26
22	12.100	17.861	21.645	26.186	38.142	55.206	113.57	228.36	449.39	866.67
23	13.552	20.362	24.891	30.376	45.008	66.247	140.83	292.30	593.20	1178.7
24	15.179	23.212	28.625	35.236	53.109	79.497	174.63	374.14	783.02	1603.0
25	17.000	26.462	32.919	40.874	62.669	95.396	216.54	478.90	1033.6	2180.1
26	19.040	30.167	37.857	47.414	73.949	114.48	268.51	613.00	1364.3	2964.9
27	21.325	34.390	43.535	55.000	87.260	137.37	332.95	784.64	1800.9	4032.3
28	23.884	39.204	50.066	63.800	102.97	164.84	412.86	1004.3	2377.2	5483.9
29	26.750	44.693	57.575	74.009	121.50	197.81	511.95	1285.6	3137.9	7458.1
30	29.960	50.950	66.212	85.850	143.37	237.38	634.82	1645.5	4142.1	10143.
40	93.051	188.88	267.86	378.72	750.38	1469.8	5455.9	19427.	66521.	*
50	289.00	700.23	1083.7	1670.7	3927.4	9100.4	46890.	*	*	*
60	897.60	2595.9	4384.0	7370.2	20555.	56348.	*	*	*	*

*FVIF > 99,999.

Table A-4
Sum of an Annuity of $1 per Period for n Periods

$$FVIFA_{k,n} = \sum_{t=1}^{n} (1 + k)^{n-t} = \frac{(1 + k)^n - 1}{k}$$

Number of Periods	1%	2%	3%	4%	5%	6%	7%	8%	9%	10%
1	1.0000	1.0000	1.0000	1.0000	1.0000	1.0000	1.0000	1.0000	1.0000	1.0000
2	2.0100	2.0200	2.0300	2.0400	2.0500	2.0600	2.0700	2.0800	2.0900	2.1000
3	3.0301	3.0604	3.0909	3.1216	3.1525	3.1836	3.2149	3.2464	3.2781	3.3100
4	4.0604	4.1216	4.1836	4.2465	4.3101	4.3746	4.4399	4.5061	4.5731	4.6410
5	5.1010	5.2040	5.3091	5.4163	5.5256	5.6371	5.7507	5.8666	5.9847	6.1051
6	6.1520	6.3081	6.4684	6.6330	6.8019	6.9753	7.1533	7.3359	7.5233	7.7156
7	7.2135	7.4343	7.6625	7.8983	8.1420	8.3938	8.6540	8.9228	9.2004	9.4872
8	8.2857	8.5830	8.8923	9.2142	9.5491	9.8975	10.260	10.637	11.028	11.436
9	9.3685	9.7546	10.159	10.583	11.027	11.491	11.978	12.488	13.021	13.579
10	10.462	10.950	11.464	12.006	12.578	13.181	13.816	14.487	15.193	15.937
11	11.567	12.169	12.808	13.486	14.207	14.972	15.784	16.645	17.560	18.531
12	12.683	13.412	14.192	15.026	15.917	16.870	17.888	18.977	20.141	21.384
13	13.809	14.680	15.618	16.627	17.713	18.882	20.141	21.495	22.953	24.523
14	14.947	15.974	17.086	18.292	19.599	21.015	22.550	24.215	26.019	27.975
15	16.097	17.293	18.599	20.024	21.579	23.276	25.129	27.152	29.361	31.772
16	17.258	18.639	20.157	21.825	23.657	25.673	27.888	30.324	33.003	35.950
17	18.430	20.012	21.762	23.698	25.840	28.213	30.840	33.750	36.974	40.545
18	19.615	21.412	23.414	25.645	28.132	30.906	33.999	37.450	41.301	45.599
19	20.811	22.841	25.117	27.671	30.539	33.760	37.379	41.446	46.018	51.159
20	22.019	24.297	26.870	29.778	33.066	36.786	40.995	45.762	51.160	57.275
21	23.239	25.783	28.676	31.969	35.719	39.993	44.865	50.423	56.765	64.002
22	24.472	27.299	30.537	34.248	38.505	43.392	49.006	55.457	62.873	71.403
23	25.716	28.845	32.453	36.618	41.430	46.996	53.436	60.893	69.532	79.543
24	26.973	30.422	34.426	39.083	44.502	50.816	58.177	66.765	76.790	88.497
25	28.243	32.030	36.459	41.646	47.727	54.865	63.249	73.106	84.701	98.347
26	29.526	33.671	38.553	44.312	51.113	59.156	68.676	79.954	93.324	109.18
27	30.821	35.344	40.710	47.084	54.669	63.706	74.484	87.351	102.72	121.10
28	32.129	37.051	42.931	49.968	58.403	68.528	80.698	95.339	112.97	134.21
29	33.450	38.792	45.219	52.966	62.323	73.640	87.347	103.97	124.14	148.63
30	34.785	40.568	47.575	56.085	66.439	79.058	94.461	113.28	136.31	164.49
40	48.886	60.402	75.401	95.026	120.80	154.76	199.64	259.06	337.88	442.59
50	64.463	84.579	112.80	152.67	209.35	290.34	406.53	573.77	815.08	1163.9
60	81.670	114.05	163.05	237.99	353.58	533.13	813.52	1253.2	1944.8	3034.8

Table A-4
Continued

Number of Periods	12%	14%	15%	16%	18%	20%	24%	28%	32%	36%
1	1.0000	1.0000	1.0000	1.0000	1.0000	1.0000	1.0000	1.0000	1.0000	1.0000
2	2.1200	2.1400	2.1500	2.1600	2.1800	2.2000	2.2400	2.2800	2.3200	2.3600
3	3.3744	3.4396	3.4725	3.5056	3.5724	3.6400	3.7776	3.9184	4.0624	4.2096
4	4.7793	4.9211	4.9934	5.0665	5.2154	5.3680	5.6842	6.0156	6.3624	6.7251
5	6.3528	6.6101	6.7424	6.8771	7.1542	7.4416	8.0484	8.6999	9.3983	10.146
6	8.1152	8.5355	8.7537	8.9775	9.4420	9.9299	10.980	12.136	13.406	14.799
7	10.089	10.730	11.067	11.414	12.142	12.916	14.615	16.534	18.696	21.126
8	12.300	13.233	13.727	14.240	15.327	16.499	19.123	22.163	25.678	29.732
9	14.776	16.085	16.786	17.519	19.086	20.799	24.712	29.369	34.895	41.435
10	17.549	19.337	20.304	21.321	23.521	25.959	31.643	38.593	47.062	57.352
11	20.655	23.045	24.349	25.733	28.755	32.150	40.238	50.398	63.122	78.998
12	24.133	27.271	29.002	30.850	34.931	39.581	50.895	65.510	84.320	108.44
13	28.029	32.089	34.352	36.786	42.219	48.497	64.110	84.853	112.30	148.47
14	32.393	37.581	40.505	43.672	50.818	59.196	80.496	109.61	149.24	202.93
15	37.280	43.842	47.580	51.660	60.965	72.035	100.82	141.30	198.00	276.98
16	42.753	50.980	55.717	60.925	72.939	87.442	126.01	181.87	262.36	377.69
17	48.884	59.118	65.075	71.673	87.068	105.93	157.25	233.79	347.31	514.66
18	55.750	68.394	75.836	84.141	103.74	128.12	195.99	300.25	459.45	700.94
19	63.440	78.969	88.212	98.603	123.41	154.74	244.03	385.32	607.47	954.28
20	72.052	91.025	102.44	115.38	146.63	186.69	303.60	494.21	802.86	1298.8
21	81.699	104.77	118.81	134.84	174.02	225.03	377.46	633.59	1060.8	1767.4
22	92.503	120.44	137.63	157.41	206.34	271.03	469.06	812.00	1401.2	2404.7
23	104.60	138.30	159.28	183.60	244.49	326.24	582.63	1040.4	1850.6	3271.3
24	118.16	158.66	184.17	213.98	289.49	392.48	723.46	1332.7	2443.8	4450.0
25	133.33	181.87	212.79	249.21	342.60	471.98	898.09	1706.8	3226.8	6053.0
26	150.33	208.33	245.71	290.09	405.27	567.38	1114.6	2185.7	4260.4	8233.1
27	169.37	238.50	283.57	337.50	479.22	681.85	1383.1	2798.7	5624.8	11198.0
28	190.70	272.89	327.10	392.50	566.48	819.22	1716.1	3583.3	7425.7	15230.3
29	214.58	312.09	377.17	456.30	669.45	984.07	2129.0	4587.7	9802.9	20714.2
30	241.33	356.79	434.75	530.31	790.95	1181.9	2640.9	5873.2	12941.	28172.3
40	767.09	1342.0	1779.1	2360.8	4163.2	7343.9	22729.	69377.	*	*
50	2400.0	4994.5	7217.7	10436.	21813.	45497.	*	*	*	*
60	7471.6	18535.	29220.	46058.	*	*	*	*	*	*

*FVIFA > 99,999.

Table A-5
Values of the Areas under the
Standard Normal Distribution Function

z	0.00	0.01	0.02	0.03	0.04	0.05	0.06	0.07	0.08	0.09
0.0	.0000	.0040	.0080	.0120	.0160	.0199	.0239	.0279	.0319	.0359
0.1	.0398	.0438	.0478	.0517	.0557	.0596	.0636	.0675	.0714	.0753
0.2	.0793	.0832	.0871	.0910	.0948	.0987	.1026	.1064	.1103	.1141
0.3	.1179	.1217	.1255	.1293	.1331	.1368	.1406	.1443	.1480	.1517
0.4	.1554	.1591	.1628	.1664	.1700	.1736	.1772	.1808	.1844	.1879
0.5	.1915	.1950	.1985	.2019	.2054	.2088	.2123	.2157	.2190	.2224
0.6	.2257	.2291	.2324	.2357	.2389	.2422	.2454	.2486	.2517	.2549
0.7	.2580	.2611	.2642	.2673	.2704	.2734	.2764	.2794	.2823	.2852
0.8	.2881	.2910	.2939	.2967	.2995	.3023	.3051	.3078	.3106	.3133
0.9	.3159	.3186	.3212	.3238	.3264	.3289	.3315	.3340	.3365	.3389
1.0	.3413	.3438	.3461	.3485	.3508	.3531	.3554	.3577	.3599	.3621
1.1	.3643	.3665	.3686	.3708	.3729	.3749	.3770	.3790	.3810	.3830
1.2	.3849	.3869	.3888	.3907	.3925	.3944	.3962	.3980	.3997	.4015
1.3	.4032	.4049	.4066	.4082	.4099	.4115	.4131	.4147	.4162	.4177
1.4	.4192	.4207	.4222	.4236	.4251	.4265	.4279	.4292	.4306	.4319
1.5	.4332	.4345	.4357	.4370	.4382	.4394	.4406	.4418	.4429	.4441
1.6	.4452	.4463	.4474	.4484	.4495	.4505	.4515	.4525	.4535	.4545
1.7	.4554	.4564	.4573	.4582	.4591	.4599	.4608	.4616	.4625	.4633
1.8	.4641	.4649	.4656	.4664	.4671	.4678	.4686	.4693	.4699	.4706
1.9	.4713	.4719	.4726	.4732	.4738	.4744	.4750	.4756	.4761	.4767
2.0	.4773	.4778	.4783	.4788	.4793	.4798	.4803	.4808	.4812	.4817
2.1	.4821	.4826	.4830	.4834	.4838	.4842	.4846	.4850	.4854	.4857
2.2	.4861	.4864	.4868	.4871	.4875	.4878	.4881	.4884	.4887	.4890
2.3	.4893	.4896	.4898	.4901	.4904	.4906	.4909	.4911	.4913	.4916
2.4	.4918	.4920	.4922	.4925	.4927	.4929	.4931	.4932	.4934	.4936
2.5	.4938	.4940	.4941	.4943	.4945	.4946	.4948	.4949	.4951	.4952
2.6	.4953	.4955	.4956	.4957	.4959	.4960	.4961	.4962	.4963	.4964
2.7	.4965	.4966	.4967	.4968	.4969	.4970	.4971	.4972	.4973	.4974
2.8	.4974	.4975	.4976	.4977	.4977	.4978	.4979	.4979	.4980	.4981
2.9	.4981	.4982	.4982	.4982	.4984	.4984	.4985	.4985	.4986	.4986
3.0	.4987	.4987	.4987	.4988	.4988	.4989	.4989	.4989	.4990	.4990

Answers to Selected End-of-Chapter Problems

We present here some of the intermediate steps and final answers to selected end-of-chapter problems. These are provided to aid the student in determining whether he or she is on the right track in the solution process. The primary limitation of this approach is that some of the problems may have *more than one* correct solution, depending upon which of several equally appropriate assumptions are made in the solution. Furthermore, there are often differences in answers due to rounding errors or other computational considerations. Many of the problems involve some verbal discussion as well as numerical calculations. This verbal material is *not* presented here.

2-2 a. Tax = $71,750.

b. $9,200.

c. $1,380.

2-4 a. Advantage as a corporation,

1985 = $1,535; 1986 = $5,690; 1987 = $10,486.

2-6 a. $14,250; $20,900; $19,950; $19,950; $19,950.

Section 179 expense = $5,000.

3-4 k = 6.86%;

rate of inflation drops from 10% to 4.86%.

3-6 $I_1 = 12\%$, $I_2 = 8\%$, $I_3 = 6\%$.

4-2 b. $518.74.

d. $200.00.

4-4 b. $552.56.

d. $1,000.00.

4-6 a. $PV_A = \$729.32$.

   $PV_B = \$786.96$.

   b. $PV_A = PV_B = \$1,000.00$.

4-8 a. $k = 14.87\% \approx 15\%$.

4-10 $k = 20\%$.

4-12 $k = 8\%$ for a 5-year annuity.

4-14 a. $PV = \$23,184.70$.

   b. (1) $\$18,039.48$.

      (2) Zero after last withdrawal.

4-16 a. $PV = \$146.14$.

   b. $PV = \$145.68$.

   c. $PV = \$177.48$.

4-18 a. First National Bank, effective rate $= 13\%$.

4-20 $PMT = \$8,042.14$.

4-22 $PMT = \$5,097$.

4A-2 $k = 12\%$.

5-2 a. (1) $YTM_1 \approx 8\%$.

      (2) $YTM_2 \approx 6\%$.

   b. Yes.

5-4 a. $D_1 = \$1.05$; $D_2 = \$1.10$; $D_3 = \$1.16$.

   c. $\$18.26$.

   e. $\hat{P}_0 = \$21.00$.

5-6 a. (2) $\hat{P}_0 = \$6.25$.

      (4) $\hat{P}_0 = \$115.00$.

5-8 $\hat{P}_0 = \$21.60$.

5-10 a. $\hat{P}_0 = \$36.46$.

   Dividend yield $= 6.86\%$.

   Capital gains yield $= 7.16\%$.

   $k_s = 14.02\% \approx 14\%$.

6-2 a. $k_A = 15.6\%$.

   c. (1) k_M increases to 15%, $k_A = 17\%$.

      (2) k_M decreases to 12%, $k_A = 12.8\%$.

6-4 a. $k_X = 17\%$.

   $\hat{P}_0 = \$20.83$.

   c. $k_X = 14.6\%$.

   $\hat{P}_0 = \$26.04$.

6-6 a. $k_C = 10.6\%$.

   $k_D = 7\%$.

b. $\hat{P}_C = \$22.73$.

   $\hat{k}_c = 10.0\%$.

6A-2 a. $Beta_A = 1.0$.

   $Beta_B = 0.5$.

c. $k_A = 15\%$.

   $k_B = 12.15\%$.

6B-2 a. $\hat{k}_A = 15\%$; $\sigma_A = 12.8\%$.

h. $b_A = 0.74$; $b_B = 1.47$.

7-2 $k_s = 10.25\%$.

7-4 a. $k_d(1 - T) = 4.80\%$.

   $k_s = 12.30\%$.

b. $k_a = 10.05\%$.

d. $k_e = 12.8\%$; $k_a = 10.4\%$.

7-6 a. $g = 8.0\%$.

c. $k_s = 12\%$.

e. \$15 million.

8-2 b. $IRR_A = 18.1\%$.

   $IRR_B = 24.0\%$.

d. Crossover rate $= 14.53\%$.

8-4 a. Plan B will forego \$10,250,000 in Year 1 but will receive \$1,750,000 per year in Years 2-20.

9-2 a. Net cost $= \$117,800$.

b. Net cash flows:

   Year 1 $= \$34,986$; Year 2 $= \$41,947$; Year 3 $= \$41,411$.

c. \$32,000.

d. Yes, NPV $= \$3,827$.

9-6 a. $k_n = 11.6\%$.

   $k_r = 5.28\%$.

b. Relevant real cash flows:

t = 0	t = 1	t = 2	t = 3
(\$18,800)	\$7,040	\$8,049	\$7,971

c. NPV $= \$1,980$.

d. Nominal cash flows:

t = 0	t = 1	t = 2	t = 3
($18,800)	$7,346	$8,680	$8,945

NPV = $1,187.

10-2 Oil-fueled plant.

10-4 k_a (before break point) = 9.0%.

k_a (after break point) = 10.5%.

Optimal capital budget = $6 million.

11-2 a. V_U = $12,000,000; V_L = $16,000,000.

11-4 a. With zero debt, V = $20,000,000.

With $6,000,000 debt at 6%, V = $20,000,000.

c. Zero debt V = $12,000,000.

$6 million debt V = $14,400,000.

11-6 a. $10,000,000.

12-2 a. V = $3,000,000 (D = $0).

V = $3,283,636 (D = $900,000).

b. P = $16.42 (D = $900,000).

c. EPS = $1.81.

12-4 a. k_s = 14%.

c. V = $78.57 million; stock price falls to $28.57.

e. S = $33.25 million at t = 30%, and D = $70 million. This assumes the old debt is a perpetuity.

13-2 b. No.

d. The firm that reduced its payout (followed the residual policy) had the steep IOS.

13-4 Total assets = Total claims = $1,979.20 (millions of dollars).

14-1 a.

	1979	1984
EPS	$8,160	$12,000
DPS	4,200	6,000
BV/share		90,000

d.

	1979	1984
EPS	$2.04	$ 3.00
DPS	1.05	1.50
BV/share		22.50

g.

	ROE
Sonnet	15.00%
Mailers	13.64%
Callaway	13.33%

k. Callaway's price,

Based on Sonnet: $P_0 = \$21.54$.

Based on Mailers: $P_0 = \$33.38$.

15-4 a. Price of zero coupon bond = $269.74.

Number of bonds that must be sold to raise $500 million is 1,853,637.

b. (1) Zero coupon, 14%; annual coupon, 15%.

(2) Zero coupon, 6.51%; annual coupon, 7.5%.

15A-2 a. PV of total investment = $-\$5,226,334$.

PV of savings = $6,391,678.

NPV = $1,165,344.

b. Refunding should take place now.

16-2 a. P = $20, FV = $-\$5$.

P = $25, FV = $0.

P = $30, FV = $5.

P = $100, FV = $75.

16-4 a. 14.1%.

b. $12 million.

d. The value of the bonds would have fallen below $1000.

16-6 b. $\hat{k}_c = 11.65\%$.

d. (1) 59% decline in stock's price.

(2) 28% drop in bond's price.

17-2 a. Cost of owning = $784,585.

Cost of leasing = $803,802.

Therefore Silverton should *buy*.

b. Yes, NPV of lease investment = $1,265.

18-2 a. Expand payables.

      b. Impact on trade creditors of a 30-day delay.

18-4 Approximate cost = 14.69%; effective cost = 15.65%.

18-6 a. Total assets = $1,752,200.

      b. Total dollar cost = $160,800.

          Effective annual interest rate = 15.12%.

	Cost of Goods Sold	Ending Inventory Value
19-2 a.		
Specific identification	$ 34.8 million	$33.8 million
FIFO	36.0	32.6
LIFO	32.6	36.0
Weighted average	34.3	34.3

      b. LIFO; FIFO.

      c. LIFO.

      d. All four methods are identical.

19-4 a. Expected shortage cost = $160.

          Carrying cost = $0.

          Total costs = $160.

      b. $39.17.

      c. $16.67.

      d. 4,000 units.

20-2 a. July surplus cash = $426,000.

          December surplus cash = $799,750.

      d. Yes.

20-4 a. $10,000; $1,000.

      b. $10,000; $600.

20-6 a. March = −$4,500; April = −$21,600.

      b. $36,300, yes.

21-2 a. ΔI = $883,333.33.

          ΔP = $4,333.33.

      b. ΔI = −$533,333.33.

          ΔP = $62,666.67.

      c. Proposal 2 would increase profits $58,333.34 more than Proposal 1.

21-4 a. $ACP_0 = 22$ days, $ACP_N = 30$ days.

b. $\Delta I = \$27,222.22$.

c. $\Delta P = \$20,032.78$; yes.

d. $\Delta I = \$22,222.22$.

$\Delta P = -\$5,162.22$.

22-2 a. Current ratio $= 2.73\times$.

ROA $= 5.0\%$.

ROE $= 7.1\%$.

Debt to total assets $= 30\%$.

Net profit on sales $= 2.8\%$.

Sales to inventories $= 5\times$.

Sales to total assets $= 1.77\times$.

ACP $= 30$ days.

22-4 a. 16%.

b. ROE $= 20.99\%$.

23-2 a. Total assets $=$ Total claims $= \$78,480,000$.

b. 25%.

23-4 a. External funding requirement $= \$52,000$.

Long-term debt $= \$31,200$.

Equity $= \$20,800$.

24-2 a. $k_s = 19.8\%$.

b. $V = \$273,100$.

25-2 a. $0.

b. First mortgage holders, $300,000.

Second mortgage holders, $100,000.

c. Trustee's expenses, $50,000.

Wages due, $30,000.

Taxes due, $40,000.

25-4 a. $3,200,000; $7,000,000; no.

26-2 4.546 francs.

26-4 Gain of $400,000.

27-2 a. Alpha = $\bar{k} - k = 18.0\% - 17.2\% = 0.8\%$.

27-4 a.

	V_A	V_B
12/31/80	$10,000,000	$10,000,000
12/31/84	24,676,650	26,201,250

  b. Manager A's total return = 146.8%;

  Geometric average return = 25.3%.

  Manager B's total return = 162.0%;

  Geometric average return = 27.2%.

  c. Total return = 22.3%;

  Geometric average return = 5.2%.

Index